HUGH JOHNSON'S

WINE COMPANION

HUGH JOHNSON'S

WINE COMPANION

THE ENCYCLOPEDIA OF WINES, VINEYARDS & WINEMAKERS

Fully revised and updated by Stephen Brook

6TH EDITION

Hugh Johnson's Wine Companion
Fully revised and updated by Stephen Brook

First published in Great Britain in 1983 by Mitchell Beazley, an imprint of Octopus Publishing Group Limited, 2–4 Heron Quays, London E14 4JP.

An Hachette Livre UK Company
www.hachettelivre.co.uk

Distributed in the USA and Canada by Octopus Books USA: c/o Hachette Book Group USA, 237 Park Avenue, New York, NY 10017

Revised editions 1987, 1991, 1997, 2003, 2009
Copyright © Octopus Publishing Group Ltd 1987, 1991, 1997, 2003, 2009
Text copyright © Hugh Johnson 1987, 1991, 1997, 2003, 2009

A CIP catalogue record for this book is available from the British Library.

ISBN: 978 1 84533 457 4

The author and publishers will be grateful for any information which will assist them in keeping future editions up-to-date. Although all reasonable care has been taken in the preparation of this book, neither the publishers nor the author can accept any liability for any consequences arising from the use thereof, or the information contained therein.

For this edition:
Editorial Director Tracey Smith
Commissioning Editor Becca Spry
Project Manager Jo Wilson
Editor Margaret Rand
Art Director Tim Foster/ Pene Parker
Design Colin Goody
Production Lucy Carter
Proofreader Hilary Azzam
Index Isobel McLean

Original cartography Clyde Surveys Ltd
Printed and bound by
Toppan Printing Company in China

Author's acknowledgements

Many growers' associations either facilitated trips to their regions or sent me wine samples. Among these are Elisabeth Pasquier of Vinea in Switzerland; Léna Martin of CIVA in Alsace; Cécile Niehouser in Madiran; Willi Klinger and Susanne Staggl of the Austrian Wine Marketing Board; John McLaren, Venla Freeman, and Diane Berardi of the California Wine Institute; Ruben Gil of the Consejo de Toro; Maria José Sevilla, Victoria Dillon, and Maite Hernandez of Wines of Spain; Jo Mason and Su Birch of Wines of South Africa; Kirsten Moore and Doug Neal of Wine Australia; Anna Noble of Phipps PR and the Rioja consejo; Well Com PR in Alba, Italy; Dorli Muhr of Austria's Wine & Partners; Emily Gorton of Jam PR in San Francisco; Céline Bouteiller and Natalie Jeune of Focus PR and the CIVR of Roussillon; and Stephany Boettner of the Oregon Wine Advsory Board.

I would like to thank Yair Kornblum and Michal Neeman who facilitated my visit to the Tel Aviv wine fair in 2008; Baron Jakob Kripp who provided information about Romania's wines and Peter Schleimer alerted me to rising stars in Austria. Thanks also to Lisa Shara Hall at the Pinot Noir Conference in Oregon, and Whitney Schubert and to the press office of ProWein in Düsseldorf. Thank you Cécile Mathiaud of the BIVB in Burgundy and Francoise Peretti of the Champagne Bureau. I am grateful to Stuart Piggott and Joel Payne; Great Western Wines; Louis Guntrum of Rheinhessen; and the Domäne Wachau in Austria. Jose Manuel Ortega was lavish with his hospitality and with extensive tastings in Argentina and Spain. Rodrigo Redmont brilliantly organised extensive visits to Abruzzo and Friuli, and Chandra Kurt made valuable contributions to the Swiss section.

Margaret Rand, with her usual impeccable professionalism, has edited this book, and contributed her own expert knowledge to many entries. Joanne Wilson has been the efficient house editor at Mitchell Beazley. Lastly, Hugh Johnson has given me a free hand to ensure the book as is comprehensive and thorough as space permits, while at the same time he has cast his ultra-knowledgeable eye over every line. His steady encouragement has made the whole task much easier, and his kindly and authoritative spirit continues to infuse this new edition of the *Wine Companion*.

Stephen Brook

Contents

Introduction

It has been 25 years since the first publication of this book: beyond argument, the most eventful quarter-century in the history of wine. Five previous editions have done their best to keep up with ever accelerating change. For this and the previous edition I have recruited one of the best-informed and most polished minds in the world of wine: Stephen Brook, himself the author of 12 books on the subject, to scan all my accumulated work and correct and update it for the twenty-first century with all the resources at the publisher's disposal. I have been involved all the way through, making corrections of my own, but the task of describing – even sketching – the modern wine world, its methods, and its personnel is too much for one person.

For all its air of seamless and senior tradition, its classifications and regulations, nothing ever stands still in the world of wine. It is a constant fascination that every vintage is different, and then keeps changing in barrel or bottle with every year of maturity – and not, by any means, at a predictable pace. It has all the excitement of a moving target. But much more is on the move than just vintage quality and maturity. The ownership of vineyards and wineries, laws and regulations, winemakers and their techniques and philosophies are all in constant flux, and with them the quality of what they produce.

There is one constant in all this: – the terroir; the soil – but more than that; the whole natural environment in which the vines grow and the wine is made and cellared. Terroir is the ultimate factor in deciding both character and quality. Not at all constant, however, is the market. Today, wine drinkers – their tastes, perceptions, and demands – have a major role in the ever-changing scene that must be added to all the other factors.

All these are potent reasons why a *Wine Companion* published in 2009 is a changed animal from the editions that went before. In 1983 I compared recent changes with those that led the nineteenth-century writer Cyrus Redding to coin the term "modern wine". To Redding, the word "modern" distinguished the wines of his time from those of the Ancients. His "modern" methods are now old-fashioned – even antediluvian. They created most of the wines now referred to as "classics", but history has moved on again. Modern wine to us is the creation of the technology evolved in the last years of the twentieth century and the first of the twenty-first (though perhaps the word technology is too

brutal). The way the great winemakers proceed today could be described as scientific philosophy.

This modern world began with such radical discoveries as the effects of different temperatures on fermentation. (We should remember that the nature of fermentation itself was discovered by Pasteur only in the 1860s.) The ability to slow down fermentation by refrigeration was the first great breakthrough. Without it, the New World of wine, essentially those regions whose Mediterranean climates had limited their potential in the past, would never have challenged the Old.

Their challenge, though, from the mid-1960s on, has made the Old World look again at its entrenched ideas, has made it modify, adapt, and discard old dogma to the point where the simple concept of Old World and New has only a geographical meaning. Old World and New, in fact, have met in what is becoming the global wine village.

Such neighbourliness carries its dangers. The first is the inclination to make the same sort of wine as everyone else: the principal trend of the latter years of the twentieth century and still a danger, but happily less inexorable than it was. Its most obvious manifestation was the near-universal planting of Cabernet Sauvignon and Chardonnay. A more insidious one was the fashion of using oak, not as it was originally intended – for conditioning the wine ready for bottling – but actually to flavour it like a dash of ketchup by adding oak chips or even essence. A generation grew up under the delusion that Chardonnay actually tastes of oak – while in reality if it does, it is either badly made or not ready to drink.

At the beginning of the present century, it appears, too, that a fundamental difference in taste threatens to divide consumers on the two sides of the Atlantic. To simplify, influential American critics are judging wines more for the impact they make than for those traits that make them good companions: the power to tempt and beguile, to accompany food, and quench thirst. Europe so far has only partly succumbed to the American criteria, but it is a question to follow with interest.

This book is a portrait of this world of modern wine: its methods, its planting of vineyards and cellars, and above all, its practitioners. It is designed to be a practical companion in choices that become more varied and challenging all the time. Like any portrait, it tries to capture the reality of a single moment. The moment is past as soon as the shutter has clicked. The closer the focus and the greater the detail the more there is to change and grow out of date. This edition has been revised and updated to reflect the reality of 2009.

To make it a practical companion we try to give the essential information about each wine country and wine region you are likely to encounter or which is worth making an effort to know. We have shunned a catalogue of the legislation that surrounds the wine business increasingly each year. It casts little light and does nothing to add to the pleasure of our subject – which is, after all, either a pleasure or a failure.

The essentials, it seems to us, are the names and, as far as possible (which is not very far), descriptions of the world's worthwhile wines: who makes them, how much there is of them, how well they keep, and where they fit into our lives – which are too short, alas, to do justice to anything like all of them. You will also find answers to the recurring questions about grape varieties, production methods, and the ways of the wine trade. You will not find a historical survey or a technical treatise, but just enough information, we hope, to indicate essential differences and the trends of change in winemaking today.

The heart of the book is arranged by countries on the same system as Hugh Johnson's annual *Pocket Wine Book*, with the Index as the alphabetical alternative to find a name you cannot immediately place in a national or regional context. The *Wine Companion* is updated far less frequently than its annual pocket-sized stablemate, leaving to its more ephemeral editions the questions of current vintages, their quality, and maturity. Both will be much clearer if you possess the current (sixth) edition of *The World Atlas of Wine*, in which the regions are geographically displayed in the greatest detail.

Each section provides the essential background information about the wines in question, then lists the principal producers with succinct details. In a few well-trodden areas the lists make themselves. In most others, a complete catalogue would be as unhelpful as it would be unmanageable. Our method, then, is to consult first our own experience, then the advice of friends, local brokers, and officials whom we have reason to respect. We have corresponded with as many producers as possible, asking them specific questions about their properties or firms, their methods, products, and philosophies. Often, unfortunately, the exigencies of space have forced us to leave out good producers we would have liked to include. We have tasted as many of the wines described as we could (which is why some specific tasting notes go back ten years or more).

The enjoyment of wine is a very personal thing. Yet if you love it, and spend your life among wine-lovers, you will find a remarkable consensus about which wines have the power to really thrill and satisfy us. Prejudice and narrow-mindedness have no place; preferences are what it is all about. We have not tried to hide ours among the fabulous variety described in this book.

How to Follow the Star-Rating System

The *Wine Companion* has introduced a new star-rating system for each producer listed.

☆☆☆☆	Exceptionally fine or great quality, consistent over many vintages
☆☆☆	Consistently high quality
☆☆	At least good quality
☆	Sound and steady wines

Any rating given in red denotes particular good value. No rating is given to new producers whose wines are too new or too few to allow assessment; or to wineries that have recently changed hands.

Modern Wine

At its simplest, wine is made by crushing grapes and allowing the yeast naturally present on the skins to convert the sugar in their juice to alcohol. This is the process of fermentation. No more human intervention is needed than to separate the juice from the skins by pressing. Crushed and fermented like this, white grapes make white wine, and red grapes red.

The art of the winemaker can be equally simply expressed. It is to choose good grapes, to carry out the crushing, fermenting, and pressing with scrupulous care and hygiene, and to prepare the wine for drinking by cleaning it of yeasts and all foreign bodies. For some sorts of wine this entails ageing it as well; for others, the quicker it gets to market the better.

These are the eternal verities of wine and winemaking, well-understood for hundreds of years. They can be carried to perfection with no modern scientific knowledge or equipment whatever – with luck. Great wines came to be made in the places where nature, on balance, was kindest. Given a ripe crop of grapes in a healthy state, the element that determined success more than any other was the temperature of the cellar during and after the fermentation. France (but not the south), Germany, the Alps, and Hungary had these conditions. The Mediterranean and places with a similar climate did not.

If there is one innovation that has made the most difference between old and modern winemaking, it is refrigeration. Refrigeration and air-conditioning have added the whole zone of Mediterranean climate to the world of potentially fine wine. Yet technology has advanced on a broad front. Every aspect of grape-growing and winemaking is now under a degree of control undreamed of before. These controls are now common practice in almost all the bigger and newer wineries where wine is made. Its scientific basis is widely understood even in traditional areas and among small properties. One California professor confesses that winemakers now have more possible controls than they know how to use. In leading edge California, white winemaking is so clinically perfected that one of the main problems is deciding what sort of wine you want to make. On the other hand, as Professor Emile Peynaud of Bordeaux University has said, "The ultimate goal of modern oenology is to avoid having to treat the wine at all."

The following pages summarize some of the more important modern techniques and currently held views on the many factors that affect the qualities of wine. They follow the processes of grape growing and winemaking more or less sequentially, so that they can be read as an account or referred to as a glossary. Some processes apply to white wine only, some to red, some to both.

The Vine

A wine-grower in the Clos de Vougeot has no choice about what grapes to plant. It has been a sea of Pinot Noir for centuries. Nothing else is permitted. A wine-grower in the Médoc has an important choice to make: half a dozen varieties are allowed. The emphasis he places on the harsher or the smoother varieties is the basis of his house style.

A wine-grower in the New World is as free as the air. His own taste and his view of the market are his only guide. This choice, together with the debates it has started, has made all wine-lovers far more grape conscious than ever before. Not only are more wines named by their grape varieties, but this very fact has made the clear ascendancy of some varieties over others public knowledge.

What is a grape variety? It is a selection from among the infinity of forms a plant takes by natural mutation. In the basic economy of viticulture, a wine-grower looks first for fruitfulness, hardiness, and resistance to disease in his plants. Then he looks for the ability to ripen its fruit before the end of the warm autumn weather. Lastly, he looks for flavour and character.

There has been plenty of time since the discovery of wine to try out and develop different varieties. In the botanical genus Vitis, the vine, there are more than 20 species. The wine vine is only one: a wild woodland plant of Europe and eastern Asia, *Vitis vinifera*. It was scrambling through the treetops of France long before the idea of crushing and fermenting its grapes was imported, via Greece, from the near East.

Nobody knows the precise origins of any of the varieties of vine that were developed locally in France, Italy, Spain, along the Danube, and in the rest of wine growing Europe. But the assumption is that they started as selections by trial from local vine varieties, possibly interbreeding with imported ones of special quality. In Germany, for instance, the Romans made the brilliant discovery of a grape variety with habits perfectly adapted to the cool northern climate: the Riesling, or its ancestor. Selections, adaptations, or descendants from it have become all the other grapes in the German style.

There are now 4,000 or more named varieties of wine grape on earth. Perhaps 100 have really recognizable flavour and character. Of these, a bare dozen have moved into international circulation, and the dozen can be narrowed again to those that have personalities so definite (and so good) that they form the basis of a whole international category of wine. They are the principal red and white grapes of Bordeaux, the same of Burgundy, the Riesling of Germany, the Gewurztraminer of Alsace, the Syrah of the Rhône, and the grandfather of them all: the Muscat. Today, there is an increasing temptation to plant the champion grapes everywhere. It is a difficult argument between quality and that most precious attribute of wine – variety.

The Nebbiolo grape, known as the great grape of Piedmont

Classic Grapes

Riesling

Johannisberg Riesling, Rhine Riesling, White Riesling

The classic grape of Germany competes with Chardonnay for the title of the world's best white grape. The Riesling produces wines of crisp fruity acidity and transparent clarity of flavour. Even the aromas it gives off are refreshing.

In Germany, it ranges from pale green, fragile, and sharp on the Mosel to golden, exotically luscious wines, especially in the Rheinpfalz. It is remarkably versatile in warmer climates, perhaps at its most typical in Alsace, Austria, Oregon, and Australia, becoming more buxom when grown in California, where it ages more rapidly to its unique mature bouquet of lemons and petrol. It is also one of the few varieties that is delectable both as a dry wine and as an intensely sweet one. Germany's great Rieslings add another dimension found in almost no other white wine: they mature for as long as almost any reds.

Chardonnay

The white burgundy grape makes fatter, more winey, and potent-feeling wine than Riesling, less aromatic when young, maturing to a rich and broad, sometimes buttery, sometimes smoky or musky smell or flavour. The finesse of *blanc de blancs* Champagne, the mineral smell of Chablis, the nuttiness of Meursault, the ripe-fruit smells of Sonoma Valley wines show its unique versatility. It is a grape that is adapting superbly to Australia, California, New Zealand, and northern Italy.

Cabernet Sauvignon

The Médoc grape. Most recognizable and most versatile of red grapes, apparently able to make first-class wine in any warm soil, in just about any wine-growing region of the world. Small, dark, rather late-ripening berries yield an intense colour, a strong blackcurrant and sometimes herbal aroma, and much tannin, which makes it the slowest wine to mature. It needs age in oak and bottle, and is best of all blended with Merlot, etc., as in Bordeaux. Outside Bordeaux, it is still common to find examples of pure varietal Cabernet, but increasingly winemakers in areas as diverse as California, South Africa, Chile, and Italy are opting for more subtle claret style blends.

Pinot Noir

This is the red burgundy and Champagne grape. So far, it is apparently less adaptable to foreign vineyards, where the fine burgundian balance is very hard to achieve. Sweeter, less tannic, and richer-textured than Cabernet, and therefore enjoyable at a far younger age. It is rarely blended, except in Champagne. It has proved especially successful in Oregon, California, and New Zealand, less so in Mediterranean countries.

Syrah or Shiraz

Widespread, and the great grape of the Rhône Valley. Makes tannic, peppery, dark wine, which can mature superbly. It is very important as Shiraz in Australia. Grown increasingly in the Midi, and in South Africa, Chile, and California.

Gewu(ü)rztraminer

The beginner's grape due to its forthright spicy smell and flavour. Once almost unique to Alsace (without the umlaut), but now also encountered in Italy, Austria, Germany, New Zealand, and North America.

Sauvignon Blanc

The name derives from sauvage – wild – which could well describe its grassy or gooseberry flavour. It is widespread in Bordeaux, where it is blended with Sémillon for both sweet and dry wines, but is most characteristic in Sancerre. A successful transplant to the New World, New Zealand, and South Africa in particular: it can be light and aromatic, or as full-bodied as Chardonnay. Its ultimate value is constrained by its short lifespan.

Harvesting Chardonnay grapes at Chittering Estate, Western Australia

Muscat

Muscat Blanc à Petits Grains, Moscato Canelli
The finest of the ancient tribe of Muscats is the "small white" used for sweet *vins doux naturels* from the south of France and for Asti Spumante. Most of the dry Muscats of Alsace come from a more regular yielding variety, Muscat d'Ottonel.

Europe's Principal Grapes

France

All eight classic grapes are grown to perfection in France. The Muscat, Riesling, and Gewurztraminer are long-established imports, but the remaining five, the reds and whites of Burgundy, the Rhône, and Bordeaux, appear to be natives of France, representing an eastern and a western tradition: that of the Alps and that of the Atlantic. (They meet on the Loire.)

Nobody can say with any confidence how many other grapes make up this great tradition. A single variety might have four or five different names in different areas quite close together – or indeed, the grape may be a local strain and not quite the same variety. These local characters range from such common plants as the red Carignan of the Midi to the delicate white Viognier, once restricted to the Rhône, but now being more widely used for *vins de pays*; and such rare ones as the white Tresallier (limited to one tiny zone in the upper reaches of the Loire).

Red Grape Varieties

Aleatico red Muscat variety of Corsica. Makes a wine of the same name.
Aramon high-yielding southern table-wine variety, now in decline.
Auxerrois synonym of Malbec in Cahors.
Braquet main variety of Bellet, near Nice.
Cabernet Franc high-quality cousin of Cabernet Sauvignon used in Bordeaux (especially St-Emilion) and in the Loire.
Cabernet Sauvignon see page 10.
Carignan leading bulk-wine producer of the Midi; dull other than very old vines. Greatly improved by carbonic maceration.
Carmenère old Bordeaux variety, now rare; flourishing in Chile.
Cinsaut (or Cinsault) prominent southern Rhône variety, used in Châteauneuf-du-Pape etc., and the Midi, often for rosé.
Cot synonym of Malbec in the Loire.
Counoise peppery grape of the south; rare but good.
Duras local Gaillac variety.
Fer (or Fer Servadou) used in several wines of the southwest , notably Marcillac.
Gamay Beaujolais grape: juicy, light, and fragrant. Also grown in the Loire, especially Touraine, and in central France.
Grenache powerful red used in Châteauneuf-du-Pape and Côtes du Rhône, and for rosés (eg. Tavel) and dessert wines in Roussillon.
Grolleau (or Groslot) common Loire red used in, for example, Anjou Rosé.

Malbec important variety now fading from the best Bordeaux, but central to Cahors.
Merlot essential element in fine Bordeaux; the dominant grape of Pomerol.
Mondeuse chief red of Savoie.
Mourvèdre key variety of Bandol in Provence, found widely in the Midi and southern Rhône.
Négrette variety peculiar to Frontonnais and Gaillac.
Nielluccio sturdy Corsican variety, now thought identical to Sangiovese.
Petit Verdot high-quality subsidiary grape of Bordeaux.
Pineau d'Aunis local to the Loire Valley, especially Anjou and Touraine.
Pinot Meunier (or Meunier) inferior "dusty-leaved" version of Pinot Noir "tolerated" in Champagne, but nonetheless used in some of the greatest wines.
Pinot Noir see page 10.
Poulsard palered Jura variety.
Sciacarello light, peppery Corsican variety.
Syrah see page 10.
Tannat tannic variety of the southwest, especially Madiran.
Trousseau majority grape in Jura reds, inferior to Poulsard.

White Grape Varieties

Aligoté secondary Burgundy grape of high acidity. Wines for drinking young.
Altesse Savoie variety. Wines are often sold as "Roussette".
Arrufiac Béarnais variety (Pacherenc du Vic-Bilh).
Auvergnat (or Auvernat) Loire term for the Pinot family.
Baroque used in Béarn to make Tursan.
Beurot synonym in Burgundy of Pinot Gris.
Blanc Fumé synonym of Sauvignon Blanc at Pouilly-sur-Loire.
Blanquette synonym of Mauzac Blanc and Clairette Blanc.
Bourboulenc Midi (Minervois, La Clape) variety, also goes into (red and white) Châteauneuf-du-Pape. Brings richness and acidity to a blend.
Chardonnay see page 10.
Chasselas neutral variety used in Savoie, Pouilly-sur-Loire, and Alsace.
Chenin Blanc versatile, high quality variety of the Loire.
Clairette common neutral-flavoured Midi grape, also makes sparkling Rhône Clairette de Die.
Colombard Low-acid grape found in western France, popular for *vins de pays*. Also distilled for Cognac and Armagnac.
Courbu Jurançon variety (alias Sarreat).
Folle Blanche formerly the chief Cognac grape, also grown in Bordeaux and Brittany.
Gewurztraminer see page 10.
Grenache Blanc dull, workhorse grape of the south.
Gros Manseng one of the main grapes of Jurançon; intensely flavoured.
Gros Plant synonym of Folle Blanche in the western Loire.
Jacquère the grape of Apremont and Chignin in Savoie.
Jurançon Blanc minor Armagnac variety (not in Jurançon).
Klevner name used for Pinot Blanc in Alsace.
Len-de-l'El (or Loin de l'Oeil) variety used in Gaillac.
Maccabeu (or Maccabéo) Catalan variety used in Roussillon for dessert *vins doux naturel*.

Malvoisie synonym of Bourboulenc in the Languedoc, of Torbato in Roussillon, and Vermentino in Corsica.

Marsanne with Roussanne, the white grape of Hermitage and the Northern Rhône.

Mauzac used in Blanquette de Limoux and Gaillac.

Muscadelle minor, slightly Muscat-flavoured variety used in Sauternes and some dry white Bordeaux.

Muscadet gives its name to the wine of the western Loire. Also called Melon de Bourgogne.

Muscat see page 11.

Petit Manseng excellent, aromatic, southwest variety used in the wines of Jurançon, etc.

Picpoul synonym of Folle Blanche in Armagnac; in the Southern Rhône and the Midi (Picpoul de Pinet) it is a different variety: Picpoul Blanc.

Pineau de la Loire synonym in the Loire of Chenin Blanc (not a Pinot).

Pinot Blanc white version of Pinot Noir, grown in Alsace and a bit in Burgundy .

Pinot Gris pink-skinned, aromatic mutation of Pinot Noir, widespread in Alsace.

Piquepoul see Picpoul.

Riesling see page 10.

Rolle Italian Vermentino in Provence.

Romorantin grown only at Cheverny; dry, often sharp wine.

Roussanne (with Marsanne) makes white Hermitage.

Roussette synonym of Altesse in Savoie.

Sacy minor variety of the Yonne.

St-Emilion synonym of Ugni Blanc in Cognac.

Sauvignon Blanc see page 10.

Sauvignon Gris; pink-skinned version of S. Blanc, less aromatic but interesting, and used in some fine Graves.

Savagnin the "yellow wine" grape of Château-Chalon (Jura).

Sémillon great Bordeaux grape, key to Sauternes; also important in dry white Bordeaux.

Sylvaner the workhorse light-wine grape of Alsace.

Traminer see Gewurztraminer.

Tresallier variety of the extreme upper Loire (St-Pourçain-sur-Sioule) now fading.

Ugni Blanc common grape of the west and south; Italy's Trebbiano; "St-Emilion" in Cognac.

Vermentino Italian grape, known in Provence as Rolle.

Viognier aromatic grape of Condrieu in the Northern Rhône. Increasingly common in the Midi, especially as a varietal *vin de pays*.

Italy

Italy's grape catalogue is probably one of the longest of all. With wine-growing so universal a factor of Italian life, uninterrupted for millennia before phylloxera, local selection has completely blurred the origins and relationships of many varieties beyond recall. Similarly, is the fish caught off Tunisia and called by an Arab name the same as a similar one caught in the Adriatic and called by a name peculiar to the Romagna? In truth, Italian grapes are scarcely less slippery a subject.

In general, their selection has been on the grounds of productivity and good health, along with adaptability to the soil and reliable ripening, rather than great qualities of flavour or ability to age. The mass of Italian grapes are, therefore, sound rather than inspiring, their flavours muted or neutral. The only international classic to (maybe) come from Italy is the (Gewürz) Traminer, from the South Tyrol.

But once you start to list the exceptions, the Italian grapes with personality and potentially excellent quality, it does seem strange that more of them have not yet made a real name for themselves in the world. Nebbiolo, Barbera, Teroldego, Sangiovese, Sagrantino, Montepulciano, Nero d'Avola, and Aglianico are reds with much to offer. There are fewer first-class whites, but Ribolla, Friulano, Cortese, Fiano, Falanghina, Greco, Verdicchio, and Vermentino all make original contributions, and the Moscato of Piedmont, while not exclusively Italian, is a very Italian interpretation of the most ancient of grapes. At the same time, more and more is being heard of Cabernet, Merlot, Pinot Bianco, and even Chardonnay and Riesling, while Pinot Grigio has become wildly popular in Germany and North America. The northeast is now almost as international in its ampelography as any of the wine areas of the New World. The appearance of Cabernet Sauvignon, Syrah, and Chardonnay in Tuscany in recent years is a trend that has somewhat slackened, as growers in the classic regions recognize the value of their indigenous varieties.

The central question over the future of Italian wine is how far she will defend her traditions (which is the purpose of the DOC legislation) in sticking to her indigenous grapes, and how far she will bow to the international trend – as she is tending to do in winemaking techniques. The world has begun to appreciate just what variety Italy has to offer. She will do well to develop her native flavours to the full. They include as wide a range as the wines of any country – France included.

There is no general rule on the mention of grape varieties on labels; local custom dictates whether the wine is labelled by place, grape, or a name entirely unrelated to either. With the current increase in variety consciousness, however, it does seem likely that producers will start to make more of the grape varieties in future – at least on wines destined for export.

Red Grape Varieties

Aglianico source of full-bodied Taurasi in Campania, and Aglianico del Vulture in Basilicata.

Aleatico Muscat-flavoured grape used for dark dessert wines in Elba, Latium, Apulia, and elsewhere.

Barbera dark, acidic Piedmont variety widely grown in the northwest.

Bombino Nero used in Apulia's Castel del Monte *rosato*.

Bonarda minor variety widespread in Lombardy and Piedmont.

Brachetto makes fizzy, perfumed Piedmont wines.

Brunello di Montalcino local name for Sangiovese, and once (though no longer) thought to be a separate strain.

Cabernet (Franc and Sauvignon) widespread in the northeast; increasing elsewhere.

Calabrese synonym of Sicilian Nero d'Avola.

Cannonau leading dark variety of Sardinia for DOC wines, the Grenache of France.

Carignano (French Carignan), prominent in Sardinia.

Cesanese good Latium red.
Chiavennasca Nebbiolo in Valtellina, Lombardy.
Corvina Veronese main grape of Valpolicella.
Corvinone now known to be a separate variety to Corvina, with which it shares many vineyards in Valpolicella. Makes dark, tannic wines for ageing.
Croatina much used in Lombardy's Oltrepò Pavese and in Emilia-Romagna.
Dolcetto low-acid Piedmont variety.
Freisa Piedmont variety, makes sweet, often fizzy wines, and occasional dry ones.
Gaglioppo source of most Calabrian reds, including Cirò.
Grignolino makes light, pleasant wines around Asti in Piedmont.
Guarnaccia red variety of Campania, especially Ischia.
Lacrima rose-scented, acidic variety of central Italy.
Lagrein grown in Alto Adige: faintly bitter reds and dark rosés.
Lambrusco prolific source of Emilia's effervescent wines.
Malbec seen occasionally in Apulia and Venezia.
Malvasia Nera makes sweet, fragrant, sometimes sparkling reds in Piedmont; also a fine dessert wine in Apulia.
Marzemino dark grape grown in Trentino and Lombardy.
Merlot Bordeaux native widely grown in Italy, especially in the northeast.
Molinara light ingredient of Valpolicella.
Monica makes Sardinian reds, dry and sweet.
Montepulciano dark variety of central Italy, widely planted.
Nebbiolo the great grape of Piedmont, the base of Barolo, Barbaresco, Gattinara, etc. Its wine can be challenging, being high in acidity, tannin, and alcohol.
Negroamaro potent Apulian variety of the Salento peninsula.
Nerello Mascalese Sicilian grape, for Etna reds and rosés.
Nero d'Avola dark, soft, rich reds from the south.
Petit Rouge used in some Valle d'Aosta reds.
Piedirosso (or Per'e Palummo) features in Campania reds.
Pignolo tannic Friulian red, now being revived.
Pinot Nero Burgundy's Pinot Noir (see page 10), grown in much of northeast Italy.
Primitivo Apulian grape, the same as Zinfandel.
Raboso worthy, if tannic, Veneto native.
Refosco source of dry, full-bodied Friuli reds. Known as Mondeuse in France.
Rondinella perfumed ingredient of Valpolicella.
Rosenmuskateller rose-scented pink Muscat of the north.
Rossese fine Ligurian variety, makes DOC at Dolceacqua.
Sagrantino good, pungent variety found in Umbria.
Sangiovese mainstay of Chianti and one of Italy's most widely planted vines, with many clones. At best magnificent, astringent but full-bodied, ageing many years.
Schiava widespread in Alto Adige.
Spanna synonym for Nebbiolo.
Syrah making inroads in many parts.
Teroldego unique to Trentino, makes characterful Teroldego Rotaliano.
Tocai Rosso (or Tocai Nero) makes DOC red in Veneto's Colli Berici.
Uva di Troia main grape of several DOC wines in north Apulia.
Vespolina often blended with Nebbiolo in east Piedmont.

White Grape Varieties

Albana Romagna makes dry and semi-sweet wines.
Arneis Piedmont variety that is enjoying a revival.
Biancolella native of Ischia.
Blanc de Valdigne source in Valle d'Aosta of Blanc de Morgex, Blanc de la Salle.
Bombino Bianco main grape of Apulia and Abruzzo, where it is known as Trebbiano d'Abruzzo.
Bosco in Liguria, the main ingredient of Cinqueterre.
Catarratto widely grown in west Sicily, often used in Marsala.
Chardonnay grown in Trentino-Alto Adige, Veneto, and Friuli and now found throughout the country, from Piedmont to Sicily.
Cortese used in south Piedmont's finest whites: found also in Lombardy's Oltrepò Pavese.
Falanghina increasingly fashionable white grape of Campania.
Fiano in Campania makes Fiano di Avellino.
Forestera partners Biancolella in Ischia Bianco.

Nebbiolo vines on pergolas, Carema, Piedmont

Friulano formerly known as Tocai and used for DOC whites in Lombardy and Veneto, as well as in its native Friuli.

Garganega main and best grape of Soave.

Grechetto variety of Umbria, important in Orvieto.

Greco Campania's best white.

Grillo figures, usually with Catarratto, in Marsala.

Inzolia used in Sicilian whites, as well as Marsala.

Malvasia common for both dry and sweet wines, especially in Latium (for Frascati etc.).

Moscato (Muscat, see page 11) widespread in sparkling wines (eg. Asti Spumante) and dessert wines (eg. Moscatos of Sicily).

Müller-Thurgau encountered in Friuli, Trentino-Alto Adige.

Nuragus ancient Sardinian grape.

Pecorino characterful variety of the Marches and Abruzzo, being revived.

Picolit source of Italy's most expensive dessert wines from Friuli.

Pigato grown only in southwest Liguria; good table wine.

Pinot Bianco Burgundy's Pinot Blanc, grown all over north Italy. Weisser Burgunder in Alto Adige.

Prosecco prominent in Veneto, mainly for sparkling wines.

Rheinriesling see Riesling Renano.

Riesling Italico Welschriesling; not a true Riesling, probably native to the northeast.

Riesling Renano Rhine Riesling, and thus authentic.

Sauvignon Blanc grown in parts of the northeast, and exceptional in Friuli.

Tocai see Friulano.

Trebbiano Italian workhorse grape, the Ugni Blanc of France. Trebbiano d'Abruzzo (alias Bombino Bianco) is a separate variety.

Verdeca Apulian grape used in southern whites.

Verdicchio main grape of the Marches.

Verduzzo Friulian variety used also in the Veneto for both dry and dessert wines.

Vermentino source of DOC white in Sardinia, and good table wines in Liguria.

Vernaccia name given to different, unrelated vines in different places. Racy in San Gimignano, sherry-like in Oristano, Sardinia.

Zibibbo Sicilian name for Muscat of Alexandria. See Muscat, page 11.

Germany

The international reputation of German wine for a unique effect of flowery elegance is based on one grape alone: Riesling. But the widespread use of Riesling as we know it is probably no more than 200 or 300 years old. Germany has several old varieties of local importance, which continue to hold their own. More significantly, her vine-breeders have been struggling for a century to produce new vines that offer Riesling quality without its inherent disadvantage: ripening so late in the autumn that every vintage is a cliffhanger. The centenary of the first important Riesling cross (with Silvaner) was celebrated in 1982. The past 100 years have seen its fruit, the Müller-Thurgau, become so prolific that, for a time, it surpassed Riesling as Germany's most popular grape.

Yet none of the new varieties, not even Müller-Thurgau, has supplanted Riesling in the best and warmest vineyards. None has achieved more than either a sketch or a caricature of its brilliant balance and finesse. Nor have any survived such ultimate tests of hardiness as January 1979, when the temperature dropped by 40 degrees to -20°F (-29°C) in 24 hours. Thousands of vines were killed. Riesling survived.

The major advance in Germany in recent times has been the improvement of red wines, most of all of Spätburgunder. Global warming shares the credit with determined and imaginative winemaking. Wines that used to be pale and weedy are often now plump and structured, joining the few interpretations of Pinot Noir in the world that can hold up their heads with Burgundy.

Sixty-three per cent of the German vineyard is white. Of the 37 per cent that is red, Spätburgunder (Pinot Noir) long ago overtook the inferior Portugieser.

Red & White Grape Varieties

Albalonga Rieslaner x Silvaner. Should be ultra-ripe. Now in decline.

Bacchus an early ripening cross of (Silvaner x Riesling) x Müller-Thurgau. Spicy but rather soft wines, best as Auslesen, frequently used as Süssreserve.

Blauburgunder synonym for Pinot Noir.

Cabernet Cubin One of a number of Cabernet crosses developed in the 1990s in Franken. Dark-red wines with high ripeness levels. Being adopted with caution.

Domina Pinot Noir x Portugieser. A deep coloured cross, gradually being planted in the Ahr and southern Germany.

Dornfelder A complex cross, developed in the 1950s, but only widely planted in the 1990s, especially in the Pfalz. Gives dark, quaffable red wines even from high yields.

Ehrenfelser Riesling x Silvaner. A good cross, between Müller-Thurgau and Riesling in quality.

Elbling once the chief grape of the Mosel, now only grown high upriver. Neutral and acidic, but clean and good in sparkling wine.

Faber Weissburgunder x Müller-Thurgau, with a certain following in Rheinhessen and the Nahe.

Frühburgunder A small-berried mutation of Pinot Noir. It ripens earlier and has lower acidity. Good quality.

Gewürztraminer see page 10.

Grauburgunder or Grauerburgunder Ruländer, alias Pinot Gris rich, spicy wine in the Pfalz, Baden, and Rheinhessen.

Gutedel south Baden name for the Chasselas, or Swiss Fendant. Light, refreshing, but short-lived wine.

Huxelrebe Gutedel x Courtiller Musqué. A prolific variety, very aromatic, with good sugar and acidity. Popular in Rheinhessen, but in gradual decline.

Kerner Trollinger x Riesling. One of the better new varieties, widely planted. When not overcropped, it tastes like a blend of Silvaner and Riesling.

Lemberger synonym for Austrian Blaufränkisch. Gives complex wine with good acidity in Württemberg.

Morio-Muskat it is hard to believe that this early ripening cross of Silvaner and Weisser Burgunder has no Muscat blood.

Müller-Thurgau Riesling x Sylvaner. Created in 1882, but only widely planted after 1930. Immensely popular, despite suffering chronic insipidity, unless yields are heavily reduced. Also known as Rivaner.

Optima Silvaner x Riesling x Müller-Thurgau. This is an improvement on Bacchus. Delicately spicy.

Ortega Müller-Thurgau x Siegerrebe. Very early ripening, aromatic, and spicy with superb balance. Planted in the Mosel and in Franken. Gives rather cloying, sweet wines, however.

Perle Gewürztraminer x Müller-Thurgau. An aromatic new cross, planted in Rheinhessen and Franken. In decline.

Portugieser very popular, high-yielding red grape; is insipid.

Regent one of the better new red varieties, becoming popular in the Pfalz and Rheinhessen.

Reichensteiner Müller-Thurgau x (Madeleine Angevine x Calabreser Fröhlich). A Euro-cross, slightly better for both sugar and acid than Müller-Thurgau.

Rieslaner Silvaner x Riesling. A brilliant variety, created in 1921, but hard to grow. Gives superb sweet wines with higher acidity even than Riesling.

Riesling see page 10.

Ruländer synonym for Grauburgunder.

Samtrot a mutation of Pinot Meunier found in Württemberg. Soft, but elegant wines.

Scheurebe the second cross Silvaner x Riesling to become celebrated. Well-established (Rheinhessen, Rheinpfalz) for highly aromatic, often unsubtle wine. At its best when made sweet.

Schwarzriesling German synonym for Pinot Meunier. Found in Baden and Württemberg.

Silvaner a late-ripener like the Riesling, also badly affected by drought in light or thin soils, steadily giving ground to Müller-Thurgau and others. Scarcely noble, but at its best (in Franken and Rheinhessen) the true yeoman: blunt, trustworthy, with unsuspected depths.

Spätburgunder (Pinot Noir) long established in Germany; the best these days can give burgundy a run for its money.

Trollinger the favourite grape of Württemberg, giving light red wine consumed in industrial quantities within the region, and regarded with bafflement outside it.

Weisser Burgunder or Weissburgunder (Pinot Blanc) makes good fresh, full-bodied wine in Baden.

Autumnal Riesling vines, Wurzgarten vineyard, on the Mosel

Spain & Portugal

Spain and Portugal have been net exporters, rather than importers, of grape varieties. A few of the international varieties have been planted, but they have certainly not yet taken hold in a way that radically alters the wine, whereas their grapes exported to the world include the Palomino (to California, South Africa, and Australia), the Verdelho (to Australia), and, probably, the Carignan, much the most widespread red grape of the south of France. Traditionally, there were few varietals wines in Spain and Portugal, although, as with elsewhere, this is changing . Red wines in Rioja, Ribera del Duero, and Toro are often pure Tempranillo; Bierzo is pure Mencía. Other regions have a tradition of blending. The most notable exceptions are the four varietals of Madeira: Sercial, Verdelho, Bual, and Malmsey.

Red Grape Varieties

Agua Santa early ripening red of Bairrada, giving stronger wine than the Baga.

Alfrocheiro Preto prized red variety in Dão and Alentejo.

Alvarelhão Dão variety, and grown for port. Also found in Galicia.

Aragonez synonym of Tempranillo, popular in Alentejo.

Azal Tinto red grape with high acid, used for Vinho Verde.

Baga dark, tannic, potentially noble grape of Bairrada. Gives berry fruit flavours.

Bastardo a rather pale and low-acid, but aromatic and well-balanced, grape, used for port and in Dão.

Bobal sturdy grape of southeast Spain, juicy if made well.

Borraçal red Vinho Verde grape providing high malic acidity.

Cabernet Sauvignon (see page 11) increasingly being planted in Spain.

Cariñena Carignan in France, originated in Cariñena (Aragón) but now more grown in Catalonia.

Castelão a minor Bairrada red, soft and neutral.

Castelão France's preferred synonym of Periquita since 2002; widely planted grape of southern Portugal.

Cencibel synonym in La Mancha and Valdepeñas for Tempranillo.

Garró old Penedès variety used by Torres in Gran Muralles: dark and tannic.

Garnacha Tinta used in Rioja Baja for powerful, if pale Riojas, also Penedès, and Navarra, where it dominates. French synonym is Grenache Noir.

Graciano the most elegant and aromatic of Rioja grapes; gives quick maturing wine. Now being revived.

Jaen a constituent of red Dão. Could be Spain's Mencía.

Listán Negro blending grape of the Canaries. The white version is the same as Palomino.

Mazuelo a Riojan red grape, a synonym for Cariñena.

Mencía used in Léon and Galicia for fresh, perfumed reds.

Monastrell a widely grown red of good colour and texture, especially in Penedès, the Levante, and Valdepeñas.

Periquita see Castelão Frances.

Pinot Noir (see page 11) Torres grows Pinot for his red Santa Digna. Also found in Navarra.

Ramisco the tannic, blue-black secret of Colares. Needs very long ageing.

Roriz or Tinta Roriz Tempranillo in the Douro Valley. Rich, intense ingredient of port.

Samsó Penedès variety.

Souzão deeply coloured and excellent port grape.

Tempranillo fine, aromatic, early ripening, and basis for Rioja. Grown throughout Spain under a variety of synonyms, and in Portugal as Roriz or Aragonez.

Terrantez rare but excellent Madeira grape.

Tinta Barroca high-yielding but robust port grape.

Tinto Cão low-yielding red variety used for port and Dão.

Tinta Negra Mole high-yielding, workhorse Madeira grape.

Tinta Pinheira minor Bairrada variety; pale, low acid, alcoholic.

Touriga Franca perfumed red used for port; previously called Touriga Francesa.

Touriga Nacional deep-coloured, low-yielding port variety, also used in Dão.

Trincadeira gives rich reds in Alentejo; known in the Douro as Tinta Amarela.

Ull de Llebre Penedès synonym for Tempranillo.

Vinhão Vinho verde red grown for its relatively high alcohol.

White Grape Varieties

Airén the main white grape of Valdepeñas and La Mancha.

Albariño the best Galician variety for clean, dry, fragrant and often *pétillant* whites; also grown in Portugal (Alvarinho) for Vinho Verde.

Albillo used, with red grapes, in Vega Sicilia.

Arinto used for lemony white Dão and Bairrada and to make the rare, dry Bucelas and sweet Carcavelos.

Barcelos recommended white Dão variety.

Bical fragrant and fine Bairrada white, complementary to the sharper Arinto.

Bual or Boal sweet Madeira grape, with luscious flavours, also used in Carcavelos and Alentejo.

Chardonnay (see page 10) becoming more established in Spain with wines from Penedès, Somontano, and elsewhere. Also the occasional Portuguese example.

Esgana Cão the name given to the Sercial of Madeira on the Portuguese mainland. The name means "dog strangler".

Encruzado main white grape of Dão. Not madly interesting.

Fernão Pires widely planted aromatic Portuguese white.

Godello aromatic Spanish grape, probably the same as Portugal's Verdelho.

Gouveio minor white port variety.

Lairén see Airén.

Listan synonym of Palomino.

Loureiro high-yielding, aromatic grape for Vinho Verde.

Macabeo synonym of Viura. For sparkling wines.

Malvasia important white grape in port, Rioja, Navarra, Catalonia, and the Canary Islands.

Maria Gomes the principal white grape of Bairrada.

Moscatel widespread sweet wine grape.

Palomino the main grape of sherry; makes surprisingly dull table wine that needs technical wizardry to make it palatable.

Pansa quite aromatic when grown in Alella. Synonym of Xarel-lo of Penedès.

Parellada used in Penedès for delicately fruity whites and sparklers.

Pedro Ximénez grown for blending in Jerez, Málaga, and the principal grape in Montilla: dried, it adds intense sweetness and colour.
Sercial fine, acidic grape grown for the Madeira of the same name.
Traminer used (with Moscatel) by Torres for Viña Esmeralda.
Treixadura light, lemony grape of Galicia and (as Trajadura) Vinho Verde.
Verdejo quite aromatic grape of Rueda.
Verdelho white Dão variety, better known in Madeira.
Viosinho well-structured variety of northern Portugal.
Viura (alias Macabeo) the principal grape of white Rioja, also Navarra and Rueda.
Xarel-lo Catalan grape, important in Penedès.
Zalema main variety in *vino generoso* of Huelva, being replaced by Palomino.

Southeast & Central Europe

The grape varieties of southeast Europe and the countries fringing the Black Sea are as old as those of the west. The Romans colonized the Danube at the same time as the Rhine. Under the Austro-Hungarian Empire, the only wines to reach international fame were those of Hungary, led by Tokaji. The local grapes, therefore, evolved slowly on their own course, making spicy, often sweetish whites and dry, tannic reds. The eastern fringes of the Alps in Slovenia, Austria, and north into Bohemia (Czech Republic) are essentially white wine country, dominated by their low key namesake, the Welschriesling (variously known as Italian Riesling, Olasz Rizling, or Laski Rizling), and Austria by its sappy, vigorous Grüner Veltliner.

Hungary is most prolific in native white grapes of strength and style, led by the Furmint of Tokaji. Its red, the Kadarka, is widespread in the Balkans, more recently joined by the Pinot Noir and Gamay. Warmer climates near the Adriatic and Black Seas have reds and sweet whites. The last two decades have seen an invasion of classics from the west.

Red & White Grape Varieties

Blauburger straightforward Austrian red variety, Portugieser x Blaufrankisch.
Blaufränkisch lovely fresh Austrian red variety, Kékfrankos in Hungary, Lemberger in Germany.
Bouvier used for sweet wines in Austria's Burgenland.
Ezerjó a white variety making fine wine at Mór, in Hungary. Also a bulk producer from the Serbian border region with Hungary and Romania. One of the best Hungarian dry whites.
Featasca Albă important Romanian white grape, now surpassed by its descendant Fetească Regală. Mostly soft wines.
Furmint classic white grape of Tokaji. (Sipon in Slovenia.) Its (very successful) use for dry wines is a recent trend.
Grasa makes rich, nobly rotten whites in Romania.
Grüner Veltliner versatile white grape of Austria, rightly fashionable. Also found in Hungary and Czech Republic.
Hárslevelü second main variety for making Tokaji. Full and aromatic.
Juhfark rare but invigorating Hungarian white variety with high acidity, found only in Somló.

Kadarka the common red grape of Hungary, but it is widespread throughout the region, producing a stiff, spicy red that is built especially for ageing. Known as Gamza in Bulgaria.
Kékfrankos (Austrian Blaufränkisch) more reliable than Kadarka and hence being planted as a substitute, especially in Hungary.
Kéknyelü white low-yielding variety of Hungary's vineyards north of Lake Balaton, makes concentrated, golden-green wines.
Kraski Teran the Refosco of Italy, makes crisp, tangy red in Slovenia.
Leányka delicate, dry white especially from Eger in the north of Hungary.
Lunel (or Yellow) Muscat Sargamuskotály in Hungarian. One of the four grape varieties permitted for use in Tokaji.
Mavrud makes Bulgaria's best red, dark and plummy, can last 20 years.
Melnik robust red vine of Bulgaria.
Mezesfehér Hungarian white grape ("little honey") but less grown now.
Misket indigenous to Bulgaria, both red and white often used to make a fatter blend.
Muscat Ottonel the East European Muscat, a specialty of Romania.
Olaszrizling Hungarian name for Riesling Italico. Widely planted. Grasevina in Slovenia and Croatia.
Plovdina dark-skinned red grape, native to Macedonia.
Prokupac red grape of Serbia and Macedonia, blended to make Zupsko Crno, and much used to make rosé.
Rebula (or Ribolla) an Italian export that makes slightly creamy, yellow wine in Slovenia.
Rkatsiteli Russian variety that is good for strong white wines, preferred sweet by local market. Also used in northeast Bulgaria.
St Laurent deep-coloured variety, possibly of Alsatian origin, but now found only in Austria and Germany.
Saperavi variety indigenous to Georgia, giving intense, peppery wines akin to Syrah.
Smederevka chief white of Serbia and Kosovo for fresh dry whites.
Szürkebarát a form of Pinot Gris grown in the Badacsonyi region of Hungary for rich, not necessarily sweet, wine.
Tamiioasa Romanian name for Muscat (see page 11).
Vranac makes vigorous reds in Montenegro.
Wildbacher acidic red variety grown in Austria's Weststeiermark for Schilcher.
Zéta new name for white Oremus, Furmint x Bouvier and part of the Tokaji blend since 1994.
Zilavka white variety with faint apricot flavour, grown in southern Serbia.
Zweigelt red grape making deep-coloured, pleasantly scented, spicy wine, especially in Austria.

In the Vineyard

Grape Varieties

The choice of grape varieties is the most fundamental decision of all. See pages 10–17

Source of Grapes

For a winemaker there are arguments both for and against growing your own grapes. Those in favour are that you have total control over the management of the vineyard, and thus decide the quality of the grapes. The argument against is that a winemaker can pick and choose among the best grapes of specialist growers in different areas – if he has the money.

In France, and throughout most of Europe, almost all quality wine (except for most Champagne) is "home-grown". In California and Australia, the debate is more open. Winemakers who buy their grapes (almost always from the same suppliers) include some of the very best. It is becoming more common for wineries to work on a contract basis with suppliers, dictating crucial factors such as yields and picking dates – and guaranteeing a higher price.

Virus-free Vines

Certain authorities (notably at the University of California at Davis) are convinced that the only way to achieve a healthy vineyard is to "clean" the vine stocks in it of all virus infections. Until recently, the beautiful red colour of vine leaves in autumn was not known to be a symptom of a virus infected plant. The South Africans have been struggling for decades to reduce virus infection in their vineyards, as it can lead to insufficient maturation and hard, "green" flavours.

Plants can now be propagated free of virus infection by growing them very fast in a hot greenhouse, then using the growing tips as mini-cuttings (or micro-cuttings, growing minute pieces of the plant tissue in a nutrient jelly). The virus is always one pace behind the new growth, which is thus "clean" and will have all its natural vigour.

Virus elimination is no substitute for selection of the best vines. The Office International du Vin declared in 1980 that "It is a fantasy to try to establish a vineyard free of all virus diseases", and recommended its members to "Select clones resistant to dangerous virus diseases and which will still be capable, after infection, of producing a satisfactory crop both as to quality and quantity" (see Cloning, below).

Cloning

Close observation of a vine will show that some branches are inherently more vigorous, bear more fruit, ripen earlier, or have other desirable characteristics. These branches (and their buds) are "mutations": genetically slightly different from the parent plant. The longer a variety has been in cultivation the more "degenerate" and thus genetically unstable it will be, and the more mutations it will have. The Pinot family is extremely ancient and notoriously mutable. A recent technique is to select such a branch and propagate exclusively from its cuttings. A whole vineyard can then be planted with what is, in effect, one identical individual plant, known as a clone. There is thus not one single Pinot Noir variety in Burgundy, but scores of clones selected for different attributes. Growers who plant highly productive clones will never achieve the best quality wine. Those who choose a shy-bearing, small-berried clone for colour and flavour must reckon on smaller crops.

One advantage of a single-clone vineyard is that all its grapes will ripen together. A disadvantage is that one problem, pest, or disease will affect them all equally. Common sense seems to indicate that the traditional method of selecting cuttings from as many different healthy vines as possible (known as "massal selection") rather than one individual, carries a better chance of long term success.

The Choice of Rootstocks

The majority of modern vineyards are of a selected variety of European vine, grafted onto a selected American rootstock, which has inbuilt resistance to phylloxera. Compatible rootstocks have been chosen and/or bred and virus-freed to be ideal for specific types of soil. Some are recommended for acid-to-neutral soils (such as most in California), while others flourish on the limey or alkaline soils common to most of Europe's vineyards. Some parts of the world, notably South America, are free of phylloxera, so it is possible to plant vines on their own roots.

Grafting

The grafting of a "scion" of the chosen vine variety onto an appropriate rootstock is either done at the nursery before planting ("bench grafting") or onto an already-planted rootstock in the vineyard ("field grafting"). Recently, in California, it has become common practice for growers to change their minds after a vine has been in production for several years, deciding that they want (say) less Zinfandel and more Chardonnay. In this case they simply saw off the Zinfandel vine at rootstock level, just above the ground, and "T-bud" graft a Chardonnay scion in its place. Within two years they will have white wine instead of red. Not only do growers lose less production, but they also take advantage of the well-established root system of the mature vines.

Hybrid Vines

After the phylloxera epidemic in Europe a century ago, some French biologists started breeding hybrid vines by marrying the European classics to phylloxera-resistant American species. Once the technique of grafting the French originals onto American roots was well-established, the French establishment rejected these *producteurs directes*, or "PDs" (so-called because they produced "directly" via their own roots).

Good, hardy, and productive as many of them are, they are banned from all French appellation areas, however they are highly suitable for use in the eastern United States, where

hardiness is a perpetual problem. These hybrid vines were also once popular in New Zealand, and some of the better ones are quite extensively planted in England.

New Crossings of European Vines

Germany is the centre of a breeding programme that aims to find, within the genetic pool of varieties of *Vitis vinifera*, a combination of desirable qualities that could supplant, in particular, the Riesling. It is Germany's finest vine, but Riesling ripens relatively late, thus carrying a high risk element at vintage time. So far, no cross has even remotely challenged Riesling for flavour or hardiness – though many have for productivity, strongly aromatic juice, and early ripening. Müller-Thurgau was the first, and is still, the best-known example.

The University of California also has a vinifera breeding programme that has produced some useful additions, particularly in the form of high-yielding grapes for hot areas, capable of retaining good aromas and acidity. The best-known examples resulting from this programme include Ruby Cabernet (Cabernet Sauvignon/Carignan); Carnelian and Centurion (Cabernet Sauvignon/Grenache); Carmine (Cabernet Sauvignon/ Merlot); Emerald Riesling (Riesling/Muscadelle); and Flora (Gewürztraminer/Sémillon), all produced by Dr. Harold Olmo at Davis.

South Africa has produced the Pinotage, said to be a cross between Pinot Noir and Cinsaut (though, unfortunately, with few of the qualities of the former). With over 3,000 named varieties already in circulation to choose from, there seems to be a limited point in breeding for the sake of breeding.

Genetic Modification (GM)

Viticulture is not free of the debates that make this such a controversial topic in agricultural planning, and for much of the same reasons. The commercial planting of GM vines is not authorized, but research is taking place in Germany, France, and elsewhere. There is much fierce opposition from quality-conscious growers, who fear cross-contamination. Research is also advanced in producing genetically modified yeasts with a view to a more predictable fermentation, but here, too, there is opposition from growers and winemakers who worry about standardization replacing individuality.

Soil

Soil is always given pride of place in French discussions of wine quality. It is considered from two aspects: its chemical and its physical properties. Current thinking is that the latter is much the more important. Most soils contain all the chemical elements the vine needs.

The physical factors that affect quality are texture, porosity, drainage, depth, and even colour. In cool climates, anything that tends to make the soil warm (ie. absorb and store heat from the sun) is good. Stones on the surface store heat and radiate it at night. Darker soil absorbs more radiation. In Germany, vine

Autumn Tempranillo vines on the limestone / clay soil of Remelluri estate, Labastida, Alava, Spain

rows are oriented to expose the soil to maximum sunlight. Dry soil warms up faster. Another important advantage of good deep drainage (eg. on Médoc gravel) is that it makes the vine root dig deep to find moisture. Deep roots are in a stable environment: a sudden downpour just before harvest will not instantly inflate the grapes with water. On the other hand, recent experiments at Davis, California, have shown that where the soil is cooler than the above-ground parts of the vine, the effect can be deep-coloured red wine. (Château Pétrus on the iron-rich clay of Pomerol would seem to bear this out. St-Estèphe also has more clay, and its wines often more colour, than the rest of the Médoc.)

In California, clay also seems to produce stable white wines that resist oxidation and therefore have a greater ability to mature. But here also, overrapid ripening often leads to wines that are low in acidity and easily oxidized. The cool of clay might simply be slowing the ripening process: the very opposite of the effect required in, say, Germany.

A reasonable conclusion would be that the best soil is the soil that results in the grapes coming steadily to maturity: warm in cool areas, reasonably cool in hot areas. It should be deep enough for the roots to have constant access to moisture, since a vine under acute stress of drought closes the pores of its leaves. Photosynthesis stops, and the grapes cannot develop or ripen fully. Expert opinion seems to be that if the soils of the great vineyards (eg. Bordeaux First Growths) have more available nutrients and minerals (especially potassium), it is because over the years their owners have invested more in them.

Scrutiny of the Côte d'Or has not revealed any chemical differences between the soils of the different *crus*, which would account for their acknowledged differences of flavour.

Sites, Slopes, & Microclimates

It is conventional wisdom that wine from slopes is better. The words *côtes* and *coteaux* – meaning slopes – constantly recur in France. The obvious reasons are the increased solar radiation on a surface tipped toward the sun (meaning warmer soil), and the improved cold-air drainage, reducing the risk of frost. A south-facing slope (in the northern hemisphere) is almost always the ideal, but local conditions can modify this. In areas with autumn morning fog, a westerly slope is preferable, since the sun does not normally burn through the fog until the afternoon. The best slopes of the Rheingau are good examples. But, in Burgundy and Alsace, easterly slopes have the advantage of sun all morning to warm the ground, which stores the heat while the angle of the sun decreases during the afternoon. Alsace also benefits from a particularly sunny climate caused by the "rain shadow" of the Vosges mountains to its west.

Many of the best Old World vineyards (eg. in Germany, the Rhône Valley, the Douro Valley) were terraced on steep slopes to combine the advantages of slope with some depth of soil. Being inaccessible to machinery, terraces are largely being abolished. In Germany, huge earth-moving projects have rebuilt whole hills to allow tractors to operate. The Douro Valley is being remodelled with wide, sloping terraces instead

of the old, narrow, flat ones. Experiments with "vertical" planting on the steep Douro slopes – doing away with terraces altogether – have been inconclusive. Heavy rains can wash soil nutrients to the bottom of the slope. A flat valley floor (as in the Napa Valley, parts of Washington State, and much of Ribera del Duero) is the most risky place to plant vines, because cold air drains into it on spring nights, at a time when the vines have tender shoots (see Frost Protection, below).

It is noteworthy that, in Burgundy, the *grands crus* vineyards have a lower incidence of frost damage than the *premiers crus* – presumably because growers have observed the cold spots and lavished their attentions on the safer ones. The same distinction is even true of the incidence of hail. The term microclimate refers to the immediate surroundings of the vine. The slightest difference can become important in the long period between bud-break and harvest. In the Rheingau, wind is considered a principal enemy, since it can blow out accumulated warmth from the rows – which are therefore planted across the prevailing summer southwesterly wind.

Another factor is the shade and possible build-up of humidity under a dense canopy of leaves (see Training & Trellising, below). Yet another is the greater incidence of frost over soil covered with herbage than over bare earth, which makes it worth cultivating the vine rows in spring. Microclimatic factors are difficult to pin down with exactitude, but exposure to sun and wind, elevation and luminosity, susceptibility to frost or erosion, are all vital factors in defining not only the quality, but also the flavour of wines.

Frost Protection

A dormant vinifera vine in winter can survive temperatures down to -28°C (-18°F). In regions where lower temperatures regularly occur, it is common practice to bury the lower half of the vines by "earthing-up" in late autumn. A vine is most vulnerable to frost in spring, when its new growth is green and sappy. The only old means of protection was to light stoves (or "smudge pots") in the vineyards on clear spring nights, although this is now discouraged for environmental reasons. It was often a forlorn hope. An improvement introduced in the frost-prone areas of California, for example, was a giant fan to keep the air in the vineyard moving and prevent cold air accumulating, but it has proved ineffectual without heaters. Helicopters are also an efficient, if expensive, way of circulating freezing air to prevent frost damage. Then there is the sprinkler, which simply rains heavily on the almost-freezing vine. The water freezes on contact with young shoots forming a protective layer of ice, which acts as insulation against frosts. Such sprinklers can be an excellent investment, doubling as a (somewhat crude) method of irrigation during dry, hot summers.

Training & Trellising

Most vineyards used to consist of innumerable individual bushes, "head"- or "gobelet"-pruned to a few buds from the short trunk after each harvest. With a few famous exceptions (among them the Mosel, parts of the Rhône, and Beaujolais) most modern vineyards are "cordoned" – that is, with the vines

trained onto one or more wires parallel to the ground, supported at intervals by stakes. The wish to use mechanical harvesters has encouraged the use of higher trellising systems, often designed to spread the foliage at the top by means of a crossbar supporting two parallel wires 1.2 metres (four feet) apart. The first such trellis was developed in Austria in the 1930s by Lenz Moser. High trellises are not suitable for cool areas such as Germany, where heat radiation from the ground is essential for ripening. On the other hand, they have been used immemorially in northern Portugal to produce deliberately acidic wine. Widespread "curtains" of foliage, or "double curtains" where the vine is made to branch onto two high supporting wires, have several advantages in warm areas, but there are some doubts about the quality of the resulting wine. They expose a larger leaf surface for photosynthesis, at the same time as shading bunches of grapes from direct sunlight. In fertile soils that can support vigorous growth, the so-called "lyre" system, spreading the vine top into two mounds of foliage, is very successful – if not for top-quality wine, at least for good quantities of ripe grapes.

Canopy Management

Viticulturists have become much more aware of the concept of canopy management. They appreciate how it is possible to manipulate the vine, to give the grapes more or less direct exposure to sunlight, and control the amount of vegetation, so that humidity within the canopy does not cause disease. Any number of ingenious trellising methods are being developed (especially by the Australian guru of the canopy, Dr. Richard Smart), not only the "double curtain" and "lyre" system, but also Scott Henry and Sylvoz, all with the same intent of obtaining the best fruit without curtailing yields to uneconomic levels.

Pruning Methods

Pruning methods have been adapted to new methods of vine training. The most significant development is mechanical pruning, which dispenses with the skilled but laborious handwork in the depths of winter, by treating the vine row as a hedge. Aesthetically appalling, results (initially in Australia) show that a system of small circular saws straddling the vine and cutting all wood extending beyond a certain narrow compass can be as satisfactory as the practised eye and hand. Although some hand pruning may be necessary it is certain to become more common in vineyards. Experience in California, for example, has shown that mechanical pruning costs as little as 15 per cent of the cost of hand pruning.

Growth Regulators

For many years it has been customary to trim excessively long, leafy shoots from the tops and sides of vines in summer. The growth regulating spray, a chemical that slowly releases ethylene gas, inhibits further leaf growth, prevents the canopy from becoming too dense, and encourages the plant to make its carbohydrate reserves available to the fruit, instead of allowing it to waste them on useless long shoots. It apparently also encour-

Overhead trellising of grape vines, Marlborough, New Zealand

ages ripening, and makes it easier for a mechanical harvester to detach the grapes from their stems. Excessive vigour is a problem and can be combated with various trellising and pruning methods. Good vineyard management also helps. So does the increasingly widespread use of a cover crop: planting chicory or other greenery between the vine rows. The outcome is competition with the vine for available water; reducing vine vigour.

Systemic Sprays

The traditional protection against fungal diseases such as mildew in the vineyard is "Bordeaux mixture", a bright-blue copper-sulphate solution, sprayed from a long-legged tractor (but washed off again by the next rain). New "systemic" sprays are absorbed into the sap-stream of the plants and destroy their fungal (or insect) victim from inside the leaf or grape.

Unfortunately, fungal diseases, and such pests as red-spider mites, can rapidly develop resistance, making it necessary for manufacturers to vary the formula (at great expense). The best-known systemic fungicide, Benomyl, is now of limited use for this reason. Environmentally conscious growers now look for "pest management" schemes that seek to combat insect damage by introducing other natural predators – in Western Australia for instance, guinea fowl gobble up destructive mites.

Organic Cultivation

Wine can be grown by organic methods, just as any other crop. This cuts out artificial fertilizers, insecticides, and other sprays. Three years must pass since the vineyard was last artificially fertilized before that vineyard can be certified as "organic". Some sprays can be used – old-fashioned copper-sulphate is one. The organic logic must also be followed through into the winery. In Europe there is no such thing as organic wine, only wine that is produced from organically farmed grapes. In the United States wine may be labeled as "organic" is certain wine-making practices are renounced, notably the use of sulphur dioxide, but the results are often flawed.

Biodyamism

More exacting than organic is Biodynamic viticulture, which follows principles laid down by a guru of the 1930s, Rudolph Steiner. There is a complete viticultural calendar, which advises on the most appropriate time to treat the vines, based on the phases of the moon, among other criteria. The treatments are produced from herbs, flowers, and even dung, which are then concentrated and aged, and then employed in homeopathic doses. Compost production is also regulated to guarantee its effectiveness. Some see Biodynamism as a return to nature, others as almost a witchcraft, but what is hard to dispute is that such practices return a rich microbial life to the soil.

The system has been adopted by many first-class estates in France, California, and Australia, and with such splendid results that none can ignore it. Labour costs are high, but practitioners save on expensive and harmful chemical treatments that have, over many decades, done much damage to the health of the world's vineyards.

Making Wine

Controlling Yield

Higher quantity means lower quality. Acceptance of this golden rule is built into the appellation regulations of most European wine producing nations. In France, some areas limit the yield to 35 hectolitres per hectare (about two tons per acre) or even less, although Bordeaux is cropped at a more generous 50–60 hectolitres per hectare. *Vins de pays* are allowed to produce up to 80 hl or even more. In Italy, the limits are expressed as so many *quintals* (100kg) of grapes per hectare, with a limit on the amount of juice that may be extracted from each *quintal*. It is widely accepted that in parts of Germany and Italy, officially sanctioned yields are too high for good quality, and the best growers' associations, such as Germany's VDP, insist on far lower yields for their members.

The New World, as yet, has no regulations in this regard – which, in view of its *laissez-faire* philosophy, is not surprising. However, conscientious growers are keenly aware of the detrimental effect of too high a yield, and many, if their crop looks like being excessive, will carry out a green harvest come summer. This entails the removal of part of the potential crop so that the vine concentrates its energy on ripening what is left. Others may suggest that this upsets the natural balance of the vine, and ideally the crop should be regulated by intelligent pruning. Nonetheless, global warming and the planting of productive rootstocks and clones often oblige even the most conscientious growers to green harvest. The practice has additional advantages: the remaining bunches will ripen earlier (useful where rain or hail can occur during harvest) and the better spaced grapes will be less susceptible to rot in wet weather.

Irrigation

Irrigation used to be considered utterly incompatible with quality wine. But such important regions as Argentina, Chile, Washington State, and large parts of Australia could not grow grapes at all without it. No one can deny the quality of their best wines. Once again, it is a question of understanding the metabolism of the vine and using intelligence and moderation. Computerized weather stations within the vineyards give producers highly detailed data. Modern viticulturists can use techniques such as neutron probes and "pressure bombs" to ensure the vines receive the right amount of water at the right time. Sensible irrigation can give better results than the natural but random downpours of rain that are the sole recourse in regions where the practice is forbidden.

Mechanical Harvesting

A machine for picking grapes, saving the stiff backs (and high wages) of the tens of thousands who turn out to the harvest each year, only became a reality in the 1960s (in New York State, picking Concord grapes). By the 1980s, machines harvested a third of all America's wine grapes, and the percentage is now

higher still. The mechanical harvester has gained wide acceptance in big vineyards, though some quality areas still resist, especially where steep terrain makes the use of a machine impractical. The machine works by straddling the vine row and violently shaking the trunks, while slapping at the extremities of the vine with flexible paddles or striker bars. The grapes fall onto a conveyor belt, which carries them to a chute above the vine tops. Here they pass in front of a fan, which blows away any loose leaves, and the grapes are then shot into a hopper towed by a tractor. In many cases, the hopper leads straight to a crusher, and the crusher to a closed tank, so that the grapes leave the vineyard already crushed, sheltered from sunlight and insects, and dosed with sulphur dioxide (SO_2) to prevent oxidation.

The harvester has many advantages. Firstly, it can operate at night, when the grapes are cool, and secondly, it needs only two operators. Whereas a traditional team may have to start while some grapes are still unripe, and finish when some are overripe, the machine works fast enough to pick a whole vineyard at ideal maturity. The harvesting rate in California is up to 150 tons (or up to about 16 hectares) a day. The disadvantages of the harvester include the need for especially robust trellising, the loss of perhaps ten per cent of the crop, and the slight risk of including leaves, insects, and other unwanted matter in the crush. In addition, skin contact is inevitable, and for this reason machines are not permitted in Champagne, or in Beaujolais, where whole bunches are essential to the vinification process.

Botrytis Infection

The benevolent aspect of the fungus mould *Botrytis cinerea*, as the noble rot that produces great sweet wines, receives so much publicity that its malevolent appearance in the vineyard at the wrong time (when it gets the less romantic name of grey rot) can be forgotten. In some regions its prevalence has made it the most serious and widespread disease the grower has to confront. The more fertile the vineyard and luxuriant the vine, the more likely it is to strike at the unripe or (most vulnerable) semi-ripe grapes and rot the bunch. It starts by attacking grapes punctured by insects or grape worm; controlling the bugs is therefore the most effective protection. Some growers use modern sprays to deter the onset of botrytis; others oppose the practice. Only when the sugar content in the grapes has reached about 70° Oechsle or 17° Brix (enough to make wine of about nine per cent natural alcohol) does evil rot become noble rot (see page 75). Some New World regions have experimented with inducing botrytis infection artificially by spraying spores onto the vineyards. Results are inconclusive, though some good sweet wines have been produced by this method.

Sugar & Acid Levels

The crucial decision of when to pick the grapes depends on the measurement of their sugar and acid contents. As they ripen,

Machine harvesting of Sauvignon Blanc grapes in vineyard of Cloudy Bay, Marlborough, New Zealand

sugar increases and acid decreases. For each type of wine there is an ideal moment when the ratio is just right. Ripening starts at the moment called *véraison*, when the grape, which has been growing slowly by cell division, still hard and bright green, grows rapidly by the enlargement of each cell. This is when red grapes begin to change colour.

Sugar content is usually measured with a handheld refractometer. A drop of juice is held between two prisms. Light passing through it bends at a different angle according to its sugar content; the angle is read off on a scale calibrated as degrees Brix, Oechsle, or Baumé; the American, German, and French systems, respectively, for measuring ripeness.

In warm weather, sugar content may increase by up to 0.4° Brix a day, while there may be a significant drop in acidity. "Ripe" grapes vary between about 18 and 26 degrees Brix (ie. with a potential alcohol level of 9.3–14 degrees). Different levels of acidity are considered ideal for different styles of wine. In Germany, acid levels as high as 0.9 per cent would be commendable for a wine of 11.3 degrees of potential alcohol (90 degrees Oechsle). In France or California, the recommended acidity level for grapes with the same sugar content would be approximately 0.7 per cent for white wine and slightly lower for red. One risk in hotter regions is rapidly rising sugar levels, which induce growers to pick before the whole grape is fully mature, resulting in harsh, green, tannic flavours. The trick is to achieve phenolic ripeness (ie. ripe seeds and tannins) before sugar levels become so high that hot, over-alcoholic wines result. It is easier said than done.

The third variable taken into account is the pH of the juice. This is a measure of the strength, rather than volume, of its acidity. The lower the figure, the sharper the juice. Normal pH in wine is in the range 2.8–3.8. Low pH readings are desirable for stability and (in red wines) good colour. The modern trend to pick overripe grapes can result in red wines with a pH little short of 4.0, which can threaten the stability and longevity of the wine. This is often the case with Californian reds; Australians, growing grapes in equally hot regions, avoid the risk by adding acidity during fermentation, a technique that also draws criticism. There are no easy answers, other than to pick grapes at optimal rather than excessive maturity. Although scientific measurements can be invaluable aids in deciding when to pick, many growers cling to the time-honoured method of sampling the grapes throughout the vineyard, relying on taste above all.

Handling the Fruit

A good winemaker will not accept grapes that have been badly damaged on the way from the vineyard, or with a high proportion of mouldy bunches, or what the Californians call MOG (matter other than grapes, eg. leaves, stones, and soil). For winemaking at the highest standard the bunches are picked over by hand – *triage* – and rotten grapes thrown out. Some producers do this in the vineyard, but most have conveyor belts at the winery, where a team of sharp-eyed workers can spot and remove unworthy fruit. With large quantities, a degree of imperfection must be accepted. Several regions of Europe specify the size and design of container that must be used for

bringing in the grapes. The object here is to prevent the weight of large quantities from crushing the grapes at the bottom. The huge "gondolas" often used for transporting grapes in industrial-scale vineyards, frequently under a hot sun, have the drawback in that many of the grapes at the bottom will be broken and macerating in juice long before they even reach the hygienic conditions of the winery.

Sulphur Dioxide

The first step in winemaking procedures is usually the addition of a small dose of sulphur dioxide (SO_2) to the crushed grapes, or must. Nothing has supplanted this universal and age-old antiseptic of the winemaker in protecting the must from premature or wild fermentation, and both must and wine from oxidation, though some winemakers use very little and strive to use none – putting instead inert gases between the juice or wine and the oxygen in the atmosphere.

The amount of SO_2 allowed is regulated by law. Wine with too much has a sharp, brimstone smell and leaves a burning feeling in the throat – a common occurrence in the past, particularly in semi-sweet wines where sulphur was used to prevent refermentation in the bottle. Sterile filters have now eliminated the need for this, and the consumer should be unaware that wine's old preservative is used at all. Some people may suffer ill-effects from SO_2: hence the USA regulation that labels state "contains sulfites". Sweet wines need higher levels of SO_2 at bottling than dry ones, and wines made using botrytis much higher levels, since sulphur combines with their high concentration of dry extract, and it is only free, or unbound, sulphur that is effective in preventing refermentation.

White Wine: Skin Contact?

Light, fresh, and fruity white wines are made by pressing the grapes as soon as possible after picking. The aim is to prevent the juice from picking up any flavours ("extract") from the skin. The grapes are crushed, just hard enough to break their skins. This pomace is loaded into the press. In wineries looking for maximum freshness, the juice or the grapes may be chilled.

Many bigger wineries now use a de-juicer between the crusher and the press. This may consist of a mesh screen, sometimes in the form of a conveyor belt, through which the free juice falls. A de-juicer reduces the number of times the press has to be laboriously filled and emptied, but it increases the chance of oxidation of the juice. One de-juicer that avoids oxidation is a stainless-steel tank with a central cylinder formed of a mesh screen. The crushed pomace is loaded into the space around this cylinder and carbon dioxide (CO_2) is pumped under pressure into the headspace. The free juice is gently forced to drain out via the central cylinder, leaving relatively little pomace to be pressed. Up to 70 per cent can be free-run juice, leaving only 30 per cent to be extracted by pressing.

Fuller, more robust wines with more flavour and tannins to preserve them while they age, are made by holding the skins in contact with the juice in a tank for up to 24 hours after crushing. This maceration (at low temperature, before fermentation starts) extracts some of the elements that are present in the

Muscadet grapes in the press, Clisson, Loire-Atlantique, France

skins but not the juice. The pomace is then de-juiced and pressed as usual. Skin contact has fallen from fashion, since it is only beneficial when the grapes are in perfect health. Modern winemakers worry that skin contact can impart a phenolic or tannic flavour and texture to a wine, diminishing its freshness.

White Wine: Stems or No Stems

White grapes are usually pressed with their stems, unless they are machine harvested. The reason is that unfermented grape flesh and juice are full of pectins and sugar, making them slippery and sticky. The stems make the operation of the press easier, particularly when it comes to breaking up the "cake" to press a second time. The press should not be used at a high enough pressure to squeeze any bitter juice out of stems or pips. Many top-quality wines are now being made by whole-bunch pressing, with no crushing or destemming. The technique helps to retain aroma and maintain a low pH.

Types of Press

There is a wide choice of types of press, ranging from the old-fashioned vertical (or hydraulic or basket) model, in which a plate is forced down onto the pomace contained in a cylindrical cage of vertical slots, to the mass-production continuous press. The first is the most labour intensive, but still produces the clearest juice; the second is very cheap and easy to run, but cannot make better than medium grade wine.

Until the 1980s, many wineries chose a horizontal press, which works on a principle similar to the old vertical press, squeezing the pomace by means of plates that are brought together by a central screw. However, the quality of the juice is inferior and most quality-conscious wineries have now invested in a "bladder" or pneumatic press. This contains a long rubber balloon which, when inflated, squeezes the pomace against the surrounding fine grille. Both are batch presses, meaning that they have to be filled and emptied anew for each batch of pomace, whereas the continuous press spews forth an unending stream of juice below, and a cake of pomace at the end.

White Wine: Cold Fermentation

The most revolutionary invention in modern winemaking is controlled-temperature fermentation, particularly for white wines, which used to be flat and low in acid, in warm climates. What was done naturally by using small barrels in the cold cellars of Europe is now practised industrially in California, Australia, and elsewhere by chilling the contents of often huge, stainless steel vats. Most vats are double-skinned or jacketed, with a layer of glycol or ammonia as a cooling agent between the skins. Another technique is to dribble cold water down the outside surface. A second-best method is to circulate the wine through a heat exchanger (or a coil submerged in cold water) outside the vat.

Each winemaker has their own idea about the ideal temperature for fermentation. Long, cool fermentation draws out the primary fruit in a wine, though when practised to extremes on certain grapes – particularly non-aromatic sorts – it seems to

leave its mark on the wine as a "pear drop" smell. A number of modern Italian white wines, and even occasionally red ones, are spoilt by overenthusiastic refrigeration. If the temperature is forced down too far, the fermentation will "stick" and the yeasts cease to function. It can be difficult to start again, and the wine will almost certainly suffer in the process.

A completely different approach is used to make big, richer, smoother, and more heavy-bodied wines, from Chardonnay and sometimes Sauvignon Blanc. They are fermented at between 15°–20°C (59°–68°F), or, in barrels, even as high as 25°C (77°F). However, the small volumes in a wooden barrel mean that temperatures will never rise to excessive levels.

White Wine: Clarifying the Juice

Modern presses are more efficient than old models but often produce juice with a higher proportion of suspended solids (pieces of grape skins, flesh, pips, or dirt). Fermentation of white wine with these solids tends to produce bitterness, so the juice must be cleaned first. This can be done by holding it for a day or more in a settling tank, at a cool temperature, allowing particles to sink to the bottom; by filtering through a powerful vacuum filter; or (fastest) by use of a centrifuge pump, which uses centrifugal force to throw out all foreign bodies. Overcentrifuged wine can be stripped of desirable as well as undesirable constituents; great care is needed, and many wineries once equipped with the technology have abandoned it.

White Wine: Adjusting Acidity

Either de- or re-acidification of white wine must be necessary, depending on the ripeness of the crop. Overacid juice is de-acidified by adding calcium carbonate (chalk) to remove tartaric acid, or a substance called Acidex, which removes malic acid as well by double-salt precipitation. In Germany, the addition of sugar and (up to 15 per cent) water to wines of QbA level (see page 243) and below naturally lowers the proportion of acidity. In France, *chaptalization* with dry sugar (permitted in the centre and north) has the same effect to a lesser degree. In the south of France, however, only concentrated must, not sugar, is allowed for raising the alcoholic degree; it naturally raises the acid level at the same time. In Australia and other warm countries where the usual problem is too little acid, it is permitted to add one of the acids that naturally occur in grapes: malic, citric, and tartaric. Tartaric is preferred, since it has no detectable flavour and also helps towards tartrate stability (see Cold Stabilization, page 28). But it is more expensive.

Tanks & Vats

The grandeur of traditional fermenting vats of oak (or sometimes chestnut, acacia, or redwood) is accompanied by many disadvantages. Most important are the problems of disinfecting them and keeping them watertight between vintages.

Early in the twentieth century, concrete began to replace them in newer and bigger wineries. It is strong, permanent, and easy to clean. Moreover, it can be made in any shape to fit odd corners and save space. Although considered obsolete after the installation of stainless-steel vats in recent decades, winemakers are coming to respect the advantages of concrete, in which the wine is never subjected to extremes of temperature. In 2003, a new winery, kitted out with new concrete tanks, opened in Argentina, and some new Bordeaux wineries have also invested in this once despised medium.

Nonetheless, in almost all modern wineries, stainless steel is the king. It is strong, inert, simple to clean and to cool. Moreover, it is also extremely versatile; the same tank can be used for fermentation and, later in the year, for storage, ageing, or blending. Its high initial cost is thus quite quickly recouped.

To make good wine, a winery must have ample capacity. It often happens that in an abundant vintage there is a shortage of space. Grapes cannot be stored, so the only answer is to cut short the fermenting time of the early batches. With red wines this will mean shorter maceration and thus lighter wine. Well-designed wineries not only have plenty of tank space, they have tanks in a variety of sizes to avoid leaving small lots of wine in half-full containers or being obliged to mix them.

Wooden fermenters are also making a comeback. Mondavi installed them, at great expense, in its new winery. They are expensive to maintain, but purists insist they are still the ideal medium for prolonged, even fermentation. It has become a common sight, even in hi-tech wineries, to see some wooden vats reserved for the finest lots.

Yeasts

There are yeasts naturally present in every vineyard and winery, which will cause fermentation if they are allowed to. Some consider them part of the stamp, or personality, of their locality, and believe they help to give their wine its individuality. Indeed, an experiment in swapping the yeasts of different Bordeaux château showed how distinct each strain was: Graves could be made to resemble Pauillac. Many of the largest modern wineries, wanting to keep total control, take care to remove the natural yeast (by filtering or centrifuging), or at least to render it helpless with a strong dose of SO_2. Some even flash-pasteurize the juice by heating it to 55°C (131°F) to kill off bacteria and inhibit the wild yeasts. They then proceed to inoculate the must with a cultured yeast of their choice, which is known to multiply actively at the temperature they choose for fermentation. Some of the most popular yeasts in California go by the promising names of "Montrachet", "Champagne", and "Steinberg". The secret is to start the fermentation with a generous amount of active yeast; once the whole vat is fermenting, such problems as oxidation can temporarily be forgotten.

The activity of yeast increases rapidly with rising temperature. For each additional degree Celsius, yeast transforms ten per cent more sugar into alcohol in a given time. The ceiling to this frantic activity occurs at about 30°–35°C (86°–95°F) when the yeasts are overcome by heat. A runaway fermentation can stick at this temperature, just as most yeasts will not function below about 10°C (50°F).

There is no doubt that using cultivated yeasts is less risky than relying on natural yeasts. But there are drawbacks. The use of the same yeast for every wine can impart a uniform flavour to those wines. Moreover, some cultivated yeasts are so effective that their conversion rate of sugar into alcohol can be very high, resulting in wines with worryingly high alcohol levels. Many winemakers will allow fermentation to begin naturally but will intervene with cultivated yeasts should there be any signs that the indigenous yeasts are falling down on the job.

On a more specialized note, the use of flor yeast for producing sherry is now greatly advanced. New ways have been found to produce the sherry effect much faster and with more certainty than the traditional way of leaving the naturally occurring layer of flor floating on the wine.

White Wine: Malolactic Fermentation

Secondary or malolactic fermentation (see Red Wine: Malolactic Fermentation) is less common with white wine than with red. It is sometimes encouraged, to reduce excess acidity in wines from cool climates (eg. Chablis and other parts of Burgundy, Loire, Switzerland, but less commonly in Germany). Its complex biological nature may help to add complexity to flavours. In warmer regions where acidity tends to be low, malolactic fermentation in white wines is often avoided.

White Wine: Residual Sugar

A completed natural fermentation makes a totally dry wine, all its sugar converted to alcohol. The only exceptions are wines made of grapes so sweet that either the alcohol level or the sugar, or both, prevents the yeasts from functioning. To make light, sweet wines, either the fermentation has to be artificially interrupted or sweet juice has to be blended with dry wine. The former was the old way. It needed a strong dose of SO_2 to stop the fermentation, and more in the bottle to prevent it starting again. The invention of filters fine enough to remove all yeasts, and means of bottling in conditions of complete sterility, now solve the sulphur problem.

Some winemakers in Germany used to prefer a different method: blending with "sweet reserve". The method used is to sterilize a portion of the juice instead of fermenting it. The majority of the wine is made in the normal way, fermented until no sugar is left. The sweet reserve (in German, *süssreserve*) is then added to taste, and the blend bottled under sterile conditions. The addition of unfermented juice naturally lowers the alcohol content of the wine. At top estates in Germany, *Süssreserve* is no longer used. Instead, wines are allowed to cease fermentation naturally, with varying degrees of residual sugar, and different lots are then blended to produce the best balanced wine. Although it is fashionable to prefer dry wines to sweet, many consumers would be surprised to know that many so-called dry wines, such as a large number of New World Chardonnays, contain a small amount of residual sugar. The sweetness may not be discernible, but adds roundness and texture to the wine.

White Wine: After Fermentation

After white wine has fermented, it must be clarified. The traditional method was to allow it to settle and then rack it off its lees (composed largely of dead yeast cells). When Muscadet is bottled *sur lie* this is exactly what is happening. Modern wineries, however, tend to use a filter, if necessary with the additional precaution of fining with a powdery clay from Wyoming called bentonite, which removes excess proteins: potential causes of later trouble in the form of cloudy wine. Bentonite fining is also sometimes used before fermentation.

White wines not intended for ageing (ie. most light commercial wines) then need only to be stabilized and filtered before they can be bottled. Those intended for ageing are usually transferred into barrel for clarification, so that they enjoy the same benefits of barrel ageing as red wines. They may be left for several months on the fine lees, which may be regularly stirred up, in a process called *bâtonnage*, so that the wine benefits from the effects of yeast autolysis, whereby the lees, including dead yeast, impart extra complexity to the flavour.

White Wine: Cold Stabilization

Tartaric acid, which is a vital ingredient in the balance and flavour of all wines, has an unfortunate habit of forming crystals in combination with either potassium (quite big sugary grains) or calcium (finer and whiter, powdery crystals). In former times, wine was kept for several years in cool cellars, and these crystals formed a hard deposit on the walls of their casks, known in Germany as *weinstein* – "wine stone". With faster, modern methods, most large wineries consider it essential to prevent the crystals forming after the wine is bottled. Although the crystals have no flavour at all, and are totally natural and harmless, there are ignorant and querulous customers who will send back a bottle with any sign of deposit.

Unfortunately, it is a costly business to remove the risk of tartrate crystals. The simplest way is to chill the wine to just above freezing point in a tank for several days. The process is accelerated by seeding with added tartrate crystals to act as nuclei for more crystals to form. More efficient ways of achieving this strictly unnecessary object will keep research chemists busy for years to come.

Red Wine: Stems or No Stems

Each red winemaker has his own view about whether the grape stems should be included, wholly or in part – and it changes with the vintage. In the Rhône, the stems are sometimes included; in Burgundy rarely; in Bordeaux few or none; in Chinon on the Loire, the stems are left on the vine. Outside Europe, stems are usually excluded. However, a vogue has developed for partial or total "whole-bunch fermentation" of Pinot Noir, which, some believe, adds complexity to the wine.

The argument for destemming is that stalks add astringency, lower the alcohol content, reduce the colour, and take up valuable space in the vat. The argument for keeping some of them in is that they help the process of fermentation by aerating the mass, they lower the acidity, and they make pressing easier. In any case, the stems must be thoroughly ripe, or they will add green flavours to the wine.

Must Concentration

In the late 1980s, French oenologists developed systems for removing water from grapes harvested in wet conditions. The most popular technology was reverse osmosis. Its careful use could eliminate the dilution that water, on or beneath the skins, could cause. It could also increase the potential alcohol of the concentrated must, so European authorities would not allow concentrated must to be *chaptalized*. Must concentrators are now clearly part of the standard equipment at many wineries.

The technique remains controversial, as it is open to abuse. It can encourage lazy growers to pick too early or during wet spells, on the grounds that they can then correct any deficiencies by concentration. This reasoning is flawed, since the technology concentrates all components in the wine, and any unripe flavours would only be augmented. But used with care and discretion, must concentration can be a positive development in improving overall wine quality in difficult vintages.

Red Wine: Pumping Over

When a vat of red wine ferments, the grape skins float to the surface, buoyed up by bubbles of CO_2 that attach themselves to solid matter. The "cap" (French, *chapeau*, Spanish, *sombrero*) that they form contains all the essential colouring matter – and is prone to overheating and being attacked by bacteria. It is therefore essential to keep mixing the cap back into the liquid below. There are several methods.

In Bordeaux, the cap is often pushed under by men with long poles. In Burgundy, with smaller vats, it is trodden under (*pigeage*) by men, formerly naked, who jump into the vat. Another widespread method is to fit a grille below the filling level, which holds the cap immersed (*chapeau immergé*). Mechanical plungers are also used. But the most widespread method now used is "pumping over": taking wine by a hose from the bottom of the vat and spraying it over the cap, usually several times a day.

Several ingenious alternatives have been invented. The Rototank is a closed horizontal cylinder that slowly rotates, continually mixing the liquids and solids inside. Its advantage is speed of extraction, but most quality-conscious winemakers prefer a slower fermentation with frequent pumping-over. An automatic system developed in Portugal, where the traditional way of extracting the colour was night-long stomping by all the village lads to the sound of accordions, involves an ingenious gusher device activated by the build-up of CO_2 pressure in a sealed tank.

Dealing with the cap is a crucial part of the winemaking process. It is important to extract the colour, tannin, and flavour that will give the wine its individuality; it is equally important to avoid extracting more than the grapes are able to yield. Overextraction can give bitter, tough wines; under-extraction will result in a lack of colour, stuffing, and structure. That is why many winemakers opt for a variety of techniques to ensure the degree of extraction is exactly right for the grapes.

Micro-oxygenation

This controversial technique was developed in Madiran in the late 1980s by wine producer Patrick Ducournau. Madiran wine is produced from the notoriously tannic Tannat grape, and the technique was aimed at softening those tannins by introducing a controlled dose of oxygen during fermentation and/or during the ageing process in barrels. There seems no doubt that the technique works, and that its use can greatly subdue harsh tannins and unripe flavours. Micro-oxygenation has become a useful weapon in the armoury of industrial winemakers.

However, it is also widely used at some of the top properties in Bordeaux and elsewhere. The idea of dosing the wine during barrel maturation is to lessen the need for racking, which, the proponents of micro-oxygenation argue, is a more brutal and less controllable method of introducing oxygen into the wine. This may be so, but what is still unknown is the overall effect of the technique on the ageing potential of wines that are intended to be kept for years or decades before being drunk.

Red Wine: Pressing

By the time fermentation is finished, or nearly finished and merely simmering slightly, most (up to 85 per cent) of the red wine is separated from the solid matter and will run freely from the vat. This free run wine, or *vin de goutte*, is siphoned out of the vat into either barrels or another tank. The remaining *marc* is pressed. Red wine is pressed in the same types of presses as white, but after fermentation the pulp and skins have partly disintegrated and offer less resistance.

Relatively gentle pressure will release very good quality *vin de presse*, which is richer in desirable extracts and flavours than the *vin de goutte*. It might need such treatment as fining, to reduce astringency and remove solids, but in most cases it will be a positive addition and make better wine for longer keeping. Wine from a second, more vigorous, pressing will almost always be too astringent, and will be sold separately, or used in a cheap blend. The amount of press wine blended into the free run will vary from vintage to vintage, and be affected by the stylistic preference of the winemaker.

The Value of Barrels

The development of winemaking in the New World, with its more questioning approach, has drawn attention to what has long been known, but taken for granted: that new barrels have a profound effect on the flavour of wine stored in them – and even more on wine fermented in them. California Chardonnays, fermented in the same French oak as white burgundy, can have an uncanny resemblance to its flavour. Barrels were invented (probably by the Gauls) of necessity as the most durable and transportable of containers, supplanting the amphora and the goatskin in regions that could afford them. They have developed to their standard sizes and shapes over centuries of experience. The 200-odd-litre barrels of Bordeaux, Burgundy, and Rioja are the largest that one man can easily roll or two men carry – but they also happen to present the greatest surface area of wood to wine of any practicable size.

The advantages of this contact lie partly in the very slow transfer of oxygen through the planks of the barrel, and partly through the tannin and other substances that the wine dissolves from the wood itself. The most easily identified (by taste or smell) of these is vanillin, which has the flavour of vanilla. Oak tannin is useful in augmenting and slightly varying the tannins naturally present in wine as preservatives. Other scents and flavours are harder to define, but can be well-enough expressed as the "smell of a carpenter's shop". Which wines benefit from this addition of extraneous flavours? Only those with strong characters and constitutions of their own. It would be disastrous to a fragile Mosel or a Beaujolais Nouveau. The bigger the wine and the longer it is to be matured, the more oak it can take.

New barrels are extremely expensive and add significantly to the final cost, and price, of a wine. The full impact of their oak flavour diminishes rapidly after the first two or three years' use, but there is a lively trade in secondhand barrels, particularly those that have contained great wines. Barrels can also be renewed to full pungency by shaving the wine-leached interior down to fresh wood. A cheap but effective way of adding oak flavour to wine is to use oak chips or staves. These are still strictly forbidden in France – and indeed, considered shocking – but chips are widely accepted in the New World for cheaper wines, and it seems only a matter of time before commercial pressure sees their adoption in France, too. Chips vary in size from sawdust granules to matchsticks, and must be properly seasoned to avoid any harsh flavours. Winemakers must

Oak barrels such as these in Italy are making a comeback

calculate how much they need, according to the volume of the wine and the desired degree of oakiness, and the chips are added to the wine in a muslin bag. Properly used, they are very effective in flavouring both Chardonnay and red wine for those who like the extraneous flavour of oak (I don't). The use of toasted wooden staves introduced into the fermentation tank is a better if still questionable method.

A quite different role is played by the huge permanent oak barrels (*foudres*, or *demi-muids* in French, *fuders* or *stücks* in German), which are common in southern France, Alsace, Germany, Italy, Spain, and eastern Europe. Their oak flavour has been minimized or neutralized by constant impregnation with wine, and often by a thick layer of tartrate crystals. Their value seems to lie in offering an ideal environment, with very gradual oxidation, for the maturing and slow stabilizing of wine. Before the advent of sterile bottling, an oak vat was simply the safest place for a grower to store wine, sometimes for years, topped up with fresh wine as necessary.

Cooperage has become something of a fetish. Winemakers frequently compare the same wine aged in oak from different French forests, even from the same forest but different barrel makers. The names of Demptos and Nadalié of Bordeaux, of Taransaud and Séguin-Moreau of Cognac, and François Frères and the Tonnelleries de Bourgogne of Burgundy are just as familiar in the Napa Valley as in France. (Seventy per cent of all French barrels are exported.) Current opinion seems to be that the tighter-grained oaks of the forests of the Massif Central, Tronçais, Allier, and Nevers, and from the Vosges, provide the most refined flavours for both red and white wines. American white oak, uncharred, Bourbon barrels are also used. They offer less flavour and tannin but a higher tannin:flavour ratio – good for Cabernet and Zinfandel, less so for white wines. American oak is significantly cheaper than French oak, which has encouraged some French coopers to establish cooperages in California, where they use French methods to treat American oak, with some success.

Baltic, Balkan, and other oaks are also used, and much has been written about their relative merits. Since there is no visual difference, and a cooper's shop contains oak from many sources, one may well be sceptical about such fine distinctions in any case. Other factors, such as the thickness of the staves, whether they have been split or sawn, air-dried or kiln-dried, steamed or "toasted" with varying degrees of toasting, even whether the barrel is washed in hot water or cold, can all start arguments among the initiated. Consequently, some people place more emphasis on the type of oak, while others attach more importance to the individual cooper.

Red Wine: Carbonic Maceration

The technique of fermenting uncrushed grapes, known as *macération carbonique*, has been developed in France since 1935 by Professor Michel Flanzy and others. The method is described on pages 142–43. It began to make a real impact in the early 1970s in dramatically improving the quality of the better Midi wines, especially from intrinsically tough grape varieties such as Carignan. It is now well-established in France as the best way to produce fruity, supple, richly coloured reds

for drinking young, but its acceptance has been surprisingly slow in other countries. Low acidity tends to make such wines short lived, which is inappropriate for the finest growths. But a proportion can be a valuable element in a blend with a particularly tannic and/or acidic red component.

Racking

Once the lees, or sediment, in a barrel or vat have sunk to the bottom, the wine is racked off them simply by pouring the clear liquid from a tap above the level of the solids. In wines that are kept over a length of time in barrels, racking is repeated every few months, as more solids are precipitated. The most traditional Rioja cellars sometimes rack a wine again and again for years on end. If the wine is judged to need more oxygen, racking is done via an open basin; if not, it is done by a hose linking one barrel directly to another.

Red Wine: Malolactic Fermentation

Growers have always been aware of a fresh activity in their barrels of new wine in the spring following the vintage. Folklore put it down to a natural sympathy between the wine and the rising sap in the vineyards. It seemed to be a further fermentation, but it happened in wine that had no sugar left to ferment.

It is a form of fermentation carried on by bacteria, not yeasts, which are feeding on malic ("apple") acid in the wine and converting it to lactic ("milk") acid, giving off CO_2 bubbles in the process. It has several results: a lowering of the quantity of acidity and of its sharpness (lactic acid is milder to the taste than malic); and increase of stability, and a less quantifiable smoothing and complicating of the wine's flavour. For almost all red wines, therefore, it is highly desirable, and winemakers take steps to make sure that it takes place.

In most cases, a gentle raising of the temperature in the cellar to about 20°C (68°F) is sufficient. Sometimes it is necessary to import the right bacteria, and it is now possible to seed the malolactic fermentation artificially. Sometimes, the malolactic fermentation can be encouraged to happen concurrently with the first (alcoholic) fermentation.

Blending for Complexity

Champagne, red and white Bordeaux, southern Rhône reds, Chianti, Rioja, and port, are all examples of wines made, more often than not, of a mixture of grapes. Burgundy, Barolo, sherry, German and Alsace wines are examples of one grape wines. American varietal-consciousness initially put a premium on the simplistic idea that "100 per cent is best". But recent research has shown that, even among wines of humble quality, a mixture of two is often better than the lesser of the two, and generally better than either. This is taken to prove that complexity is in itself a desirable quality in wine; that one variety can season another, as butter and salt do eggs.

There is a general trend in Bordeaux-admiring regions, such as California and Tuscany, towards claret-style blending of Merlot and other varieties with Cabernet. On the other hand, no other grape has been shown to improve Pinot Noir,

Chardonnay, or Riesling. Added complexity in their already delicious flavours either comes with the help of barrel ageing, in Riesling with noble rot, or simply with years in bottle.

Fining

The ancient technique of pouring whipped egg whites, gelatin, isinglass (fish gelatin), blood, or other coagulants into wine is still widely used both on must and finished wine, despite modern filtration systems. Its object is to clean the liquid of the finest suspended solids (which are too light to sink) and to reduce excessively high tannins. The fining agent, poured onto the surface, slowly sinks like a superfine screen, carrying any solids to the bottom. Certain finings such as bentonite (see White Wine – After Fermentation, pages 27–8) are specific to certain undesirable constituents. "Blue" fining (potassium ferrocyanide) removes excess iron from the wine.

Filtration

German and Italian companies have been enthusiastically developing ever finer and finer filters capable of removing almost everything, even the flavour, from wine if they are not used with discretion. Most filters consist of a series of pads alternating with plates, through which the wine is forced under pressure. The degree of filtration depends on the pore size of the pads. At 0.65 microns they remove yeast, at 0.45 bacteria as well. To avoid having to change them frequently, wine is nearly always clarified by such other means as fining, before filtration.

Wine critics such as Robert Parker have been adamantly opposed to routine filtration. He is right to the extent that if the wine, especially red wine, is sufficiently clarified after lengthy barrel ageing, then filtration is hardly necessary and can only detract from the quality of the wine. However, "unfiltered" has become a mantra, and some wines that ought to be lightly filtered, such as white wines in which the lees remain in suspension, are bottled without intervention. The result is a cloudy white wine that is biologically unstable – and this does the consumer no favours. To filter or not to filter should be a pragmatic, not a dogmatic, decision.

Pasteurization

Louis Pasteur, the great French chemist of the late nineteenth century who discovered the relationship of oxygen to wine, and hence the cause of vinegar, gave his name to the process of sterilization by heating to kill off harmful organisms. In wine, this means any yeast and bacteria that might start it re-fermenting. A temperature of 60°C (140°F) for about 30 minutes is needed – although an alternative preferred today (for bulk wine only) is flash pasteurization at a much higher temperature – 85°C (185°F) – for up to one minute.

Normally, pasteurization is used only on cheap wines not intended to mature further, although there is evidence that it does not permanently inhibit further development. Modern sterile handling and filtration is steadily phasing out pasteurization from modern wineries.

Ageing

There are two separate and distinct ways in which wine can age: oxidative ageing in contact with oxygen, and reductive ageing, when the oxygen supply is cut off. Barrel ageing is oxidative; it encourages numerous complex reactions between the acids, sugars, tannins, pigments, and multifarious polysyllabic constituents of wine.

Bottle ageing is reductive. Once the wine is bottled, the only oxygen available is the limited amount dissolved in the liquid or trapped between the liquid and the cork. In wines with a high CO_2 content (eg. Champagne) there is not even this much oxygen. Life-forms depending on oxygen are therefore very limited in their scope for activity. "Reductive" means that the oxygen is reduced – eventually to zero. In these conditions different complex reactions between the same constituents occur at a much slower rate.

The ultimate quality and complexity in most wines is arrived at only by a combination of these two forms of ageing, though the proportions of each can vary widely. Many white wines are bottled very young, but improve enormously in bottle. Champagne and vintage port are matured almost entirely in bottle. Fine red wines might spend up to three years in barrel, and then perhaps two or three times as long in bottle. Tawny port and sherry are matured entirely in barrel, and are not normally intended for any further bottle-age.

Closures

The traditional way of sealing a bottle has always been with a cork. The closure it achieves is just about perfect, permitting age-worthy wines to mature in bottle over years or even decades. Unfortunately, many corks do come impregnated with a taint known as TCA (trichloroanisole), which can either render the wine entirely undrinkable or, at best, mute its aromas and flavours. Whether TCA is the consequence of chance or negligence is hotly debated, and cannot be resolved here.

However, the high incidence of TCA has led to experimentation with alternative closures such as crown caps, plastic "corks", and screwcaps. The latter have been adopted with enthusiasm by Australian Riesling producers and producers of the majority of wines in New Zealand. Comparative tastings of the same wine bottled with various closures seem to confirm that screwcaps (also known as Stelvin closures) work best. What is uncertain is how such closures will affect the long-term development of great red wines, such as burgundy and Bordeaux.

Bottling

The question of where, and by whom, wine should be bottled has always been much debated, but since the introduction in France of the mobile bottling unit in the 1960s, it has become the rule, rather than the exception, for producers even on a small scale to bottle their own wine. The bottling unit is simply a lorry equipped as a modern semi-automatic bottling plant. Its arrival meant that the evocative words *mis en bouteille au château* or *au domaine*, widely supposed (especially in America) to be a guarantee of authenticity and even quality, could be used by all the little properties that used to rely on merchants to bottle for them. The change rubbed both ways: some merchants' names were a guarantee of well-chosen, well-handled wine; others were not.

Modern automatic bottling lines can be like a cross between an operating theatre and a space shuttle, with airlock doors for total antiseptic sterility. The wine is often "sparged", or flushed out with CO_2 or an inert gas such as nitrogen, to remove any oxygen. The bottle is first filled with nitrogen, and the wine filled into it through a long nozzle to the bottom, pushing out the gas as the level rises. The cost (both to the purse and the environment) of transporting so much glass between continents may well lead to more shipping in bulk and bottling in the market-place in future, at least for everyday wines.

Many light white, rosé, and occasionally red wines benefit greatly from being bottled with a small degree of CO_2 dissolved in them – just enough for a few faint bubbles to appear at the brim or the bottom of the glass. In many wines, this is a natural occurrence. In others, it is an easy and effective way of giving a slight prickle of refreshing sharpness to wines that would otherwise be dull, soft, and/or neutral.

Cooperatives

Arguably the most important development for the majority of winemakers in Europe has been the rise of the cooperative movement. By pooling resources and qualifying for generous government grants and loans, the peasant wine-farmers of the past are now nearly all grape-growers who deliver their whole harvest to a well-equipped central winery. Most are now up-to-date, with vats, presses, and bottling lines far better than the district would otherwise have, and a qualified oenologist.

A few are outright leaders in their regions; nobody else can afford such investment. It is hard to fault the quality of the wines from the cooperatives in Chablis, St-Emilion, and many villages in the Alto Adige. Nearly all use premiums to encourage farmers to produce riper, healthier, cleaner grapes and charge fines for rot, leaves, and soil in the crop.

However, cooperatives are run for, and sometimes by, their members, who can be stubbornly conservative in their refusal to adapt their vineyards to the requirements of the market. In the absence of firm management, some cooperatives, especially in regions such as the Languedoc, still allow their members to produce vast quantities of overcropped and unsaleable wine.

Flying Winemakers

The trend for what are now called "flying winemakers" first began among the co-ops of southern France and Italy, which have greatly benefited from an input of New World technology and know-how, particularly concerning hygiene and temperature control. The concept (and the term) were invented by the pioneering English wine merchant, Tony Laithwaite.

Many of the young graduates in Australia begin their wine-making experience by clocking up as many vintages as possible on both sides of the world. Central and Eastern Europe, in particular, have benefited from their input. Often the graduates are employed by established flying winemakers (among them Kym Milne and Jacques Lurton) to produce a specific wine for a specific customer, more often than not for a British supermarket. There is disquiet that some flying winemakers will simply impose a formula, thus standardizing the wines, but this risk has been overstated. The wines will reflect the quality and character of the grapes from which they are made – however perfect the technology.

Chemical Analysis

Whoever coined the phrase "a chemical symphony" described wine perfectly. (There are, of course, string quartets, too.) Good wine gets its infinitely intriguing flavour from the interweaving of innumerable organic and inorganic substances, in amounts so small that they have hitherto been untraceable. But this is no longer the case. A gas chromatograph is an instrument capable of identifying and measuring up to 250 different substances in wine so far. It (and similar instruments) can produce a graphic chemical profile. University of California researchers are playing the fascinating computer game of trying to match the sensory (eg. smell and taste) perception of teams of tasters with the drawings of the chromatograph to discover which substance is responsible for which taste – the idea presumably being that once we know, vineyards and grapes will become obsolete.

At a more humdrum level, it is normal to do simple laboratory checks on about 20 constituents, from alcohol and acidity to sugar and sulphur, before giving any wine a clean bill of health. Technical advances have allowed wineries to invest in ever more efficacious instruments that can analyse wines and ensure, in theory, that nothing that is faulty or questionable is allowed onto the bottling line.

The Critical Audience

A catalogue of the influences and advances in modern wine would be one-sided without a mention of the consumer. At least as striking as the technological changes of the past 25 years has been the snowballing interest in wine. This snowballing began in Britain, but has spread rapidly throughout the world. Countries as diverse as Canada, Sweden, and Korea have a choice of wine magazines, access to tastings and winemaker dinners, and wine tourism companies that bring consumers to the source. The spirit of rivalry and the friendly confrontation between producer and consumer might be the most important driving force of all. We are all the beneficiaries.

Wine Styles

Wine is simply fermented grape juice. The basic stages in making white and red wines have already been explained; variations on the main theme are explained here.

Dry White Wines

Plain dry wine of no special character, fully fermented, not intended to be aged. Usually made with non-aromatic grapes, especially in Italy, southern France, Spain, and California. Outstanding examples are Muscadet, Torrontés from Argentina, and Soave. Winemaking is standard, with increasing emphasis on freshness by excluding oxygen and fermenting cool. Fresh, fruity, dry to semi-sweet wines for drinking young are made from aromatic grape varieties: eg. Riesling, Sauvignon Blanc, Gewürztraminer, Muscat Blanc. Extreme emphasis on picking at the right moment, clean juice, cool fermentation, and early bottling. Dry but full-bodied and smooth whites are usually made with a degree of skin contact, fermented at higher temperatures, sometimes in barrels, bottled after a minimum of nine months and intended for further ageing.

Chardonnay from Burgundy is the classic, which the New World aspires to emulate. Sauvignon Blanc and Chenin Blanc are occasionally treated in this way. Some wines defy the categories: Albariño aged for many years on its lees in tanks; heady white Rhône varietals vinified in a variety of ways; unoaked but long-lived Greco di Tufo from Italy and Semillon from Hunter Valley.

Sweet White Wines

Fresh, fruity, light in alcohol, semi-sweet to sweet. Sometimes made by fermenting to dryness and "back-blending" with unfermented juice. The same style, but made by stopping fermentation while some sugar remains, usually has higher alcohol and a more winey, less obviously grapey flavour. Most French, Spanish, Italian, and many New World medium-sweet wines are found in this category. Botrytis (noble rot) wines have a balance of either low alcohol with very high sugar (German style), or very high alcohol and fairly high sugar (Sauternes style). Hungary's Tokaji Aszú lies in the middle, balancing high sugar and moderate alcohol with high acidity. Very sweet wines are made from extremely ripe or partially raisined grapes, where the sugars are concentrated by drying the grapes after harvesting. French *vin de paille*, Italian *vin santo* and *passito* wines, and many Muscats are classic examples.

Rosé Wines

Pale rosé is made from red grapes pressed immediately to extract juice with little colour, sometimes called *vin gris* ("grey wine") or *blanc de noirs* in the case of sparkling wines. Rosé with more colour is made from red grapes crushed and *saigné* (or bled), so that the juice is run off the skins after a short red wine-type maceration or vatting, then pressed and fermented like white wine. This is the method used for Tavel Rosé, Anjou Rosé, Italian Chiaretto, and *vin d'une nuit*. Rosé Champagne is made in two ways: the maceration process is when skins of black grapes are left in contact with the juice during the initial fermentation, producing a delicate, pale pink wine. The wine undergoes a second fermentation in the bottle to produce the sparkle. The second method is to blend still red and still white wines together after the initial fermentation.

Red Wines

Light, fruity wines made with minimum tannin by a short maceration period. Should be drunk early, as the extract, pigments, and tannin necessary for maturation are absent. Softer, richer, more savoury and deep-coloured wines (but still low in tannin) are made by carbonic maceration, or interior fermentation of the grapes, before pressing. Heating the must is another if increas-ingly discredited method of producing colour and smoothness. Full-blooded reds for maturing (known as *vins de garde*) are made by long contact of the skins with the juice to extract pigments, tannins, phenols, etc. All great red wines are made this way.

Fortified Wines

Vin doux naturel is naturally very sweet wine, its fermentation stopped (*muté*) by adding spirits, leaving residual sugar and high alcohol (15–16 per cent). Port follows the *vin doux naturel* procedure, but fermentation is stopped earlier, at four to six per cent, by a larger dose of spirits: one-fifth of the volume. Final alcohol is also higher at 19–20 degrees. Sherry is naturally strong white wine fully fermented to dryness. Then a small quantity of spirits is added to stabilize it while it matures in contact with air. Madeira is white wine with naturally high acidity. Sweeter styles have their fermentation arrested with the addition of alcohol, before it stops of its own accord. Then it is heated before being aged in barrels or big glass jars.

Sparkling Wines

White (or sometimes red) wines made to ferment a second time by the addition of yeast and sugar. The gas from the second fermentation dissolves in the wine under pressure. In the classic Champagne method the second fermentation takes place in the bottle in which the wine is sold, involving complicated and laborious processing, which inevitably makes it expensive. The *méthode champenoise* (or classic method as we must now call it, since the Champenois have properly claimed the term as belonging to their region) is not susceptible to many short cuts or labour saving devices, although machines have been devised for most of the laborious hand work involved.

The most notable is an automatic "riddling rack" to replace the unremitting chore of shaking and turning each bottle regularly. The massive framework, which vibrates and tips automatically at intervals, is known in France as a *gyropalette*, in the USA simply as a "VLM" – Very Large Machine. Wines from elsewhere, however good, can only be described as being made by the "classic method" or, in French, *méthode traditionnelle*. Cheaper methods, none of which achieves the same degree of dissolved gas as the classic method, include:

The transfer process. Wine is transferred, via a filter, under pressure to another bottle.

Cuve close or Charmat. The second fermentation takes place in a tank; the wine is then filtered under pressure and bottled.

Carbonization. CO_2 is pumped into still wine (although the bubbles are scarcely long lived).

France

It is hard to find anyone who denies the primacy of France as the country that set the international standards by which wine is judged. Fine wine as it is understood today was simply a French invention, a product of the same national genius that produced France's varied, ingenious, and (at its best) sublime cuisine. The only non-French wines accepted as universal models are Germany's Rieslings, Spain's sherry, and Portugal's port.

This is not to invalidate other originals: Chianti or Barolo or Rioja; but they remained vernacular styles long after Bordeaux, Burgundy, Champagne, and certain Loire, Rhône, and Alsace wines were targets that winemakers everywhere aimed at – in the first instance by planting their grape varieties. A form of natural selection gave France her inspired ideas of what wine can be. Her first vineyards were planted in the Midi in the sixth or seventh centuries BC. The Romans established what are now the highest-quality areas – Burgundy, Bordeaux, Champagne, the Rhône and Loire valleys, and Alsace. They chose them for their promising-looking slopes near centres of population with reasonable transport facilities; ideally water but failing that by main trade routes. At first they probably tried Italian and Greek vines, but trial and error produced better indigenous candidates, natives of the woods of Gaul, Spain, the Rhineland and the Alps. It is fairly certain today's vines are their descendants. France's soils, climate, and natural conditions of cellarage have not changed. We can speculate, then, that with allowances for different techniques and tastes, French wines have honed their identities over almost 2,000 years. Identity and fame once established, there is the inevitable problem of maintaining standards, not to mention preventing fraud. For every person who knows what a given wine ought to taste like, there are a hundred who are ready to pay for something they will be unable to identify.

The problem is age-old. Many laws have been passed to regulate wine – how much, when, where, by whom, of what grapes, and under what name. At the start of the twentieth century the problem was acute. Phylloxera had left Europe with a serious shortage and fraud of every kind was rife. The need for a national system of control was clear and in 1932 the Institut National des Appellations d'Origine (INAO) was founded to regulate the entire quality wine industry. The first ACs were created in 1936. This has become the model for other countries' systems of regulation, such as the Italian DOC and the Spanish DO.

French wine is classified into three categories: and the Office National Interprofessionnel des Vins de Table was founded to keep order. These distinctions are now central to the whole wine system in Europe. In EU terms every wine is either a Vin de Qualité Produit dans Une Région Determinée (VQPRD) or a *vin de table* – an absurd choice of category, incidentally, almost all wines are made to be drunk at table, and it is perfectly fair to say that Château Lafite is a table wine. The French system itself has become more elaborate. Apart from *vin de consommation courante*, where the price depends solely on the alcoholic degree, there are three classification categories for all the wines of France.

Appellation (d'Origine) Contrôlée (AC or AOC)

A more or less strict control of origin, grape varieties and methods used, alcoholic strength, and quantity produced. Most AC wines are limited to a basic production in the region that ranges approximately from 25 to

50 hectolitres per hectare but a complicated system of annual reassessment usually allows more, sometimes considerably more. Among the 457 existing ACs, the nature of appellation control varies. In Bordeaux, the most specific and restricted appellation is a whole village, within which individual properties (châteaux) are given liberties to plant where, and what (within the regional tradition) they like. In the best sites of Burgundy, by contrast, each vineyard has its own appellation. In Champagne the appellation covers the whole region and its method of working. Each region has its own logic. The number of ACs is constantly expanding as regions subdivide and local growers petition for their own AC, sometimes successfully. The AC system was not instituted to provide quality control, only guarantees of origin and authenticity. Quality control by compulsory tasting has now been introduced, at least in theory. In practice, as much as 97 per cent of wines submitted for tasting are nodded through: relations between growers and inspectors are far too close for the good of the system. This is a problem of which the INAO has been well aware, but has been slow to resolve. The consequence is the whole AC system is under question. Even though the system guarantees origin and no more than a basic level of quality, consumers understandably but erroneously assume an AC name on the label does imply a decent level of quality. They will be frequently disappointed.

Vins Délimités de Qualité Supérieure (VDQS)

The second rank of appellations was instituted in 1945 for regions with worthwhile identities and traditions producing "minor" wines. It has similar systems of control, and in practice became a sort of training ground for true ACs. This tier has become of minor importance, and by 2005 less than one per cent of French wine production was VDQS. EU reforms will lead to the disappearance of the category after 2011.

Vins de Pays

Vins de pays are now in reality the dynamic second tier after AC. The notion of "country wines" was crystallized in 1979, organized like ACs on several levels of precision; the regional being the broadest, the departmental the most precise, usually with the highest standards. There are six regional *vins de pays*, of which the best known are the Jardin de la France for the Loire Valley, and d'Oc for the entire Midi. Some 50 *départements* give their names to *vins de pays* grown within their borders and (up to a point) their viticultural traditions. As many as 100 defined districts, with a great concentration in the Midi, produce Vins de Pays de Zone, most of them obscure. Times are changing rapidly, though. Under the aegis of the EU the entire system is likely to be radically overhauled. In France the category of *vignobles de France* will replace *vin de table*. Such wines will be unashamedly technological, produced from high-yielding vines, using concentrators, oak chips, sweetening with concentrated must, and any other techniques the producer fancies. This will allow for European wineries to create brands to compete with better known brands from the New World.

The second tier will be the IGP: *indication géographique protégée*, which is intended as a replacement for *vin de pays* and will place no restriction on varieties planted and will allow cross-regional blending. The top tier, replacing AC, will be AP (*appellation d'origine protégée*). New bodies called Organismes de Défense et de Gestion will replace existing Syndicats and define the rules for each AP. Similar changes will be made across Europe, with each country reporting its new codes of production to the EU in 2009.

Well, that's the theory. Many producers and regions, with little appetite for reform and more bureaucracy, seem to be keeping quiet while hoping the whole thing will go away. Germany proposes to maintain its own system until at least 2011; the Italians are faced with the reduction of their 470 denominations (DOC, DOCG, and IGT) to a mere 182. Enquiries made of national regulatory bodies at the time of going to press did not elicit clear replies, and it is doubtful that the new system will come into place as rapidly as EU officials would like to think. If it does come into being as EU administrators and politicians intend, it is far from clear that the new model, other than permitting mass production techniques, will correct the deficiencies of the old. Whatever the intricacies of regulatory systems, present or future, it remains the fact that the greatest French wines are the models to which others aspire. There would be no Rhône Rangers in California without Côte-Rôtie and Hermitage, no Screaming Eagle without Mouton or Margaux, no Giaconda Chardonnay without Corton-Charlemagne, no Masseto without Pétrus. That supremacy, based on centuries of experience, is set to continue.

Bordeaux

Four factors make Bordeaux the most important vineyard region of all: its quality, size, variety, and unity. The last two are not contradictory but complementary. They are the reason we keep coming back for more. Although the range of styles and types of Bordeaux is seemingly inexhaustible, yet there is an unmistakable identity among all of them, a clean-cut, appetizing, easily digestible, and stimulating quality that only Bordeaux offers.

The Bordeaux character comes as much from grapes and climate as from the soil (which varies from gravel to limestone to clay). And, of course, it comes from traditions of making, handling, and enjoying wine in a certain way, an amalgam of the tastes of the French and their northern neighbours, the British, Belgians, Dutch, Germans, and Scandinavians, who have paid the piper since the Middle Ages.

In the early 2000s it was agreed that too much wine, much of it mediocre, was being produced in Bordeaux; very low prices, especially for simple white wines, persuaded the authorities that the least valued vineyards should be grubbed up, with compensation paid to the growers. Consequently the total area under vine has declined, though by far less than anticipated, and by 2006 there were 121,496 hectares of vineyards (2,000 fewer than the previous year).

In 2007, 32 per cent of Bordeaux production was exported. But the proportion among the best growths (Pauillac, Graves, and Margaux, for example) is considerably higher. More than ever, Bordeaux is a region dominated by red grapes, with white grapes accounting for no more than 11 per cent of plantings. Bordeaux supplies four basic styles of wine: light, everyday red; fine red; dry white; and sweet, "liquorous" white. There is not a great deal to be said about the first, except that there is a vast supply, varying from the excitingly tasty to the merely passable or occasionally poor and watery. It may be offered under a brand name or as the production of a *petit* château.

There is a degree of overlap between this everyday red and "fine" red, where the former excels itself or the latter lets the side down, but the fine red is really a distinct product, a more concentrated wine matured in oak and intended to be cellared for a few years until it reaches maturity. This is where the distinctions between different soils and situations produce remarkable differences of flavour and keeping qualities, more or less accurately reflected in the system of appellations and of classifications within the appellations. The total quantity available in this category is even more impressive for this class of wine: approaching one bottle for every two of the everyday red.

The dry whites belong, in the main, alongside the light reds. But a growing number, mostly from the Pessac-Léognan region just south of the city, rise to the level of fine white Burgundy. Exacting viticulture is teasing great character from Bordeaux's traditional white grapes, and fermenting in oak is adding to their stature. The sweet whites are a drop in the ocean, only about one bottle in 60, but a precious specialty capable of superlative quality, and much appreciated in Bordeaux even at a humble level as an apéritif. Although the gap in price between prestigious Bordeaux and humble Bordeaux seems to grow wider with each passing year, the gap in quality between these two poles is surely narrowing. The same viticultural and wine-making techniques that raised the standard of top Bordeaux wines are now being applied to more modest appellations. Bordeaux lovers dismayed by ever-rising prices should turn their attention to up-and-coming subregions such as the Côtes de Castillon, Fronsac, Lalande-de-Pomerol, and the Graves, which can often offer fine quality at an eminently affordable price. Every Bordeaux vintage is subject to the most fickle of climates. Overriding all other considerations is the unpredictable maritime weather. A great vintage such as 2005 will give even the commonest wines an uncommon vitality, but conversely, the category of fine wines can be sadly depleted by a really bad one, and the sweet whites can be eliminated altogether. This shifting pattern of vintages against the already complex background of appellations and properties, and the long lifespan of the good wines, make the appreciation of Bordeaux a mesmerically fascinating pursuit.

Classifications

The appellations of Bordeaux are themselves a sort of preliminary classification of its wines by quality, on the basis that the

---

BORDEAUX IN ROUND FIGURES

Over the 30 years from 1963 to 1993, the total area of *appellation contrôlée* vineyards in Bordeaux dwindled for a while, then recently began to increase. In 2007 it reached 123,334 hectares, producing 5.7 million hectolitres. (This growth occured despite plans to eliminate the worst situated vineyards which were not economically viable.) Red wine accounts for 89 per cent of Bordeaux's production, while white wine has dropped dramatically as a proportion of this total – from 60 per cent in the 1950s to 11 per cent by 2007. Around 25 per cent of all wine production was undertaken by 52 cooperatives. Meanwhile, the number of individual properties steadily decreases. In 1950 the total was 60,327 and in 1994 it was just 13,957: a drop of 77 per cent. By 2007 it had dwindled to about 10,000. With this concentration of ownership, efficiency has improved. Vintages of the 1950s (admittedly including a disastrous frost in 1956) produced an average crop of 30 hectolitres per hectare; the decade 1985 to 1994, an average of 52. But disastrous years can still occur, as in 1991 when spring frosts eliminated around two-thirds of the crop. In healthy vineyards, growers aim for yields of between 40 and 50 hectolitres per hectare in prestigious sites, and between 50 to 60 in sites producing wines of lesser quality.

more narrowly they are defined, the higher the general level of the district. This is as far as overall grading has ever (officially) gone. More precise classifications are all local to one area, without cross-referencing.

The most effective way of comparing the standing of châteaux within different areas is by price – the method used for the first and most famous of all classifications, that done for the Médoc for the Paris Exhibition of 1855.

In 1855, the criterion was the price each wine fetched, averaged over a long period, up to 100 years, but taking into account its recent standing, and the current condition of the property. The list is still so widely used that it is essential for reference over 150 years later.

A few châteaux have fallen by the wayside; the majority have profited by their notoriety to expand their vineyards, swallowing lesser neighbours. It is certain that the original classification located most of the best land in the Médoc and gave credit to the proprietors who had planted it.

What they subsequently did with it has proved to be less important than the innate superiority of the gravel banks they chose to plant.

The Concept of a Château

The unit of classification in Bordeaux is not the land (as in Burgundy) but the property on the land, the estate or château. It is the château that is either a First or a Fourth Growth or a *cru bourgeois*. A proprietor can buy land from a neighbour of greater or lesser standing, add it to his own and, given that it is suitable, it will take his rank. Vineyards go up or down the scale according to who owns them.

An example. Château Gloria is an estate of high quality in St-Julien, formed since World War II by buying parcels of land from neighbouring *crus classés*. When the land changed hands it was "classed", but because the buyer had no classed château, the vines were demoted to *cru bourgeois*.

Conversely, many classed growths have added to their holdings by buying neighbouring *cru bourgeois* vines. When the Rothschilds of Château Lafite bought the adjacent Château Duhart-Milon, they could theoretically have made all its wine as Lafite.

The justification for this apparent injustice is that a château is considered more as a *marque* than a plot of ground. Its identity and continuity depend so much on the repeated choices the owner has to make, of precisely when and how to perform every operation from planting to bottling, that he has to be trusted with the final decision of what the château wine consists of. A recent sign of how seriously owners take this is the proliferation of "second labels" for batches of wine that fail to meet self-imposed standards. Only the Médoc, along with Château Haut-Brion in Graves, were classified in 1855. The list is divided into five classes, but stresses that the order within each class is not to be considered significant. Only one official change has been made since: the promotion in 1973 of Château Mouton-Rothschild from Second to First Growth.

This is the Médoc method. St-Emilion is different. Some of its châteaux, the *grands crus classés*, including the superior *premiers grands crus*, have a semi-permanent classification reviewed every ten years – and last reviewed in 2006. Some owners of demoted properties challenged the new classification in the courts, which led to suspension until it was restored some months later.

Crus Bourgeois and Petits Châteaux

The best of the non-classified estates in the Médoc were grouped together in 1932 as *crus bourgeois*. Over the decades their ranks became swollen and the words *crus bourgeois* on a label ceased to be a reliable guide to a level of quality. The same was true of the terms *cru artisan* and *cru paysan*, which are sometimes used for properties below *crus bourgeois* in size and/or quality.

In the early 2000s, the entire concept of the *crus bourgeois* was being re-examined, and a panel composed of various sectors of the Bordeaux wine trade set about determining which of the 419 *crus bourgeois* were truly worthy of that status. In 2001, the ministry of agriculture decreed that there should be three categories: *crus bourgeois*, *crus bourgeois supérieurs*, and *crus bourgeois exceptionnels*, membership of each being subject to revision every ten years.

The panel announced the new classification in 2003. Their pruning had been severe, and only 240 properties were approved as *crus bourgeois*, of which 86 were *crus bourgeois supérieurs*, and an elite corps of nine properties (Chasse-Spleen, Haut-Marbuzet, Labégorce-Zédé, Ormes de Pez, Phélan Segur, Potensac, Poujeaux, and Siran) were hailed as *crus bourgeois exceptionnels*. Some of the rejected properties claimed that the panel had not followed the correct procedures, and launched a legal challenge. After much to-ing and fro-ing in the courts, a judgment was made in 2007 that threw out the entire 2003 classifcation, in effect reinstating the discredited 1932 classification.

The *crus bourgeois* properties formed an organization called the Alliance, which set about establishing new rules that would, it was hoped, lead to a fresh classification in 2009.

For many markets it is of little interest whether a wine is classified as a *cru bourgeois* or not. Most purchasers of Château Potensac buy the wine because of its outstanding track record, not because it is, or was, a *cru bourgeois exceptionnel*. But within other markets, including France, the words still count for something, which explains why many proprietors are so keen to see a new classification in place. To add to the confusion, a number of estates in the Côtes de Bourg and Côtes de Blaye also used the term *cru bourgeois*, which the Médocains had

The gates to Château Cos d'Estournel, St-Estèphe

always assumed was their exclusivity. The Médocains took the matter to court, and lost.

A great number of the thousands of lesser châteaux that used to exist are now allied to the *caves coopératives*, but more and more sought out by wine merchants and given the dignity of their own labels. There is no object in listing their endless names, however evocative, but to the claret-lover with an open mind they are always worth exploring, offering some of the best bargains in France. In good vintages, drunk at no more than three or four years old, they can be both delicious and reasonable in price. The system still flourishes, with slight modifications. Most châteaux now bottle their own wines, and there has been a growth in direct sales to consumers, especially in less prestigious regions such as Côtes de Bourg and the St-Emilion satellite districts. Nonetheless, the descendants of those ancient families – the Lawtons and Schylers and many others – are still deeply involved in the Bordeaux wine trade. In good times, everyone profits, and the consumer, at the end of the line, pays.

The Red Grapes of Bordeaux

The particulars given in the following pages of each of the principal Bordeaux châteaux include the proportions of the different grape varieties in their vineyards, as far as they are known. The classic Bordeaux red-wine varieties are all related, probably descended from the ancient Biturica. Before phylloxera destroyed most of the Bordeaux vineyards, many varieties were cultivated, often in a more or less random mixture, but very few of them were chosen for the epic replanting that followed the scourge. Five principal varieties have been selected for a combination of fertility, disease resistance, flavour, and adaptability to the Bordeaux soils.

Cabernet Sauvignon is dominant in the Médoc. It is the most highly flavoured, with small berries making dark, tannic wine

that demands ageing, but then has both depth and "cut" of flavour. It flowers well and evenly, and ripens a modest crop relatively late, resisting rot better than softer and thinner-skinned varieties. Being a late ripener it needs warm soil. Gravel suits it well, but the colder clay of Pomerol is unsatisfactory.

Its close cousin, the Cabernet Franc, is a bigger, juicier grape. Before the introduction of Cabernet Sauvignon in the eighteenth century, it was the mainstay of Bordeaux, and is still widely planted, particularly in Pomerol and St-Emilion, where it is sometimes known as the Bouchet. Cabernet Franc wines have delicious, soft-fruit flavours (which are also vividly seen in Chinon and Bourgueil, wines made from this grape on the Loire) but less tannin and depth. Less regular flowering, a thinner skin, and some poor clonal selections are also drawbacks, at least in the Médoc. More important today is the Merlot, a precocious grape that buds, flowers, and ripens early, making it more vulnerable in spring but ready to pick sooner, with an extra degree of alcohol in its higher sugar. Unfortunately, at harvest, its tight bunches need only a little rain to start them rotting.

Merlot wine has good colour and an equally spicy but softer flavour than Cabernet Sauvignon, making wine that matures sooner. In the Médoc, a judicious but steadily growing proportion – sometimes up to 50 per cent – is used; rather more in the Graves; more in St-Emilion, and in Pomerol up to 100 per cent. This is the grape that gives Château Pétrus its opulent texture and flavour. A fourth red grape that is still used in small amounts in the Médoc is the Petit Verdot, another Cabernet cousin. It ripens late with good flavour and ageing qualities, but flowers irregularly and has other quirks. A little in the vineyard is nonetheless a source of added complexity and "backbone" in the wine. It is quite widely planted in Margaux.

A fifth variety, once important but now found principally in St-Emilion and the Côtes de Bourg, is the Malbec (alias

THE UNIQUE BORDEAUX WINE MARKET

With few exceptions, you cannot buy a bottle of wine direct from a top Bordeaux estate. (Lesser estates may be different.) There are none of the tasting rooms and picnic tables so common in the Californian and Australian wine regions. This is because, for over two centuries, Bordeaux proprietors did not wish to be involved with such tawdry matters as commerce. They preferred to entrust the selling of their wine to specialist merchants (négociants) based in the city of Bordeaux itself.

The system has been maintained, more or less intact, to this day. Proprietors were often politicians or bankers or noblemen who lacked or scorned the commercial contacts that would facilitate the selling of large quantities of wine. Merchant

houses, often founded by the English or Irish, the Dutch or Germans, had access to distribution networks throughout Europe and were prepared to undertake the job on behalf of the château owners. They would also nurture the young wine in barrel in their own warehouses, and then bottle it.

Today, as centuries ago, the owner decides in the spring following the vintage on an opening price for the new wine. A broker, known in France as a courtier, acts as a go-between for owners and merchants alike and negotiates the transaction. The merchant will then sell his allocation to a network of importers, retailers, restaurateurs, and so forth.

Most of the time, the system works well. The proprietors gain a good deal of

cash fast, and can be reasonably sure that their wine is widely distributed; moreover, they can dispense with a sales force and the irksome overheads that entails. The courtier pockets his two-per cent commission for doing – well, not very much. And the merchants make as much money as they can get away with.

The balance of power shifted from time to time; sometimes the merchants had the whip hand, sometimes the proprietors. The strength of the system is that the merchants would usually undertake to buy wine from all vintages, good or bad. Failure to do so could be punished by the proprietor, who could deny the merchant access to the next really good vintage.

Pressac), a big, juicy, early ripening grape, which has serious flowering problems (*coulure*; see Glossary). It is grown in the Gironde more for quantity than quality. Paradoxically, under its synonym Auxerrois (or Cot), it is the grape of the historically famous "black wines" of Cahors. The arid climate of the Argentine Andes suits it better than either. In the long run, a château proprietor designs his wine by the choice and proportions of varieties he plants – though it remains true that some vintages favour one variety, some another, whatever the proprietor's taste.

The White Grapes of Bordeaux

The classic white-wine vineyard in Bordeaux is a mixture of two principal varieties, and one or two subsidiary ones as variable in proportions as the red.

Sauvignon Blanc and Sémillon make up at least 90 per cent of the best vineyards, Sauvignon for its distinct, incisive flavour and good acidity, Sémillon for its richness and its susceptibility to noble rot. Thus the sweet-wine vineyards of Sauternes tend to have more Sémillon, and often a small plot of the more highly flavoured Muscadelle.

Unfortunately, Sauvignon Blanc has flowering problems in Bordeaux, which makes it an irregular producer; to keep a constant proportion of its grapes means having a disproportionate number of vines. A variant known as Sauvignon Gris is also interesting, and has been planted at some top estates in Pessac-Léognan and Graves. Recently, some excellent fresh, dry white has been made entirely of Sémillon. Other white grapes include Ugni Blanc, Folle Blanche, Colombard, and, unofficially, Folle Blanche and Colombard.

The Wine Trade in Bordeaux

Since Roman times, when a "negotiator britannicus" was reported buying wine in Burdigala, Bordeaux's overseas trade has been one of the mainstays of the life of the city. In the Middle Ages, the chief customer was England. From the seventeenth century, it became the Dutch, and later the Germans, then the English again, and latterly the Americans. In the 1980s, the Japanese joined in, followed in the present century by the Chinese and Indians. The north of France, and above all Belgium, however, still absorb the biggest share, much of it by direct sales.

For two centuries up to the 1960s, the trade was largely in the hands of a group of négociants, nearly all of foreign origin, with their offices and cellars on the Quai des Chartrons, on the river just north of the centre of the city. The oldest firm still in business is the Dutch Beyermann, founded in 1620. The "Chartronnais" families, including Cruse, Calvet, Barton & Guestier, Johnston, and Eschenauer, were household names, and their power was considerable.

Most of these firms have been taken over or their names absorbed, their importance diminished with the growth of

---

THE BORDEAUX CLASSIFICATION OF 1855

First Growths (*premiers crus*)
Château Lafite-Rothschild, Pauillac
Château Latour, Pauillac
Château Margaux, Margaux
Château Haut-Brion, Pessac-Léognan
Château Mouton-Rothschild, Pauillac
(elevated to First Growth in 1973)

Second Growths (*deuxièmes crus*)
Château Rauzan-Ségla, Margaux
Château Rauzan-Gassies, Margaux
Château Léoville-Las-Cases, St-Julien
Château Léoville-Poyferré, St-Julien
Château Léoville-Barton, St-Julien
Château Durfort-Vivens, Margaux
Château Lascombes, Margaux
Château Gruaud-Larose, St-Julien
Château Brane-Cantenac, Cantenac-Margaux
Château Pichon-Longueville, Pauillac
Château Pichon-Lalande, Pauillac
Château Ducru-Beaucaillou, St-Julien
Château Cos d'Estournel, St-Estèphe
Château Montrose, St-Estèphe

Third Growths (*troisièmes crus*)
Château Giscours, Labarde-Margaux
Château Kirwan, Cantenac-Margaux
Château d'Issan, Cantenac-Margaux
Château Lagrange, St-Julien
Château Langoa-Barton, St-Julien
Château Malescot-St-Exupéry, Margaux
Château Cantenac-Brown, Cantenac-Margaux
Château Palmer, Cantenac-Margaux
Château la Lagune, Ludon
Château Desmirail, Margaux
Château Calon-Ségur, St-Estèphe
Château Ferrière, Margaux
Château Marquis d'Alesme Becker, Margaux
Château Boyd-Cantenac, Cantenac-Margaux

Fourth Growths (*quatrièmes crus*)
Château St-Pierre, St-Julien
Château Branaire, St-Julien
Château Talbot, St-Julien
Château Duhart-Milon-Rothschild, Pauillac
Château Pouget, Cantenac-Margaux
Château la Tour-Carnet, St-Laurent

Château Lafon-Rochet, St-Estèphe
Château Beychevelle, St-Julien
Château Prieuré-Lichine, Cantenac-Margaux
Château Marquis-de-Terme, Margaux

Fifth Growths (*cinquièmes crus*)
Château Pontet-Canet, Pauillac
Château Batailley, Pauillac
Château Grand-Puy-Lacoste, Pauillac
Château Grand-Puy-Ducasse, Pauillac
Château Haut-Batailley, Pauillac
Château Lynch-Bages, Pauillac
Château Lynch-Moussas, Pauillac
Château Dauzac, Labarde-Margaux
Château d'Armailhac, Pauillac
(formerly known as Mouton d'Armailhacq and Mouton Baronne-Philippe)
Château du Tertre, Arsac-Margaux
Château Haut-Bages-Libéral, Pauillac
Château Pedesclaux, Pauillac
Château Belgrave, St-Laurent
Château de Camensac, St-Laurent
Château Cos-Labory, St-Estèphe
Château Clerc-Milon-Rothschild, Pauillac
Château Croizet-Bages, Pauillac
Château Cantemerle, Macau

direct sales from lesser châteaux, of bottling at the châteaux, and above all, with the sheer cost of holding stock. New ways of selling new kinds of brand name wines to fewer but more powerful retailers have created a new class of trade. Most of them have also moved out of Bordeaux to more accessible warehouses. Many of the most important merchants do not deal directly with the consumer, so their names are unknown outside the wine trade. The following enjoy some public recognition.

Barton et Guestier
Blanquefort. Winemaker: Laurent Prada
www.barton-guestier.com
Owned by Diageo. Only a third of the business is now Bordeaux and the connection with the original firm, founded in 1725 by an Irishman whose descendants still own Château Langoa-Barton, is only in the name.

Borie-Manoux
Bordeaux. Principal: Philippe Castéja
Major supplier of Bordeaux to hotels, restaurants, and specialist retailers on the home market. Owner of the popular Beau Rivage Bordeaux brand; controls over 240 hectares of vines in the major appellations: Châteaux Batailley, Lynch-Moussas, Haut-Bages-Monpelou, Beau-Site, Trottevieille, Bergat, Domaine de l'Eglise.

Calvet SA
Bordeaux. www.calvet.com
Founded in 1870, and known for numerous brands from all over France. Its most popular Bordeaux bottling is Réserve Rouge. After some difficult years, the company was bought in 2006 by Grands Chais de France.

Castel Frères
Blanquefort. Principal: Pierre Castel
www.groupe-castel.com
A shipper with enormous turnover, but wine sales are overshadowed by those of beer and water. Castel owns, among many other properties, Château d'Arcins in the Haut-Médoc and Domaines Virginie in the Languedoc. Also owns leading Bordeaux brand Malesan and major retailer Nicolas.

Cheval Quancard
Principal: Roland Quancard.
Carbon Blanc. www.chevalquancard.com
Family firm that owns brand Le Chai de Bordes. Firm owns 15 *petits* châteaux in Bordeaux and exports to 60 countries.

Cordier-Mestrezat
Principal: Claude Marsolat
Bordeaux. www.cordier-wines.com
Numerous changes have led to the sales of the prestigious châteaux once owned by the Cordier family. Brands such as Prestige and Collection Privée are still produced and distributed to 120 countries. Former Calvet winemaker Paz Espejo is responsible for production.

C.V.B.G. (Consortium Vinicole de Bordeaux et de Gironde)
Parempuyre. Principal: Patrick Jestin
www.cvbg.com
Including Dourthe and Kressmann, this major player on the Bordeaux scene owns Châteaux Pey La Tour, Belgrave, and La Garde, and has developed successful brands such as Beau Mayne, Dourthe Numéro Un, and Essence.

Dulong
Floirac. Principal: Eric Dulong
www.dulong.com
A family company founded in 1873 and exporting substantial quantities of Bordeaux brands and table wines.

Robert Giraud
St André de Cubzac. Principal: Philippe Giraud
www.robertgiraud.com
A major player on the French market with its Blason Timberlay brand. Owns 150 ha of Bordeaux vineyards.

Nathaniel Johnston & Fils
Bordeaux.
www.nath-johnston.com
Family firm, founded 1734. Denis and Archibald Johnston are the ninth generation. Mostly trades in fine wines but also produces brands such as Reserve Claret.

Mähler-Besse
Bordeaux. Principal: Franck Mähler-Besse
www.mahler-besse.com
A family firm of Dutch origins, with a major holding in Château Palmer and a formidable stock of old vintages. Brands include Cheval Noir and Le Vieux Moulin.

Yvon Mau
Gironde sur Dropt. Principal: Jean-Francois Mau
www.ymau.com
Dynamic producer, acquired by Spanish drinks giant Freixenet in 2001. Commercially astute policy of brand and château exclusivities has brought success with major retailers. Yvescourt and Premius are good-quality brands. Also own Châteaux Preuillac and Brown.

Millésima
Bordeaux. Principal: Patrick Bernard
www.millesima.com
An atypical merchant, specializing in direct mail-order sales of *crus classés* to the public.

J.-P. Moueix
Libourne. Principal: Christian Moueix
www.moueix.com
A leading Right Bank merchant house, but better known as part-owner of Château Pétrus and owner of numerous other top estates in Pomerol and St-Emilion. In 2000, Moueix sold all the properties he owned in Fronsac in favour of further purchases in Pomerol.

Baron Philippe de Rothschild SA
Pauillac. Principal: Baronne Philippine de Rothschild
www.bpdr.com
Based in the Médoc, the company commercializes Bordeaux's best-known brand Mouton Cadet and the Baron Philippe range, and has an estate in the Languedoc. It is co-owner of the Napa wine, Opus One, and the Chilean Almaviva.

Schröder & Schÿler
Bordeaux. Principal: Yann Schÿler
www.schroder-schyler.com
Founded in 1739, this is a fine all-round négociant,
owning Château Kirwan and distributing many top wines,
as well as its own brands Signatures de Bordeaux and
Private Reserve.

Sichel
Bordeaux. Principal: Allan Sichel
www.sichel.fr
Part-owner of Château Palmer, and sole owner of Château
d'Angludet. Its own winery makes fruity modern claret and
"Sirius", a brand of excellent, barrel-fermented white and
oak-aged red Bordeaux.

Thunevin
St-Emilion. Principal: Jean-Luc Thunevin
A newcomer to Bordeaux 20 years ago, Thunevin is the owner
of Château Valandraud and other properties, consultant to the
Fayat group, French distributor of wines such as Pingus and
Harlan Estate, and now creator of a Merlot-dominated brand
called Bad Boy.

Médoc

The Médoc is the whole of the wedge of land north of
Bordeaux between the Atlantic and the wide estuary of the
Gironde, the united rivers Garonne and Dordogne. Its vineyards all lie within a few miles of its eastern estuarine shore, on
a series of low hills, or rather plateaux, of more or less stony soil
separated by creeks known as jalles, their bottom land filled
with alluvial silt. Dutch engineers in the seventeenth century
cut these jalles to drain the new vineyards. Their role is vital in
keeping the water table down inland.

The proportion of graves (big gravel or small shingle) in the
soil is highest in the Graves region, upstream of Bordeaux, and
gradually declines as you go downstream along the Médoc. But
such deposits are always uneven, and the soil and subsoil both
have varying proportions of sand, gravel, and clay. The downstream limit of the Haut-Médoc is where the clay content really
begins to dominate the gravel, north of St-Estèphe.

The planting of the croupes, the gravel plateaux, took place
in a century of great prosperity for Bordeaux under its par-
lement, whose noble members' names are remembered in many
of the estates they planted between 1650 and 1750. The Médoc
was the Napa Valley of the time, and the Pichons, Rauzans,
Ségurs, and Léovilles were the periwigged Krugs, Martinis, de
la Tours, and Beringers.

The style and weight of wine these grandees developed have
no precise parallel anywhere else. In some marvellous way, the
leanness of the soil, the vigour of the vines, the softness of the
air, and even the pearly seaside light seem to be implicated. Of
course, it is a coincidence (besides being a terrible pun) that
"clarity" is so close to "claret" – but it does sound right for the
colour, smell, texture, weight, and savour of the Médoc.

The centuries have only confirmed what the original
investors apparently instinctively knew: that the riverside gravel
banks produce the finest wine. The names that started first have
always stayed ahead. The notion of "First Growths" is as old as
the estates themselves.

Today, the Médoc is divided into eight appellations: five of
them limited to one commune (St-Estèphe, Pauillac, Moulis,
Listrac, and St-Julien), one (Margaux) to a group of five small
communes, one (Haut-Médoc) a portmanteau for parts of equal
merit outside the first six, and the last, Médoc, for the northern tip
of the promontory.

Margaux

The Margaux appellation covers a much wider area than the
village: vineyards in the Margaux commune, plus neighbouring
communes Cantenac, Labarde, Arsac and Soussans – a total of
1,408 hectares, rather more than Pauillac or St-Estèphe, with
more crus classés than any other, and far more high-ranking
ones. in the late 20th century many of these crus were clearly
under-performing, but now the disappointments diminish with
every passing vintage.

Margaux is a big, sleepy village, with a little maison du vin to
direct tourists. Wine from Margaux itself comes from the lightest, most gravelly land in the Médoc, and is considered
potentially the finest, most fragrant of all. That of Cantenac, in
theory, has slightly more body, and that of Soussans, on
marginally heavier, lower-lying land going north, less class.
The châteaux of Margaux tend to huddle together in the village, with their land much divided into parcels scattered around
the parish.

Margaux Premier Cru

Château Margaux ☆☆☆☆
Owner: Corinne Mentzelopoulos 78 ha of which 12 white.
Red grapes: Cab.Sauv. 75%, Merlot 20%, Petit Verdot
and Cab.Fr. 5%. White grapes: Sauv. 100%.
www.chateau-margaux.com
With Château Lafite, the most stylish and obviously
aristocratic of the First Growths, both in its wine and its lordly
premises. The wine is never blunt or beefy, even in great years;
at its best, it is as fluidly muscular as a racehorse and as
sweetly perfumed as any claret – the very taste and smell of elegance.

Like Lafite, Margaux emerged in the late 1970s from
15-odd years of unworthy vintages. The late André
Mentzelopoulos, whose daughter Corinne directs the estate
today, bought the property (for 60 million francs) in 1977,
and invested huge sums in a total overhaul of château,
vineyards, and winemaking facilities. His ambition for
perfection showed immediately with the excellent 1978.
Professor Peynaud advised the sweeping changes that put
Château Margaux back at the very top. In 1983, the young
Paul Pontallier became general manager of the estate, an
inspired appointment that has ensured that Margaux is always
one of the top wines of any vintage.

The château is a porticoed mansion of the first empire,
unique in the Médoc; the chais and cellars, pillared and
lofty, are in keeping. Magnificent avenues of plane trees
lead through the estate. Some vineyards further inland are

planted with white (Sauvignon) grapes to make a powerful but polished dry wine, Pavillon Blanc. The second label for red is Pavillon Rouge.

Margaux Crus Classés

Châteaux Boyd-Cantenac ☆☆
3ème Cru Classé. Owner: Lucien Guillemet. 17 ha. Grapes: Cab.Sauv. 60%, Cab.Fr. 8%, Merlot 25%, Petit Verdot 7%. www.boyd-cantenac.fr
The strange name, like that of Cantenac-Brown, came from a nineteenth century English owner. A small property not widely seen, nor much acclaimed, can be long-lasting and highly flavoured but can lack depth and polish. Recent vintages suggest quality is improving.

Château Brane-Cantenac ☆☆–☆☆☆
2ème Cru Classé. Owner: Henri Lurton. 90 ha. Grapes: Cab.Sauv. 65%, Cab.Fr. 5%, Merlot 30%. www.brane-cantenac.com
A very big and well-run property on a distinct, pale gravel plateau. The wine is generally enjoyable and supple at a fairly early stage, but lasts well. Good vintages of the '80s hold their own among the good Second Growths, and since 1995 they have become even better. After Lucien Lurton turned over the estate to his son Henri in 1992, the latter returned to manual harvesting and improved the cuverie. The second label is Baron de Brane.

Château Cantenac-Brown ☆☆–☆☆☆
3ème Cru Classé. Owner: Simon Halabi. 42 ha. Grapes: Cab.Sauv. 65%, Cab.Fr. 5%, Merlot 30%. www.cantenacbrown.com
A great, prim pile of a building, like an English public school, on the road south from Margaux. Conservative wines capable of terrific flavour. It went through a bad patch, until in 1987 a new owner, AXA Millesimes, invested heavily in the vineyards and cellar. Scattered vineyards account for some inconsistencies. Its 2006 purchase by a wealthy businessman may herald a new era. The second label is Brio du Ch. Cantenac-Brown.

Château Dauzac ☆☆–☆☆☆
5ème Cru Classé. Owner: MAIF insurance group. 40 ha. Grapes: Cab.Sauv. 58%, Cab.Fr. 5%, Merlot 37%. www.andrelurton.com
In 1992, MAIF brought in André Lurton of La Louvière to advise, and a new cellar was built in 1994. Has been reliably smooth if uninspiring, but recent vintages have seen a striking improvement in quality, and the wines remains very reasonably priced. Lurton's daughter Christine now administers the property. Second wine is La Bastide Dauzac.

Château Desmirail ☆☆
3ème Cru Classé. Owner: Denis Lurton. 32 ha. Grapes: Cab.Sauv. 60% Cab.Fr. 1%, Merlot 39%. www.chateau-desmirail.com
A Third Growth that disappeared for many years into the vineyards and vats of Châteaux Palmer and Brane-Cantenac. It was reborn in 1981. Lurton is aiming for perfume and elegance, but Desmirail still lacks distinction. Second label: Initial de Desmirail.

Château Durfort-Vivens ☆☆
2ème Cru Classé. Owner: Gonzague Lurton. 30 ha. Grapes: Cab.Sauv. 65%, Cab.Fr. 12%, Merlot 23%. www.durfort-vivens.com
The name of Durfort, suggesting hardness and strength,

The avenue, Château Margaux, Margaux

used to sum up the character of this wine – which seemed to want keeping for ever. The new generation took over in 1992 and increased the proportion of Merlot. Lurton seeks refinement more than weight or flesh, but Durfort can still seem undernourished. Second label is Le Second de Durfort.

Château Ferrière ☆☆–☆☆☆
3ème Cru Classé. Owner: Claire Villars/Merlaut family. 8 ha. Grapes: Cab.Sauv. 75%, Merlot 20%, Petit Verdot 5%. www.ferriere.com
From 1952 to 1991, Ferrière was leased to Lascombes. Now it is in the same capable hands as Haut-Bages-Libéral. Exciting, uncompromising quality from old vines since 1995.

Château Giscours ☆☆–☆☆☆
3ème Cru Classé. Owner: Eric Albada Jelgersma. 80 ha. Grapes: Cab.Sauv. 53%, Cab.Fr. and Petit Verdot 5%, Merlot 42%. www.chateau-giscours.fr
A success story of the 1970s when it made an outstanding '70 and much better '75 than most. The '80s were decidedly shaky. The vast Victorian property was virtually remade since the 1950s by the Tari family, including making a large lake to alter the microclimate. By creating turbulence between the vines and the neighbouring woodland, it helps to ward off spring frosts. The wines are tannic, robustly fruity, often dry, but at best full of the pent-up energy that marks first-class claret – not the suavely delicate style of Margaux. Since 1995, under new Dutch owners, the wine has become more consistent. Second wine: Sirène de Giscours.

Château d'Issan ☆☆–☆☆☆
3ème Cru Classé. Owner: Emmanuel Cruse. 30 ha. Grapes: Cab.Sauv. 65%, Merlot 35%. www.chateau-issan.com
One of the (few) magic spots of the Médoc: a moated seventeenth-century mansion down among the poplars, where the slope of the vineyard meets the riverside meadows. Issan is never a big wine, but old vintages have been wonderfully, smoothly persistent. The 1980s were disappointing here, and the 1990s patchy, but recent vintages have been more concentrated and refined.

Château Kirwan ☆☆☆
3ème Cru Classé. Owner: the Schÿler family and partners. 35 ha. Grapes: Cab.Sauv. 40%, Cab.Fr. 20%, Merlot 30%, Petit Verdot 10%. www.chateau-kirwan.com
The Third Growth neighbour to Brane-Cantenac. Until recently, Kirwan had few friends among the critics, although it is carefully run and often made elegant, feminine claret. Michel Rolland consulted here from 1992 to 2005, and the wine gained fruit, weight, and oak. Recent vintages have been exemplary.

Château Lascombes ☆☆
2ème Cru Classé. Owner: Colony Capital. 83 ha. Grapes: Merlot 50%, Cab.Sauv. 45%, Petit Verdot 5%. www.chateau-lascombes.com
A potentially superb property (one of the biggest in the Médoc) restored by the energy of Alexis Lichine in the 1950s to making delectable, smooth, and flavoury claret. Some of the

vineyards Lichine assembled were far from Second Growth standard. Changes in consultants and over-ambitious pricing led to inconsistencies in style and quality that are not entirely resolved. The second label is Chevalier de Lascombes.

Château Malescot-St-Exupéry ☆☆–☆☆☆
3ème Cru Classé. Owner: Jean-Luc Zuger. 24 ha. Grapes: Cab.Sauv. 50%, Cab.Fr. 10%, Merlot 35%, Petit Verdot 5%. www.malescot.com
A handsome house in the main street of Margaux, with vineyards scattered north of the town. Confidently run by the owner, with advice from Michel Rolland, Malescot opts for a rich, oaky, mouth-filling style. Fine wine, but not always that typical of Margaux.

Château Marquis d'Alesme Becker ☆☆
3ème Cru Classé. Owner: Perrodo family 16 ha. Grapes: Cab.Sauv. 30%, Cab.Fr. 15%, Merlot 45%, Petit Verdot 10%.
A small vineyard in Soussans, owned until 2006 by the same family as Château Malescot (q.v.), but now has the same proprietor as Ch Labégorce. The Zugers made rugged, even coarse wines, but the Perrodo team are set to change that for the better.

Château Marquis de Terme ☆☆
4ème Cru Classé. Owner: Philippe Sénéclauze. 38 ha. Grapes: Cab.Sauv. 55%, Cab.Fr. 3%, Merlot 35%, Petit Verdot 7%. www.chateau-marquis-de-terme.com
A respected old name, popular among French consumers. It is made notably tannic for very long life, although since 2000 the wine shows more overt fruitiness.

Château Palmer ☆☆☆☆
3ème Cru Classé. Owner: Société Civile du Château Palmer. 52 ha. Grapes: Cab.Sauv. 46%, Merlot 46%, Petit Verdot 8%. www.chateau-palmer.com
In quality, hot on the heels of Château Margaux. The best vintages ('61, '66, '70, '83, '86, '88, '90, '95, '96, 2000, '05) set the running for the whole Médoc. They combine finesse with most voluptuous ripeness, the result of a superb situation on the gravel rise just above Château Margaux, and skilful winemaking and selection, with a judicious use of new barrels. Second wine Alter Ego, first made in '98, has established its own identity as a modern-style claret.

Château Pouget ☆
4ème Cru Classé. Owner: Pierre Guillemet. 10 ha. Grapes: Cab.Sauv. 60%, Merlot 30%, Cab.Fr. 10%. www.chateau-pouget.com
Under the same ownership, and with the same mostly lacklustre results, as Boyd-Cantenac.

Château Prieuré-Lichine ☆☆–☆☆☆
4ème Cru Classé. Owner: Ballande group. 70 ha, of which 2 white. Red grapes: Cab.Sauv. 50%, Merlot 45%, Petit Verdot 5%. White grapes: Sauv. 80%, Sém. 20%.
The personal achievement of the late Alexis Lichine, who assembled a wide scattering of little plots around Margaux in the 1950s and created a reliable and satisfying modern Margaux. Then things slid.

Sacha Lichine sold in 1999, now St-Emilion-based consultant Stéphane Derenoncourt supervizes winemaking. A well-defined new style has yet to emerge, as the wine often lacks Margaux typicity.

Château Rauzan-Gassies ☆–☆☆
2eme Cru Classé. Owner: Jean-Michel Quié. 30 ha. Grapes: Cab.Sauv. 65%, Cab.Fr. 10%, Merlot 25%.
Disappointing for decades, but signs of improvement since 1996. The owners seem to like it as it is, although the arrival of a new generation may herald a change for the better.

Château Rauzan-Ségla ☆☆☆
2ème Cru Classé. Owner: Wertheimer family (Chanel). 51 ha. Grapes: Cab.Sauv. 54%, Merlot 41%, Cab.Fr. 1%, Petit Verdot 4%. www.rauzan-segla.com
The larger of the two parts of the estate that used to be second only to Château Margaux, but lagged behind from the '50s to the '90s. New owners (since 1994) have restored the property and improved quality beyond recognition, in a style focusing on finesse and drinkability rather than power. The second label is Ségla.

Château du Tertre
5ème Cru Classé. Owner: Eric Albada Jelgersma. 52 ha. Grapes: Cab.Sauv. 40%, Cab.Fr. 20%, Merlot 35%, Petit Verdot 5%.
This backwoods vineyard at Arsac has performed spottily in the past, but new owners since 1997 have invested heavily, with palpable results. It has joined the list of Margaux to follow.

Other Margaux Châteaux

Château d'Angludet
Cantenac. Owner: Benjamin Sichel. 34 ha. www.chateau-angludet.fr
Located on the western edge of the appellation, Angludet produces firm wines that take time to show their unquestionable class and elegance.

Château d'Arsac ☆
Arsac. Owner: Philippe Raoux. 112 ha. www.chateau-arsac.com
Raoux successfully petitioned to have 40 ha of this large inland estate reclassified as Margaux, but the wines seem too oaky and dense.

Clos des Quatre Vents ☆☆–☆☆☆
Soussans. Owner: Luc Thienpont. 2 ha.
Now that he has left Château Labégorce-Zédé, Thienpont is devoting himself to this tiny property, rich in old vines. Concentrated and flamboyant wines.

Château Deyrem-Valentin ☆☆
Soussans. Owner: Jean Sorge. 14 ha.
Elegant, mid-weight Margaux. Very consistent wines for medium-term drinking.

Château la Gurgue ☆☆
Margaux. Owner: Claire Villars/Merlaut family. 10 ha. www.lagurgue.com
A formerly run-down property with well-located vineyards.

Since 1979 under the same ownership as Château Chasse-Spleen. Fully and fruity yet well structured too.

Château Labégorce ☆–☆☆☆
Margaux. Owner: Perrodo family. 36 ha. www.chateau-labegorce.fr
Forward wines with less than real Margaux elegance, but clear signs of improvement since the excellent 2000.

Château Labégorce-Zédé ☆☆
Soussans. Owner: Perrodo family. 36 ha. www.labegorce-zede.com
Very well run by Luc Thienpont until 2005, when bought by rich neighbours at Château Labégorce. The two properties may yet be reunited.

Château Marojallia ☆☆–☆☆☆
Arsac. Owner: Philippe Porcheron. 2.5 ha. www.marojallia.com
Margaux's first *vin de garage*. The brainchild of Jean-Luc Thunevin, with advice from Michel Rolland. Good if atypical wines. Second label is Clos Margalaine.

Château Monbrison ☆☆
Arsac. Owner: Vonderheyden family. 21 ha
Jean-Luc Vonderheyden, who died too young, made a reputation for this property in the '80s with wines of density and finesse. His brother maintains this tradition.

Château Paveil de Luze ☆–☆☆
Soussans. Owner: Baron Frédéric de Luze. 32 ha. www.chateaupaveildeluze.com
A gentlemanly estate with smooth, well-mannered wine to match. For drinking relatively young.

Château Siran ☆☆–☆☆☆
Labarde. Owner: William Alain Miailhe. 24 ha. www.chateausiran.com
Fine estate, making most attractive and consistent wine invariably of classed-growth status. Under advice from Michel Rolland, Siran was muscular and well structured; under new consultant Denis Dubourdieu (since 2004) Siran shows more finesse.

Château La Tour de Bessan ☆–☆☆
Soussans. Owner: Marie-Laure Lurton. 19 ha. www.vignobles-marielaurelurton.com
Close to Château du Tertre, this property produces Margaux of elegance and charm.

Château la Tour de Mons ☆–☆☆
Soussans. Owner: consortium of investors. 43 ha.
Romantic, old-fashioned property producing rounded wines with much Merlot. Dependable but not exciting.

Moulis & Listrac

Moulis and Listrac are two communes of the central Haut-Médoc whose appellations (each commune has its own individual one) are more stalwart than glamorous. Between Margaux and St-Julien, the main gravel banks lie farther back from the river with heavier soil. No château here was classified in 1855, but a dozen *crus bourgeois* make admirable wine of the more austere kind that suits certain perhaps old-fashioned palates – mine incuded. The best soil is on a great dune of gravel stretching from Grand Poujeaux in Moulis (where Châteaux Chasse-Spleen and Poujeaux are both among the Haut-Médoc's best value) inland through Listrac. The total area of vines is 635 hectares in Moulis, 670 in Listrac. Both saw rapid expansion in the heady atmosphere of the 1980s. Lean years can be a tough testing ground for these inland Médoc châteaux, where Cabernet ripens later than in vineyards close to the Gironde, but recent warm vintages have delivered some richer wines. Closer to the river, the villages of Arcins, Lamarque, and Cussac have only the appellation Haut-Médoc.

Moulis & Listrac Châteaux

Château Anthonic ☆–☆☆
Moulis. Owner: Cordonnier family. 29 ha.
Traditional wines from the Grand Poujeaux plateau and other parcels, in a light and brisk style.

Château Baudan ☆☆
Listrac. Owner: Alain Blasquez. 6 ha.
Small property that sells concentrated wine directly to restaurants and retailers.

Château Biston-Brillette ☆☆–☆☆☆
Moulis. Owner: Michel Barbarin. 25 ha.
www.chateaubistonbrillette.com
Elegant, medium-bodied wine of high, consistent quality.

Château Branas Grand Poujeaux ☆☆–☆☆☆
Moulis. Owner: Justin Onclin. 12 ha.
www.branasgrandpoujeaux.com
A new owner from 2002 has reduced yields to make rich, concentrated, oaky wines in a frankly *garagiste* style.

Château Brillette ☆☆
Moulis. Owner: Jean-Louis Flageul. 40 ha.
www.chateau-brillette.fr
Located on the next plateau to the various Poujeaux, Brillette's wine is supple and gently oaky. Shows greater richness since 2001.

Château Cap Léon Veyrin ☆–☆☆
Listrac. Owner: Alain Meyre. 23 ha
An improving property, boasting vineyards with an average age of 25 years.

Château Chasse-Spleen ☆☆–☆☆☆
Moulis. Owner: Merlaut family. 113 ha.
www.chasse-spleen.com
A big property, and even bigger since the purchase in 2003 of Château Gressier-Grand-Poujeaux. Regularly compared with *crus classés* for style and durability. Expertly made and highly consistent wines for a ten-year haul.

Château Clarke ☆☆
Listrac. Owner: Baron Benjamin de Rothschild. 55 ha.
www.lcf-rothschild.com
Completely replanted in the late 1970s, Clarke, despite the

investment, has had difficulty producing consistent wines. In some vintages they are delicious: in others, tough and tannic. Michel Rolland's advice since '99 has made Clarke more user-friendly.

Château Ducluzeau ☆☆
Listrac. Owner: Borie family. 5 ha.
Tiny production, but admirable, 90%-Merlot wine, made by the owner of Ducru-Beaucaillou.

Château Duplessis ☆
Moulis. Owner: Marie-Laure Lurton-Roux. 20 ha.
Lighter, more easy-going wine than most here.

Château Dutruch Grand Poujeaux ☆☆
Moulis. Owner: François Cordonnier. 25 ha.
Under same ownership as Anthonic, delivering well-structured wine typical of Moulis, for long maturing.

Château Fonréaud ☆–☆☆
Listrac. Owner: Jean Chanfreau. 3 ha.
www.chateau-fonreaud.com
Well-known property, but the wines are often astringent and charmless. 2004 and 2005 show more fruit and succulence. Fonréaud's Le Cygne is one of the best Médoc whites.

Château Fourcas-Dupré ☆☆
Listrac (Part of the vineyard is in Moulis). Owner: Patrice Pagès. 47 ha. www.chateaufourcasdupre.com
Sound wine, often with succulent fruit, but sometimes afflicted with hard tannins.

Château Fourcas-Hosten ☆☆
Listrac. Owner: Laurent and Rénaud Momméja. 44 ha.
www.chateaufourcashosten.com
Marked by cassis and oak, but tends towards austerity. Needs bottle-age for its tannins to become more supple. New owners from 2006 have, from their Hermès company, the resources to make this a leading property in Listrac.

Château Lestage ☆
Listrac. Owner: Chanfreau family. 44 ha.
www.chateau-fonreaud.com
Same owners as Château Fonréaud. Well-known; unremarkable.

Château Maucaillou ☆☆–☆☆☆
Moulis. Owner: Philippe Dourthe. 68 ha.
www.chateau-maucaillou.com
Important property with a winemaking museum. Good, deep wine: velvety, chewy, and essentially fruity.

Château Mayne-Lalande ☆☆
Listrac. Owner: Bernard Lartigue. 16 ha.
Full-bodied wine and a sometimes exceptional Grande Réserve, given longer barrel-ageing.

Château Moulin à Vent ☆–☆☆
Moulis. Owner: Dominique Hessel. 25 ha.
www.moulin-a-vent.com
Sound, fruity wine, steadily improving.

Château Peyre-Lebade ☆–☆☆
Listrac. Owner: Baron Benjamin de Rothschild. 56 ha.

Once home of the painter Odilon Redon, replanted in 1989. Neighbour to Château Clarke.

Château Poujeaux ☆☆☆
Moulis. Owner: Philippe Cuvelier. 52 ha.
www.chateaupoujeaux.com
Principal property of the Poujeaux plateau. Vies with Chasse-Spleen as the leading wine of its commune. Recent vintages increasingly and consistently fine. Bought in 2008 by proprietor of Clos Fourtet in St-Emilion.

Château Ruat-Petit-Poujeaux ☆
Moulis. Owner: Pierre Goffre-Viaud. 16 ha.
Rather rustic wines.

Château Saransot-Dupré ☆–☆☆
Listrac. Owner: Yves Raymond. 17 ha.
www.saransot-dupre.com
Full-bodied, Merlot-based. Also two ha of Bordeaux Blanc.

Château Sémeillan Mazeau ☆
Listrac. Owner: Jander family. 8 ha.
www.vignobles-jander.com
Rich, burly wine that needs a few years to become accessible.

St-Julien

St-Julien, with a high proportion of *crus classés*, is the smallest of the top-level Médoc appellations. It has only 910 hectares, but 80 per cent of this is classed Second, Third, or Fourth Growth (no First and no Fifth, and very little *cru bourgeois*). Its prominent gravel plateau by the river announces itself as one of the prime sites of Bordeaux.

St-Julien harmonizes force and fragrance with singular suavity to make the benchmark for all red Bordeaux, if not the pinnacle. Farther inland, towards the next village, St-Laurent, the wine is less finely tuned. The two villages of St-Julien and Beychevelle are scarcely big enough to make you slow your car.

St-Julien Crus Classés

Château Beychevelle ☆☆☆
4ème Cru Classé. Owner: Grands Millésimes de France and Suntory. 75 ha. Grapes: Cab.Sauv. 62%, Merlot 31%,
Cab.Fr. 5%, Petit Verdot 2%. www.beychevelle.com
A regal château built in the seventeenth century, with riverside vineyards on the slope running up to St-Julien from the south. Its silky, supple wine is the one I most associate with the better class of English country house; Blandings must have bulged with it. Famous vintages of the '50s and '60s were touchstones of the sort today's corporate ownership does not match. The curious boat on the label commemorates its admiral founder, to whose rank passing boats on the Gironde used to *baisse les voiles* – hence, they say, the name. Since 1995 director Philippe Blanc has reduced yields and made stricter selections, and purchasers are rewarded with wines that are more fleshy, concentrated, and refined. The second label is Amiral de Beychevelle.

Château Branaire-Ducru ☆☆☆
4ème Cru Classé. Owner: Patrick Maroteau. 50 ha.
Grapes: Cab.Sauv. 70%, Cab.Fr. 5%, Merlot 22%,
Petit Verdot 3%. www.branaire.com
Vineyards in several parts of the commune; the château opposite Beychevelle. Model St-Julien, relying more on flavour than force; notably fragrant and attractive wine with a track-record of reliability. Former manager Philippe Dhalluin, until snatched away by Mouton-Rothschild, significantly raised the quality of this exceptionally pure, dignified wine. Jean-Dominique Videau continues the good work. The second label is Château Duluc.

Château Ducru-Beaucaillou ☆☆☆–☆☆☆☆
2ème Cru Classé. Owner: Bruno Borie. 72 ha.
Grapes: Cab.Sauv. 70%, Merlot 30%.
www.chateau-ducru-beaucaillou.com
Riverside neighbour of Château Beychevelle, with a château almost rivalling it in grandeur, if not in beauty. The Borie family also owns Ch'x Grand-Puy-Lacoste and Haut-Batailley in Pauillac. After a bad patch around 1990, the estate has been back on top form since '95, with the firm but seductive flavour of the best St-Juliens.

Château Gruaud-Larose ☆☆☆–☆☆☆☆
2ème Cru Classé. Owner: Jean Merlaut. 82 ha.
Grapes: Cab.Sauv. 57%, Cab.Fr. 7%, Merlot 32%,
Petit Verdot 4%. www.gruaud-larose.com

COMMANDERIE DU BONTEMPS DE MÉDOC ET DES GRAVES

The Médoc unites with the Graves in its ceremonial and promotional body, the Commanderie du Bontemps de Médoc et des Graves. In its modern manifestation it dates from 1950, when a group of energetic château proprietors, on the initiative of the regional deputy, Emile Liquard, donned splendid red velvet robes and started to "enthrone" dignitaries and celebrities, wine merchants, and journalists at a series of protracted and very jolly banquets held in the *chais* of the bigger châteaux. The Commanderie claims descent from an organization of the Knights-Templar of the Order of Malta at St-Laurent in the Médoc in 1154 – a somewhat tenuous link. Its three annual banquets are the festivals of St Vincent (the patron saint of wine) in January, the Fête de la Fleur (when the vines flower) in June, and the Ban des Vendanges, the official proclamation of the opening of the vintage, in September. Male recruits to the Commanderie are usually entitled Commandeur d'Honneur, and female, Gourmettes – a pun meaning both a woman gourmet and the little silver chain used for hanging a cork around the neck of a decanter. The Commanderie cleverly blends a knack for wine promotion with a refusal to take itself or its members too seriously.

This magnificent vineyard on the south slope of St-Julien was long the pride of the merchant house Cordier, until its sale in 1997. Manager Georges Pauli remains in charge. Consistently one of the fruitiest, smoothest, easiest to enjoy of the great Bordeaux, although as long-lived as most, and better value than almost any. Bankable high quality since 1995. Second wine: Sarget de Gruaud-Larose.

Château Lagrange ☆☆–☆☆☆
3ème Cru Classé. Owner: Suntory. 113 ha, of which 4 white. Red grapes: Cab.Sauv. 67%, Merlot 26%, Petit Verdot 7%. White grapes: Sauv. 60%, Sém. 30%, Muscadelle 10%.
www.chateau-lagrange.com
A magnificent wooded estate inland from St-Julien. The Japanese owners took over in 1983, and started to expand and re-equip. Now the largest St-Julien producer. Discreet, supple wines, always enjoyable, rarely thrilling. Recent vintages show greater structure. The second label is Les Fiefs-de-Lagrange.

Château Langoa-Barton ☆☆☆
3ème Cru Classé. Owner: Barton family. 17 ha. Grapes: Cab.Sauv. 72%, Cab.Fr. 8%, Merlot 20%.
www.leoville-barton.com
The noble sister château of Léoville-Barton and home of the Bartons. Similar excellent wine, although always a short head behind the Léoville. But famously good value, and it ages well.

Château Léoville-Barton ☆☆☆–☆☆☆☆
2ème Cru Classé. Owner: Barton family. 45 ha. Grapes: Cab.Sauv. 72%, Cab.Fr. 8%, Merlot 20%.
www.leoville-barton.com
This third of the original Léoville estate has been owned by the Irish Barton family since 1821. One of the finest and most typical St-Juliens, robust but never extracted, made by a principled, straight-talking Irishman in old-oak vats at the splendid eighteenth-century Château Langoa. Utterly reliable, highly consistent. A cornerstone of the Anglo-Saxon cellar.

Château Léoville-Las-Cases ☆☆☆☆
2ème Cru Classé. Owner: Jean-Hubert Delon. 97 ha. Grapes: Cab.Sauv. 65%, Cab.Fr. 12%, Merlot 20%, Petit Verdot 3%. www.leoville-las-cases.com
The largest third of the ancient Léoville estate on the boundary of Pauillac, adjacent to Château Latour. A top-flight Second Growth and a favourite of the critics, consistently producing connoisseur's claret, extremely high-flavoured and dry for a St-Julien, needing long maturing and leaning towards austerity. The vineyard's stone gateway is a landmark, but the *chais* are in the centre of St-Julien beside the château, which belongs to Léoville-Poyferré. Severe selection means that the *grand vin* often represents less than half the total. The second wine is Clos du Marquis. See also Château Potensac (Médoc).

Château Léoville-Poyferré ☆☆☆
2ème Cru Classé. Owner: Cuvelier family. 80 ha. Grapes: Cab.Sauv. 65%, Merlot 25%, Petit Verdot 8%, Cab.Fr. 2%. www.leoville-poyferre.fr
The central portion of the Léoville estate, including the château. Potentially as great a wine as Léoville-Las-Cases, and Didier Cuvelier is set on rivalling his neighbour with oenologist Michel Rolland's help. The resulting wine is voluptuous and oaky. The second wine takes the name of a *cru bourgeois*, Château Moulin-Riche.

Château St-Pierre ☆☆
4ème Cru Classé. Owner: Francoise Triaud. 17 ha. Grapes: Cab.Sauv. 65%, Cab.Fr. 10%, Merlot 25%.
The smallest and least-known St-Julien classed growth. The property was bought in 1982 by Henri Martin of Château Gloria (q.v.), who then purchased the historic vineyards and reconstituted much of the original estate. It is now run by his son-in-law, Jean-Louis Triaud. Rather lean wines from old vines.

Château Talbot ☆☆☆
4ème Cru Classé. Owners: Nancy Bignon and Lorraine Rustmann. 107 ha, of which 5 white. Red grapes: Cab.Sauv. 66%, Cab.Fr. 3%, Merlot 24%, Petit Verdot 5%, Malbec 2%. White grapes: Sauv. 80%, Sém. 20%. www.chateau-talbot.com
One of the biggest and most productive Bordeaux vineyards, just inland from the Léovilles. Despite the sale of most Cordier properties, Talbot remains in the hands of Jean Cordier's daughters. Like Gruaud-Larose, a rich, fruity, smooth wine, but without the same plumpness or structure. The dry white Caillou Blanc, once lacklustre, is much improved and ages well for four to five years. Second label is "Connétable de Talbot".

Other St-Julien Châteaux

Château la Bridane ☆☆
Owner: Bruno Saintout. 15 ha.
www.vignobles-saintout.com
Solid wine, with blackcurrant fruit. Very attractive wine for medium-term drinking.

Château du Glana ☆☆
Owner: Vignobles Meffre. 43 ha.
www.chateau-du-glana.com
Oddly unrenowned as one of St-Julien's only two big unclassed growths. The owner is a wine merchant with several properties, who built a giant *chai* more like a warehouse. His splendidly sited vineyards produce respectable wine from grapes picked mostly by machine. Quality is improving now that two brothers from the next generation are running the property.

The sculpted lion at Château Léoville-Las-Cases, St-Julien

Château Gloria ☆☆–☆☆☆
Owner: Francoise Triaud. 44 ha. www.chateaugloria.com
The classic example of the unranked château of exceptional quality, the creation of the illustrious mayor of St-Julien, Henri Martin, who assembled the vineyard in the 1940s with parcels of land from neighbouring *crus classés*. The wine is rich and long-lasting but distinctly tannic.

Château Lalande Borie ☆☆
Owner: Borie family. 18 ha
A vineyard created from part of the old Lagrange in 1970 by the owner of Château Ducru-Beaucaillou, where the wine is made. In effect, a baby brother of Ducru.

Château Moulin de la Rose ☆☆
Owner: Guy Delon. 4.5 ha
A little-known property surrounded by *crus classé* vineyards. Well-made wines.

Château Terrey-Gros-Caillou & Château Hortevie ☆☆
Owner: Borie family. 14 ha.
A union of two small properties, producing very creditable St-Julien. Bought in 2005 by the owners of Ducru-Beaucaillou.

Pauillac

Pauillac is a rather sleepy little town on the banks of the Gironde. Most of the town's few hotels and restaurants face the estuary across a tree-lined quay and a modest marina. Only the *maison du vin* (worth a visit) on the quay gives a hint of this town's world renown. That, and the famous names on signs everywhere you look in the open steppe of the vineyards.

The wine of Pauillac epitomizes the qualities of all red Bordeaux. It is the virile aesthete; a hypnotizing concurrence of force and finesse. It can lean to an extreme either way (Latour and Lafite representing the poles) but at its best, strikes such a perfect balance that no evening is long enough to do it justice. There are 1,215 hectares of vineyards with more *crus classés* than any other commune except Margaux, surprisingly weighted towards Fifth Growths – some of which are worth much better than that.

Pauillac has been given a new lease of life by the indefatigable Jean-Michel Cazes, who has restored the moribund hamlet of Bages just south of the town, and created a superlative bakery and bistro to supplement his more luxurious hotel and restaurant at Château Cordeillan-Bages nearby.

Pauillac Premiers Crus

Château Lafite-Rothschild ☆☆☆☆
Owner: Domaines Baron de Rothschild. 100 ha.
Grapes: Cab.Sauv. 70%, Cab.Fr. 3%, Merlot 25%,
Petit Verdot 2%. www.lafite.com
See The Making of a Great Claret, page 51

Château Latour ☆☆☆☆
Owner: Francois Pinault. 66 ha. Grapes: Cab.Sauv. 78%,
Cab.Fr. 4%, Merlot 16%, Petit Verdot 2%.
www.chateau-latour.com
Château Latour is in every way complementary to Château Lafite. They make their wines on different soils in different ways; the quality of each is set in relief by the very different qualities of the other. Lafite is a tenor; Latour a bass. Lafite is a lyric; Latour an epic. Lafite is a dance; Latour a parade.

Latour lies on the southern, St-Julien limit of the commune on the last low hill of river-deposited gravel, before the flood plain and the stream that divides the two parishes. The ancient vineyard, taking its name from a riverside fortress of the Middle Ages, surrounds the modest mansion, its famous domed stone tower and the big, square, stable-like block of its *chais*. Two other small patches of vineyard lie inland near Château Batailley.

For nearly three centuries the estate was in the same family (and up to 1760, connected with Lafite). Its modern history began in 1963, when the de Beaumonts sold the majority share to an English group headed by the banker Lord Cowdray, and including the wine merchant Harveys of Bristol. They set in hand a total modernization, starting with temperature-controlled, stainless-steel fermenting vats in place of the ancient oak. Combined English and French talent has since rationalized and perfected every inch of the property, setting such standards that Latour has, rather unfairly, become almost more famous for the quality of its lesser vintages than for the splendour of such years as 1961, '66, '70, '78, '82, '86, '90, '95, '96, 2000, and 2005. Its consistency and deep, resonant style extends into its second label, Les Forts de Latour, which fetches a price comparable to a Second Growth château. Les Forts comes partly from vats of less than the *grand vin* standard, but mainly from two small vineyards (18 hectares) farther inland towards Batailley. These were replanted in 1966, and their wine first used in the blend in the early 1970s. There is also (unusually) a third wine, modestly labelled "Pauillac", which by no means disgraces its big brothers.

In 1989, Allied-Lyons Ltd (owners of Harveys) bought the Cowdray-Pearson share, but the 30-year English occupation ended when Allied-Lyons sold Latour in 1994 to the French entrepreneur François Pinault. Pinault's lieutenant, Frédéric Engerer, has supervised another complete rebuilding and modernization of the winemaking facilities, completed in 2002. He is also playing a large part in the winemaking process, which is unusual for an estate director. There is no sign of compromise.

Château Mouton-Rothschild ☆☆☆☆
Owner: Baronne Philippine de Rothschild. 82 ha,
of which 5 white. Red grapes: Cab.Sauv. 80%,
Cab.Fr. 10%, Merlot 8%, Petit Verdot 2%. White grapes:
Sém. 50%, Sauv. 48%, Muscadelle 2%. www.bpdr.com
Mouton-Rothschild is geographically neighbour to Lafite, but gastronomically closer to Latour. Its hallmark is a deep concentration of the flavour of Cabernet Sauvignon, often described as resembling blackcurrants, held as though between the poles of a magnet in the tension of its tannin – a balancing act that can go on for decades, increasing in fascination and grace all the time. In 1976, I noted of the 1949 Mouton: "Deep, unfaded red; huge, almost California-style nose; resin and spice; still taut with tannin, but overwhelming in its succulence and sweetness. In every way magnificent."

More than any other château, Mouton-Rothschild is identified with one man, the late Baron Philippe de Rothschild, who came to take it over as a neglected property of his (the English) branch of the Rothschild family in 1922, and died in 1989. This remarkable man of many talents (poet, dramatist, racing-driver among them) determined to raise Mouton from being first in the 1855 list of Second Growths to parity with Lafite. It took him 51 years of effort, argument, publicity, and above all, perfectionist winemaking. He gained official promotion in 1973, the only change ever made to the 1855 classification.

Baron Philippe and his American wife, Pauline, created a completely new house in the stone stable block and collected in the same building a great museum of works of art relating to wine, displayed with unique flair (and open to the public by appointment). He was succeeded in 1989 by his daughter Philippine, who has inherited her father's unquenchable zest for life, and has brilliantly nurtured the New World empire he inaugurated with Robert Mondavi in the 1980s.

The baron's love of the arts (and knack for publicity) led him to commission a different famous artist to design the top panel of the Mouton label every year from 1945 on. Consequently some vintages are as sought after for their labels as for their contents. The baron's Bordeaux domaine expanded over the years to include Châteaux d'Armailhac and Clerc-Milon, and la Baronnie, the company that produces and markets Mouton-Cadet, the celebrated branded Bordeaux. Mouton itself had no second label until the launch in 1994 of Le Petit Mouton. Since 1991, a small quantity of intense, dry white, Aile d'Argent, has been made. It has yet to prove itself.

In 2003 the modest but extremely able Philippe Dhalluin was hired as tecnnical director of the three Pauillac estates, and the results have been swift: the 2006 Mouton is one of the top wines of a difficult vintage.

Pauillac Crus Classés

Château d'Armailhac ☆☆–☆☆☆
5ème Cru Classé. Owner: Baronne Philippine de Rothschild. 50 ha. Grapes: Cab.Sauv. 52%, Cab.Fr. 20%, Merlot 26%, Petit Vedot 2%. www.bpdr.com
Originally Mouton-d'Armailhacq, bought in 1933 by Baron Philippe de Rothschild and twice renamed. The vineyard is south of Mouton, next to Pontet-Canet, on lighter, even sandy soil, which, with a higher proportion of both Cabernet Franc and Merlot, gives a rather lighter, quicker-maturing wine, but a star nonetheless, made to the customary Mouton standards.

Château Batailley ☆☆–☆☆☆
5ème Cru Classé. Owner: Castéja family. 55 ha. Grapes: Cab.Sauv. 70%, Cab.Fr. 3%, Merlot 25%, Petit Verdot 2%.
The name of the estate, another of those divided into easily confusable parts, comes from an Anglo-French disagreement in the fifteenth century. Charles II's favourite wine merchant was called Joseph Batailhé – I like to think he was a son of this soil, the wooded inland part of Pauillac. Batailley is the larger property and retains the lovely little mid-nineteenth-century château in its "English" park. Its wine is tannic, never exactly graceful, but eventually balancing its austerity with sweetness; old (20-year) bottles keep great nerve and vigour. These are the Pauillacs that approach St-Estèphe in style. The wine is usually excellent value.

Château Clerc-Milon ☆☆☆
5ème Cru Classé. Owner: Baronne Philippine de Rothschild. 32 ha. Grapes: Cab.Sauv. 46%, Cab.Fr 15%, Merlot 35%, Petit Verdot 3%, Carmenère 1%. www.bpdr.com
An obscure little estate known as Clerc-Milon-Mondon until 1970, when it was bought by Baron Philippe de Rothschild. The scattered vineyards are promisingly positioned close to Château Lafite and Château Mouton-Rothschild. Typical Rothschild perfectionism, energy, and money have made a series of good vintages, starting with a remarkably fine 1970. After an uneven patch, Clerc-Milon has since 2000 been classic and consistent.

Château Croizet-Bages ☆–☆☆
5ème Cru Classé. Owner: Jean-Michel Quié. 28 ha. Grapes: Cab.Sauv. 58%, Cab.Fr. 7%, Merlot 35%.
A property belonging to the owners of Château Rauzan-Gassies, Margaux (q.v.). No château, but vineyards on the Bages plateau between Lynch-Bages and Grand-Puy-Lacoste. Vintages of the '80s and '90s were mostly feeble, but there are at long last signs of greater succulence and grip in the 2000s.

Château Duhart-Milon-Rothschild ☆☆☆
4ème Cru Classé. Owner: Domaines Baron de Rothschild. 67 ha. Grapes: Cab.Sauv. 70%, Merlot 30%. www.lafite.com
The little sister of Château Lafite, on the next hillock inland, known as Carruades, bought by the Rothschilds in 1964 and since then completely replanted and enlarged. Its track record was for hard wine of no great subtlety, but as the young vines age, this is becoming a great château again, making long-living claret. The second label is Moulin de Duhart.

Château Grand-Puy-Ducasse ☆☆
5ème Cru Classé. Owner: Crédit Agricole Grands Crus. 40 ha. Grapes: Cab.Sauv. 60%, Merlot 40%.
Three widely separated plots of vineyard, one next to Grand-Puy-Lacoste, one by Pontet-Canet, the third nearer Batailley, and *chais* and château on the Pauillac waterfront. Much replanted and renovated, but already known for big, well-built, and long-lived wine (e.g. '61, '64, '66, '67, '70). The 1986 and 1989 vintages were stars of the '80s, but the wines have often lacked flair. The 1996 and 2000 are welcome exceptions.

Château Grand-Puy-Lacoste ☆☆☆–☆☆☆☆
5ème Cru Classé. Owner: Borie family. 55 ha. Grapes: Cab.Sauv. 70%, Cab.Fr. 5%, Merlot 25%.
Sold in 1978 by the Médoc's greatest gastronome, Raymond Dupin, to one of its most dedicated proprietors, Jean-Eugène Borie (of Ducru-Beaucaillou, Haut-Batailley, etc.), whose son, François-Xavier, lives at the château and runs it. Rather remote but attractive property with an extraordinary romantic garden, a thousand miles from the Médoc in spirit, on the next

"hill" inland from the Bages plateau. The wine has tremendous attack, colour, structure, and class. The second label is Lacoste-Borie.

Château Haut-Bages-Libéral ☆☆–☆☆☆
5ème Cru Classé. Owner: Claire Villars/Merlaut family. 28 ha. Grapes: Cab.Sauv. 80%, Merlot 17%, Petit Verdot 3%. www.hautbagesliberal.com

A vineyard bordering Château Latour to the north. The Merlaut family has invested heavily here, and this property is making much better wine than its rather limited reputation suggests. It is a true Pauillac: forthright, tannic, and long-lived. The second label is Chapelle de Bages.

Château Haut-Batailley ☆☆–☆☆☆
5ème Cru Classé. Owner: Borie family. 22 ha. Grapes: Cab.Sauv. 65%, Cab.Fr. 10%, Merlot 25%.

A wine of charm rather than weight, as much St-Julien in style as Pauillac. For sheer tastiness there are few wines you can choose with more confidence. The second label is La Tour l'Aspic.

Château Lynch-Bages ☆☆☆–☆☆☆☆
5ème Cru Classé. Owner: Cazes family. 100 ha, of which 5 white. Red grapes: Cab.Sauv. 75%, Cab.Fr. 10%, Merlot 15%. White grapes: Sauv. 45%, Sém. 40%, Muscadelle 15%. www.lynchbages.com

An important estate, fondly known to its many English friends as "lunch-bags"; a perennial favourite for sweet and meaty, strongly Cabernet-flavoured wine, epitomizing Pauillac at its most hearty. The Bages plateau, south of the town, has relatively strong soil over clay subsoil. The best vintages ('82, '85, '86, '88, '89, '90, and all vintages from '95 onwards) are very long-lived. Jean-Michel Cazes, who doubled as Pauillac's leading insurance broker, rebuilt the crumbling château and the gloomy *chais* in the '80s and raised the name of his property to new heights. He was also the founding director of the AXA wine estates, until he retired from that position in 2001. His family's other properties include Les Ormes-de-Pez in St-Estèphe. The second label is Haut-Bages-Averous.

Château Lynch-Moussas ☆–☆☆
5ème Cru Classé. Owner: Castéja family. 55 ha. Grapes: Cab.Sauv. 75%, Merlot 25%.

Stablemate since 1969 of its neighbour Château Batailley. Stalky and light in the '80s and '90s, this peppery wine has, under the watchful eye of Philippe Castéja, grown in concentration and seriousness.

Château Pedesclaux ☆☆
5ème Cru Classé. Owner: Jugla family. 12 ha. Grapes: Cab.Sauv. 50%, Cab.Fr. 5%, Merlot 45%. www.chateau-pedesclaux.com

Until recently, the least renowned classed growth of Pauillac,

scattered around the commune like Grand-Puy-Ducasse. Complacently underperforming and dim, until in the late '90s a new family team, Denis and Brigitte Jugla, took the reins, renovated the winery, and improved selection. Now worthy of its status again, with an exceptional 2005.

Château Pichon-Longueville ☆☆☆–☆☆☆☆
2ème Cru Classé. Owner: AXA Millésimes. 70 ha. Grapes: Cab.Sauv. 60%, Cab.Fr. 4%, Merlot 35%, Petit Verdot 1%. www.pichonlongueville.com

The following entry gives the background to the unwieldy name. A new owner (the insurance company AXA) since 1987 set lustily about competing with the Comtesse across the road, which for years had made much better wine. With Jean-Michel Cazes (see Château Lynch-Bages) as director, and a seemingly bottomless purse, an aggressive building programme transformed the place. From 1988 onwards the wine became an earnest contender with its neighbour, and more full-bloodedly Pauillac in style, with its preponderance of Cabernet. Second wine is Les Tourelles de Longueville.

Château Pichon-Longueville, Comtesse de Lalande ☆☆☆–☆☆☆☆
2ème Cru Classé. Owner: Champagne Louis Roederer. 84 ha. Grapes: Cab.Sauv. 45%, Cab.Fr. 12%, Merlot 35%, Petit Verdot 8%. www.pichon-lalande.com

Two châteaux share the splendid estate that was planted in the seventeenth century by the same pioneer who planted the Rauzan estate in Margaux. The châteaux were long owned by his descendants, the various sons and daughters of the Barons de Pichon-Longueville. Two-thirds of the estate eventually fell to a daughter who was Comtesse de Lalande – hence the lengthy name, which is usually shortened to Pichon-Lalande.

The mansion lies in the vineyards of Château Latour, but most of its vineyard is across the road, on gravelly soil with clay below, surrounded by the vines of the other Pichon château and parts of the vineyards of Châteaux Latour, Ducru-Beaucaillou, and Léoville-Las-Cases. The southern portion of the vineyard is actually in St-Julien. With its relatively generous proportion of Merlot, the wine lacks the concentrated vigour of Château Latour, but adds a persuasive perfumed smoothness that makes it one of the most fashionable Second Growths.

Under previous owner May-Eliane de Lencquesaing the estate produced fabulously good wine of the kind everyone wants: stylish Pauillac of the St-Julien persuasion, not so rigid with tannin and extract that it takes decades to mature. Vintages since 1975 have been among the best of their year. Pressure from shareholders led the tireless but octogenarian Mme. de Lencquesaing to put Pichon-Lalande on the market, where it was acquired by a worthy successor. The second label is Réserve de la Comtesse.

The Tour d'Aspic, Château Haut-Batailley, Pauillac

Château Pontet-Canet ☆☆☆–☆☆☆☆
5ème Cru Classé. Owner: Alfred Tesseron. 79 ha.
Grapes: Cab.Sauv. 62%, Cab.Fr. 6%, Merlot 32%.
www.pontet-canet.com

Sheer size has helped Pontet-Canet to become one of Bordeaux's most familiar names. That, and over a century of ownership by the shippers Cruse & Fils Frères. Its situation near Mouton promises top quality; the 1929 was considered

---

CHÂTEAU LAFITE-ROTHSCHILD – THE MAKING OF A GREAT CLARET

This is the place to study the author's control of his superlatives. Wine for intelligent millionaires has been made by this estate for well over 200 years, and when a random selection of 36 vintages, going back to 1799, was drunk and compared in recent times, the company was awed by the consistency of the performance. Underlying the differences in quality, style, and maturity of the vintages, there was an uncanny resemblance between wines made even a century and a half apart.

It is easy to doubt, because it is difficult to understand the concept of a Bordeaux cru. As an amalgam of soil and situation with tradition and professionalism, its stability depends heavily on the human factor. Sometimes even Homer nods. Lafite had its bad patch in the 1960s and early 1970s. Since 1976, it has once again epitomized the traditional Bordeaux château at its best.

As a mansion, Lafite is impeccably chic rather than grand; a substantial but unclassical 18th -century villa, on a terrace above the most businesslike and best vegetable garden in the Médoc. There are no great rooms; the red drawing room, the pale-blue dining room, and the dark-green library are comfortably cluttered and personal. The Rothschild family of the Paris bank bought the estate in 1868. It has been the apple of their corporate eye ever since. In 1974, the 34 -year-old Baron Eric de Rothschild took over responsibility for the estate.

Grandeur starts in the cuvier, the vat house, and low barns of the chais, where the barrels make marvellous perspectives of dwindling hoops seemingly for ever. In 1989, a unique and spectacular new circular chai, dug out of the vineyards and supported by columns to test Samson, was inaugurated. History is most evident in the shadowy, moss-encrusted bottle cellars, where the collection stretches back to 1797 – probably the first Bordeaux ever to be château-bottled, still in its original bin.

Quality starts with the soil: deep, gravel dunes over limestone.
It depends on the age of the vines: at Lafite an average of 40 years. It depends even more on restricting their production: the figure of 40 to 45 hectolitres is achieved by stern pruning.

Vintage in the Médoc starts at any time between early September and late October. Picking teams, some 250-strong, begin with the Merlot, which ripens first, and move as quickly as they can.

The vital work of selection starts in the vineyard, discarding bunches that are unevenly ripe or infected with rot. It continues at the cuvier, where they are inspected before being tipped in the destemmer. The crushed grapes, each variety separately, are pumped either into steel tanks or into large upright oak vats for fermentation, usually with the natural yeasts from the vineyard or winery. If the grapes lack sufficient natural sugar, the must will be chaptalized. The temperature of fermentation is controlled to rise no higher than 30°C (85°F) – enough to extract the maximum colour from the skins; not enough to inhibit the yeasts and stop a steady fermentation.

Fermentation can take from one to three weeks, depending on the yeasts, the ripeness of the grapes, and the weather. The wine may be left on the skins for up to 21 days, if necessary, to leach the maximum colour and flavour. The juice is run off into new 225-litre barriques made at the château of oak from the forest of Tronçais in the Allier in central France. The remaining marc of skins and pips is pressed in a hydraulic press. Some of this, exaggeratedly tannic, can be blended if necessary, usually between ten per cent and none at all.

The barriques, up to 1,100 of them in a plentiful year, stand in rows in the chai, loosely bunged at the top, while the malolactic fermentation finishes. Early in the new year, the proprietor, his manager, the maître de chai, and consultant oenologist (Jacques Boissenot) taste the

inky, biting new wine to make the essential selection: which barrels are good enough for the château's grand vin, which are fit for the second wine, Carruades de Lafite, and which will be bottled as mere Pauillac. This is the moment for the assemblage of the wines of the four different varieties, up to now still separate. Once assembled, the wines are put back into clean barrels.

For a further year they stand with loose bungs, being topped up weekly to make good any "ullage", or loss by evaporation. During this year they will be racked into clean casks two or three times and fined with beaten egg whites. The white froth poured onto the top coagulates and sinks, taking any floating particles with it to the bottom. When the year is up, the bungs are tapped tight and the casks turned bondes de côte – with their bungs to the side. From now on the only way to sample them is through a tiny spiggot hole plugged with wood at the end of the cask.

At Lafite, the wine is kept in cask for a further nine to 12 months, until the second summer or autumn after the vintage, then racked into a vat, which feeds the bottling machine.

Complicated as it is to relate, there is no simpler or more natural way of making wine. The Lafite team is wary of the latest hi-tech or fashionable methods, although many of them are rigorously tested to see if they could be beneficial. The factors that distinguish First Growth winemaking from more modest enterprises are the time it takes, the number of manoeuvres, and the rigorous selection.

In recent years, Rothschild enterprise has been at work to use the technical (as well as financial) strength of Lafite in new fields both near and far. The neighbouring Château Duhart-Milon has been bought and renovated; Château Rieussec in Sauternes and leading Pomerol Château L'Evangile acquired, as well as a large property in the Languedoc; and joint ventures started in Chile (1988), Portugal (1992), and Argentina (1999).

better than the Mouton of that great year. But after 1961 quality slipped, and in 1975, the estate was sold to Guy Tesseron, a Cognac producer. The 1980s saw steady improvement, and fanatical selection brought the wines to an impressive new level by the late 1990s. They have swagger, power, and concentration, and recent vintages have been of superb quality. The double-decker *cuvier*, *chais*, and bottle cellars are on an enormous scale, even by Médoc standards. The second label is Les Hauts de Pontet.

Other Pauillac Châteaux

Château la Bécasse ☆–☆☆
Owner: Roland Fonteneau. 4.2 ha.
Tiny but admirable estate making deep-flavoured Pauillac in good years.

Château Bellegrave ☆☆
Owner: Jean-Paul Meffre. 7 ha.
www.chateau-bellegrave.fr
Same ownership as Château du Glana in St Julien, but the wines have more stuffing.

Château Colombier Monpelou ☆
Owner: Bernard Jugla. 24 ha.
Light and evidently underperforming wines from well-located vines.

Château Cordeillan Bages ☆☆
Owner: J.M. Cazes. 2 ha. www.cordeillanbages.com
A mere 1,000 cases from the château hotel vineyard.

Château La Fleur Peyrabon ☆–☆☆
Owner: Patrick Bernard. 5 ha.
Négociant Bernard's Haut-Médoc property Château Peyrabon contains a sector within Pauillac, bottled separately.

Château Fonbadet ☆☆–☆☆☆
Owner: Pierre Peyronie. 20 ha.
www.chateaufonbadet.com
A good growth, producing rich, dense, traditional wines from very old vines. Can be outstanding in top years.

Les Forts de Latour ☆☆☆
See Château Latour.
The first of the "second" wines of the Médoc, and still the best.

Château Haut-Bages Monpelou ☆–☆☆
Owner: Castéja family. 15 ha.
Until 1948, part of Château Duhart-Milon, now in the same hands as Château Batailley and effectively its second wine.

Château Pibran ☆☆–☆☆☆
Owner: AXA Millésimes. 17 ha.
Fleshy, robust, at times opulent wine. In 2001, neighbour Château Tour Pibran was purchased and incorporated.

Cave Coopérative la Rose Pauillac ☆–☆☆
www.la-rose-pauillac.com
Shrinking growers' cooperative drawing on 60 ha. Well-made, if rustic, Pauillac.

St-Estèphe

St-Estèphe is more pleasantly rural than Pauillac; a scattering of six hamlets with some steepish slopes and (at Marbuzet) wooded parks. It has 1,255 ha of vineyards, mainly *crus bourgeois*, on heavier soil planted with, as a rule, a higher proportion of Merlot to Cabernet than the communes to the south. Typical St-Estèphe keeps a strong colour for a long time, is slow to show its virtues, has less perfume, and a coarser, more hearty flavour than Pauillac, with less of the tingling vitality that marks the very best Médocs. With a few brilliant exceptions, the St-Estèphes are the foot soldiers of this aristocratic army.

St-Estèphe Crus Classés

Château Calon-Ségur ☆☆☆
3ème Cru Classé. Owner: Mme. Denise Capbern-Gasqueton. 55 ha. Grapes: Cab.Sauv. 65%, Cab.Fr. 15%, Merlot 20%.
The northernmost classed growth of the Médoc, named after the eighteenth century Comte de Ségur, who also owned Lafite and Latour, but whose "heart was at Calon" – and is remembered by a red one on the label. After years when the wine was somewhat dour and tannic, quality leapt ahead in the mid-1990s, and Calon-Ségur is now indisputably one of the top wines of the region. The walled vineyard surrounds the fine château.

Château Cos d'Estournel ☆☆☆–☆☆☆☆
2ème Cru Classé. Owner: Michel Reybier. 64 ha. Grapes: Cab.Sauv. 58%, Cab.Fr. 2%, Merlot 38%, Petit Verdot 2%. www.cosdestournel.com
Superbly sited vineyard sloping south towards Château Lafite. No house, but a bizarre *chinoiserie chai*. The most (perhaps the only) glamorous St-Estèphe, one of the top Second Growths with both the flesh and the bone of great claret and a fine record for consistency. Despite changes of ownership since 1998, Jean-Guillaume Prats, the son of the previous owner, remains at the helm. This is one of the finest modern-style clarets, with the estate using all the technology at its disposal to focus on quality. It remains a powerful, long-lived wine with an abundance of fruit and oak. Fifteen to years is a good age to drink it. The second label is Les Pagodes de Cos. The "s" of Cos is sounded, like most final consonants in southwest France.

Château Cos-Labory ☆☆–☆☆☆
5ème Cru Classé. Owner: Bernard Audoy. 18 ha. Grapes: Cab.Sauv. 55%, Cab.Fr. 10%, Merlot 35%.
A businesslike little classed growth next door to Cos d'Estournel, but only geographically. The rather scattered vineyards make a blunt, honest St-Estèphe, relatively soft and fruity for drinking in four or five years. What the wines lack is finesse.

Château Lafon-Rochet ☆☆☆
4ème Cru Classé. Owner: Michel Tesseron. 45 ha. Grapes: Cab.Sauv. 55%, Merlot 41%, Cab.Fr. 4%.
www.lafon-rochet.com
A single block of vineyard sloping south towards the back of

Château Lafite on the south bank of St-Estèphe. The château was rebuilt in the 1960s by the Cognac merchant, Guy Tesseron, whose son Michel (brother of Alfred Tesseron of Château Pontet-Canet), spares no expense to make good wine, and has greatly improved the property. He makes full-bodied, lush, powerful wine, which is worth keeping for smoothness, but does not seem to find great finesse. Recent vintages, even 2006, show a steady progression in quality.

Château Montrose ☆☆☆–☆☆☆☆
2ème Cru Classé. Owner: Martin Bouygues. 95 ha. Grapes: Cab.Sauv. 65%, Cab.Fr. 10%, Merlot 25%. www.chateau-montrose.com
Isolated, seemingly remote property overlooking the Gironde north of St-Estèphe with a style of its own; traditionally one of the firmest of all Bordeaux, hard and forbidding for a long time, notably powerful in flavour even when mature. The deep colour and flavour of the wine probably come from the clay subsoil under reddish, iron-rich gravel. Being right on the river also helps the grapes to early ripeness. Wines from 1978–85 let the standard drop, but in the early '90s the tone has again been sterner, tempting some to call Montrose the "Latour of St-Estèphe" (Its situation overlooking the river encourages the comparison.) Superb in '90, '95, '96, 2000, '03, and '05. In 2006 the Charmolüe family, who had owned Montrose since 1896, sold the estate to a construction tycoon, who immediately expanded the property. Second label is La Dame de Montrose.

Château Cos d'Estournel, St-Estèphe

Other St-Estèphe Châteaux
Château Andron-Blanquet ☆
Owner: Bernard Audoy. 16 ha.
Made at Cos-Labory (q.v.). Inexpensive but lacklustre.

Château Beau-Site ☆☆
Owner: Castéja family. 35 ha.
A fine situation close to Calon-Ségur. Good, sturdy wines, but most enjoyable fairly young.

Château le Boscq ☆☆
Owner: Union Francaise de Gestion. 18 ha.
Very good, supple wines for medium-term drinking, though the '96 still drinks well in 2008.

Château Capbern-Gasqueton ☆–☆☆
Owner: Mme. Denise Capbern-Gasqueton. 41 ha.
Rich, burly wine from same stable as Château Calon-Ségur.

Château Chambert-Marbuzet ☆–☆☆
See Château Haut-Marbuzet.

Château Clauzet
Owner: Baron Maurice Velge. 28 ha. www.chateauclauzet.com
The new Belgian proprietor bought Clauzet and Château de Côme nearby in 1997 and is producing sound if rather dense wines.

Château Coutelin-Merville ☆–☆☆
Owner: Bernard Estager. 23 ha.
Light yet somewhat rustic wines, though 2003 is sumptuous.

Château le Crock ☆☆
Owner: Cuvelier family. 33 ha. www.cuvelier-bordeaux.com
Classical mansion; same ownership as Château Léoville-Poyferré (see St-Julien). Consistent and well-made, with ample density and fruit. Can be enjoyed quite young.

Château Haut-Beauséjour ☆☆
Owner: Champagne Louis Roederer. 20 ha.
A property re-created in 1992 by Jean-Claude Rouzaud, who also owns Château de Pez (q.v.).

Château Haut-Marbuzet ☆☆☆
Owner: Henri Duboscq. 58 ha.
Today the outstanding *cru bourgeois* of St-Estèphe: oaky, fleshy, luxurious, and instantly appealing. Châteaux Chambert-Marbuzet and Tour de Marbuzet are lesser but still attractive wines from the same stable.

Château Lilian Ladouys ☆☆
Owner: Martin Bouygues. 45 ha. www.chateau-lilian-ladouys.com
New owners in 1989 made substantial investments, and initial vintages were splendid, if very oaky. Composed of dozens of scattered parcels, the property proved difficult to manage and experienced financial difficulties, relieved in 2006 by its sale to the owner of Château Montrose.

Château Marbuzet ☆☆
Owner: Michel Reybier. 11 ha. www.cosestournel.com

Until 1995 the second label of Cos d'Estournel (q.v.) and subsequently released as an independent wine produced by the same team.

Château Meyney ☆☆
Owner: Crédit Agricole Grands Crus. 51 ha.
One of the best-sited and most long-lived of the many reliable *cru bourgeois* in St-Estèphe. Firm, dark wine, often tough, and never quite living up to the vineyards' potential.

Château Les Ormes-de-Pez ☆☆–☆☆☆
Owner: Cazes family. 33 ha. www.ormesdepez.com
Extremely popular and highly regarded property. Deservedly so, as the wine is rich, fleshy, elegant, and beautifully balanced.

Chateau Petit Bocq
Owner: Dr Gaëtan Lagneaux. 15 ha.
www.chateau-petit-bocq.com
Rich, savoury, oaky wines produced since 1993 by a Belgian doctor.

Château de Pez ☆☆
Owner: Champagne Louis Roederer. 26 ha.
Potentially noble, very long-lived wine, occasionally of classed growth standard. At 20 years, the 1970 was magnificent. Since Roederer bought the property in 1995, the wine has become softer and more elegant.

Château Phélan-Ségur ☆☆–☆☆☆
Owner: Thierry Gardinier. 90 ha. www.phelansegur.com
Important property, totally rebuilt, and full of ambition since the Gardiniers (former owners of Pommery) bought it in 1985. Sometimes underrated, as the wine is elegant rather than powerful or dramatic. Best enjoyed within ten years.

Château Pomys ☆
Owner: François Arnaud. 12 ha. www.chateaupomys.com
A well-known property (and hotel) producing classic but rather dull St-Estèphe.

Château Ségur de Cabanac ☆☆
Owner: Guy Delon. 7 ha
Only 3,000 cases of very good quality.

Château Sérilhan ☆☆
Owner: Didier Marcelis. 20 ha.
www.chateau-serilhan.com
Marcelis was hauled back from a career in hi-tech industries to run the family properties, which he is doing with flair, intelligence, and determination.

Château Tour de Pez ☆–☆☆
Owner: Philippe Bouchara. 30 ha.
Improving property, producing wine with ample fruit and reasonable intensity.

Château Tour des Termes
Owner: Christophe Anney. 16 ha.
www.chateautourdestermes.com
Rich ripe wines, vivid and enjoyable.

Château Tronquoy-Lalande ☆☆
Owner: Martin Bouygues. 17 ha.

Once dark and tannic, the wine has become more supple in the 1990s – a change in style rather than quality. Now under the same ownership as Château Montrose, so its future direction is uncertain.

Haut-Médoc

Haut-Médoc is the catch-all appellation for the fringes of the area that includes the most famous communes. It varies in quality from equal to some of the best in the very south, where Château la Lagune in Ludon and Château Cantemerle are out on a limb, to a level only notionally higher than the best of the lower, northerly end of the Médoc. Some of this land lies along the river in the middle of the appellation, in the low-lying communes of Arcins, Lamarque, and Cussac – which also, it must be said, have some very good gravel. Some lies back inland along the edge of the pine forest.

With a total of 4,380 hectares, the Haut-Médoc appellation is only an indication of high quality – not a guarantee.

Haut-Médoc Crus Classés

Château Belgrave ☆☆–☆☆☆
5ème Cru Classé. Owner: private consortium but managed by CVBG. 60 ha. Grapes: Cab.Sauv. 45%, Cab.Fr. 8%, Merlot 42%, Petit Verdot 5%. www.cvbg.com
A lost property until 1980, and since then it has produced consistently attractive wine. In the late 1990s, quality improved further, and the wine has much more intensity and class.

Château de Camensac ☆
5ème Cru Classé. Owner: Jean Merlaut and Céline Villars-Foubet. 70 ha. Grapes: Cab.Sauv. 60%, Cab.Fr. 5%, Merlot 35%.
Neighbour of Châteaux Belgrave, la Tour-Carnet, and Lagrange (qq.v.) in the St-Laurent group, inland from St-Julien. Humdrum wines under the former owners, the Forner family, but purchase in 2005 by the experienced Merlauts should bring long-awaited improvement.

Château Cantemerle ☆☆
5ème Cru Classé. Owner: SMABTP group. 90 ha. Grapes: Cab.Sauv. 50%, Cab.Fr. 5%, Merlot 40%, Petit Verdot 5%. www.cantemerle.com
The next château north from la Lagune, within a wooded park of mysterious beauty. The tree beside the house on the pretty engraved label is a plane that now dominates the house completely – a monster. The vineyards, with light soil and a good deal of Merlot, yield wine of charm yet formidable stability. Vintages of the '50s and '60s were marvellous; those of the '70s not quite so good, but quality was regained in the '80s. Today rather patchy and lacking in backbone and finesse. Second wine: Les Allées de Cantemerle.

Château la Lagune ☆☆–☆☆☆
3ème Cru Classé. Owner: Jean-Jacques Frey. 75 ha. Grapes: Cab.Sauv. 60%, Merlot 30%, Petit Verdot 10%. www.chateau-lalagune.com

The nearest important Médoc château to Bordeaux, and a charming eighteenth-century villa. The vineyard had almost disappeared in the 1950s, when it was totally replanted and equipped with the latest steel vats and pipes. Through numerous changes in ownership, the wine retained its sweetness, spiciness, and fleshiness. Since 1999 the new owner, also a major Champagne proprietor, has invested heavily (the new *cuvier* is magnificent), and daughter Caroline, trained by Denis Dubourdieu, makes the ever more refined wine.

Château la Tour-Carnet ☆☆–☆☆☆
4ème Cru Classé. Owner: Bernard Magrez. 65 ha, of which 1 white. Red grapes: Cab.Sauv. 40%, Cab.Fr. 7%, Merlot 50%, Petit Verdot 3%. White grapes: Sauv. 35%, Sém. 35%, Sauv. Gris 30%. www.latour-carnet.com
A moated medieval castle in the relatively rolling, wooded back country of St-Laurent, but négociant Bernard Magrez acquired the estate in 1997 and moved swiftly to improve quality in the vineyard and winery. Excellent quality since 1998, and a new white wine from 2003.

Other Haut-Médoc Châteaux

Château d'Agassac ☆☆
Ludon. Owner: Groupama. 38 ha. www.agassac.com
The Médoc's most romantic château, medieval, moated, and deep in the woods. The Groupama insurance company bought Agassac in 1996 and invested substantially. The wines are fleshy, but fresh and balanced.

Château d'Arche ☆–☆☆
Ludon. Owner: Mähler-Besse. 9 ha. www.mahler-besse.com
A good wine with pure fruit and sweet oak.

Château Arnauld ☆–☆☆
Arcins. Owner: Nathalie Roggy and Rrancois Theil. 38ha.
A good but inconsistent wine.

Château Beaumont ☆–☆☆
Cussac. Owner: GMF. 105 ha. www.chateau-beaumont.com
Grand château on the Cussac plateau, in some of the same hands as Beychevelle (q.v.), making stylish, good-value claret for early drinking.

Château Belle-Vue
Owner: Vincent Mulliez. 10 ha. www.chateau-belle-vue.com
A lush, ripe, modern claret from vineyards near Giscours.

Château Bel-Orme-Tronquoy-de-Lalande ☆
St-Seurin. Owner: Jean-Michel Quié. 28 ha.
Well-sited property of the family that owns Châteaux Rauzan-Gassies and Croizet-Bages (qq.v.). A tough, tannic wine in the '70s and '80s; more supple since mid-'90s.

Château Bernardotte ☆☆
Owner: Champagne Louis Roederer. 39 ha. www.chateau-bernadotte.com
Property on the fringes of Pauillac, acquired by Château Pichon-Lalande in '97, since when quality, already sound, has improved further. Now under the same new ownership as Pichon-Lalande.

Château Cambon-la-Pelouse ☆☆
Macau. Owner: Jean-Pierre Marie. 65 ha. www.cambon-la-pelouse.com
Large estate between Cantemerle and Giscours (qq.v.), with 50% of the vineyard planted with Merlot. Increasingly substantial wines for medium-term drinking.

Château Caronne-Ste-Gemme ☆–☆☆
St-Laurent. Owner: François Nony. 45 ha. www.chateau-caronne-ste-gemme.com
A substantial property delivering well-made, somewhat lean wine, capable of charm with time.

Château Charmail ☆☆
St-Seurin. Owner: Olivier Sèze. 22 ha.
Full, fruity claret with a silky texture and good ageing potential.

Château Cissac ☆–☆☆
Cissac. Owner: Louis Vialard. 50 ha. www.chateau-cissac.com
A pillar of the bourgeoisie. Reliable, robust, if old-fashioned Médoc; best after ten years or so (it used to take 20), thanks to the preponderance of Cabernet Sauvignon in the wine.

Château Citran ☆☆
Avensan. Owner: Antoine Merlaut. 90 ha. www.citran.com
Round, full wine (42% Merlot) with ageing potential, benefited from Japanese investment from 1987 until bought by Merlaut (of the Taillan group) in 1996.

Château Clément Pichon ☆–☆☆
Parempuyre. Owner: Clément Fayat. 25 ha. www.vignobles.fayat.com
Formerly exhibited a bland, upfront style, but since mid-'90s has gained in weight and complexity. Delicious 2005.

Château Coufran ☆☆
St-Seurin. Owner: Miailhe family. 75 ha. www.chateau-coufran.com
The northernmost estate of the Haut-Médoc, it is unusual in being 85% Merlot to make softer, more "fleshy" wine than its neighbouring sister – Château Verdignan (q.v.).

Château Fontesteau ☆
St-Sauveur. Owner: Dominique Fouin and partners. 32 ha. www.fontesteau.com
A conservative wine in the classic Médoc style, for long keeping, but recent vintages have been inconsistent.

Château de Gironville ☆
Macau. Owner: Vincent Mulliez. 10 ha. www.scgironville.com
Replanted in '87, and now under same ownership as Belle-Vue (q.v.) and made in a similar style.

Château Hanteillan ☆–☆☆
Cissac. Owner: Catherine Blasco. 82 ha. www.chateau-hanteillan.com
Old property, lavishly restored and replanted since 1973. Easygoing, well-balanced wine for early drinking.

Château Lachesnaye ☆–☆☆
Owner: Bouteiller family. 20 ha. www.lachesnaye.com
Next door to better known Château Lanessan (q.v.), and under the same ownership. Robust wines that can age well.

Château de Lamarque ☆☆
Lamarque. Owner: Pierre-Gilles Gromand. 35 ha.
www.chateaudelamarque.com
The finest remaining medieval fortress in the Médoc, in the village where the ferry leaves for Blaye. The wine is supple and spicy, with a flavour of blackberries; it establishes the potential of the central Médoc. But don't expect elegance.

Château Lamothe-Bergeron ☆–☆☆
Cussac. Owner: Crédit Agricole Grands Crus. 66 ha.
Gently herbaceous wine, Merlot-dominated, for early drinking.

Château Lamothe-Cissac ☆
Cissac. Owner: Vincent Fabre. 33 ha.
A fairly austere wine, lacking finesse. The Vieilles Vignes bottling is superior.

Château Lanessan ☆☆–☆☆☆
Cussac. Owner: Bouteiller family. 40 ha.
www.lanessan.com
An extravagant Victorian mansion and park with a popular carriage museum. The best-known estate in Cussac, which occasionally reaches *cru classé* quality. Polished rather than exciting wine. Ages well.

Château Larose-Trintaudon ☆
St-Laurent. Owner: Assurances Générales de France.
175 ha. www.larose-trintaudon.com
The biggest estate in the Médoc, planted since 1965, built up by the Spanish Forner family until its sale in '86. Quantity does not seem to impede steady, enjoyable quality, even if the wine is essentially bland. The top selection is bottled as Château Larose-Perganson.

Château Lestage Simon ☆–☆☆
St-Seurin. Owner: Vignobles Leprince. 40 ha.
Concentrated, fruity, and reliable.

Château Lieujean ☆
St-Sauveur. Owner: Jean-Michel Lapalu and Patrice Ricard. 38 ha. www.domaines-lapalu.com.
A simple but attractive wine from the Lapalu stable.

Château Liversan ☆–☆☆
St-Sauveur. Owner: Domaines Lapalu. 40 ha.
www.domaines-lapalu.com
Charming property including Château Fonpiqueyre. Conscientious winemaking backed by new investment.

Château Magnol ☆
Blanquefort. Owner: Barton et Guestier. 17 ha.
www.barton-guestier.com
Half Cabernet, half Merlot; supple and medium-bodied.

Château Malescasse ☆☆
Lamarque. Owner: Alcatel Alsthom. 37 ha.
www.malescasse.com

Replanted in the 1970s by the Tesseron family, who sold the property in '92. Inexpensive but well-made wines that lack some personality.

Château de Malleret ☆
Le Pian. Owner: Not disclosed. 50 ha.
Lean and undistinguished wines, but a new owner in 2006 might turn things around.

Château Maucamps ☆–☆☆
Macau. Owner: Alain Tessandier. 14 ha.
A gentle wine of some finesse for medium-term drinking.

Château le Meynieu ☆
Vertheuil. Owner: Jacques Pédro. 20 ha.
A burly wine, with ample tannin and oak, if little elegance.

Château Meyre ☆–☆☆
Avensan. Owner: Corinne Bonne. 18 ha.
Sound wine but eclipsed by the special cuvée called Optima.

Château Mille Roses ☆–☆☆
Macau. Owner: David Faure. 10 ha.
A fairly new property, producing lively wines that so far lack finesse.

Château du Moulin Rouge ☆
Cussac. Owner: Guy Pelon. 16 ha.
A hefty, well-structured wine.

Château Paloumey ☆☆
Ludon. Owner: Martine Cazeneuve. 32 ha.
www.chateaupaloumey.com
One of a group of properties ownd by the ambitious Mme. Cazeneuve, and making consistently good wines since 2001.

Château Peyrabon ☆–☆☆
St-Sauveur. Owner: Patrick Bernard. 50 ha.
www.chateaupeyrabon.com
Bought in 1998 by Patrick Bernard of Millésima, the wine has yet to shed a distinct gawkiness. The property also releases a small quantity of Pauillac called Château La Fleur-Peyrabon (q.v.)

Château Puy-Castéra ☆
Cissac. Owner: Alix Marès. 28 ha. www.puycastera.com
After complete renovation in '73, the property has steadily produced sound but simple wine.

Château Ramage la Batisse ☆
St-Sauveur. Owner: MACIF. 66 ha.
A vineyard developed since 1961. The estate employs modern methods to make a traditional yet rapidly maturing style of wine.

Château de Retout ☆–☆☆
Cussac. Owner: Gérard Kopp. 33 ha.
www.chateau-de-retout.com
Robust and full-bodied claret, though far from elegant.

Château Reysson ☆
Vertheuil. Owner: Mercian Corporation. 70 ha.
Japanese owners since 1987 favour an easygoing style for early drinking, although the Réserve bottling has more stuffing.

Château Saint-Ahon ☆
Blanquefort. Owner: Comte Bernard de Colbert. 31 ha.
www.saintahon.com
Sleek, enjoyable wine; not too extracted.

Château St-Paul ☆–☆☆
St-Seurin. Owner: consortium of investors. 20 ha.
Formerly rustic wines, but improved since Olivier Sèze of
neighbouring Château Charmail (q.v.) took over winemaking.

Château Sénéjac ☆☆
Le Pian. Owner: Thierry Rustmann. 40 ha.
Sénéjac had a good reputation for its white wine, but these
vines were grubbed up by the new owner in 1999. The *prestige
cuvée* Karolus was discontinued after 2004, as it had become
only marginally superior to the regular Sénéjac.

Château Senilhac ☆
St-Seurin. Owner: Jean-Luc Grassin. 23 ha.
Straightforward, sometimes astringent, for early consumption.

Château Sociando-Mallet ☆☆☆
St-Seurin. Owner: Jean Gautreau. 74 ha.
Bought by Jean Gautreau in '69, and by the early '80s a major
success, thanks to excellent location of the vineyards and
exacting winemaking. Recent vintages, needing long
maturation, have outshone many crus classés. Second wine:
Demoiselle de Sociando-Mallet.

Château Soudars ☆–☆☆
St-Seurin. Owner: Eric Miailhe. 23 ha.
www.chateausoudars.com
Essentially a new estate, created by Jean Miailhe's son since
'73. Well-made, supple wine, with an abundance of ripe fruit.

Using a traditional hand press to crush grapes

Château Tour du Haut Moulin ☆–☆☆
Cussac. Owner: Lionel Poitou. 32 ha.
Full-flavoured wine (50% Merlot) from an estate near
Beaumont; deservedly enjoys a wide following.

Château la Tour St-Joseph ☆
Cissac. Owne: Quancard family. 10 ha.
www.chevalquancard.com
Sturdy wine, with a fair amount of oak.

Château Verdignan ☆–☆☆
St-Seurin. Owner: Miailhe family. 60 ha.
In contrast to its sister-château Coufran (q.v.), Verdignan has
the classic Médoc proportion of Cabernet, and needs keeping
two or three years longer.

Château de Villegeorge ☆–☆☆
Avensan. Owner: Marie-Laure Lurton-Roux. 20 ha.
www.vignobles-marielurtonroux.com.
Another Lurton property. Lean wines that often fail to live up
to their former reputation.

Appellation Médoc

The lower Médoc (being farther down the Gironde) was
formerly called Bas-Médoc, which made it clear that it was this
area and not the whole peninsula under discussion. The soils,
and therefore the wines, are considered inferior here. The last
of the big-calibre gravel has been deposited by glaciers between
Graves and St-Estèphe.

Although the ground continues to heave gently, the humps
become more scattered and their soil much heavier, with a high
proportion of pale, cold clay, suited to Merlot rather than
Cabernet (although patches of sandier soil persist).

The wine has distinctly less finesse and perfume, but good
body and structure with some of the tannic "cut" that makes all
Médocs such good wines at table. Good vintages last well in
bottle, without developing the sweet complexities of the Haut-
Médoc at its best.

The last decade has seen a great revival of interest in this
productive area. Half a dozen big properties have already made
the running and now offer a good deal, if not an absolute
bargain. In 1972, there were 1,836 hectares in production in the
appellation Médoc. By 2006, this figure had risen to 5,580
hectares.

Much the most important commune is Bégadan, with several
of the most prominent estates. Nearly a third of the whole
appellation comes from the one parish. Next, in order of
production, come St-Yzans, Prignac, Ordonnac, Blaignan, St-
Christoly, and St-Germain.

The principal producers are given here in alphabetical order,
followed by the names of their communes. The central town
for the whole area is Lesparre.

Leading Lower Médoc Châteaux

Château Blaignan ☆
Blaignan. Owner: Crédit Agricole Grands Crus. 87 ha.
Blaignan's largest vineyard, yielding easygoing wines for early
drinking.

Château Bournac ☆
Civrac. Owner: Bruno Secret. 14 ha.
Solid, even rustic wines.

Château La Breuil-Renaissance ☆–☆☆
Blaignan. Owner: Philippe Bérard. 27 ha.
www.lebreuil-renaissance.com
Dense, plump wines, especially the Cuvée Prestige.

Château la Cardonne ☆☆
Blaignan. Owner: Guy Charloux. 86 ha.
www.domaines-cgr.com
This estate was restructured in the early 1970s by the
Rothschilds. This provided a great boost to the lower
Médoc with its prestige and predictably well-made wine.
However, the property has changed hands repeatedly and
is now grouped with Châteaux Ramafort and Grivière (qq.v.).
Frankly commercial: machine-picked and never sold *en
primeur*. Nonetheless, it does produce well-focused wines,
impeccably made.

Château la Clare ☆☆
Bégadan. Owner: Jean Guyon. 20 ha.
www.rollandeby.com.
Energetic and oaky wines from same stable as Château Rollan
de By (q.v.)

Château d'Escurac ☆☆–☆☆☆
Civrac. Owner: Jean-Marc Landureau. 18 ha
Has only bottled its wines since '90. Brilliant wine in '96, and
high standards maintained ever since.

Château Fontis ☆
Ordonnac. Owner: Vincent Boivert. 10 ha
The parental property is Château Les Ormes-Sorbet (q.v.),
and these wines, though light, are made with similar flair.

Château La Gorce
Blaignan. Owner: Denis Fabre. 44 ha.
www.chateaulagorce.com
Solid and satisfying traditional Médoc.

Château les Grands Chênes ☆☆
St. Christoly. Owner: Bernard Magrez. 11 ha.
Since 1998, Magrez and his team have lavished their resources
and skill on this already elegant wine. The Cuvée Prestige has
been discontinued since it no longer marks a significant
improvement on the regular wine.

Château Greysac ☆☆
Bégadan. Owner: Domaines Codem. 60 ha.
www.greysac.com
Big, efficient property making sound wine, well-known in the
USA. Greysac is approachable young but capable of ageing.

Château Grivière ☆–☆☆
Blaignan. Owner: Guy Charloux. 18 ha.
www.domaines-cgr.com
(See Château la Cardonne.)
A rounded and fruity wine, with almost 60% Merlot.

Haut-Condissas ☆☆–☆☆☆
Bégadan. Owner: Jean Guyon. 5 ha. www.rollandeby.com
A parcel within Rollan de By, given luxury treatment, and
a very high price.

Château Haut-Maurac ☆☆
St Yzans. Owner: Olivier Decelle. 28 ha.
Frozen-food tycoon Decelle owns Mas Amiel in Roussillon
and other properties in Bordeaux. Fine gravelly terroir here
results in stylish wines.

Château Laujac ☆
Bégadan. Owner: Bernard Cruse. 30 ha.
A home of the famous family of shippers, hence well-known
abroad long before most of the other châteaux in the district.
The wine is straightforward but lacks concentration.

Château Loudenne ☆☆
St-Yzans. Owner: Jean-Paul Lafragette. 65 ha.
www.lafragette.com
A low, pale pink château on a hill of gravelly clay overlooking
the river. Loudenne was in English hands (it was Gilbey's
French HQ) for over a century, an informal clubhouse for
visiting merchants and journalists. The estate produced well-
balanced and long-lived wine until it changed hands in 1999.
Under the new owner, Loudenne has become more polished,
and a new-oaked *prestige cuvée*, Hippocampus, was introduced.

Château Lousteauneuf ☆☆
Valeyrac. Owner: Bruno Segond. 22 ha.
www.chateau-lousteauneuf.com
Impressive modern-style with considerable power in top years.

Château Les-Ormes-Sorbet ☆☆
Couquèques. Owner: Hélène Boivert. 22 ha.
Rich, highly oaked wines with fine depth of fruit.

Château Patache d'Aux ☆☆
Bégadan. Owner: Jean-Michel Lapalu. 43 ha.
www.domaines-lapalu.com
Popular, full-flavoured Médoc with 60% Cabernet
Sauvignon, now linked with the aristocratic Château
Liversan (q.v.).

Racking wine in the Victorian chai, Château Loudenne, Medoc

Château Potensac ☆☆☆
Ordonnac. Owner: Jean-Hubert Delon. 67 ha.
www.chateau-potensac.com
A very successful enterprise of the Delons of Château
Léoville-Las-Cases, who have owned Potensac for two
centuries. Well-made, fruity, structured claret with a stylish
flavour of oak and surprising longevity.

Château Preuillac ☆☆
Lesparre. Owner: Yvon Mau and the
Dirkzwager company. 30 ha.
www.chateau-preuillac.com
Acquired by the Mau négociant company in 1998. The
terroir is not exceptional, but scrupulous work in vineyard
and winery is delivering steadily improving results.

Château Ramafort ☆☆
Blaignan. Owner: Guy Charloux. 20 ha.
www.domaines-cgr.com
Another property in the group based at La Cardonne (q.v.).
Stylish wines with some complexity.

Château Rolland de By ☆☆–☆☆☆
Bégadan. Owner: Jean Guyon. 44 ha.
www.rollandeby.com
Guyon's determination to produce something exceptional
in the Médoc shows through in this tightly structured,
oaky wine. See also Haut-Condissas.

Château Le Temple ☆–☆☆
Valeyrac. Owner: Denis Bergey. 18 ha.
Solid fleshy wines, and a Cuvée Prestige in top years.

Château Tour-Blanche ☆
St-Christoly. Owner: Bernard Magrez. 39 ha.
www.bernard-magrez.com
New ownership has brought the services of oenologist Michel
Rolland, so there should be better quality to come.

Château La Tour-de-By ☆☆
Bégadan. Owner: Marc Pagés. 74 ha.
www.la-tour-de-by.com
Extremely successful estate with a high reputation for
enjoyable and durable, if not literally fine, wine.

Château Tour-Haut-Caussan ☆☆–☆☆☆
Blaignan. Owner: Philippe Courrian. 17 ha.
Fine off-vintages give this property one of the best records in
the Médoc. Utterly traditional winemaking, with consistently
satisfying results.

Vieux-Château Landon ☆☆
Bégadan. Owner: Cyril Gillet. 38 ha.
www.vieux-chateau-landon.com
An energetic proprietor with ambitions. Sound, lively wine.

Château Vieux-Robin ☆☆
Bégadan. Owner: Maryse Roba. 18 ha.
www.chateau-vieux-robin.com
Cuvée Bois de Lunier, aged in partly new oak, is better than
the regular wine. Conscientious winemaking, often
impressive results.

Graves

Wine was first made at Bordeaux in what is now the city and the
suburbs, immediately across the river and to the south. Graves
was the name given to the whole of the left (city) bank of the
Garonne for as far as 65 kilometres (40 miles) upstream,
beyond the little town of Langon, and back away from the river
into the pine forests of the Landes – an area not much different
in size from the wine-growing Médoc, but more cut up with
woodland and farms and containing few extensive vineyards or
big châteaux.

VISITING CHÂTEAUX

Visitors to the Médoc will have no
difficulty in finding châteaux willing to
show them how they make their wine, and
to let them taste it from the barrel. One
way of arranging a château visit is to call
at one of the offices called *maison du vin*.

The principal one is in the heart of
Bordeaux near the Grand Théâtre.
Margaux, Pauillac, St-Estèphe, and
several other villages have local ones.
They will suggest an itinerary and, if
necessary, make contacts. This is the best
method of arranging a visit, as you can be
sure of a proper welcome when you arrive.
An even simpler method, but only really
practicable for those who speak some
French, is to stop at any of the many

châteaux that advertise "dégustation"
(tasting) and "vente directe" – direct
sales – on roadside signs. They include
some important châteaux as well as many
modest ones, and the less prestigious the
region, the greater the opportunities to
visit and taste. You will fare better in
Fronsac or Entre-Deux-Mers than in St-
Julien. At any reasonable time (ie. not
during the harvest and not from noon to
two o'clock) you can expect a more or less
friendly welcome. Clearly the idea of
vente directe is that you should buy a
bottle or two, but you need not feel
obliged. In response to the complaint
that Médoc châteaux in particular are
reluctant to receive visitors, more and

more properties are offering tours and
visits. A fee is usually charged but
includes a tasting as well as a properly
organized visit, often in the language of
your choice. Estates such as Mouton-
Rothschild, Lynch-Bages, and Pichon-
Longueville all offer this kind of tour.

It pays to contact an estate to make
an appointment, especially if its wine
is much sought after. Bordeaux wine
properties are not set up to receive
passing visitors, but a polite letter, fax, or
phone call should secure an appointment
at even the grandest property. Do not
expect a lavish tasting: wine professionals
are rarely offered more than a barrel
sample or the latest release.

Graves' distinguishing feature (hence its name) is its open, gravelly soil, the relic of Pyrénéan glaciers in the ice ages. In fact, the soil varies within the region just as much as that of the Médoc. Sand is common. Pale clay and red clay are both present. But, as in the Médoc, it is pretty certain that by now most of the potentially good vineyard land is being put to good use. In all, there are some 5,040 hectares of vineyards. In 1983, it was 1,494. But Graves is too diffuse to grasp easily.

There are subregions. In the north, where all the *crus classés* are situated, the AC Pessac-Léognan was established after years of intense lobbying. Despite the cumbersome name, the region, and its wines, have proved a success. Less content were the growers to the south, whose wines are only entitled to the AC Graves appellation. An enclave in the south of the region has quite different styles – of landscape, ownership, and wine. This is Sauternes.

Although Graves is divided between two-thirds red wine and one-third white, most of the top-quality wine is red. The words commonly used to explain how red Graves differs from Médoc make it sound less fine; "earthy", "soft", "maturing sooner" all sound more homely than inspiring. The late Maurice Healey got it in one when he said that Médoc and Graves were like glossy and matt prints of the same photograph. The matt picture can be equally beautiful, but less crisp and sharp-edged, with less glittering colours.

White Graves, at its best, is a rare experience – and an expensive one. Very few estates even aim for the unique combination of fullness and drive that comes to white Graves with time. The best is equal in quality to the great white burgundies. Opinion is divided even on the grapes to make it with. Some favour all Sémillon, some all Sauvignon Blanc, and some a mixture, in various proportions. Over the last 15 years a variant of Sauvignon Blanc called Sauvignon Gris has been quite widely planted to give more spice to the blend.

Some make the wine in stainless steel and bottle it in the early spring. Others (including the best) make it and mature it, at least briefly, in new-oak barrels. The tendency among the lesser growths making dry wine has been to pick too early to obtain full ripeness. Sauvignon Blanc in any case tends to ripen unevenly here. The best makers now concentrate on getting full ripeness and a complete fermentation to give clean, dry wine with plenty of flavour.

The communes of the northern Graves are as follows, starting in the north on the doorstep of Bordeaux: Pessac and Talence (in the suburbs); Gradignan and Villenave-d'Ornon (with very little wine today); Léognan, the most extensive, with six classed growths; Cadaujac, St Médard d'Eyrans, Canéjan, Mérignac, and Martillac. Up to 1987, all shared the single appellation Graves. In that year, the new AC Pessac-Léognan was created, to include 55 châteaux and domaines in ten communes; a total of around 1,500 hectares. South of this district, but increasingly important for similar wine, is Portets. Cérons, on the threshold of Barsac and Sauternes, makes both sweet and dry white wine, the dry now gaining in quality and popularity. Red has been steadily increasing at the expense of white, whether dry or sweet.

The châteaux of Graves were first classified in 1953 and 1959 in a blunt yes-or-no fashion, which gives little guidance.

Château Haut-Brion having been included in the Médoc classification 100 years earlier (in 1855), 12 other châteaux were designated *crus classés* for their red wine, in alphabetical order.

In 1959, six of them and two additional châteaux were designated *crus classés* for white wine. There has been talk of a regular revision of the classification, but after the fiascos of the *crus bourgeois* and St-Emilion classification a few years ago, any such plan has been indefinitely postponed.

Graves Premier Cru

Château Haut-Brion ☆☆☆☆
Pessac. Owner: Domaine Clarence Dillon. AC: Pessac-Léognan. 46 ha, of which 43 white. Red grapes: Cab.Sauv. 45%, Cab.Fr. 18%, Merlot 37%. White grapes: Sém. 60%, Sauv. 40%. www.haut-brion.com
The first wine château to be known by name, late in the seventeenth century, and although now surrounded by the suburbs of Bordeaux, still one of the best, regularly earning its official place beside the four First Growths of the Médoc.

The situation of the sixteenth-century manor house of the Pontacs is no longer particularly impressive, but its nine-metre- (30-foot-) deep gravel soil gives deep-flavoured wine that holds a remarkable balance of fruity and earthy flavours for decades. Mouton has resonance, Margaux has coloratura; Haut-Brion just has harmony – between strength and finesse, firmness and sweetness. I shall never forget the taste of an Impériale of the 1899 – the most spellbinding claret I have ever drunk.

The present owners, the descendants of American banker Clarence Dillon, bought the estate in a near-derelict condition in 1935. In 1983, they added the next-door Château La Mission-Haut-Brion (q.v.). The current president is Dillon's great-grandson, Prince Robert de Luxembourg.

It was the estate's good fortune to have at its helm since 1960 Jean-Bernard Delmas. It was he who surprised his neighbours by being one of the first to instal stainless-steel vats for the quite quick and relatively warm fermentation. Delmas also undertook a prolonged research project to determine the best rootstocks and clones, which contribute their diversity and subtlety to the wine. This, and the fairly high proportion of Cabernet Franc, contribute complexity and harmony. Delmas retired in 2004, but was succeeded by his son Jean-Philippe.

As for age, Haut-Brion demands it. The good vintages of the 1970s – '71, '75, '78, '79 – only recently reached their peak; the apogee of the 1980s is still some time away. The '89 Haut-Brion is already a legend. A tiny quantity of superlative white Graves is also made and sold at an extravagant price. The second wine of Haut-Brion underwent a change of name in 2007, when the hard to pronounce Bahans-Haut-Brion was replaced by Clarence de Haut-Brion.

Graves Crus Classés

Château Bouscaut ☆☆
Cadaujac. Owner: Sophie Lurton. AC: Pessac-Léognan. 47 ha, of which 7 white. Red grapes: Merlot 55%,

Cab.Sauv. 40%, Malbec 5%. White grapes: Sém. 50%, Sauv. 50%. www.chateau-bouscaut.com

A handsome (though rebuilt) eighteenth-century house with rather low-lying vineyards, which was bought from its American owners in 1979 by Lucien of the ubiquitous Lurton family. The style is rather understated and there was a tendency to overproduce, but recent vintages have been much better, although the white can have quite fierce acidity.

Château Carbonnieux ☆☆–☆☆☆

Léognan. Owner: Antony Perrin. AC: Pessac-Léognan. 90 ha, of which 43 white. Red grapes: Cab.Sauv. 60%, Merlot 30%, Cab.Fr. 7%, Malbec 2%, Petit Verdot 1%. White grapes: Sauv. 65%, Sém. 35%. www.carbonnieux.com

An old embattled monastery built around a courtyard, restored and run by a family who left Algeria in the 1950s. Bigger, and hence better known, than most Graves properties, particularly for its white wine, one of the flag-carriers for white Graves. The white is aged for ten months in partly new oak barriques, then bottled young, thus keeping freshness while getting some of the proper oak flavour. Quality took a marked step forward during the late '80s. Three or four years in bottle are needed to perfect it. The red faces more competition, but is well-made typical Graves, dry, and persistent.

Château le Sartre (q.v.) is one of a number of Graves properties in the hands of the Perrins. Tour Léognan is the second wine.

Domaine de Chevalier ☆☆☆–☆☆☆☆

Léognan. Owner: Olivier Bernard. AC: Pessac-Léognan. 40 ha, of which 5 white. Red grapes: Cab.Sauv. 64%, Cab.Fr. 3%, Merlot 30%, Petit Verdot 3%. White grapes: Sauv. 70%, Sém. 30%. www.domainedechevalier.com

This is rather a strange place to find a vineyard, in the middle of a frost-prone wood. Total rebuilding, however, revolutionized a sombre old place in the 1980s. The soil and the style of the red wine are similar to the nearby Haut-Bailly (q.v.); starting stern, maturing dense and savoury, and capable of a long old age. The red epitomizes finesse, not fat, and often fares poorly in blind tastings. But it's hard to think of a wine that gives more pleasure at the dinner table.

The white wine is second only to Laville-Haut-Brion in quality and is designed for an astonishingly long life. It is made with the care of a great Sauternes, fermented and matured in barrels. To drink it before five years is a waste, and the flavours of a 15-year-old bottle can be breathtaking.

Château Couhins ☆–☆☆

Villenave-d'Ornon. Owner: Institut National de la Recherche Agronomique (INRA). 24 ha, of which 7 white. Red grapes: Cab.Sauv. 50%, Cab.Fr. 10%, Merlot 40%.

White grapes: Sauv. 84%, Sém. 15%, Sauv. Gris 1%. www.chateau-couhins.fr

The Institut National de la Recherche Agronomique bought the land in 1968 for viticultural research, and first made wine in 1981. The whites are far more interesting than the austere reds.

Château Couhins-Lurton ☆☆–☆☆☆

Léognan. Owner: André Lurton. AC: Pessac-Léognan. 25 ha, of which 7 white. Red grapes: Merlot 77%, Cab.Sauv. 23%. White grapes: 100% Sauv. www.andrelurton.com

In 1970, André Lurton bought six hectares of this classed growth which he had farmed since 1967. The wine, unusually, is pure Sauvignon, fermented and aged in oak. It rewards keeping five to ten years. The Lurtons also bought the château and original cellar in 1992. The red, with an unusually high proportion of Merlot, was introduced in 2002.

Château de Fieuzal ☆☆–☆☆☆

Léognan. Owner: Lochlann Quinn. AC: Pessac-Léognan. 48 ha, of which 8 white. Red grapes: Cab.Sauv. 48%, Cab.Fr. 2.5%, Merlot 48%, Petit Verdot 1.5%. White grapes: Sauv. 50%, Sém. 50%. www.fieuzal.com

Until its sale in 2001, Fieuzal had been nurtured by Gérard Gribelin to tune the masculine, tannic, earthy style of the region to fine harmony; since the mid-1980s a regular top performer. The production of white is not technically "classé" although it is better than some that are. Quality stumbled in recent years, but a new director is determined to develop its full and remarkable potential.

Château Haut-Bailly ☆☆☆

Léognan. Owner: Robert Wilmers. AC: Pessac-Léognan. 28 ha. Grapes: Cab.Sauv. 65%, Cab.Fr. 10%, Merlot 25%. www.chateau-haut-bailly.com

Until 1998 the property of the Belgian Sanders family, and generally considered one of the top five châteaux of (red) Graves. It makes no white wine. One-quarter of the vineyard is a mixed plantation of very old vines. Relatively shallow, stony soil over hard clay is an unusual site for a great vineyard, and the result can be problems during drought.

The great years ('66, '70, '78, '79, '86, '88, '89, '90, '96, '98, 2000, '05) I can best describe as nourishing, like long-simmered stock; deep, earthy, and round. I love them. Second label: "La Parde de Haut Bailly". Despite the change of ownership, the Sanders family, who have cared for this property so deeply, stay on to run the estate. Véronique Sanders, the granddaughter of Jean, is competent and committed.

Château Latour-Martillac ☆☆–☆☆☆

Martillac. Owner: Kressmann family. AC: Pessac-Léognan. 45 ha, of which 9 white. Red grapes: Cab.Sauv. 60%, Merlot 35%, Petit Verdot 5%. White grapes:

Château Bouscaut, Pessac-Léognan

Sém 55%, Sauv. 40%, Muscadelle 5%.
www.latour-martillac.com
A property once in the Montesquieu family (who owned the magnificent moated la Brède nearby). The Kressmanns, a Bordeaux négociant family, patiently cultivate old vines for quality. The white wine is classic Graves, vigorous and toasty and best with bottle-age; the red is a good example of the robust, savoury style of the region.

Château Laville-Haut-Brion ✩✩✩✩
Talence. Owner: Domaine Clarence Dillon. AC: Pessac-Léognan. 3.5 ha. Grapes: Sém. 70%, Sauv. 27%, Muscadelle 3%. www.haut-brion.com
The white wine of la Mission-Haut-Brion (q.v.), first made in 1928 on a patch where former owner M. Woltner decided the soil was too heavy for red. Bordeaux's best dry white wine. Drunk young, its quality may go unnoticed – and its price will certainly seem excessive. The wine is fermented in new oak barriques, and bottled from them the following spring. Its qualities – apart from an increasingly haunting flavour as the years go by – are concentration and the same sort of rich-yet-dry character as "Ygrec", the dry wine of Château d'Yquem, used to have, but with more grace. Stunning quality since 1985. No rush to drink: '66 and '75 were going strong in 2008.

Château Malartic-Lagravière ✩✩✩
Léognan. Owner: Alfred-Alexandre Bonnie. 53 ha, of which 7 white. Red grapes: Cab.Sauv. 45%, Cab.Fr. 8%, Merlot 45%, Petit Verdot 2%. White grapes: Sauv. 80%, Sém. 20%. www.malartic-lagraviere.com
A square stone house, though doubled in size by its new owner and set in a typical Graves landscape, patched with woods and gently tilted vineyards. The red is a firm, austere, dark-coloured *vin de garde*, finishing fine rather than fleshy, though since 1994 the style appears rounder.

The white (mostly Sauvignon) is dazzling when young, but becomes even better – and more typical of Graves – with five or ten years in bottle. Enormous investments by M. Bonnie are already paying off in terms of even higher quality and finesse.

Château La Mission-Haut-Brion ✩✩✩✩
Talence. Owner: Domaine Clarence Dillon. AC: Pessac-Léognan. 21 ha. Grapes: Cab.Sauv. 48%, Cab.Fr. 7%, Merlot 45%. www.haut-brion.com
The immediate neighbour and former rival to Haut-Brion, equally in the Bordeaux suburbs of Pessac and Talence with the Paris-Madrid railway running in a cutting (good for the drainage) through the vineyard. Owned since 1983 by the proprietors of Haut-Brion, and run as meticulously as the First Growth. The claim is that the urban surroundings give the advantage of 1°C (1.8°F) higher temperature than the open country, and also a large harvesting force at short notice.

The wines show the effect of warm and dry conditions: concentration and force. Beside Haut-Brion, which is no weakling, they can appear almost butch. Michael Broadbent makes use of the words "iron", "earth", "beef", and "pepper" in his notes on various vintages. After due time (often 20 years or more), they combine warmth with sweetness in organ-like tones that make it a "super second" in quality. A tasting of over 50 vintages in 2008 exceeded (high) expectations, and like only the very finest growths, La Mission often excelled in difficult years. The white wine, Laville-Haut-Brion, is discussed separately.

Château Olivier ✩✩–✩✩✩
Léognan. Owner: Jean-Jacques de Bethmann. AC: Pessac-Léognan. 55 ha, of which 9 white. Red grapes: Cab.Sauv. 45%, Cab.Fr. 5%, Merlot 50%. White grapes: Sém. 50%, Sauv. 50%. www.chateau-olivier.com
A moated fortress with vineyards, operated for the owner until 1981 by the shipper Eschenauer & Co, but now under the control of the family again. Until the late 1990s the wine was uninspired, and uninspiring, but costly analyses of the vineyards have resulted in grubbing up vines in poor sectors, and replanting in those with the best potential. The results are already clear: sharper, crisper whites, and more succulent reds.

Château Pape-Clément ✩✩✩
Pessac. Owner: Bernard Magrez. AC: Pessac-Léognan. 33 ha, of which 3 white. Red grapes: Cab.Sauv. 60%, Merlot 40%. White grapes : Sém. 45%, Sauv. 45%, Muscadelle 10%. www.pape-clement.com
One-time property of Bertrand de Goth, the fourteenth-century Bishop of Bordeaux who, as Clement V, brought the papacy to Avignon. The vineyard lies within the Bordeaux suburbs and is planted in quite varied soils, though gravel dominates. No Cabernet Franc in the vineyard, but a high proportion of Merlot. New barrels are used for 70–95 per cent of the crop, depending on the vintage. Wines used to be lacklustre, but in the 1990s quality improved beyond recognition, and the 2000, 2005, and 2006 are magnificent. The property also makes a tiny quantity of spicy, oaky white.

Château Smith-Haut-Lafitte ✩✩✩
Martillac. Owner: Florence and Daniel Cathiard. AC: Pessac-Léognan. 55 ha, of which 10 white. Red grapes: Cab.Sauv. 55%, Cab.Fr. 10%, Merlot 33%, Petit Verdot 2%. White grapes: Sauv. 90%, Sém. 5%, Sauv. Gris 5%. www.smith-haut-lafitte.com
With cash from their sportswear business and considerable flair and enthusiasm, the Cathiards have, since 1990, transformed the reputation of their famous old estate with modernization of vineyard, cellar, château, and wine. The white (not a classed growth) is one of the best (and most frankly oaky) of the region, and the red improves steadily. The second wine is the good-value Les Hauts de Smith. The property includes a hotel, restaurant, and luxury spa.

Château la Tour-Haut-Brion ✩✩–✩✩✩
Talence. Owner: Domaine Clarence Dillon. AC: Pessac-Léognan. 5 ha. Grapes: Cab.Sauv. 42%, Cab.Fr. 35%, Merlot 23%. www.haut-brion.com
Formerly the second label of Chateau la Mission-Haut-Brion (q.v.), the property was then run as a separate vineyard. But from 2006 onwards, the label was discontinued, and the wine blended, if good enough, with La Mission.

Other Graves Châteaux

Château d'Archambeau ☆
Illats. Owner: Jean-Philippe Dubourdieu. 28 ha.
Easygoing dry white, and fragrant, barrel-aged reds.

Château L'Avocat ☆☆
Cérons. Owner: Robert and Susan Watts. 8 ha.
www.chateauduseuil.com
Same ownership as Château du Seuil (q.v.) and similar quality,
although whites may to be too oaky for some tastes.

Château Baret ☆☆
Villenave-d'Ornon. Owner: Ballande family.
AC: Pessac-Léognan. 22 ha.
Property just south of the Bordeaux ring road, producing
variable reds but dependable whites. An exclusivity of
Borie-Manoux.

Château Branon ☆☆–☆☆☆
Léognan. Owner: Sylviane Garcin-Cathiard.
AC Pessac-Léognan. 6 ha.
Same ownership as Château Haut-Bergey, but a very
different style: dense reds, quite extracted and formidable.
A *garagiste* Graves.

Château Brondelle ☆☆
Langon. Owner: Jean-Noël Belloc and Philippe Rochet.
40 ha. www.chateaubrondelle.com
One of the most serious Graves estates, with special *cuvées*
for oak-aged red and whites. The white Cuvée Anais has
complexity and minerality.

Château Brown ☆☆
Léognan. Owner: Yvon Mau and the Dirkzwager
company. AC: Pessac-Léognan. 28 ha.
www.chateau-brown.com
Elegant and well-balanced whites and reds, but new manager
Jean-Christophe Mau and consultant Stéphane Derenoncourt
are keen to raise quality higher.

Château Cabannieux ☆–☆☆
Porets. Owner: Régine Dudignac. 22 ha.
www.chateaucabannieux.com
Utterly traditional Graves, unpretentious and full of honest
pleasure.

Château Cantelys ☆☆
Martillac. Owner: Florence and Daniel Cathiard.
AC: Pessac-Léognan. 30 ha. www.smith-haut-lafitte.com
Owned since 1994 by the Cathiards, who make the wine at
Ch. Smith-Haut-Lafitte (q.v.). Less complex than the classed
growth, but well-made and good for medium-term drinking.

Château les Carmes Haut-Brion ☆☆
Pessac. Owner: Didier Furt. AC: Pessac-Léognan. 5 ha.
www.les-carmes-haut-brion.com
A miniature neighbour of Haut-Brion with a new lease of life
since Furt took over in 1986. Good, savoury wine that has yet
to attain. finesse.

Château de Castres ☆☆
Castres. Owner: José Rodriguez-Lalande. 30 ha.

Renovated in 1996 by a new owner, who is an ambitious
oenologist already producing silky, savoury reds and lush
whites.

Château de Chantegrive ☆☆–☆☆☆
Podensac. Owner: Henri and Françoise Lévêque. 90 ha.
www.chantegrive.com
A substantial property, using modern methods. Reliable wines,
especially the opulently oaky white Cuvée Caroline.

Château Crabitey ☆☆–☆☆☆
Portets. Owner: Amis de la Chartreuse de Seillon. 27 ha.
www.vignobles-seillon.com
Monastic property, expertly run by Arnaud de Butler,
producing opulent reds.

Château de Cruzeau ☆☆
St-Médard-d'Eyrans. Owner: André Lurton.
AC: Pessac-Léognan. 60 ha. www.andrelurton.com
A Lurton property bought and replanted in 1973. The red is
medium-bodied and the white plump and spicy, both best
drunk young.

Château d'Eck ☆–☆☆
Martillac. Owner: Michel Gonet. AC: Pessac-Léognan.
5 ha.
Young vines near the *autoroute* yield flashy red wines.

Château Ferran ☆☆
Martillac. Owner: Hervé Béraud-Sudreau. AC: Pessac-
Léognan. 22 ha. www.chateauferran.com
Typical, slightly herbaceous Graves, riper and more elegant
since 2000.

Château Ferrande ☆–☆☆
Castres. Owner: Castel Frères. 86 ha
Very large property just north of Portets. Red and white wines
for drinking young.

Clos Floridène ☆☆–☆☆☆
Bequey. Owner: Denis and Florence Dubourdieu. 30 ha.
www.denisdubourdieu.com
Original, full, and richly characterful white made by Denis
Dubourdieu, who has done for Bordeaux whites what Emile
Peynaud did for reds. Keeps for five years. Attractive red, too.

Château de France ☆☆–☆☆☆
Léognan. Owner: Bernard Thomassin. AC: Pessac-
Léognan. 38 ha. www.chateau-de-france.com
A large, often underrated property among some of the best of
the district, modernized and enlarged since 1971. Investments
paid off in the late 1990s, when the wines, both red and white,
gained in flesh and complexity.

Domaine de Gaillat ☆
Langon. Owner: Hélène Bertrand-Coste. 8 ha.
A plump, savoury red for early drinking. Recent vintages have
been rather gamey.

Château la Garde ☆☆–☆☆☆
Martillac. Owner: Dourthe-Kressman. AC: Pessac-
Léognan. 59 ha. www.cvbg.com
The red, in good vintages, is robust and flavoury. The white is

grapey and oaky. Quality, however, has much improved since mid-1990s.

Château Gazin-Rocquencourt ☆
Léognan. Owner: Alfred-Alexandre Bonnie. AC: Pessac-Léognan. 22 ha.
Since 2006 under the same ownershop as Malartic-Lagravière, so quality will surely improve. It certainly needs to.

Château Grandmaison ☆–☆☆
Léognan. Owner: Jean Bouquier. AC: Pessac-Léognan. 19 ha. www.domaine-de-grandmaison.fr
Little known property that makes attractive wines, and sometimes remarkable wines.

Château du Grand Abord ☆–☆☆
Portets. Owner: Marc Dugoua. 20 ha
Succulent red wine, almost pure Merlot, and a fragrant, lemony white.

Grand Enclos du Château de Cérons ☆☆
Cérons. Owner: Giorgio Cavanna. 26 ha.
An ancient property now in Tuscan hands, and making rich, spicy whites, and aromatic reds.

Château Haut-Bergey ☆☆
Léognan. Owner: Sylviane Garcin-Cathiard. AC: Pessac-Léognan. 26 ha. www.chateau-haut-bergey.com
The sister of Daniel Cathiard of Château Smith-Haut-Lafitte (q.v.) bought this property in 1991. Steadily improving smoky reds, and grapefruity whites.

Château Haut-Gardère ☆☆
Léognan. Owner: Lachlann Quinn. AC: Pessac-Léognan. 25 ha.
Reborn in 1979, this property adjoining Fieuzal and under the same ownership makes sound, oaky reds and toasty whites.

Château Haut-Lagrange ☆☆
Léognan. Owner: Francis Boutemy. AC: Pessac-Léognan. 20 ha. www.hautlagrange.com
Completely replanted in the early 1990s, so full potential has yet to be realized. Boutemy defies modern trends by ageing mostly in tank. The reds are supple, the whites markedly citric.

Château Haut-Nouchet ☆
Martillac. Owner: Louis Lurton. AC: Pessac-Léognan. 38 ha. www.louis-lurton.fr
Pleasant, inexpensive wines from rather young vines. Organic viticulture, eccentric winemaking, no always successful.

Château Haut-Selve ☆–☆☆
St Selve. Owner: Laubade et Domaines Associés. 42 ha. www.voignobles-lesgourgues.com.
A large property, making medium-bodied wines; the white is fresher and more lively than the sturdy, hard-edged red.

Château de l'Hospital ☆☆
Portets. Owner: M.Lafragette. 20 ha. www.lafragette.com

Sémillon-dominated whites and Merlot-dominated reds from a property owned from 1998 to 2008 by the owner of La Loudenne in the Médoc.

Château Lafont-Menaut ☆–☆☆
Martillac. Owner: Philibert Perrin. 10 ha. www.carbonnieux.com
Inexpensive but well-crafted wines from the Carbonnieux stable.

Château Larrivet-Haut-Brion ☆☆
Léognan. Owner: Philippe Gervoson. AC: Pessac-Léognan. 56 ha.
Energetically run property by Christine Gervoson, supported by Michel Rolland as a consultant. Lean, racy whites and fairly tannic, chocolatey reds.

Château Léhoul ☆☆
Langon. Owner: Eric Fonta. 10 ha.
Ambitious and concentrated wines from the southern Graves.

Château la Louvière ☆☆–☆☆☆

Léognan. Owner: André Lurton. AC: Pessac-Léognan. 48 ha. www.andrewlurton.com
The show place of M. Lurton's considerable estates, a noble eighteenth century mansion where he makes avant-garde dry white, Sauvignon-dominated, of Loire-like freshness; and typically masculine, earthy red of *cru classé* standard.

Château Luchey-Halde ☆–☆☆
Mérignac. Owner: Mérignac Agricultural College. AC: Pessac-Leognan. 22 ha. www.luchey-halde.com
A historic vineyard, grassed over as a military sports ground, but revived and replanted in 2000. Expensive wine given the adolescent vines.

Château Magneau ☆☆
La Brède. Owner: Henri Ardurats. 41 ha. www.chateau-magneau.com
Very consistent and good-value wines, of which the best is the barrique-aged white Cuvée Julien.

Château Le Pape ☆☆
Léognan. Owner: Patrick Monjanel. AC: Pessac-Leognan. 6 ha. www.chateaulepape.com
Dense red wines from a small but potentially fine property.

Château Pique-Caillou ☆☆
Mérignac. Owner: Isabelle and Paulin Calvet. AC: Pessac-Léognan. 20 ha
Suburban property recently bisected by a new road. Fairly tannic wines with black-cherry flavours, and refreshing whites.

Château de Portets ☆
Portets. Owner: Jean-Pierre Théron. 25 ha. www.chateau-de-portets.com

Château la Louvière, Pessac-Léognan

Beautifully located riverside property, but the wines are often lean and green.

Château Rahoul ☆☆
Portets. Owner: Alain Thienot. 40 ha. www.thienot.com
Estate with a deserved reputation for stylish, wood-aged reds and crisp whites.

Château de Respide ☆☆
Langon. Owner: Franck Bonnet. 35 ha.
www.chateau-de-respide.com
Long-established vineyards on the sandy soil of Langon, producing wines of some complexity, especially the barrique-aged Cuvée Callipyge.

Château Respide-Médeville ☆☆
Toulenne. Owner: Christian Médeville. 15 ha.
www.respide-medeville.com
A small property that has, for many years, been producing red wines with depth and concentration, and whites with a pronounced citric character. Drink within five years.

Château de Rochemorin ☆☆
Martillac. Owner: André Lurton. AC: Pessac-Léognan.
60 ha. www.andrelurton.com
A major old estate abandoned in the 1930s, replanted since 1973 by M. Lurton. Modern, fruity reds and dry, aromatic whites.

Château Roquetaillade la Grange ☆–☆☆
Mazères. Owner: Guignard family. 75 ha.
A very reliable property, established for many years. Simple but well-made wines.

Château de Rouillac ☆☆
Canéjan. Owner: M.Lafragette.19 ha. www.lafragette.com
A handsome but neglected property until bought by Lafragette in 1996. Revived with advice from Michel Rolland, but in 2008 the property was put on the market. Powerful, spicy wines, white and red.

Château St-Robert ☆☆–☆☆☆
Pujols. Owner: Crédit Foncier de France. 40 ha.
www.saint-robert.com
Same ownership as Chateaux Bastor-Lamontagne in nearby Sauternes, this is a very reliable property, and the top *cuvée*, Poncet Deville, both red and white, is confidently oaky.

Château le Sartre ☆☆
Léognan. Owner: Marie-Josée Lariche. AC: Pessac-Léognan. 35 ha. www.chateau-le-sartre.com
Owned by sister of Antony Perrin of Château Carbonnieux. Made in a similar but lighter style. But improved since 2004.

Château du Seuil ☆☆–☆☆☆
Cérons. Owner: Robert and Susan Watts. 15 ha.
www.chateauduseuil.com
British owners, New Zealand winemaker. Stylish and ambitious wines. See also Château L'Avocat.

Domaine de la Solitude ☆☆
Martillac. Owner: Soeurs de la Ste-Famille. AC: Pessac-Léognan. 30 ha. www.domainedelasolitude.com

Monastic property leased to Olivier Bernard of Domaine de Chevalier, who is still struggling to restore the neglected vines. Robust but inconsistent wines.

Château Le Thil-Comte Clary ☆☆
Léognan. Owner: Jean de Laitre and Guillaume de Tastes. AC: Pessac-Léognan. 17 ha. www.chateau-le-thil.com
Replanted from 1990, Le Thil has had a complex history, and is mostly on clay-limestone rather than gravel soils. Thus far the whites succeed more often than the reds.

Château Tourteau-Chollet ☆–☆☆
Arbanats. Owner: Maxime Bontoux. 55 ha.
Large property, that used to produce pleasant, commercial red and white wines. Since 2001 new owner Bontoux has invested heavily and the whites are much improved.

Château le Tuquet ☆☆
Beautiran. Owner: Paul Ragon. 56 ha.
This is Beautiran's principal property on the main Bordeaux to Langon road. In ripe years, the red is supple and charming.

Vieux-Château Gaubert ☆☆–☆☆☆
Portets. Owner: Dominique Haverlan. 34 ha.
Ever since Haverlan bought this property in 1988, he has made excellent wines, both white and red, and both unusually intense and complex.

Villa Bel Air ☆☆
St-Morillon. Owner: Jean-Michel Cazes. 46 ha.
www.villabelair.com
These are wines designed for immediate pleasure: medium-bodied red, and ripe, barrique-fermented whites.

Sauternes

Towards the south of the Bordeaux region, red winemaking dwindles to insignificance compared with white. A slightly warmer and drier climate, and very limey soil, are ideal for white grapes; the wine naturally has what the French call great *sève* – sap – a combination of body and vitality.

The best of the region is the relatively hilly enclave of Sauternes, an appellation that applies to four villages just south of a little stream called the Ciron. On the other side of the Ciron, on flatter land, lies Barsac, which also has the right to the Sauternes appellation. In all, 2,300 hectares. As the cold waters of the Ciron meet the warmer flow of the Garonne, autumnal mists develop, conditions that give rise to the famous noble rot, and the possibility of *vin liquoreux*. For the last 250 years, Sauternes has specialized in this extraordinarily concentrated, golden dessert wine. However, noble rot is fickle, and good wines cannot be made every year. The early 1990s were disastrous, but since 1995 conditions have been excellent.

Unlike most of the Graves region, Sauternes has big estates in the manner of the Médoc. Historically, its position on the inland route up the Garonne gave it military importance. Later, its fine climate and its good wine made it a desirable spot to replace castles with mansions. A score of these were already famous for their "sappy" white wine when the 1855 classification was made for the Paris Exhibition. They were classified in three ranks, with Château d'Yquem alone in the first, nine classed as *premiers crus*, and another nine as *deuxièmes crus* – which is, broadly speaking, still a fair classification, except that divisions of property have increased the *premiers crus* to 11 and the *deuxièmes* to 14.

The laborious procedure for making great Sauternes is described on the opposite page. With sweet wines out of fashion in the '60s and '70s, it became unrealistic for most proprietors, who could not afford the labour needed to pick single grapes at a time, or the new barrels, or the years of waiting. But fashion, and apparently climate, have both changed so radically recently that Sauternes is entering a new golden age.

The ultimate short cut, used by many of the humbler growers, is simply to wait for fully ripe grapes (hoping that at least a few are "nobly rotten"), pick them all together, add sugar to bring the potential alcohol up to about 18 degrees, then stop the fermentation with SO_2 when the fermentation has produced 13 or 14 actual degrees, leaving the wine sweet. It is a bastard approach to winemaking, with predictably mediocre results. The wine has none of the classic Sauternes flavour and should, in fairness, be called something else.

What is the classic flavour? It depends on the vintage. In some it is forceful, hot, and treacly. In others, it is rich and stiff with flavour, but almost literally sappy and not sweet. In the best, with all the grapes nobly rotten, it is thick with sugar yet gentle, creamy, nutty, honeyed. Barsacs tend to be a little less rich than Sauternes, but can produce their own spellbinding equilibrium of the rich and the brisk. Bottles can be better than ever after as much as 40 or 50 years.

Yields of Sauternes vary worryingly according to the weather. An average harvest, even in a good year, might give 30 dozen bottles per hectare, whereas a St-Julien classed growth for example, will make about 95 dozen per hectare with much less trouble.

Sauternes Premier Cru Supérieur

Château d'Yquem ☆☆☆☆
Sauternes. Owner: LVMH. 103 ha. Grapes: Sém. 80%, Sauv. 20%. www.yquem.fr
Indisputably the greatest sweet wine of France, but also recognized as the best white wine of Bordeaux long before the fashion for sweet wine was initiated in the nineteenth century. The extreme pains that go into its making are described in detail on the previous page.

After centuries of ownership by the Lur-Saluces family, the property was sold to luxury-goods group LVMH in 1999. The struggle for control was a bitter one, but resolved amicably, with Comte Alexandre de Lur-Saluces continuing to manage the estate until 2004, when he was replaced by Pierre Lurton, who also directs Cheval Blanc. See also page 71.

In certain vintages, Château d'Yquem also makes Y (which is pronounced "Ygrec"), its rare dry wine. It has some of the concentration of Yquem, and the same alcohol content, but only a trace of sweetness for balance.

Sauternes Premiers Crus

Château Climens ☆☆☆☆
Barsac. Owner: Bérénice Lurton. 30 ha. Grapes: Sém. 100%. www.chateau-climens.fr
Barsac's sweetest and richest wine, made painstakingly from a crop nearly as derisory as that at Yquem, giving it almost caramel concentration as it ages, yet with an elegant lightness of touch typical of Barsac at its best. Often excels in years such as 1991 when others struggle to produce drinkable wine. The locals pronounce the final "ns" emphatically, with a sort of honking effect. The second label is Les Cyprès de Climens.

Château Coutet ☆☆☆–☆☆☆☆
Barsac. Owner: Baly family. 39 ha. Grapes: Sém. 75%, Sauv. 23%, Muscadelle 2%. www.chateaucoutet.com
With Château Climens, the leading growth of Barsac, using traditional barrel fermentation to make exceptionally fine and stylish wine. The old manor house dates back to the English rule of Aquitaine. In the best years, a selection of the richest wine is labelled "Cuvée Madame", but production rarely exceeds 1,500 bottles.

Château Guiraud ☆☆☆
Sauternes. Owner: Xavier Planty, Stefan von Neipperg, Olivier Bernard, and Robert Peugeot. 83 ha. Grapes: Sém. 65%, Sauv. 35%. www.chateau-guiraud.fr
The southern neighbour of Yquem, but distinctive in having a fairly high proportion of Sauvignon in the vineyard. Vintages of the 1980s had mixed success: power sometimes outweighed finesse. Guiraud is now hitting its stride under long-term winemaker Xavier Planty, who successfully rounded up some high-profile co-investors to buy the property in 2006.

Château Clos Haut-Peyraguey ☆☆☆
Bommes. Owner: Martine Langlais-Pauly. 12 ha. Grapes: Sém. 90%, Sauv. 10%. www.closhautpeyraguey.com
Formerly the upper part of the same estate as Château Laufaurie-Peyraguey, separated in 1879 and in the Pauly family since 1914. A modest estate, making relatively light but extremely elegant wine. Château Haut-Bommes has the same owner and has effectively become the second wine.

Château Lafaurie-Peyraguey ☆☆☆–☆☆☆☆
Bommes. Owner: the Suez company. 40 ha. Grapes: Sém. 90%, Sauv. 8%, Muscadelle 2%.
A fortress to challenge Yquem – militarily, that is – with a fine reputation for beautifully structured, long-lived Sauternes, especially since 1979. The 1983 was the first of great run.

Château Rabaud-Promis ☆☆–☆☆☆
Bommes. Owner: Philippe Dejean. 33 ha. Grapes: Sém. 80%, Sauv. 18%, Muscadelle 2%.
The larger part of the formerly important Rabaud estate, making rich wine, fat without being heavy. Since 1986, a reliably good property to follow, but rarely exceptional.

Château Rayne-Vigneau ☆☆–☆☆☆
Bommes. Owner: Crédit Agricole Grands Crus. 80 ha. Grapes: Sém. 80%, Sauv. 20%.
A big estate, now detached from its château but celebrated in history for its soil being – literally – full of precious stones.

CHÂTEAU D'YQUEM – THE MAKING OF A GREAT SAUTERNES

Wine has few legends more imposing than the hilltop fortress of Yquem and its golden nectar. Only France could produce such a monument to aristocratic craftsmanship.

In 1785, Josephine Sauvage d'Yquem, whose family would retain the estate for over 200 years, married the Comte de Lur Saluces. Two years later Thomas Jefferson paid a famous visit to the château and rated the wines so highly that he ordered a consignment for America. Whether the wine he so admired was as liquorous and intensely sweet as Yquem is today remains a mystery. It was certainly as sweet as possible. The question is when it became worth using the pains and patience that now make the wine so extraordinary. Today, the painstaking care at Yquem is difficult to exaggerate. A description of its methods is a description of the ideal – which other châteaux approximate to a greater or lesser degree.

The principle must first be understood. Under certain autumnal conditions of misty mornings and sunny afternoons, one of the forms of mould common in vineyards reverses its role; instead of ruining the grapes, it is entirely beneficial. Given a healthy, ripe, and undamaged crop without other fungus infections, it begins to feed on the sugar and the tartaric acid in each grape,

probing with roots so fine that they penetrate the microscopic pores of the grapeskin. The grapes rapidly shrivel, turning first grey with fungus spores, then warm, violet-brown, their skins mere pulp. By this time they have lost more than half their weight, but less than half their sugar. Their juice is concentrated, extremely sweet, and rich in glycerine. If conditions are perfect (as they were in 1967, 1989, and 2001) the process is sudden and complete; not a grape in the bunch is recognizable. They are a repulsive sight.

Unfortunately, in most years the process is gradual; the berries rot patchily – even one by one. At Yquem, the pickers, 140 strong, move through the vines at a snail's pace gathering the grapes, if necessary, one at a time, then going back over the same vines again and again, up to 10 (once up to 11) times. The final crop amounts to about one glass of wine per vine.

In the cuvier the grapes are slightly sulphured, put through a gentle wooden fouloir (crusher), then immediately pressed in old-fashioned vertical presses three times, the "cake" being cut up with shovels and thrown into a mill to remove the stalks between pressings. The whole day's picking – up to 40 barrels – is assembled together in one vat, then

poured straight into new-oak barriques, filling them three quarters full, to ferment. As fermentation and then ageing proceeds, each barrel is tasted again and again to see whether it has the qualities of the grand vin.

If it does not, it will be sold to the trade as anonymous Sauternes. There is no court of appeal, no second wine, at Yquem.

When the wine reaches around 14 degrees of alcohol, the yeasts gradually stop working, leaving up to 120 grammes of sugar to a litre. The sums are critical here. Twenty-per-cent total sugar ("potential alcohol") in the juice is ideal. With 25 per cent, the fermentation might stop at nine to 10 degrees – as in Trockenbeerenauslese. (The extreme example is Tokaji Essencia, with so much sugar that the potential alcohol content is 35 degrees but fermentation barely starts at all.)

Château d'Yquem used to be kept for no fewer than 3.5 years in cask, but under Pierre Lurton and consultant Professor Denis Dubourdieu that period is being slightly shortened. The "new" Yquem may be slightly different from the Lur-Saluces Yquem, but so far there is no sign whatever that standards are being allowed to slip.

Château d'Yquem, Sauternes

The fortunate Vicomte de Roton (a Pontac, whose descendants still have the château) found himself picking up sapphires, topaz, amethysts, and opals by the thousand. (The rest of the soil is gravel.) Modern methods produce rich and good, but not the most ambitious, Sauternes, and a little "Rayne-Vigneau Sec".

Château Rieussec ☆☆☆☆
Fargues. Owner: Domaines Barons de Rothschild. 90 ha. Grapes: Sém. 90%, Sauv. 8%, Muscadelle, 2%. www.lafite.com

Yquem's eastern neighbour, perched even higher on the same line of hills. Rieussec, traditionally aromatic, elegant yet powerful, changed significantly in the '70s under its previous owner, when it became darker and richer with a honeyed, botrytis character. A dry white, inspired by Yquem's "Y", is called "R".

The Lafite-Rothschilds bought the property in 1985, and the style became more classic and less tarry. Vintages since the late 1990s have been outstanding. The second wine is Carmes de Rieussec.

Château Sigalas Rabaud ☆☆☆
Bommes. Owner: Comte Gérard de Lambert des Granges. 14 ha. Grapes: Sém. 80%, Sauv. 20%.

One-third of the former Rabaud estate, descended for over a century in the Sigalas family. The wine was mainly made and aged in tanks until 1988 to avoid oaky flavours; thereafter more oak was used, but the emphasis was always on retaining the wine's freshness and fruit.

In 1994, the owners of Château Lafaurie-Peyraguey (q.v.) leased the property and the wine has gained in complexity without losing its distinctive character.

Château Suduiraut ☆☆☆–☆☆☆☆
Preignac. Owner: AXA Millésimes. 92 ha. Grapes: Sém. 90%, Sauv. 10%. www.suduiraut.com

A château of great splendour within equally splendid park-land and the next vineyard to Yquem, going north. One of the most respected names, despite a period of relative neglect in the early 1970s. AXA has converted the buildings into a kind of corporate hotel but the focus on wine production remains complete under director Pierre Montegut.

Suduiraut at its best ('67, '76, '82, '88, '90, '97, '99, and 2001) is plump and unctuous, truly *liquoreux*; the poor man's Yquem. Second wine since '93: Castelnau de Suduiraut.

Château la Tour Blanche ☆☆☆
Bommes. Owner: Ministère de l'Agriculture. 37 ha. Grapes: Sém. 80%, Sauv. 15%, Muscadelle 5%. www.tourblanche.com

Probably the first estate on which sweet Sauternes was made, and placed first after Yquem in the 1855 classification. Bequeathed to the French state in 1912 by M. Osiris (an umbrella tycoon), whose name still appears on the label. The vineyard slopes steeply westwards towards the River Ciron.

Since 1989, the entire crop has been fermented in new oak – before 1983 it was all in steel tank. There is a college of viticulture here, but clearly separated from the wine estate. The style of the wine is increasingly unctuous.

Sauternes Deuxièmes Crus

Château d'Arche ☆☆–☆☆☆
Sauternes. Owner: consortium of investors. 27 ha. Grapes: Sém. 90%, Sauv. 10%. www.chateaudarche-sauternes.com

Exceedingly luscious, sometimes heavy Sauternes at its best ('83, '90, and 2001). Jean Perromat directed from 1980 to 2003, when he handed the reins to his son-in-law Jérôme Cosson.

Château Broustet ☆☆
Barsac. Owner: Didier Laulan. 16 ha. Grapes: Sém. 80%, Sauv. 16%, Muscadelle 4%.

Owned for many years by the Fourniers, who also owned the great Château Canon, St-Emilion. But they made a rather coarse wine at Broustet. Didier Laulan has profited from the string of good vintages since 1996 to improve quality considerably, although the wine can still lack concentration.

Château Caillou ☆–☆☆☆
Barsac. Owner: Marie-Josée Pierre. 13 ha. Grapes: Sém. 90%, Sauv. 10%. www.chateaucaillou.fr

A very businesslike property on the higher ground of "Haut" Barsac, near Château Climens. A small amount of superior Cuvée Prestige (known until 2001 as Private Cuvée) is produced in top years, as well as the even more restricted and expensive Cuvée Reine. Humdrum quality in the 1980s and unfortunate family rows meant that this estate was seriously underperforming for many years, but since the mid-1990s there has been a welcome improvement, although the basic bottling can lack excitement.

Château Doisy-Daëne ☆☆☆
Barsac. Owner: Denis Dubourdieu. 15 ha. Grapes: Sém. 80%, Sauv. 20%.

Doisy-Daëne is in the forefront of modern winemaking with sophisticated use of steel and new oak to make fresh, lively sweet wines of real class. In top vintages, tiny quantities of truly extreme wine, rightly called L'Extravagant and priced accordingly, are produced. The estate also produces excellent dry Graves.

Château Doisy-Dubroca ☆–☆☆
Barsac. Owner: Louis Lurton. 4 ha. Grapes: Sém. 100%. www.louis-lurton.fr

A small property linked for a century to the neighbouring Château Climens. Under Louis Lurton the wine has become inconsistent. Vintages are held back for a few years before release.

Château Doisy-Védrines ☆☆☆
Barsac. Owner: Olivier Castéja. 30 ha. Grapes: Sém. 80%, Sauv. 15%, Muscadelle 5%

One of the richer Barsacs, fermented in barrels and built for a good long life.

Château Filhot ☆–☆☆
Sauternes. Owner: Gabriel de Vaucelles. 62 ha. Grapes: Sém. 60%, Sauv. 35%, Muscadelle 5%. www.filhot.com

A palace, or nearly, built by the Lur Saluces family in the early nineteenth century on the edge of the woods south of Sauternes. The big vineyard on sandy soil produces wines that

are distinctively light by classical Sauternes standards.
A reluctance to age the wines in wood diminished their
complexity, but in the mid-1990s this began to change.
Yet the wines still lack concentration and succulence.

Château Lamothe ☆
**Sauternes. Owner: Guy Despujols. 7.5 ha. Grapes:
Sém. 85%, Sauv. 10%, Muscadelle 5%.**
www.guy-despujols.free.fr
Minor Sauternes, best drunk young. In top years an expensive
Sélection Exceptionelle is produced.

Château Lamothe Guignard ☆–☆☆
**Sauternes. Owner: Philippe and Jacques Guignard. 19 ha.
Grapes: Sém. 90%, Sauv. Gris 5%, Muscadelle 5%**
The Guignards, a winemaking family from the Graves,
bought this part of the vineyard from the proprietor of
Château d'Arche (q.v.) in 1981. They were soon producing
excellent, spicily fruity, luscious Sauternes at a fair price, but
for some reason quality has unfortunately slipped throughout
the 1990s. But the 2001 is excellent.

Château de Malle ☆☆–☆☆☆
**Preignac. Owner: Comtesse Nancy de Bournazel. 27 ha.
Grapes white: Sém. 75%, Sauv. 23%, Muscadelle 2%.**
www.chateau-de-malle.fr
The most beautiful house and garden in Sauternes – possibly
in Bordeaux – and much appreciated by tourists. Built for
the owner's family (related to the Lur Saluces) around 1600.
Italian gardens were added 100 years later. The vineyard,
on light sandy soil, is in Sauternes and Graves, and produces
roughly equal quantities of sweet white and red. Until the late
1980s, quality was sound rather than distinguished, but the
wine has gained in richness and complexity throughout the
1990s. The second wine is Château de Sainte-Hélène, and
the excellent white Graves is M de Malle.

Château de Myrat ☆–☆☆
**Barsac. Owner: de Pontac family. 22 ha. Grapes: Sém.
88%, Sauv. 8%, Muscadelle 4%.**
The father of the present owners uprooted all the vines in
1976. The vineyard was replanted in 1988, but the first
vintages were the disastrous years of the early '90s. The better
vintages of the late '90s produced good but inconsistent wines.

Château Nairac ☆☆☆
**Barsac. Owner: Nicolas Heeter-Tari. 16 ha. Grapes: Sém.
90%, Sauv. 6%, Muscadelle 4%. www.chateau-nairac.com**
A young American, Tom Heeter, made this formerly run-down
estate one of the leaders of the district, with wines of the racy,
less sticky Barsac style that bear keeping ten years or more.
The wine is now made by his perfectionist son – harvesting
only truly botrytized grapes and ruthlessly selling off barrels
that don't please him. The resulting wine is highly
concentrated and of imposing quality.

Château Romer ☆–☆☆
Fargues. Owner: Anne Farges. 6.5 ha.
www.chateau-romer.com
Leased by Château Romer-du-Hayot (q.v.) until 2002.
The 2003 was impressive.

Château Romer-du-Hayot ☆–☆☆☆
**Fargues. Owner: Markus de Hayot. 11 ha. Grapes:
Sém. 75%, Sauv. 25%.**
The château was demolished for the new *autoroute*, and the
wine is made at the owner's Château Guiteronde in Barsac.
For many years the wine has been simple, having been aged
only in tanks, but now barrique-ageing has given them more
complexity, though the wines can lack freshness.

Château Suau ☆
**Barsac. Owner: Corinne Dubourdieu. 8 ha. Grapes:
Sém. 80%, Sauv. 10%, Muscadelle 10%.**
The relic of a more important property, near the Garonne
sited on heavier soil than the best growths. Careless quality
until 2002, when a new generation took over and swiftly made
changes that will, in time, surely result in better wines.

Other Sauternes Producers

Château d'Armajan des Ormes ☆
Preignac. Owner: Perromat family. 15 ha.
Apricotty but unexciting wine, and a Crème de Tête
bottling in top years.

Château Bastor-Lamontagne ☆☆
Preignac. Owner: Crédit Foncier. 58 ha.
www.bastor-lamontagne.com
Despite corporate ownership, this property has been well
administered by Michel Garat, with a history of good
vintages to substantiate its claim to be "as good as a Second
Growth". In 2000 the single-vineyard Cru Bordenave was
added to the range.

Château Cantegril ☆–☆☆
Barsac. Owner: Denis Dubourdieu. 18 ha.
www.denisdubourdieu.com
Part of the former Château de Myrat (q.v.) vineyard,
beautifully kept but rather unambitious until 1988. A wine of
charm rather than depth.

Clos Dady ☆☆–☆☆☆
**Preignac. Owner: Catherine and Christophe Gachet.
6 ha. www.clos-dady.com**
Old vines and scrupulous winemaking result in rich,
flamboyant wines. There is a prestige cuvée called Dolce Vita,
insufficiently superior to the regular wine to justify its very
high price.

Château Closiot ☆–☆☆☆
Barsac. Owner: Françoise Sirot-Soizeau. 5 ha.
Sound and often lush Barsac, but the new-oaked Cuvée
Passion is more distinguished.

Château La Clotte-Cazalis ☆☆
Barsac. Owner: Bernadette Lacoste. 5 ha.
www.laclotte.com
Ungainly name but delicious wines, first made from this
formerly leased property in 2001.

Cru Barréjats ☆☆☆
Barsac. Owner: Dr. Mireille Daret. 5 ha.
www.cru-barrejats.com

Tiny, high-quality estate between Climens and Caillou, which went live in 1990.

Château de Fargues ☆☆☆–☆☆☆☆
Fargues. Owner: Comte Alexandre de Lur Saluces. 15 ha.
www.chateau-de-fargues.com
A proud castle in ruins, with a diminutive vineyard, but the perfectionist standards of Yquem. Glorious and consistent quality under winemaker Francois Amirault.

Château Gilette ☆–☆☆☆
Preignac. Owner: Christian Médeville. 5 ha.
A unique producer of long-aged Sauternes of great splendour, aged in large tanks and not bottled until its idealistic owner considers it ready to drink – at 25 years or so. M. Médeville also produces the far more conventional Château les Justices.

Château Haut-Bergeron ☆☆–☆☆☆
Preignac. Owner: Robert Lamothe. 16 ha.
Sumptuous peachy wines of classed growth quality.

Château Liot ☆
Barsac. Owner: Jean Gérard David. 20 ha.
Large property on the best slopes in Barsac. The general level is "good commercial", always satisfactory, never beguiling.

Château Massereau ☆☆–☆☆☆
Barsac. Owner: Jean-Francois and Philippe Chaigneau. 1.2 ha.
A *garagiste* Barsac, first made in 2000, impressive quality but bewilderingly expensive.

Château Piada ☆–☆☆
Barsac. Owner: Frédéric Lalande. 10 ha.
One of the better-known lesser Barsacs, reliable if unambitious.

Château Raymond-Lafon ☆☆☆
Sauternes. Owner: Meslier family. 16 ha.
www.chateau-raymond-lafon.fr
Bought in 1972 by the then manager of Château d'Yquem, and made with similar care and aged three years in oak. Lush, majestic, and long-lived.

Château de Rolland ☆–☆☆
Barsac. Owner: Francois Guignard. 18 ha.
www.chateauderolland.com
Attractive wines, honeyed but somehow lacking in elegance and complexity.

Château Roumieu-Lacoste ☆–☆☆
Barsac. Owner: Hervé Dubourdieu. 12 ha.
The nephew of the owner of the excellent Doisy-Daëne makes good, rich wine here.

Château St-Amand ☆–☆☆
Preignac. Owner: Anne-Marie Facchetti-Ricard. 20 ha.
Admirable quality in the style of Barsac, with the emphasis on fruit rather than oak or complexity. Sold by Sichel as La Chartreuse.

St-Emilion

As a town, every wine-lover's idea of heaven; as an appellation, much the biggest for high-quality wine in France, producing not much less than the whole of the Côte d'Or of Burgundy. Nowhere is the civic and even the spiritual life of a little city so deeply imbued with the passion for making good wine.

St-Emilion, curled into its sheltered corner of the hill, cannot expand. Where other such towns have spread their nondescript streets over the countryside, around St-Emilion there are priceless vineyards, most of its very best, lapping up to its walls, which prevent any sprawl. It burrows into its yielding limestone to find building blocks and store its wine – even to solemnize its rites. Its old church is a vast-vaulted cave, now used for the meeting of the Jurade, St-Emilion's ceremonial organization (see below).

The vineyards envelop several distinct soils and aspects, while maintaining a certain common character. St-Emilion wines are a degree stronger than Médocs, with less tannin. Accessible, solid tastiness is their stamp, maturing to warm, gratifying sweetness. They are less of a puzzle than Médocs when young and mature faster, but are no less capable of asking unsolvable questions as they age.

The best St-Emilions come from the relatively steep *côtes*, the hillside vineyards and the cap of the escarpment around the town, and from an isolated patch of gravel soil on the plateau about 1.5 km (two miles) northwest, almost in Pomerol. The *côtes* wines are the more smiling, in degrees from enigmatic to beaming; the wines of the graves more earnest and searching. Michael Broadbent defines the difference as "open" (*côtes*) and "firm" (graves). But they can easily be confused with one another, with Médocs, with Graves, and even with Burgundy. And some of the same qualities are found in vineyards on substantially different soils, both down in the sandy (sables) region in the Dordogne Valley below St-Emilion town itself, and in the five "satellite" villages to the north and east.

The classification of St-Emilion follows a pattern of its own. It was settled in 1954 and is the only one regularly revised, the latest revision having been declared in 2006.

There are now, since the 1985 vintage, two appellations, simple AC St-Emilion and AC St-Emilion Grand Cru. The *crus classés* come in two classes: *premier grand cru classé* and *grand cru classé*. The top class is divided into two: "A" and "B". The current classification names two châteaux (Cheval Blanc and Ausone) as premiers *grands crus classés* "A", and 13 as "B". Bs are the approximate equivalent in value to Médoc Second and Third Growths. Then come 46 *grands crus classes*.

Obviously, St-Emilion is not an area of big estates. The average size of holding is about eight hectares, the biggest not much more than 40, and many are as small as two or three, making a mere few hundred cases. In fact "grand cru" in St-Emilion, unqualified, is the same broad category as *crus bourgeois* in the Médoc.

Since the early 1990s, there has been an unsubtle transformation in the style of many St-Emilion wines. Nowhere else in Bordeaux have techniques such as must concentration and micro-oxygenation been adopted with such enthusiasm.

Applied to wine cropped at very low yields, the result is opaque colour, immense concentration and power, high alcohol, and jammy flavours. There is no doubt that there is a wide following for such wines, especially among American wine critics, but others might argue that

St-Emilion is in danger of losing not just its elegance, but also its typicité.

St-Emilion Premiers Grands Crus

Château Ausone ☆☆☆☆
Owner: Alain Vauthier. 7 ha. Grapes: Merlot 45%, Cab.Fr. 55%. www.chateau-ausone.com

If you were looking for the most obviously promising vineyard site in the whole Bordeaux area, this would be first choice. No wonder its name is associated with the Roman poet Ausonius (also connoisseur of the Moselle). It slopes south and east from the rim of the St-Emilion escarpment, whose limestone cap has been quarried for building and provides perfect cool, commodious cellars. The soil is pale alkaline clay, in a shallow layer over permeable limestone (which vine roots love).

Ausone went through a long eclipse when its wine was good, but not good enough. Its neighbours seemed to dim their lamps at the same time. Different branches of the owning family squabbled so deeply that even decisions such as when to begin the harvest had to be resolved in the local courts. Under such conditions investments in the property ground to a halt.

In 1995 one of the protagonists, Alain Vauthier, took over the estate, and ever since quality has soared. Today Ausone is rich and seductive, with a revelatory density and complexity repeated in every subsequent vintage, culminating in the superb 2000 and 2005.

Winemaking here is exactly the same in principle as in the Médoc. New barrels are used for the whole, pathetically small crop. The wine's whole evolution to drinkability is slightly quicker than a top Médoc, yet its potential lifespan, judging by rare old bottles, is no shorter. The final result is the pure magic of claret: sweet, lively harmony with unfathomable depths.

Château Cheval Blanc ☆☆☆☆
**Owner: Bernard Arnault and Albert Frère. 37 ha.
Grapes: Cab.Fr. 58%, Merlot 42%.
www.chateau-cheval-blanc.com**

Although it shares the first place in St-Emilion with Ausone, the soil and situation (and tradition) of Cheval Blanc are totally different. It lies back on the plateau near the boundary of Pomerol on much deeper soil, an irregular mixture of gravel, sand, and clay with clay subsoil. The main grape is Cabernet Franc (known in these parts as Bouchet).

There is no white horse here, and the château is an unfanciful, cream-painted residence that for some reason always reminds me of Virginia. The new *chais* make a more imposing building. The same family had owned the property since its nineteenth-century beginning, but in 1998, a private partnership of two very rich businessmen altered all that.

Cheval Blanc is the Mouton of St-Emilion: the blockbuster that somehow refers straight back to its grapes. The 1947 is a legend, a wine of heroic style and proportions, with the combined qualities of claret, port, sculpture, and Hermès or Gucci – or is this *lèse-majesté*? The '61 proved is a tough piece of beef that needed to marinate for years. Not all vintages are so awe-inspiring: but '75, '82, '83, '89, '90, '95, '98, 2000, and '05 are in the grandest tradition. Pierre Lurton has been running the property since 1991 and has not put a foot wrong. The second wine is "Le Petit Cheval".

Vineyards close to St-Emilion

Château Angélus ☆☆☆☆
Owner: Boüard de Laforest family. 23 ha. Grapes: Merlot 50%, Cab.Fr. 47%, Cab.Sauv. 3%. www.angelus.com
On the slope below Château Beauséjour where the soil is heavy. The owners' passionate pursuit of excellence caused Angélus's promotion in 1996 after a series of high-grade vintages in the second half of the '80s and the more difficult early '90s. The wine is as opulent and explosive as any in Bordeaux.

Château Beau-Séjour-Bécot ☆☆☆
Owner: Gérard and Dominique Bécot. 17 ha. Grapes: Merlot 70%, Cab.Fr. 24%, Cab.Sauv. 6%. www.beausejour-becot.com
Two-thirds of an estate that was divided in 1869 (the smaller part got the house). The vineyard slopes west from the crest behind Château Ausone. Since 1969, the property has been modernized, with a complete new *cuvier*, and its dimmed reputation restored to that of a leader in the tight circle of the St-Emilion *côtes*, making the sort of rich wine for the medium term (say, ten years) that makes St-Emilion so popular. Demoted in the 1985 classification because M. Bécot had extended the property by buying two other vineyards, but rightly reinstated in 1996. The flavours are lush, almost plummy, and all recent vintages have been excellent.

Château Beauséjour (Duffau-Lagarrosse) ☆☆–☆☆☆
Owner: Jean Duffau-Lagarrosse. 7 ha. Grapes: Merlot 70%, Cab.Fr. 20%, Cab.Sauv. 10%.
The smaller part of Beauséjour, but with the charming house and garden. Run in the traditional, small, family château style; full-bodied, well-extracted, but tending to be short of finesse, though the '90 has a sensational reputation. '95, 2000, and '04 are all very good.

Château Bélair ☆☆–☆☆☆
Owner: Etablissements Jean-Pierre Moueix. 12.5 ha. Grapes: Merlot 80%, Cab.Fr. 20%. www.chateaubelair.com
Until 1995, the bigger but junior brother of Château Ausone with the same owner. Part of the same sloping vineyard, plus a patch on the flat top of the hill behind. Winemaker Pascal Delbeck inherited Bélair in 2003, but tax and other problems forced him to sell in 2008. After almost 25 years with Delbeck at the helm, Bélair became a controversial wine: light, elegant but often insubstantial. Nonetheless the good vintages aged remarkably well.

Château Canon ☆☆–☆☆☆
Owner: Wertheimer family (Chanel). 18 ha. Grapes: Merlot 75%, Cab.Fr. 25%. 65%, Cab.Fr. 35%. www.chateau-canon.com
My instinct is to spell the name with two "n"s: a great bronze gun-barrel (rather than a genteel cleric) expresses the style of Canon nicely: generous, masculine, not too aggressive young, but magnificent with 20 years in bottle.

The Fournier family sold to the Wertheimers of Chanel, also owners of Château Rauzan-Ségla (q.v.), in 1997. Much of the vineyard needed to be replanted, and, rather to the surprise of some in St-Emilion, the INAO permitted the vineyards of Château Curé-Bon, another property purchased by the Wertheimers, to be promoted in status and incorporated into those of Canon. With so many changes, it is still hard to discern the true Canon style of the present century.

Château Figeac ☆☆☆–☆☆☆☆
Owner: Thierry Manoncourt. 40 ha. Grapes: Cab.Sauv. 35%, Cab.Fr. 35%, Merlot 30%. www.chateau-figeac.com
Château Figeac has the aristocratic air of a Médoc *cru classé* and

THE CONSULTANTS

Few Bordeaux châteaux, even the grandest, dispense with a consultant oenologist. The *maître de chai* is the man, or woman, on the spot, supervising the daily operations of the winery. The consultant gives an outside view, often advising on viticulture as well as winemaking and blending. The first such consultant, from the 1950s to 1990, was Emile Peynaud. A former director of the Station Oenologique of the University of Bordeaux, he acquired an astonishing list of clients among the châteaux of Bordeaux.

He encouraged his clients to be selective in harvesting, which should only begin when the grapes are as ripe as possible, and to add to the "free-run" wine at least some of the more tannic, pressed wine to give a firm, tannic structure. He was also the first oenologist

to understand the complexities of malolactic fermentation. His advice was based on solid research undertaken at the university. Others followed in his footsteps, such as Pascal Ribéreau-Gayon and Denis Dubourdieu. Dubourdieu is the master of white-wine fermentation, having conducted research projects into skin contact, aroma, and lees-stirring.

Bordeaux as a whole – and indeed the wider world of wine – has benefited immeasurably from the contributions of its academic oenologists, some of whom have developed techniques, such as must concentration, that have kept Bordeaux at the forefront of oenological innovation. Bordeaux proprietors like to affect a certain disdain for "technological" wines (shorthand for Australian), but no region is more adept at technology than Bordeaux itself. Other consultant

oenologists are almost as influential, although they do not hold academic appointments. Michel Rolland is known throughout the world, and regularly advises estates worldwide, as well as Bordeaux. Others, such as Jacques Boissenot and Gilles Pauquet, stay closer to home. Stéphane Derenoncourt, self-taught and sympathetic to Biodynamics, has become, together with Rolland, the current consultant of choice on the Right Bank, although he has extended his client list into the Médoc and further afield. Hubert de Boüard, proprietor of Château Angélus, and Jean-Luc Thunevin, proprietor of Château Valandraud, have also begun to consult for some important estates. Nor are these top oenologists airy theoreticians. Their understanding of winemaking is rooted in the terroir of Bordeaux, and refined in the laboratory.

once had an estate on the grand Médoc scale, including what is now Château Cheval Blanc. The house could be called a mansion and the park has a seigneurial feeling absent in most of the Libournais. The present vineyard, still among the biggest in St-Emilion, has stonier ground and a higher proportion of Cabernet Sauvignon than the others – which may account for its different style from Cheval Blanc. Figeac is more welcoming, less dense and compact; closer to a Médoc (again) in its structure of sweet flesh around a firm spine. It is big but not strapping, maturing relatively early and beautifully sweet in maturity – always individual. Deceptively easy-drinking when young, Figeac shows its true refinement after ten or more years. The 1950 won a standing ovation when poured at a St-Emilion dinner in 2007.

Clos Fourtet ☆☆–☆☆☆
Owner: Philippe Cuvelier. 20 ha. Grapes: Merlot 85%, Cab.Fr. 5%, Cab.Sauv. 10%. www.closfourtet.com
The first *cru classé* that visitors stumble on as they walk out of the lovely old walled town into the vineyards. A modest-looking place, but with a warren of limestone cellars. (The old quarry-cellars are said to run for miles, one château's cellars connecting with another. Paradise for an oenospeleologist-burglar.) Old vintages of Clos Fourtet were tough going for many years. More recently, the wine has been made a bit kindlier, but without reaching the peaks of quality or price. The year in which the property was sold by the Lurton family to a genial businessman, Philippe Cuvelier – 2000 – turned out to be a magnificent vintage here.

Château la Gaffelière ☆☆☆
Owner: Comte Léo de Malet-Roquefort. 22 ha. Grapes: Merlot 80%, Cab.Fr. 10%, Cab.Sauv. 10%, www.chateau-la-gaffeliere.com
The tall Gothic building at the foot of the hill up to St-Emilion, with vineyards at the foot of Ausone and Pavie. Three centuries have passed in the de Malet-Roquefort family, a history of noble vintages which aged well and gracefully ('55 was a favourite). Recent experience has been less consistent, but both '82 and '83 are fine wines. From 1995, when Michel Rolland was hired as a consultant, the wine showed more overt cassis and blackberry fruit, but by 2000, Rolland was no longer involved. Stéphane Derenoncourt took over as consultant in 2004, a very successful vintage here.

Château Magdelaine ☆☆☆
Owner: Etablissements Jean-Pierre Moueix. 11 ha. Grapes: Merlot 95%, Cab.Fr. 5%.
An impeccable little property situated next to Château Belair, with a vineyard on the plateau and another on the south slope. Its high proportion of Merlot makes it almost a Pomerol, but less plummy, with the "meat" of St-Emilion and great finesse. There can scarcely be a more reliable or fascinating St-Emilion to watch vintage by vintage. And it needs a decade to unfurl.

Château Pavie ☆☆☆
Owner: Gérard Perse. 42 ha. Grapes: Merlot 60%, Cab.Fr. 30%, Cab. Sauv. 10%. www.vignobles-perse.com
A priceless site, the whole south-by-west slope of the central St-Emilion *côtes*; the biggest vineyard on the hill, with the advantage of both top and bottom as well. Pavie was formerly known for warm, round claret of medium weight, more delicious than deeply serious. Since supermarket tycoon Gérard Perse bought the property (and its neighbour Château Pavie-Decesse), the changes have been radical. A splendid new *chai* was built, but more importantly, Perse opted for low yields, and maximum ripeness and concentration. In the course of a few vintages, the price trebled. The wine world is now divided in its opinion. Generally speaking, the Americans adore it, the Brits deplore its atypical fat.

Château Pavie-Macquin ☆☆☆
Owner: Corre-Macquin family. 15 ha. Grapes: Merlot 70%, Cab.Fr. 25%, Cab.Sauv. 5%.
Organically farmed vineyard and fine winemaking by Nicolas Thienpont and Stéphane Derenoncourt. A sumptuous and highly concentrated wine, built for long ageing. Promoted in 2006.

Château Troplong-Mondot ☆☆☆
Owner: Christine Valette. 30 ha. Grapes: Merlot 90%, Cab.Fr. 5%, Cab.Sauv. 5%. www.chateau-troplong-mondot.com
A famous vineyard on the crest of the *côtes* east of the town, above Château Pavie. Reliably good in the '80s and, since '88, powerfully concentrated, oaky wines. Enthusiastic following. Predictably won promotion in 2006.

Château Trottevieille ☆☆–☆☆☆
Owner: Castéja family. 10 ha. Grapes: Merlot 55%, Cab.Fr. 35%, Cab.Sauv. 10%.
Detached from the solid block of *crus classés* along the *côtes*, on the plateau east of the town, on richer-looking but still shallow clay with pebbles over limestone. Full-flavoured wine with plenty of character, and better since 2000 as a result of stricter selection in vineyard and cellar. Philippe Castéja knows the wine in the past has lacked flair, and is using Denis Dubourdieu and Gilles Pauquet to restore its reputation. The results are beginning to show.

St-Emilion Grands Crus Classés

Château L'Arrosée ☆☆–☆☆☆
Owner: Roger Caille. 9 ha. Grapes: Merlot 60%, Cab.Sauv. 20%, Cab.Fr. 20%. www.chateaularrosee.com
At the bottom of the *côtes* near the town. The name "l'Arrosée" means "watered" (by springs). The wine itself, on the contrary, is medium-bodied but concentrated and serious, if not entirely consistent. New winery, and huge new investment in the latest technology, is giving the wine more flesh and opulence.

Château Balestard la Tonnelle ☆☆
Owners: the Capdemourlin family. 11 ha. Grapes: Merlot 70%, Cab.Fr. 25%, Cab.Sauv. 5%. www.vignoblescapdemourlin.com
The Capdemourlin family has owned this property since the seventeenth century, when the poet Villon described its wine as "le divin nectar". I have been more prosaically satisfied with this full-bodied, meaty wine. It's robust but not always elegant.

Château Bellefont-Belcier ☆☆–☆☆☆
Owner: a trio of investors. 13 ha. Grapes: Merlot 70%, Cab.Fr. 20%, Cab.Sauv. 10%. www.bellefont-belcier.com
Vineyards below Pavie-Decesse and Troplong-Mondot are well located. That promise is being fulfilled since the late'90s, with wines of opulence and occasional exoticism. Promoted in 2006.

Château Bergat ☆–☆☆
Owner: Castéja family. 4 ha. Grapes: Merlot 50%, Cab.Fr. 40%, Cab.Sauv. 10%.
Tiny vineyard in the sheltered gully east of the town, linked by ownership with Château Trottevieille (q.v.).

Château Berliquet ☆☆–☆☆☆
Owner: Vicomte Patrick de Lesquen. 9 ha. Grapes: Merlot 72%, Cab.Fr. 20%, Cab.Sauv. 8%.
Old estate modernized in the 1970s, promoted in 1985, and made and marketed by the St-Emilion cooperative until the early 1990s. Since 1997, consultant winemaker Patrick Valette has given the wine more oak and concentration.

Château Cadet-Piola ☆☆
Owner: Alain Jabiol. 7 ha. Grapes: Merlot 51%, Cab.Sauv. 28%, Cab.Fr. 18%, Malbec 3%. www.chateaucadetpiola.com
Memorable as the only Bordeaux label to portray (prettily) the female bosom. But a sturdy, even masculine, wine.

Château Canon-La-Gaffelière ☆☆☆
Owner: Graf Stephan von Neipperg. 19 ha. Grapes: Merlot 55%, Cab.Fr. 40%, Cab.Sauv. 5%. www.neipperg.com
German-owned property on sandy soil by the railway under the *côtes*. Total renovation in 1985 brought some startlingly good wines. Manager Stephan von Neipperg and his winemaker, Stéphane Derenoncourt, occupies the forefront of modern winemaking in St-Emilion, favouring very low yields and harvests at optimal ripeness; also ardent believers in the virtues of micro-oxygenation. Wines are rich, plump, and velvety, sumptuous but possibly a tad too voluptuous to give pleasure to the last drop. See also La Mondotte.

Château Cap-de-Mourlin ☆☆
Owner: Capdemourlin family (see Château Balestard). 14 ha. Grapes: Merlot 65%, Cab.Fr. 25%, Cab.Sauv. 10%. www.vignoblescapdemourlin.com
Situated half a kilometre or so (one mile) north of town on clay soil. For several years until 1982 this estate was divided, but is now one again, and is making high-flavoured wine that can be austere when young.

Château Chauvin ☆☆–☆☆☆
Owner: Marie-France Février and Béatrice Ondet. 15 ha. Grapes: Merlot 75%, Cab.Fr. 20%, Cab.Sauv. 5%. www.chateauchauvin.com

Fragmented property but with some very old vines. Much improved since 1995, though still rather inconsistent.

Château Clos des Jacobins ☆☆
Owner: Bernard Decoster. 8.5 ha. Grapes: Merlot 75%, Cab.Fr. 23%, Cab.Sauv. 2%.
Located in the centre of the commune where *côtes* begins to shade into graves. After years of ownership by the house of Cordier, the Clos was sold in 2001, and again in 2004. Hubert de Bouard of Château Angélus supervises the winemaking, and the style is, therefore, likely to change. Splendid wine in 2005.

Clos de l'Oratoire ☆☆–☆☆☆
Owner: Graf Stephan von Neipperg. 10 ha. Grapes: Merlot 90%, Cab.Sauv. 5%, Cab.Fr. 5%. www.neipperg.com
Acquired by the owner of Château Canon-La-Gaffelière in 1991. The high proportion of Merlot gives a sumptuous, forward, hedonistic wine.

Clos St Martin ☆☆–☆☆☆
Owner: Reiffers family. 1.3 ha. Grapes: Merlot 70%, Cab.Fr. 20%, Cab.Sauv. 10%. www.vignoblesreiffers.com
The smallest of the *grands crus classés*. Minute production: essentially a garage wine, made by Sophie Fourcade.

Château la Clotte ☆☆–☆☆☆
Owner: Nelly Moulierac. 4 ha. Grapes: Merlot 80%, Cab.Fr. 15%, Cab.Sauv. 5%. www.chateaulaclotte.com
Beautifully situated in the fold of the hill east of the town. Delightful wines since 2001.

Château la Clusière ☆☆
Owner: Gérard Perse. 2.5 ha. Grapes: Merlot 100%.
This small vineyard adjoins Château Pavie (q.v.), and since 2002 Perse has incorporated its crop into Pavie. Thus La Clusière no longer exists.

Château Corbin ☆☆
Owner: Annabelle Cruse Bardinet and sisters. 13 ha. Grapes: Merlot 80%, Cab.Fr. 20%.
Corbin is the northern hamlet of graves St-Emilion, near the Pomerol boundary and sloping gently northeast. Supple wines, improved since 2001.

Château Corbin-Michotte ☆☆
Owner: Jean Noël Boidron. 7 ha. Grapes: Merlot 65%, Cab.Fr. 30%, Cab.Sauv. 5%.
Spicy, oaky wines for medium-term drinking.

Château la Couspaude ☆☆–☆☆☆
Owner: Jean-Claude Aubert. 7 ha. Grapes: Merlot 70%, Cab.Fr. 20%, Cab.Sauv.10%. www.la-couspaude.com
Re-established in the classification in 1996. Aubert works closely with Michel Rolland, so not surprisingly this is a rich, oaky, plummy wine with a lot of heft and a fairly high price.

Fermentation tanks, Château Bellefont-Belcier, St. Emilion

Château Couvent-des-Jacobins ☆☆
Owners: the Joinaud-Borde family. 11 ha. Grapes:
Merlot 75%, Cab.Fr. 25%.
Excellent *côtes* vineyard right under the town walls to the east,
with venerable cellars in the town centre. The wine is well-
structured, ripe, and juicy, though angular in difficult vintages.

Château Dassault ☆☆–☆☆☆
Owner: Laurent Dassault. 24 ha. Grapes: Merlot 70%,
Cab.Fr 25%, Cab.Sauv. 5%. www.chateaudassault.com
One of the biggest graves vineyards, northeast of the town.
Steady rather than distinguished, although since 1995 the
wines show more concentration and elegance.

Château Destieux ☆☆☆
Owner: Christian Dauriac. 8 ha. Grapes: Merlot 70%,
Cab.Fr. 15%, Cab. Sauv. 15%.
www.vignobles-dauriac.com
Medical technician Dauriac is a fanatical and finicky
winemaker, guided by his schoolfriend Michel Rolland.
Richness, concentration, and even majesty (in 2005) secured
deserved promotion in 2006.

Château la Dominique ☆☆–☆☆☆
Owner: Clément Fayat. 23 ha. Grapes: Merlot 86%,
Cab.Fr. 12%, Cab.Sauv 2%. www.vignobles-fayat.com
This is the neighbour of Château Cheval Blanc (q.v.) reflecting
its privileged position in an almost unbroken sequence of
concentrated, fleshy, wines, with the Michel Rolland touch. In
2006 Jean-Luc Thunevin was brought in to run La Dominique
and Fayat's other properties in Pomerol and the Médoc.

Château Fleur-Cardinale ☆☆–☆☆☆
Owner: Dominique Decoster. 18 ha. Grapes: Merlot 70%,
Cab.Fr. 20%, Cab.Sauv. 10%.
www.chateau-fleurcardinale.com
From the moment Decoster bought this property in 2001, he
was determined, with assistance from Michel Rolland, to win
promotion to *grand cru classé*. Five years later he succeeded, and
deservedly. Firm but succulent wines from a late-ripening site.

Château Fonplégade ☆☆–☆☆☆
Owner: Stephen Adams. 18 ha. Grapes: Merlot 91%,
Cab.Fr. 7%, Cab.Sauv. 2%.
One of the grander châteaux, on the *côtes* among the very best,
yet never one of the great names. A new American owner since
2004 has invested mightily to produce fleshy, vibrant, modern-
style wines.

Château Fonroque ☆☆
Owner: Alain Moueix. 18 ha. Grapes: Merlot 88%,
Cab.Fr. 12%. www.chateaufonroque.com
Alain Moueix took over here in 2001, and converted Fonroque
to Biodynamism. Fonroque is dark, firm wine, occasionally
tough, but it ages well.

Château Franc-Mayne ☆☆
Owner: Hervé and Griet Laviale. 7 ha. Grapes: Merlot
90%, Cab.Sauv. 10%. www.chateaufrancmayne.com
A serious little property, with a small hotel, on the western
côtes. New young owners since 2005 have the resources and

energy to bring more distinction to the wine, which surely has
considerable potential.

Château Grand Corbin ☆–☆☆
Owner: Giraud family. 15 ha. Grapes: Merlot 68%,
Cab.Fr. 27%, Cab. Sauv. 5%. www.grand-corbin.com
Rather modest wines from the Corbin sector, but managed
to gain promotion in 2006.

Château Grand-Corbin-Despagne ☆☆–☆☆☆
Owner: Francois Despagne. 27 ha. Grapes: Merlot
75%, Cab.Fr. 25%. www.grand-corbin-despagne.com
Rightly demoted in 1996, but then Despagne took over,
determined to win reinstatement. He succeeded in 2006.
Well-made wines that always reflect the vintage.

Château Grand Mayne ☆☆☆
Owner: Marie-Francoise Nony. 17 ha. Grapes: Merlot
76%, Cab.Fr. 13%, Cab.Sauv. 11%.
www.chateau-grand-mayne.com
A well-placed property realizing its considerable potential for
rich-tasting, serious claret.

Château Grand-Pontet ☆☆–☆☆☆
Owner: Sylvie Pourquet. 14 ha. Grapes: Merlot 75%,
Cab.Fr. 15%, Cab.Sauv. 10%.
Next to Beau-Séjour Becot and, like it, revitalized since 1985.
Showy wine, sometimes too extracted. Nonetheless,
underrated.

Château Les Grandes Murailles ☆☆
Owner: Reiffers family. 2 ha. Grapes: Merlot 100%.
www.vignoblesreiffers.com
Rather effortful wines from a tiny plot below the ruined wall
of the thirteenth-century Dominican church, a well-known
local landmark outside the town.

Château Haut-Corbin ☆–☆☆
Owner: SMABTP insurance company. 6 ha. Grapes:
Merlot 65%, Cab. Sauv. 25%, Cab.Fr. 10%.
www.hautcorbin.com
The least of the Corbins up near the Pomerol border, often
surly and dull.

Château Haut-Sarpe ☆–☆☆
Owner: Jean-Francois Janoueix. 21 ha. Grapes: Merlot
70%, Cab.Fr. 30%. www.j-janoueix-bordeaux.com
The Janoueix family are merchants in Libourne with
properties in Pomerol. Haut-Sarpe lies east of St-Emilion. Its
mansion is more impressive than the wine, which can be
hollow. 2005 was a fine exception.

Château Laniote ☆–☆☆
Owner: Arnaud de la Filolie. 5 ha. Grapes: Merlot 75%,
Cab.Fr. 20%, Cab.Sauv. 5%. www.laniote.com
One of the many little properties so appreciated in Belgium
that they are unknown elsewhere. Rather rustic wine, but a
welcoming estate with the owner given to outbursts of song.

Château Larcis-Ducasse ☆☆–☆☆☆
Owner: Jacques-Olivier Gratiot. 11 ha. Grapes: Merlot
75%, Cab.Fr. 20%, Cab.Sauv. 5%. www.larcis-ducasse.com

The best vineyard of St-Laurent-des-Combes, splendidly sited on the *côtes* just east of Château Pavie (q.v.). Elegant wine that needs patience before it shows its complexity. Exceptional in 2000 and '05, thanks to the involvement of manager Nicolas Thienpont and oenologist Stéphane Derenoncourt. A property to watch.

Château Larmande ☆☆
Owner: Groupe d'Assurance la Mondiale. 25 ha. Grapes: Merlot 65%, Cab.Fr. 30%, Cab.Sauv. 5%.
www.chateau-larmande.com
Lovely wines in the 1980s ('83, '85, '86, and '88) made its reputation, which was then enhanced by new ownership in 1991. In the late 1990s and early 2000s, the wines seemed very tannic and extracted, but they may well become harmonious with time.

Château Laroque ☆☆
Owner: Beaumartin family. 61 ha. Grapes: Merlot 87%, Cab.Fr. 11%, Cab.Sauv. 2%.
www.chateau-laroque.com
A substantial property on the St-Emilion *côtes* in St-Christophe. A reliable, medium-bodied wine.

Château Laroze ☆☆–☆☆☆
Owner: Guy Meslin. 27 ha. Grapes: Merlot 68%, Cab.Fr. 26%, Cab.Sauv. 6%. www.laroze.com
Lying low on the western *côtes* on sandy soil. Not one of the outstanding vineyards, but modern and well-managed, and capable of very good classic wines for medium-term enjoyment.

Château Matras ☆–☆☆
Owner: Véronique Gaboriaud-Bernard. 8 ha. Grapes: Merlot 34%, Cab.Fr. 33%, Cab.Sauv. 33%.
Beautifully sited château at the foot of the western *côtes* near Château Angélus (q.v.). Vigorous wines with good concentration of flavour.

Château Monbousquet ☆☆–☆☆☆
Owner: Gérard Perse. 31 ha. Grapes: Merlot 70%, Cab.Fr. 20%, Cab.Sauv. 10%. www.vignobles-perse.com
Everyone acknowledges that most of the vineyard is on mediocre land near the river, but after Gérard Perse bought the property in '93, quality soared, thanks in large part to advice from Michel Rolland and very low yields. Promoted in 2006.

Château Moulin du Cadet ☆☆
Owner: Isabelle Blois Moueix. 5 ha. Grapes: Merlot 100%.
Run Biodynamically by Alain Moueix of neighbouring Château Fonroque (q.v.). A combination of clay soil and a *côtes* situation gives solidity and sweetness.

Château Pavie-Decesse ☆☆☆
Owner: Gérard Perse. 3.5 ha. Grapes: Merlot 90%, Cab.Fr. 10%. www.vignobles-perse.com
The junior partner of Château Pavie, from the flatter land at the top of the *côtes*. The estate was bought by Perse in 1997, and is now made in the same way as Pavie, with the same controversial results.

Château Petit-Faurie-de-Soutard ☆–☆☆
Owner: Capdemourlin family. 8 ha. Grapes: Merlot 65%, Cab.Fr. 30%, Cab.Sauv. 5%.
www.vignoblescapdemourlin.com
Neighbour of Cap-de-Mourlin. Readily confused with nextdoor Faurie-de-Souchard. Technically *côtes* wines, but like Château Soutard (of which it was once a part) harder to penetrate.

Château le Prieuré ☆☆
Owner: Guichard family. 6 ha. Grapes: Merlot 90%, Cab.Fr. 10%.
On the eastern *côtes* in an ideal situation. Much improved since 2001, and from 2006 Stéphane Derenoncourt is advising.

Château Ripeau ☆☆
Owner: Françoise de Wilde. 15 ha. Grapes: Merlot 60%, Cab.Fr. 30%, Cab.Sauv. 10%
A well-known graves château in the past, considered on a par with Château la Dominique (q.v.). Less prominent recently, but heading for a revival, although still inconsistent.

Château St-Georges (Côte-Pavie) ☆☆
Owner: Jacques Masson. 5.5 ha. Grapes: Merlot 80%, Cab.Fr. 20%.
An enviable spot between Châteaux Pavie and la Gaffelière. In 2004 the owner entrusted the management to the Milhade négociant house, and quality improved overnight.

Château la Serre ☆☆
Owner: Luc d'Arfeuille. 7 ha. Grapes: Merlot 80%, Cab.Fr. 20%.
Just outside the town on the *côtes* to the east. Despite its surprisingly high proportion of Merlot, this used to lack charm, but since 2001 things seem to be looking up.

Château Soutard
Owner: Groupe d'Assurance la Mondiale. 22 ha. Grapes: Merlot 70%, Cab.Fr. 30%.
An important property on a rocky outcrop northeast of the town. Can be well-made, warm, and powerful wine. The great vintages are long-keeping classics. Sold in 2006 but too soon to see any results.

Château la Tour Figeac ☆☆–☆☆☆
Owner: Otto Rettenmaier. 15 ha. Grapes: Merlot 65%, Cab.Fr. 35%. www.latourfigeac.com
Formerly part of Château Figeac, now owned and run on Biodynamic principles, with the help of Stéphane Derenoncourt. Worthy wine, voluptuous and concentrated.

St-Emilion Grands Crus & Other Châteaux

The quality of such a number of châteaux obviously varies very widely. Only those with particularly high and consistent standards are listed, together with some of the *vins de garage* that became fashionable from the mid-1990s.

Château Barde-Haute ☆☆–☆☆☆
Owner: Sylviane Garcin-Cathiard. 17 ha.

Property next to Château Troplong-Mondot. Acquired in 2000 by the owner of Château Haut-Bergey in the Graves. Enjoyable and energetic wines.

Château Bellevue ✩✩
Owner: Hubert de Boüard. 6 ha. Grapes: Merlot 80%, Cab.Fr. 20%.
Well named for its situation high on the west slope of the *côtes*. In 2000, Stéphane Derenoncourt (see Château Canon-La-Gaffalière) became consultant winemaker, and Nicolas Thienpont (see Château Pavie-Macquin). There was a dramatic change, for the better, from the light, fruity '99s to the dark, dense exotic 2000. Nonetheless, Bellevue was demoted from *grand cru classé* in 2006. Hubert de Boüard was undeterred from taking a controlling interest in 2008.

Château Bellevue-Mondotte ✩✩–✩✩✩
Owner: Gérard Perse. 2.5 ha. www.vignobles-perse.com
Bought in 2001 by Perse; well-located old vines, and extremely low yields result in a wine with more density than drinkability.

Château Boutisse ✩–✩✩
Owner: Milhade family. 24 ha.
A large property in St Christophe, and late-ripening. Sound, fruity wines of few pretensions.

Château Cadet-Bon ✩✩
Owner: Guy Richard. 6 ha. Grapes: Merlot 70%, Cab.Fr. 30%. www.cadet-bon.com
The terroir here doesn't permit enormous richness, but recent vintages have shown good fruit and ample finesse. It changed hands in 2001, and the new owner invested heavily, but to little avail. He was punished by vintages he hadn't made, and Cadet-Bon was demoted in 2006.

Château Carteau-Côtes-Daugay ✩–✩✩
Owner: Jacques Bertrand. 16 ha.
A traditional wine, though supple and accessible.

Cave Coopérative: Union des Producteurs de St-Emilion ✩–✩✩
Very well run co-op, and a superbly equipped, if rather ugly, winery. Top *cuvées* include Galius and Aurélius.

Clos Badon Thunevin ✩✩
Owner: Jean-Luc Thunevin. 6.5 ha. www.thunevin.com
Supert-ripe, oaky wines for fairly rapid consumption.

Clos St Julien ✩✩
Owner: Catherine Papon-Nouvelle. 1.2 ha.
Tiny property just outside the town. Half Merlot, half Cabernet Franc, and aged in new oak. Intense wines, sometimes a touch overwrought.

Le Dôme ✩✩✩
Owner: Jonathan Maltus. 3 ha. www.teyssier.fr
Costly, new-oaked wine from mostly Cabernet Franc vines planted near Angélus.

Château Faugères ✩✩
Owner: Silvio Denz. 49 ha. www.chateau-faugeres.com
A complex property, since about half of it lies within the Côte de Castillon. A small sector of the St-Emilion vineyard is used

to make the ultra-concentrated Péby-Faugères. The property changed hands in 2005, and the new owner commissioned a winery from renowned architect Mario Botta, and plans to introduce a white wine.

Château Faurie-de-Souchard ✩✩
Owner: Francoise Sciard. 11 ha. Grapes: Merlot 65%, Cab.Fr. 26%, Cab.Sauv. 9%.
www.chateau-faurie-de-souchard.net
Confusingly, the neighbour of Petit-Faurie-de-Soutard (q.v.). Robust wines, often too tannic. Demoted in 2006, prompting the hiring of consultant Stéphane Derenoncourt to turn things around.

Château de Ferrand ✩–✩✩
Owner: Bich family. 30 ha. www.chateauferrand.com
A fine property – the wine is more modest, though well made.

Château La Fleur ✩✩
Owner: Laurent Dassault. 6 ha.
Small property adjoining Château Dassault (q.v.). Superripe wines with a good deal of oak.

Château La Fleur Morange ✩–✩✩✩
Owner: Jean-Francois Julien. 3.5 ha.
Very old vines feed this *garagiste* winery. Impressive if excessively massive wines.

Château Fombrauge ✩✩–✩✩✩
Owner: Bernard Magrez. 52 ha. www.fombrauge.com
Fombrauge is a large property that changed hands in 1999. Quality was previously humdrum, but Magrez and Michel Rolland have invested heavily, with some very impressive results. A tiny amount of garage wine, Magrez-Fombrauge, is now produced, although at a very high price. The regular bottling is better balanced.

Chateau de Fonbel ✩–✩✩
Owner: Alain Vauthier. 19 ha. www.chateau-ausone.com
Can't afford Ausone? This comes from the same stable, but is a simple, accessible wine of considerable charm.

Château La Gomerie ✩✩✩
Owner: Gérard and Dominique Bécot. 2.5 ha.
A no-holds-barred wine produced since '95 by the owners of neighbouring Château Beau-Séjour-Bécot. Voluptuous, and from 2000 of outstanding quality. Expensive.

Château Gracia ✩✩–✩✩✩
Owner: Michel Gracia. 2.6 ha.
Garagiste wines – "Angelots" is another label from Gracia – produced in the heart of the village by building contractor Gracia and his well-trained daughters. Lush wines, but well balanced.

Château Guadet ✩✩
Owner: Guy-Pétrus Lignac. 6 ha. Grapes: Merlot 75%, Cab.Fr. 25%. www.guadet.com
Vineyard just out of town to the north. Delicate wines with finesse. Demoted in 2006, to the fury of its owner.

Château Haut Brisson ✩✩
Owner: Peter Kwok. 13 ha.

Under new ownership; the wine is becoming more fleshy and concentrated.

Château Haut-Rocher ☆–☆☆
Owner: Jean de Monteil. 9 ha.
www.vins-jean-de-monteil.com
Ancient property in eastern St-Emilion. Easy-drinking wines.

Château Jean Faure ☆☆
Owner: Olivier Decelle. 18 ha.
Well-located property near Château La Dominique, now being revived by food industrialist Decelle, with advice from Michel Rolland.

Château Laforge ☆☆–☆☆☆
Owner: Jonathan Maltus. 4.5 ha.
www.teyssier.fr
A *garagiste* wine, mostly Merlot, aged in a good deal of new oak. Ripe and concentrated but less individual than its stablemate Le Dôme (q.v.).

La Mondotte ☆☆☆–☆☆☆☆
Owner: Graf Stephan von Neipperg. 4.5 ha. www.neipperg.com
Neipperg was refused permission by INAO to incorporate these few hectares of well-located vines into Château Canon-la-Gaffelière, so in '96 he created a kind of garage wine from its production. Inky, voluptuous wines, sometimes flirting with overripeness. Magnificent in 2001 and 2005.

Château Moulin St-Georges ☆☆–☆☆☆
Owner: Alain Vauthier. 8 ha.
Excellent new-oaked wines from a small property under the same ownership as, and just across the valley from, Château Ausone (q.v.).

Château de Pressac ☆☆
Owner: Jean-Francois Quenin. 36 ha.
Located on a knoll near Château Faugères, this imposing property's vineyards have been extensively renovated by the new owner since '97. Noir de Pressac is a synonym for Malbec, which was planted here in the 1730s. Quenin has paid homage to the past by replanting it. It's cool here, so grapes can struggle to ripen, but steady progress is being made.

Château Quinault ☆☆
Owner: Bernard Arnault and Albert Frère. 15 ha.
www.chateau-quinault.com
From 1997 Dr Alain Raynaud developed this property in Libourne with some critical acclaim. The wine was made in the same way as a garage wine for maximum concentration. In 2008, lacking the means to see the property classified, Raynaud sold it to the owners of Cheval Blanc.

Château Rochebelle ☆☆–☆☆☆
Owner: Philippe Faniest. 3 ha.
A rising star since the superb '98 and 2001. Fleshy wines of arresting sensuality.

Château Rol Valentin ☆☆–☆☆☆
Owner: Eric Prissette. 8 ha. www.rolvalentin.com
Small property near Cheval Blanc, vinified by Stéphane Derenoncourt with intense attention to detail. Owes its notoriety both to its owner (a famous footballer) and to its undoubted quality.

Château Sansonnet ☆–☆☆
Owner: François d'Aulan. 7.5 ha. www.edoniawines.com
An estate near Château Trottevieille (q.v.), under new ownership since '99. Despite much attention to the vineyards, the wines remain lacklustre.

Château Tertre-Daugay ☆☆
Owner: Comte Léo de Malet-Roquefort. 16 ha.
www.chateau-tertre-daugay.com
Spectacularly well-sited on the final promontory of the *côtes* west of Château Ausone, in disarray for some years, but since 1978 in the same hands as Château la Gaffelière and replanted. Some recent vintages have shown the true class of the property, so demotion in 2006 was arguably undeserved.

Château Tertre-Rôteboeuf ☆☆☆
Owner: François Mitjaville. 6 ha.
www.tertre-roteboeuf.com
As a pioneer of very late harvesting, and an opponent of green-harvesting, Mitjaville follows his own path. The wines are oaky, dense, and exotic, in a category of their own. High prices.

Château Teyssier ☆–☆☆
Owner: Jonathan Maltus. 21 ha. www.teyssier.fr
On the plain near Vignonet, Teyssier makes an easy-drinking wine of no pretensions. Maltus has parcels elsewhere in St-Emilion, from which he produces two very expensive and admired wines: Laforge and Le Dôme (qq.v.), and, since 2004, Château Grand Destieu on the sandy plain.

Château la Tour-du-Pin-Figeac
Owner: Bernard Arnault and Albert Frère. 9 ha.
Bland wines from a privileged situation among the great plateau vineyards. Demoted in 2006, then snapped up by the owners of neighbouring Château Cheval Blanc.

Château la Tour-du-Pin-Figeac (Giraud-Bélivier) ☆
Owner: André Giraud. 11 ha.
www.vins.giraud-belivier.com
A vineyard, beside Cheval Blanc, but the wines are dim. Demoted in 2006.

Chateau Trianon ☆☆
Owner: trio of investors. 10 ha.
www.chateau-trianon.com
Under same ownership as Château Bellefont-Belcier, and run with flair by Dominique Hébrard. Old Carmenère vines give this wine its individuality. Medium-bodied, supple wines.

Château de Pressac, St. Emilion

Château Valandraud ☆☆☆
Owner: Jean-Luc Thunevin. 8 ha. www.thunevin.com
The archetypal garage wine: some undistinguished parcels (and some on much better soil) cropped very low and vinified for maximum sumptuousness. But overpriced.

Château Vieux Fortin ☆☆
Owner: Claude Sellan. 5.5 ha.
Obscure property, but with well-placed old vines near Château La Dominique. Lush and invigorating wines, aged in new oak.

Château Villemaurine ☆
Owner: Justin Onclin. 7 ha.
At the gates of the town, a *côtes* vineyard with splendid cellars but seriously disappointing wines. Demoted in 2006, shortly after it was purchased by the new owner.

Château Yon-Figeac ☆☆
Owner: Alain Chateau. 25 ha.
For 20 years this was run by Bernard Germain, who owns properties in Bordeaux and Anjou; then sold to 2005 to a paper magnate. The Gemain wines were enjoyable in the medium term.

The St-Emilion Satellites

Apart from the five saintly villages (St-Emilion, St-Laurent, St-Christophe, St-Etienne, and St-Hippolyte) that are considered part of the appellation St-Emilion, four more to the north and east are granted the privilege of adding St-Emilion to their names. They are known as the satellites.

They lie just north of the little River Barbanne, which forms the northern boundary of glory and renown. Their citizens argue that the formation of the valley gives two of them, St-Georges (170) and Montagne (1,064), a better situation than some of St-Emilion.

Be that as it may, those two, plus Puisseguin (725) and Lussac (1,440), are honoured. Proprietors in St-Georges may call their wines Montagne St-Emilion if they wish. St-Georges has a splendid château that gives it pride in its own name. Its wine is indeed like St-Emilion and can be made almost equally meaty and long-lived. More growers, however, prefer using a good deal of Merlot and making softer (still strong) wine that can be delicious in two or three years. Unfortunately, many properties are still producing decidedly rustic wines.

Leading Puisseguin-St-Emilion Châteaux

Château Branda ☆☆
Owner: Arnaud Delaire and Yves Blanc. 10 ha.
Oaky and concentrated wines, stylish in good years.

Château des Laurets ☆
Owner: Baron Benjamin de Rothschild. 86 ha.
Numerous changes of ownership until the Rothschilds arrived in 2003. The team is still coming to terms with a large, complex vineyard, part of which lies in Montagne.

La Mauriane ☆☆–☆☆☆
Owner: Pierre Taix. 3.5 ha. www.lamauriane.com
Vin de garage from very old vines. Careful selection has brought the wine to a high standard: generous and challenging.

Château Rigaud ☆☆
Owner: Pierre Taix. 8 ha. www.lamauriane.com
Same ownership as La Mauriane (q.v.) and a more conventional and less oaky wine.

Château Soleil
Owner: Graf Stephan von Neipperg. 20 ha. www.neipperg.com
Located on a limestine plateau, Soleil was acquired by Neipperg and other investors in 2005.

Leading Lussac-St-Emilion Châteaux

Château de Barbe Blanche ☆–☆☆
Owner: André Lurton. 28 ha. www.andrelurton.com
The regular bottling, confusingly called Réserve shows the influence of new oak. Steady progress now that the vineyards have been restored.

Château Bel-Air ☆☆
Owner: Jean-Noel Roi. 21 ha.
Half the wine is aged in oak, but in 1998 Roi launched his Cuvée Jean-Gabriel, aged solely in new barriques.

Château de Bellevue ☆
Owner: André Chatenoud. 12 ha. www.chateau-de-bellevue.com
Chatenoud has worked in Australia and Napa, but the Bellevue wines are a mixed bag.

THE JURADE DE ST-EMILION

The ceremonial and promotional organization of St-Emilion is probably the oldest in France. The Jurade de St-Emilion was formally instituted by King John of England and France in 1199, as the body of elders to govern the little city and its district – a dignity granted to few regions at the time. Nobody seriously pretends that the modern institution is a linear descendant, but its impressive processions to Mass in the great parish church and to its own candle-lit solemnities in the cloisters cut out of the solid limestone in the centre of the town, are full of dignity as well as good humour. The Jurade also played an important role in the control of quality and administration of the various categories of châteaux. Its annual tastings give a boost to St-Emilion quality in a similar way to the tastevinage undertaken by the Chevaliers de Tastevin in Burgundy. On a memorable autumn weekend in 1981, the Jurade visited the great medieval city of York, arriving by river in a state barge, to process to the Minster for a service conducted by the archbishop, and to dine in the splendour of Castle Howard. They do these things with style.

Château du Courlat ☆☆
Owner: Pierre Bourotte. 17 ha.
The best wine here, from old Merlot vines, is Cuvée Jean-Baptiste.

Château La Grande Clotte ☆☆
Owner: Malaterre family, but leased to Michel Rolland. 8.5 ha. www.rollandcollection.com
The red is unoaked and straightforward, but the Rollands delight in the new-oaked white (AC Bordeaux), which is both delicious and structured.

Château Lucas ☆–☆☆
Owner: Frédéric Vauthier. 19 ha.
An old monastic property with vines on the limestone plateau. Two special bottlings: the Cuvée Prestige, and the new-oaked L'Esprit, only made in top years. The regular wine and the Prestige are rather simple; L'Esprit is too oaky.

Château de Lussac ☆☆
Owner: Hervé and Griet Laviale. 23 ha.
www.chateaudelussac.com
Since 2000 under same ownership as Château Franc-Mayne (q.v.) in St-Emilion. Good spicy wines, thanks to strict selection.

Château Lyonnat ☆–☆☆
Owner: Milhade family. 52 ha. www.milhade.com
Large property, and until recently unmemorable wines. With advice from Rhône winemaker Jean-Luc Colombo, quality has improved, especially for the old-vine Réserve.

Château Mayne-Blanc ☆–☆☆
Owner: Jean Boncheau. 17 ha.
Cuvée Tradition is aged in used barrels, Cuvée St Vincent (from old vines) in mostly new barriques, L'Essentiel from the oldest vines. Sound wines across the board.

Leading Montagne-St-Emilion Châteaux

Château Beauséjour ☆☆
Owner: Pierre Bernault. 12 ha.
www.chateau-beausejour.com
Under new ownership since 2004, with Stéphane Derenoncourt consulting. The Clos de l'Eglise is a Merlot-dominated wine from old vines.

Château Calon ☆
Owner: Jean-Noël Boidron. 28 ha.
Old vines and natural winemaking, yet the wines are unremarkable.

Château de la Couronne ☆☆–☆☆☆
Owner: Thomas Thiou. 11 ha.
Thiou is a self-taught winemaker who believes in minimal intervention. The top *cuvée* is the concentrated and powerful Reclos.

Château Faizeau ☆☆
Owner: Chantal Lebreton. 12 ha.
www.chateau-faizeau.com

Same ownership as Château Croix de Gay in Pomerol (q.v.). Aged in 50% new oak, this is a ripe, plummy wine from an abundance of old Merlot vines.

Château Maison Blanche ☆☆
Owner: Nicolas Despagne. 32 ha.
Most of the wine is aged in older barrels, but Cuvée Louis Rapin is aged in new oak. Full-bodied wines of high quality.

Château Messile Aubert ☆☆
Owner: Jean-Claude Aubert. 10 ha.
www.la-couspaude.com
Powerful oaky wines that benefit from bottle age.

Château Montaiguillon ☆–☆☆
Owner: Chantal Amart Ternault. 28 ha.
www.montaiguillon.com
A well-known property making good, spicy wines for medium-term drinking.

Château Roc de Calon ☆–☆☆
Owner: Bernard Laydis. 24 ha.
The best wine here is the elegant Cuvée Prestige.

Château Roudier ☆–☆☆
Owner: Jacques Capdemourlin. 30 ha.
www.vignoblescapdemourlin.com
Traditional, long-lived wine, with best grapes going into the cuvée called L'As de Roudier.

Vieux-Château St-André ☆☆
Owner: Jean-Claude Berrouet. 10 ha.
The personal property of the recently retired winemaker at Pétrus. Fruity, well-balanced wines.

Leading St-Georges-St-Emilion Châteaux

Château Belair St Georges ☆–☆☆
Owner: Nadine Pocci. 10 ha.
Easygoing but well made wines.

Château Macquin ☆☆
Owner: Denis Corre-Macquin. 31 ha.
Low-lying vineyards near the Barbanne River. Succulent and vigorous wines.

Château St Georges ☆–☆☆
Owner: Georges Desbois. 45 ha.
www.chateau-saint-georges.com
The eighteenth-century mansion here is one of the showplaces of the region. The wines can't match the grandeur of the house, although at their best they can stylish and long-lived.

Château Tour du Pas St-Georges ☆☆
Owner: Pascal Delbeck. 15 ha.
A pleasingly old-fashioned and restrained wine, and occasionally a pure-Merlot Cuvée Eugenie. They age well.

Pomerol

If there are doubters (and there are) about the differences that different soils make to wine, they should study Pomerol. In this little area, flanked by the huge spread of St-Emilion like a market-garden to Libourne on the north bank of the Dordogne, there are wines as potent and majestic as any in France, cheek by jowl with wines of wispy, fleeting fruitiness and charm – and dull ones, too.

The soil grades from shingly sand around the town of Libourne through increasingly heavy stages to a climactic plateau, where the clay subsoil is very near the surface. A yard down, the clay is near-solid and packed with nuggets of iron. This, at the giddy height of 15 metres (50 feet) above its surroundings, is in every sense the summit of Pomerol. But there is gravel here too, contributing finesse to wines such as La Conseillante and La Fleur Pétrus. Even the finest Pomerol is far from uniform.

Despite its international renown, Pomerol will always be an abstruse, *recherché* corner of the wine world. Its whole vineyard area of 780 ha is no larger than St-Julien, the smallest of the great communes of the Médoc. Perhaps half of this (as against two-thirds of St-Julien) is of truly distinctive, classed-growth standard.

The size of the properties is correspondingly small, with the biggest estate at just under 50 ha. The total annual production is about 350,000 cases entitled to the appellation. There is no cooperative; small growers tend to make their wine and sell it directly to consumers all over France, and particularly to Belgium.

It is only 100 years since the name of Pomerol was first heard outside its immediate area, yet tradition has already provided it with a clear identity. Its best soil is clay; therefore cold. The early ripening Merlot does better than the later Cabernet, and of the Cabernets, the Franc (alias Bouchet) rather than the Sauvignon. The mellow, brambly Merlot and the lively, raspberryish Bouchet pick up the iron from the clay, are matured in fragrant oak – and *voilà*, you have a greatly over-simplified recipe for Pomerol.

Where does it get its singular texture of velvet, its chewy flesh, its smell of ripe plums and even cream, and even honey? Wherever, it was more than an edict from the bureaucracy that fixes appellations. Authorities put Pomerol between St-Emilion and the Médoc in style. To me, it is closer to St-Emilion: broader, more savoury, and with less "nerve" than Médocs of similar value, maturing in five years as much as Médocs do in ten – hence tending to overlay them at tastings, as California wines do French. Great Pomerols, however, show no sign of being short-lived.

No official classification of Pomerol has ever been made. Were there to be one, the many under-performers might have an incentive to improve. But the best estates are well known, with price establishing a crude but surprisingly reliable hierarchy, headed, without doubt, by Pétrus.

Pomerol First Growth

Château Pétrus ☆☆☆☆
Owner: Ets. J.-P. Moueix. 11 ha. Grapes: Merlot 95%, Cab.Fr. 5%.
See Pétrus, Pomerol's First Growth, page 84.

Leading Pomerol Châteaux

Château Beauregard ☆☆–☆☆☆☆
Owner: Credit Foncier. 17 ha. Grapes: Merlot 70%, Cab.Fr. 30%. www.chateau-beauregard.com
In contrast to most of the modest châteaux of Pomerol, the seventeenth-century Château Beauregard is so desirable that Mrs Daniel Guggenheim had it copied stone-for-stone on Long Island. Rich, fruity, elegant wines since '98, increasingly reliable and confident.

Château Bellegrave ☆☆
Owner: Jean-Marie Bouldy. 8 ha. Grapes: Merlot 75%, Cab.Fr. 25%.
Gravel and clay soils, but not in the best sector. Nonetheless Bouldy makes honest and sometimes excellent wine that is easily underrated.

Château Bonalgue ☆☆–☆☆☆☆
Owner: Pierre Bourotte. 6.5 ha. Grapes: Merlot 90%, Cab.Fr. 10%
Full-bodied wines of good consistency, if not among the most elegant of Pomerol.

Château le Bon-Pasteur ☆☆☆
Owner: Michel Rolland. 7 ha. Grapes: Merlot 80%, Cab.Fr. 20%. www.rollandcollection.com
At his own property in the Maillet sector, Michel Rolland demonstrates the richly sensuous style of Merlot-based wines that he has helped so many other Right Bank properties to achieve.

Château Bourgneuf-Vayron ☆☆–☆☆☆☆
Owner: Xavier Vayron. 9 ha. Grapes: Merlot 90%, Cab.Fr. 10%
Within the heart of Pomerol, lying between Trotanoy and Latour. Potent, plummy wine; not the most stylish, although there are signs of more finesse and harmony in the later 1990s. It ages very well.

Château la Cabanne ☆☆
Owner: Jean-Pierre Estager. 10 ha. Grapes: Merlot 92%, Cab.Fr. 8%. www.estager.com
The name means "the hut" or the "shanty", which seems excessively modest for an estate situated in the heart of Pomerol with Trotanoy as a neighbour. The soil gravel and clay; the wine is not remarkable, and can be rustic.

Château Cantelauze ☆☆–☆☆☆☆
Owner: Jean-Noel Boidron. 1.5 ha. Grapes: Merlot 90%, Cab.Fr. 10%
Tiny vineyard, tiny production, but what there is of Cantelauze is elegant and balanced.

Château Certan de May ☆☆☆
Owner: Mme. Barreau-Badar. 5 ha. Grapes: Merlot 70%, Cab.Fr. 25%, Cab.Sauv. 5%.
Formerly called Château Certan. Perfectly sited next to Vieux-Château-Certan and Pétrus (qq.v.); but verging more towards Pétrus in richness and concentration. Recent vintages have been inconsistent but quality has been impeccable since 2004.

Château Certan-Giraud
See Hosanna.

Château Certan-Marzelle ☆☆–☆☆☆
Owner: Ets. J.-P. Moueix. 3.3 ha. Grapes: Merlot 100%.
This formed part of Château Certan-Giraud, until acquired and renamed by Christian Moueix in '98. Soft and approachable wines since 2001.

La Clémence ☆☆–☆☆☆
Owner: Christian Dauriac. 3 ha. Grapes: Merlot 85%, Cab.Fr. 15%.
Dr Dauriac, owner of Château Destieux (q.v.) in St-Emilion, has six parcels in Pomerol, from which he blends a single wine. Superripe, opulent, new-oaked style that very much reflects the philosophy of consultant Michel Rolland. But very expensive wines.

Château Clinet ☆☆☆
Owner: Jean-Louis Laborde. 9 ha. Grapes: Merlot 85%, Cab.Sauv. 10%, Cab.Fr. 5%. www.chateauclinet.com
Close to Pétrus and Lafleur. Formerly a lean, almost Médoc-style wine, but recently much fatter. Late harvesting gives the wines their richness and power, perhaps at the expense of some finesse.

Clos du Clocher ☆☆–☆☆☆
Owner: Pierre Bourotte. 6 ha. Grapes: Merlot 75%, Cab.Fr. 25%.
Central vineyard close to Trotanoy, making well-balanced, middle-weight wine with plenty of flavour.

Clos L'Eglise ☆☆☆
Owner: Sylviane Garcin-Cathiard. 6 ha. Grapes: Merlot 70%, Cab.Fr. 30%. www.vignoblesgarcin.com
A superb little vineyard located on the north rim of the plateau, bought in 1997 as part of a shopping spree that took in estates in the Graves and St-Emilion. Old Clos l'Eglise vintages were backward, long-lived wines. The new style is very concentrated, lush, and oaky.

Clos René ☆☆
Owner: Jean-Marie Garde. 18 ha. Grapes: Merlot 70%, Cab.Fr. 20%, Malbec 10%.
Unpretentious and on the unfashionable (western) side of the commune, yet good and often long-lived Pomerol, though at the lighter end of the spectrum.

Château la Conseillante ☆☆☆–☆☆☆☆
Owners: Nicolas family. 12 ha. Grapes: Merlot 80%, Cab.Fr. 20%.
The splendid silver-on-white label is designed around an "N" for the family that has owned the château for more than a century. Coincidentally, London's Café Royal has the same motif for the same reason. La Conseillante lies between Pétrus and Cheval Blanc, but makes a more delicate, high-pitched wine – sometimes as fine and fragrant as any Pomerol, but less plummy and fat. Recent vintages are first-class.

Château la Croix ☆–☆☆
Owner: J. Janoueix family. 10 ha. Grapes: Merlot 60%, Cab.Sauv. 20%, Cab.Fr. 20%. www.j-janoueix.bordeaux.com
Another 2 ha is la Croix-Toulifaut, which gives a lighter wine. These crosses are in the south of the commune on relatively light soil with a high iron content, not to be confused with la Croix-de-Gay on the northern edge. Sturdy, generous wine not noted for great finesse but repaying bottle age. The same firm owns the 4-ha Château la Croix-St-Georges.

Château la Croix-du-Casse ☆☆
Owner: Philippe Castéja. 9 ha. Grapes: Merlot 90%, Cab.Fr. 10%.
Grown on light soils, this is a ripe, fleshy wine, made until his death in 2001 by Jean-Michel Arcaute of Château Clinet.

Château la Croix-de-Gay ☆☆–☆☆☆
Owner: Chantal Lebreton. 10 ha. Grapes: Merlot 95%, Cab.Fr. 5%. www.chateaulacroixdegay.com
A well-run vineyard on the gravelly clay sloping north down to the River Barbanne. As in so many Pomerol properties, its wines are being made with more care for a more demanding market. There is (since 1982) a costly 100% Merlot *cuvée prestige* Fleur du Gay that is the best part (about 1,200 cases) of the crop. The regular wine suffers, it seems, as a consequence.

Château du Domaine de l'Eglise ☆☆
Owner: Castéja family. 7 ha. Grapes: Merlot 95%, Cab.Fr. 5%
Medium-bodied wine with a marked flavour of oak. But much improved since 2001.

Château L'Eglise-Clinet ☆☆☆–☆☆☆☆
Owner: Denis Durantou. 6 ha. Grapes: Merlot 75%, Cab.Fr. 20%, Malbec 5%. www.durantou.com
Generally rated above Clinet; a stouter production with tannin, even brawn. Recently reaching higher: luscious deep wines of top class. Second label La Petite Eglise is from young vines, some from other properties.

Château l'Enclos ☆☆
Owner: Stephen Adams. 9 ha. Grapes: Merlot 82%,

Statue of St. Peter, Château Pétrus, Pomerol

Cab.Fr. 17%, Malbec 1%. www.chateau-lenclos.com
With Clos René, one of the most respected châteaux of the
western half of Pomerol, with the sort of deeply fruity and
rewarding wine that impresses you while young, yet ages well.
Bought in 2006 by the owner of Château Fonplégade in St-
Emilion, so changes are likely.

Château l'Evangile ☆☆☆
**Owner: Domaines Baron de Rothschild. 14 ha. Grapes:
Merlot 70%, Cab.Fr. 30%. www.lafite.com**
In the top ten of Pomerol for quality and size. At its best (eg.
'90, '95, '98, 2001, '05) a voluptuous, concentrated wine for a
long life. The (Lafite) Rothschilds bought a majority share in
1990, but only won complete control of the property after
2000. Its situation between Pétrus and Cheval Blanc is
propitious, and the new winery is impressive.

Château Feytit-Clinet ☆☆–☆☆☆
**Owner: Jérémy Chasseuil. 6 ha. Grapes: Merlot 90%,
Cab.Fr. 10%.**
I have had some wonderful old wines from this little château,
across the road from the illustrious Château Latour à Pomerol
(q.v.). Faltered under Moueix management from '66, but the
family is back in control since 2000, and quality is returning.
Even the 2002 was exceptional.

Château la Fleur-Pétrus ☆☆☆
**Owner: Ets. J.-P. Moueix. 12 ha. Grapes: Merlot 80%,
Cab.Fr. 20%.**
The third-best Moueix Pomerol – which is high praise indeed.
The vineyard is more gravelly than Pétrus and Trotanoy,
the wine less fat and fleshy with more obvious tannin at first,
poised, taut, asking to be aged. Enlarged in 1985 to take in
4 ha that had belonged to its neighbour, le Gay, planted with
very old vines.

Château Franc-Maillet ☆☆
**Owner: Gérard Arpin. 6 ha. Grapes: Merlot 80%, Cab.Fr.
20%. www.vignobles-arpin.com**
Owned by the Arpin family since 1919, this is a solid, tannic
wine. The Cuvée Jean-Baptiste is aged in new oak. Not great
Pomerol, but fairly priced.

Château le Gay ☆☆–☆☆☆
**Owner: Catherine Péré-Vergé. 10 ha. Grapes: Merlot
90%, Cab.Fr. 10%. www.montviel.com**
For 60 years the Robin sisters owned this property, vinified
and commercialized by Moueix. In 2002 it was sold to the
present owner, who invested a fortune in the estate and its
buildings. With advice from Michel Rolland, le Gay has been
transformed into a lush, oaky, modern Pomerol with a strong
hedonistic appeal. Only since 2005 has the wine seemed
worthy of its reputation and price.

Château Gazin ☆☆☆
**Owner: De Bailliencourt family. 24 ha. Grapes: Merlot
90%, Cab.Fr. 3%, Cab.Sauv. 7%. www.chateau-gazin.com**
One of the biggest Pomerol properties, despite selling a
section to its neighbour, Château Pétrus, in 1970. The
quality record used to be uneven; at best a fittingly fruity,
concentrated wine, but usually a shade full. Then, in 1987,
machine-harvesting was abandoned and the grapes began to
be picked at higher ripeness levels. The '89 seemed to mark a
turning point toward an excellent long-term wine, and the last
two decades have been excitingly good. Nor is the price as
elevated as the quality might suggest.

Château Gombaude-Guillot ☆☆
**Owner: Laval family. 7 ha. Grapes: Merlot 80%,
Cab.Fr. 20%**
An organically cultivated property right in the centre near the
church. Used to be a lean but harmonious wine, though recent
vintages have shown more weight and richness.

Château La Grave à Pomerol ☆☆–☆☆☆
**Owner: Ets. J.-P. Moueix. 9 ha. Grapes: Merlot 90%,
Cab.Fr. 10%.**
A fabulous wine in the 1920s, but the Moueix family acquired
some of the best parcels for la Fleur Pétrus and other
properties. Today, not the most full-bodied Pomerol, but
particularly well-balanced and stylish with tannin to encourage
long development. The soil here is graves, not clay – hence
finesse rather than flesh.

Château Hosanna ☆☆☆
**Owner: Ets. J.-P. Moueix. 4.5 ha. Grapes: Merlot 70%,
Cab.Fr. 30%.**
This is part of the former Château Certan-Giraud, which
Moueix bought in 1999, restructured, and renamed.
Wonderful terroir near Lafleur yields silky wine that gains
intensity from the old Cabernet Franc vines.

Château Lafleur ☆☆☆☆
**Owner: Jacques and Sylvie Guinadeau. 4.5 ha. Grapes:
Merlot 50%, Cab.Fr. 50%**
Lafleur (next to la Fleur-Pétrus, q.v.) is a model of balance,
body with finesse, and considerable style. Very complex soils
give complexity, Cabernet Franc gives lift and freshness, and
the harmonious whole ages as superbly as any Pomerol.
Second wine is Les Pensées de Lafleur.

BORDEAUX TRADE MEASURES

For official and statistical purposes, all
French wine production is measured in
hectolitres, but each region has its
traditional measures for maturing and
selling its wine. In Bordeaux, the measure
is the *tonneau*, a notional container since
such big barrels are no longer made.

A *tonneau* consists of four barriques –
the barrels used at the châteaux, and still
sometimes for shipping. A barrique
bordelaise must by law contain 225
litres, which makes 25 cases of a dozen
75cl bottles each. The *tonneau* is
therefore a simple and memorable
measure: 100 cases of wine.

Château Lafleur-Gazin ☆☆
Owner: Mme. Delfour Borderie. 8 ha. Grapes: Merlot 80%, Cab.Fr. 20%.
Northern neighbour of Château Gazin, making elegant, smooth, well-bred wine. The property is managed and the wine vinified by J.-P. Moueix.

Château Latour à Pomerol ☆☆☆
Owner: Foyer de Charité Châteauneuf de Galaure. 8 ha. Grapes: Merlot 90%, Cab.Fr. 10%.
The property is run by the house of Moueix. It shows a fuller, fruitier style than la Fleur-Pétrus: more fat, less sinew – words can be very misleading. Paradoxically, it is a graves wine, from westwards of the fat band of clay. Very long-lived.

Château Mazeyres ☆☆
Owner: Société Générale. 22 ha. Grapes: Merlot 80%, Cab.Fr. 20%. www.mazeyres.com
Located close to Libourne, this large property is managed by Alain Moueix (see Château Fonroque in St-Emilion). The sandy, gravelly soils give wines of elegance rather than power.

Château Montviel ☆☆
Owner: Catherine Péré-Vergé. 5 ha. Grapes: Merlot 80%, Cab.Fr. 20%.
A modest wine from dispersed vineyards, but well-made and consistently pleasurable. For medium-term drinking.

Château Le Moulin ☆☆
Owner: Michel Querre. 2.4 ha. Grapes: Merlot 20%, Cab.Fr. 20%. www.querre.com
A *garagiste* wine from modest sandy gravel soils. Very low yields, rigorous sorting, and a good deal of new oak gives a sweet, opulent, generous wine.

CHÂTEAU PÉTRUS – POMEROL'S FIRST GROWTH

As Château d'Yquem is to Sauternes, so Château Pétrus is to Pomerol; the perfect model of the region and its aspirations. Like its region, Pétrus is a miniature; there are 3,000 cases in a good year, and often less. Among First Growths it is unique in that it has never been officially classified, nor does its eminence date back much more than a century. The Loubat family were the promoters of its quality and status, and from 1943 the négociant Etablissements J.-P. Moueix became its sole agent. In 1969 Moueix became the majority shareholder, although this remained a secret until the late 1990s. From 1964 until his retirement in 2007, Jean-Claude Berrouet was the highly respected winemaker not only of Pétrus but of the other properties in the Moueix portfolio.

Pétrus is the flagship. Outwardly it is a modest little place, although recently spruced up by Christian Moueix. The *cuvier* is a cramped space between batteries of narrow concrete vats. The *chais*, recently rebuilt, are more spacious, but by no means grand.

The magic lies in the soil. No golf course or wicket is more meticulously tended. When one section of ancient vines (the average age is 40 years) was being replaced I was astonished to see the shallow topsoil bulldozed aside from the whole patch and the subsoil being carefully graded to an almost imperceptible slope to give a shade more drainage. It was a remarkable opportunity to see how uninviting this famous clay is.

The principle of winemaking at Pétrus is perfect ripeness, then ruthless selection. If the October sun is kind, the Merlot is left to cook in it. It is never picked before lunch, to avoid diluting the juice with dew. The crop is small, the new wine so dark and concentrated that new oak, for all its powerful smell, seems to make no impression on it. At a year old the wine smells of blackcurrant. At two, a note of tobacco edges in. But any such exact reference is a misleading simplification. Why Pétrus (or any great wine) commands attention is by its almost architectural sense of structure; of counterpoised weights and matched stresses. How can there be such tannin and yet such tenderness?

Because Pétrus is fat, fleshy, not rigorous and penetrating like a Médoc but dense in texture like a Napa Cabernet, it appears to be "ready" in ten years or less. Cigar smokers probably should (and anyway do) drink it while it is in full vigour. To my mind it takes longer to become claret. In a sense the great vintages never do.

Checking Pomerol's first growth

Château Moulinet ☆–☆☆
Owner: Marie-José Moueix. 18 ha. Grapes: Merlot 70%, Cab.Sauv. 20%, Cab.Fr. 10%.
An isolated estate on the northern edge of Pomerol where both the soil and the wine are lighter; the wine is stylish notwithstanding. Recent investments may lead to improvements.

Château Nénin ☆☆
Owner: Jean-Hubert Delon. 32 ha. Grapes: Merlot 70%, Cab.Fr. 30%.
One of the biggest properties, lying between Châteaux Trotanoy and la Pointe (qq.v.), but lacklustre for many years. The Delons of Château Léoville-Las-Cases bought Château Nénin in 1997 and restored the neglected vineyards. Quality will surely rise, but progress has been slow.

Château Petit-Village ☆☆–☆☆☆
Owner: AXA Millésimes. 11 ha. Grapes: Merlot 75%, Cab.Sauv. 17%, Cab.Fr. 8%. www.petit-village.com
Pomerol from the Cheval-Blanc zone. It has taken some years for the AXA team, more experienced on the Left Bank than the Right, to learn how to handle the property, but since 2004 the wine has been impressive and stylish.

Le Pin ☆☆☆–☆☆☆☆
Owner: Jacques Thienpont. 2.3 ha. Grapes: Merlot 88%, Cab.Fr. 12%.
The Thienponts, sensing the quality of the terroir, bought this tiny property on top of the Pomerol plateau next to Certan de May in 1979. They have achieved superb results, with the '82 being a top wine of the vintage and recent vintages selling (mainly in Asia) for prices to make you blanch. Sumptuous, mocha-tinged wine, with a beguiling Burgundian character.

Château Plince ☆–☆☆
Owner: Michel Moreau. 9 ha. Grapes: Merlot 70%, Cab.Fr. 30%. www.chateauplince.com
A suave, fruity wine with immediate appeal if little complexity.

Château la Pointe ☆☆
Owner: Generali insurance company (Italy). 22 ha. Grapes: Merlot 80%, Cab.Fr. 15%, Cab.Sauv. 5%.
The vineyard is on the doorstep of Libourne, on gravel and sand over the famous iron-bearing clay. Much improved through the 1990s, but it passed into corporate hands in 2007.

Château Providence ☆☆–☆☆☆
Owner: Ets. J.-P. Moueix. 2.7 ha. Grapes: Merlot, 98%, Cab.Fr. 2%.
A shareholder since '99, and owner since 2002, Moueix has swiftly transformed a rather rustic wine from an excellent location into one that is sleek and sensuous yet vigorous.

Château Rouget ☆☆–☆☆☆
Owner: Jean-Pierre Labruyère. 17.5 ha. Grapes: Merlot 85%, Cab.Fr. 15%. www.chateau-rouget.com
I cast envious eyes on Château Rouget each time I pass; it has the prettiest site in Pomerol in a grove of trees leading down to the River Barbanne. Since 1997 Michel Rolland has helped shape it into a ripe, opulent wine with considerable density.

Château de Sales ☆–☆☆
Owner: Bruno de Lambert. 47 ha. Grapes: Merlot 70%, Cab.Fr. 15%, Cab.Sauv. 15%. www.chateau-de-sales.com
The only noble château of Pomerol, remote down long avenues to the northwest, then rather disconcertingly having the railway line running right through the garden. The big vineyard is beautifully run and the wine increasingly well-made, yet without the concentration and sheer personality of the great Pomerols.

Château du Tailhas ☆–☆☆
Owner: Luc Nebout. 11 ha. Grapes: Merlot 80%, Cab.Fr. 10%, Cab.Sauv. 10%. www.tailhas.com
This is the southernmost Pomerol vineyard, a stone's throw from the edge of the sandy riverside area of St-Emilion. It still has Pomerol's iron-rich clay subsoil, yet the wine is rather light and lacking in substance.

Château Taillefer ☆☆
Owner: Catherine Moueix. 12 ha. Grapes: Merlot 75%, Cab.Fr. 25%. www.chateautaillefer.com
Owned by the Moueix family since 1923. Unremarkable for many years, Taillefer is, since the later 1990s and with advice from Denis Dubourdieu, showing much more finesse.

Château Trotanoy ☆☆☆☆
Owner: Ets. J.-P. Moueix. 7.5 ha. Grapes: Merlot 90%, Cab.Fr. 10%.
Generally allowed to be the runner-up to Château Pétrus, made by the same hands to the same Rolls-Royce standards. The little vineyard is on the western slope (such as it is) of the central plateau. The vines are old, the yield low, the darkly concentrated wine matured in new barriques (which lend it a near-Médoc smell in youth). For ten years or more the best vintages have a thick, almost California-Cabernet texture in your mouth. Tannin and iron show through the velvet glove.

Vieux-Château-Certan ☆☆☆–☆☆☆☆
Owner: Alexandre Thienpont. 14 ha. Grapes: Merlot 60%, Cab.Fr. 30%, Cab.Sauv. 10%. www.vieux-chateau-certan.com
The first great name of Pomerol, though overtaken at a canter by Pétrus in the last 30 or 40 years. The style is quite different: drier and less fleshy but balanced in a Médoc or Graves manner. At early tastings, substance can seem to be lacking, to emerge triumphantly later. The handsome old château lies halfway between Pétrus and Cheval Blanc. Its Belgian owners take intense and fully justified pride in its unique personality.

Château Vieux Maillet ☆☆
Owner: Hervé and Griet Laviale. 7 ha. Grapes; Merlot 90%, Cab.Fr. 10%. www.chateauvieuxmaillet.com
The owners of Château Franc-Mayne in St-Emilion bought and expanded this property in 2003. Richly fruity wines with a promising future.

Château La Violette ☆☆–☆☆☆
Owner: Catherine Péré-Vergé. 2 ha. Grapes: Merlot 100%.
Micro-property near Trotanoy acquired in 2006 by the owner of Château le Gay (q.v.). Is this the first barrel-fermented Pomerol? Her initial vintages were certainly impressive.

Château Vray-Croix-de-Gay ☆☆
**Owner: Guichard family. 3.2 ha. Grapes: Merlot 90%,
Cab.Fr. 10%. www.baronneguichard.com**
The name means "the real Croix-de-Gay", implying that the
neighbours pinched the name. Jockeying for position seems
appropriate here on the northern rim of the precious plateau.
Over recent years considerable efforts and investment have
been made here, including taking on Stéphane Derenoncourt
as consultant, and the wines from 2004 onwards show much
more verve.

Lalande-de-Pomerol

On the northern boundary of Pomerol is the little river of
Barbanne. The two communes on its other bank, Lalande and
Néac, share the right to the name Lalande-de-Pomerol for red
wine which, at its best, is certainly of junior Pomerol class.
Traditionally, they have grown more of the Malbec (or Pressac),
a difficult grape, which is now going out of fashion. But the
gravel-over-clay in parts is good, and some châteaux have high
reputations. Altogether there are 1,120 hectares of vines owned
by 180 growers (without a cooperative) make an average total of
600,000 cases.

Leading Lalande-de-Pomerol Châteaux

Château de Bel-Air ☆–☆☆
Lalande-de-Pomerol. Owner: Stephen Adams. 15 ha.
This is fairly tannic wine that requires a few years ageing to
become harmonious. Lost its way in recent years but the new
American owner is likely to make the most of a property with
very good potential.

Château Bertineau St-Vincent ☆☆
Néac. Owner: Michel Rolland. 6 ha.
Elegant wines that are vinified at Michel Rolland's main
property at Château le Bon-Pasteur in Pomerol (q.v.).

Château La Borderie-Mondésir ☆–☆☆
Lalande-de-Pomerol. Owner: Laurent Rousseau. 2.2 ha.
Old vines on gravelly soils, yet the wines, including the new-
oaked Cuvée Excellence seem rather extracted.

Château de Chambrun ☆☆
Néac. Owner: Silvio Denz. 1.7 ha.
Vin de garage owned by the Janoueix family until 2008, when
sold to the owner of Château Faugères in St-Emilion.

Château de Cruzelles ☆☆
Lalande-de-Pomerol. Owner: Christian Pichon. 10 ha.
Leased by Denis Durantou of Château Clinet (q.v.) in
Pomerol. Structured wines for the appellation.

Château la Fleur de Boüard ☆☆–☆☆☆
**Néac. Owner: Hubert de Boüard de Laforest. 20 ha.
www.lafleurdebouard.com**
De Boüard, of Château Angélus, bought this property in 1998
and gave it its present name. Rich, dark wine that sets new
standards for the appellation. Le Plus is the special *cuvée*, but
the regular wine is better balanced.

Château Garraud ☆☆
Néac. Owner: Jean-Marc Nony. 19 ha. www.vln.fr
Low yields and serious winemaking have ensured a high
standard here for some years.

Château Grand Ormeau ☆☆
Lalande-de-Pomerol. Owner: Jean-Claude Beton. 14 ha.
Since the 1980s, this estate has produced rich, well-structured
wines, especially the old-vine Cuvée Madeleine.

Château La Gravière ☆☆
**Néac. Owner: Catherine Péré-Vergé. 7 ha.
www.montviel.com**
Smoky, modern-style wines from the owner of Château le Gay
(q.v.) in Pomerol.

Château Haut-Chaigneau ☆☆
Néac. Owner: André Chatonnet. 28 ha.
Chatonnet is a skilled winemaker, and it shows in this supple
wine packed with fruit.

Château les Hauts-Conseillants ☆☆
Néac. Lalande-de-Pomerol. Owner: Pierre Bourotte. 10 ha.
Oaky but supple and balanced wine from Château Bonalgue
owner in Pomerol (q.v.).

Château Jean de Gué ☆☆
**Musset. Owner: Jean-Claude Aubert. 10 ha.
www.la-couspaude.com**
Ripe, tannic wines that benefit from some bottle age.

Château Pavillon Bel-Air ☆–☆☆
Néac. Owner: Crédit Foncier. 8 ha
Since 2003 under the same ownership as Château Beauregard
(q.v.) in Pomerol. Attractive well-made wines, especially the
special *cuvée* called Le Chapelain.

Château Perron
Lalande. Owner: Bertrand Massonie. 15 ha.
Well-made, sensibly priced wines, and, from 1997, a more
complex *cuvée* called La Fleur.

Château la Sergue ☆☆
Néac. Owner: André Chatonnet. 5 ha.
Made mostly from Merlot, vinified in wooden vats, and aged
in new oak. Intense wine.

Château Siaurac ☆–☆☆
**Néac. Owner: Guichard family. 59 ha.
www.baronneguichgard.com**
Home to the Guichard family, who own several properties in
the Libournais. Quality has been sound but unremarkable, but
the new generation are determined to do better.

Château Tournefeuille ☆☆–☆☆☆
**Néac. Owner: Francois Petit. 15 ha.
www.chateau-tournefeuille.com**
Superbly located near the church on the plateau, and since
2001 the wines have been among the best of the appellation.

Château de Viaud ☆–☆☆
Lalande-de-Pomerol. Owner: Philippe Raoux. 21 ha.
Sound, well-balanced wines from owner of Château d'Arsac (q.v.).

Bordeaux's Minor Regions

The vast extent of the Gironde vineyards begins to sink in when you look at the number and size of growers' cooperative cellars dotted over the *département*. Most communes have one or two well-established châteaux: old manor houses whose wine has long been made in the manner of a not-very-ambitious family business. In many cases, the small grower has sold his vineyard to the bigger grower as an alternative to joining the co-op. A number of well-run larger châteaux are thereby adding to their hectarage and seeking to produce wines with more personality and, arguably, commercial appeal. Several now offer a proportion of their best vats as a top *cuvée* – aged in oak and at a higher price than their basic wine. Unquestionably, a new understanding of winemaking techniques, coupled with a far more demanding generation of wine-buyers and -drinkers, is transforming these outlying regions. Wine-loving investors have found affordable properties here, and many small estates that used to sell fruit to the cooperatives are now producing wine of improving quality under their own label. These wines are little-known, as neither the producer nor the region can afford to promote them properly. It's not hard to find bargains.

Fronsac & Canon-Fronsac

The town of Libourne lies on the Dordogne at the mouth of its little northern tributary, the Isle. It has Pomerol as its back garden, St-Emilion as its eastern neighbour, and only half a kilometre so (about a mile) to the west another, surprisingly different, little wine area.

Fronsac is a village on the Dordogne, at the foot of a jumble of steep bumps and hollows, and a miniature range of hills up to 90 metres (292 feet). Several of the châteaux were obviously built as country villas rather than as plain farms. Under it all there is limestone. The vines are nearly all red, the usual Bordeaux varieties, traditionally with more stress on the soft and juicy Malbec than elsewhere. Merlot, however, dominates, with 78 per cent of the plantings. Having plenty of colour and

alcohol, Fronsac wine has been much used in the past as *vin médecin* for weaklings from more famous places.

Historically, Fronsac took precedence over Pomerol. During the eighteenth century, its wines were even drunk at court. Circumstances gave Pomerol the advantage it has exploited well, and it is only over the past 20 years that Fronsac has begun to climb back – and only in the past 15 years that real investment has been able to change its image.

There are 1,130 hectares of vineyards. Over two-thirds of the hills (the lower parts) are AC Fronsac; the rest, where the soil is thinner with more lime, is AC Canon-Fronsac. Its wines can be delectable, full of vigour and spice, hard enough to resemble Graves or St-Emilion more than Pomerol, and worth a good five years' ageing. The style has been changing, bringing these wines into line with the prevailing trend on the Right Bank towards fatter, plumper, oakier wines – sometimes at the expense of acidity and finesse.

Leading Fronsac & Canon-Fronsac Chateaux

Château Barrabaque ✰✰
Canon-Fronsac. Owner: Bernard Noel. 9 ha.
Pleasant, rounded, harmonious wines, and an oakier *cuvée prestige*.

Château Canon-de-Brem ✰–✰✰
Canon-Fronsac. Owner: Jean Halley. 4.5 ha.
www.chateau-dauphine.com
Since 2006 the crop has been blended into Château de La Dauphine (q.v.).

Château de Carles ✰✰–✰✰✰
Saillans. Owner: Constance Droulers. 20 ha.
Supple, enjoyable wines, although the best fruit goes into the more flamboyant and exciting Château Haut Carles.

Château Cassagne-Haut-Canon ✰–✰✰
St-Michel de Fronsac. Owner: Jean-Jacques Dubois. 13 ha
Soft, oaky wines, ripe, but lacking in vigour. La Truffière is the special *cuvée*.

GARAGE WINES

In the early 1990s a new phenomenon occurred: the *vin de garage*. As the name implied, these were wines made in an artisanal fashion in tiny quantities. The scale of the operation allowed for a fanatical attention to detail – very low yields, exhaustive selection, destemming by hand, and so forth – which supposedly resulted in wines of exceptional quality.

Le Pin in Pomerol has often been described as Bordeaux's first garage wine. Although a small property with a rudimentary winery, Le Pin is a proper, reasonably homogeneous estate. The

prototype for a garage wine is surely Valandraud (q.v.) in St-Emilion, which was, as its creator happily confesses, made from vines planted on mediocre terroir. A mixture of extreme concentration and lashings of new oak helped the wine to gain recognition and, like Le Pin, it sold for very high prices. This set a trend. More and more growers would separate a small section of their vineyard, or purchase a small undistinguished parcel, and crop and vinify in the *garagiste* manner. Minuscule quantities were used to

justify a very high price. By 2000, however, there were at least 60 *vins de garage* and the novelty was wearing off. It also contradicted the very foundation of Bordeaux: the notion that exceptional terroir produces exceptional wine.

Vins de garage are a specialty of the Right Bank. The proprietors of the much larger estates of the Médoc and Graves are opposed to the whole idea. In the end, the consumer will decide whether the wines are worth the prices being demanded for them.

Chateau Chadenne ☆
St Aignan. Owner: Philippe Jean. 5 ha.
Old vines and a good deal of new oak characterize the wines, yet recent vintages have failed to excite.

Château Coustolle ☆–☆☆
Canon-Fronsac. Owner: Alain Roux. 20 ha.
www.chateaup-coustolle.com
Large property; produces wines with some tannic grip.

Château Dalem ☆☆
Saillans. Owner: Michel Rullier. 14 ha.
Soft, juicy, velvety wines, moderately concentrated.

Château de la Dauphine ☆–☆☆
Fronsac. Owner: Jean Halley. 18 ha.
www.chateau-dauphine.com
Formerly owned by Moueix, but sold in 2000. Medium-bodied wines with a soft texture.

Château Fontenil ☆☆–☆☆☆
Saillans. Owner: Michel Rolland. 9 ha.
www.rollandcollection.com
Lush, fruity, occasionally jammy wines, aged in 60% new oak. The regular wine is better balanced than the usually overripe special *cuvée* Le Défi.

Château du Gaby ☆☆
Canon-Fronsac. Owner: David Curl. 11 ha. www.chateau-du-gaby.com
A new owner since 2006, who should continue to make fine wine in a prime site.

Château Grand Renouil ☆☆
Canon-Fronsac. Owner: Michel Ponty. 11 ha.
Full-bodied wines of considerable complexity. Also makes one of the few white wines of the region.

Château Mayne-Vieil ☆–☆☆
Saillans. Owner: Sèze family. 32 ha.
Two *cuvées*, of which the better is Aliénor.

Château Mazeris-Bellevue ☆
St-Michel-de-Fronsac. Owner: Jacques Bussier. 9 ha.
Rather light wines, with supple, raspberry fruit.

Château Moulin Haut Laroque ☆☆–☆☆☆
Saillans. Owner: Jean-Noël Hervé. 15 ha.
www.moulinhautlaroque.com
Vineyards on the plateau and careful sorting give impeccably made wines with abundant fruit and a discreet structure.

Château Moulin Pey-Labrie ☆☆–☆☆☆
Fronsac. Owner: Grégoire Hubau. 6.5 ha.
www.moulinpeylabrie.com
Rich, oaky wines of consistent quality.

Château du Pavillon ☆☆
Canon-Fronsac. Owner: Michel Ponty. 4 ha.

Same ownership as Château Gramd Renouil (q.v.) and similar quality and consistency.

Château Richelieu ☆☆
Fronsac. Owner: Arjen Pen. 12 ha.
www.chateau-richelieu.com
Stéphane Derenoncourt has been called in by a new owner to improve quality, and appears to be succeeding.

Château de la Rivière ☆☆
La Rivière. Owner: James Grégoire. 59 ha.
www.chateau-de-la-riviere.com
The region's most important estate, with an opera-set château producing well-balanced wines that age well. Numerous changes in ownership have unsettled the style, but Grégoire accepts the full potential of the superb property has yet to be realised.

Château la Rousselle ☆–☆☆
La Rivière. Owner: Jacques Davau. 4.5 ha.
Oaky, fleshy wines for drinking fairly young.

Château Tour du Moulin ☆☆
Saillans. Owner: Vincent Dupuch. 7 ha.

Vigorous wines, especially the Cuvée Particulière with its well integrated oakiness.

Château les Trois Croix ☆☆–☆☆☆
Fronsac. Owner: Patrick Léon. 14 ha.
The personal property of the former winemaker of Château Mouton-Rothschild. Rich, well-structured wines.

Château la Vieille Cure ☆–☆☆
Saillans. Owner: Colin Ferenbach and associates. 18 ha.
This estate is American-owned. Producing very ripe wines with good concentration and ageing potential.

Château Villars ☆☆–☆☆☆
Saillans. Owner: Jean-Claude Gaudrie. 30 ha.
Some impressive wines with ripe toastiness being balanced by fine tannins.

Côtes de Castillon & Côtes de Francs

Two areas adjoining the St-Emilion satellites to the east, still within the general appellation area of Bordeaux, were granted their own independent *appellations d'origine contrôlée* in 1989. The larger is the Côtes de Castillon in the hills to the north of the Dordogne valley overlooking Castillon-la-Bataille, where the French defeated the English forces in 1452 and ended English rule in Aquitaine. Ten communes are planted with some 3,000 hectares of vines. To its north, the Côtes de Francs is much smaller, with 512 hectares under vine and an annual production of almost 4 million bottles. The appellation takes in parts of the communes of Francs, Les Salles, St-Cibard, and Tayac; tranquil and remote country long known as a good

Château Villars, Saillans

producer of Bordeaux Supérieur, but only now recognized on its distinctive merits. Côtes de Castillon and Côtes de Francs wines in general are like lightweight St-Emilions, especially in cool years when the grapes can struggle to ripen. Many wines have only remained rustic because the property owners could not afford necessary investments. But these regions should not be dismissed out of hand. Several châteaux, many owned by shrewd outsiders such as Stephan von Neipperg and the Bécot family of St-Emilion, are beginning to show real ambition and are making wine to mature five years or more.

Leading Côtes de Castillon Châteaux

Château d'Aiguilhe ☆☆–☆☆☆
St-Philippe-d'Aiguilhe. Owner: Stephan von Neipperg. 50 ha. www.neipperg.com
Under the same ownership as Château Canon-La-Gaffelière (q.v.). Going from strength to strength.

Château d'Ampélia ☆☆
St-Philippe d'Aiguille. Owner: François Despagne. 5 ha.
Quite tannic, robust wines, with less finesse than Despagne's Château Grand-Corbin-Despagne (q.v.) in St-Emilion.

Château Cap de Faugères ☆☆
Ste-Colombe. Owner: Silvio Denz. 31 ha.
The extension of Château Faugères in St-Emilion (q.v.). Attractive wines for medium-term consumption.

Château la Clarière-Laithwaite ☆☆–☆☆☆
Ste-Colombe. Owner: Tony Laithwaite. 5 ha.
Perfectionist wines since 1998, sold mostly through Laithwaite's Direct Wines company in Britain. Le Presbytère is a splendid old-vines *cuvée*.

Clos Puy-Arnaud ☆☆–☆☆☆
Belvès. Owner: Thierry Valette. 12 ha.
The Valettes are the former owners of Château Pavie in St-Emilion. Thierry Valette bought this property in '99, and now makes some of the region's most stylish wines. Château Pervenche Puy Arnaud is the reliable second wine.

Château Côte Montpezat ☆
Belvès. Owner: Dominique Bessineau. 30 ha. www.cote-montpezat.com
Charming, easy-drinking wines.

Château Joanin-Bécot ☆☆–☆☆☆
St Philippe d'Aiguilhe. Owner: Bécot family. 5 ha. www.beausejour-becot.com
Gérard Bécot's daughter Juliette runs this property, purchased in 2001. Bold, full-flavoured wines.

Château Lapeyronie ☆–☆☆☆
Ste-Colombe. Owner: Jean-Frédéric Lapeyronie. 8 ha.
Rich, supple wines of consistent quality.

Château Pervenche Puy Arnaud ☆
Belvès-de-Castillon. Owner: Thierry Valette. 8 ha.
Organic property, with Stéphane Derenoncourt as consultant.

Château Peyrou ☆☆
St Magne. Owner: Catherine Papon-Nouvel. 4.5 ha.
Old vines on the border with St-Emilion. Fruity but polished wines.

Château de Pitray ☆☆
Gardegan. Owner: Comtesse de Boigne. 31 ha. www.pitray.com
Powerful, cherry-scented wines. The regular wine is aged in tanks, the Premier Vin in barriques.

Château Veyry ☆☆–☆☆☆
Castillon. Owner: Christian Veyry. 4 ha.
Veyry is a consultant for many properties in the St-Emilion area and Fronsac. His own property produces very concentrated and rather expensive wines of good quality.

Domaine de l'A ☆☆–☆☆☆
Ste-Colombe. Owner: Stéphane Derenoncourt. 8 ha. www.vigneronsconsultants.com
The personal property of one of Bordeaux's top winemakers. Cultivated biodynamically. In effect, a private, experimental station for Derenoncourt to try out his ideas.

BUYING WINES "EN PRIMEUR"

In the 1980s a new way of buying wine became fashionable. Instead of buying wines once they were in bottle, it was possible to buy the wine about six months after the vintage, and many more months before it was bottled. The advantage to the consumer was, supposedly, an opportunity to buy the wine at a cheaper price, and, of equal importance, to secure a case or two of rare wine (eg. Pomerol) that might be harder or impossible to find after its release. For the château proprietor and négociant, the advantage was cash flow: instead of waiting two or three years for their money, they could bank cheques after six months. In some vintages the system worked well. Anyone who bought the 1995 vintage en primeur (or, in American parlance, as futures) would have secured some bargains. In other years, such as 1997, when quality was modest but prices very high, the consumer lost out.

Bordeaux loves the en primeur system. It creates a buzz of excitement around almost every new vintage. However, all judgments, whether by the trade or the press, on the new wines must be based on cask samples, drawn from barrel without any monitoring or control. Most proprietors are honest, but the temptation to show the best or richest barrel is surely high. Buying en primeur is risky, if only because the wine is still in an unfinished state when assessed and purchased. It only makes sense when the wine is good and offered at an appealing price. In years such as 2007, when quality was mostly modest yet prices were high, there is no real reason for the consumer to part with his cash until the wine is bottled and can be properly assessed.

Vieux-Château-Champs de Mars ☆–☆☆
Les Salles de Castillon. Owner: Régis Moro. 17 ha.
Nothing rustic about these perfumed wines. Good value
except for costly Cuvée Johanna. Also makes Côtes de Francs
(Château Pelan Bellevue).

Leading Côtes de Francs Châteaux

Château les Charmes-Godard ☆–☆☆
**St-Cibard. Owner: Nicolas Thienpont. 14.5 ha, of which
1.5 white. www.nicolas-thienpont.com**
Small property, producing good white as well as rich red.
Thienpont, who manages some top estates in St-Emilion,
owns a number of properties here.

Château Franc-Cardinal ☆
Tayac. Owner: Philip Holzberg. 10 ha.
Attractive Merlot-based wines.

Château de Francs ☆☆
Francs. Owner: Hébrard and de Boüard families. 35 ha.
Sumptuous wines for medium-term drinking. The top wine is
the oakier Les Cerisiers.

Château Marsau ☆–☆☆
Francs. Owner: Jean-Marie Chadronnier. 15 ha.
All-Merlot property belonging to the former boss of CVBG.

Château La Prade ☆–☆☆
**St-Cibard. Owner: Nicolas Thienpont. 4.5 ha.
www.nicolas-thienpont.com**
Oaky wines from old vines on the limestone plateau.

Château Puyguéraud ☆☆
**St-Cibard. Owner: Nicolas Thienpont. 35 ha.
www.nicolas-thienpont.com**
Sturdy but not inelegant wines, they are among the best of the
region. The top wine is Cuvée George.

Côtes de Bourg

The right bank of the Gironde was a thriving vineyard long
before the Médoc across the water was planted. Bourg, lying to
the north of the Dordogne where it joins the Garonne (the two
form the Gironde), is like another and bigger Fronsac: hills
rising steeply from the water to 60 metres (180 feet) or more,
but unlike the hills of Fronsac, almost solidly vine covered. The
Côtes de Bourg (3,000 hectares) makes as much wine as the
lower Médoc – as does its immediate neighbour to the north,
the Côtes de Blaye (5,600 hectares). Bourg specializes in red
wine of a respectable standard, made largely of Merlot and
Cabernet Franc, round, full-bodied and ready to drink at four
or five years – but certainly not in a hurry. The châteaux that
line the riverbank have, to all appearances, a perfect situation.
The potential is considerable and is gradually being realized.

Leading Côtes de Bourg Châteaux

Château Brûlesécaille ☆☆
**Tauriac. Owner: Jacques Rodet. 25 ha.
ww.brulesecaille.com**

Sound red wines for medium-term drinking and a small
amount of full-bodied Sauvignon Blanc.

Château Le Clos du Notaire ☆☆
**Bourg. Owner: Roland Charbonnier. 20 ha.
www.clos-du-notaire.com**
Yes, this did once belong to a notary, and the present owner
is a descendant. Two wines: the self-explanatory Tradition
and the very oaky Notaris.

Château Falfas ☆☆
Bayon. Owner: John Cochrane. 22 ha.
Biodynamic estate, producing quite tannic wines. The top
wine, Cuvée Chevalier, is made from 70-year vines and aged
in new oak.

Château Fougas ☆☆–☆☆☆
**Lansac. Owner: Jean-Yves Béchet. 13 ha.
www.vignoblesbechet.com**
Impeccable viticulture and winemaking at this organic
property results in some of the most stylish and reliable wines
of the Côtes. Cuvée Maldoror is especially elegant.

Château de la Grave ☆–☆☆
**Bourg. Owner: Philippe Bassereau. 45 ha.
www.chateaudelagrave.com**
This estate makes quite stylish wines and a special *cuvée*
ambitiously named Nectar.

Château Guerry ☆☆
Tauriac. Owner: Bernard Magrez. 22 ha.
Robust, flavoury wine of consistent quality with a fair
proportion of Malbec.

Château Guionne ☆–☆☆
**Lansac. Owner: Alain Fabre. 21 ha.
www.chateauguionne.com**
Three bottlings: one unwooded, the others oaked. The most
interesting is Cuvée Renaissance, which is 50% Malbec.

Château Labadie ☆
Mombrier. Owner: Joel Dupuy. 42 ha.
Large commercial property, mechanically harvested. Various
cuvées, all of sound quality.

Château Martinat ☆☆
Lansac. Owner: Stéphane Donze. 10 ha.
Two *cuvées* from this ambitious property: the regular bottling
and the new-oaked Epicuréa. The difference is more in style
than quality.

Château Nodoz ☆–☆☆
Tauriac. Owner: Jean-Louis Magdeleine. 42 ha.
Three red wines of varying concentration and oakiness, but
all well made.

Château Peychaud ☆☆
**Teuillac. Owner: Bernard Germain. 29 ha.
www.germain-saincrit.com**
The Cuvée Maisonneuve is fleshy and oaky.

Château le Roc des Cambes ☆☆☆
Bourg. Owner: Francois Mitjaville. 10 ha.

The best and costliest wine of the region, from the same stable as Château Tertre-Rôteboeuf (q.v.). Dense and concentrated.

Château Tayac ☆☆–☆☆☆
Bourg. Owner: Pierre Saturny. 30 ha. www.chateau-tayac
A riverside property with excellent vineyards and numerous *cuvées*. Forceful, tannic wines that benefit from cellaring.

Premières Côtes de Blaye

Two miles of water, the widening Gironde, separates Blaye from the heart of the Médoc. Blaye is the northernmost vineyard of the "Right Bank"; the last place, going up this coast, where good red wine is made. North of this is white-wine country; the fringes of Cognac. Blaye already makes about one third white wine, including some delightful but short-lived Colombard-based wines. Premières Côtes de Blaye is the appellation reserved for better vineyards, nearly all red, whose wine is to all intents like that of Bourg – although generally considered not as good or full-bodied. A new AC Blaye was created in 2000, requiring slightly higher minimal ripeness and more rigorous quality controls. Unfortunately, the name gives the impression that it is a basic rather than superior appellation, and not all estates are using it.

Leading Premières Côtes de Blaye Châteaux

Château Bel Air La Royère ☆☆–☆☆☆
Cars. Owner: Xavier and Corinne Loriaud. 23 ha.
Fine quality here, thanks to skilled winemaking and some old-vine Malbec that gives spice and character.

Château Bellevue-Gazin ☆☆
Plassac. Owner: Alain Lancereau-Burthey. 15 ha.
www.chateau-bellevue-gazin.com
Newcomers working old vines on gravelly clay. Stylish red wines, and a charming clairet.

Châteaux Bertinerie and Haut-Bertinerie ☆☆
Cubnezais. Owner: Bantegnies family. 58 ha.
www.chateaubertinerie.com
Very well-run property with immediately appealing wines, white and red. The Haut-Bertinerie label is used for the best wines, and priced accordingly.

Château les Bertrands ☆
Reignac. Owner: Laurent Dubois. 86 ha.
www.chateau-les-bertrands.com
Large commercial property, all machine-harvested. Cleanly made if frequently dilute wines, with the exception of the *prestige cuvée* "Nectar".

Château Cantinot ☆–☆☆
Cars. Owner: Yann Bouscasse. 12 ha.
www.chateaucantinot.com
New owners since 2002, busily restoring the vineyards and aiming for good quality.

Château Charron ☆☆
St-Martin-Lacaussade. Owner: Bernard Germain. 18 ha.
www.germain-saincrit.com

Many old vines on the property give wines, white as well as red, of considerable weight and richness. The Cuvée Acacia is the best white, and "Les Gruppes" the most impressive red.

Château Gigault ☆☆
Owner: Christophe Reboul-Salze. 14 ha.
www.the-wine-merchant.com
Cuvée Viva is the top wine here. Negociant Reboul-Salze is also a shareholder in Château Grands Maréchaux (q.v.).

Château du Grand Barrail ☆–☆☆☆
Plassac. Owner: Denis Lafon. 35 ha.
Since 1998, Lafon has produced Cuvée Renaissance, from the oldest vines and aged, perhaps excessively, in new oak.

Château Grands Maréchaux ☆☆
St Grions d'Aiguevives. Owner: Christophe Reboul-Salze. 20 ha. www.the-wine-mechant.com
Dark, concentrated wines, made with advice from Stéphane Derenoncourt.

Domaine des Graves d'Ardonneau ☆–☆☆
St Mariens. Owner: Christian Rey. 34 ha.
Inland property producing attractive reds – especially the Grand Vin – and zesty whites.

Château les Jonqueyres ☆☆
St-Paul. Owner: Pascal Montaut. 15 ha.
www.chateaulesjonqueres.com
Montaut is credited with Blaye's revival in quality, and his own wines are medium-bodied and well balanced.

Château Monconseil-Gazin ☆–☆☆
Plassac. Owner: Jean-Michel Baudet. 24 ha.
Good AC Blaye wines.

Château Mondésir-Gazin ☆☆–☆☆☆
Plassac. Owner: Marc Pasquet. 14 ha.
www.mondesir-gazin.com
This is a serious property run by an equally serious man. Concentrated wines are produced, and good Côtes de Bourg.

Château Pérenne ☆☆
St Genès. Owner: Bernard Magrez. 70 ha.
www.bernardmagrez.com
Large property producing very good wine, white as well as red. The top *cuvée*, La Croix de Pérenne, can be excessively oaky and over-alcoholic.

Château Peyredoulle ☆–☆☆
Berson. Owner: Josette Germain. 22 ha.
www,.germain-saincrit.com
The top wine, from a 2-ha parcel, is Maine Criquau.

Château Puynard ☆–☆☆
Berson. Owner: Nicolas Grégoire. 16 ha.
Sold in bulk until the new owner arrived in 2002. Ripe reds and a delicate clairet.

Château Roland la Garde ☆☆–☆☆☆
St-Seurin. Owner: Bruno Martin. 28 ha.
www.chateau-roland-la-garde.com
Martin produces three wines, including the majestic Grand Vin.

Château La Rose Bellevue ☆–☆☆
St Palais. Owner: Jérôme Eymas. 45 ha.
www.chateau-larosebellevue.com
Well-crafted wines at a fair price.

Château Segonzac ☆–☆☆
St-Genès. Owner: Jacques Marmet. 33 ha.
www.chateau-segonzac.com
Swiss-owned since '90. The top wine is Héritage, aged in new barriques.

Château des Tourtes ☆–☆☆
St-Caprais. Owners: the Raguenot family. 47 ha.
The *cuvée prestige* whites and reds are supple wines for short-term drinking.

Premières Côtes de Bordeaux

A long, narrow strip of the east bank of the Garonne facing Graves enjoys the doubtful prestige of this appellation. Its hinterland is Entre-Deux-Mers. At their northern end they were some of Bordeaux's Roman and medieval vineyards – now buried under houses. At their southern end, at Cadillac and into Ste-Croix-du-Mont, they are known for sweet wines, at their best up to Sauternes standards. Along the way the mix is about 80 per cent red and 20 per cent white, the white recently made much drier and fresher than formerly. (Château Reynon is perhaps the best example.) Red Premières Côtes is potentially much better than plain Bordeaux Supérieur from less well-placed vineyards, and this is beginning to be recognized. Some of the best estates pursue a sensible policy of producing balanced, enjoyable wines for relatively early consumption, a style of wine that can and should compete with simpler New World wines that are often more expensive and less interesting. In general, the 3,400 hectares of vineyards here are not going to deliver powerful and structured wines.

Leading Châteaux of the Premières Côtes

Château Carignan ☆☆–☆☆☆
Carignan. Owner: Philippe Pieraerts. 67 ha.
www.chateau-carignan.com
A huge property on the edge of the city. The regular wine can be austere, and the best grapes are used for Prima, which, from 2006, is pure Merlot.

Château Carsin ☆–☆☆
Rions. Owner: Juha Berglund. 27 ha. www.carsin.com
Good modern-style wines from a Finnish-owned estate, though recent vintages have shown some inconsistency.

Clos Ste-Anne ☆☆
Capian. Owner: Sylvie and Marie Courselle. 7.5 ha.
The daughters of Château Thieuley own this gravelly property, producing a substantial red and some Cadillac.

Château Le Doyenné ☆–☆☆
St Caprais. Owner: Domonique Watrin. 9 ha.
www.chateauledoyenne.fr.
Firm red wines with a touch of austerity. Moderately priced.

Château Fayau ☆–☆☆
Cadillac. Owner: Jean Médeville. 140 ha.
Substantial family-run property, offering a wide range of wines, including a long-lived Cadillac.

Château Haut-Rian ☆
Rions. Owner: Michel Dietrich. 76 ha.
Crisp modern wines; Cadillac, too.

Château Lagarosse ☆–☆☆
Tabanac. Owner: Stephen Adams. 25 ha.
Sound, Merlot-dominated wines.

Château Lamothe de Haux ☆–☆☆
Haux. Owner: Fabrice Néel. 80 ha.
www.chateau-lamothe.com
Cuvée Valentine, red and white, are the best wines at this well-run property.

Château Lezongars ☆☆
Villenave de Rions. Owner: Russell Iles. 48 ha.
www.chateau-lezongars.com
British owners produce a range of enjoyable wines at varying quality levels.

Château Plaisance ☆☆–☆☆☆
Capian. Owner: Patrick Bayle. 25 ha.
www.chateauplaisance.com
Serious wines, red and white, some showing plenty of oak, especially the excellent Cuvée Alix.

Château Reynon ☆☆
Béguey. Owner: Denis and Florence Dubourdieu. 35 ha.
www.denisdubourdieu.com
Sound light reds, and very good whites, especially the "Cuvée Vieilles Vignes".

Château Suau ☆☆
Capian. Owner: Monique Bonnet. 60 ha.
www.chateausuau.com.
Well-run estate produces a range of wines with commercial appeal. The new-oaked Prestige is admirable.

Entre-Deux-Mers

The two "seas" in question are the rivers Dordogne and Garonne, whose converging courses more or less define the limits of this big, wedge-shaped region; the most diffuse and, territorially, the most important in Bordeaux, with some 23,000 hectares under vine. The appellation Entre-Deux-Mers is now reserved for dry white wine only, although there are moves to allow it for red wines too. Growers tend to declare their best white wines as Entre-Deux-Mers, while other wines they produce are given the Bordeaux or Bordeaux Supérieur appellation, which are, of course, shared with the whole Bordeaux region. Three-quarters of production is red, also sold as Bordeaux or Bordeaux Supérieur.

The south of the region is relaxed patchwork countryside with as much woodland and pasture as vineyard. The north is almost a monoculture of the vine. Its biggest cooperative, at Rauzan, makes 1.2 million cases a year. The 14 cooperatives make a third of the production of Bordeaux dry white.

Entre-Deux-Mers is the one wine Bordeaux has succeeded in redesigning in modern marketing terms. The region was bogged down with cheap, sweet wine nobody wanted any more. Some bright spark thought of the catch-phrase "Entre deux huitres, Entre-Deux-Mers" ("Between two oysters," etc…) and a rosy future opened up for dry white: the Muscadet of the south-west. I have yet to taste an Entre-Deux-Mers of the sort of quality that would win medals in California – but the world needs its staples. It varies from the briskly appetizing to the thoroughly boring, but in ways that are hard to predict. A good cooperative is as likely to produce a clean and bracing example as a property with a long name. A handful of private growers, like Francis Courselle of Thieuley, and Jean-Louis Despagne of Tour de Mirambeau (qq.v.) set a standard that others emulate.

No sooner had the growers adroitly replanted their vineyards with white varieties than the "French paradox" was propounded, and demand switched from white to red wines worldwide. This has led to the bizarre situation whereby Bordeaux produces some of the world's most expensive red wine, and some of the cheapest white. The basic Bordeaux and Bordeaux Supérieur appellations underlying all the more specific and grander names of Bordeaux are available to any-one using the approved grapes, achieving a certain degree of alcohol, and limiting the harvest to a statutory maximum (which varies from year to year). Bordeaux Supérieur must be cropped at lower yields than AC Bordeaux, and must be a touch higher in alcohol – and thus body. Much of it is produced within Entre-Deux-Mers, as well as in districts just beyond its borders.

Leading Entre-Deux-Mers Châteaux

(and properties using the Bordeaux appellation)

Château L'Abbaye der Ste-Ferme ☆☆
Ste Ferme. Owner: Baron Arnaud de Raignac. 50 ha.
The owner seeks to make red wines of flair and intensity.

Château Bauduc ☆–☆☆
Créon. Owner: Gavin Quinney. 30 ha. www.bauduc.com
Charming, floral white wines, and improving reds, especially Clos des Quinze. Attractive pricing has ensured considerable commercial success, especially in England.

Château Beaulieu ☆☆
Salignac. Owner: Comte Guillaume de Tastes. 15 ha.
Oaky Bordeaux Supérieur from vineyards north of Libourne.

Château Bel-Air Perponcher ☆☆
Naujan et Postiac. Owner: Jean-Louis Despagne. 61 ha. www.despagne.fr
Excellent white wines, with unusual complexity for the region. The red Grande Cuvée is intensely fragrant.

Château Bonnet ☆☆
Grézillac. Owner: André Lurton. 250 ha. www.andrelurton.com

André Lurton has demonstrated for many years that it is possible to make simple but delicious wines, white and red, from Entre-Deux-Mers vineyards. In 2000, he launched a special *cuvée* called Divinus.

Château de Camarsac ☆–☆☆
Camarsac. Owner: Thierry Lurton. 60 ha.
Delicate wines from the vineyards of this medieval fortress.

Château Chapelle Maracan ☆☆
Mouliets-et-Villemartin. Owner: Alexandre de Malet Roquefort. 15 ha. www.malet-roquefort.com
Acquired in 2000, this fine property near Castillon makes the spicy, succulent Bordeaux Supérieur, La Chapelle d'Aliénor.

Clos Nardian ☆☆
St Aubin-de-Branne. Owner: Jonathan Maltus. 1 ha. www.teyssier.fr
Just across from his base at Château Teyssier in St-Emilion are ancient white vines which he translates into a huge, viscous, New-World-style blend. Expensive.

Château Dubois-Challon ☆☆
Baigneaux. Owner: Pascal Delbeck. 11 ha.
Best known for its floral, amiable white, Fleur Amandine.

Château Ducla ☆–☆☆
Gironde-sur-Dropt. Owner: Yvon Mau. 80 ha. www.chateau-ducla.com
Sound if rather unexciting wines from a conscientious négociant house.

Château de Fontenille ☆–☆☆
La Sauve Majeure. Owner: Stéphane Defraine. 42 ha. www.chateau-fontenille.com
Fontenille produces a plump white, an easygong red, and a charming clairet from mostly Cabernet Franc.

Girolate ☆☆–☆☆☆
Naujan et Postiac. Owner: Jean-Louis Despagne. 10 ha. www.girolate.com
Flagship, some would say *garagiste*, wine from the Despagne group: pure Merlot, hand-crafted.

Château Grée Larroque ☆☆–☆☆☆
St Ciers d'Abzac. Owner: Arnaud Benoit de Nyvenheim. 2 ha.
Delicious Bordeaux Supérieur from vines north of Libourne.

Château Launay ☆–☆☆
Soussac. Owner: Baron Arnaud de Raignac. 60 ha.
Bought in '99 by the owner of Château de l'Abbaye de Ste-Ferme (q.v.). Fat, heavy whites and over-extracted reds, modish but hard to enjoy.

Château Bonnet, Grézillac

Château Marjosse ☆
Tizac de Curton. Owner: Pierre Lurton. 37 ha.
When not making fabulous wine at Château Cheval Blanc (q.v.), Lurton relaxes by producing fresh, simple wines from his personal property.

Château Pénin ☆☆
Génissac. Owner: Patrick Carteyron. 40 ha.
www.chateaupenin.com
Numerous *cuvées*, of which the Grande Sélection is fresh, fruity, and balanced.

Château Pey La Tour ☆–☆☆
Salleboeuf. Owner: Dourthe-Kressmann. 142 ha.
www.cvbg.com
Immense property producing classically styled, good-value Réserve reds.

Château Rauzan-Despagne ☆☆
Naujan-et-Postiac. Owner: Jean-Louis. Despagne. 64 ha.
www.despagne.fr
Some remarkable red wines are made here, notably the old-vine Grande Réserve, which is built to last. And a delightful Sauvignon Blanc and clairet.

Château de Reignac ☆☆–☆☆☆
St Loubès. Owner: Yves Vatelot. 80 ha. www.reignac.com
Vatelot sometimes makes lunch guests taste his wines blind against Médoc First Growths. That's asking for trouble, but his best reds – Reignac and Balthus – have remarkable complexity and staying power. Vatelot gives the credit to soils flattering to both Merlot and Cabernet.

Château Sainte-Marie ☆☆
Targon. Owner: Gilles Dupuch. 80 ha.
www.chateau.sainte.marie.com
Two fine white wines: one (Madlys) oaked, the other not. The reds, of which there are three *cuvées*, are enjoyable but less characterful.

Château de Seguin ☆
Lignan. Owner: Michael Carl. 121 ha.
www.chateau-seguin.com
Vast and much expanded property, developed by a Danish family. Good but unexciting wines.

Château Thieuley ☆☆–☆☆☆
La Sauve. Owner: Francis Courselle. 83 ha.
www.thieuley.com
One of the outstanding producers of the region. The top white wine is the Cuvée Francis Courselle, fermented and aged in new barriques; the best red the Réserve. A special *cuvée* called Héritage seems tailored for the tasting bench more than the dining table.

Château Tour de Mirambeau ☆☆
Naujan-et-Postiac. Owner: Jean-Louis Despagne. 88 ha.
www.despagne.fr
A huge supply of very consistent wines, red and white. British Airways has bought them for years.

Ste-Croix-du-Mont & Loupiac

The southern end of the Premières Côtes de Bordeaux faces Barsac and Sauternes across the Garonne. From Cadillac southwards the specialty is sweet white wine, growing more "liquorous" the nearer it gets to Sauternes. Ste-Croix-du-Mont gazes across at the hills of Sauternes from its higher riverbank and often shares the same autumnal conditions that lead to noble rot and sticky wines. Without quite the same perfection of soil, or pride of tradition, it cannot afford the enormous investment in labour needed to make the greatest wines, but it succeeds remarkably often in producing wine at least as good as run-of-the-mill Sauternes, and often better. And they are a good deal less expensive than Sauternes.

The only difference in the regulations between Sauternes and these Right-Bank wines is the quantity allowed. The same grapes and alcohol content are required, but the grower is allowed 40 hectolitres per hectare as against only 25 for Sauternes. This is not to say that perfectionist growers make their full quota. They also make dry wines of potentially fine quality, and a little light red sold as Bordeaux. There are 429 hectares of vines with about 100 estates, but in 2004 only 324 hectares were declared as producing Ste-Croix-du-Mont. Loupiac is not quite so well-placed, and makes slightly less liquorous wines on 330 hectares. About 58 properties make Loupiac, though not all bottle their own production. Growers make dry: white and red.

Leading Ste-Croix-du-Mont Châteaux

Château Bel-Air ☆–☆☆
Owner: Jean-Guy Méric. 25 ha.
An ancient property, from which Méric makes three sweet wines. The best is the Prestige, only made in top vintages.

Château Crabitan-Bellevue ☆
Owner: Bernard Solane. 22 ha.
Orangey but one-dimensional wines, and in top vintages an excellent barrique-aged Cuvée Spéciale.

Château la Grave ☆☆
Owner: Jean-Marie Tinon. 15 ha.
Oaked and unoaked styles here, and Château Grand Peyrot from a different soil.

Château Loubens ☆☆–☆☆☆
Owner: Arnaud de Sèze. 16 ha.
Exceedingly rich, sometimes rather alcoholic wines, that see no oak.

Château Lousteau-Vieil ☆
Owner: Martine Sessacq. 17 ha.
A long-established estate. Wines lack real concentration.

Château des Mailles ☆–☆☆
Owner: Daniel Larrieu. 2 ha.
Many old vines contribute to this lush wine. In top vintages an oaked *cuvée* is produced.

Château du Mont ☆☆
Owner: Hervé Chouvac. 14 ha.
Sensuous wines of good quality, especially Cuvée Pierre.

Château du Pavillon ☆☆
Owner: Alain Fertal. 8 ha.
An ambitious estate, aiming for fully botrytized wines whenever possible.

Château la Rame ☆☆–☆☆☆
Owner: Yves Armand. 40 ha (20 in Ste-Croix).
The top producer here. The honey-scented, oaked Réserve could easily be mistaken for a fine Barsac.

Leading Loupiac Châteaux

Clos Jean ☆
Owner. Lionel Bord. 11 ha. www.vignoblesbord.com
Well-known property that produces commercial wines with little noble-rot character.

Château du Cros ☆☆
Owner: Michel Boyer. 35 ha. www.chateauducros.com
An enthusiastic producer of good-quality Loupiac, partially barrel-aged. In 2004 he introduced Cuvée Tradition, from centenarian vines.

Château Grand Peyruchet ☆
Owner: Bernard Queyrens. 8 ha.
Half the wine is aged in barriques. It has a fresh apricot character.

Château Loupiac-Gaudet ☆☆
Owner: Marc Ducau. 26 ha.
www.chateau-loupiacguadet.com
Good, straightforward wine, now set to become more complex since barrel-ageing was adopted in 1998.

Domaine de Noble ☆☆–☆☆☆
Owner: Patrick Dejean. 17 ha.
The leading producer in this area, producing both oaked and unoaked wines with good concentration and a zesty acidity.

Château de Ricaud ☆
Owner: Alain Thiénot. 70 ha (20 in Loupiac).
Medium-bodied wines, from a property owned by a leading Champagne producer.

Château les Roques ☆☆
Owner: Alain Fertal. 4 ha.
Same ownership as Château du Pavillon in Ste-Croix (q.v.). Cuvée Frantz is from the oldest vines.

Graves de Vayres & Ste-Foy-Bordeaux

Within the same block of vineyard, two smaller zones have separate appellations defined with Gallic precision: one on the basis of its soil and potential for something out of the rut, the other, I suspect, for political reasons.

Graves de Vayres (700 hectares), across the river from Libourne, has more gravel than its surroundings. Unfortunately, its name invites comparison with Graves, which it cannot sustain. Whites are sometimes made sweeter than Entre-Deux-Mers. The quickly maturing reds have been compared in a charitable moment to minor Pomerols. The other appellation, Ste-Foy-Bordeaux (400 hectares), looks like

a natural part of the Bergerac region cobbled on to Bordeaux. Its wines are not notably different from the wines of Bergerac, and its history is identical. For centuries, the Dutch came for the two commodities most in demand: sweet wine and wine for distilling. But it is home to some serious properties.

Leading Châteaux

Château Champ des Treilles ☆☆–☆☆☆
Margueron (Ste-Foy). Owner: Jean-Michel and Corinne Comme. 10 ha. www.champdestreilles.com
Comme is the winemaker at Château Pontet-Canet, so he knows what he's about, although his wife Corinne manages this property, which is farmed Biodynamically. Numerous wines, some of exceptional quality.

Château des Chapelains ☆–☆☆
St André-et-Appelles (Ste-Foy). Owner: Pierre Charlot. 35 ha. www.chateaudeschapelains.com
Inexpensive but somewhat inconsistent wines. Les Temps Modernes is usually the best red wine.

Château Goudichaud ☆
St Germain-du-Puch (Graves de Vayres). Owner: Yves Glotin. 48 ha.
Light wines to drink young.

Château Hostens-Picant ☆☆
Les Lèves (Ste-Foy). Owner: Yves Picant. 42 ha.
www.chateauhostens-picant.fr
Suave whites and reds, especially the oaked *cuvées*. Stéphane Derenoncourt advises.

Château Lesparre ☆
Beychau et Caillou (Graves de Vayres). Owner: Michel Gonet. 180 ha. www.chateaulesparre.com
Commercial, uncomplicated, dependable.

Côtes de Bordeaux St-Macaire

Ten villages beyond Ste-Croix-du-Mont rejoice in this appellation for semi-sweet wine, a trickle of which finds its way to Belgium. Red sold as Bordeaux or Bordeaux Supérieur is much more important.

Cérons

Cérons applies to the three Graves villages (Podensac and Illats are the other two) that abut Barsac on the north and have a natural tendency to make sweet wines. Their wines often incline to be *moelleux*, the grey area which is sweet but not *liquoreux*. Occasionally they attain *liquoreux* stickiness. All depends on the autumn and the vinification, which previously used sulphur as its crutch and left much to be desired. Modern methods can mean much cleaner and better wine, as the growing reputations of some of the properties indicate.

Production of Cérons has been in decline, as growers have the option to produce dry white wine (Graves) from the same vineyards, without all of the risks attendant upon sweet wine production and at higher yields. In 2005 only 41 hectares declared their crop as Cérons. Only 20 producers bottle Cérons; even good examples fetch only a moderate price. France consumes nearly all of it.

Leading Cérons Châteaux

Château de Cérons ☆☆–☆☆☆
Cérons. Owner: Jean Perromat. 12 ha.
www.chateaudecerons.com
Jean Perromat is a passionate defender of the appellation and produces one of its best wines, with a pronounced apricot or citric character. Age becomes it as well as it does good Sauternes.

Château de Chantegrive ☆☆
Podensac (see Graves).
Not made every year. Wines of finesse and concentration.

Château Haura ☆☆
Illats. Owner: Bernard Leppert. 2 ha.
www.denisdubourdieu.com
Leased by Denis Dubourdieu, who makes unctuous wines from here.

Grand Enclos du Château de Cérons ☆☆–☆☆☆
Cérons. See Graves.
Fine quality, but not produced every year.

Burgundy

Burgundy has the best-situated shop window in France, if not in Europe. The powerful, the influential, the enterprising, and the curious have been filing by for two millennia along the central highway of France, from Paris to Lyon and the south, from the Rhine and the Low Countries to Italy. Every prince, merchant, soldier, or scholar has seen the Côte d'Or, rested at Beaune or Dijon, tasted, and been told tall tales about the fabulous wine of this narrow, scrubby hillside.

Whether any other hillside could do what the Côte d'Or can is a fascinating speculation – without an answer. What it does is to provide scraps of land and scattered episodes of weather that bring two grape varieties to a perfection not found anywhere else. In certain sites and in certain years only, the Pinot Noir and Chardonnay achieve flavours valued as highly as any flavour on earth.

So specific are the sites and the conditions needed that the odds are stacked quite strongly against them. It is an uncertain way to make a living. So Burgundy has organized itself into a system that makes allowances – for crop failures, for human errors, for frailties of all kinds. Its legislation is a delicate structure that tries to keep the Burgundian one jump ahead of his clients without them tumbling to the fact.

Yet it is more than mere jurisprudence. The marshalling of Burgundy's vineyards reflects the accumulated wisdom of at least 1,000 years of vine-growing, established by generations of patient monks who came to understand every nuance of slope and exposure, breeze and soil. No single factor can explain the supremacy of one vineyard, or the inferiority of its neighbour.

The Classification of Burgundy

Bordeaux classifies its properties; Burgundy classifies its individual vineyards. Every vineyard in the Côte d'Or and Chablis (although not in Beaujolais and the Mâconnais) is precisely ranked by its appellation. Starting at the top, there are over 40 *grands crus* which have their own individual appellations. They do not (except in Chablis) use the names of their communes. They are simply and grandly Le Corton, Le Musigny, Le Montrachet. In the ninteenth century, the villages that were the proud possessors of this land added the *grand cru* name to their own, so that Aloxe became Aloxe-Corton; Chambolle, Chambolle-Musigny; Puligny and Chassagne both added Montrachet to their names. Hence the apparent anomaly that in general the shorter name means the better wine.

In parentheses it must be said that the decisions about which sites are are old and, in a few cases, unfair. They were taken on observations of performance over many years. Their soil, in different ways, is ideal. They are generally the places that suffer least from spring frost, summer hail, and autumn rot. But they can be well or badly farmed. There are certainly some of the next rank, *premier cru*, which reach or exceed the level of several *grands crus*. The rank of *premier cru* is given with much deliberation over detail to 562 plots of land in the best non-*grand cru* vineyards of all the best communes. For several years a review was in progress that entailed nit-picking over minute parcels of vines. It was only finally completed in 1984. The upshot is, for example, that in the Pommard vineyard (or climat) of Les Petits Epenots plots two to eight and 13 to 29 are classed as *premier cru*, while plots nine to 12 are not. I give this instance not to confuse the issue, but to show how extremely seriously the authorities take the matter.

Politics played its part too. Certain villages, such as Nuits-St-Georges, decided not to submit a request to have its best sites classified as *grand cru*. Few growers can recall why this was so, but it appears to have been bound up with the unwelcome prospect of higher taxation applied to *grands crus*. So we are left with the anomaly that everyone accepts that vineyards such as Les St-Georges in Nuits or Clos des Chênes in Volnay can give wines of *grand cru* quality, but they remain classified as *premiers crus*.

The biggest and best *premiers crus* have reputations of their own, particularly in the Côte de Beaune (where Le Corton is the only red *grand cru*). Such vineyards as Volnay Caillerets and Pommard Rugiens can be expected to produce fabulously good wine under good conditions. In such cases the producer proudly uses the name of the vineyard. The law allows the vineyard name to be printed on the label in characters the same size as the commune name. There are smaller *premiers crus*, however, without the means to acquire a great reputation, whose wine is sometimes just sold as, for example, Volnay Premier Cru. Often a grower's holdings in some vineyards are so small that he is obliged to mix the grapes of several holdings in order to have a vatful to ferment. This wine will have to settle for an unspecific name.

The *grands crus* and *premiers crus* form an almost unbroken band of vineyards occupying most of the east-facing Côte d'Or slope, perfectly exposed to the morning sun. The villages with their evocative names – Gevrey-Chambertin, Aloxe-Corton, Pommard – generally sit at the foot of the slope, encompassing in their parish boundaries both the best (upper) land and some less good (or even distinctly inferior) either on the flat at the bottom or in angles of the hills that face the "wrong" way. This also is classed. The best of it, but not up to *premier cru* standard, is entitled to use the name of the village and the vineyard. In practice not many vineyards below *premier cru* rank are cited on labels. The law in this case demands that a vineyard name be printed in characters only half the size of the commune name. This allows a distinction on the labels of a grower such as, say, Denis Mortet between his estate's Gevrey-Chambertin Champeaux (a *premier cru*) and Gevrey-Chambertin Matrot (a village vineyard or *lieu-dit*). The *appellation contrôlée* here applies to the village name, not the vineyard. In the descriptions of properties that follow, I refer to these as "village" wines. Inferior land within a village is not even allowed the village name. It falls under the rubric of *appellations régionales*: the most specific name it can have is

Bourgogne (when it is made from the classic grapes, red and white, of the region), Bourgogne Passe-tout-grain, Bourgogne Aligoté, or Bourgogne Grand Ordinaire. These terms are explained on page 100.

Grapes & Wine

Burgundy is easier wine to taste than Bordeaux, but harder to judge and understand. The Pinot Noir, which gives all the good reds of the Côte d'Or, has a singular and memorable smell and taste, sometimes described as pepperminty, sometimes as showing aromas of raspberries or violets, yet also rooty, as in beetroot, and warm as in alcohol, but in any case beyond the reach of my vocabulary.

Singular as it is, it varies in pitch more than most grapes from one site to another and one vintage to another. In unripe years it smells mean, pinched, and watery (German red wines of the old school give a good idea of the effect). At the other extreme it roasts to a raisiny character, as happened in the torrid 2003 vintage, when the most sun-drenched sites (usually the *grands crus*) were the worst affected.

The ideal young red burgundy has the ripe-grape smell with neither of these defects, recognizably but lightly overlain with the smell of oak. And it tastes very much as it smells: a little too astringent for total pleasure but with none of the impenetrable tannin of a great young Bordeaux. Good burgundy tastes good from birth.

The object of keeping it in barrels is not simply to add a flavour of oak, but to bolster the tannins, to encourage a gentle oxidation, and to allow the wine to stabilize naturally. The object of maturing it in bottle is to achieve softness of texture and a complex alliance of flavours that arise from the grape, yet seem to have little to do with it. Fine old red burgundy arrives at an intense, regal red with a note of orange (the decorator's "burgundy" colour is that of young wine). It caresses the mouth with a velvet touch that loses nothing of vigour by being soft. And it smells and tastes of a moment of spring or autumn just beyond the grasp of your memory.

The inetrnational style of heavy-handed winemaking promoted by U.S. magazines has had less impact in Burgundy than in many regions. Indeed it may have provoked a reaction, leading growers and consumers to appreciate the finesse that is burgundy's true glory.

Strange to say, white burgundy can have a distinct resemblance to red – not exactly in smell or taste, but in its texture and weight, and the way that it evolves.

Chardonnay wine is not markedly perfumed when it is new: just brisk and, if anything, appley. The traditional Burgundian method of fermenting it in small barrels adds the smell of oak immediately, but a skilled winemaker will ensure that the oak influence is integrated and harmonious, not overwhelming. Thereafter, the way the wine develops in barrel and bottle

Church and vineyards, Domaine Brocard, Chablis

depends very much on which district it comes from, and on the acid/alcohol ratio of the particular vintage.

An ideally balanced vintage such as '90, '95,'99, or 2002 keeps a tension between the increasingly rich flavours of maturity and a central steeliness, year after year. A sharp, barely ripe vintage such as '87 leans too far towards the steel – and not very springy steel at that. A very ripe vintage such as '92 or 2005 produced many wines that were too fat and lacked "cut". All in all, however, the success rate of white burgundy vintages is very much higher than that of red.

How Burgundy is Made

As soon as the grapes arrive at the winery, they are sorted with varying degrees of rigour, depending on whether rot or uneven ripening are present. Then the grapes are lightly crushed and often destemmed, before being dispatched into an open-topped cylindrical vat filled to about two-thirds of its capacity. Every grower has his own theory of how many or few of the stems should be included, depending on the ripeness of the grapes (and of their stalks), and whether he wants to make a tannic *vin de garde* or a softer wine to mature more quickly. Ultra-conservative growers still tend to include all or most of the stalks.

Many growers today favour "cold maceration" – keeping the skins in the juice at a low temperature that prevents fermentation for a few days but extracts fruity flavours and colour.

To start the pulpy mass fermenting, it is sometimes necessary to add a measure of actively fermenting wine from another vat, with a teeming yeast population – known as a *pied de cuve*. In an account of the Côte d'Or in 1862 by Agoston Haraszthy, reporting to the government of California, "Five days is generally sufficient for the fermenting of wine in this part, unless it is cold weather, when the overseer sends his men in a couple of times more in their costume à l'Adam to create the necessary warmth." He adds that "This, in my eyes, rather dirty procedure could be avoided by throwing in heated stones or using pipes filled with steam or hot water." And indeed it is. Pinot Noir needs a warm fermentation to extract all the colour and flavour from the skins.

The operation of *pigeage*, or mixing the floating cap of skins with the fermenting juice, is still sometimes performed in small cellars by the vigneron or his sons, scrupulously hosed down, in bathing shorts, but more up-to-date establishments use a manual or mechanical plunger to perform the operation. In addition, or as an alternative, some producers will either pump the juice from the bottom of the vat over the *chapeau* (*remontage*) or use a grille which prevents the cap from floating to the top (*chapeau immergé*). I am told by practitioners that it is the positively physical rubbing of the *marc* by *pigeage* that is important. It liberates elements that *remontage* or *chapeau immergé* cannot possibly obtain.

Individual ideas on the right duration of this maceration of the skins in the cuve vary from a very few days to up to almost three weeks, depending to a large extent on the degree and kind of extraction sought by the winemaker. The free-run wine is then drawn off and the *marc* pressed. The wine of the first pressing is usually added to the free-run juice and the ensemble filled into barrels, old or new according to the means and motives of the proprietor, to settle down and undergo its quiet secondary – malolactic – fermentation. The malolactic fermentation is often encouraged by raising the cellar temperature, but many growers are in no rush, and it's not unusual to hear the wine perking away well into the spring following the vintage. Once they have finished this infantile fretting they are racked into clean barrels.

Fine red burgundies are usually kept in barrel for between 12 and 18 months. Unlike Bordeaux, they are racked as little as possible to avoid contact with the air. Two months before bottling they may need to be fined to remove the very faintest haze. Some cellars use filters to clarify the wine, but other producers avoid this.

Making White Burgundy

The procedure for making all dry white wines, white burgundy included, is virtually standardized today (see page 33). The object is maximum freshness, achieved by minimum contact with the air. Careful, clean, and cool handling of the grapes is followed by a quick pressing and slow, cool fermentation.

Basic Chablis and Mâcon will usually be fermented efficiently in stainless steel tanks. Chablis, having more acidity and a more distinctive flavour, can then benefit from maturing on its fine lees in a steel or concrete vat and then in bottle for a considerable time. The simpler, rounder taste of Mâcon wines has little to gain by keeping.

But the classic white burgundies of the Côte d'Or are another matter. They are fermented in small oak barrels. A *grand cru* or top *premier cru* will often be aged in a high proportion of new oak, but there are no firm rules. The pungent smell of new oak is part of the personality of the wine from the start, but should moderate with age. The majority of growers, those with good but not the finest land, settle for older barrels, perhaps replacing a few each year. In this case, the oak has less of the obvious carpenter's-shop effect on the wine; the barrel

Warming the must the traditional way

is simply the ideal size and shape of container for maintaining fermentation at an even, low temperature, cooled by the humid ambience of the cellar. A greater volume of wine would generate too much heat as fermentation progresses.

Fermentation over, the wine stays in the barrel, on its yeasty sediment, or lees. The tradition in Burgundy is to stir those lees regularly so that the wine can "feed" off the nutrients they contain and gain in body and richness. According to the winemaker's judgment, it is then racked off the lees into clean barrels and kept until the maker deems it ready for bottling. What he is doing is allowing a gentle and controlled oxidation of the wine to introduce nuances and breadth of flavour that would otherwise not develop. It is then ready for drinking – unless the buyer wants to continue the ageing process in the bottle. To me, the possibility of this reductive ageing is the whole point of buying the great white burgundies. No other white wines (with the exception of Riesling) reward patience so well.

Adding Sugar

It is regular practice in Burgundy, as in most of France, to add sugar to the unfermented grape juice. The long experience of growers has shown that slightly more than the natural degree of sugar can produce a better fermentation and a more satisfactory final wine. It is not purely the extra one to two degrees of alcohol but the evolution and final balance of the wine that is affected (they say). Climatic changes over recent years have reduced the need for routine *chaptalization*, but it remains the rule rather than the exception. All *chaptalization* is strictly controlled by law. Nobody in any appellation may add more than two degrees alcohol to any wine by adding sugar. (There is a temptation to add the maximum; sugar makes the wine easier to sell. The extra alcohol makes it taste more impressive and flattering in its youth when buyers come to the cellar to taste.)

It has always been illegal to add acidity to a *chaptalized* wine. You can follow either procedure but not both. However, it has been an open secret that most Burgundian winemakers frequently perform both, not to cut corners but to produce a better-balanced wine. When one of Burgundy's most celebrated winemakers admitted to the practice in the late 1990s, all hell broke loose, but he won the moral argument simply by admitting to a procedure widely practised. (Winemakers could legally *chaptalize* one vat, and add acidity to another, and then blend the two – thus demonstrating that the law is an ass.)

The Burgundy Revolution

This fine-tuning during vinification and ageing pales in comparison with the major changes in viticulture over the past decade or so. There has been a widespread recognition that, during the 1960s and 1970s, serious errors were made: too much fertilizer was used, and clones adapted for productivity rather than quality were planted. Today there are few quality-oriented growers who do not accept that the choice of plant material – whether massal or clonal selection – is of crucial importance. The routine use of herbicides has also declined, severe pruning or green harvesting (or both) are employed to keep yields low, and sorting the grapes arriving at the winery, considered a novelty in the late 1980s, is now commonplace.

BIODYNAMISM

It was the Loire producer Nicolas Joly who first became convinced that the ideas of educationalist and theorist Rudolf Steiner were applicable to grape farming. Biodynamics is hard to explain because of its mystical elements. It counsels an approach to viticulture that is essentially organic, but with some added ingredients. Biodynamism argues that cosmic forces such as lunar positions have a direct influence on natural growing seasons here on earth. This is hardly a cranky idea, since such processes as racking and bottling were traditionally performed according to the position of the moon, which growers knew could affect the turbidity of the wine.

Biodynamism also demands a return to ploughing the soil, the use of precisely composed compost, and the addition of homeopathic doses of minerals or materials such as manure buried within a cow's horn for a specified time. Treatments are dissolved in a solution and ritually stirred (or "dynamized") before being applied at precisely prescribed times of the day (or night) and month. This is the mumbo-jumbo aspect of Biodynamism that many conscientious growers find hard to swallow. Yet some of the most prestigious (and hard-headed) of Burgundy's growers – including Leflaive, Leroy, and Lafon – have fervently adopted the system. Some of them admit they don't really understand how it functions, yet they find that their vineyards are healthier. Micro-organisms and nutrient elements in the soil begin to multiply, and because the soil is enjoying optimal health, so the proponents of Biodynamism argue, the fruit, too, will be healthier and more intense in flavour. In some vintages Biodynamic vineyards can be more susceptible to diseases such as mildew; in other years they seem to resist disease better than vines farmed conventionally. Burgundy poses a unique challenge to practitioners of Biodynamism, since an estate's holdings are not, as in California, a entire vineyard, but, in some cases, just a few rows. It seems hard to see how Biodynamism can triumph in just a few rows when the immediately neighbouring vines may be conventionally (ie. chemically) farmed. Biodynamism is fast winning converts, not just in Burgundy but throughout France. You can divide practitioners into three schools. First, the true converts, whose aim is to create a harmonious and natural ecosystem governed by Biodynamic principles. Second, those who admit they can't easily understand the mystical elements underlying the system yet find its practices benefit their vines and wines. Thirdly, those for whom the label Biodynamism is a marketing tool. The last category is small, given the costs and complexities of applying the rules.

Many leading estates have also adopted Biodynamism (see box on page 99). The consequence of all these developments is that the overall quality of Burgundy's wines has risen sharply in recent years, and is no longer confined to a handful of top estates.

General Appellations

There are four appellations that are available to growers in the whole of Burgundy with certain provisos:

Bourgogne

Red, white, or rosé wines. The whites must be Chardonnay, or Pinot Beurot. The reds must be Pinot Noir, except in the Yonne, where the César and the Tressot are traditional and are admitted, and the *crus* of Beaujolais, whose Gamay may be sold as Bourgogne. A few villages, such as Epineuil and Chitry, have the right to add their name to Bourgogne on the label. There are also separate appellations for Bourgogne Côte Chalonnaise and Bourgogne Côte du Couchois.

The maximum crop is 55 hectolitres per hectare for red and rosé, 60 for white. Minimum natural strength: 10 degrees for red and rosé, 10.5 degrees for white. It is worth ageing Bourgogne Rouge at least two years. Bourgogne AC made by top growers in the major villages from vines grown just outside the village boundaries represent the best-value wine. In Burgundy, the name of the producer is everything.

Bourgogne Passe-tout-grains

Red or rosé wines from any area made of up to two-thirds Gamay and at least one-third Pinot Noir fermented together. Maximum crop: 55 hectolitres per hectare. Minimum natural strength: 9.5 degrees. Bourgogne Passe-tout-grains can be delicious after at least one-year's ageing, and is not as heady as Beaujolais. It also makes rather a good rosé. But it is rarely encountered these days.

Bourgogne Aligoté

White wine of Aligoté grapes, with up to 15 per cent Chardonnay, from anywhere in Burgundy. Maximum crop 60 hectolitres per hectare. Minimum natural strength 9.5 degrees. One commune, Bouzeron in the Côte Chalonnaise, has gained its own appellation for Aligoté; the permitted maximum crop is 45 hectolitres per hectare. Aligoté often makes a sharp wine with considerable local character when young – the classic base for a *vin blanc* cassis, or Kir.

Bourgogne Grand Ordinaire (or Bourgogne Ordinaire)

Red, white, or rosé from any of the permitted Burgundy grape varieties. Maximum crop is 55 hectolitres per hectare for red and rosé, 60 for white. Minimum natural strength nine degrees for red and rosé, 9.5 degrees for white. This appellation is now not often used.

A new AC was approved in 2002 – St-Bris. This is an oddity among Burgundian appellations, since its 106 hectares are dedicated to Sauvignon Blanc and not to Chardonnay. Its vineyards and producers are located in five villages of the Yonne: St-Bris, Chitry, Irancy, Quenne, and Vincelottes.

Burgundy in round figures

"Greater Burgundy", the region including not only the Côte d'Or but Beaujolais, the Mâconnais, Mercurey, and the Yonne (Chablis), now produces 15 per cent of all *appellation contrôlée* wines. In Burgundy (excluding Beaujolais), there are some 29,500 hectares of AC vineyards under vine, and a further 22,500 in Beaujolais. While red wine production has remained fairly stable, white wine production has expanded, especially in Chablis and the Mâconnais.

The trend in Burgundy, as in Bordeaux and elsewhere in France, has been towards more specialization and fewer but bigger holdings of vines. Today the total production in the region, including Beaujolais, is 2.9 million hectolitres (the equivalent of almost 30 million cases). The average annual production for the five years 2003 to 2007 is summarized below for the principal brackets of Burgundy appellations.

White wines	Hectolitres	Cases
Côte d'Or *grands crus*	3,745	41,570
Côte d'Or *premiers crus*	23,522	261,090
Côte d'Or other (village) wines	62,455	693,200
Chablis	263,800	2,927,330
Côte Chalonnaise	38,840	430,735
Mâcon Villages	197,926	2,195,000
Mâcon Blanc (other)	108,155	1,199,450
Crémant	104,485	1,158,740
Beaujolais	13,119	142,000
Regional appellations (simple Bourgogne, etc.)	188,325	2,088,525
Total production of white wines	1,004,400	11,138,500

Red wines	Hectolitres	Cases
Côte d'Or *grands crus*	12,037	133,490
Côte d'Or *premiers crus*	56,076	621,880
Côte d'Or other (village) wines	162,960	1,807,230
Côte Chalonnaise	38,495	426,900
Mâcon	36,691	406,900
Beaujolais and Beaujolais-Villages	754,574	8,358,300
Beaujolais crus (eg. Fleurie)	324,800	3,562,500
Regional appellations (simple Bourgogne, etc.)	218,020	2,417,800
Total production of red wines	1,603,650	17,784,500
Total production, red & white	2,608,050	28,923,270

Chablis

Chablis and the few other scattered vineyards of the Yonne *département* are a tiny remnant of what was once the biggest vineyard area in France. It was the 40,000 hectares of the Yonne, centred around the city of Auxerre, that supplied the population of Paris with its daily wine before the building of the railways brought them unbeatable competition from the Midi. Whether one is to draw any conclusion from the fact that its best vineyard was called La Migraine is hard to say.

Any vineyard so far north is a high-risk enterprise. When falling sales were followed by the phylloxera disaster, Auxerre turned to other forms of agriculture. Chablis dwindled yet held on. When it was first delineated as an appellation in the 1930s, there was not much more than 400 hectares, but they included the hillside of the seven *grands crus*. Nobody could ignore the quality of their wine. I remember a 45-year-old half-bottle of Les Clos 1923 as being one of the best white wines I ever drank.

It was the merchants of Beaune who made Chablis famous. In the simple old days when Beaune, being a nice, easy name to remember, meant red burgundy, Chablis meant white. The name was picked up and echoed around the wine-growing world as a synonym for dry white wine. But the real thing remained a rarity. Year after year, spring frosts devastated the Chablis vineyards and discouraged replanting. Only in the 1960s did new methods of frost control turn the scales.

The introduction of sprinkler systems to replace stoves among the vines on cold spring nights finally made Chablis profitable. Within a decade, the planted area doubled, with each hectare yielding far more wine more reliably than ever before. It continues to grow. Today there are about 4,500 hectares . Inevitably, the old guard strongly resisted the granting of the appellation to so much new land, especially since the area of *premiers crus* was also expanded. Today, however, the *grands* and *premiers crus* are more or less sacrosanct. What typifies the best Chablisienne terroir is the so-called Kimmeridgian soil, a mix of limestone and clay with fossilized shells. Post-expansion Chablis grown on lesser soils may yield attractive wine but without the bite and raciness of true Chablis.

Unqualified village Chablis, as it is generally made today, is sharp, dry, and clean. A good example is distinctly fruity with a quality that only Chardonnay gives. A poor one is simply neutral and either too acidic or too flabby. A small amount of wine from inferior plots is only allowed the appellation Petit Chablis. A good Petit Chablis has the regional style, can even be gentle and juicy; but you must find a first-class maker. Many say it should not be called Chablis at all.

Premier cru and *grand cru* Chablis are different wines; there are distinct steps upward in body, flavour, and individuality. Some people find the best *premiers crus* the most satisfyingly typical, with plenty of flavour and a distinctive "cut" of acidity. The *grands crus* add a richness and strength which round them out; occasionally too much so. To be seen at their best, the *grands crus* need at least four and sometimes up to ten years ageing in bottle.

In the 1980s, the fashion for ageing in new oak came to Chablis. Opinions were sharply divided, as much among producers as among their customers. Fortunately, the trend is in retreat, and estates that once aged their *grands crus* in 100 per cent new oak are now more judicious. Certainly a skilful use of barriques, including a proportion of new barrels, can add complexity and structure to the wine. The trick is not to end up with a wine that, however splendid and attention-grabbing, has lost its Chablisienne *typicité*. Many growers ignored the trend altogether and still vinify and age the wine entirely in steel tanks, with no evident loss in quality.

The scent and flavour that develop are the quintessence of an elusive character you can miss if you only ever drink Chablis young. I can only define it as combining the fragrances of apples and hay with a taste of boiled sweets and an underlying mineral note that seems to have been mined from the bowels of the earth. A good vintage in due course gains a golden richness that reminds me of Sauternes. The price of Chablis has not kept pace with its value. Grand Cru Chablis, although considerably more expensive than in the past, is happily in much better supply than Bâtard-Montrachet. Otherwise, it could well fetch as high a price. *Premier cru* Chablis from a good grower is the best value in white burgundy. In 2001, 18 top growers formed an association called the Union des Grands Crus. The idea was to impose stricter controls than the AC rules require, and thus enhance the image and quality (and no doubt price) of *grand cru* Chablis. After much debate, the Union members agreed to outlaw machine-picking on *grand cru* sites, the main surprise being that it was ever permitted in the first place. (Machine-picking remains common in the lesser appellations.)

Leading Chablis Producers

Barat ☆–☆☆
Milly.
Early bottled, unoaked wine from a clutch of *premiers crus*: clean, fresh, and lively, if not especially complex.

Jean-Claude Bessin ☆☆–☆☆☆
La Chapelle Vaupelteigne.
Small property with outstanding wines from *premiers crus* Fourchaume and Montmains.

Billaud-Simon ☆☆☆
Chablis. www.billaud-simon.com
Most of the estate's 20 hectares are *premiers* or *grands crus*, the latter including 1.7 hectares in Les Clos, Les Preuses, and Vaudésir. Many of the wines are unoaked, spend a long time in vat or barrel before being bottled, and have a steely brilliance.

Pascal Bouchard ☆☆–☆☆☆
Chablis. www.pascalbouchard.com
Both a large domaine and a négociant house, Bouchard maintains high standards, balancing richness and minerality.

Jean-Marc Brocard ☆☆–☆☆☆
Préhy. www.brocard.fr
Brocard is a self-made man who has built up a large domaine of 135 hectares, partly Biodynamic. He is also a négociant, buying in about two-thirds of his requirements. The range of wines is very extensive and generally reliable and good value. In addition to Chablis, he produces some fascinating Bourgogne Blancs, each from a different soil type and labelled accordingly. The Chablis wines are unoaked, but the top wines can age very well, although they are styled to be enjoyable young.

Cave Coopérative la Chablisienne ☆☆–☆☆☆
Chablis. www.chablisienne.com
A quarter of all Chablis comes from this cooperative, founded in 1923. Of the *grands crus* vineyards, the most significant are 3.3 hectares of Les Preuses, and the 7.2-hectare monopoly known as Château Grenouille, owned by the cooperative since

2000. Fourchaume is much its most important *premier cru*. Its methods are modern and its wine well-made, clean, and surprisingly sophisticated. Vinification and ageing are adapted to the *crus* and fruit quality, with no firm rules about barrique-ageing. Oak fans should look out for the Grande Cuvée, a *premier cru* blend that is barrel-fermented. So is the (*grand cru*) Château Grenouille.

Daniel Dampt ☆☆
Milly. www.dampt-defaix.com
Classic, unoaked Chablis with spice and minerality.

Vincent Dauvissat ☆☆☆☆
Chablis.
Vincent Dauvissat's great-great-grandfather was a cooper, so it is no surprise that his cellars, unlike many in Chablis today, are still full of barrels, including the traditional *feuillettes*, which are smaller than regular Burgundian barrels. Dauvissat ages the wine from his 12 hectares for about eight months in mostly older wood in the old style. His best wines are the *grands crus* Les Clos and Les Preuses. His remaining vineyards are mostly *premier cru*. This is an utterly reliable source of exceptional Chablis.

Etienne Defaix ☆☆
Château de Milly. www.chablisdefaix.com
About half this estate, 26 hectares, is in *premier cru* sites, with many parcels of old vines. The *premiers crus*, unusually, are aged in tanks for up to three years, with lees-stirring to enrich the wine. The Defaix family insists that this is a traditional method. Interestingly, it gives the wine a character akin to oakiness.

Jean-Paul Droin ☆☆–☆☆☆☆
Chablis. www.jeanpaul-droin.fr
Droin's great-grandfather presented his wines to Napoléon III when he visited Auxerre in 1866. His cellars have not changed overmuch. Droin, now working with his son Benoit, is fortunate enough to own 11 hectares of *premiers crus* (mainly

Vaillons), as well as parcels in five *grands crus*. Once a champion of new-oak fermentation and ageing, he has moderated his views, and the wines since the mid-1990s are much better balanced. They are some of the finest Chablis around.

Joseph Drouhin ☆☆☆
Beaune. www.drouhin.com
The famous Beaune négociant makes immaculate, beautifully tender, and aristocratic wine from the *grands crus* Vaudésir, Les Clos, Les Preuses, and vividly typical *premier cru* from a number of sites.

Jean Durup ☆☆–☆☆☆☆
Maligny.
The huge estate of Jean Durup, president of the lobby that favours expanding the appellation Chablis. He has 180 hectares, of which 35 are in *premiers crus* (principally Fourchaume and Vau de Vey). All the wines are unoaked. An impeccable modern winery whose wines appear under the names Domaine de l'Eglantière and Château de Maligny.

William Fèvre ☆☆☆☆
Chablis. www.williamfevre.com
Fèvre was the largest owner of *grands crus* and a fervent advocate of new-oak fermentation. The estate's 16 hectares of *grands crus* include four of Les Clos, six of Bougros, and three of Les Preuses, with smaller but significant parcels in Valmur, Vaudésir, and Grenouilles. There is a similar amount of *premiers crus*, split among seven vineyards, and 20 hectares of Chablis "simple". In 1998, the property was purchased by Bouchard Père et Fils of Beaune (q.v.). From 1999, yields were diminished, hand-picking was made *de rigueur*, and the amount of new oak was severely reduced. The wines could scarcely be better.

Alain Geoffroy ☆☆
Beines. www.chablis-geoffroy.com
A third of the 45-hectare domaine is *premier cru*, mainly

THE VINEYARDS OF CHABLIS

Chablis comes in four tiers: Chablis AC (also known as village; 3077 hectares), Petit Chablis (680), *premier cru* 760, and *grand cru* (102). *Premier cru* vineyard names (listed here) are sometimes used in conjunction with *premier cru* names. In the 1990s, new vines were planted at such a rate that by 2006 the area exceeded 4,620 hectares (there were only 2,280 as recently as 1988). Total production is around 30 million bottles.

Premiers Crus
Premier cru Chablis may be sold either with the names of individual vineyards or those of certain vineyards grouped

together. The latter is generally the case, so in practice there are only a small number of names. In alphabetical order, together with the names of the vineyards that have the right to use the name in question (since 1986): Les Beauregards (Côte de Cuissy); Beauroy (Troesmes, Côte de Savant); Berdiot; Chaume de Talvat; Fourchaume (Vaupulent, Côte de Fontenay, l'Homme Mort, Vaulorent); Les Fourneaux (Morein, Côte des Près-Girots); Côte de Jouan; Les Landes et Verjuts; Côte de Léchet; Mont de Milieu; Montée de Tonnerre (Chapelot, Pied d'Aloup, Côte de Bréchain); Montmains (Forêts, Butteaux); Vaillons (Châtains, Séchet,

Beugnons, Les Lys, Mélinots, Roncières, les Epinottes); Côtes de Vaubarousse; Vaucoupin; Vau de Vey (Vaux Ragons); Vau Ligneau; and Vosgros (Vaugiraut).

Grands Crus
Blanchot (13 hectares); Bougros (16); Les Clos (27); Grenouilles (10); Preuses (11.5); Valmur (13); and Vaudésir (16 hectares). La Moutonne is a vineyard of 2.5 hectares within Vaudésir and Les Preuses. Learning the differences between them is one of life's sustaining pleasures.

Beauroy (seven hectares), as well as vines in *grands crus* Les Clos and Vaudésir. Geoffroy is no fan of wood, and likes to bottle young to preserve the wines' freshness and *typicité*.

Jean-Pierre & Corinne Grossot ☆☆–☆☆☆
Fleys.
Enthusiastic growers with 18 hectares, including holdings in *premiers crus* Fourchaume, Vaucoupin, Mont de Milieu, and the rarely encountered Côte de Troemes. Vinification is mostly in stainless steel, although some oak is used for the better wines.

Domaine Laroche ☆☆–☆☆☆☆
Chablis. www.larochewines.com
Michel Laroche is the fifth-generation owner of an estate of 130 hectares. There are six hectares of Chablis Grand Cru, notably Les Blanchots, and 30 of *premier cru*. Modern equipment makes Chablis in an austere, vigorous style, though some new oak is used for the *grands* and *premiers crus*. The *grands crus* should be kept for between three and eight years. The top wine is a selection from old Blanchot vines labelled Réserve de l'Obédiencerie. The name Laroche also appears on a wide range of non-domaine wines, including a good brand of simple Chablis, St Martin. Laroche remains a keen defender of the appellation and was the driving force behind the new Union des Grands Crus.

Long-Depaquit ☆☆☆
Chablis. www.albertbichot.com
This family estate was bought in 1967 by the négociant Bichot (q.v.) of Beaune. Of its 65 hectares, 20 are *premiers crus* and nine *grands crus*, including over two of Vaudésir. The most famous property is the two-hectare Moutonne vineyard, a part of the *grands crus* Vaudésir and Les Preuses, whose history goes back to the Abbey of Pontigny and its monks, who apparently skipped like young sheep under its inspiration. Long-Depaquit wines are very thoughtfully and professionally made with modern methods, but not for instant drinking. Since 1993, there has been a very cautious use of oak-ageing for the *grands crus*.

Domaine des Malandes ☆☆–☆☆☆
Chablis. www.domainedesmalandes.com
A 25-hectare domaine with 0.9 hectares in *grand cru* Vaudésir, and seven hectares of *premiers crus* including Fourchaume and Montmains. Modern-style Chablis: bright, fresh, and untouched by oak.

Louis Michel & Fils ☆☆–☆☆☆
Chablis. www.louismicheletfils.com
The late Louis Michel and son Jean-Loup built up a sizeable estate from small beginnings. Jean-Loup now has 20 hectares, 13 in *premiers crus* (some in Montmains and Montée de Tonnerre) and two in *grands crus* (Vaudésir, Grenouilles, and Les Clos). He believes in letting the wine make itself as far as possible. He uses no barrels, but by modest yields

and careful handling makes concentrated wines that repay years of bottle-age.

Christian Moreau ☆☆–☆☆☆
Chablis. www.domainechristianmoreau.com
After losing control of their company to the négociant Boisset, Christian Moreau and his son Fabien wrested back their vineyards in 2002. Minimal oak-ageing gives wines of great precision and vigour.

Louis Moreau ☆☆–☆☆☆
Beines. www.louismoreau.com
The former Jean-Claude Dauvissat estate. Impressively concentrated *grands crus*.

Pinson ☆☆
Chablis. www.domaine-pinson.com
Traditional producer with 12 well-located hectares. Quality slipped in the '90s but the Pinson brothers are now back on form.

Jean-Marie Raveneau ☆☆☆☆
Chablis.
A 7.5-hectare domaine entirely composed of *grands crus* (Blanchots, Valmur, Les Clos) and *premiers crus*, considered by some to be the best in Chablis. The wines are fermented in tanks, but aged in barrels of various sizes and ages for at least one year. They can be austere and minerally when young but age superbly, arriving at facinating, unpredicted conclusions.

Olivier Savary ☆☆
Chablis. www.chablis-savary.com
Mostly unoaked wines include an exemplary village bottling and a pure, elegant *premier cru* Fourchaume.

Simonnet-Febvre & Fils ☆☆
Chablis. www.simmonet-febvre.com
This small domaine of four hectares is better known as a négociant going back five generations. The *grand cru* Preuses and a range of *premiers crus* is oak-aged. Bought by Beaune négociant Louis Latour in 2003.

Robert Vocoret ☆☆
Chablis. www.vocoret.com
A century-old family domaine of 50 hectares, four in *grands crus* (Les Clos, Valmur, Blanchots) and 15 in *premiers crus*. Some of the better wines are aged in large casks but bottled fairly young. The result is wine with less of the immediately appealing fruit but a firm grip that rewards keeping.

Other Chablis Producers

Other leading Chablis producers include: Domaine du Chardonnay, Jean Collet, Gérard Duplessis, Nathalie and Gilles Fèvre, Lamblin, Bernard Legland, Sylvain Mosnier, Gilbert Picq, Denis Race, Servin, Gérard Tremblay, Tribut-Dauvissat, Domaine de Vauroux, and Château de Viviers.

Château Long-Depaquit, Chablis

The Côte d'Or – Cote de Nuits

The heart of Burgundy is the 48-kilometre (30-mile) line of hills running south from Marsannay on the southern outskirts of Dijon, inclining westwards as it goes and presenting a broadening band of southeast-facing slopes until it stops at Santenay. The eight villages of the northern sector, ending at Prémeaux, are the Côte de Nuits. The 20 villages running south from Aloxe-Corton are the Côte de Beaune. The Côte de Nuits is almost exclusively devoted to red wine – almost all Pinot Noir. On these steep slopes, but particularly their middle curves, the most potently flavoured, concentrated, eventually smooth and perfumed wines are made.

The villages are listed here from north to south. Each is briefly described with an appreciation of its wine and a list of its *grands crus* (if any) and *premiers crus*. Growers are no longer listed under each village entry, as they have become too numerous, but there is an expanded section listing the major Côte d'Or growers, beginning on page 115.

(NB: all *grands/premiers crus* entries include hectare figures in brackets.)

Marsannay-la-Côte

Formerly known only for its excellent Rosé de Marsannay, this village now has, uniquely in Burgundy, an appellation for all three colours. The whites are greatly improved, the rosés are deliciously perfumed and elegant, the reds sometimes light, sometimes structured and ageworthy. Marsannay also covers the few remaining vineyards (eg. Clos du Roy) of Chenove, which is now a light industrial suburb of Dijon. Marsannay covers 250 hectares. In 2005 the Syndicat commissioned a detailed geological study of the vineyards to support its application to promote the best sites to *premier cru*.

Fixin

The *premiers crus* are splendidly situated and capable of wines as good as those of Gevrey-Chambertin. Even the village wines are stout-hearted and long-lived. The commune has 109 hectares under vine. Between Fixin and Gevrey-Chambertin, the village of Brochon has no appellation of its own. Its better vineyards are included in Gevrey-Chambertin. The lesser ones are plain Côte de Nuits-Villages.

Premiers Crus

Arvelets (5)	Clos de la Perrière (4.5)
Clos du Chapitre (4.8)	Hervelets (5)
Clos Napoléon (1.8)	

Gevrey-Chambertin

There is a very wide range of quality in the production of Gevrey – the biggest of any of the villages of the Côte d'Or. Some of its flat vineyards beyond the valley road are of middling quality only. But there is no questioning the potential of its constellation of *grands crus*. Chambertin and the Clos de Bèze are acknowledged to lead them; an extra charge of fiery concentration gives them the edge. The seven others must always keep the Chambertin after their names; Clos de Bèze may put it before, or indeed simply label itself Chambertin. They are all stern, essentially male (since everything in France has a gender) wines that I cannot imagine even Astérix himself tossing back in bumpers (Obélix, perhaps). French critics claim for Chambertin the delicacy of Musigny allied to the strength of a Corton, the velvet of a Romanée and the perfume of the Clos Vougeot. I have certainly tasted fabulous complexity, but delicacy is not the word I would choose. Great age is probably the key. Among the *premiers crus* on the hill behind the village, Clos St-Jacques is widely thought to be on the same level of quality as the bevy of hyphenated Chambertins.

Grands Crus

Chambertin (12.9)	Griotte-Chambertin (2.7)
Chambertin Clos de Bèze (15.4)	Latricières-Chambertin (7.4)
	Mazis-Chambertin (9)
Chapelle-Chambertin (5.4)	Ruchottes-Chambertin (3.3)
Charmes-(and/or Mazoyères) Chambertin (30.7)	

Premiers Crus

Bel Air (2.6)	Corbeaux (3.2)
La Boissière (0.45)	Craipillot (2.7)
Cazetiers (9)	Ergot (1.2)
Champeaux (6.7)	Estournelles St Jacques (2.3)
Champitonnois (also called Petite Chapelle) (4)	Fonteny (3.6)
	Goulots (1.8)
Champonnets (3.4)	Issarts (0.6)
Cherbaudes (2.2)	Lavaux St Jacques (9.5)
Clos du Chapitre (1)	Petits Cazetiers (0.95)
Clos Prieur (part) (2)	Poissenot (2.2)
Clos St-Jacques (6.7)	Clos Prieur-Haut (2)
Clos des Varoilles (6)	La Romanée (1)
Closeau (0.5)	**Appellation communale:**
Combe-aux-Moines (4.7)	**330 hectares**
Combottes (4.5)	

Morey-St-Denis

Although not among the best-known of the Côte de Nuits villages, Morey has four to its name and part of a fifth. Clos de la Roche is capable of making wine with the martial tread of a Chambertin; Clos St-Denis marginally less so; Clos des Lambrays is unusually opulent; Clos de Tart was much lighter, but has taken on weight, as well as lovely fragrance, in recent vintages. All the wines are worth a study, for authenticity and, other than the *grands crus*, the chance of a bargain. Only 95 hectares in all.

Grands Crus

Bonnes Mares (a small part) (1.5)	Clos de la Roche 17
	Clos St-Denis (6.6)
Clos des Lambrays (8.6)	Clos de Tart (7.5)

Premiers Crus

Blanchards (2)	Façonnières (1.7)
Chaffots (2.6)	Genavrières (1.2)
Charmes (1.2)	Gruenchers (0.5)
Charrières (2.3)	Les Millandes (4.2)
Chénevery (3)	Monts-Luisants (5.4)
Chéseaux (1.5)	Riotte (2.5)
Clos Baulet (0.9)	Ruchots (2.6)
Clos de la Bussière (2.6)	Les Sorbès (2.6)
Clos des Ormes (3.2)	Le Village (0.9)
Clos Sorbé (3.5)	**Appellation communale:**
Côte Rôtie (1.2)	**53 hectares**

Chambolle-Musigny

The lilt of the name is perfectly appropriate for the wines of this parish – as is the apparent evocation of the muse. It is hard to restrain oneself from competing in similes with the much-quoted sages of Burgundy, but Gaston Roupnel seems to have it precisely right. Musigny, he says, "has the scent of a dewy garden… of the rose and the violet at dawn." Le Musigny is my favourite red burgundy, closely followed by premiers crus Les Amoureuses and Les Charmes, and the other *grand cru*, Bonnes Mares. A contributory reason is that some particularly good winemakers own this land.

Grands Crus

Bonnes Mares (13.5)	Musigny (10.7)
(see also Morey-St-Denis)	

Premiers Crus

Amoureuses (5.4)	Echanges
Les Baudes (3.4)	Feusselottes (4.5)
Aux Beaux Bruns (1.5)	Fuées (4.4)
Borniques (1.4)	Groseilles (1.3)
Carrières	Gruenchers (2.8)
Chabiots (1.5)	Hauts Doix
Charmes (9.5)	Lavrottes (0.9)
Châtelots (3)	Noirots (2.8)
Combe d'Orveau (2.4)	Plantes (2.6)
Combottes (1.6)	Sentiers (4.9)
Aux Combottes (2)	Véroilles (0.37)
Cras (3.4)	**Appellation communale:**
Derrière la Grange (0.4)	**98 hectares**

Vougeot

The great vineyard of the Clos (de) Vougeot has the most resounding reputation in Burgundy. Fifty hectares within a single wall built by the fourteenth-century monks of Cîteaux add a certain presence. The land at the top of the slope, next to Musigny and Grands-Echezeaux, is equal to the best in Burgundy, but with its present fragmented ownership among 80 growers it is not easy to meet a bottle that answers this description. Classical references always stress its perfume. My impression is of a more meaty, extremely satisfying but less exotic wine than those of its great neighbours.

Grand Cru

Clos de Vougeot (50)

Premiers Crus Red

Clos de la Perrière (2.2)	Petits Vougeots (3.5)
Cras (3)	La Vigne Blanche

Premier Cru White

Clos Blanc (3)
Appellation communale:
 4 hectares

Flagey-Echézeaux

Exists as a village but not as an appellation, despite the fact that it has two *grands crus* in the parish. They are effectively treated as being in Vosne-Romanée, having the right to declassify their wine under the Vosne name. In reality, Grands-Echézeaux is at *grand cru* level – an ideal site adjacent to the best part of the Clos Vougeot. Its wines can have all the flair and the persuasive depths of the greatest burgundy. But the huge 34-hectare Les Echézeaux would be more realistically classified as one or several *premiers crus*. Its lack of any readily spotted identity joined with its apparently unmanageable name means that it sells for a reasonable price. There is a lightness of touch, a gentle sweetness, and airy fragrance about a good Echézeaux which make it less of a challenge than the biggest burgundies.

Vosne-Romanée

If Chambertin has the dignity, the name of Romanée has the glamour. Only the very rich and their guests have ever even tasted La Romanée-Conti. The Domaine de la Romanée-Conti, sole owner of that vineyard and the next greatest, La Tâche, casts its exotic aura equally over Richebourg, Romanée-St-Vivant, and Grands-Echézeaux, where it also owns property. The domaine's wines are marked with a character that seems to be their own, rather than that of Vosne-Romanée as a whole. Out of the torrent of words that has poured around Vosne and its sacred ground over the centuries I would pick three: "fire", "velvet", and "balance".

In the excitement of the *grands crus*, the *premiers crus* of Vosne-Romanée can be unwisely overlooked. They can be among the most complex and long-lived of burgundies.

Grands Crus

Echézeaux (37.7)	La Romanée (1.8)
Grande Rue (1.6)	Romanée-Conti (1.8)
Grands-Echézeaux (9)	Romanée-St-Vivant (9.3)
Richebourg (8)	La Tâche (6)

Premiers Crus

Beaux Monts (11.4)	En Orveaux (1.8)
Aux Brûlées (4.5)	Petits Monts (3.7)
Chaumes (6.5)	Reignots (1.6)
Clos de Réas (2.1)	Rouges (2.6)
Croix Rameau (0.6)	Suchots (13)
Cros Parantoux (1)	**Appellation communale:**
Gaudichots (1)	**97 hectares, of which 13.3**
Malconsorts (7)	**are in Flagey-Echézeaux**

Nuits-St-Georges

As a town, Nuits-St-Georges does not bear comparison with the alluring city of Beaune; its walls have long gone and it has no great public monuments. But it is the trading centre of the Côte de Nuits, the seat of a dozen négociants, its endless silent cellars maturing countless big-bellied *pièces*. In another way, too, it echoes Beaune; its long hill of vines produces highly prized and famous wine without a single peak. If Nuits had a *grand cru*, it would be Les St-Georges, and possibly Les Vaucrains, Les Cailles, and Les Porrets on the slope above and beside it. But none of these vineyards has convinced the world that its wine alone rises consistently above the *premier cru* level.

Compared with the wines of Beaune, those of Nuits-St-Georges are tougher and less fruity and giving in their youth – often for many years. It is hard to understand why they should be so popular in Anglo-Saxon countries, since ten years is often needed to turn toughness to warmth of flavour. The best Nuits has marvellous reserves of elusive character that demand leisurely investigation.

Prémeaux, the village to the south, is part of the appellation Nuits-St-Georges and itself has a run of *premiers crus* of equal merit, squeezed on to a steep and narrow slope between the road and the woods.

Premiers Crus

Aux Argillas (3)
Les Argillières and Clos des
   Argillières Prémeaux (4.2)
Boudots (6.2)
Bousselots (5)
Cailles (7)
Chaboeufs (3)
Chaignots (5.8)
Chaines-Carteaux (2)
Champs Perdrix (0.7)
Château Gris (3.5)
Clos de l'Arlot,
   Prémeaux (5.4)
Clos des Forêts St-Georges,
   Prémeaux (7)
Clos des Grandes Vignes,
   Prémeaux (2.1)
Clos de la Maréchale,
   Prémeaux (9.5)
Clos St Marc, Prémeaux (3.5)
Corvées and Clos des
   Corvées, Prémeaux 5.1
Corvées Pagets,
   Prémeaux (2.3)
Cras (3)
Crots (1.2)

Damodes (8.5)
Didiers, Prémeaux (2.5)
Haut-Pruliers (0.4)
Murgers (5)
Aux Perdrix, Prémeaux (3.5)
Perrières (2.5)
Perrière-Noblot (0.3)
Porrets and Clos des
   Porrets (7.3)
Poulettes (2)
Procès (1.4)
Pruliers (7)
Richemone (2)
Roncières (1)
Rue de Chaux (2)
Les St-Georges (7.5)
Aux Thorey and Clos de
   Thorey (5)
Terres Blanches, Prémeaux
   (0.9)
Vallerots (0.8)
Vaucrains (6)
Vignes Rondes (3.8)
**Appellation communale:
163 hectares**

Wooden press and cylindrical vats in a Burgundy winery

Côte de Nuits-Villages

This appellation is a consolation prize for the parishes at either end of the main *côtes*: Prissey, Comblanchien, and Corgoloin next to Prémeaux on the road south, and Fixin, Brochon, and Marsannay on the Dijon road beyond Gevrey-Chambertin. Fixin and Marsannay have appellations of their own.

For the others this is the highest aspiration. Stone quarries are more in evidence than vineyards on the road to Beaune. The marble from the hill here is some of France's best. Only one important vineyard stands out as a *premier cru manqué*: the Clos des Langres, property of la Reine Pédauque, at the extreme southern tip of the Côte de Nuits.

The Côte d'Or – Côte de Beaune

The heartland of great white Burgundy, home to the fabulous vineyards of Corton-Charlemagne, Meursault, and Montrachet. But its red wines are distinguished too, from the powerful wines of Pommard, the refined Volnays, and the consistently underrated vineyards around Beaune itself. It is also a good region for bargain-hunters to explore, with increas-ingly elegant and substantial wines from lesser-known villages such as Savigny, Monthelie, and St Aubin.

Nonetheless its most treasured wines are likely to remain its rich, buttery Meursaults, the racy wines of Puligny and Chassagne, the high-powered minerally whites of Corton, and the mighty *grands crus* of Bâtard-Montrachet and Montrachet itself.

Ladoix-Serrigny

The Côte de Beaune starts with its most famous landmark, the oval dome (if you can have such a thing) of the hill of Corton. The dome wears a beret of woods but its south, east, and west flanks are all vines, forming parts of three different parishes: (in order from the north) Ladoix-Serrigny, Aloxe-Corton, and – tucked round the corner out of sight – Pernand-Vergelesses. The best vineyards of all three are those on the mid- and upper slopes of the hill, which share the appellation Corton Grand Cru (the only red *grand cru* of the Côte de Beaune) and in parts, for white wine, Corton-Charlemagne.

Ladoix-Serrigny has the smallest part of Corton, and not the best, in its vineyards of Rognet-Corton and Les Vergennes, names which are rarely encountered but often subsumed in the general title of Corton, as all the *grand cru* territory can be. Similarly the village wines of Ladoix, which few people have

---

ROMANEE-CONTI – A GREAT BURGUNDY ESTATE

All the conundrums of wine come to a head at this extraordinary property. It has been accepted for at least three centuries that wine of inimitable style and fascination comes from one small patch of hill, and different wine, marginally but consistently less fascinating, from the sites around it. Romanée-Conti sounds like a super-successful public relations exercise. In some ways it is even organized as one. But there is no trick. On such a small scale, and with millionaires eager for every drop, it is possible to practise total perfectionism. Without the soil and the site, the opportunity would not be there; without the laborious pursuit of perfection, it would be lost.

A great vineyard like this is largely man-made, the practice in the days of the eighteenth century. Prince de Conti, who gave it his name, brought fresh loam up from the pastures of the Saône Valley in wagonloads to give new life to the soil. Ironically, today the authorities would forbid so much as a bucketful from outside the appellation. Does this condemn the great vineyard to a gradual decline? The co-proprietors of the domaine today are the Leroy and de Villaine families. Aubert de Villaine manages the estate; his home is at Bouzeron, near Chagny, where he makes particularly good Aligoté. After a spectacular in-house row and court case in 1992, Mme. Bize-Leroy was removed from her role within the company and replaced by her nephew Henry-Frédéric Roch. Pierre de Benoist, who is Aubert de Villaine's nephew, will join the management team after de Villaine's expected retirement in 2009.

The vineyards are cultivated organically, with Biodynamic trials in some parcels. New plant material is carefully selected from existing vines so as to preserve their unique footprint. The domaine's policy is to delay picking until the grapes are consummately ripe, running the gauntlet of the autumn storms and the risk of rot, simply rejecting all the grapes that have succumbed. The proportion of stems put in the vat depends on the season.

Fermentation is very long: from three weeks to even a full month. All the wine is matured in new barrels every year. There is a minimum of racking and filtration. It is indeed the grapes that do it. As the prices of the domaine's wines are spectacularly high, one expects to find them exceptional in character and in perfect condition. They are essentially wines for very long bottle-ageing. It is almost the hallmark of DRC wines that they are instantly recognizable by their exotic opulence. It used to be the case that bottles were filled directly from each barrel, which led to inconsistencies and some frankly poor bottles. These errors have been corrected, and since 1993 the domaine has hardly put a foot wrong. The holdings, and average production figures, of the domaine are as follows:

La Romanée-Conti
1.8 hectares, 6,000 bottles
La Tâche
6 hectares, 17,000 bottles
Richebourg
3.5 hectares, 13,000 bottles
Grands-Echézeaux
3.5 hectares, 13,000 bottles
Echézeaux
4.67 hectares, 19,000 bottles
Romanée-St-Vivant
5.28 hectares, 21,000 bottles
Le Montrachet
0.67 hectares, 3,500 bottles

ever heard of, often take advantage of the appellation Côte de Beaune-Villages.

Grands Crus

Corton-Charlemagne white wines only:	Hautes-Mourottes (1.8)
	Le Rognet-et-Corton (3.2)
Basses Mourottes (1)	

Corton red and white:

Les Carrières (0.4)	Le Rognet et Corton (8.4)
Les Grandes Lolières (3)	La Toppe au Vert (0.1)
Les Moutottes (0.8)	Les Vergennes (3.4)

Premiers Crus

Total area 25 hectares:

Basses Mourottes (0.9)	Les Joyeuses (0.8)
Bois Roussot (1.8)	Petites Lolières
Les Buis	La Micaude (1.6)
Le Clou d'Orge (1.6)	En Naget
La Corvée (7)	Le Rognet et Corton
Les Grêchons et Foutrières	**Appellation communale:**
Hautes-Mourottes (0.6)	**98 hectares**

Aloxe-Corton

The major part of the *grands crus* Corton and Corton-Charlemagne dominates this parish, but still leaves a substantial amount of lower land with the appellation Aloxe-Corton, both *premier cru* and village. It is important to remember that Corton *tout-court* is always a superior appellation to Aloxe-Corton.

It is almost impossible (and, in any case, not really essential) to grasp the legalities of the *grands crus* here. Corton embraces a dozen different adjacent vineyards, the top of which is actually called Le Corton. The others may be labelled either Corton, or, for example, Corton-Clos du Roi, Corton-Bressandes. On such a big hillside there is inevitably a wide range of style and quality. Bressandes, lowest of the *grands crus*, is considered to produce richer wine (from richer soil) than Clos du Roi above it… and so on. There are 120 hectares of *grand cru* in Aloxe-Corton, of which 49 are entitled to produce Corton-Charlemagne. But growers have the right to plant red grapes within Corton-Charlemagne if they wish, though few do so. This makes it impossible to give precise figures for areas planted, as we have done for other communes. But it may be useful to know that about two-thirds of *grand cru* vineyards are released as red Corton (including its sub-vineyards such as Les Bressandes), about one-third as Corton-Charlemagne, and just over one per cent as white Corton.

Corton-Charlemagne is a white *grand cru* from some of the same vineyards as red Corton: those on the south slope and the top ones where the soil is paler and more impregnated with lime. Perversely enough, there is also an appellation for white *grand cru* Corton, although this is rarely seen.

True to their national inclinations, the French rate (red) Corton the best wine of the hill, comparing it for sheer force of personality with Chambertin, whereas the British speak of Corton-Charlemagne in the same breath as Le Montrachet. It expresses great driving vigour of a kind closer to a *grand cru*

Chablis made in oak, though with more spice, even earth, and correspondingly less of the simple magic of ripe fruit. Because the terroir is so varied, as is the competence of the growers here, it should not surprise us that while the greatest Corton-Charlemagne is as magnificent and long-lived as any white burgundy, there are also some dispiriting and lack-lustre examples.

It is in the nature of Corton-Charlemagne to hide its qualities and show only its power, as red wines do, for as many as seven or eight years. Red Corton needs keeping as long as the *grands crus* of the Côte de Nuits.

The dominant name among Corton growers, both red and white, is that of Louis Latour, whose press house and cellars are cut into the foot of the hill itself and who gives the name of his château, Grancey, to a selection of Corton of even greater than usual power.

Grands Crus

Lieu-dits for red Corton (7)	Perrières (10)
Bressandes (17.4)	Renardes (14.3)
Maréchaudes (4.2)	Clos du Roi (10.7)

Parts (smaller than 4 hectares) of Chaumes and Voirosses, Combes, Fiètres, Grèves, Meix, Meix Lallemand, Pauland, Le Village, and La Vigne au Saint in Aloxe-Corton.

Premiers Crus

Chaillots (4.6)	Paulands (1.6)
Clos des Maréchaudes (1.4)	Les Valozières (6.6)
Clos du Chapitre	Les Vercots (4.2)
Les Fournières (5.5)	**Appellation communale:**
Les Guérets (2.5)	**84 hectares**
Les Maréchaudes (2.3)	

Pernand-Vergelesses

The *grand cru* of Pernand-Vergelesses is Corton-Charlemagne; there is no red Corton on the western slope of the hill (the only western slope in the whole of the Côte d'Or). But its *premiers crus* are in a completely different situation, directly facing Corton-Charlemagne across the narrow valley that leads up to this hidden village. The premiers crus are red; they continue the best vineyards of neighbouring Savigny, and in a sense those of Beaune.

Grand Cru

Charlemagne (white only) and Corton (red only) are both in the same parcel.

Premiers Crus

Caradeux (14.4)	Ile des Vergelesses (9)
Clos Berthet (1.5)	Sous Frétille
Clos Le Village	Les Vergelesses (18)
Creux de la Net (3.4)	**Appellation communale:**
Fichots (11)	**74 hectares**

Savigny-lès-Beaune

Savigny, like Pernand-Vergelesses, stops the head of a little valley cut back into the *côte* and grows vines on both sides of it. On the Pernand side they face south, on the Beaune side north-east. The best are at the extremities of the parish, where both incline most to the east: respectively, Les Vergelesses and Lavières, and La Dominode and Marconnets.

Savigny has a substantial château, a great number of good growers, and best of all a tendency to more moderate prices than its neighbours. Its wines could be called light classics, apt to age if only for the medium term, yet never ultra-chic. They need a good vintage to bring them up to their full strength – but whose do not?

Premiers Crus

Bas Marconnets (3)	Jarrons (1.4)
Basses Vergelesses (1.7)	Lavières (17)
Bataillere (1.8)	Narbantons (9.5)
Champ-Chevrey (1.5)	Petits Godeaux (0.7)
Charmières (2)	Peuillets (16)
Clous (10)	Redrescul (0.5)
Dominode (8)	Rouvrettes (2.8)
Fourneaux (6.4)	Serpentières (12)
Gravains (6)	Talmettes (3)
Guettes (14)	Aux Vergelesses (15)
Hauts-Jarrons (4.5)	**Appellations communales:**
Hauts-Marconnets (5.4)	**212 hectares**

Beaune

Beaune offers more temptation than any town to turn a wine encyclopedia into a guide book. It begs to be visited. Walking its wobbly streets between its soothing cellars is one of the great joys. The oldest, biggest, grandest, and most of the best négociants have their warrens here. They also own the greater part of its wide spread of vineyards. Do not look to Beaune for the most stately or the most flighty wines. "Franc de gout" is the classic description, which is almost impossible to translate. Franc signifies straight, candid, open, real, downright, forthright, and upright. Not dull, though. Young Beaune is already good to drink; as it ages, it softens and broadens its bouquet.

If there is a pecking order among the premiers crus, the following are near the top of it: Les Grèves, Fèves, Cras, Teurons, Marconnets, and Clos des Mouches (which also produces an excellent white wine). But nobody would claim to be able to distinguish them all, and more depends on the

Vaulted cellars of Beaune, dating from the Middle Ages

maker than the site. For this reason, the various monopoles of the négociants are usually worth their premium. Their names are usually prefixed with the word clos. The three biggest landowners are Bouchard Père & Fils, Chanson, and the Hospices de Beaune.

Where no area is specified in the list below, it is because it is not possible to give a definitive figure.

Premiers Crus

Aigrots (18 ha)	Fèves (4.5)
Avaux (11.5)	En Genèt (4.5)
Bas Teurons (6.3)	Grèves (32)
Bélissand (5)	Marconnets (9.5)
Blanches Fleurs (0.4)	Mignotte (2.4)
Boucherottes (8.5)	Montée Rouge (3.7)
Bressandes (17)	Montrevenots (8)
Cent Vignes (24)	En l'Orme (2)
Champs Pimont (16)	Perrières (3.2)
Chouacheux (5)	Pertuisots (5.2)
Clos des Avaux (3.7)	Reversées (4.8)
Clos de l'Ecu (2.4)	Sceaux
Clos de la Féguine (1.9)	Sizies (8.6)
Clos St-Landry (2)	Sur les Grèves (3)
Clos des Mouches (25)	Sur Les Grèves Clos Sainte
Clos de la Mousse (3.4)	Anne (0.7)
Clos du Roi (8.4)	Teurons (21)
Clos des Ursules (2.7)	Toussaints (6.5)
Coucherias (7.7)	Tuvilains (9)
Cras (5)	Vignes Franches (10)
A l'Ecu (2.6)	**Appellation communale:**
Epenottes (8)	**95 hectares**

Chorey-lès-Beaune

The little appellation of Chorey-lès-Beaune slips off the map down into the plain. The wines can be delicious (some excellent growers live here) but should be drunk young.

Côte de Beaune

This appellation was instituted, as it seems, to discover who was dozing during the complexities of Côte de Beaune-Villages (see page). It applies only to wine from along the upper slopes of the Montagne de Beaune just above the *premiers crus*. There are only 33 hectares in production, white as well as red, so it's not often seen.

Pommard

In the war of words that continually tries to distinguish one village from another, the wines of Pommard seem to have been labelled "loyaux et marchands", which translates as "loyal and commercial". The suggestion is not of poetic flights. Pommard makes solid, close-grained wines of strong colour, aggressive at first, bending little even with age. Les Rugiens, with its iron-red soil, is the vineyard with most of these qualities, considered the best of the village. Les Epenots, on the edge of Beaune, gives rather easier wine. There are some proud and decidedly loyal growers in the parish, but few of them have mastered the art of taming the Pommard tannins.

Premiers Crus

Arvelets (8.5)	Fremiers (5)
Bertins (3.5)	Grands-Epenots (10)
Boucherottes (1.5)	Les Jarollières (3.2)
Chanière (2.8)	En Largillière (4)
Chanlins Bas (4.4)	Petits Epenots (15)
Chaponnières (2.8)	Pézerolles (6)
Charmots (9.7)	Platière (2.5)
Clos Blanc (4.2)	Poutures (4.1)
Clos de la Commaraine (3.8)	Refène (2.3)
Clos des Epeneaux (5.2)	Rugiens-Bas (5.8)
Clos Micot (or Micault) (2.8)	Rugiens-Hauts (6.8)
Clos de Verger (2)	Saussilles (or Saucilles) (3.9)
Combes-Dessus (2.7)	**Appellation communale:**
Croix Noires (1.3)	**206 hectares**
Derrière Saint-Jean (0.3)	

Volnay

Corton and Volnay are the extremes of style of the Côte de Beaune: the first regal, robust, deep-coloured, and destined to dominate; the second ideally tender, "lacy", a lighter red with a soft-fruit scent, all harmony and delight. The dictum goes that Volnay is the Chambolle-Musigny of the Côte de Beaune. Personally, I find it exact: each is my favourite from its area. To shift the ground a little, Château Latour answers to Corton; Lafite lovers will want Volnay – though a few Volnay growers are carried away with the search for power and extract these days. A pity.

The lovely little village hangs higher in the hills than its neighbours, its 135 hectares of *premiers crus* on the mid-slopes below. The long ramp of vines that leads down to Meursault contains Les Caillerets, probably the closest any Volnay

---

ENJOYING BURGUNDY

White burgundy is incomparable as the wine to accompany the first course of a formal meal and pave the way for a fine red – of Burgundy or Bordeaux. The lighter and more acid wines are excellent with charcuterie; mature, full-bodied ones are as satisfying with poultry or veal.

Red burgundy can be so delicate that it begs to be appreciated alone. In contrast, it can also be so massive in flavour and vinosity that the pungency of well-hung game is not too much for it. Lighter wines benefit from being served cool. Only full-scale, well-matured burgundies should be

served at the room temperature of Bordeaux. In Burgundy, red wine is seldom decanted. The Burgundian habit of serving the finest reds with strong cheese, even Epoisses, seems frankly eccentric.

Premier Cru gets to *grand cru* quality. Champans, beside it under the village, reaches the same class, as does Clos des Chênes. There is no clear division between Volnay and its southern neighbours, Meursault in the valley and Monthélie on the hill. The same style of wine, even the same vineyard names continue. Meursault is allowed to use the name of Volnay for red wine grown in its part of Santenots, Plures, and Les Vignes Blanches (as long as it uses Pinot Noir). To taste them beside the white *premiers crus* of Meursault is to discover that red and white wine are by no means chalk and cheese. Where no area is specified, it is because it is not possible to give a definitive figure.

Premiers Crus

Angles (3.4)	Clos du Château des Ducs (0.6)
Aussy (1.7) From 2007	Clos des Chênes (15)
became part of Ronceret	Clos de la Cave des Ducs (0.6)
Brouillards (5.6)	Clos des Ducs (2.4)
Caillerets (14.4)	Clos de la Rougeotte (0.5)
Carelle Sous la Chapelle (3.7)	Clos du Verseuil (0.7)
From 2007 became part	En l'Ormeau (4.3) From 2007
of Carelles-Dessous	became part of Mitans
La Chapelle	Frémiets (7.4)
Carelles Dessous (1.5).	Gigotte (0.5)
From 2007 became part	Grand-Champs (0.2)
of Carelles-Dessous	Lassolle (0.2)
La Chapelle	Lurets (2)
Carelles-Dessous La	Mitans (8)
Chapelle (5.2)	Pitures (7)
Champans (11)	Pointes d'Angles (1.2)
Chanlins (2.9) From 2007	Robardelle (3)
became part of Pitures.	Ronceret (3.6)
Chevret (6.4)	Santenots (22)
Clos de l'Audignac (1.1)	Taille Pieds (7)
Clos de la Barre (1.3)	Le Village (2.9)
Clos de la Bousse d'Or (2.2)	**Appellation communale:**
Clos de la Chapelle (0.57)	**92 hectares**

Monthélie

Just as Corton-Charlemagne goes on round the corner into Pernand-Vergelesses, so the best Volnay vineyard flows into the lesser-known Monthélie. It changes its name to Les Champs Fulliot. The centre of interest in the village of Monthélie is its château, the property of one of its most distinguished growers: Eric de Suremain. Good Monthélie has the charm of Volnay but is less structured and long-lived.

Premiers Crus

Les Barbières (1)	Meix-Bataille (2.3)
Cas Rougeot (0.6)	Riottes (0.7)
Champs Fulliot (8)	Sur la Velle (6)
Château Gaillard (0.5)	Taupine (1.5)
Clos Gauthey (1.8)	Vignes Rondes (2.7)
Clos des Toisières (0.43)	Le Village (0.2)
Le Clou des Chênes (1.5)	**Appellation communale:**
Les Cloux (3)	**106 hectares**
Duresses (6.7)	

Meursault

If Meursault has convinced itself that it is a town, it fails to convince visitors looking for amenities – still less action. Its streets are a bewildering forest of hoardings to cajole the tourist into the cellars that are its whole *raison d'être*.

There is a mass of Meursault, and it is mixed. Its model is a drink that makes me thirsty even to think of it: a meeting of softness and succulence with thirst-quenching clarity and "cut". A village Meursault will be mild; the higher up the ladder you go the more authority and cut the wine will have. With age comes rounding out, the onset of flavours people have described with words like "oatmeal" and "hazelnuts", and "butter"; things that are rich but bland.

The white wine vineyards of Meursault are those that continue unbroken into Puligny-Montrachet to the south, and the best are those that are nearest to the parish line: Les Perrières, Les Charmes, Les Genevrières. The hamlet of Blagny, higher on the same hill, also contains Meursault Premiers Crus of the top quality: Sous le Dos d'Ane and La Pièce Sous le Bois – names that seem to express a rustic crudity, which is far from being the case. Blagny's elevation results in wines with more austerity and bite than those from lower sites. The same is true from village wines from high on the hill (Les Tillets, Les Narvaux). They can be excellent, with sharper acidity, and, like Blagny, they are slow to develop. The best red wines of Meursault sell as Volnay-Santenots.

Premiers Crus

Bouchères (4.4)	La Pièce Sous le Bois (11)
Caillerets (1)	Plures (10.5)
Charmes (31)	Poruzots (11.4)
Clos des Perrières (1)	Ravelles (1.3)
Cras (3.5)	Santenots (22)
Genevrières (16.5)	Sous Blagny (2.2)
Gouttes d'Or (5.4)	Sous le Dos d'Ane (5)
Jeunelotte (5)	**Appellation communale:**
Perrières (Dessous and	**288 hectares**
Dessus) (13.7)	

Blagny

Blagny has no appellation of its own, but possesses excellent vineyards in both Meursault and Puligny-Montrachet.

Puligny-Montrachet Premiers Crus

La Garenne (10)	**Appellation communale:**
Hameau de Blagny (4.2)	**8 hectares**
Sous le Puits (6.8)	

Meursault Premiers Crus

La Jeunelotte (5)	Sous le Dos d'Ane (5)
La Pièce Sous le Bois (11)	**Appellation communale:**
Sous Blagny (2.2)	**2 hectares**

Auxey-Duresses

This is the village above and behind Meursault where a valley at right angles to the *côte* provides a south slope at the correct mid-point of the hill for a limited patch of *premier cru* vineyard, mostly planted with Pinot Noir. The white can resemble a very crisp Meursault, which I find more exciting than Auxey red, which can be quite rustic. The village also shelters the fabulous stocks of Mme. Bize-Leroy, the "Gardienne des Grands Millésimes" (see Maison Leroy).

Premiers Crus

Bas des Duresses (2.4)	Ecusseaux (3.1)
Bréterins (1.7)	Grands Champs (4)
Chapelle (1.3)	Reugne (2)
Climat du Val (8.4)	**Appellation communale:**
Clos du Val (1)	**102 hectares**
Duresses (8)	

St-Romain

A pretty little village lurking in the second wave of hills, behind Auxey-Duresses. It has no *premier cru* land, being too high on the hills, and from its 100 hectares makes more and better white wine than red. In cool years the wines can be too sharp for comfort.

Puligny-Montrachet

Puligny and Chassagne appear at first sight like Siamese twins linked by their shared grand cru, Le Montrachet. But the impression is a false one. Puligny is a dedicated white-wine parish. Chassagne, despite the Montrachet of its name, used to earn most of its living from red, and about 30 per cent of the vineyards are still planted with Pinot Noir.

There is no magic by which white wine from Meursault Charmes must taste different from the Puligny Les Combettes, which meets it at the boundary. Yet I would expect the Puligny-Montrachet to have a slightly more lively taste of fruit, a bit more bite, and perhaps a floweriness which is not a Meursault characteristic. Sheaves of old tasting notes tend to contradict each other, so my description is pure impressionism – all that airy metaphor in dabs of paint representing orchards does seem to have something to do with the taste I cannot describe.

What is more tangible is the superiority of the *premiers crus*. Those of Combettes and Champs Canet at the Meursault end of Puligny, and the part of Blagny that lies in this parish with the appellation Blagny Premier Cru, can be expected to be closer to Meursault in style. A slightly higher premium is normally put on the ones that border the *grands crus*: Cailleret and Pucelles.

Two of the *grands crus* that are the white-wine climax of Burgundy lie entirely within Puligny-Montrachet: Chevalier-Montrachet (the strip of hill above Montrachet), and Bienvenues-Bâtard-Montrachet: half the shallower slope

Château de Meursault, Beaune

below. The accepted appreciation of Chevalier is that it has the fine flavour of Montrachet but in less-concentrated form (concentration being the hallmark of this grandest of all white wines). The critics do not normally distinguish between Bienvenues and Bâtard (to shorten their unwieldy names). Any such generalization is inevitably overturned by the next tasting of a different vintage or a different grower's wine.

As for Puligny-Montrachet village without frills – it is still expensive. Is it worth more than Meursault? Probably not, as there is more excitement to be had from the better village wines of Meursault. The Puligny-Montrachet is likely to be slightly the more expensive of the two.

Grands Crus

Bâtard-Montrachet (6)	Chevalier-Montrachet (7.36)
Bienvenues-Bâtard- Montrachet (3.6)	Montrachet (4)

Premiers Crus

Caillerets (3.4)	Folatières (17.7)
Chalumeaux (5.8)	Garenne (10)
Champs Canet (4)	Hameau de Blagny (4.3)
Champ Gain (10.7)	Perrières (8.4)
Clavoillon (5.6)	Pucelles (5.1)
Clos de la Garenne (1.5)	Referts (5.5)
Clos de la Mouchère	Sous le Puits (6.8)
Combettes (6.8)	Truffière (2.5)
Demoiselles (0.6)	**Appellation communale:** **114 hectares**

Chassagne-Montrachet

Almost half of the *grands crus* Le Montrachet and Bâtard-Montrachet and the whole of Criots-Bâtard-Montrachet occupy the hill corner that ends the parish to the north. Unfortunately, the steep south-facing slope that runs at right angles to them, along the road to St-Aubin in the hills, has not enough soil for vines. If this were the Douro, there would be terraces. Between here and the village there is some *premier cru* land, but the famous wines begin again where the *côte* picks up its momentum and its tilt in the Clos St-Jean above the little township. Caillerets, Ruchottes, and Morgeot are names seen on expensive and memorable white bottles. Other vineyards, such as Clos St-Jean, stress red.

Any association of ideas that suggests that red Chassagne should be a light wine is quite wrong. Far from being a gentle fade-out from Volnay, Chassagne returns to the meat and muscle of Corton or the Côte de Nuits. Red Chassagne, moreover, sells at the price of the lesser-known villages – much cheaper than the grand names of the Côte de Nuits. It can sometimes be every bit as satisfying. Lesser examples can be coarse.

Many of the *premiers crus* can be bottled under the names of better-known premiers, which is why some of the names are rarely, or never, glimpsed on labels.

Where no area is specified in the list below, it is because it is not possible to give a definitive figure.

Grands Crus

Bâtard-Montrachet (6)	Montrachet (4)
Criots-Bâtard-Montrachet (1.6)	

Premiers Crus

Abbaye de Morgeot (4)	Dents de Chien (0.65)

Baudines (3.6) (part of Bois
  des Chassagne)
	Embrazées/Embazées (5.2)
	  (part of Bois de Chassagne)

Blanchot Dessus (1.2)	Fairendes (7.2)
Bois de Chassagne (4.8)	(part of Morgeot)

Bondues (1.7) (part of
  Chenevottes)
	Francemont (2.4) (part of
	  Morgeot)

Boudriotte (part of	Grande Borne (1.7)
Morgeots) (2.2)	Grande Montagne (2.8)
Brussonnes (part of	Grandes Ruchottes (2.1) (part
Morgeots) (2.9)	of Grande Montagne)
Caillerets (6.1)	Grands Clos (4) (part of
Cardeuse (1) (part of Morgeot)	Morgeot)
Champs Gains (4.6)	Guerchères (2.2) (part of
Champs Jendreau (2.1)	Morgeot)
(part of Morgeot)	Macherelles (5.2)
La Chapelle (4.6) (part of	Maltroie (4)
Morgeot)	Morgeot (54)
Chassagne (1.1) (part of	Murées (1.6) (part of Clos
Cailleret)	St Jean)
Chassagne (2.9) (part of	Pasquelles (2.4) (part of
Maltroie)	Vergers)
Chassagne du Clos St Jean (2)	Petingerets (1.7) (part of
(part of Clos St Jean)	Vergers)
Chaumées (7.5)	Petits Clos (5) (part
Chaumes (2.7) (part of	of Morgeot)
Morgeot)	Petits Fairendes (0.8)
Chenevottes (8.2)	(part of Morgeot)
Clos Chareau (2) (part of	Les Places (2.4)
Morgeot)	(part of Maltroie)
Clos du Château (3)	Les Rebichets (5.5)
Clos de la Chapelle (part of	(part of Clos St Jean)
Morgeot)	En Remilly (1.6)
Clos de la Maltroie (part of	Romanée (3.4) (part of
Maltroie)	Grande Montagne)
Clos des Murées (part of	Roquemaure (0.6)
Clos St Jean)	(part of Morgeot)
Clos Pitois (3) (part of	Tête du Clos (2.1)
Morgeot)	(part of Morgeot)
Clos St Jean (5)	Vergers (5.2)
Combards (0.65) (part of	Vide-Bourse (1.2)
Caillerets)	Vigne Blanche (2.2) (part
Commes (1) (part of	of Morgeot)
Chenevottes)	Vigne Derrière (3.7)
Ez Crets (2.3) (part of	(part of Caillerets)
Maltroie)	En Virondot (2.3)
Ez Crottes (2.3)	(part of Grande Montagne)
(part of Morgeot)	

Appellation communale:
157 hectares

St-Aubin

St-Aubin is a twin to St-Romain, a village tucked into the first valley behind the *côte* but with a slight advantage of situation that gives it some *premiers crus*, if slightly more than the terroir warrants. The village of Gamay (the presumed source of the grape that makes Beaujolais, which is a taint to the Côte d'Or) contributes about half the land in this appellation. The whites show more flair than the reds. They exhibit a sub-Puligny (or is it sub-Meursault?) style, and most of the best sites (En Remilly, Murgers des Dents de Chien, Chatenière, and Charmots) border those of Puligny and Chassagne. The wines have improved greatly in recent years and can be excellent value. The area under vine is 161 hectares, of which 12 are *premiers crus*.

Where no area is specified in the list below, it is because it is not possible to give a definitive figure.

Premiers Crus

Les Castets	En Montceau
Champlots.	Les Murgers des Dents
Charmois (15)	de Chien (16)
Chatenière.	Perrieres
Les Combes.	Pitangeret
Les Cortons	Le Puits
En Créot	En Remilly (22)
Derrière Chez Edouard	Sous Roche Dumay
Derrière la Tour	Sur le Sentier du Clou
Frionnes.	Vignes Moingeon
Sur Gamay	Le Village

Santenay

It is a conceit, I know, but I have always found the names of the villages of Burgundy to be a useful clue to the nature of their wines. Chambertin has a drum-roll sound, Chambolle-Musigny a lyrical note; Pommard sounds precisely right for its tough, red wine, and so does Volnay for its more silky produce. Santenay sounds like good health. (Funnily enough, it has a far-from-fashionable spa for the treatment of rheumatism and gout.)

Healthiness seems just the right sort of image to attach to the wines of Santenay. They are rather plain, even-flavoured, with no great perfume or thrills but good, solid drinking.

At their best, in Les Gravières, La Comme, and Le Clos de Tavannes, they are in the same class as Chassagne-Montrachet: weighty and long-lived. Other parts of the parish with stonier, more limey soil have paler reds and a little white wine of increasing interest.

Premiers Crus

Beauregard (18)	Fourneaux (6)
Beaurepaire (15.5)	Grand Clos Rousseau (7.7)
Clos Faubard (5.2)	Gravières (24)
Clos des Mouches (1.5)	Maladière (13.5)
Clos Rousseau (10)	Passe Temps (11.5)
Clos de Tavannes (5.3)	**Appellation communale:**
Comme (22)	**203 hectares**

Maranges

This new (1989) appellation covers the three rather forlorn little villages which share the vineyard Les Maranges, along the hill just west of Santenay and to their regret, just over the *département* line of the Côte d'Or, in the outer darkness of Saône-et-Loire. Their names are Sampigny, Dezuze, and Cheilly. The wines are well-structured with deep colour, and are generally quite tannic. They age well and make splendid drinking when eight years old, as the local clientele buying direct has proved time and again. There are 82 hectares of *premiers crus*.

Cheilly-les-Maranges Premiers Crus
Boutières, Fussière, and Clos Roussots

Dezize-les-Maranges Premier Cru
Fussière, Clos de la Fussière, Croix aux Moines

Sampigny-les-Maranges Premiers Crus
Clos Roussots, Clos des Rois, Clos des Loyères

Côte de Beaune-Villages

All the villages of the Côte de Beaune, with the exception of Beaune, Pommard, Volnay, and Aloxe-Corton, have this as a fall-back appellation in red wine (only).

Leading Côte d'Or Producers

The almost literally priceless land of the Côte d'Or is broken up into innumerable small units of ownership, variously expressed as ares (a hundredth of a hectare) or as *ouvrées* (an old measure that is one twenty-fourth of a hectare, or about a tenth of an acre). These little plots have come about by the French system of inheritance, by the amount of capital needed to buy more, and by the dread of local disasters, which make it inadvisable to put all your eggs in one basket. They mean that a grower

---

LE MONTRACHET

All critics agree the best Montrachet is the best white burgundy. In it all the properties that make the mouth water in memory and anticipation are brought to a resounding climax. The first quality that proclaims it at a tasting with its neighbours is a concentration of flavour. I have wondered how much this is due to its singular site and its soil and how much to the regulations (and common sense) that keep its crop to a minimum. There is little doubt that other good vineyards could pack more punch if their keepers kept them more meanly pruned and fertilized, picked late, and used only the best bunches. Such economics only work for a vineyard whose wine is as good as sold before it is made, at any price. The principal owners of Le Montrachet are the Marquis de Laguiche (whose wine is handled by Drouhin), Comtes Lafon, Baron Thénard, Bouchard Père & Fils, Jacques Prieur, Ramonet, and the Domaine de la Romanée-Conti.

who has, say, ten hectares may well have them in 30 different places – often just a few rows of vines separated from his others in the same vineyard.

The precious land is also divided by ancient custom into a jigsaw of climats, or fields, sometimes with natural and obvious boundaries, sometimes apparently at random. Each climat is a known local character with a meaning and value to the farmers that is hard for an outsider to grasp.

Overlay the one pattern on the other and you have the fragmentation of ownership that bedevils buyers of burgundy. Whereas in Bordeaux a château is a consistent unit doing one or, at most, two things on a reasonably large scale, a Burgundy domaine is often a man and his family coping with a dozen or more different wines with different needs and problems. If he is a good husbandman of vines, his talent does not necessarily extend to the craftsmanship of the cellar – or vice versa. For any number of reasons, inconsistency is almost inevitable.

There are major exceptions in the form of bigger vineyards with richer owners. But the concept of the little man trying to do everything is fundamental. It explains the importance of the négociants or shippers, whose traditional role is to buy the grower's grapes or newly made wine, mature it, and blend it with others of the same vineyard or village or district to make marketable quantities of something consistent.

It takes little imagination to see that an unscrupulous merchant could get away with almost anything under these conditions. Matters were worse four years ago, when you could safely assume that certain merchants were blending in wines from outside the region – a semi-legal semi-fraud that is now strictly outlawed. But there is still plenty of room for manoeuvre in the area of quality. There are inspections but nobody pretends they are comprehensive or effective.

When most consumers hear that merchants are venal, their reaction is to look directly for authenticity from the growers. Bottling at the domaine has been presented as the answer. It brings us back, though, to the basic question: who is more competent and more conscientious? Ownership of a corner of a fine and famous field does not carry with it a technical degree in winemaking or *élevage* – the bringing up of wine in the cellar – or bottling. That is why it is essential to learn who is making the best wine. Fortunately the list is growing rather than shrinking, thanks to the growing competence of a younger generation of growers, well-schooled and innovative, who are often making far better wine than Burgundy has probably ever seen. They are more conscious than many of their fathers of the need to return to a balanced viticulture, free from a dependency on fertilizers, productive clones, and yields pushed to the maximum.

Ambroise ☆☆–☆☆☆
Nuits-St-Georges. www.ambroise.com
The exuberant Bertrand Ambroise approaches winemaking with gusto. Ten of the 30 hectares he works are leased, and he also buys in grapes. There are dense, cherryish wines from Nuits (especially the splendid *vieilles vignes*), as well as *grands crus*, white and red, from Corton. Ambroise ages almost all his wines in new oak, but is now using 400-litre barrels so as to diminish the wines' overt oakiness.

Guy Amiot ☆☆–☆☆☆
Chassagne-Montrachet.
www.grands-crus-amiot-et-fils.com
This little-known estate owns 12 hectares in numerous *premiers crus* of Chassagne, with most vines older than 30 years. The style is solid, oaky, powerful, and minerally, with Baudines and Caillerets often among the best *crus*.

Pierre Amiot ☆☆
Morey-St-Denis.
A traditionalist grower with small plots totalling 8.5 hectares in *grands crus* Clos de la Roche and Clos St-Denis as well as Gevrey-Chambertin Les Combottes and Chambolle-Musigny. Pierre's two sons now run the estate, and quality has improved since the late 1990s.

Robert Ampeau ☆☆–☆☆☆
Meursault.
Outstanding ten-hectare domaine respected particularly for its white wines. The best-known are from Meursault Perrières, Charmes, and La Pièce Sous le Bois (partly in Blagny), and a parcel in Puligny Combettes. The reds, which are less consistent, include Beaune Clos du Roi, Savigny Premier Cru (Lavières and Fourneaux), Pommard, and Volnay Santenots.

Unusually, Ampeau only sells wines well-bottle-aged in his own cellars. Since Ampeau's death in 2004, his son Michel has been running the property.

Corton André ☆–☆☆
Aloxe-Corton. www.corton-andre.com
Négociant and grower on the largest scale. Pierre André founded La Reine Pédauque. His château at Corton is the centre for the estate, which includes six hectares of Corton. These Cortons are easily the best wines. The company was bought by the Ballande group in 2002 and sells the wines under the Corton André and Reine Pédauque labels.

Marquis d'Angerville ☆☆☆
Volnay. www.domainedangerville.fr
An impeccable domaine of 15 hectares mostly in Volnay. The present Marquis's grandfather was a pioneer of domaine-bottling as a way of countering fraudulent practice by négociants abusing the good name of Volnay.

The monopole Clos des Ducs is an unusual, steep, and chalky 2.4-hectare vineyard whose wine tends to miss the velvet of the best Volnay, but can age magnificently. I prefer the more sumptuous Champans (produced from four hectares) and Caillerets. After some disappointing vintages, the estate has been back on form since 2004.

Clos de la Roche, Morey-St-Denis

Domaine d'Ardhuy ☆☆
Corgoloin. www.ardhuy.com
The former owners of Reine Pédauque and Corton-André
(q.v.) retain some important vineyards. Good Cortons, and
a fine Clos des Langres in Côte de Nuits-Villages.

Hervé Arlaud ☆☆–☆☆☆
Morey-St-Denis. www.domainearlaud.com
Since 1998, Cyprien Arlaud has been making the wines at this
15-hectare estate, aiming for a fruity, supple style without too
much extraction. He has got the balance right: voluptuous
fruit and ripe tannins.

Domaine de l'Arlot ☆☆–☆☆☆
Nuits-St-Georges.
The insurance company AXA owns this Prémeaux estate,
but it has been run (and co-owned) for over 15 years by
Jean-Pierre de Smet. Olivier Leriche directs the winemaking.
The Clos de l'Arlot is a monopole site (four hectares), as
is the seven-hectare Clos des Forêts St-Georges. The wines
are elegant and appear a touch light. Yet they retain their
poise, and their fruit, for many years.

Comte Armand ☆☆☆
Pommard. www.domaines-comte-armand.com
New life was breathed into this domaine, which owns the
excellent monopoly vineyard, Clos des Epeneaux, when the
young Québecois Pascal Marchand was put in charge in 1985.
  Since 1995 the domaine has added vineyards in Auxey-
Duresses (red and white), Volnay, and Meursault through
share-cropping agreements. In 1999, Marchand moved on
and his place here taken by young Benjamin Leroux, who
seems equally competent. Since 2002, the estate has been
cultivated Biodynamically. These are deeply coloured,
intense wines, which require significant ageing.

Robert Arnoux ☆☆–☆☆☆☆
Vosne-Romanée.
Arnoux died in 1995, but his son-in-law, Pascal Lachaux,
runs this 14-hectare estate, which is endowed with *grands crus*
Echézeaux, Romanée-St-Vivant, and Clos de Vougeot, as
well as a parade of premiers crus in Nuits and Vosne. The
best wines are often the Vosne Suchots and the Romanée-St-
Vivant. The style is elegant and oaky, and although the wines
are extremely expensive, they are certainly among the best in
the village.

Domaine d'Auvenay ☆☆☆☆
Auxey-Duresses.
This small, four-hectare domaine is the personal property
of the Leroy family, and is separate from the more recent
Domaine Leroy (q.v.). But the wines are made in the same
way, with tiny yields, especially from the *grands crus* such
as Chevalier-Montrachet. The wines are superb, all but
unobtainable, and very expensive.

Denis Bachelet ☆☆☆
Gevrey-Chambertin.
One man's tiny enterprise in Gevrey-Chambertin, *premier
cru* Les Corbeaux, and Charmes-Chambertin. But brilliantly
stylish wines.

Ghislaine Barthod ☆☆☆
Chambolle-Musigny.
From seven hectares of mostly *premiers crus*, Ghislaine Barthod
makes a fine range of wines that achieve the right balance
between structure and seductiveness. The new oak
is held in check, rarely exceeding 30 per cent. Les Cras and
Charmes are often the best of the *crus*.

Domaine des Beaumont ☆☆
Morey-St-Denis. www.domaine-des-beaumont.com
A rarity in Burgundy, a new estate, with its first vintage in
1999 from five hectares of mostly *premiers crus* in Morey
and Chambolle. The style is ripe, oaky, and svelte.

Roger Belland ☆
Santenay. www.domaine-belland-roger.com
Belland offers a wide range of wines from all over the Côte
de Beaune. It is best to focus on the wines of Santenay and
Maranges, which are rich but never rustic.

Domaine Bertagna ☆☆☆
Vougeot. www.domainebertagna.com
Owners of some Vougeot *premier cru* (white as well as red),
including the monopole Clos de la Perrière (two hectares), the
hill just below Le Musigny. Bertagna has a total of 21 hectares,
with a fair selection of *grands crus* such as Chambertin, Clos St-
Denis, Corton, and Corton-Charlemagne. Quality, once
patchy, has gained in rigour and consistency.

Albert Bichot ☆–☆☆☆
Beaune. www.albert-bichot.com
Founded in Beaune in 1831. As a grower, Bichot owns three
domaines: Domaine du Pavillon in Pommard, Clos Frantin in
Nuits, and Long-Depaquit (q.v.) in Chablis. At the top levels,
especially from their own domaines, quality can be high.

Simon Bize ☆☆–☆☆☆
Savigny.
A domaine of 22 hectares almost entirely in Savigny (there
are parcels of Chevalier-Montrachet and Corton-Charlemagne
too), with holdings in the *premiers crus* Vergelesses, Guettes,
and Marconnets. These are perfumed wines of great purity.

Blain-Gagnard ☆☆☆
Chassagne-Montrachet.
Jean-Marc Blain is an utterly reliable grower, and all his
Chassagne Premiers Crus are aged in about 30 per cent new
oak. Boudriottes and Cailleret can be exceptional. Blain also
has small parcels of Bâtard-Montrachet, Criots, and, since
2000, Montrachet itself.

Henri Boillot ☆☆–☆☆☆
Volnay.
Until 2005 this major domaine was known as Jean Boillot.
Henri Boillot has holdings not only in Volnay, but also in
Puligny-Montrachet (four hectares, including the monopole
Clos de la Mouchère), Beaune *premiers crus*, and Pommard.
The Volnays are unusually rich. Boillot's négociant business
uses the name Maison Henri Boillot.

Jean-Marc Boillot ☆☆–☆☆☆
Pommard.

Jean-Marc, the brother of Henri Boillot (q.v.), came into his inheritance in 1988. He is equally at home making richly oaked white wines from various vineyards mostly in Puligny-Montrachet, or clearly defined reds from Volnay and Pommard. He also runs a négociant business; the labels for these wines omit the word *propriétaire*.

Lucien Boillot ☆☆
Gevrey-Chambertin.
Two grandchildren of Henri Boillot, Louis and Pierre, inherited this flourishing 14-hectare domaine, with its scattered holdings in Gevrey, Nuits, and Volnay. Later the property was divided up and is now owned solely by Pierre.

Jean-Claude Boisset ☆–☆☆☆
Nuits-St-Georges. www.boisset.com
A recent (in Burgundian terms – 1961) foundation which has since swallowed up many long-established names, including Charles Viénot, Bouchard Aîné, Pierre Ponnelle, Jaffelin, Ropiteau, J. Moreau in Chablis, and the Cellier des Samsons in Beaujolais. Boisset was more praised for commercial skills and marketing acumen than for attaining peaks of quality with its wines. However, under the dynamic Jean-Charles Boisset, two new high-quality ventures were developed: the family holdings at Domaine de la Vougeraie (q.v.), and the J.C. Boisset wines, made to the same exacting standards from purchased grapes.

Bonneau du Martray ☆☆☆☆
Pernand-Vergelesses. www.bonneaudumartray.com
The largest producer of the inimitable Corton-Charlemagne, with a solid block of 9.5 hectares of old vines, and an adjacent 1.5 in Corton (red). The famous Cuvée François de Salins, the costliest wine of the Hospices de Beaune, comes from the same prime hill corner site. This is the only estate in Burgundy, other than Domaine de la Romanée-Conti, to own nothing but *grand cru* vineyards. In 1994 Jean-Charles Le Bault de la Morinière succeeded his father and raised high standards even higher. The Corton-Charlemagne behaves more like a red, ageing majestically. It reaches its sublime peak at ten years and can be kept longer. After lagging behind the white wine for many years his red Corton is now looking good too.

Bouchard Père & Fils ☆☆–☆☆☆☆
Beaune. www.bouchard-pereetfils.com
The biggest domaine in Burgundy, with 130 hectares in the Côte d'Or alone, and one of the best négociants, run by Bouchards from father to son since 1731, until the company was sold to Henriot (of Champagne fame) in 1995. Joseph Henriot immediately set in train a series of measures to raise the standing of the wines, including the declassification of some *grand cru* stocks which he thought not up to scratch – a move typical of the complex character of a man who is at once an agile businessman and a passionate guardian of quality.

Bouchard's biggest holdings are in Beaune, where its *premiers crus* include the monopoles of the famous four-hectare Grèves Vigne de l'Enfant Jésus, the 3.5-hectare Clos de la Mousse, and the two-hectare Clos St Landry. It is also the largest proprietor of vineyards in Meursault. Inevitably, it has some impressive *grands crus* in its portfolio: Montrachet, of course, but also two hectares of Chevalier-Montrachet, and

substantial parcels in Corton. Other notable wines are Volnay Caillerets labelled as Ancienne Cuvée Carnot, atypically foursquare and long-lived Volnay from very old vines.

In the early 1990s, the firm was going through a very bad patch, beset by scandal and a dwindling reputation. In just a few years Henriot restored this great name, and the prestigious wines are once again all that they should be. Henriot has also acquired Domaine William Fèvre (q.v.) in Chablis, and overseen a similar miraculous transformation.

René Bouvier ☆☆
Marsannay.
Highlights include the delicious Le Clos white and the vibrant red Ouzeloy. Fine Gevreys too.

Michel Bouzereau ☆☆☆
Meursault.
Michel and his son, Jean-Baptiste, produce rich, spicy *premiers crus* from Genevrières and Charmes, but the village wines from Teurons and Limozins can be very fine, too, with a discreet oaky fragrance. Even his Aligoté is notable.

Alain Burguet ☆☆
Gevrey-Chambertin.
Eight hectares of mostly village vines, made remarkable by the fact that their average age is 50 years. The Cuvée Vieilles Vignes is as good as some *premiers crus* in the village. Burguet's only *premier cru* in Gevrey is Champeaux. Burguet runs a small négociant business too, purchasing grapes from Clos de Bèze and other vineyards.

Louis Carillon ☆☆
Puligny-Montrachet. www.louis-carillon.com
A proud family domaine of 12 hectares, going back 350 years, now run by Louis with his two sons. The vineyards include a little patch of Bienvenues-Bâtard-Montrachet. The Pulignys have an attractive citric quality and plenty of zest. Little new oak is used, so the fruit comes shining through.

Carré-Courbin ☆☆
Volnay.
A small 4.5-hectare estate, but with fine vineyards in Volnay and Pommard *premiers crus*. The wines are gently oaky and well-balanced, and succulent.

Sylvain Cathiard ☆☆☆
Vosne-Romanée.
A small five-hectare property with fine sites in Nuits-St-Georges and Chambolle as well as Vosne Malconsorts. Magnificent wines in recent vintages, powerful and spicy, and richly oaked. Awesome prices.

Champy ☆☆–☆☆☆
Beaune. www.champy.com
Probably Beaune's oldest négociant house, founded in 1720, Champy was sold in 1990 to respected wine broker Henri Meurgey and his son, Pierre. They now own 17 hectares, but still buy in most of their requirements and offer some 60 different wines. Quality is high, level with many fine domaines.

Domaine Chandon de Briailles ☆☆–☆☆☆
Savigny-lès-Beaune. www.chandondebriailles.com

An important 13-hectare property, largely in the best red-wine vineyards of Savigny (Les Lavières) and the neighbouring Ile des Vergelesses in Pernand, run by mother and daughter to a very high standard. Also considerable owners in Corton, with 1.7 hectares in Bressandes, plus Clos du Roi and a little Corton Blanc. These are discreet, ultra-refined wines, poised and elegant. Biodynamic since 2005.

Chanson Père & Fils ☆–☆☆☆
Beaune. www.vins-chanson.com
Négociant and grower (founded 1750) with a fine domaine of 45 hectares, many of them in Beaune *premiers crus*, and substantial holdings in Savigny and Pernand-Vergelesses. Its best wines are perhaps its Beaune Clos des Fèves (3.8 hectares) and Clos des Mouches. Wines tasted in 2002 from the early decades of the twentieth century showed how marvellously the supposedly lightweight wines of Beaune could age. However, towards the end of the century quality had slipped, and in 1999 the company was bought by Bollinger. The new team moved rapidly to lower yields and to eliminate practices such as machine-harvesting. The wines showed an immediate improvement that has subsequently been maintained. The whites in particular (eg. Auxey-Duresses) are models.

Philippe Charlopin ☆☆☆
Gevrey-Chambertin.
The boisterous Charlopin's success with wines from Gevrey and Marsannay has allowed him to expand his 16-hectare domaine, already endowed with Clos St-Denis and Chambertin, with small parcels in Charmes-Chambertin and Clos Vougeot. Charlopin picks as late as possible, and produces rich, fleshy, even voluptuous, wines.

Chauvenet ☆☆
Nuits-St-Georges.
Christophe Drag has made the wines here since 1994, and has a good collection of *premiers crus* to work with. All are rich and assertive, and Vaucrains is often the best of them.

Alain Chavy ☆☆
Puligny-Montrachet.
Gérard Chavy's well-known domaine was divided in 2003 between brothers Alain and Jean-Louis. Both have inherited their father's skill, but Alain's *premiers crus* are especially elegant.

Chevalier Père et Fils ☆☆
Buisson. www.domaine-chevalier.com
Lively white Ladoix as well as more imposing Cortons.

Robert Chevillon ☆☆☆
Nuits-St-Georges.
A typical, family run 13-hectare estate, part owned and part rented. Very old vines and outstanding winemaking produce splendid *premier cru* Nuits-St-Georges from (especially) Les Cailles, Les St-Georges, Les Vaucrains, etc. A little white Nuits.

Bruno Clair ☆☆–☆☆☆☆
Marsannay. www.bruno-clair.com
This domaine was created after Domaine Clair Daü was divided in 1985. Bruno Clair himself received 21 very dispersed hectares. He has just under one hectare of Chambertin Clos de Bèze with some 90-year-old vines, and 3.5 hectares of *premiers crus* in Gevrey-Chambertin (including Clos St Jacques) and Savigny-lès-Beaune (the excellent Les Dominodes). There are also 5.5 hectares of red Marsannay, from which he makes three single-vineyard wines that are among the finest of the village. He also leases some vines in Corton-Charlemagne. A very reliable source across the range.

Denis Clair ☆☆
Santenay.
Although based in Santenay, most of Clair's 11 hectares of vineyards are located in good sites in St-Aubin. These are excellent wines, with the rich minerality of good white burgundy, and they are attractively priced.

Bruno Clavelier ☆☆
Vosne-Romanée.
Clavelier farms six hectares of organic vineyards in Vosne, Chambolle, and Gevrey-Chambertin. These are full-bodied, well-structured wines, sometimes ungainly, but rich and full of fruit.

Christian Clerget ☆☆–☆☆☆
Vougeot.
A small six-hectare domaine with some very old vines in Chambolle and Echézeaux as well as Vougeot. Ripeness and tannin can wage war when the wines are young, but this is red burgundy with considerable density and stuffing.

Yves Clerget ☆☆–☆☆☆
Volnay. www.domaine-clerget.com
A domaine of six hectares with an incredibly long history: the Clergets apparently were making wine in Volnay in 1268. The pride of the house is its resounding Pommard Rugiens. The Volnay parcels are in the *premiers crus* Carelle Sous la Chapelle, the monopole Clos du Verseuil, and Caillerets. For some reason this is a seriously underestimated estate.

Domaine des Clos ☆☆
Beaune.
Founded in 1995 and now Biodynamic, this is a new source of well-made wines from Beaune and Nuits-St-Georges.

Clos de Tart ☆☆☆☆
Morey-St-Denis. www.closdetart.com
This famous 7.5-hectare monopole *grand cru* has been owned since 1932 by the Beaujolais growers Mommessin. Quality was disappointing until Sylvain Pitiot was appointed as director in 1995. The vines are organically cultivated and yields are kept low; the wine is aged at least 18 months in new oak. Pitiot's methods have paid off, and the wine is sumptuous and concentrated, if very oaky in its youth.

Old wooden wine press and premiers crus vineyards, Chassagne-Montrachet

Jean-François Coche-Dury ☆☆☆–☆☆☆☆
Meursault.
Jean-François is the third generation to own this 11-hectare domaine that has both vineyards in Meursault and in Corton-Charlemagne. He has an almost fanatical following for his powerful white wines – even his Bourgogne Blanc. The Corton-Charlemagnes fetch extravagant prices at auction. Superb quality, but there is better value elsewhere.

Marc Colin ☆☆–☆☆☆
St-Aubin.
Half Colin's 17 hectares of vineyards are in St-Aubin, where he makes firm, well-structured, but nonetheless fruity white wines. There are also vines in *premiers crus* in Chassagne- and Puligny-Montrachet, and a little Montrachet as the icing on the cake. The property is now run by his sons.

Jean-Jacques Confuron ☆☆–☆☆☆
Nuits-St-Georges. www.jjconfuron.com
A Confuron daughter married Alain Meunier, who has run the estate since 1988. The wines are expressive and very well-made. The 8-hectare domaine owns two *grand cru* sites: Romanée-St-Vivant and Clos de Vougeot.

Confuron-Coteditot ☆☆–☆☆☆
Vosne-Romanée.
This 11-hectare domaine embraces a wide range of appellations, from Chambolle to Charmes-Chambertin. The wines are not that dense or extracted, but they have a natural ease of expression that is very satisfying. Dependable quality.

Coste-Caumartin ☆–☆☆
Pommard. www.costecaumartin.neuf.fr
A good source of full-bodied yet not over-tannic Pommard, especially from the monopoly *premier cru*, Clos des Boucherottes.

Domaine de Courcel ☆☆–☆☆☆
Pommard. www.domaine-de-courcel.com
The Courcels have made Pommard here for 400 years. Their eight-hectare domaine includes the five-hectare Grand Clos des Epenots within the *premier cru* Epenots, and one hectare of Rugiens. These *premiers crus* need a decade of cellaring to shed their stubborn tannins and subdued fruit. In great vintages such as 2005 the wines are stunning, but lesser years can be too extracted for their – and our – good.

Pierre Damoy ☆☆–☆☆☆
Gevrey-Chambertin. www.domaine-pierre-damoy.com
The biggest single share of Chambertin and Clos de Bèze (six hectares) belongs to the Damoy family. Yet the wines were indifferent until Pierre Damoy took over in 1992 and ended the domaine's Rip van Winkle phase. He ruthlessly cut yields and moved towards Biodynamism. The result was dense tannic wines that were impressive but severe. Over the years the style has moderated and has more vigour, although some 2004s and 2005s were marred by discernible alcohol. As well as a host of *grands crus*, Damoy makes excellent village wine from his monopole Clos du Tamisot.

Vincent Dancer ☆☆–☆☆☆
Chassagne-Montrachet. www.vincentdancer.com
Dancer's vineyards are equally divided between Chassagne, Meursault, and Pommard – and he is equally adept in all three. A fine source.

Deux Montille ☆☆–☆☆☆
Volnay.
Négociant house set up in 2003 by Etienne de Montille (see Domaine de Montille) and his sister Alix. Intense and concentrated wines, mostly Côte de Beaune.

Doudet-Naudin ☆☆
Savigny. www.doudet-naudin.com
A house associated with old-fashioned, very dark-coloured, concentrated, almost jammy wines that have had a great following in Britain in the past. They last, and 20-year-old bottles can be richly velvety and full of character. Lately the style has been more in tune with today's taste for greater freshness. Its organic 12-hectare domaine includes *premiers crus* in Savigny and Beaune Clos du Roi, and *grands crus* in Corton-Charlemagne and Corton-Maréchaudes.

Joseph Drouhin ☆☆–☆☆☆☆
Beaune. www.drouhin.com
A leading négociant (founded in 1880) with one of the biggest domaines in Burgundy, with 31 hectares of *grands* and *premiers crus* in the Côte d'Or and a further 38 in Chablis. By 2007 all but a handful of Chablis vineyards were being cultivated Biodynamically. Robert Drouhin has now ceded control to his very able children. The whole gamut of Drouhin wines is made very conscientiously, rising to the appropriate peaks and never falling below fine quality in the *grands crus*. The speciality of the house is the excellent Beaune Clos des Mouches: long-lived, full-bodied wine, red and white. Drouhin also has sole rights on the superb Montrachet of the Marquis de Laguiche.

MARC DE BOURGOGNE & CASSIS

The pulpy residue of skins, pips, and stalks left in the press after the juice has been run off is often distilled to produce a spirit known as *marc*. The clear spirit is matured in oak to give it colour and, with luck, a little finesse. Most *marc* is made by growers for private consumption. Some of the larger houses, such as Bouchard Père & Fils and Louis Latour, make carefully aged commercial versions. There are also high-priced versions aged for many years in new oak, from prestigious domaines such as de Vogüé. Cassis is an alcoholic blackcurrant liqueur that softens the sharpness of white wine – in Burgundy, usually Aligoté – in a proportion of one of cassis to three or four of wine. The resulting drink is sometimes called Kir after a brand of cassis developed by Canon Félix Kir, one-time mayor of Dijon.

The Drouhins are wary about excessive new oak, and take the *élevage* very seriously, air-drying their own wood before cooperage. The house style gives preference to finesse, so those more used to rich, extracted red burgundies are sometimes disappointed by the Drouhin wines. But they age very well and gain in complexity, as anyone who has tasted a mature Griottes-Chambertin or Musigny can confirm. Drouhin was the first Burgundian to plant Pinot Noir in the USA – in Oregon's Willamette Valley (q.v.).

Drouhin-Laroze ☆☆☆
Gevrey-Chambertin. www.drouhin-laroze.com
Since 2001 Philippe Drouhin has been making the most of a great collection of *grands crus* including Clos de Bèze, Clos de Vougeot, Bonnes Mares, and Chapelle-Chambertin.

David Duband ☆☆
Chavannes.
Ambitious and oaky wines from a palatte of Côte de Nuits vineyards.

Robert Dubois ☆
Nuits-St-Georges.
A family estate with 22 hectares, including Clos de Vougeot and the *premiers crus* Les Porêts and Clos des Argillières. The wines can be chunky and tough.

Dubreuil-Fontaine ☆–☆☆
Pernand-Vergelesses. www.dubreuil-fontaine.com
The Dubreuils have run this 20-hectare family property for generations, and Christine Gruère-Dubreuil is the latest generation. Rich in Corton *grands crus*, red and white, Pommard Epenots, and the one-hectare Clos Berthet in the village of Pernand.

Claude Dugat ☆☆☆
Gevrey-Chambertin.
Claude Dugat has a 3.5-hectare domaine making wines of the highest class. *Premiers* and *grands crus* (Griottes-Chambertin, Charmes-Chambertin) are aged entirely in new oak.

Dugat-Py ☆☆☆☆
Gevrey-Chambertin. www.dugat-py.com
Bernard Dugat makes impressive wine from seven hectares of mostly very old vines from Vosne-Romanée to Gevrey, where he has *grands crus* in Mazis and Charmes-Chambertin. Like his cousin Claude (q.v.), he ages his top wines entirely in new oak.

Dujac ☆☆☆–☆☆☆☆
Morey-St-Denis. www.dujac.com
Jacques Seysses is the "Jac" of the name. Rather to his surprise, since he is an ex-banker who turned winemaker in 1969, he is widely regarded as a mentor by dozens of Burgundy's best winemakers. Clos de la Roche, where he has two hectares, is usually the best wine, but Bonnes Mares is becoming better with every year, as the vines age. There are also *premiers crus* from Chambolle and Gevrey-Chambertin, plus *grands crus* Charmes-Chambertin and Echézeaux. In 2005 parcels were purchased in Vosne Malconsorts, Romanée-St Vivant, and Clos de Bèze. There is also a smidgin of rare white Morey Monts Luisants.

Seysses has always experimented tirelessly, in the vineyard as well as the winery, and has few preconceived ideas. His methods are essentially noninterventionist: retaining stems in most vintages, using new barrels, never filtering. The result is elegance with depth, as red burgundy should be. Dujac wines are never overtly tannic or dark, as Seysses favours finesse over extraction. The wines seem too exquisite to age well, but 30-year-old bottles have remained fresh and delightful. The Seysses sons are now continuing the meticulous tradition established almost 40 years ago.

René Engel
See Domaine d'Eugénie.

Sylvie Esmonin ☆☆–☆☆☆
Gevrey-Chambertin.
This estate only began bottling in 1989, after Sylvie completed her studies and returned to the family domaine. The top wine is Clos St Jacques, where she owns 1.6 hectares.

Domaine d'Eugénie
Vosne-Romanée.
The former Domaine Engel until Philippe Engel's unexpected death in 2005. A year later the property was bought by Francois Pinault of Château Latour. The domaine of seven hectares includes 1.5 in Clos Vougeot and plots in Grands-Echézeaux, Echézeaux, and Vosne-Romanée. The Engel wines were fine, masculine, and powerful; the Eugénie wines have yet to be tasted.

Faiveley ☆☆–☆☆☆☆
Nuits-St-Georges. www.bourgognes-faiveley.com
The Faiveleys, an unbroken family succession since 1825, own one of the biggest domaines in Burgundy: some 130 hectares divided among 35 appellations in the Côte d'Or alone. Seventy-five hectares are in Rully and Mercurey, where their 6.3 hectare monopole Clos des Myglands is their best-known wine, and Clos du Roi usually their best wine. As for *grands crus*, Faiveley can boast of substantial holdings in Mazis, Latricières, and Clos de Bèze, well as Clos Vougeot, Corton-Charlemagne, and Corton. Recent acquisitions have given Faiveley substantial holdings in Puligny-Montrachet, but the négociant arm of the business continues to flourish. During the early 1990s the wines seemed almost too dense and solidly structured, but today the balance is much finer. These are wines built to last, and they do. In 2006 François Faiveley handed over the domaine to his son Erwan.

Jean-Philippe Fichet ☆☆–☆☆☆
Meursault.
Mostly village wines but made with uncompromising purity and concentration. Tesson is usually the top wine.

Fougeray de Beauclair ☆
Marsannay.
Although based far to the north, this estate owns 1.5 hectares of Bonnes Mares, from which it produces a good but usually not outstanding wine, imbued with new oak.

Jean-Marie Fourrier ☆☆–☆☆☆
Gevrey-Chambertin.

A change of generations in 1997 led to a marked improvement at this ten-hectare domaine. The one *grand cru* (Griottes-Chambertin, with 90-year-old vines) is often rivalled by the svelte and concentrated Clos St Jacques. Recent vintages have been outstanding, with great depth of fruit.

Jean-Noël Gagnard ☆☆☆–☆☆☆☆
Chassagne-Montrachet. www.domaine-gagnard.com
Gagnard's daughter Caroline Lestimé makes the wines here, from 7.5 hectares of splendid Chassagne vineyards, including a fine parcel of Bâtard. They are utterly consistent, with a vigorous, limey character that is appealing young, yet the wines age very well. An excellent source.

Alex Gambal ☆☆
Beaune. www.alexgambal.com
Gambal, from Washington DC, came to Burgundy in the early 1990s and in 1996 set up his own small négociant business, which is flourishing. At present his best wines tend to be from Chassagne-Montrachet.

Jean-Michel Gaunoux ☆☆
Meursault. www.gaunoux.com
Jean-Michel's ten-hectare domaine includes *premier cru* Goutte d'Or, as well as Volnay Clos des Chênes. The Meursaults are pure and not too oaky.

Michel Gaunoux ☆☆
Pommard.
Half of Gaunoux's ten hectares are in Pommard *premier cru* with the biggest part in Epenots and the best in Rugiens. The wine is firm, robust, and long-lived.

Géantet-Pansiot ☆☆☆
Gevrey-Chambertin. www.geantet-pansiot.com
Vincent Géantet presides over a 15-hectare domaine endowed with many very old vines. He sees little point in using a high proportion of new oak to age the wine, which are ripe and fleshy, with the one *grand cru*, Charmes-Chambertin, showing additional layers of elegance and length of flavour.

Pierre Gelin ☆
Fixin. www.domaine-pierregelin.com
Gelin has ownership of parcels in Clos de Bèze and Mazis-Chambertin, as well as the Fixin monopole Clos Napoléon. Quality has been middling in recent vintages.

Germain Père et Fils ☆☆–☆☆☆
Chorey-lès-Beaune. www.chateau-de-chorey.com
Benoit Germain's turreted medieval château, just north of Beaune, has five hectares in Chorey and seven in Beaune *premier cru*, where some parcels date from 1948. His Beaune includes Teurons, Cent Vignes, Vignes Franches, Cras, and Boucherottes. These are surprisingly serious and long-lived wines from these often overlooked sites. The proportion of new oak is high, even for the Chorey. Cuvée Tante Berthe is a selection of old vines from the *premiers crus*, aged entirely in new oak.

Vincent Girardin ☆☆–☆☆☆
Santenay. www.vincentgirardin.com
Girardin owns 18 hectares in appellations as varied as Rully,

Echézeaux, and Corton-Charlemagne, as well as Santenay itself. In addition he buys in grapes for his flourishing négociant business. These are modern-style burgundies, with a large dose of new oak, even for simpler wines such as Bourgogne Blanc. But Girardin is a skilled winemaker, and these offer great satisfaction.

Camille Giroud ☆☆☆
Beaune. www.camillegiroud.com
An extraordinary house founded in Beaune in 1865 and specializing in wines intended for very long ageing. In 2002, the company was bought by a group of American investors, with David Croix as the skilled winemaker.

The range has been expanded to include *grands crus* such as Corton Clos du Roi and Chambertin. Superb quality since 2004.

Henri Gouges ☆☆☆–☆☆☆☆
Nuits-St-Georges. www.gouges.com
In many minds and for many years the top grower of Nuits, with almost all his 15 hectares in the *premiers crus*, including the whole of the Clos des Porrets. During the 1980s, the property went through a bad patch, but has fully recovered, often producing wines close to *grand cru* quality: powerful, slow to develop, and long in the finish. There is also a rare white Pinot Noir from vines that have mutated in the vineyard.

Alain Gras ☆
St-Romain.
From his 12-hectare domaine, Alain Gras produces some of the best wines – red and white – from this often forgotten village.

Albert Grivault ☆☆☆
Meursault.
A small five-hectare domaine focused around the monopole Clos des Perrières, which gives rich but racy wines with a strong personality.

Jean Grivot ☆☆☆–☆☆☆☆
Vosne-Romanée. www.domainegrivot.fr
Etienne Grivot (son of Jean) is a deeply dedicated grower with a number of small parcels of exceptionally good land – 16 hectares in 21 appellations. The holdings include 1.9 hectares in Clos Vougeot and four in Vosne-Romanée, notably the excellent *premier cru* Beaumonts and bits of Suchots and Brûlées, which are sandwiched between the *grands crus* Richebourg and Echézeaux.

In the late 1980s, the wines were too dense and extracted and even lacked *typicité*, but Etienne Grivot has corrected this, and they are now superb: very concentrated, yet not too heavy or dense. The fruit quality is vivid without flashiness, and these are clearly wines that will age very well.

Robert Groffier ☆☆☆
Morey-St-Denis.
An excellent eight-hectare domaine in the best sites of Bonnes Mares, Clos de Bèze, and above all the owner's favourite: Chambolle-Musigny Les Amoureuses and Les Sentiers. Delicious wines but very expensive.

Anne Gros ☆☆☆–☆☆☆☆
Vosne-Romanée. www.anne-gros.com
A small domaine of only six hectares, but the vineyards are fabulous: 0.6 hectares of Richebourg, 0.9 of Clos Vougeot, and a little Echézeaux and Chambolle-Musigny. So are the wines, which are unctuous and toasty yet with underlying finesse.

Michel Gros ☆☆☆
Vosne-Romanée. www.domaine-michel-gros.com
After Jean Gros retired in 1995, his son Michel took over running this domaine. At the same time another son, Bernard, became responsible for Domaine Gros Frère et Soeur, while daughter Anne-Françoise (at Domaine A-F Gros) and niece Anne (q.v.) began to make excellent wines at their share of the domaine. Here the best-known wine is the monopole Clos des Réas, a walled vineyard of over two hectares. These are wines of ripeness and charm rather than power.

Antonin Guyon ☆–☆☆
Savigny-lès-Beaune. www.guyon-bourgogne.com
A very substantial domaine of 50 hectares, with a remarkable spread of good sites, so it is strange that the name is not better known. Its Cortons are its particular pride. The wines can be hard-edged when young, but age well.

Hudelot-Noëllat ☆☆–☆☆☆
Chambolle-Musigny.
Well-reputed 11-hectare estate, endowed with parcels in Clos Vougeot, Richebourg, and Romanée-St-Vivant, and *premiers crus* in Chambolle-Musigny and Nuits. These are perfumed, concentrated, and well balanced wines.

Louis Jadot ☆☆–☆☆☆☆
Beaune. www.louisjadot.com
Although the American concern Kobrand owns this firm, the previous owners, the Gagey family, continue to run the property. The domaine of Louis Jadot now covers 78 hectares, including the original holding, the 2.7 hectare Clos des Ursules in Les Vignes Franches.

In Beaune, it also has substantial holdings in various other *premiers crus*. In Aloxe-Corton it has vineyards in Corton Pougets (*grand cru*) and Corton-Charlemagne; in Puligny-Montrachet parcels of Les Folatières and Chevalier-Montrachet. Jadot also controls 70 hectares in Beaujolais, producing wines of excellent quality including oak-aged examples. Since 1985, the company has purchased the Chassagne grapes of Domaine du Duc de Magenta, and the wine is sold under that label. The brilliant white wines are the greatest pride: especially the Corton-Charlemagne or Chevalier-Montrachet.

Jadot reds are equally reliable, thanks to the passionate care since 1970 of winemaker Jacques Lardière, shining example of a grower-cum-négociant.

Patrick Javillier ☆☆
Meursault. www.patrickjavillier.com
Ten hectares of mostly village wines and impressive Corton-Charlemagne. The various Bourgogne Blanc wines have a lot of personality and should not be overlooked.

Jayer-Gilles ☆☆–☆☆☆
Magny-les-Villers.
Gilles Jayer is the most acclaimed grower of the Hautes-Côtes, with a fondness for new oak.

Jessiaume ☆
Santenay. www.domaine-jessiaume.com
A 14-hectare estate with vines in *premiers crus* in Volnay and Beaune as well as Santenay. In 2006 the property was bought by Scotsman Sir David Murray, and the 2007s are fresh and distinctive.

François Jobard ☆☆☆
Meursault.
Everybody in Meursault has great respect for the quiet, lean, wiry François Jobard, than whom no grower is more meticulous. Superb Meursault from such vineyards as Poruzots, Charmes, and Genevrières. The wines are naturally high in acidity, and the cellars are exceptionally cool, which means that these bottles are slow to evolve, and definitely repay keeping.

Rémi Jobard ☆☆☆
Meursault.
Since François's nephew, Rémi, took over in 1997, quality has soared, with brilliant Meursault *premiers crus* from Genevrières and Charmes. Rapidly becoming as reliable a source for long-lived wines as François Jobard (q.v.).

Vincent and Francois Jouard ☆☆
Chassagne-Montrachet.
Eleven hectares of choice vineyards, the finest being Clos de la Truffière and Bâtard-Montrachet.

DOMAINES V. NÉGOCIANTS

Ambitious and successful estates find themselves in a quandary. Demand now exceeds supply, as the average domaine's holdings are finite, and it is difficult to expand production to meet that growing demand. The price of land has long been too high for estates to buy more than the occasional few rows. Nor do properties come on the market very often.

The solution is to buy grapes from other growers and set up a small négociant business alongside the domaine's estate-bottled production. There is nothing wrong with this, except it can be difficult for a consumer to know whether he is buying, and drinking, an estate wine or a négociant wine. Some producers have created a separate label for their négociant wines. Morey Blanc is the négociant label for Pierre Morey in Meursault, and Dujac Père et Fils the equivalent for Domaine Dujac. However, some properties simply integrate the purchased grapes into the domaine's production. This may not affect the quality of the wine, but as a commercial procedure it does lack transparency.

Labouré-Roi ☆–☆☆
Nuits-St-Georges.
A négociant with a reputation as one of the most consistent and reliable at quite modest prices. But the wines do not dazzle.

Michel Lafarge ☆☆☆☆
Volnay.
An old family estate that survived the doldrums of Burgundy in the mid-1930s by the initiative of Michel Lafarge's grandfather, who bottled his wine and attacked the Paris market with it in person. Of the 12 hectares, most are in Volnay, but there are also some in Meursault and Beaune Grèves. The *premiers crus* include Clos des Chênes (always outstanding here) and the monopole site Clos du Château des Ducs. Painstaking viticulture and vinification, and a judicious use of one-third new barrels produce elegant and long-lived wines, surely the best in Volnay. Since 2000, the estate has been Biodynamic and is now run by Michel's son, Frédéric.

Comtes Lafon ☆☆☆☆
Meursault. www.comtes-lafon.fr
One of the rare producers to excel with both red and white wines. Dominique Lafon took over as full-time winemaker here in 1984, producing sublime Meursault from the *premier cru* Charmes, Genevrières, and Perrières vineyards plus their own "back garden", Clos de la Barre, and a tiny amount of *grand cru* Montrachet.

Since 1999 the vineyards have all been Biodynamically cultivated. His reds are mostly from Volnay: Champans, Clos des Chênes, and especially a large holding of Santenots-du-Milieu, to which some Monthélie has been added. Other red burgundies can match, even surpass, Lafon's, excellent though they are, but when it comes to white burgundy there is surely no one to match Dominique Lafon.

Laleure Piot ☆–☆☆
Pernand-Vergelesses. www.laleure-piot.com
The best wines from this ten-hectare domaine are usually the Cortons, red and white.

Lamarche ☆☆–☆☆☆
Vosne-Romanée. www.domaine-lamarche.com
A fourth-generation family domaine with the good fortune to own the monopole of La Grande Rue, a narrow strip of 1.6 hectares running up the hill between Romanée-Conti and La Tâche. A bottle of the 1961 at 21 years old was a miracle of subtle sensuality: understated beside La Tâche, but in its quieter way among the great bottles of my experience. The rest of the 11-hectare property includes parcels of Clos de Vougeot, Grands-Echézeaux and the Vosne-Romanée *premiers crus* Malconsorts and Suchots. Dull wines until the mid-1990s, when, perhaps stimulated by the promotion of La Grande Rue to *grand cru* status in 1990, quality improved significantly.

Domaine des Lambrays ☆☆☆☆
Morey-St-Denis. www.lambrays.com
The domaine owns almost the entire *grand cru* Clos des Lambrays. Thierry Brouin makes the wine, with the encouragement of German tycoon Gunter Freund, who bought the property in 1996. Since 1996, quality has been stellar. The domaine also produces small quantities of Puligny Folatières and Cailleret, superb but expensive.

Hubert and Olivier Lamy ☆☆–☆☆☆☆
St-Aubin.
www.domainehubertlamy.com
Ever since Olivier Lamy took over the family domaine in 1995, quality has soared. Even the red wines from St-Aubin, rarely exceptional, are very good here, though not quite at the level of the delicious white *premiers crus*. Around 30 per cent new oak is employed.

Louis Latour ☆–☆☆☆
Beaune. www.louislatour.com
One of Burgundy's names to conjure with, founded in 1797 and since 1867 owned and directed, father-to-son, by Latours called Louis. The centre of its domaine is the Château de Grancey at Aloxe-Corton, one of the first large-scale, purpose-built wineries in France. The domaine totals 50 hectares, of which 35 are in Corton and Aloxe-Corton, including 10 of Corton-Charlemagne and a two-hectare monopole of *grand cru* Clos de la Vigne au Saint. Other *grands crus* include Romanée-St-Vivant and 0.5 hectares of Chevalier-Montrachet Les Demoiselles.

Latour is most celebrated for its white wines, above all Corton-Charlemagne. They are powerful and must be kept. Latour stubbornly continues to employ an unusual method of vinification for the reds, subjecting the must briefly to a form of flash pasteurization. This may account for the fact that the red wines are considerably lighter and less complex than the splendid whites.

Domaine wines account for one-tenth of its production. Latour's selections of other wines, particularly whites, are reliable. Montagny is a specialty to look out for, and the Chardonnay Vin de Pays de l'Ardèche is remarkable in character and volume.

Dominique Laurent ☆☆☆
Nuits-St-Georges.
This former *pâtissier* is passionate about what he considers authentic burgundy: wines made from old and unproductive vines. To this end, this unusual négociant works very closely with proprietors who own exceptional parcels of vines, and pays top prices. Although Laurent has started to participate in the winemaking at some estates, his real gift is as an *éleveur*. He has his own cooperage, and his wines spend at least 18 months on the fine lees in barrels, with a high percentage of new oak. Bottling is done directly from barrel.

Romanée-Conti vineyard, Vosne Romanée

This is old-fashioned winemaking at its best, and the results are impressive: concentrated, rich, and dense, with numerous *cuvées* that demonstrate the variety to be found in a single commune such as Nuits-St-Georges.

Production of each wine tends to be tiny. Laurent has developed a cult following, and although some doubt has been cast about the ageing potential of some of the wines, they are nonetheless bold and personal expressions of burgundy.

Domaine Leflaive ☆☆☆☆
Puligny-Montrachet. www.leflaive.fr
The grand old man of Puligny-Montrachet, Vincent Leflaive, established a fabulous reputation for his Puligny-Montrachet from such vineyards as Clavoillons, Combettes, and Pucelles plus *grands crus* Bâtard-, Bienvenue-Bâtard-, and Chevalier-Montrachet. The jewel in the crown, Le Montrachet, has now been added.

In Vincent's later days quality slipped, but his daughter, Anne-Claude, assisted by a revitalized team and a firm belief in Biodynamic methods, has rapidly restored the image of this great domaine. As a leader of the Biodynamic movement, she also puts her name to some out-of-the-way examples of the creed – even in Muscadet. All are worth trying.

Olivier Leflaive ☆☆–☆☆☆
Puligny-Montrachet. www.olivier-leflaive.com
Nephew of Vincent Leflaive, Olivier is now the most highly regarded négociant in the area, thanks to winemaker Franck Grux, with brilliant Pulignys and excellent St-Romain, St-Aubin, Auxey-Duresses, etc. – model wines from the Côte de Beaune. Leflaive is best-known for his stylish white wines, and deservedly so, but the red wines, mostly found on the domestic market, can be good, too.

Domaine Leroy ☆☆☆☆
Vosne-Romanée. www.domaineleroy.com
Mme. Lalou Bize-Leroy, a restless and ambitious woman of extraordinary energy, was already co-directing the Domaine de la Romanée-Conti, as well as running her family's négociant business Maison Leroy (q.v.), when she began to acquire excellent vineyards by buying up moribund domaines such as Charles Noëllat.

The expansion of her domaine (it now encompasses 22.5 hectares) was a contributory factor to her bust-up with and eventual dismissal from the DRC in 1992. Undaunted, she continued in her purpose of establishing a great domaine.

She now has a range of *grands crus* scarcely matched by any other property in Burgundy, and a quiver-full of excellent premiers crus. Since the early 1990s, she has adopted Biodynamism with a passion, and insists on yields so low that they can scarcely be economical. Most of the wines are aged for 18 months in new oak, yet such is their concentration that oakiness is not an obvious characteristic of the wines.

A few hours tasting the entire range in her cellars, a privilege granted to few, is a dazzling and humbling experience, as one perfect wine succeeds another. If Domaine Leroy is now among the very top domaines of France, you can be sure that the prices reflect this.

Maison Leroy ☆☆☆
Auxey-Duresses.
Mme. Lalou Bize-Leroy inherited this family négociant business in 1955, and specialized in releasing wines only when fully mature. They need patience, and they cost a fortune. The self-styled "Gardienne des Grands Millésimes" is believed to have a stock of 2.5 million bottles. Bottle variation can lead to some disappointments.

Chantal Lescure ☆☆–☆☆☆
Nuits-St-Georges. www.domaine-lescure.com
This estate was founded in 1975 and has 18 hectares of vineyards from Chambolle to Volnay. It used to be allied to the négociant house Labouré-Roi, but that arrangement ceased in 1996, when a new team took over. In 1999, a new winery was built. The investments have paid off and the wines are now very impressive, the Vosne Suchots often outshining the Clos Vougeot.

Domaine du Comte Liger-Belair ☆☆☆
Vosne-Romanée. www.liger-belair.fr
Until 2000, the wines of this estate were marketed by Bouchard Père & Fils (q.v.), but now the domaine is making and distributing its wines itself. The nine hectares of vineyards are mostly in Vosne, and include a monopole site, the Clos du Château. Magnificent *grand cru* La Romanée and Echézeaux, but wildly expensive.

Thibault Liger-Belair ☆☆–☆☆☆
Nuits-St-Georges. www.domaine-liger-belair.com
Not to be confused with the grander Domaine du Comte Liger-Belair (q.v.), owned by a distant relative. But with each vintage the wines here, which are produced Biodynamically, grow in confidence and personality. Splendid Richebourg.

Hubert Lignier
Morey-St-Denis.
Until his untimely death in 2003, Hubert Lignier's son Romain made great strides, producing wines that were rich and concentrated, and underpinned by a fair amount of new oak. Disagreements between Romain's widow and Hubert will need to be settled before the estate can be re-assessed.

Château de la Maltroye ☆☆☆
Chassagne-Montrachet.
The source of some outstanding white Chassagne under the monopole label of the château. In addition, the 15-hectare estate has a small piece of Bâtard-Montrachet as well as red-wine vineyards in Chassagne Clos St-Jean.

Matrot ☆☆–☆☆☆
Meursault. www.matrot.com
A 19-hectare domaine now run by Thierry Matrot. It is best-known for its whites from the Meursault section of Blagny, and for Meursault *premiers crus* Charmes and Perrières, and Puligny *premiers crus* Combettes and Chalumeaux. There are also 1.5 hectares of red Volnay-Santenots and an unusual red Blagny from La Pièce Sous le Bois, which makes a vivid, somewhat harsh wine, as a change from the gentler Volnay.

The whites can be austere in their youth, but with age they become harmonious and complex.

Louis Max ☆–☆☆☆
Nuits-St-Georges. www.louismax.com
A négociant house founded in 1859 by Russian immigrant
Louis Max, and now run by his descendant Laurent Max.
In the 1990s, the company improved its performance and
packaging and began building up a portfolio of its own
vineyards. *Grands crus* such as Charmes-Chambertin can
be impressive.

Méo-Camuzet ☆☆☆–☆☆☆☆
Vosne-Romanée. www.meo-camuzet.com
For many years, Jean Méo leased out his vineyards, but since
1983 they have been back in family hands, and his son, Jean-
Nicolas, at first advised by legendary winemaker Henri Jayer,
has been turning out majestic and very rich wines from some
outstanding vineyards.

The *grands crus* here are Richebourg, Echézeaux, Clos
Vougeot, and Corton. There are two *premiers crus* in Nuits,
and three in Vosne, including the rare and wondrous Cros
Parantoux. Numerous tastings since the late 1980s have shown
how well these wines can age, and how complex they become.

Prince Florent de Mérode ☆☆
Ladoix-Serrigny.
Although based in Serrigny, most of this domaine's holdings
are in Corton, with nearly four hectares of *grands crus*. After
many years of mediocrity, these wines are now made in a rich,
full-bodied style.

Château de Meursault ☆☆
Meursault. www.meursault.com
A 60-hectare domaine bought in 1973 by the négociant
Patriarche of Beaune and turned into a showplace for visitors.
The Meursault *premiers crus* are blended and sold as Château
de Meursault. There are also red wines from *premiers crus* in
Pommard, Savigny, and Beaune. Prices are high.

Moillard
Nuits-St-Georges.
This respectable firm went through complex changes over
the past few years, with the sale of some of its excellent vine-
yards, and then in 2008 the sale of the négociant business to
Vincent Sauvestre.

Mongeard-Mugneret ☆☆–☆☆☆
Vosne-Romanée. www.mongeard.com
A 30-hectare estate making sound and long-lived Vosne
Suchots, Echézeaux, Grands-Echézeaux, Vougeot, and
Richebourg, as well as a slate of *premiers crus* from Vosne,
Nuits, Vougeot, and Savigny.

René Monnier ☆☆
Meursault.
The Monnier family has substantial holdings in Meursault
Chevalières and the *premiers crus* Charmes, Beaune Cent
Vignes, and Toussaints and Puligny Folatières. In general,
the whites have more bite and character than the reds.

Hubert de Montille ☆☆☆
Volnay.
This 15-hectare property owned by a Dijon lawyer is now run

by his son, Etienne. The vineyards are scattered among the
best vineyards of Volnay (Champans, Taille-Pieds, Mitans),
Pommard (Epenots, Rugiens, Pézerolles), Corton, and
Puligny-Montrachet. Both the Pommard and Volnay are
richly coloured, flavoursome, wines that age well.

De Montille opposes *chaptalization*, so the character of the
wines can be lean and rather tough in their youth. More than
any other Volnays, they need ten years in bottle to develop
their remarkable complexity – a useful lesson.

Strength does not equal longevity. Under Etienne de
Montille the farming is Biodynamic and the style of the wines
has become less austere but no less flavoury and elegant.

Bernard Morey ☆☆
Chassagne-Montrachet.
An old family domaine of 15 hectares, largely in Chassagne
and almost equally divided between white and red wines.
The wines are fruity and reliable, but not the most elegant.

Marc Morey ☆☆–☆☆☆
Chassagne-Montrachet.
Morey's son-in-law, Bernard Mollard, has been making
he wines here for 15 years. There are a number of *premiers
crus*, and small parcels in Bâtard-Montrachet and Chevalier-
Montrachet. In general, the style of the wines is fruity,
balanced, and accessible.

Pierre Morey ☆☆☆
Meursault. www.morey-meursault.com
Morey has been the winemaker for Domaine Leflaive (q.v.)
since 1989, and produces fine Meursault and Bâtard-
Montrachet from his own Biodynamic 11 hectares. He
also buys in grapes for his négociant label, Morey Blanc.

Albert Morot ☆☆–☆☆☆
Beaune.
Seven hectares of Beaune *premiers crus* in Teurons, Grèves,
Cent Vignes, Toussaints, Bressandes, and Marconnets and
two at Savigny-Vergelesses Clos la Bataillère. Since 2000
quality has improved, with greater selection at harvest and
up to 50 per cent new oak. A fine property through which
to discover the characters of top-level Beaune.

Denis Mortet ☆☆☆–☆☆☆☆
Gevrey-Chambertin. www.denis-mortet.com
Denis Mortet was probably the best of the modernist
winemakers of the village, practising essentially organic
viticulture, harvesting only very ripe grapes, and using
a great deal of new oak. The wines were rich, dark,
concentrated, and finely balanced, and all benefitting from
cellaring. Mortet committed suicide in 2006, but his son
Arnaud is maintaining high standards.

Thierry Mortet ☆☆
Gevrey-Chambertin. www.domainethierrymortet.fr
Thierry has been somewhat overshadowed by the success of
his older brother, Denis (the family domaine was divided in
1992). The wines are good, with sweet fruit and spiciness.

Mugneret-Gibourg ☆☆☆
Vosne-Romanée. www.mugneret-gibourg.com

Of the seven Mugneret estates in Vosne, this is probably the finest. After the death of Georges Mugneret (some wines still appear under his label), the property has been managed by his widow Jacqueline and her two daughters. Yields are low at this nine-hectare domaine, and the proportion of new oak barrels varies. These are succulent wines: firm Vosne, delicious Feussellottes with all the charm of Chambolle, exotic Echézeaux, more tannic Clos Vougeot, and some rich Ruchottes-Chambertin. An impeccable source.

Lucien Muzard ☆–☆☆
Santenay. www.domainemuzard.com
This family estate of 16 hectares produces splendid, gently oaky wines at a fair price.

Michel Niellon ☆☆–☆☆☆
Chassagne-Montrachet.
A small but highly regarded estate, much in demand in the United States. The style is ripe and rounded, but, other than the *grands crus*, these are rarely wines for long cellaring.

Domaine Parent ☆☆
Pommard. www.parent-pommard.com
A 15-hectare domaine founded in 1750, and best-known for its firm Pommards and medium-bodied wines from Volnay and Beaune. In 1999, the domaine was split, with François Parent vinifying his one-third share separately. He also makes the wines for his wife's domaine, A-F Gros in Vosne-Romanée.

Patriarche ☆–☆☆
Beaune. www.patriarche.com
Possibly the biggest firm in Burgundy (it claims to have the biggest cellars) with a history going back to 1780 and an annual production of 20 million bottles. Patriarche has a paradoxical image: on one hand, proprietor of the Château de Meursault (q.v.) and the Château de Marsannay, domaines that amount to 110 hectares, and regularly a major buyer at the Hospices de Beaune auctions; and on the other a brand which the snob in me would describe as definitely downmarket.

Its greatest success must be Kriter Brut de Brut, created in the early 1960s as a high-quality, non-appellation sparkling wine. Brand names include Père Patriarche and Cuvée Jean Baptiste.

Pavelot ☆☆
Savigny. www.domainepavelot.com
The Pavelots have been growers in Savigny since the eighteenth century. Their domaine comprises 12 hectares, a little under half of it in the *premier cru* vineyards of the slopes, with very old vines in Dominode. The wines are soundly made and consistent, but lack some excitement.

Domaine des Perdrix ☆☆–☆☆☆
Nuits-St-Georges. www.domaines-devillard.com
Rich, voluptuous, and often extracted wines from a 12-hectare domaine. Includes monopole site Aux Perdrix and Echézeaux.

Domaine de la Perrière ☆☆
Fixin.
The five-hectare domaine produces only one wine: the famous Fixin Clos de la Perrière, established by the Cistercian monks of Citeaux in the twelfth century. The original manor, its cellars, and the great press, 700 years old, are still here. Since 2005 owner Bénigne Joliet strives to reduce yields and realize the full potential of a vineyard reputed to be the equal of a Gevrey-Chambertin *grand cru*.

Perrot-Minot ☆☆–☆☆☆☆
Morey-St-Denis. www.perrot-minot.com
The finest site of this 14-hectare domaine is the 1.5-hectare parcel in Charmes-Chambertin, and there are two *premiers crus* in Chambolle-Musigny: Fuées and Combe d'Orveau. Christophe Perrot-Minot is a modernist, and his wines are fleshy and hedonistic – perhaps not very subtle, but undoubtedly concentrated.

Château de Pommard ☆–☆☆
Pommard. www.chateaudepommard.com
Since 2003 the property, with its renowned 20-hectare walled vineyard, has been owned by Maurice Giraud. He hired Philippe Charlopin of Gevrey-Chambertin as consultant winemaker.

Ponsot ☆☆–☆☆☆☆
Morey-St-Denis. www.domaine-ponsot.com
As well as top sites in Morey-St-Denis, this 12-hectare domaine has parcels in Chambertin, Charmes-Chambertin, and Clos de Vougeot. The top wine is the splendid Clos de

la Roche, concentrated, long-lived wine without recourse to new oak. White *premier cru* Morey Monts-Luisants is Ponsot's other specialty, made mostly from venerable Aligoté vines. Its high acidity demands bottle-age. At their best, Ponsot's wines are remarkable, but they can be dismayingly inconsistent.

Nicolas Potel ☆☆–☆☆☆☆
Nuits-St-Georges.
www.nicolas-potel.fr
Nicolas Potel grew up in Volnay as the heir-apparent of the Domaine Pousse d'Or (q.v.). But the premature death of his father and the sale of the estate in 1997 led to his departure. With a reservoir of goodwill among the growers of Burgundy, and their confidence in his rare skills as a winemaker with international experience, Potel set himself up as a négociant. In 2003 the négociant Labouré-Roi bought the company, but left Potel in charge. The winemaking is non-interventionist, and he seeks out parcels of old vines whenever possible, paying good prices. A huge range of wines means that quality can vary, but at his best Potel provides ripe, sensuous wines at a fair price.

Domaine de la Pousse d'Or ☆☆
Volnay. www.la-pousse-d-or.fr
A 15-hectare domaine focused on the *premiers crus* of Volnay, Pommard, and Santenay; recently supplemented with red

Traditional wine barrel, Château de Pommard, Pommard

grands crus in Corton. Its reputation, as high as any in the Côte de Beaune, was made by Gérard Potel. In 1997, Potel died unexpectedly and the domaine was sold. It has three monopoles in Volnay: Clos de la Bousse [sic] d'Or, Clos des 60 Ouvrées, and Clos d'Audignac. The new owner, Patrick Landanger, knew from the outset that Potel would be a hard act to follow, and his first vintages were disappointing. But quality is now improving, if not yet at the supremely elegant level established by Potel.

Jacques Prieur ☆☆☆
Meursault. www.prieur.com
One of Burgundy's most remarkable properties, with almost all its 21 hectares in great vineyards. In 1988 Jacques Prieur's grandson Martin teamed up with Maison Rodet to revive the property, but in the early 2000s Jean-Pierre Labruyère took control, retaining the gifted winemaker Nadine Gublin. The estate is lavishly endowed with vineyards in Clos Vougeot, Echezeaux, Chambertin, Musigny, Chevalier Montrachet, and Le Montrachet itself. Gublin's style is for powerful, extracted reds, and whites of dazzling intensity.

Château de Puligny-Montrachet ☆☆–☆☆☆
Puligny-Montrachet. www.chateaudepuligny.com
Since 2001 Etienne de Montille (of Domaine de Montille) has been given a free hand to run this handsome 20-hectare property with 23 appellations. The walled Clos du Château is a mere Bourgogne Blanc, but of fine quality, although inevitably surpassed by the *premiers crus* and the Chevalier-Montrachet.

Ramonet ☆☆☆
Chassagne-Montrachet.
A distinguished old name in Chassagne. This 17-hectare domaine produces long-lived Bâtard-, Bienvenues-Bâtard-Montrachet, and Le Montrachet, racy premier cru Chassagne from Les Ruchottes and other sites, and Chassagne village. The red wines are less famous but remarkably fine; Clos de la Boudriotte, Clos St-Jean, and red Chassagne village are as good as any red wines of the southern Côte de Beaune. The grand old man, Pierre Ramonet, died in 1995 and his grandsons, Noël and Jean-Claude, now make the wine.

Rapet ☆
Pernand-Vergelesses. www.domaine-rapet.com
A highly reputed 18-hectare domaine including parcels of Corton-Charlemagne and (red) *grand cru* Corton, and *premier cru* Pernand-Vergelesses. Dependable rather than stellar.

Remoissenet ☆☆
Beaune. www.remoissenet.com
Founded in 1877, a négociant house with a mixed reputation – whites generally better than reds – and sold to new American owners in 2005. The most prized wine is the Montrachet entrusted to Remoissenet by Baron Thénard, the second largest landowner in this supreme site.

Remoriquet ☆☆
Nuits-St-Georges. www.domaine-remoriquet.fr
The Remoriquets are an established family of growers (now headed by Gilles Remoriquet) in Nuits with *premiers crus* Les St-Georges, Rue de Chaux, Les Bousselots, and Les Damodes. This is a conservative domaine, using little new oak; but the wines are robust and age well.

Daniel Rion ☆☆
Nuits-St-Georges. www.domaine-daniel-rion.com
A 19-hectare domaine with a solid reputation, with vineyards in Vosne-Romanée, Chambolle-Musigny, and Clos Vougeot, as well as Nuits.

CRÉMANT

Three high-quality French white-wine regions successfully established a new appellation for their best-quality sparkling wine. The term crémant, originally used in Champagne for wines produced at about half the full sparkling-wine pressure, thus gently fizzing instead of frothing in the glass, has been borrowed (with the consent of Champagne, where the term is no longer in use) as a controlled term for these full-sparklers of high quality.

A new term was needed because the old one, mousseux, had acquired a pejorative ring; any old fizz made by industrial methods could (and can) use it. In contrast, crémant from Burgundy, the Loire, and Alsace have to be made with Champagne-type controls. Specifically, they concern the grape varieties used, the size of the crop, the way it is delivered to the press-house with the bunches undamaged, and the pressure that should be applied (with a limit of two-thirds of the weight of the grapes being extracted as juice). Thereafter, the Champagne-method rules apply, with the minimum time in bottle with the yeast being specified as nine months in Burgundy and Alsace and 12 in the Loire.

The result of these controls is a category of sparkling wine of good if rarely exceptional quality. The wines tend to be made from grapes of insufficient quality to fetch a decent price for still wines such as Bourgogne Blanc. Crémant from southern Burgundy tends to be fuller and richer than examples from northern areas such as the Yonne, just as Montagny is broader than Chablis. In 2005, total Crémant de Bourgogne production was over 12 million bottles: confirmation that the term crémant, in its new meaning, is well understood. Quality ranges from bland to rustic to stylish, and a number of producers, such as Albert Sounit in Rully, are making more serious *cuvées*.

Among the hundred or so concerns producing Crémant de Bourgogne are: Ambroise, Nuits-St-Georges; Blason de Bourgogne, Beaune; André Bonhomme, Mâcon; Louis Bouillot, Nuits-St-Georges; Cave d'Azé, Azé; Caves de Bailly, St-Bris-le-Vineux; Cave de Lugny, Lugny; Cave de Viré, Viré; Paul Chollet, Savigny; Bernard Cros, Cercot; Deliance; André Delorme, Rully; Roger Luquet, Fuissé; Moingeon, Beaune; Picamelot, Rully; Simonnet-Febvre, Chablis; Albert Sounit, Rully; Verret, St Bris-le-Vineux; Veuve Ambal, Beaune; Vitteau-Alberti, Rully

Patrice Rion ☆☆–☆☆☆
Nuits-St-Georges. www.patricerion.com
Established in 2001, when Rion sold his share of the family property, Daniel Rion (q.v.), to his brothers and set up on his own. The six hectares of vines are supplemented by a négociant business.

Domaine de la Romanée-Conti ☆☆☆☆
Vosne-Romanée.
See Romanée-Conti – A Great Burgundy Estate, page 107.

Nicolas Rossignol ☆☆–☆☆☆
Volnay. www.nicolas-rossignol.com

THE HOSPICES DE BEAUNE

The Hospices de Beaune has a unique role as a symbol of the continuity, the wealth, and the general benevolence of Burgundy. It was founded as a hospital for the sick, poor, and aged of Beaune in 1443 by the Chancellor to the Duke of Burgundy, Nicolas Rolin, and his wife Guigone de Salins. They endowed it with land in the Côte de Beaune for its income; a practice that has been followed ever since by rich growers, merchants, and other citizens. The Hospices now owns 62 hectares of vineyards and much more farmland. The wine from its scattered vineyard plots is made in *cuvées*, not necessarily consisting of the wine of a single climat but designed to be practicable to make and agreeable to drink. Each *cuvée* is named after an important benefactor of the Hospices.

There are 38 *cuvées*, all but one in the Côte de Beaune.

The wine is sold, *cuvée* by *cuvée* and cask by cask, at a public auction on the third Sunday of November in the market hall opposite the Hospices. The profits are spent on running the hospital, which now has every sort of modern equipment. Its original wards, chapel, and works of art are open to the public.

Buyers include merchants, restaurants, individuals, and syndicates from all over the world, who are attracted by the idea of supporting this ancient charity, and the publicity that accompanies it. The winemaking of the Hospices was much criticized in the early 1990s but is now back on course. However, it is exceedingly difficult to judge the wines so soon after the harvest, when buyers have to make

their choice. After the sale the wine passes into the hands of local merchants, who are responsible for its *élevage*. Not surprisingly, the upbringing of the wine is a major factor in its eventual quality.

The third weekend in November is the most important date in the Burgundy calendar, known as Les Trois Glorieuses from the three feasts which make it a stiff endurance test. On Saturday the "Chevaliers de Tastevin" hold a gala dinner at the Clos de Vougeot. On Sunday after the auction the dinner is at the Hospices, and Monday lunch is a wine-growers' feast known as the Paulée at Meursault: this last a gigantic bottle party, at which even the guests are expected to bring something interesting for all their neighbours to share.

Hospices de Beaune, Beaune

A new star in Volnay, with 12 hectares of excellent sites. A wonderfully vibrant collection in 2006.

Rossignol-Trapet ☆☆
Gevrey-Chambertin. www.rossignol-trapet.com
When Domaine Trapet (q.v.) was split in 1990, the Rossignols kept 14 hectares of superb vineyards, including 1.6 hectares of Chambertin. Sound and stylish wines, yet they never quite seem to do justice to the splendour of the domaine's *grands crus*.

Joseph Roty ☆☆☆
Gevrey-Chambertin
Reclusive and uncommunicative owners make lush, full-bodied wines from eight hectares of very old vines, almost all in Gevrey. His *grands crus* are all aged in new oak.

Emmanuel Rouget ☆☆☆
Flagey-Echézeaux
The nephew and inheritor of Henri Jayer's legendary estate, including *grand cru* Echézeaux, Vosne-Romanée *premiers crus* Beaumonts and Cros Parantoux, and Nuits-St-Georges. These are splendid wines (especially the Cros Parantoux), but very expensive.

Guy Roulot ☆☆–☆☆☆
Meursault. www.domaineroulot.com
This is a family domaine that owns 12 hectares, mostly in Meursault, including *premiers crus* Charmes and Perrières, but also village wines from excellent sites such as Tessons, Luchets, and Les Meix Chavaux. There are also vineyards in Auxey-Duresses and Monthélie. These are serious, well-judged wines, made with growing confidence and excellence since 1989 by Jean-Marc Roulot.

Georges Roumier ☆☆–☆☆☆☆
Chambolle-Musigny. www.roumier.com
Christophe Roumier took over the family property in 1982, and has raised it to the highest level. There are 12 hectares, mostly in Chambolle, but there is also a monopole *premier cru* in Morey-St-Denis (Clos de la Bussière), and some small parcels in Ruchottes- and Charmes-Chambertin. Although all his wines are classics of depth and harmony, his finest effort is invariably the Bonnes Mares, where he owns various parcels that amount to 1.45 hectares.

Armand Rousseau ☆☆☆☆
Gevrey-Chambertin. www.domaine-rousseau.com
Charles Rousseau is unquestionably the most respected grower of Chambertin. The 14-hectare property, now run by his son Eric, includes 2.2 hectares in Chambertin, 1.5 in Clos de Bèze, as well as parcels in Mazis and Charmes-Chambertin and in the Clos de la Roche in Morey, and (his particular pride) 2.2 hectares of Gevrey Clos St-Jacques. The wines might not be the most powerful in Burgundy, but their perfume and finesse are incomparable.

Etienne Sauzet ☆☆–☆☆☆☆
Puligny-Montrachet. www.etienne-sauzet.com
Etienne Sauzet died in 1975 and for almost 30 years the nine-hectare domaine has been run by his son-in-law,

Gérard Boudot. Family feuding among Sauzet's grandchildren led to the original domaine being divided, so Boudot has had to buy in grapes to make up for the loss of some vineyards.

The house style is to keep the wines on their lees for a year to develop flavour and fat. The main holding is in Puligny *premiers crus*, with about 1.5 hectares each of Combettes (the best-known wine) and Champ-Canet; and a small parcel of Bâtard-Montrachet. Although enjoyable young, the Sauzet Pulignys are even better at five or more years of age.

Comte Senard ☆☆
Beaune. www.domainesenard.com
Philippe Senard's nine-hectare domaine includes substantial holdings in Corton's *grands crus* of Corton, Clos du Roi, and Bressandes, and the entire two-hectare "Clos Meix". After a bad patch in the early 1990s, the wines are now fresh and vigorous, benefitting from a new modern winery.

Château de Monthelie ☆
Monthelie.
A small, old-fashioned but famous estate whose 11 hectares of old vines in Monthélie, long farmed Biodynamically, produce a red wine comparable with good Volnays. At their best, they are perfumed and elegant.

Tollot-Beaut ☆☆
Chorey-lès-Beaune.
A family property since 1880 with impeccable standards. Of a total of 24 hectares, one-third at Chorey and the remainder divided among various *premiers crus* of Beaune, Savigny, and Aloxe-Corton, with *grands crus from* Corton-Bressandes, Le Corton, and Corton-Charlemagne. No secrets here, but careful, traditional winemaking. The special pride of the house is in the Corton-Bressandes and Beaune Clos du Roi. The wines can seem light initially but they age well.

Château de la Tour ☆☆–☆☆☆
Vougeot. www.chateaudelatour.com
With six hectares in Clos de Vougeot, François Labet is by far its largest proprietor. As well as the regular bottling, there is a Cuvée Vieilles Vignes from vines planted in 1910. Often the regular wine is less dense and extracted.

Trapet ☆☆–☆☆☆
Gevrey-Chambertin. www.domaine-trapet.com
Jean Trapet and his son, Jean-Louis, now own half of the original Louis Trapet domaine which was divided in 1990. The viticulture has been Biodynamic since 1997. The pride of the house is still its Chambertin, made in the traditional way, and showing great delicacy and finesse.

Domaine des Varoilles ☆☆–☆☆☆
Gevrey-Chambertin. www.domaine-varoilles.com
A ten-hectare domaine once known for serious *vins de garde* that really must be matured. It takes its name from its *premier cru* Clos des Varoilles, planted by monks on the south-facing hill above Gevrey. The Clos du Couvent, Clos du Meix des Ouches, and La Romanée are other monopoles in Gevrey, besides parcels of Charmes- and Mazoyères-Chambertin, Bonnes Mares, and Clos de Vougeot. In recent vintages the wines have acquired more flesh to balance the firm tannins.

Michel Voarick ☆
Aloxe-Corton.
www.domaine-michel-voarick.com
A nine-hectare family domaine which includes farming
the famous Corton Cuvée Dr. Peste for the Hospices de
Beaune. Voarick owns 2.5 hectares of *grand cru* Corton
(Clos du Roi, Bressandes, Languettes, Renardes) and one
of Corton-Charlemagne, besides vineyards in Pernand-
Vergelesses and Aloxe-Corton. Robust but rustic wines
that often lack finesse.

Domaine Comte Georges de Vogüé ☆☆☆☆
Chambolle-Musigny.
This ancient domaine has descended by inheritance since
1450. The name "de Vogüé" appears in 1766. Splendid
vaulted cellars under the fifteenth-century house hold the
production of 12 hectares, of which 7.2 are in Musigny,
2.7 in Bonnes Mares, 0.6 in the *premier cru* Les Amoureuses,
and two in the appellation Chambolle-Musigny. Some
3,000 Chardonnay vines in Musigny produce a minute
quantity of a unique Musigny Blanc.

The estate replanted these vines in 1994, and is selling
the wine as a costly Bourgogne Blanc until the vines are
old enough to merit the *grand cru* appellation. There is
no appellation to allow the white to be declassified to a
premier cru, which is why it is now released
as a humble Bourgogne.

After a flat patch in the 1970s
and 1980s, the wines are once again
superlative. The Amoureuses is the
most seductive wine, but the greatest
is the sublime Musigny Vieilles Vignes.
It's indicative of the exacting standards
of this estate that Musigny vines under
20 years of age are bottled as Chambolle
Premier Cru.

Domaine de la Vougeraie ☆☆–☆☆☆
Nuits-St-Georges.
www.domainedelavougeraie.com
This new domaine was established by
the négociant house Boisset (q.v.) as a
way of unifying the substantial 34 hectares
of vineyards it had collected over the
years. Winemaker Pascal Marchand
established the style, which is forthright,
and his successor Pierre Vincent is maintaining quality.

The domaine can offer a splendid range of organic
vineyards, from old vines in village appellations to the noblest
of *grands crus* such as Corton-Charlemagne and Musigny.

Côte Chalonnaise

Santenay brings the Côte d'Or to a close at its southern end.
There is scarcely time for lunch at the luxurious Lameloise at
Chagny before the wine scout has to be alert again for the five
villages that make up the Côte Chalonnaise. Chalon-sur-Saône
has little to do with the district today, but in antiquity it was one
of the great wine ports of the empire. It was the point where
wine coming or going north to or from Paris or the Moselle had
to be trans-shipped from river to road – 25,000 amphoras were
found in one dredging operation in the Saône at Chalon.

A new appellation, Bourgogne Côte Chalonnaise, was
introduced in 1990, which distinguishes the wines of the Côte
Chalonnaise from the rather large and undefined appellation of
Bourgogne itself. The Côte from Chagny southwards is less
distinct and consistent than from Santenay northwards. So is its
wine. Rising demand and prices have only recently made wine-
growing profitable rather than marginal, and encouraged
replanting of land abandoned after phylloxera. About 1,600
hectares are planted, although the appellation authorizes the
planting of considerably more. Pinot Noir dominates, but there
are villages such as Montagny or Bouzeron where white grapes
are more important. Although its best wines are up to minor
Côte de Beaune standards, it is difficult to pin them down with
a regional character. They vary remarkably
from village to village.

Mercurey and Givry are dedicated 90
per cent to red wine, which should be firm
and tasty Pinot Noir at least on a level with,
say, a good Côte de Beaune-Villages; if
anything harder and leaner, with Givry,
traditionally the bigger, demanding longer
keeping. The tannins, especially in
Mercurey, can have an earthy edge to
them, but more modern winemaking
techniques are now producing wines that
are considerably less rustic than in the past.

Two-thirds of Rully's vineyards now produce white wine, which, at its best, is marvellously brisk, with a touch of real class.
The red, at least as most growers make it
today, can be rather thin compared with
Mercurey. High acidity in Rully whites
makes them ideal for sparkling wines.

Montagny is entirely a white wine appellation, with the
peculiarity that two-thirds of its vineyards are entitled to be
labelled *premier cru* – which seems scarcely fair to the carefully
limited *premiers crus* of the other villages. Montagny whites tend
to have a little more body and less finesse than those of Rully.
They are certainly more in fashion.

The fifth appellation of the Côte Chalonnaise is the only
specific one of the Aligoté grape in Burgundy. The village of
Bouzeron, between Rully and Chagny, has made a specialty of
what is elsewhere a plain, sharp café wine. In 1979, it was
granted the appellation Bourgogne Aligoté de Bouzeron.

The other regional specialty is Crémant de Bourgogne,
sparkling wine that is growing in commercial importance.

Tasting from the cask

(See box on page 127.) Three sizeable producers account for most of the *crémant* production. They are Delorme at Rully, R. Chevillard at La Rochepot on the road to Paris, and Parigot-Richard at Savigny-lès-Beaune.

The region in round figures

Appellation		Average Annual Production	
Bouzeron	2,790 hl	30,100 cases	(white)
Rully	10,500 hl	116,500 cases	(white)
	5,300 hl	60,000 cases	(red)
Mercurey	23,800 hl	264,000 cases	(red)
	3,600 hl	40,000 cases	(white)
Givry	10,400 hl	115,000 cases	(red)
	2,250 hl	25,000 cases	(white)
Montagny	17,000 hl	190,000 cases	(white)

Leading Côte Chalonnaise Producers

Brintet ☆
Mercurey. www.domaine-brintet.com
This estate produces good, solid reds from a wide range of vineyards, including monopole *premier cru* La Levrière.

Château de Chamirey ☆☆
Mercurey. www.chamirey.com
Formerly distributed by Rodet (q.v.), as co-owner Betrand Devillard was the head of that company. A large domaine of 37 hectares, once known for sturdy wines with more substance than refinement, but now more harmonious and nuanced.

Clos Salomon ☆☆
Givry
This is one of the most historic and best-known vineyards of Givry, and its renown has been restored by the Gardin family. Grapefruity whites and firm reds.

Domaine de la Renarde (Jean-François Delorme) ☆–☆☆
Rully. www.domaineanneetjeanfrancoisdelorme.com
The most remarkable enterprise in the region; a 65-hectare estate built from scratch over recent decades, largely by reclaiming vineyards abandoned long ago. Delorme is equally well-known as one of Burgundy's best sparkling wine specialists. The Rully monopole Varot is the 17-hectare vineyard that gives his best white, notable for freshness and finesse.

Dureuil-Janthial ☆–☆☆
Rully.
This is a 17-hectare organic domaine and it produces both white and red wines in more or less equal quantities. The quality of the wines is sound.

Domaine de la Folie ☆–☆☆
Rully. www.domainedelafolie.com
A substantial property with 1,000 years of history. The 18 hectares are in one block around the house, with Chardonnay in a majority, producing Rully Blanc Clos St-Jacques, plus Rully Rouge Clos de Bellecroix, and a smaller patch of Aligoté. The wines, especially the whites, have a good reputation.

Michel Goubard ☆
St-Désert.
An example of how good Bourgogne Côte Chalonnaise without a specific appellation can be in this part of the *côtes*.

Paul & Henri Jacqueson ☆☆–☆☆☆
Rully.
Father and son together take great pride in this 11-hectare domaine. The best wines are the *premiers crus*, notably Les Pucelles (white) and Les Clous (red). No corners are cut here: for instance, oak staves for their barrels are dried at the winery to ensure optimal quality. Excellent value.

Joblot ☆☆–☆☆☆
Givry.
Jean-Marc Joblot's 13 hectares, with nine of *premiers crus*, produce some of the best and most concentrated wines of the Côte Chalonnaise.

Michel Juillot ☆☆
Mercurey. www.domaine-michel-juillot.fr
For many years Juillot has been one of Mercurey's best winemakers, winning acclaim for his red Clos des Barraults and Champs Martin from his 30 hectares. He also produces Corton Perrières and Corton-Charlemagne. Nowadays Michel's son Laurent is in charge.

Lorenzon ☆–☆☆
Mercurey.
Splendid if somewhat oaky wines from Champs Martin, the top *cuvée* from this five-hectare domaine.

Lumpp ☆–☆☆
Givry. www.francoislumpp.com
Red and white wines of little weight but impeccable balance.

Jean Maréchal ☆
Mercurey. www.jeanmarechal.fr
Maréchals have made Mercurey for 300 years. Most of their ten hectares are *premiers crus*, almost all red. These are long-lived wines.

Ragot ☆☆
Givry. www.domaine-ragot.com
A nine-hectare domaine with a dignified château. The proportion of white is unusually high for Givry, and the keeping qualities of the wine are remarkable – particularly in years of high acidity. The reds have charm rather than weight.

Francois Raquillet ☆☆–☆☆☆
Mercurey. www.domaineraquillet.free.fr
Robust wines from various *crus*. Clos l'Eveque is often the best of them.

Antonin Rodet ☆☆–☆☆☆
Mercurey. www.rodet.com
A négociant developed to a high level of quality by Bertrand Devillard. Now under new ownership, it no longer has a controlling interest in the Château de Chamirey (q.v.) or Domaine Jacques Prieur (q.v.), but still owns Château de Rully and Château de Mercey. It has also bought the négociant house of Dufouleur in Nuits-St-Georges. Rodet deals in wines

from all parts of Burgundy, taking special pride in its Bourgogne Rodet, Mercurey, Meursault, and Gevrey-Chambertin. The very best wines from any appellation are labelled Cave Privé.

Domaine de Suremain ☆☆
Mercurey. www.domaine-de-suremain.com
Yves de Suremain is a leading proprietor whose 20 hectares, all in Mercurey, deliver concentrated and age-worthy wines.

Caves des Vignerons de Buxy ☆–☆☆
Buxy. www.vigneronsdebuxy.com
Important and very modern growers' co-op for Buxy and Montagny, founded in 1931. Its 120 members own 750 hectares of vines, less than half with generic appellations (Bourgogne Rouge, Passe-tout-grains, and Aligoté are its main productions.) The remainder include white Montagny, Rully, red Côte Chalonnaise, and Crémant de Bourgogne.

A & P de Villaine ☆☆–☆☆☆
Bouzeron. www.de-villaine.com
Aubert de Villaine, better known as co-proprietor of the Domaine de la Romanée-Conti, is equally proud to have helped win the formerly obscure Bouzeron its own appellation for Aligoté in 1979. This forthright wine remains the flagship of this organically farmed property, but there is also exceptional Bourgogne Côte Chalonnaise called La Digoine, white Rully and red Mercurey.

Mâconnais

Say Mâconnais to most wine-drinkers today and their knee-jerk response will be "blanc". The region is riding high on the reliability and uncomplicated pleasantness of its Chardonnay whites. They have the advantage of being recognizably white burgundy but far cheaper than Côte d'Or wines, and marvellously easy to choose – since most of them are made by skilful cooperatives which welcome visitors.

The Mâconnais is a widespread and disjointed region, taking its name from the important commercial city on the Saône just outside its limits to the east. It has little of the monoculture of Beaujolais; its mixed farming land is more attractive, and in places geologically spectacular. Pouilly-Fuissé is its only appellation with *grand vin* aspirations.

Most Mâcon wine used to be red, made of Gamay, but grown on heavy chalky soil which prevented it from ripening to Beaujolais softness and vitality. Mâcon Rouge was indeed merely *vin ordinaire* with an appellation until Beaujolais methods of fermentation were introduced. Recently, there have been some much better wines up to Beaujolais-Villages standards. Pinot Noir from the Mâconnais can aspire no higher than the appellation Bourgogne Rouge or (mixed with Gamay) Passe-tout-grains. High yields are common, and much of the wine is thin and boring The temptation for all but the most conscientious growers is to pick at minimum ripeness levels and *chaptalize* to the maximum – not a formula for good winemaking.

Chardonnay now occupies at least three-quarters of the vineyards, including (in the more northerly communes in particular) a strain of Chardonnay known as the "Musqué" for its decidedly richer, melony-musky flavour. Used to excess it can produce a blowzy, unsubtle wine. In due proportion it adds a hint of richness to otherwise rather straight, dry white: undoubtedly an element in the popularity of Mâcon-Villages or Mâcon with the name of a particular village.

Pouilly-Fuissé rises higher in the quality league for local reasons of soil and situation – but not always as high as its price implies. The four villages in the appellation area have been prominent over the centuries, partly for their proximity to Mâcon, partly as a tourist attraction for the mighty limestone bluffs that dominate them and the prehistoric traces that litter the district, partly for the chalky clay and sunny slopes that make their wine at least as good as any south Burgundy white. Generalizations about Pouilly-Fuissé are risky, as the wine varies greatly according to the precise location of the vineyard in a country that is all bumps and dips.

The fact that wines of more or less equal value are produced in the surrounding area has given rise to two other appellations. The smaller Pouilly-Vinzelles (which includes Pouilly-Loché) has somehow failed to catch the public's eye. The much larger St-Véran, which scoops in seven communes, including the northern fringe of the Beaujolais country, was added in 1971 and now offers extremely good value.

Throughout the 1990s there was a discernible change in style. Whereas most Mâcon was fresh and unpretentious, some growers in the more prestigious appellations now harvest as late as possible to obtain high potential alcohol levels, and age the wine in new-oak barrels with *bâtonnage*. The result is a fat, opulent wine, certainly rich but sometimes vulgar and blowzy. Such wines can be excellent, but often lack the sustaining acidity that underpins the richness of a top Côte de Beaune white. Nonetheless the top growers of the region have acted as locomotives, hauling behind them aspiring estates and providing an incentive to improve quality and concentration. The result is an even wider choice of good wines at a fair price.

The Appellations of Mâconnais

The Mâconnais has seven appellations of its own and shares the right to five more with the rest of Burgundy. Its own appellations are:

For White Wines
Mâcon Blanc. Chardonnay wine from 12 communes not within the Villages zone.
Mâcon-Villages (or Mâcon- followed by the name of one of 26 villages in the eastern half of the region). The best-known of these – Clessé and Viré – were awarded their own AC in 1999: Viré-Clessé, with almost 400 hectares in production. The minimum degree is 11, as for Mâcon Supérieur. All the Mâcon appellations together amount to 3,330 hectares.
St-Véran. 660 hectares. The same as for Mâcon-Villages but from seven of the southernmost communes, overlapping into Beaujolais at St-Amour: Chânes, Chasselas, Davayé, Leynes, Prissé, Solutré-Pouilly, and St-Vérand. Davayé and Prissé lie to

the north and are based on classic Burgundian limestone, which gives the wines weight and concentration, the rest are to the south of Pouilly-Fuissé on the granitic sand of the Beaujolais, which is much less suited to white wine production. They offer lighter, thinner wines, which can also be sold as Beaujolais Blanc, Mâcon-Villages, or Bourgogne Blanc if the customer prefers one of these names. If a particular vineyard is named on the label, the minimum degree is 12, with the implication that the wine is better and more concentrated.

Pouilly-Fuissé. 767 hectares. Chardonnay from specified parts of the villages of Pouilly, Fuissé, Solutré, Vergisson, and Chaintré. If a vineyard name is used, it must have 12 degrees.

Pouilly-Loché. 32 hectares. May be sold as itself or labelled as...

Pouilly-Vinzelles. 53 hectares. The same rules as for Pouilly-Fuissé, but for wine from the two villages of Vinzelles and Loché to the east – marginally less good but more than marginally cheaper.

For Red Wines

Mâcon Rouge. From Gamay or Pinot Noir. It can also be made pink and offered as Mâcon Rosé.

Mâcon- (followed by one of 20 village names). The two appellations together account for 580 hectares.

General Appellations

Aligoté. As in the rest of Burgundy.

Bourgogne. For Chardonnay whites and Pinot Noir reds.

Crémant de Bourgogne. As in the rest of Burgundy.

Passe-tout-grains. For Gamay and Pinot Noir (2:1) reds.

Leading Mâconnais Producers

The great bulk of Mâcon, both white and red, is produced by the 18 growers' cooperatives of the area. The best-known are those of Chaintré (for Pouilly-Fuissé), Lugny (for Mâcon-Lugny and Mâcon Rouge Supérieur), Mancey (red and white Mâcon), Prissé (Mâcon-Prissé and St-Véran), and Viré (Viré-Clessé). The following are the few individual producers with more than a local reputation.

Auvigue ☆☆–☆☆☆
Charnay.
Numerous bottlings from this five-hectare domaine. The Pouilly-Fuissés are exceptionally elegant and well balanced.

Daniel Barraud ☆☆
Vergisson. www.domainebarraud.com
Numerous *cuvées*, some barrique-fermented. Silky, concentrated wines with vigour and freshness.

Domaine de la Bongran
See Jean Thévenet.

André Bonhomme ☆☆
Viré.
A dependable source, offering three *cuvées* of Viré-Clessé.

Christophe Cordier ☆☆–☆☆☆
Fuissé.

The best wines come from his vineyards in Pouilly-Fuissé and Milly-Lamartine, all barrel-fermented and serious.

Cornin ☆☆
Chaintré. www.cornin.net
The Mâcon wines are outclassed by the opulent but vigorous Pouilly-Fuissés.

Domaine Corsin ☆–☆☆
Davayé. www.domaine-corsin.com
Exuberant wines from St-Véran and Pouilly-Fuissé.

Domaine de la Croix Senaillet ☆☆
Davayé. www.domainecroixsenaillet.com
Organic vineyards provide delicious St-Vérans.

Domaine des Deux Roches ☆☆
Davayé. www.collovrayterrier.com
This large property produces discreetly oaky Pouilly-Fuissés and refreshing St-Véran.

Ferret ☆☆☆
Fuissé. www.louisjadot.com
Fifteen hectares of mostly old vines permit the Ferrets to produce numerous *cuvées* of Pouilly-Fuissé with varying degrees of new-oak ageing. Bought by Beaune négociant Jadot in 2008.

Château de Fuissé ☆☆–☆☆☆
Fuissé. www.chateau-fuisse.fr
Long-established family property, producing a complex range of Pouilly-Fuissé. Fine quality but facing ever stronger competition from neighbours.

Guffens-Heynen ☆☆–☆☆☆
Vergisson. www.verget-sa.com
Exacting, mineral wines from Mâcon-Pierreclos and Pouilly-Fuissé.

Domaine des Heritiers des Comtes Lafon ☆☆–☆☆☆
Milly-Lamartine.
Dominique Lafon has acquired a domaine here from which he produces an expanding range of wines. 2001 was the first vintage. Quality is high, but prices are reasonable.

Lassarat ☆☆
Vergisson. www.roger-lassarat.com
Lush Chardonnays from St-Véran and Pouilly-Fuissé.

Olivier Merlin ☆–☆☆
La Roche Vineuse
Twelve hectares, scrupulously tended and vinified. Some fine Pouilly-Fuissé, too.

Domaine Rijckaert ☆☆
Viré-Clessé
Lean, elegant wines, quite different in style from the sometimes bloated southern Mâcon style. Domaine wines carry a green label, as Rijckaert also buys fruit.

Saumaize-Michelin ☆☆–☆☆☆
Vergisson.
Biodynamic wines of great richness. The Pouilly-Fuissés are the best of them, but the Mâcon-Villages can come close.

Robert-Denogent ☆☆
Fuissé. www.robert-denogent.com
Pouilly-Fuissé on steroids, yet not clumsy.

Domaine de la Soufrandière ☆☆
Davayé. www.bretbrothers.com
A range of Biodynamic wines from a variety of appellations.

Domaine de la Soufrandise ☆–☆☆
Fuissé.
Small property that also produces an unusual late-harvest wine.

Jean Thévenet ☆☆☆
Quintaine-Clessé. www.bongran.com
Also produces remarkable sweet wines from botrytized Chardonnay. Labels include Domaine Emilian Gillet and Domaine de la Bongran.

Domaine Valette ☆☆–☆☆☆
Chaintré
Splendid range of wines from some of the appellation's best sites.

Verget ☆☆–☆☆☆
Sologny. www.verget-sa.com
Founded by Belgian broker Jean-Marie Guffens in 1991 as a high-quality négociant house. See also Guffens-Heynen

Beaujolais

The Beaujolais region is no more complex than its light-hearted wine. Twelve appellations take care of the whole 22,500 hectares. They could really be reduced to half a dozen without greatly grieving anyone but the gastronomes of Lyon. What is needed is a grasp of the essential grades of quality and a good address list – which need not be long.

The great majority of Beaujolais is made either by a growers' cooperative or by tiny properties. There are almost 3,000 estates, with average holdings varying from five to ten hectares. Inevitably, few of those properties can bottle and market their wines, so they earn their living by selling grapes or wines to the many large merchant houses within the region. No more than 17 per cent of the crop is domaine-bottled; the rest is bottled and marketed by merchants and 18 cooperatives.

The world's perception of Beaujolais today is very different from what it was 30 years ago. Beyond its own region and Paris, where it was the café wine, Beaujolais used to be traded as a cut-price burgundy, imitating the weight of the Pinot Noirs of the Côte d'Or, by dint of picking as ripe as possible and adding plenty of sugar, achieving strength without grace. I have always been mystified by mid-nineteenth century figures showing Beaujolais *crus* with 15 degrees of alcohol (while Médocs had nine or ten degrees). Very few red wines need anything like that strength, and least of all Gamay, which lacks the flavour to countenance it. The Gamay of Beaujolais has no great fruity flavour; well-made and in the modern manner, it lures you in with its sappy smell and a combination of soft juiciness and a slight nip – the perfect recipe for quenching thirst.

Beaujolais, or its image, has lost much of its lustre in recent years, and the former vogue for industrially produced *nouveau* styles, although still going strong in Japan, has generally diminished, which is no bad thing. There is now a glut of production, and some major changes in the structure of the region's vineyards may be imminent. In 2002, over 100,000 hectolitres were ordered to be sent for distillation in order to stabilize prices, since so much wine from the two previous vintages remained unsold. In subsequent vintages a proportion of the crop has been dispatched to the distilleries. Growers had routinely produced the maximum yields at the expense of vinosity and quality, and many of them had remained complacently unaware that the market for dilute and rapidly ageing red Beaujolais was shrinking. There is certainly a decline in the amount of wine being made by carbonic maceration (see below) as the leading growers do their best to show that, on these slopes, Gamay is capable of producing serious red wine. Recent investment by major players from the Cote d'Or, including Jadot and Latour, has also raised morale and standards.

How Beaujolais is Made

The secret of the fresh, grapey fruitiness of Beaujolais lies in the way the Gamay grape – a variety of modest pretensions to quality – is handled and fermented. Winemaking in the Beaujolais combines the classic method of making burgundy with *macération carbonique*: the activity of enzymes inside an uncrushed grape, which, provided it is surrounded by CO_2, causes an internal fermentation and the extraction of colour and flavour from the inner skin. The trick is to fill the fermentation vat with whole bunches, stalks and all, with as few grapes crushed and damaged as possible. The weight of the upper grapes crushes the lower ones, which start a normal fermentation with their natural yeasts. The CO_2 given off by this process (helped along with gas from a bottle, if necessary) blankets off the air from the uncrushed upper layers. Here the grapes quietly feed on themselves, many of them splitting in the process. After six or seven days of spontaneous fermentation, the vat is about one-third full of juice, known as "free-run". This is run off, and the solid matter pressed to extract the remaining juice. The two products are blended together, and fermentation continues to completion. In normal red-winemaking, the *vin de presse* is in a minority (and may not be used at all). In the Beaujolais method it accounts for between two-thirds and three-quarters of the total, and the resulting wines tend to be softer and less astringent than those fermented traditionally.

At this stage, the juice still has unfermented sugar in it. Fermentation has to finish before the juice is stable enough to be called wine. The law regulating Beaujolais Nouveau says that this will happen by the third Thursday in November, although in years with a late harvest, some brutal methods of stabilization are needed to "finish" the wine in time. Not all growers accept this method. Some appeal to a different tradition, which requires more old-fashioned methods, scarcely distinguishable from those further north in the Côte d'Or.

The resulting wines have more structure and complexity, especially if barrique-aged, but lack the exuberant *typicité* of a fresh, youthful Beaujolais-Villages. However, more and more of the top growers are adopting these Burgundian methods. Both approaches have their partisans. If Gamay made by carbonic maceration can sometimes seem too simply hedonistic for wine fanciers who value seriousness and extraction, Burgundian-method Beaujolais can seem a touch too worked and solemn for so joyful a grape as Gamay.

The Appellations of Beaujolais

The most basic Beaujolais is from the southern half of the region, south of Villefranche, where the Gamay is encouraged to produce large quantities on heavy soil (although there is nothing to stop growers anywhere in Beaujolais using the appellation). This is a now-or-never wine, originally destined to be sold on draught in local cafés and by the carafe in restaurants. It is best drunk as young as possible. The term *nouveau* really only means the wine of the last harvest, until the next. The minimum alcoholic degree is nine, but this is regularly exceeded, either naturally or by *chaptalizing*. "Beaujolais" applies to red, white, or rosé, but only one per cent is white. Total area is 9,100 hectares.

Beaujolais-Villages

Beaujolais-Villages AC has a total of 6,300 hectares. The northern half of the region, or Haut-Beaujolais, has steeper hills, warmer soil (because it is lighter and more sandy), and makes better wine. Beaujolais-Villages is the appellation that covers the whole of this area, 38 villages in all, but ten small zones in the north, identified by combinations of slopes and soils that are peculiar to themselves, are singled out as the Beaujolais *crus* – the aristocrats.

Beaujolais-Villages makes a better *vin de primeur* than plain Beaujolais, except in atypically hot vintages. It has a minimum of 10 degrees alcohol and more backing of fruit and body – more flavour, in fact – to complement the rasp of new fruit juice. It is almost always worth its fairly modest premium both *en primeur* and even more when it has been, or will be, kept. Good Beaujolais-Villages is at its best in the summer after the vintage, and can hold for another year. Besides the *crus*, the region as a whole has some producers whose wines are regularly up to *cru* standards.

The Beaujolais Crus

Between the railway along the Saône Valley and the 450-metre (1,463-foot) contour line in the Beaujolais mountains to the west, from just south of Belleville to the boundary with the Mâconnais, the vine has the landscape to itself. Sandy, stony, or schistose granite-based soils without lime give the Gamay a roundness and depth of flavour it lacks elsewhere. Here it is pruned hard, and the plants are trimmed individually. Minimum natural strength of the wine is 10 degrees, but when it is sold with a vineyard name the required minimum is a degree higher. It will almost always be *chaptalized* up to 13 degrees or more.

Cru Beaujolais can be offered *en primeur*, but not until a month after Beaujolais and Beaujolais-Villages, from December 15. It would be a pity to prevent it being poured for Christmas. The best *crus* are never treated in this way; they are kept in barrel or vat until at least the March after the vintage. Their full individuality and sweet, juicy smoothness take anything from six months to six years in bottle to develop. Three of the *crus* – Morgon, Chénas, and above all Moulin-à-Vent – are looked on as *vins de garde*, at least by Beaujolais standards.

Brouilly 1,300 hectares. The southernmost and the largest of the *crus*, enveloping areas in six villages (Odenas, St-Lager, Cercié, Charentay, St-Etienne-la-Varenne, and Quincié) grouped around the isolated Mont de Brouilly (see Côtes de Brouilly). The word "typical" is most often used for Brouilly – not surprising for the biggest-producing *cru* lying in the very heart of the region. This means the wine is full of grapey flavour and vigour, but is not aggressive in its first year.

Chénas 285 hectares. The smallest *cru*, sheltered from the west by a wooded hill (Chénas is derived from *chêne*, meaning oak) and including part of the commune of La Chapelle-de-Guinchay. Certain Chénas wines achieve formidable strengths, but its vineyard sites are too varied for the appellation to be readily identifiable, or its style reliable.

Chiroubles 358 hectares. All the vineyards are southeast-facing on the higher slopes, making some of the best-balanced and most prized Beaujolais, in limited quantities. In some years, the elevation can mean that the vines struggle to ripen fully. This is the first *cru* to be "supple and tender" for the eager restaurateurs of Paris.

Côte de Brouilly 312 hectares. The slopes of the Mont de Brouilly give a stronger, more concentrated wine than the surrounding appellation Brouilly, but in smaller quantities. The minimum degree here is 10.5 – the highest in Beaujolais. The wines are said to develop the high-toned scent of violets after two to three years in bottle. After warm vintages, they benefit from keeping that long.

Fleurie 875 hectares. The pretty name, a substantial supply, and a singular freshness of flavour all contribute to making this the most memorable and popular Beaujolais *cru* emanating from red, granitic, sandstone soils. Fleurie is often irresistible in its first year, with the result that the full, sweet silkiness of its maturity at three or four years is little-known. Juliénas 578 hectares. With St-Amour, the northernmost *cru* (the *département* boundary of Rhône and Saône-et-Loire runs between them). Substance, strong colour, and vigour, even tannin, mean that Juliénas needs two years or more to age. It is generally considered to be a mealtime Beaujolais rather than a thirst quencher. Morgon 1,115 hectares. The spread of vineyards around Villié-Morgon, between the *crus* Brouilly and Fleurie, are credited with a character so peculiar that morgonner has become a verb for a way that other wines sometimes (when they are lucky) behave. The soil is schistose, and the peculiarity is described as a flavour of wild cherries. I have not found them so identifiable, but they are among the bigger and longest-lasting wines of Beaujolais.

Moulin-à-Vent 655 hectares. There is no village of Moulin-à-Vent, but a sail-less windmill among the hamlets between Romanèche-Thorins and Chénas gives its name to the most "serious" and expensive Beaujolais appellation. Moulin-à-Vent *en primeur* is almost a contradiction in terms. It should be a firm, meaty, and savoury wine that has less of the surging scent of Beaujolais in its first year, but builds up a bouquet resembling burgundy in bottle. Some authorities attribute its power to the presence of manganese in the soil. Some growers age it briefly in small oak barrels to add to its structure and longevity. Moulin-à-Vent is always served last in a Beaujolais meal, often with the cheeses, which will dominate the lighter wines.

Régnié 393 hectares. The newest Beaujolais *cru*, to the west of Brouilly and Morgon from the commune of Régnié-Durette. While it shows a particular resemblance to Brouilly, it nonetheless has a personality of its own, with its well-defined aroma of red fruits. The soils of Régnié are sandier than the other *crus*. The *cru* has had difficulty establishing a reputation for itself, and bulk prices have sometimes dipped below those for Beaujolais-Villages.

St-Amour 323 hectares. The one Beaujolais appellation in the Mâconnais – its white wine is entitled to the appellation St-Véran. The power of suggestion is strong. Its name may have some bearing on my predilection for this wine. I find it next to Fleurie and Chiroubles in delicacy and sweetness – pleading to be drunk young, yet tasting even better after two or three years in bottle. As one of the smaller areas it is not often seen.

Enjoying Beaujolais

Beaujolais Nouveau is often served alone, slightly chilled, as a party wine, but it can be very fatiguing and thirst-making –

especially when its alcoholic degree is very high. Its cheerful properties are better appreciated with terrines or cheeses, picnic or buffet food. Beaujolais *crus* of good vintages, aged three or four years in bottle, often begin to resemble fine Rhône wines or, more rarely, Côte d'Or wines. They are best served at the same temperature as red burgundy and with similar food. An increasing number of these wines are being aged in barriques. They can be highly rated by wine critics and are capable of fetching high prices, but whether you enjoy the combination of Gamay fruitiness and new oak barrels is very much a matter of personal taste.

Leading Beaujolais Producers

Domaine Noël Aucoeur ☆–☆☆
Villié-Morgon. www.domaineaucoeur.com
A good property in Morgon, with a good Beaujolais-Villages and an oaked "Cuvée Jean-Claude Aucoeur" from Morgon. The property also offers wines from other *crus*.

Paul Beaudet ☆–☆☆
La Chapelle-de-Guinchay.
Négociant firm, well-known in top restaurants and in the USA for about ten *cru* bottlings as well as other good wines.

Christian Bernard ☆–☆☆
Fleurie.
Lush, highly approachable wines from Moulin-à-Vent and Fleurie.

Daniel Bouland ☆☆–☆☆☆
Villie-Morgon. 6 ha.
Exemplary Morgon and Côte de Brouilly from very old vines are the hallmark of this perfectionist estate.

Jean-Marc Burgaud ☆☆
Villié-Morgon. 17 ha. www.jean-marc-burgaud.com
Burgaud is based in Morgon, where he makes powerful wines from the Côtes du Puy. But he has more to offer: a rounder Morgon Charmes, a fruity Beaujolais-Villages, and an example of a striking complex wine from Régnié.

F & J Calot ☆☆
Villié-Morgon. 10 ha.
Jean Calot has little time for carbonic maceration, declaring that his aim is to make structured wines. He is aided by the ownership of some very old vines, and his "Cuvée Vieilles Vignes" is made from vines at least 70 years old. It's a spicy, concentrated wine with aromas of blackberries. Also memorable is the plummy "Cuvée Jeanne", picked slightly overripe.

Château de la Chaize ☆
Odenas. 99 ha. www.chateaudelachaize.com
This is the largest private estate in Beaujolais, with a château and gardens that draw many visitors. The Brouilly wines, while correct, don't quite match the grandeur of the surroundings.

Emile Cheysson ☆☆
Chiroubles. 26 ha
Extensive vineyards allow Jean-Pierre Large to compose his

Chiroubles blends with care. The basic wine shows to the full the charm of which Chiroubles is capable, while the oak-aged Prestige has greater weight and complexity, but perhaps at the expense of *typicité*.

Michel Chignard ☆☆
Fleurie. 8 ha.
Rich, seductive wines, among the finest from this popular *cru*. The "Cuvée Spéciale" will be too oaky for many Beaujolais enthusiasts. Prices are relatively high.

Clos de la Roilette ☆☆–☆☆☆
Fleurie. 9 ha.
The Coudert family makes lush Fleurie from very old vines.

Louis-Claude Desvignes ☆☆–☆☆☆
Villié-Morgon. 13 ha. www.louis-claude-desvignes.com
A respected and resolutely traditional producer of Morgon, making wines with fruit and depth, especially the Côtes du Py. They invariably benefit from a few years in bottle.

Bernard Diochon ☆☆
Romanèche-Thorins.
Small property focused on very old vines in Moulin-à-Vent.

Jean Foillard ☆☆
Villié-Morgon. 11 ha.
A small domaine, but Foillard is fortunate to have vines in the Côte du Puy, one of the best vineyards in the region. This is a wine made at optimal ripeness levels and aged in older barrels that don't impart any oaky flavours, and it repays ageing.

Domaine du Granit ☆–☆☆
Chénas. 8 ha.
A small estate based in Chénas but producing robust Moulin-à-Vent.

Château des Jacques ☆☆☆
Romanèche-Thorins. 41 ha. www.louis-jadot.com
The Burgundy négociant, Jadot, bought this large Moulin-à-Vent estate in 1996. It is divided into five separate sites (plus vineyards in Mâcon-Villages and Beaujolais-Villages) that are vinified and sometimes marketed separately. The vinification is essentially Burgundian, and the grapes are de-stemmed. These are dense, complex wines, with little initial primary fruit, so they need time to age. The best *cru*, Clos des Rochegrès, is a wine to contemplate after seven or eight years.

Paul and Eric Janin ☆☆–☆☆☆
Romanèche-Thorins. 12 ha.
One-third of this estate is in Beaujolais-Villages, the rest in Moulin-à-Vent. Part of the property is farmed Biodynamically. Janin ferments his wines at a high temperature and ages them either in tanks or large casks. The result is dense wines with varying aromas of cherries and liquorice, and the best of them is either the "Clos du Tremblay" or the new *prestige cuvée* called Séduction. The Beaujolais-Villages vines lie just across the border from the *cru*, they give wines of surprising guts and structure.

Jean-Claude Lapalu ☆☆
St-Etienne-la-Varenne. 12 ha.
Brouilly and Beaujolais-Villages of great charm and purity, especially the old-vine Broullly Croix des Rameaux.

The hills of Beaujolais rise from the plain of the Saône to a height of more than 1,500 ft

Hubert Lapierre ☆☆
La Chapelle-de-Guinchay. 7.5 ha.
www.domaine-lapierre.com
Lapierre's estate is divided almost equally between Chénas and Moulin-à-Vent. The wines are given a fairly long fermentation, and aged in tanks, with the exception of one *cuvée* of Chénas, which is aged in oak for ten months. It is arguable whether it is actually superior to the unoaked wines. The wines, made from some very old vines, all age well.

Marcel Lapierre ☆☆
La Chapelle-de-Guinchay. 11 ha.
www.marcel-lapierre.com
Intense yet fruit-packed wines from his organic vineyards in Morgon.

Domaine de la Madone ☆–☆☆
Fleurie. 13 ha. www.domaine-de-la-madone.com
Jean-Marc Després from de la Madone produces both a regular Fleurie and a "Cuvée Vieilles Vignes", which has considerably more concentration. The Cuvée Prestige combines very old vines with barrel-ageing. The estate is in no rush to release its wines, so purchasers have the benefit from at least a year's bottle-ageing.

Domaine des Marrans ☆☆
Fleurie. 10 ha.
The Mélinand family have vines with an average age of 40 years. They also produce Chiroubles and Juliénas, and their top wines have rich, dense, black-fruit flavours.

Dominique Piron ☆☆–☆☆☆
Villié-Morgon. 26 ha. www.domaines-piron.fr
In addition to his own vineyards, Dominique Piron farms smallholdings that belong to owners with other careers, and then he purchases their grapes, giving him access to around 60 hectares. His crus include Morgon, Chénas, and Moulin-à-Vent.

Jean-Charles Pivot ☆☆
Quincié. 4 ha.
A good grower in the Côte de Brouilly, who is also well-known for his Beaujolais-Villages. This is Beaujolais at the hedonistic end of the spectrum.

Domaine des Terres Dorées ☆☆☆
Crière. 17 ha.
Jean-Paul Brun is certainly the most original and creative winemaker of the region, though some may dismiss him as a mere eccentric. It was he who led what has now become a fashion: to return to traditional methods of vinification far removed from the carbonic maceration and flashy fruitiness of most Beaujolais production. So much of Brun's wine is denied the AC, which does not seem to bother him greatly.

He also produces weighty white wines, both unoaked and oaked, from Chardonnay, and first-rate Morgon and Moulin-à-Vent from recently acquired vineyards. All his wines have remarkable concentration and finesse that mark them out as among the most interesting and characterful of all the wines of Beaujolais.

Michel Tête ☆☆–☆☆☆
Juliénas. 13 ha.
Half the estate lies within Juliénas, the rest in St-Amour and Beaujolais-Villages. The latter is planted on granitic soils, so it is a wine with some stuffing. In 1990, he introduced a Juliénas Cuvée Prestige, half of which is oak-aged. The crisp, cherryish St-Amour is consistently good.

Château Thivin ☆☆–☆☆☆
Odenas. 26 ha. www.chateau-thivin.com
The Beaujolais-Villages is the bargain here, but the best wines are certainly the impressive *cuvées* from the Côte de Brouilly, which have depth of flavour without excessive extraction. Cuvée Zacharie is aged in barriques.

Domaine du Vissoux ☆☆–☆☆☆
Fleurie. 30 ha. www.chermette.fr
Pierre-Marie Chermette vinifies his wines with minimum manipulation, avoiding *chaptalization* and the addition of cultivated yeasts whenever possible. He produces two bottlings of Fleurie, and a good Moulin-à-Vent. The various *cuvées* of simple Beaujolais are bargains, for drinking young.

Leading Beaujolais Merchants

Georges Duboeuf ☆–☆☆☆
Romanèche-Thorin. www.duboeuf.com
Duboeuf's family has been embedded in the region for four centuries. Beaujolais is in his blood. In the early 1950s, he made wine from his brother's vineyards and sold it to local restaurants. The chef, Georges Blanc, bought the wine with enthusiasm and over the decades, his small winery has expanded into an extremely slick and successful company, buying in wines from 400 growers and 15 cooperatives, mostly in the Beaujolais and Mâconnais, but also from the Rhône.

Now in his seventies, Georges, aided by his son Franck effortlessly combines excellent winemaking and blending with first-rate marketing. His Hameau du Vin in Romanèche-Thorin is one of France's most lovely wine museums.

Eventail de Vignerons Producteurs
Corcelles.
A marketing group, working with the production of a large number of mostly good-quality independent estates. Not rated as a group of producers.

Henry Fessy ☆–☆☆
St-Jean-d'Ardières. 11 ha. www.vins-henry-fessy.com
Fessy produces a very wide range of wines from all over Beaujolais, and at all quality levels. The basic Beaujolais bottlings have drive and excellent fruit, the *crus* are inevitably more varied in quality and subtle in expression. All wines are vinified by the Fessy team, and production is around two million bottles. In 2008 the house was bought by Burgundy négociant Louis Latour.

Loron & Fils ☆–☆☆
Fleurie. www.loron-et-fils.com
A large, high-quality family business, formerly mainly dealing in bulk but now selling more and more in bottle, under several

brand names. Offers some good domaine wines and a range of Crémants de Bourgogne.

Mommessin ☆–☆☆
Quincié. www.mommessin.com
Until recently this was a very traditional family business. Now it is diversifying into *vins de marque* and Rhône wines as well as Beaujolais, where it has exclusive arrangements with several good domaines.

Potel-Aviron ☆☆
La Chapelle de Guinchay. www.nicolas-potel.fr
An unusual joint venture between Burgundy négociant Nicolas Potel and Stéphane Aviron, from a Beaujolais wine-broking family. Their aim is to produce wines made in the true Burgundian fashion. Although these are wines with unusual structure and depth of fruit, their ten months in oak robs them, some argue, of *typicité*.

Louis Tête ☆☆
St-Didier sur Beaujeu. 16 ha. www.tete-beaujolais.com
A specialist in the high-class restaurant trade, particularly well-known in Britain and Switzerland. The properties it markets include Château des Alouettes in Beaujolais-Villages and Domaine de la Chapelle in Brouilly.

Jura

Connoisseurs of the French countryside each have their favourite corner. I hope never to be forced to make a final choice, but I have a shortlist ready, and the Jura is on it. These limestone mountains (they give their name to a whole epoch of geology, the Jurassic) roll up towards Switzerland from the plain of the Saône in Burgundy. Halfway in a straight line from Beaune to Geneva you come to the delicious timbered and tiled little town of Arbois (where Pasteur lived), then Poligny, then Château-Chalon, the heart of a completely original wine country. The Jura vineyards are small (much smaller than they once were; currently 1,800 hectares). But their origins are as old as Burgundy's, their climate and soil singular, and their grapes their own.

Jura producers are fond of making a wide range of wines, from *méthode traditionnelle* sparkling to the unique, flor-induced *vin jaune*. The overall appellation is Côtes du Jura. This straggling appellation covers a long strip of country from north of Arbois to south of Cousance. Arbois is another general AC with higher alcohol stipulated. L'Etoile covers whites and *vins de paille* from the valley around the village of L'Etoile to the south. As an AC, the 48-hectare Château-Chalon is exclusively for *vin jaune*.

The vineyard sits on a band of heavy clay, rich in lime, exposed along the mountain slopes between 275 and 410 metres (885 and 1,165 feet) high. Woods, bovine pastures, and limestone cliffs constantly interrupt the continuity of the vines. Unlike Alsace to the north, which lies in the rain shadow of the Vosges, the west-facing Jura is often deluged by summer rain. Hail is a frequent problem here, but September and October are usually sunny. Jura grapes have been selected because they thrive in deep, damp soil, given a good, sun-warmed slope. The most widespread is the Poulsard (confusingly referred to as Plousard in the Pupillin region): a pale red, which is the nearest thing to a rosé grape. Another obscure red, the tannic Trousseau, is grown with it to stiffen its too "supple" wine. Pinot Noir is increasingly added to give more colour and backbone to red wine – but red is in a minority here; most of the wine is rosé, fermented on its pale skins as though intended to be red. Nowadays, the Chardonnay is the standard grape for light white wines; it performs well (occasionally under the alias of Melon d'Arbois or Gamay Blanc) but certainly not spectacularly. Much of it is made into sparkling wine. But the real specialty is Savagnin or Naturé. Savagnin is the same as the Heida grape of Swizerland's Valais. It is said to be related to the Alsatian Traminer, but doesn't taste much like it. Savagnin It is a late ripener and a small cropper, but its wine is powerful in alcohol and flavour. Used merely for topping up barrels of Chardonnay it gives them, as they age, a marvellously rustic style, sometimes described as *vin typé*. Vinified on its own, it delivers a salty, nutty wine of great personality. Purists, however, insist that pure Savagnin as a dry table wine is not a traditional Jura style.

Savagnin's true destiny is to produce a strange wine that has a strong resemblance to fino sherry. This is the oxidative *vin jaune*, which can only be made from vines cropped at no more than 20 hectolitres per hectare. The young wine is left in old barrels with a history of making *vin jaune*, not filled to the top but in the normally perilous state of "ullage". A flor yeast, presumably residing in the barrel wood, rapidly grows as a film on the surface of the wine, excluding direct contact with oxygen. The wine is left thus for a statutory minimum of six years and three months, without being topped up. At the end of this ageing period, it has lost 30 per cent of its volume, but a miraculous stability has (or should have) come over it. A finished *vin jaune* is an impressive apéritif, intense in flavour, obviously slightly oxidized (there is not the thick covering of flor that there is in Jerez), but long and fine and altogether worthwhile. The village (not château) of Château-Chalon and a few adjacent communes are famous for the best, although good *vins jaunes* are made all over the area.

Wine produced in such restricted quantities (and by no means every year) and by such drawn-out methods is inevitably expensive. Like Tokaji, *vin jaune* comes in smaller-than-standard bottles that help to disguise the price. (The *clavelin* of the Jura, long-necked and hunch-shouldered, holds 62 centilitres.) I cannot pretend it is anything like as good value, as reliable, or even as delicious, as a first-class fino sherry. But it exists – and as wine-lovers, we should be grateful for variety and support it, especially in such time-honoured forms as this. Another time-honoured regional specialty, *vin de paille*, was under threat of extinction but has been revived. It is made by hanging bunches of grapes in the rafters (or laying them on straw – *paille* – mats) to dry and concentrate their sweetness in the manner of Italian *vin santo*. The drying requires at least two months, and then the wine must be barrel-aged for at least three years; the tradition was ten. The result is a wine with 15.5 to 16 degrees of alcohol and around 100 grams of residual sugar. The Jura vineyard was decimated by phylloxera and took many years to recover. Today it thrives – largely on the tourist trade and faithful private customers in France. There are 230 growers, but only a few who cultivate more than 13 hectares. One of the biggest is merchant-grower Henri Mair; advertisements for its Vin Fou adorn thousands of roadside shacks.

A local specialty is MacVin, which is not an offshoot of a well-known fast-food chain, but a blend of two-thirds grape juice with one-third *marc*, aged up to 30 months in casks. Since 1991, this product has had its own AC. Despite, or perhaps because of, the singularity of the Jura wines, a number of young growers have founded small properties in recent years, so the future of this fascinating region seems assured. These remain wines to be sought out from the best producers. Those set as bait for thirsty skiers on their way to or from Alpine resorts rarely do the region much credit.

Leading Jura Producers

Château d'Arlay ☆–☆☆
Arlay. 30 ha. www.arlay.com
The Jura's one lordly estate, descended in the same family since the twelfth century, when it was a Hapsburg stronghold. The present owner, Comte Alain de Laguiche, has family ties with the Marquis de Laguiche of Montrachet, the de Vogüés of Champagne and Chambolle-Musigny, and the Ladoucettes of Pouilly-Fumé. Château d'Arlay uses traditional Jura varieties to produce an excellent range of wines, including Corail, an unusual, dark-coloured red blend of Poulsard, Trousseau, and Pinot Noir, and an excellent nut- and spice-filled *vin jaune*, as well as *vin de paille*.

Berthet-Bondet ☆–☆☆
Château-Chalon. 10 ha. www.berthet-bondet.net
This domaine was only created in 1985. It makes earthy Chardonnay and rather austere Savagnin, and an unusually elegant *vin jaune*.

Jean Bourdy ☆☆
Arlay. 10 ha
A cornerstone of the Jura wine industry, dating back to the sixteenth century, with bottles of centenarian wines still offered for sale. Jean Bourdy retired in 1979 after 52 years, and today the property is run by his grandson Jean-Philippe. Their model Jura wines come from Savagnin grown in Château-Chalon and Arlay, where they make red, rosé, and Chardonnay white as well as superlative *vin jaune*.

Caveau des Jacobins ☆–☆☆
Poligny. 35 ha.
Small cooperative producing a range of Côtes du Jura wines and good *crémant*. Its traditional Poulsard has a good following. Also good Chardonnay aged in barriques.

Château de l'Etoile ☆–☆☆
L'Etoile. 25 ha. www.chateau-etoile.com
The Château de l'Etoile exists no more, but the name has been used by the Vendelle family since 1883. Famous for its *crémants*, *vin jaune* with tremendous attack, and Côtes du Jura white. A small amount of red is also produced.

Fruitière Vinicole d'Arbois ☆–☆☆☆
Arbois. 210 ha. www.chateau-bethanie.com
Founded in 1906, it has 120 members, making it the oldest and biggest of the Jura co-ops, producing red, white, and jaune wines, all AC, both still and sparkling. Good Savagnin and Chardonnay, and a Cuvée Bethanie that blends the two. The largest producer of *vin jaune*, the cooperative also began making *vin de paille* in 1989.

Fruitière Vinicole de Pupillin ☆☆
Pupillin. 28 ha. www.pupillin.com
A small co-op producing especially interesting whites; also known for special barrels of spicy *vin jaune*. Pupillin is a perfect example of a Jura country village, with some 200 inhabitants, all living by and for the vine.

Ganevat ☆☆
Rotalier. 8 ha.
A good source of Pinot Noir, but it's the plump, spicy Chardonnays that make the deepest impression.

Michel Geneletti ☆–☆☆
L'Etoile. 13 ha. www.domaine-geneletti.net
Mostly Chardonnay produced here, toasty and spicy. But the *crémant*, Savagnin and *vin jaune* are also fine.

Julien Labet ☆☆–☆☆☆
Rotalier. 3 ha.
In 2003 Alain Labet gave some of his vineyards to his son Julien, who now uses his own name. He specializes in very rich Côtes du Jura whites, especially Chardonnay, from single vineyards.

Jean Macle ☆☆–☆☆☆
Château-Chalon. 12 ha.
A major producer of Château-Chalon of exceptional quality, and a fine Côtes du Jura white.

Henri Maire ☆–☆☆
Château-Montfort, Arbois. 300 ha. www.henri-maire.fr
Very much the biggest producer of Jura wines, with six separate domains at its disposal, furnishing all the Jura appellations. The company's imaginative and aggressive sales strategy has made Maire a household name. His modern domaines produce a vast range of wines under all the Jura appellations, plus many other wines. Sparkling Vin Fou is perhaps the best-known, if not the most distinguished. Some of the reds are distinctly sweet – not to my taste.

François Mossu ☆☆
Voiteur, Château-Chalon. 4 ha.
Passionately committed producer, with a finely balanced *vin jaune* with a distinctive seawater tang, and rather alcoholic *vin de paille* tinged with iodine, barley sugar, and caramelized orange.

Pierre Overnoy ☆
Pupillin. 7 ha
Organic estate, producing fine Chardonnay and aromatic Savagnin. But the reds, made without SO_2, can be weird. Overnoy retired in 2001 and today the wines are made by Emanuel Houillon.

Désiré Petit ☆
Pupillin. 12 ha.
An old family property scattered within the sheltered coomb of Pupillin, making reds, whites, and rosés that with the exception of the minerally Chardonnay are fashioned to be drunk young.

Pignier ☆–☆☆
Montaigu. 15 ha. www.domaine-pignier.com
Since 2002 the Pignier vineyards have been farmed Biodynamically, and the wines are exquisitely cellared in a former Carthusian monastery. Most of the wines are varietal, and the whites, which spend a long time in barrels, can be rather heavy and oily. Very citric *vin jaune*.

Domaine de la Pinte ☆–☆☆☆
Arbois. 34 ha. www.lapinte.fr
A large, modern estate created by Roger Martin in 1955 on abandoned vineyard land of the chalky clay loved by the Savagnin, which occupies almost half the vineyards. This organic domaine occupies some of the best terroir in Arboisand produces a complete range of Arbois wines, and both the *vin jaune* and *vin de paille* are exceptional.

Jacques Puffeney ☆☆–☆☆☆
Montigny-lès-Arsures. 7.5 ha.
Exceptional nutty white Arbois, and the reds are greatly improved. The *vin jaune* can show considerable richness.

Domaine de la Renardière ☆☆
Pupillin. 6 ha.
Jean-Michel Petit, who has worked in Napa Valley, created this small domaine in 1990, and has proved as adept with red wines as with white.

Xavier Reverchon ☆–☆☆☆
Poligny. 6 ha.
Xavier Reverchon produces a typically wide range of hand-made wines in small quantities – including intense *vins jaunes*, *méthode traditionnelle*, and MacVin (red and white), as well as many small lots of red, white, and rosé. Rather woody Chardonnay, but deliciously pure Savagnin, traditionally made and aged without topping up. A house speciality is Les Freins, produced from barrels intended for *vin jaune* but which failed to develop flor: thus, midway in style between pure Savagnin and oxidative *vin jaune*.

Domaine Rijckaert ☆☆
Leynes. 5 ha.
Jean Rijckaert is better known for his estate at Viré-Clessé in the Mâconnais, but here in Arbois he turns his hand with great success to the local Chardonnay. These are wines of remarkable purity and focus, as he deliberately eschews an oxidative style.

The town of Arbois, home of Louis Pasteur

Domaine Rolet ☆☆–☆☆☆
Arbois. 65 ha. www.rolet-arbois.com
One of the most important producers in the Jura after Henri Maire (q.v.), making consistently fine wines in all the major appellations. Concentrates on single-grape-variety wines including Chardonnay, Poulsard, and a Trousseau built to last. Experiments with a shorter vinification period for the Poulsard have produced a fresh, fruity rosé, something of a departure from the traditional Jura style. The Tradition whites blend Savagnin and Chardonnay and are aged up to 36 months in barrel; the result is tangy and minerally. Powerful *vin jaune*, too.

Stéphane Tissot ☆☆–☆☆☆
Montigny-lès-Arsures. 37 ha. www.stephane-tissot.com
Organic family domaine making exceptional if expensive Arbois and Côtes wines of all colours including nutty *vin jaune*, and a sumptuous, honeyed *vin de paille* from all four traditional varieties. The whites, especially the Arbois Chardonnay, are exemplary.

Jacques Tissot ☆–☆☆
Arbois. 30 ha. www.domaine-jacques-tissot.fr
Louis Pasteur made some of his fermentation experiments in this *chai* in the centre of Arbois. All Jacques Tissot's wines are well-made, but his red-berry-scented Trousseau is especially good. Rich, full *vin jaune*, with an alluring aroma of mango.

Domaine de la Tournelle ☆☆
Arbois. 6 ha. www.domainedelatournelle.com
Pascal Clairet worked for years as the oenologist of the chamber of commerce and, in 1991, founded his own property. Wines include very powerful Savagnin, and pretty, strawberry-scented Poulsard, as well as *vin jaune* and *vin de paille*.

Savoie

The wine country of Savoie follows the River Rhône south from the Lake of Geneva, then lines the Lac du Bourget (the biggest lake in France) around Aix-les-Bains, then hugs the sides of the valley south of Chambéry and turns the corner eastwards into the Val d'Isère. The whole wine zone is affected by the proximity of the Alps. It exists more as opportunistic outbreaks occurring in four *départements* than as a cohesive vineyard. Its appellations, encompassing 1,800 hectares of vineyards, have an intimidating complexity – in sharp contrast to its simple, fresh, and invigorating wine.

Over three-quarters of Savoie wine is white, based on half a dozen different grapes. Along the south shore of Lake Geneva (Haute-Savoie) it is the Chasselas, the grape the Swiss know as Fendant. Crépy is the best-known *cru*, with Marignan, Ripaille, and Marin, all light and often sharp wines. Crépy is an all-white appellation that might have disappeared but for the efforts of Léon Mercier and his son Louis. The better wines are bottled *sur lie*, giving them a slight spritz. Ayze, too, has a name for its sharpish *pétillant*.

Seyssel is your chance to win a bet. Few people realize or remember that it is France's northernmost Rhône wine. The grapes here are Roussette (alias Altesse) for still wines and Molette for fizz. Roussette, the aristocrat, reaches a relatively high degree of sugar, body, and flavour; Molette is a mild little thing. Seyssel has built an international reputation by developing its naturally fizzy tendency into fully fledged, classic-method sparkling. The specialist is Varichon & Clerc. Still or *pétillant*, dry or sometimes slightly sweet, Roussette wines with local reputations are made along the Rhône valley and Lac du Bourget at Frangy, Marestel, Monterminod, and Monthoux. Occasional super-vintages put them on a level with Vouvray.

The third principal white grape, and the commonest of the region, is the Jacquère. South of Seyssel, still on the Rhône, the district of Chautagne, centred on its cooperative at Ruffieux, makes Jacquère white, and the grape dominates the vineyards south of Chambéry: Chignin, Apremont, Abymes, and Montmélian. Chignin has the best southern hillside exposure. Its Jacquère fetches slightly a *franc* (remember them?) or two more a bottle than its neighbours, Apremont and Les Abymes. Red Gamay, Pinot Noir, and Mondeuse are also important.

Suburbia is invading these lovely vineyards fast. Montmélian, a little Alpine village a few years ago, is now hideous with housing estates. So far the red-wine vineyards on the slopes of the Val d'Isère are almost intact, but for how long? Their centre is the cave coopérative at Cruet, serving Cruet, Arbin, Montmélian, and St-Jean de la Porte. Much its best wine, to my mind, is its Mondeuse (especially that of Arbin). Gamay costs a little more, and Pinot Noir more again, but Mondeuse is the character: a dark, slightly tannic, smooth, but intensely lively wine that reminds me a little of Chinon, the "raspberry" red of the Loire.

There are other local specialties too: Roussette is the highest priced white of the Cruet cooperative; a yellow, full-bodied, slightly bitter wine you might take for an Italian. And Chignin grows the Bergeron, either a rare local grape or (say many) the Roussanne of the (lower) Rhône. This is the only Savoyard white wine that ages with distinction.

Savoie's ACs are shadowed by the VDQS Bugey to the west on the way to Lyon, a mere 240 hectares with an even more complex set of names, which is hard to justify in reality. The white VDQS is Roussette de Bugey, which from 2008 must be a pure Roussette, without additional grapes such as Chardonnay. Jacquère, Aligoté, and Chardonnay are allowed in Vin de Bugey Blanc. VDQS Vin de Bugey is red, rosé, or white and also has its *crus*: Virieu-Le-Grand, Montagnieu, Manicle, Machuraz, and Cerdon. Cerdon, in turn, is also an individual VDQS for *mousseux*, including a rosé, and merely fizzy *pétillant*.

Leading Savoie Producers

Abymes

Cave Coopérative le Vigneron Savoyard ☆
Apremont.
A small cooperative with eight members. (Also for Apremont, Gamay, Mondeuse, Vin de Pays de Grésivaudan.)

Pierre Boniface ☆☆
Les Marches. 7 ha.
Good reputation for Jacquère and sparkling wine.

Michel Magne ☆☆
Chapareillan.
Lush Apremont Tête de Cuvée.

Jean Perrier ☆–☆☆
Apremont. 23 ha. www.vins-perrier.com
Good-value wines from Apremont.

Gilbert Tardy ☆–☆☆
Apremont.
Flowery wines.

Ayze

Domaine Belluard ☆–☆☆
Ayze. 13 ha.
A Biodynamic property that specializes in *méthode traditionnelle* and a rare white from the Gringet grape, said to be related to the Savagnin of the Jura. Dominique Belluard has eight hectares of the variety, which you are unlikely to find anywhere else in Savoie.

Chautagne

Cave Coopérative de Chautagne ☆
Ruffieux. 185 ha.
www.cave-de-chautagne.com
This cooperative, uniting 130 growers, specializes in red wines from Mondeuse, Pinot Noir, and Gamay, although a quarter of the production is of white wines.

Chignin and Chignin-Bergeron

**Domaine La Combe des Grand'
Vignes** ☆–☆☆
Chignon. 8 ha. www.chignin.com
Brothers Denis and Didier Berthollier are known for their excellent Chignin Bergeron.

The Quénard Family ☆☆
Chignin.
(Five separate branches: André and son Michel, Claude, Jean-Pierre and Jean-Francois, Raymond and son Pascal, René.) Pascal, with six hectares, is often regarded as the best, with André and Michel (22 hectares) hot on his heels. However, all the branches maintain high standards.

Crépy

Domaine de la Grande Cave de Crépy ☆–☆☆
Douvaine.
Specialties here include wines from vines over 40 years old, and a rare late-harvest Chasselas.

Cruet

Cave des Vins Fins ☆
Cruet. 360 ha. www.cavedecruet.com
Founded in 1939, this cooperative is responsible for one fifth of all Savoie wine, and offers a range of 35 different bottlings.

Domaine de l'Idylle ☆–☆☆
Cruet. 18 ha.
Good Jacquère and Mondeuse from the Tiollier brothers.

Frangy

Domaine Dupasquier "Aimavigne" ☆☆–☆☆☆
Jongieux. 12 ha.
Excellent Roussette and other wines, which are bottle-aged before release.

Monthoux

Michel Millon Rousseau ☆☆
St-Jean-de-Chevelu. 2 ha
Fine whites wines, especially Jacquère, on the Coteau de Monthoux.

Montmelian

Louis Magnin ☆☆–☆☆☆
Arbin. 6 ha.
www.domainelouismagnin.fr
Excellent Roussanne and Mondeuse, the latter capable of ageing. Even the more modest Gamay is very well made.

Charles Trosset ☆☆
Arbin. 4 ha,
Two brothers, Joseph and Louis, run this small property, which specializes in Mondeuse.

Ripaille

Château de Ripaille ☆–☆☆
Thonon-les-Bains. 22 ha. www.ripaille.fr
Good Chasselas, and nothing but Chasselas.

Seyssel

Maison Mollex ☆☆
Corbonod. 25 ha. www.maison-mollex.com
This estate is a major producer in the appellation, producing fine *méthode traditionnelle* wines as well as a wide range of still wines from Apremont and elsewhere.

Varichon & Clerc ☆
Seyssel. www.boisset.com
Owned by Burgundian négociant Boisset, this is a general négociant for sparkling Savoie wines.

Weighing grapes at a cave coopérative, Savoie

The Loire Valley

It is marvellous with what felicity, what gastronomic *savoir-vivre*, the rivers Rhône and Loire counter-balance one another on their passage through France. For 160 kilometres (100 miles) or so they even run parallel, flowing in opposite directions 48 kilometres (30 miles) apart.

They decline the notion of rivalry: in every way they are complementary. The Rhône gives France its soothing, warming, satisfying, winter-weight wines. The Loire provides the summer drinking.

The Loire rises within 160 kilometres (99 miles) of the Mediterranean. Wine is made in earnest along some 400 kilometres (248 miles) of its course and on the banks of its lower tributaries. It is a big stretch of country, and one might expect a wide variety of wines. The long list of the appellations (there are 63 ACs) encourages the idea, but it is not difficult to simplify into half-a-dozen dominant styles based on the grape varieties.

The Loire has three principal white and two red grapes (but only one that gives fine wine). Among the whites, the centre stage is held by the Chenin Blanc (alias Pineau de la Loire). It dominates in Touraine and even more so in Anjou, its produce ranging from neutral/acidic base material for sparkling Saumur to toffee-rich, apparently immortal, dessert wines. It is so versatile because it has such subtle flavours (quince, citrus fruits, green apples); its qualities lie more in balance and vitality. It keeps a high acid content even when it ripens (which it can do) to extremely high levels of sugar. Aromatically it is non-committal – until it matures. Even then, it has fruit salad and crème brûlée both within its repertoire.

Downstream from Anjou the dominant white grape is the Muscadet – again a low-profile variety. Early ripening and (in contrast) low acidity, rather than any great aroma, make it ideal for instant drinking with *fruits de mer*.

Upstream in Touraine, east of Vouvray-Montlouis and beyond to Pouilly and Sancerre, is the country of the Sauvignon Blanc, in this climate one of the most intensely aromatic grapes in France.

The Cabernet Franc is the quality red grape of the Loire, at its very best at Chinon in Touraine and almost equally successful in parts of Anjou. It is shadowed everywhere by the Gamay, which is made into juicy, fresh, light-to-medium-bodied reds that can be delicious. Both, along with Grolleau, are responsible for large quantities of more or less amiable rosé, one of the region's great money-spinners.

A number of grapes are named on Loire labels: the white Gros Plant of the Muscadet region (a sharp grape that might be described as its Aligoté); the Pinot Noir, grown to make red wine in Sancerre; Chardonnay in Haut-Poitou. A couple are traditional and accepted; a white variety called Romorantin gives the thin wine of Cheverny. A great number of ignoble plants used to be grown, but in the last 30-odd years they have been slowly ousted from the vineyards in favour of the principal types and an understudy cast of Cabernet Sauvignon, Malbec (here called Cot, although from 2006 producers can use the name Malbec on their labels), Pinot Meunier, and such local characters as Arbois (now known as Orbois, to avoid confusion with the Jura wine) and Pineau d'Aunis, and even Furmint from Hungary and Verdelho from Madeira.

As with its grapes, so with its regions, the Loire is simply divisible into its upper waters, above Orléans, which – together with their hinterland near Bourges – are best-known for producing whites from Sauvignon Blanc; its famous slow-moving centre, where it passes in infinite procession among the many châteaux of Touraine and Anjou; and its broad maritime reaches, where the wind carries the hint of shrimps far inland.

Wine Areas of the Loire Valley

All Loire AC and VDQS wines are listed below. (Remember that the VDQS category is due to be phased out at the end of 2011. Most will apply for AOP status, with the one exception of Gros Plant, which is happy to be translated into an IGP, allowing it to retain higher yields and the possibility of blending with other varieties.) There is a total vineyard area of 73,000 hectares, cultivated by 13,000 growers. The production figures given refer to the 2000 vintage.

Coteaux d'Ancenis (red, white, and rosé) VDQS. Lower Loire. 262 ha. Light Gamay, occasionally Cabernet, reds and rosés from the north bank opposite Muscadet. The white is marginal, and is produced from Chenin Blanc and a minuscule quantity of Malvoisie (Pinot Gris).

Anjou (red and white) AC. West-Central. Light, mainly Cabernet Franc, reds from a wide area (an alternative to Saumur). Slightly less white is produced: mainly Chenin Blanc and often slightly sweet. There is no special quality.

Anjou-Coteaux de la Loire (white) AC. West-Central. 120 ha. A limited area along both banks of the river west of Angers. Chenin Blanc of variable quality, but often quite delicious off-dry or sweet wines. Only a handful of producers.

Anjou Gamay (red) AC. West-Central. 320 ha. Light yet tasty reds for first-year drinking, which can often have more character than many a Beaujolais.

Anjou Mousseux (white and rosé) AC. West-Central. Made throughout the entire Anjou zone. Chenin Blanc is the base of the whites though Cabernet, Cot, Gamay, Grolleau, and Pineau d'Aunis are permitted (to a maximum of 60 per cent). A small quantity of rosé is made from Cabernet, Cot, Gamay, Grolleau, and Pineau d'Aunis.

Anjou-Villages (red) AC. West-Central. 270 ha. There are 46 communes entitled to this appellation for the production of Cabernet Franc and Cabernet Sauvignon. The wines cannot be sold before the September after the harvest. Since 1998, about a dozen producers cultivating 85 hectares can use the appellation Anjou-Villages Brissac, named after one of the best-known villages.

Cabernet d'Anjou (rosé) AC. West-Central. 2,600 ha. The best-quality rosé, normally rather sweet; at its best from Martigné-Briand, Tigné, and La Fosse-Tigné in the Coteaux du Layon.

Rosé d'Anjou (rosé) AC. West-Central. 2,200 ha. Pale, sweet rosé mainly from Grolleau.

Coteaux de l'Aubance (white) AC. West-Central. 160 ha. Chenin Blanc, in a range of styles from off-dry to *doux*, from shallow schist soils on the south bank opposite Angers, north of the (not automatically superior) Coteaux du Layon. Quality is increasing steadily.

Côtes d'Auvergne (red, white, and rosé) VDQS. Extreme upper Loire. 1,000 ha, of which only 400 are cultivated commercially, the remainder being for family consumption. Near Clermont-Ferrand. Chanturgues, Châteaugay, Corent, Boudes, and Madargues are considered *crus* and their names are used on the labels. Easy-drinking wines made principally from Gamay and Pinot Noir. The white is relatively unimportant: a very light Chardonnay.

Bonnezeaux (white) AC. West-Central. 120 ha. Superlative *cru* of Chenin Blanc in the Coteaux du Layon, Anjou. In fine years, when noble rot is abundant, a great sweet wine with Sauternes-like concentration, since yields are restricted to a maximum of 25 hl/ha.

Bourgueil (red and rosé) AC. Central. 1,400 ha. Excellent red of Cabernet Franc (up to ten per cent Cabernet Sauvignon is permitted, but its use is rare) from the north bank facing Chinon, Touraine. For drinking young and cool or maturing like Bordeaux.

Châteaumeillant (red and rosé) VDQS. Upper Loire. 98 ha. Minor area of Gamay and Pinot Noir south of Bourges. Light reds or very pale *gris* rosés.

Chaume (white) AC. West-Central. 70 ha. A superior appellation for Coteaux du Layon from an exceptional terroir. The wine must have an extra degree of ripeness to that required for a Coteaux du Layon.

Cheverny (red, white, and rosé) AC. East-Central. 490 ha. Small but growing supply of light Gamay and Pinot Noir blends with up to 15 per cent Cabernet or Cot for the red, and pure or blended Gamay for the rosé. The white is mainly quite sharp Sauvignon with a dash of Chardonnay from south of Blois.

Chinon (red, white, and rosé) AC. Central. 2,100 ha. Fine Cabernet Franc red, sometimes superb and capable of ageing many years, but generally drunk young and cool. The most important Loire red. A small quantity of white is produced from Chenin Blanc.

Cour-Cheverny (white) AC. 45 ha. A pungently vinous wine made from the local Romorantin grape in the heart of the Cheverny zone.

Fiefs Vendéens (red, white, and rosé) VDQS. West. 380 ha. Light reds and rosés made principally from Gamay, Pinot Noir, and Cabernet. About one-quarter of production is white, mostly quaffable Chenin Blanc.

Côtes du Forez (red and rosé) AC. Extreme Upper Loire. 200 ha. The southernmost Loire vineyards, south of Lyon: Gamay, Beaujolais-style.

Coteaux du Giennois (red, white, and rosé) AC. Upper Loire. 191 ha. Light- to medium-bodied reds from just downstream of Pouilly/Sancerre towards Gien. Well-made, they can be delicious. A recent ruling states they must be a Pinot Noir and Gamay blend. Half of the production is white, solely from Sauvignon.

Haut-Poitou (Vin du) (red, white, and rosé) VDQS. South-Central. 700 ha. Flourishing vineyard south of Anjou, mainly Gamay and Cabernet Sauvignon, with some Merlot, Pinot Noir, Cot, and Grolleau. There is an expanding production of Sauvignon Blanc, Chardonnay, Chenin Blanc, and Pinot Blanc.

Jasnières (white) AC. North-Central. 60 ha. A *cru* within Coteaux du Loir. Small Chenin Blanc area north of Tours. Wine like Vouvray, if less rich. Ages very well.

Coteaux du Layon (white) AC. West-Central. 1,350 ha. The biggest area of quality Chenin Blanc, south of Angers, generally fully sweet, *moelleux* or *liquoreux*; it includes the *grands crus* Quarts de Chaume and Bonnezeaux.

Coteaux du Layon-Villages must have an extra degree of ripeness and come from 350 hectares distributed among six communes: Beaulieu-sur-Layon, Faye-d'Anjou, Rochefort-sur-Loire, Rablay-sur-Layon, St-Aubin-de-Luigné, and St-Lambert-du-Lattay.

Coteaux du Loir (red, white, and rosé) AC. North-Central. 78 ha. Small area of Pineau d'Aunis and Gamay with some Cot and Cabernet north of Tours on the Loir, a tributary of the Loire. About one-third is white from Chenin Blanc.

Crémant de Loire (white and rosé) AC. Anjou-Saumur-Touraine. 550 ha. Appellation for high-quality sparkling wine, which must be aged at least 12 months on the yeasts.

Rosé de Loire (rosé) AC. Anjou-Saumur-Touraine. 750 ha. An appellation for dry rosés with 30 per cent Cabernet – not widely used, but can be good.

Menetou-Salon (red, white, and rosé) AC. Upper Loire. 458 ha. Red and rosé rival to Sancerre, with similar light Pinot Noir. The more important white production is Sauvignon, like Sancerre.

Montlouis (white) AC. East-Central. 350 ha. The reflected image of Vouvray across the Loire: dry, semi-sweet, and occasionally sweet wines. Also made as *pétillant* and *mousseux* sparkling wines.

Muscadet (white) AC. Lower Loire. 3,424 ha. A large area but a small part of Muscadet production (see Muscadet de Sèvre-et-Maine).

Muscadet Coteaux de la Loire (white) AC. Lower Loire. 200 ha. The smallest section of Muscadet, upstream of Muscadet de Sèvre-et-Maine.

Muscadet Côtes de Grand Lieu (white) AC. Lower Loire. 290 ha. The newest Muscadet subregion stretches west of Nantes airport.

Muscadet de Sèvre-et-Maine (white) AC. Lower Loire. 8,217 ha. Much the biggest Loire AC: the best part of Muscadet, east and south of Nantes.

Gros Plant du Pays Nantais (white) VDQS. Lower Loire. 2,000 ha. Sharp white of Gros Plant (or Folle Blanche) from the Muscadet area.

Orléanais (Vin de l') (red, white, and rosé) VDQS. Upper Loire. 150 ha. Very light reds of Pinot Meunier, Cabernet Franc, and Pinot Noir. The white wine is a light-style Chardonnay.

Pouilly-Fumé (white) AC. Upper Loire 1,200 ha. Powerful, aromatic Sauvignon Blanc from opposite Sancerre.

Pouilly-sur-Loire (white) AC. Upper Loire. 40 ha. Neutral white of Chasselas from the same vineyards as Pouilly-Fumé – must be drunk young.

Quarts de Chaume (white) AC. West-Central. 50 ha. *Grand cru* of the Coteaux du Layon, with maximum yields set at 20 hl/ha. In certain years, glorious rich wines of Chenin Blanc.

Quincy (white) AC. Upper Loire. 175 ha. Small source of attractive Sauvignon Blanc west of Bourges.

Reuilly (red, white, and rosé) AC. Upper Loire. 160 ha. White from Sauvignon Blanc; Pinot Noir and Pinot Gris reds and rosés.

Côte Roannaise (red and rosé) AC. Extreme Upper Loire. 180 ha. Gradually expanding Gamay region not far from Beaujolais, in distance or style. There are some 30 growers.

St-Nicolas-de-Bourgueil (red and rosé) AC. Central. 1,000 ha. Neighbour to Bourgueil with similar excellent Cabernet Franc.

St-Pourçain-sur-Sioule (red, white, and rosé) VDQS. Extreme upper Loire. 600 ha. The well-known local wine of Vichy: Gamay and Pinot Noir from chalk soil – good café wine. A great deal is very pale rosé. The white, which can be better, is made from Tressallier, Chardonnay, and Sauvignon. Commendable country wines.

Sancerre (red, white, and rosé) AC. Upper Loire. 2,500 ha. Light Pinot Noir red and rosé from chalky soil have their followers, but the area is better known for white. Making real

progress: the best wines are richer and longer-lived. About five times as much white is produced: fresh, eminently fruity and aromatic Sauvignon Blanc.

Saumur (red and white) AC. West-Central. 1,450 ha. Light Cabernet reds from south of Saumur – can also be sold as Anjou. The white is crisp Chenin Blanc with up to 20 per cent Chardonnay and/or Sauvignon. About one third of the grapes are made into sparkling wine.

Cabernet de Saumur (rosé) AC. West-Central. 75 ha. Upstream, slightly drier, equivalent of Cabernet d'Anjou. Wines must be vinified by a method that direct presses for early consumption.

Saumur-Champigny (red) AC. West-Central. 1,400 ha. Possibly the best Cabernet reds of Anjou, from the northern part of the Saumur area just east of the city.

Coteaux de Saumur (white) AC. West-Central. 12 ha. Almost extinct Chenin Blanc, often off-dry, sometimes *moelleux*, from a similar but slightly more widespread area than Saumur-Champigny.

Saumur Mousseux AC. West-Central. 1,285 ha. *Méthode traditionnelle* rosé of Cabernet, Gamay, Grolleau, Pinot Noir, and d'Aunis. The white is mostly Chenin Blanc (though up to 60 per cent can be Grolleau, Pinots Noir, and d'Aunis). Increasingly popular and sometimes excellent.

Savennières (white) AC. West-Central. 124 ha. Sometimes splendid, powerful, long-lived, dry Chenin Blanc from west of

Mechanized harvesting has taken place in some vineyards since the 1960s

Angers. It includes the Grands crus Roche aux Moines (17 ha) and Coulée de Serrant (6.8 ha).

Vins de Thouarsais (red, white, and rosé) VDQS. West-Central. 20 ha. Vineyards in the Thouet Valley south of Saumur make red and rosé from Gamay, and white from Chenin Blanc.

Touraine (red, white, and rosé) AC. East-Central. 5,500 ha. Principal grapes for red and rosé are Gamay, Cabernet, and Cot (the label will name the grape). Gamays can outshine many a Beaujolais – at least in warm years. In west Touraine, pure Cabernet is generally bottled; in the east, the authorities are encouraging blends. For rosés, Pineau d'Aunis and Grolleau may also be used. The white is usually Sauvignon Blanc, in a tolerable imitation of Sancerre. Chenin Blanc, Menu Pineau (alias Arbois), and Chardonnay now play a supporting role. Semi- and full-sparkling versions are of some importance. Whites are based on Chenin Blanc with up to 30 per cent black grapes, including Cabernet, Pinots Noir, Gris, and Meunier, Pineau d'Aunis, Cot, and Grolleau. Reds from Cabernet Franc; rosés from Cabernet Franc, Cot, Gamay, and Grolleau.

Touraine-Amboise (red, white, and rosé) AC. East-Central. 220 ha. Light reds made from Gamay, Cabernet, and Cot from just east of Vouvray. The white is Chenin Blanc, sometimes capable of Vouvray-like quality.

Touraine-Azay-Le-Rideau (white and rosé) AC. East-Central. 90 ha. Small Chenin Blanc area that occasionally produces wines as rich as Vouvray. The rosé is a minor outpost of Grolleau with some Gamay, Cot, or Cabernet, made between Tours and Chinon.

Touraine-Mesland (red, white, and rosé) AC. East-Central. 110 ha. Rather good blends of Gamay, Cabernet Franc, and Cot for the red, and 80 per cent Gamay for the rosé, from the north bank of the Loire opposite Chaumont. Less important is the dry white chiefly of Chenin Blanc, sometimes blended with Chardonnay and Sauvignon.

Touraine Noble Joué (rosé) AC. East-Central. 24 ha. An almost extinct historic appellation that has been recently revived. Small production of rosé from Pinot Meunier, Pinot Noir, and/or Pinot Gris.

Valençay (red, white, and rosé) VDQS. Upper Loire. 150 ha. Dry white of Chenin Blanc, Sauvignon, and others. Reds and rosés are an outpost of Gamay on the eastern border of Touraine.

Coteaux du Vendômois (red, white, and rosé) AC. North-Central. 152 ha. The wines, particularly the rosés, are made chiefly from Pineau d'Aunis supported by Gamay, Cabernet, and Pinot Noir. The white is Chenin Blanc, pure or blended with Chardonnay.

Vouvray (white) AC. East-Central. 2,000 ha. Dry, semi-sweet, or sweet Chenin Blanc of potentially superb quality, according to the vintage. There are also sparkling versions.

Muscadet

It is hard to resist the notion of Muscadet as Neptune's own vineyard. Nowhere is the gastronomic equation quite so simple and clear-cut – or appetizing. Brittany provides the *fruits de mer*; the vineyards clustering south and east of Nantes provide oceans of the ideal white wine.

Muscadet is both the grape and the wine – as well as the zone. The grape came from Burgundy (where it is still sometimes found as the Melon de Bourgogne) as an early ripener that was satisfied with thin, stony soil. Early ripening (about September 15) gets it in before the autumn rain in this often cloudy and windswept vineyard. The Muscadet (or Melon) has low natural acidity that makes it particularly vulnerable in contact with air. To avoid oxidation and to bottle the wine as fresh and tasty as possible, the local tradition is to leave the new wine in its tank or barrel at the end of fermentation, lying on its own yeasty sediment (*sur lie*) and to bottle it in March or April from the barrel – racking it, as it were, straight into bottles without fining or filtering. A certain amount of CO_2 is still dissolved in the wine and helps to make it fresh and sometimes faintly prickly to the tongue.

With modern quantities and economics, such careful bottling barrel by barrel is becoming rare, but the aim is still the same – except among certain growers who look for a more fully developed wine for further ageing. Regulation changes have effectively made bottling *sur lie* an appellation in itself: now there are generic Muscadets and generic Muscadets *sur lie*, Muscadets de Sèvre-et-Maine and Muscadets de Sèvre-et-Maine *sur lie*, etc. The key differences are in the yield and in the timing of bottling following the harvest. Yields for *sur lie* wines, for example, cannot exceed 55 hectolitres per hectare (for generic Muscadets the yield can be up to 65 hectolitres per hectare). As from 1997, *sur lie* wine must be bottled off its lees in the cellar in which it was vinified.

Thus there are different styles of Muscadet, but it is hard to pin them down except by tasting each producer's wares. The extremes are a light, fruity but essentially rather mild wine or, by contrast, one with a pungently vegetable and somehow "wild" flavour, that can be very exciting with oysters or clams. The latter style can mature surprisingly well: I have had a five-year-old bottle that had achieved a sort of quintessential soft dryness I found delectable with turbot. Wines that have been bottle-aged can be marketed by their producers with the words Muscadet Haute Expression on the label.

Much the greatest concentration of Muscadet vineyards is just east of Nantes and south of the Loire, in the area named for the rivers Sèvre and Maine. About 75 per cent of the 12,000 hectares of vineyards are Sèvre-et-Maine; the rest is divided among the Coteaux de la Loire scattered eastwards towards Anjou, Côtes de Grand Lieu, and plain Muscadet with over 3,400 hectares dotted over a wide area south of Nantes.

All four appellations are interspersed with 2,000 hectares planted with the secondary white grape of the area, the Gros Plant or Folle Blanche, which stands in relation to Muscadet as Aligoté does to Chardonnay: an acknowledged poor relation, but with a faithful following of its own. Gros Plant du Pays

Nantais is always sharp, often "green", sometimes coarse, but can be made by a sensitive hand into a very fresh if fragile wine. It would be a natural Breton progression to drink a bottle of Gros Plant with oysters, then Muscadet with a sole. Gros Plant has a maximum alcoholic degree of 11; Muscadet a maximum of 12. Controlling the maximum degree is unusual, but particularly necessary in a region where *chaptalization* is normal and natural acidity low. Over-sugared Muscadet would be a graceless brute.

So, some would argue, is Muscadet aged in new oak. This fad gained some ground in the late 1990s, but has not really caught on. It should not be dismissed out of hand as an aberration, but it does seem an unnecessary embellishment of a wine that has won friends with its uncomplicated charm. A more subtle tendency among some producers is deliberately to bottle the wine with some residual sugar.

But Muscadet is not flourishing. There was a time, about 30 years ago, when Muscadet was a staple offering at every British wine bar: cheap, uncomplicated, refreshing. But modern drinkers look for more overt fruit than classic Muscadet can deliver. Moreover, the expansion of the area under vine during those boom years led to many poor quality wines reaching international markets – and failing to find favour. Sales have slumped, and the local authorities have been obliged to decree the grubbing up of less popular Gros Plant vineyards, for a start. This is a shame, as authentic Muscadet has its place, both as an apéritif, and as a satisfying wine with which to wash down fresh and simply prepared fish and seafood.

For red wine, the region has little to offer: 262 hectares among the Muscadet vineyards of the Coteaux de la Loire, around the town of Ancenis, grow Gamay and a little Cabernet for light red and rosé, sold as VDQS Coteaux d'Ancenis. There is also Malvoisie (Pinot Gris), an off-dry specialty of Ancenis, which can make an excellent apéritif. Blends of Cabernet, Gamay, and Pinot Noir are used in the up-and-coming VDQS wines known as Fiefs-Vendéens, from the Atlantic coast region La Vendée, just south of Muscadet.

The name Vin de Pays du Val de Loire (it used to be called Vin de Pays du Jardin de la France) is increasingly used for wines such as Chardonnay and Gamay from a wide area, which covers 13 *départements*. Other *vin de pays* may put the name of the region on the label, including Marches de Bretagne, Retz, or the *département* name, such as Vin de Pays de Loire-Atlantique.

Leading Muscadet Producers

Domaine du Bois-Joly ☆☆
Le Pallet. 30 ha. www.domaineduboisjoly.com
The Bouchard family produces invigorating *sur lie* wines, especially the *cuvée* Harmonie and a *cuvée* released after up to seven years of bottle-age. This is also a reliable source for Gros Plant and light Gamay rosé.

Boullault & Fils ☆–☆☆
Château La Touche, Vallet. 40 ha. www.boullault-fils.com
A fine sloping vineyard, run with great care by the Boullault family since 1930. The wines sell under the labels Domaine

des Dorices or Château la Touche, depending on the market. There is no difference between them. The domaine distinguishes three *cuvées*, however. The first, Cuvée Choisie, which represents the major part of the production, is made for drinking young. The Hermine d'Or selection, and in great vintages, the Cuvée Grande Garde (which is kept up to 20 months on its lees), benefit from three years or more of cellaring.

Château de Briacé ☆–☆☆
Le Landreau. 15 ha. www.chateau-briace.com.
The château is a private wine college, at which the students of viticulture and oenology work the vines. The Muscadet de Sèvre-et-Maine, Gros Plant, and various varietal *vins de pays* are invariably clean, correct, and nicely made.

Chéreau-Carré ☆☆
St Fiacre-sur-Maine. 120 ha. www.chereau-carre.fr
The Chéreau family is one of Muscadet's largest proprietors as well as an important négociant house specializing in Loire wine. It markets four million bottles yearly, half from purchased wines, half from estates belonging to various family members. The domaines include Château de Chasseloir, which serves as Chéreau-Carré's HQ. A 25-hectare property on the banks of the River Maine, it includes a three-hectare parcel of century-old vines vinified separately as Comte Leloup de Chasseloir.

Domaine du Bois Bruley is a 13-hectare vineyard in Basse Goulaine. This property supplies Chéreau's Gros Plant du Pays Nantais as well as Muscadet de Sèvre-et-Maine *sur lie*. Château de l'Oiselinière de la Ramée is a 10-hectare vineyard in Vertou. The old-vines *cuvée* here is called L'Aigle d'Or. See also Domaines V. Günther-Chéreau.

Xavier Coirier ☆
Pissote. 20 ha.
A dedicated grower in the VDQS Fiefs-Vendéens. Fresh, fragrant whites, rosés, and reds for summer quaffing.

Donatien-Bahuaud ☆–☆☆
La Chapelle-Heulin. 12 ha. www.donatien-bahuaud.fr
A large négociant-grower, Donatien-Bahuaud markets ten million bottles of Loire wine a year, of which 25 per cent is Muscadet. The firm's most famous Muscadet is Le Master de Donatien, which represents *cuvées* selected after blind tasting by food and wine professionals. The selected *cuvées* are bottled at the property of the individual growers and are presented in seriographed bottles.

Donatien-Bahuaud also produces Muscadet from its own vines at Château de la Cassemichère as well as other Muscadets, including the early drinking Fringant. In 2007 the company was acquired by the Rhône négociant Gabriel Meffre, and the once extensive range has been somewhat reduced.

Domaine de l'Ecu ☆☆☆
La Bretonnière, Le Landreau. 21 ha.
Guy Bossard's estate pioneered organic and then Biodynamic cultivation in the Sèvre-et-Maine. Bossard produces a wide range of wines from his medium-sized domaine. A fairly recent venture has been the coaxing of distinct and distinctive *cuvées*

from different soil types: Gneiss, Orthogneiss, and Granit. The richly textured, mineral Hermine d'Or *cuvée* shows the ability of his wines to develop in bottle. Other wines include a very fine Gros Plant du Pays Nantais, and a nuanced *méthode traditionnelle* made chiefly from Gros Plant.

Domaine de la Foliette ☆☆
La Haye-Fouassière. 38 ha.
A large, traditional estate producing rich, appley Muscadet de Sèvre-et-Maine sur lie.

Marquis de Goulaine ☆–☆☆
Château de Goulaine, Basse-Goulaine. 50 ha.
www.chateau.goulaine.online.fr
The showplace of Muscadet; westernmost of the great Renaissance châteaux of the Loire. The Château de Goulaine, inhabited by the same family for 2,000 years, is now an efficient example of the stately home trade. Estate-grown grapes plus bought-in wine supply a wide range of wines: Gros Plant and Chardonnay as well as three different Muscadets, all bottled *sur lie*. The Cuvée du Millénaire, the domaine's best wine, is a Muscadet made from 50-year-old vines from Goulaine's four-hectare Clos la Tâche, blended with wines from several growers.

Guilbaud Frères ☆–☆☆
Gorges. 30 ha. www.guilbaud-muscadet.com
Négociant company founded in 1927 producing three million bottles of above-average Muscadets under various names, including its own wines from Domaine de la Moutonnière and Château de la Pingossière. The Clos du Pont, from La Moutonnière, is Guilbaud's finest wine; Château de la Pingossière is also commendable. Le Soleil Nantais, Guilbaud's top-of-the-range négociant wine, maintains a good standard.

Domaine Guindon ☆☆
St-Géréon. 28 ha.
Pierre Guindon offers three qualities of Muscadet des Coteaux de la Loire, as well as Gros Plant and Coteaux d'Ancenis (Gamay red and rosé) and unusual off-dry Malvoisie (Pinot Gris). A specialty here is a Muscadet given extensive skin-contact before fermentation.

Bringing in the harvest at the Château de Chasseloir

Domaines V. Günther-Chéreau ☆☆
Château du Coing, St-Fiacre-sur-Maine. 65 ha.
www.chateau-du-coing.com
This offshoot of Maison Chereau-Carré (q.v.) is owned by
Bernard Chéreau's daughter Véronique. Château du Coing
is a 50-hectare estate on the confluence of the Sèvre and the
Maine. The most impressive *cuvée* is called L'Ancestrale, which
spends over two years *sur lie*. For new-oak addicts there is also
a *cuvée* from very old vines fermented in new barrels. She also
owns two other properties. Grand Fief de la Cormeraie is
a five-hectare vineyard in the commune of Monnière.
"Commandeur" is the name of the splendid old-vines bottling.
Château de la Gravelle is a 12-hectare vineyard in Gorges. Its
two *cuvées* of Muscadet de Sèvre-et-Maine include an old-vines
bottling labelled "Don Quichotte".

Domaine de la Haute-Févrie ☆☆
La Févrie, Maisdon-sur-Sèvre. 26 ha.
Sebastien Branger produces elegant Muscadet de Sèvre-et-
Maine sur lie. L'Excellence is the name of his bottling from
vines at least 50 years old. Clos Joubert is aged in barriques.
A new addition to the range is Fiefs du Pagatine, from 55-
year-old vines and aged *sur lie* for 14 months. These are classic,
fully dry Muscadets.

Domaine des Herbauges ☆☆
Bouaye. 40 ha. www.domaine-des-herbauges.com
Jérôme Choblet makes superior Muscadet Côtes de Grand
Lieu from vineyards west of Nantes airport. Clos de la
Sénaigerie and Clos de la Fine are two notable single-vineyard
bottlings. Choblet also produces pleasant Gros Plant du Pays
Nantais and *vin de pays* from Chardonnay and Gamay.

Domaine de la Louvetrie ☆☆–☆☆☆
Les Brandières, La Haye-Fouassière. 45 ha.
www.domaines-landron.com
Joseph Landron is an exciting organic grower who bottles
his wines by soil type. His lightest *cuvée*, Amphibolite, is
named after its soils and is made to be drunk within the year.
The Hermine d'Or and Fief du Breil bottlings come from
harder soils – silica-streaked orthogneiss – and benefit from
a year or more of cellaring. The latter, the domaine's prestige
bottling, issues from old vines on a slope well-exposed to
the south.

Pierre Luneau-Papin ☆☆–☆☆☆
Le Landreau. 35 ha.
A skilled winemaker and dedicated grower, Pierre Luneau
produces a range of Muscadet *sur lie*: a lean, elegant Muscadet
des Coteaux de la Loire and numerous Muscadets de Sèvre-et-
Maine *sur lie*, including two single-vineyard bottlings: Les
Allées (from old vines) and Les Pierres Blanches from even
older, 60-year vines. There are also a barrel-fermented Manoir
la Grange and the new-oaked *cuvée* Le "L" d'Or.

Louis Métaireau ☆☆–☆☆☆
La Févrie, Maisdon-sur-Sèvre. 29 ha.
www.muscadet-grandmouton.com
All Métaireau wines are classic, fresh Muscadets without
exaggerated flavour. He insists on finesse. The two deluxe

bottlings, Cuvée LM and Number One, exemplify this style.
Métaireau also co-owns the 23-hectare Domaine du Grand
Mouton. Grapes from this property are picked slightly
underripe; the wines are *très sauvage* for the first one or
two years (when they go well with shellfish). At three or four
years they mellow enough to partner sole. Métaireau bottles
about ten per cent of Grand Mouton directly off its lees,
without filtration.

A tireless innovator, he introduced two Vin de Pays de
Loire-Atlantique, made from Melon, as well as two Muscadets
de Sèvre-et-Maine *sur lie* – Premier Jour and "10.5". The first
is made from grapes picked on the first day of harvest; the
second is low in alcohol. The company is now run by his
daughter Marie-Luce.

Château la Noë ☆–☆☆☆
Vallet. 100 ha.
A lordly domaine, unusual in Muscadet, with a stately
neoclassical mansion. The family of the Comte de Malestroit
has owned it since 1740. The estate produces a full-bodied
Muscadet from low yields.

Henri Poiron & Fils ☆☆
Les Quatre Routes, Maisdon-sur-Sèvre. 36 ha.
A grower with two properties producing three bottlings of
meaty Muscadet de Sèvre-et-Maine sur lie, Domaine des
Quatre Routes, Domaine du Manoir, and Château des
Grandes Noëlles. Gros Plant du Pays Nantais, Cabernet and
Gamay Vin de Pays du Jardin de la France, and a *méthode
traditionnelle* complete the selection.

Château de la Ragotière ☆☆
La-Regrippière. 68 ha. www.freres-coulliaud.com
This estate, traceable back to medieval times, was acquired
by the Coulliaud brothers in 1979. They produce a range of
Muscadets from the 28-hectare La Ragotière, of which the
most rich is often the Vieilles Vignes, and some varietal wines,
such as the Chardonnay. The brothers also own the 40-hectare
Château de la Morinière.

Marcel Sautejeau ☆–☆☆
Domaine de l'Hyvernière, Le Pallet. 150 ha.
www.marcel-sautejeau.fr
One of the larger Loire-Atlantique négociants, family-run.
The Domaine de l'Hyvernière is owned by Marcel Sautejeau
and the Château de la Botinière is owned by associate Jean
Beauquin. The Muscadet is mechanically harvested and
bottled *sur lie* to be drunk within two years. The Clos des
Orfeuilles comes from a plot within L'Hyvernière.
L'Exceptionnel is the firm's deluxe négociant bottling.
Total turnover of wine from the whole of the Loire valley
is more than 17 million bottles a year.

Sauvion & Fils ☆☆
Château du Cléray, Vallet. 38 ha. www.sauvion.fr
A flourishing family firm of growers and négociants, based
at the historic Château du Cléray. The domaine *sur lie* wine
is light and attractive, though the firm's special bottlings,
grouped under the Haute Culture range, often upstage it.
Allégorie du Cléray is Muscadet fermented and aged in

new-oak barrels. Cardinal Richard is the proprietary name Sauvion gives to a grower's wine that has been placed first after several juried tastings.

Les Vignerons de la Noëlle ☆–☆☆
Ancenis. 600 ha. www.vignerons-de-la-noelle.com
Founded in 1955, this cooperative has 150 growers with vineyards spanning the Nantais and the western rim of Anjou. The majority of production is Muscadet, both Sèvre-et-Maine and Coteaux de la Loire, including estate-bottlings in each appellation: Domaine la Mallonière and Domaine des Hautes-Noëlles in Sèvre-et-Maine, and a Muscadet from the Coteaux de la Loire. It also produces Gros Plant du Pays Nantais, Gamay-Coteaux d'Ancenis (red and rosé), Anjou Coteaux de la Loire, Anjou Rouge and -Villages, and Crémant de Loire.

Daniel & Gérard Vinet ☆☆
La Quilla, La Haye-Fouassière. 60 ha.
www.muscadet-vinet.fr
The Vinet brothers are ambitious young growers producing prime Muscadet de Sèvre-et-Maine *sur lie*. Domaine de la Quilla is their fine base Muscadet; Clos de la Houssaie comes from a small parcel of 0.7 hectares, producing 5,000 bottles annually. The *prestige cuvée*, Le Muscadet, is an assemblage of the Vinets' best *cuvées*, selected after numerous tastings, and releassd after five years of bottle age.

Anjou-Saumur

Muscadet is the most single-minded of all French vineyards. Anjou, its neighbour to the east, has a gamut of wines as complete as any region of France. Its biggest turnover used to be in rosé, before spring frosts caused damage. However, Anjou's sparkling wine industry at Saumur is second only to Champagne in size, its best reds are considerable Cabernets, and its finest wines of all, sweet and dry Chenin Blanc whites, rank among the great apéritif and dessert wines of France.

Rosé d'Anjou is a sweetish, light pink from which nobody expects very much – a blend of mainly Grolleau with Cabernet, Cot, Gamay, and the local Pineau d'Aunis. It has not recovered its former hold on the export market – though it seems to play well in French supermarkets. Cabernet d'Anjou, whose market is primarily national, is fighting back. It is also rosé (not red) but an appellation to treat with more respect. The Europe-wide resurgence in rosé wines since 2003 has not greatly aided these Anjou wines, as the competition, especially for drier, more refreshing wines, has become fierce. Cabernet Franc (here often called the Breton) is the best red-wine grape of the Loire; its rosé is dry and can be full of its raspberry-evoking flavour, too. The best examples come from Martigné-Briand, Tigné, and La Fosse-Tigné in what is known as Haut-Layon – part of the Coteaux du Layon – which is also the most important district for Chenin Blanc white wines with an inclination to sweetness.

With one exception, all the considerable vineyards of Anjou lie along the south bank of the Loire and astride its tributaries, the Layon, the Aubance, and the Thouet. The exception is Savennières, the local vineyard of the city of Angers, which interprets the Chenin Blanc in its own way: as a forceful and intense dry wine. Savennières contains two small *grands crus*: La Roche aux Moines and La Coulée de Serrant. The wines of these, or of any of the top-quality Savennières growers, are awkward and angular at first, with high acidity and biting concentration of flavour. In their youth they can seem hard and ungiving. They need age, sometimes up to 15 years, to develop their honey-scented potential. Drunk younger, they need accompanying food. It does seem that many producers are now making Savennières in a more accessible style, a commercial imperative, perhaps, but one that risks a loss of *typicité*.

Savennières faces Rochefort-sur-Loire across the broad river, complicated with islands. Rochefort is the gateway to the long valley of the Layon, where the Chenin Blanc may be dry (and acid and pernicious), but where all the fine wines are at least crisply sweet like an apple, and the best deeply and creamily sweet with the succulence of Sauternes.

The district of Coteaux de Layon contains two substantial *grands crus*, Quarts de Chaume and Bonnezeaux, where noble rot is a fairly frequent occurrence (less so than in Sauternes) and sheer concentration pushes the strength of the wine up to 13 to 14 degrees. Some great Layons are also made when the grapes

---

ENJOYING LOIRE WINES

The wide range of Loire wines covers almost any gastronomic eventuality. For apéritifs there are excellent sparkling wines, and even better *crémants* (*demi-sec* or young *moelleux* are also served by the locals as an apéritif) of Saumur and Vouvray, or the pungent, dry Chenin Blanc wines of Savennières. Mature *moelleux* may be rich enough to match foie gras.

For seafood, there is the incomparable match of Muscadet; for charcuterie Gros Plant du Pays Nantais, a young Pouilly-Fumé, Chenin Blanc, a light cool red,

or a dry to off-dry rosé; for richer fish dishes with sauces, either more and better Muscadet or a Sancerre or Pouilly-Fumé two or three years old.

For *entrées*, Chinon, Bourgueil, and Saumur-Champigny provide either Beaujolais-style young wines, freshly fruity, or the weight of riper vintages with five or six years' maturity. Mature Savennières or Vouvray *sec* or *demi-sec* can make an interesting alternative to white burgundy for certain richly sauced creamy dishes.

Sancerre is the inevitable local choice with strong cheeses; with milder ones the sweet wines of the Coteaux du Layon can be excellent. Light, young Coteaux du Layon, appley, sweet and very cold, can be a remarkable picnic wine.

The nobly rotten sweet wines of Bonnezeaux and Quarts de Chaume are some of France's finest dessert wines. Like the great German sweet wines, they are complete in themselves – perhaps better alone than with any food.

are picked *passerillés* (shrivelled), or normally overripe. There is a return to harvesting grapes by *tri* and those from the Layon and the Aubance that meet certain specifications may carry the designation Sélection de Grains Nobles on their labels. Some, but by no means all, of these sweet wines are aged in barrels. They are, in a sense, the vintage port of white wines: like vintage port, bottled young to undergo all their development with minimum-possible access to oxygen. The eventual bouquet is consequently as clean, flowery, and fresh-fruity as the grape itself, with the resonance and honeyed warmth of age. Great old Vouvray is so similar that it would be a brave man (or a native) who could claim to know them apart. Like German wines of fine vintages, they perform a balancing-act between sweetness and sustaining acidity. But few German wines of modern times can hold their balance for half as long.

Trends in the sweet-wine industry are being matched by progress in the production of the other styles of wine made in Anjou. The dry whites (Anjou Blanc) and the reds (both Anjou Rouge and Anjou-Villages) are similarly displaying a real improvement in quality. Anjou-Villages is the appellation which the top four-dozen red-wine communes are entitled to use.

Saumur is the centre of eastern Anjou, with a set of appellations of its own for dry or medium-dry white wines of Chenin Blanc (which is increasingly being bottled pure, though it can still be blended with up to 20 per cent Chardonnay and/or Sauvignon), and for *mousseux* versions of the same. Saumur's sparkling wine industry is built upon Chenin Blanc, which has the acidity to produce successful *méthode traditionnelle* wines. The main producers, many of whom are also négociants dealing in a range of Loire wines, are listed on the following pages. Many grapes are permitted in *crémants*, including a number of black ones, but not Sauvignon Blanc. There are also appellations in Saumur for red and rosé wines of Cabernet Franc and Pineau d'Aunis. The red-wine vineyards are scattered to the south of the city. Saumur-Champigny has enjoyed a recent leap to fame and fashion, with its light, savoury, herby reds. They come into their own in the ripest vintages; in lesser years, concentration and depth of flavour can be hard to attain.

Leading Anjou-Saumur Producers

Domaine de Bablut ☆☆–☆☆☆
Brissac-Quincé. 50 ha. www.vignobles-daviau.fr
Under the stewardship of Christophe Daviau, this long-established family estate is taking exciting new directions, particularly in the production of Coteaux de l'Aubance and in pursuing Biodynamic viticulture. The top bottlings are Vin Noble and Grandpierre, from botrytized grapes partially fermented and aged in new-oak barrels. They are as delicious

as they are nuanced. The domaine also produces the rest of the Anjou roster of wines – the pure Cabernet Franc called Pietra Alba is an imposing wine – and makes those of nearby Château de Brissac as well.

Domaine des Baumard ☆☆–☆☆☆
Rochefort-sur-Loire. 37 ha.
www.baumard.fr
Jean Baumard is a senior figure of the Loire, and a former professor of viticulture at Angers. His son, Florent, took over the domaine 20 years ago. His vineyards are dispersed, with significant holdings in Quarts de Chaume, Savennières (including part of the Clos du Papillon), and Coteaux du Layon (Clos de Ste-Catherine). Five hectares of Cabernet Franc and five of Cabernet Sauvignon make Anjou Rouge Logis de la Giraudière. Chardonnay is grown, along with Chenin, to make Crémant de Loire, and a house speciality is Vert de l'Or, a Verdelho made in dry and sweet versions. The Baumards use no wood as they prefer a reductive style. The Clos de Ste-Catherine is hard to classify: neither sweet nor dry but very lively – recommended with summer fruit or as an apéritif. The best wine is certainly the noble and elegant Quarts de Chaume.

Château de Bellerive ☆☆–☆☆☆
Rochefort-sur-Loire. 22 ha.
www.vignobles-alainchateau.fr
A major estate of the Grand Cru Quarts de Chaume, which has changed hands frequently in recent years. The current owner is Alain Château, who has bought a quiver of properties in the Loire and Bordeaux. Almost Yquem-like methods are adopted, which means accepting a tiny crop from old vines and picking only nobly rotten grapes in successive *tris* around the vineyard. Fermentation, which takes place in barrels, requires most of the winter.

The great difference between this and Sauternes (apart from the grapes) is that bottling is done at the end of April "when the moon is waxing", and all maturation takes place in bottle rather than barrel. The wine can scarcely be appreciated for five, sometimes ten, years – and it lasts for 50.

Château du Breuil ☆☆
Beaulieu-sur-Layon. 24 ha.
A good source of Coteaux du Layon-Beaulieu, the deluxe bottling of which is the Vieilles Vignes, matured in new oak barrels. However, the property was sold in 2006.

Domaine de Brizé ☆☆
Martigné-Briand. 40 ha. www.domainedebrize.free.fr
A fine family winery, run by fifth-generation Delhumeaus. The spectrum of Anjou wines is made, among them a sturdy Anjou-Villages called Clos Médecin, textbook Layon, dazzling Anjou-Gamay, and award-winning Crémant de Loire.

The Château of Saumur on the Loire

Philippe Cady ☆☆–☆☆☆
St-Aubin-de-Luigné. 20 ha. www.domainecady.fr
Luscious, honeyed Coteaux du Layon-St-Aubin and some
Chaume. The richest *cuvées* are called Volupté, and the most
concentrated is usually the Cuvée Eléonore.

Cave des Vignerons de Saumur ☆
St-Cyr-en-Bourg. 1,400 ha .
The cave coopérative, with 300 members, makes the gamut
of Saumur sparkling wines, including Saumur Brut (under
a variety of labels), Saumur Rosé Brut, Crémant de Loire
Cuvée de la Chevalerie Brut and Rosé, and a Rouge Mousseux
demi-sec. In all, this accounts for around 30 per cent of the
production of each appellation. The white Saumur also has
a good reputation.

Château de Chaintres ☆☆
Dampierre-sur-Loire. 20 ha. www.chaintres.com
Owned by Baron Gaël de Tigny, this is a charming old
country house. It was once a priory, and a notable producer
of Saumur-Champigny from walled vineyards. The Cuvée
Oratoriens is the only wine that is oak-aged.

Clos de Coulaine ☆☆
Savennières. 7 ha.
A respected producer of fresh, floral Savennières and silky
Anjou Rouge and -Villages. Since 1992, the domaine has
been run by Claude Papin, a top producer of Coteaux du
Layon (see Château Pierre-Bise).

Clos Rougeard ☆☆☆
Chacé. 10 ha.
The Foucault family, now in its eighth generation here,
produce three *cuvées* of Saumur-Champigny. Les Poyeux is an
outstanding vineyard, and the wine is aged in one-year-old
barrels; Le Bourg, in contrast, is aged in new oak. There is also
a minute production of the all but extinct sweet wines from
Coteaux de Saumur. Profound, long-lived wines.

Domaine du Closel ☆☆
Savennières. 16 ha. www.savenieres-closel.com
An estate, long run by women, producing classic white
Savennières, concentrated wine fermented mostly in tank,
then aged in wood (excepting some *cuvées*, such as Clos du
Papillon, which still ferment in barrel), and a little Cabernet
for Anjou or Anjou-Villages. Les Caillardières is a Savennières
made in an off-dry style.

Château de la Coulée de Serrant ☆☆–☆☆☆☆
Château de la Roche-aux-Moines, Savennières. 15 ha.
www.coulee-de-serrant.com
A beautiful little estate in an outstanding situation, chosen by
monks in the twelfth century. The main vineyard is the Clos
de la Coulée de Serrant, run by Nicolas Joly, whose highly
individual methods of growing vines and making wine are
based around the theory of Biodynamism, of which he is
regarded as a high priest by countless acolytes. He uses no
fertilizers or artificial pesticides and no modern technological
equipment; the results are wines of unusual ageing qualities.
Joly also owns three hectares of La Roche aux Moines called
the Clos de la Bergerie, and some parcels of Cabernet for

Château de la Roche. Another *cuvée* from Savennières, Les
Vieux Clos, has recently been added to the Joly stable. Chenin
Blanc here makes some of its most intense dry (or off-dry)
wines of extraordinary savour and longevity. With a yield of
only about 1,700 cases, the top wine is on allocation at a
suitably high price. No one questions Nicolas Joly's zeal, but
some questions have been raised about the oxidative character
some vintages acquire with ageing; Joly, however, insists the
wine needs to be decanted for 24 hours to achieve its full
grandeur and complexity, and that once open, the wine will
continue to develop positively for many days.

Philippe Delesvaux ☆☆–☆☆☆☆
St-Aubin-de-Luigné. 15 ha.
An ambitious grower who lived in Paris until he came here in
1983. He produces pleasant Anjou Blanc *sec* and tasty Anjou
Rouge, but pulls out all the stops with his Layon, particularly
the *cuvées* from the *lieux-dits* La Moque and Clos du Pavillon,
and the luscious Sélection de Grains Nobles. These are among
the most concentrated of all the sweet wines of France, crafted
by a grower who has the patience and courage to wait for the
maximum concentration each year.

Château de Fesles ☆☆–☆☆☆☆
Thouarcé. 35 ha. www.fesles.com
An historic property, reputed for its remarkable Bonnezeaux
from 14 hectares. Long owned by the Boivin family, which
had, quite literally, created the appellation, it has passed
through different hands in the 1990s, and is one of many
estates now owned by Bernard Germain in Bordeaux and
Anjou. All the white wines, dry and sweet, are fermented in
400-litre barrels. Although the estate produces a range of
Anjou wines, the Bonnezeaux is the most sought-after:
sumptuous and peachy, and marked by botrytis, it remains
fresh for decades thanks to its vibrant but ripe acidity.

Domaine des Forges ☆☆–☆☆☆
St-Aubin-de-Luigné. 42 ha.
Claude Branchereau makes the gamut of Anjou wines, and
has added some Savennières to his portfolio, but his heart is in
his Coteaux du Layon, of which he makes several marvellous
cuvées, including an old-vines bottling from the Chaume *lieu-
dit* Les Onnis (also spelled "Aunis"). The richest wines are
the numerous Sélections de Grains Nobles, but the simpler
wines can be just as enjoyable with their freshness and bright,
appley fruit.

Château de la Genaiserie ☆☆–☆☆☆
St-Aubin-de-Luigné. 24 ha. www.genaiserie.com
In 1990, Yves Soulez purchased a rambling old château with
prime Layon vineyards after selling his share of the family
domaine in Savennières. Of his many *cuvées* of Layon, the
richest, most concentrated, and finest came from low-yielding
old vines in the *lieux-dits* Les Petits Houx, Les Simonelles, and
La Roche. In 2003 Soulez sold the property to Frédéric Julia,
who this far has maintained the standards of his predecessor.

Domaine aux Moines ☆☆
Savennières. 8 ha.
This property is a major proprietor in the top Savennières *cru*

of La Roche-aux-Moines. The dry wines are traditional and long-lived. In suitable vintages the domaine produces wines with a distinct sweetness called Cuvée des Nonnes or Cuvée de l'Abbesse.

Domaine des Petits Quarts ☆☆–☆☆☆
Faye. 60 ha.
Jean-Pascal Godineau makes a wide range of wines, but his pride and joy is Bonnezeaux, producing five different *cuvées*, three of which are from single vineyards. In some vintages he is able to produce an astonishingly sweet and concentrated *cuvée* called Quintessence.

Château Pierre-Bise ☆☆☆
Beaulieu-sur-Layon. 53 ha.
One of the top producers of Coteaux du Layon, Claude Papin is fascinated by the notion of terroir and bottles Layon by soil type, offering numerous different *cuvées*, including Layon-Chaume and Quarts de Chaume. Papin also produces excellent Anjou Blanc , Anjou-Villages, and Anjou-Gamay, as well as Savennières from Clos de Coulaine (q.v.).

Domaine des Rochelles ☆☆
St Jean des Mauvets. 52 ha.
www.domainedesrochelles.com.
The Lebretons deservedly enjoy a fine reputation, above all for their reds from Brissac. The Cuvée Croix du Mission has an unusually high proportion of Cabernet Sauvignon.

Domaine des Roches Neuves ☆☆–☆☆☆
Varrains. 22 ha. www.rochesneuves.com
Thierry Germain, a young Bordelais from a well-established family of growers and merchants, purchased this property in 1991 and ever since has been turning out flavoursome Saumur-Champigny, the two most concentrated being the Cuvée Vieilles Vignes Terres Chaudes and the Cuvée Marginale, the latter aged in new oak. There is also an impressive white called L'Insolite, from very old Chenin Blanc vines.

Domaine de la Sansonnière ☆☆☆
Thouarcé. 8 ha.
Mark Angeli goes his own way. A firm believer in Biodynamic viticulture and high-density planting, he makes mostly white wines, of which the most striking are his superlative rich Anjous and, in suitable vintages, Bonnezeaux.

Château Soucherie ☆–☆☆
Beaulieu-sur-Layon. 30 ha. www.soucherie.com
The property of the Tijou family since 1952, but in 2007 Pierre-Yves Tijou retired and the property was sold to industrialist Roger Beguinot, who appointed a new winemaker with the aim of improving quality, which had declined in recent years. Most of the estate is in Coteaux du Layon planted with Chenin Blanc, with Cabernet and Gamay for red and rosé. The best Layons are often the Vieilles Vignes, the Chaume, and Beaulieu Cuvée de la Tour, from 90-year-old vines. Since 1991 the property has included two hectares in Savennières called Clos des Perrières.

Domaine Pierre Soulez ☆☆–☆☆☆
Château de Chamboureau, Savennières. 18 ha.

Substantial producer of Savennières, both dry and *moelleux*. The best of them often come from his parcel within Roche-aux-Moines. The red and rosé are of lesser interest. In 2006 Soulez, with retirement in view, sold some parcels to Philippe Fournier, who is also the new owner of Domaine Jo Pithon (q.v.). The range is likely to shrink further.

Château de Suronde ☆☆☆
Rochefort-sur-Loire. 8 ha. www.suronde.fr
In 1995 Francis Poirel, a maritime economist, acquired this property and became a passionate producer of superb Quarts de Chaume. Yields from his organic vineyards were minute, and in some years the top *cuvée* was made by picking botrytized berries one by one. In 2005, however, he sold the property, although the vintage that year signalled no change of direction.

Château de Targé ☆☆
Parnay. 25 ha. www.chateaudetarge.fr
A four-towered manoir, in the Pisani-Ferry family since 1655, producing acclaimed Saumur-Champigny, especially the Cuvée Ferry and Quintessence.

Château la Varière ☆☆–☆☆☆
Brissac. 95 ha. www.chateaulavariere.com
Jacques Beaujeau is well-known for his robust Anjou-Villages, but he also makes sumptuous Bonnezeaux and Quarts de Chaume in top vintages such as 1997.

Château de Villeneuve ☆☆☆
Souzay-Champigny. 28 ha.
www.chateau-de-villeneuve.com
Excellent family domaine run by Jean-Pierre Chevallier. The most powerful of the *cuvées* of Saumur-Champigny is the barrel-aged old-vines bottling from the *lieu-dit* Le Grand Clos. There are two *cuvées* of Saumur Blanc, including Les Cormiers, which is fermented and aged in new-oak barrels.

Château Yvonne ☆☆
Parnay. 5 ha.
This property is unusual in having as many white vines as red. At present the former are prized more than the latter.

Sparkling Saumur

The in-built acidity of Chenin Blanc is the cause and justification of the Saumur sparkling wine industry, which is based in the chalk caves of St-Hilaire-St-Florent, just west of Saumur. It uses the classic method to produce cleanly fruity, usually very dry wines at substantially less than Champagne prices, less characterful and complex, but just as stimulating.
However, an increasing number of producers are now making Crémant de Loire; and there is a corresponding number of deluxe *cuvées*. A few of these begin to approach Champagne prices and, at times, Champagne quality (relatively speaking).

Leading Producers of Sparkling Saumur

Ackerman-Laurance ☆–☆☆
Saumur. www.ackerman-remypannier.com
The original firm, founded in 1811 when Ackerman, a Belgian,

introduced the *méthode traditionnelle* to the Loire. Still a leader with the new extra-quality Crémant de Loire. The company also offers a wide range of still wines. Owned by Rémy Pannier

Bouvet-Ladubay ☆☆–☆☆☆
St-Hilaire-St-Florent, Saumur.
www.bouvet-ladubay.fr
The second-oldest (1851) of the sparkling wine houses, Bouvet-Ladubay became part of the Taittinger group in 1974 until its sale in 2006 to United Breweries of India. Excellent sparkling Saumurs include Bouvet Brut, Saphir (a vintage *brut*), Rubis (an off-dry red based on Cabernet), and three deluxe *cuvées*, each partially or entirely fermented in barrel: Trésor, Trésor Rosé, and a *demi-sec* Grand Vin de Dessert.

An interesting new departure is the serious and concentrated Nonpareils range, controversial because of its use of new oak. Overall, annual production exceeds three million bottles.

Gratien & Meyer ☆–☆☆
Saumur. 20 ha. www.gratienmeyer.com
A twin company to the Champagne house of Alfred Gratien. Twenty hectares of vineyards (Chenin Blanc and Cabernet) can be found over the cellars. Products include Saumur Brut, Saumur Rosé Brut, Blanc de Noirs, Crémant de Loire Brut, and Flamme d'Or – the top-drawer Saumur Brut.

Langlois-Château ☆☆
St-Hilaire-St-Florent, Saumur. 73 ha.
www.langlois-chateau.com
This old house was bought by Bollinger in 1973. Principally it is a producer of fine sparkling Crémant de Loire (*blanc*, rosé, and vintage), including a complex prestige bottling called Quadrille, but also of still Loire wines from Muscadet to Sancerre.

The best of these come from the firm's own vineyards, Château de Fontaine Audon in Sancerre, and Domaine Langlois-Château for Saumur red and white. Château de Varrains is a Saumur-Champigny aged in new-oak puncheons.

De Neuville ☆
St-Hilaire-St-Florent.
www.ackermanremypannier.com
A firm producing sparkling Saumur and Crémant de Loire. Now belongs to Rémy Pannier (q.v.).

Other Anjou-Saumur Producers

Veuve Amiot ☆
St-Hilaire-St-Florent. www.veuve-amiot.com
Founded 1884, now owned by Martini & Rossi, this is an important producer of sparkling Saumur, Anjou, and Crémant de Loire.

Patrick Baudouin ☆☆☆
Chaudefonds-sur-Layon. 8 ha.
www.patrick-baudouin-layon.com
Produces Coteaux du Layon from very low yields. The top *cuvées* are Maria Juby and Après Minuit. Both are very intense, very sweet, and very expensive.

Château d'Epiré ☆☆–☆☆☆
St-Georges-sur-Loire. 9 ha. www.chateau-epire.com
Family ownership of this estate dates back to 1749, and today it is run by Luc Bizard. The aim is Savennières made for long ageing, and the estate also pioneered an off-dry style.

Domaine Filliatreau ☆☆
Chaintres. 45 ha.
Paul Filliatreau was the grower who put Saumur-Champigny on the map, but quality has been overtaken by other estates in recent years. However, the Cuvée Vieilles Vignes and Cuvée des Douze are still impressive wines.

Domaine les Grandes Vignes ☆–☆☆
Thouarcé. 51 ha. www.domainelesgrandesvignes.com
Large, reliable estate producing a sound range of dry Anjou wines in all styles. The holdings include 1.5 hectares of Bonnezeaux.

Château de la Guimonière ☆☆–☆☆☆
Rochefort-sur-Loire. 23 ha.
Bernard Germain bought this property in 1996, along with Château de Fesles (q.v.), but sold it in 2005 to Alain Château, the owner of Château Bellerive. With 15 hectares in Chaume, he produces creamy, plump, sweet wines from one of the top properties in the region.

Domaine de Haute-Perche ☆–☆☆
St-Melaine-sur-Aubance. 34 ha.
www.domainehauteperche.com
Christian Papin's estate has expanded in recent years. He makes the entire range of Anjou wines. The best tend to be his warm, supple Anjou-Villages, honeyed Coteaux de l'Aubance, and delicious Anjou-Gamay.

Château du Hureau ☆☆–☆☆☆
Dampierre-sur-Loire. 19 ha. www.domaine-hureau.fr
Philippe Vatan produces five exemplary *cuvées* of Saumur-Champigny, finely balanced between fruit and oak, and a sumptuous sweet Coteaux de Saumur.

Domaine de Juchepie ☆☆
Faye. 7 ha. www.juchepie.com
Equally fine dry and nobly sweet wines from this Biodynamic property in Coteaux du Layon.

Domaine de Montgilet ☆☆
Juigné-sur-Loire. 37 ha. www.montgilet.com
Vincent and Victor Lebreton are very good producers of Coteaux de l'Aubance. The best *cuvées* are Le Tertereaux and Les Trois Schistes.

Sparkling wine in the cellars of Saumur

Domaine Musset-Rouillier ☆–☆☆
Le Pelican, La Pommeraye. 28 ha.
Gilles Musset, a serious grower, joined forces with Serge Rouillier, another good young producer, in 1994. They produce exemplary Anjou Coteaux de la Loire, as well as admirable Anjou Blanc *sec* and Anjou-Villages.

Domaine Ogereau ☆☆
St-Lambert-du-Lattay. 20 ha. www.domaineogereau.com
Medium-bodied Coteaux du Layon-St-Lambert, deliberately made without extreme concentration. Best is the single-vineyard Clos des Bonnes Blanches. The white, rosé, and red Anjou are also of impressive quality, and the latest addition to the range is a Savennières from Clos du Grand Beaupréau.

Château de Passavant ☆
Passavant-sur-Layon. 42 ha. www.passavant.net
Traditional producer of Anjou white, red, and rosé, as well as Coteaux du Layon. Organic since 1998.

Domaine du Petit Métris ☆
St Aubin. 30 ha. www.domaine-petit-metris.com
The Renou brothers have vines in Chaume and two parcels, often sold as two different *cuvées*, in Savennières. Sound rather than exciting wines.

Domaine du Petit Val ☆☆
Chavagnes. 44 ha. www.domainedupetitval.com
Denis Goizil makes a full range of Anjou wines in all colours as well as very rich Bonnezeaux that is sometimes marred by high alcohol.

Jo Pithon ☆☆–☆☆☆☆
St-Lambert-du-Lattay. 27 ha.
www.domaine-jopithon.com
Enthusiast for ultra-concentrated Coteaux du Layon and Quarts de Chaume, but also makes fine, dry white Anjou and Savennières. In 2005 Philippe Fournier, an Angers buisinessman, bought the property and expanded it by purchasing new vineyards. He also brought in Bordeaux consultant Stéphane Derenoncourt to advise, unusually, on white wine production.

Château de Plaisance ☆☆
Rochefort. 20 ha. www.chateaudeplaisance.com
Guy Rochais produces two *cuvées* of Savennières, but is better known for his fine wines from Chaume and Quarts de Chaume.

René Renou ☆–☆☆☆
Thouarcé. 10 ha
Until his untimely death in 2006, René Renou was the head of INAO, charged with defending the *typicité* of France's wine regions. His estate specializes in Bonnezeaux wines. The basic *cuvées* are dull, but Anne and Zenith are silky and elegant. His widow and son are now running the estate.

Domaine Richou ☆–☆☆
Mozé-sur-Louet. 30 ha. www.domainerichou.fr
Good Coteaux de l'Aubance, especially the Trois Demoiselles and Pavillon, both from old vines. And very good examples of *crémant*, Anjou Gamay and Anjou-Villages.

Château de la Roulerie ☆☆
St-Aubin. 21 ha. www.vgas.com
Like Château de Fesles, owned since 1996 by Bernard Germain, and made in the same way as Fesles (q.v.). Good Chaume and Anjou Sec.

Domaine de St-Just ☆–☆☆
St Just-sur-Dive. 40 ha. www.st-just.net
Good modern-style, fruit-driven Saumur-Champigny and white Saumur.

Domaine du Sauveroy ☆–☆☆
St-Lambert-du-Lattay. 26 ha.
www.sauveroy.com
Pascal Cailleau is winemaker at this family estate, using modern winemaking techniques to produce the Anjou reds and often outstanding Coteaux du Layon-St-Lambert Cuvée Nectar.

Château de Tigné ☆☆
Tigné. 50 ha. www.chateaudetigne.com
A substantial organic estate owned by actor Gérard Depardieu. The top *cuvées* are the Vieilles Vignes and Cyrano.

Château de Varennes ☆☆
Savennières. 7 ha. www.vignobles-alainchateau.com
Owned by Bernard Germain since 1996, until its sale in 2005 to paper magnate Alain Château, who also owns Château Bellerive (q.v.). The Savennières is atypical in that it is made in an accessible style for drinking fairly young.

Domaine des Varinelles ☆–☆☆
Varrains. 42 ha. www.daheuiller.com
The Daheuillers are a long-established family of predominantly red winemakers in Saumur-Champigny. The Cuvée Larivale is aged in new oak.

Touraine

It is hard to define Touraine more precisely than as the eastern half of the central Loire, with the city of Tours at its heart and a trio of goodly rivers – the Cher, the Indre, and the Vienne – joining the majestic main stream from the south. Almost on its border with Anjou it produces the best red wines of the Loire. Chinon and Bourgueil lie on the latitude of the Côte de Beaune and the longitude of St-Emilion – a situation that produces a kind of claret capable of stunning vitality and charm. The Cabernet Franc, with very little, if any, Cabernet Sauvignon, achieves a sort of pastel sketch of a great Médoc, smelling of raspberries, begging to be drunk cellar-cool in its first summer, light and sometimes astringent, yet surprisingly solid in its construction: ripe vintages age almost like Bordeaux, at least to seven or eight years.

Much depends on the soil. Sand and gravel near the river produce lighter, faster-maturing wine than clay over tuffeau limestone on the slopes (*coteaux*). These differences seem greater than those between Chinon and Bourgueil, certainly than any between Bourgueil and its immediate neighbour on the north bank, St-Nicolas-de-Bourgueil, although this has a separate appellation of its own. Touraine's other famous wine is Vouvray, potentially the most luscious and longest lived of all the sweet Chenin Blanc whites, though, like German wines, depending more on the vintage than the site for the decisive degree of sugar that determines its character. The best vineyards are on the warm, chalky, tuffeau slopes near the river and in sheltered corners of side valleys. A warm, dry autumn (1989, 1997, and 2005 were optimal) can overripen the grapes here by sheer heat; a warm, misty one can bring on noble rot to shrivel them. In either case, great sweet Vouvray will be possible, with or without the peculiar smell and taste of *Botrytis cinerea*.

Cool years make wines of indeterminate (though often very smooth and pleasant) semi-sweetness, or dry wines – all with the built-in acidity that always keeps Chenin Blanc lively (if not always very easy to drink). One solution to overacid wines here, as in Saumur, is to make them sparkle by the *méthode traditionnelle*. The other is the production of a style known as *sec tendre*, which in practice means midway between truly dry and *demi-sec*.

It is an odd coincidence that each of the great Loire wines comes with a pair across the river: Savennières with Coteaux du Layon, Bourgueil with Chinon, Sancerre with Pouilly, and Vouvray with Montlouis. Montlouis, squeezed between the Loire's south bank and the Cher's north bank, is not regarded, except by those who make it, as having quite the authority and "attack" of great Vouvray. Its sites are slightly less favoured, its wines softer and more tentative. They can sparkle just as briskly, though, and ripen almost as sweet.

Outside these four appellations, Touraine, with its simple but all-purpose AC Touraine, has only a modest reputation, although these wines continue to improve.

I suggest that the future lies with the general (and self-explanatory) Sauvignon and Gamay de Touraine; some of the top *cuvées* of Sauvignon and Gamay can give, respectively, Sancerre and Beaujolais a run for their money. They are not as fine as either, but an awful lot cheaper. Increasingly, the wine authorities are encouraging (indeed, in the case of Touraine-Mesland mandating) blends of Gamay, Cabernet, and Cot.

Leading Touraine Producers

Domaine Philippe Alliet ☆☆☆
Cravant-les-Côteaux. 17 ha.
Low yields are the clue to the impressive record of this small Chinon estate, where the vines are planted on deep gravel soils. All three of his *cuvées* are complex wines, all given long macerations, then aged in barriques, and bottled without filtration; they show suave textures and an unusual depth of fruit.

Domaine Yannick Amirault ☆☆–☆☆☆
Bourgueil. 19 ha.
Amirault produces St-Nicolas-de-Bourgueil as well as three *cuvées* of Bourgueil. All the wines are reliable, but vary in weight and style. The most concentrated is usually the splendid old-vine Bourgueil La Petite Cave, but Le Grand Clos and Les Quartiers, also from Bourgueil, often rival it. Almost all the wines repay keeping for three to five years.

Domaine des Aubuisières ☆☆–☆☆☆
Vouvray. 25 ha. www.vouvrayfouquet.com
Bernard Fouquet produces sublime *secs*, *demi-secs*, and *moelleux* from three different vineyards, Le Marigny, Les Girardières, and Le Bouchet. In certain vintages there is an ultra-rich *moelleux* selection called Cuvée Alexandre. His sparkling Vouvray is full-bodied and flavoursome.

Audebert & Fils ☆–☆☆
Bourgueil. 42 ha. www.audebert.fr
One of the biggest négociant-growers in Bourgueil, St-Nicolas-de-Bourgueil, and Chinon. Domaine du Grand Clos and La Marquise are special *cuvées* from specific vineyards – easy wines for drinking cool in their youthful prime, although the Grand Clos has some tannic structure and can age.

Bernard Baudry ☆☆–☆☆☆
Cravant-les-Côteaux. 30 ha.
Baudry and his son Mathieu release up to five separate *cuvées* of Chinon according to the provenance of the wine. Thus Les Granges and Haies Martels are from young vines, while Les Grézeaux comes from old vines on clay-gravel soils. The top bottling is usually Cuvée Croix Boissée, which is powerful and long-lived. Baudry also produces an attractive white Chinon.

Domaine Catherine & Pierre Breton ☆☆
Restigné. 15 ha. www.domainebreton.net
Founded in 1982, this organic estate has been a leader in Bourgueil from the outset. There are various *cuvées*, but all the wines are made from vines cropped at no more than 40 hl/ha. Clos Sénéchal is usually the most elegant, the oak-aged Les Perrièresusually the most lush. Red wines only.

Cave du Haut-Poitou ☆–☆☆
Neuville de Poitou. 900 ha. www.cavehautpoitou.free.fr
The VDQS zone of Haut-Poitou is well south of the Loire on the road to Poitiers, where 47 communes on the chalky soil of a plateau used to supply distilling wine to Cognac. In 1948, a cooperative was founded and succeeded in raising standards to the point where, in 1970, the region was promoted to VDQS.

In September 1995, Georges Duboeuf of Beaujolais purchased 40 per cent of the business. He ended its days as a cooperative and bought himself a useful source of varietal wines – Sauvignon Blanc, Chardonnay, Gamay, and Cabernet. More recent additions to the range are a Pinot Noir and an oak-aged Chardonnay. Ninety per cent of the appellation's wine is produced by the cave.

Cave des Producteurs la Vallée Coquette ☆–☆☆
Vouvray. 400 ha. www.cp-vouvray.com
Founded in 1953, this cooperative vinifies about 15 per cent of the appellation. It specializes in sound sparkling Vouvray, *pétillant* and *méthode traditionnelle*, but the *moelleux* can be remarkably good.

Domaine Champalou ☆☆–☆☆☆
Vouvray. 20 ha.
Dider and Catherine Champalou, both oenologists, created this estate in 1985. Their wines, dry, *sec tendre* and sweet, are consistently good, and in top vintages they produce a Trie de

Vendange from the ripest botrytis grapes. The result is creamy and intense, and probably indestructible.

Domaine de la Chevalerie ☆–☆☆
Restigné. 33 ha. www.domaine-de-la-chevalerie.com
Pierre Caslot is the thirteenth generation of his family to farm Cabernet vines, from which he makes numerous *cuvées* of firm, deep-toned Bourgueil, aged up to 18 months in wood. The Cuvée des Busardières is made from 50-year-old vines and is intended to age for five or more years.

François Chidaine ☆☆–☆☆☆
Husseau, Montlouis. 30 ha.
www.cave-insolite-chidaine.com
One of Montlouis's top producers, whose Biodynamically farmed holdings were augmented in 2002 when he acquired the Clos Baudouin vineyard in Vouvray that used to belong to Prince Poniatowski. His superb sweet Montlouis, Les Lys, is made from vines that are 60 to 90 years old, picked grape by grape. He also makes firm dry wines.

Clos Baudoin
Vallée de Nouy, Vouvray. 14 ha.
Over many decades Prince Poniatowski made some remarkable and long-lived Vouvrays from three sites, but in 2003 he leased the entire property to François Chidaine (q.v.).

Clos Naudin ☆☆☆–☆☆☆☆☆
Vouvray. 12 ha.
Philippe Foreau is a perfectionist: no herbicides, very low yields, no added yeasts, no *chaptalization*, and all the wines are fermented in 300-litre barrels, but not in new oak. The dry wines can be very good here, but it's the supremely elegant *moelleux* wines that are truly memorable, with their flavours of apricots, pears, and dried fruits. The word Réserve on the label signifies that the grapes were nobly rotten. The 2005s are of spectacular quality.

Couly-Dutheil ☆☆–☆☆☆
Chinon. 97 ha. www.coulydutheil-chinon.com
A grower of Chinon and Saumur-Champigny and a négociant for other Loire wines, founded in 1910 by B. Dutheil, developed by René Couly, and now run by René's sons and grandson. Their vineyards are divided between wines of plain and plateau, sold as Les Gravières (the lightest) and Domaine René Couly, and the (better) wines of the *coteaux*, the Clos de l'Echo and Clos de l'Olive. La Diligence is a new bottling from a recently purchased south-facing vineyard – for mid-term drinking. Another top wine is a selection labelled Baronnie Madeleine, though the two Clos wines are usually superior. Most *cuvées* can be drunk young, but the *coteaux* wines can age for years into a harmonious mellowness.

Pierre-Jacques Druet ☆☆☆
Benais. 22 ha.
One of Bourgueil's most skilful and thoughtful producers,

Druet offers numerous *cuvées* of Bourgueil and two of Chinon, including the Clos du Danzay. In Bourgueil he produces a meaty, barrel-fermented rosé and, in order of age-worthiness, Les Cents Boissellées, Beauvais, Le Grand Mont and the often magnificent Vaumoreau.

Domaine du Four à Chaux ☆☆
Thoré la Rochette. 29 ha.
www.domaine-four-a-chaux.com
Dominique Norguet makes the best wine in VDQS Coteaux du Vendômois, particularly *vin gris* of Pineau d'Aunis and red blends, either of Gamay and Pineau d'Aunis or of Pinot Noir and Pineau d'Aunis.

Château Gaudrelle ☆–☆☆☆
Vouvray. ha. www.chateaugaudrelle.com
Alexandre Monmousseau makes a wide range of Vouvrays: *sec tendre*, sparkling, and *moelleux*. Moelleux Réserve Spéciale is a less concentrated style thanRéserve Personnelle, which is made from grapes picked at Sauternes-style levels of sugar.

Domaine Guiberteau ☆☆
St Just-dur-Divey. 9 ha
A small organic property in Saumur with most of its vines on the excellent soils of the Brézé hill. As well as two *cuvées* of reds, there is a white Saumur of considerable weight and power.

Domaine des Huards ☆☆
Cour-Cheverny. 34 ha.
www.gendrier.com
The Gendrier family vineyards are in AC Cheverny and in AC Cour-Cheverny. In Cheverny they produce estimable Sauvignon-based dry whites and Gamay- and Cabernet-based reds and rosés; in the latter they make some of the best examples of a dry white from the local Romorantin grape.

Domaine Huet ☆☆☆–☆☆☆☆☆
Vouvray. 35 ha. www.huet-echansonne.com
Gaston Huet was perhaps the most respected name in Vouvray. In 1997, a few years before his death, he was still pouring his 1937 for admirers. Huet came from a family of growers which for generations had been making wine of the highest quality from three vineyards: Le Haut-Lieu, Le Mont, and Le Clos du Bourg – sweet or dry, still or sparkling – according to the season. Son-in-law Noël Pinguet is the winemaker and has converted the domaine to Biodynamic viticulture. In 2003 the property was bought by the American financier Anthony Hwang, who also has interests in Tokaj.

Charles Joguet ☆–☆☆☆
Sazilly. 40 ha. www.charlesjoguet.com
An artist as well as one of Chinon's best winemakers Joguet retired from active participation in the domaine in 1997. Joguet's best vines, over 80 years old, are in the two-hectare Clos de la Dioterie. Clos du Chêne Vert, also two hectares, is another noted vineyard. It is worth paying the slight premium

Oak barrel ageing and fermentation, Domaine Huet, Vouvray

for the top *cuvées*, as the other bottlings can be slight. Although quality declined in the late 1990s, recent vintages are more reminiscent of Joguet's best old vintages.

Domaine Frédéric Mabileau ☆☆
St-Nicolas-de-Bourgueil. 27 ha.
www.fredericmabileau.com
Mabileau has been running this family domaine since 1991, and the wines have gained in quality. In 2007 the vineyards became fully organic. Of the four *cuvées* from St-Nicolas, only Cuvée Eclipse spends time in new oak. The sole Bourgueil, Racines is aged in larger barrels. With age, the wines develop a seductive gaminess.

Domaine Henry Marionnet ☆☆☆
Soings en Sologne. 60 ha. www.henry-marionnet.com
Henry Marionnet at Domaine de la Charmoise is a modern-minded grower who has shown the true potential of Gamay and Sauvignon Blanc in Touraine. At the same time he has revived near-extinct indigenous varieties such as Romorantin and Gamay de Bouze, and experimented with ungrafted vines. The special bottlings include Première Vendange, hand-harvested Gamay with no added sulphur, sugar or yeast; and the grapefruity Provignage, a very rare bottling from Romorantin vines planted in 1850.

Domaine Jacky Marteau ☆☆
Pouillé. 25 ha. www.domainejackymarteau.free.fr
A reliable producer of superb Crémant de Loire, Gamay de Touraine, Marteau also makes fine Sauvignon de Touraine, Cabernet, and rosé of Pineau d'Aunis.

Domaine des Ouches ☆☆–☆☆☆
Ingrandes-de-Touraine. 16 ha.
www.domainedesouches.com
The Gambier family has been making excellent wines here for decades. The top bottling is usually the Vieilles Vignes, aged, like most of the other wines, in old barriques. These are wines that can be quite austere in their youth and that benefit from a few years in bottle.

Jean-Maurice Raffault ☆☆
Savigny-en-Véron. 55 ha.
The Raffaults have steadily expanded their domaine with holdings in seven communes, all within Chinon. Rodolphe Raffault makes the wines of different soils separately. Les Galluches, a light Chinon, comes from sandy soils; his longest-lived Chinons from the *lieux-dits* Les Picasses and Isoré.

Olga Raffault ☆☆
Savigny-en-Véron. 25 ha. www.olga-raffault.com
One of several Raffaults, not necessarily related, in and around this village at the western end of the Chinon appellation. (Another, Raymond, owns Domaine du Raffault). The estate, now run by Olga's granddaughter Sylvie de la Vigerie, keeps the wine of different sites separate.

Clients can choose from a range of fruity and fairly full-bodied wines, of which the longest-lived *cuvée* is Les Picasses Vieilles Vignes. Raffault also makes a tiny amount of Chinon Blanc.

Domaine de la Taille aux Loups ☆☆☆
Husseau, Montlouis. 25 ha. www.jackyblot.fr
Jacky Blot founded this estate in 1988 and picks selectively at very low yields. He likes to use new oak on certain wines, such as dry Cuvée Remus. Its sweet counterpart, Cuvée Romulus, is a rich mouthful of apples and honey with a spicy finish. A small quantity of dry and sweet Vouvray is produced from the Clos des Venise, and the no-*dosage pétillant* called Triple Zéro is also of interest. All the wines, whatever their style, can be enthusiastically recommended as among the most characterful of the region.

Domaine Taluau & Foltzenlogel ☆☆
Chevrette, St-Nicolas-de-Bourgueil. 27 ha.
www.vins-taluau-foltzenlogel.com
Joel Taluau has teamed up with Thierry Foltzenlogel and thus expanded his production. Vineyards in St-Nicolas and a few within Bourgueil produce fragrant and charming light red wines. Taluau used to ferment everything in stainless steel, but now produces a small *cuvée* called l'Insoumise, a batch of Cuvée Vieilles Vignes aged in older oak. Freshness and charm take precedence over power and intensity.

Vigneau-Chevreau ☆☆–☆☆☆
Chancay. 28 ha. www.vigneau-chevreau.com
A Biodynamic estate. Half the production is of sparkling wine. The *demi-sec* is often more harmonious than the austere *sec*, and the *moelleux* is intense, stylish, and tangy.

Other Touraine Producers

Ampelidae ☆–☆☆
Marigny-Brizay. 41 ha. www.ampelidae.com
This Poitou estate dispenses with appellations and sells its wide range of mostly varietal wines as Vin de Pays de la Vienne. But the approach is serious, with manual harvesting and no *chaptalization*.

Baudry-Dutour ☆☆–☆☆☆
Panzoult. 86 ha. www.baudry-dutour.fr
This venture came into being in 2004 when Christophe Baudry of the Domaine de la Perrière teamed up with Jean-Martin Dutour of Domaine du Roncée. The range is much as before, with sound basic bottlings and a handful of single-vineyard wines of greater complexity, and prices are very reasonable for the quality.

Domaine de Bellivière ☆☆
Lhomme. 13 ha. www.belliviere.com
Excellent source of Jasnières and Coteaux du Loir. Very low yields justify high prices, but reds are austere in youth.

Bourillon Dorleans ☆–☆☆
Vouvray. 26 ha. www.bourillon.com
Frédéric Bourillon has experimented with malolactic fermentation to give his dry wines greater softness – perhaps not a direction to pursue. Good *moelleux* wines, especially the top *cuvée* Coulée d'Or.

Marc Brédif ☆
Rochecorbon. 20 ha.

Négociant-grower with hospitable cellars in the rock caves below Rochecorbon. The firm belongs to the de Ladoucette concern of Pouilly. The firm offers a complete range of Vouvrays, in both still and sparkling forms. Brédif invented Vouvray *pétillant* in the 1920s. Some Chinon is also produced.

Domaine de Cézin ☆☆
Marçon. 12 ha. www.fresneau.fr
The Fresnau family has vineyards in Jasnières and more substantial holdings in the Coteaux du Loir. The Jasnières and the Pineau d'Aunis Rouge are rustic and personalized and have immense charm.

Château de Chenonceaux ☆
Chenonceaux. 35 ha.
The estate belongs to what must be the most beautiful of Loire showplace châteaux, complete with a well-equipped little winery in a courtyard. A wide range of Touraine wines is made.

Clos de la Briderie ☆–☆☆
Monteaux. 10 ha.
Vincent Girault makes some of the most attractive wines in Touraine-Mesland, including barrel-fermented white.

Clos de Nouys ☆☆
Vouvray. 25 ha. ww.closdenouys.com
Excellent wines across the board from carefully tended old vineyards. The top *moelleux* is Grains Dorés.

Clos des Quarterons ☆–☆☆
St-Nicolas-de-Bourgueil. 29 ha
Thierry Amirault's property is well-distributed on the lighter soils of St-Nicolas. Fruity wines, with no wood influence except for Cuvée Vieilles Vignes.

Clos Roche Blanche ☆☆
Mareuil-sur-Cher. 18 ha.
It isn't easy to be a successful producer within the basic Touraine appellation, as low prices don't encourage high quality. This organic property is one of the exceptions, releasing stylish varietal wines, such as Sauvignon and Cot.

Lydie et Max Cognard ☆–☆☆
St-Nicolas-de-Bourgueil. 12 ha.
www.vins-stnicolas-bourgueil-cognard.com.
Good wines, with the delicacy and balance expected from St-Nicolas-de-Bourgueil.

Château de Coulaine ☆–☆☆
Beaumont-en-Véron, Chinon. 18 ha.
Etienne de Bonnaventure pays close attention to the nuances of terroir in his various *cuvées*, of which the most impressive is often the barrique-aged Les Picasses.

Deletang ☆
Montlouis. 17 ha. www.domaine-deletang.com
Good Montlouis and *méthode traditionnelle* Chenin Blancs.

Domaine Dutertre ☆–☆☆
Limeray. 37 ha.
A family property producing Cabernet, Malbec, and Gamay for red and rosé Touraine-Amboise. The Dutertres also make sparkling and still dry whites in their rock-cut cellar.

Domaine de la Fontainerie ☆☆
Vouvray. 6 ha.
Catherine Dhoye-Deruet stamps her personality on her wines, which are made without added yeasts and without *chaptalization*. Firm *sec*, and a range of *moelleux* and sparkling wines.

Château Gaillard ☆–☆☆
Mesland. 45 ha.
Vincent Girault has long cultivated his vines according to the principles of Biodynamics. These are uncomplicated but well made wines that offer excellent value. Girault has recently taken over his parents' property at Clos de la Briderie (q.v.).

Domaine de la Garrelière ☆
Razines. 20 ha. www.garreliere.com
This Biodynamic property produces excellent Sauvignon, and the reds are certainly not without interest.

Domaine des Geslets ☆☆
Bourgueil. 16 ha.
A fine source of elegant Cabernets from both Bourgueil and St-Nicolas-de-Bourgueil.

Domaine La Grange Tiphaine ☆☆
Amboise. 11 ha. www.lagrangetiphaine.com
Damien Delecheneau's estate has a dual identity, with vines in Touraine Amboise and also in Montlouis. The latter are made in different styles, while the Amboise range focuses, unusually, on red varieties such as Malbec and Cabernet Franc.

Jean-Pierre Laisement ☆–☆☆
Vouvray. 13 ha.
All his wines are made in 600-litre casks, stored in his chilly cellars. Good *moelleux*, sometimes with an unusual touch of austerity.

Domaine Levasseur-Alex Mathur ☆☆
Montlouis. 13 ha.
In 1998 Claude Levasseur sold his property to its present owner, Eric Gougeat, who makes an oaked *sec* called, alarmingly, Requiem, as well as Amadeus, a succulent *moelleux* with flavours of apple and quince.

Domaine des Liards ☆
Montlouis. 19 ha.
A third-generation property run by the Berger family, 80 per cent is planted with Chenin Blanc for still, sparkling, and *pétillant* Montlouis, the rest with Sauvignon for Touraine Blanc, and Cabernet Franc for Touraine Rouge.

Dominique Moyer ☆☆
Husseau, Montlouis. 12 ha. www.domaine-moyer.com
A respected old family of growers (since 1830) with many very old vines (30 per cent are over 70 years old). The Moyers go to the length of successive pickings to crush nothing but ripe grapes, making *sec* and *demi-sec* as ripe and round as possible. A little sparkling wine now made.

Domaine Pichot ☆☆
Vouvray. 27 ha.
Christophe and Jean-Claude Pichot have secured a good

reputation for their wines, which succeed in all styles, from *sec* to the ultra-concentrated called Les Larmes de Bacchus.

François Pinon ☆–☆☆
Vallée de Cousse, Vernou-sur-Brenne. 13 ha.
Pinon is scrupulous in vineyard and cellar, producing high-quality Vouvray in all styles. His regular bottling, Cuvée Tradition, is a *demi-sec*. The *moelleux* is quite stylish, with appley overtones, but lacks intensity.

The Upper Loire

It might well surprise the vignerons of Sancerre and Pouilly, the uppermost of the mainstream Loire vineyards, to learn what a profound influence their produce has had on forming modern tastes in white wine. It has an easily recognizable style of wine, pungent and cutting, with the smell and acidity of Sauvignon Blanc grown in a cool climate. Although Sauvignon is planted on a far larger scale in Bordeaux, its wine never smelt and tasted so powerfully characteristic there as it does on the Loire, since the Bordeaux tradition was (less so, now) to blend it with the smoother and more neutral Sémillon. One might say that the world discovered the Sauvignon Blanc and its singular flavour through the vineyards of Sancerre and Pouilly-sur-Loire. What is the flavour? It starts with the powerful aroma, which needs no second sniff. "Gunflint", the smell of sparks when flint strikes metal, is one way to characterize it. In unripe vintages tasters talk of cat's pee, and I am reminded of wet wool.

Successful Sancerres and Pouilly-Fumés have an attractive smell and taste of fresh blackcurrants, leaves and all, and a natural high acidity that makes them distinctly bracing. Sancerre usually has more body and "drive" (and acidity) than Pouilly-Fumé; consequently it can benefit from two or three years' ageing. Pouilly needs only a year or so, although there are exceptions. Although there is no formal vineyard classification in Sancerre, some sites are widely recognized as exceptional, and their names sometimes appear on labels. The best-known are Le Chêne Marchand and Monts Damnés.

For reasons of tradition, the Pouilly vineyards also contain a few vineyards planted with the neutral Chasselas grape, which cannot be sold as "Fumé", only as Pouilly-sur-Loire: a pale, adequate, rather pointless wine, which must be drunk very young. Sancerre, on the other hand, is almost as proud of its Pinot Noir red and rosé as its Sauvignon white. They never achieve the flavour and texture of great burgundy, although those being made by the best producers can match lighter red burgundies. More commonly, they have the faintly watery style of German Spätburgunder (the same grape). Nor do they age so satisfactorily – at best for five to ten years. But they are highly appreciated at source.

Leading Sancerre Producers

Bailly-Reverdy ☆☆
Bué. 20 ha.
A distinguished traditional grower with vineyards in no fewer than 15 sites. The bottling from the famous Clos du Chêne

Marchand is now called Caillottes. White from other vineyards is called Domaine de la Mercy Dieu; there is also a bottling from Monts Damnés. He looks for (and finds) a balance of fruit and finesse, particularly in his whites. The red Sancerre, which is succulent and tastes of cherries, accounts for around one third of production

Joseph Balland-Chapuis ☆–☆☆
Bué. 34 ha. www.balland-chapuis.com
A well-established estate, owned since 1997 by the Guy Saget group, which controls seven substantial domaines in the Loire. The vines are mostly in Sancerre but also in VDQS Coteaux du Giennois and a small parcel in Pouilly. Many *cuvées* of Sancerre, including two excellent whites, Chêne Marchand (aged in about 50 per cent new oak) and Comte Thibault. The deluxe red, Comte Thibault Vieilles Vignes, matures in new oak. Cuvée Pierre and Cuvée Marguerite Marceau (a Giennois) are late-harvest Sauvignons, sweet to varying degrees and fermented in new oak.

Henri Bourgeois ☆☆–☆☆☆
Bué. 69 ha. www.bourgeois-sancerre.com
One of the most important grower-négociants in Sancerre. In addition to its vineyards, the firm acts as a négociant in Sancerre, Pouilly, Menetou-Salon, and Quincy. Bourgeois offers numerous *cuvées*, including La Bourgeoise (red and white), Grande Réserve, Etienne Henri, and Les Monts Damnés, all of high quality. Overall, these are delectable wines, varying from *cuvée* to *cuvée*, yet all unmistakably Sancerre. The Bougeois family has also taken on the opposition by developing a vineyard in New Zealand, Clos Henri.

Cave Coopérative des Vins de Sancerre ☆
Sancerre. 200 ha. www.vins-sancerre.com
Founded in 1963 and producing nothing but Sancerre. Eighty per cent of production is of white, the remainder divided between red and rosé. The cooperative, which unites 110 growers, moved into new cellars in 2001. A serious producer of typical Sancerre under a variety of labels. The prestige bottling is "Le Duc de Tarente".

François Cotat ☆☆☆
Chavignol. 4 ha.
A very small, totally traditional, and most prestigious grower. François Cotat does everything himself, uses an old basket press, ferments in casks with natural yeasts, and neither fines nor filters. The vineyards are close to those of his cousin Pascal (q.v.) and just as distinguished.

Pascal Cotat ☆☆
Chavignol. 2 ha.
A tiny property on the slopes of Monts Damnés. The emphasis is firmly on quality, but the search for maximum ripeness does mean that in some years the wines retain some residual sugar. On the other hand they age far better than most Sancerres.

Francois Crochet ☆☆
Bué. 11 ha.
A young grower who excels with red Sancrere as much as white. The top Sauvignon is from Chêne Marchand.

Domaine Lucien Crochet ☆☆–☆☆☆☆
Bué. 39 ha. www.lucien-crochet.fr
A family holding, three-quarters of it Sauvignon, the rest Pinot Noir. Classic methods produce excellent wine, particularly his Clos du Chêne Marchand from his five hectares there. Bottlings include La Croix du Roy (both red and white) and the Cuvée Prestige LC (likewise), an old-vines bottling often released several years after the vintage. The Cuvée Prestige is oak-aged.

Domaine Vincent Delaporte ☆–☆☆
Chavignol. 23 ha. www.domaine-vincent-delaporte.com
About one-fifth of the production of Delaporte and son Jean-Yves is of Pinot Noir. Most wines ferment in stainless-steel tanks, although Cuvée Maxime is a limited-production oaked Sancerre from the oldest vines. The reds age in oak.

André Dezat ☆☆
Verdigny. 38 ha.
Simon and Louis, sons of the old-school grower André Dezat, have vines in Pouilly as well as Sancerre. His whites are extremely pure and elegant, and the red and rosé also have a loyal following.

Gitton Père & Fils ☆☆
Ménétréol. 27 ha. www.gitton.fr
A family estate in Sancerre, supplemented by vineyards in Pouilly, Côteaux du Giennois, and the Côtes de Duras. The wines are made in many different batches according to different soils – at least 15 different Sancerre *cuvées* with different labels – Les Belles Dames, Le Gelinot, Les Romains, and so on – and five Pouilly-Fumés. Altogether an original house, with a rich, supple style of its own.

Pascal Jolivet ☆☆–☆☆☆
Sancerre. 30 ha. www.pascal-jolivet.com
A dynamic grower and négociant with vineyards divided between Sancerre and Pouilly (q.v.). Jolivet does buy grapes and wine, but puts out a number of domaine bottlings. In Sancerre these include Le Chêne Marchand and La Grande Cuvée, an old-vines bottling made only in good years. No oak is used for the white wines. In 2006, Jolivet introduced his Sauvage, from organic vines; its red counterpart is aged in one-third new oak.

Château de Maimbray ☆
Sury-en-Vaux. 7 ha.
Matthias Roblin produces sound, sturdy Sancerres grown on soils with a high clay content, which makes them fuller and richer than most.

Alphonse Mellot ☆☆☆
Sancerre. 48 ha. www.mellot.com
Growers, négociants, and propagandists for Sancerre with an important holding in good sites, mostly in La Moussière. The Mellot family date back to the sixteenth century, and it has been a family tradition for 19 generations that the head of the family is named Alphonse, as indeed is the present owner.
   Yields are modest here, and the wines are impeccable across the range, if among the most expensive of the region. His deluxe bottlings are Cuvée Edmon – partly aged in new oak,

and Génération XIX, which appears in both a red and a toasty white version. Mellot aims to produce wines that are capable of ageing, but are nonetheless accessible young. The company has also developed a vineyard in the Coteaux Charitois called Les Pénitents, which is planted with Chardonnay and Pinot Noir.

Thierry Merlin-Cherrier ☆☆
Bué. 13 ha.
Full-bodied whites, especially from Chêne Marchand, with power balanced by lively acidity.

Henry Natter ☆☆
Montigny. 20 ha. www.henrynatter.fr
Founded in 1974, the estate soon acquired a fine reputation for its deft, fruity wines, especially the zesty whites. The best wine is made from old vines and called Cuvée François de la Grange, and for those in a celebratory mood, Natter produces L'Expression de Cécile, bottled solely in magnums.

Vincent Pinard ☆☆–☆☆☆☆
Bué. 15 ha.
A small estate that produces a number of different *cuvées*, all from hand-picked fruit. There is a strong emphasis on red wines, though the whites are rich and elegant.

Pierre Prieur & Fils ☆☆
Verdigny. 20 ha.
A prominent family of growers for generations with several good sites, including Les Monts-Damnés (which is chalky clay) and the stonier Pichon, where an unusually high proportion of the property is Pinot Noir. The white is made to age two or three years; the rosé of Pinot Noir mysteriously seems to share its quality – even its Sauvignon flavour. The red, which is aged half in tanks, half in oak, resembles very light burgundy.

Jean Reverdy & Fils ☆–☆☆
Verdigny. 12 ha.
A succession of Reverdys since 1646 have farmed here. They make fine, classic wines, particularly the Clos de la Reine Blanche white, which can mature for three or four years.

Pascal & Nicolas Reverdy ☆☆
Maimbray. 14 ha.
A small estate producing elegant citric Sancerres. The Cuvée Angelots (which used to be known as Vieilles Vignes) is from 60-year-old vines and bottled unfiltered. The red is unusually rich for Sancerre. Sadly, Nicolas Reverdy died in an accident in late 2007.

Claude Riffault ☆–☆☆
Sury-en-Vaux. 13 ha.
Claude's son Stéphane makes zesty wines for relatively early drinking. The most striking *cuvée* is Les Pierrottes grown on flinty soils.

Jean-Max Roger ☆☆
Bué. 27 ha. www.jean-max-roger.fr
Jean-Max Roger is an important grower-négociant with vineyards in Sancerre and Menetou-Salon. He has long specialized in *cuvees* from some of the best vineyards in the region, such as Clos Derveau, Chêne Marchand, and, most

importantly, Grand Chemarin, where he owns six hectares. Roger, now aided by his sons Etienne and Thibault, is no partisan of oaked Sancerre, although his Vieilles Vignes is partly fermented in 400-litre barrels.

Domaine Vacheron ☆☆☆
Sancerre. 43 ha.
A particularly welcoming family of growers whose wines can be tasted in summer in the centre of Sancerre at Le Grenier à Sel. They offer white Le Paradis, red Belle Dame, and rosé Les Romains. Since 2004 the vineyards have been farmed Biodynamically. Their equipment and ideas are modern, but the red ages a year in burgundian casks and is bottled without fining or filtration. Yields are restrained, and the red Sancerre in particular is one of the most concentrated and complex of the region.

André Vatan ☆☆
Verdigny. 10 ha.
Flowery white Sancerre and delicate red and rosé from a long-established grower.

Leading Pouilly Producers

Chatelain ☆–☆☆
St-Andelain. 30 ha. www.domaine-chatelain.fr
A leading grower-négociant, releasing numerous bottlings, including St-Laurent-l'Abbaye, Les Chailloux, The old-vine Prestige, and the late-harvested but dry Pilou, which is barrel-fermented. Jean-Claude Chatelain and son Vincent are also shareholders in a new vineyard in the La Charité-sur-Loire area south of Pouilly, where they make Chardonnay and Pinot Noir.

Didier Dagueneau ☆☆☆☆
St-Andelain. 12 ha.
The appellation's best winemaker by far, although his dazzling career was cut short by his death in a flying accident in 2008. The impassioned Dagueneau made four decisive *cuvées* of Pouilly-Fumé: Blanc Fumé de Pouilly (formerly En Chailloux), Buisson Ménard, Pur Sang, and Silex. The last two ferment and age in new-oak barrels of various sizes. There are also mini-*cuvées*: Clos du Calvaire from vines planted to a density of 11,000 vines per hectare, and the late-harvested L'Astéroïde, made from ungrafted vines.

Astonished many years ago by the quality of venerable bottles of Pouilly in private cellars, he changed his vinification and style from an easy-drinking white for early consumption to a well-structured, oak-aged wine capable of evolving fruitfully over many years. The style remains controversial, but Dagueneau was its master, and no other producer can rival the elegance and power of his wines. They brilliantly combine richness and minerality.

Serge Dagueneau & Filles ☆☆
St-Andelain. 15 ha. www.s-dagueneau-filles.fr
A vineyard with a high reputation for typically fruity and full-flavoured Pouilly-Fumé and Pouilly-sur-Loire. His old-vines *cuvée* is Clos des Chaudoux which is aged for 18 months on its fine lees. He also has a property in the obscure Coteaux Charitois, where he produces Chardonnay, Pinot Noir, and Gamay.

Pascal Jolivet ☆☆
Sancerre. 20 ha. www.pascal-jolivet.com
Pascal Jolivet is based in Sancerre but also has vines in Pouilly

Bringing in the the harvest by horse, Pouilly-sur-Loire: a rare sight today

from which he produces numerous bottlings, including Les Griottes and La Grande Cuvée, made from old vines in good vintages.

Domaine Masson-Blondelet ☆☆–☆☆☆
Pouilly-sur-Loire. 21 ha. www.masson-blondelet.com
The Masson and Blondelet families (united by marriage in 1974) grow mainly Sauvignon and a small amount of Chasselas and Sancerre. Their best parcels are vinified separately: Les Angelots from limestone, Villa Paulus from marne, and, from the oldest vines, Tradition Cullus. Since 2004 there has been an additional *cuvée*, Les Pierres de Pierre from clay-flint soils.

Château du Nozet ☆☆
Pouilly-sur-Loire. 65 ha.
The major producer and promoter of the fine wines of Pouilly, both from company-owned vineyards and from purchased wine. Baron Patrick de Ladoucette is the head of the family firm, which has three labels: Pouilly-Fumé de Ladoucette, Sancerre Comte Lafond (from bought-in grapes), and a *prestige cuvée* Pouilly-Fumé Baron de L.

The Baron also owns vineyards on La Poussie in Sancerre. The Pouilly-Fumé wines are inexplicably expensive, and always have been.

Michel Redde ☆–☆☆☆
La Moynerie, St-Andelain. 40 ha.
www.michel-redde.fr
One of the best-known producers of Pouilly-Fumé, now in its seventh generation under Thierry Redde. There are no fewer than six *cuvées*, reflecting different soil types, as well as two Sancerres. Cuvée Majorum is the top wine from old vines, but Redde is adamantly opposed to oak-ageing. Pouilly-sur-Loire is also produced.

Guy Saget ☆–☆☆
Pouilly-sur-Loire. 10 ha. www.guy-saget.com
A fifth-generation growers' family affair run by the brothers Saget, expanded since 1976 into a négociant business. It now sells four million bottles of Loire wines annually, from 25 different appellations. Their technique is long cool fermentation with minimum disturbance of the wine and no malolactic fermentation to reduce the high natural fruity acidity. See also Balland-Chapuis.

Château de Tracy ☆☆
Tracy-sur-Loire. 31 ha.
www.chateau-de-tracy.com.
The family of the Comte d'Estutt d'Assay has owned the Château, on the Loire just downstream from Pouilly, since the sixteenth century. The style is fairly rounded, and the wines are best enjoyed young. After a dull patch, the wines from the late 1990s show more concentration and precision.

The Minor Regions

The success of Sancerre and Pouilly has encouraged what were dwindling outposts of vineyards in less-favoured situations to the west of the Loire to expand their plantings. The names of Menetou-Salon (465 hectares), Quincy (224 hectares), and Reuilly (186 hectares) are now accepted as Sancerre substitutes at slightly lower prices (but longer odds against a fine, ripe bottle). Three other regions of the upper Loire have now gained VDQS status: Coteaux du Giennois, the tiny Châteaumeillant (good for its rosé), and Vins de l'Orléanais.

Much higher up the river where it cuts through the Massif Central, several scattered vineyard areas relate less to the Loire than to southern Burgundy and the Rhône. The most famous is St-Pourçain-sur-Sioule (650 hectares), once a monastic vineyard. Its wine is almost all consumed today to mitigate the effects of treatment at the spa of Vichy – but it is hard to see how it could ever have had more than a local following. Price remains the main thing in favour of the remaining areas of the heights of the Loire, but the quality is improving. The Côte Roannaises (now AC), and the AC Côtes du Forez and the VDQS Côtes d'Auvergne grow the right grapes for quality – Gamay, Chardonnay, some Pinot Noir, and Syrah.

Reuilly

Henri Beurdin ☆
Reuilly. 16 ha.
Jean-Louis Beurdin produces classic Sauvignon that is citric, bone-dry, and well balanced.

Claude Lafond ☆☆
Le Bois St-Denis, Reuilly. 15 ha.
www.claudelafond.com
An energetic young grower, Lafond makes some of the best wine in the appellation, including a dry white Clos des Messieurs, a dry rosé La Grande Pièce, and a light Pinot Noir called Les Grandes Vignes. He also directs the 13-hectare Domaine des Seigneurs, which unites over 100 shareholders, and is co-owner of the two-hectare Château Gaillard.

Menetou-Salon

Domaine de Chatenoy ☆–☆☆
Menetou-Salon. 60 ha. www.clement-chatenoy.com
The ancestors of Pierre Clément have owned this estate since 1560, and he now produces red, white, and rosé. Cuvée Pierre Alexandre is fermented and aged in 50 per cent new oak.

Philippe Gilbert ☆☆
Les Faucards. 27 ha. www.domainephilippegilbert.fr
A relatively new property, Domaine Gilbert has been Biodynamic since 2006. As well as classic unwooded Menetou-Salon, Philippe Gilbert also produces the oak-aged Renardières, both white and red.

Henry Pellé ☆–☆☆☆
Morogues. 40 ha. www.henry-pelle.com
A family winery producing vigorous whites and pleasant, light reds. The top white *cuvée* is Clos des Blanchais, made from old

vines. Morogues, which abuts the Sancerre zone, is the only commune that may attach its name to that of Menetou-Salon on the label. The domaine also produces some négociant wines, and for these the name Morogues is suppressed. There is also a small production of Sancerre.

La Tour Saint-Martin ☆☆
Crosses. 16 ha.
Over the past 20 years Bertrand Minchin has steadily improved the quality at this estate, and has taken a particular interest in Pinot Noir, with which almost half the property is planted. The Cuvée Célestin is the top Pinot, and surprisingly structured.

Quincy

Domaine Mardon ☆–☆☆☆
Quincy. 14 ha. www.domainemardon.com
A good family winery producing brisk whites – among the best in the appellation. And a small quantity of red Reuilly for good measure.

Coteaux du Giennois

Alain Paulat ☆☆
Villemoison. 5 ha.
Alain Paulat is a passionate young grower who cultivates his vines organically. He produces toothsome light reds from Gamay and Pinot Noir.

Balland-Chapuis & Gitton (q.v.) ☆☆
Sancerre.
Also makes reliable Coteaux du Giennois.

Vin de l'Orléanais

Clos St-Fiacre ☆
Mareau-aux-Près. 18 ha
Engaging light reds from Pinot Meunier and Pinot Noir as well as light Chardonnays and somewhat vegetal Cabernets.

Châteaumeillant

Domaine du Chaillot ☆
Dun-sur-Auron. 7 ha.
www.domaine.du.chaillot.free.fr
Pierre Picot makes just one wine each vintage: a fruity yet subtle Gamay.

Patrick Lanoix ☆
Châteaumeillant. 19 ha.
The estate produces pleasant reds and rosés (predominantly Gamay) under two labels: Domaine du Feuillat and Cellier du Chêne Combeau.

Côtes d'Auvergne

Cave St-Verny ☆
Veyre-Monton. www.saint-verny.com
Founded in 1950 as a cooperative, the cave was purchased in 1991 by Limagrain, Europe's largest seed specialist. It produces nearly half the wine in the appellation in ultra-modern cellars, turning out clean whites, rosés (those from Corent are particularly noteworthy) and light red wines

based on Gamay and Pinot Noir. The deluxe bottling is called Première Cuvée, while the oak-aged wines are labelled Privilège.

Côtes du Forez

les Vignerons Foreziens ☆
Trelins. 200 ha. www.vigneronsforeziens.fr
The cooperative produces 98 per cent of AC Côtes du Forez and 60 per cent of the Vin de Pays d'Urfe. The former is Gamay; the latter predominantly Chardonnay.

Côte Roannaise

Paul Lapandéry & Fils ☆–☆☆
St-Haon-le-Vieux. 8 ha.
A family winery with vineyards pitched at a vertiginous 72° angle. Lapandéry's highly personalized light reds, from Gamay and Pinot Noir, are based on very low yields and very long barrel-age.

Domaine de la Perrière ☆–☆☆
Ambierle. 5 ha.
Owned until 2003 by Alain Demon, this estate, with its steep vineyards above the Loire, is now the property of Philippe Peulet. The wines are Gamays of character, and the Réserve is made from vines over 50 years old.

St-Pourçain

Union des Vignerons ☆
St-Pourçain-sur-Sioule. 300 ha.
www.vignerons-saintpourcain.com
The cooperative (founded 1952), with 160 members, handles two-thirds of the production from this once-famous central vineyard, formerly a monastic stronghold. The principal varieties grown are Chardonnay and Tresallier for whites, and Pinot Noir and Gamay for reds. Special bottlings include its popular Ficelle, an easy-drinking Gamay; Réserve Spéciale (white and red); red and white wines from two estates and Domaine de Chinière and Domaine de la Croix d'Or. A number of independent growers are also making great efforts and some progress.

Champagne

Champagne is the wine grown in the northernmost vineyards of France: the local wine of Paris. The Champagne method (or traditional method, as Brussels insists that we now call it) is something that is done to the wine to make it sparkle – and can be done to any wine. Those who make wine sparkle in other regions would like us to believe that the method is all that matters. What really matters is the wine. It was one of the best in France long before the method was invented. The difference between the best Champagne and the merely good is almost entirely a matter of the choice and treatment of grapes, their variety, their ripeness, their handling, and the soil that bears them.

Outside France, the Champagne market is largely controlled by the Grandes Marques: the 20 or so great firms with the widest distribution. These great merchants actually own only a small percentage of the vineyards, and have to rely on about 15,000 small farmers to provide them with grapes. Many growers in Champagne also sell their crop to cooperatives, though some – the *récoltants-manipulants* – make small amounts of Champagne of their own. All told, growers are responsible for 5,000 brands, though these are not necessarily vinified by them. The best of these independent growers are described in detail here.

Any merchant buying Champagne can think up a name (a "buyer's own brand") and print a label, so there is no limit to the number of brands. In itself this lends strength to the Grandes Marques with the best-known names, which are often bought simply as safe bets. But reputation and wealth also allow them to buy the best materials, employ the best staff, and stock their wine longest. (Time is vital to develop the flavours.) The great houses push to the limit the polishing and perfecting of an agricultural product.

The "method" began 200 years ago with the genius of a Benedictine monk, Dom Pérignon of Hautvillers, apparently the first man to "design" a wine by blending the qualities of different grapes from different varieties and vineyards to make a whole greater, more subtle, more satisfying than any of its parts. This blend, known as the *cuvée*, is traditionally the secret patent of each maker, though cellarmasters today will sometimes invite the wine trade and press to observe the blending process first-hand.

The best blends are astonishingly complex, with as many as 30 or 40 ingredient wines of different origins and ages, selected by nose and palate alone. Houses with their own vineyards stress the character of the grapes they grow themselves; the heavier Pinot Noir of the Montagne de Reims or the lighter Chardonnay of the Côte des Blancs – each village is subtly different. But few have enough to supply their own needs. Grape-prices are fixed by a percentage system.

It was not Dom Pérignon but his contemporaries who discovered how to make their wine sparkling by a second fermentation in a tightly corked bottle – a process with dangers and complications that took another century to master completely. The principle of making Champagne is outlined on page 33. The sparkle is caused by the large amounts of CO_2 dissolved in the wine. The "mousse", or froth in the glass, is only part of it – you swallow the greater part. CO_2 is instantly absorbed by the stomach wall. Once in the bloodstream it accelerates the circulation, and with it the movement of alcohol to the brain. This is where Champagne gets its reputation as the wine of wit and the choice for celebrations. Other sparkling wines made by the same method can claim to have the same effect, but rarely the same taste.

Leading Champagne Producers

Besserat de Bellefon ☆☆
Epernay. Owner: Boizel Chanoine group. Visits: appt. only. NV: Grande Tradition. NV Cuvée des Moines: Brut, Brut Rosé, Blanc de Blancs. Vintage: Clos des Moines. www.besseratdebellefon.com
A family business until 1959, the firm has had several corporate owners since then, the most recent being the dynamic Boizel Chanoine group. The Besserat house style is for very fine, light wines much appreciated in top French restaurants. The Cuvée des Moines Blanc de Blancs with its gentle sparkle and creamy flavour makes a good apéritif, while the Cuvée des Moines Rosé has great finesse.

Billecart-Salmon ☆☆☆
Mareuil-sur-Aÿ. Owner: Roland-Billecart family. 6 ha. Visits: appt. only. NV: Brut Réserve, Brut Rosé, Demi-Sec. Vintages: Cuvée Nicolas-François Billecart, Blanc de Blancs, Cuvée Elisabeth Salmon Rosé, Grande Cuvée, Clos St Hilaire Blanc de Noirs. www.champagne-billecart.fr
A small, highly respected Grand Marque, this family firm is currently producing exquisite Champagnes of the light and elegant kind. Always respectful of the traditional composition of its *cuvées*, Billecart nonetheless uses modern vinification techniques that involve a natural cold settling of the must and long, cool fermentations. The result is wine of floral aromas and delicate flavours that belie its ability to live a long and distinguished life. The Brut Réserve is quite exceptional; although dominated by the two Pinots, its 30% Chardonnay content gives an extra dimension of finesse and elegance.

Outstanding vintage wines have a perfect balance of freshness and maturity, especially the late-disgorged Grande Cuvée, the same wine as the vintage but given ten years' ageing on the yeasts. A recent innovation is

Mixing in the dosage to make Champagne

Clos St Hilaire, a Blanc de Noirs from a one-hectare site near the house; production is tiny, the price great.

Bollinger ☆☆☆–☆☆☆☆

Aÿ. Owner: Bizot family. Associated companies: Ayala, Langlois-Château (Loire), Chanson (Burgundy). 160 ha. Visits: appt. only. NV: Special Cuvée Brut. Vintages: Grande Année Brut and Rosé, RD, Vieilles Vignes Françaises. Still wines: Aÿ, Côte aux Enfants. www.champagne-bollinger.fr

One of the "greats" of Champagne, a traditionalist house making muscular wine with body, length, depth, and every other dimension. Much of the harvest is barrel-fermented and wines are kept on their yeast as long as possible; in the case of RD "recently disgorged" about ten years, giving extra breadth of flavour.

A tiny patch of ungrafted pre-phylloxera Pinot Noir in Aÿ and Bouzy gives Vieilles Vignes Françaises: very rare and expensive, "combining the power of the New World with the elegance of the Old", in the words of Guy Bizot, great nephew of Madame Lily Bollinger. Sixty per cent of grapes come from Bollinger's own vineyards, the remainder is bought from Côte des Blancs and Verteuil in the Marne Valley. The vintage wines certainly benefit from bottle age, but the same is true for the non-vintage over two to three years.

Delamotte ☆☆–☆☆☆

Le Mesnil-sur-Oger. Owner: Laurent-Perrier. 11 ha. Visits: appt. only. NV: Brut, Blanc de Blancs, Rosé. Vintage: Blanc de Blancs Vintage. www.salondelamotte.com

The sixth oldest Champagne house, founded in 1760. Since Laurent-Perrier's purchase of Salon (q.v.) in 1989, the two firms, housed in adjacent eighteenth-century premises, have been managed jointly. The firm has some *grand cru* Chardonnay in Le Mesnil which, though producing only about 25 per cent of the company's needs, certainly shapes the Chardonnay-led style of the Champagnes; fresh, aromatic, and long-lived. The vintage-dated Blanc de Blancs is the most interesting: rich, peach-like, and refreshed by a lean length of flavour.

Deutz ☆☆☆

Aÿ. Owner: Louis Roederer. 42 ha. Visits: appt. only. NV: Brut Classic. Vintages: Brut, Blanc de Blancs, Rosé. Prestige: Cuvée William Deutz Brut and Rosé, Amour de Deutz. www.champagne-deutz.com

Like many great Champagne firms, this house was founded by German immigrants. Although the Lallier-Deutz family are still involved in the business, a majority stake was acquired by Roederer in 1993, since when quality has soared.

The Roederer investment shows to good effect in the new Brut Classic, a first-rate non-vintage *cuvée*, creamy, rich, yet decidedly dry in the Deutz tradition. The vintage-dated *blanc de blancs* Amour de Deutz made from *grand cru* grapes is exquisite, as is the Cuvée William Deutz, a prestige blend of great vinous subtlety and weight.

Drappier ☆☆–☆☆☆☆

Urville. Owner: Drappier family. 75 ha. Visits: appt. only. NV: Brut Nature, Carte d'Or Brut, Carte Blanche,

---

CHOOSING CHAMPAGNE

The knowledge essential for buying Champagne to your own taste is the style and standing of the house and the range of its wines. The major houses offer reliability and quality that ranges from the humdrum to the exceptional; they are not to be slighted. Smaller growers can offer characterful wines from a single prestigious village such as Mesnil or Aÿ, but some producers are less than exacting in their production methods. Elements that affect the style and taste of the Champagne – the composition of the blend, the richness of the *dosage*, the date of disgorgement – are rarely disclosed on the label.

Most houses offer wines in the following categories:

Non-vintage (NV) A *cuvée* maintained, as nearly as possible, to an exact standard year after year: usually fairly young. Standard gauge of "house style". Essentially apéritif wines.

Vintage Best-quality wine of a vintage whose intrinsic quality is considered too good to be hidden in a non-vintage *cuvée*. Normally aged longer on the yeast than non-vintage, more full-bodied and tasty, with the potential to improve for several more years. Their greater body makes them better at table.

Rosé A small quantity of still red wine from one of the Pinot Noir villages (often Aÿ or Bouzy) is blended with still white wine. This blend undergoes a second fermentation, which creates the bubbles. A very few producers, such as Krug, make rosé by a brief maceration of the grapes, but this is much harder to control than blending in red wine. In many cases, entrancingly fruity and fine, and one of the house's best *cuvées*.

Blanc de blancs A *cuvée* of Chardonnay grapes only, with great grace and less weight than traditional Champagne, but lacking the dimensions of harmony in a classic blend.

Blanc de noirs A *cuvée* of black grapes only, sometimes faintly pink or *gris*, and invariably rich and flavoury.

Cuvée de prestige (under many names) A super-Champagne on the hang-the-expense principle. Moët's Dom Pérignon was the first; now most houses have one. Fabulously good though most of them are, there is a strong argument for two bottles of non-vintage for the price of one *cuvée* de prestige. (See page 178.)

Coteaux Champenois Still white or red wine of the Champagne vineyards, made in limited quantities when supplies of grapes allow. Naturally high in acidity, but can be exquisitely fine.

Brut, extra dry, etc. What little consistency there is about these indications of sweetness or otherwise is shown on page 180.

Dry Nature, Rosé Brut, Signature Blanc de Blancs. Vintage: Grande Sendrée Brut. www.champagne-drappier.com

Vignerons in the Aube since the time of Napoléon, this is a dynamic merchant-grower house producing hedonistic Champagne of great character. The heart of the business is the domaine planted mainly with Pinot Noir on the southern limestone slopes of Urville.

Meticulous winemaking in a pristine *cuverie* above cool, twelfth-century Cistercian cellars results in some memorable bottles: the Carte d'Or Brut suffused with aromas and flavours of red fruits (the Drappier style); the impressive Brut Nature – powerful, uncompromising, bone-dry, but in no way astringent or bitter; the prestige Grande Sendrée – mouth-filling, magnificent, and very Pinot, but with exactly the right amount of Chardonnay to add an extra touch of definition and refinement.

Duval-Leroy ☆–☆☆☆
Vertus. Owner: Carol Duval. 190 ha. Visits: appt. only. NV: Fleur de Champagne Brut, Rosé de Saignée, Lady Rose, Demi-Sec. Vintage: Femme de Champagne, Extra Brut, Blanc de Chardonnay, Cuvée Leroy Neiman, Authentis. www.duval-leroy.com

A quality-conscious family firm, which benefitted enormously from the acquisition of choice Chardonnay vineyards mainly on the Côte des Blancs. Until recently, much of the company's export business was in supplying "buyer's own brand" Champagnes to merchants in Britain, Belgium, and Germany. But in the late 1990s, the marketing strategy sought to establish the brand on world markets, and under the leadership of the current head of the company, Carol Duval, a formidably strong-willed widow, that ambition was largely achieved.

The style of the Champagne is subtle, fresh, aromatic, and well illustrated by the Chardonnay-dominated Fleur de Champagne. The superb *blanc de blancs* is a vintage wine, the classic 1990 a model of its kind. The latest additions to the range are the three Authentis single-vineyard Champagnes. The house also wins plaudits for being one of the few which still makes a half-litre size (bizarrely illegal in the EU, but not in the US) – in my view a great lack elsewhere.

Gosset ☆☆–☆☆☆
Aÿ. Owner: Frapin Cognac. 100 ha. Visits: appt. only. NV: Brut Excellence, Grande Réserve, Grand Rosé. Vintage: Grand Millésime. Prestige: Célebris Brut, Blanc de Blancs, and Rosé. Still wine: Bouzy Rouge. www.champagne-gosset.com

Founded in 1584, Gosset has good claim to being the oldest wine house in the Marne, though Ruinart (q.v.) was the first to make sparkling Champagne on a serious scale. After 410 years of Gosset ownership, control of the firm passed to the quality-conscious Cointreau family of Frapin Cognac in 1994.

The new Brut Excellence is a brisk, racy wine dominated by Chardonnay (61 per cent), and is ideal as an apéritif. The real stars of the range are the floral, rich, and complex Grande Réserve, a classic blend of Pinot and Chardonnay, and the lustrous rosé: full, velvet-smooth and very elegant. Gosset Champagnes are built to last, the malolactic fermentation

deliberately avoided to ensure a long life. Usually rich and satisfying, Gosset Champagnes can sometimes err on the side of heaviness.

Alfred Gratien ☆☆–☆☆☆
Epernay. Owner: Seydoux family of Gratien & Meyer (Saumur). No vineyards. Visits: appt. only. NV: Brut, Brut Rosé, Blanc de Blancs. Vintage: Brut. Prestige: Cuvée Paradis Brut, Cuvée Paradis Rosé. www.alfredgratien.com

Small traditionalist house, making 250,000 bottles per annum of excellent, very dry wines vinified in small barrels; the malolactic fermentation is avoided to ensure maximum vitality and long life. The vintage wines have an unusually high Chardonnay content, though the house style also favours a significant amount of Pinot Meunier in the blends in order to add notes of spices and luxuriant fruit. The Cuvée Paradis ranks among the very greatest Champagnes, at once elegant and exotic; unlike many prestige bottlings, it is a non-vintage blend from the best vineyards.

Charles Heidsieck ☆☆☆
Reims. Owner: Rémy-Cointreau. 70 ha (shared with Piper-Heidsieck). Visits: appt only. NV: Brut Réserve, Mis en Cave. Vintage: Brut and Rosé. Prestige: Blanc de Millénaire, Oenothéque. www.charlesheidsieck.com

The original Charles Heidsieck was the "Champagne Charlie" of the song, who made a fortune in the USA but almost lost it in the Civil War. The late Daniel Thibault was appointed winemaker in 1985, and within a few years the quality of the wines had improved greatly, especially the Brut Réserve. Its outstanding character owes everything to natural vinification, technical treatments of the wine being kept to a minimum, and to the complexity of the blend, which is composed of 300 components with at least 40 per cent reserve wines. Honeyed, fleshy, yet with a discreet vinosity, this is a Champagne *par excellence* to accompany fine cuisine.

The prestige Blanc des Millénaires is a magnificent *blanc de blancs*, a high-wire act of sharply defined, mature Chardonnay flavours and exotic fruitiness. An interesting initiative was the "mis en cave" ("bottled in cellar") programme, launched with the 1992 vintage. These are non-vintage wines, and the date refers to the year each bottling began its ageing process in the cellars. The extra bottle-age, and perhaps a superior blend, shows in round and toasty flavours.

Henriot ☆☆–☆☆☆
Reims. Owner: Joseph Henriot. Associated companies: Bouchard Père et Fils, William Fèvre. Visits: appt. only. NV: Brut Souverain, Brut Souverain Pure Chardonnay, Rosé. Vintage: Brut. Prestige: Cuvée des Enchanteleurs. www.champagne-henriot.com

Rémois merchants and wine-growers since the seventeenth century, the Henriots are as Champenois as the windmill of Verzenay. In 1994, Joseph Henriot took the firm back into family ownership. The price of independence from the LVMH group was the loss of the family's very fine, 100-hectare vineyards located mainly on the Côte des Blancs, though grapes are still sourced from these exceptional sites on a long-lease basis.

Henriot Champagnes are very dry, pure-flavoured, and based exclusively on Pinot Noir and Chardonnay, the latter seemingly, if not actually, dominant. The Pure Chardonnay is a model of incisive but persistent Chardonnay flavours. The Cuvée des Enchanteleurs is a *prestige cuvée* that ages beautifully. In 1995, Joseph Henriot bought the Burgundy house of Bouchard Père et Fils (q.v.).

Jacquesson ☆☆☆–☆☆☆☆

Dizy. Owner: Chiquet family. 26 ha. Visits: appt. only. NV: Cuvée 731, Rosé. Vintage: Brut, Rosé, Avize Grand Cru, various single vineyard bottlings. www.champagnejacquesson.com

Johann Joseph Krug, founder of the *ne plus* ultra of Champagne houses, learned blending at Jacquesson, and this low-key firm is still one of the best exponents of classic Champagne-making.

Subtly cask-aged reserve wines contribute significantly to the supple, rich, yet structured house style of the finished Champagnes. The Chiquet family's 95 per-cent-rated vineyards at Dizy, Aÿ, Hautvillers, and Avize account for 40 per cent of their requirements. The much-loved Perfection Brut has been replaced by the Cuvée series; succeeding numbers reflect the vintage on which the wine is based. The Signature range is also no more, having been replaced by the magnificent vintage-dated Grand Cru from Avize (pure Chardonnay), and a beguiling range of rare single-vineyard wines from Aÿ and Dizy. Quality has never been higher, and Jacquesson has ascended to the top ranks of Champagne houses.

Krug ☆☆☆☆

Reims. Owner: Moët Hennessy-Louis Vuitton group (LVMH). 20 ha. Visits: appt. only. NV: Grande Cuvée, Rosé. Vintage: Clos du Mesnil, Clos d'Ambonnay. www.krug.com

The house of Krug sees itself as something apart from other Champagnes, and indeed its wines are quite unlike any other. All are fermented in small oak barrels and then aged on the cork for an uncommonly long time before sale.

The Grande Cuvée has a high proportion of Chardonnay brilliantly assembled with Pinot Noir and Pinot Meunier into a masterly blend composed of seven up to ten vintages and 20 to 25 different growths. It has good claim to be among the finest of all Champagnes, very dry, elusively fruity, gentle yet authoritative at the same time. The Krug Rosé, first introduced in 1983, is another masterpiece of fruit and savour and is intended to accompany the finest culinary creations.

The vintage is not generally released until it is nine years old; these wines need long ageing, sometimes 15, 20, even 25 years to reach their peak. This is especially true of the single-vineyard vintage Clos du Mesnil, a pure Chardonnay Champagne, austere when young but with the potential to taste like a Corton Charlemagne with bubbles after a quarter of a century in bottle. The Krugs value the Clos because it reflects a remarkable terroir; they do not claim it is always superior to the vintage. In 2007 the Krugs launched another Clos, that of Ambonnay, a 1995 Blanc de Noirs at a price that makes Clos du Mesnil look cheap.

Lanson ☆–☆☆☆

Reims. Owner: Boizel Chanoine group. No vineyards. Visits: appt. only. NV: Black Label Brut, Demi-Sec, Rosé, Noble Cuvée Rose. Vintage: Brut, Blanc de Blancs. Prestige: Noble Cuvée. www.lanson.fr

This ancient house has gone through tumultuous times, but its future should be secure now that it has been acquired by Bruno Paillard and his Boizel Chanoine group. The range remains much the same, although a rosé has been added to the Noble Cuvée tier. The vivid, tingling style of the Black Label is shaped by a lot of Pinot Noir (50 per cent) in the blend, and the avoidance of any malolactic fermentation, thus increasing the fruity character of the wine. Lanson vintage, dominated by Pinot Noir, is broad-shouldered, deep in flavour. Chardonnay (70 per cent) is the motor of the Noble Cuvée: floral, supremely elegant, but with a firm, durable structure.

Laurent-Perrier ☆☆–☆☆☆

Tours-sur-Marne. Owner: Nonancourt family. 154 ha. Associated companies: Salon, Delamotte, de Castellane. Visits: during working hours. NV: Brut, Ultra Brut, Rosé Brut, Demi-Sec. Vintage: Brut. Prestige: Grand Siècle NV and Vintage, Grand Siècle Alexandra Rosé. www.laurent-perrier.co.uk

Laurent-Perrier non-vintage brut is now a consistent Champagne, fresh, racy, with a Chablis-like mineral character. Ultra Brut is a dry, sugarless wine, but with no hint of the hair shirt as it is always made from grapes of a ripe year. The hugely successful rosé is made the hard way – by putting the Pinot Noir grape skins in contact with the juice to obtain the right colour, and then ageing the wine for four years.

The real triumph of the house, though, is the Cuvée Grand Siècle. Sumptuous, stylish, and long-maturing, it is a blend of three vintages, though it was occasionally sold with a vintage label until 1997. The vineyards, either owned or under long-term contract, are in the best sites of the Montagne de Reims, the Côte des Blancs, and the Marne Valley.

Mercier ☆

Epernay. Founded 1858. Owner: LVMH group. 218 ha. Visits: at regular hours. NV: Brut, Rosé, Demi-Sec. Vintage: Brut Millésimé. www.champagnemercier.fr

Mercier, like the rest of the Moët group, has the virtue of size and consistency of supply meaning reliability. The stress is on dry, brut Champagne in a soft, black grapes style. Quality, while sound, is far from exciting.

Eugène Mercier, the founder, was the pace-setter in bringing Champagne to ordinary French people during the late nineteenth century. For the Universal Exhibition held in Paris in 1889, he built a huge wine barrel; it took a team of 24 oxen three weeks to tow the cask to the capital. But his most enduring memorial is the labyrinth of cellars beneath the crest of the hill on Epernay's Avenue de Champagne – 16 kilometres (ten miles) long and connected by miniature electric train.

Moët & Chandon ☆☆–☆☆☆☆

Epernay. Owner: LVMH group. 630 ha. Associated companies: Mercier, Ruinart, Domaine Chandon in

THE RISE OF THE CUVEE DE PRESTIGE

The success of Champagne has always been based on shrewd marketing, ensuring its reputation worldwide as the only suitable wine for any celebration. Individual Champagne houses go to great lengths to establish their own image. Veuve Clicquot sponsors fashionable events in the English season; Krug throws lavish and well-publicized parties instead.

When a Champagne house needs a shot in the arm, one way to supply it is to create a new product. Dom Pérignon was launched by Moët & Chandon for the first time in 1936, although the wine was made from the 1921 vintage. Its success has been colossal, though fully justified by the quality of the wine.

Where Moët led, others soon followed. In the 1950s Taittinger created a luxury *blanc de blancs*, Comtes de Champagne; and Laurent-Perrier launched its Grand Siècle. The 1960s saw the introduction of Perrier-Jouët's Belle Epoque in its unmistakable enamelled bottle, and Veuve Clicquot's Grande Dame. Roederer's ultra-chic Cristal was originally created in the 1870s for the Russian court, and can plausibly claim to be the granddaddy of them all.

A *prestige cuvée*, by definition, is associated with luxury and rarity, so the price is high. With rare exceptions, such as Laurent-Perrier's Grand Siècle and Gratien's Cuvée Paradis, the wines are from a single vintage, begging the question of whether there is any significant difference between the vintage and the *prestige cuvées*. The answer is usually yes. Some houses will aim for an ultra-rich style. Charles Heidsieck's Blancs de Millenaires is in a powerfully toasty style, for example.

Other producers aim for the maximum finesse. This would be true of Grande Dame and even of Dom Pérignon. Veuve Clicquot and Moët work hard to ensure there is a clear stylistic distinction between their excellent vintage Champagnes and their *prestige cuvées*. But even they would admit that in certain exceptional years, such as 1988 and 1990, the difference in quality between the two is fairly narrow, although the stylistic difference remains.

Krug would argue that its basic Champagne is the best possible "multi-vintage" blend and thus a *prestige cuvée* by price and definition. When Krug decided on new products, it opted for

single-vineyard wines from Clos du Mesnil and Clos d'Ambonnay. Very few other producers have opted for single-vineyard wines, although Philipponnat's Clos des Goisses is a noble exception, and Leclerc-Briant has persevered with this approach. Jacquesson has recently begun to move in the same direction. The great majority of producers, however, remain true to the concept of Champagne as a wine based on the art of blending.

Although some of these *cuvées* really are produced in very small quantities, being based on the most severe selection of grapes from the very finest of *grand cru* sites, others, notably Dom Pérignon, are produced in surprising quantities. These Champagnes are not always as rare as their producers would like us to believe. For the last decade, exports of *prestige cuvées* have been at between five to six per cent of total Champagne exports, with the lion's share going to the USA.

There can be no disputing that many *cuvées de prestige* are exceptional Champagnes. Others, however, substitute heavyhandedness and vulgar packaging for real quality. The borderline between true distinction and slick marketing is, in Champagne, razor-thin.

The church at Villedommage on the Montagne de Reims

California, Australia, Spain, Argentina, and Brazil. **Visits: regular hours. NV: Brut Impérial, Rosé Impérial, Nectar Impériale. Vintage: Grand Vintage, Grand Vintage Rosé. Prestige: Dom Pérignon Blanc and Rosé. www.moet.com**

Moët's traditional style is elegant, light, and easy to appreciate but also rounds out nicely with age. Very wide sources of supply ensure consistency of the huge quantities of Brut Impérial. The vintage is a true Champenois blend of the three principal grapes, and from the 2000 vintage is intended to be a daring and extreme expression of the year. The NV, according to the Moët *chef de caves*, might also become more characterful in future.

Exceptional winemaking by Richard Geoffroy, a former medical doctor, means that Dom Pérignon has been as fine as its reputation in recent vintages, distinctly luxurious yet also discreet and elegant. The Dom Pérignon Rosé – peach-coloured, subtle, nuancé – is outstanding. The Moët group owns parcels in ten out of 17 *grand cru* vineyards. Grapes from these vineyards supply Ruinart (q.v.) as well as Moët.

Mumm ☆–☆☆

Reims. Owner: Pernod Ricard. 218 ha. Visits: at regular hours. NV: Cordon Rouge, Rosé. Demi-Sec, Mumm de Cramant. Vintage: Brut. Prestige, Grand Cru, Cuvée R. Lalou. www.mumm.com

It is hard to be categoric about the overall quality and style of Mumm Champagnes, as the range is very diverse and there have been numerous changes of ownership in recent years. The wines made from a preponderance of Pinot Noir are mainly solid and straightforward. Cordon Rouge non-vintage remains bland, lacking a little character. The lightly sparkling Mumm de Cramant, made from Chardonnay grapes from the village of Cramant, is excellent. From 1998 the *prestige cuvees* René Lalou and Grand Cordon, have been replaced by Cuvée R. Lalou, a 50/50 blend of Pinot Noir and Chardonnay. Its vineyards produce 20 per cent of its needs. Annual production is about nine million bottles. Since 1971, Mumm has been a leader of viticultural research in Champagne.

Bruno Paillard ☆☆–☆☆☆

Reims. Owner: Paillard family. 25 ha. Visits: appt. only. Associated companies: Boizel, De Venoge, Lanson, Philipponnat, Chanoine, Alexandre Bonnet. NV: Première Cuvée, Première Cuvée Rosé, Blanc de Blancs Réserve Privée. Vintage: Brut. Prestige: Ne Plus Ultra. www.mumm.com

The youngest classic Champagne house, founded in 1981 by the perfectionist Paillard, a broker with deep roots in the industry. His wines are consistent models of elegance and refinement, very dry, almost austere, and built to last. The first-rate Première Cuvée is now partially fermented in wood, the Réserve Privée made by the old method for *crémant* (lightly sparkling Champagne). Paillard vintage wines are beautifully labelled, and should be applauded for always specifying the date of disgorging. In 2000, Paillard launched a *prestige* wine called Ne Plus Ultra, from barrel-fermented *grand cru* grapes, aged eight years before disgorgement. Sales are around 600,000 bottles a year.

Joseph Perrier ☆☆–☆☆☆

Châlons-en-Champagne. Owner: Alain Thiénot. 21 ha. Visits: appt. only. NV: Cuvée Royale, Blanc de Blancs, Cuvée Royale Rosé, Demi-Sec. Vintage: Cuvée Royale. Prestige: Cuvée Joséphine. www.joseph-perrier.com

The stylish, fruit-laden wines of the sole Grande Marque in Châlons go from strength to strength. The Cuvée Royale non-vintage is a benchmark of succulent, ripe Pinots (both Noir and Meunier) brilliantly blended with 35 per cent Chardonnay. The Chardonnay-led prestige Cuvée Joséphine is usually a memorable bottle. Its vineyards at Cumières, Damery, Hautvillers, and Verneuil supply one-third of the firm's requirements. Sales are around 650,000 bottles a year. Vintage wines are not released until they are seven or eight years old.

Perrier-Jouët ☆☆–☆☆☆

Epernay. Owner: Pernod Ricard. 66 ha. Visits: appt. only. NV: Brut. Vintage: Brut, Rosé. Prestige: NV Blason de France Blanc and Rosé, Belle Epoque Blanc and Rosé, By & For. www.perrier-jouet.com

Long respected for first-class, very fresh and crisp (but by no means light) non-vintage and luxury *cuvées* with plenty of flavour. Blason de France, a blend of good vintages, is its rarest wine, complex and age-worthy. The much better-known Belle Epoque, in its flower-painted bottle, is the flagship of the house: a *prestige cuvée* of consistently rich and harmonious style. In 2008 a special *cuvée*, By & For, was launched: 100 cases of "bespoke" Champagne tailored to the tastes of the purchaser for a mere £35,000 per case.

SERVING & ENJOYING CHAMPAGNE

When
For celebrations any time, as an apéritif, occasionally with light meals, with dessert (sweet/*demi-sec* only), in emergencies, as a tonic.

How
At 7°C–10°C (45°F–50°F), colder for inexpensive Champagne, up to 13°C (54°F) for very fine, mature ones.

In a tall, clear glass, not a broad, shallow one. To preserve the bubbles, pour slowly into a slightly tilted glass.

How much
Allow half a bottle (three glasses) per head for an all-Champagne party. Allow half as much when it is served as an apéritif before another wine.

What to look for
Plenty of pressure behind the cork, total clarity, abundance of fine bubbles lasting indefinitely, powerful but clean flavour and finish, and balance – not mouth-puckeringly dry or acid, not cloyingly sweet. Above all, it should be moreish.

The choice vineyards include superb Chardonnay sites in Cramant and Avize, and Pinot sites in Aÿ. It is these that shape the hazelnut and creamy flavours of the excellent vintage wines. Grapes also come from 30 other *crus*. Sales average 3.3 million bottles from stocks of around ten million. In 2005, Perrier-Jouët, together with its sister house of Mumm, was purchased by Pernod Ricard.

Piper-Heidsieck ☆–☆☆
Reims. Owner: Rémy-Cointreau. 70 ha (shared with Charles-Heidsieck). Visits: regular hours. NV: Brut, Brut Divin (Blanc de Blancs), Rosé Sauvage, Cuvée Sublime Demi-Sec. Vintage: Brut. Prestige: Cuvée Rare. www.piper-heidsieck.com
These well-regarded, very dry wines have changed a little in style since the firm was bought by Rémy-Cointreau in 1989. Although still very fresh, they now have an extra dimension of floweriness on the nose and fruitiness on the palate. Brut Sauvage, a very dry style with practically no *dosage*, has now been phased out. The Chardonnay-led Cuvée Rare is exceptional, with long, citrus-like flavours and the potential to develop in bottle for up to 15 years.

Pol Roger ☆☆☆
Epernay. Owner: Pol Roger family. 85 ha. Visits: appt. only. NV: Brut Réserve, Pure, Rich. Vintage: Brut, Blanc de Blancs, Rosé. Prestige: Sir Winston Churchill, Réserve Spéciale PR. www.polroger.co.uk
Smallish Grand Marque consistently regarded among the best half-dozen and a personal favourite of mine for nearly 50 years. Outstandingly clean, floral, and crisp NV; stylish, long-lived vintage; one of the best rosés; and fragrant, exquisite Blanc de Blancs. The Pinot-led Sir Winston Churchill (in homage to a family friend) is shamelessly sumptuous, exotically scented, and satin-textured.

The Réserve Spéciale PR is supremely elegant, being 50 per cent Chardonnay; all the grapes come from *grand cru* vineyards. Pure is an undosed *cuvée* made of equal parts of Chardonnay, Pinot Noir, and Pinot Meunier. The cellars are said to be the coldest and deepest in the region. The firm's vineyards are mainly in the Côte des Blancs.

Pommery ☆–☆☆
Reims. Owner: Vranken. Visits: at regular hours. NV: Brut Royal, Brut Apanage, Brut Rosé, Wintertime (Blanc de Noirs), Springtime (Rosé), Summertime (Blanc de Blancs, Falltime (Blanc de Blancs), Dry Elixir Demi-Sec. Vintage: Brut. Prestige: Louise Brut and Rosé, Flacons d'Exception. www.pommery.fr
In 2002 this historic house was sold to the Vranken group, not exactly renowned for exceptional quality. Moreover, the previous owners, LVMH, retained the magnificently sited Pommery vineyards. However, cellarmaster Thierry Gasco remained in place, so some continuity has been guaranteed.

The best-known Champagne is Brut Royal, an elegant, pure-flavoured wine of low dosage. Delicacy and refinement are the hallmark of the vintage wines. Louise Pommery (since 1979) has been a revelation of Pommery quality: stylish, crisp, deeply winey, and well structured. Since 1996, mature vintage Champagnes in magnums, the Flacons d'Exception, have been released in tiny quantities to connoisseurs. On receipt of the order, the wine is disgorged and delivered to the recipient's address within one month, for optimal freshness in the finished Champagne.

Louis Roederer ☆☆☆–☆☆☆☆
Reims. Owner: Frédéric Rouzaud. 210 ha. Associated companies: Roederer Estate, California, Ramos Pinto, Portugal, Château Pichon-Lalande and Château de Pez (Bordeaux), Delas (Rhône). Visits: appt. only. NV: Brut Premier, Rich. Vintage: Brut, Blanc de Blancs, Rosé. Prestige: Cristal Brut, Cristal Rosé. www.champagne-roederer.com
A very great family owned Champagne house whose peerless reputation rests on its marvellous vineyards (supplying 70 per cent of its needs), and scarcely rivalled collection of reserve wines to maintain the highest standards for Brut Premier. The house style is notably smooth and mature, epitomized by the excellent, full-bodied Brut Premier and the fabulous Cristal, one of the most luscious Champagnes, racy but deeply flavoured. Recent vintages such as '85, '89, '90, '95, and 2000 are among the greatest Cristals ever released.

Ruinart ☆☆☆
Reims. Owner: LVMH group. 17 ha. Visits: appt. only. NV: R de Ruinart Brut, Blanc de Blancs, and Rosé. Prestige: Dom Ruinart Blanc de Blancs, Dom Ruinart Rosé. www.ruinart.com
Founded in 1729, making Ruinart the oldest recorded Champagne-making firm. Napoléon's Josephine enjoyed Ruinart – but, alas, refused, after her divorce, to honour the bills she ran up as empress. It is extremely stylish among the lighter Champagnes, both in non-vintage and vintage. The luxury Dom Ruinart is among the most notable *blanc*

DOSAGE, DRYNESS, & SWEETNESS

When Champagne is disgorged, the loss of the frozen plug of sediment needs making good to fill the bottle. At this stage the sweetness of the finished wine is adjusted by topping up (*dosage*) with a *liqueur d'expédition* of wine mixed with sugar and sometimes brandy. A few firms make a totally dry wine, topped up with wine only, and known by names such as Brut Natur or Brut Intégral. The great majority have some sugar added. The following are the usual amounts (g/l) of sugar in the *dosage* for each style (although they vary from house to house): Extra brut: 0–6g/l, bone-dry. Brut: 3–15g/l, very dry. Extra sec: 12–20g/l, dry. Sec: 17–35g/l, slightly sweet. Demi-sec: 33–50g/l, distinctly sweet. Doux: over 50g/l, very sweet. Late-disgorged wines, such as Bollinger's RD, usually need no more than a minimal *dosage*.

de blancs: uniquely fleshy and rounded owing to the Montagne de Reims Chardonnay grapes in the blend, and on a winning streak in recent vintages ('82, '85, '88, '89, '93, '96). Dom Ruinart Rosé is equally outstanding. The firm owns Chardonnay vines in the Montagne *grands crus* of Sillery and Puisieulx, the grapes are reserved for the Dom Ruinart *cuvées*.

Salon ☆☆☆☆
Le Mesnil-sur-Oger. Owner: Laurent-Perrier. 1 ha. www.salondelamotte.com
This unique house produces only vintage *blanc de blancs* Champagne from the village of Mesnil. Since 1920, vintages have been declared about three times a decade. Salon pioneered *blanc de blancs* wines and still leads in quality if not quantity, since production per vintage never exceeds 80,000 bottles. These are subtly rich and very dry wines, hand-crafted and comparable in weight and complexity to *grand cru* burgundy. Not for those who like a fresh filly of a wine. Fifteen years is a good age for them. Few other Champagnes are aged so long before release: the 1990 only came onto the market in 2001.

Salon's single hectare of vines only supplies about ten per cent of its needs; the rest of the grapes are bought in from growers owning *grand cru* Mesnil plots in the village, these sources virtually unchanged since the 1920s. Salon only releases around 30,000 bottles per year, yet stock is around 270,000 bottles (nine years' supply), which means it has one of the biggest sales/stock ratios in Champagne.

Jacques Selosse ☆☆☆–☆☆☆☆
Avize. Owner: Anselme Selosse. 6 ha. Visits: appt. only. NV: Initial, Version Original, Substance, Exquise (Sec), Contraste (Blanc de Noirs), Rosé. Vintage: Brut.
Original grower, farming biodynamically and fermenting all his wines in wood, in some cases new wood. Some wines, such as the remarkable Substance, are produced using a complex solera system (see glossary). Only natural yeasts are used for fermentation, and the *dosage* is very low. Opinions were once divided on whether these Champagnes are great or merely weird, but the balance has now swung decisively in Selosse's favour. No more than 55,000 bottles produced annually, so prices are high.

Taittinger ☆☆–☆☆☆
Reims. Owner: Taittinger family. 289 ha. Visits: regular hours. Associated company: Domaine Carneros. NV: Brut Réserve, Demi-Sec, Prestige Rosé, Nocturne Sec, Prélude Grand Cru. Vintage: Brut. Prestige: Comtes de Champagne, Comtes de Champagne Rosé, Collection. www.taittinger.com
An important force in the Champagne world since 1945, and controlled by a consortium of investors, of which the family has the largest share. The style of the *brut* wines derives from the dominance of Chardonnay in the blend. Extra time in bottle greatly improved the NV in the late 1990s, although the *dosage* can be quite high. Comtes de Champagne is one of the most ageworthy, exquisitely luxurious *prestige cuvées*.

Taittinger Collection, a range packaged in designer-created bottles, is essentially the same wine as the vintage, released as a collector's item. Half the vineyards are planted with Chardonnay, and supply around half the house's needs. The main sources of grapes are Avize, Chouilly, Cramant, Mesnil, and Oger.

Veuve Clicquot-Ponsardin ☆☆☆
Reims. Owner: LVMH group. 286 ha. Visits: appt. only. Associated wine companies: Cape Mentelle, Cloudy Bay. NV: Yellow Label Brut, Demi-Sec, Rosé. Vintage: Gold Label, Rosé, Rich Réserve. Prestige: La Grande Dame, La Grande Dame Rosé. www.veuve-clicquot.com
Large, prestigious, and influential house making excellent classic Champagnes in a firm, rich, full-flavoured, and relatively heavy style. The company's success was founded by "The Widow" Clicquot, who took over the business in 1805 at the age of 27, when her husband died. She invented the now universal *remuage* system for clarifying the wine, and produced the first rosé Champagne. Since 1928, there have been only five winemakers, the present *chef de caves* being Dominique Demarville (since 2006). Notwithstanding its respect for tradition, winemaking is thoroughly modern, and no wood has been used since 1961. The prestige La Grande Dame is a masterpiece of balanced body and finesse, and since its first release in 1996, La Grande Dame Rosé has been lauded as one of the best pink Champagnes. The vineyards are very evenly spread across the classic districts.

CHAMPAGNE: A NEW BEGINNING

In the early 1990s, the Champagne industry was stricken by the worst economic crisis since the 1930s. The sharp fall in sales led to a collapse in prices and a swelling of stocks, compounded by bumper crops between 1989 and 1996. All types of Champagne producer – houses, co-ops, growers – were hit hard and huge losses were incurred.

By the end of the 1990s, the worst was over. Catastrophe was avoided by draconian measures, initiated by the Champagne authorities in 1992, to reduce yields in the vineyard and improve procedures for the pressing of the harvest – a critical stage in the making of Champagne. Only two pressings of the grapes (the *cuvée* and the *taille*) are now allowed. A third pressing has been effectively abolished, and rightly so, for with each successive press the quality of the juice diminishes. The wines are now generally aged for longer on the yeasts (three years for a non-vintage from a good house); the result is a leap in quality in the finished wines.

This emphasis on quality has paid off commercially. Even in mid-2008, when fears about an impending global economic crisis were curtailing spending, the demand for top-level Champagne remained stronger than ever.

Other Champagne Producers

Includes grower-Champagne makers, the cooperatives, and merchant houses.

Agrapart ☆☆
Avize. 10 ha. www.champagne-agrapart.com
Many of the Agrapart Champagnes are partly or wholly barrel-fermented. Blanc de blancs is the house specialty, a wine of raciness and elegance. Fine rosé too.

Aubry ☆☆
Jouy lès Reims.
Family house growing old grape varieties, unused by others, to unique effect; very pretty rosé, too.

Ayala ☆☆–☆☆☆
Aÿ. 51 ha. www.champagne-ayala.com
Changes in ownership in recent years have left Bollinger as the proprietor since 2005. Specialities include two non-*dosé* Champagnes. The *cuvee de prestige* Perle uses the same base wine as the Blanc de Blancs but adds 20 per cent Pinot Noir. Overall quality is improving fast.

Paul Bara ☆☆
Bouzy. 11 ha. www.champagnepaulbara.com
Leading *récoltant-manipulant* in Bouzy, making ample Pinot-led Champagnes. The Grand Rosé is exceptional.

Edmond Barnaut ☆–☆☆
Bouzy. 18 ha. www.champagne-barnaut.com
Secondé, the fifth-generation owner, has developed an unusual solera system for his non-vintage wines: bottling two-thirds of the new wine and adding the rest to the solera after a third has been drawn out and bottled. Also produces Bouzy Rouge and a rare Bouzy Rosé.

Beaumont des Crayères ☆–☆☆
Mardeuil. 80 ha. www.beaumont-des-crayeres.com
Little co-op, just west of Epernay, makes good Champagne at reasonable prices. Fresh and fruity; Pinot Meunier-dominated.

Boizel ☆☆
Epernay. www.champagne-boizel.fr
Family business founded in 1834, and since 1994 part of Bruno Paillard's Boizel-Chanoine group. Well-made, fruity wines; kind prices.

Alexandre Bonnet ☆☆
Les Riceys. 65 ha. www.alexandrebonnet.com
Champagne grower and maker of the rare Rosé des Riceys.

The family became merchants in 1932, and since 1998, this quality-conscious (and good-value) house has been owned by Bruno Paillard (q.v.). The grapes come from its own vineyards around Les Riceys and the Marne's top growths, especially the Côte des Blancs. The vintage Cuvée Madrigal can be sumptuous.

Bricout ☆–☆☆
Avize.
In 2003 this small house, known for its light, racy Champagnes, was acquired jointly by Vranken and LVMH. The Chardonnay-led *prestige cuvée* Arthur Bricout is by far the best wine.

Canard-Duchêne ☆–☆☆
Ludes. www.canard-duchene.fr
One of the less exciting but commercially important Grandes Marques, specializing in Pinot-based NV with delicate fruitiness, and the rich prestige Charles VII. Owned by LVMH until 2003, when sold to Alain Thiénot.

de Castellane ☆
Epernay. www.castellane.com
An old-established house with a grand past, symbolized by its extravagant crenellated tower. Now owned by Laurent-Perrier. Produces a sound, rather light NV and a more substantial vintage Cuvée Commodore.

Delbeck ☆☆
Reims.
A fine, small Champagne house that, like Champagne Bricout, was bought in 2003 by Vranken and LVMH. Grand cru Champagnes are produced from different villages such as Aÿ and Cramant. Fine vintage wines, too.

Dehours ☆☆
Cerseuil.
Small house specializing in barrel-fermented single-vineyard wines of real distinction, especially pure Pinot Noir.

Daniel Dumont ☆–☆☆
Rilly-la-Montagne. 10 ha.
Excellent Champagnes, especially the well-aged Pinot-dominated Grande Réserve, and the fine demi-sec.

Egly-Ouriet ☆☆–☆☆☆
Ambonnay. Owner: Francis Egly. 12 ha.
Most of the Egly vineyards are in *grand cru sites*, and the grapes reach high natural sugar levels at harvest. These are predictably rich wines, Pinot Noir-dominated, and there is one curiosity: Les Vignes de Vrigny, a pure Pinot Meunier Champagne.

THE MYSTERIES OF THE LABEL

The Champagne industry uses a number of codes on the label to identify the source of the wine:
NM *négociant-manipulant* A producer who makes Champagne from purchased grapes.
RM *récoltant-manipulant* A producer who makes Champagne from his own grapes.
CM *coopérative-manipulant* Cooperative producer.
ND *négociant-distributeur* A company that sells, but does not produce Champagne.
SR *société de récoltants* A partnership, usually between family members.
MA *marque d'achateur* Champagne sold under the name of the seller, usually a supermarket as in a buyer's own brand (BOB).

Nicolas Feuillatte ☆–☆☆
Chouilly. www.feuillatte.com
This brand was created in 1976 by the
eponymous M Feuillate, a globetrotting
promoter, and sold by him in 1986 to the
Centre Vinicole de la Champagne (CVC),
the largest cooperative in the region.
Very modern winemaking and "correct"
quality, with the occasional exceptional
cuvée, such as the vintage Palme d'Or. In
2001, it enterprisingly released bottlings
from four different *grand cru* sites.

Georges Gardet ☆–☆☆
Chigny-les-Roses. 7 ha.
www.chateau-gardet.com
Family firm producing rich, well-aged
wines made mainly with Pinot Noir grapes
from the Montagne de Reims. All the
Champagnes are marked with the date
of disgorging.

Gatinois ☆☆–☆☆☆
Aÿ. 7 ha.
Grower, making tiny quantities of
concentrated, Pinot Noir-based
Champagne from *grand cru* sites and
still red Coteaux Champenois in good
years. High quality.

René Geoffroy ☆☆
Cumières. 13 ha.
www.champagnegeoffroy.com
Jean-Baptiste Geoffroy, like his father
René, shows the independent grower at his best, offering a
highly individual range of well-crafted Champagnes, partly
barrel-fermented, and a good Coteaux Champenois from
Pinot Noir.

Pierre Gimonnet & Fils ☆☆–☆☆☆
Cuis. 26 ha.
www.champagne-gimonnet.com.
The Gimonnets have been growing grapes in Cuis for
250 years, and their vineyards are stuffed with old vines –
all Chardonnay. The very dry and racy Extra-Brut, with
no *dosage* to disguise any failings, is a triumphant testament
to the Gimmonet's skill.

Emile Hamm ☆–☆☆
Aÿ. www.champagne-hamm-ay.com
Formerly an Aÿ grower and a merchant
house since 1930. Excellent, very dry
Champagne. Prestige Signature is the
top wine.

Heidsieck Monopole ☆
Epernay. www.vranken.fr
One of the oldest Champagne houses
(founded 1777), this Grande Marque was
sold by Mumm to the Vranken group in
1996. *Cuvées* are named like milk bottles:
NV is Blue Top, vintage is Gold Top.
Stylistically bland.

Jacquart ☆–☆☆
Reims. www.jacquart-champagne.fr
This cooperative-turned-merchant is
owned by Alliance Champagne, giving it
access to 2,600 hectares, and sells ten
million bottles a year. The crisp, incisive
Brut Mosaique (50 per cent Chardonnay)
is a bargain. Top range is called Nominée.

Larmandier-Bernier ☆☆–☆☆☆
Vertus. 15 ha. www.larmandier.com
Excellent Chardonnay sites, farmed
organically, on the Côte des Blancs and
Pierre Larmandier's own talent combine
to create some of the most pure-flavoured
blanc de blancs. Exceptional Cramant Grand
Cru and ultra-dry, non-*dosé* Vertus
Premier Cru.

Leclerc-Briant ☆☆
Epernay. 30 ha. www.leclercbriant.com
In the 1990s this firm took the innovative decision to produce
Les Authentiques: four single-vineyard Champagnes from
premier cru sites. It is also converting to Biodynamic viticulture.

R & L Legras ☆☆
Chouilly. 40 ha. www.champagne-legras.fr
Growers since the eighteenth century, and now a fashionable
small house, with a niche market among France's Michelin-
starred restaurants for its lovely *grand cru blanc de blancs*.

ROSE DES RICEYS

Within the borders of Champagne lies
one of France's most esoteric little
appellations, specifically for an ageworthy
Pinot Noir rosé. Les Riceys is in the
extreme south of Champagne. Most of its
production is Champagne, but in good,
ripe vintages the best Pinot Noir grapes
from an authorised 100 hectares are

selected. The floor of an open wooden
vat is first covered with grapes trodden
by foot. Then the vat is filled with whole
unbroken bunches. Fermentation starts
at the bottom and the fermenting juice
is pumped over the whole grapes.
    At a skilfully judged moment, the
juice is run off, the grapes pressed,

and the results "assembled" to make
a dark rosé of a unique sunset tint and,
as its makers describe it, a flavour of
gooseberries. The principal practitioner
used to be Alexandre Bonnet (q.v.); his
sons now continue this tradition. Also
made by Defrance and Henri Abelé.

Bringing in the harvest in the Champagne region

A R Lenoble ☆–☆☆
Damery. 18 ha. www.champagne-lenoble.com
Family firm employing some barrel-fermentation since 2000.
Fine *blanc de blancs*.

Mailly Grand Cru ☆☆
Mailly. 70 ha. www.chateau-mailly.com
Small and exclusive cooperative, each of its 70 member-
growers own *grand cru* vines in Mailly on the Montagne de
Reims. Full, muscular Champagnes (with at least 75 per cent
Pinot Noir) that need a minimum of four years on the cork to
show their paces.

Serge Mathieu ☆☆–☆☆☆
Avirey-Ligney. 11 ha.
www.champagne-serge-mathieu.com
Top-flight grower of the Aube, making Champagnes that
are rich yet super fine. Superb rosé.

Pierre Moncuit ☆☆–☆☆☆
Le Mesnil-sur-Oger. 19 ha. www.pierre-moncuit.fr
First-rate *blanc de blancs* from one of the best villages on
the Côte des Blancs.

Philipponnat ☆☆–☆☆☆
Mareuil-sur-Aÿ. 17 ha. www.philipponnat.com
Small, traditionalist house, now part of the Bruno Paillard
group (q.v.), making well-constituted wines built to last.
Especially fine and weighty single-vineyard, 5.5-hectare Clos
des Goisses: a marvel of Pinot Noir concentration, made only
in top vintages such as '88, '89, '90, '95, '96, and '99.

Alain Robert ☆–☆☆☆
Le Mesnil-sur-Oger. 10 ha.
Outstanding Mesnil grower and perfectionist Champagne-
maker. His Mesnil Sélection, never less than 12 years old,
is a great *blanc de blancs*. Many of his wines are only disgorged
on receipt of orders. Not to be confused with Champagne
A Robert of Fossoy.

Tarlant ☆☆
Oeuilly. 13 ha. www.tarlant.com
Top-flight grower who ferments each individual vineyard's
wine separately in wood to give best expression to their
respective soils. The Krug-like Cuvée Louis is outstanding.

Alain Thiénot ☆☆–☆☆☆
**Reims. 14 ha. Associated wine companies: Champagnes
Joseph Perrier and Marie Stuart. www.thienot.com**
Formerly a broker from an old Champenois family, Alain
Thiénot is a Champagne merchant on the move, having
acquired other houses such as Joseph Perrier (q.v.). The
non-vintage is fresh and sprightly, yet with a good touch
of maturity. The exceptional Grande Cuvée allies beautiful,
supple fruitiness with considerable complexity.

de Venoge ☆–☆☆
Epernay. www.champagnedevenoge.com
Now controlled by the Bruno Paillard group (q.v.), sizeable
house making pleasant, soft, and supple Champagnes in a full
range of styles. Very good vintage *blanc de blancs*. Quality can be
inconsistent.

Vilmart ☆☆–☆☆☆
Rilly-la-Montagne. 11 ha. www.champagnevilmart.fr
Small firm producing 100,000 bottles per year of very high-
quality wines fermented in wood and aged for a long time
in bottle. The top wine is usually the Coeur de Cuvée from
very old vines.

Vrancken ☆
Epernay. www.vranken.fr
Demoiselle is the leading brand of this Champagne group,
which was created in 1976 by Paul-François Vranken, a
Belgian marketing man. Light, Chardonnay-dominant wines
of fair quality. Veuve Monnier and Charles Lafitte are other
labels. The group gained control of Barancourt in 1994,
Heidsieck Monopole in 1996, and Pommery in 2002 (qq.v.).

CHAMPAGNE & FOOD

There is no single classic dish for accompanying Champagne, but Champagne makers like to encourage the idea that their wine goes with almost any dish (even game and cheese). Vintage Champagne certainly has the fullness of flavour to go with most food – but many people find sparkling wine indigestible with food. Champagne is the apéritif wine par excellence, but can be marvellously refreshing after a rich meal. As an alternative to sparkling wine, still Coteaux Champenois, white or red (notably Bouzy rouge) can offer the refinement of Champagne in a non-fizzy form.

Alsace

After all the regions of France whose appellation systems seem to have been devised by medieval theologians, Alsace is a simple fairy tale. A single appellation, Alsace, takes care of the whole region. Alsace grand cru is for chosen sites.

Nor are there Germanic complications of degrees of ripeness to worry about. Alsace labelling is as simple as Californian: maker's name and grape variety are the nub. The difference is that in Alsace a host of strictly enforced laws means that there are few surprises. Varietal wines must be made purely from the variety identified on the label. The wines are correspondingly predictable and reliable. Their makers would like them to be considered more glamorous. In order to have their wines named among the "greats", they place increasing emphasis on late picking, on wines from *grand cru* and selected sites.

What matters more to most drinkers is that Alsace guarantees a certain quality and a style more surely than almost any wine region. It makes brilliantly appetizing, clean-cut, and aromatic wine to go with food, and at a reasonable price. The only uncertainty the buyer has to face is the degree of sweetness. What could be ideal food wines, crisp and grapey, are too often over-massive and over-sweet. Technically late-picked wines are so labelled, but many growers are in the habit of picking later than they used to, with sometimes confusing results. See note on page 190.

The region is 113 kilometres long by two or three kilometres wide (70 miles long by one or two miles wide). It forms the eastern flank of the Vosges Mountains in the *départements* of the Haut-Rhin and the Bas-Rhin where the foothills, between 180 and about 360 metres (600 to 1,200 feet), provide well-drained southeast- and south-facing slopes under the protection of the peaks and forests of the mountains. The whole region is in their rain-shadow, which gives it some of France's lowest rainfall and most sustained sunshine.

On the principle that watersheds are natural boundaries, Alsace should be in Germany. It has been, but even since the Rhine became the frontier, it has been French. Its language and architecture remain Germanic. Its grape varieties are Germanic, too – but handled in the French manner they produce a different drink. What is the difference? The vineyards across the river in Germany can produce similar wines from similar varieties, but in general they have a different structure.

The Baden Rieslings are racy rather than rich, and the Pinot Gris is often smothered in oak rather than allowed to express its glorious, musky spiciness without the distraction of wood. German Pinot Blanc is often aged in barrels, too. Although many of the best Alsace wines are still fermented in oak, the barrels are antiques, thickly lined with tartrate crystals that prevent any flavours of wood or oxidation. Thus the aromatic (or otherwise) character of its grapes stands out cleanly and clearly. Alsace wines are bottled as soon as possible in the spring (or latest in the autumn) after the vintage. Most are drunk young – which is a pity. Bottle-ageing introduces the elements of complexity, which are otherwise lacking. A good Riesling or Gewurztraminer (no umlaut used in Alsace) or Pinot Gris is worth keeping at least four years in bottle and often up to ten. This is especially true of the sweeter wines that are being produced in ever larger quantities (see page 186). Sweet wines fetch higher prices, but they are no substitute for the combination of full and crisp flavours, which the region's best dry wines can deliver.

The centre of the finest area in Alsace lies in the Haut-Rhin, in the group of villages north and south of Colmar, with Riquewihr, an extravagantly half-timbered and flower-decked little town, as its natural wine capital: a sort of St-Emilion of the Vosges. The climate is warmest and driest in the south, but scarcely different enough to justify the popular inference that Haut-Rhin is parallel to, let us say, Haut-Médoc. There is no suggestion of lower quality in the name Bas-Rhin; it is simply lower down the River Rhine. Even farther down, going directly north, are the German Palatinate vineyards. These produce the richest and some of the greatest of all the German Rieslings.

More important are the individual vineyard sites with the best soils and microclimates. Thirty or 40 Vosges hillsides have individual reputations, which in Burgundy would long ago have been enshrined in law, but in Alsace only became so in 1983. After hovering on the brink of listing certain vineyards as *grands crus* for many years, by the mid-1970s many growers felt that the time had come to make a proper classification of the great slopes of Alsace. A list of 94 *lieux-dits*, or possible sites, was drawn up, and from these, the first 25 received full *grand cru* status in 1983, followed by a further 23 in 1985, and subsequently three more, the latest promotion being Kaefferkopf in 2007. This total of 51 will probably not be exceeded for some time. The *grands crus* represent 5.5 per cent of the total vineyard area of Alsace, but only represent four per cent of production. This is both because of lower yields imposed on the *grands crus* and because some growers blend their *grands crus* and do not declare them as such.

A few of the *grand cru* names are well-established on labels. Schoenenbourg at Riquewihr is particularly noted for its Riesling; Kaysersberg's Schlossberg, Guebwiller's Kitterlé, Turckheim's Eichberg and Brand, and Thann's Rangen are other examples. Ownership of these vineyards is noted in the following list of producers, see overleaf.

Grand cru wines must come from specifically delimited slopes and may only be single-variety wines of ("noble") Riesling, Gewurztraminer, Pinot Gris, Muscat, and (since 2001) Sylvaner. They have a lower permitted yield and a higher minimum alcoholic strength than other Alsace wines. Since 2001, proprietors within any *grand cru* have the right to set their own tougher rules and regulations than the basic AC requirements. Growers say that the *grand cru* legislation gives them the chance to demonstrate the terroir character of their best wines, but not all the great houses agree with this, and some (Trimbach, Beyer, Hugel) choose not to use *grand cru* names on their labels. Trimbach, however, is now making an exception for wine from the 2.7-hectare *grand cru* Geisberg, which it leases from the Couvent de Ribeauvillé.

Another great success story in Alsace has been the remarkable growth in popularity of Crémant d'Alsace, produced since the turn of the century, but that is only recently seeing some success. Crémant is a *méthode traditionnelle* sparkling wine that may come from any Alsace grape – although in practice Muscat and Gewurztraminer are found to be too aromatic. Pinot Blanc is the most used, and some Chardonnay may also be added (although not permitted for the still wines).

Crémant rosé is 100 per cent Pinot Noir. The last ten years have also seen red wines re-emerging. They mean more, perversely, to Alsace growers and consumers than perhaps they do to outsiders who have the world's reds to choose from. Pinot Noir is the grape of choice. In the past, it has been a struggle to find colour and substance in it here, but careful selection of Pinot Noir clones combined with careful colour and flavour extraction are making fuller, more characterful reds. On occasion, indeed, something akin to fine Burgundy.

Growers & Cooperatives

The vineyards of Alsace are even more fragmented in ownership than those of the rest of France. With 5,150 growers sharing the total of 15,450 hectares, the average individual holding is a mere three hectares. (Although in truth, 90 per cent of the volume produced is commercialized by 220 growers or firms.)

The chances of history established a score or more leading families with larger estates – still rarely as much as 40 hectares. With what seems like improbable regularity, they trace their roots back to the seventeenth century, when the Thirty Years War tore the province apart. In the restructuring of the industry after the two World Wars last century, these families grouped smaller growers around them in a peculiar pattern consisting of their own domaine plus a winemaking and

merchanting business. They contract to buy the small growers' grapes and make their wine – very often using their own domaine wines as their top-quality range. The small grower's alternative to a contract with a grower-négociant (or just a négociant) is to join the local cooperative. Alsace established the first group in France, at the turn of the century, and it now has one of the strongest wine cooperative movements in the world. Their standards can be extremely high, and they often provide the best bargains in the region. However, just as elsewhere in France, more and more growers are bottling their own wines.

Leading Alsace Producers

Domaine Agapé ☆–☆☆
Riquewihr. 9 ha. www.alsace-agape.fr
Vincent Sipp set up his own winery in 2007, and offers a full range of well-balanced zesty wines, the best being the Riesling *grands crus*.

Lucien Albrecht ☆☆
Orschwihr. 30 ha. www.lucien-albrecht.fr
Jean Albrecht is the most important proprietor in *grand cru* Pfingstberg, from which he produces impressive Riesling, Pinot Gris, and Gewurztraminer. The more basic wines are fine and fruity, and always good value.

Jean Becker ☆–☆☆
Zellenberg. 18 ha.
The Beckers have been growers and merchants at Riquewihr since 1618. One quarter of their vineyards are *grand cru* (Froehn at Zellenberg and Sonnenglanz at Beblenheim),

---

VENDANGE TARDIVE

Late picking, Vendange Tardive, is the means by which Alsace growers are scaling the heights of prestige, which Burgundy and Bordeaux have so far monopolized. A hot summer and autumn (1989, 1990, 1994, 1998, 2002, and 2005) provide such high sugar readings in the grapes that fermentation can stop with considerable natural sweetness still remaining. The wines reach an alcohol level usually greater than that of a German Auslese. The resulting combination of strength, sweetness, and concentrated fruity flavour is still peculiar to Alsace.

The Hugels of Riquewihr were instrumental in creating what has become the Vendange Tardive legislation. Very ripe grapes with exceptionally high sugar

concentration, usually attained with the help of noble rot, produce wines of enormous power, which are classified as Sélection de Grains Nobles (SGN).

In 2001, the rules were tightened, and the minimum potential alcohol for each grape variety was increased. For Vendange Tardive, Muscat and Riesling must be picked at a potential alcohol of at least 14 degrees (up from 13.1 degrees), Pinot Gris and Gewurztraminer at 15.3 degrees (up from 14.4 degrees). For SGN, Muscat and Riesling must be picked at a minimum of 16.4 degrees, Pinot Gris and Gewurztraminer at 18.2 degrees plus.

Such changes were long overdue. With crop-thinning and the phenomenon of global warming, it was not difficult

for growers to attain high must weights. In short, far too much Vendange Tardive and even SGN was being produced. The best growers always exceeded the legal requirements and focused on quality; but some merchant houses and cooperatives simply obeyed the letter of the law and produced wines that fell far short of the standards originally set by the Hugels and others.

So the wines are likely to become richer and sweeter, and there will be a greater contrast between a *grand cru* Pinot Gris and a Pinot Gris Vendange Tardive of the future. It will be a pity if growers carry their passion for late harvesting to the point where their dry wines become second best.

Wine producer's sign, Ribbeauville, Alsace

with other vineyards in Riquewihr, Ribeauvillé, and Hunnawihr. The Beckers seem to have a knack for excellent Gewurztraminer.

Léon Beyer ☆☆–☆☆☆
Eguisheim. 21 ha. www.leonbeyer.fr
A family firm founded in 1867, although the Beyers have been making wine in Alsace since 1580. Their vines are all in Eguisheim. Beyer's best wines are full-bodied, powerful, and dry, clearly designed to go with food and often seen in top restaurants in France. Their finest wines are bottled under the Cuvée des Comtes d'Eguisheim label, and age extremely well.

Domaine Paul Blanck & Fils ☆☆☆
Kientzheim. 38 ha. www.blanck.com
Top-quality estate founded in 1922. The holdings include part of the Kientzheim *grands crus*, Schlossberg and Furstentum – the Blancks have been registered Schlossberg owners since 1620 – and *grands crus* Winneck-Schlossberg, Sommerberg, and Mambourg. The estate is close to organic, and all grapes are hand-picked. Fermentation is in stainless steel and temperature controlled, with splendid results. Furstentum tends to give the richest wines, and many of the wines from here contain some residual sugar. Schlossberg, in contrast, has a more mineral character, and tastes (and usually is) drier. All Blanck wines are beautifully made at all levels.

Léon Boesch ☆–☆☆
Westhalten. 13 ha. www.domaine-boesch.com
Young Mathieu Boesch runs this organic property; its sole *grand cru*, and the source of the best wines, is Zinnkoepfle. Riesling is sound, Gewurztraminer can be exceptional.

Bott-Geyl ☆☆
Beblenheim. 14 ha. www.bott-geyl.com
This Biodynamic estate is run by Jean-Christophe Bott, and produces a good range of rich, ultra-ripe, spicy, though occasionally flabby wines from all the principal varieties. The grand cru sites here are Furstentum and Sonnenglanz, which deliver very exotic Pinot Gris.

Albert Boxler ☆☆–☆☆☆
Niedermorschwihr. 13 ha.
Jean Boxler's pride and joy are the *grands crus* Sommerberg and Brand, from which he produces Rieslings, especially, of great richness and finesse. Rather confusingly, he often bottles different parcels of Sommerberg separately, to display the terroir character within the *grand cru*.

Ernest Burn ☆☆–☆☆☆
Gueberschwihr. 10 ha. www.domaine-burn.fr
Francis and Joseph Burn run this fine estate. Half the vineyards are in Clos St Imer with *grand cru* Goldert; it has been in the family since 1934. The Pinot Gris can be remarkable: plenty of spice and honey, but never blowzy, and Muscat from the *clos* can be unusually elegant.

Cave de Cleebourg ☆
Cleebourg. Founded in 1946. 192 members with 180 ha. www.cave-cleebourg.com
This cooperative specializes in Pinots, especially Auxerrois, but all other varieties are offered too.

Marcel Deiss ☆☆☆–☆☆☆☆
Bergheim. 27 ha. www.marceldeiss.com
The Deiss family have been vignerons in Alsace since 1744, and founded the present domaine in 1949. Its best sites include 2.5 hectares of *grand cru* Altenberg de Bergheim, and holdings within *grands crus* Schoenenbourg and, since 1998, Mambourg. From 1998 onwards the estate has been fully Biodynamic.

Jean-Michel Deiss is determined that his wines should above all reflect their terroir, which he considers far more important than mere varietal character. So his top wines are in fact blends, thus flying in the face of usual Alsace practice. Low yields and late harvesting means, however, that many of his wines are distinctly sweet – too much so for some tasters.

Dirler-Cadé ☆☆–☆☆☆
Bergholz. 18 ha.
Together with Schlumberger (q.v.), one of the best estates (Biodynamic since 1998) of southern Alsace, with holdings in *grand cru* Saering, Spiegel, Kitterlé, and Kessler. Jean Dirler makes varietal wines from all of them, so it is possible to compare their different characters. These are very serious wines, essentially dry and with plenty of fire and extract.

Dopff & Irion ☆
Riquewihr. 32 ha. www.dopff-irion.com
One of the biggest grower/merchants of Alsace, but now part of the Pfaffenheim cooperative. The best wines are often the Rieslings from Schoenenbourg and, in a weightier style, Vorbourg.

Dopff au Moulin ☆
Riquewihr. 76 ha. www.dopff-au-moulin.fr
A family firm of seventeenth century origins, with substantial vineyard holdings, principally in the Schoenenbourg at Riquewihr for Riesling, and Eichberg at Turckheim for Gewurztraminer, with Pinot Blanc grown near Colmar specifically for Crémant d'Alsace, which Dopff pioneered in 1900. Crémant remains the house speciality. Riesling from Schoenenbourg can be excellent, but overall quality is patchy.

Caves d'Eguisheim ☆
Eguisheim. Founded 1902. 750 members with 1,350 ha. www.wolfberger.com
Alsace's largest cooperative sells its wine under the brand name Wolfberger. Dependable if uninspired.

Paul Ginglinger ☆☆
Eguisheim. 12 ha. www.paul-ginglinger.fr
Paul's son Michel, with experience in South Africa and Australia under his belt, has continued the domaine's focus on pure-flavoured and incisive wines from mostly old vines.

Willy Gisselbrecht
Dambach. 17 ha. www.vins-gisselbrecht.com
A family firm of merchants, specializing in Riesling but producing a full range of dependable wines, although they don't reach great heights.

Rémy Gresser ☆☆
Andlau. 10 ha. www.gresser.fr

Rieslings from three *grands crus* (Moenchberg, Kastelberg, Wiebelsberg) dominate this Biodynamic estate. Kastelberg is often the most complex, but all the wines are well made.

Hugel & Fils ☆–☆☆☆
Riquewihr. 126 ha. www.hugel.fr
The best-known Alsace label in the Anglo-Saxon world. A combination of grower and grape négociant, in the family since 1639, with vineyards in Riquewihr producing its top wines, mostly from *grands crus* Schoenenbourg and Sporen. The Hugels, however, do not label any of their wines as *grands crus*. The house style is full, round, and supple, fermented dry but less apparently so than some. The Hugels pioneered late-harvested wines, which first won international acclaim in 1976.

The quality ladder for Riesling, Gewurztraminer, etc., goes Regular, Tradition, Jubilée, Vendange Tardive, and in certain years SGN. For blended wines made from purchased grapes, Hugel use registered names such as "Fleur d'Alsace" and "Gentil d'Alsace", which is a revival of the traditional "Edelzwicker" blend using quality grapes. The firm produces about 100,000 cases a year.

Cave Vinicole de Hunawihr ☆
Hunawihr. Founded 1954. 110 members with 200 ha, including 10 ha *grand cru*. www.cave-hunawihr.com
Specialties: Riesling and Gewurztraminer from *lieu-dit* Muehlforst, of which it is particularly proud, and *grand cru* Rieslings from Schoenenbourg and Rosacker.

Josmeyer ☆☆
Wintzenheim. 25 ha. www.josmeyer.com
Grower and négociant since 1854, with Biodynamically farmed vineyards at Wintzenheim and Turkheim (including five hectares of *grand cru* Hengst and Brand). The full-flavoured Gewurztraminers and vigorous Rieslings are particularly successful, but this house is most noted for its wide range of grapes, including Pinot Blanc, the latter *unchaptalized* to produce a light, refreshing wine.

Cave de Kientzheim-Kaysersberg ☆–☆☆
Kientzheim. Founded 1955. 150 members with 180 ha, including 20 ha *grand cru*. 140,000 cases. www.vinsalsace-kaysersberg.com

---

ALSACE GRAPES

Area of grapes occupied is expressed as a percentage of the total Alsace vineyard.
Auxerrois This is a member of the Pinot family, but its precise identity is unknown. Wines from Auxerrois are richer and broader than its cousin Pinot Blanc. The area planted with Auxerrois in Alsace is not specified in official statistics but is less than 1%.
Chasselas (9%) (In Germany Gutedel, in Switzerland Fendant.) Formerly one of the commonest grapes, rarely if ever named on a label, but used for its mildness in everyday blends, including the so-called "noble" Edelzwicker.
Clevner or Klevner A local name for the Pinot Blanc (q.v.).
Gewurztraminer (18.6%) Much the most easily recognized of all. Alsace grapes, with a special spicy aroma and bite that epitomize Alsace wine. Most Alsace Gewurztraminer is made off-dry and intensely fruity, even to the point of slight fierceness when young. With age, remarkable scents of rose petals and citrus fruit often suggesting grapefruit and lychees, intensify. Gewurztraminer of a fine vintage, whether made dry or in the sweet, Vendange Tardive style, is worth maturing almost as long as Riesling. The fault of a poor Gewurztraminer is softness and lack of definition, or alternatively a heady heaviness without elegance. In a range of Alsace wines, Gewurztraminer should be served last, after Rieslings and Pinots.
Pinot Blanc (21.1%) An increasingly popular grape, giving the lightest of the "noble" wines; simply fresh and appetizing without great complexity. Now seen as Alsace's answer to Chardonnay. This is the base wine for most Crémant d'Alsace.
Pinot Gris, formerly Tokay d'Alsace (14.7%) After Riesling and Gewurztraminer, the third potentially great wine grape of the region. First-class Pinot Gris has a dense, stiff, intriguing smell and taste – the very opposite of the fresh and fruity Pinot Blanc.

It is almost frustrating to taste, as though it were concealing a secret flavour you will never quite identify. Pinots Gris mature magnificently into broad, rich, deep-bosomed wines whose only fault is that they are not refreshing. Plantings have increased in response to strong demand. The name "Tokay" has been reclaimed by Hungary for its nobly sweet wine. The Hungarian wine is spelled Tokaji but pronounced the same.
Pinot Noir (9.6%) A grape that is made into both red and rosé in Alsace, but it is sometimes necessary to read the label to know which is which. The must is often heated to extract colour, but the result in the past has been rarely more than a light wine, without the classic Pinot flavour found in, for example, Bouzy Rouge from Champagne. A growing number of fuller-bodied examples are emerging, including some extracted wines aged in barriques.
Riesling (21.8%) The finest wine grape of Alsace, as it is of Germany, but here interpreted in a totally different way. Alsace Rieslings are fully ripened and have a firmer structure than German wines. Dryness and the intensity of their fruit flavour make them seem rather harsh to some people. In fact, they range from light refreshment in certain years to some of the most aromatic, authoritative, and longest-lasting of all white wines. In recent years there has been a regrettable tendency to leave residual sugar in Riesling, but top producers such as Trimbach and Beyer are resisting the trend fiercely.
Muscat (2.3%) Until recently, Alsace was the only wine region to make Muscat grapes into dry wine. The aroma is still hothouse sweet, but the flavour is crisp and very clean, sometimes with a hint of nut kernels. It is light enough to make an excellent apéritif.
Sylvaner (9.3%) Steadily being pushed out by Pinot Noir and Pinot Blanc, but at its best (at Mittelbergheim, for example) a classy, slightly "pétillant", faintly vegetal but flavoursome wine, which ages well.

Specialties include *crémant*, Riesling Kaefferkopf, Gewurztraminer Altenberg, and Riesling from Furstentum and Schlossberg.

André Kientzler ☆☆–☆☆☆
Ribeauvillé. 13 ha. www.vinskientzler.com
Four hectares lie within the *grands crus* of Geisberg, Osterberg, and Kirchberg. Osterberg gives the driest, most pungent Rieslings; those from Geisberg are richer. Auxerrois and Chasselas from this domaine are among the best in Alsace, and the Pinot Gris and Muscat are of high quality, too.

Marc Kreydenweiss ☆☆–☆☆☆
Andlau. 13 ha. www.kreydenweiss.com
From holdings in the *grands crus* Wiebelsberg, Kastelberg, and Moenchberg, Kreydenweiss produces beautifully made, concentrated wines. The Rieslings from old vines in the steep Kastelberg site are made to last. Unusually, the domaine produces a late-picked Pinot Blanc, offered under the vineyard name Kritt, and a blend, Clos du Val d'Eleon, from 70% Riesling and 30% Pinot Gris. In the 1980s, the wines were very austere, but since Kreydenweiss adopted Biodynamic viticulture in 1989, they have gained in weight, in part because some of them go through malolactic fermentation.

Kuentz-Bas ☆–☆☆☆
Husseren-les-Châteaux. 11 ha. www.kuentz-bas.fr
A family firm of growers and négociants, with vineyards in

Husseren, Eguisheim, and Obermorschwihr. There are holdings in the *grands crus* Eichberg and Pfersigberg at Eguisheim. These are firm, dry wines, well-balanced and elegant. The wines have excellent acidity, and the Vendange Tardive wines are superb. At Kuentz-Bas, the Vendange Tardive wines are labelled Cuvée Caroline, the SGNs Cuvée Jeremy. Collection Rare bottlings come from old vines and special parcels that are not *grand cru*.

Seppi Landmann ☆☆
Soultzmatt. 8 ha. www.seppi-landmann.fr
The pride and joy of this small estate are the parcels in *grand cru* Zinnkoepflé, which has limestone soils and gives wines that age very well. Landmann is one of the rare specialists in the underrated Sylvaner, producing the variety in all conceivable styles, whether legally sanctioned or not.

Albert Mann ☆☆–☆☆☆
Wettolsheim. 22 ha. www.albertmann.com
Maurice and Jacky Barthelmé run this fine property, with grand cru vineyards in Furstentum, Schlossberg, and Altenberg. They excel with lush, ultra-ripe Vendange Tardive and SGN from Gewurztraminer and Pinot Gris, and sometimes from Riesling. In recent years they have extended their expertise to Pinot Noir, of which they make numerous *cuvees*.

Meyer-Fonné ☆☆
Katzenthal. 10 ha.
Riesling and Pinot Gris are usually the best wines produced at Felix Meyer's steadily improving estate. The most basic bottlings are excellent value, but the *grands crus* (Kaefferkopf, Winneck-Schlossberg) have far more personality.

Muré ☆☆–☆☆☆
Rouffach. 22 ha. www.mure.com
A family of growers now in its twelfth generation. The heart of this organic domaine is the monastic Clos St-Landelin,

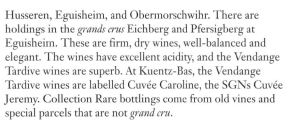

Bringing in the harvest at Hunawihr

a 15-hectare parcel within *grand cru* Vorbourg, which the Murés bought in 1935. The *clos* has warm, stony, and limey soil and notably low rainfall, and yields are kept very low. Its wines are full in character and round in style, intended as *vins de garde*.

The Pinot Noir and Muscat are some of the deepest and fullest in Alsace; the Riesling and Gewurztraminer are extremely rich, even a touch broad. Like Jean-Michel Deiss (see Marcel Deiss), René Muré believes terroir matters more than grape variety, so since 1998 the domaine has developed a blended wine from the *clos*. Wines made from purchased grapes are bottled under the Côte de Rouffach label.

Domaine Ostertag ☆☆
Epfig. 14 ha.

Biodynamic estate with a two-hectare holding in the Muenchberg *grand cru* vineyard (Riesling and Pinot Gris). The peculiarity of the estate is that some of its Pinot Blanc and Gris is aged in barriques (some of them new), in defiance of usual Alsace practice. The results, not surprisingly, have proved controversial, but André Ostertag courageously sticks to his guns. Other specialties are Sylvaner *vieilles vignes* and Riesling from Muenchberg.

Cave Vinicole de Pfaffenheim ☆–☆☆
Pfaffenheim. Founded 1957. 200 members with 240 ha. www.pfaffenheim.com

Specialties include Pinot Noir, Pinot Gris Cuvée Rabelais, Chasselas Cuvée Lafayette, and a Gewurztraminer from the *grand cru* Goldert. Dry wines with reasonable concentration.

Cave Vinicole de Ribeauvillé ☆–☆☆
Ribeauvillé. Founded 1895. 40 members with 262 ha. www.cave-ribeauville.com

The oldest growers' cooperative in France. Specialties are Le Clos du Zahnacker, (blending Riesling, Gewurztraminer, and Pinot Gris in equal proportions), and Rieslings from Altenberg, Schlossberg, and Osterberg.

Rolly Gassmann ☆
Rorschwihr. Founded in 1676, this estate is mainly in Rorschwihr and partly in Bergheim and Rodern.

Many of the wines are rounded with residual sugar, sometimes excessively so.

Martin Schaetzel ☆☆–☆☆☆
Ammerschwihr. 7.5 ha.

A fine property, rich in *grands crus*, that has shrunk as a consequence of the owner's divorce. Riesling from Schlossberg and Gewurztraminer from Kaefferkopf are excellent, but the mightiest wine is the Riesling from Rangen.

Domaines Schlumberger ☆–☆☆☆
Guebwiller. 140 ha. www.domaines-schlumberger.com

The biggest domaine in Alsace, family owned, with vineyards at Guebwiller and Rouffach at the southern end of the region. Half of the estate is of *grand cru* vineyards: Kitterlé, Saering, and Kessler. Guebwiller's warm climate, sandy soil, and sheltered sites, allied with old-style methods, relatively small crops and ageing in wood, make Schlumberger wines some of the richest and roundest of Alsace, with sweet and earthy flavours of their own.

The best are from the Kitterlé vineyard and repay several years' bottle-ageing. The Vendange Tardive and SGN bottlings are named Anne, Christine, and Clarice after various family members, and are among the most refined examples of these styles in Alsace.

Schoffit ☆☆☆
Colmar. 16 ha.

Bernard Schoffit's most important site is the Clos St Théobald, within *grand cru* Rangen at Thann. The wines are rich and silky, and because of the high ripeness levels of the most favoured sites, they sometimes contain residual sugar. Outstanding Riesling from Rangen, old-vine Chasselas, and spicy, concentrated Pinot Gris, with exceptional length. Stunning, and very expensive, Gewurztraminer and Pinot Gris Sélection de Grains Nobles, also from Rangen.

Bruno Sorg ☆☆
Eguisheim. 10 ha. www.domaine-bruno-sorg.com

François Sorg is an exemplary grower, striving to achieve a balance between optimal ripeness and sensible alcohol levels. The basic wines, such as Sylvaner and Muscat, are delicious but, predictably, the most noble wines are the Rieslings and Pinot Gris from *grands crus* Florimont and Pfersigberg.

Spielmann ☆–☆☆
Bergheim. 8 ha. www.sylviespielmann.com

STYLE WARS

Some decades ago you could be sure that an Alsace Riesling would taste dry. That is no longer the case. It is quite common for many Rieslings, especially from *grands crus*, to have some residual sugar and to taste distinctly sweet. *Grands crus* such as Altenberg in Bergheim easily succumb to botrytis, so residual sugar is hard to avoid; other sites such as Schlossberg tend to produce Rieslings that ferment to complete dryness.

Unfortunately there is rarely anything on the label to guide the consumer. The authorities have recommended that growers indicate on the label sweetness levels on a scale of one to ten, but few have heeded. Growers explain that with reduced yields and long, warm autumns grapes reach exceptional ripeness levels, so that fermentation staggers to a halt while the wine still contains unfermented sugar. The result: 20 grams of perceptible

sugar. Some producers, notably Trimbach, will manage the winemaking to ensure their wines are fully dry. Others such as Zind-Humbrecht, Deiss, or Muré prefer to let nature take its course and live with the results. The consequence is that many wines that are technically Vendange Tardive are now released as regular Rieslings, but without explaining to consumers the style of wine within the bottle.

Sylvie Spielmann worked in Burgundy, California, and Australia before returning to the family property in Bergheim in 1988. Lush Pinot Gris from Blosenberg and refined Riesling from *grand cru* Kanzlerberg.

Marc Tempé ☆–☆☆
Zellenberg. 8 ha.
The first vintage here was 1995, and the estate became Biodynamic the following year. All the wines are vinified in casks, and most of them stay on the lees without racking for up to two years. Tempé, a former technician with INAO, has become a fashionable source, but the wines can be erratic.

F E Trimbach ☆☆☆–☆☆☆☆
Ribeauvillé. 25 ha. www.maison-trimbach.fr
A historic (1626) family domaine and négociant house, with the highest reputation for particularly fine and racy dry wines. Its special pride is the Hunawihr Riesling Clos Ste-Hune, indisputably the finest Riesling produced in Alsace. Sadly, they produce no more than 7,000 bottles.

A fascinating tasting of old vintages showed it at its best after about seven years. Each variety is made in the recently modernized cellar at three quality levels: standard (vintage), Réserve, and Réserve Personnelle, the latter always coming from its own vineyards. The glorious Riesling Cuvée Frédéric Emile is sourced from Osterberg and Eichberg, though Trimbach doesn't use the term *grand cru* on the label. Gewurztraminer Cuvée des Seigneurs de Ribeaupierre is at the same quality level.

Cave Vinicole de Turckheim ☆☆
Turckheim. Founded 1955. 216 members with 340 ha, including 18 *grand cru*. www.cave-turckheim.com
Specialties are Gewurztraminer Baron de Turckheim, the Terroirs d'Alsace varietal range, Pinot Noir Fut de Chêne, and Crémant Meyerling. The cooperative resists the temptation to vinify in large lots, and there are numerous varietal wines from specified *lieux-dits* and *grands crus*, of which the finest is Brand.

Domaine Weinbach ☆☆☆–☆☆☆☆
Kaysersberg. 28 ha. www.domaineweinbach.com
A distinguished domaine of former monastic land, the Clos des Capucins was founded in 1898. Now run by the widow and daughters of the late Théo Faller, who is buried among his vines. Laurence Faller is in charge of the winemaking,

Catherine the marketing. The family policy is to harvest as late as possible and use full maturity to give the wines maximum character, structure, length on the palate, and the potential to age. Ten years is not too much for the Rieslings. Réserve Particulière is the standard label for Riesling and Gewurztraminer, with various *cuvées* named after family members to single out special pickings or styles.

Riesling from *grand cru* Schlossberg is often seen as the epitome of elegance. Not content with Vendange Tardive and SGN in suitable vintages, the domaine, since 1989, has also produced a super-SGN called Quintessence, which is literally picked berry by berry.

Domaine Zind-Humbrecht ☆☆☆☆
Turckheim. 40 ha. www.zind-humbrecht.fr
The domaines of the Humbrechts of Gueberschwihr (since 1620) and the Zinds of Wintzenheim united in 1959. Léonard Humbrecht made wonderful Rieslings until the early 1990s, when his son Olivier, a Master of Wine, took over. Olivier is a fanatic for the individuality of each vineyard. He makes distinctive wines from four *grand cru* vineyards: Brand at Turckheim (opulent, sometimes exotic Riesling), Goldert at Gueberschwihr (full-bodied Gewurztraminer), Hengst at Wintzenheim (more full-bodied *vin de garde*), and Rangen at Thann, where his four-hectare Clos St-Urbain gives magnificent Rieslings.

Over 30 wines are made in order to capture the very best aspects of terroir, all from specific *lieux-dits* such as Clos Windsbuhl and Clos Jebsal. Humbrecht insists on optimal ripeness and natural fermentation in large casks. Consequently some of the wines have residual sugar, but often there is so much power and extract that the sweetness is not detectable.

Valentin Zusslin
Orschwihr. 13 ha. www.zusslin.com
Spicy elegant Riesling from the *grand cru* Pfingstberg, but *lieux-dits* such as Clos Liebenberg and Bollenberg can come close in quality. Biodynamic since 1997.

ALSACE APPELLATIONS

The name of the grape, or the term "Edelzwicker", meaning a blend of different grapes, is usually the most prominent word on Alsace labels. These days, however, Edelzwicker is seen less and less: partly it's the result of the trend towards quality, and partly because abroad, at least, recognizable grape names sell.

Appellation Alsace (including Crémant d'Alsace)
Wine from any permitted grape variety, with a maximum crop of 80 hectolitres per hectare.

Appellation Alsace Grand Cru
Wine from one of the noble grape varieties (Riesling, Gewurztraminer, Pinot Gris, or Muscat), growing in

a designated *grand cru* site, with a maximum crop of 55 hectolitres per hectare (but with a PLC allowing a maximum of 66!) and a minimum natural potential alcohol degree of ten for Riesling and Muscat, 12 for Gewurztraminer and Pinot Gris.

The Rhône Valley

In the late 1980s, after many years of virtually ignoring the Rhône Valley and its wines, the wine trade began to discover in it all sorts of virtues. More, perhaps, than stood up to dispassionate examination. The two great classic vineyards of the Northern Rhône, Hermitage and Côte-Rôtie, whose extraordinary qualities were the well-nurtured secret of a few, were "discovered" by Robert Parker. Their virtues were then imputed to all sorts of Rhône wines (from the south as well as the north) that bore them little or no relation. In the next decade or so, great quantities of what were scarcely more than high-strength *vins de table* climbed to the price of Bordeaux, and even beyond. True, some had scarcity on their side: entire appellations such as Côte-Rôtie and Cornas are scarcely the size of a Médoc *cru classé*. The positive side to this price hike was that it facilitated some much-needed investment in the region, especially in the Northern Rhône.

More exposure led to more opportunities, and questioning of the common grapes in use and the extravagant yields farmers expected. Now the world's eye is on them things are looking much better. At their best, they are grown in soil that exalts their qualities, by men of great taste who are fully aware of the flavours they are producing. Where the well-worn eulogies of scents of truffles and woodlands, violets, and raspberries were usually wishful thinking, wines of real vigour are offering the world an alternative well worth exploring. Standards are rising fast. The qualities of earthy energy and welcome warmth are common, and searching will find you much more. Even the truffley woodland floor.

Northern Rhône

The characteristic of the Northern Rhône is dogged single-mindedness: one red grape, the noble Syrah, a darkly tannic variety with concentrated, fruity flavour, grown on rocky slopes that need terracing to hold the soil. It reaches its climax in Côte-Rôtie.

Côte-Rôtie used to be a mere 100 hectares of terraced hill above the village of Ampuis. Not without controversy, the appellation has been enlarged to include over 100 hectares of plateau land behind the *côte* proper. Côte-Rôtie means "roasted hill"; two sections of the hill, one with paler (more chalky) soil, and the other considerably darker, are known respectively as the "Côte Blonde" and the "Côte Brune". Their wines are normally blended by growers who have only a few hectares in total. There is rather more wine labelled "Côte" than can theoretically be produced – some growers appear to be using the terms blonde and brune as indicators of lighter or heavier styles, as there is no legal constraint on its use.

The Syrah here was in the past grown and mixed with up to 20 per cent (but usually less and sometimes none) of Viognier. Partly from this aromatic component, but probably more from the singular soils or coolest microclimate of the hill, it draws a delicacy that makes Côte-Rôtie the finest, if not the most powerful. This is the northernmost region in which Syrah will ripen, and, as is true of other grapes in other regions, this marginality gives the wines their tension, spice, and depth. One explanation for the presence of Viognier in some vineyards here, apart from the likelihood that some vines have migrated from neighbouring Condrieu, is that the white grape would reliably ripen to at least 13 degrees of potential alcohol, where Syrah here often struggled to surpass 12. In short, Viognier provides a natural form of *chaptalization* in difficult vintages.

Between ten and 20 years of age, Côte-Rôtie moves closer to great Bordeaux than any other French wine, with an open, soft, fruity, perhaps raspberry bouquet that recalls the Médoc, yet with a warmer texture. Recent developments include perhaps more stress on new-oak flavours than the wine will stand.

Condrieu, where the once rare Viognier makes white wine, is only five kilometres (three miles) downstream from Ampuis, on the same south-facing right bank. Cloning has much improved this temperamental grape, which is now far more reliable. It is therefore enjoying a renaissance in the Rhône (and riding to fame in the south of France, California, Australia, and elsewhere).

St-Joseph covers a 50-kilometre (30-mile), stretch of the same riverbank and its immediate hinterland, with some very good sites but no consistency. About 1,000 hectares are planted, with some Roussanne and Marsanne as well as Syrah. Indeed it is permitted to include up to 15 per cent of white grapes in the red wine, although most red St-Joseph is likely to be pure Syrah. Legislation in 1992 has changed the territory covered by the appellation, to force a move off the plateau and valley floor back onto the slopes – although growers have until 2022 to make the move! A good example is clean, dark, and sufficiently fruity Syrah, without the grip or depth of Hermitage: wine to drink at four or five years. Vineyards from the southern half of the zone end to give spicier, more structured wines than those in the north.

The same in general is true of Crozes-Hermitage, the appellation for the east bank around Tain-l'Hermitage, without the advantage of the great upstanding mass of granite to help grill its grapes. It is the biggest AC of the Northern Rhône, with 1,400 hectares of Syrah under vine, and the least expensive, so its wines are often the consumer's introduction to Rhône wines. Growers such as Jaboulet and Graillot have shown what can be achieved here.

Few famous vineyards are as consistent as Hermitage. Its whole 130-hectare surface faces full south, at an angle that maximizes the warmth of the sun. Four-fifths are planted with Syrah, the rest with two white grapes, Roussanne and Marsanne, which produce a wine as splendid in its way as the red. A century ago, white Hermitage (then all Roussanne) was reckoned the best and most long-lived white wine in France keeping, it was written, "much longer than the red, even to the extent of a century". It is surprising to find white wine of apparently low acidity keeping well at all. Yet at ten years (a good age for it today) it has a haunting combination of breadth and depth with some delicate, intriguing, lemony zest.

St-Joseph and Crozes-Hermitage, incidentally, also make white wines of the same grapes, which can be excellent, though they do not share the longevity of white Hermitage. Red

Hermitage has the frankest, most forthright, unfumbling attack of any of the Rhône wines. Young, it is massively purple-black, frequently uncomplicated by smells of new oak, powerfully fruity, almost sweet, beneath a cloak of tannin, and it takes years to lose its opacity. Many people enjoy it in this state – or so it seems, because mature bottles are rare.

Cornas concludes the red-wine appellations of the Northern Rhône, with a sort of country cousin to Hermitage – another dark Syrah wine of macho vigour which only becomes a drink for fastidious palates after years in bottle. Only 110 hectares are currently planted, almost all on the steep slopes behind the village. South of Cornas the appellation St-Péray is a surprising one for a *méthode traditionnelle* sparkling wine made from Marsanne and Roussanne grapes, which, providing you forget the finesse of Champagne or the *crémants* of northern France, has much to be said for it. It is a heavy-duty sparkler of almost sticky texture, even when it is dry. With age, it develops a very pleasant, almost nutty flavour. There is also a still St-Péray.

Leading Northern Rhône Producers

Thierry Allemand ☆☆–☆☆☆
Cornas. 3.5 ha.
Allemand's best wine is Cuvée Reynard, made from vines over 30 years old. Small production, high quality.

Gilles Barge ☆☆
Ampuis. 7 ha.
Forward-looking grower of fine Côte-Rôtie and a little Condrieu. Good, sometimes excellent wines, needing ten years or so. Quality has been steadily improving, and the wines are gaining in finesse. The top wine is his Cuvée du Plessy.

Bernard Burgaud ☆☆☆
Ampuis. 4 ha.
The forthright Burgaud believes in big, well-structured wines, scorning the inclusion of Viognier and the fad for multiple *cuvées*. He uses 20 per cent new oak each year, and the wines are neither fined nor filtered. Impeccable quality.

Caves de Tain-l'Hermitage ☆–☆☆☆
Tain-l'Hermitage. 1,120 ha.
www.cavedetain.com
A very large but high-quality co-op, offering excellent Crozes-Hermitage, Hermitage, St-Joseph, and Cornas. In 2001, a new director ordered immense investments in the winery to improve quality further. Some of the top *cuvées*, such as Crozes Les Hauts de Fief and Hermitage Gombert de Loche are among the best within their appellations.

Emile Champet ☆–☆☆
Ampuis. 2 ha.
An old-fashioned estate producing rather old-fashioned, tannic Côte-Rôties that often retain a rustic edge.

Chapoutier ☆☆–☆☆☆☆
Tain l'Hermitage. 300 ha (85 ha in Northern Rhône).
www.chapoutier.com
Founded in 1808, this is one of the most distinguished names of the Rhône, both as grower and négociant. It is the largest proprietor of Hermitage, with 35 hectares, and has significant holdings of Côte-Rôtie, Crozes-Hermitages, St-Joseph, and Châteauneuf-du-Pape.

When Michel Chapoutier took over the family firm in the late 1980s, he audaciously reversed the habits of decades. Old chestnut casks were replaced by barriques; yields were cut so severely that production was more than halved. Much of the domaine was converted to Biodynamic viticulture. New luxury *cuvées* were introduced in each appellation, while maintaining the brands for which Chapoutier was best-known, such as Crozes Meysonniers and the white Hermitage Chante Alouette.

While all these changes were taking place at home, at the same time, Chapoutier bought and developed properties in Provence, Roussillon, and Australia. Some of the developments at Chapoutier have been controversial, but it is impossible to question the dedication to quality, the scrupulous attention to terroir, and the brilliant marketing of the house, which had been resting on its laurels for far too long.

Gérard Chave ☆☆☆☆
Mauves. 20 ha.
In 1981, Gérard Chave celebrated 500 years of direct succession in Hermitage, and today the next generation is in place in the form of his able son Jean-Louis. Chave red and white are among the best and longest-lived wines in France, composed from seven different terroirs within Hermitage, so each vintage requires careful blending to achieve the best

results. In the late 1980s, a special *cuvée* was introduced, Cuvée Cathelin, but the "standard" Hermitage is so fine that it is rarely worth paying the considerable premium for Cathelin. There is also a modest production of more affordable St-Joseph and a small négociant business called J L Selections.

Auguste Clape ☆☆–☆☆☆
Cornas. 7 ha.
Pierre-Marie Clape's Cornas is dark-purple, almost black, and intensely tannic. Techniques are very traditional: ageing in old casks, no fining, and no filtration. The wines are very long-lived. There is also a bargain Côtes du Rhône, a pure Syrah from vines just outside the appellation, and the pure Marsanne St-Péray.

Clusel-Roch ☆☆
Verenay, Ampuis. 5 ha. www.domaine-clusel-roch.fr
There are three *cuvées* of Côte-Rôtie from this excellent property, the finest being Les Grandes Places. There is no exaggeration here: no excessive alcohol, no over-indulgence in new oak. The wines are tight, balanced, and elegant.

Chapoutier vineyard, below the chapel on the hill of Hermitage

Domaine du Colombier ☆☆
Mercurol. 15 ha.
Florent Viale makes delicious wines from old parcels of vines in Crozes-Hermitage. The top *cuvée* is Gaby, which is aged in older, 500-litre barrels. These are quite tannic, gamey wines that gain in complexity with age, and the white is peachy and exotic. There is also a small quantity of Hermitage.

Jean-Luc Colombo ☆☆–☆☆☆
Cornas. 110 ha. www.vinsjlcolombo.com
A consulting oenologist for many big names throughout southern France, the impassioned Jean-Luc Colombo makes big, plummy Cornas, built for long ageing (Les Ruchets is the top *cuvée*) from his own domaine. Under his négociant label, he produces a range of exciting wines from all the northern Rhône appellations including Hermitage, as well as Côtes du Rhône, and wines from a domaine near Marseille called "Côte Bleue". All his wines share certain characteristics: full ripeness, complete destemming, and a generous proportion of new oak.

Domaine Combier ☆☆–☆☆☆
Pont de l'Isère. 20 ha.
Laurent Combier doubles as a fruit farmer. Fruitiness is also a hallmark of his Crozes-Hermitage, red and white. The top *cuvée* is Clos des Grives, which shows wonderfully pure Syrah fruit and is one of the most hedonistic of all Crozes-Hermitage wines. The white Clos des Grives is mostly Roussanne and is unusually spicy.

Courbis ☆☆–☆☆☆
Châteaubourg. 32 ha. www.vins-courbis-rhone.com
Serious property, carefully vinifying separate parcels from its vineyards in both St-Joseph and Cornas. Dominique Courbis manages to give his wines considerable density and power without any loss of finesse. Top St-Joseph bottling is Les Royes.

Pierre and Jérôme Coursodon ☆–☆☆
Mauves. 15 ha.
Family property of very old vines on the better slopes of St-Joseph. Both reds and whites demand to be aged. The arrival of the young Jérôme Coursodon in 1998 has given the estate a shot in the arm.

Yves Cuilleron ☆☆–☆☆☆
Chavanay. 46 ha. www.cuilleron.com
Since Yves took over the domaine from his father in 1986, he has made spectacular improvements. Better vineyard practice, selective picking, and careful winemaking have resulted in superb Condrieus – particularly his unusual late-harvested Ayguets. He also makes three *cuvées* of St-Joseph, of which the most intense is Les Serines from 60-year-old vines, and a small quantity of Côte-Rôtie. In recent years Cuilleron has expanded his estate considerably, but without any decline in quality.

Delas Frères ☆–☆☆☆
St-Jean-de-Muzols. 30 ha. www.delas.com
Long-established grower and négociant, now owned by Deutz Champagne (and thus Louis Roederer). It has ten hectares in Hermitage (red and white), and buys from growers in most appellations. The change in ownership revitalized the company, and new ideas, together with new investments, have increased quality dramatically since the late 1990s. The red wines in particular have gained in rich fruitiness, without losing their capacity to age and evolve.

Ferraton ☆☆–☆☆☆
Tain l'Hermitage. 7 ha.
Four hectares of Hermitage, plus vines in Crozes and St-Joseph, making solid, traditional wines. The red Hermitage spends at least two years in wood. For some years the domaine has been working closely with Chapoutier (q.v.), adopting Biodynamic viticulture and producing more stylish wines.

Pierre Gaillard ☆☆☆
Malleval. 21 ha.
Gaillard is based in St-Joseph, but also owns parcels in Côte-Rôtie and Condrieu. He makes excellent, fairly oaky wines from all these appellations. By selling off wines he feels are not up to standard, in bulk, Gaillard maintains a consistently high level of quality.

Gerin ☆☆☆
Verenay, Ampuis. 10 ha. www.domaine-gerin.fr
Jean-Michel Gerin founded his domaine in 1990, and has gone from strength to strength. There are three *cuvées* of Côte-Rôtie, with Les Grandes Places and La Landonne aged entirely in new oak. These are modern, sleek, stylish wines in the Guigal mode, and have a devoted following. His Condrieu can also be excellent. In 2002 Gerin started a joint venture in Priorat called Trio Infernal (q.v.).

Alain Graillot ☆☆–☆☆☆
La Roche de Glun. 20 ha.
Few northern Rhône producers are as consistent as Graillot, whose Crozes-Hermitage (both red and white) routinely sets a high standard. Yields are deliberately low and the grapes picked when fully ripe to produce very stylish white and red wines that repay some bottle-ageing, especially the top red *cuvée* La Guiraude. Small quantities of St-Joseph and Hermitage are also produced.

Château Grillet ☆☆–☆☆☆
Verin. 3.8 ha.
The smallest property in France with its own *appellation contrôlée*, owned by the Neyret-Gachet family since 1840. The vineyard consists of perilous terraces forming a suntrap 150 metres (570 feet) above the bank of the Rhône. Some 22,000 Viognier vines yield on average 800 cases a year of highly aromatic wine, which is aged for at least 18 months in oak. Opinions are divided about whether any sort of ageing improves Viognier wine, but this does seem to be an exception. For some time, Château Grillet's reputation has wobbled, although prices have remained very high. Quality has certainly improved since Bordeaux oenologist Denis Dubourdieu was hired as a consultant.

Bernard Gripa ☆–☆☆
Mauves. 14 ha.
A traditionalist producer of St-Joseph, partly fermented with stems and aged a year in wood. The resulting wines are dense and well-structured. His whites are 90 per cent Marsanne.

Guigal ☆☆☆☆
Ampuis. 56 ha. www.guigal.com
The Guigal family are the leading producers of Côte-Rôtie, which they grow themselves on 20 hectares, and also buy in as grapes from many other small growers. They age their single-vineyard Côte-Rôties in new-oak barrels for three years, avoiding both fining and filtration if possible. The object is extremely long-lived wine. From 2003 onwards the barrels have come from their own cooperage.

The regular bottling is Côtes Brune et Blonde; in addition there are four *crus*: La Mouline, La Landonne, La Turque, and (from 1995) Château d'Ampuis. Whether Guigal's oak-scented style is true to the nature and traditions of Côte-Rôtie is a question on which I feel differently from the majority. It certainly attracts extravagant praise, worldwide demand, and dizzying prices. In 1985, the Guigals bought the firm of Vidal-Fleury (q.v.), and since then have absorbed De Vallouit and Jean-Louis Grippat, bringing the firm much sought-after St-Joseph and Hermitage sites. Guigal also produces sumptuous Condrieu and robust Hermitage, as well as good Gigondas and some of the very best Côtes du Rhône.

Paul Jaboulet Aîné ☆☆–☆☆☆
Tain l'Hermitage. 100 ha. www.jaboulet.com
After 170 years of existence as an important family of growers and négociants, the company was sold to the Swiss financier Jean-Jacques Frey, whose daughter Caroline is now responsible for the winemaking, just as she is at their other property Château La Lagune (q.v.) in the Médoc. At both properties she takes advice from her former teacher Professor Denis Dubourdieu. Few would dispute that quality slipped badly here in the 1990s and the company was in need of a shot in the arm. The domaine is focused on Hermitage and Crozes-Hermitage, and it produces a number of *cuvées* from each.

The red Hermitage La Chapelle in great vintages is one of France's greatest wines, maturing over 25 years or more. The white Hermitage Le Chevalier de Sterimberg is also memorable. Crozes-Hermitage Domaine de Thalabert is as fine as any wine from that appellation; likewise, the white Crozes Mule Blanche.

Other excellent wines are St-Joseph Le Grand Pompée, Côte-Rôtie Les Jumelles, Cornas St Pierre, Châteauneuf-du-Pape Les Cèdres, and a very full and fruity Côtes du Rhône Parallèle 45. In the late 1990s, Jaboulet bought the Domaine Roure in Crozes, thus acquiring some of that appellation's best sites.

Joseph Jamet ☆☆☆
Ampuis. 7 ha.
This domaine, of brothers Jean-Paul and Jean-Luc, comprises 25 separate plots in Côte-Rôtie. Its wine exhibits fine fruit and good structure, even in difficult years. Quality, high and consistent, has soared in recent years.

Robert Jasmin ☆☆
Ampuis. 5 ha.
A famous name, though a small property, with vines averaging 30 years of age . Since the death of Robert Jasmin in 1999, the estate has been run by son Patrick. It retains a very traditional

style of vinification, with five per cent Viognier added to the black Syrah, and ageing in older barrels for 12 to 18 months. The wines are not especially structured, and are best enjoyed around five years after bottling.

Ogier ☆☆–☆☆☆
Ampuis. 11 ha.
This family property in Côte-Rôtie is run with great energy by young Stéphane Ogier. The regular bottling is a splendid wine, infused with black fruits and liquorice. The top, new-oaked *cuvée*, Belle Hélène, is far more massive; whether it is better is another question.

Vincent Paris ☆☆–☆☆☆
Cornas. 4 ha.
Paris is the nephew of Robert Michel, whose wines were well known in the 1980s and 1990s. In 2007 he retired, and Paris took over. Initial releases of his two *cuvees*, Granit 30 and Granit 60, were highly impressive.

Pochon ☆☆
Château de Curson, Chanos-Curson. 15 ha.
There are two ranges of Crozes-Hermitage at this very dependable estate. The regular bottling is under the Pochon label, the best selections under the Château de Curson label. The latter is very much the more interesting wine, with an appealing juicy richness. Delicious whites, with more personality than most white Crozes.

Gilles Robin ☆☆
Mercurol. 11 ha.
A rising star in Crozes-Hermitage, with his first vintage b eing 1996. Robin wants to make wines in the same way his grandfather did: ploughing the vines, minimal treatments, and long fermentations. The results are sumptuous, fruity wines, with a characteristic Syrah gaminess.

René Rostaing ☆☆☆
Ampuis. 8 ha.
A splendid estate with some of the best vineyards in Côte-Rôtie (La Viallière, La Landonne). René Rostaing makes elegant, deeply coloured wines, as did his father-in-law (Albert Dervieux-Thaize) and uncle (Marius Gentaz-Dervieux) who left him their prime vineyards on their retirement in 1990 and 1993. First-rate Condrieu.

Marc Sorrel ☆☆–☆☆☆
Tain l'Hermitage. 4 ha. www.marcsorrel.com
Marc Sorrel's white Hermitage Les Rocoules, and top red Hermitage *cuvée* Le Gréal are often some of the best and most long-lived of the commune. The Crozes-Hermitage is more modest.

Georges Vernay ☆☆☆
Condrieu. 16 ha. www.georges-vernay.fr
The leading figure in Condrieu, with vineyards mostly planted on reclaimed abandoned terraces. His wine is bottled in its first spring (or even winter) for freshness – and because demand outstrips supply. A small amount, from the oldest vines, spends longer in wood and becomes Les Terrasses de l'Empire, Coteau de Vernon and Chaillées de l'Enfer, both

distinctly superior wines. He also has two hectares of Côte-Rôtie and small vineyards in St-Joseph and Côtes du Rhône. There are two wines from Côte-Rôtie: the regular bottling and Cuvée Maison Rouge, which is oaky and peppery. Since 1997, the property has been run by his daughter, Christine.

J Vidal-Fleury ☆–☆☆
Ampuis. 12 ha.
The oldest (established 1781) and biggest domaine of Côte-Rôtie terraces, bought in 1985 by the Guigal family (q.v.) but run independently. The range is strong on wines from the Southern Rhône, although the Côte-Rôtie is far from negligible.

François Villard ☆☆–☆☆☆
St-Michel-sur-Rhône. 25 ha.
This former chef has been making waves with his opulent wines from Condrieu, red and white St-Joseph, and two Côte-Rôties, including the sometimes spectacular La Brocarde. He has followed the trend to produce late-harvested Condrieu, and his impressive version is called Quintessence. He is also a partner in Vins de Vienne (q.v.).

Vins de Vienne ☆☆–☆☆☆
Seyssuel. 25 ha.
A joint venture among three St-Joseph growers; François Villard, Yves Cuilleron, and Pierre Gaillard (qq.v.). Essentially a négociant business, but they have also planted vineyards near Vienne with Syrah and Viognier. The wines, first made in 1999, come from the major Rhône appellations, and are oaky and expensive.

Alain Voge ☆–☆☆
Cornas. 7 ha.
The Voge family, which is in its fourth generation here, makes Cornas by traditional methods, and sparkling St-Péray by the classic method.

Other Northern Rhône Producers

Franck Balthazar ☆☆
Cornas. 4 ha.
Very old vines and traditional vinification and ageing in large casks give Cornas of density and drive.

Albert Belle ☆☆
Larnage. 24 ha.
Philippe Belle is a sound producer of Crozes-Hermitage and St-Joseph who also makes a very small quantity of red Hermitage.

Bonnefond ☆☆
Ampuis. 7 ha.
Patrick and Christophe Bonnefond only started bottling Côte-Rôtie and Condrieu in the 1990s, and have acquired a fine reputation for them.

J F Chaboud ☆
St-Péray. 13 ha
Almost all the production here is classic-method St-Péray.

Yann Chave ☆☆
Mercurol. 16 ha

A reliable source of plummy red Crozes-Hermitage, and a white from ultra-ripe grapes. Very good, modern-style wines.

Collonge ☆
Mercurol. 30 ha.
Formerly, a reliable producer of Crozes-Hermitage and St-Joseph, red and white. Bought in 2006 by Philippe and Vincent Jaboulet.

Domaine de la Côte Ste-Epine ☆–☆☆
St Jean de Muzols. 6 ha.
The grapes from these very old St-Joseph vines used to be sold to Guigal, but for some years the domaine has released its own wines, both red and white. This is a property on the rise.

Duclaux ☆☆
Tupin-et-Semons. 5.5 ha.
www.coterotie-duclaux.com
Brothers Benjamin and David Duclaux have taken over their family domaine on the Côte Blonde and are making refined wines without too much recourse to new oak.

Durand ☆–☆☆
Châteaubourg. 12 ha.
Brothers Eric and Joël have a growing reputation not only for St-Joseph but for Cornas, from which they produce three *cuvées*.

Domaine des Entrefaux ☆–☆☆
Chanos-Curson. 26 ha.
Some years ago family disputes muddied the waters at this Crozes-Hermitage estate, but stability has now returned. The best wine is the red Les Machonnières with its blackberry fruit.

Garon ☆☆
Ampuis. 2.5 ha.
Until 1995, the Garons sold their Côte-Rôtie grapes to Guigal, but now produce small quantities of bright, spicy, plummy wine.

Gonon ☆–☆☆
Mauves. 10 ha.
Pierre Gonon, now assisted by his son Pierre, has made progress at this St-Joseph estate, and the wines have gained in density.

Domaine des Hautes-Chassis ☆☆
La Roche de Glun. 14 ha.
Franck Faugier produces three *cuvées* of Crozes-Hermitage, of which Galets and Les Chassis are the best. They're all very well made wines, and prices are reasonable.

Lionnet ☆–☆☆
Cornas. 8 ha.
Jean Lionnet retired in 2005, when his lease on his Domaine de Rochepertuis, his flagship wine, expired. The remaining vines are now farmed and vinified by his daughter Corinne, and her first vintage was 2003.

Niero-Pinchon ☆☆
Condrieu. 5 ha.
A small estate, from which Robert Niero coaxes two bottlings of Condrieu, and one of Côte-Rôtie.

André Perret ☆–☆☆
Chavanay. 11 ha.
Reliable producer of St-Joseph and rich *cuvées* of Condrieu.

Domaine des Remizières ☆–☆☆
Mercurol. 30 ha.
A well-established domaine belonging to the Desmeure family. Numerous *cuvées* of slightly rustic Crozes-Hermitage and St-Joseph. A little Hermitage is also produced.

Jean-Michel Stephan ☆☆–☆☆☆
Ampuis. 4.5 ha.
The first vintage here was in 1994, and today the small parcels of Côte-Rôtie vines are cultivated Biodynamically. The Vieilles Vignes bottling includes wine from centenarian vines.

Domaine du Tunnel ☆☆
St-Péray. 7 ha.
Stéphane Robert founded the property in 1994 and has made swift progress, especially with his opulent Cornas.

Southern Rhône

The catch-all appellation for the huge spread of Southern Rhône vineyards is Côtes du Rhône. It is not a very exigent title – the equivalent of AC Bordeaux Rouge. The area covers a total of 49,000 hectares of vineyards in 171 communes north of Avignon, describing a rough circle among the low hills surrounding the widening Rhône. It leaves out only the alluvial bottom land around the river itself. In an average year, it makes over twice as much wine as the appellation Beaujolais – indeed, not far short of the whole of Burgundy. Ninety-seven per cent of it is red or rosé.

In such an ocean of wine there are several estates that set standards of their own, and good négociants choose and blend well. The thing to bear in mind is that most Côtes du Rhône is for drinking young, while it is reasonably fruity.

Côtes du Rhône-Villages is the inner circle. Over 40 years ago, growers in two communes east of the valley, Gigondas and Cairanne, and two to the west, Chusclan and Laudun, raised their sights to making stronger, more concentrated *vin de garde*, modelling their wines on the *crus* of the Southern Rhône (Grenache base plus Syrah, Mourvèdre, and Cinsault). Limiting their crop to 38 hectolitres per hectare (plus PLC, as always; see Glossary) and ripening their grapes to give 12 degrees alcohol they made better wine, and got better prices.

A number of their neighbours followed suit. In 1967, the appellation Côtes du Rhône-Villages was decreed for a group of what has now risen to 18 communes totalling 6,600 hectares. The village name is permitted on the label for this group, but a total of 76 villages, covering 3,000 hectares, are still entitled to use "Côtes du Rhône-Villages" where the wine is not exclusively from the named village. Gigondas, Vacqueyras, Beaumes-de-Venise, Vinsobres, and Rasteau (for its fortified wines) have AC status, and this seems likely to happen to others in the group as they establish their identity and build their markets. Certainly, Vacqueyras deserved its promotion to AC. As an example of the style of the area it might be compared with Gigondas. Tasted together, the Gigondas is fuller and rounder, with more "stuffing"; the Vacqueyras is more "nervous": harsh at first but developing a very pleasant, dusty, slightly spicy, bouquet. The wines from the best producers in both Vacqueyras and Gigondas are emphatically *vins de garde*; at five or six years they still need decanting – or keeping another three years.

There are outlying regions that belong administratively to the Rhône, although some are quite distant from the valley itself. These are the Coteaux du Tricastin, Côtes du Ventoux, Côtes du Vivarais, Côtes du Luberon, and Costières de Nîmes. Many of these regions lie high up and the wines tend to be lighter than the brawnier Côtes du Rhône. They are discussed in more detail later in this chapter, as are the very different wines of Châteauneuf-du-Pape. With the exception of Costières de Nîmes, which in any case has more in common with the Languedoc than the Rhône Valley, these large appellations are dominated by cooperatives, although a handful of estates have made names for themselves by producing more individual and concentrated wine than the lacklustre norm.

There is a small production of fortified wine in the Côtes du Rhône, of which by far the best known is the delicious Muscat from Beaumes-de-Venise, which manages to retain remarkable freshness and delicacy, despite its high alcohol. The wine, especially examples from the cooperative and from négociants such as Jaboulet, was extremely popular in the 1980s, but the fad has mysteriously faded away, even though the wine remains as delectable as ever. There is also some excellent *vins doux naturels* in Rasteau, mostly from Grenache.

Leading Southern Rhône Producers

Daniel & Denis Alary ☆☆
Cairanne. 25 St Péray
There are excellent red wines made here, especially Cuvée Font d'Estévenas.

Pierre Amadieu ☆
Gigondas. 140 ha. www.pierre-amadieu.com
The largest estate in the region, producing wines from a range of appellations. The Gigondas Grande-Romane, the hallmark wine, is rather tannic and leathery.

Domaine des Bernardins ☆
Beaumes-de-Venise. 22 ha.
A good source of straightforward Beaumes-de-Venise, but it's the elegant Muscat that is worth seeking out here.

Domaine Brusset ☆☆
Cairanne. 86 ha. www.domainebrusset.fr
Daniel Brusset's Cuvée des Templiers is a traditional Cairanne and one of the village's best, made only in top vintages. This estate also has a fine reputation for its Gigondas, especially Les Hauts de Montmirail, which is aged in partly new barriques.

Domaine de Cabasse ☆☆
Séguret. 20 ha. www.domaine-de-cabasse.fr
This Swiss-owned property produces modern, sleek Gigondas and Côtes du Rhône Séguret. Fine rosé, too.

Cave de Cairanne ☆☆
Cairanne. 1,250 ha. www.cave-cairanne.fr
Founded in 1929, this cooperative has 80 members, who offer as wide and constantly changing range of wines. But two red wines have become Cairanne classics: Cuvée Antique from 80-year-old vines, and the smoky, concentrated Réserve des Voconces.

Domaine du Cayron ☆☆☆
Gigondas. 16 ha. www.domaine-cayron.com
Michel Faraud and his three daughters makes one of the finest Gigondas, from 45-year-old vines scattered all over the appellation. The winemaking is completely traditional: no destemming, no added yeasts, ageing in large casks, and bottling without fining or filtration.

Didier Charavin ☆–☆☆
Rasteau. 50 ha.
A family property going back to the years of the French Revolution, making classic, sweet Rasteau entirely from Grenache, and an old-style red from Grenache, Syrah, and Carignan, aged for one year in oak barrels. The top wine is usually the vigorous Cuvée Parpaïouns.

Clos des Cazaux ☆☆–☆☆☆
Vacqueyras. 40 ha. www.closdescazaux.fr
Enthusiastically run by the Archimbaud-Vache family, this estate produces a range of excellent Vacqueyras. St Roch is a traditional style, tasting of black-cherries; Cuvée des Templiers is almost pure Syrah – less typical but delicious. The Gigondas, overwhelmingly Grenache from old vines, is released under the label Tour Sarrazine, and is consistently fine and complex.

A negociant assesses the crop

Vignerons de Chusclan ☆–☆☆
Chusclan. www.vigneronsdechusclan.com
This is rosé country, and this co-operative produces excellent examples, as well as sound red wines based on old-vine Grenache.

Domaine Le Couroulu ☆☆
Vacqueyras. 20 ha.
Guy Ricard makes some splendid Vieilles Vignes Vacqueyras from 60-year-old Grenache, enlivened with some almost equally old Syrah.

Domaine de Deurre ☆–☆☆
Vinsobres. 50 ha. www.domaine-de-deurre.com
These Côtes du Rhône wines have a marked acidic structure. All are unoaked except for Cuvée Jean-Marie Valayer. Hubert Valayer also makes wine from St Maurice.

Domaine de Durban ☆–☆☆
Beaumes-de-Venise. 57 ha.
The Leydiers are excellent producers of both Muscat de Beaumes-de-Venise and red Côtes du Rhône-Villages.

Domaine des Escaravailles ☆☆–☆☆☆
Rasteau. 65 ha.
Gilles Ferran's property is divided between Rasteau and Cairanne. Quality here is very high, and the best *cuvées* include Cairanne Ventabren and Rasteau La Ponce, both of which are elegant and persistent in flavour.

Domaine La Fourmone ☆–☆☆
Vacqueyras. 37 ha. www.domaine-la-fourmone.com
Owned by the Combe family, this is a reliable producer of Vacqueyras and Gigondas (under the Oustau Fouquet label) for medium-term drinking.

Domaine les Goubert ☆–☆☆
Gigondas. 23 ha. www.lesgoubert.fr
Jean-Pierre Cartier's vineyards are spread over various appellations. His Beaumes-de-Venise is always good value, but his best wine is his Gigondas. This wine comes in two versions; the first traditional, the other, Cuvée Florence, barrique-aged. And it was one of the first wines oaked in Gigondas, a style that remains controversial, although it has proved very successful on the American market.

Domaine du Gour de Chaulé ☆☆
Gigondas. 10 ha.
Owner Mme. Aline Bonfils makes powerful yet elegant wines for medium-term drinking.

Domaine Gourt de Mautens ☆☆–☆☆☆
Rasteau. 14 ha. www.gourtdemautens.com
Jérôme Bressy is a rising star in Rasteau, where he makes unusually concentrated red and white wines, sold at considerably high prices.

Domaine Gramenon ☆☆–☆☆☆
Monbrison-sur-Lez. 29 ha.
Superb Côtes du Rhône from the Drôme region, mostly from extremely old Grenache and Syrah wines. Delicious Viognier too.

Domaine du Grand Montmirail ☆–☆☆
Gigondas. 35 ha.
Gigondas estate owned by Yves Cheron. The previously low
production from old Grenache vines has been adapted with
more Syrah, while Mourvèdre is now also used to make more
assertive wines. Cheron also produces Vacqueyras.

Château du Grand Moulas ☆–☆☆
Mornas. 34 ha. www.grand-moulas.com
From his vineyards in the Côtes du Rhône, Marc Ryckwaert
and his son Nicolas make three reds (the top label is the
Syrah-dominated Cuvée de l'Ecu) and a white, all very fine
examples of the appellation.

Domaine du Grapillon d'Or ☆☆
Gigondas. 20 ha. www.domainegrapillondor.com
Burly Gigondas with power rather than finesse, and peppery,
plummy Vacqueyras. A recent innovation is Cuvée Excellence,
a Gigondas from the oldest vines.

Domaine Les Hautes Cances ☆☆
Cairanne. 16 ha. www.hautescances.9business.fr
Organic estate that made its first wine in 1995. Old vines and
low yields ensure high average quality, and the Vieilles Vignes
can be exceptional.

Gabriel Meffre ☆☆
Gigondas. 71 ha. www.gabriel-meffre.fr
In 1936, Meffre founded a domaine that grew to become the
largest in France, with 800 hectares of vineyards. After his
death, the property went through numerous changes, but since
1997 has been owned by former general manager Bertrand
Bonnet with a selection of other investors.

The vineyards (Domaines des Bosquets, Raspail, and la
Daysse in Gigondas) remained with the Meffre family, so the
company now buys in grapes. However, it also owns Château
de Longue Toque in Gigondas and Château Grand Escalion
in Costières de Nîmes. The company's chief brand is Laurus,
which draws on fruit from most of the principal appellations
of the Rhône Valley.

Domaine de la Monardière ☆☆
Vacqueyras. 20 ha.
Christian Vache took over this estate in 1987, overhauled
it, and began producing good wines with ample weight and
fruit. The Vieilles Vignes, from 60-year-old vines, can be
exceptional.

Domaine de l'Oratoire St-Martin ☆☆–☆☆☆
Cairanne. 25 ha. www.oratoirestmartin.fr
Frédéric and François Alary run one of the very best estates
in this increasingly prized appellation, and have farmed
organically for some years. Their best wines are the unoaked
Cuvée Prestige from old vines, and the oaky Cuvée Haut-
Coustias, red and white. These are modern wines with sleek
tannins and purity of fruit.

Domaine Les Pallières ☆☆
Gigondas. 25 ha. www.vignoblesbrunier.fr
The Roux family made wine in the manner of Châteauneuf-
du-Pape in Gigondas for 500 years. With no heirs, it was sold

in 1998 to the Bruniers of Vieux Télégraphe (q.v.). Their
version of the wine is less rustic, but perhaps less individual,
than those of the Roux'.

Domaine Pelaquié ☆
Laudun. 70 ha. www.domaine-pelaquie.com
A large property, producing good but uninspired wines from
this Côtes du Rhône village, as well as from Lirac and Tavel,
which lie just to the south of here.

Maison Perrin ☆☆
Orange. 85 ha. www.domaineperrin.com
La Vieille Ferme is the well-known négociant brand of the
Perrin family, famous for its Châteauneuf-du-Pape Château
de Beaucastel. The excellent red is made as a *vin de garde*
from the Côtes du Ventoux, and the delicate, fresh white
from high vineyards on the Montagne de Lubéron. Both
are exceptional value. Recently the range has expanded
to include more serious wines from Gigondas, Vacqueyras,
and other appellations.

Domaine du Pesquier ☆☆–☆☆☆
Gigondas. 16 ha.
Traditional winemaking in tanks and large casks, and no
filtration, giving sumptuous, gamey Gigondas with a silky
texture.

Domaine de Piaugier ☆☆
Sablet. 30 ha.
Jean-Marc Autran makes serious Sablet and Gigondas from
single vineyards. Some of them are quite unusual, such as
Cuvée Ténébi, which has at least 50 per cent of the rare
Counoise variety in the blend.

Domaine Rabasse-Charavin ☆☆
Cairanne. 68 ha.
A top producer of Cairanne, Corinne Couturier makes several
wines, including a straight Syrah, and the Cuvée d'Estevenas
from very old Grenache vines.

Domaine Raspail-Ay ☆☆☆
Gigondas. 18 ha.
One of the best domaines in Gigondas. Dominique Ay
produces a very well-structured and fruity wine from his
estate, where the average age of the vines is 30 years. This
is Gigondas as it should be: built to last.

Domaine La Réméjeanne ☆–☆☆
Cadignac. 38 ha. www.laremejeanne.com
Fresh wines from near Bagnols in the Côtes du Rhône.
Numerous *cuvées*, including a particularly attractive Syrah
called Les Eglantiers.

Domaine Richaud ☆☆☆
Cairanne. 46 ha.
Marcel Richaud may well be the best producer in Cairanne.
The basic red is lively and fresh, and one of his best wines
is the Cuvée L'Ebrescade, from 100-year-old Mourvèdre,
Syrah, and Grenache vines. The other red is Les Estrambords,
which he selects as the best wine of the vintage, usually a pure
Grenache or pure Mourvèdre.

Château de Rouanne ☆☆
Vinsobres. 85 ha.
Marc Ferrentino only began bottling wines from this vast property in 1998, and he continues to sell most of the production in bulk. He retains the best lots for two excellent Côtes du Rhône-Villages wines: Vinsobres and Plan de Dieu.

Château de St-Cosme ☆☆☆
Gigondas. 15 ha. www.saintcosme.com
Louis Barruol is fortunate in owning vineyards with an average age of 60 years. The standard Gigondas is ripe and supple, and in top years Barruol makes Cuvée Valbelle, aged in 50 per cent new oak, magnificent in the 1998 vintage. There is also a small but high-quality négociant business.

Château St-Estève d'Uchaux ☆–☆☆
Uchaux. 60 ha. www.chateau-st-esteve-d-uchaux.com
The Français-Monier family have owned this estate since 1809. Uchaux lies on a sandy ridge north of Orange, which gives ripe, warm wines with body and character. The property produces three red wines, and no fewer than three Viogniers, including the rare Cuvée Thérèse.

Domaine St-Gayan ☆☆–☆☆☆
Gigondas. 38 ha. ww.saintgayan.com
Jean-Pierre Meffre has 400 years of Gigondas vigneron forebears. He produces much-appreciated, tannic Gigondas up to 14.5 degrees of alcohol, reeking of crushed fruit, from ancient vines. Also big-scale Côtes du Rhône-Villages in Sablet and Rasteau. In addition, there is an oaked Gigondas called Fontmaria, made in response to American demand for this style.

Domaine Sainte-Anne ☆–☆☆
St-Gervais. 33 ha.
The Steinmaier family makes concentrated Côtes du Rhône and -Villages, red and white; and good Viognier.

Domaine Le Sang des Cailloux ☆☆
Sarrians. 17 ha. www.sangdescailloux.com
Bought by Serge Férigoule in 1990, this is a source of good Vacqueyras, especially the rich Cuvée Lopy from 80-year-old Grenache vines and aged in 450-litre barrels. These are wines that benefit from bottle age.

Domaine de Santa Duc ☆☆☆
Gigondas. 21 ha. www.santaduc.fr
Yves Gras makes superlative Gigondas from dispersed vineyards, cultivated in an essentially organic way. The top bottling is the Cuvée Hautes Garrigues, a blend of Grenache and Mourvèdre. Gras uses a good deal of new oak, but he dislikes the cult of overtly oaky wines, and insists that barriques are a tool to give greater complexity and texture.

Château La Soumade ☆☆–☆☆☆
Rasteau. 26 ha.
André Romero is the most dynamic of the Rasteau producers. He makes wines for long ageing, and both Cuvée Fleur and the rare Cuvée Confiance are from very old Grenache vines. The Rasteau Doux is a vintage wine, from 90 per cent Grenache. All Romero's wines have high alcohol,

and are not for the faint-hearted. However, since Stéphane Derenoncourt came on board as a consultant, the wines have gained in refinement.

Tardieu-Laurent ☆☆☆
Lourmarin. (No vineyards.)
www.tardieu-laurent.com
This négociant business is a joint venture between Dominique Laurent (q.v.) of Nuits-St-Georges, and Michel Tardieu. They buy wine from growers with very old vines, then age the wines in their own cellars. New oak is used for Syrah-based wines; one-year-old barrels for Grenache-based wines. Rich, dense wines, from the northern Rhône as well as all the southern appellations, too extracted and formidable for some tastes but undeniably impressive. Expensive.

Château des Tours ☆
Sarrians. 39 ha.
This estate belongs to Emmanuel Reynaud, proprietor of Château Rayas in Châteauneuf (q.v.). Here, too, Grenache reigns, giving supple Côtes du Rhône and Vacqueyras.

Domaine du Trapadis ☆–☆☆
Rasteau. 23 ha. www.domainedutrapadis.com
Robust, sometimes porty red wines are the forte of this estate, and the fortified wine is successful too.

Château du Trignon ☆☆
Sablet. 68 ha.
An old (1898) family estate with modern ideas, making excellent wine. The vineyards are divided between Gigondas, Sablet, and Rateau. In 2006 owner Charles Roux sold the property to Jérôme Quiot, so the style may change in the future.

Domaine Viret ☆☆
St Maurice sur Eygues. 30 ha.
www.domaine-viret.com
Despite an attachment to a system the Virets call "cosmoculture", which embraces elements from Aztec culture as well as Biodynamism, the wines here are rich and packed with fruit.

Tavel & Lirac

A similar area to Châteauneuf-du-Pape a few miles west, on the other side of the Rhône, has traditionally been famous for its rosé, made with the same grapes. Tavel has a unique reputation for full-bodied dry rosé, made not by fermenting the wine briefly on its (red) grape skins, as most other rosés are made, but by a period of up to two days of maceration before fermentation starts. (The yeasts have to be inhibited by SO_2, or in modern cellars by cooling.) The wine is then pressed and fermented like white wine.

I have never been attracted by this powerful, dry, rather orange-pink wine, any more than by similar rosés from Provence. It is regarded, though, as one of the classics. Like Racine, it should be re-read from time to time. Lirac, the northern neighbour to Tavel, has been specializing more recently in red wines, which at their best can be very pleasantly fruity and lively, and in other cases, strong and dull.

Leading Tavel & Lirac Producers

Château d'Aquéria ☆–☆☆
Tavel. 65 ha. www.aqueria.com
An immense seventeenth-century property, offering lush, fruity Lirac as well as a classic Tavel.

Domaine Lafond-Roc-Epine ☆–☆☆
Tavel. 75 ha. www.roc-epine.com
Sound, fruity wines in three colours, and a significant production of Châteauneuf-du-Pape as well.

Domaine Maby ☆–☆☆
Tavel. 60 ha. www.domainemaby.fr
A large and well-established family property in Tavel and Lirac. The Liracs, both white and red, are especially good. The red La Fermade has about 45 per cent Mourvèdre, which gives the wine its backbone.

Domaine de la Mordorée ☆☆–☆☆☆
Lirac. 55 ha. www.domaine-mordoree.com
A forward-looking, organic estate, producing gently aromatic white, as well as robust Lirac and Tavel. Its best-known wine, however, is probably the Châteauneuf Cuvée Reine des Bois.

Château St-Roch ☆☆
Roquemaure. 45 ha. www.chateau-saint-roch.com
This substantial Lirac property of Antoine Verda changed hands in 1998, when it was acquired by Château de la Gardine (q.v.) of Châteauneuf-du-Pape. Despite La Gardine's fondness for barriques, the St-Roch wines remain unoaked and traditional.

Château de Trinquevedel ☆☆
Tavel. 31 ha.
François Demoulin is one of the leading growers of Tavel, with interesting ideas on adapting his methods to the state of the crop, using partly old techniques and partly new (chilling and *macération carbonique*). He believes a little bottle-age improves his Tavel, which, for rosé, is dark and robust.

Ventoux & Lubéron

Where the Rhône Valley merges with Provence to the east, the appellation Côtes du Ventoux has forged ahead in volume, now far out-producing the united Côtes du Rhône-Villages. Among some very reasonable reds, one of the outstanding wines is La Vieille Ferme (q.v.) of Jean-Pierre Perrin, brother of the owner of Château de Beaucastel (q.v.). Not long ago Ventoux was largely the preserve of cooperatives and a few négociants, but today there is a growing number of enterprising private estates.

The same is true of the Côtes du Lubéron, the hills along the north of the Durance Valley (famous throughout France for its asparagus). Its reds, mostly from Grenache and Syrah, and whites may appeal more for their crisp, well-defined flavours than some of the more pedestrian efforts of the Rhône.

Cool Alpine air encourages wines that are relatively light in body but that can have considerable finesse. Further north, between the Côtes du Rhône and the town of Montélimar, lies the Coteaux du Tricastin, a windy and cool region that also gives lightweight wines.

Leading Ventoux & Lubéron Producers

Domaine des Anges ☆–☆☆
Mormoiron. 18 ha. www.domainedesanges.com
Irishman Gay McGuinness owns this estate, which produces a fruity Côtes du Ventoux from Grenache and a Syrah especially for drinking young. The white is made mostly from Marsanne and Roussanne. The best wines are bottled as "Archanges": a Syrah-dominated red, and a pure Roussanne white.

Domaine de la Citadelle ☆–☆☆
Ménerbes. 40 ha. www.domaine-citadelle.com
A serious property in the Côtes du Lubéron, offering a wide range of wines. The best is the barrique-aged Cuvée Le Gouverneur, a Syrah/Grenache blend.

Château de Clapier ☆–☆☆
Mirabeau. 40 ha. www.chateau-de-clapier.com
This Côtes du Lubéron estate has been owned by the same family since 1880. Rather than trying to produce wines with weight and stuffing, Thomas Montagne rightly focuses on freshness and approachability, and largely succeeds. It is worth paying the slight premium for the Cuvée Soprano, white and red.

Domaine de Fondrèche ☆–☆☆
Mazan. 35 ha. www.fondreche.com
Owner Sébastien Vincenti produces a wide range of ambitious Côtes du Ventoux wines, both red and white. The reds consist of varying blends of Grenache, Syrah, and Mourvèdre, with a generous use of oak that can sometimes seem excessive.

Château Pesquié ☆☆
Mormoiron. 72 ha. www.chateaupesquie.com
The Chaudière brothers offer two distinct styles at this immense Côtes du Ventoux property: fresh fruity wines under the Terrasses range, and denser, oak-aged Syrah-dominated reds under the Quintessence label. Consistent quality.

Château Valcombe ☆☆
St-Pierre-de-Vassols. 23 ha.
www.vignobles-paul-jeune.com
A high-quality estate in the Côtes du Ventoux. Sumptuous oaked white La Sereine is from Grenache Blanc and Roussanne; its red counterpart is dominated by Syrah, and can display remarkable density of fruit.

Châteauneuf-du-Pape

Châteauneuf-du-Pape is much the biggest and most important specific southern Rhône appellation. If its 3,150 hectares of vines produced as plentifully as those of its neighbours, there would be almost as much Châteauneuf-du-Pape as Côtes du Rhône-Villages. But small crops are mandatory: the yield of Châteauneuf-du-Pape is on average 33 hectolitres per hectare; for Côtes du Rhône-Villages it can be up to 42 hectolitres per hectare. Concentration is the very essence of this wine. Its vines grow in what looks like a shingle beach of big, smooth, oval stones – known as galets – that often cover the whole surface of the vineyard. Each vine is an individual low bush.

Where all other French appellations specify one or two, at

most four, grape varieties of similar character, the tradition in Châteauneuf-du-Pape is to grow up to 13 with widely different characteristics. It is not clear whether this is primarily an insurance policy, or simply accumulated tradition. Some growers assert that each of them, even the coarse or simply neutral ones, adds to the complexity of the wine.

New plantations, however, are tending to cut down the number to four or five. The base, always in the majority and sometimes as much as 80 to 100 per cent, is Grenache. Cinsault, Syrah, and Mourvèdre are also important. Varieties that could be described as optional are (red) Counoise, Muscardin, Vaccarèse, and Terret Noir and (white) Picardan, Clairette, Picpoul, Roussanne, and Bourboulenc. The white varieties were once used in the red wine, as well as made into white Châteauneuf-du-Pape on their own; these days there is a new demand for the white version.

Grenache and Cinsault are described as providing strength, warmth, and softness; Mourvèdre, Syrah, Muscardin, and Vaccarèse as adding structure, colour, "cut", and refreshment to the flavour, as well as the ability to live for long enough to develop a bouquet. Although the legal minimum is 12.5 degrees of alcohol, 13.5 degrees is considered the lowest acceptable by the best growers, and 14.5 degrees or more is not unusual.

And the result? We have all had great, dull, headachey wines called Châteauneuf-du-Pape. There is no distinct varietal handle by which to grasp either the aroma or the flavour. The best estates, however, make magnificent *vins de garde* that start to open up after five years, and develop after ten or more. When a bouquet starts to develop, it is still elusive. It is rather part of a glowing, roast-chestnut warmth about the whole wine. With growing maturity, aromas of tobacco, leather, and exotic spices characterize the wines. Eventually, in the best examples, latent finesse and the essential sweetness of a great wine will emerge. The best I have ever drunk was a 1937, still in perfect condition in 1997.

Recent vintages set to age splendidly include 1990, 1998, and 2005. But a word of caution: the great years for Châteauneuf are mostly the very ripe years, and in some cases alcohol levels can go through the roof. White Châteauneuf-du-Pape, formerly a long-lived wine – rich and elusive, is now more often made for drinking within three years at most. From certain estates, the white can age for ten or more years. How this is possible is mysterious, given the low acidity of the wine.

Leading Châteauneuf-du-Pape Producers

Château de Beaucastel ☆☆☆–☆☆☆☆
Courthézon. 100 ha. www.beaucastel.com
Brothers Jean-Pierre and François, the fourth generation of the Perrin family, make one of the best wines of the region on this big property, dating back to the seventeenth century. Their Châteauneuf vineyard is supplemented by Côtes du Rhône located just across the appellation boundary.

All 13 authorized grapes, with relatively high proportions of Grenache and Mourvèdre, a low crop, 15-day fermentation in square stone vats, and 18 months' ageing in oak give the wine depth and durability. Organic methods are used in the vineyards, and the wine is bottled unfiltered, leading to some glorious bottles, but also occasionally to farmyard smells. In top vintages the property releases a special *cuvée* called Hommage à Jacques Perrin, with all the qualities of a great Beaucastel taken to an even higher pitch.

A small amount of delicious white Châteauneuf is made of 85 per cent Roussanne and 15 per cent Grenache Blanc. Even better is the magnificent Cuvée Roussanne Vieilles Vignes, one of France's great white wines. Their Côtes du Rhône (a notable bargain for this quality) is called Cru de Coudoulet de Beaucastel. Also look out for their Côtes du Ventoux La Vieille Ferme.

Domaine de Beaurenard ☆☆
Châteauneuf-du-Pape. 32 ha. www.beaurenard.fr
Paul Coulon represents the seventh generation on this family property. He also owns 25 hectares of Côtes du Rhône at Rasteau. Both are planted with the same mixture of 70 per cent Grenache and ten per cent each of Syrah, Cinsault, and Mourvèdre. He stresses careful, bunch-by-bunch selection in the vineyard and *cuvaison à l'ancienne* – long, carefully controlled vatting – in the cellar. For a while, the estate favoured carbonic maceration, but has changed. The top *cuvée* is called Boisrenard: rich and massive but sometimes ungainly.

Domaine Bois de Boursan ☆☆☆
Châteauneuf-du-Pape. 15 ha.
Jean-Paul Versino has been enjoying great success with this property, founded by his Piedmontese father in 1955 and planted with all 13 authorised varieties. In top years he

---

CLAIRETTE DE DIE

Clairette de Die, a region of 1,500 hectares east of Valence, is like a sorbet between the substantial main dishes of the Northern and Southern Rhône. The energy of the local cooperative has revived a fading appellation. Clairette de Die is at its best when made sparkling, but one or two traditional growers make a satisfying, nutty still wine. Sparkling Clairette must have 75 per cent Muscat,

whereas Crémant de Die, once pure Clairette, may now include Aligoté and Muscat. There is also a still dry wine from Clairette called Coteaux de Die.

Cave de Die Jalliance
Much of the appellation is handled by the 232 members of this forward-looking cooperative, which also offers *crémants* from Bordeaux and Burgundy thanks to

links with those regions. There is also a new range of organically grown wines.

The brut is a dry, sparkling wine with an aroma of lilac and lavender, it's claimed. Tradition is a sweet fizz of Muscat de Frontignan. The method involves fermentation in bottle (but, unlike Champagne, of the original grape-sugar), then filtering and decanting to another bottle under pressure.

produces Cuvée des Félix, which is aged in older barriques to give a ripe, intense wine, with fruity rather than meaty or leathery flavours.

Henri Bonneau ☆☆☆
Châteauneuf-du-Pape. 6 ha.
From labyrinthine cellars in the village, Bonneau, a resolute traditionalist, produces Cuvée Marie Beurier and the Réserve des Célestins, solid, spicy, often massive reds that are aged for many years in old barrels. The overall style is powerful and concentrated, sometimes funky. Prices are exceedingly high.

Domaine Bosquet des Papes ☆☆–☆☆☆
Châteauneuf-du-Pape. 27 ha.
Maurice Boiron and son Nicolas produce traditional wine from very old vines. Since 1990, they have also made Cuvée Chante Le Merle from 90-year-old vines, a splendid wine with overtones of coffee and leather.

Domaine Chante-Cigale ☆☆–☆☆☆
Châteauneuf-du-Pape. 46 ha. www.chantecigale.com
The name means "the song of the cicada" – if song is the appropriate word. This traditional property is owned by Christian Favier, and his son Alexandre has been making the wines since 2006. Old-style vinification and up to two years in cask make serious *vin de garde*, especially the Cuvée Vieilles Vignes, made from vines between 80 and 100 years old.

Domaine Chante-Perdrix ☆☆
Châteauneuf-du-Pape. 18 ha. www.chante-perdrix.com
A property south of Châteauneuf, not far from the Rhône River. Medium-bodied wine, shows finesse rather than power.

Domaine de la Charbonnière ☆☆
Châteauneuf-du-Pape. 24 ha.
Michel Maret has been making steadily improving wines at this property, with his Vieilles Vignes bottling a particularly pure expression of old-vine Grenache.

Domaine Les Clefs d'Or ☆–☆☆
Châteauneuf-du-Pape. 26 ha. www.lesclefsdor.fr
The Deydiers are a modest family and they have no truck with the fad for multiple *cuvées*. Instead, they offer an honest, entirely typical Châteauneuf at a moderate price. But the wines can be inconsistent in lesser vintages.

Domaine Clos du Caillou ☆☆–☆☆☆
Courthézon. 53 ha.
Sylvie Vacheron's estate is divided between sandy sectors and slopes rich in galets. The resulting wines are sleek and fruity, with a distinct touch of oak that places them firmly in the modern camp.

Clos du Mont Olivet ☆☆–☆☆☆
Châteauneuf-du-Pape. 40 ha.
The three sons of Joseph Sabon are the fourth generation to make utterly traditional wine . The top *cuvée*, made only in outstanding vintages, is called Papet, from old vines with very small yields. The wines are tannic and need plenty of ageing. eight hectares at Bollène (Vaucluse) produce Côtes du Rhône.

Clos des Papes ☆☆☆–☆☆☆☆
Châteauneuf-du-Pape. 32 ha. www.closdespapes.fr
A property in direct descent from father to son for more than 300 years. The vineyards are planted with 65 per cent Grenache, 20 per cent Mourvèdre, plus Syrah, Muscardin, and Vaccarèse. Vincent Avril makes wines that balance power and structure against finesse. Not only the reds, but whites, too, are capable of long life in bottle.

Domaine Font de Michelle ☆☆
Bedarrides. 48 ha. www.font-de-michelle.com
Both red and white Châteauneuf-du-Pape are made at this domaine owned by the brothers Gonnet. The red is elegant rather than powerful: the white fresh and attractive. The top *cuvée* is named Etienne Gonnet after their father.

Château Fortia ☆
Châteauneuf-du-Pape. 30 ha. www.chateau-fortia.com
The family estate of the instigator of the system of *appellations contrôlées*, Baron Le Roy, who in 1923 first defined the best vineyard land of the region in terms of the wild plants, thyme, and lavender – growing together – an early ecologist. Despite the domaine's reputation, quality slipped badly in the 1990s, although recent vintages have shown more concentration and stylishness.

Château de la Gardine ☆☆–☆☆☆
Châteauneuf-du-Pape. 54 ha. www.gardine.com
The Brunels aim for a reasonably fruity and elegant wine rather than a pugilist. The top wine, the Cuvée des Générations, is aged partly in new oak. The Brunels have been using barriques since 1980, so they know how to moderate overt oak influence. However, the white Générations is far too oaky, and the regular *cuvée*, which is delicious, is surely preferable. The Brunels also own Château St-Roch in Lirac (q.v.).

Domaine Grand Veneur ☆☆☆
Châteauneuf-du-Pape. 55 ha. www.domaine-grand-veneur.com
A large estate, with most of its vineyards in the Côtes du Rhône and Lirac. In recent years, the Jaume family have made tremendous efforts here, especially with the rich, oaky Cuvée les Origines, with flavours of chocolate and black fruits. There is also a soft, plump, all-Roussanne white called La Fontaine.

Domaine de la Janasse ☆☆☆
Courthézon. 50 ha. www.lajanasse.com
Christophe Sabon produces Côtes du Rhône and Châteauneuf-du-Pape from his domaine, planted mostly with old vines (some 80 to 100 years old in Châteauneuf). Low yields and a long *cuvaison* ensure very powerful wines, now among the best of the appellation. Top labels are Cuvée Chaupin (usually 100 per cent Grenache) and Vieilles Vignes (85 per cent Grenache). Also exceptional white wine, and, since 1996, a *cuvée prestige* aged in predominantly new oak, and containing 70 per cent Roussanne.

Domaine de Marcoux ☆–☆☆☆
Châteauneuf-du-Pape. 18 ha.
This, the first Biodynamic estate in the region, has won a loyal following, but the wines have never been consistently

convincing. However, the Cuvée Vieilles Vignes has been most impressive in recent vintages.

Château Mont-Redon ☆☆
Châteauneuf-du-Pape. 145 ha. www.chateaumontredon.fr
The biggest single vineyard in Châteauneuf, with a long history ("Mourredon", part of the episcopal estate, had vines in 1334), bought in 1921 by Henri Plantin and now run by his grandsons, Jean Abeille and Didier Fabre. Its immensely stony ground used to produce a benchmark Châteauneuf for endless ageing. Today it is a good middle-weight. Mont-Redon is the largest producer of white Châteauneuf, which is enjoyable young for its nutty freshness. The estate also includes vineyards in Lirac and the Côtes du Rhône at Roquemaure.

Domaine de Nalys ☆
Châteauneuf-du-Pape. 50 ha. www.domainedenalys.com
Nalys, which is owned by the French insurance company Groupama, makes one of the fresher examples of Châteauneuf, at one time using carbonic maceration, and ageing the wine only up to a year in wood before bottling. The red remains mediocre, but the estate also makes notably good unoaked white wine for fairly early drinking.

Château de la Nerthe ☆☆☆
Châteauneuf-du-Pape. 90 ha. www.chateaulanerthe.fr
One of the great names of Châteauneuf, quoted in the nineteenth century as being a separate and slightly better wine than Châteauneuf itself. All 13 authorised varieties are planted in is vineyards. Director Alain Dugas combines scientific rigour with a deep understanding of his vineyards, and the wines have been gaining steadily in depth and sophistication – and, alas, in price too. The top *cuvées*, called Cadettes (red) and Beauvenir (white), have been outstanding, despite a generous use of new oak. La Nerthe successfully attains complete ripeness without excessive alcohol.

Domaine du Pegaü ☆☆
Châteauneuf-du-Pape. 22 ha. www.pegau.com
Paul Féraud set up the domaine in 1987, and early acclaim seems to have gone to his head. There is, in addition to a good, leathery, basic wine, a plethora of special *cuvées*, mostly barrique-aged, and sold at extremely high prices. Yet, in my opinion, the wines can skirt perilously close to oxidation .

Château Rayas ☆☆☆
Châteauneuf-du-Pape. 13 ha.

Château des Fines-Roches, Châteauneuf-du-Pape

A small but outstanding property, which is often cited as the best of Châteauneuf. Emmanuel Reynaud's estate is on slightly atypical clay soils and is overwhelmingly planted with ancient Grenache. He ages the red for two or three years in old casks, depending on the vintage. Although there have been rich and profound vintages of Rayas, white as well as red, over many decades, quality can fluctuate wildly, although since Emmanuel Reynaud took over from his secretive uncle Jacques in 1997, the hand at the helm has been steadier. The wine often disappoints when young, but gains in complexity and depth as it ages. Reynaud uses "Pignan" as a second label. Château Fonsalette (a top Côtes du Rhône) is made at Rayas, but the Fonsalette Cuvée Syrah, often delectable, is now not produced.

Domaine Roger Sabon ☆–☆☆☆
Châteauneuf-du-Pape. 17 ha. www.roger-sabon.com
Four different Châteauneufs are made, and inevitably the most basic, Les Olivets, lacks weight. The top wine is the scarce Les Secrets de Sabon from 100-year-old vines.

Pierre Usseglio ☆☆
Châteauneuf-du-Pape. 23 ha. www.domaine-usseglio.com
Thierry Usseglio has won praise for his top wines, Mon Aeuil and Deux Frères, but they can suffer from very high alcohol and burly tannins.

Domaine de la Vieille Julienne ☆☆–☆☆☆
Les Grès, Orange. 32 ha. www.vieillejulienne.com
Jean-Paul Daumen's vineyards lie in the northern part of the region and are dominated by Grenache. His top Cuvée Réservé, first produced in 1994, is not made every year, but it's a wine, essentially traditional, that shows magnificent concentration and dense fruit. In some vintages, however, it can be marred by very high alcohol.

Vieux Donjon ☆☆–☆☆☆
Châteauneuf-du-Pape. 14 ha.
A classic estate, producing a ripe, slightly smoky white, and a single powerful red from 80 per cent Grenache. The reds are firm and tannic, but always seem to have a core of ripe fruit. If the wines seem somewhat formidable when tasted young, they age beautifully, delivering sweet, brambly fruit.

Domaine du Vieux Télégraphe ☆☆☆
Bédarrides. 70 ha. www.vignoblesbrunier.fr
A long-established estate that takes its name from the old signal tower that once stood on the hill. It is worked by two brothers of the Brunier family who make a rather conservative, dark, peppery, and intense Châteauneuf. The vines are 65 per cent Grenache, 15 per cent Syrah, and 15 per cent Mourvèdre. The stony soil, low yields, and long fermentation of the whole bunches account for the deep concentration of the wine. They are also owners of another property, Domaine de la Roquette.

Domaine de Villeneuve ☆☆
Courthézon. 9 ha. www.domainedevilleneuve.com
A rising star since new owners took over the domaine in 1993 and converted its vineyards to Biodyamism. The age of the vines ranges from 30 to 100 years, yet the wines have finesse as well as concentration of fruit. No more than 20 per cent of the wine is aged in wood.

Provence

Times have changed in Provence, and continue to change. Now that pink wine is fashionable Provence wants to be up there showing the world what it can do; more than two-thirds of its wine is rosé, typically ultra-pale in colour, with good balance but often surprising firmness of flavour. Indeed, delicacy of colour is no guide to flavour here: these wraith-like glassfuls taste like proper wines. They aim at mineral, terroir-driven flavours rather than frivolous fruit jam; and making rosé is the main aim in a cellar, not a mere by-product of red, or a quick and cynical way of removing money from cash-rich tourists.

Although without tourists, where would Provence rosé be? The prices, compared to those of other rosés, can be eye-watering. Yes, there is a difference made these days between rosé for early drinking (often made from Cinsault and Syrah) and more powerful wines (often Mourvèdre or Cabernet Sauvignon), and there's even a small trend for oak-aged rosé intended to go better with food. The wines can be delicious, but the prices still require a certain sun-soaked befuddlement on the part of the buyer. The impetus for some of this change has come from outside. Provence has new settlers, many of them stars in other spheres. Replanting the vines and rebuilding the *chai* is a bagatelle when you are restoring a considerable château – and skilful advice is easy to find. The result is not just greatly improved rosés, but also a much greater number of serious reds, and more well-made whites. There are sometimes aromas of herbs and pines: the heady, sun-baked smell of the land. Individual growers have capitalized on the California-like climate and the wider availability of classic grape varieties.

In Provence, the estate or grower's name is all. Appellations are now a much more reliable guide to quality, too; Coteaux d'Aix-en-Provence and especially Les Baux-de-Provence have become serious contenders in the quality stakes. Areas of Côtes de Provence, such as Mont Ste-Victoire, now also have a number of good producers, especially of red wines. The western extension of the Côtes de Provence has its own appellation: the Coteaux Varois, more elevated and with a later, cooler ripening season. Whites and Syrah do well here, but Cabernet Sauvignon can finish the season still tasting green. Within the Côtes the wines of the Ste-Victoire area now rejoice in their own AC. Indeed, the number of appellations seems to be increasing exponentially, in direct opposition to the rationalization promised by the new EU wine regime. Fréjus has its own AC, as does La Londe, and in 2010 or later St-Tropez and Vallée Interieure will follow.

The old Côtes de Provence was an alarmingly wide area for a single appellation, including the coast from St-Tropez to beyond Toulon to the west, and a great stretch of country inland, north of the Massif des Maures, back to Draguignan and the first foothills of the Alps. Within this there have long been four little local appellations where the wine was considered consistently above-average. The biggest and unquestionably the best – indeed, it must be included among France's most splendid reds – comes from Bandol, a 16-kilometre (ten-mile) stretch of coast and its hinterland just west of Toulon, with

1,500 hectares of vineyards. Good Bandol red has a quality that has traditionally been rare in Provence: tannic firmness that makes it a three-year wine at the very least, lasting without problems, but maturing in splendour up to ten years or more. The law requires Bandol vines to be at least eight years old for the wine to qualify for appellation status, and the wine must be aged at least 18 months in cask. The reason is a high proportion (the legal minimum is 50 per cent, but many of the best estates will now use 100 per cent) of Mourvèdre, which appreciates the heat of rocky terraces. Local lore has it that Bandol from nearer the sea, hence sometimes misty, is finer than that from further inland. There is also fine Bandol rosé, especially from Mourvèdre, and less consistent white. Farther west along the coast, almost in the outskirts of Marseille, the fishing port/resort of Cassis, with 165 hectares of vines, is known for its (relatively) lively and aromatic white, for which the bouillabaisse restaurants of Marseille see fit to charge *grand vin* prices.

The wines of the district of Aix-en-Provence, north of Marseille, come under the AC Coteaux d'Aix-en-Provence (3,500 hectares). The microscopic 40-hectare enclave of Palette, an appellation area just east of Aix, is dominated by Château Simone (q.v.). Les Baux, with 325 hectares of vines, has achieved appellation status for its reds and rosés: Les Baux-de-Provence (for the present, the whites remain under the more general Coteaux d'Aix appellation). Many of the top-quality producers in Les Baux are using some Cabernet Sauvignon, and most adopt organic methods to grow their vines. Behind Nice in the hills at the extreme other end of Provence, the 40-hectare appellation of Bellet is justified by wine that is considerably better than the generally pretty ordinary prevailing standard of its neighbours; the whites being better than the reds. The Côte d'Azur seems to disprove the theory that a sophisticated clientele spurs winemakers to make fine wine. Some 20 estates in Provence use the title *cru classé*. This dates to the 1950s and an attempt to raise local quality standards. It was originally used by producers who were the first to bottle their wines at the estate. The term should not be taken too seriously. Some of the estates' wines, on the other hand, can bear close scrutiny these days.

Leading Provence Producers

Bandol

Domaine La Bastide Blanche ☆☆
Le Castellet. 28 ha.
The estate produces three different *cuvées* from its dispersed Biodynamic vineyards. They show aromatic complexity and considerable verve and power.

Domaine de la Bégude ☆☆
Le Camp-du-Castellet. 15 ha.
Bégude belongs to the Tari family, former owners of Château Giscours in Margaux. These are Bandol's highest vineyards, which gives the wines freshness and aroma without any loss of *typicité*. The estate is also much admired for its rosé.

Domaines Bunan ☆☆–☆☆☆
La Cadière d'Azur. 67 ha. www.bunan.com
The brothers Bunan, Paul and Pierre and Paul's son, Laurent,

own steep vineyards at La Cadière (Moulin des Costes) and at nearby Le Castellet (Mas de la Rouvière).

Some excellent and increasingly important, long-lived red (mostly Mourvèdre, plus Grenache and some Syrah) is made, and in exceptional years, a special pure-Mourvèdre *cuvée* is produced under the Château de la Rouvière label. The top wine from Moulin des Costes is the oak-aged Cuvée Charriage. The Bunans also rent the 12-hectare Domaine de Bélouvé in the Côtes de Provence.

Jean-Pierre Gaussen ☆☆
La Cadière d'Azur. 14 ha.
Mourvèdre rules at this property, especially in the Cuvée Longue Garde which, as the name suggests, is intended to improve and soften with considerable bottle-age. (Until 2000 the estate was known as Domaine de la Noblesse.)

Domaine du Gros'Noré ☆–☆☆
La Cadière d'Azur. 9 ha. www.gros-nore.com
Alain Pascal, a former boxer, uses 80 per cent Mourvèdre in his red Bandol, which, like him, knows how to pack a punch.

Domaine Lafran-Veyrolles ☆☆
La Cadière d'Azur. 10 ha.
Reliable red and rosé from Bandol, and an often exceptional Cuvée Spéciale.

Domaine de Pibarnon ☆☆☆
La Cadière d'Azur. 48 ha. www.pibarnon.fr
In 1977, Comte Henri de St-Victor gave up his day job in Paris and bought this run-down estate, and within ten years had developed it into one of Bandol's top properties. Today it is run by his son Eric. The red is almost pure Mourvèdre, and the rosé, which is from 50 per cent Mourvèdre, can be surprisingly long-lived. When young, Pibarnon smells of violets and blueberries; with age, like other Bandols, it takes on overtones of tobacco and truffles.

Domaine Pradeaux ☆☆–☆☆☆
St-Cyr. 26 ha.
A highly traditional Bandol property, making robust wines that, with age, can resemble good Bordeaux but with more gaminess. The vines are close to 50 years old, and low yields give the wines power and richness. But in their youth they often seem tough and austere, so patience is demanded, and usually rewarded.

Château Romassan ☆–☆☆
Le Castellet. 66 ha. www.domaines-ott.com
In 2004 this large estate was acquired by the Champagne house Louis Roederer, who brought in Denis Dubourdieu as a consultant. At present the range developed by the Ott family has been retained, as have the scarcely justifiable high prices demanded for all the wines. In top vintages a red Cuvée Longue Garde can be impressive.

Domaine Tempier ☆☆☆–☆☆☆☆
Le Plan-du-Castellet. 29 ha. www.domainetempier.com
Lucien Peyraud is widely regarded as the "father of the Bandol appellation", for his part in rescuing it from decline. His sons and grandson, assisted by winemaker Daniel Ravier, make the

finest wines of Bandol, hence of Provence: superbly flavoury and long-lived red and rosé.

Many of the vines are up to 70 years old; the average age is 35 years. The red (two-thirds of production) has at least 60 per cent Mourvèdre, the rest Grenache, Syrah, Cinsault, and a little Carignan from very old vines. The outstanding Cuvée Cabassaou is 100 per cent Mourvèdre, and the two single-vineyard wines, La Tourtine and Le Migoua, are of comparable quality.

Domaine de la Tour du Bon ☆☆
Le Brûlat-du-Castellet. 12 ha. www.tourdubon.com
Agnès Henri-Hocquard runs this fine domaine, with its plump rosé and a rich red from 70 per cent Mourvèdre. The Cuvée St Ferréol is made from pure Mourvèdre, and partly aged in new oak.

Château Vannières ☆☆–☆☆☆
La Cadière d'Azur. 31 ha. www.chateauvannieres.com
A leading Bandol producer, on an estate dating back to 1532. The stylish, medium-bodied red is made of 90 per cent Mourvèdre and given long ageing in large casks.

Domaine de la Vivonne ☆☆–☆☆☆
Le Castellet. 15 ha. www.vivonne.com
One of the leading lights in the Bandol appellation, Walter Gilpin makes robust wines in a traditional way, though sometimes a few new barriques supplement the casks. The wines are very deep in colour, and rich in black-cherry succulence.

Les Baux-de-Provence

Mas de la Dame ☆☆
Maussanne. 57 ha. www.masdeladame.com
Mmes. Poniatowski and Missoffe produce one of the best wines in Les Baux from their organic estate. Since the late 1990s, consultant oenologist Jean-Luc Colombo has overhauled wine production, releasing as a top *cuvée* the Coin Caché from Grenache and Syrah: in its youth a tough and oaky red. It joins the other concentrated red, La Stèle. A new *cuvée*, Le Vallon des Amants, is a curiosity, being almost pure Mourvèdre.

Domaine d'Eole ☆☆
Eygalières. 16 ha. www.domainedeole.com
A forward-looking organic estate producing white wines under the Vin de Pays des Alpilles label, as well as a range of three red wines, of which the top *cuvée* is Léa, with its unobtrusive oakiness.

Château d'Estoublon ☆–☆☆
Fontvieille. 17 ha. www.estoublon.com
Estoublon produced very dull and dilute wines until it was bought by the Schneider family in 1999. They shrewdly hired Eloi Durrbach of Trévallon to advise winemaker Rémy Reboul. The property has been transformed. Out, for example, went Grenache Blanc and Ugni, in came Marsanne and Roussanne. The vines began to be farmed organically. Quality, for red and white, is very much on the rise.

Mas de la Gourgonnier ☆
Mouriès. 45 ha. www.gourgonnier.com
A traditional though organic estate run for decades by the Cartier family in the heart of the Les Baux mountains. Both the rosé and red are hearty, rich in fruit, and spicy. No great sophistication here but honest and consistent wines.

Domaine Hauvette ☆
St-Rémy-de-Provence. 17 ha.
A one-woman organic property run with rigour by former skiing instructor Dominique Hauvette. The red suffers from inconsistency: fleshy but refined in some vintages, baked and bland in others.

Domaine de Lauzières ☆–☆☆☆
Mouriès. 32 ha. www.lauzieres.com
The Lauzières wines were rustic in the 1980s, but in 1993 the property was bought by a dynamic Swiss lawyer, who converted the vines to organic viticulture and, rather oddly, planted a good deal of Petit Verdot. This is blended with Grenache to produce a *vin de table* called Sine Nomine. Convention returns in the form of two Baux wines, Solstice and Equinoxe.

Château Romanin ☆☆
St-Rémy. 55 ha. www.romanin.com
Romanin began as a joint venture between financier Jean-Pierre Reynaud and Jean-Andre Charial, owner of two top restaurants in Les Baux. The estate has been Biodynamic from the outset, and the winery is conceived as a cathedral to Biodynamic principles. The wines have not always matched the ambition, though. In 2006 the property was bought by Jean-Louis Charmolüe after he sold Château Montrose in St-Estèphe.

Domaine de Trévallon ☆☆☆–☆☆☆☆
St Etienne-des-Grès. 17 ha.
www.domainedetrevallon.com
The rich, intense, half-Cabernet Sauvignon, half-Syrah blend is the best wine in the district of Les Baux, but is not entitled to the appellation, as the INAO allows only 20 per cent Cabernet Sauvignon. Consequently, since 1994, Eloi Durrbach produces his superlative wine as a red Vin de Pays des Bouches-du-Rhône, and he also makes a tiny amount of sumptuous white from 60 per cent Marsanne and 40 per cent Roussanne. In this case, the law is undeniably an ass.

Other Provence Producers

Château L'Arnaude ☆
Lorgues. 30 ha. www.chataudarnaude.com
For 20 years this Côtes de Provence property was well run by the Knapp family, then sold in 2005 to Mats Wallin, who swiftly invested in sorting tables, new tanks, and 300-litre barrels for the best wines. Quality is set to rise, although 70 per cent of production is still of rosé.

Domaine du Bagnol ☆–☆☆
Cassis. 7 ha.
Michelle Génovési's small estate produces a good Marsanne-dominated white and an excellent rosé.

Château Bas ☆☆
Vernègues. 72 ha. www.chateaubas.com
A new team took over the running of this Coteaux d'Aix property in the late 1990s, with the aim of improving quality. The top bottling is the Cuvée du Temple: a heavy white from mostly Rolle, and a sometimes extracted red from Syrah.

Domaine les Bastides ☆☆–☆☆☆
Le Puy-Ste-Réparade. 30 ha.
Jean Salen and daughter Carole produce a splendid Cuvée Valéria from Cabernet Sauvignon and Grenache, a complex wine made without recourse to small oak barrels. The rosé is unusually full-bodied.

Domaine des Béates ☆☆–☆☆☆
Lambesc. 52 ha. www.domaine-des-beates.com
A Biodynamic Coteaux d'Aix property owned since 1996 by the Chapoutier family from the Rhône. The estate wine is a dark, rich, vigorous blend of Cabernet, Syrah, and Grenache, and the top (and wildly expensive) Cuvée Terra d'Or is a blend of Cabernet and Syrah, aged in barriques and intended for long ageing.

Château du Beaupré ☆
St-Cannat. 36 ha. www.beaupre.fr
Since the mid-1990s, the Double family have been improving the quality of their wines, using more barriques for the best, which are released under the Collection label. However, the wines, though reliable, can lack concentration.

Château de Bellet ☆–☆☆
Nice. 8 ha.
Ghislain de Charnacé's property is one of just three in the tiny AC Bellet. The others are Château de Crémat and Clos St-Vincent (qq.v.). The white is almost entirely Rolle (Vermentino), and the red a blend of local varieties Folle Noir and Braquet. The best wines are bottled under the Cuvée Baron G label.

Château de Berne ☆
Lorgues. 80 ha. www.chateauberne.com
Despite the initial resemblance to Hollywood among the Provençal pine trees, this British-owned estate is producing some good-quality, modern-style Côtes de Provence.

Mas de Cadenet ☆☆
Trets. 45 ha. www.masdecadenet.com
A fine property within the Ste-Victoire AC. The top wine, from the oldest vines, is the spicy, concentrated Mas Négrel from Grenache and Syrah, and there is also a traditional sweet wine of Provence, a *vin cuit*.

Château Calissanne ☆☆–☆☆☆
Lançonde Provence. 100 ha. www.calissanne.fr
This large estate was bought in 2001 by industrialist Philippe Kessler. He died in 2008, but his widow continues his good work. There are two excellent bottlings: the château range, and Clos Victoire, which is aged in barrels of varying ages and sizes. The red Victoire is a fine blend of old-vine Cabernet Sauvignon and Syrah, and the rosé a vivid blend of Syrah and Grenache.

Clos Ste-Magdelaine ☆☆
Cassis. 12 ha.
A reliable white-wine property overlooking the Mediterranean, probably the best in Cassis, with ripe, lively, floral wines.

Clos St-Vincent ☆☆–☆☆☆
Nice. 5 ha.
A tiny organic property in AC Bellet. Sumptuous wines in all three colours, using mostly Rolle for the white and Folle Noire for the red. But prices are clearly aimed at the villa dwellers of the Côte d'Azur.

Clos Val Bruyère ☆
Cassis. 7.5 ha. www.chateau-barbanau.com
Fruity whites from Clairette, Marsanne, and Ugni Blanc. A sister property is the Château Barbanau in the Côtes de Provence.

Commanderie de Peyrassol ☆–☆☆
Flassans-sur-Issole. 65 ha. www.peyrassol.com
The Commanderie was founded by the Templars in 1204, and acquired by the Rigord family in 1790, then sold in 2001 to Philippe Austruy. The new owner simplified the range: the basic wines under the Commanderie label, the top wines, aged in new oak, under the Château Peyrassol label. Both reds are blends of Cabernet Sauvignon, Syrah, and Grenache.

Château la Coste ☆☆
Le Puy-Ste-Réparade. 148 ha.
www.chateau-la-coste.com
One of the largest estates in Provence. Matthieu Coste has revamped the property, converting it to Biodynamism, and built a new winery. There are numerous bottlings, and the top range is Cuvée Premium: the red from Grenache and Syrah, the white from Vermentino and Chardonnay. Quality is steady but prices, once at bargain level, have risen.

Domaine de la Courtade ☆☆–☆☆☆
Ile de Porquerolles. 30 ha. www.lacourtade.com
An outpost of experimentation on an exceptionally sunny island west of Toulon, begun in 1983. The concentrated reds are almost pure Mourvèdre; the barrique-aged whites are from Rolle. Quality is very high, as are prices. The second label is L'Alycastre.

Château de Crémat ☆☆
Nice. 12 ha. www.chateau-cremat.com
This is a leading property in the tiny appellation Bellet in the hills above Nice, well-known to habitués of the Côte d'Azur. The previous owner, Jean-Pierre Pisoni, invested heavily in the neglected vineyards before selling the property to the current owner, Cornelis Kamerbeek.

Domaine de la Cressonnière ☆–☆☆
Pignans. 25 ha. www.cressonniere.com
Robust, sometimes tannic red wines, blended into different *cuvées*. Carignanne, unsurprisingly, is mostly Carignan, made by carbonic maceration. More structured is Mataro, and even though Mataro is a synonym for Mourvèdre, the wine is mostly Syrah, aged in new oak.

Domaine du Deffends ☆☆
St-Maximin. 14 ha. www.deffends.com
One of the best estates in the sometimes overlooked Coteaux Varois. A *vin de pays* white is made from Rolle and Viognier, but red wine dominates production. The top *cuvée* is Clos de la Truffière: a blend of Cabernet and Syrah, as much red fruit as truffle in its aromas.

Château d'Esclans ☆☆–☆☆☆
La Motte. 35 ha. www.chateaudesclans.com
A daring new venture, since in 2006 this beautiful property was bought by Sasha Lichine, son of the late Alexis, who hired former Mouton-Rothschild winemaker Patrick Léon to make the wines. What is unusual is that almost the entire range is rosé, with the top *cuvées*, especially Garrus, being fermented and aged in new oak. Prices make the Ott rosés look cheap, but these are beautifully scented rosés of immense refinement and vigour.

Domaine Ferme Blanche ☆
Cassis. 20 ha.
A leading property in this fashionable village, producing relatively floral white and a light, dry rosé.

Château de Fonscolombe ☆
Le Puy-Ste-Réparade. 144 ha.
The aristocratic Saporta family has two Coteaux d'Aix properties north of Aix – this noble Renaissance château (88 hectares) and the Domaine de la Crémade (59 hectares). The wines are well made, employing modern techniques for whites and rosés, and traditional oak vinification for reds. The Cuvée Spéciale red is 15 to 20 per cent Cabernet. Overall, the wines lack concentration, but are highly drinkable.

Château du Galoupet ☆
La Londe-les-Maures. 72 ha.
www.galoupet.com
A property that aims to combine traditional grape varieties of the Côtes de Provence region with current winemaking techniques. The château dates back to Louis XIV, and the older part of the cellar is Roman.

Château Gassier ☆–☆☆
Puyloubier. 40 ha.
Pretty, mineral, balanced rosé and some red from an estate owned by the négociant Jeanjean.

Domaine Gavoty ☆☆☆
Cabasse. 25 ha. www.gavoty.com
Bernard Gavoty was the music critic for Le Figaro in the 1970s. Today, this property, a producer of excellent Côtes de Provence, is run by Roselyne Gavoty. Bernard's pen-name was Clarendon, and the top *cuvée*, the often sumptuous Cuvée Clarendon, is a fitting tribute. The red is mostly Syrah, the rosé mostly Grenache.

Château la Gordonne ☆
Pierrefeu du Var. 180 ha. www.listel.fr
An enormous estate owned by Domaines Listel, producing red, white, and rosé Côtes de Provence from shale soil on the Maures foothills.

Château Léoube ☆–☆☆
Bormes-les-Mimosas. 62 ha.
Run by Romain Ott, son of the original family of Domaines Ott (q.v.), this estate is under the same ownership as Daylesford Organic, which in turn is owned by the man who founded the construction equipment company JCB. The vineyard is part of a 560-ha estate by the sea and is aiming for organic accreditation. The wines are quite low in acidity, sleek and distinctive.

Les Maîtres Vignerons de la Presqu'île de St-Tropez ☆☆
Gassin. 750 ha. www.mavigne.com
This unusual enterprise unites nine domaines, each of which vinifies its own wines, which are then bottled and marketed by the vignerons, who, from 2001, teamed up with other wineries to form a more efficient marketing group, Terres de Mer. Château de Pampelonne is the top label. Good-value reds and rosés are bottled under Cuvée du Chasseur, Carte Noire, and other labels.

Château Minuty ☆
Gassin. 65 ha.
Jean-Etienne Matton runs this sizeable property near St-Tropez, which has a serious reputation for its rosés.

Domaines Ott ☆☆
Le Castellet. 156 ha. www.domaines-ott.com
Founded in 1896 by a native of Alsace, the former Ott domaines consist of three properties producing good, if high-priced, Provence wines by traditional, organic methods: limited yield, no sulphur, oak-ageing. Estates owned are Clos Mireille (Côtes de Provence; white wines only), Château Romassan (Bandol; q.v.), and Château de Selle (Côtes de Provence). The wines appeared to have been trading on their reputation for some years, but in 2004 all three properties were sold to Champagne Louis Roederer, and improvements are in hand in both vineyards and cellars.

Domaine Rabiega ☆☆
Flayosc. 10 ha. www.rabiega.com
A small, Swedish-owned estate producing impressive, ripe oaky wines: Clos d'Ière No 1 (mostly Syrah), and No 2, (a blend of Grenache, Carignan, and Cabernet Sauvignon).

Château Réal Martin ☆☆
Le Val. 37 ha. www.chateau-real-martin.com
This always dependable property for red and white Côtes de Provence changed hands in 2001, when it was purchased by businessman Jean-Marie Paul. The top range is now called

Vaulted cellars, Château Romanin, St. Remy

Prestige, and Paul has planted some Cabernet Sauvignon, to which the previous owners were sternly opposed.

Château Revelette ☆☆
Jouques. 25 ha. www.revelette.fr
Owner Peter Fischer trained at UC Davis in California before acquiring this now organic property in 1985. It lies high in the Coteaux d'Aix at 400 metres (1,300 feet), so the wines can have a certain austerity when young. The elevation also means that his Chardonnay has freshness as well as oakiness; the red Grand Vin, from Cabernet Sauvignon and Syrah, has intense berry fruit.

Domaine Richeaume ☆☆
Puyloubier. 25 ha.
German proprietor Henning Hoesch, now succeeded by his son Sylvain, makes a red from Cabernet Sauvignon and Syrah, which is aged for two years in wood, and maintains that even his rosé and white are wines for keeping. Hoesch also produces unblended Syrah and a rosé *de saignée* from Grenache.

Domaine de Rimauresq ☆☆
Pignans. 57 ha. www.rimauresq.fr
This property has been under Scottish ownership since 1988. The property has some vines up to 70 years old, which are used to make the special Cuvée "R". In top vintages winemaker Pierre Duffort fashions a super-*cuvée* called Quintessence du "R".

Château Routas ☆☆
Bras, Coteaux Varois, 44 ha. www.chateauroutas.com
The reds and rosé of this estate were well-known in the USA before Scots tycoon Sir David Murray bought it in 2005. The new policy is site-specific Syrah, Cabernet, Viognier and Chardonnay from the high exposed limestone; increasingly fine wines.

Domaine de St-André de Figuière ☆☆
La Londe-les-Maures. 42 ha.
www.figuiere-provence.com
Alain Combard's organic estate lies between St-Tropez and Toulon, producing good red and rosé from its schist soils. There are various levels of quality, the best being the Vieilles Vignes, closely followed by the red Reserve, which is a focused, barrique-aged Mourvèdre. Good rosé, too.

Château de St-Martin ☆
Taradeau. 40 ha. www.chateaudesaintmartin.com
A handsome old house with deep cellars, in the same family since the seventeenth century. The proprietor, Mme. du Barry, makes reliable Côtes de Provence and stocks older vintages for sale.

Château Ste-Roseline ☆☆
Les Arcs-sur-Argens. 108 ha. www.sainte-roseline.com
Property developer Bernard Teillaud bought and renovated this ancient monastic estate in 1994, replanting and expanding many of the vineyards. The Mourvèdre-dominated red Cuvée Prieure is the best wine made at this Côtes de Provence estate, and there is an extensive range of rosés, made from Tibouren, Mourvèdre, and Syrah. The top wines do not come cheap.

Château du Seuil ☆☆
Puyricard. 55 ha. www.chateauduseuil.fr
A large property quite high in the Coteaux d'Aix and prone to spring frost. The best wines are the Grand Seuil range. Quality improved dramatically in the late 1990s.

Château Simone ☆☆
Palette, Meyreuil. 17 ha. www.chateau-simone.fr
One of two properties in the tiny AC Palette, and owned by the sixth generation of the Rougier family. The estate provides local restaurants with a very satisfactory specialty: slightly but agreeably rustic wines that really taste of the herbs and pines of the countryside.

On average, the vines are 60 years old. The red ages well; the Clairette-dominated white could be considered an acquired taste, but often gains in grandeur after a few years in bottle. The rosé is lovely.

Châteaux Elie Sumeire ☆
Trets. 140 ha. www.chateaux-elie-sumeire.fr
The Sumeire family owns three estates (Château Coussin Ste-Victoire, Château de Maupague, and Château l'Afrique), in different parts of the Côtes de Provence appellation, making it one of the appellation's largest landowners . Whites and rosés are sold young, but they make a practice of ageing reds for a period of between six months and two years.

Domaine de Triennes ☆–☆☆
Nans-les-Pins. 44 ha. www.triennes.com
This estate in Coteaux Varois has distinguished Burgundian co-owners: the de Villaines of Romanée-Conti and the Seysses of Domaine Dujac. Since Dujac ages its wines in new oak, the domaine provides a useful outlet for those used but good-quality barrels. Viognier and Syrah are the top wines here, together with the St-Auguste blend of Cabernet, Merlot, and Syrah.

Château Les Valentines ☆–☆☆
La Londes-les-Maures. 40 ha.
www.lesvalentines.com
Until 1997 the crop from this domaine between Toulon and St-Tropez was sold to the local cooperative. The top *cuvée* Les Bagnards carries a good deal of oak, and many will find the simpler, fruiter blends more appealing.

Château Vignelaure ☆
Rians. 60 ha. www.vignelaure.com
The first estate to show that inland Provence could produce very good wines of more than local interest. Georges Brunet arrived from the Médoc in the 1960s and planted Cabernet with the local vines. Although seen as making the best wine in the Coteaux d'Aix, Brunet sold the property in the mid-1980s, and thereafter quality declined as a succession of new owners arrived.

In 1998, the Irish O'Brien family became sole owners, having previously benefitted from the advice of co-owner and itinerant winemaker, Hugh Ryman. Strict selection restored quality, and O'Brien introduced La Colline de Vignelaure, a rich, new-oaked Merlot. However, in 2008 the property was sold to a new Swedish owner, Bengt Sundström.

The Midi

The arc of country from the Spanish border to the mouth of the Rhône may well be France's oldest vineyard. It is certainly its biggest. Until about 15 years ago, uncountable quantities of unwanted wine were pumped from its plains, to the despair of politicians all over Europe. Traditions of better wine-growing had persisted in the hills, but at such economic disadvantage that there seemed little future for them.

But times have changed. The best local traditions, and varieties, are being retained but are being grafted onto new techniques to produce – at last – some memorable Midi wines. Interest and investment from, among other places, Australia has made the locals sit up and take notice. The region is now coming to life again: the Languedoc hills, Corbières and Minervois, and also Roussillon.

Not until the 1960s did far-sighted growers and investors realize that the soils and climate of these sun-drenched slopes had enormous potential. The penny dropped at the same time as California rose from its slumber. In the Midi, low morale, bureaucracy, peasant conservatism, and typically complicated land ownership have all been brakes on progress. The French way is to move cautiously along established lines: to improve wines, not to change them. A major impediment to improvement has been the power, now in decline, of the cooperatives. Its members had grown used to harvesting as early as possible, tractoring the grapes over to the co-op, and then going hunting for the rest of the year. The fact that their grapes were poor and the wines unsaleable troubled them not a bit. To this day, these stubborn growers refuse to recognise the reality of competition from more dynamic regions and wineries, especially from their southern neighbour, Spain.

Upgrading started with the winemaking process, and then spread to the marketing of its produce. The introduction of *macération carbonique* was the vital first step. It extracted from dull grapes, such as Carignan, juicy flavours that nobody knew were there. The process is now a long way down the road, and a handsome list has emerged of properties and cooperatives with good wine to offer, from the "aromatic" grapes that the public want. It is now the estates rather than the cooperatives that lead the way in quality, although the best co-ops are tailoring their production and packaging to a generation of wine-drinkers seeking good, fruity wines at fair prices.

The Midi of quality wine divides into four distinct regions. Following the right-hand curve of the coast north from the Spanish border, they are: Roussillon in the Pyrénéan foothills, once famous for sweet apéritif and dessert wines but now gaining a reputation for some forceful and impressive reds; Corbières, red wine country; Minervois in the southernmost foothills of the Cévennes, also best-known for red wine; and the scattered Coteaux du Languedoc, producing red, white, and rosé in quality ranging from dire *vin ordinaire* to magnificent.

Precisely what constitutes a quality area and which are the "right" grapes for it are studied here with as much Gallic precision as on the slopes of Beaune. It is not long since VDQS was the senior rank in these parts. Now many areas have been promoted to AC as their true potential becomes evident. Unfortunately the downside is that this proliferation of appellations and sub-appellations has left even wine professionals, not to mention consumers, confused. This is also the country of the *vin de pays*. Pages 238–41 give details of the innumerable "country-wine" districts.

But to sell your wine as a *vin de pays* is also an interesting alternative to growers who find the panoply of appellation too oppressive. There is a danger of the situation arising, which Italy already knows, where the bright pioneer believes (and rightly) that his wine is more important than its label. Some of the best wines of the Midi are sold as *vin de pays* simply because Cabernet or Merlot is not cricket under the existing rules. Many estates pursue a policy of compromise: retaining AC labelling for their traditional wines, while opting for more commercial varietal wines, picked at higher yields, for their *vin de pays* ranges.

Roussillon

The wines of the baking Roussillon enjoy the prestige of an ancient and unique product, its *vin doux naturel*, practically unknown outside France, but so proud of its origins that it sees port (the equivalent) as an imposter. Unfortunately these immense quantities of Muscat and fortified Grenache are difficult to sell. Even wines kept to mellow maturity in large casks for 20 years or more have to be offered at ridiculously low prices. What has been drawing new investors, and not only from France, to Roussillon is the enormous potential for red wines. The soils, often schist, are remarkable, giving wines of great virility and character.

The sheltered seaside hills around Perpignan, and inland up the valleys of the Agly and the Tet, make some formidable reds. The best examples, based on Grenache, Syrah, Mourvèdre, and old Carignan, can have some of the structure of, for example, Châteauneuf-du-Pape, though with more roundness and a softer texture. More and more growers are deliberately ageing in oak and sometimes in bottle, too, to add complexity to beef.

The best wines are entitled to the Côtes du Roussillon (5,745 hectares) or the Côtes du Roussillon-Villages (2,190 hectares divided among 32 communes) ACs. Rosés remain commercially important – an astonishing 60 per cent of Côtes du Roussillon production is still rosé – even if quality often leaves much to be desired. At the same time, growers such as Gérard Gauby (q.v.) and Domaine des Chênes are showing what can be done with white grapes, even in this very hot region. Recent years have seen a growth in sub-appellations, largely at the behest of cooperatives. The following villages now have the right to attach their names to Côtes du Roussillon-Villages: Aspres, Caramany, Latour de France, Lesquerde, and Tautavel. Each comes complete with a complex set of rules and regulations. This may explain why so many leading properties are now choosing to bottle their wines as Vin de Pays Côtes Catalanes.

One small, red-wine area at the seaside resort of Collioure (600 hectares) on the Spanish border, has had its own appellation since 1949 for a singular, concentrated wine in which

Carignan plays little part: a blend principally of Mourvèdre and Grenache Noir, with intense flavours unlike anything else north of the Spanish border. From 2003 INAO authorized the inclusion of white wines within the AC.

The *vins doux naturels* apparently owe their origin to the revered figure of Arnaldo da Villanova, the thirteenth-century sage and doctor of Montpellier, who introduced the still from Moorish Spain. It was he who first added *eau de vie* to naturally strong wine to stop the fermentation and maintain a high degree of natural sugar – hence the term *doux naturels*. But whereas in port, the *eau de vie* represents a fifth of the volume and more than half the alcoholic strength, in *vins doux naturels* it is limited to ten per cent of the volume, while the natural strength of the wine has, by law, to reach no less than 15 degrees. It is not for a foreigner, with the privilege of an education in port, to hold forth on the qualities of *vins doux naturels*. Aged, they acquire an oxidized flavour known by the Spanish term *rancio*. Traditional producers age them in 30-litre, pear-shaped glass jars known as *bonbonnes* (again, from the Spanish: *bombonas*). *Vin doux naturel* is made in many different styles and varying degrees of sweetness and age. Some esteemed examples can be aged for as long as 20 years or more in large casks. As well as Grenache blends sold as Rivesaltes (5,590 hectares), Banyuls (1,173 hectares), or Maury (507 hectares), or as the single-varietal Muscat de Rivesaltes (5,117 hectares), there is a growing fashion for "vintage" styles, closely modelled on vintage port. These are often called *rimage*.

Leading Roussillon Producers

Cave de l'Abbé Rous ☆–☆☆☆
Banyuls-sur-Mer. www.abberous.com
A cooperative twinned with the Cellier des Templiers (q.v.) that specializes in high-quality Collioure and Banyuls in a full range of styles. The primary market is retailers and restaurants, whereas the Cellier furnishes private customers.

Agly Brothers ☆☆
Latour de France. 7 ha.
A collaboration that began in 2003 between Michel Chapoutier of the Rhône and Ron Laughton of Jasper Hill (q.v.) in Victoria. The backbone of the one wine is Carignan planted in 1902, plus Grenache and Syrah. Stirring stuff: with fine red-fruits aromas, and stylish tannins.

Mas Amiel ☆☆☆
Maury. 155 ha,
The appellation's best producer, offering traditional, cask-aged Maury, as well as the modern vintage style. Under Charles Dupuy, quality improved steadily throughout the 1990s. After his death in 1999, Mas Amiel was bought by Olivier Decelle, a frozen-food tycoon who also owns a number of properties in Bordeaux. At Mas Amiel he has expanded the range without compromising the quality. As well as the superb fortified wines, he is now producing excellent Côtes du Roussillon, white and red, including the powerful, oak-aged Cuvée Carérades.

Cave des Vignerons de Baixas ☆–☆☆☆
Baixas. 2,100 ha. www.dom-brial.com
Founded in 1923, this is an important cooperative, producing a comprehensive range of wines from all permitted styles, still and fortified. Dom Brial is its brand name, Château Les Pins its top label. By far the largest producer of Muscat de Rivesaltes.

Mas Baux ☆
Canet-en-Roussillon. 12 ha. www.mas-baux.com
Almost entirely replanted in 1999, this relatively new property keeps yields low to compensate for the youth of most of the vines. Supple wines for medium-term drinking. Soleil Rouge is the best Côtes du Roussillon, and is aged in 500-litre barrels for a year.

Domaine Bila-Haut ☆☆
Latour de France. 65 ha.
Michel Chapoutier's Biodynamic property produces two good-value Côtes du Roussillon-Villages: one unoaked and the other, Occultus Lapidem, a partly oak-aged blend of Grenache, Carignan, and Syrah.

Domaine Boudau ☆–☆☆☆
Rivesaltes. 52 ha. www.domaineboudau.fr
A large property best known for its Muscat and Rivesaltes, although in recent years the range of Côtes du Roussillon has been expanding. Dependable quality.

Château de Caladroy ☆
Bélesta. 130 ha. www.caladroy.com
A large estate, with a beautiful twelfth-century castle. It produced humdrum wines until the late 1990s, when quality took a turn for the better and some oak-ageing was introduced.

Domaine Calvet-Thunevin ☆☆–☆☆☆
Maury. 16 ha. www.thunevin.com
In 2000 Jean-Luc Thunevin of St-Emilion teamed up with local grower Jean-Roger Calvet to acquire some vineyards on outstanding schist soils. Quality is high, but so are the prices. Most of the wines are Côtes du Roussillon-Villages, made to maximum concentration.

Château de Casenove ☆☆–☆☆☆
Trouillas. 50 ha.
Owned by former press photographer Etienne Montès, who has worked closely with oenologist Jean-Luc Colombo to improve quality. The white Côtes du Roussillon is good, if not especially aromatic, and benefits from bottle-age.

Domaine Tour Vieille, Collioure

The top red is usually Cuvée Jaubert: a pure Syrah, partly barrique-aged.

Domaine Cazes ☆☆–☆☆☆
Rivesaltes. 160 ha. www.cazes-rivesaltes.com
The Cazes brothers, leading producers for decades, have continued to modernize their winery and replant their substantial vineyards with Grenache, Syrah, Mourvèdre, and Malvoisie. Their Rivesaltes and Muscat de Rivesaltes are utterly reliable, and the old-cask-aged bottlings such as Cuvée Aimé Cazes are well worth their cost.

In recent years the Cazes have made great progress with their red Côtes du Roussillon and Côtes du Roussillon-Villages. In 1993, they launched Credo, a Cabernet Sauvignon and Merlot *vin de pays*, designed, successfully, to show how well the Bordeaux grapes work in the region. Nonetheless, this remains a better address for *vin doux naturel* than for red wines.

Domaine des Chênes ☆☆–☆☆☆
Vingrau. 30 ha.
Alain Razungles is an oenology professor at Montpellier, so you would expect him to make good wine at the family domaine. And indeed he does, with some rich *cuvées* of Côtes du Roussillon-Villages and some excellent whites based on Grenache Blanc. A fine and consistent range of *vins doux naturels* confirms Razungles' versatility.

Domaine du Clos des Fées ☆☆–☆☆☆
Vingrau. 25 ha. www.closdesfees.com
This ambitious and recently expanded estate focuses on intense and very oaky red Côtes du Roussillon-Villages, using modern techniques such as lees-stirring and micro-oxygenation. The owner, Hervé Bizeuil, was once a sommelier, and clearly has his eye on selling to top restaurants. Fine quality and high prices. Collectors of cult wines might take notice of Petite Sibérie, an old-vine Grenache with a price tag of over €200.

Coume del Mas ☆–☆☆☆
Banyuls-sur-Mer. 10 ha.
The personal property since 2000 of viticulturalist Philippe Gard. The wines include a super-ripe Banyuls aged in 50 per cent new oak called Quintessence, and a Collioure called Quadratur from Gard's top vineyard.

Domaine de la Coume du Roy ☆☆–☆☆☆
Maury. 25 ha. www.lacoumeduroy.com
An old property that specializes in concentrated *vins doux naturels*, and still offers vintages back to the 1920s.

L'Etoile ☆–☆☆☆
Banyuls-sur-Mer. 152 ha.
This cooperative was founded in 1921, and produces an enormous range of Banyuls and red and rosé Collioure. Most of the wines are cask-aged, and older examples are aromatic and subtle, with echoes of orange, coffee, and caramel. Vintage styles are also made, but not every year.

Domaine Ferrer-Ribière ☆–☆☆
Terrats. 44 ha.

A large property producing a very complete range of wines, with the reds so far more convincing than the whites. The top wines are the most traditional, being made from old vines of Grenache and Carignan.

Domaine Fontanel ☆–☆☆
Tautavel. 35 ha.
A wide and competently made range of wines from a forward-looking estate. Le Prieuré is particularly stylish, combining Syrah and Grenache and being aged in new oak for 18 months.

Domaine Força-Réal ☆☆
Millas. 40 ha. www.forca-real.com
In a spectacular mountainside setting, Jean-Paul Henríques produces red and white Côtes du Roussillon and Rivesaltes from a vineyard that he has restored and replanted since 1989.

The second wine of the estate is the easy-drinking Mas de la Garrigue, while the top wine is the wood-aged Les Hauts de Força-Réal. His pride is a caramel-and-coffee-flavoured Rivesaltes Hors d'Age.

Domaine Gardiès ☆☆–☆☆☆
Vingrau. 30 ha. www.domaine-gardies.fr
Since the early 1990s, Jean Gardiès has produced some delicious Côtes du Roussillon-Villages, especially the Grenache-dominated Tautavel. The estate takes pride in its Cuvée La Torre, given tannic backbone by its high proportion of Mourvèdre.

Domaine Gauby ☆☆☆–☆☆☆☆
Calce. 42 ha.
Gérard Gauby makes a fascinating collection of wines, including red and white Côtes du Roussillon in various blends, and *vin de pays*, some of them partially aged in new barriques. The white Vin de Pays des Côtes Catalanes (a blend of Carignan Blanc, Grenache Blanc, and Maccabéo) sells for more than the Côtes du Roussillon.

Vines that are 50 years old produce Vieilles Vignes. Muntada is Roussillon's most remarkable Syrah, infused with flavours of red fruits. Production is limited to around 7,000 cases, as Gauby's selection policy dispatches 60 per cent of the crop to the local cooperative.

Château de Jau ☆☆
Cases de Péné. 134 ha.
The Dauré family own a trio of excellent properties in the region. At Jau, they make some of the best Côtes du Roussillon, plus outstanding Muscat, and good whites of Malvoisie and Maccabéo. The Côtes du Roussillon-Villages is a blend dominated by Syrah and Mourvèdre. Their other estates are the 80-hectare Clos des Paulilles, which produces Collioure and Banyuls, and Mas Cristine, which focuses on Rivesaltes.

Domaine de Madeloc ☆☆
Banyuls-sur-Mer. 24 ha.
The Roussillon outpost of northern Rhône winemaker Pierre Gaillard. Although some Banyuls is made, the focus here is on different *cuvées* of Collioure, white as well as red.

Domaine du Mas Blanc ☆☆☆
Banyuls-sur-Mer. 21 ha. www.domainedumasblanc.com

The late Dr. André Parcé was for many years the leading producer of Banyuls and Collioure (and in his role as a member of the INAO inner circles, notorious for his opposition to the promotion of Château Mouton-Rothschild to *premier cru* status). The property is now run by his son, Jean-Michel. Its range of wines is still traditional, and includes rare styles such as Banyuls Blanc, Banyuls Dry, and a solera-aged wine. In the 1980s, Dr. Parcé re-terraced his Collioure vineyards at immense cost, and the estate produces a number of different *cuvées* of this powerful red wine.

Domaine du Mas Crémat ☆☆–☆☆☆
Espira de l'Agly. 30 ha. www.mascremat.com
Owned by the Burgundian Jeannin-Mongeard family since 1990, this estate produces white and red Côtes du Roussillon from dark schist and limestone soils. The barrique-fermented Grenache Blanc is remarkable.

Domaine Matassa ☆☆
Fenouillèdes. 16 ha.
New Zealander Sam Harrop, a consultant winemaker, and South African Tom Lubbe, who worked at Domaine Gauby (q.v.) and is now the owner's son-in-law, teamed up to produce wines from various parcels of vines, which they farm Biodynamically. Both red and white are sold as *vin de pays*, the red mostly Grenache, the white a blend of Grenache Blanc and Maccabéo. The winemakers rein in the new oak so as to allow the splendid vineyards to shine through in the wines.

Vignerons de Maury ☆–☆☆
Maury. 400 ha.
www.vigneronsdemaury.com
Founded 1910, this substantial cooperative produces much of the Maury output, and first introduced the vintage style of Maury in 1982. The top *cuvée*, the vintage Chabert, is predominantly Grenache. A large volume of Côtes du Roussillon and *vins de pays* is also made.

Vignerons de Pézilla ☆
Pézilla-La-Rivière. 600 ha.
www.vins-roussillon-pezilla.com
One of the more dynamic cooperatives in the region, producing a fascinating selection of *vins de pays* (including Chardonnay and Viognier) as well as Côtes du Roussillon and a range of Rivesaltes at very modest prices.

Domaine Piétri-Géraud ☆☆
Collioure. 28 ha.
A small, mother-and-daughter estate producing unfiltered Collioure from Grenache and Syrah, as well as cask-aged Banyuls and Muscat de Rivesaltes.

Domaine Piquemal ☆–☆☆
Espira de l'Agly. 50 ha.
www.domaine-piquemal.com
In a series of cellars in the centre of Espira de l'Agly, Pierre Piquemal makes a wide range of wines, including a Merlot-dominated red, rosé, and a Muscat Sec. Recent vintages of Côtes du Roussillon have been vinified in wood and emphasize soft tannins and ripe fruit. Some of the wines have lacked character in recent vintages. Also Rivesaltes.

Olivier Pithon ☆☆
Calce. 15 ha. www.domaineolivierpithon.com
Since the late 1990s Pithon has acquired vineyards close to those of his friend and mentor Gérard Gauby. The labelling system, for *vins de pays* as well as Côtes du Roussillon, is needlessly complicated here, but the wines are first-rate, thanks to exceptionally low yields and a winemaking style that avoids excess.

Domaine La Pleiade ☆☆
St Paul de Fenouillet. 12 ha.
www.domaine.la.pleiade.free.fr
A small property, owned by the former director of the Maury cooperative. As well as Maury from pure Grenache Noir, there is a little Côtes du Roussillon-Villages.

Domaine Pouderoux ☆☆
Maury. 16 ha.
A well-established property that shows mastery of Maury in various styles, vintage as well as traditionally aged.

La Préceptorie de Centernach ☆☆–☆☆☆
St-Arnac. 28 ha. www.la-rectorie.com
A joint venture between local grower Vincent Legrand and La Rectorie (q.v.), allowing the latter to work with the superb vineyards of Maury as well as its local Collioure soils. The vintage Maury, Aurélie Pereira, is superb, its power moderated by peppery vigour, and the white and red Côtes du Roussillon also reach considerable heights.

Domaine de la Rectorie ☆☆–☆☆☆
Banyuls-sur-Mer. 25 ha.
www.la-rectorie.com
Marc and Thierry Parcé run this excellent estate, which produces some of the finest Collioure and a range of Banyuls. There are also some *vin de pays* using varieties and blends not authorized for AC wines. Two unusual wines are the l'Oriental, from superripe grapes without the addition of spirit; and Fleur de Pierre, a dry, *rancio* style made by a solera system.

Domaine Sarda-Malet ☆☆–☆☆☆
Perpignan. 50 ha.
www.sarda-malet.com
This estate, run by the dynamic Suzy Malet and her son Jérôme, specializes in Côtes du Roussillon and Rivesaltes *vin doux naturel*. There are two Côtes du Roussillon whites, made from a blend of Grenache, Roussanne, Marsanne, Malvoisie, and Maccabéo grapes – one is tank-fermented and the other (Terroir Mailloles) is vinified in wood. The top wine is a Syrah/Mourvèdre blend, also called Terroir Mailloles, that is aged in new oak. The include a fine vintage Rivesaltes, La Carbasse, and Muscat de Rivesaltes.

Domaine des Schistes ☆☆
Estagel. 45 ha. www.domaine-des-schistes.com
Jacques Sire left the local cooperative in 1989. Since going solo, he has made some truly remarkable red wines from his schist soils. The best wine is Les Terrasses from 60 per cent Syrah, plus Carignan, and Grenache, which is aged in 30 per cent new oak.

Domaine Le Soula ☆☆–☆☆☆
St Martin-de-Fenouillet. 19 ha.
A joint venture between Gerard Gauby (q.v.) and partners that include British wine merchant Roy Richards. The range is simple: two *vins de pays*, white and red, from organic vineyards. These are mountain wines from steep slopes that are farmed Biodynamically. Although they are aged in 50 per cent new oak, the wood is scarcely perceptible thanks to their concentration and intensity of fruit.

Les Maîtres Vignerons de Tautavel ☆
Tautavel. 330 ha.
www.vignerons-tautavel.com
Founded in 1927, this cooperative makes, among other wines, fine Côtes du Roussillon-Villages red, including an oak-aged version, and rich Rivesaltes.

Cellier des Templiers ☆–☆☆☆
Banyuls-sur-Mer. 1,200 ha. www.banyuls.com
This is a large-scale operation, uniting eight cooperatives. Consequently, it dominates the Collioure and Banyuls areas. Together with its sister operation, Abbé Rous (q.v.), it produces and markets about 80 per cent of the two appellations. Unlike Abbé Rous, the Cellier markets its wines primarily to private customers. There has been considerable investment in equipment, and the general quality is good. There are 19 different styles of Banyuls on offer, mostly traditional but also *rimage*, and 15 Collioures.

Domaine Tour Vieille ☆☆–☆☆☆
Collioure. 13 ha.
Christine Campadieu and Vincent Cantié have together developed one of the best estates in the region. There are usually two *cuvées* of Collioure: one a Grenache/Syrah blend, the other from Grenache and Mourvèdre.
A specialty is Cap de Creus, a dry, *rancio* style which Mme. Campadieu says is one of the traditional wines of the region: dry and very strong.

Domaine Vaquer ☆–☆☆
Tresserre. 30 ha.
The unusual specialty here is a white Maccabéo that can age for 15 years without difficulty. The top red wines are L'Exception and Cuvée Fernand Vaquer, which is mostly old-vine Carignan aged two years in oak. All the wines are *vin de pays*.

Domaine des Vents ☆☆
St Paul-de-Fenouillet. 16 ha.
Although only established in 2004, this domaine has already won great acclaim for its Côtes du Roussillon Clos des Vents, an oak-aged blend of Grenache and Carignan, with a dash of Syrah.

Domaine Vial Magnères ☆☆
Banyuls-sur-Mer. 10 ha.
This small estate is run by a former food chemist, Bernard Sapéras, and his son Olivier. It produces good Collioure as well as various styles of Banyuls. His best wine is usually Al Tragou, a *rancio* wine from Grenache Noir, made by a partial solera method.

Corbières

Corbières is a huge region, stretching from Narbonne inland almost to Carcassonne, and the same distance south to the borders of Roussillon. It rises and rolls in parched hills of pale limestone, suddenly embroidered in bold patterns with the green stitches of vines. The neutral Carignan grape has long been dominant, but must not now exceed 50 per cent of the blend. Syrah, Mourvèdre, and Grenache are blended with it.

A good site, combined with restraint in cropping and careful winemaking, make solid enough wines, but all too often they lack flavour and flair. Improvements are taking the form of winemaking with *macération carbonique* to coax at least an illusion of fruitiness from the grapes, and – more radically – replanting with varieties with more personality than Carignan. (Old-vine Carignan, however, is much prized). There is also greater use of wood (for fermenting and maturing) to add an extra taste component and structure to the wines. A small but significant growth of white wine in the region is notable, some of it barrel-fermented and oak-aged. However, red wine still accounts for 95 per cent of production, with three per cent being rosé and only two per cent white.

There are some big properties as well as the thousands of growers who contribute to the cooperatives. Two areas in the southeast corner of Corbières, largely co-op country, have long enjoyed the appellation Fitou for their reds on the grounds that they are more ageworthy than the rest. There are 2,600 hectares entitled to the Fitou AC, though the wines can be labelled Corbières should the producers so wish.

There has also been a more recent division of the Corbières appellation into 11 different zones to highlight the varying terroir; the climate ranges from maritime to arid. These are Montagne d'Alaric, St Victor, Fontfroide, Queribus, Boutenac, Termenès, Lézignan, Lagrasse, Sigean, Durban, and Serviès.

The main challenge to growers is combating rusticity. Although the region is vast and varied, much of it is dry and harsh, and finesse in the wines can be hard to achieve. Naturally there are exceptions, and a growing number of them, but it still seems to be the case that Corbières as a whole is lagging behind Roussillon, St Chinian, and parts of the Coteaux du Languedoc. On the other hand, growers have resisted the temptation to produce micro-*cuvées* at inflated prices, and the wines are among the most reasonably priced of southern France.

Leading Corbières Producers

Château Aiguilloux ☆–☆☆
Thézan-des-Corbières. 38 ha.
www.chateau-aiguillou.com
The self-taught François Lemarié runs this estate, employing carbonic maceration to produce structured, tannic red and fresh, fruity rosé.

Château d'Aussières ☆–☆☆
Narbonne. 158 ha. www.lafite.com
The Rothschilds of Château Lafite own this immense property, which they have replanted since 1999. These are

attracting medium-term wines with some finesse, and the white *vin de pays* is pure, unoaked Chardonnay.

Domaine Bertrand-Bergé ☆☆
Paziols. 33 ha. www.bertrand-berge.com
This Fitou estate was already commercialising its wines in the nineteenth century, so it is not surprising that the average age of its vines is 60 years. Four different *cuvées* are produced, from the unoaked Tradition to the excellent barrique-aged Jean Sirven, which is half composed of old-vine Carignan.

Château Borde-Rouge ☆☆
Lagrasse. 23 ha. www.borde-rouge.com
This property, which has always aimed at high quality, changed hands in 2005 and the range has been revamped. The basic wines are called Rubellis, the prestige range Carminal, and the top wine is Ange, first made in 2002 and well received.

Cave des Vignerons de Camplong ☆–☆☆
Camplong-d'Aude. 300 ha. www.camplong.com
A cooperative, intelligently run for many years by Odile Denat, that makes the best use of its members' mostly Grenache and Carignan vines, skilfully supplemented with Syrah and Mourvèdre. Peyres Nobles is the principal range, made in all three colours and sold at a very reasonable price.

Château de Caraguilhes ☆☆
St-Laurent-de-la-Cabrerisse. 135 ha. www.caraguilhes.fr
A large organic estate bought in 2005 by Pierre Gabison. As well as a standard Corbières, the property produces two special *cuvées*: Prestige and Solus. The Prestige spends nine months in barriques; Solus is a special selection, half of it Carignan. The top *cuvées* used to be over-oaked, but recent vintages show more fruit.

Château Cascadais ☆☆
St-Laurent-de-la-Cabrerisse. 34 ha.
This property is owned by Philippe Courrian of Château Tour Haut-Caussan (q.v.) in the Médoc. The red is given some cautious ageing in new oak.

Clos de l'Anhel ☆☆
Lagrasse. 10 ha. www.anhel.fr
Philippe Matthias is the winemaker of Château Pech-Latt (q.v.), and since 2000 this has been his personal property. "Anhel", incidentally, is local dialect for "agneau" or lamb. The various *cuvées* are stylish and avoid the pitfalls of over-extraction. Matthias favours micro-oxygenation during vinification, and little new oak is used, except for a proportion of the top *cuvée*, Les Dimanches.

Cave d'Embres et Castelmaure ☆–☆☆
Embres-et-Castelmaure. 340 ha.
A well-run co-op, using modern techniques such as micro-oxygenation to moderate the rusticity of the Carignan. The best wines include the Cuvée Pompadour, aged in barrique but without new oak, and the Grande Cuvée from Syrah and Grenache. In an enterprising move, the co-op has taken on Michel Tardieu of Tardieu-Laurent (q.v.) as a consultant.

Château Etang des Colombes ☆☆
Lézignan. 77 ha. www.etangdescolombes.com

At an estate well stocked with old vines, Christophe Gualco produces a variety of wines, of which the best is the barrique-aged Cuvée Bois des Dames .

Domaine de Fontsainte ☆☆–☆☆☆
Boutenac. 45 ha. www.fontsainte.com
Yves Laboucarié was one of the region's most dedicated and scrupulous winemakers, benefiting from excellent and varied vineyards. He is now succeeded by his son Bruno. The Domaine wine has limited oak-ageing, and the Réserve La Demoiselle is made from centenarian vines and aged in older barriques for 12 months. In 1999 he introduced Clos du Centurion, mostly from old Carignan, and also aged in barriques.

Château Gléon-Montanié ☆☆–☆☆☆
Villesèque-des-Corbières. 50 ha.
www.gleon-montanie.com
The Montanié family's wines are marked by their vigour and liveliness. The top Cuvée Gascon Bonnes is more extracted, with rich fruit and dense tannins. But it is hard to beat the regular Corbières for vivid, peppery character.

Domaine du Grand Arc ☆☆–☆☆☆
Padern. 14 ha. www.domaine-grand-arc.com
Owner/winemaker Bruno Schenk comes from Alsace, which could hardly be more different from this region. He offers numerous bottlings. Réserve is unoaked, as is La Fleurine, which contains 65 per cent Carignan; Cuvée des Quarante is mostly Grenache and Syrah, aged in oak. His *vin de garde* is Aux Temps d'Histoire, an opulent pure Carignan.

Château du Grand Caumont ☆☆
Lézignan. 100 ha. www.grandcaumont.com
The Rigal family's old estate near the River Orbieu has been energetically modernized. The Cuvée Tradition is made by carbonic maceration, and the St Paul Cuvée Prestige is based on a selection of old Carignan vines.

Domaine du Grand Crès ☆☆–☆☆☆
Ferrals. 15 ha.
Hervé Leferrer is no fan of carbonic maceration and all his red grapes are de-stemmed. The Cuvée Classique is aged in older barrels. The ripe, fleshy Cuvée Majeureis made from low-yielding Syrah and Grenache, and aged in 25 per cent new oak which confers some discreet, deft, oak character. The estate also makes one of Corbières' better whites, an unwooded *vin de pays* from Viognier and Roussanne.

Château Grand Moulin ☆☆–☆☆☆
Lézignan. 60 ha. www.chateau-grand-moulim.com
Jean-Noel Bousquet started bottling his own wines from 1988. All the reds are de-stemmed. The two top reds are the Fûts de Chêne Vieilles Vignes; and Terres Rouges, with a higher proportion of Syrah in the blend. Both are aged in up to 50 per cent new oak. The result are supple, but peppery and smoky reds, with a great deal of character and concentration. The oaked white is heavy.

Château Haut-Gléon ☆☆–☆☆☆
Villesèque-des-Corbières. 29 ha. www.hautgleon.com

The Duhamel family are keen on oak-ageing for their best wines. The result is a rather clumsy white from Bourboulenc and Roussanne, but the Syrah-dominated Cuvée Cairo is very fine: slightly gamey on the nose, but with sleek red fruits on the palate. The buildings of the estate include a twelfth-century chapel, but the winery itself is thoroughly modern.

Château Hélène ☆☆
Barbaira. 40 ha.
Marie-Hélène Gau was a reliable producer of Corbières for many years. Her wines were named after Greek heroes and heroines: Cuvée Penelope had a good dose of Syrah; Cuvée Ulysse was a more traditional blend, aged in older barriques; and Cuvée Hélène de Troie was mostly Syrah, aged in new oak. There was also a white Hélène de Troie from Grenache Blanc and Roussanne. In 2001, Mme. Gau sold the estate to Robert Baudoin, who has maintained her classical range.

Château de Lastours ☆☆–☆☆☆
Portel-des-Corbières. 100 ha.
www.chateaudelastours.com
This remarkable estate is based around a centre for the mentally handicapped, most of whom are employed on the estate. The vines are planted in a kind of sheltered bowl surrounded by rugged hills that provided the former director with tracks for four-wheel-drive races. But the wines are serious. The Cuvée Simone Descamps and Arnaud de Berre are complex reds with ageing potential. In top vintages it produces a very powerful, barrique-aged red, called simply Château de Lastours. In 2004 the property was bought by the Filhet-Allard insurance group, which has invested in new equipment but, so far, has left range and quality unaltered.

Château Mansenoble ☆☆☆
Moux. 20 ha. www.mansenoble.com
Guido Jansegers abandoned his career as a journalist in Belgium in 1992 in order to pursue his love of wine. Mansenoble is now one of the region's top estates, which Jansegers attributes to his fanatical selective harvesting, ensuring that only fully ripe grapes are picked. No carbonic maceration is used. Cuvée Marie-Annick is based on Grenache and Syrah but has a good dose of Mourvèdre in the blend. Many of the wines receive some oak-ageing but Jansegers is careful to retain a proportion in tanks to preserve freshness.

Domaine de Montjoie ☆
St-André-de-la-Cabrerisse. 40 ha.
Replanting has improved the vineyards, which deliver a stylish, full-flavoured red and a light rosé.

Château de Nouvelles ☆
Tuchan. 76 ha. www.chateaudenouvelles.com
This Fitou estate, half of which is planted with Carignan, was once known for solid and rather rustic wines. A new generation has refreshed the range, adding a Cuvée Gabrielle

aged in new oak, although there is still a substantial production of Muscat and Rivesaltes too.

Château les Ollieux Romanis ☆–☆☆
Boutenac. 95 ha. www.chateaudesollieux.com
This estate has grown by absorbing its neighbour, Château des Ollieux, in 2006. The range is fairly classic, with an unoaked Classique bottling, and a wooded Cuvée d'Or, with various compromises in between. But quality is set to improve.

Château les Palais ☆–☆☆
St-Laurent-de-la-Cabrerisse. 100 ha.
This estate made a name for itself when it pioneered the use of carbonic maceration for Corbières back in the 1960s. It continues to make soft, fresh, fruity Carignan-dominated wines, which have made it one of the most familiar Corbières names.

Château Pech Latt ☆☆
Lagrasse. 120 ha.
A fine, former monastic property, owned by Burgundy négociant Louis Max, with a wide range of red, rosé, and white wines. The basic white is pure Marsanne and lacks excitement. Among the reds, the best is Cuvée Alix from 50-year-old vines, with its soft, black fruits richness. However, the reliable oak-aged Vieilles Vignes is good value.

Domaine des Pensées Sauvages
Albas. 11 ha.
This estate, bought in 1989 by English anthropologist Nick Bradford, concentrated mostly on one wine: a red Corbières aged in barriques and larger wood. In 2008 he retired and the future of the property is uncertain.

Roque Sestiére ☆–☆☆
Luc-sur-Orbieu. 10 ha.
Roland Lagarde focuses mostly on well-crafted white wines from local varieties such as Grenache Blanc Malvoisie, and Maccabéo.

Château St-Auriol ☆☆–☆☆☆
Lagrasse. 40 ha. www.saint-auriol.com
Red Corbières is the principal wine from this highly regarded estate run by Claude Vialade. She is a great proponent of the different terroirs of Corbières, as she also owns three other properties in the region. The wines are generous and fruity with no rusticity. In the late 1990s, a new *cuvée* was introduced: La Folie de St-Auriol, aged in mostly new oak, but balanced by refreshing acidity.

Château de Vaugelas ☆
Camplong. 110 ha. www.chateauvaugelas.com
Substantial estate owned by the Bonfils family. The top wine, aged in oak for 12 months, is simply called "V".

Les Vignerons du Mont Tauch ☆☆–☆☆☆☆
Tuchan. 1,950 ha. www.mont-tauch.com

Château la Voulte-Gasparets, Boutenac

This very successful cooperative has recently swallowed up some of its neighbouring co-ops such as Paziols and Fitou. Quality is ensured by ruthless selection once the grapes arrive at the winery. There are many wines from single domaines, such as the excellent Château de Ségures, and impressive *prestige cuvées* such as L'Exception, aged 21 months in oak. A range of individual village and individual vineyard wines has been added to an already extensive list.

Domaine de Villemajou ☆–☆☆
Boutenac. 140 ha. www.gerard-bertrand.com
One of many properties owned by the enterprising Gérard Bertrand. The mainstay of the estate is the supple, enjoyable red, but Bertrand has introduced an expensive *garagiste* wine called La Forge for those who seek a more extracted style.

Château la Voulte-Gasparets ☆☆☆
Boutenac. 56 ha.
Ideal soil, together with careful use of carbonic maceration and wood-ageing, results in rich, supple wines. The Cuvée Romain Pauc is the best and most elegant wine, made mostly from very old Carignan, and given a mere touch of new-oak ageing. Quality from this admired estate, run by Patrick Reverdy and his son Laurent, has been highly consistent for many years.

Crémant de Limoux

The most unexpected and original of all the wines of the Midi is the high-quality sparkling wine of Limoux, tucked away behind Corbières on the upper reaches of the River Aude above Carcassonne. There is substantial evidence that this lonely area of hilly farms produced France's first sparkling wine, about 200 years before Champagne. Local lore pins its origin down to 1531. The wine used to be called Blanquette de Limoux – Blanquette coming not from the colour of the wine but from the white down that covers the underside of the leaves of the Mauzac (alias Blanquette) grape.

Mauzac is the white grape with a slight smell of cider that is the base for the rustic bubbly of Gaillac. (Gaillac was a Roman wine town; its antiquity may be immense.) Whatever its origins, the traditional Limoux formula was Mauzac for sprightliness plus Clairette for mildness, originally just *pétillant*, but now made by the *méthode traditionnelle* to full pressure and extremely high standards of delicate blending. Clairette has dropped out of the blend, having made way for Chenin Blanc and, more importantly, for Chardonnay. The Burgundian grape contributes its full flavour to the best *cuvées*; if Blanquette has a fault, it is a slightly pinched, lemony leanness, which can benefit by plumping out.

There are a number of different styles within Limoux. Crémant de Limoux is a sparkling version, which must have 90 per cent Chenin and Chardonnay; a dash of Mauzac or Pinot Noir is also permitted but rare. The wine must be aged for at least 15 months on its lees. Blanquette must have at least 90 per cent Mauzac, with up to ten per cent Chardonnay; the less frequently encountered Blanquette *méthode ancestrale* is pure Mauzac.

Finally, still wines are permitted under the Limoux AC appellation, which was created in 1993; in 2003, Limoux Rouge was also given AC rank, and must contain at least 50 per cent

Merlot. Unlike the wines of Champagne and Burgundy, those from Limoux are best drunk within a year or two of production.

Seventy per cent of the entire production of the 2,800 hectares under vines is in the hands of the vast and ultra-modern cooperative, the Caves du Sieur d'Arques. Founded in 1946, the co-op now has some 400 members. As well as sparkling wines, it releases numerous Chardonnays from different terroirs and different vineyards, as well as a red blend of Mediterranean and Bordeaux varieties called Occursus. This dynamic cooperative sells some 14 million bottles per year. There are also a number of good individual producers, such as the Domaine de l'Aigle, Château d'Autugnac, Domaine Collin, Jean-Louis Denois, and Domaine Mouscaillo.

Minervois

The River Aude parts the last wrinkles of the Pyrenees from the first of the Massif Central, and Corbières from the Minervois. The Minervois is a 60-five kilometre (40-mile) stretch of its north bank, encompassing both the gravelly flats along the river and the very different hills behind, topped by a plateau at 180 metres (600 feet). Rivers have cut deep ravines in its soft brown rock, in one place leaving a mid-river island for the tiny town of Minerve. The plateau is dry, treeless *garrigue* where the vine struggles, and even the Carignan makes wine with nerves and sinews.

Modern winemaking in the high Minervois has produced some deliciously vital, well-engineered wines with a structure not of old oak beams, as the word *charpente* seems to imply, but more like an air-frame: delicately robust. Some white wines are made here from southern French varieties, but they represent only two per cent of production. The commercial centre of the region is below, on the plain.

AC status was granted to Minervois in 1985, and complex rules defining the varietal make-up of its wines were set in place. More recently, in 1998, Minervois La Livinière was granted its own AC, for red wines only. The defined area covers 2,600 hectares, but at present only 200 are planted; the wine must be aged for at least 15 months before release.

Total area: 18,000 hectares (of which 5,000 are in production) with around 220 private producers and 30 cooperatives. Also produced within the Minervois is the deliciously sweet Muscat de St-Jean-de-Minervois *vin doux naturel* from 195 hectares.

Leading Minervois Producers

Domaine des Aires Hautes ☆☆
Siran. 27 ha.
The vineyard was substantially replanted in the 1970s, but only began bottling its wines in 1991. Syrah is the dominant variety in the two top *cuvées*: Sélection and the plummy Clos de l'Escandil, which is aged in 30 per cent new oak. A house specialty is a pure Malbec.

Domaine de Barroubio ☆☆
St-Jean-de-Minervois. 27 ha. www.barroubio.fr
The estate produces a simple Minervois, but is better known

for its splendid Muscats, especially the very rich, raisiny Cuvée Nicolas, aged two years in wood.

Château Borie du Maurel ☆☆–☆☆☆
Félines-Minervois. 30 ha. www.boriedumaurel.com
Owner Michel Escande believes in keeping yields below 30 hl/ha. The grapes, which are planted in a kind of amphitheatre, are picked at optimal ripeness, so the whites can be both alcoholic and a touch sweet. The regular Minervois is soft and simple; the Cuvée la Féline a sleek wine from 70 per cent Syrah. Cuvée Sylla is pure Syrah in a rather austere style that sells for a high price.

Château Cesseras ☆–☆☆
Cesseras. 65 ha.
The Ournac brothers produce two ranges of wines from this substantial property: *vins de pays* under the Domaine Coudoulet label, and Minervois, rich in Syrah, under the château name. Their La Livinière has delightful freshness of fruit. Bizarrely, some Sangiovese has been planted here.

Clos Centeilles ☆☆–☆☆☆
Siran. 15 ha. www.clos-centeilles.fr
Patricia Boyer-Domergue is passionately committed to this atypical property, which fashions what she regards as highly traditional wines. Carignanissime is a pure old-vine Carignan; Cuvée Capitelle a rare, plummy Cinsault from low-yielding vines. Clos Centeilles itself is a walled vineyard with old Carignan, Syrah, Grenache, and Mourvèdre; its wine is aged two years in older barrels. Sometimes she produces a Pinot Noir, and a botrytis wine from Grenache Gris called Erme de Centeilles.

Clos du Gravillas ☆☆–☆☆☆
St-Jean-de-Minervois. 6.5 ha.
www.closdugravillas.com
John Bojanowski comes from Kentucky and since 1999 has thrown himself with great enthusiasm into cultivating his organic estate. He is a fan of old-vine Carignan, which is used for two of his wines, while his white l'Innattendu is a Grenache Gris, partly fermented in new oak. Not everything succeeds here, but the Carignans and the old-vine blend called Le Rendez-Vous du Soleil are both juicy and concentrated.

Château Coupe-Roses ☆☆
La Caunette. 32 ha. www.coupe-roses.com
Françoise Le Calvez is both owner and winemaker of this property implanted on the sunny hillside of La Caunette. She produces four *cuvées* of Minervois, including two Grenache-dominated wines, Cuvée Granaxa and the sumptuous Cuvée Prestige. Her Cuvée Orience is a leaner, more elegant wine, mostly from Syrah.

Château du Donjon ☆–☆☆
Bagnoles. 45 ha. www.chateau-du-donjon.com
An old family property, now run by Jean Panis. The best wine is the cherryish Cuvée Prestige, a barrique-aged Syrah/Grenache blend. Under the La Gardinière label, he bottles varietal wines from Carignan, Merlot, and Cabernet Sauvignon.

Château de Fabas ☆☆
Laure-Minervois. 55 ha. www.chateaufabas.com
Roland Augustin bought this well-regarded property in 1996. Syrah and Mourvèdre are vital components in most of the cuvées. The top wine, the Mourvèdre-dominated Alexandre has been replaced by Le Mourral, which is Syrah and Grenache, and also aged in oak. The white Seigneur Blanc is a fleshy blend of Vermentino and Roussanne.

Château Faîteau ☆☆
La Livinière. 7 ha. www.chateau-faiteau.leminervois.com
A quality-conscious estate run by Jean-Michel Arnaud, whose Syrah-dominated and barrique-aged La Livinière is exceptionally poised.

Château de Gourgazaud ☆–☆☆
La Livinière. 90 ha. www.gourgazaud.com
Highly influential property that pioneered carbonic maceration in the region. Carignan has more or less disappeared from the vineyards, and been replaced by Syrah and Mourvèdre. Cuvée Mathilde has 80 per cent Syrah; the Réserve is the same wine but aged in new oak. There is also a wide range of *vin de pays* from Cabernet, Chardonnay, Viognier, and other varieties.Roger Piquet died in 2005, and the property is now run by his two daughters, who are determined to maintain his dynamism.

Château la Grave ☆
Badens. 45 ha. www.chateau-la-grave.net
A large property belonging to the Orosquette family, making supple, Syrah-marked blends and aromatic whites. A recent innovation has been an almost pure Grenache called Marie.

Domaine Lignon ☆
Aigues-Vives. 26 ha.
The leading wine is a rounded Syrah called Les Vignes d'Antan made by carbonic maceration.

Château Maris ☆☆–☆☆☆
La Livinière. 40 ha. www.mariswine.com
This important and forward-looking property belongs to Bertie Eden, an enthusiast for Biodynamic farming. As well as a fine La Livinière from Syrah and Grenache, Eden produces two excellent Vieilles Vignes bottlings; one from Carignan, the other, aged in new oak, from Syrah.

L'Ostal Cazes ☆☆
La Livinière. 55 ha.
Jean-Michel Cazes of Château-Bages has developed this substantial property since its first vintage in 2003. As well as the Syrah-dominated La Livinière, there is a less complex and ambitious Minervois, Estibals, with more Grenache and Carignan. Varietals and *vin de pays* are bottled under the Circus brand.

Château d'Oupia ☆☆
Oupia. 40 ha.
André Iche and his daughter Marie have created a range of red wines with more structure than most, as well as a good white from Marsanne and Roussanne. The Cuvée Nobilis, half Syrah and the remainder Grenache and Carignan, is particularly successful and ages well.

Domaine L'Oustal Blanc ☆☆
Creissan. 10 ha.
Powerful and dramatic wines from Claude Fonquerle,
who worked for some years in the Côtes du Ventoux, He
is particularly admired for his whites, which can be a bit
overpowering. Prices are high.

Domaine Piccinini ☆☆
La Livinière. 35 ha. www.domaine-piccinini.com
Maurice Piccinini took a major part in establishing the
La Livinière AC. His own estate is now run by his son,
Jean-Christophe. The regular Minervois is reliable and
fruity, but the best wine is the Syrah-dominated Cuvée
Line et Laetitia.

Domaine La Rouviole ☆–☆☆
Siran. 24 ha.
Red wines only from this Siran property, with a La Livinière
bottling, half Grenache, half Syrah, of particular finesse
at the head of the range.

Château Ste-Eulalie ☆☆
La Livinière. 34 ha.
www.chateausainteeulalie.com
Bought and run by an oenologist couple since 1996, this
fine estate, with its particularly stony soils, produces the
lively Cuvée Cantilène, aged in 40 per cent new oak and
constructed for medium-term drinking.

Jean-Baptiste Senat ☆☆
Trausse-Minervois. 16 ha.
Senat only makes red wines from the estate he has been
running since 1996. La Nine is an unoaked blend of Grenache
and Carignan, whereas his top wine, Le Bois des Merveilles,
blends Grenache with Mourvèdre, discreetly aged in 500-
litre barrels.

Domaine la Tour Boisée ☆☆
Laure-Minervois. 84 ha.
www.domainelatourboisee.com
The energetic Jean-Louis Poudou divides production
between AC wines and single-varietal *vin de pays* directed
mostly at the export market. The most vigorous of the white
wines is the Cuvée Marie-Claude from old vines of local
varieties. Its red counterpart is a Carignan and Syrah in
a round, slightly jammy style.

Château de Villerambert-Julien ☆☆–☆☆☆
Caunes-Minervois. 75 ha.
www.villerambert-julien.com
The Julien family has been working this estate since 1852,
and is a passionate promoter of AC wines. The use of
carbonic maceration was phased out some years ago,
and most of the wines are aged in barriques, though
the Juliens are very sparing in their use of new oak.

The basic range, which is good value, is called Opéra;
the red is warm and supple, the rosé unusually lively and
fresh. The top *cuvée* was formerly called Trianon and
now bears the name of the château, and is usually based
on Syrah. The new *cuvée*, Ourdivieille, is pure Grenache.

Languedoc

The Langudeoc AC, created in 2007, includes the whole of
Roussillon. This section deals with the former Coteaux du
Languedoc, which has disappeared and been replaced either by
the super-AC of Languedoc (so large as to be no more than a
geographical indicator), or by numerous regional appellations.
The latter belong to the villages on the slopes, where all the
best vineyards lie. The plains of the Languedoc between
Narbonne and Montpellier have been a notorious source of
calamitous quantities of low-strength blending wine. The area
is, however, shrinking as growers begin to realize that Europe
no longer has any use for a bottomless wine lake. But certain of
its hillsides have a comparable potential for quality as Corbières
and Roussillon. A dozen areas, which are rather confusingly
scattered across the map, produce worthwhile wines. In the
1980s, one domaine showed what could be done in terms of
extraordinary quality: the highly individual Mas de Daumas
Gassac at Aniane. Now, many other properties are rivalling
Daumas Gassac for renown, quality, and price. The region is
vast, with around around 45,000 hectares within the former
Coteaux du Languedoc.

Even though the Coteaux no longer exists as an official
entity, its numerous sub-appellations do. Certain villages are
recognised as having sufficient identity of their own (in theory)
to justify appending their names to the Languedoc label. They
are: Cabrières, La Méjanelle, Montpeyroux, Picpoul de Pinet,
Quatourze, St-Christol, St-Drézéry, St-Georges-d'Orques,
St-Saturnin and Vérargues. Some of these are now agitating
for independent AC status comparable to that enjoyed by
Faugères, St-Chinian, and Clairette du Languedoc. In addition,
the regulations confusingly recognize "climatic regions", such as
the Terres de Sommières, Terrasses du Larzac, Pézenas, La Clape,
Terrasses de Béziers, Pic-St-Loup, and Grès de Montpellier.

The main concentration of vineyards is to the north of
Béziers, in the first foothills of the Cévennes where the River
Hérault leaves its torrents to become placid and poplar-lined.
Cabrières, Faugères, St-Saturnin are such foothill vineyards.
The best-known of them are Faugères and St-Chinian, in the
hills to the west towards Minervois. Their reds can be full-
bodied, distinctly savoury wines. St-Chinian, partly on chalky
clay and partly on dark-purple schist full of manganese, is worth
careful study.

The variety of soils in these hills gives character to their
wine. The Berlou Valley, on the schist soils, is outstanding
for riper, rounder reds than the rest of the region. The most
individual, and an area with plenty of exciting potential, is La
Clape, the isolated limestone *massif* like a beached island at the
mouth of the River Aude, between Narbonne and the sea. The
soil and climatic conditions on La Clape have shown that they
can produce highly distinctive white wines. Cool sea breezes
give the hills a microclimate of their own. Several domaines
have planted Chardonnay.

St-Saturnin also makes stylish wines, often with a significant
proportion of Syrah. Many growers in the Coteaux now make
use of the *vin de pays* regulations to make such non-conforming
wine as Merlots and Chardonnays, which can be excellent: look

for "domaine" names on labels otherwise identical to those of reputable châteaux. By law "château" must not appear on a *vin de pays* label. Early hopes that such varietal wines would offer a serious challenge to similar wines from the New World have yet to be realized, in part because the regulations permit high yields, giving rise to a sea of fruity but commercial wines with little staying power. The estates listed below are organized in terms, first, of AC regions, and then of the sub-appellations of the Languedoc.

Leading Faugères Producers

This westernmost of the Cévennes foothill districts has some very competent producers of red and rosé. It has been an AC since 1982, covering 2,000 hectares. Rules insist on at least 20 per cent Syrah or Mourvèdre, and a maximum of 40 per cent Carignan. Private estates are important here, and only about half the production pours from the two cooperatives. Quality from the top properties is high, but Faugères is still struggling to assert its own identity within the region as a whole.

Abbaye de Sylva Plana ☆☆
Laurens. 54 ha.
www.vignoblesbouchard.com
Since 2000, excellent Cuvée Songe d'Abbé from old Syrah vines in Faugères.

Domaine Jean-Michel Alquier ☆☆☆
Faugères. 27 ha.
Jean-Michel Alquier runs this impeccable property, which his father founded in the 1950s. (It should not be confused with Domaine Gilbert Alquier, which is run by his brother Frédéric.) Two *cuvées*, Maison Jaune and the Syrah-dominated Les Bastides, are carefully aged in up to 50 per cent new oak. There is nothing exaggerated about these wines, which are among the most elegant of the Languedoc. Impressive white and rosé, too.

Domaine Léon Barral ☆☆–☆☆☆☆
Lentheric. 30 ha.
Didier Barral has been running the family domaine since the early 1990s and has given close attention to his vineyards, drawing on Biodynamic practices without opting for certification. Syrah and Mourvèdre are the mainstays of his best wines, although Grenache and Carignan play their part too. His basic Faugères is designed to be drunk young, whereas *cuvées* Jadis and above all Valinière are structured and powerful and intended to be aged.

Château des Estanilles ☆☆☆
Lenthéric. 35 ha.
Michel Louison is something of a maverick, producing wines to suit his fancy and not too bothered about the niceties of AC regulations. Although his regular Faugères bottlings are very good, he is rightly renowned for his pure Syrah, and for a

remarkable barrique-fermented rosé from Mourvèdre. His daughter, Sophie, is increasingly involved.

Château Grézan ☆–☆☆
Laurens. 10 ha. www.chateau-grezan.fr
A very large property that produces a number of different *cuvées*, mostly oak-aged. Les Schistes Dorés is predominantly Syrah, aged two years in oak, but the Cuvée Vieilles Vignes, which is half Grenache, shows a lighter touch.

Château la Liquière ☆–☆☆☆
Cabrerolles. 60 ha. www.chateaulaliquiere.com
The Vidal family has been producing high-quality wines for many years. Bernard Vidal has been a fan of Carignan from old vines, but only when vinified by carbonic maceration. His best wine, with a high proportion of Syrah, is the concentrated and almost jammy Cuvée Cistus. It is now rivalled by Tucade, which puts Mourvèdre in the foreground.

Domaine de Météore ☆☆
Cabrerolles. 20 ha.
With all its vines planted on schist soils, Météore makes spicy liquorice-scented wines with the emphasis on fruit and vigour rather than striving for complexity. Syrah and Mourvèdre dominate the various *cuvées*.

Château Moulin de Ciffre ☆☆
Autignac. 40 ha.
The Lésineau family were proprietors in Pessac-Léognan before moving here in 1998. From the outset they were able to produce a svelte, elegant Faugères with a touch of eucalyptus; and an even more stylish and concentrated special *cuvée* called Eole.

St-Chinian

In the Cévennes foothills, to the west, lies this important zone promoted to AC in 1982. There are 3,300 hectares, cultivated by 104 private estate and nine co-ops. Quality has been improving steadily, and some of the best estates of the Languedoc are located here. 90 per cent of the wines are red, the remainder rosé. Since 2004 INAO has granted AC status to the region's white wines (from Roussanne, Marsanne, Grenache, and Vermentino), so clearly their proportion will grow slightly in the years ahead. In the same year appellations were conferred on Berlou and Roquebrun. Both regions have around 250 hectares entitled to the appellation, all planted on schist soils.

Leading St-Chinian Producers

Château Borie La Vitarèle ☆–☆☆
Causses et Veyran. 15 ha www.borielavitarele.fr
Jean-François Izarn grows his St-Chinian on schist soils; his Coteaux on limestone. Two wines stand out: Les Schistes, a

St-Chinian, Herault region

blend of Grenache and Syrah, and Cuvée Les Crès, which is is unusual in that the vineyard is exceptionally stony. The wines are rich but earthy, and they age successfully for a few years.

Domaine Canet Valette ☆☆–☆☆☆
Cessenon. 18 ha. www.canetvalette.com
This is an organic estate run by the perfectionist Marc Valette. Mille et Une Nuits is a gamey blend of traditional varieties; Maghani, a low-cropped blend of Grenache and Syrah; and Les Galejades, a remarkable late-harvested red with flavours of cherry compôte. All highly individual.

Cave Les Vins de Roquebrun ☆☆
Roquebrun. 500 ha. www.cave-roquebrun.fr
Best of the St-Chinian cooperatives, with some impressive whites from Roussanne, and Mourvèdre-dominated reds.

Château Cazal-Viel ☆☆–☆☆☆
Cessenon. 150 ha. www.laurent-miquel.com
An important estate, run by the Miquel family. Syrah dominates all the red wines. The principal white is Finesse, a blend of Sauvignon Blanc, Chardonnay, Viognier, and Muscat. Scion Laurent Miquel has for some years developed his own range of wines from the same vineyards. Thus the new-oaked Larmes des Fées, which used to be released under the Cazal-Viel label, now appears under his. Consequently the range of Cazal-Viel wines has been trimmed down. But quality remains high.

Mas Champart ☆☆☆
Bramefan. 12 ha.
Varied soil types define the *cuvées* here. All the wines are excellent, including the flowery white , but the star turn is Clos de la Simonette, only made in top years and containing 70 per cent Mourvèdre – a meaty wine built for the long haul. The Causse du Bouquet, with its similar proportion of Syrah, is also noteworthy.

Clos Bagatelle ☆☆
St-Chinian. 45 ha. www.closbagatelle.com
Good St-Chinian wines, especially the svelte new-oaked Cuvée Gloire de Mon Père.

Château Coujan ☆–☆☆
Murviel. 100 ha. www.chateau-coujan.com
Florence Guy runs this large domaine in St-Chinian. The best St-Chinian wine is the Cuvée Gabrielle de Spinola, with 50 per cent Mourvèdre, but the estate is even better known for its wide range of varietal wines.

Domaine Fontaine Marcousse ☆☆
Puisserguier. 10 ha.
www.domaine-fontainemarcousse.com
The domaine only started bottling its St-Chinian wines in 1999. Cuvée Quercus is the most concentrated wine, aged in 50 per cent new oak, and Carignan fans should note the supple Cuvée Capellou.

Domaine des Jougla ☆
Prades-sur-Vernasobres. 27 ha.
A family estate founded centuries ago in the Cévennes foothills. Sound St-Chinian, mostly from schist soils.

Domaine La Madura ☆☆
St-Chinian. 14 ha. www.lamadura.com
Cyril Bourgne was the cellarmaster at Château Fieuzal in Bordeaux before launching this venture in St-Chinian. The range is simple: an unoaked Tradition, and Grand Vin, a meaty blend of Syrah and Mouvèdre with a dash of Grenache, aged in oak. Lush whites too.

Château Maurel Fonsalade ☆☆
Causses et Veyran. 27 ha.
An exceptionally beautiful estate in St-Chinian, producing sleek wines with no trace of rusticity. The black-fruited Cuvée Vieilles Vignes, made from Syrah, Grenache, and a little Mourvèdre, is the most consistent wine.

Laurent Miquel
See Château Cazal-Viel.

Domaine Moulinier ☆☆–☆☆☆
Pierrerue. 24 ha.
Pascal Moulinier says Pierrerue is one of the hottest corners of St-Chinian, so he is careful not to pick his grapes when overripe. His Terrasses Grillées, mostly Syrah aged in a good proportion of new oak, is consistently delicious.

Vignoble de Berlou ☆–☆☆
Berlou. 590 ha. www.berloup.com
This well-run cooperative completely dominates the Berlou region. Almost half the vineyards are planted with Carignan, so the co-op produces a number of vesions, such as the old-vine Calisso, made by carbonic maceration. Schisteil is the basic wine, consistently fruity and enjoyable.

Coteaux du Languedoc Districts
Cabardès

This area was promoted to AC in 1999: 400 hectares, cultivated by 25 private estates and the members of five cooperatives. The wines are ingeniously divided stylistically into Vent d'Est (Mediterranean varieties such as Syrah and Grenache) and Vent d'Ouest (Atlantic varieties such as Cabernet and Merlot). The AC rules require the use of 40 per cent of each family of grape varieties.

Domaine de Cabrol ☆☆
Aragon. 21 ha. www.domaine-le-cabrol.com
From the highest vineyards in Cabardès, Claude Carayol produces both Vent d'Est and the more succulent Vent d'Ouest, and La Dérive, a blend of all four varieties, aged two years in 500-litre barrels. Powerful wines that benefit from some ageing.

Château de Pennautier ☆☆
Pennautier. 146 ha. www.vignobles-lorgeril.com
Pennautier, with a sumptuous Louis XIII château, is just one of three Languedoc properties owned by the Lorgerils. Not surprisingly, the range of wines is extensive, with *vin de pays* as well as Cabardès. The top wine is the Syrah-dominated L'Esprit de Pennautier, which is aged in new oak. The Lorgerils also own Château La Bastide Rougepeyre, also in Cabardès.

Cabrières

In the Clermont l'Hérault region of the Cévennes foothills, close to Faugères. Best-known for the light rosé, made without pressing, but the schist soils are also suitable for producing Syrah-spiced reds. About 400 hectares are in production, most of them vinified by the cooperative.

Société Coopérative Agricole des Vins de Cabrières ☆
Clermont-l'Hérault. 400 ha. www.cabrieres.com
By far the most important producer, this co-op makes Cabrières and Clairette du Languedoc. Top range is called Variations.

Clairette du Languedoc

A scarcely merited *appellation contrôlée* uniting 275 hectares for a generally dull and dispiriting dry white from Clairette grapes grown in several communes along the Hérault. Much of it is fortified as a cheap apéritif and sold under such names as "Amber Dry". But some producers are attempting to make the most of what Clairette can offer, and some sweet versions are also produced. The best producers include Domaine de Clovallon (q.v.) in the Coteaux du Languedoc and Château St-André at Pézenas. The most important producer, inevitably, is the co-op: the Caves Coopérative de La Clairette d'Adissan at Adissan.

La Clape

A 1,000-hectare coastal area of limestone hills between Narbonne and the shore. Elevation and the constant wind give good acidity and refreshing whites, but red wines are improving fast, which is just as well since they account for 80 per cent of production. AC rules are complex, but focus on typical southern French varieties. The region has 36 private producers and four cooperatives.

Château d'Angles ☆☆
St Pierre-la-Mer. 36 ha. www.chateaudangles.com
Eric Fabre was once technical director of Château Lafite and brings his expertise to bear on this estate, with its varied soils. The white La Clape is mostly Bourboulenc, the red blends Syrah, Carignan, Mourvèdre, and Grenache. These are among the most refined wines of the area.

Château Camplazens ☆☆
Armissan. 39 ha. www.camplazens.com
This estate has been through many changes of ownership, but seems to have stabilized since 2002 under the hand of Peter Close from Britain. Red wines are the strong suit here, and as well as blends of the traditional varieties, there are also varietal wines from Viognier, Syrah, and Grenache. The wines are good, showing less overt oakiness than in the 1990s.

Château de Capitoul ☆☆–☆☆☆
Narbonne. 64 ha. www.chateau-capitoul.com
Charles Mock runs one of the largest properties in the region. In the 1990s, he restructured the vineyards and modernized the winery. The standard range is called Lavandines, and Les Rocailles is a selection of wines from older vines. Both lines are very well-made, especially the creamy, apricotty whites. The Viognier *vin de pays* is one of southern France's best, and in some years there is a rather oxidative late-harvest version. A new *prestige cuvée*, Maelma, is a selection of the best lots and is aged two years in barriques.

Languedoc's famous landmark, La Clape

Domaine de l'Hospitalet ☆–☆☆
Narbonne. 82 ha.
www.gerard-bertrand.com
Not so much a wine estate as a tourist complex, with
restaurants and museums. Founded by the Ribourel family,
it was sold in 2002 to the Corbières-based négociant, Gérard
Bertrand, who owns properties throughout the Languedoc.
It has taken a while for Bertrand to find a place for Hospitalet
within his immense portfolio, but the wines are now of sound
quality, especially the whites.

Château de la Négly ☆☆–☆☆☆
Fleury d'Aude. 66 ha.
Until 1992 the wines were sold to a cooperative. After
substantial replanting, Jean-Paul Rosset began bottling his
wines in 1997. He has launched various bottlings, of which
the best appears to be La Falaise from Syrah and Grenache.
He has attracted much publicity by producing some single-
vineyard wines in minute quantities, at prices to which most
Burgundy *grands crus* merely aspire. However, his basic red
wine, La Côte, offers good value.

Château Pech-Celeyran ☆☆
Salles d'Aude. 95 ha. www.pech-celeyran.com
Large property, owned for generations by the St-Exupéry
family, divided between La Clape and *vin de pays* sites.
Known for Viognier, Chardonnay, and barrique-aged reds.
The oaked wines are released under the Céleste label.

Domaine de Pech-Redon ☆–☆☆☆
Narbonne. 42 ha.
Restored old organic estate in a lovely situation high on the
hills at La Clape, near the sea. Christophe Bousquet runs
it with energy. As well as good AC wines, there are atypical
offerings such as an unoaked Alicante, and a Mourvèdre
and Cabernet Sauvignon (rather dry). The best wine is often
La Centaurée, mostly Syrah and first made in 1998.

Château Ricardelle ☆☆–☆☆☆
Narbonne. 43 ha.
www.chateau-ricardelle.com
Bruno Pellgrini has made major efforts to improve quality
here. Two fine reds: Closablières and the very oaky Blason.
The former seems more vigorous and better-balanced.

Château de Rouquette-sur-Mer ☆☆–☆☆☆
Narbonne. 55 ha. www.chateaurouquette.com
A remarkable site, once a hunting reserve, situated on the
rocky slopes of La Clape near the sea. Modern winemaking
results in fresh, well-crafted red, white, and rosé. Cuvée
Henri Lapierre is the top range, the white being a traditional
Bourboulenc. Two small-volume, oak-aged wines have been
added to the range: Clos de la Tour and L'Absolu, both of
which are among the best reds of La Clape.

Montpeyroux

Northern district for full-bodied, chewy reds from the foothills
of the Larzac Mountains, near the famous Gorges de l'Hérault.
The clay soil known as *marne bleu* is said to explain the power
and heft of many of the wines.

Domaine de l'Aiguilière ☆☆☆
Montpeyroux. 25 ha.
The domaine produces two exceptionally rich and opulent
reds: Côte Dorée and Côte Rousse, the former more
structured, the latter more seductive.

Domaine d'Aupilhac ☆☆☆
Montpeyroux. 25 ha. www.aupilhac.com
Sylvain Fadat is one of the Languedoc's most respected
winemakers. His standard Montpeyroux is a highly traditional
wine with good tannic backbone, but Fadat delights in variety,
also producing a dense blackberry-toned pure Carignan, a
pure Cinsault from 100-year-old vines called Les Servières,
and a *vin de pays* Plôs de Baumes from Bordeaux varieties.
Perhaps the best wine of all is a new and highly structured
Montpeyroux called Le Boda, a blend of Mourvèdre and Syrah
aged in 300-litre barrels for two years.

Domaine Alain Chabanon ☆☆–☆☆☆
Lagamas. 20 ha. www.domainechabanon.com
Alan Chabanon sells one-third of his crop to the cooperative
in order to maintain quality. The regular Montpeyroux is free
of rusticity, and he also produces special *cuvées* such as a pure
Merlot (Le Petit Merle) and a sweet Chenin (Le Villard). In
2002, the estate officially became Biodynamic.

Domaine des Grécaux ☆–☆☆
St Jean-de-Fos. 11 ha.
Alain Caujolle-Gazet's first vintage was 1999, and he produces
two wines: Terra Solis for early drinking, and the more
structured L'Hêméra.

Pic-St-Loup

A 600-metre (1,800-foot) peak due north of Montpellier. The
AC here requires at least two of the principal varieties –
Grenache, Syrah, and Mourvèdre – to be present in the blend.
In practice Syrah and Mourvèdre are the varieties of choice.
There are 1,500 hectares under vine. Only nine per cent of pro-
duction is white, which must be sold as Coteaux du Languedoc.

Mas Bruguière ☆☆
Valflaunès. 20 ha. www.mas-bruguiere.com
Planted near Domaine de l'Hortus (q.v.) in a narrow valley,
the well-drained vineyards are refreshed and kept healthy by
steady breezes. The tank-aged L'Arbouse is a spicy, full-bodied
blend of Grenache and Syrah. La Grenadière is the oaked
version: stylish, and developing gamey aromas with age.
In 2003 Guihem Bruguière made the first vintage of a pure
Syrah called Le Septième at a very high price.

Château de Cazeneuve ☆☆
Lauret. 25 ha. www.cazeneuve.net
Belgian André Leenhardt bought this property in 1988, and
his first vintage was in 1992. For some years it has been one
of the region's most dependable estates. The white, mostly
Roussanne, has become rich and complex . The estate's best
cuvée, Roc des Mates, is mostly Syrah, aged in 40 per cent new
oak. Les Calcaires is less weighty, but sometimes better-
balanced. Leenhardt has recently launched a new Syrah-
dominated blend, Le Sang du Calcaire.

Clos Marie ☆☆–☆☆☆
Lauret. 20 ha.
Obtrusive oak and aggressive tannins sometimes marred the wine from this ambitious estate, but they have become much more harmonious. The top *cuvées*, Simon and Les Glorieuses are sumptuous, but the pricing is as ambitious as the wines.

L'Ermitage du Pic-St-Loup ☆☆–☆☆☆
St Mathieu-de-Treviers. 44 ha.
The *cuvées* Tradition and St Agnès are delicious distillations of black fruits, which some may find preferable to the heavily oaked Guilhem Gaucelm.

Château L'Euzière ☆☆
Fontanès. 23 ha. www.chateauleuziere.fr
Michel Causse produces a range of wines, of which the most alluring is the perfumed, elegant Syrah-dominated Les Escarbouches.

Domaine de l'Hortus ☆☆☆
Valflaunès. 55 ha. ww.vignobles-orliac.com
It was Jean Orliac who put this region on the map. Since the 1980s he has made excellent wines, especially reds. Both the basic Bergerie de l'Hortus and the oaked Grande Cuvée are exemplary. The oak is perfectly judged and the wines always in balance. The whites are unoaked blends of Chardonnay, Viognier, and Roussanne.

Château de Lancyre ☆–☆☆
Valflaunès. 80 ha. www.chateaudelancyre.com
The largest property in Pic-St-Loup makes sound wines – especially the Grande Cuvée and Vieilles Vignes – at a fair price.

Château de Lascaux ☆–☆☆
Vacquières. 45 ha. www.chateau-lascaux.com
Jean-Benoît Cavalier's vineyards lie close against the foothills of the Cévennes. The top wine, Nobles Pierres, is a relatively light, cherry-scented wine (mostly Syrah), and its white counterpart, Les Pierres d'Argent, has a tendency to be overwhelmed by oak; indeed the unoaked version, also from Roussanne, Marsanne, and Vermentino, is quite often preferable. Consistent and sensibly priced wines overall, but they can lack concentration.

Mas de Mortiès ☆☆
St-Jean-de-Cuculles. 23 ha. www.morties.com
A good chunky Pic-St-Loup, a more supple but very enjoyable red Coteaux du Languedoc, and, disarmingly, a *prestige cuvée* called Jamais Content, with a sweet, oaky nose and well integrated tannins.

Château La Roque ☆☆
Fontanès. 32 ha. www.chateau-laroque.eu
A former Benedictine estate, it was bought by Jack Boutin in 1985, and then sold in 2007 to Normandy industrialist Jacques Figuette, who has continued investments in the property. Sound, mostly unoaked wines, with a solid, leathery Cuvée Tradition. The top wine, Cupa Numismae, is Mourvèdre and Syrah, aged in 50 per cent new barriques: menthol, cherries, and hefty tannins.

Château de Valflaunès ☆☆–☆☆☆
Valflaunès. 13 ha. www.chateaudevalflaunes.com
Numerous *cuvées* juggle with Grenache and Syrah and, in the case of Un Peu de Toi, with 75 per cent Carignan. Tem Tem is Syrah with a dash of Grenache. Despite the air of whimsy, these are serious wines, with an unusual intensity and elegance for the Languedoc.

Picpoul de Pinet

The vines of Pinet, overlooking the Etang de Thau, produce the Picpoul grapes for a pleasant, dry white with 12 per cent alcohol and a touch of freshness. Whether by design or chance, these wines are the perfect accompaniment to the oysters farmed in the nearby lagoons: the Muscadet of the Midi, in fact. There are 1,300 hectares, worked by around 25 private estates and coops. The co-ops remain important, being responsible for 82 per cent of production. A regrettable fad for oaked versions, fueled by foreign visitors, has fortunately been slow to catch on.

Cave de l'Ormarine ☆–☆☆
Pinet. 910 ha. www.cave-ormarine.com
This co-op accounts for half the sales of the region. The basic *cuvée* is Carte Noire, with its fresh, lemon-grass scent. The more selective Duc de Morny bottling, however, is better.

Domaine Félines Jourdan ☆–☆☆
Mèze. 110 ha. www.felines-jourdan.com
A good producer of Picpoul, with vibrant, crisp wines.

Domaine Gaujal ☆
Pinet. 45 ha. www.gaujal.fr
As well as crisp, aromatic Picpoul, this property produces varietal Chardonnay and Merlot.

Other Coteaux du Languedoc (and Vin de Pays) Producers

Abbaye de Valmagne ☆–☆☆
Villeveyrac. 75 ha. www.valmagne.com
A spectacular Cistercian abbey, its nave full of vast casks, and a more modern Coteaux du Languedoc vineyard, producing rich whites from Roussanne and Viognier, and spicy reds from the Grès de Montpellier district.

Bessière ☆–☆☆
Mèze. www.bessiere.fr
Founded in 1902, a conscientious, family-owned négociant house, working with some 30 different domaines across the Languedoc.

Château Capion ☆☆
Gignac. 45 ha. www.chateaucapion.com
Owned by Adrian Buhrer, who also owns Saxenburg in South Africa. Both the Syrah-dominated château wine and Le Juge, a Rhône-style blend, are aged in mostly new oak.

Cave Coopérative de St-Saturnin ☆–☆☆
St-Saturnin. 650 ha.
www.vins-saint-saturnin.com
Vineyards in the *garrigue* of the Cévennes foothills with a gamey, cherryish *cuvée* called Seigneur des Deux Vierges.

Mas la Chevalière ☆–☆☆
Béziers. 42 ha. www.mas-la-chevaliere.com
A replanted property acquired by Chablis producer M Laroche in 1997. Most of the wines are made from purchased grapes. The top blend, made only in exceptional years, is La Croix Chevalière.

Mas de Chimères ☆–☆☆
Octon. 18 ha.
Good-value wines from the Terrasse du Larzac: these are scented and fleshy expressions of Grenache and Syrah.

Domaine Clavel ☆☆–☆☆☆
Assas. 44 ha. www.vins-clavel.fr
Jean Clavel was a prime mover in establishing the Coteaux AC, and his son Pierre continues his father's dedication to quality. Their regular bottling is the juicy Les Garrigues from Syrah and Grenache, but Clavel has won most acclaim for its Copa Santa, a Syrah/Mourvèdre blend, aged in oak for 15 months and unfiltered. Robust and ripe, the wine has smoky aromas and remarkable length of flavour.

Domaine de Clovallon ☆–☆☆
Bédarieux. 10 ha.
Catherine Roque produces a large range of wines, including the rare Clairette du Languedoc.

Mas de Daumas Gassac ☆☆☆
Aniane. 50 ha. www.daumas-gassac.com
The only begetter of this inspired estate, Aimé Guibert, can justly be said to have brought pride to the Languedoc for the first time. After he bought the undulating property on volcanic terrain, consultants from Bordeaux raved about the quality of the soil. They were right. Guibert's Cabernet Sauvignon is a massive, long-lived wine, with the structure of Bordeaux and the wild quality of the Languedoc *garrigue*.

The white is a blend of Chardonnay and Viognier; a fatly aromatic wine. Guibert has also worked closely with local cooperatives to produce large-volume wines of good quality at fair prices. In 2003 Guibert handed the properties to three of his sons, who are maintaining the very high standards their father set.

Mas de l'Ecriture ☆☆–☆☆☆
Jonquières. 13 ha. www.masdelecriture.com
Since 1999 Pascal Fulla has been producing sumptuous wines, especially the Syrah-rich L'Ecriture from the Terrasses du Larzac. But prices are high.

Château de Flaugergues ☆–☆☆
Montpellier. 30 ha. www.flaugergues.com
The best property in the small gravelly region of Méjanelle, in the hands of the Comtes de Colbert for three centuries. Good blends from Grenache and Syrah.

Foncalieu ☆–☆☆
Arzens. www.foncalieuvignobles.com
A company founded in 1967 to market the production of 18 cooperatives farming 9,000 hectares. Most of the wines are sold as *vin de pays*, and the firm has a range of brands and an annual production of two million cases.

Domaine de la Garance ☆☆☆
Caux. 8 ha.
Owner-winemaker Pierre Quinonero coaxes wonderful fruit from his Carignan and other varieties, some of which are over a century old. The white can be oxidative, but the red Les Claviers Carignan and A Coline Grenache show the splendid potential of these varieties when planted in the right habitat.

Domaine Les Grandes Costes ☆–☆☆
Vacquières. 10 ha. www.grandes-costes.com
The vines lie close to Pic-St-Loup, and the wines share the fragrance and elegance of those from that region. The Cuvée Grandes Costes also has weight and concentration.

Domaine La Grange des Pères ☆☆☆
Aniane. 14 ha.
Laurent Vallié worked at some of the top estates of southern France before planting his own vineyards, which came on stream in 1992. Yields are minute, so ripeness levels are high. The wines, sold as *vin de pays*, are aged in wood for at least two years, share the power of their neighbour at Daumas Gassac, and far exceed their prices. The red is from Cabernet, Syrah, and Mourvèdre; the white mostly from Roussanne and Chardonnay.

Domaine La Grange de Quatre Sous ☆☆
Assignan. 8 ha.
A wide range of wines from a small property. By releasing them as *vin de pays*, Swiss owner Hildegard Horat can juggle with varieties such as Chardonnay, Cabernet Sauvignon, and Cabernet Franc.

Domaine Henry ☆–☆☆
St-Georges-d'Orques. 15 ha.
www.domaine-henry.com
The top wine from this domaine is the Cuvée St-Georges-d'Orques. It has surprising delicacy, with flavours of strawberries and cherries.

Maison Jeanjean ☆
St-Felix-de-Lodez. 300 ha. www.jeanjean.fr
A huge, family-owned négociant house with wines drawn from the whole of southern France.

Château de Jonquières ☆☆
Jonquières. 9 ha. www.chateau-jonquieres.com
This medieval château on the plateau of Larzac produces small quantities of excellent wines. The reds are traditional blends of Syrah, Grenache, Mourvèdre, and Carignan, and the best fruit is preserved for the stylish La Naronnie.

Mas Jullien ☆☆–☆☆☆
Jonquières. 16 ha.
Olivier Jullien runs this innovative, Biodynamic estate in the Terrasses du Larzac. He combines experimentation with a respect for tradition, using local varieties despite the commercial difficulties in selling them.

The range of wines used to be wide, but in recent years Jullien has settled for simplicity, with his principal red a blend of Syrah and Carignan, and a lighter red called Etats d'Ame; and a pair of elegant whites.

Domaine Lacroix-Vanel ☆☆–☆☆☆
Caux. 11 ha.
A serious property near Pézenas, aiming for structured and long-lived wines, with Syrah and Mourvèdre to the fore.

Listel ☆
Sète. 1,800 ha.
A huge company producing salt as well as good-value wines. It is now owned by the Champagne producer Vranken. It is best known for its rosé or Gris de Gris.

Domaine de Montcalmès ☆☆
Puéchabon. 20 ha.
Since 1999 Frédéric Pourtalié has focused on producing a single Syrah-dominated blend, supported with Grenache and Mourvèdre, and aged in oak for two years.

Domaine de Nizas ☆–☆☆
Caux. 44 ha.
www.domainedenizas
A large property bought in 1998 by John Goelet, the owner of Clos du Val (q.v.) in Napa. The range includes a pure old-vine Carignan and an unusual Reserve from Petit Verdot, Cabernet Sauvignon, and Syrah.

Château Notre Dame du Quatourze ☆
Narbonne. 32 ha.
The leading property in the Quatourze near Narbonne. Full-bodied Carignan thrives on the quartz soils.

Domaine Peyre Rose ☆☆☆
St-Pargoire. 25 ha.
In a remote spot high on the *garrigue*, Marlène Soria makes just two red wines, both of them mostly from Syrah but from different vineyards: Clos Léone and Clos des Cistes. Yields are extremely low, at around 20 hl/ha, and the wines are aged in tanks and large casks, a welcome change from the prevailing trend for new oak with everything.

(A cellar problem, now resolved, meant that vintages from 1999 to 2001 were not bottled.) Both wines are opulent, powerful, and long-lived, the Clos des Cistes denser and more tannic, the Léone with more immediately appealing berry fruit. There is also a minuscule production of white wine called Oro.

Prieuré de St-Jean-de-Bébian ☆☆–☆☆☆
Pézenas. 33 ha. www.bebian.com
The former owner, Alain Roux, brought cuttings here from the finest estates of the Rhône, and as the vines matured, he began to fashion his own long-lived and powerful wines. In 1994, the property was bought by wine writer Chantel Lecouty and her husband, Jean-Claude Le Brun.

Together, they modified the vinification and introduced barrique-ageing. Although the wine is perhaps more elegant, it unfortunately may have lost some of its wild individuality. Expensive.

Domaine de la Prose ☆☆–☆☆☆
Pignan. 18 ha. www.domainedelaprose.com
Alexandre de Mortillet bought this property in 1990, and built modern cellars in 2000. The red is pure Syrah given prolonged ageing in new barriques; the white, from Vermentino and Grenache Blanc, is barrel-fermented and emerges as rather leaden. But the red Grande Cuvée and its less oaky counterpart, Cuvée d'Embruns, are very successful.

Château Puech-Haut ☆☆–☆☆☆
St-Drézery. 100 ha. www.chateau-puech-haut.com
Since 1995, this estate has been making really excellent wines. The red Prestige is mostly Grenache and, to be honest, rather earthy, but the top offering, the new-oaked Tête de Cuvée, which is 60 per cent Syrah, is extremely intense. Very good white wine, too, mostly from Roussanne and Marsanne.

Domaine Roc d'Anglade ☆☆
Langlade. 8 ha.
Although Rémy Pedreno prefers to release his rather expensive wines as *vin de pays* as it gives him greater liberty, that does not mean that he opts for high yields or eccentric blends. The red is a solid, discreetly oaked blend of Syrah, Grenache, and Carignan, and the white is spicy and vivacious.

Château St-Martin-de-la-Garrigue ☆☆
Montagnac. 60 ha.
There are 17 varieties planted on Jean-Claude Zabalia's estate, so the range of wines is considerable. Both Cuvée St-Martin, from Syrah and Mourvèdre, and Cuvée Bronzinelle (a Rhône-style blend) are excellent.

Skalli ☆–☆☆☆
Sète. www.vinsfamilleskalli.com. 250 ha.
The Skalli family have proved revolutionary producers of *vins de pays* from international varieties. Fortant de France is the best known brand, but the range is vast. The company is also active in Corsica and Napa Valley, where it owns Chateau St-Supéry.

Domaine de Terre Mégère ☆–☆☆
Cournonsec. 22 ha.
An estate with a rising reputation west of Montpellier. Good white blend La Galopine from Viognier and Chardonnay, and reliable red *vin de pays*.

The Muscats of Languedoc

Three small zones along the central south coast, between the wine port of Sète and the marshes of the Camargue, have appellations (and an antique reputation) for sweet Muscat *vins doux naturels* – 1,380 hectares in all. Frontignan, with 800 hectares, is the biggest and best-known. Its vineyards stretch along the coast through Mireval (the second appellation, with 260 hectares) towards Montpellier. The sole permitted grape is the

Château de Jonquières, Jonquières

Muscat à Petits Grains; its wine powerfully aromatic, golden and sticky, but lacking (at least as it is made today) the freshness and finesse of Muscat de Beaumes-de-Venise. Since the early 1980s, an independent producer, Yves Pastourel at Château de la Peyrade, has worked to improve this situation and succeeded in producing a lighter and more refined wine. The third area, with 320 hectares, is Lunel, halfway between Montpellier and Nîmes, just inland from the Carmargue.

The cooperatives of Frontignan and Lunel are the major producers, and the cooperative at Vérargues also makes Muscat. High-quality private estates are few and far between. Other than La Peyrade, there is the Mas de Bellevue at Lunel, and Domaine Lacoste, also at Lunel, which also produces an unusual late-harvested version from grapes that have raisined on the vine.

Costières de Nîmes

This rapidly improving region has for some time been in the throes of an identity crisis, unable to decide whether it forms part of the Languedoc or Provence. Its location, just south of Nîmes on undulating slopes with a view onto the Mediterranean, suggests the latter, but it is generally recognized as belonging to the former. It's a hot, stony region, with some slight maritime influence. It is also large, declaring production from 4,185 hectares, cultivated by almost 100 private estates and 17 cooperatives.

The traditional varieties here are the usual suspects of the Midi, but in recent years much more Syrah has been planted, and with happy results. Syrah here gives intense, pure wines of great charm. Charm and suppleness are the present hallmarks of the Costières. This is not a region that shapes wines of great depth or complexity, though some producers see no reason why such styles should not emerge in the future.

There is one other AC tucked within the Costières: the obscure 40-hectare Clairette de Bellegarde. Why these wines, which need to be drunk young before their fruit fades, should rejoice in their own AC is a mystery. More attractive whites are being made from Viognier, Marsanne, and Roussanne, not necessarily as AC wines. About a quarter of production is of rosé wines. Estates tend to be large and many vineyards are picked by machine. Thus costs are relatively low, and this is reflected in the reasonable prices charged for even the best wines.

Château Beaubois ☆☆
Franquevaux. 55 ha. www.chateau-beaubois.com
The Boyer family took over this property in 1985 and produces a well-balanced Cuvée Tradition and, in certain vintages, an oaked Cuvée Elegance. Initially over-oaked, Elegance is now more harmonious. Fragrant white from Roussanne and Viognier.

Château de Beck ☆–☆☆
Vauvert. 50 ha. www.chateaudebeck.com
Industrialist Jean-Francois Herbinger has revitalized this fine estate, with all its vines planted in a single south-facing block. Both whites and reds are made from traditional varieties, other than a Viognier vin de pays.

Château de Belle Coste ☆☆
Caissargues. 65 ha.
This serious property is just outside Nîmes. The regular red is made from Grenache and Syrah; the top Cuvée St Marc has Mourvèdre to give the blend more backbone. The white has always contained a good deal of Viognier, which was permitted here on an "experimental" basis in the late 1980s, and has been in the wine ever since.

Mas de Bressades ☆☆–☆☆☆☆
Manduel. 25 ha. www.masdebressades.com
Production here is divided between the Cuvée Tradition and Cuvée Excellence. The white Excellence is mostly Roussanne fermented in new oak, and has a spicy, citric character. The red is mostly Syrah with some Grenache and can, in certain vintages, be a tannic wine. Excellent rosé.

Château de Campuget ☆☆
Manduel. 160 ha. www.campuget.com
The Dalle family own two good properties: Campuget and Château L'Amarine a few miles away. The winery is modern and well-equipped. Standard cuvées can lack concentration. The Prestige bottling is better, and the Cuvée Sommelière, a pure Syrah aged in new 500-litre barrels, is first-rate, with a lovely red-fruit character and fine length of flavour.

Mas Carlot ☆
Bellegarde. 72 ha.
Owned by a Paris restaurateur, Mas Carlot, and run by his daughter Natalie. The estate also bottles its oaked wines as Château Paul Blanc, and is also a significant producer of Clairette de Bellegarde.

Château Grande Cassagne ☆☆–☆☆☆☆
St-Gilles. 32 ha.
Since 1994, the Dardé brothers have made deliciously fruity red, white, and rosé. Rapid commercial success allowed them to be more selective, and in recent years they have introduced some new cuvées. The white Hippolyte is mostly Roussanne, vinified in oak, and the red Hippolyte is a selection of their best Syrah, aged in new barriques. Cuvée Civette, in contrast, is mainly Grenache.

Domaine des Grimaudes ☆☆
Manduel. 6 ha.
Since 1999, this has been the southern retreat of Marc Kreydenweiss (q.v.) from Alsace, and it is run by his daughter Emmanuelle. Here too the farming is Biodynamic.

Château Masneuf ☆☆–☆☆☆☆
Vauvert. 62 ha. www.chateau-mas-neuf.com
The previous owner, Olivier Gibelin, was an ebullient character but his wines were inconsistent. Since 2000 the new owner, Luc Baudet, has refined the range, adding some small-volume bottlings of very high quality, such as Aves des Si from Syrah, and a Mourvèdre/Grenache blend called, perhaps predictably, Mourvache.

Château Mourgues du Grès ☆☆–☆☆☆☆
Beaucaire. 55 ha. www.mourguesdugres.com
François Collard favours a very ripe style for his red Costières.

Sometimes it verges towards the jammy end of the spectrum, but usually it has lovely purity of fruit, reflecting the high proportion of Syrah he favours. His best selections are bottled as Terre d'Argence, and there is also an oaked *cuvée*, Les Capitelles, that offers a different interpretation of the same excellent fruit. The rosé is one of the region's finest, with delicate strawberry aromas. There is also a rosé, Capitelles, mostly from Mourvèdre. Since 1999 Collard has produced two white wines of comparable quality.

Mas de Tourelles ☆
Beaucaire. 90 ha. www.tourelles.com

Hervé Durand's property is less remarkable for its Costières wines than for its painstaking re-creation of a Roman winery, complete with Roman-style wines aromatized with honey and seawater.

Château de la Tuilerie ☆–☆☆
Route de St-Gilles, Nîmes. 98 ha.
www.chateautuilerie.com

An immaculately maintained estate owned by Mme. Chantal Comte. She produces many bottlings from this substantial property. The Vieilles Vignes is very reliable, but the Cuvée Eole wines, both white and red, are also oak-aged but show more concentration. Occasionally she produces L'Un de Sens, a pure Syrah aged in new barrels. These are among the more expensive wines of the region.

Corsica

The importance of France's dramatically mountainous island of Corsica used to be almost entirely as a producer of bulk material for table-wine blends and of robust rosés to quench the thirst of holiday-makers. When France lost Algeria, its wine-growers flooded into the island to plant the plains of the east coast with the basic grapes of Algeria and the Midi: Carignan, Grenache, and Cinsault. In the 1960s, the island's vineyards expanded from 8,000 to 31,000 hectares. A scandal erupted in 1974, with accusations of fraud and illegal practices, and this resulted in a period of retrenchment. Thereafter the vineyards were restructured: many small properties vanished, and there was a growth in relatively big properties farmed for quantity rather than quality.

The appellation Vin de Corse was instituted in 1976 as an encouragement to limit crops. However, only 31 per cent of Corsican wine is AC. There are eight more specific ACs, mostly related to regions, such as: Ajaccio, Patrimonio, Calvi, Sartène, Figari, Porto Vecchio, and Coteaux du Cap Corse. In addition there is an appellation for Muscat du Cap Corse. The regional appellations retain traditional grape varieties. These include the red Nielluccio (Italy's Sangiovese) and Sciaccarello, which may be unique to Corsica, and the white Vermentino. (Local dialect opts for different spellings, which may be seen on some labels: Niellucciu, Sciaccarellu, and Vermentinu.) Just over half the island's production from the present 7,000 hectares is rosé wine; 40 per cent is red, and only ten per cent white.

Corsica: known as L'Ile de Beauté

The local preference is to drink rosé rather than white with fish. Southern French varieties such as Syrah and Mourvèdre have also been planted, along with Chardonnay and Merlot, which flourish in the Vins de Corse vineyards along the coast.

Patrimonio, in La Conca d'Oro in the north of the island, is relatively long-established for rosé and red made primarily of Nielluccio and whites from Vermentino, with one degree higher minimum alcohol (12.5) than the rest of the island's wines. Ajaccio, the capital, has Sciaccarello red and rosé and Vermentino white. Calvi and the region of Balagne in the northwest have a relatively high proportion of AC wine. Cap Corse specializes in dessert wines, including sweet Muscat.

Porto-Vecchio and Figari, and the flat southeast, have more vineyards, but using a good proportion of Nielluccio. Sartène, around Propriano in the southwest, is the area with the highest proportion of appellation wines, of Corsican grapes – mainly Sciaccarello – and of traditional-style, small growers working on good hill slopes. Plantings of Cabernet Sauvignon, Merlot, Chardonnay, and Chenin Blanc on the eastern plain south of Bastia are included in increasingly interesting Vin de Pays de L'Ile de Beauté. Production is dominated by two large co-ops: the UVAL and UVIB, and by large companies such as Skalli, which uses the Coteaux de Diana label.

The principal quality-focused domaines are listed below. In Ajaccio, other producers of interest include Clos d'Alzeto, Alain Courreges, Domaine de Peraldi (good Sciaccarello), and Domaine de Pratavone (leathery, raspberry-toned reds; floral whites). In Calvi, the top properties include Domaine d'Alzipratu and Clos Culumbu (both producing peppery rosés), and Domaine Maestracci. In Figari the leading estates include Domaine de la Murta (rich rosé), Domaine Petra Bianca, and Domaine de Tanella (especially Cuvée Alexandra).

Patrimonio has a number of quality-conscious estates: Antoine Arena (serious reds and late-harvest Vermentino), Clos de Bernardi, Domaine du Catarelli, Clos Marfisi, Domaine San Quilico, and Domaine de Pastricciola.

Leading Corsica Producers

Comte Abbatucci ☆☆
Casalabriva, Ajaccio. 18 ha.
www.domaine-come-abbatucci.com
One of the few Biodynamic properties in Corsica, Abbatucci is planted with local varieties, and excels with white wines.

Antoine Aréna ☆☆–☆☆☆
Morta Maïo, Patrimonio. 13 ha.
The voluble, intelligent Aréna is one of the island's top producers. The vineyards are farmed Biodynamically. The range is broad, but the focus is firmly on indigenous varieties, and includes an excellent Muscat du Cap Corse and an unusual white from the rare Bianco Gentile grape.

Clos d'Alzeto ☆–☆☆
Sari d'Orcino. 43 ha. www.closdalzeto.com
Founded in 1800, this Ajaccio estate, the highest in Corsica, remains resolutely traditional in its choice of grape varieties. Thanks to the elevation, the wines have perfume and finesse rather than weight or power.

Clos Capitoro ☆–☆☆
Pisciatella, Ajaccio. 50 ha. www.clos-capitoro.com
This family estate was founded in 1856. Sciaccarello dominates the rosé and red. Jacques Bianchetti is not a fan of oak-ageing, but does nonetheless produce a few wines, white and red, that spend some time in wood.

Domaine d'E Croce ☆☆
Poggio d'Oletta. 15 ha. www.yves-leccia.com
Yves Leccia, a well-known winemaker, left the family domaine in 2005 to found his own Patrimonio property. The white is a vivacious Vermentino, the red a spicy Nielluccio. This is unoaked, as is the Cuvée YL, which is mostly Grenache.

Domaine Fiumicicoli ☆☆
Sartène. 70 ha. www.domaine-fiumicicoli.com
This large southerly estate excels across the range, with a flowery white, a firm rosé from Sciaccarello, and a Nielluccio-dominated red Cuvée Vassilla, aged in one-year-old barrels.

Domaine Gentile ☆–☆☆
St Florent, Patrimonio. 30 ha.
www.domaine-gentile.com
An organic estate known for its Muscats and also for Rappu, a sweet wine that revives an ancient tradition, being composed of a lightly fortified blend of Nielluccio, Vermentino, and Muscat.

Domaine Leccia ☆–☆☆
Poggio d'Oletta. 10 ha.
www.domaine-leccia.com
Since the departure of Yves Leccia to create his own domaine, the family property has been run by Annette Leccia. Sound red, rosé, and Muscat from traditional varieties.

Domaine Orenga de Gaffory ☆–☆☆
Patrimonio. 60 ha.
www.domaine-orengadegoffroy.com
One of the largest properties in Patrimonio, it is best known for the oak-aged Cuvée des Gouveneurs and the excellent Muscat.

Domaine de Torraccia ☆–☆☆
Porto Vecchio. 25 ha.
Christian Imbert has been a passionate defender of traditional Corsican wines. His own domaine is organic, and its strength lies in red wine, especially Cuvée Oriu, which is mostly Nielluccio. The style is robust, and some vintages require bottle age for the tannins to soften.

The Southwest

The southwest corner of France exists in calm self-sufficiency. Its rich food and notable wines seem, like its beauty and tranquillity, to be its private business. To the east lie the great vineyards of the Languedoc; to the north Bordeaux; Spain lies beyond the towering Pyrénées to the south. In their foothills and the river valleys of the Tarn, the Garonne, the Lot, the Gers, the Adour, and the Gave, a different race of wines is grown, bearing no relation to the Midi and, with some exceptions, remarkably distinct from Bordeaux. Historically, some of these wines, notably Cahors and Gaillac, were exported via Bordeaux and known as the wines of the Hauts-Pays: the high country. A variety of grapes with extraordinary local names, some of them Basque, gives a range of flavours found nowhere else. In the 1990s, the world began to discover them and encourage the expansion of what was a depleted vineyard.

Regions such as Madiran, once renowned for the stern rusticity of its wines, have learned to tame the wines' natural tannins without any loss of typicity. Gaillac has rediscovered its ancient varieties. Idiosyncrasies flourish in the southwest, although the international wine-buying public has been slow to latch on to what the region has to offer.

Bergerac

The vineyards of Bergerac flank the River Dordogne, which joins the Garonne downstream from Bordeaux. The growers could thus escape the greedy clutches of the Bordeaux merchants who controlled the passage of wines from other Hauts-Pays such as Cahors and Gaillac. Bergerac had free access to overseas markets – above all to the prosperous Dutch. The region's attachment to the Protestant religion caused many Huguenots to flee to Holland after the suppression of the reformed religion in 1698, and this reinforced Bergerac exports to that country. The Dutch preferred sweet white wines, which thus became and remained the pride of the Bergerac region. Monbazillac is its most famous name. But in the twentieth century, this style of wine was hard to sell. So the Bergeraçois tried red. Demand has switched to and fro between red and white, with Bergerac tending to be a step behind.

The varieties planted are the Bordeaux red grapes, which perform excellently here, with Merlot in the majority. To call them claret is to ignore historical and political boundaries, but not gastronomic ones. White grapes also do well here, and almost 40 per cent of production is now of white wines. The presence of a prosperous ex-pat community and the fact that foie gras could be considered the local sport should be incentives for the region to acquire more renown. Yet it has remained very much in the shadow of Bordeaux, with only a small handful of estates with any fame outside the area. Bergerac is not one simple appellation but, like Bordeaux, an all-embracing one with 13 subsections determined by slopes, soil, microclimates, and wine styles.

Red Bergerac unqualified is light, unmistakably claret-like by nature: an indistinguishable substitute for many light Bordeaux reds at a markedly lower price. Côtes de Bergerac are bigger, and more so still are the wines from the chalky eastern part of the region with its own appellation, Pécharmant (390 hectares), which, like claret, improve with ageing. The dry white is sold as Bergerac Sec. Some growers exercise the option of introducing the flavour of Sauvignon into wine that is still predominantly Sémillon and, to a lesser extent, Muscadelle. Indeed, mono-varietal white wines are not permitted under the local rules. A new generation of winemakers is working with barrique-ageing for their richest wines, but there is a genuine taste for the semi-sweet here that can produce wines of great charm to the open-minded, although excessive yields and clumsy winemaking can rob many a Côtes de Bergerac *moelleux* of its potential.

No fewer than five inner regions of Bergerac enjoy appellations for sweet and semi-sweet whites (which rely on Sémillon and hope for a degree of "noble rot"). Just south of the town of Bergerac, Monbazillac (3,600 hectares – in theory only, since not all sites within the appellation can deliver sweet wines of quality), with its operatic château (the property of the local cooperative), is capable of truly luscious and powerful wines after the style of Sauternes. The best now share the miraculous harmony of fruity acidity that makes a great Sauternes – and their lives are no shorter. I have lingered long over 40-year-old Monbazillac that had turned a fine tobacco colour. Saussignac is a small appellation (900 hectares in all, though in practice fewer than 100 would be used for sweet wines) for wines that range from the semi-sweet to a handful as rich as those of Monbazillac, though often with fresher acidity. Dry wines from the Saussignac area are sold as Bergerac Sec, while the AC Saussignac is reserved for *moelleux* or sweet wines from botrytis-affected fruit.

North of the Dordogne lies Montravel. Some 1,747 hectares of red vines and 1,463 of white are in theory entitled to the appellation, although wines from fewer than 400 hectares actually claim the appellation. Plain Montravel is a dry white scarcely distinguishable from Bergerac Sec. However, the distinctions between the appellations Côtes de Montravel (*moelleux*), and Haut-Montravel (fully sweet) complicate an already complex situation for the Montravel growers, whose red wines previously could not be called Montravel (they had to be called Bergerac). The rules were changed in 2001, when the growers finally won the right to their own Montravel Rouge AC. Rosette, an almost lost appellation barely clinging to life, is another medium-sweet white, produced in the hills just north and west of Bergerac town.

Finally, Côtes de Bergerac, when applied to white wines, denotes a *moelleux* style with sweetness levels that range from four to 54 grams of residual sugar. Quality is rarely special.

Leading Bergerac, Pécharmant and Monbazillac Producers

Domaine de l'Ancienne Cure ☆☆–☆☆☆☆
Colombier. 42 ha. www.domaine-anciennecure.fr
The owner and winemaker of this estate, Christian Roche, has clarified his already extensive range of Bergerac and

Monbazillac. The basic wine is without pretension. Far more interesting is Cuvée Abbaye from more carefully selected grapes and with some oak-ageing. In exceptional years he also produces L'Extase, including an unusual Bergerac Sec made from overripe grapes and aged in 60 per cent new oak. Many of the white wines, sweet and dry, contain around one third Muscadelle, which differentiates them from comparable styles from Bordeaux.

Château Beauportail ☆☆
Pécharmant, Bergerac. 10 ha.
Fabrice Feytout's fairly small property close to the town produces a rich, discreetly oaky wine that should keep well.

Château Bélingard ☆–☆☆
Pomport. 90 ha. www.chateaubelingard.com
Laurent de Bosredon is an enthusiastic producer of red and white Bergerac of reliable, if unexceptional, quality, and some fine, rich Monbazillac called Blanche de Bosredon. He favours a racy, elegant style of Monbazillac in preference to a wine that is too weighty and tarry.

Domaine de Bertranoux ☆☆
Pécharmant. 5 ha.
Owned by Daniel Hecquet of Château Puy-Servain (q.v.) in Montravel, Bertranoux produces two *cuvées* of barrique-aged Pécharmant.

Château la Borderie ☆–☆☆☆
Sigoulès. 70 ha.
Armand Vidal was for decades a leading producer of Monbazillac and Bergerac, and his estates are now run by his daughter Elisabeth. The Monbazillac is of the highest quality, especially the Cuvée Prestige, which is aged in barrels for 18 months. The Vidals also own nearby Château Treuil de Nailhac, their older, smaller estate. Treuil de Nailhac has a distinct Muscat taste, due to the high proportion of Muscadelle grapes.

Château Caillavel ☆–☆☆
Pomport. 19 ha.
Since 1996, M Lacoste, Caillavel's owner, has been fermenting his sweet wine in new oak, the wood imparting a certain creaminess. Cheaper and more commercial Monbazillac is sold under the name of another of his properties, Château Haut-Theulet.

Château Champarel ☆
Pécharmant. 8 ha.
Good, sturdy wine that needs a few years for its tannins and fruit to integrate.

Clos des Terrasses ☆☆
Sigoulès. 15 ha. www.closdesterrraces.com
The crop from this property was sold to the cooperative until 2001, when it was bought by Fabrice de Suyrot. He brought sound practice to the viticulture here, and was soon producing wines of good quality. The regular red, mostly from Merlot, is aged for 12 months in oak; the Cuvée Le Clos is from the oldest vines and spends about 15 months in new barrels.

Château de la Colline ☆☆
Thénac. 18 ha. www.la-colline.com
A new English-owned property established in 1994. The red is overwhelmingly Merlot, and appropriately succulent. It is aged for 18 months in barriques, as is the Sémillon-dominated white. Martin also produces pure varietal Sémillon and Merlot for early drinking.

Cave Coopérative de Monbazillac ☆
Sigoulès. 800 ha. www.chateau-monbazillac.com
About one half of the cooperative's production is of sweet wine. The best usually comes from the 22 hectares of the Château de Monbazillac, but other properties include Châteaux Septy, and Versant du Haut-Poulvère. In the 2000s efforts have been made to improve quality, including the decision to ferment the prestigious Château de Monbazillac in oak.

Château le Fagé ☆–☆☆
Pomport. 40 ha. www.chateau-le-fage.com
Although François Gérardin likes to think of himself as an all-rounder, it is his Monbazillac that attracts the plaudits, made from a high 90 per cent Sémillon, with a fermentation at low temperature and long ageing in enamelled cement. In top vintages he makes a Grande Réserve, which is aged for over two years in barrels.

Château Fonmourgues ☆☆–☆☆☆
Monbazillac. 19 ha.
Dominique Vidal makes a richer, more opulent style of Monbazillac than his father did at Château la Borderie (q.v.). He also makes red and dry white Bergerac of good quality.

Château de Panisseau, Thénac

Domaine Grande Maison ☆☆☆
Monbazillac. 20 ha.
Thierry Després took over this property in 1990 and promptly replanted much of the vineyards, which are cultivated organically. He uses individual techniques, such as chilling the botrytized bunches before fermentation. The basic wine is the Cuvée des Anges, there is an unusual Monbazillac from Sauvignon Gris and Sauvignon Blanc called Cuvée Exotique, and the top oak-aged wine is bizarrely called Les Monstres and sells for a very high price, since it is produced from minuscule yields.

Château Grinou ☆☆
Monestier. 35 ha.
Guy Cuisset is an all-rounder making good red Bergerac, especially the oak-aged Reserve, a pure Merlot, as well as both dry white Bergerac and fine Saussignac.

Château Haut-Bernasse ☆☆–☆☆☆
Monbazillac. 27 ha. www.haut-bernasse.com
Jacques Blais is a cellist and self-taught winemaker, whose wines steadily improved through the 1990s. In 2002 he sold the property to Jules Villette, who has maintained standards for fine oak-aged Monbazillac and rich if oaky red Côtes de Bergerac.

Domaine du Haut-Pécharmant ☆☆
Bergerac. 23 ha. www.haut-pecharmant.com
The second-largest Pécharmant vineyard. Owner, Michel Roches, makes his long-lived wine in a traditional manner, with only the Cuvée Prestige being aged in oak. His most distinctive wine is Cuvée Veuve Roches, made from 70 per cent Cabernet Franc.

Domaine de la Jaubertie
Colombier. 52 ha.
A splendid property in disarray for many years. Nick Ryman developed the estate in the 1970s, and his son Hugh, later the best-known of all the flying winemakers, cut his teeth by making balanced and elegant reds and delicious whites, including a rare pure Muscadelle. Hugh Ryman sold Jaubertie in 2000, and although the estate continues to produce wine, it is rarely seen.

Château Masburel ☆☆
Fougueyrolles. 23 ha. www.chateau-masburel.com
Neil and Olivia Donnan have opted for a rich, powerful style of red Bergerac. Lady Masburel is a lighter range, and the Donnans also make a barrel-fermented Montravel, which is mostly Sauvignon Blanc.

Domaine la Métairie ☆
Creyssensac-et-Pissot. 6 ha.
An oak-aged Pécharmant, and all the better for it. In recent years, the proportion of Merlot in the blend has been increasing. In 2005 the property as bought by Daniel Hecquet.

Château Monestier La Tour ☆☆
Monestier. 34 ha. www.chateaumonestierlatour.com
Philip de Haseth-Möller bought and restored this handsome house and its vineyards. Today, with advice from Stéphane Derenoncourt, he produces a full range of white and red Bergerac, and a little Saussignac to ice the cake.

Château Poulvère ☆
Sigoulès. 86 ha. www.poulvere.com
A large estate producing a full range of Bergerac styles, including an unoaked Pécharmant under the Domaine les Grangettes label. The Monbazillac is good but not exceptional.

Château La Robertie ☆–☆☆
Rouffignac-des-Sigoulès. 16 ha.
www.chateau-larobertie.com
Jean-Philippe Soulier bought this run-down property in 1999 and has made swift progress. The top wine is La Robertie Haute, a red from the best sector of the vineyard; it is aged in new oak. The domaine also produces a pair of Monbazillacs, of which the more concentrated is the oak-aged Vendanges de Brumaire.

Château Thénac
Thénac. 80 ha. www.chateau-thenac.com
A large property just east of Bergerac that has been restored and renovated under owner Eugene Shvidler. Ludwig Vanneron, former assistant to Michel Rolland, is the winemaker. The top wines appear under the chateau label, and there is an easy-drinking style called Fleur du Périgord.

Château Theulet ☆–☆☆
Monbazillac. 50 ha.
An estate that goes back to the time of the special relationship with Holland. Owner Pierre Alard makes supple, highly drinkable red Bergerac and good Monbazillac Cuvée Prestige, aged in 50 per cent new oak.

Château Tirecul la Gravière ☆☆☆–☆☆☆☆
Monbazillac. 9 ha. www.vinibilancini.com
This perfectionist estate is owned by oenologist Bruno Bilancini. The property is unusual in that half the vines are Muscadelle. Bilancini works as though this were a top Sauternes property: selective harvesting, high sugar levels, and a good deal of new oak for barrel fermentation. The wines are marked by their richness and intensity. The almost syrupy top *cuvée* is called Cuvée Madame. It is far more expensive than the regular Monbazillac, which is itself among the best of the region.

Château Tiregand ☆☆
Creysse. 43 ha. www.chateau-de-tiregand.com
The biggest Pécharmant property, replanted after the 1956 frosts by the St-Exupéry family. Iron in the soil gives a structure in the wine that calls for ageing in bottle. Wine from young vines is much lighter and sold as Clos de la Montalbanie, while the best parcels are aged in 50 per cent new oak and sold as Grand Millésime.

Château la Tour des Gendres ☆☆☆
Ribagnac. 50 ha.
Made from mostly Biodynamic vineyards on diverse soils just south of Monbazillac, Luc de Conti makes stylish and distinctive wines. As well as a white Bergerac called Moulin des Dames, Cuvée des Conti is mostly Sémillon, aged briefly in new oak. The wine has a distinct flavour of citrus fruits. A special *cuvée* called Anthologia is made from late-picked

Sauvignon, aged in oak. In 2005 a rare pure Muscadelle was added to the range. The red Anthologia is made by the severely artisanal method of fermenting in 500-litre barrels. The red wines, aged on their fine lees, are the most expensive in Bergerac: especially Anthologia. Better value are the excellent, skilfully oaked wines labelled Gloire de Mon Père.

Domaine les Verdots ☆☆–☆☆☆
Conne-de-Labarde. 35 ha. www.verdots.com
At this beautifully equipped estate David Fourtout produces a bewildering range of wines under a variety of labels. The mid-range wines are labelled Les Tour des Verdots, while the top wines confirm the owner's pride in them: Selon David Fourtout. There is also a small quantity of Monbazillac made from leased vineyards, and what must be the only Bergerac *moelleux* aged partially in new oak.

Saussignac

Clos d'Yvigne ☆☆–☆☆☆
Gageac-et-Rouillac. 20 ha. www.cdywine.com
Half the production here is of red wine and a little good Merlot rosé, but it takes second place to the magnificent Saussignac. Owner Patricia Atkinson often waits into mid-November before harvesting to ensure the grapes are as botrytized and concentrated as possible. The wine is 90 per cent Sémillon and aged in new oak. It is honeyed, tastes of dried apricots, and fetches a good price.

Château Court-les-Mûts ☆–☆☆
Razac. 68 ha.
Pierre-Jean Sadoux is an oenologist who did much to keep the Saussignac flame burning after growers had abandoned its production. He also produces a full range of Bergerac, notably one of the best of the Bergerac reds from 50 per cent Merlot and the two Cabernets.

Château la Maurigne ☆☆–☆☆☆
Razac de Saussignac. 7 ha. www.chateaulamaurigne.com
Patrick and Chantal Gérardin bought this property in 1996 and have worked hard to make wines of high quality. They produce red and white Bergerac of sound quality, but the main focus is Saussignac. Three versions are produced, reflecting ever stricter selection. The top wine is Florilège, which spends years in new oak before bottling.

Château les Miaudoux ☆☆
Saussignac. 26 ha.
Gérard Cuisset was one of the pioneers of the new-style, ultra-sweet Saussignac white wines, taking their cue from neighbouring Monbazillacs. The wine is fermented and aged in about one-third new oak. Cuisset also produces a full range of Bergerac styles, all at reasonable prices.

Domaine Richard ☆☆–☆☆☆
Monestier. 18 ha.
The owner is Richard Doughty. Yes, an Englishman, also passionate about *liquoreux* Saussignac. Like Gérard Cuisset at les Miaudoux, he relies on his dry white Bergerac for a living, but his heart is in the sweet wine. The estate is farmed organically.

Montravel

Château Jonc-Blanc ☆–☆☆☆
Velines. 13 ha.
A leading producer of red Montravel called Rubis, as well as fruity red Bergerac.

Château Moulin Caressse ☆–☆☆☆
St Antoine-de-Breuilh. 27 ha.
Apart from a few simple Bergeracs, the focus here is on Montravel and Haut-Montravel. The top range, called Cent pour 100, consists of barrel-aged dry white and red.

Château Pique-Segue ☆☆
Port Ste-Foy. 76 ha.
A large estate, so some of the oaked wines appear under the Dauzan La Vergne label; these include a very oaky Merlot. The Dauzan La Vergne Haut-Montravel is almost pure Sémillon, barrel-fermented and aged for around eight months. The wine is attractive and balanced, but not hugely concentrated.

Château Puy-Servain ☆☆
Port Ste-Foy. 20 ha. www.puy-servain.com
Owner Daniel Hecquet has been the leading grower pressing for higher quality and a shift to a sweeter, richer style of *liquoreux*. The whites here are the thing. The wines from a second Hecquet property, Château Calabre, are made without wood, while Puy-Servain is oaked. The dry white is very dry, the oaked version (called Marjolaine) having plenty of body and fat. The Haut-Montravel sweet wines reflect the current styles in Monbazillac and Saussignac, but as yet do not quite reach the level of the best from those two areas.

Rosette

Very few estates still produce this apéritif wine. As a *moelleux* rather than a *liquoreux*, it competes with difficulty against the far richer wines from Monbazillac and Saussignac. Among the properties producing acceptable versions are Château Monplaisir and Domaine de Coutancie.

Cahors

Cahors is certainly the most celebrated red wine of the scattered regions of the southwest. The ancient town on the River Lot with its famous fortified bridge is linked in the public mind with dramatic-sounding "black wine". This was because so much of the wine made in Bordeaux was thin and travelled badly, and merchants needed something to give strength and body to their exports. The position at the commanding mouth of the Garonne enabled them to call the tune at Cahors, whose growers they encouraged to produce a thick, dark brew by boiling some of their wine, even fortifying it. This was the famous "black wine", so celebrated, at least in myth, that Crimean winemakers produced a "Cahorski" in tribute.

Real Cahors wine has always been quite different, although the traditional methods of long fermentation and the universal use of the Malbec grape (called Auxerrois in Cahors) always produced a darker and more rustic wine than claret. Perhaps this explains why Cahors is still trying to live down the reputation it earned from its "black wine". Cahors was destroyed by phylloxera in the 1880s, and nearly a second time by the great frost of 1956. It struggled back very slowly until the 1960s and '70s, when a business-like cooperative and a handful of old-time growers pulled the region together. It was promoted to appellation status in 1971 – not for a revival of its "black wine", but for well-balanced, vigorous, and agreeable reds. A minimum of 70 per cent Auxerrois may now be blended with the softer Merlot as well as Tannat (the grape of Madiran). No other varieties are allowed today.

Most of the 4,100 hectares are now on the alluvial valley land, which is very gravelly in places, although there are some expanding plantings on the *causses*, the limestone plateaux above the river. Despite the difference in the two terroirs, there is less distinction than might be imagined between the styles of *causse* and valley wines. Local growers suggest that the plateaux yield more elegant wines, and that the alluvial vineyards are more variable in quality. The real contrast is between the traditional methods of vinification and those adopted by the newcomers, the négociants turned vignerons and the financial entrepreneurs who have spent fortunes in creating modern wineries. All too often these provide textbook examples of the law of diminishing returns. The best Cahors today are still mostly produced by the long-established growers and a few younger ones from the region who, like their counterparts in Madiran, understand the importance of keeping the *typicité* of their own wine. That *typicité* includes a certain robustness and vigour, power but not necessarily weight, and a hint of gaminess as the wine matures.

The popularity and quality of Malbec from Argentina seem to have provoked the growers of Cahors to aim higher and do better. Over the past decade there has been an astonishing leap in quality, confirming that the post-phylloxera plantings of Malbec here (in contrast to the pre-phylloxera cuttings taken to Argentina) are fully capable of making excellent wine. In addition, new generations of growers and winemakers have honed their winemaking skills and the coarse, rustic wines of the 1970s and 1980s now seem a thing of the past. There is a tendency to assume that wines aged in new oak are intrinsically superior to those aged in tanks or older barrels. In fact, there is a place for all styles of Cahors. A fruit-packed, tank-aged wine can give great pleasure at a modest price for a few years, while the more costly oak-aged wines will satisfy those who seek a more international style. This is not to disparage the best oaked Cahors, which can be of tremendous quality.

Leading Cahors Producers

Château de la Bérangeraie ☆☆
Grezels. 28 ha.
Located up on the limestone plateau, this is a fine source of inexpensive unoaked Cahors. Cuvée Maurin is forthright and packed with fruit, while devotees of barrel-aged Cahors can find a sumptuous example in Matthis Bacchus.

Domaine Le Bout du Lieu ☆☆
St Vincent-Rive-d'Olt. 17 ha.
A family producing three interpretations of pure Malbec. Although aged in new barriques, their Cuvée Empyrée is well balanced, with spicy, cherry fruit and a persistent finish.

Château la Caminade ☆☆
Parnac. 35 ha. www.chateau-caminade.com
The Ressès family's estate is worth a visit for the architecture alone; a fine example of a Quercynois presbytery, turrets and

The bridge over the River Lot at Cahors

all, now given over to high-class viticulture. In addition to its mainstream wine, the Château la Caminade produces an oaked premium wine called La Commendary from pure Malbec, as well as a lighter and unwooded style called Coste Peyrouse. There is also a full-blown, new-oaked bottling of pure Malbec called L'Esprit, but overall La Commendary seems better balanced and more satisfying.

Cave Coopérative les Côtes d'Olt ☆–☆☆
Parnac. 900 ha.
250 growers participate in this forward-looking cooperative. The range of wines is large, and overall standards are sound. Unwooded wines include Comte André der Monpezat and Château Vignals; the oaked cuvées are "Impernal" and "Château les Bouysses". "Impernal" is pure Malbec, whereas les Bouysses has 20 per cent Merlot. Both are aged in 5 0 per cent new oak. Impernal is the more discreet and structured of the two.

Château du Cèdre ☆☆☆
Vire-sur-Lot. 27 ha.
Pascal and Jean-Marc Verhaeghe are certainly among the finest winemakers in the appellation. With more Malbec in their vineyards than most, the basic wine is finished with some Merlot, while in the Cuvée Prestige the Merlot is replaced by Tannat. Both wines are made using micro-oxygenation, and the Prestige is aged in about one-third new oak. There is also a new-oaked luxury *cuvée* called, simply, Le Cèdre, and in 2000 yet another *cuvée*, GC, was introduced. It's a massive wine, built to impress, and many drinkers will prefer the more digestible Prestige or Le Cèdre.

Château de Chambert ☆–☆☆
Floressas. 62 ha. www.chateaudechambert.com
There were vineyards here in the eighteenth century, but the entire property was replanted in 1974. In 2007 the property, which hitherto had produced medium-bodied, elegant wines, was sold to a young businessman Philippe Lejeune, who has hired consultant Stéphane Derenoncourt to lift the wines to a higher level.

Clos la Coutale ☆–☆☆
Vire. 55 ha.
The Bernèdes have been making wine here since before the Revolution. Today, the wine is noted for its rich fruit underpinned by firm tannins, and is often successful in difficult years. It's an old-fashioned style with a slight rusticity, but it can age well.

Clos de Gamot & Château de Cayrou ☆☆
Prayssac and Puy l'Evêque. 40 ha.
The colourful Jean Jouffreau, who died in 1996, was a hard act to follow at these two properties, but his son-in-law, Yves Hermann-Jouffreau is determined to maintain standards. The Clos de Gamot vineyard has been in the family since 1610 and is planted exclusively with Malbec. Château de Cayrou was bought in 1971 and is planted with a more modern mix that includes some Merlot and Tannat. The wines from both properties enjoy ultra-traditional production from a modern winery. The Gamot, a chewy, concentrated wine, can last as long as great claret in a good year. Cayrou is a little lighter in style, with considerable elegance.

Clos Triguedina ☆☆☆
Vire. 65 ha. www.jlbaldes.com
Dating back to 1830, this large estate, owned by Jean-Luc Baldès, makes wines that need some ageing. In addition to the mainstream wine (from 80 per cent Malbec), there is a special old-vine *cuvée* called Prince Probus, which is generously oaked, and a lighter wine sold as Domaine Labrande for earlier drinking. In the mid-1990s, the winery re-created the black wine of Cahors, heating the must in tanks for 30 minutes, and ageing the wine is new oak. The result is tannic and jammy, and by no means preferable to the splendid Probus.

Clos d'Un Jour ☆☆–☆☆☆
Duravel. 7 ha.
Owner/winemaker Stéphane Azemar allows you to compare two styles of Cahors. Un Jour is pure Malbec aged in 50 per cent new oak; Un Jour Sur Terre is similar but aged in terracotta jars. Tasted side by side the former seems to have more panache and intensity, but both are of exceptional quality.

Domaine Cosse Maisonneuve ☆☆
Fargues. 20 ha.
Matthieu Cosse and Catherine Maisonneuve teamed up in 1999 to create a new domaine, which is cultivated Biodynamically with high-density plantings. They produce five wines, playing with combinations of terroir and winemaking style. The finest is probably Les Laquets, which has sufficient density to cope with prolonged barrel-ageing. Clearly a domaine on the rise.

Domaine du Garinet ☆–☆☆
Le Boulvé. 3 ha. www.domainedugarinet.moncuq.com
This tiny British-owned estate produces two wines: an unoaked Classique and, using the same base wine, the oak-aged Fûts de Chêne. Often the former has great vibrancy, but both are vibrant and juicy.

Château de Gaudou ☆☆
Vire. 35 ha. www.chateaudegaudou.com
Four *cuvées* are produced here from varied soils: the Tradition, aged in large casks; the 85 per cent Malbec barrique-aged Grande Lignée; and the oaky but vigorous pure-Malbec Renaissance. A recent addition to the range is the Réserve de Caillou in an unashamedly *garagiste* style that is overbearing.

Château Haut-Monplaisir ☆☆–☆☆☆
Lacapelle-Cabanac. 27 ha.
The Fourniés own excellent vineyards on high gravelly terraces, and have taken on Pascal Verhaeghe of Château du Cèdre (q.v.) as an advisor. Like many other forward-looking properties in Cahors, they produce three versions of the wine: an unoaked, a Prestige aged partially in new oak; and Pur Plaisir, aged in new 500-litre barrels. All three are excellent, being marked by great vibrancy and freshness.

Château de Haute-Serre ☆–☆☆
Cieurac. 66 ha. www.g-vigouroux.fr
These are the highest vineyards in Cahors, located on the

plateau in a single stony parcel. A well-known property in the nineteenth century, says owner Georges Vigouroux, but it was entirely replanted in 1972. Just one-third of the wine is aged in barriques to avoid overtly oaky flavours. There is also a special selection, Géron Dadine, aged in 400-litre barrels and often showing a pronounced flavour of black-cherries.

Château d'Homs ☆☆
Saux. 10 ha. www.domainedhoms-cahors.fr
A small property that produces a number of *cuvées*, the best being from the oldest vines. The Prestige is marked by red-fruits flavours, whereas Chevalier d'Homs has more spice and a black-fruits character. These are very well made wines.

Château Lagrézette ☆☆–☆☆☆
Caillac. 65 ha. www.chateau-lagrezette.tm.fr
The estate that led the revival of the region in the 1980s. The owner, Alain-Dominique Perrin, is the head of Cartier and has spared no expense to make wine that is both concentrated and elegant. The winemakers, overseen by consultant Michel Rolland, employ modern techniques, such as cold maceration and micro-oxygenation, to obtain the desired results. The flagship wines are Le Pigeonnier, a pure Auxerrois from yields of 20 hl/ha and given prolonged ageing in oak, and Dame Honneur. These are rich, sumptuous wines, perhaps not entirely typical of Cahors, and their price structure is ambitious.

Château Lamartine ☆☆
Soturac. 30 ha. www.cahorslamartine.com
A long-established property that uses very modern techniques to produce supple, oaky wines that give a great deal of pleasure, as well as the richer, more extracted Cuvée Expression.

Château de Mercuès ☆–☆☆
Mercuès. 40 ha. www.g-vigouroux.fr
A luxury hotel as well as a wine estate, owned by the ubiquitous Vigouroux family. Supple, slightly chocolatey wines, plus a full-bodied special Cuvée 6666 – the number refers to the density of vines per hectare - aged entirely in new oak.

Château Pineraie ☆☆☆
Puy-l'Evêque. www.chateaupineraie.com
The Burc family have owned this property since 1456. Their best wine, Cuvée Authentique, is pure Malbec from the ground that rises up towards the *causse*. Although aged in new oak, Authentique has superb fruit and structure that push the oak into the background.

Prieuré de Cénac ☆☆–☆☆☆
Parnac. 35 ha. www.rigal.fr
Owned by the Rigal family since 1979, a property on varied soils, with about 80 per cent Auxerrois and low yields. After a dull patch, this property is now back on form with a sleek, superripe Cuvée La Vierge.

Château La Reyne ☆☆–☆☆☆
Leygues. 20 ha.
Johan Vidal produces four wines from La Reyne, of which the most sensational is the tangy, oaky, blackberry-flavoured Vent d'Anges.

Aveyron & The Upper Lot

One hundred and twelve kilometres (70 miles) upstream from Cahors, the rolling limestone *causses* give way to the foothills of the Massif Central, and the landscape starts to close in on the River Lot. Wine has been made in this area for centuries, from grapes grown on almost perpendicular slopes, terraced and walled with back-breaking effort. At Marcillac, the rich burghers of Rodez had their country homes where they employed resident winemakers to supply their needs; later, after the phylloxera epidemic, the wine was made to slake the thirst of the coalminers of Decazeville.

When the mines were closed down in the 1950s, the Marcillac growers formed themselves into a cooperative to raise standards of production and to find a new market for their wine. It is highly original, made almost entirely from the Fer Servadou grape, called locally Mansois. It has a slight resemblance to Cabernet Franc: the same grassiness and flavour of soft, red fruits, redcurrants and blackcurrants, and sometimes blackberries. There is only red and rosé Marcillac. The 180 hectares have enjoyed *appellation contrôlée* status since 1990. The local white wine comes from further up the river from nine hectares at Entraygues, where the Lot is joined by the Truyère, and at Estaing (a mere seven hectares). Here the Chenin Blanc grape is used to make a bone-dry, stylish, and surprisingly modern-tasting wine; at Estaing some Mauzac is also used. The production is very small, but locally important; the wines are seldom seen outside the area, but are on the lists of all the local restaurants.

Red wine, too, is made at both towns. Entraygues and Estaing both enjoy VDQS status, as do the wines grown in the upper valley of the Tarn in the vicinity of the town of Millau. Entraygues has no cooperative, and only six producers, but Estaing and Côtes de Millau both have small cooperatives in addition to a handful of private growers. Entraygues would be heading for extinction, were it not for the stubborn perseverance of a handful of growers such as François Avallon and Jean-Marc Viguier and the loyalty of some local restaurateurs. The same is true of Estaing, which is dominated – if that is the right word for such a tiny region – by Les Vignerons d'Olt.

At Millau, the only significant producers are the Cave des Vignerons des Gorges du Tarn and Domaine du Vieux Noyer.

Leading Aveyron Producers
Marcillac

Cave des Vignerons du Vallon ☆☆
Valady. 110 ha. www.vigneronsduvallon.com
By far the largest producer, responsible for over half the production of Marcillac's wine. Most, but not all, of the wines are unoaked. Quality is high, and the wines, whatever their style, manage to show delicacy and persistence. The oaked Cuvée Exception has surprising finesse.

Domaine du Cros ☆–☆☆
Goutrens. 26 ha. www.domaine-du-cros.com
Philippe Teulier has doggedly expanded his holdings. Wines of substance, especially the Cuvée Vieilles Vignes.

Domaine Laurens ☆
Clairvaux d'Aveyron. 21 ha. www.domaine-laurens.com
A producer of local *eau-de-vie* as well as of medium-bodied, unoaked red and rosé.

Jean-Luc Matha ☆–☆☆
Bruéjouls. 13 ha.
Two principal wines, one unoaked, the other the cask-aged Cuvée Spéciale. Both have charm and a discreet minerality.

Gaillac

Gaillac is one of the most productive and economically important of the scattered vineyards of the southwest. Historically, it has supplied not only Albi, the capital of its *département*, the Tarn, but places much further away – its reds having a name for amazing transportability and longevity. It was established as a vineyard during the first century after Christ, during the Roman occupation of the Midi, and long before vines were planted at Bordeaux.

Its unheard-of indigenous grape varieties, the bane of some modern producers but the pride and joy of others, encourage the idea of extreme antiquity. Its reds are the Duras (nothing to do with the wine area of that name) and the Braucol, the local name for Fer Servadou; its whites are Mauzac, Len de l'El (or Loin de l'Oeil), and Ondenc. Ondenc had almost completely disappeared until it was revived by Robert Plageoles, who replanted two hectares in 1983.

A century ago, just before phylloxera struck, the production of Gaillac was almost entirely of red wine. The little white that was made was either sweet or sparkling or both, or else of a style not unlike that of a light sherry. The reds were big and sturdy, mostly sold down the river to Bordeaux for blending. When the vineyard was replanted, the emphasis changed to white wine because of the competition in reds from the Midi.

The traditional white Gaillac grape, Mauzac, was exploited to produce sweet wines with an appley character. AC status was granted for the white wines in 1938. The red wines were only recognized in 1970, largely because the growers had failed to replant post-phylloxera with good-quality varieties and had stuck to the old, rather commonplace stocks. The modern reconstruction of the industry, sparked off by big cooperatives, has opted for more standardized production. A tradition of bottling white wine before its first fermentation was over was dropped in favour of the Champagne method, despite the fact that the Gaillac process ante-dated the Champagne technique by several centuries. Sauvignon, Merlot, Gamay, and Syrah have been brought in, and where they are used, the wines are lighter and more neutral than they used to be.

In addition to the three cooperatives, there are today about 100 private producers, which is ten times as many as there were in 1970. Some 2,500 hectares are under vine. Most of the best producers are going back to the old Gaillac grapes in a search for *typicité* and distinctiveness. The modern range of Gaillac is thus bewildering; there are plain, dry white wines, or *perlé* – that is, dry with a slight prickle induced by keeping them on their lees; there are dry and *demi-sec* sparkling wines; and there are more-or-less sweet still wines. There are oaked and unoaked reds and a *vin de l'année* after the style of, and often much better than, Beaujolais Nouveau. There are also rosé wines, of course. In terms of quality, there are marked variations, and the situation is complicated by the fact that some growers inevitably excel in some styles more than others.

Leading Gaillac Producers

Domaine de Balagès ☆–☆☆
Lagrave. 14 ha.
An atypical estate, in that only red wines are produced, notably the barrel-aged Cuvée Rêveline.

Domaine de Causse-Marines ☆☆–☆☆☆
Vieux. 15 ha. www.causse-marines.com
Patrice Lescarret is known for his outstanding sweet wines. They are given proprietary names such as Délires d'Automne (an oxidative style) and Grain de Folie, have varying degrees of intensity and are based on different blends. He also makes a wine under a flor-like layer of yeast which he calls Mystère and which resembles *vin jaune*. These are fascinating, if sometimes weird, wines.

Domaine d'Escausses ☆☆
Ste Croix. 34 ha.
www.domainedescausses.com
Jean-Marc Balaran offes up the usual eclectic range from Gaillac: a barrel-fermented Sauvignon and Mauzac (Vigne de l'Oubli), a blend of Fer Servadou, Syrah, and Cabernet Sauvignon (La Croix Petite), and a splendid oak-aged Fer Servadou (La Vigne Mythique). All at modest prices.

Domaine de Gineste ☆–☆☆
Técou. 16 ha.
www.domainedegineste.com
This estate, now owned by Emmanuel Maugeais, is best-known for a wine called La Coulée d'Or. Despite the muddle of the Gaillac AC rules, this wine doesn't qualify, as it is a late-harvest blend of Chardonnay and Mauzac. The dry red and white wines are not quite at the same level.

Domaine de Labarthe ☆☆
Castanet. 48 ha.
Jean-Paul Albert does not disappoint. To be recommended are his white *perlé* from Mauzac, his sweet white from Len de l'El called Grains d'Or, his basic red wine, and his top-of-the-range red, Cuvée Guillaume, which is quite markedly oaked.

Statue of Bacchus, Palais de la Berbie, Albi

Mas Pignou ☆
Laborie. 35 ha.
A property with a complete range of wine as well as the best view of Gaillac town and the valley of the Tarn. His dry white (50 per cent Sauvignon, 50 per cent Len de l'El) ages well. The prestige red is Cuvée Mélanie, but the basic red is excellent, too.

Domaine de Mazou ☆–☆☆
Lisle sur Tarn. 35 ha. www.mazou.com
Jean-Marc Boyals excels with red wines. Despite its name, the Tradition is oak-aged, and a wine with weight, freshness, and persistence.

Robert Plageoles ☆☆☆
Cahuzac-sur-Vere. 20 ha
At his Domaine des Très Cantous, Robert Plageoles and son Bernard produce an astonishing range of varietal wines. Almost all are from the traditional Gaillac varieties: a 100 per cent Duras, a Gamay, dry and sweet whites exclusively from Mauzac, a dry sparkler made according to the old Gaillac method, sweet wines from 100 per cent Ondenc, and another from Muscadelle. The very sweet and honeyed Vin d'Autan and Grain d'Autan are made from late-harvested Ondenc, the latter from botrytized grapes. The range is rounded off with Vin de Voile, very similar in character to a *vin jaune* from the Jura, though made from Mauzac. The entire region owes the Plageoles a great deal.

Domaine Rotier ☆☆–☆☆☆
Cadalen. 36 ha. www.domaine-rotier.com
The quality-conscious Rotiers make a good range of wines in all the main styles found in Gaillac: red wine, barrel-aged white wines, and, of course, sweet wine. The best are labelled Renaissance, and the barrique-aged Doux, from botrytis-affected Loin d'Oeil, is packed with delicious quince fruit.

Cave Coopérative de Técou ☆
Técou. 850 ha. www.cavedetecou.fr
The best all-rounder of the three co-ops. The 220 members do not have the best terrain; most of the vineyards are on the south bank in the plain. But the quality of the winemaking is all the more remarkable for that. The top red is Gaillac Passion: a blend of Braucol and Merlot aged in mostly new oak.

Fronton

The slopes around Fronton and Villaudric, 24-kilometres (15-miles) north of Toulouse and 32-kilometres (20-miles) west of Gaillac, achieved AC status in 1975 for their ripely fruity red and rosé wines, which until then had been a secret kept by the people of Toulouse. The local grape is Négrette, brought back from Cyprus at the time of the Crusades by the Knights Templar, who owned much of the land covered by today's vineyards at Fronton. For those who cannot resist the complications of ampelography, I should add that the Négrette turns up in the Charente (of all places) as Le Petit Noir. Its only appellation appearance is, however, in the Frontonnais. In 2005 the name of the appellation was changed from Côtes du Frontonnais to Fronton. Some 2,300 hectares are cultivated.

Négrette, which by law must form at least 50 per cent of every Fronton vineyard, is, as its name implies, very dark-skinned and its juice is dark, too. The grapes are small and the skins are thin, which has encouraged at least one good grower to vinify by *macération carbonique*. The bouquet of Négrette is said to suggest violets, red fruits, and/or liquorice; the flavour often brings to mind cherries and almonds.

The problem with the Négrette grape, though, is that it is liable to grey rot, but given that the climate of Toulouse is hot and dry during the growing season, it flourishes well there. It is a very adaptable grape; on its own its low tannin and acidity can make a light quaffing style of wine of considerable character; and blended with the two Cabernets, Gamay, and/or Syrah, it can make a bigger wine, capable of four or five years' ageing.

Leading Frontonnais Producers

Château Baudare ☆–☆☆
Labastide-St-Pierre. 35 ha. www.chateaubaudare.com
As well as Négrette, grapes such as Gamay and Syrah are also planted in Claude and David Vigouroux's vineyards. The result is a range of enjoyable medium-bodied wines to drink young, supplemented by *vins de pays*. The Cuvée Prestige has 50 per cent Cabernet Sauvignon and is mellowed by ageing in large casks.

Château Bellevue-la-Forêt ☆–☆☆
Fronton. 115 ha. www.chateaubellevuelaforet.com
Patrick Germain is one of the biggest private producers in the southwest. He started from scratch in 1975, with advice from Emile Peynaud. His wines include a 100 per cent light Négrette called Ce Vin, originally styled by local restaurateur André Daguin, and a traditional red, his biggest seller, as well as some oaked prestige wines such as Optimum, which, unusually, has more Syrah than Négrette. (Oak is controversial in Fronton, most growers believing that it does not suit the grape variety.) The rosé from this estate is popular and very good.

Château Cahuzac ☆
Fabas. 55 ha.
A long-established property owned by the Ferran family. Their most expensive wine, the Fleuron de Guillaume, follows the fad for ageing in new oak and is not necessarily superior to their silky red, L'Authentique.

Domaine de Callory ☆
Labastide-St-Pierre. 27 ha.
A traditional estate that eschews wood-ageing but makes a sound blend of Négrette, Syrah, and Cabernet Sauvignon.

Château Clamens ☆–☆☆
Fronton. 20 ha. www.chateau-clamens.fr
A property that made its debut in 1998. Owner Jean-Michel Begue favours oak-ageing for his top wines, and Cuvée Julie has 70 per cent Cabernet Sauvignon.

Château la Colombière ☆☆
Villaudric. 20 ha. www.chateaulacolombiere.com
A well-crafted range of wines from Philip Cauvin's Biodynamic

estate, including Coste Rouge, a pure Négrette, and the blended Baron de D, made from 50-year-old vines.

Château Coutinel ☆
Labastide-St-Pierre. 44 ha. www.arbeau.com
A large well-run property. The oak-aged *cuvées* such as Elixir seems less successful than the supple, fruity standard bottlings.

Château Cransac ☆
Fronton. 40 ha. www.chateaucransac.com
The unoaked Tradition has sleek cherry fruit, while the oak-aged Renaissance is unusual in containing 50 per cent Cabernet Franc.

Château Joliet ☆–☆☆
Fronton. 20 ha. wwwchateau-joliet.com
Owners François and Marie-Claire Daubert specialize in an all-Négrette red, Fantaisie, which is among the best of its style in the region. There is no such thing as white Fronton, but Daubert makes a delicious, sweet *vin de pays* from the Mauzac grape.

Château Marguerite ☆
Campsas. 75 ha.
A very large property producing medium-bodied red wines and a surprisingly rich rosé.

Château Montauriol ☆–☆☆
Villematiuer. 35 ha. www.vignobles-nicolasgelis.com
A change in ownership in 1998 has led to improved quality in traditional-style wines made with at least 50 per cent Négrette.

Château Plaisance ☆☆
Vacquiers. 24 ha. www.chateau-plaisance.fr
Marc Pénavayre makes four styles of Fronton, in addition to a good rosé: a so-called Vin de Printemps, whose style speaks for itself; an excellent mainstream red; an oaked Cuvée Thibault de Plaisance, which has 40 per cent Syrah in the blend, and the surprisingly well-balanced Tot co ou Cal, which is only made in outstanding years and aged in new oak.

Château le Roc ☆☆
Fronton. 25 ha. www.leroc-fronton.com
Frédéric Ribes makes wines that are more structured than most, and need some cellarage. Since 1995, he has selected the best Négrette and Syrah grapes for his Cuvée Don Quichotte, which is both of high quality and fairly priced.

Château St-Louis ☆
Labastide-St-Pierre. 35 ha. www.chateausaintlouis.fr
Good, rounded wines, and a fleshy, plump Cuvée l'Esprit, which is mostly Négrette and aged in oak.

The Bordeaux Satellites

Côtes de Duras

The Côtes de Duras has the misfortune, like Bergerac, to lie just over the departmental boundary from Bordeaux – more particularly from Entre-Deux-Mers. The climate is marginally warmer and drier than that of Bordeaux. Its wine is in every way comparable: the dry white is made increasingly from Sauvignon, though Sémillon and Muscadelle are widely grown. The red wines have as much as 60 per cent Cabernet Sauvignon, 30 per cent Merlot, and a little Cabernet Franc and Malbec. Cooperatives are important here, but the best wines come from a handful among the 50 or so independent producers. There are just under 2,000 hectares under vine, two-thirds of which are planted with red grapes.

Leading Côtes de Duras Producers

Domaine Amblard ☆
St-Sernin-de-Duras. 120 ha.
Guy Pauvert runs a huge property producing sound wines, all of which are aged in tanks.

Vignerons Landerrouat-Duras Berticot ☆
Duras. 1,000 ha. www.cave-landerrouat-duras.com
Probably the best of the cooperatives, making a huge range of fairly basic wines.

Château la Grave-Béchade ☆☆
Baleyssagues. 64 ha. www.lagravebechade.fr
Daniel Amar's comfortable *gentilhommière* is the only winemaking property in the region aspiring to the status of a real château. Equipped with ultra-modern technology, it is making wines worthy of bourgeois-château status in Bordeaux terms. A red-wine estate, with both oaked and unoaked bottlings from Cabernet and Merlot.

Domaine Lafon ☆☆
Loubès-Bernac. 13 ha. www.gitton.fr
Well-exposed vineyards give very ripe wines, often released as varietal bottlings from Merlot and even Malbec. There is also a small production of *moelleux* wine. The Gittons also own properties in Sancerre and Pouilly-Fumé.

Domaine de Laulan ☆–☆☆
Duras. 35 ha. www.domainelaulan.com
The Geoffroys are originally from Chablis, but are well implanted now in Duras. Both white and red wines are made in unwooded and oaked versions. The Sauvignon is deliciously fruity, thus demonstrating how different this grape can be at a southern latitude.

Domaine Mouthes Le Bihan ☆☆
St Jean-de-Duras. 12 ha.
An organic estate, producing red and white wines of considerable sophistication.

Côtes du Marmandais

The 1,320-hectare Côtes du Marmandais lies right on the fringes of Bordeaux. Its light red (its major product) could for many years come under the heading of "claret", and its Sauvignon/Sémillon white is comparable to everyday Bordeaux Blanc. En route to AC status, granted in 1990, growers were required, with a view to ensuring *typicité* for Marmandais, to grow whatever they might choose from a list of grapes specific to the southwest, including Malbec, Fer Servadou, and particularly a rare and local specialty called Abouriou. In this way,

Marmande wine has begun to acquire a character of its own, while retaining a fresh and fruity style. Two rival co-ops of roughly equal size used to make nearly all the wine, one to represent right-bank growers at Beaupuy, the other on the left bank at Cocumont. They subsequently merged to form the Cave du Marmandais. There are 11 private estates.

Leading Marmandais Producers

Château de Beaulieu ☆☆
St-Sauveur-de-Meilhan. 29 ha.
www.chateaudebeaulieu.net
The varieties planted here are Bordelais (with the addition of Syrah), and so, in general, is the style of the wine. Quality is consistently good, and there is a richer and very oaky Cuvée de l'Oratoire.

Cave du Marmandais ☆
Cocumont. 1,260 ha. www.origine-marmandais.fr
After the Vignerons de Beaupuy fused with the Cave de Cocumont, the newly formed mega-co-op was producing 92 per cent of Marmandais wines. The top ranges, each from a different bank of the river, are Béroy and Confidentiel.

Elian Da Ros ☆–☆☆☆
Cocumont. 21 ha.
Da Ros worked for some years at Domaine Zind-Humbrecht in Alsace, which may explain his penchant for rich, full-flavoured wines that certainly stand out from the frequently anodyne wines of the region. So far the reds show more strongly than the whites.

Buzet

When Bordeaux was firmly limited to the *département* of the Gironde, one of the up-country sources of claret to be hardest-hit was the hills south of the Garonne to the north of the Armagnac country, the Buzet. Happily, white wine for distillation was an alternative crop, but the gravel and chalky clay on good southeast slopes had long produced very satisfactory red wine. In the last 30 years, they have been reconstituted and are doing better than ever.

The Vignerons de Buzet cooperative dominates the 2,000-hectare area, making red wine to good Bordeaux standards. There are though, a handful of excellent private growers, continuing to contribute beneficial competition.

Leading Buzet Producers

Domaine du Pech ☆–☆☆
Ste-Colombe-en-Bruilhois. 17 ha.
www.chateaudupech.com.
Magali Tissot converted her domaine to Biodynamism in 2004. The unoaked wine is fresh and straightforward, and the oaked La Badinerie has more structure, though neither is intended for long ageing.

Château Sauvagnères ☆
Ste-Colombe-en-Bruilhois. 20 ha.

Sound if unexciting red wines from the three principal Bordeaux varieties.

Les Vignerons de Buzet ☆☆
Buzet-sur-Baise. 1,600 ha. www.vignerons-buzet.fr
The overwhelming majority of Buzet comes from this model cooperative (with its own cooper), which has steadily expanded and improved the vineyards of the area since 1955, and can claim the credit for its promotion to appellation status in 1973.

The red wines are aged in the homemade barrels, the new wood being given to the top range called Baron d'Ardeuil. The least expensive range is called Tradition, and small amounts of white and rosé wines complement the range.

The co-op also makes wines for a number of individual properties, including Domaine Padère and the 80-hectare Château de Gueyze (the best wine from this co-op), and Châteaux du Bouchet, de Pils, Balesté, Mazelière, and Tauzia. There is tension between the co-op and some of the private growers. The former makes no secret of its aim to establish a monopoly, which is a pity, because the latter are making wines with often more local character.

Côtes du Brulhois

This 312-hectare VDQS area adjoins Buzet to the east, but makes more rustic wines. Brulhois may, for example, contain Tannat, Malbec, and Fer Servadou in addition to the two Cabernets and Merlot. Some local growers have more rustic grapes still, but are not allowed to keep these and at the same time declare in a VDQS area, so many have given up altogether. Production has long been almost entirely in the hands of two cooperatives that have now merged: the Vignerons du Brulhois and the Cave de Donzac.

Madiran & Pacherenc

Madiran is the wine that came back from the dead. By 1948, the vineyard in the Vic-Bilh hills on the southern edge of the Armagnac country, 40-kilometres (25-miles) north of Pau, had dwindled to 50 hectares.

Today there are 1,400 and some would claim that Madiran is the best red of the southwest, Cahors included. If it lacked the advantages of Cahors (fame and accessibility), it also avoided the identity crisis that still until recently afflicted the better-known wine. But it is not an easy wine to understand and drink. Its tannins can be punishing, its density oppressive. Yet a good Madiran, given a few years in bottle, develops the same kind of complexity as a mature Bandol or, dare one say it, Médoc. Its peculiar quality is to start life with a disconcerting bite, then to mellow quite rapidly into a wine with a most singular style and texture. When I was looking for the right word for a nine-year-old from the main cooperative of the region, I was so struck by its silkiness on the tongue that I hesitated over the rather lame "liquid", then tried "limpid". Later I looked Madiran up in Paul de Cassagnac's *French Wines*, a little-known but extremely rewarding work of 1936. "An infinitely fluid savour" were the first words that struck my eye. So Madiran is consistent, despite its near demise; across 55 years it still caresses the palate in a seductively swallowable way.

This is the more odd in that de Cassagnac fulminates against "the inferior Tannat", a "common grape" being introduced to replace the Cabernet in the region for the sake of its bigger crop. All real Madiran, he says, is Cabernet. Yet today its producers tell us the secret of its character is the grape that sounds like tannin, and gives all the harshness its name implies; a smaller-berried cousin of the Malbec. A high proportion of Tannat, they say, is essential. Many growers use Tannat alone, at least for their top *cuvées*. The best-known grower in the region, Alain Brumont, goes one stage further and believes that all other varieties should be banned from the appellation – and he should know.

The technique known as micro-oxygenation – the injection of controlled doses of oxygen into the wine during either fermentation or ageing – was developed here by Patrick Ducournau. It originated as a means of moderating the fierce tannins of Tannat. It seems to work well, and allows the wine to be broached and drunk at a younger age than before. (When applied to less robust varieties such as Merlot in St-Emilion, the technique is more controversial.)

The Vic-Bilh hills, a sort of piano rehearsal for the soaring Pyrénées, parallel to the south, give their name to the white wine called Pacherenc: a dialect equivalent of the French *piquets en rangs*, or "stakes in rows". Pacherenc sometimes lends itself as an alternative title to the Arrufiac grape, traditionally an important element in the wine. Gros and Petit Manseng and Petit Courbu are other grapes used. Traditionally, like Vouvray, it was as sweet a wine as the autumn permitted, but most growers today try to make a dry and a sweet version by adopting different proportions of the grape varieties. Pacherenc was always a tiny local production, but nowadays most Madiran growers like to make some. The area planted with white grapes is now 280 hectares.

Leading Madiran & Pacherenc Producers

Château d'Aydie (Domaines Laplace) ☆–☆☆☆
Aydie. 65 ha.
The Laplace family is one of the few who never gave up on Madiran, and there are still some pre-phylloxera vines to prove it. Château d'Aydie is where the family now lives, and it gives its name to their prestige wine, from pure Tannat, aged in 50 per cent new oak. A less-structured red is named after grandfather Frédéric Laplace and has 60 per cent Tannat with equal quantities of the two Cabernets. Midway in style

between the two is Odé d'Aydie, which has 80 per cent Tannat and is far from shy and retiring. All these wines are completely faithful to the *typicité* of Tannat and thus of Madiran. The family think highly of the future for Pacherenc, and their own superb version of the sweeter style is made from grapes usually picked well into November and fermented in new oak.

Château Barréjat ☆☆☆
Maumusson. 16 ha.
Denis Capmartin has been the owner of this property since 1992, and he has enthusiastically taken up the technique of micro-oxygenation. Until recently his top *cuvée* has been Vieux Ceps from 80 per cent Tannat; most of the vines are exceedingly old. The general style is supple with a depth of blackberry fruit that is impressive and beguiling. Capmartin has also introduced a pure Tannat, aged in new barriques, fittingly called Extrême. Fortunately the wine is less intimidating than its name, and it has a voluptuousness and finesse rare in Madiran.

Domaine Berthoumieu ☆☆–☆☆☆
Viella. 24 ha. www.domaine-berthoumieu.com
There is something immediately attractive about Didier Barré's Madirans. They are much less stern and forbidding than some, and seem to come round more quickly than many, even though the prestige red Charles de Batz contains 90 per cent Tannat and is aged in new oak. Barré selectively harvests his white grapes three times, and his sweet Pacherenc is made from the last three pickings.

Domaine des Bories ☆–☆☆
Crouseilles. 15 ha.
Two *cuvées*: a supple and accessible Tradition and the more extracted and not necessarily preferable Vieilles Vignes, which is 80 per cent Tannat and aged in new oak.

Domaine Guy Capmartin ☆☆
Maumusson. 16 ha.
Owned by Guy, the brother of Denis Capmartin (see Château Barréjat). The Cuvée Tradition is relatively accessible when young, but the oakier and more structured Cuvée du Couvent benefits from five years in bottle. It is a chunky, robust wine that attains harmony and texture with age.

Chapelle Lenclos ☆☆
Maumusson-Laguian. 23 ha.
Patrick Ducournau is the think-tank of Madiran, much admired as one of the bright young hopes of the southwest. Although

---

THE GERS: ARMAGNAC COUNTRY

Although a full range of wines is today made in the Armagnac area, it is the dry white wines largely from the Colombard grape that have attracted much popularity. There are typical inexpensive examples produced at co-ops such as Condom and Nogaro,

as well as the Plaimont trio, though none to merit particular attention. Most are sold as the Vin de Pays Côtes de Gascogne. Some independent growers are, however, producing wines of better class, of the sort that a buyer is likely to find in a good wine bar.

Growers include: The Grassa family: Château de Tariquet; Domaine de Rieux; Domaine de Planterieu; Château d'Aydie; Domaine de la Jalousie; Domaine de Pagny; Domaine Mesté-Duran; Domaine de Lahitte; Domaine le Puts; Domaine de Bergerayre.

a devotee of 100 per cent Tannat wines – his premium wine Chapelle Lenclos, for example – he is also keen to soften its tannins and round its edges. This he does by applying the technique of micro-oxygenation that he pioneered. His wines are very enjoyable, but perhaps lack the uncompromising *typicité* of those from Brumont and others.

Ducournau's problem is that he is in such demand as a brilliant wine technician that he lacks the time to look after his two properties, the second and lesser being Domaine Mouréou. In 2002 he appointed a winemaker and gave him a free hand, but a few years later he handed over responsibility for viticulture and winemaking to the Laplace family from Château d'Aydie (q.v.).

Clos Basté ☆☆–☆☆☆
Moncaup. 10 ha.
A former winemaker at Château L'Aydie, Philippe Mur set up his own domaine in 1998. His main Madiran is pure Tannat, aged in 50 per cent new oak. It is steeped in black fruits yet there is no lack of spiciness and vigour. The Pacherenc Moelleux is a triumph.

Domaine du Crampilh ☆☆
Aurions-Idernes. 30 ha.
A well-known estate that has improved in quality through the 1990s. Alain Oulié employs micro-oxygenation to produce a range of flavoury wines, of which the most concentrated is the Pure Tannat Vieilles Vignes.

La Cave de Crouseilles ☆–☆☆
Crouseilles. 600 ha.
A first-class co-op whose top bottling, Château de Crouseilles (a property which they own), can be among the best wines of the region. The mainstream Madirans and Pacherencs are good, too.

Domaine Damiens ☆–☆☆
Aydie. 15 ha.
The wines here used to be quite rustic, and still retain a certain gawkiness, but in recent years the top *cuvée* St Jean has been rich, plummy, and suave.

Domaine Labranche-Laffont ☆☆
Maumusson. 20 ha.
The Dupuy family, or at least its female members, are rapidly making a name for themselves in this male-dominated appellation. The Cuvée Vieilles Vignes comes from a small parcel of pre-phylloxera vines. These are rich, full-bodied wines, subtly softened by micro-oxygenation.

Château Laffitte-Teston ☆☆
Maumusson. 40 ha.
www.chateau-laffitte-teston.com
Jean-Marc Laffitte's red Madirans are among the best the region has to offer, and include a 100 per cent Tannat Vieilles Vignes bottling. Both his Pacherencs are consistently delicious too. Laffitte prides himself on the fact that his wines are supple and can be approached young, but the price to be paid for this admirable accessibility is that the wines can sometimes lack stuffing.

Château Montus and Domaine Bouscassé ☆☆–☆☆☆☆
Maumusson. 140 ha.
Alain Brumont is the high priest of the Tannat grape. The premium wines from his two properties (Montus Prestige and Bouscassé Vieilles Vignes) are both 100 per cent Tannat, and are vinified for five weeks before being aged in new barriques. Not surprisingly they take several years to mature.

At gravelly soiled Montus, the mainstream wine is 80 per cent Tannat and 20 per cent Cabernet Sauvignon, while at Bouscassé, where the soil is clay and limestone, 65 per cent Tannat is complemented by 25 per cent Cabernet Sauvignon and 10 per cent Cabernet Franc. A third wine, Domaine Meinjarre, is half Tannat, half Cabernet Franc and is priced at bargain level, and a fourth, Torus, described as "charnu, profond, puissant, chatoyant, fruit noir, cassis, mure" (but not expensive) was introduced with the 2000 vintage.

There is a range of Pacherenc, too, in varying degrees of sweetness depending on the date of harvesting. Brumont is not above making good *vin de pays* and launched a range of varietal wines, many of them from obscure local varieties, in the mid-1990s. At the other extreme he is always seeking to push the limits of his Madiran. Montus la Tyre is a heavyweight Tannat grown in the region's highest vineyards, and in 1994 and 2000 he was moved to age some of his Tannat for 2,000 days in barriques. Despite the popularity of micro-oxygenation within Madiran, Brumont does not use the technique. Brumont experienced major financial difficulties in 2004 and the company was restructured, although it remains in his control. Some of the more basic wines were dropped from the portfolio, but that decision may not turn out to be permanent.

Domaine Laougué ☆☆–☆☆☆
Viella. 17 ha. www.domaine-laougue.fr
Three *cuvées* of Madiran from Pierre Dabadie: the unoaked Clos Camy, fresh and unoaked, Excellence de Marty from 80 per cent Tannat and aged in 50 per cent new oak, and the all-Tannat, all-new-oak Passion Charles Clément. Tasted side by side, the wonderfully complex Excellence makes the deepest impression.

Château Peyros ☆–☆☆
Lembeye. 20 ha. www.vignobles-lesgourgues.com
A property run on sound commercial lines, with, for example, machine harvesting. But quality can be good, although in some years there are signs of unripe tannins. The Vieilles Vignes is generally preferable to the oakier Cuvée Greenwich.

Domaine Tailleurguet ☆☆
Maumusson. 9 ha.
An estate now emerging from obscurity under the skilful hands of François Bouby. Both the basic *cuvée* and the more assertive Fûts de Chêne have opulent fruit, great concentration, and no trace of excessive extraction. A property to watch.

Côtes de St-Mont & Leading Producer

In 1974, André Dubosc created a cooperative of growers in the valley of the Adour, north of Madiran and south of Armagnac. There are three branches at Plaisance, St-Aignan, and St-Mont. The co-op is thus called Plaimont. The object was to find an alternative market for the dry white wine locally produced for distillation into Armagnac, because the demand for Armagnac had started to decline. Dubosc had hit on a winner, because it was not long (1981) before he had created almost single-handedly his own VDQS under the name of Côtes de St-Mont, for wines of all three colours. He was also to attract members from the Côtes de Gascogne, whom he persuaded to improve standards with the Colombard grape. He attracted growers, too, from the northern part of the Madiran AC. Another cooperative, the Vignoble de Gascogne at Riscle, has followed the lead of Plaimont.

Producteurs Plaimont ☆☆
St-Mont. 2,500 ha (of which 1,000 are St-Mont).
www.plaimont.com
Today the co-op produces Madiran and Pacherenc, both of excellent quality; St-Mont reds and whites, basically from the same grapes as Madiran and Pacherenc; and a full range of Vins de Pays Côtes de Gascogne that have become hugely popular: a sort of sub-Sauvignon style at a good price.

In the 1990s, Dubosc developed new ranges of St-Mont wines, such as Le Faite de St-Mont, from local varieties only, including some that were in danger of extinction, such as Pinenc. A similar zest for innovation led to the creation of more original wines: a light easy-drinking Madiran called Rive-Haute, a more powerful style from slightly overripe grapes called Plénitude, and fine old-vine Madiran called Arte Benedicte.

Tursan & Leading Producer

The leading vineyard of the *département* of Landes. Almost the entire production comes from the cooperative at Geaune, Les Vignerons Landais, which has 250 members owning about 350 hectares out of a total area of 460 hectares of vines. The wines won VDQS status in 1958, although half of the production is still of Vin de Pays des Landes. The reds are mostly Cabernet Franc with a little Tannat, while the whites are made principally from an obscure local variety called Baroque, with a little enlivening Sauvignon and Gros Manseng. There are Cabernet-based rosés, too. The style is aimed at the holiday-makers of the Atlantic coast: light, fruity, and easy to drink, short *cuvaisons* at not too high a temperature for the reds, while the whites are given a cool fermentation. Total production does not exceed 1.5 million bottles.

Other Tursan Producers

Château de Bachen ☆☆
Duhort-Bachen. 17 ha.
The celebrated chef Michel Guérard has his elegant home here since 1983, and has built an architect-designed winery. Many of the wines are sold in his restaurants at Eugénie-lès-Bains. He specializes in white wine and the vineyard is 50 per

cent Baroque, plus Gros Manseng, Petit Manseng, Sauvignon, and Sémillon. There are two grades of dry white, Château de Bachen and Baron de Bachen, the latter well oaked. The wines are high-class, but hardly typical of the Tursan appellation. The reds are very simple.

Domaine de Perchade ☆
Payros-Cazautets. 20 ha.
Alain Dulucq produces a white that is 90 to 100 per cent Baroque, a rosé mostly from Cabernet Franc, and a red from a mixture of Tannat and the two Cabernets.

Béarn & the Pyrénées

Béarn

Country-style wines have been made in the Béarn district for centuries. In recent times they rose to prominence largely on account of their rosé, which became fashionable throughout France in the middle of the twentieth century. Today the red wines are overshadowed by Madiran and Irouléguy, and the whites by Jurançon, but good wines throughout the range are made from 160 hectares of vines at the cooperative at Bellocq near the pretty town of Salies-de-Béarn. The reds are from old local varieties, plus Tannat and the Cabernets. Growers in Madiran sell their rosé as Béarn AC, while those in Jurançon such as Clos Guirouilh sell Béarn red. Just one independent estate in Béarn proper makes very good wine: the Domaine Lapeyre on the outskirts of Salies. It also uses the name Domaine Guilhémas. The Jurançon cooperative at Gan also makes Béarn.

Jurançon

All references to Jurançon start with the story of the infant King Henri IV, whose lips at birth were brushed with a clove of garlic and moistened with Jurançon wine – a custom said still to be followed in the Bourbon family, though without such spectacular results. The point is that Jurançon is strong, not just in alcohol but in character. Its highly aromatic grapes ripen on the Pyrénéan foothills south of Pau in autumns warmed by the south winds from Spain. Its flavour is enhanced by small crops, in particular for the sweet wines. These should be made by harvesting very late, in November, when hot days and freezing nights have shrivelled the grapes (*passerillage*) and concentrated their juice.

The two principal grape varieties are the Gros and Petit Manseng, the latter not only smaller but with a much higher sugar content. Both give wines of high alcohol degree with a remarkably "stiff" and positive structure in the mouth, almost fierce when young but maturing to scents and flavours variously likened to such exotic fruits and spices as mangoes, guavas, and cinnamon. The best sweet wines are made from pure Petit Manseng, whereas Gros Manseng is more commonly used for the dry wines. Some growers also use a little Petit Courbu in their dry wines to give them bite. Colette provided tasting notes I will not presume to rival: "I was a girl when

I met this prince; aroused, imperious, treacherous as all great seducers are – Jurançon."

There are two appellations: Jurançon Sec and Jurançon, the latter applicable only to wines ranging from half-sweet to *liquoreux*. There is an important co-op at Gan, and about 60 private producers. Generally they make three styles of wine: *sec*, *moelleux*, and ultra-sweet, sometimes oaked. The dry wines used to be distinctly tart. The high acidity that gives such verve to the sweet wine can be searing in a dry version. Over the past ten years growers have learnt how to retain that essential freshness in the dry wine while using late harvesting to give more body and fruit. That same acidity in the sweet wines means that the less concentrated versions make excellent apéritifs in the local restaurants. Many growers make repeated pickings, and consequently a succession of bottlings from grapes picked in October, November, and December at ever higher sweetness levels.

In the 1980s, production had declined and the wine had become little known. Fortunately, a few energetic growers boosted the region, and plantings doubled in about 15 years to just over 1,000 hectares. Today the best wines are much admired and in great demand. Many wine-drinkers who find the sweet wines of Sauternes and the Sélection de Grains Nobles from Alsace simply too rich and unctuous take particular pleasure in the racy freshness of the best Jurançons.

Leading Jurançon Producers

Domaine Bellegarde ☆–☆☆☆
Monein. 18 ha.
Pascal Labasse is the prototype new-wave Jurançon grower, remaining open-minded on the use of new wood. He makes a bone-dry *sec* that ages well, a *moelleux* from Petit Manseng called Cuvée Thibault, and an ultra-sweet Sélection, from grapes picked in December; aged in new oak, it is only made in outstanding vintages.

Domaine Bordenave ☆–☆☆
Monein. 8 ha.
This old property began bottling its wines in 1993. The best wine is the oak-aged Cercle des Amis from pure Petit Manseng. Some other sweet *cuvées* are made from Gros Manseng, which is less satisfactory.

Domaine Bru-Baché ☆☆–☆☆☆
Monein. 10 ha.
Claude Loustalot took over from his uncle Georges Bru-Baché in 1994 and continues the same eccentric approach to sweet Jurançon, producing *cuvées* of increasing intensity. Quintessence is Petit Manseng aged in around 50 per cent new oak, and exhibiting lovely flavours of apricot and quince. L'Eminence, first made in 1991, is Petit Manseng picked in December and aged entirely in new oak.

Domaine Camin Larrédya ☆☆–☆☆☆
La Chapelle-de-Rousse. 10 ha.
www.caminlarredya.com
Jean-Marc Grussaute runs his property with great energy, although his attachment to the local *patois* does lead to unpronounceable labels. The *sec* is unoaked, but the three tiers of sweet wine all receive varying degrees of oak-ageing. The top sweet wines are pure Petit Manseng. Au Capcèu is the delicious and racy mid-tier wine. The finest is A Sólhevat (previously known as "François"), only made in top years and aged for two years in barriques: spicy and very concentrated with a passionfruit tang.

Domaine Cauhapé ☆☆–☆☆☆☆
Monein. 40 ha. www.cauhape.com
Henri Ramonteu is the best-known private grower of Jurançon, with the second-largest vineyard. He produces three dry wines, of which the finest is La Canopée, made from Petit Manseng and aged in oak. There are three very good *moelleux* wines, but Ramonteu takes extreme risks with two *prestige cuvées*. Quintessence du Petit Manseng is made by snipping off raisined bunches and suspending them on wires from the vines, allowing them to attain even greater concentration. It is a wine of extraordinary intensity, with flavours of dried fruits and a discreet smokiness. Folie de Janvier is made in part from grapes picked in January; the wine spends two years in new oak. These two top *cuvées* are exceedingly expensive, but the lesser *moelleux* are more reasonably priced and also of high quality.

Cave des Producteurs de Jurançon ☆–☆☆
Gan. 750 ha. www.cavedejurancon.com
Most of the production at this cooperative is of dry wine, of which there are three grades. There are three unoaked *moelleux* also, of which the top of the range, Prestige d'Automne, is excellent.

Clos Guirouilh ☆☆
Lasseube. 10 ha.
Jean Guirouilh's *sec* has tremendous style and elegance, the taste of apples and pears giving way to citrus fruits with age. The *moelleux* is made of roughly equal parts of each of the Mansengs, the Petit being given some new oak. In good years he will make a *liquoreux* entirely from Petit Manseng.

Clos Lapeyre ☆☆–☆☆☆☆
La Chapelle-de-Rousse. 17 ha. www.jurancon-lapeyre.com
As well as the usual *sec*, Jean-Bernard Larrieu produces a special dry *cuvée* from old Gros Manseng called Vitatge Vielh [*sic*], kept one year in wood and needing some ageing. More unusual, and not made every year, is the *sec* called Mantoulan, which contains the rare indigenous variety Camaralet. The finest of the sweet wines is La Magendia, a superb 100 per cent Petit Manseng with delightful flavours of mango and lemon.

Clos Uroulat ☆☆–☆☆☆
Monein. 16 ha.
Charles Hours has always been an enthusiast for the wines of the region, and is himself a producer of elegant and stylish, rather than fat and luscious wines. His superb *sec*, Cuvée Marie, has both crispness and weight. He uses some new wood for his sweet wine from Petit Manseng. In 2007 he launched a cheerfully packaged range bizarrely called Trendy Happy Hours in an attempt to woo younger drinkers away from beer and cola.

Château Jolys ☆–☆☆
La Chapelle-de-Rousse. 36 ha.
Pierre-Yves Latrille helped revitalize the region in the 1980s. The vineyards of la Chapelle-de-Rousse are on much higher ground than those of Monein, usually in amphitheatre-like folds of the hills called *cirques*. Latrille has planted in vertical rows rather than on terraces. His wines are good middle-of-the-road Jurançon, the *sec* from Gros Manseng; the *moelleux*, 50 per cent Gros and 50 per cent Petit, and his *liquoreux* Vendanges Tardives all from the Petit.

Cru Lamouroux ☆–☆☆
La Chapelle-de-Rousse. 6 ha.
Richard Ziemeck-Chigé, who now makes the wines at his former father-in-law's property, does not believe in Jurançon Sec. His top *cuvées* are called Amélie-Jean and Nathalie, both from Petit Manseng and aged, respectively, for two and four years in oak.

Domaine de Souch ☆☆–☆☆☆
Laroin. 7 ha.
Biodynamic estate belonging to Yvonne Hégoburu. The basic *moelleux* is delicious and fresh if not especially complex, and the best wine is Marie-Kattalin, a pure Petit Manseng of delicacy and intensity. In top vintages she also produces a high-priced Vendange Tardive from grapes picked extremely late. Many different bottlings make selection difficult, but most of the wines are flowery with good acidity and length.

Irouléguy

The Basque growers make wines to match the taste of their fellow-countrymen for rugby and bullfights; big, sturdy wines, trying to outdo Madiran, and a perfect match for the local cuisine. They are based, like Madiran, on the Tannat grape, plus the two Cabernets. The vines are grown on steep terraces at up to 400 metres (1,300 feet), so all picking is done by hand.

Yields are small and the wines need time in bottle. The rosé is excellent, and there has been a small renaissance of the white wine, based on the Jurançon grape varieties. For many years the excellent cooperative had it all its own way, but there are now some good independent producers. With 250 hectares planted, this is an appellation to watch.

Leading Irouléguy Producers

Domaine Arretxea ☆☆
Irouléguy. 8 ha.
A small, Biodynamic estate, with a powerful, oaked Cuvée Haitza from a large majority of Tannat. It needs to be aged for its spicy, berry aromas to emerge. The excellent white from the Jurançon varieties is called Hegoxuri.

Domaine Brana ☆☆
St-Jean Pied-de-Port. 23 ha. www.brana.fr
The Branas were the first growers to introduce white wines to the region. Theirs are based on Gros Manseng and unoaked. Scenically magnificent – the splendid winery is hewn out of the mountainside – with breathtaking views, the vines are planted in terraced rows on almost vertical slopes. Yields are tiny, and the wine expensive. There is only 30 per cent Tannat, the rest of the red vineyard being divided more or less equally between the two Cabernets – the wines are very drinkable when young. Axeria is pure Cabernet Franc but more rough-hewn than its Touraine counterparts.

Domaine Etxegaraya ☆☆
St-Etienne-de-Baïgorry. 7 ha.
The Hillau family began bottling their wines, which are all unoaked, in 1994. The standard red is very good, even lush, and the remarkable Cuvée Lehengoa is made from 100-year-old Tannat.

Domaine Ilarria ☆–☆☆
Irouléguy. 10 ha.
These wines from organic vineyards are a benchmark for true Irouléguy. The basic red is Cabernet-dominated, whereas Bixintxo has 55 per cent Tannat and more spice and vigour. Two reds, made from 80 and 100 per cent Tannat, are serious propositions. The latter is called Cuvée Bixintxo (the Basque name for St Vincent). Cuvaisons are long, and the wines aged in a mixture of new and old wood for 18 months.

La Cave Irouléguy ☆–☆☆
St-Etienne-de-Baïgorry. 150 ha.
www.cave-irouleguy.com
Cooperative founded in 1952 with 140 members, so many holdings are tiny. Much of the production is of rosé, the basic version of which rejoices in the Basque name Argi d'Ansa; the better version, containing half each Tannat and Cabernet is called Axeridoy. The basic red is Gorri d'Ansa, but there are special *cuvées*: Domaine de Mignaberry (from old vines) and the oakier, more structured Omenaldi.

Vins de Pays

In the early 1980s the rules and regulations for the newly coined *vin de pays* were set out. The object was to give pride to local production that had hitherto had no identity. Since that time, the junior rank of French country wines has undergone nothing short of a revolution. Wines that were previously used entirely for blending, or dispatched label-less to the local bars, are now made to minimum standards and in regulated quantities. Eventually some 140 *vins de pays* were created, although some would always remain obscure. Outside interest, not least investment from New World wine countries, flying winemakers, and foreign supermarket wine-buyers, raised standards and broke the mould of generations of cautious vignerons. The results are many of the best value-for-money wines of France. Some producers, however, took advantage of the regulations to produce ranges of dilute, characterless wines that often found a market among the most undiscriminating supermarkets and consumers.

The category can be confusing, since *vin de pays* vary enormously in size and importance. Some are as local as three or four parishes; some are departmental (Vins de Pays de Loire

Atlantique, for instance); some as sweeping as the whole of the Midi (Vins de Pays d'Oc) or the Loire Valley (Vins de Pays du Jardin de la France). The last regional *vins de pays*, of which there are four, were intended to give new life to traditional winemaking areas and be used as the vehicle for experimentation and new ideas – which they have done.

The second control is over the grape varieties to be grown. In some cases one or more classic grapes are prescribed as obligatory, while a number of others are tolerated up to a percentage. Some areas do not specify varieties at all. The most successful new *vins de pays* allow single-grape productions – 85 per cent from the Midi – and are generally seen as France's riposte to the varietals of the New World. The rules specify yields, which tend to be far more generous than those for AC or VDQS wines. With a Europe-wide restructuring of wine appellations imminent, the whole category may disappear, or be reborn in some other guise. Consequently, only the most important *vins de pays* are listed below.

Rhône & Provence

Most of the wine-growing areas of the Rhône and Provence are entitled to the wide-ranging appellations Côtes du Rhône or Provence. The *vins de pays* cover outlying, often interesting districts and one or two zones within the AC areas themselves. The wines, mostly red, are usually blends of the traditional grapes of the south, but increasingly the Bordeaux varieties are featuring.

Alpes-de-Haute-Provence Provence. Mostly reds grown in the Durance Valley. Also some rosé.

l'Ardèche Fourteen communes in the Ardèche and Chassezac valleys. Mainly reds from local and international varieties, and whites from southern French varieties plus Chardonnay.

Bouches-du-Rhône The wines come from three distinct but very large zones: the Aix-en-Provence area, the main Côtes de Provence vineyards in the east of the *département*, and the Camargue. Most are red, made from the southern grape varieties, with some Cabernet.

Collines Rhodaniennes Includes the entire northern Rhône.

Comtés Rhodaniens One of the four regional *vin de pays* designations covering eight *départements* (the Ain, Ardèche, Drôme, Isère, Loire, Rhône, Savoie, and the Haute-Savoie).

Coteaux du Verdon Provence. From the northern Var, and mostly red and rosé from local varieties and/or Cabernet Sauvignon.

Drôme The eastern part of the Rhône Valley, south of Valence and east of Montélimar. Over 80 per cent is red, made from Carignan, Cinsault, and Syrah, supplemented by Gamay, Cabernet Sauvignon, and Merlot.

Mont-Caume Provence. Twelve communes around Bandol. One of the best such wines is the pure Cabernet Sauvignon from Bunan.

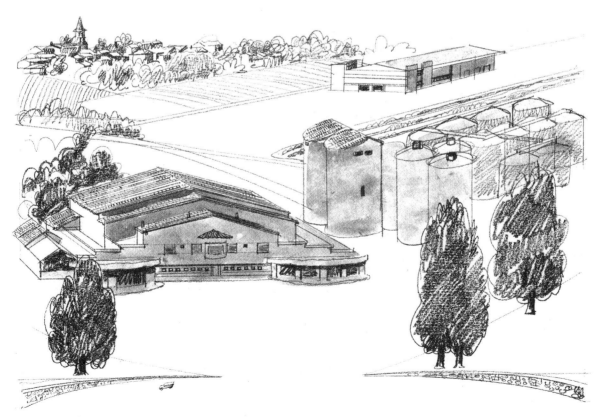

Caves cooperatives in the vins de pays district

Principauté d'Orange Around Bollène, Orange, Vaison-la-Romaine, and Valréas, east of the Rhône in the Côtes du Rhône-Villages and Châteauneuf-du-Pape country. Many Grenache-dominated reds are produced.

Var The most important *vin de pays* region in Provence, covering the whole of the Var *département*. Much rosé and red made here from Grenache, Cinsault, Carignan, Syrah, and other varieties, including Cabernet Sauvignon.

Vaucluse Includes the eastern part of the Côtes du Rhône and Côtes du Ventoux. Similar reds to Côtes du Rhône, although the blend includes Cabernet Sauvignon. The unmemorable white is from Ugni Blanc.

The Gard

The *département* of the Gard stretches from the Rhône at Avignon west into the hills of the Cévennes. The chief town is Nîmes. Most of the *département* is wine-growing country, and there is a *vin de pays* for the whole area: Vin de Pays du Gard. Other *vins de pays*, covering areas of varying size, are listed below. There are no specified grape varieties.

Coteaux du Pont-du-Gard Nineteen communes around Remoulins, between Nîmes and Avignon.

Sables-du-Golfe-du-Lion Sand dunes and coastal strips in parts of 12 communes in the Camargue west of the mouth of the Rhône.

Hérault

This is France's biggest wine-producing *département*. Vin de Pays de l'Hérault covers the whole area. Twenty-seven local districts have their own sets of regulations. Some of the areas cover land in the St-Chinian and Minervois ACs, others include communes entitled to the Coteaux du Languedoc AC. The presence of one of the Midi's top estates – Mas de Daumas Gassac – proves that this is not only an area of inexpensive wines.

Côtes du Brian Thirteen communes in the eastern Minervois. Best-known producer is Clos des Centeilles for some more daring wines.

Collines de la Moure Twenty-seven communes around Frontagnan and Mireval. Widely used by private estates and co-ops alike.

Coteaux de Murviel The eastern part of St-Chinian, with Château Coujan the best-known producer.

Côtes de Thongue Hérault. Red and white. Fourteen communes around Pézenas and Béziers. Quite commonly encountered.

Aude

The entire *département* of the Aude, which stretches inland from Narbonne, is entitled to call the wines produced Vin de Pays de l'Aude.

Coteaux de Miramont Nine communes around Capendu east of Carcassone.

Val d'Orbieu This consists of 12 communes in the Orbieu Valley situated west of Narbonne. Grapes, red and rosé: Carignan, Cinsault, Grenache, Alicante-Bouschet, Picpoul, Terret Noir. White: Clairette, Macabeu, Bourboulenc, Carignan Blanc, Grenache Blanc.

Coteaux de Peyriac Seventeen communes in the western Minervois.

Roussillon & Corbières

Vins de Pays des Pyrénées-Orientales is the name used for the predominantly red wines produced in most areas of the *département*, except the southeast. The country to the south, consisting of plains and the foothills of the Pyrénées, uses the Catalan name for its two defined districts.

Catalan Roussillon. Area stretching inland from Perpignan and Argelès.

Côtes Catalanes Roussillon. North and west of Perpignan.

Côte Vermeille Roussillon. The area around Banyuls and Collioure along the coast.

The Southwest

Nearly all of the southwest is included in one or other of the many *vins de pays* now proliferating. The best tend to be produced by growers for whom they are their first and only wines, rather than a bolt-on to wines of superior appellation.

l'Agenais Covers the whole of Lot-et-Garonne from the Armagnac to Cahors boundaries. It is mostly for red wines made by cooperatives.

Bigorre Hautes-Pyrénées. Certain communes around Madiran and Vic-de-Bigorre to the south. The Plaimont Producteurs and Brumont at Madiran (q.v.) also use Bigorre to describe some varietal wines.

Charentais Charente and Charente-Maritime. Entire *départements*. Usually lean and rustic.

Côtes de Gascogne Almost the entire *département* of the Gers (Armagnac country). Wide range of traditional and quality grape varieties.

Gers Covers the whole *département*, overlapping Côtes de Gascogne. Many whites from Ugni Blanc and Colombard.

Coteaux du Quercy The area used to be called Bas-Quercy, the *causses* stretching south from Cahors. In the north, the Cahors grapes, Malbec, Merlot, and Tannat dominate, but further south Cabernet Franc, Gamay, and some Cabernet Sauvignon are also used.

Côtes du Tarn Covers the Gaillac AC area and land to the south as far as the River Agout. Large and important production of dry white, rosé, and red wine.

Comté Tolosan Capable of designating most of the

southwest, but in practice mostly used for the area of Toulouse, north to Montauban, and south towards Pamiers. Can be just about anything.

Pyrénées-Atlantiques Covers the whole *département*, but mainly for wines grown in Béarn and Jurançon areas. Mostly red and rosé.

Terroirs Landais This covers the whole of the *département* of Landes. Used mostly for wines of the Gascon style (Colombard and Ugni Blanc for the whites, Tannat and Cabernets for the reds) produced over the border from the Gers; also smaller productions in the west of the *département*, mostly from Cabernet Franc, grown near the Atlantic coast.

Loire

Coteaux Charitois Area around la Charité-sur-Loire, south of Pouilly-sur-Loire. Mostly Sauvignon Blanc.

Jardin de la France Most of the lower and mid-Loire basin. The vast zone covers 13 *départements*. A successful appellation, often seen used for simple Chardonnays, for example, though Chenin and Sauvignon are also allowed.

Loire-Atlantique From the Muscadet region. Reds and rosés are made from Gamay and Grolleau; whites from Muscadet, Gros Plant, and Chardonnay.

Burgundy

l'Yonne Usually Chardonnay from the northern stretches of Burgundy around Auxerre. This is the sole Burgundian *vin de pays* anyone is likely to encounter.

Midi & Corsica

Pays d'Oc Covers the whole of Languedoc-Roussillon. This *vin de pays* is used for wines made from varieties not traditional to the region. Seventy per cent of production is of varietal wines. Many of the most interesting of the new wave of southern French wines are being made using this *vin de pays* name. Top producers include Skalli Fortant de France and La Baume.

L'Ile de Beauté Corsica. Mostly red wines from a wide range of varieties, though Carignan and Cinsault may not exceed 25 per cent and 50 per cent, respectively, of the planted area. Some good wines are made.

Germany

The quality of Germany's top wines has never been better. A focus on her traditionally outstanding grapes, mostly Riesling, a grape of more expressivity and complexity than any other white and an insistence on the importance of terroir have raised her prestige sky-high, at least in Germany. In the USA, too, Germany's star is rising. But in Britain, once the most loyal of markets, memories of the cheap wines of the 1970s and 1980s still linger.

Until the 1970s, it was generally accepted that Germany made the world's finest white wines, with white burgundy as its only peer. No great dinner could begin without its Mosel (then known Moselle) or Rhine Spätlese. The Riesling was universally hailed as the queen of white grapes (while few people, believe it or not, had even heard of Chardonnay). However, while the international reputation or renown of every single wine-producing country has improved, that of Germany has remained in the doldrums, even though the quality of the top wines has never been better. The slide began with the German Wine Law of 1971, ironically coinciding with a truly magnificent vintage. The law came down firmly on the side of the little man, the cooperative member – whose vote, one can be forgiven for thinking, the politicians were eager to attract. The new law allowed him to label his wine with grand names that bore almost no relation to its origin. It permitted the use of the word "quality" where it meant the opposite, while debasing such vital descriptive terms as Auslese to a mere matter of grams of sugar. It placed no restriction on yields, with the consequence that many, even most, wines soon came to taste like sugar water (with the stress on the water). All vineyards were regarded as being of equal quality, in defiance of centuries of Burgundian-style appreciation of the differences in character and quality between one site and its neighbour. Plummeting quality in turn forced the price of German wine down to some of Europe's lowest levels.

The best German producers, and prestigious growers' associations such as the VDP (Verband Deutscher Prädikats-und Qualitätsweingüter, or Federation of German Prädikats and Qualitäts wine estates), have been well aware of this wretched state of affairs for many years, and have willingly adopted an independent attitude, effectively bypassing legal minimum standards, which they regard as dismally permissive. The VDP, as well as a number of independent and quality-conscious producers, has made great strides in re-establishing the once glorious reputation of German wine, often in the face of accusations of elitism. But since there is no legal framework, such as the Italian DOC or the French AC, that can lay down rules and regulations that apply to all, they have had no choice. Few would now dispute that the quality of German wines at the top level is outstanding, even if certain markets, including the British one, seem determined to ignore the fact.

Most German vineyards are in northerly parts of Europe, and that makes vineyard location absolutely crucial. Think of the great loops of the River Mosel, where the sunshine on the vineyard varies with the shape, the steepness, and the exposure more than anywhere on earth. Free-draining slate or schist is vital for ripening Riesling here; the qualities of the best vineyards are known to everyone – and so is the impossibility of making fine wine on north-facing slopes or flat alluvial land.

Compare the Côte d'Or of Burgundy. Over centuries, it has been minutely divided into its *grands crus*, *premiers crus*, and villages sites. Its world fame rests on this classification; it simply works. The official German line is that such pinpointing of natural quality is "elitist" and undemocratic. Moreover, even though with its fabulously versatile Riesling Germany has a trump card to play, the authorities have connived with large-scale producers and cooperatives to permit wines labelled with historic names such as "Bernkasteler" or "Piesporter" to be made from inferior varieties such as Müller-Thurgau and not a drop of Riesling. If a region does not protect its own good name, nobody else will do it. Any French *syndicat* defines its role as the protection of its appellation; in Germany there is, alas, no appellation to protect. Hence the current débâcle. On the other hand, what is true for the Mosel or the Rheingau, the regions where Riesling is the essential classic grape, is not necessarily true, or not true at all, for the Pfalz, or Baden in the south, or Franconia, where Silvaner comes into its own. Different soils and different traditions, not to mention longer growing seasons, offer other possibilities that thinking wine-growers -must embrace.

In German thinking, and for understandable reasons, ripeness is everything. All German quality criteria (at least the government-regulated ones) are based on the accumulated sugar in the grapes at harvest time. With the single exception of the Rheingau, there is no official ranking of vineyards as in France, no specific recipes for varieties of grapes as in Italy. German labels, at least those of quality wines, make unequivocal statements, although the overload of information can sometimes be more bewildering than illuminating.

Since 1971, the wine laws have been subject to further revisions. But their strategy remains unaltered. They divide all German wine into three strata. The lowest, Tafelwein, ("table wine") subject to relatively few controls, is correspondingly barred from claiming any specific vineyard origin. It is assumed to be a blend of wines that have required additional sugar. The only technical point to remember is the difference between Deutscher Tafelwein, which must be German in origin, and Tafelwein without the qualification, which may contain wine from other European countries (formerly Italy, now more often Eastern Europe). A low-strength neutral base wine is easily cleaned up and given some superficial German characteristics by using very aromatic *süssreserve* ("sweet reserve": unfermented grape juice that may legally be added to finished wine). The use of heavily Gothic labels is obviously intended to encourage the innocent to believe that the wine is indeed German. A new category of Tafelwein, called Landwein, ("land" or "county" wine) with stricter rules, was introduced in 1982 as a sort of German *vin de pays*. But Landwein is far from matching its French counterparts in popularity or enterprise. More significant is the rebellious use of the Tafelwein designation by a handful of proud growers who have despaired of official categories and consider their freedom to use their own judgement more important than official recognition.

The second category of German wine was christened Qualitätswein bestimmter Anbaugebiete: QbA for short. The term means "quality wine from a designated region". The use of the word "quality" in this context is really meaningless. Nonetheless, to a German, the difference between this and the top category of wine, Qualitätswein mit Prädikat, (QmP) is doubtless clear and simple. Unfortunately, the legislators did not take non-Germans into account, drinkers who are unaware that the two classes of Qualitätswein are far apart, distinguished by a basic difference.

Distinctions of Quality

Qba wines may be *chaptalized* during fermentation, as some added sugar will boost the alcohol level; QmP wines are what used (before 1971) to be called, much more directly and succinctly, *natur* or *naturrein*; in other words the grapes had enough natural sugar to make wine. Mit Prädikat is hard to translate. "With special attributes" is the stilted official version. It certainly does not reflect the status of QmP wines as the top category in which, almost without exception, all the best wines of Germany are included. (The exceptions occur in vintages where the grapes did not ripen fully; in such cases light *chaptalization* may improve a wine that might otherwise taste thin and undernourished.) Qualitätswein mit Prädikat carry a designation of maturity of their grapes as part of their full names, in the following order; simply ripe grapes of the normal harvest are Kabinett; late-gathered (therefore riper) are Spätlese; selected very ripe grapes are Auslese. The precise sugar content (or "must weight") and therefore potential alcohol required for each category, in each region, is stipulated in the regulations.

At this point most wines begin to retain distinct natural sweetness. If an Auslese is fermented fully dry, it will be noticeably high in alcohol – often throwing it off-balance. Two levels of ripeness and selectivity beyond Auslese remain: Beerenauslese (BA), in which the individual berries are selected for extreme ripeness and concentration, and Trockenbeerenauslese (TBA), in which only berries dried and shrivelled by noble rot (occasionally by unseasonal heat) are selected. Sugar levels in such wines are commonly so high that fermentation is seriously hampered, and may take months to attain a modest degree of alcohol. TBAs are usually a stable conjunction of very modest alcohol level (usually around 5.5 per cent) and startlingly high sugar. They are less than half as strong in alcohol as Château d'Yquem, which is made in much the same way, and correspondingly twice as sweet (although great TBAs may be even more concentrated and intense than Yquem – but not necessarily better).

One further category of QmP wine deserves to be considered separately because of the way it is made. Eiswein is made by crushing grapes that have frozen solid on the vine. Crushing before they thaw means that the almost pure water, which constitutes the ice, is separated from the sugar, acids, and other constituents, which have a lower freezing point. The result, like a TBA, is intensely concentrated, but usually much less ripe and invariably more acidic. It can be extraordinary, its high acid giving it the potential for almost limitless ageing.

The name and ranking of a QmP wine is conventionally set forth on its label in the same order. First is the Gemeinde (town or village) name; then the vineyard; then the grape; then the category of ripeness – Kabinett, Spätlese, and so on. In addition there may also be a stylistic guide: *trocken* or *halbtrocken*, which are explained below.

A further complicating factor, and the major fault in the 1971 German law, prevents this formula from being crystal clear. It is the concept of the Grosslage, or extended vineyard. Unfortunately, labels do not, and are not allowed to, distinguish between a single-vineyard site, known as an Einzellage, and a group of such sites with very much less specificity: a Grosslage. Grosslage groupings were made with the idea of simplifying the sales of wines from lesser-known Einzellagen. Notoriety comes more easily to bigger units. But their names are in no way distinguishable from Einzellage names and I have never met a person who claims to have memorized them. The consumer is therefore deprived of a vital piece of information. As a further confusing factor, in some areas, Einzellagen are also groups of separate vineyards deemed to have a common personality. There is thus no truly clear-cut distinction between the categories. At their worst, Grosslage names are a con. Two well-known examples are Nierstein's Gutes Domtal and Piesport's Michelsberg. In both cases, these Grosslagen need contain not a drop of wine from the village identified on the label; indeed, it is almost certain that a Gutes Domtal will contain nothing more than Müller-Thurgau grown on flat land better suited for potato growing. An exact French parallel would be that any Médoc could be sold as Margaux.

The often-quoted rule of thumb, based on the Kabinett-Spätlese-Auslese scale, is "the sweeter the wine, the higher the quality". While it is still true to say that quality is directly related to ripeness, the question of sweetness is now very much at the discretion of the winemaker (and the consumer). It became easy for growers to plant modern crossings such as Albalonga and Optima that would deliver very sweet wines almost every year. However, these wines were usually deficient in acidity and cloying. Fortunately, the fashion, such as it was, for these sugary concoctions has dwindled. Their existence did no favours to many wines from the Mosel and Nahe, among other regions, in which the sweetness was natural and pure, and in perfect balance with the refreshing acidity of the wines.

The great change in German wine fashion over the past 20 years has been the demand for fully dry, unsweetened wines, to accompany food. To be so described as *trocken*, on the label, these must contain less than nine grams of sugar per litre. The taste for *trocken* wines has grown with, and in turn boosted, the use of what are typically French grapes, mainly of the Pinot family, to make true "table" or "food" wines of a kind Germany has traditionally lacked. It has fundamentally shifted the emphasis southward from the northernmost vineyards, where Riesling reigns, to such regions as the Pfalz and Baden, where the Pinots and similar grapes are fully at home. In tasting *trocken* wines of Riesling, it soon becomes clear how much a little natural sweetness adds to the charm, balance, and drinkability of most German wines; they have to have unusually good figures to survive such naked scrutiny. On the other hand, this is the area in which the most progress has recently been made by the most ambitious producers, especially in warmer Riesling regions such as the Pfalz. A halfway category, *halbtrocken*, with up to 18 grams of sugar per litre, more often achieves the right balance of fullness and bite to make satisfactory mealtime wine. The undoubted tendency towards global warming has made it easier than in the past to produce well-balanced drier styles of Riesling in particular. Not only the VDP, but the leading growers of the Rheingau, have worked hard to ensure that dry wines, especially Rieslings, are only made from properly ripe fruit. Consequently, the tart, fierce wines that passed for "dry" in the 1980s are mostly a thing of the past. The VDP lays down explicit stylistic parameters for its Grosses Gewächs wines from outstanding vineyards; in the Rheingau, the Erstes Gewächs system, which is enshrined in regional wine law, lays down minimal ripeness levels from specific sites but does not impose stylistic regulations.

German growers produce astonishing quantities. France, Italy, and other countries make low yields a pre-condition for their best appellations. In Germany, only sugar levels count. Average crops have grown from 25 hectolitres per hectare in 1900, to 40 in 1939, and in the 1970s were averaging over 100. The year 1982 hit a record: a 173 hectolitres per hectare average, with a maximum close to 400. But this is the national average, including cooperatives, where anything goes. Since 1989, there has been a tightening of the law to prevent such ludicrously high yields, although the regulations still remain very generous and are scarcely compatible with the production of good-quality wine. In 2006, the average yield in the Rheingau was 72 hectolitres per hectare, and in Württemberg 105. On the other hand many have doubted the serious intent of a law that permits overproduction in one vintage to be held over to the next. It appears that the political will to frustrate overproduction is far from resolute. Meanwhile, all serious growers attempting high-quality wines impose their own limits at a level well below the legal maximum. The average figure for Maximin Grünhaus and Robert Weil, for example, is 55 hectolitres per hectare; Dr. Loosen harvests at 50 hectolitres per hectare; and Egon Müller and Schlossgut Diel at 45 hectolitres per hectare.

Another serious concern is that the current law, in setting simple minimum ripeness standards for Auslesen and the other top categories, simply invites growers to achieve that minimum and no more. The old rules allowed eager winemakers to differentiate between their standard and better-than-standard Auslesen, such terms as Feine or Feinste Auslese carrying considerable premiums. If the terms were open to abuse, they also rewarded the patient and ambitious perfectionist. Today he will still signal to his clients which are his best casks of wine, but often in an obscure semaphore of gold capsules and long gold capsules, no less open to abuse because it is closed to the uninitiated. The official answer to any doubts about the standards or authenticity of QbA and QmP German wines is that each wine is both analyzed and tasted officially before being issued with a unique Amtliche Prüfungsnummer (AP: "official inspection number"), which appears on every label. The pass-mark for any wine at AP tastings is 1.5 out of 5, suggesting the examination is far from rigorous. All official tastings employ a points scheme, which is also used for the awarding of the gold, silver, and bronze medals at both national (DLG) and regional levels.

But here again it is the self-imposed criteria of top growers that really set the standard. It is here that the VDP has firmly taken the lead in setting far stricter quality criteria than the government. Membership of the VDP is open to growers (there are about 200 at present) who sign up for self-discipline. Its standards are well policed and laggards lose their membership. The VDP imposes maxima of production and minima of must-weight far stricter than those decreed by government. The VDP has also supported a long overdue, though still unofficial, classification of the German vineyards (see box below). It is on the VDP and the pride of its members that the future of Germany's high-quality wine industry depends.

German Wine Regions

Germany's finest wines come from hillside vineyards facing the southern half of the compass. In this northern climate the extra radiation on land tilted toward the sun is often essential for

THE NEW CLASSIFICATION

In the 1980s, progressive growers, especially in the Rheingau, sought to undo some of the damage inflicted by the 1971 wine law, by restoring the notion of a vineyard hierarchy. It was argued that no one could possibly memorize 3,000 individual sites. Better instead to highlight the best sites, and suppress the names of the lesser ones, by blending their production as a village or estate wine. The basis for vineyard classification throughout Germany would be the nineteenth century maps showing the tax band for each site: the better the vineyard, the higher the tax band. Not an infallible guide, but a sound starting point for classification.

The Rheingau proposals made sense, but encountered understandable opposition, especially from good growers not blessed with outstanding sites. Nonetheless, by the late 1990s, the Rheingau had evolved a system of vineyard classification (Erstes Gewächs, or First Growth) that was legally approved. Unfortunately, the system of classification resulted in about one-third of the Rheingau being certified as First Growth, which is clearly far too high. The fatal error was to apply a complicated formula to vineyards based on the ripeness usually attained in those sites. This tended to benefit warmer and more precocious sites near the river, and penalize those further inland and higher up. To the dismay of some producers, some ordinary sites emerged as Erstes Gewächs, while others with a better track record were omitted.

Thus far, only a small percentage of vineyards entitled to be labelled Erstes Gewächs are bottled as such. In practice, the estates are using the label as a kind of signal to identify their very top wines, produced according to the Erstes Gewächs rules and regulations. A few top growers protest that there is no stylistic definition attached to Erstes Gewächs and that *chaptalization* is permitted for what is intended to be great wine.

In other regions – notably the Pfalz, Rheinhessen, and Nahe – different criteria were adopted in 2002 for a VDP initiative to classify dry wines from certain sites as First Growths (known here as Grosses Gewächs). It seems probable that these are the criteria that will be adopted in almost all German wine regions in the years ahead. The exceptions are regions such as the Mosel, where dry wines are the exception rather than the rule. Criteria vary slightly from region to region, but those for Grosses Gewächs are as follows:
• Wines must be dry (up to eight grams of sugar). Nobly sweet wines such as BA or TBA are recognized as being of outstanding quality, but may not be labelled as Grosses Gewächs.
• Grape varieties must be traditional to the region.
• Maximum yield 50 hectolitres per hectare.
• Sugar content of grapes at harvest must be at least Spätlese level.
• Classified vineyards to be inspected regularly, and wines subjected to a tasting panel for approval.
• Special bottle and logo.

A second tier of vineyards is recognized as Klassifizierte Lagenweine. These are not First Growths, but are accepted as being high quality sites. The main difference from Grosses Gewächs is that yields may be 65 hectolitres per hectare.

All other wines must be sold as estate or village wines without any vineyard designation on the label. Although this is a VDP initiative, it is intended that the system will be open to all producers who accept the quality criteria.

ripeness. Other factors also come into account: the climate-moderating presence of water; shelter from wind; and fast-draining and heat-retentive soil. Fine German wines, in fact, come from almost every type of soil, from slate to limestone, clay to sand – given other optimal conditions. The effects of different soils on the character of wines from one grape, the Riesling, is a fascinating sub-plot of German oenology. But climate and microclimate, orientation, and angle of hill come first.

The 13 principal wine regions fall into five broad divisions. The most important is the Rhine Valley, including its lesser tributaries, from the Pfalz (the Palatinate) in the south, past Rheinhessen, the Hessische Bergstrasse, the Rheingau and the Nahe, the Mittelrhein, and finally to the little tributary Ahr near Bonn in the north. Second comes the Mosel, flowing north with its tributaries the Saar and the Ruwer to meet the Rhine at Koblenz. Third comes the vast but scattered region of Baden in the south, from Heidelberg all the way to the Swiss border. Fourth comes Franken (or Franconia), the vineyards of the Main Valley in northern Bavaria. Fifth, and rarely spoken of outside Germany, comes the disjointed and diverse region of Württemberg.

Foreigners tend to meet German wine either as a commercial blend (like Liebfraumilch) or as the produce of one of the many great historic estates of the Rhine or Mosel. (Liebfraumilch is a hazy category, required merely to have between 18 and 40 grams of residual sugar, and to be made from certain grape varieties from the most productive of Germany's wine regions.) The wines of the small local grower, often produced to supply family and friends and by the glass to guests at their own cheerful little Weinstube, are rarely sold outside the region, but can epitomize the style and vitality of his region. His wines are generally less fine than those of sophisticated noble estates. But they have character, often charm, and sometimes, brilliant dash and fire.

Mosel

The Mosel twists and turns its way more than 193 kilometres (120 miles) from the German-French- Luxembourg border to its confluence with the Rhine at Koblenz. It cuts deep into the hill country of the Eifel and Hunsrück; a huge mass of slate, 400 million years of age, that weathers to give the stony grey soil. On the steep sides of its narrow valley, and those of its tributaries, the Saar and Ruwer, grow the brightest, briskest, most aromatic, and hauntingly subtle of all German Rieslings. This is essentially Riesling country, and no soil or situation brings out the thrilling and fascinating personality of the finest of all white grapes to better effect.

The complex topography and the cool, northerly climate result in huge microclimatic variations between vineyards that lie only a stone's throw from one another. The steep, south-facing slopes in sheltered positions give noble Rieslings that are expressive and elegant, while the flat vineyards on heavy soil produce mean, watery wines from high-yielding grape varieties such as Müller-Thurgau and Kerner. Unfortunately, the German wine law does nothing to differentiate between these two worlds; indeed, it confuses the two. Cheap generic wines are sold under plausible sounding Grosslage names such as Piesporter Michelsberg and Ürziger Schwarzlay, although little or none of the wine in the bottle originates from the towns named. These wines are a world away from Rieslings that grew in the great Piesporter Goldtröpfchen and Ürziger Würzgarten sites.

The Mosel encounters its first few tentative vineyards in France, flows through Luxembourg, then enters Germany near Trier, once the effective capital of the Roman Empire. On either side of the city, it is joined by the Rivers Saar and Ruwer.

GERMANY IN ROUND FIGURES

The total vineyard area of Germany is 102,000 hectares, dispersed among 13 regions that differ enormously in size. The following table shows the vineyard area in hectares per region, and in the line below the most important grape variety in that region, and the proportion of the area it occupies.

Mosel	9.080
Riesling (58%)	
Ahr	544
Pinot Noir (62%)	
Mittelrhein	465
Riesling (68%)	
Rheingau	3,106
Riesling (78%)	
Nahe	4,199
Riesling (25%)	

Rheinhessen	26,327
Müller-Thurgau (16%)	
Pfalz	23,363
Riesling (21%)	
Hessische Bergstrasse	436
Riesling (50%)	
Franken	6,072
Müller-Thurgau (32%)	
Württemberg	11,515
Trollinger (22%)	
Baden	16,000
Pinot Noir (36%)	
Saale-Unstrut	658
Müller-Thurgau (20%)	
Sachsen	411
Müller-Thurgau (20%)	

The following are the most widely planted grape varieties throughout Germany, followed by the percentage of plantings.

Riesling	20.8%
Müller-Thurgau	13.7%
Pinot Noir	11.6%
Dornfelder	8.1%
Silvaner	5.2%
Portugieser	4.6%
Kerner	3.9%
Pinot Gris	4.3%
Pinot Blanc	3.4%
Bacchus	2.9%
Trollinger	2.5%
Pinot Meunier	2.4%
Regent	2.1%
Scheurebe	1.7%
Lemberger	1.6%
Chardonnay	1.1%
Other	10%

It is their side valleys, rather than the main stream, that have the first great Mosel vineyards. Upper Mosel (Obermosel) wines are at best light and refreshing. The ancient Elbling grape dominates here, giving appley, pleasantly tart, dry wines. Riesling also has difficulty ripening on the Saar and Ruwer, although global warming has made it less difficult than in the past. But when it does ripen, on the best slopes, the results are unsurpassed anywhere on earth: quintessential Riesling, clean as steel, with the evocative qualities of remembered scents or distant music.

The Mosel valley below Trier divides into two sub-regions, the Middle Mosel with its succession of famous vineyards strung along the river's course like pearls on a necklace. The wines are slightly fuller and more effusively aromatic than those of the Saar and Ruwer, but are equally long-living. The border between the Middle Mosel and the Terrassen Mosel ("Terraced Mosel" or Untermosel) has long been disputed, but Zell is the logical dividing line. Below this, the vines tend to be planted on narrow terraces, rather than directly climbing the precipitous slopes as elsewhere in the region (although there are some significant exceptions, such as the Bremmer Calmont). Here grow the fullest, most supple Mosel Rieslings, resulting in a growing number of convincing dry wines. In 2007 the name of the region was simplified from the former name of Mosel-Saar-Ruwer.

Saar Vineyards

Ayler Kupp Some of the most charming and immediately appealing Saar wines. Most important owners: Bischöfliche Weingüter, Peter Lauer, Johann Peter Reinert, Dr. Wagner.

Filzener Pulchen Sleek, steely wines with delicate apple and berry aromas. Most important owner: Piedmont.

Kanzemer Altenberg Very classic Saar Rieslings, subtlety and refinement married to racy acidity. Most important owners: Bischöfliche Weingüter, von Othegraven, Vereinigte Hospitien.

Oberemmeler Hütte Monopoly site of the von Hövel estate. Elegant, long-living wines with pronounced floral aromas.

Ockfener Bockstein Sadly, substantially enlarged recently. Rieslings combining the forthright Mosel aromas with the steel of the Saar. Most important owners: Dr. Fischer, von Kesselstatt, von Othegraven, Sankt Urbanshof, Dr. Wagner, Zilliken.

Saarburger Rausch Slow-developing, long-living wines with a pronounced citrus and mineral character. Most important owners: Dr. Wagner, Zilliken.

Scharzhofberg The greatest and most famous vineyard on the Saar, giving wines of the highest elegance and nobility in superior vintages. Their ageing potential is legendary,

The Mosel landscape

even Kabinett wines keeping for 25 years and more. This status was not ignored by the 1971 law, which made the 28-hectare vineyard an Ortsteil of Wiltingen; hence the village name does not appear on the label. Most important owners: Bischöfliche Weingüter (Hohe Domkirche), von Hövel, von Kesselstatt, Egon Müller-Scharzhof, van Volxem, Vereinigte Hospitien.

Serriger Schloss Saarstein Monopoly site of the Schloss Saarstein estate. Piercing acidity and a blackcurrant aroma make these very distinctive Saar wines. Very long-lived.

Wiltinger Gottesfüß A small site yielding intense, succulent wines with a pineapple note that occures in good vintages. Most important owners: van Volxem, von Kesselstatt, Reverchon.

Wiltinger Braune Kupp Monopoly Riesling site of the Le Gallais estate, yielding substantial wines that often show a herbal character. Only QmP wines are sold as Braune Kupp; the Grosslage name Scharzberg is for QbA wine, some of which is from Egon Müller's own estate. Kabinetts are light; higher qualities aromatic and spicy.

Ruwer Vineyards

Eitelsbacher Karthäuserhofberg The monopoly site of the Tyrell family's formerly monastic Karthäuserhof estate. Almost explosively aromatic wines that have a positively piquant interplay of fruit and acidity are produced here.

Kaseler Kehrnagel Sleeker than the Nies'chen wines, but otherwise with similar character. Most important owners: Bischöfliche Weingüter, Karlsmühle.

Kaseler Nies'chen Complex wines with a pronounced blackcurrant aroma and more body than most Ruwer Rieslings. Most important owners: Bischöfliche Weingüter, Karlsmühle, von Kesselstatt, von Beulwitz.

Maximin Grünhäuser Abtsberg This site forms the heart of the famous Grünhaus estate's vineyards. Like the Herrenberg, it is a monopoly of the von Schubert family. The wines are exceptionally elegant and refined, possessing decades of ageing potential.

Maximin Grünhäuser Herrenberg The red-slate soil of this famous site produces slightly leaner and more aromatic wines than those of its great neighbour, the Abtsberg. The names of the Grünhäuser sites recall the estate's monastic past; Herrenberg wines were made for the lord while those of Abtsberg, as the name suggests, were reserved for the abbot. The monks made do with wines from the Brudersberg.

Middle Mosel Vineyards

Bernkasteler Badstube (Alte Badstube am Doctorberg, Bratenhöfchen, Graben, Lay,) Small Grosslage composed only of superior sites. Generally, sleek, racy wines that are the epitome of Mosel Riesling. In top vintages the Lay and Graben can give magnificent wines. Most important owners: Dr. Pauly-Bergweiler, Dr. Loosen, Dr. Thanisch, Heribert

Kerpen, Joh. Jos. Prüm, S.A. Prüm, Selbach-Oster, Studert-Prüm, J. Wegeler, Dr. Weins-Prüm.

Bernkasteler Doctor Tiny, legendary 3.26-hectare site, which towers above the roofs of old Bernkastel. Intense, sleek wines that are capable of great finesse. Many experts claim to detect a smoky aroma. Most important owners: von Kesselstatt, Dr. Thanisch, J. Wegeler (Deinhard).

Brauneberger Juffer Large site surrounding the great Juffer-Sonnenuhr, giving slightly less refined wines with similar body and minerally character. Most important owners: Fritz Haag, Willi Haag, Paulinshof, Max Ferd. Richter.

Brauneberger Juffer-Sonnenuhr For centuries, the combination of minerally power and racy elegance made the wines from Brauneberg's top site the most sought-after Mosel Rieslings. Their reputation is once again on the rise. Most important owners: Fritz Haag, Willi Haag, Paulinshof, Max Ferd. Richter, Dr. Thanisch.

Dhroner Hofberg Little-known site, the best part of which yields extremely juicy, appealing wines that show well from an early age. Most important owners: A.J. Adam, Clüsserath, Bischöfliche Weingüter.

Erdener Prälat Nestling between massive red-slate cliffs and the bank of the river, the tiny Prälat site enjoys the warmest microclimate in the entire Mosel region. The result is rich wines with lavish almond, apricot, and exotic-fruit aromas, and great ageing potential. Most important owners: Bischöfliche Weingüter, Jos. Christoffel, Dr. Loosen, Mönchhof, Dr. Weins-Prüm.

Erdener Treppchen The Treppchen wines bear a family resemblance to those of the Prälat, but are more restrained and racy, many would say more classical. The eastern part of this site is the best. Most important owners: Bischöfliche Weingüter, Joh. Jos. Christoffel, Jos. Christoffel, Erbes, Dr. Loosen, Merkelbach, Meulenhof, Mönchhof, Peter Nicolay, Schmitges.

Graacher Domprobst The deep slate soil of Graach's finest vineyard gives firm, intensely minerally Riesling, with a

Egon Müller

pronounced blackcurrant aroma. In hot years they are extremely long living. Most important owners: Friedrich-Wilhelm-Gymnasium, Kees-Kieren, Heribert Kerpen, Markus Molitor, S.A.Prüm, Max Ferd. Richter, Willi Schaefer, Selbach-Oster, Dr. Weins-Prüm.

Graacher Himmelreich Large site encompassing vineyards of variable quality. More charming and supple wines than those from the neighbouring Domprobst. Most important owners: Dr. Pauly-Bergweiler, Friedrich-Wilhelm Gymnasium, Kees-Kieren, Dr. Loosen, Markus Molitor, Joh. Jos. Prüm, S.A. Prüm, Max. Ferd. Richter, Willi Schaefer, Studert-Prüm, Dr. Weins-Prüm.

Josephshöfer 4.7-hectare monopoly site of the Kesselstatt estate yielding substantial Rieslings with a pronounced earthy note and excellent ageing potential.

Leiwener Laurentiuslay With the quality renaissance in Leiwen, this site's abilities to give Mosel Rieslings that are at once rich and refined has become more widely appreciated. Many old vines. Most important owners: Grans-Fassian, Carl Loewen, Rosch, Sankt Urbans-Hof.

Lieserer Niederberg-Helden This once famous site gives wines with a strong family resemblance to those from the nearby Brauneberg. Most important owners: Sybille Kuntz, Schloss Lieser.

Piesporter Domherr This small site within the famous Goldtröpfchen makes more delicate, but equally great Rieslings, which show their class when young and mature. Most important owners: von Kesselstatt, Reinhold Haart, Kurt Hain.

Piesporter Goldtröpfchen The extremely deep slate soils of this site yield the most baroque of all Mosel Rieslings. When young, their explosive blackcurrant, citrus-fruit, and peach aromas may be too exotic for some, but with ageing they acquire great elegance. In hot years many of the best Mosel wines come from here. Most important owners: von Kesselstatt, Joh. Haart, Reinhold Haart, Kurt Hain, Lehnert-Veit, Reuscher-Haart, Sankt Urbans-Hof, Vereinigte Hospitien.

Pündericher Marienburg The steep slopes below the Marienburg castle give the finest and richest Rieslings in this stretch of the Mosel valley. Most important owner: Clemens Busch.

Thörnicher Ritsch Little-known site with excellent exposure, capable of yielding Rieslings with a Saar-like purity and steely intensity. Most important owner: Carl Loewen.

Trittenheimer Apotheke The best parts of this site are precipitously steep, with stony slate soil, giving wines with considerable elegance and subtlety. Most important owners: Ansgar Clüsserath, Ernst Clüsserath, Clüsserath-Eifel, Clüsserath-Weiler, F.J. Eifel, Grans-Fassian, Milz, Rosch.

Trittenheimer Leiterchen Tiny one-hectare monopoly site of the Milz estate in the heart of the Apotheke. The very rocky soil often gives wines with a herbal note.

Urziger Würzgarten Its red sandstone soil results in astonishingly powerful, spicy Mosel Rieslings that need many years of ageing to reach their peak. Only the heart of this site is rated as first class. Most important owners:

EGON MULLER – A GREAT SAAR ESTATE

German winemaking at its highest level can best be described as wine for wine's sake. In a fine vintage the producer is almost passive, like a painter before a sunset. Rather than try to mould the vintage to his preconceived ideal, he is dedicated to interpreting what nature provides. If one estate embodies this approach to wine it is that of Egon Müller-Scharzhof. Egon Müller IV's family has owned the Scharzhof manor at Wiltingen on the Saar, and eight hectares of the steep Scharzhofberg above it, since 1797. Their late-picked wines have frequently achieved world record-prices at the annual auction of the Grosser Ring, or Great Ring, of leading Mosel-growers at Trier.

Egon Müller's great-great-great-grandfather bought the estate, formerly church land like so much of Germany's best, after it was secularized under Napoleon. It is very much the old family

house, its hall lined with trophies of the chase, and its library with leather-bound books. A tasting of the new vintage with Egon Müller takes place in the half-light of the hall, standing at a round table of black marble with a ring of green bottles, and elegant tasting glasses. The Riesling that he grows on the grey slate of the Scharzhofberg is Riesling in its naked purity. As the harvest proceeds, each picking is fermented apart in its own cask. The samples at the tasting are of different casks. As the end of the harvest approaches, the differences between casks increase. The Kabinetts are often bottled as one wine, but Spätlesen are usually kept in separate lots, and there may be five or six different Auslesen as each day's ripening intensifies the honeyed sweetness of the latest wines. A Gold Cap Auslese (a gold capsule replaces the words Feinste Auslese) from Egon Müller has as much penetrating

perfume, vitality, and "breeding" as any wine in Germany. Its measured sweetness is matched with such racy acidity that the young wine may almost make you wince. Yet time harmonizes the extremes into a perfectly pitched unity, a teasing, tingling lusciousness that only Riesling, only the Saar, only the Scharzhofberg can achieve. As for the rare TBA, its quality and scarcity are such that only the richest collectors can afford it. A case of the 1994 TBA fetched the equivalent of $42,000 when auctioned in 2001, while a single bottle of 2002 Eiswein was sold for €1,715.

Egon Müller jointly owns (with Gerard Villanova) a second Saar estate, the four-hectare Le Gallais, which makes up the entire Wiltinger Braune Kupp site. Its wines, vinified in the Scharzhof cellars, are richer but less fine than the Scharzhofbergers. He also runs his wife's family's Château Belá in Slovakia.

Bischöfliche Weingüter, Joh. Jos. Christoffel, Karl Erbes, Dr. Loosen, Merkelbach, Mönchhof, Dr. Pauly-Bergweiler, Dr. Weins-Prüm.

Wehlener Sonnenuhr The stony slate soil of this, the most famous of all Mosel vineyards, results in wines of almost supernatural grace and delicacy. Usually they are extremely charming from an early age, yet long living. The highest lying parts of this large site are the best. Most important owners: Dr. Pauly-Bergweiler, Heribert Kerpen, Dr. Loosen, Joh. Jos. Prüm, S.A. Prüm, Max Ferd. Richter, Selbach-Oster, Studert-Prüm, J. Wegeler, Dr. Weins-Prüm.

Zeltinger Sonnenuhr The best corners of this site are a match for the directly neighbouring and more famous Sonnenuhr vineyard of Wehlen. However, slightly richer soils result in more weighty, firmer wines. Most important owners: Markus Molitor, Joh. Jos. Prüm, Selbach-Oster.

Terrassen Mosel Vineyards

Bremmer Calmont This great amphitheatre of vines is the steepest vineyard in all of Europe. Its narrow terraces yield firmly structured Rieslings with pronounced minerally character. Most important owner: Reinhold Franzen.

Neefer Frauenberg Much more floral, charming wines than Calmont. Most important owner: Reinhold Franzen.

Winninger Röttgen The aromatic, silky wines from this site, just downstream from the village of Winningen, have been famous for centuries. Most important owners: von Heddesdorf, Heymann-Löwenstein, Knebel, R. Richter.

Winninger Uhlen The great soaring wall of narrow terraced vineyards which forms the Uhlen is one of the most imposing vineyards on the entire Mosel – an impressive sight from the autobahn bridge where it crosses the river here. The firmly structured, minerally Rieslings produced from the Winninger Uhlen are arguably the finest of the Terrassen Mosel. Most important owners: von Heddesdorf, Heymann-Löwenstein, Knebel.

Leading Mosel Producers

Bastgen ☆☆
Kesten. www.weingut-bastgen.de
Since Mona Bastgen and Armin Vogel took over this tiny five-hectare estate, it has begun to prove the true potential of sites such as the Kestener Paulinshofberg. These are substantial wines, with plenty of fruit and character.

Von Beulwitz ☆☆–☆☆☆☆
Mertesdorf
In 1982, Herbert Weis bought a hotel and a six-hectare wine estate in the Ruwer, and continues to manage both. His best wines come from ungrafted vines in Kaseler Nies'chen, and are intensely fruity, though they can lack some zest.

Bischöfliche Weingüter ☆–☆☆
Trier. www.bwgtrier.de
This, the largest estate under a single management in the

Mosel, was formed by the union in 1966 of three independent charitable properties: the Priesterseminar (Bishop's Seminary); the Domkirche (Trier Cathedral) estates; and the Bischöfliches Konvikt (Bishop's Hostel). In 2003 it acquired another charitable property, the Friedrich-Wilhelm Gymnasium, but sold off many of its vineyards.

In all, the property consists of 107 hectares, with excellent vineyards in Scharzhofberg, Kaseler Nies'chen, and Trittenheimer Apotheke. The charities maintain separate press houses; after pressing, all the juice is brought together in the venerable central cellar in Trier for fermentation and cask-ageing. Ninety-eight per cent of the whole estate is Riesling, mostly vinified in a *trocken* or *halbtrocken* style. After a period of unexciting performance during the 1980s, quality improved during the early 1990s but seems lacklustre given the resources at the estates' disposal.

Clemens Busch ☆☆–☆☆☆☆
Pünderich. www.clemens-busch.de
Busch, who took over the seven-hectare family estate in 1991, introduced organic viticulture and has triumphantly validated the quality of the splendid Pündericher Marienburg site. Most of the wines are lime-scented, invigorating, and dry, though sometimes their alcohol is a touch too evident. In certain vintages the Auslesen are noteworthy.

Joh. Jos. Christoffel ☆☆☆
Ürzig.
In 2001, Hans-Leo Christoffel, the owner of this tiny but highly regarded estate, retired, leasing his vineyards to his neighbour at Mönchhof (q.v.). They continue to be released under the Christoffel label. These have long been among the most polished, elegant Rieslings in this dramatic section of the Middle Mosel. Stars on the label (between one and five, the more indicating the better quality) are used to differentiate between the different bottlings of Würzgarten Auslese in fine vintages.

Ansgar Clüsserath ☆–☆☆
Trittenheim.
Ansgar is the latest of the many Clüsseraths to set up shop here. The Apotheke is the source of his best wines, which can be mineral to the point of earthiness.

Ernst Clüsserath ☆☆
Trittenheim. www.weingut-ernst-cluesserath.de
A tiny three-hectare estate whose wines have already won serious young owner/winemaker Ernst Clüsserath much acclaim. The yields here are very low, and the wines, whether dry or naturally sweet, are delicate and penetrating.

Clüsserath-Weiler ☆☆☆
Trittenheim. www.cluesserath-weiler.de
Half of Helmut Clüsserath's vineyards are in the Apotheke, and he is especially proud of a tiny parcel, planted with 100-year-old vines, called Fährfels, which is bottled separately. All the wines are elegant, minerally, and medium-bodied, and a star system differentiates the different Auslese qualities.

Reinhold Franzen ☆☆
Bremm. www.weingut-franzen.de

This would be a celebrated estate simply because the Bremmer Calmont is Europe's steepest vineyard. However, Franzen also coaxes exceedingly good wines, mostly dry, from its precipitous slopes.

Friedrich-Wilhelm Gymnasium
See Bischöfliche Weingüter.

Grans-Fassian ☆☆☆
Leiwen. www.grans-fassian.de
The urbane Gerhard Grans has been running the nine-hectare family estate for a quarter of a century now, and has always insisted on low yields to give his wines their crystalline character. He is fortunate to have excellent vineyards not only in Leiwen but in Trittenheimer Apotheke and Piesporter Goldtröpfchen. Unerring quality across the range, and some of the best Eiswein of the region.

Fritz Haag ☆☆☆–☆☆☆☆
Brauneberg.
www.weingut-fritz-haag.de
This distinguished estate can trace its history back to 1605. It has long been one of the top addresses for perfectly made, elegant, cask-matured Riesling wines, especially from Juffer-Sonnenuhr. Wilhelm Haag has rebuilt their once supreme reputation, although replantings in the early 1990s meant that the usual balance of the estate was disturbed, as there were too many young vines. At their best, the wines have a bracing minerality and power, without a trace of heaviness. In vintages such as 2005 and 2007 he unleashes numerous *cuvées* between Auslese and (sublime) TBA.

Willi Haag ☆☆
Brauneberg. www.willi-haag.de
Family problems caused a lapse in quality here, but this estate is back on form under Markus Haag, producing clean, attractive Rieslings from the best sites in Brauneberg.

Reinhold Haart ☆☆☆–☆☆☆☆
Piesport. www.haart.de
The quietly determined Theo Haart runs Piesport's leading estate, producing wines that combine the extravagant personality of these top-site vineyards with charm and delicacy. He also makes impressive wines from vines in the unclassified Wintricher Ohligsberg, which he purchased in 1990. His Gutsriesling is labelled Haart to Heart.

Kurt Hain ☆☆–☆☆☆
Piesport. www.piesportergoldtroepfchen.de
Gernot Hain took over this well-established, five-hectare estate in 1988, and makes delicious wines, dry and naturally sweet, from the Goldtröpfchen.

Heymann-Löwenstein ☆☆–☆☆☆☆
Winningen. www.heymann-loewenstein.com
Reinhard Löwenstein's reputation as a rebel is well-deserved,

not least because of the fanaticism with which he has pursued top quality, in an area where mediocrity is still largely the norm. He also scorns the use of such winemaking aids as cultivated yeasts, enzymes, and bentonite. His unusually full-bodied, dry Rieslings, rich in weight and flavour from prolonged ageing on the lees, are among the best examples of this style in the region. As well as prized single-vineyard wines, there are appealing blends from slate soils called Schiefferterrassen and Vom Blauen Schieffer. He also produces some imposing if costly late harvest wines.

Von Hövel ☆☆
Konz-Oberemmel. www.weingut-vonhoevel.de
The jovial Eherhard von Kunow makes some of the most immediately appealing Saar Rieslings. Rich and aromatic as young wines, they gain in elegance as they age. The Scharzhofberg wines are slightly more opulent than those from the estate's Hütte monopoly, from which many superb

Auslese and higher Prädikat wines are made. At Kabinett and Spätlese level, the estate's wines offer excellent value.

Immich-Batterieberg ☆☆
Enkirch. www.batterieberg.de
Gert Basten bought this property, including a mansion that dates to the ninth century, in 1989. The monopoly Batterieberg was created by dynamiting the slate cliffs in 1844. Yields are low, so the grapes attain high ripeness levels conducive to dry wine production, which can be outstanding here.

Albert Kallfelz ☆–☆☆
Zell-Merl. www.kallfelz.de
This estate, at the boundary between the Middle Mosel and the Terrassen Mosel, has expanded rapidly to its present 43 hectares. His best wines come from Merler Königslay-Terrassen, two-thirds of which are owned by the estate. Almost all the wines are *trocken* or *halbtrocken*.

Karlsmühle ☆☆
Mertesdorf. www.weingut-karlsmuehle.de
Peter Geiben abandoned his former profession of hotelier to devote all his time to his vineyards in Kasel and his monopoly Lorenzhöfer vineyards. He makes Ruwer wines of tremendous personality, whether dry and pungent, or sweet and racy.

Karthäuserhof ☆☆☆–☆☆☆☆
Trier-Eitelsbach. www.karthaeuserhof.com
A beautiful old manor of the Carthusian monks in a side valley of the Ruwer, bought in 1811 by the ancestor of the present owner when Napoleon secularized church land. It stands at the foot of the steep Eitelsbacher Karthäuserhofberg vineyard, which is entirely owned by the estate. Since Christoph Tyrell took control of the estate in 1986, quality has improved in leaps and bounds. Today, the estate's dry and naturally sweet Rieslings are among the Mosel's finest. Intense blackcurrant and peach aromas and racy acidity are

Wine drinking scene decorates a fountain, Bernkastel

their hallmark. The bottle is unmistakable, with only a narrow label on the neck and none on the body.

Heribert Kerpen ☆☆
Wehlen. www.weingut-kerpen.de
Martin Kerpen is fortunate enough to own three hectares of mostly ungrafted vines in Wehlener Sonnenuhr. He was a pioneer of dry wines in the Mosel, but his elegant floral Spätlese and Auslese wines with natural sweetness are consistently impressive.

Reichsgraf von Kesselstatt ☆☆–☆☆☆
Morscheid. www.kesselstatt.com
This was the greatest private estate of the Mosel-Saar-Ruwer when it was bought in 1978 by Günther Reh. Since 1983, the estate has been directed by his daughter, Annegret. The entire estate covers some of the greatest sites of the region: Scharzhofberg, Piesporter Goldtröpfchen, Kaseler Nies'chen, and the monopoly site Josephshöfer in Graach, and is planted with 100% Riesling. Annegret Reh-Gartner's strategy has been to sell or lease out the lesser sites and focus on the top vineyards. Many of the wines are *trocken* or *halbtrocken*, including the high-quality estate Riesling called Palais Kesselstatt. Regardless of style, the wines are packed with fruit and have a vibrant, but never dominant, acidity.

Reinhard Knebel ☆☆☆
Winningen.
A family split led to the creation of this excellent Terrassen Mosel estate in 1990. Tragedy struck in 2004, with Reinhard Knebel's suicide, but his widow Beate has not allowed quality to slip. The Riesling *halbtrocken* wines are very good here, and the Auslesen from Uhlen are exceptional. Knebel also makes some fabulous TBAs from Röttgen, but in minute quantities.

Sybille Kuntz ☆☆
Lieser. www.sybillekuntz.de
Many of the Kuntz wines are dry, and strong by Mosel standards, and the best of them is usually the *cuvée* called Gold-Quadrat, made from ungrafted vines. There is no Kabinett or Spätlese, but when conditions permit, Kuntz also likes to produce ultra-sweet botrytis wines.

Peter Lauer ☆☆
Ayl. www.riesling-weine.de
A numbered sequence of wines explores every nuance and expression of the great Ayler Kupp vineyard.

Schloss Lieser ☆☆☆
Lieser. www.weingut-schloss-lieser.de
Thomas Haag, son of Wilhelm Haag of Brauneberg, moved to the next village in 1992 to run the former Freiherr von Schorlemer estate. In 1997, he was able to buy the property, from which he produces concentrated, long lived wines. Not wines of tremendous power, but they have charm, raciness, and exceptional length of flavour. The 2005 and 2007 vintages raised quality, already very fine, a notch higher.

Carl Loewen ☆☆
Leiwen. www.weingut-loewen.de
Karl-Josef Loewen is something of a visionary by rescuing forgotten vineyard sites such as Thörnicher Ritsch. The *trocken* and *halbtrocken* wines are good, but by far the best wines are the Auslesen from Leiwener Laurentiuslay.

Dr. Loosen ☆☆☆☆
Bernkastel. www.drloosen.de
From old, ungrafted vines in great vineyards from Bernkastel to Erden, the dynamic Ernst Loosen produces some of the finest Rieslings made in the Mosel – and Germany – today. Their hallmarks are concentration, complex mineral, herb, and spice flavours, and a distinctly drier balance than the norm for the region. The character of each site is extremely distinct. The crowning glory of the peaks in the estate's wide range are the majesterial Auslese wines from the Erdener Prälat. His standard wines are also fully representative and good value. See also J J Wolf in the Pfalz.

Alfred Merkelbach ☆–☆☆
Ürzig.
A minuscule property but a reliable source of modestly priced wines from Urziger Würzgarten.

Milz ☆–☆☆
Trittenheim.
Founded in the seventeenth century, this estate is blessed not only with good parcels in the Apotheke, but with two monopoly sites in Trittenheim: Felsenkopf and Leiterchen. Quality varies from sound to excellent.

Markus Molitor ☆☆☆
Wehlen. www.markusmolitor.com
With 38 hectares, this is the largest estate on the Middle Mosel. Not all the sites are outstanding, but Markus Molitor has excellent parcels in Zeltinger Sonnenuhr. About half the production is of dry wines, but for many wine-lovers, it's the exquisite Auslesen from Wehlener Klosterberg and Sonnenuhr that are the most appealing. Look out, too, for sensational, and very expensive, nobly sweet wines.

Mönchhof ☆☆
Urzig. www.moenchhof.de
The old manor house of Mönchhof is a landmark at Urzig, and in its sixteenth-century cellars repose classic Rieslings from Urzig and Erden. Very little dry wine is made. Dependable if not always thrilling quality from the mid-1990s make this an excellent source for these wines. In 2001, the owner, Robert Eymael, leased the neighbouring Joh. Jos. Christoffel estate (q.v.).

Egon Müller – Scharzhof ☆☆☆☆
See box on page 249.

Von Othegraven ☆☆–☆☆☆
Kanzem. www.von-othegraven.de
Since Dr. Heidi Kegel took control of this historic estate in the late 1990s, quality has soared, with exquisite wines from Ockfener Bockstein and, especially, Kanzemer Altenberg. She has restored the renown of one of the Saar's greatest vineyards.

Paulinshof ☆☆–☆☆☆
Kesten. www.paulinshof.de
This former monastic property has been owned by the

Jüngling family since 1969. Klaus Jüngling and his son Oliver have specialized in dry wines, picking as late as possible so as to have lower acidity levels. These dry and off-dry wines, especially from Brauneberger Juffer-Sonnenuhr and their monopoly site Brauneberger Kammer, are first-rate. As, indeed, are their nobly sweet wines.

Dr. Pauly-Bergweiler & Peter Nicolay ☆☆–☆☆☆
Bernkastel-Kues. www.pauly-bergweiler.com
The marriage between Dr. Peter Pauly and Helga Pauly-Berres united some of the best vineyards in the Middle Mosel, including Bernkasteler Alte Badstube am Doctorberg, Graacher Domprobst and Graacher Himmelreich, Wehlener Sonnenuhr, Erdener Prälat, and Urziger Goldwingert (monopoly). In top vintages, Stefan Pauly, who now runs the estate, produces some fabulous sweet wines, such as sumptuous TBAs from Urziger Würzgarten and Eiswein from Bernkasteler Lay. The stars of the Nicolay range are usually the rich wines from the Urziger Goldwingert.

J.J. Prüm ☆☆☆☆
Wehlen. www.jjpruem.com
The most famous estate of many belonging to the most famous family of growers of the Middle Mosel. The estate house, down by the river, looks across the water up to the great Sonnenuhr vineyard, of which it has one of the largest holdings. The huge sundials among the vines here and in Zeltingen were built by an earlier Prüm.

The estate's signature is wine of glorious fruity ripeness, setting off the exquisite raciness of Riesling grown on slate, with deep notes of spice and honey. As very young wines, they often retain a yeasty aroma from fermentation, but this quickly dispenses. Their ageing potential is legendary: Spätlese and Auslese often needing ten years and more to reach their peak. An Auslese and Feinste Auslese from 1949 were still fresh and persistent in 2008. Even the entry-level Prüm Riesling is a fine wine to age several years. Dr. Manfred Prüm's daughter Katharina is now at his side.

S.A. Prüm ☆☆
Wehlen. www.sapruem.com
Part of the great Prüm estate, which was originally divided among seven children in 1911. Since 1971, Raimund Prüm has made vigorous wines, especially from Wehlener Sonnenuhr. The Prüms as a whole are very conservative winemakers, but Raimund Prüm has had no qualms about using brightly designed labels to match the freshness of his wines. Depending on the vintage, up to 70 per cent of his wines are *trocken* or *halbtrocken*.

Johann Peter Reinert ☆
Kanzem. www.weingut-reinert.de
Johann Peter Reinert makes fruity wines of considerable charm from this four hectare estate. The finest of these come from the Kanzemer Altenberg.

Max Ferd. Richter ☆☆–☆☆☆
Mülheim. www.maxferdrichter.com
This substantial estate, with holdings scattered through the Middle Mosel, is an extremely consistent producer of classic

Mosel Rieslings, both in the dry and naturally sweet styles. Dirk Richter's finest wines are the powerful, minerally Rieslings from the top sites of Brauneberg, while Eiswein is made almost every year from his monopoly site, the Mülheimer Helenenkloster. Dr. Richter also runs a merchant business; the vinification is equally traditional and scrupulous, the only difference being that the grapes are purchased, mostly from growers with whom he has long term contracts.

Josef Rosch ☆☆–☆☆☆
Leiwen.
Werner Rosch is one of a number of growers behind the renaissance of the vineyards of Leiwen and Trittenheim. Although most of his wines are dry and somewhat austere, he also produces fine, naturally sweet wine, especially Auslesen of great elegance.

Sankt Urbans-Hof ☆☆☆
Leiwen. www.weingut-st-urbans-hof.de
Hermann Weis is a nurseryman who, with his son Nik, directs the third-largest privately owned wine estate in the Mosel. The dry Rieslings from Leiwener Laurentiuslay are very good, but outclassed by the mouth-watering naturally sweet wines from Piesporter Goldtröpfchen and Ockfener Bockstein.

Schloss Saarstein ☆☆
Serrig. www.saarstein.de
The charming and dedicated Christian and Andrea Ebert run one of the most consistent wine estates on the Saar. Most of the wines come from their monopoly of Serriger Schloss Saarstein. Absolute purity of flavour and steely intensity are the qualities that typify both the dry wines and those with natural sweetness. The BA, TBA, and Eiswein are among the greatest in the entire Mosel, with enormous ageing potential.

Willi Schaefer ☆☆☆–☆☆☆☆
Graach.
This miniature estate in the Middle Mosel, with a mere 2.7 hectares of vineyards, regularly produces the finest of Rieslings from the most excellent vineyards of Graach. This combination of extremely limited production and high demand means that the Auslese and higher Prädikat wines sell out almost instantaneously. It would be difficult to find Mosels with better ageing potential than these beautifully crafted, sleek, racy wines.

C. von Schubert, Maximin Grünhaus ☆☆☆☆
Grünhaus/Trier. www.vonschubert.com
This outstanding estate of the Ruwer is also one of Germany's finest. Acquired by the ancestors of Dr. Carl von Schubert in 1882, the vineyards consist of a unique undivided hill dominating the beautiful, formerly Benedictine-owned manor house, with its cellars dating back to Roman times. The estate's three vineyards, Herrenberg, Abtsberg, and the less well-exposed Bruderberg, produce distinctly different wines.

Since the early twentieth century, the estate's miraculously delicate wines have been sold under an extravagant art nouveau label. In spite of their lightness of body, even the "simplest"

Grünhaus Rieslings age magnificently – the epitome of great German Riesling. The naturally sweet Auslesen of good vintages are sublime: infinitely subtle but surprisingly spicy and powerful, ageing 20 years or more. The estate is also one of the most reliable producers of dry Rieslings in the Mosel area.

Selbach-Oster ☆☆☆
Zeltingen. www.selbach-oster.de
Johannes Selbach follows in his late father Hans's footsteps by making beautifully crafted Mosel Rieslings from 16 hectares. Below Auslese level the wines have a distinctly dry finish. The finest wines almost invariably come from Zeltinger Sonnenuhr, which gives wines that combine richness with great subtlety, and possess excellent ageing potential. The family also runs a high-quality merchant house under the name J & H Selbach.

Studert-Prüm ☆☆
Wehlen.
www.weingut-studert-pruem.de
The Studert family, which has been growing vines since the sixteenth century, acquired the Wehlen vineyard holdings of the Benedictine St Maximin Abbey in Trier in 1805. Since the early 1990s, quality has taken a significant jump up here. The dry wines can be tart, but the naturally sweet Wehlener Sonnenuhr bottlings are delicious and make up the bulk of production.

Wwe Dr. H Thanisch – Erben Müller-Burggraef ☆☆
Bernkastel.
The Thanisch estate, which produced the legendary 1921 TBA from Bernkasteler Doctor, was divided between two branches of the family in the late 1980s. This is the larger of the two. Despite excellent vineyard holdings in Brauneberg and Wehlen as well as Bernkastel, quality was unexciting until the late 1990s, when it began to produce some excellent sweet wines. They have flamboyance rather than finesse.

Wwe Dr. H Thanisch – Erben Thanisch ☆☆–☆☆☆
Bernkastel.
This is the smaller of the Thanisch properties, and can be distinguished from the other by the VDP logo. Almost all the wines are naturally sweet, with some superb ranges from the Doctor vineyard. Their renown means they are very expensive, but the wines from other sites, such as Bernkasteler Badstube, are both very good and far less costly.

Vereinigte Hospitien ☆
Trier. www.weingut.vereinigtehospitien.de
This is one of the great charitable institutions of Trier, occupying Germany's oldest cellars, built as a Roman warehouse. The charity still runs a free hospital, largely financed by vineyards and other considerable estates.

Although the Hospitien owns excellent sites in Scharzhofberg and Goldtröpfchen and throughout the Saar, the wines are disappointing.

Van Volxem ☆☆☆
Wiltingen. www.vanvolxem.de
In 2000 this troubled property was bought by Roman Niewodniczanski, heir to a brewery fortune. His mission has been to revive the tradition of great dry Rieslings from the Saar. He ignores the Prädikat system, fitting the style of the wine to the vineyard and grapes that produced it. These wines, from an expanding collection of top sites such as Scharzhofberg and Wiltinger Gottesfüß, are not bone-dry, but taste dry thanks to their natural high acidity.

Niewodniczanski also makes some resplendent sweet wines. He imposes extremely low yields, which account for the wines' power and concentration.

Dr. Heinz Wagner ☆☆–☆☆☆
Saarburg. www.weingutdrwagner.de
In the cavernous cellars below his imposing nineteenth century mansion close to Saarburg's railway station, Heinz Wagner produces unusually substantial Saar wines. The wines from the Bockstein are both subtle and seductive, while those from the Rausch are deep and long-living. A reliable source for dry wine, too.

J Wegeler ☆☆–☆☆☆
Bernkastel. www.wegeler.com
The Mosel estate of the once-famous Koblenz wine merchants started in 1900, with the sensational purchase of part of the Doctor vineyard. Today it owns 14 hectares, mostly in outstanding sites. In 2001, Oliver Haag, brother of Thomas Haag of Schloss Lieser (q.v.), took over running the estate, and recent vintages have seen a marked improvement in quality.

Dr. F Weins-Prüm ☆☆☆
Wehlen
The shy Bert Selbach makes light but vivid Mosel Rieslings from a whole range of excellent vineyards. Almost all the wines are naturally sweet, and have a classic balance of fruit and acidity. Those from the Erdener Prälat and Wehlener Sonnenuhr usually have most character. They greatly repay ageing for five years or more.

Forstmeister Geltz Zilliken ☆☆☆
Saarburg. www.zilliken-vdp.de
The family estate of the much-respected Ferdinand Geltz (1851–1925), Master Forester of the King of Prussia, is run by his great-grandson, Hans-Joachim Zilliken. The wines are made very traditionally, in casks, and are designed for long age in bottle. The intensely minerally, racy wines from the Rausch are among the finest in the entire Saar. The Eiswein can be especially brilliant.

Statue of St. Jacobus, Vereinigte Hospitien, Trier

Ahr & Mittelrhein

Ahr

Perverse as it may seem, one of Germany's northernmost wine regions specializes in red wine. The Ahr valley is an appealing landscape of steeply terraced vineyards, wooded hills, and rocky terrain. The Ahr is a western tributary of the Mittelrhein and is not far south of Bonn. The valley's steep sides are clothed almost continuously in vines for 16 kilometres (10 miles): 540 hectares, of which almost two-thirds are Spätburgunder (Pinot Noir), Portugieser, and other red grapes. The remainder is planted with white grapes – Riesling and Müller-Thurgau are the most important. In its most sheltered corners, temperatures soar when the sun shines, and in a good summer Spätburgunder grapes ripen fully. The pale, thin, sweet-sour wines of the past came primarily from misconceived winemaking. Since the late 1980s, a handful of pioneers, working with proper maceration techniques and skilful barrel ageing, have proved that "real" red wines can also be made. Perfume and grace, rather than power and richness, are their strengths. The region's whites are usually dry, but are seldom capable of competing with those of the Mittelrhein or the Mosel.

Leading Ahr Producers

J.J. Adeneuer ☆☆
Ahrweiler. www.adeneuer.de
The Adeneuers are relative newcomers to high-quality red-wine production, but have learned fast. Most of the wines are aged in large casks, but the top *cuvées* are aged in up to one-third new barriques. Their top site is Walporzheimer Gärkammer; it is bottled separately. Their other outstanding bottling is their Spätburgunder No.1. These are wines to be enjoyed fairly young, at between three and five years.

Deutzerhof ☆☆☆
Mayschoss. www.deutzerhof.de
At no other Ahr estate has the quality improved so dramatically during the last decade as here. These are deep-coloured Spätburgunders, with a judicious touch of new oak. The top wines come from Altenahrer Eck, but there are also exceptional blends such as Caspar C and Grand Duc. Some white wines, the late-harvest Rieslings, especially, are also remarkable, but the reds are the wines to follow.

Winzergenossenschaft Mayschoss-Altenahr I-II
Mayschoss. www.winzergnossenschaft-mayschoss.de
This cooperative controls almost a quarter of the valley's vineyards, so it is an important player. The wines have been steadily improving, and includes a range of Frühburgunder as well as Spätburgunder wines.

Weingut Meyer-Näkel ☆☆☆
Dernau. www.meyer-naekel.de
Ex-high-school teacher and self-taught winemaker, Werner Näkel was the dynamo of the red-winemaking revolution of the 1980s. He makes the most elegant and sophisticated Spätburgunder red wines in the region, and also makes excellent wines from the rare Frühburgunder variety. His subtle use of new oak is cautious and precisely judged. Werner Näkel's wines should have dispelled any remaining scepticism about the need to take the Ahr seriously.

Nelles ☆
Bad Neuenahr. www.weingut-nelles.de
Thomas Nelles enjoys making a wide range of wines from varieties such as Domina, Riesling, and Grauburgunder, which may explain why, except at the top level, the Spätburgunder seems a touch superficial.

Jean Stodden ☆☆–☆☆☆
Rech. www.stodden.de
Most of Gerhard Stodden's six-hectare estate is planted on steep terraces. The best wines, from Grosses Gewächs sites in Rech and Bad Neuenahr, are aged in barriques, and tend to be very tannic. They are very expensive but enjoy a keen following in Germany.

Outstanding Mittelrhein Vineyards

Mention the Rhine and images immediately come to mind of the river coursing through the narrow gorge between Bingen and Koblenz, with its castles and vines clinging precariously to precipitous slopes. This, and the scattered vineyards between Koblenz and Bonn, make up the little-known Mittelrhein region. In wine terms, "Lower Rhine" might be a more appropriate name, since these are the last vineyards along the river's course.

Since 1950, the vineyard area has shrunk from 1,200 hectares to a mere 465; they continue to dwindle at an alarming rate, which is most regrettable, because the most favoured vineyards here give Rieslings that are quite a match for those of the western Rheingau, and it has often been the best and steepest vineyards that have been abandoned. Fully 68 per cent of the region's vineyards are planted with the noble Riesling grape. The elegant, medium-bodied dry and naturally sweet Rieslings, made by the region's leading producers in recent years, have resulted in a renaissance of interest in Mittelrhein wines. So far, this has concentrated itself around Bacharach in the south, but competition is also beginning to hot up further north, around Boppard.

Bacharacher Hahn Arguably the best site in the southern Mittelrhein. Its stony, slate soil gives full-bodied Rieslings with rich, peachy fruit. The Hahn is virtually a monopoly site of the Toni Jost estate.

Bacharacher Posten Like Hahn, the Posten enjoys the warmth of the Rhine and can show richness and refinement. Most important owners: Fritz Bastian, Mades, Ratzenberger.

Bacharacher Wolfshöhle Archetypal Bacharach Rieslings: sleek, racy wines with a strong minerally character from the slate soil. Most important owners: Fritz Bastian, Kauer, Mades, Ratzenberger.

Bopparder Hamm This giant amphitheatre of vines divides into five sites. Of them, the Feuerlay, Mandelstein, and

Ohlenberg can all give magnificent Rieslings, but only a few local growers regularly realize this potential. Most important owners: Didinger, Lorenz, Müller, August Perll, Walter Perll, Weingart.

Steeger St Jost This site yields steely Rieslings with the most intense bouquet of all Mittelrhein wines. Most important owners: Mades, Ratzenberger.

Leading Mittelrhein Producers

Bastian ☆☆
Bacharach. www.weingut-bastian.de
A small estate specializing in firm steely Rieslings from top sites in the village. Very impressive Grosses Gewächs wines from Posten and Wolfshöhle.

Didinger ☆–☆☆
Osterspai. www.weingut-didinger.de
Jens Didinger produces a substantial proportion of dry and off-dry wines, but quality is steady across the board. The wines are little known, but can be sampled at the estate's inn.

Toni Jost ☆☆
Bacharach. www.tonijost.de
Peter Jost's richly fruity, dry, and naturally sweet Rieslings are real charmers. Their exuberance seems to match his own. Best are the concentrated late-harvest wines from the superb Hahn site. They can offer the finest Rheingau wines tough competition.

Dr. Randolf Kauer ☆
Bacharach. www.weingut-dr-kauer.de
Dr. Kauer is a professor at the Geisenheim wine college. His organic three-hectare estate makes racy, Mosel-like Rieslings that need time to show their best. Few Kauer vines are in celebrated sites, yet the standard is high, except in cool years when the grapes don't always ripen fully.

Lanius-Knab ☆☆–☆☆☆
Oberwesel. www.lanius-knab.de
Until the quality renaissance at this estate during the early 1990s, Oberwesel's wines were completely overshadowed by those of neighbouring Bacharach. Jörg Lanius's wines

(dry and naturally sweet) are racy Mittelrhein Rieslings of crystalline purity.

Matthias Müller ☆☆
Spay. www.weingut-matthiasmueller.de
Young Matthias Müller has already proved that he can make wines that reflect the true class of the Bopparder Hamm vineyards. The emphasis here is always on ripe fruit, freshness, and harmonious acidity.

August Perll ☆
Boppard. www.perll.de
Thomas Perll makes surprisingly rich, somewhat exotic wines that have fruit rather than freshness.

Ratzenberger ☆☆–☆☆☆
Bacharach. www.weingut-ratzenberger.de
Jochen Ratzenberger maintains the high standards his father set. Yields here are low, thanks to selective harvesting. These are classic, racy Mittelrhein Rieslings with singing minerality, and remarkably long-lived. His Sekt, aged three years on the yeast, is excellent.

Weingart ☆☆
Spay. www.weingut-weingart.de
The Weingart wines used to be rather light, but recent vintages have had more heft and complexity thanks to lower yields.

Rheingau

The Rheingau is the region that established Germany's reputation for world-class white wines in the early nineteenth century. A compact region, it lies on the right bank of the Rhine during the 32 kilometres (20 miles) it flows from east to west from Wiesbaden to Bingen. Most of its vineyards lie on gentle slopes, with southerly exposure, that are well-protected from northerly air streams by the mass of the Taunus Mountains. Here, on soils ranging from slate to loess and marl, the Riesling vine can yield wines that are as aristocratic as the region's famous estates. It accounts for 78 per cent of the vineyard area; next is

---

SEKT

Germany has found a way of turning her awkward excess of underripe wine, the inevitable result of her northerly situation, into pleasure and profit. They are turned into the national sparkling wine: Sekt.

Sekt may be either fermented in bottle or in tank, may be made from any grapes from any region, and may even include imported wines. The wine can only be labelled as Deutscher Sekt if the grapes are entirely German grown. Many of the best specify that they are entirely Riesling

wines, and some specify their exact origins. There is, however, a growing number of fine Sekts being produced from Pinot varieties in southern Germany.

The range of quality is enormous, as 95 per cent of Sekt is produced by the Charmat method and mostly banal. The best examples have nothing in common with Champagne except bubbles: their flavour is essentially flowery and fruity, with the inimitable Riesling aroma in place of Champagne's

greater depth of fruit and yeastiness. Leading specialists: Heymann-Löwenstein, Kesselstatt, Selbach-Oster, Dr. Wagner (Mosel); Ratzenberger (Mittelrhein); Diel (Nahe); Hans Barth, Georg Breuer, Johannishof, Schloss Reinhartshausen (Rheingau); Raumland (Rheinhessen); Bergdolt, von Buhl, Koehler-Ruprecht, Rebholz, Wilhelmshof (Pfalz); Schloss Sommerhausen (Franken); Bernhard Huber, Franz Keller, Schloss Neuweier (Baden).

Spätburgunder with 13 per cent.

This unique combination of natural and human factors makes the recent problems of the region hard to understand. Since the mid-1980s, a number of famous estates with glorious traditions have experienced difficulties, several changing hands and one closing its doors forever (Schloss Groenesteyn). Poor quality has been the main problem of the big estates, most of whom have been overtaken by a handful of ambitious young winemakers at the head of small, family run estates. Thankfully, the combination of press criticism and competition from less famous neighbours has shaken most of the region's large estates out of their slumbers. Slowly but surely, the Rheingau is beginning to prove again that its white wines can be among the greatest anywhere in the world.

The Rheingau led the drive for vineyard classification, but regrettably made a botched job of it, with the result that one third of the vineyards are entitled to be produced, subject to various conditions, as Erstes Gewächs. In practice the proportion is far, far lower, as estates realize that the accolade of First Growth should only be bestowed on truly outstanding wines.

The region can be divided into several sub-areas. The first of these sub-areas is the island of vines at Hochheim on the River Main between Wiesbaden and Frankfurt, whose vineyards yield big, intense wines. The relatively fertile soils of the villages that lie close to the bank of the Rhine between Walluf and Winkel give the most typical Rheingau wines: elegant and subtle to the point of a slight austerity. Higher up, close to the Taunus Forest, the wines are more racy, with a pronounced minerally character from the soil. The wines from Johannisberg and Rüdesheim in the west share this general character, but are fuller-bodied. Assmannshausen is famous for its Spätburgunder red wine.

Outstanding Rheingau Vineyards

Assmannshauser Höllenberg The stony, slate soil of the 55-hectare Höllenberg yields light, elegant, perfumed Spätburgunder reds that nonetheless can be long lived. Most important owners: August Kesseler, König, Hotel Krone, Staatsweingut.

Eltville Sonnenberg Medium-bodied Rieslings with ample fruit and supple acidity that drink well from an early age, but also mature well. Most important owner: Langwerth von Simmern.

Erbacher Hohenrain/Steinmorgen Racy Rieslings with firm acidity that need several years to unfold and reveal their class. Most important owners: Jakob Jung, von Knyphausen.

Erbacher Marcobrunn/Schlossberg/Siegelsberg The famous Marcobrunn gives the most powerful of all Rheingau Rieslings, its heavy marl soil giving them rich fruit, a firm structure, and long ageing potential. The neighbouring sites yield slightly lighter wines with a similar character. Most important owners: August Eser, Schloss Reinhartshausen (Schlossberg monopoly), Schloss Schönborn, Langwerth von Simmern, Staatsweingüter.

Geisenheimer Fuchsberg/Kläuserweg With their heavy marl soils, these two sites give substantial Rieslings with assertive acidity, that need several years' ageing to reveal their full depths. Most important owner: H H Eser, Johannishof, Wegeler.

Geisenheimer Rothenberg A century ago, one of the Rheingau's most renowned vineyards. Its red-slate soil gives lavishly aromatic wines, often with exotic fruit aromas, with a beautiful fruit/acidity balance. Most important owner: Wegeler.

Hallgartener Schönhell The fullest and most harmonious of Hallgarten wines come from this site. Even so, the acidity can be pronounced in young wines. Most important owners: Fürst Löwenstein, Prinz, Querbach.

Hattenheimer Nussbrunnen/Wisselbrunnen/ Mannberg The famous Nussbrunnen yields full, aromatic wines whose ample fruit often masks their acidity, while the wines from the precocious Wisselbrunnen are sleeker and more elegant. Mannberg gives lighter, racy wines. Most important owners: August Eser, Schloss Reinhartshausen, Ress, Schloss Schönborn, Langerth von Simmern.

Hattenheimer Pfaffenberg Monopoly of Schloss Schönborn. Its light, sandy soil yields full, aromatic Rieslings with a particularly elegant acidity.

Hochheimer Domdechaney/ Kirchenstück The two most famous vineyards of Hochheim yield dramatically contrasting wines. The Domdechaney's heavy marl gives powerful, earthy wines; while the lighter soil of the Kirchenstück yields elegant, refined wines. Most important owners: Künstler, Schloss Schönborn, Staatsweingüter, Domdechant Werner.

Hochheimer Hölle/Königin-Victoria-Berg Situated directly on the bank of the Main, these sites have an exceptional microclimate and deep marl-clay soils. This combination gives powerful, highly structured Rieslings. Most important owners: Hupfeld (Königin-Victoria-Berg monopoly), Künstler, Domdechant Werner.

Johannisberger Hölle/Klaus The Hölle's deep, stony soil gives firm, substantial wines with excellent ageing potential; those from the Klaus are more filigree and elegant. Most important owners: Prinz von Hessen, Hupfeld, Johannishof, von Mumm, Trenz.

Kiedricher Gräfenberg/Wasseros The stony phyllite slate soils of these steeply sloping sites give rich, aromatic wines with elegant acidity and enormous ageing potential. Most important owner: Weil.

Martinsthaler This site has similar soil and exposition to Rauenthal. Elegant, racy wines that drink well early.

Mittelheimer St Nikolaus The light soil and riverbank situation of this site results in ripe, juicy wines with plenty of charm. Most important owners: Kühn, Schönleber.

Oestricher Doosberg/Lenchen The deep loess soils of Oestrich result in full-bodied, juicy wines with firm acidity;

the Lenchen wines are slightly lighter and more elegant; the Doosberg wines are the more powerful, and often better than Lenchen in dry years. Most important owners: Eser, Hupfeld, Kühn, Querbach, Spreitzer, Wegeler.

Rauenthaler Baiken/Gehrn/Nonnenberg/ Rothenberg/Wulfen The Rieslings from the Rauenthaler Berg are among the most sought-after of all Rheingaus. The phyllite slate and excellent exposition high above the river result in extremely elegant, racy wines with pronounced "spice" and great ageing potential. The finest of all are those from the Baiken, the most vivacious those from the Rothenberg. Most important owners: Breuer (Nonnenberg monopoly), Eser, von Simmern, Staatsweingüter.

Rüdesheimer Berg-Rottland/ Roseneck/Schlossberg
The steep vineyards of the Rüdesheimer Berg climb dramatically from the bank of the Rhine where its course turns north again. Here the Riesling grape gives rich, supple wines, which nonetheless need long ageing to show their best. Most important owners: Breuer, Johannishof, Kesseler, Leitz, Ress, Schloss Schönborn, Staatsweingüter, Wegeler.

Schloss Johannisberg Monopoly site of the eponymous estate. One of the greatest vineyard sites on the entire course of the Rhine. Its wines may not be the richest, but at their best they possess a sublime elegance.

Schloss Vollrads Set well back from the Rhine, this monopoly of the eponymous estate has underperformed for many years. With a new team in place since 1999, there are welcome signs of improvement.

Steinberg Planted in the twelfth century by the monks of Eberbach, this legendary walled vineyard in Hattenheim is comparable to the Clos Vougeot of Burgundy. At their best, its wines are racy, intense, and refined. It is a monopoly of the Staatsweingüter.

Wallufer Walkenberg This little-known site gives powerful, firm wines that need many years of ageing to show their best. Most important owners: J.B. Becker, Toni Jost.

Winkeler Hasensprung/Jesuitengarten Directly next to the vineyards of Schloss Johannisberg, the Hasensprung gives similar but rather more succulent wines that develop more quickly. The Jesuitengarten wines from vines close to the riverbank are sleeker and more racy. Most important owners: Allendorf, August Eser, Hamm, Hupfeld, Johannishof, Wegeler.

Leading Rheingau Producers

Fritz Allendorf ☆
Winkel. www.allendorf.de
A substantial estate with 58 hectares in production, including a major holding in Winkeler Jesuitengarten. The wines are light and generally dry or medium-dry. They can be assertive and noticeably high in acidity.

Hans Barth ☆☆
Hattenheim. www.weingut-barth.de
This 12-hectare estate is best-known for its Sekt, including the excellent Ultra. The still, generally dry, Rieslings are more variable, but there are some excellent nobly sweet wines.

J.B. Becker ☆☆–☆☆☆
Walluf.
The Becker estate was founded in 1893, and since 1971 has been run by the flamboyant but thoughtful Hans-Josef and his sister Maria. Their vineyards include substantial holdings in the excellent Wallufer Walkenberg, from where he makes powerful, dry wines. Indeed, the Auslese Trocken is often too powerful for its own good. He also produces good Spätburgunder, which was first planted in the Walkenberg in 1903. One peculiarity here is Becker's penchant for BA with high alcohol and relatively low residual sugar. This is an acquired taste.

Georg Breuer ☆☆☆☆
Rüdesheim. www.georg-breuer.com
During the early 1990s, winemaker Hermann Schmoranz and director Bernhard Breuer made this one of the top Rheingau wine producers, and it remains at the top. A founding member of the Charta association of Rheingau estates, Bernhard Breuer was an outspoken promoter of a vineyard classification for the Rheingau.

At his own estate an internal classification was introduced long ago; only the best dry and dessert wines from the very top sites (Berg Schlossberg and the monopoly site Rauenthaler Nonnenberg) are sold with a vineyard designation. Excellent wines are also sold under the names of Rüdesheim and Rauenthal. The Sekt is serious and expensive, the Pinot Noir rather tough. While still in his fifties, Breuer died unexpectedly in 2004, but the estate remains in the reliable hands of his brother Heinrich and cellarmaster Schmoranz.

August Eser ☆–☆☆
Oestrich. www.eser-wein.de
At this 10-hectare estate, owned by the family since 1759, Joachim Eser makes a full range, from dry to sweet. He maintains a generally high standard in all styles, but the estate needs a top vintage to really shine.

Schloss Vollrads, Oestrich-Winkel

Joachim Flick ☆☆
Flörsheim-Wicke. www.flick-wein.de
Reiner Flick makes some of the best wines from the eastern end of the Rheingau, although he owns few vines in top sites other than Hochheimer Hölle. The emphasis is on rounded accessible Rieslings, mostly dry but there can be spectacular TBAs in suitable vintages such as 2003.

Prinz von Hessen ☆☆
Geisenheim. www.prinz-von-hessen.com
The princely Landgraf of Hessen bought this large estate in 1958. Director Markus Sieben improved quality convincingly in the 1990s, and his successor, Clemens Kiefer, is following the same path by focusing prinicpally on the best sites. Many of the wines are dry, and there is also, unusually, some Merlot.

Hupfeld ☆
Oestrich-Winkel. www.weingut-hupfeld.de
The Hupfeld family is best known as the owner of the well-known Königin Victoriaberg vineyard at Hochheim, where Queen Victoria stopped to watch the vintage in 1850. The original owners, the Pabstmann family, were not slow to commemorate the visit, getting the Queen's permission to rename the vineyard after her, erecting a Gothic monument and designing the most tinselly (now quite irresistible) label. It is not Hochheim's finest, but is full, soft, and flowery, and just what Queen Victoria might well have enjoyed. The family also owns vineyards in Oestrich-Winkel.

Schloss Johannisberg ☆☆–☆☆☆
Johannisberg. www.schloss-johannisberg.de
This marvellously situated property is surely the most famous estate of the Rhine, its name almost synonymous with the true Riesling vine. The first monastery was built on this hill-top commanding the Rhine in 1100; full flowering came in the eighteenth century under the Prince-Abbot of Fulda. Its vintage of 1775 was the first to be gathered overripe (the Abbot's messenger having arrived late with permission to pick); the term Spätlese and the appreciation of noble rot are said to have started with this incident, although such wines were already well-known in other parts of Europe.

The estate was secularized under Napoléon, and in 1816 it was presented by the Austrian Emperor to his Chancellor, Prince Metternich, for his diplomatic services. In 1942, the Johannisberg monastery-castle (but not its cellar) was destroyed in an air raid, and has since been totally rebuilt. The vineyard, in one block on the ideally sloping skirts of the castle hill, has been planted entirely with Riesling for 250 years. Technically it is an Ortsteil – a local entity which needs no Einzellage name.

At their best, the wines of Schloss Johannisberg are extraordinarily firm in structure, concentrated, and long-lived, with every quality of classic Riesling grown on an exceptional site. An 1862 TBA, tasted in 2001, was still remarkably fresh and persistent. However, in 1992 the estate was acquired by the huge Henkell & Söhnlein wine company, and the wines, except at the highest Prädikat levels, lost much of their flair. However, recent vintages have shown more concentration and style, especially in the sweet and nobly sweet categories.

Johannishof ☆☆–☆☆☆
Johannisberg. www.weingut-johannishof.de
Johannes Eser comes from an old growers' family and has made a reputation for racy and full-flavoured wines, including the finest Johannisberg Rieslings. The deep cellars, nine metres (30 feet) under the hill, are traditional: cold and damp with dark, oval casks for maturing wine of character. Augmented some years ago by six hectares in Rüdesheim, Johannishof has the raw materials to produce ever more impressive wines.

Jakob Jung ☆☆–☆☆☆
Erbach. www.weingut-jakob-jung.de
Ludwig Jung's generally dry Rieslings offer rare value for money in an expensive region. Best are the elegant Erstes Gewächs wines from the Erbacher Hohenrain and Steinmorgen.

Graf von Kanitz ☆☆–☆☆☆
Lorch. www.weingut-graf-von-kanitz.de
The noble von Kanitz family has only owned this property since 1926. The vineyards are planted on steep slopes at the northeastern extremity of the region. The wines are lively and assertive, with ample fruit, and age well. The Kapellenberg Erstes Gewächs has exceptional drive and purity in good vintages.

August Kesseler ☆☆☆
Assmannshausen. www.august-kesseler.de
A remarkable young estate, which is producing outstandingly successful, deep-coloured Assmannshausen Spätburgunder matured in barriques and sophisticated Rüdesheim Riesling, both Erstes Gewächs and with natural sweetness. Prices are high, but the wines have been taken up enthusiastically by top-quality restaurants and private customers.

Baron Knyphausen ☆☆
Erbach. www.knyphausen.de
This former monastic estate was bought in 1818 by the baron's forebears. The property is run on traditional lines, making full-flavoured wines, 70 per cent dry or medium-dry. The quality here is consistent, but some wines lack the grip and concentration of the very finest from the Rheingau.

Robert König ☆☆
Assmannshausen.
www.weingut-robert-koenig.de
A rarity in the Rheingau: an estate that is almost entirely dedicated to red wine, from Spätburgunder and Frühburgunder. These are cask-matured wines that are traditional in style, but possess plenty of character.

Krone ☆☆–☆☆☆
Assmannshausen. www.weingut-krone.de
This is the estate of probably the most famous hotel on the Rhine, the Krone. Since the arrival of young winemaker Peter Perabo in 1995, the Spätburgunders have begun to challenge those of neighbour August Kesseler (q.v.). There are numerous *cuvées*, best sampled at the hotel's restaurant, which carries 1,300 wines on its list.

Peter Jakob Kühn ☆☆☆–☆☆☆☆
Oestrich. www.weingutpjkuehn.de
Oestricher Lenchen and Doosberg may not be the Rheingau's most celebrated sites, but Peter Kühn makes marvellous wines, 80 per cent of them dry, from these vineyards, which have been farmed Biodynamically since 2005. Kühn is a tireless experimenter, adopting and adapting techniques he observes on his travels. Full fruit and harmonious acidity are the qualities to be found right through the range. The Lenchen TBAs can be sensational.

Franz Künstler ☆☆☆–☆☆☆☆☆
Hochheim. www.weingut-kuenstler.de
Gunter Künstler is one of the most talented young winemakers on the entire Rhine. His powerful, minerally, dry Rieslings catapulted him to fame during the late 1980s and continue to win blind tastings. However, his less well-known Auslese and higher Prädikat dessert wines also deserve the highest praise. In 1996, Künstler almost tripled his holdings by purchasing the renowned Aschrott estate in Hochheim, giving him access to more top sites. His Spätburgunder can be impressive, if priced too ambitiously.

Hans Lang ☆☆
Hattenheim. www.lang-wein.com
This versatile grower produces light but elegant Rieslings, and a range of other wines: a pretty Silvaner, and barrel-fermented Weisser Burgunder. There's Spätburgunder, too, but it can be rather extracted. The Rieslings are the best wines, with plenty of character and acidity.

Freiherr Langwerth von Simmern ☆☆–☆☆☆
Eltville. www.weingut-langwerth-von-simmern.de
This aristocratic estate, which dates from 1464, is based at the beautiful Renaissance Langwerther Hof in the ancient centre of Eltville – one of the loveliest spots in the Rheingau. The richly heraldic (if scarcely legible) red label used to be one of the most reliable in Germany for classic Riesling, but standards slipped badly in the 1990s. At the end of the 1990s, a family member returned to take charge, a new winemaker, Dirk Roth, was appointed, and quality is rising fast.

Josef Leitz ☆☆☆–☆☆☆☆
Rüdesheim. www.leitz-wein.de
When Johannes Leitz began making wine here in the mid-1980s, he followed the hi-tech model of the time. But he was unhappy with the results, and in the 1990s opted for low yields, natural yeasts, and ageing the wine on the fine lees after a slow fermentation. The improvement in quality was immediate. Leitz is now in the first rank of Rheingau growers, producing Rieslings of great individuality and elegance. Leitz is equally adept with dry and nobly sweet wines.

Fürst Löwenstein ☆☆
Hallgarten. www.loewenstein.de
This princely estate is divided between Franken and the Rheingau. If it is less well-known than it deserves, that may be because until 1997 it was leased to Graf Matuschka of Schloss Vollrads (q.v.). The dry wines, especially the Erstes Gewächs, are crisp and racy, if lacking some depth.

Prinz ☆☆
Hallgarten.
From six hectares, Fred Prinz, the former production manager for the Staatsweingüter makes impressive dry and naturally sweet Rieslings from Hallgarten vineyards.

Querbach ☆☆
Winkel. www.querbach.com
In 1998, the Querbachs launched their own rather bizarre system of classification. No.2 for *chaptalized* Kabinett, No.1 for Spätlese Trocken; there is also an Erstes Gewächs from Oestricher Doosberg. They have also bravely abandoned cork closures for their wines. Quality is good throughout the range, which also offers excellent value.

Schloss Reinhartshausen ☆☆☆
Erbach. www.schloss-reinhartshausen.de
For more than a century, and until 1988, this large 76-hectare estate was owned by the Prussian royal family. Today it is owned by a consortium. Despite the size of the property, quality across the board is reliable. Best of all are the powerful, aristocratic wines from Erbacher Marcobrun and the racy wines from Hattenheimer Wisselbrunnen. Their drawback is their high price. Sekt is an important specialty here and is among the best in the Rheingau. Quality improved decisely after the appointment of Walter Bibo as director in 2003, and the 2005 TBAs are of dazzling quality.

Balthasar Ress ☆☆
Hattenheim. www.ress-wine.com
Stefan Ress, now assisted by his son Christian, is a well-established merchant and grower, producing a wide range of wines from throughout the region. In 1978 he leased the four-hectare Schloss Reichartshausen, originally a Cistercian property but latterly rather neglected. This estate's wines are unashamedly modern in style, vinified in stainless steel and bottled early for maximum freshness. Quality is rather variable; most wines are best drunk young.

Schloss Schönborn ☆☆–☆☆☆☆
Hattenheim. www.schoenborn.de
Since 1349, this vast, privately owned estate in the Rheingau, 50 hectares of mostly excellent sites, has been in the hands of a family of great political and cultural influence. Critics are divided over the recent performance of Schönborn wines. Some have described them as the "Rubens of the Rheingau", while others have found them too heavy and clumsy. They come in vast variety, from the central Marcobrunn to Lorch at the extreme west of the region and Hochheim at the extreme east. The problem has been of inconsistency, and although that has yet to be fully rectified, the wines do seem to be steadily improving.

Josef Spreitzer ☆☆☆
Oestrich. www.weingut-spreitzer.de
Brothers Andreas and Bernd look after this 11-hectare family property with flair and competence. Good sweet wines come primarily from Lennchen, which, along with Hattenheimer Wisselbrunnen, is also the source of their elegant Erstes Gewächs wines. Balance is their hallmark.

Staatsweingüter Kloster Erbach ☆–☆☆☆
Eltville. www.staatsweingueterhessen.de

The State of Hessen's domain at Eltville is based on monastic vineyards ceded to the Duke of Nassau under Napoleon; then they passed to the Kingdom of Prussia, and eventually to the State of Hessen, whose capital is nearby Wiesbaden. For its ceremonial HQ, the domain has the magnificent and perfectly preserved Cistercian abbey of Kloster Eberbach (1135) in a wooded valley behind Hattenheim, and the most famous of its vineyards, the Steinberg, comparable to a walled Burgundian *clos*. Kloster Eberbach is also the scene of prestigious annual wine auctions. It was here that the word "cabinet" was first used (for the vintage of 1712) to designate reserve-quality wine – a meaning totally altered by modern laws.

The estates, 193 hectares in all, include properties in Assmannshausen and the Hessische Bergstrasse, which are discussed separately. Despite the weight of tradition, the wines are now made in a sparkling new winery at the Steinberg vineyard, which has a capacity of over two million litres of wine, stored mostly in steel tanks as well as wooden vats. From the mid-1970s, this great estate's performance underwent a steady decline, despite owning some of the best sites in the region. The director since 2000, Dieter Greiner, understands precisely what needs to be done to restore the domain to its former excellence. Whether the politicians who are his masters will allow him to get on with the job remains to be seen. There can still be dismaying inconsistency, with both mediocre and superb Erstes Gewächs and nobly sweet wines from the same vintage.

Schloss Vollrads ☆☆–☆☆☆
Oestrich-Winkel. www.schlossvollrads.com

Few men did more to promote the Rheingau and its wines than Graf Erwein Matuschka-Greiffenclau, who presided over this magnificent old estate in the hills above Winkel, the latest in a long line of aristocrats who have inhabited Winkel since at least 1100. Their vineyards have been accepted as an Ortsteil, a separate entity that uses no commune or Einzellage name. Schloss Vollrads specialized in dry wines with minimal residual sugar, and Graf Matuschka also leased the Weingut Fürst Löwenstein (q.v.) in Hallgarten.

But the wines were rarely as good as they should have been, and practices such as machine harvesting were tolerated at Vollrads. Graf Matuschka's dedication to official bodies such as the VDP may have allowed him to ignore the indifferent quality of his own wines. Growing financial difficulties throughout the 1990s culminated in his suicide in 1997. The estate passed into the hands of his bankers, but after some anxious years, when it was feared that Vollrads might be split up, the Nassauische Sparkasse decided to keep the property intact and hired the experienced Dr. Rowald Hepp, to manage the property. Since 1999, there has been a distinct improvement in quality, but the wines have yet to realize the full potential of the property.

J Wegeler ☆☆
Oestrich-Winkel. www.wegeler.com

In the 1990s, this substantial 48-hectare estate, once linked to the Koblenz merchant house of Deinhard, was cruising on its former reputation. The Wegeler vineyards are superb: Oestricher Lenchen, Winkeler Hasensprung, Geisenheimer Rothenberg, and the Rüdesheimer Berg. A new management team has been turning things around, and while the focus has been on drier styles of Riesling, vintages such as 2005 produced a superb set of nobly sweet wines as well.

Weingut Robert Weil ☆☆–☆☆☆☆
Kiedrich.
www.weingut-robert-weil.com

The historic Weil estate has been owned since 1988 by Japanese drinks giant Suntory, which made huge investments, including more than doubling the estate's vineyard area and building the most modern winemaking facility in the region. Important as these steps were, it is the work of director Wilhelm Weil that was decisive in pushing the estate back to the forefront of the region. Its late-harvested Riesling Auslese, BA, and TBA and Eiswein from the Kiedricher Gräfenberg are among the greatest wines of this style made in Germany.

The grapes are harvested with repeated selections and must weights far exceed the legal minima, leading some to suggest that the Weil wines, while splendid, are exaggerated. The constant demand for the wines, despite their high prices, suggests the consumer is happy with them as they are. While the dry wines are of good quality, they do not begin to scale these heights.

Domdechant Werner'sches Weingut ☆☆–☆☆☆
Hochheim. www.domdechantwerner.com

The Werner family bought this superbly sited manor, overlooking the junction of the Rhine and Main, from the Duke of York in 1780. The buyer's son, Dr. Franz Werner, was the famous Dean (Domdechant) of Mainz who saved the cathedral from destruction by the French.

The same family (now called Michel) still owns and runs the estate, making serious, full-flavoured Hochheimers from some of its best vineyards. Traditional barrel-ageing is employed for both dry and naturally sweet wines, which are both flavourful and long-lived.

Tasting from the cask

Nahe

The River Nahe is a minor tributary of the Rhine, flowing north to join it at Bingen with ideal sites for Riesling on its west bank. The best wines from its 4,120 hectares of vineyards are the equals in quality to anything in Germany. Yet the region is relatively unknown, either at home or abroad.

Since the Nahe's vineyards lie between those of the Mosel and the Rheingau, the conventional way of describing Nahe wines is as being transitional between Mosel and Rhine; some say specifically between Saar and Rheingau. This is true of the weight and balance, body and structure of the fine wines of the Middle Nahe; they do have the "nerve", the backbone, of the Saar, together with some of the meat of the weightiest and more densely flavoured Rheingau. The volcanic soil, however, adds something quite unique; to me the great Nahe wines often have a delicate hint of blackcurrant, with delicious and fascinating mineral undertones. In their delicacy yet completeness they make hypnotic sipping.

The greatest and most renowned vineyards of the Nahe lie in the rocky, winding stretch of the valley upstream from its capital town, the spa of Bad Kreuznach, particularly those of Niederhausen, Norheim, Traisen, and Schlossböckelheim. Their wines frequently achieve that miraculous balancing act between ripeness and freshness, of which only the Riesling grape is capable. Further upstream, where the valley is wider and more gently undulating, Monzingen has the best sites. Bad Kreuznach's wines come from heavier, more fertile soils, and are consequently more generous and juicy. In years with hot summers they can be bombastic; in less extreme years the epitome of charm and harmony. Downstream, towards the Nahe's confluence with the Rhine, the landscape again becomes punctuated with south-facing cliffs and steep slopes in side valleys. Here, from Lower Nahe villages such as Münster-Sarmsheim and Dorsheim, the wines have similar minerally character to those of the Middle Nahe, but are fuller and more imposing.

Outstanding Nahe Vineyards

Dorsheimer Burgberg/Goldloch/Pittermännchen The reddish slate soil of the Goldloch and Burgberg gives full Rieslings with apricot fruit and a firm structure, while the grey slate of the Pittermännchen yields sleek, racy wines that possess an extraordinary resemblance to fine Mosel Rieslings. Most important owner: Diel.

Kreuznacher Brückes/Kahlenberg/Krotenpfühl Bad Kreuznach's finest vineyards all enjoy sheltered positions on the outskirts of the town. The deep loam soils overlying reddish slate result in rich, fleshy wines. Most important owners: von Plettenberg, Staatsweingut Bad Kreuznach.

Langenlonsheimer Rothenberg/Löhrer Berg The loam and reddish slate soils here yield medium-bodied Rieslings, full of ripe fruit, that drink well from an early age. Most important owners: Schweinhardt, Wilhelm Sitzius, Tesch.

Laubenheimer Karthäuser/St Remigiusberg Just north of Langenlonsheim, these vineyards have mostly loam soils, on which Riesling attains high ripeness levels, making it an excellent site for dry wines. Most important owner: Tesch.

Monzinger Frühlingsplätzchen/Halenberg These steep sloping sites have contrasting soils. The Frühlingsplätzchen is reddish slate, giving more immediately appealing, supple wines, while the blue slate of the Halenberg gives very elegant, racy Rieslings. Most important owners: Emrich-Schönleber, Schäfer-Frohlich, Udo Weber.

Münsterer Dautenpflänzer/Kapellenberg/ Pittersberg The graceful sweep of these excellent vineyards can be viewed from the A61 *autobahn* as it crosses the Nahe. The slate over loess-loam subsoils on these sites gives intensely aromatic, racy Rieslings; those from the Dautenpflänzer have the most power, and the Pittersberg wines are the most elegant. Most important owners: Göttelmann, Kruger Rumpf.

Niederhäuser Hermannsberg/Oberhäuser Brücke These sites cover a single slope with southwesterly exposure and a stony porphyry-based soil. They are renowned for intense, minerally Rieslings. Most important owners: Dönnhoff (Brücke monopoly), Gutsverwaltung Niederhausen-Schlossböckelheim (Hermmansberg monopoly).

Niederhäuser Hermannshöhle Since the Prussian classification of the Nahe vineyards (published in map form in 1901) this has been regarded as the greatest vineyard on the Nahe. Perfect exposure and an extremely stony soil composed of a complex mix of all the local soil types results in Riesling wines with the highest elegance and aromatic complexity. Most important owners: Dönnhoff, Mathern, Jakob Schneider, Wilhelm Sitzius, Gutsverwaltung Niederhausen-Schlossböckelheim.

Niederhäuser Kertz/Klamm/Rosenheck Though these are not the greatest of Niederhausen's vineyards, they nonetheless give sophisticated, racy Rieslings with a strong minerally character from the porphyry soil. Most important owners: Mathern, Jakob Schneider.

Norheimer Dellchen/Kafels/Kirschheck Extremely steep, terraced vineyards, with stony, porphyry soil, these are the least well-known top sites of the Middle Nahe, yet they have the potential to challenge Niederhausen and Schlossböckelheim. Most important owners: Crusius, Dönnhoff, Mathern, Jakob Schneider, Staatsweingut Bad Kreuznach.

Roxheimer Berg/Birkenberg/Höllenpfad/ Hüttenberg/Mühlenberg To the northwest of Bad Kreuznach, the best sites of Roxheim lie outside the Nahe valley, but the combination of a southerly exposure and reddish slate soil gives ripe, aromatic wines of elegant acidity. Most important owner: Prinz zu Salm-Dalberg (Schloss Wallhausen).

Schlossböckelheimer Felsenberg/Kupfergrube The two great Schlossböckelheim sites stand side by side, but yield contrasting wines. The Felsenberg has been cultivated for centuries; its very stony, melaphry soil yields richly aromatic Rieslings with a silky acidity. The Kupfergrube was created out of a former copper mine in 1902, and yields sleeker, intensely racy wines which have remarkable ageing potential. Most important owners: Crusius, Dönnhoff, Gutsverwaltung Niederhausen-Schlossböckelheim.

Schlossböckelheimer In den Felsen/Königsfels The wines seldom match those of Schlossböckelheim's greatest sites, but they, too, give racy Rieslings with an extremely pronounced minerally character. Most important owners: Hexamer, Korrell.

Traiser Bastei/Rotenfels The famous Bastei vineyard lies between the bank of the Nahe and the 180-metre- (600-foot-) high mass of the Rotenfels cliffs. Extremely stony porphyry soil yields powerful, pungently minerally wines. The neighbouring Rotenfels site gives similar, but less extreme wines. Most important owners: Crusius, Gutsverwaltung Niederhausen-Schlossböckelheim.

Wallhäuser Felseneck/ Johannisberg/Pastorenberg Commanding a sheltered position high up the Gräfenbach valley these steep vineyards with their slate-rich soils give remarkably Mosel-like Rieslings. Most important owner: Schloss Wallhausen.

Leading Nahe Producers

Hans Crusius ☆☆–☆☆☆
Traisen. www.weingut-crusius.de
Hans Crusius did wonders for the profile of the Nahe wines, and his seventeenth-hectare estate is now run by his son Dr. Peter Crusius. The Rieslings are very clean and quite beautifully crafted, and those from the Traiser Bastei and Rotenfels have force and personality.

Schlossgut Diel ☆☆☆
Burg Layen. www.schlossgut-diel.com
Wine-grower, wine journalist, restaurant critic, and television presenter, the multi-talented Armin Diel is one of the outstanding personalities on the German wine scene today. His substantial holdings in all three of Dorsheim's top vineyards make this the leading estate of the Lower Nahe.

Dry and late-harvested Rieslings with natural sweetness form the bulk of the production, although the new-oak-aged Weisser Burgunder, Grauer Burgunder, and Victor (a powerful blend of the two) also enjoy a high reputation, as does the Sekt. Tastings, often blind, of every vintage since 2004 confirm that the Diel wines are now better than ever. Diel's daughter Caroline is now taking a greater role in running the estate.

Hermann Dönnhoff ☆☆☆☆
Oberhausen. www.doennhoff.com
Helmut Dönnhoff's Rieslings are the most perfect expressions of the great vineyards of the Middle Nahe. Behind his reserved manner lies a fanatical commitment to quality, and a remarkable natural talent for winemaking. Virtually every barrel from this cellar (and wood is an article of faith for Dönnhoff) is bottled separately, resulting in a confusingly wide range. However, such is the consistency and quality that this

hardly matters. The most powerful wines are those from the Oberhäuser Brücke, while those from the Hermannshöhle represent the ultimate in elegance and complexity. Dönnhoff's Eiswein is regularly among Germany's best.

Emrich-Schönleber ☆☆☆
Monzingen. www.emrich-schoenleber.com
Since the late 1980s, the Schönlebers' estate leapt into the top ranks of Nahe producers. Its Rieslings, in both the dry and naturally sweet styles, are very pure and expressive, with vibrant fruit and racy acidity. The wines from the Halenberg are the more refined, those from the Frühlingsplätzchen more generous. Schönleber's Eiswein often rivals those from Dönnhoff for splendour and intensity.

Göttelmann ☆–☆☆
Münster-Sarmsheim.
Götz Blessing married into the Göttelmann family, and since 1984 has run the estate and made the wines. The dry Riesling and Grauer Burgunder are often better than the naturally sweet wines, which can show some flabbiness. Quality is variable, but the best wines are very good indeed.

Hahnmühle ☆
Mannweiler-Cölln. www.weingut-hahnmuehle.de
Peter Linxweiler is best-known for sleek, steely, dry Rieslings from the rocky vineyards of the Alsenz Valley. Only half the domaine is planted with Riesling, so Linxweiler can also offer wines from Silvaner, Traminer, and Chardonnay.

Korrell ☆☆
Bad Kreuznach. www.korrell.com
Martin Korrell has transformed this once obscure property into the best estate in Bad Kreuznach. Only half the vines are Riesling, so the range includes dry Gelber Muskateller, Weissburgunder, and Chardonnay. But the Rieslings, from Schlossböckelheim as well as Kreuznach, are very good, both dry and sweet.

Weingut Kruger-Rumpf ☆☆–☆☆☆
Münster-Sarmsheim. www.kruger-rumpf.com
This estate, with many of the best sites in Münster-Sarmsheim among its 19 hectares, is deservedly admired for its firm, dry wines of great style from Riesling, Silvaner, Weisser Burgunder, and Spätburgunder. In 2001, Stefan Rumpf crossed the border into Rheinhessen and purchased vines in the Binger Scharlachberg. All the wines can be tasted in the estate's excellent wine restaurant, which offers some of the best regional cooking in the Nahe.

Mathern ☆
Niederhausen. www.mathernweine.de
The estate is endowed with a fine selection of steep sites in Niederhausen and Norheim, and until his untimely death in 2002 Helmuth Mathern had been making the most of them. Recent vintages have shown less concentration and flair.

Gutsverwaltung Niederhausen-Schlossböckelheim ☆☆
Niederhausen. www.riesling-domaene.de
The former Nahe State Domain, once considered the finest in Germany, was founded in 1902 by Kaiser Wilhelm II. Its

foundation pioneered viticulture on the steep slopes above the now-famous site of a former copper mine (the Kupfergrube) to grow Riesling. By 1920, its wines were acknowledged to be superlative and remained so into the 1980s.

After a period of rather erratic performance in the early 1990s, the whole property was bought by the agricultural products manufacturer Erich Maurer. Despite his good intentions, the wines have yet to attain the greatness of the past, and the dry wines in particular can be too austere. At their best, the Schlossböckelheimers are the most stylish and delicate; the Niederhäusers are fuller and more seductive; the Traisers big, ripe, and long-lived. The wines from 2005 onwards show more finesse.

Prinz zu Salm-Dalberg'sches Weingut Schloss Wallhausen ☆
Wallhausen. www.salm-salm.de
The organic estate belonging to Michael Prinz zu Salm-Salm, the former president of the wine estate association known as the VDP, lies in a little-known and unspoiled corner of the Nahe region.

The most serious wines are single-vineyard bottlings from the estate. The dry Rieslings have an austere finesse, while the sweeter styles can sometimes lack concentration.

J B Schäfer ☆☆
Burg Layen. www.jbs-wein.de
Young Sebastian Schäfer has invested considerably in the estate he has been running since 1997, and we are now seeing the results. He is aided by vines in some of the best sites in Dorsheim, Goldloch, and Pittermännchen, from which he produces good dry wines and some exceptional sweet ones.

Schäfer-Fröhlich ☆☆☆
Bockenau. www.weingut-schaefer-froehlich.de
Tim Fröhlich took over running the family estate in 1995, and its ascent into the top ranks of Nahe wines has been swift. The nobly sweet wines, especially the array of TBAs crafted by Fröhlich, are simply dazzling, but he seems equally at home with dry Grosses Gewächs from sites including the great Kupfergrube.

Willi Schweinhardt ☆☆
Langenlonsheim. www.schweinhardt.de
This long-established family of growers produces medium-sweet Rieslings and Scheurebes as well as full-bodied dry Chardonnay, Weisser Burgunder, and Grauer Burgunders. The grapey, light, and charming wines are best drunk quite young. This is a reliable and sensibly priced source of Riesling Auslese.

Sitzius ☆–☆☆
Langenlonsheim. www.sitzius.de
Only just over half of the vineyards here are planted with Riesling. The basic wines lack excitement, but the top dry

wines can be good, especially the ones from Niederhäuser Hermannshöhle. The Spätburgunder, aged in German oak, can be very appealing.

Tesch ☆☆–☆☆☆
Langenlonsheim. www.weingut-tesch.de
Founded in 1723, this used to be a highly regarded estate, and the new generation, in the form of Dr. Martin Tesch, has successfully restored its reputation. The best wines here are the dry Rieslings from Langenlonsheim and Laubenheim, sites that give good ripeness levels. The wines are generous, fruity, and quite broad-structured, but that also means they are approachable young. Tesch's best sweet wines come from Laubenheimer St Remigiusberg.

Rheinhessen

Anonymity behind the *nom de verre* of Liebfraumilch and other washed-out blends is the fate of most Rheinhessen wine. In volume terms, production is dominated by bland, gently flowery Müller-Thurgau; blunt, rustic Silvaner; and superficial, spicy wines from new varieties.

Only ten per cent of the 26,230-hectare vineyard is Riesling, concentrated in a few outstanding sites. The most important of these lie around Nackenheim, Nierstein, and Oppenheim, just south of Mainz; the rather unfortunately named "Rhine Front". The steep vineyards here give some of Germany's richest Rieslings, wines with the body and spice to take on the best of Alsace and Austria. In Bingen, at the region's northwestern extremity, vineyards with a similar quality potential – not always realized – yield more restrained and classical Rieslings.

Among the sea of vines covering the hill country that forms the bulk of Rheinhessen, are vineyards that can yield good dry Riesling, Weisser Burgunder, Grauer Burgunder, and traditional dry Silvaner. There can be some pleasant surprises from Gewürztraminer, Scheurebe, and Auxerrois, though less consistently. Efforts to give the best wines of the Rheinhessen more profile was accelerated by the introduction of the Grosses Gewächs vineyard classification. However, the success of a handful of dedicated producers on the Rhine Front and in the "Hinterland" is doing just as much to change the region's image.

There is a long way to go. Even growers anxious to improve their wines and move upmarket, find they are hampered by the low prices Rheinhessen wines usually fetch, which means that they cannot afford the necessary investment to improve their viticultural and winemaking standards. Fortunately, the success of growers such as Keller and Wittmann show what can be achieved – and that includes higher prices – so, with luck, steady improvement seems inevitable.

Using a refractometer to measure sugar levels of ripening grapes

Outstanding Rheinhessen Vineyards

Binger Scharlachberg Elegant, refined Rieslings from the Taunus quarzite soil of this terraced, south-facing 27-hectare site. The historic heart of the vineyard was grubbed up in the 1980s and has not been replanted. Most important owners: Kruger-Rumpf (Nahe), Riffel, Villa Sachsen.

Dalsheimer Bürgel A 30-hectare site with some limestone soil, and planted with a good deal of Spätburgunder. Keller owns two hectares here.

Dalsheimer Hubacker Clay with some limestone. The best parcel gives Keller excellent Rieslings.

Nackenheimer Rothenberg The northern tip of the "Roter Hang", and a precipitously steep site with stony, reddish slate soil, and excellent exposure. It gives some of the most seductively aromatic and longest-living Rieslings on the entire Rhine. Virtually a monopoly of the Gunderloch estate, although Kühling-Gillot and Heyl zu Herrnsheim both produce a Grosses Gewächs from here.

Niersteiner Brudersberg Tiny monopoly site of Heyl zu Herrnsheim. Steep slopes, reddish, slate soil, and perfect southerly exposition make for rich and elegance Rieslings.

Niersteiner Heiligenbaum Only a small part of this site is highly regarded, due to the unremarkable loamy soil that dominates here. Most important owners: Schätzel, Seebrich.

Niersteiner Hipping Arguments rage about the merits of this site. However, all are agreed that the ripe pineapple aroma typical of its wines makes them extremely attractive from an early age. Most important owners: Braun, Gehring, Gunderloch, Schneider, Seebrich, Strub.

Niersteiner Oelberg With the deepest soil of all Nierstein's top sites, the Oelberg gives powerful wines that need a long time to reveal their depths, but are also very long-lived. Most important owners: Heinrich Braun, Gehring, Guntrum, Heyl zu Herrnsheim, Kühling-Gillot, Schneider, Seebrich, Strub.

Niersteiner Orbel This steeply sloping, stony vineyard, west of Nierstein, yields wines that combine mineral intensity with racy acidity. Most important owners: Schneider, Strub.

Niersteiner Pettenthal Although enjoying identical exposition to the Nackenheimer Rothenberg, the Pettenthal's shallow soil results in quicker developing Rieslings with a pronounced minerally character. Most important owners: Braun, Gehring, Gunderloch, Heyl zu Herrnsheim, Kühling-Gillot, Schätzel.

Oppenheimer Herrenberg/Kreuz/Sackträger The heavy marl soil of these sites gives completely different wines from Nierstein's top sites. Here, even the Riesling gives weighty, corpulent wines with a firm underlying acidity. They can be heavy and charmless if not vinified expertly. Most important owners: Braun, Guntrum, Kissinger, Kühling-Gillot, Manz.

Westhofener Morstein Clay-loam above a limestone subsoil. Well-exposed, this gives fairly minerally wines. Most important owners: Groebe, Wittmann.

Leading Rheinhessen Producers

Brüder Dr. Becker ☆☆
Ludwigshöhe. www.brueder-dr-becker.de
This organic estate, run by Lotte Pfeffer-Müller, rightly enjoys a good reputation for traditional style, cask-matured, dry Riesling and Silvaner, and vibrantly fruity, modern-style Scheurebe with natural sweetness. Some of the bottlings come from the calcareous loam of the Dienheimer Tafelstein site.

Groebe ☆☆
Biebesheim. www.weingut-k-f-groebe.de
Quality can be inconsistent here, but Friedrich Groebe's seven hectares include parcels in some of Westhofen's top vineyards, and his Grosses Gewächs wines in particular can be very good, with marked minerality.

Gunderloch ☆☆☆☆
Nackenheim. www.gunderloch.de
Since the late-1980s, Fritz Hasselbach's concentrated, explosively aromatic Rieslings from the great Nackenheimer Rothenberg vineyard have shot him to international fame. His late-harvested Auslese and higher Prädikat wines are also exceptional. The almost dry "Jean Baptiste" Riesling Kabinett is a model example of this classic German wine style.

In the dry style, his basic Gunderloch Riesling also sets a high standard. Both are excellent food wines. With the acquisition of the Balbach estate in 1996, the company doubled in size. Simpler wines aimed at a more youthful market are packaged in brightly coloured labels under the Balbach name, while the Gunderloch label remains devoted to classic styles.

Louis Guntrum ☆
Nierstein. www.guntrum.de
This family business was started in 1648, and is now directed by the eleventh generation. The estate wines can be ripe and lively with a wide range of flavours, each variety and site being bottled individually. A comprehensive tasting of the 2007 vintage revealed wines with greater clarity and fruit than in the past. Overall they offer reliability rather than excitement.

Gutzler ☆☆
Gundheim. www.gutzler.de
Gutzler's 13 hectares are dispersed among various villages of southern Rheinhessen, so most of the wines do not carry a vineyard designation. Most of the white wines, from a wide range of varieties, are dry, and the best of them is usually the Riesling Grosses Gewächs from the Liebfrauenstift. The reds are quite extracted and sometimes over-oaked, but the Spätburgunder from Westhofener Morstein shows promise.

Freiherr Heyl zu Herrnsheim ☆☆–☆☆☆
Nierstein. www.heyl-zu-herrnsheim.de
A few changes in ownership and management since the mid-1990s have done few favours to this estate, which under previous proprietor Peter von Weymarn was a pioneer of dry Rieslings in the region. Present owner Detlev Meyer has simplified the range, introducing a Rotschiefer (red slate) range for Silvaner, Weisser Burgunder, and Riesling; and imposing single-vineyard wines from the monopoly site Brudersberg and from Pettenthal and Rothenberg. Although

most of the wines are dry, there are also some rare and costly BAs and TBAs. Recent vintages have produced some powerful yet lacklustre Grosses Gewächs Rieslings.

Keller ☆☆☆☆
Flörsheim-Dalsheim. www.keller-wein.de
This 12-hectare estate has set new quality standards in the southern hill country of Rheinhessen. Its Rieslings and Rieslaners are remarkable wines, considering that Flörsheim-Dalsheim possesses no celebrated vineyards. But Klaus Keller and his son, Klaus-Peter, have identified the best parcels in vineyards such as Bürgel and Hubacker, with wonderful results. Yields are incredibly low, allowing the Kellers to make dry wines of full ripeness and intensity. Clarity, effusive fruit, and racy acidity are the hallmarks of the Keller wines, whether dry, with a touch of natural sweetness, or full-blown Rieslaner dessert wines. Keller's Spätburgunder, made in tiny quantities, is as fine as any in Germany.

Klaus Knobloch ☆☆
Ober-Flörsheim. www.weingut-klausknobloch.de
This 30-hectare estate has been organically farmed since 1988. Knobloch produces an interesting range of red wines from varieties such as St-Laurent and Lemberger, as well as Spätburgunder. Among the white wines, the best is often the rich Weisser Burgunder.

Kühling-Gillot ☆–☆☆
Bodenheim. www.kuehling-gillot.com
Roland Gillot is best-known for his powerful, opulent dessert wines, which can be among Rheinhessen's best. His dry Rieslings are less remarkable, often tending to be too plump, as the vineyards in Bodenheim and Oppenheim have heavy soils.

Michel-Pfannebecker ☆☆
Flomborn. www.michel-pfannebecker.de
The Pfannebecker brothers have eliminated inferior grape crossings from their 12-hectare estate, and now focus on Riesling, Silvaner, and Spätburgunder (plus a splash of Merlot). The Rieslings, mostly dry, have elegance and length, but the Silvaners have more personality. The Grauer Burgunder and Chardonnay can be zesty and complex.

Rappenhof ☆
Alsheim. www.weingut-rappenhof.de
With 50 hectares of vineyards, this very old family estate is one of the region's largest. Although Klaus Muth has invested great energy in experiments with Chardonnay, *nouveau*-style red wines and barrique-ageing, the quality is frequently unremarkable.

Raumland ☆☆
Flörsheim-Dalsheim. www.raumland.de
Although this ten-hectare organic property produces a little red and white dry wine, the main emphasis is on classical method Sekt, both from Riesling and from Chardonnay. They are widely rated as among Germany's finest sparkling wines.

St Antony ☆☆☆
Nierstein. www.st-antony.com
This important Nierstein estate was bought in 2005 by Detlev Meyer, the owner of Heyl zu Herrnsheim (q.v.),

and in 2008 he decided to merge the two properties, so the St Anthony label will disappear.

Schales ☆–☆☆
Flörsheim-Dalsheim. www.schales.de
This long-established family property makes a wide range of wines from the limestone soil of Dalsheim, though few of the wines are vineyard designated. The powerful, dry Grauer Burgunders and Weisser Burgunders can be impressive, though most of the wines, red as well as white, are made in a crowd-pleasing style, but are none the worse for that. The sumptuous, rather heavy, sweet wines are usually made from varieties such as Huxelrebe and Siegerrebe, although there is no shortage of Rieslings.

Georg Albrecht Schneider ☆☆
Nierstein. www.schneider-nierstein.de
By his own admission, no self-publicist or salesman, Albrecht Schneider makes elegant, finely crafted Rieslings from the top sites of Nierstein. Conscientious attention to detail in both the vineyard and cellar is the secret of the high standards set by this little known estate. In contrast, the red wines from Dornfelder and St-Laurent are of little interest.

J & H A Strub ☆
Nierstein. www.strub-nierstein.de
This is an old family estate, which has a good name for producing gentle, mellow wines from some of Nierstein's top sites. They are enjoyable, but not especially memorable.

Villa Sachsen
Bingen. www.villa-sachsen.com
After a period of instability in the late 1980s and early '90s, this renowned estate was purchased by a consortium led by Michael Prinz zu Salm-Salm of Wallhausen in the Nahe. Most of the wines are dry; Grosses Gewächs from the Binger Scharlachberg is the best of them. The sweet wines tend to be too broad.

Wagner-Stempel ☆☆☆
Siefersheim. www.wagner-stempel.de
Siefersheim is not a celebrated village, but since the early 2000s Daniel Wagner has produced some thrilling Rieslings from top sites such as the Höllberg and Heerkretz. Simpler dry wines from a wide range of varieties, red as well as white, are bottled without vineyard designation. Even in the very difficult 2006 vintage, the Grosses Gewächs Rieslings are first-rate, as are the nobly sweet wines.

Wittmann ☆☆☆–☆☆☆☆
Westhofen. www.wittmannweingut.com
Together with Weingut Keller, Wittmann is the leading estate of inland Rheinhessen. There were some disappointments in 2004, but both 2005 and 2006 yielded superb Grosses Gewächs from the three top sites: Morstein, Aulerde, and Kirchspiel. Philip Wittmann, who has been running the property since 1998 and converted it to Biodynamism in 2003, is responsible for the wines' consistency, but a recent tasting of a magnificent 1993 Morstein Spätlese Trocken demonstrated that high quality is nothing new at this fine, forward-looking estate. The Rieslings are the stars, but dry Silvaner and Weissburgunder are usually exceptional, too.

Pfalz

No wine-growing region in Germany enjoys a more generous climate than the Pfalz. Nowhere in Germany is it warmer and drier than in the band of vineyards that runs for 80 kilometres (50 miles) along the eastern flank of the Haardt mountains, from the southern border of Rheinhessen to the French frontier, where the Haardt become the Vosges.

The combination of climatic advantage and generally light, sandy soils results in many of Germany's best dry wines, and some remarkable dessert wines, too. In spite of the proximity to Alsace they have a completely different style to the wines from that area. Here the emphasis is firmly on fresh aromas and crisp acidity, rather than the savoury vinosity of Alsace – not that savoury vinosity is out of reach. With almost 23,360 hectares of vineyards, the Pfalz is second only to Rheinhessen in size, though it often produces slightly more wine due to the intensive, highly mechanized viticulture practised in the flat vineyards down on the Rhine plain. Here it is possible to produce bulk wines more efficiently than anywhere else in Germany. However, it is with wines at the opposite end of the quality scale that the Pfalz has been attracting all the attention of late.

Traditionally, quality-wine production was associated with the Mittelhaardt area of the Pfalz, centred around the town of Bad Dürkheim. Here "the three Bs" – the great estates of Dr. von Bassermann-Jordan, Reichsrat von Buhl, and Dr. Bürklin-Wolf – and a clutch of smaller estates, established the region's reputation for noble Rieslings during the nineteenth and early twentieth centuries. At this time, the rest of the region, notably the southerly Südliche Weinstrasse, was seen as fit for producing nothing more than quaffing wines.

The new generation has broken this mould, proving that the north and the south of the region can produce impressive white wines. Many of the best examples are from varieties that are relatively recent introductions: the Riesling crossings, Rieslaner and Scheurebe; the white Pinots (Weisser Burgunder and Grauer Burgunder); and the red Spätburgunder, St-Laurent, and Dornfelder. Thankfully, the leading producers of the Mittelhaardt have responded to this challenge by redoubling their efforts, and quality competition is now intense.

The enterprise of the best young growers of the Südliche Weinstrasse made the owners of the great estates of the Mittelhaardt realize that their wines were not as good as they ought to have been. In the mid-1990s, this all began to change, as complacency gave way to energy, and a clear commitment to quality. The VDP's vineyard classification was embraced fervently by almost all the top estates, and the Grosses Gewächs Rieslings and Pinot Noirs, and not just from the Mittelhaardt, are now among the greatest wines of Germany. Indeed, nowhere else in Germany can powerful, dry Rieslings be produced with such consistency.

The Pfalz may lack the dramatic scenery of the Mosel, Rheingau, or Mittelrhein, but its gently undulating, verdant country makes it one of the most charming of all Germany's wine-growing regions. The Pfälzer are renowned for their love of food and wine. This finds its fullest expression at Bad Dürkheim's famous Wurstmarkt ("sausage fair"), in September, where leading winemakers rub shoulders with local farmers while enjoying a *schoppen* (half-litre glass) of wine.

Outstanding Pfalz Vineyards

Birkweiler Kastanienbusch The only Pfalz site with stony, reddish soil that retains warmth and gives subtly aromatic Rieslings, with a silky acidity. Most important owners: Gies-Düppel, Kleinmann, Rebholz, Siener, Wehrheim.

Burrweiler Schäwer The Schäwer is the only vineyard in the region with a slate soil like that of the Mosel. This results in exceptionally refined, peachy Rieslings that are atypical for the region. Most important owners: Messmer, Sauer.

Deidesheimer Grainhübel/Hohenmorgen/ Kalkofen/Kieselberg/Langenmorgen/Leinhöhle/ Maushöhle This cluster of small sites guarantees Deidesheim's excellent reputation as a producer of rich, succulent Rieslings. Traditionally, the Grainhübel is regarded as being the greatest of them. Like the Kalkofen, it has a limestone subsoil. The wines from these vineyards are slow to develop but long-lived. With its very light, sandy soil, the Leinhöhle is particularly sensitive to drought in hot years. Most important owners: Bassermann-Jordan, Josef Biffar, von Buhl, Bürklin-Wolf, Deinhard, Mosbacher, Georg Siben, J L Wolf.

Dürkheimer Michelsberg/Spielberg/Ungsteiner Herrenberg These three fine vineyards occupy the southern, western, and eastern side of a hill immediately to the north of Bad Dürkheim. The stony, limestone soil and excellent exposition result in intense, beautifully balanced Rieslings particularly well-suited to vinification in the dry style. Most important owners: Darting, Pfeffingen, Fitz-Ritter, Karl Schaefer, Egon Schmitt.

Duttweiler Kalkberg Southeast of Neustadt, this light sand and loam site can give excellent Riesling and Pinot Noir. Most important owner: Bergdolt.

Forster Freundstück/Jesuitengarten/Kirchenstück/ Pechstein/Ungeheuer The great vineyards of Forst occupy one of the most sheltered positions in the region. This, together with a light, quickly warmed topsoil and deep, water-retentive subsoil, results in remarkable Rieslings. Those from the Pechstein (so named because of the abundance of basalt in its top soil) are the raciest; those from the Ungeheuer are rich and fleshy; while the Jesuitengarten and Kirchenstück give wines with the greatest elegance.

They have been recognized as the noblest sites of the Pfalz since at least the first half of the nineteenth century. Most important owners: Acham-Magin, Bassermann-Jordan, von Buhl, Bürklin-Wolf, Lucashof, Mosbacher, Eugen Müller, Karl Schaefer, Spindler, Deinhard, J L Wolf.

Gimmeldinger Mandelgarten Just north of Neustadt, this vineyard is of weathered sandstone. Most important owners: Christmann, Müller-Catoir.

Haardter Bürgergarten/Herrenletten/Herzog The best sites of Haardt, close to Neustadt, have unusually deep and heavy soils for the Pfalz, which yield powerful wines with a firm, acidic structure and long ageing potential. At high levels of ripeness they can possess a ravishing apricot and pineapple bouquet. Most important owners: Müller-Catoir, Weegmüller.

Kallstadter Annaberg/Saumagen The limestone soil of the Saumagen and the southern exposition in the best part of this site make for extremely powerful, highly structured wines, which need years of ageing for the characteristic passion-fruit aroma to develop fully.

The Saumagen lies in a kind of amphitheatre and is an extremely warm site. The Annaberg wines are less expansive, but in hot years they can possess a marvellous elegance, and their gunflint aroma is most distinctive. Most important owners: Henninger IV, Koehler-Ruprecht.

Königsbacher Idig Medium-bodied wines with a family resemblance to those of Ruppertsberg, but a slightly firmer structure. Most important owner: Christmann.

Mussbacher Eselshaut The very light, sandy soil here gives full-bodied wines with extravagant aromas, including exotic fruit notes. Most important owner: Müller-Catoir.

Ruppertsberger Gaisböhl/Nussbien/Reiterpfad The large area of good vineyards on the western side of Ruppertsberg generally yields Rieslings with pronounced floral aromas, which are charming from a very early age.

Those from the Reiterpfad and Nussbien tend to be deeper and more complex. Most important owners: Acham-Magin, Bassermann-Jordan, Bergdolt, Biffar, von Buhl, Bürklin-Wolf, Christmann, Deinhard.

Siebeldinger im Sonnenschein The name says it all: a stony, sandy site bathed in sunshine. A top vineyard for Rebholz and Wilhelmshof.

Ungsteiner Weilberg This well-exposed site gives extremely typical, juicy, aromatic Pfalz Rieslings, which show well from their early youth, but will also age well. Most important owner: Pfeffingen.

Wachenheimer Belz/Goldbächel/Gerümpel/ Rechbächel The top vineyards of Wachenheim yields Rieslings that combine the racy elegance of the Rheingau with the richness of the Pfalz. The Wachenheimer dry wines are every bit as impressive as the famous dessert wines. Most important owners: Biffar, Bürklin-Wolf (including the Rechbächel monopoly), J L Wolf, Zimmermann.

Leading Pfalz Producers

Acham-Magin ☆
Forst. www.acham-magin.de
This small estate has always specialized in dry wines, and so has come into its own now that such wines have become fashionable. With a palette of top vineyards in Forst, Deidesheim, and Ruppertsberg, there is potential for further improvement.

Dr. von Bassermann-Jordan ☆☆☆
Deidesheim. www.bassermann-jordan.de
Following the death of Dr. Ludwig von Basserman-Jordan in 1995, this famous and historic estate has passed to his daughter and widow. Since the early eighteenth century, when founder Andreas Jordan made the first vineyard-designated wines and the first Auslese in the region, this estate has been one of the most consistent producers of fine Pfalz Rieslings from superb vineyards in Deidesheim, Forst, and Ruppertsberg.

After an uneven period during the last years of Dr. von Basserman-Jordan's life, the appointment of talented winemaker Ulrich Mell, who made his name at Biffar (q.v.), has effected a dramatic return to top form. He put an end to practices such as centrifuging the must and machine-harvesting, and severely reduced the yields, which had been far too high. The stars of the range tend to be the dry Rieslings from the top vineyards, and the exceedingly concentrated nobly sweet wines.

Apart from the wine, the estate is worth a visit for the magnificent collection of Roman artefacts displayed in its cavernous cellars (by appointment only), among the wooden casks where the estate's wines continue to be made.

Friedrich Becker ☆☆–☆☆☆
Schweigen. www.weingut-friedrich-becker.de
Becker is best-known for the high standard of his red wines, principally Spätburgunder. There are three quality levels, the top one being immensely – indeed, excessively – expensive. The whites are more variable, but the dry Chardonnay, Weisser Burgunder, Grauer Burgunder, and Gewürztraminer often have the same combination of heady richness and ripe fruit as the red wines.

Bergdolt ☆☆–☆☆☆
Duttweiler. www.weingut-bergdolt.de
The loess-loam soils of Rainer Bergdolt's vineyards may set a limit to what he can achieve with the Riesling grape, which can be a touch neutral here, but his dry Weisser Burgunders are among the finest wines made from this underrated grape in all of Germany. The dry Spätlesen are always beautifully balanced, but the Auslese Trocken can be disagreeably alcoholic. In recent years, Bergdolt's Spätburgunders have made a big jump forward. They are made in a robust style, but have gained greatly in finesse since the late 1990s.

Bernhart ☆☆
Schweigen. www.weingut-bernhart.de
Together with Becker (q.v.), this, in Pfalz's deep south, is Schweigen's leading estate. The Spätburgunder Grosses Gewächs is understated but charming, while the Grosses Gewächs from Weissburgunder and Rieslings are more opulent.

Josef Biffar ☆☆–☆☆☆
Deidesheim. www.biffar.com
This 12-hectare estate and the family's candied-fruits company are jointly directed by Gerhard Biffar and his daughter Lilli. With a string of concentrated, beautifully polished, dry, and naturally sweet Rieslings from the top vineyard sites of Deidesheim, Wachenheim, and Ruppertsberg, Biffar was

catapulted into the first rank of Pfalz producers at the beginning of the 1990s, after Ulrich Mell was hired as cellarmaster. There were a number of changes of winemaker in the late 1990s and early 2000s, which slightly unsettled quality, but the estate seems back on course.

Reichsrat von Buhl ☆☆☆☆
Deidesheim. www.reichsrat-von-buhl.de
In the 1980s, this famous estate went through a bad patch; the grapes were harvested early to avoid risk, and yields were high. In the late 1980s, the owner, Freiherr von und zu Gutenberg, who had little interest in wine, leased the property to a group of Japanese investors. By the early 1990s, it was clear that von Buhl was still underperforming, given its portfolio of magnificent vineyards, and, in 1994, a new winemaker was taken on. Frank John had previously worked at Müller-Catoir (q.v.), and followed their non-interventionist style. He also severely reduced yields.

There were further changes in personnel after Achim Niederberger bought the property in 2005, but quality seems undiminished. Riesling continues to dominate the vineyard plantings, but Grauer Burgunder, Spätburgunder, and Scheurebe are also present. The best wines are the dry Grosses Gewächs from Forster Kirchenstuck and Pechstein. In suitable years, spectacular sweet wines, from Rieslaner as well as Riesling, are also produced, notably from the Ungeheuer.

Dr. Bürklin-Wolf ☆☆☆
Wachenheim. www.buerklin-wolf.de
With 86 hectares of vineyards, this famous estate is one of the largest in Germany in private ownership. After taking over direction of Bürklin-Wolf in 1992, Christian von Guradze, who was then married to proprietor Bettina Bürklin, instituted a programme of radical changes which rapidly restored the estate to the first rank of Pfalz wine producers. He also converted the estate to Biodynamic viticulture in 2005.

Today, only the wines from outstanding sites are sold with vineyard designations, and subtle labelling (and price) differentiates those sites considered *grand cru* from those considered *premier cru*. Although Bürklin-Wolf once enjoyed the highest reputation for its Auslesen and TBAs, it has rather lost interest in the style, preferring instead to focus primarily on powerful dry Rieslings.

Christmann ☆☆☆–☆☆☆☆
Gimmeldingen. www.weingut-christmann.de
In 1994, Steffen Christmann took over the family estate in the lower Mittelhaardt, and rapidly instituted a Burgundian-style hierarchy of wines, and also introduced organic farming. He has long been an ardent proponent of classification in the Pfalz and has succeeded Prinz Salm as head of the VDP. Christmann has selected his best sites – Ruppertberger

Reiterpfad, Königsbacher Idig, and Oelberg – for his Grosses Gewächs. The Rieslings are mostly dry, though Christmann makes Auslesen and higher qualities, usually from Idig, when conditions permit. Christmann also produces rich, elegant Spätburgunder, but yields are so low as to be scarcely economically viable.

Darting ☆–☆☆
Bad Dürkheim. www.darting.de
The Dartings have created a niche for wines made in an exuberantly fruity style, very accessible and sensibly priced. They may lack sophistication but they invariably give pleasure, if sometimes at the risk of blowsiness. In 1989, the Dartings left the local cooperative and established their own estate. Best are the Rieslings from the Ungsteiner Herrenberg, but there are also excellent Scheurebes and sweet wines from Rieslaner and Muskateller.

Dr. Deinhard ☆–☆☆
Deidesheim. www.dr-deinhard.de
A well-known estate founded in 1849 by the famous wine-producing Deinhard family of Koblenz. Although the property includes excellent vineyards in Deidesheim and Ruppertsberg, the wines are some-what lacklustre.

Fitz-Ritter ☆☆
Bad Dürkheim. www.fitz-ritter.com
Johann Fitz is the ninth generation of his family to run this estate, which, with its fine, classical eighteenth-century mansion (1785) set within a park, contains the largest maidenhair tree (*Ginkgo biloba*) in Germany. The Fitz family also started here (in 1837) one of the oldest Sekt businesses in Germany, which thrives to this day. There are two Grosses Gewächs Rieslings, from Dürkheimer Michelsberg and Ungsteiner Herrenberg.

Gies-Düppel ☆☆
Birkweiler. www.gies-dueppel.de
Over the past decade Volker Gies has worked hard to improve quality from his family's estate, and has succeeded, with first-rate Weisser Burgunder and elegant Riesling from the Kastanienbusch, too.

Knipser ☆☆–☆☆☆☆
Laumersheim. www.weingut-knipser.de
The Knipser brothers have been among the leading figures in the Pfalz's red wine revolution. Since the late 1980s, they have produced a string of impressively rich, tannic Spätburgunder, St-Laurent, and Dornfelder red wines, from the little-known vineyards of Grosskarlbach and Laumersheim. Cabernet Sauvignon and Merlot were planted here in 1991, followed by Syrah and Cabernet Franc. In general, the Spätburgunder is the best of the red range, if inconsistent, and the Bordeaux and Rhône varieties can lack typicity. Their powerful, oak-aged white wines divide critical opinion, and barrique-aged

Disused wine press, Schweigen

Silvaner and Sauvignon Gris will always be a minority taste. However, the dry Rieslings are very good, though their dry Auslesen can be overly alcoholic.

Koehler-Ruprecht ☆☆–☆☆☆☆
Kallstadt.
Koehler-Ruprecht specializes in two dramatically contrasting styles of wine. The dry Rieslings sold under the Koehler-Ruprecht label are perhaps the most traditionally vinified wines in the region, spending one or two years in wooden casks. Those from the Saumagen possess extraordinary power and ageing potential, and are among the greatest dry wines made in Germany.

The wines sold under the Philippi label are all vinified in a high proportion of new barriques in a deliberately international style. Among them, the Spätburgunder reds and Weisser Burgunder/Grauer Burgunder whites are frequently impressively concentrated and very well made. The Elysium dessert wine, made from a range of grape varieties and aged for years in new barriques, is a dead ringer for a rather alcoholic Sauternes.

Lingenfelder ☆–☆☆
Grosskarlbach. www.lingenfelder.com
This 15-hectare family estate produces rich, supple Riesling and Scheurebe in a fairly broad style that appeals to the export markets, which Rainer Lingenfelder has long cultivated. He was one of the pioneers of barrique-aged Spätburgunder in the Pfalz, but skilful vinification could not disguise the fact that the clonal material was not first rate. The estate has had much deserved success with its juicy, cheerful Dornfelder, which in top years is barrique-aged and bottled under the Onyx label.

Lucashof ☆☆
Forst. www.lucashof.de
Klaus Lucas makes clean, crisp Riesling with plenty of character. The emphasis is on dry wines, the best coming from the first-class Pechstein and Ungeheuer sites of Forst.

Herbert Messmer ☆☆–☆☆☆
Burrweiler. www.weingut-messmer.de
Founded in 1960, this 26-hectare estate has long been one of the handful of dynamic properties that have changed the image of the Südliche Weinstrasse from that of being only a bulk wine producer. Gregor Messmer is a talented young winemaker with some remarkable vineyards at his disposal, including the first-class Burrweiler Schäwer, the only Pfalz vineyard with a slate soil like that of the Mosel. The elegant and tangy dry and late-harvested Rieslings from this site are frequently among the finest wines made from this grape in the entire region. The dry Weisser Burgunder and Grauer Burgunder are much more typical Pfalz wines, but equally well crafted. Messmer's Spätburgunder has acquired finesse and balance in recent vintages. The best wines are labelled "Selection", which has nothing to do with the Wine Institute's category introduced in 2001.

Theo Minges ☆☆
Flemlingen. www.weingut-minges.com
Minges is typical of the Südliche Weinstrasse in producing a wide range of wines from many varieties, including Chardonnay, Weisser Burgunder, Riesling, and Gewürztraminer. Oak can sometimes be too prominent on the otherwise balanced Spätburgunder.

Georg Mosbacher ☆☆–☆☆☆☆
Forst. www.georg-mosbacher.de
This estate has long been a leading producer of Rieslings from the famous vineyards of Forst. Rich aromas, juicy fruit, and bright acidity are the hallmarks of the Mosbacher wines, and vintages such as 2002, 2004, and 2005 have shown a complete mastery of dry Rieslings from the four Grosses Gewächs sites.

Eugen Müller ☆☆–☆☆☆
Forst. www.weingut-eugen-mueller.de
Kurt Müller owns, among his 17 hectares of vineyards, the only old vines in Forst's top sites to survive the reorganization of the village's vineyards. The resulting wines are big, rich, and muscular. Müller's son Stephan, who has spent time working in Australia's Barossa Valley, is now working alongside his father.

Müller-Catoir ☆☆☆☆
Neustadt. www.mueller-catoir.de
Two complex personalities, owner Heinrich Catoir and winemaker Hans-Günther Schwarz, made this estate the undisputed leader in the Pfalz. (See Müller-Catoir: A Great Pfalz Estate, opposite.)

Münzberg ☆☆–☆☆☆
Godramstein. www.weingut-muenzberg.de
The Kessler family's estate, close to Landau, makes some of the Pfalz's best dry Weisser Burgunder, Chardonnay (the only white to be barrel-fermented), and Grauer Burgunder. The soils are rather heavy for Riesling, but this variety can be surprisingly fresh in the hands of the Kesslers. Their red wines have also improved dramatically in recent years. Barrique-ageing was introduced in 1989, and by 2004 the Spätburgunder from Grosses Gewächs Schlangenpfiff was attaining real stature.

Karl Pfaffmann ☆☆–☆☆☆
Walsheim. www.weingut-karl-pfaffmann.de
Markus Pfaffmann graduated from Geisenheim in 1999, and came to join his father, Helmut, at this 30-hectare estate. This is a modern, commercial estate, with most vineyards machine harvested and grapes vinified in stainless steel. The wines are very well made, and the crisp Rieslings and full, fruity Weisser Burgunders and Grauer Burgunders show purity and finesse.

Pfeffingen ☆☆☆
Bad Dürkheim-Pfeffingen. www.pfeffingen.de
This highly regarded estate gained its reputation under Karl Fuhrmann from the 1950s to the 1970s. The property is now run by his daughter, Doris. Riesling dominates in the vineyards, notably the Ungsteiner Herrenberg, but Scheurebe is important, too, and produces juicily rich wines here. Pfeffingen Rieslings, whether dry or naturally sweet, have considerable finesse. Even wines from "off" vintages age long

and gracefully, while fine years such as 2004 and 2005 deliver wines of brilliance and distinction.

Ökonomierat Rebholz ☆☆☆–☆☆☆☆
Sielbeldingen. www.oekonomierat-rebholz.de
The Rebholz family were the quality wine pioneers in the Südliche Weinstrasse, making the first BA and TBA wines in the area, when such rarities were considered the exclusive preserve of the Mittelhaardt. They are far better known, however, for their intense, dry wines. In the earlier 1990s, Hans-Jörg Rebholz's Rieslings could be very austere, but more recent vintages have been brilliant, even in the tricky 2006 vintage. Of the two Grosses Gewächs, the Kastanienbusch is laced with aromas of aniseed, while the Sonnenschein is more apricotty and opulent. Although Riesling dominates the estate's vineyards, Rebholz also excels with Weisser Burgunder, Chardonnay, Gewürztraminer, and Muskateller white wines, and Spätburgunder reds (the latter both with and without new oak ageing). All of these wines benefit from a year or two of bottle-ageing to shed their youthful assertiveness. The top wines are designated "R" on the label.

Karl Schaefer ☆–☆☆
Bad Dürkheim. www.weingutschaefer.de
A family estate established in 1843, run on traditional lines. Riesling dominates the vineyards, and the wines are fermented slowly in oak casks. After the death of the owner, Dr. Wolf Fleischmann, his daughter Gerda Lehmeyer took over running the estate. After a few disappointing vintages, since 2004 quality has improved.

Schneider ☆☆
Ellerstadt. www.weingutschneider.de
Markus Schneider is now the leading grower in this village to the east of Bad Dürkheim. He has dispensed with vineyard names, which have little resonance in this area, and with the entire Prädikat system, so all the wines are bottled as QbA. Price indicates quality. Although the Rieslings are good, Schneider seems more gripped by red wines, from old vines of Portugieser as well as Spätburgunder and Bordeaux style blends. These reds are aged in casks and have considerable weight.

Georg Siben Erben ☆–☆☆
Deidesheim. www.siben-weingut.de
Wolfgang Siben was one of the first Pfalz growers to specialize in dry Rieslings. In 1997 he retired, handing over to his son, Andreas, the tenth generation of Sibens making wine here. The wines, which are from organically farmed vines, are assertive and less opulent than many Pfalz Rieslings. The Grosses Gewächs Rieslings from 2005 show a marked improvement; lesser wines remain less convincing.

Thomas Siegrist ☆☆
Leinsweiler. www.weingut-siegrist.de
Thomas Siegrist was a pioneer of barrique-aged red wines in

MULLER-CATOIR – A GREAT PFALZ ESTATE

The Pfalz's reputation as Germany's most dynamic winegrowing region would be unthinkable without the Müller-Catoir estate. It was founded in 1744 by the Huguenot Catoir family, but only more recently has it written history.

The estate is in Haardt, a suburb of Neustadt an der Weinstrasse. None of the Haardt vineyard sites attracted attention until the arrival, in 1962, of the shy owner of Müller-Catoir, Heinrich Catoir, and his ebullient winemaker, Hans-Günther Schwarz. Together they evolved and perfected a dramatic new style of German wine from a palette of grape varieties, making the estate's wines the most thrilling in the Pfalz. What is more remarkable about the achievement is that the estate does not own vineyards in the most prestigious villages such as Deidesheim and Forst. Instead they lie close to Neustadt in Haardt and Gimmeldingen, and have never been that highly regarded. Yet every Müller-Catoir wine, dry or sweet, exhibits a strong personality. The finest of them are unique expressions of the region's generous climate.

Riesling accounts for 60 per cent of the estate's 20 hectares of vineyards and gives some of the richest and most aromatic dry wines made from this noble grape, in the whole of Germany. It is, however, with rare grapes such as Rieslaner and unfashionable ones such as Scheurebe (both crossings of Silvaner and Riesling) that Catoir and Schwarz have made their names. In their hands, Rieslaner gives Auslese and higher-quality wines a scintillating freshness and unctuous richness, while their Scheurebes are lavish and exotic, yet silky and elegant. They each account for nearly 10 per cent of the estate's vineyards. In top vintages, Grauer Burgunder and Weisser Burgunder give dry wines as bombastic as the stone façade with which the baroque estate house was fitted at the turn of the century. Muskateller is a ravishingly perfumed dry wine, made only when nature smiles upon this fickle grape.

If the brilliance of the wines here is not primarily an expression of terroir, then one has to credit the skill of the winemaker. Yet Schwarz is was no manipulator. Instead, when most German wineries were becoming ever more crowded with the latest technology and filters, Schwarz argued for minimal intervention. He had no truck with centrifuges, or de-acidification, or with cultivated yeasts, and if possible, fining was avoided, too. Schwarz was similarly exacting in the vineyard: eliminating fertilizers, ploughing the soil, and pruning severely to limit yields. He was fortunate that Heinrich Catoir was willing to support this campaign for quality with his chequebook.

The Müller-Catoir wine style and commitment to quality have inspired an entire generation of young Pfalz winegrowers. Many of the region's leading young winemakers have worked at Müller-Catoir or were advised by Schwarz. Without him, the region's quality renaissance of the past three decades would have been unthinkable. He retired in 2002 and his successor, Martin Franzen, must have stepped into his shoes with some trepidation. He has, acquitted himself well. The wines are still gripping, and the nobly sweet wines as dazzling as ever.

the Pfalz, producing his first vintage in 1985. Today, he is closely assisted by his son-in-law, Bruno Schimpf. They have created some red blends, such as "Johann Adam Hausch" (75% Spätburgunder/25% Dornfelder) and "Bergacker" (Spätburgunder/Dornfelder/Cabernet Sauvignon), but in general these are less successful than the complex Spätburgunders. These are ranked according to an in-house star system. The dry white wines, from Grauer Burgunder, Weisser Burgunder, and Riesling, have gained in weight and opulence in recent years.

Weegmüller ☆–☆☆
Neustadt. www.weegmueller-weine.de
The enthusiastic Stephanie Weegmüller is the winemaker here, producing a wide range of wines from many grape varieties. That makes it hard to discern a consistent style, and some wines seem to lack verve. Haardter Herrenletten produces some very good dry Rieslings as well as Grauer Burgunder. The sweet wines from here are opulent, but a touch heavy.

Dr. Wehrheim ☆☆☆
Birkweiler. www.weingut-wehrheim.de
Karl-Heinz Wehrheim makes some of the best dry Riesling, Weisser Burgunder, and Grauer Burgunder wines in the southern Pfalz. Rich and elegant, the best wines come from the steep slopes and stony, reddish soil of the Birkweiler Kastanienbusch, and from his other Grosses Gewächs, Birkweiler Mandelberg. Only wines from these sites bear vineyard designations.

The Weisser Burgunder is particularly successful here, and the reds are of interest, too. St-Laurent was planted here as long ago as 1974, and there is a Cabernet/Merlot blend called Carolus, first made in the mid-1990s. It has yet to attain the elegance of the Kastanienbusch Spätburgunder.

Wilhelmshof ☆☆
Siebeldingen. www.wilhelmshof.de
The Roth family specializes in Sekt production, and makes some of the best sparkling wines in all of the Pfalz. There also worthwhile reds and some full-bodied Weisser Burgunders and Grauer Burgunders from the Im Sonnenschein vineyard.

J L Wolf ☆☆☆
Wachenheim. www.drloosen.de
In 1996, this poor, underperforming estate was taken over by a consortium headed by local businessman Christoph Hindenfeld and Ernst Loosen of the Dr. Loosen estate in Bernkastel, Mosel (q.v.). It did not take Loosen long to demonstrate that he is just as skilled at producing deliciously dry Rieslings as he is at making traditional, naturally sweet Mosel Rieslings. The wines, from top sites in Wachenheim, Forst, and Deidesheim, have purity and zest, and even the more basic Rieslings are excellent.

Hessische Bergstrasse

With its 436 hectares of vines, half of them Riesling, clinging to the terraced hills to the north of Heidelberg, the Hessische Bergstrasse is one of the most beautiful wine-growing regions in Germany. However, since most of its produce is drunk within the region, or sold to weekenders from the many large towns nearby, it is hardly known outside this area. This is a shame, because the best sites here are capable of giving elegant, sophisticated Rieslings of excellent quality.

The steep slopes of the Heppenheimer Steinkopf, the Bensheimer Kalkgasse, and the Bensheimer Streichling are the three top sites of Hessische Bergstrasse. The poor sandstone soil of the Steinkopf gives very minerally, racy wines; the limestone of Kalkgasse yielding more substantial, rounder wines; the Streichling is famed for producing a delicate bouquet and subtlety. On the loess-loam soils of lower-lying vineyards grow Weisser Burgunder and Grauer Burgunder, producing medium-bodied dry wines comparable with those of northern Baden. In effect the region is a continuation of Baden's northernmost vineyards.

Leading Hessische Bergstrasse Producers

Weingut der Stadt Bensheim ☆
Bensheim. www.weingut-der-stadt-bensheim.de
The town of Bensheim has a small estate of about 13 hectares, mainly Riesling. Axel Seiberth has been the director here for over 20 years, and has stamped his style on the winery. The Rieslings are surprisingly soft, and this is due to the systematic malolactic fermentation to which the wine is subjected.

This is unusual in Germany for Riesling. It results in supple wines for immediate drinking, but the wines emerge lacking in verve and typicity. The estate also makes some pleasant Spätburgunder aged in older barriques.

Staatsweingut Bergstrasse ☆–☆☆☆
Bensheim.
www.weingut-kloster-eberbach.de
Officially, this estate is part of the vast state domain of Hessen, based at Kloster Eberbach, but it has always enjoyed a high degree of autonomy. The winery takes pride in the fact that it produced the first TBAs in the region's history in 1971, and its first Eiswein the following year. Today it is dry-style Riesling, Weisser Burgunder, and Grauer Burgunder that dominate the production, but the Eiswein can still be exceptional. Overall, this is the top estate in the region.

Simon-Bürkle ☆☆
Zwingenberg. www.simon-buerkle.de
This 12-hectare estate was created by two ambitious young graduates of the Weinsberg wine school, at the beginning of the 1990s. One of them, Kurt Simon, died in 2003 but his widow Dagmar has taken his place. Although the quality is still a little erratic, this producer remains one of the quality leaders in the region, both for Riesling and Spätburgunder.

Franken

The River Main flows west, describing a great drunken W, to meet the Rhine beyond the city of Frankfurt, 80 kilometres (50 miles) east of the Rheingau. Its course runs through the irregular limestone and red-marl hills of Franconia or Franken, the northern extremity of Bavaria.

The centre of Franken is the baroque city of Würzburg. Its most famous vineyard, Würzburger Stein, beams down on the city centre from a steep hill above the river. The name Stein was once traditionally borrowed by foreigners to describe Franconian wine generically (as the English shortened Hochheim to "hock" for all Rhein wines). "Steinwein" comes in fat, dumpy flagons called *bocksbeutel*, thus distinguishing itself from almost all other German wines, which come in elegant bottles. This is probably the extent of popular knowledge.

Franken wine enjoys local popularity, and its consistency and quality are such that drinkers are happy to pay good prices for the wines. This has prevented Franconian wines from becoming better known outside Germany.

The area, extending over 6,000 hectares, is exceptionally diffuse and hard to comprehend. Vineyards are found only on exceptional south-facing slopes. The most important sector is around Würzburg, and is known as the Maindreieck (Main triangle). Further east is the Steigerwald, which has heavier soils, and the westerly sector around Bürgstadt has a growing reputation for red wines. The Franconian climate is harsh, and serious frosts are common; the season is too short to achieve regular success with Riesling, though climatic changes in recent years have resulted in a growing number of excellent wines from this variety. Traditionally, however, Franken has made its best wine with Silvaner. Only here, and occasionally on the Rheinfront in Rheinhessen, does this variety make wine of arresting quality. Silvaner, grown in Franken, can produce full-bodied dry wines (and more rarely sweet ones) with a noble breadth and substance. They are sometimes compared with white burgundy, not for their flavour, but for their vinosity and ability to match rich food at the table.

Unfortunately, the Müller-Thurgau has now gained the upper hand, being planted in 32 per cent of the vineyards. It can work well, when not overcropped, and makes easy-going, flavourful wines, although it rarely matches the remarkable low-key stylishness of Silvaner. Scheurebe can do better. Bacchus, still planted in 12 per cent of the vineyards, tends to be aggressively aromatic, but it enjoys a local following.

In a ripe year, Rieslaner produces excellent Auslesen, with the breadth of a Silvaner and depth of a Riesling. And Rieslaner can also deliver exciting dry wines. About half the wine is made by cooperatives.

Würzburg itself, however, boasts three of the oldest, biggest, and best wine estates in Germany: the Bürgerspital, the Juliusspital, and the Staatlicher Hofkeller. But this mighty trio is being increasingly challenged by the growing ranks of small estates aiming for, and often achieving, the highest quality.

Outstanding Franken Vineyards

Bürgstadter Centgrafenberg The most western, first-class vineyard of Franken is also the warmest, lying on a sheltered south-facing slope in the small basin around the town of Miltenberg. The red-sandstone soil also combines to produce unusually aromatic and racy Franken wines. The Spätburgunder grape plays as important a role as Riesling.

Casteller Schlossberg This precipitously steep slope above the village of Castell, first documented in 1258, is one of the top sites of the Steigerwald. The combination of excellent exposure and the heavy gypsum-marl soil, results in powerful, racy wines. Rieslaner, as well as Riesling and Silvaner, scale the heights here in more senses than one.

Escherndorfer Lump The "tramp" of Escherndorf is one of the most imposing vineyards in Franken; a great amphitheatre of vines in the crook of one of the Main's most dramatic bends. It is particularly renowned for rich, succulent, dry Silvaner, although Riesling too gives excellent results.

Frickenhäuser Kapellenberg The finest vineyard of Frickenhäusen is also one of the least-known top sites of Franken. The south-facing slope lies directly adjacent to the bank of the Main. While the wines it produces may not be the most powerful in the area, they have ample fruit and lovely balance.

Homburger Kallmuth The towering wall of vines that forms the famous Kallmuth is one of very few top vineyard sites in Franken not to have been Flurbereinigt or reorganized by landscaping. Its wild flora, with a marked southern character, is famous. It was first documented in 1102. The reddish sandstone soil gives richly fruity wines with a powerful minerally character.

Iphöfer Julius-Echter-Berg/Kronsberg The vineyard named after the late sixteenth-century Prince-Bishop, Julius Echter of Mespelbrunn, is indisputably one of Franken's greatest. Situated at the southwestern tip of the Steigerwald it enjoys optimum exposure, which, together with the gypsum-marl soil, gives wines of enormous power, with a strong, earthy character. The wines from the neighbouring Kronsberg are hardly less imposing.

Randersackerer Marsberg/Pfülben/Sonnenstuhl/ Teufelskeller The old town of Randersacker is blessed with more fine vineyards than any other in Franken. However

Wine goddess and Pan, Würzburg

much body and richness these wines have, they are less muscular than some other Franken wines. Beautiful balance and a subtle spicy-smoky character are their hallmarks. The differences between these vineyards, all of which have limestone soils, are primarily of exposure. First among equals is the 15-hectare Pfülben.

Rödelseer Küchenmeister The town of Rödelseer lies just to the north of Iphofen and its finest site, the Küchenmeister lies directly next to the top sites of its neighbour. The wines are similar in character, but a touch lighter.

Volkacher Ratsherr This imposing hillside vineyard lies only eight-kilometres (five-miles) north of the famous Escherndorfer Lump and enjoys a similarly favoured location, right next to the River Main. It gives rich, substantial wines with a good acid structure. Karthäuser is another top site here.

Würzburger Abtsleite/Innere Leiste Though less famous than the Würzburger Stein, both these sites enjoy excellent locations and are capable of yielding top-class Riesling and Silvaner wines. Indeed, the Innere Leiste, situated immediately below the Marienburg fortress, yields the town's most powerful wines. What the Abtsleite wines may lack in volume they more than make up for in racy elegance.

Würzburger Stein/Stein-Harfe The Stein and its subsite the Stein-Harfe (solely owned by the Bürgerspital estate – q.v.) cover a slope that extends for more than eight kilometres (five miles) directly northwest of Würzburg. For a long time, the distinctive, smoky note of these wines was explained by the proximity of the main railway line, but since electrification it has been obvious that this character comes, in fact, from the limestone soil. No wines in Franken can excel the finest Rieslings and Silvaners from this site, in elegance or subtlety of fruit – the latter often distinctly citric, even slightly tropical.

Leading Franken Producers

Bickel-Stumpf ☆☆
Frickenhausen. www.bickel-stumpf.de
Dry wines, even simple Kabinetts from Silvaner and Müller-Thurgau, can be delicious here, often more so than the sweeter styles. On the other hand, the nobly sweet wines, from Traminer and Rieslaner, can be excellent. A 2005 innovation is called Crossover, a barrique-aged Silvaner devised by Reimund Stumpf's son Matthias.

Bürgerspital zum Heiligen Geist ☆☆
Würzburg. www.buergerspital.de
A splendid charity, founded in 1319 for the old people of Würzburg by Johannes von Steren, it is now somewhat overshadowed by the even richer ecclesiastical foundation, the Juliusspital (q.v.). It owns 110 hectares, and has more Riesling planted than any other important Franken estate. It also enjoys the greatest share of Würzburg's famous Stein and other good south facing slopes. The vineyards are 33 per cent Riesling, 29 per cent Silvaner, and 12 per cent Müller-Thurgau; the rest include Weisser Burgunder, Scheurebe, Spätburgunder, and several new varieties. The specialties of the house include Silvaner, of course, both dry and in a less successful off-dry

style called Feinherb; Riesling from the Stein, which proved splendid in 2005 but less so in 2006; and broad, rich Weisser Burgunder, also from the Stein. The wines can be sampled at the huge 500-seater Weinstube in the venerable hospital buildings. Quality has been mixed in recent years, but there are signs of improvement.

Fürstlich Castell'sches Domänenamt ☆☆–☆☆☆
Castell. www.castell.de
Castell is a tiny principality, still complete with its own prince in a palace, and the vineyards and a chain of banks and other properties remain under family ownership. Until 1806, the Castells even had their own private army. The vineyards slope up to perfectly kept oak woods – the prince's other pride.

In 1997, the present prince's son, Ferdinand, took over running the estate, and installed a new team that delivered excellent results. Müller-Thurgau and Silvaner are the most important varieties, as well as Riesling and Rieslaner, the latter producing powerful, lush, and piquant sweet wines. The Schloss Castell range cites only variety and vintage on the label; these are attractive wines for early drinking.

Far superior are the single vineyard wines, and the best of these is invariably the Schlossberg, a Grosses Gewächs. The sweet wines can be exceptional too: Silvaner Eiswein, and BA and TBA from Riesling and Rieslaner.

Michael Fröhlich ☆–☆☆
Escherndorf. www.weingut-michael-froehlich.de
Michael Fröhlich's fresh, clean wines are among the best in this part of the Main valley. The Rieslings are particularly commendable; the Muskateller a bargain.

Fürst ☆☆☆–☆☆☆☆
Bürgstadt. www.weingut-rudolf-fuerst.de
Paul Fürst is one of the most talented winemakers in Germany. As well as producing impressive, if austere, dry Rieslings, he also makes some powerful Weisser Burgunder. But he is best known, and deservedly so, for his majestic red wines: concentrated Spätburgunder and velvety rich Frühburgunder.

The best of them are labelled R, presumably for Reserve. There is also a blend of Spätburgunder and Domina called Parzifal. This range constitutes the best red wines from Franken.

Glaser-Himmelstoss ☆☆
Nordheim. www.weingut-glaser-himmelstoss.de
Twelve hectares of vineyards in Dettelbach and Nordheim, just south of Escherndorf, supply the grapes for this classic estate, with its palette of dry and sweet, sometimes nobly sweet, Riesling and Silvaner. Barrique-aged Spätburgunder is identified as Rebell on the label. For Franken, prices are reasonable.

Juliusspital-Weingut ☆☆☆
Würzburg. www.juliusspital.de
This charitable foundation, on a scale even grander than Burgundy's Hospices de Beaune, was founded in 1576 by the Prince-Bishop Julius Echter von Mespelbrunn. With 170 hectares, it is now one of the largest wine estates in Germany, supporting a magnificent hospital and other charitable institutions for the people of Würzburg.

Its low vaulted cellar, 243 metres (800 feet) long, was built in 1699 and still houses casks full of wine. The vineyards are 41 per cent Silvaner, 20 per cent Riesling, 16 per cent Müller-Thurgau. The remainder includes Gewürztraminer, Ruländer, Weisser Burgunder, Muskateller, Scheurebe, and Spätburgunder (in Bürgstadt). Today, the estate, directed by Horst Kolesch, is widely regarded as being the best of the great Würzburg estates, with vineyards in numerous Grosses Gewächs sites. Silvaner appears in many guises, mostly single vineyard bottlings, and gives vibrantly fruity, elegant wines; while the dry Rieslings demonstrate what this grape is capable of in this region. There is delicious, dry and sweet Rieslaner, and some rare BA and TBA from the Stein.

Fürst Löwenstein ☆☆–☆☆☆
Kreuzwertheim. www.loewenstein.de
After a period in the doldrums, this famous princely estate, which is under the same ownership as the estate in Hallgarten in the Rheingau (q.v.), has been enjoying a revival. The most exciting wines are the impressive, traditional-style Silvaners and Rieslings from the precipitous slopes of the exceptional Homburger Kallmuth site. Spätburgunder from the Bürgstadter Centgrafenberg can be spicy and stylish.

Roth ☆–☆☆
Wiesenbronn. www.weingut-roth.de
Gerhard Roth's organic estate in the Steigerwald is best-known for its tannic, oaky reds from Spätburgunder, Lemberger, and Domina, but its fruity, substantial dry Rieslings deserve to be taken equally seriously.

Johann Ruck ☆☆☆
Iphofen. www.ruckwein.de
Since the late 1980s, Johann Ruck has been producing some splendid and meticulously made Franken wines. They marry beautifully the earthy and herbal qualities typical of the wines from Iphofen's famous vineyards, with great freshness and racy acidity. In addition to fine dry Riesling and Silvaner, Herr Ruck also makes the most concentrated dry Grauer Burgunder in the region, from old vines in Rödelsee, and delicious sweet Rieslaner. All his wines can be tasted at the historic estate house in the centre of Iphofen.

Horst Sauer ☆☆☆–☆☆☆☆
Escherndorf. www.weingut-horst-sauer.de
This 14-hectare estate has risen swiftly to become one of the most consistent producers in Franken. The secret to Sauer's success is selective harvesting from the excellent Lump vineyard. The Silvaners are crisp and minerally, and the Rieslings too are racy and pungent. Sauer is extremely proficient at nobly sweet wines, and frequently succeeds in coaxing Silvaner Eiswein and Silvaner or Riesling TBAs from the Lump. Whether dry or ultra-sweet, these are wines of exemplary quality.

Egon Schäffer ☆
Escherndorf. www.weingut-schaeffer.de
After some disappointing vintages, this miniature three-hectare estate is back on form with some seductively rich, dry Silvaners from the slopes of the famous Lump vineyard.

Schmitt's Kinder ☆☆
Randersacker. www.schmitts-kinder.de
This estate, founded in 1710, was inherited by six sisters and one son in 1917, and rather than divide it up, they agreed to work together: hence the unusual name of this 18-hectare estate. Karl Martin Schmitt produces modern style wines, and isn't afraid to use the latest technology to ensure clean musts.

The Grosses Gewächs Silvaners and Rieslings from the Pfülben are brimming with fruit and aroma, very clean and pure in flavour. In 2005 Schmitt iced the cake with some impressive BAs.

Graf von Schönborn ☆–☆☆
Volkach. www.schoenborn.de
The Schönborn family, who own a great estate in the Rheingau, also own this 30-hectare property in Franken, which has been in the family since 1806. For some years the wines have been lacklustre, the dry wines a touch earthy, the sweeter styles rather bland, but the appointment of a new cellarmaster in 2003 is gradually paying off with more consistent wines.

Schloss Sommerhausen ☆☆
Sommerhausen. www.weingut-schloss-sommerhausen.de
The Steinmanns were once hereditary stewards of this estate belonging to the castle at Sommerhausen, and in 1968 they became the owners of this 28 hectare property. Dry Riesling and Silvaner from the Grosses Gewächs Steinbach vineyard are vibrant and minerally, but Sommerhausen is also known for its wines from the Pinot family of white grapes (Weisser Burgunder, Grauer Burgunder, Auxerrois) and Chardonnay. It also produces a range of sparkling wines, of which the vintage Auxerrois bottling is often the most interesting, and in suitable vintages such as 2005, some exciting TBAs.

Staatlicher Hofkeller ☆–☆☆
Würzburg. www.hofkeller.de
The superlative vineyards of the lordly Prince-Bishops of Würzburg, originating in the twelfth century, are now (since 1816) the Bavarian State Domain. Although the prince's palace, the baroque Residenz, was largely destroyed during World War II, the great cellar beneath survived, and remains one of the most stirring sights in the world of wine. (The great Tiepolo ceiling of the Residenz also survived, and is one of the most stirring sights in the world outside wine.) There have been frequent changes in management in recent years, so quality has been somewhat uneven, which is regrettable, given the fine range of vineyards at the winery's disposal.

Nonetheless, some of the dry Rieslings and the Rieslaners are object lessons in true Franconian style, balancing high acidity with powerful flavours. The Hofkeller is quite proud of its red wines, from Domina and Frühburgunder as well as Spätburgunder, but they can lack elegance. Unfortunately, the Hofkeller continues to lag behind the two other great estates of Würzburg.

Josef Störrlein ☆☆–☆☆☆
Randersacker. www.stoerrlein.de
This small estate has enjoyed a rapid rise since it was created out of nothing by Armin Störrlein in 1970. Störrlein knows

precisely the style of wine he likes: entirely dry, yet not too acidic. This approach seems to work better with varieties such as Weisser Burgunder than Silvaner. The top Spätburgunder is excessively oaky, but there is a softer, fruitier red blend (from Domina, Spätburgunder, and Pinot Meunier) called Casparus.

Hans Wirsching ☆☆–☆☆☆
Iphofen. www.wirsching.de
A family firm since 1630, and now run by the fourteenth generation, this is the largest estate in Iphofen, with 72 hectares of vineyards. Silvaner is the principal variety here, and the best wines, invariably dry, carry the S designation. The Rieslings are zesty, and the top bottlings have a strong mineral tone. There are good wines from Scheurebe, Gewürztraminer, and Rieslaner, which in top vintages such as 2005 is used to produce sumptuous sweet wines. The reds are surprisingly lean in style. After a dull patch, Wirsching is now producing highly satisfying and balanced Grosses Gewächs from Julius Echter Berg and Kronsberg.

Zehnthof ☆☆–☆☆☆
Sulzfeld. www.weingut-zehnthof.de
Wolfgang Luckert makes sleek, supple dry wines from a wide range of white grapes (most importantly Silvaner, Chardonnay, Riesling, and Weisser Burgunder) and superb dessert wines when conditions are right. Luckert favours natural fermentations, and ageing in traditional casks. The red wine selection has been expanded in recent years, with rather costly Cabernet and Merlot in the portfolio as well as full-bodied Spätburgunder and Frühburgunder.

Württemberg

Three centuries ago, Württemberg was far and away Germany's largest wine-growing region. But wars and vine diseases led to many sites being abandoned, and by 1963 there were only 7,000 hectares in production. Today that figure has risen to 11,500. Like those of Franken, its vineyards are very dispersed, but lie roughly between the cities of Heilbronn and Stuttgart. The region's identity derives from the fact that it is, other than the Ahr, the only one in Germany where red grapes dominate. Here they occupy 71 per cent of vineyards. Unfortunately, the red grape of choice here, with over 20 per cent of plantings, is the mediocre Trollinger. Visitors find it hard to discern the appeal of this pale, light red, but it has long been a vital part of the local Swabian diet, and is consumed in heroic quantities in the bars and restaurants of Stuttgart. However, there are other red grapes capable of producing more interesting wine. Schwarzriesling is the same as Pinot Meunier and, as one would expect, it doesn't often rise to great heights, but more serious wines are made from Lemberger, Spätburgunder, and Samtrot (a Pinot Meunier mutation).

Riesling is the most important white wine grape, but gives completely different results compared to those of the Rhine or Mosel valleys. The continental climate and gypsum-marl soils, which are so well-suited to the red grapes, yield white wines that are full, broad, and earthy. The challenge for winemakers is to give them at least a touch of elegance. The best of these come from steep, terraced vineyards in the Neckar valley.

Sadly, at present, no wine-growing region in Germany has more unrealized potential than Württemberg. The ease with which wines of solid, everyday quality can be sold within the region seems to prevent more than a handful of wine-growers working for top quality – and recognition. But their ranks are growing, and the best estates are acquiring a solid reputation within Germany, although hardly any of the wines are exported.

The wine research institute at Weinsberg has busied itself creating new red-grape crossings that will give Württemberg wines more body and colour. At present they have been planted with caution, in Pfalz and the Rheinhessen as well as here, and are used almost entirely as components in a blend. The best red-wine estates of Württemberg obtain good results by green-harvesting to ensure optimal maturity, and by getting to grips with the mysteries of barrique ageing. In the early 1990s, many Württemberg reds were too tannic, too oaky, and too clumsy, but by 2005 many estates had corrected the overenthusiasms of the past and were making well-balanced wines of character and even elegance.

The region is divided into three Bereiche. Remstal-Stuttgart has some of the best sites, but the Württembergisches Unterland, which spreads across the Neckar valley north of Stuttgart to the Bottwar valley in the east, is by far the largest. And the smallest is the northern zone of Kocher-Jagst-Tauber, which, atypically, specializes in white wine.

Leading Württemberg Producers

Graf Adelmann ☆☆☆
Kleinbottwar. www.graf-adelmann.com
One of the best-known estates in Württemberg, whose bottles are instantly recognizable by their pale-blue and red "lacy" labels, with the name Brüssele (after a former owner). The family castle, Burg Schaubeck is an enchanting but venerable stronghold, apparently with Roman origins, owned by the Adelmanns since 1914. The estate, now run by Graf Michael Adelmann, is best known for its red wines, which, in the right vintage, can be among Germany's best. The most powerful of these are the Lembergers and the Cuvée Vignette, a blend of Lemberger, Cabernet Sauvignon, and Pinot grapes. Other *cuvées* include the barrique-aged, multiple-variety Herbst im Park. After some disappointing Rieslings during the early 1990s, considerable changes were made to the vinification of the white wines in favour of more fruit and freshness. Some Auslesen are marked by high alcohol and correspondingly less residual sugar, a style that is an acquired taste.

Adelmann has also created the white *cuvée* Der Loewe von Schaubeck, which unites Riesling, Weisser Burgunder, and Grauburgunder. In the 1990s, some of the wines were overoaked, but these days the barrel-ageing is more skilfully monitored and finesse is prized more than power.

Gerhard Aldinger ☆☆☆
Fellbach. www.weingut-aldinger.de
This 22-hectare estate near Stuttgart is best known for its serious red wines, of which the blended Cuvée C and Merlot

are often the most impressive. This is a spicy, Bordeaux-style wine, aged for 16 months in new barriques. Its white counterparts are Cuvée S, a barrique-fermented Sauvignon Blanc from the Aldinger's monopoly site, Untertürkheimer Gips; and Cuvée A, initially a bizarre oaked blend of Riesling and Gewürztraminer, but now a blend of Weisser Burgunder and Chardonnay. But it's the stylish reds that have made Aldinger's reputation.

Amalienhof ☆
Heilbronn. www.weingut-amalienhof.de
Since taking over the estate, with its monopoly Beilsteiner Steinberg site, in 1969, the Strecker family has built up a very successful property. The Rieslings are cleanly made, but better still are the traditionally vinified Lemberger and Samtrot red wines, and their own strange Muskat-Lemberger crossing they call Wildmuskat. In the late 1990s, the Streckers introduced a new Bordeaux-style *cuvée* called Bariton.

Graf von Bentzel-Sturmfeder ☆
Schozach. www.sturmfeder.de
This is an estate with fourteenth-century origins and eighteenth-century cellars. Two-thirds of production here is of red wine, which is given prolonged cask-ageing. Lemberger and Samtrot are usually the most impressive wines. The Rieslings are rather broad and lack zest. The wines last well, even when the acidity is relatively low, with barrel-ageing giving them stability, but they can lack finesse.

Dautel ☆☆–☆☆☆
Bönnigheim. www.weingut-dautel.de
The Dautels have been grape farmers since the sixteenth century, but it was only in 1978 that Ernst Dautel withdrew from the local cooperative and began producing his own wines. Over the years he has established himself as one of the region's top producers of red wine, which accounts for 60 per cent of his production.

He has been using small oak barrels since 1986, employing oak from various countries. The simpler Spätburgunders lack interest, but at the top level, especially the reserve bottling labelled S, the wine is truly sumptuous, with a firm, tannic finish. In 1995, Dautel introduced a blend called Kreation from Merlot, Cabernet Sauvignon, and Lemberger, the latter variety contributing a good acidic backbone to the wine. The pure Lemberger is fine, too. The Rieslings are surprisingly vigorous, and the Weisser Burgunder is preferable to the overoaked Chardonnay.

Drautz-Able ☆☆
Heilbronn.
Richard Drautz's 17-hectare estate produces an enormous range of wines, two-thirds of which is red. Although Riesling and Trollinger account for more than half the production, it is the powerful Lembergers aged in new oak, which have rightly attracted the most attention. There is also a complex and rightly praised blend called Jodokus, formed from Cabernet Sauvignon and Lemberger, and aged two years in new oak. The white wines are good, but not spectacular.

Jürgen Ellwanger ☆☆–☆☆☆
Winterbach. www.weingut-ellwanger.de
At this estate, east of Stuttgart, Jürgen Ellwanger and his sons Jörg and Andreas cultivate 21 hectares, planted with a wide range of varieties, 60 per cent of them red. They are fans of new oak, German as well as French, but wines such as Nicodemus, a barrique-aged Kerner, are only for devotees of woodiness. The reds are more impressive, especially the fruity if tannic Zweigelt; an oaky Merlot; and the peppery, oak-aged Lemberger. The estate's Rieslings are rather less impressive.

Weingärtnergenossenschaft Grantschen ☆–☆☆
Grantschen. www.grantschen.de
This impressive cooperative has 195 members and offers a huge range of wines. The whites are disappointing, but two-thirds of the production is red wine. There's a fine, well-structured barrique-aged Lemberger, less satisfying reds from new crossings such as Cabernet Cubin, but the top wine is the Grandor, Lemberger aged in new oak: a dense, peppery wine with excellent fruit.

Karl Haidle ☆☆–☆☆☆
Kernen-Stetten. www.weingut-karl-haidle.de
If Hans Haidle's estate is not better known in Württemberg, it is because he is a white-wine specialist in a region where red wines grab most of the limelight. His dry, and occasionally nobly sweet, Rieslings are among the best in the region. The

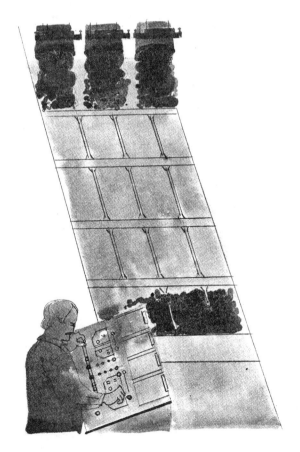

South German cooperative

reds are by no means of lesser quality. They include a plummy Zweigelt, a herbal, barrique-aged Lemberger, a consistently good *cuvée* called Ypsilon, and some elegant Spätburgunder.

Heinrich ☆–☆☆
Heilbronn. www.weingut-heinrich.de
Martin Heinrich's oaky red wines have attracted a good deal of attention. At the top of the range are the Lembergers and the powerful Wollendieb *cuvee*, which is 50 per cent Lemberger. The old-vine Trollinger is worth trying.

Schlossgut Hohenbeilstein ☆
Beilstein. www.schlossgut-hohenbeilstein.de
Hartmann Dippon took over the family estate in 1987, and promptly converted it to organic viticulture. Red wine remains the heart of the wide range, the best examples being made from Spätburgunder and Lemberger. However, many of the reds seem to lack the fruit necessary to support the barrique ageing.

Fürst zu Hohenlohe-Oehringen ☆–☆☆ ?☆☆
Oehringen. www.verrenberg.de
A princely estate since the fourteenth century, with seventeenth-century cellars, which even contain a cask dated 1702. The monopoly Verrenberg site is unusual in being a single sweep of vines, producing mostly dry whites. But the estate is best-known for its red wines, and barriques were first used here in 1983. There are varietal wines from Lemberger, Zweigelt, and Merlot, but the estate is better known for its *cuvées*, of which the best-known is the sometimes jammy Ex Flammis Orior, a blend of Lemberger, Spätburgunder, and Cabernet Sauvignon that spends two years in barriques.

Weingut des Grafen Neipperg ☆☆–☆☆☆
Schwaigern.
Documents prove the Neipperg family has been making wine here since 1248, shortly after the building of Burg Neipperg, the original castle. Two sites are monopoly vineyards:

Schwaigener Ruthe, which is terraced; and Neipperger Schlossberg around the ruinous castle. There is a story that it was the Neippergs who introduced Lemberger to make red wine of colour and tannin. Graf von Neipperg does not believe it is true, but what is certain is that Lemberger came here from Austria, where it is known as Blaufränkisch, in the seventeenth century. It remains a specialty of the estate.

Their other specialty is spicy Traminer. The Rieslings, which have high acidity, are well thought of, and there is some delicious Gelber Muskateller. As for the reds, the Graf prefers to focus on traditional varieties, since he does not believe Württemberg can compete easily on the international market with varieties such as Merlot or Syrah. Lemberger, especially from the Schlossberg, can be outstanding, and the oaked Samtrot is plump and attractive. Nobly sweet wines are rare, but occasionally Graf von Neipperg makes TBA from Gelber Muskateller. The Neippergs are also the owners of properties in St-Emilion, notably Château Canon-la-Gaffelière and La Mondotte, which are run by Stephan von Neipperg.

Schnaitmann ☆☆–☆☆☆
Fellbach. www.weingut-schnaitmann.de
Now undisputably among the top estates of the region, Rainer Schnaitmann's property produced its first vintage in 1997 from four hectares, now expanded to 11. With just a few exceptions he eschews vineyard-designated wines and prefers to label varietally, differentiating between qualities with a star system.

The Frühburgunder, Spätburgunder, and Lemberger are often outstanding, and the Riesling and Sauvignon Blanc (Schnaitmann has worked in New Zealand) are both delicious. "Simonroth" on the label denotes a wine aged in 300-litre barrels. Schnaitmann has a sure hand, producing each year ranges of high quality across the board – even Trollinger.

Schwegler ☆☆–☆☆☆
Korb. www.albrecht-schwegler.de
It would be ridiculous to include an estate of such miniscule

---

GERMAN RED WINES

Germany is best-known for its unrivalled Rieslings, and that's as it should be. But much of southern Germany enjoys a fairly warm climate, making it suitable not just for the production of dry white wines but of red wines, too. Pinot Noir, which thrives in this kind of climate, is obviously the most suitable and popular variety, but German winemakers yearn for wines with more richness and depth of colour. There are some wines made from the Bordeaux varieties, but there are few places where Cabernet Sauvignon will ripen regularly, and Merlot has only caught on in a very few places.

The German solution to this has been to invent new varieties, especially at the wine institute at Weinsberg in

Württemberg. New varieties such as Dornfelder, Regent, and Domina have become popular and often commercially successful, as a whole new wave of dark-coloured and dense crossings have come on stream. The problem is that they contribute colour and tannin, but lack elegance. That is why most growers who have planted grapes such as Domina and Cabernet Cubin tend to use them for blending.

However, southern Germany has indigenous varieties that can give perfectly acceptable red wines on their own. Württemberg's Trollinger produces pallid wines with zero international appeal, but Lemberger, Schwarzriesling (Pinot Meunier), and Samtrot are all

capable of giving lively, characterful red wines. If Californian red-wine producers have to struggle with "tannin management", their German counterparts must master "acidity management", but by picking at optimal ripeness it is perfectly possible, as the best winemakers have shown, to produce well-balanced red wines with depth of flavour and personality. It is more than a matter of simple climate, though, as the reds of the Ahr, near Bonn, can witness.

Organizations that have helped promote the best German reds are the Barrique Forum and, in Württemberg, the Hades group that unites certain barrique aged wines.

size (1.5 hectares) in a work like this, were it not for the fact that Albrecht Schwegler's rich, concentrated Granat is one of the finest red wines in Württemberg.

It is mostly Merlot. Other *cuvées* are Beryll (Lemberger and Zweigelt), and Saphir (Merlot and Zweigelt). When, in 2000, conditions permitted a TBA to be made from grapes picked at 316 Oechsle, Schwegler appropriately bottled it under the name of Monster.

Sonnenhof ☆☆
Vaihingen-Enz. www.weingutsonnenhof.de
This 34-hectare estate's vineyards are mostly on steep slopes north of Stuttgart. Most of the wines are red, and the range includes an elegant oaked Lemberger and surprisingly powerful Spätburgunder.

Wachtstetter ☆☆
Pfaffenhofen. www.wachtstetter.de
Red wines dominate production here, some aged, rather overwhelmingly, in barriques, others in traditional large casks. The Lemberger can be among the best in the region.

Staatsweingut Weinsberg ☆
Weinsberg. www.lwvo-weinsberg.de
Founded in 1868 by Karl von Württemberg as the Royal Wine School, this 40-hectare estate is still attached to one of Germany's leading wine colleges. Riesling is the most important grape, with 20 per cent of the vineyard area, but Weinsberg is best-known for its red wines, which are made both in traditional and oak aged styles.

Many new crossings have been developed here, and some of them are bottled by the college as varietal wines. Among the more appealing of the traditional reds are the Clevner (Frühburgunder) and the Lemberger.

Wöhrwag ☆☆☆
Untertürkheim. www.woehrwag.de
With the entire Untertürkheimer Herzogenberg vineyard site at his disposal, Hans-Peter Wöhrwag has consistently made some of the finest Rieslings in Württemberg in recent years. They are atypical, in the sense that they are lean and racy rather than broad. They combine finesse and power.

Wöhrwag tries to make Eiswein or TBA every year, and usually succeeds. There are two red *cuvées*, of which the better is Philipp, a blend of Lemberger and Spätburgunder. Wöhrwag is one of the few winemakers in Germany to use must concentration – and admit to it.

Herzog von Württemberg ☆☆
Ludwigsburg. www.weingut-wuerttemberg.de
Founded in 1677, this 40-hectare estate is still in the hands of the dukes of Württemberg. They own some good sites, such as Stettner Brotwasser (excellent for Riesling) and Untertürkheimner Mönchberg, where fine Lemberger and Spätburgunder are grown.

Baden

Like the Pfalz, Baden is gifted with a relatively balmy climate that makes it ideal territory for a whole range of wines, especially the Pinot varieties. By rights, it should be enjoying international renown – but it isn't. Its 16,000 hectares of vineyards, across the Rhine from Alsace, have undergone nothing other than a revolution in recent years: they have been almost entirely rationalized and remodelled and grown considerably in size.

It is Germany's warmest (although not necessarily its sunniest) wine region, with correspondingly ripe, high-alcohol, and lower acidity wines; in fact, the diametric opposite of Mosels in style and function. Baden produces good mealtime wines that have a warm vinosity that approaches the French style, and it is surely no coincidence that some of Germany's top restaurants are located here. However, the climate is slightly less favourable than the suntrap of the Vosges foothills in Alsace.

Eighty per cent of Baden's vineyards lie in a 130-kilometre (80-mile) strip running from northeast to southwest, from Baden Baden to Basel, in the foothills of the Black Forest where it meets the Rhine valley. Here the most important subregions, from north to south, are Ortenau (of which one-quarter is planted with Riesling); Breisgau; the sun-drenched volcanic Kaiserstuhl; Tuniberg; and the Chasselas-dominated Markgräflerland. The balance is of purely local importance. Other vineyards lie far to the southeast on the banks of the Bodensee (Lake Constance), north of Baden in the minor regions of the Kraichgau and Badischer Bergstrasse, respectively south and north of Heidelberg (but now united in one Bereich with both names), and far north on the border of Franken, a little region known logically enough as Bereich Badisches Frankenland. The main thrust of Baden viticulture is thus along the Rhine, from where it leaves the Bodensee to where it enters the Pfalz.

Baden is, even more than the southern Pfalz, the land of the cooperative. Around 100 of them process around 80 per cent of the crop. No fewer than 38 of these cooperatives then turn over their entire production to the huge Badischer Winzerkeller central cellars in Breisach on the Rhine. This mega-cooperative bottles some 400-500 different types of wine. Although some of the wines are well made, the domination of the region by a single producer has not helped it to win a reputation for quality and individuality.

Baden has no powerful preference for one grape variety but the Müller-Thurgau has proved to be the workhorse, with 19 per cent of the vineyard area. Perhaps surprisingly, Spätburgunder for red and light rosé (Weissherbst) is now the most widely planted variety with 29 per cent. Then come Ruländer/Grauer Burgunder (Pinot Gris), Gutedel (Chasselas), Riesling, Silvaner, Weisser Burgunder, and Gewürztraminer. Baden's taste is clearly not for the highly aromatic new varieties, as the vast majority of its white wines are made from relatively neutral grapes. The best wine, however, is made from Riesling, Weisser Burgunder, and Grauer Burgunder. Two factors account for the failure of Baden to punch its weight, especially on the international market. The first is the domination of cooperatives, most of which cater to a highly traditional local market, and are reluctant to create products that might enjoy a wider appeal. Secondly, there is an overproliferation of wine styles. It is not uncommon for a cooperative to offer ten or more different Spätburgunders – dry, lightly sweet, rosé, barrique-aged, and different quality levels of each style – which adds up to a marketing nightmare, whatever the quality of the wine. Those producers, such as Johner and Huber, who have trimmed down the range and committed themselves to high quality – justifiably charge high prices, which the domestic, but not the international, market is prepared to pay.

Outstanding Baden Vineyards

Achkarrer Schlossberg The steep slopes and stony, volcanic tuff soil of this site result in dry Weisser Burgunder and Grauer Burgunder wines that perfectly marry power with elegance.

Durbacher Plauelrain/Kapellenberg/Olberg/ Schlossberg/ Schloss Grohl/Steinberg The south-facing vineyards in the Durbach valley are some of the steepest in all Baden, and their granitic soil is ideal for Riesling, Scheurebe, and Gewürztraminer. The Plauelrain is the largest and best-known of these excellent sites.

Ihringer Winklerberg The steep, terraced Winklerberg at the southwestern tip of the Kaiserstuhl is the warmest vineyard in Germany. The volcanic tuff soil gives full-bodied, minerally, dry Grauer Burgunder and red Spätburgunder belonging to the finest Baden has to offer. The vineyard was expanded three-fold in 1971 to its present 150 hectares: quality can be inconsistent.

Neuweier Mauerberg/Schlossberg Close to Baden-Baden at the northern end of the Ortenau lie the terraced hillsides that form these fine south facing sites. Rieslings are intense and elegant, needing several years of ageing to show their best.

Oberrotweiler Eichberg/Henkenberg/Kirchberg The town of Oberrotweil, situated on the western flank of the Kaiserstuhl, boasts three first class sites, all of which give impressively rich, firmly structured, dry Weisser Burgunder and Grauer Burgunder wines.

Ortenberger Schlossberg The narrow terraces of this small site, with poor granitic soil, yield perhaps the most intensely minerally Rieslings of the Ortenau. In the sole ownership of the Schloss Ortenberg estate.

Zell-Weierbacher Abtsberg The best of the vineyards to the east of the town of Offenburg, the Abtsberg yields some of the richest wines in the Ortenau. Riesling, Grauer Burgunder, and Gewürztraminer give the best results.

The Kaiserstuhl

Leading Baden Producers

Abril ☆
Bischoffingen. www.abril.de
Hans Friedrich Abril's seven-hectare estate is a reliable source for full-bodied, dry Weisser Burgunder and Grauer Burgunder wines. Some interesting, if sometimes overpowering, Spätburgunder, too.

Winzergenossenschaft Achkarren ☆
Achkarren. www.achkarrer-wein.com
The 320 growers of this co-op produce, from 150 hectares, a wide range from some of the best sites of the Kaiserstuhl. Grauer Burgunder can be rather good, if sometimes alarmingly high in alcohol.

Bercher ☆☆☆
Burkheim. www.weingutbercher.de
Eckhardt Bercher and his brother, Rainer, run one of Baden's finest estates from an imposing seventeenth-century house in the beautifully preserved old town of Burkheim. Whether it is a simple Müller-Thurgau, sleek, dry Riesling Kabinett, or massive Weisser Burgunder Grosses Gewächs, their white wines are of a uniformly high standard. Since the late 1980s they have also made superb oak-aged Spätburgunders that are among Germany's finest red wines. Although most of the estate's wines are drunk shortly after release, everything of Spätlese or higher quality will benefit from at least five years of ageing. This is an estate where it is really possible to speak of a successful marriage of tradition and innovation. The Berchers are masters of their trade, so these are wines that can be bought and enjoyed with complete confidence.

Bercher-Schmidt ☆–☆☆
Oberrotweil. www.bercher-schmidt.de
Franz Schmidt has made a point of locating the original, and best, parcels in the much-enlarged vineyards of the Kaiserstuhl. Wines sourced from them are identified with a star system on his labels. The white wines are fresh and attractive, and see no oak. Schmidt has made great strides with Spätburgunder and has planted French clones to increase quality further.

Blankenhorn ☆
Schliengen. www.gutedel.de
Since taking over the family estate in 1989, Rosemarie Blankenhorn has restructured it and switched to organic viticulture. The estate is best-known for its Gutedel, but there are also sound dry whites from Grauer Burgunder and Weisser Burgunder. The red wines, from Spätburgunder and Bordeaux varieties, have improved considerably over recent years.

Duijn ☆☆–☆☆☆
Bühl-Kappelwindeck www.duijn.de
Dutchman Jacob Duijn, a former sommelier, specializes almost exclusively in high-priced Pinot Noir, aged in new barriques for up to 21 months and bottled without fining or filtration. From 2006, the range has been simplified and now consists of three single vineyard wines. Good clones, low yields, and careful winemaking have ensured consistently high quality here.

Winzergenossenschaft Durbach ☆☆
Durbach. www.durbacher.de
One of the best cooperatives in Germany, WG Durbach specializes in dry Rieslings and Spätburgunder. The slopes of Durbach are ideal territory for Riesling, and most of them are cultivated by the cooperative's 300 members. Sauvignon Blanc, a rarity in Baden, is a specialty here, and can be very good.

Freiherr von und zu Franckenstein ☆
Offenburg.
This estate's director/winemaker, Hubert Doll, produces juicy, elegant dry Rieslings, Grauer Burgunders, and Gewürztraminers from 14 hectares of vines on the granitic slopes of Zell-Weierbach and Berghaupten in the Ortenau. Spätburgunder, mostly aged in barriques, is far more stylish and concentrated than in the past.

Freiherr von Gleichenstein ☆☆
Oberrotweil. www.gleichenstein.de
This 24-hectare estate focuses on dry white wines from the Pinot family, which are full-bodied and rich. Quality, always sound, is set to increase after the hiring, in 1999, of a new cellarmaster, Odin Bauer. The excellent 2005s, from Spätburgunder as well as white varieties, confirm the wisdom of that appointment.

Dr. Heger ☆☆☆☆
Ihringen. www.heger-weine.de
Founded in 1935 by the country doctor Dr. Max Heger, this estate has grown rapidly in extent and reputation. Thanks to the efforts since 1992 of Dr. Heger's grandson, the dynamic Joachim Heger, it has become the best-known wine estate in Baden. This fame is primarily due to the powerful, dry Weisser Burgunder and Grauer Burgunder whites, the best of which see just a whiff of new oak. Other white varieties, such as Muskateller and Silvaner, even Riesling, can be extremely good here. The high priced Spätburgunders, aged in barriques, may not be the silkiest or most elegant Pinot Noirs in Germany, but for concentration they are hard to beat.

In 1997, Heger bought the Fischer estate in Bottingen, which in effect doubled the vineyards at his disposal. Top wines bear the Dr. Heger label; wines from lesser or leased vineyards are bottled as Weinhaus Joachim Heger and can also be of excellent quality. Somehow Joachim Heger also finds the time to harvest and produce superb TBAs in appropriate vintages such as 2005.

Reichsgraf und Marquis zu Hoensbroech ☆–☆☆
Angelbachtal-Michelfeld. www.hoensbroech.eu
Of Flemish origin, the Hoensbroechs have been in Germany since the seventeenth century, although this estate just south of Heidelberg is of much more recent origin. Their best wine is usually the powerful, dry Weisser Burgunder. The estate also has some red varieties, notably Lemberger and Schwarzriesling, more commonly encountered in Württemberg.

Bernhard Huber ☆☆☆
Malterdingen. www.weingut-huber.com
After leaving the local cooperative in 1987, Bernhard Huber swiftly acquired an unwavering reputation for his

Spätburgunder. There are numerous *cuvées*, and the best of these – the R for Reserve bottlings – are among Germany's finest red wines. For many years the red wines were blends, but in recent vintages Huber has released three single-vineyard wines, including one from the Hecklinger Schlossberg, which is planted to a very high density of 13,000 vines per hectare As for the whites, his new-oaked Malterer is an idiosyncratic blend of Pinot Blanc and the obscure local crossing Freisamer with considerable character – more than the powerful but very oaky Chardonnay.

Karl H Johner ☆☆☆
Bischoffingen. www.johner.de
Karl Heinz Johner built his estate up from scratch, and decided from the outset not to employ vineyard names. Almost all the wines are oak-aged dry varietals, and the best of them are reserve bottlings designated "S J" (Selektion Johner). The finest wines are usually the Weisser Burgunder dry whites and Spätburgunder reds. Yields are kept very low, so the wines are concentrated and powerful, with sufficient structure to absorb the oak ageing. Johner uses less new oak than in the past, although the Spätburgunder "S J" is still aged in new barrels. Johner, assisted for some years by his son Patrick, is unquestionably the most successful of the international-style producers of Baden.

Weingut Franz Keller/Schwarzer Adler ☆☆–☆☆☆
Oberbergen. www.franz-keller.de
With 50 hectares at his disposal, Fritz Keller is able to produce a wide range of wines. He has been an advocate of barrel ageing for many years, and some of his top wines, such as the Weisser Burgunder A, are aged in new 500-litre barrels. Rather than single vineyards, Keller uses letters to denote quality, A being the most concentrated, S being the second tier. The Spätburgunders are among the most intense, and

alcoholic, examples to be found from Baden. The best place to sample the wines is at the family's Schwarzer Adler restaurant, one of the best in Baden, although it's easy to be tempted by its magnificent list of French wines.

Knab ☆☆
Endingen. www.knabweingut.de
Almost all of the vines of this 15-hectare estate are planted in Endinger Engelsberg, on the eastern side of the Kaiserstuhl. All the Burgundian varieties thrive here and this has become an excellent source of robust but well-balanced wines at sensible prices.

Winzergenossenschaft Königsschaffhausen ☆–☆☆
Königsschaffhausen. www.koenigsschaffhauser-wein.de
In the 1990s this Kaiserstuhl cooperative won an excellent reputation for its wines. Sweet wines, such as majestic Ruländer TBAs, were a particular speciality, but no producer can survive on the basis of sweet wines alone, and Königsschaffhausen has also won acclaim for its dry wines from Weisser Burgunder, Grauer Burgunder, and Spätburgunder, some of them aged in barriques.

Andreas Laible ☆☆☆–☆☆☆☆
Durbach. www.weingut-laible.de
No self-publicist, Andreas Laible's winemaking talents only came to the attention of a wider public during the 1990s. His elegant, intensely fruity, dry, and naturally sweet Rieslings have almost Mosel-like character, being intense and racy. The top dry Riesling is labelled Achat. Just as impressive are his powerful Scheurebe and Traminer Auslese, and higher Prädikat dessert wines, which are among Baden's finest wines.

Lämmlin-Schindler ☆☆
Mauchen. www.laemmlin-schindler.de
This organic estate is a leading quality-wine producer of the

---

AGEING GERMAN WINES

Good-quality German wines have a much longer life span, and benefit much more from being kept in bottle, than fashion suggests or most people suppose. This does not apply, of course, to the cheap blends and the major brands, which are specifically intended to be ready to drink within months of being bottled. With the enormous crops (and hence the high water content) of these wines, there is, indeed, no gain from keeping bottles more than a few months.

But almost all the superior-grade (QmP) Rieslings, delectable as they may taste in their flowery and fruity youth, have the potential to gain another dimension of flavour with maturity. When they are first offered for sale, they are at their most brisk and lively, with acidity and fruitiness often tending to cancel

each other out in a generally tingling and exciting effect. Some fine wines (particularly Rieslings) at this stage have remarkably little aroma. Sometimes, after a year or two in bottle, the first rapture goes away without more mature flavours taking its place; the wine you bought with enthusiasm seems to be letting you down. Be patient. The subtle alchemy takes longer. It may be four or five years before the mingled savours of citrus and spice and oil emerge. The pale colour of a young Riesling will evolve into a brilliant yellow-gold, and the aromas will become more honeyed and complex.

Each vintage has its own time span, but as a generalization, Kabinett wines from a first-rate grower need at least three years in bottle, and may improve for seven or eight; Spätlesen will improve

for anything from four to ten years; and Auslesen and upwards will benefit from five or six years up to 20 or even more. The highly concentrated sweet wines – Eiswein, BA, and TBA – are more or less indestructible, but are usually at their peak at 25 years. Riesling is the most age-worthy of German wines, but varieties such as Scheurebe and Rieslaner will also improve with bottle age.

Until the 1980s, red wines were almost always made for immediate consumption, but with the adoption of Burgundian techniques such as low yields, long maceration on the skins, and a greater structure given to the best wines by ageing them in barriques, a good Spätburgunder from the Pfalz, Franken, or Baden can age for up to ten years.

Markgräflerland. Its elegant Weisser Burgunder and Grauer Burgunder are among the most sophisticated dry white wines made in Baden, and even the simple Gutedel is extremely well-crafted. Gerd Schindler was slow to get to grips with red wine production, but since 2003 quality has been much improved.

Markgraf von Baden: Schloss Staufenberg ☆☆
Durbach. www.markgraf-von-baden.de
This homely old manor on a hill, with skirting vineyards, is a place of great charm, producing delicate and sometimes distinguished dry Rieslings. Both Riesling and Traminer were planted here in the eighteenth century, so this is an estate rich in tradition. The red wines lag behind the whites in quality. The Markgraf also owns a very large wine estate in the Bodensee, but the Durbach wines are considerably more interesting.

Staatsweingut Meersburg ☆
Meersburg. www.staatsweingut-meersburg.de
Formerly the estate of the Prince-Bishops of Meersburg, this property became, in 1802, Germany's first state domain, its land largely in Meersburg, on the banks of the Bodensee (Lake Constance). The specialties are Müller-Thurgau of the gentler kind, Weisser Burgunder, and lively Spätburgunder.

Gebrüder Müller ☆
Breisach. www.weingut-gebr-mueller.de
Peter Bercher's ten-hectare estate boasts a sizeable holding in the great Ihringer Winklerberg vineyard in the Kaiserstuhl, and can claim to have made this site's reputation during the first half of the nineteenth century. Good as the dry white wines often are, it is the substantial Spätburgunder reds that rightly attract most of the attention.

Nägelsförst ☆–☆☆
Baden-Baden. www.naegelsfoerst.de
This former monastic estate was revived by Reinhard Strickler, who has focused on varietal wines rather than highlighting individual vineyards, although the renowned Neuweier Mauerberg is singled out for its fine dry Riesling. Almost all the wines, white as well as red, are barrel aged.

Schloss Neuweier ☆☆☆
Neuweier. www.weingut-schloss-neuweier.de
Since purchasing the run-down Schloss Neuweier estate in 1992, Gisela Joos and her winemaker Alexander Spinner have put this property back into the first rank of Baden's quality wine producers. The great majority of the production is dry Riesling of considerable sophistication that is capable of long ageing. Those from the Mauerberg vineyard are distinctly minerally, those from the Schlossberg are a touch weightier.

Schloss Ortenberg ☆–☆☆
Ortenberg. www.weingut-schloss-ortenberg.de
The castle of Schloss Ortenberg belongs to the German youth hostel association, and its vineyards were purchased for it in 1950 by the regional council. A merger in 1997 with another estate brought the total area of its vineyards to 46 hectares.

Ever since Winfried Köninger was appointed director in 1991, standards have improved considerably. A wide range of grapes is cultivated, with the best results coming from Riesling and Spätburgunder grapes, although the Sauvignon Blanc is also noteworthy.

Salwey ☆☆☆
Oberrotweil. www.salwey.de
As well as producing some beautifully perfumed fruit brandies, Wolf-Dietrich Salwey and his son Konrad make some of the finest white wines in the Kaiserstuhl. Although many of the white wines are still traditionally vinified, winemaker Konrad has introduced some barrique-ageing for Reserve wines designated "RS". The rich but elegant dry Weisser Burgunder and Grauer Burgunder have excellent ageing potential. Almost half the vineyards are planted with Spätburgunder, which is now the source of three splendid Grosses Gewächs wines.

His dry Spätburgunder Weissherbst wines from the Glottertal are among the finest of all German rosés. The estate's occasional dessert wines are also impressive. Only the red wines do not yet measure up to the highest standards.

Hartmut Schlumberger ☆☆
Laufen. www.schlumbergerwein.de
This old family manor, between Freiburg and Basel in the heart of the Markgräflerland, is mostly planted with Spätburgunder, Weisser Burgunder, and Gutedel. Hartmut Schlumberger has handed over the running of the estate to his son-in-law Ulrich Bernhart, who continues to produce sturdy dry wines from the Pinot varieties, white and red.

Reinhold und Cornelia Schneider ☆☆–☆☆☆☆
Endingen. www.weingutschneider.com
Reinhold Schneider runs his eight-hectare estate along more or less organic lines. His soils are varied, though not exceptional, so rather than identify individual sites on the label, he has evolved a code to indicate the soil type: volcanic, loess, or loam. Wines labelled "Trio" are a blend of all three. The wines are of a very high standard, although some recent vintages have shown punishing levels of alcohol.

Seeger ☆☆–☆☆☆☆
Leimen. www.seegerweingut.de
Located just south of Heidelberg, this small estate, which celebrated its 300th birthday in 2007, has leapt vastly in quality over recent years. Thomas Seeger's Spätburgunders, aged in a good deal of new oak, are well up there with Baden's best, although they can be very extracted and are decidedly expensive. There is also a blend called Cuvée Anna, from Spätburgunder, Lemberger, and Portugieser, which is aged 20 months – rather too long – in barriques. The estate's much improved Weisser Burgunder, Grauer Burgunder, and Riesling also deserve to be taken seriously.

Rudolf Stigler ☆☆–☆☆☆☆
Ihringen. www.weingut-stigler.de
One of the best private estates in the Kaiserstuhl, known particularly for its Riesling and Spätburgunder from the Winklerberg. These are wines with weight, minerality, and great length of flavour. Andreas Stigler's style is deliberately traditional, if not old-fashioned, emphasizing body and extract rather than the fruit itself.

Fritz Wassmer ☆☆–☆☆☆
Bad Krozingen. www.weingut-wassmer-schlatt.de
Wassmer has Burgundy in his sights, having planted French clones to a very high density in some of his 18 hectares of vineyards, two thirds of which are planted with Spätburgunder. These are probably Wassmer's best wines, but he gamely tries his hand with atypical, for Baden, varieties such as Viognier, Syrah, and Cabernet Franc. Although a fairly new estate, its ascent into the top ranks has been swift.

Graf Wolff Metternich ☆–☆☆☆
Durbach. www.weingut-metternich.de
In the late 1990s this noble estate of 36 hectares was sold to the Hurrle family. But cellarmaster Franz Schwörer remains in place, crafting fine Riesling from the best Durbach sites. A house specialty is Sauvignon Blanc, made from cuttings apparently brought here from Château d'Yquem in 1830. The wines benefit from bottle-age.

Ziereisen ☆–☆☆☆
Efringen. www.ziereisen.de
Hanspeter Ziereisen dispenses with vineyard designations and offers a wide range of varietal wines from his ten-hectare estate. Gutedel is the principal white grape, but red wines are the specialty. As well as rather extracted and oaky Spätburgunder, Ziereisen tries his hand at Syrah, which can be rather green.

Saale-Unstrut

A short distance to the south of Halle and to the west of Leipzig lie the 658 hectares of vineyards that form the Saale-Unstrut region (until 1989 they lay within East Germany). The name comes from the two idyllic river valleys that offer shelter to some of Germany's most easterly and northerly vineyards. The region itself is centred around the historic town of Naumburg, which is home to a splendid Gothic-Romanesque cathedral. It was in fact the church that brought serious viticulture to the region when the associated Cistercian monastery of Pforta was founded in 1137.

Even today, Saale-Unstrut still suffers from the hangover of the communist period. Almost half of the region's wines are made by the Freyburg cooperative to a fairly low standard. But there are clear signs that the region is now finding its feet. The area under vine has doubled since 1990, and there are now around 50 private estates, though only a handful are making noteworthy wines in reasonable quantities. They are now managing to start demonstrating that the limestone soils of the best sites are in fact capable of producing subtly aromatic, mid-weight, dry Weisser Burgunder, Riesling, and Traminer, though Müller-Thurgau is the most widely planted variety. Pinot Noir used to be a very common grape here a century ago, but it fell into disfavour in the 1960s because of difficulties with ripening and vinification; neither of these fitted into the industrial standardization of communist East Germany. Today, however, it is being revived, and Riesling, too, is on the increase.

Leading Saale-Unstrut Producers

Klaus Böhme ☆
Naumburg. www.weingut-klaus-boehme.de
Böhme was one of the first growers in the region to resume wine production, and by 1994 had assembled enough land to launch his range. Today he succeeds best with Riesling and Weisser Burgunder.

Gussek ☆–☆☆☆
Naumburg. www.winzerhof-gussek.de
André Gussek used to be the cellarmaster at Kloster Pforta (q.v.), but has been slowly establishing his own six-hectare estate. He is keen on red wines, which account for one quarter of production, and the best of these is usually the Zweigelt. The Silvaner is sound and the Weisser Burgunders surprisingly rich in alcohol.

Landesweingut Kloster Pforta ☆
Bad Kösen. www.kloster-pforta.de
This property was established in 1899 by the Prussian state, and endowed with excellent terraced vineyards along the River Saale. It has been through a period of instability, with frequent changes in management, and this has affected consistency and quality. The estate has a higher proportion of Riesling than any other in the region, and both Riesling and Weisser Burgunder can have a firm, mineral quality. Overall, quality is disappointing considering the vineyards at the estate's disposal.

Lützkendorf ☆☆
Bad Kösen. www.weingut-luetzkendorf.de
After resigning as director of the Landesweingut Kloster Pforta following German reunification in 1989, Udo Lützkendorf founded his own wine estate. It is now run by his son, Uwe, who is already setting exemplary standards: his dry Weisser Burgunder, Riesling, and Silvaner are clearly the best wines made in the region. Full of fruit, crisp acidity, and enough vigour to improve with up to five years of bottle ageing, they prove what the beautiful Saale-Unstrut region is capable of producing.

Pawis ☆☆
Freyburg. www.weingut-pawis.de
Riesling and Weisser Burgunder tend to be the best wines from this ten-hectare estate. Both varieties find their best expression as Grosses Gewächs from Freyburger Edelacker, although the acidity of these wines can be quite pronounced.

Sachsen

The 411 hectares of vineyards dotted along the Elbe valley, around the historic cities of Dresden and Meissen, form the smallest wine-growing region in Germany. During the reign of Sachsen's mighty ruler, August the Strong, in the first half of the eighteenth century, the vineyard area was far greater than it is today, and records indicate that the wines from Sachsen's top vineyard sites were regarded as being among Germany's finest. Since then, the phylloxera plague of the late nineteenth century, economic crises, war, and dictatorship came close to eradicating the region's great wine culture. As in Saale-Unstrut, the structure of the wine industry is dominated by only two producers: the cooperative of Meissen, which accounts for one-third of the region's production, and the Sächsisches Winzergenossenschaft, which makes up almost another third.

However, a growing number of independent wine-growers are now making increasingly sophisticated dry wines from a handful of grape varieties, which suggest that Sachsen may once again start producing wines of distinction. Traminer, Riesling, Weisser Burgunder, and Grauer Burgunder have the most potential. The granite and ancient igneous rock soils result in wines that are more racy and minerally than those of Saale-Unstrut.

Leading Sachsen Producers

Schloss Proschwitz ☆☆
Zadel über Meissen. www.schloss-proschwitz.de
In 1991, Dr. Georg Prinz zur Lippe bought back his family's Meissen vineyards to recreate the ancient Proschwitz estate. He has also expanded the estate so that its holdings now stand at an astonishing 70 hectares. Proschwitz succeeds well with Riesling, Scheurebe, Weisser Burgunder, and Grauer Burgunder, which are clean, tight, and polished. The red wines remain rather thin, except in superripe years such as 2003.

Vincenz Richter ☆
Meissen. www.vincenz-richter.de
Thomas Herrlich supplements his eight-hectare estate with purchases from other vineyards. The wines, from Riesling, Weisser Burgunder, and Traminer, are mostly *trocken* and *halbtrocken*.

Schloss Wackerbarth ☆–☆☆
Radebeul. www.schloss-wackerbarth.de
The best sites belonging to this 90-hectare estate lie on terraced vineyards rising up behind the baroque mansion on the outskirts of Dresden. By 1989, the estate was in terrible shape, and much effort has been expended by the local bank that owns the property on renovating the vineyards and winery. The turning point was 1999, when flabby, lacklustre wines were replaced by zestier bottlings.

A large part of the output is of sparkling wine, most of it rather sweet and ungainly. There are good Rieslings (from the Radebeuler Goldener Wagen vineyard) and Weisser Burgunder, but with the resources at its disposal, there is still room for improvement.

Klaus Zimmerling ☆☆
Pillnitz.
Sachsen's most intriguing wine estate came into existence in 1987, when Klaus Zimmerling began clearing and replanting ancient vineyard terraces with the help of friends. Despite the climate, he has opted for organic viticulture, and yields are extremely low. Today, he has a growing reputation for sophisticated, dry Rieslings, Traminers, and Grauer Burgunders. The labels are adorned with examples of his wife's sculpture, making this the most stylish packaging of any wine estate in the former East Germany.

Luxembourg

Luxembourg has some 1,250 hectares of vines along the upper Mosel, above Trier. There are about 1,000 small growers, but 65 per cent of the country's wine is made in cooperatives. The industry is highly organized and controlled. Since 1985, all wines are graded by the Institut Viti-Vinicole in one of five qualities: *non admis* (not passed), *marque nationale*, *vin classé*, *premier cru*, and *grand premier cru*. In 1991, a new appellation for Crémant du Luxembourg was created, supplementing the previous single appellation, Moselle Luxembourgeoise. These ultra-fresh sparkling wines can be bargains.

The grape varieties grown in Luxembourg are: Rivaner (Müller-Thurgau), Elbling, Riesling, Auxerrois, and, in smaller quantities, Gewürztraminer, Pinot Gris, Pinot Blanc, and Pinot Noir. However, those workhorse grapes Müller-Thurgau and Elbling are in decline, and more Chardonnay, mostly for use in sparkling wine, is being planted. Yields can easily reach 140 hectolitres per hectare, which makes its neighbour Germany look high-minded in comparison. Elbling produces very weak juice, but considerable quantities of light, often fizzy, and refreshing wines are made from a blend of Elbling and Rivaner. Rivaner is reliable; Auxerrois occasionally extremely charming – an original specialty with no real counterpart – especially from Wasserbillig; Riesling always lean but sometimes classic. Pinot Noir makes very pale but pleasant wines.

The Domaine et Tradition estates association, founded in 1988 by seven wineries, promotes quality from noble varieties, largely by restricting yields to 70 hectolitres per hectare. Major producers are Caves Bernard-Massard at Grevenmacher (good Cuvée de l'Ecusson classic-method sparkling) and Les Domaines de Vinsmoselles at Stadtbredimus (the organization of cooperatives). Others are Cep d'Or at Hëttermillen (fine *crémant* and Pinot Blanc); Alice Hartmann at Wormeldange (elegant Riesling); Kohll-Reuland at Ehnen (good *crémant*); Abi Duhr at Ahn (nutty, oak-aged Pinot Blanc); Mathis Bastian, Caves Krier Frères, Caves Gales, and Caves St Rémy at Remich (also the HQ of the Government Viticultural Station); and Henri Ruppert (good Auxerrois) and Thill Frères at Schengen.

Other good wines come from Gloden, Schumacher-Knepper (silky Riesling), Charles Decker (*vin de glace*), and Schmit-Fohl (Pinot Gris). Surprisingly, given the climate, some rather good straw wines are being made, often from Auxerrois.

Belgium

The Belgians claim to have been producing wine since the thirteenth century, although Napoleon put a stop to the industry by decreeing that the vineyards should be uprooted. However, in the 1960s there was a tentative return to viticulture. Today some 12 estates cultivate Müller-Thurgau, Kerner, all three Pinot varieties, Chardonnay, Riesling, and Auxerrois. Two of the larger properties are Clos des Agaises and Genoels Elderen.

Italy

Is there a more anarchic, inventive, fascinating wine country than Italy? The major wines of France have been schooled by export markets; Italy for years kept most of her wines to herself. Localities hugged their own specialties: even today, Italy seems an only loosely united country. But one with with an astonishing range of wine flavours, derived from a wealth of indigenous vines. The palette is extraordinary, with some 1,000 grape varieties in cultivation. Even if half of them are mere local curiosities that still gives us 500 of real interest.

It should be no surprise that some of the world's best wines come from Italy, and yet many people are still sceptical. During the two-and-a-half centuries when France was building the formidable structure and reputation of her quality-wine industry and propagating her superlative vines, Italy was doing no such thing. Wine, like loyalty, remained very much a local, even a family, affair. Like bread, it was no less important for being taken for granted. But it was not measured even by national, let alone international, standards until well into this century. And when it was, Italy was inevitably judged as a source of low-priced wine, either for cheap-and-cheerful drinking or to be passed off as something else. To this day, an almost incredible quantity slinks anonymously out of the country in tankers to other parts of the EU, and even within the country surreptitious, and illegal, inter-regional blending does the reputation of Italian wine no favours. High-quality wine depends entirely on demand, and nobody demanded it in Italy.

The Italians have not helped themselves by rejoicing in ever-more-complicated wine labels. For non-Italians, even the most interested is often blocked by a lilting litany of tuneful polysyllables in which not just the name of the wine and its maker but that of his property – and often an additional fantasy name for good measure – all appear equally important.

Recent years have seen some dramatic changes in attitude and practice, as winemakers joyfully experiment with untraditional ideas, grape varieties, and techniques. Unfortunately the result often consists of distinctive wines with designer labels (and bottles) at high-fashion prices not always justified by their quality. This producer-led revolution circumvents, or even ignores, the rules enshrined in the DOC system described below. On the other hand, this libertarian approach to wine production has also resulted, in some instances, in truly exciting wines that have become the standard-bearers for the new Italy.

New developments at official level have proved equally important. The wine-law of 1992 introduced a realization of a quality-pyramid philosophy. It peaks with wines that are subject to the strictest controls. DOCG (Denominazione di Origine Controllata e Garantita) and DOC (Denominazione di Origine Controllata) follow. There are over 325 of them, and they account for 20 per cent of Italian wine production. Half-way between the DOC wines and the next level, *vini da tavola* (table wines), are the IGT wines (Indicazione Geografica Tipica); these are wines with grape variety names, from a larger production area, and with more tolerant quality criteria than DOC wines. The IGT provides a clearer identity for much of what was the *vini da tavola* flood. It also enables greater control of this production, as IGT wines, unlike *vini da tavola*, are subject to maximum crop limitations. However, the consumer may still find himself at sea, as the IGT category includes both wines of little character and substance, and wines of exceptional quality that just happen to fall outside the criteria of the DOC/DOCG system.

The DOC was instituted in 1963 as a necessary regulatory system for Italian quality wines – an approximate equivalent to the French AC. A DOC is a very detailed legal stipulation as to the precise character, origin, grapes, crop levels, strength, methods, and ageing of a particular wine or group of wines, agreed between the consortium of its producers and an expert committee in Rome. Previous editions of this book have listed individual DOC regulations in considerable detail. In practice, however, most good producers obey those rules they believe contribute to the quality or typicity of a wine, while ignoring those (such as traditional excessive wood ageing) that are, in their view, detrimental to quality. For example, until a few years ago, it was mandatory to include a proportion of white grapes in Chianti Classico. This absurd rule benefitted growers with a lot of Trebbiano in their vineyards. But it clearly could not improve the quality of a Sangiovese-based wine, so the best growers quietly ignored it. So, DOC listings below now focus on the most important features of each DOC rather than a list of detailed regulations. Moreover, the major overhaul of wine categories and denominations planned by the EU for 2009 may well make many, if not all, existing DOCs obsolete. We will have to wait and see how Italians will react.

It is the great paradox of Italian wine today that a DOC freezes a type of wine in an historical moment. A DOC is essentially the definition of a tradition – at the very moment when wine technology has reached a pitch undreamed of before, when California (the outstanding example) is using its freedom to experiment to produce more exciting wine every year. The reader of this book, therefore, should make no absolute qualitative distinction between DOC and other wines, beyond that a DOC is "traditional" and subject to official regulation. Another step in the regulation of certain DOCs was instigated with the creation of an additional category: DOCG. The "G" stands for Garantita, implying that the wines are guaranteed as Italy's best. They are, indeed, the best geographically controlled wines. The first four DOCGs were Barbaresco, Barolo, Brunello di Montalcino, and Vino Nobile di Montepulciano. Albana di Romagna was the next to be added to the list though anyone who tastes it may be forgiven for asking how seriously the "G" is to be taken. Some more recent additions also suggest that promotion to DOCG is as much a political matter as an acknowledgment of imposing quality. It is hard to summarize the present state of Italian winemaking. Recent investments in modern equipment and new ideas have produced some wonderful results, but have also stripped old friends of their character. So far, the modern movement has succeeded in making both the most boring and the most brilliant wines. Those who feared Italy would be drowned in a tide of international varieties have been proven wrong. Although Italian producers are trying their hand at Cabernet Sauvignon, Merlot, Chardonnay, and Syrah (and why not?), they have also remained true to their traditional varieties. There is a balance to be found between tradition and technology (in grapes, cellaring, and every aspect of winemaking) and Italy is very busy looking for it.

If the present DOC/DOCG system reinforces tradition, the broad criteria of the IGT designation encourage innovation. Thus proprietors and winemakers are free, like Proust's narrator, to follow either of two paths, or both. No one would deny that the outcome has been almost wholly positive. In regions with a long history, such as Piedmont or Tuscany, quality at the top level has never been higher. In regions that were once a byword for mediocrity, such as Sicily, the full potential of the sun-drenched slopes is at last being realized. White wines, never Italy's strongest suit, now attain high international standards in Friuli and the Alto Adige, while newer regions such as Campania are snapping at their heels. The only blot on the landscape is the Italian penchant for fiddling the rules: sometimes in a good cause, as when gifted winemakers ignore DOC regulations that undermine quality, sometimes in a bad cause, when illegal blending is practised simply to improve profit margins. Overall, however, it is clear that Italy, along with Spain, has become Europe's most dynamic wine country in the current century.

The method of access to the essentials in the following pages tries to make the problems of identifying and judging Italy's wines as simple as possible. This is how it works. The country is divided into 20 regions. Each is treated separately, in two parts. First come the names and descriptions of the wines, then a wide selection of the better and bigger winemakers, with brief accounts of their standing, methods, size, and a list of the wines they offer. If you know the name of the wine or the maker but not the region, the only place to start is the index. If you know the region, go straight to the wine or the maker. Cross-referencing goes from maker to wine but not (to avoid a repetitive list) the other way round. The only list of producers, for example, of Chianti Classico is the list of winemakers in Tuscany, in which you will find that many Chianti makers also make other wines.

Piedmont

For uninhibited exploration of the varieties of grapes and what can be made from them, no part of Europe can compare with Piedmont (Piemonte in Italian). Its steep hills offer such an assortment of indigenous grapes that international varieties have scarcely been planted at all. Each of the local grapes is a character with something to offer. Each is made into wine unblended, often in several styles, and also mixed with others in brews, which may be traditional or experimental, conventional or idiosyncratic. The former are frequently blessed with DOCs and DOCGs, the latter not – but this has no bearing on their respective qualities.

The emphasis is mostly on red wine, although Moscato has a long history in the region, present in various guises but none better known than Asti Spumante. The Cortese is also a good white grape, now proving itself in Gavi, and Arneis is enjoyed a well-deserved vogue in the Langhe region, but the catechism of important Piedmont wines must start with a list of the red

ITALY IN ROUND FIGURES

1   The production by region in hectolitres (2006–2007)
2   Percentage of production registered as DOC

	1	2
Piedmont	2,724,000	84
Valle d'Aosta	18,000	23
Lombardy	1,080,000	47
Trentino-Alto Adige	1,220,000	85
Veneto	7,500,000	42
Friuli	1,020,000	65
Liguria	89,000	14
Emilia-Romagna	6,500,000	35
Tuscany	2,800,000	57
Umbria	998,000	31
Marche	1,256,000	48
Lazio	2,310,000	7
Abruzzo	3,800,000	8.5
Molise	319,000	4
Campania	1,800,000	44
Puglia	6,500,000	15
Basilicata	221,000	1.6
Calabria	406,100	21
Sicily	6,500,000	4
Sardinia	859,000	15
Italy	**48,000,000**	

grapes that enjoy the harsh climate of this sub-Alpine area.

Nebbiolo comes first in quality. It takes its name from the fog (*nebbia*) that characterizes autumn here, not only closing Milan airport regularly but also creating quintessentially mellow, fruitful pictures of gold-leaved vines tilting up to the grey hilltop villages. The 490-metre (1,592-foot) Langhe hills south of Alba on the River Tanaro provide the slopes, shelter, soil, sunshine, and humidity that bring Nebbiolo to perfection in Barolo (southwest of Alba) and Barbaresco (to its east). The style of Barolo, a wine of the maximum concentration, tannin, and alcohol, has no very ancient history but it does have conviction, and its growers' palates are ready for as much power as their vines will give them. The inexperienced, the timid, and the claret-lovers should start with Nebbiolo in its milder, less explosive manifestations, such as Nebbiolo d'Alba or Roero. Barbera comes first in quantity. But it, too, carries conviction. It can be clumsy, but good Barbera – which is to say, Barbera that has not been overcropped – is plummy and astringent in just the right measure, and its refreshing acidity makes it an admirable wine with hearty but unpretentious food.

Dolcetto is quite different. No other red grape succeeds in conveying such an impression of softness, while being sometimes startlingly dry. It sounds odd, but with rich food it makes a tantalizing meal opener; it is a marvellous complement to antipasti, especially the cold meats. Dolcetto is not normally for ageing. The village of Dogliani is its heartland, and some growers there are doing their best to give the wine a dogged seriousness by ageing it in new oak, an experiment that rarely improves on the original concept of Dolcetto as a juicy wine that is above all else fruit driven.

In complete contrast, Freisa is inclined to be fizzy and sometimes even sweet, and again in contrast, Grignolino tends to the pale, mild but teasingly bitter style of wine, which is common in northwest Italy. However, some producers, such as Vajra, make an impressive and powerful dry Freisa that can age well. Add the lively, light Bonarda and the Croatina and Vespolina and the range of possible cocktails is almost limitless.

The following list reflects the complexity of the region with more DOCs and DOCGs than any other – and lots of unofficial "table" wines besides. Regional DOCs such as Langhe, Monferrato, and Piemonte serve not only to give a legal home to huge quantities of not-yet DOC wines, but also to legalize the blending of two or more varieties, by creating new appellations for such wines.

Nowhere in Italy, it's arguable, is the use of French oak been as controversial as here. Traditionalists have always aged wines such as Barolo, Barbera, and Dolcetto in large casks, whereas modernists such as Elio Altare and Angelo Gaja began ageing their wines in barriques in the 1980s. There is little point coming down on one side or the other. There are great "traditional" Piedmontese wines, and great "modernist" ones, and these days most producers adopt the best practices from both approaches. The quality of the fruit harvested is usually of far more importance than the container used to age the wine.

Would that there were space here for more than a low bow towards the best fare of Italy: the truffles, the *fonduta*, the game, and all the simple but sensuous things that give these wines their proper context.

DOC & Other Wines

Albugnano DOC. Red and *rosato* wine. Province: Asti. Villages: four within Monferrato district. Grape: Nebbiolo (minimum 85%). Obscure appellation for a relatively light Nebbiolo.

Barbaresco DOCG. Red wine. Province: Cuneo. Villages: Barbaresco, Neive, Treiso. Grape: Nebbiolo.

The immediate neighbour of Barolo, sharing most of its qualities of power and depth, youthful harshness, and eventual perfumed sweetness. Great Barbaresco has a style and polish it is hard to define; it is tempting, though inaccurate, to call it the Côte-Rôtie to the Hermitage of Barolo. Neither lives as long or develops so sumptuously as the best Rhône wines; but many bottlings (particularly the wines from Gaja, although he is by no means alone) have added new superlatives to Italy's wine vocabulary: the most luxurious, the most vigorous, silky, incisive, and memorable.

Barbera d'Alba DOC. Red wine. Province: Cuneo. Villages: many around Alba. Grape: Barbera.

Barbera wines are ubiquitous in Piedmont, but the best of them fall into one of three DOCs. Alba is considered the best area for full-bodied Barbera apt for ageing – though the style is entirely at the producer's discretion. It is also the case that the best sites in Alba are devoted to Nebbiolo, with Barbera being planted on sites that are less well-exposed.

Barbera d'Asti DOC. Red wine. Provinces: Asti, Alessandria. Villages: from Casale Monferrato to Acqui Terme. Grape: Barbera.

Critics disagree on whether this or Alba gives the best Barbera. Over the past decade, Barbera, often planted on the best sites, since Asti is not primarily a Nebbiolo zone, yields outstanding results here.

Barbera del Monferrato DOC. Red wine. Provinces: Asti, Alessandria. Villages: a large number of the above provinces. Grapes: Barbera (85–90%), Freisa, Grignolino, Dolcetto (10–15%).

The optional addition of other grapes, and an acceptance of higher yields than for the other Barbera appellations, make this the least serious of the DOC Barberas, although some very good bottles exist.

Barolo DOCG. Red wine. Province: Cuneo. Villages: Barolo, Castiglione Falletto, Serralunga d'Alba, La Morra, Monforte d'Alba, Verduno, parts of other communes. Grape: Nebbiolo.

If Barolo gives the palate a wrestling match, it makes its eventual yielding all the more satisfying. It takes practice to understand this powerful, astringent wine. For several years all flavour and most smell is masked and inaccessible. What is hidden is an extraordinary spectrum of scents (tar, truffles, violets, faded roses, incense, plums, raspberries have all been found). With such traditional Barolos, maturity comes on quite suddenly at about ten years and little is gained by keeping bottles beyond 15. The trend, though, is for more generous, though by no means easy, wines, often barrique-aged, whose softer tannins make them more accessible sooner without shortening – indeed probably adding to – their long-term potential. In few areas anywhere has modern philosophy so successfully updated a natural classic.

The best vineyards are often signalled on the labels with the dialect words *sorì* (meaning a steep, sheltered slope) or *bricco/bric* (a ridge). La Morra makes the earliest-developing and arguably most elegant wines, Monforte and Serralunga the slowest.

Barolo Chinato A domestic tradition among Barolo growers is to brew apéritifs and cordials with their wine. This, the

14th century castle of Cavour, Piedmont

best-known *amaro*, is made bitter with an infusion of china bark and quinine. Another recipe includes green walnuts, tansy, garlic, cloves, and cinnamon.

Boca DOC. Red wine. Province: Novara. Villages: Boca, parts of four others. Grapes: Nebbiolo (Spanna, 45–70%), Vespolina, Bonarda Novarese (Uva Rara).

One of several dry reds from the hills north of Novara, where Nebbiolo is called Spanna. Blending with other grapes lightens this one. Tiny production.

Bonarda Piemontese Bonarda is a light red grape mostly grown in north Piedmont for blending. It can be fresh and pleasant on its own. Its own DOC is Piemonte Bonarda DOC.

Brachetto d'Acqui DOCG. Red wine. Provinces: Asti, Alessandria. Villages: Acqui Terme, Nizza Monferrato, 24 others. Grape: Brachetto.

A light, sweet, fizzy red, with more than a touch of Muscat in the aroma. The best have delicacy and charm and, like much Moscato d'Asti, it very low in alcohol.

Bramaterra DOC. Red wine. Province: Vercelli. Villages: Massarano, Brusnengo, Cruino Roasio, Villa del Bosco, Sostegno, Lozzolo. Grapes: Nebbiolo (Spanna, 50–70%), Croatina, Bonarda and/or Vespolina.

A big, solid, blended red from the Vercelli hills, improving with age. Sold in Bordeaux style bottles. Only 28 hectares remain.

Canavese DOC. Red, white, and *rosato* wine. Provinces: Torino, Vercelli, Biella. Numerous villages. Grapes: Nebbiolo, Barbera, Freisa, Croatina, Neretto, Erbaluce.

Fairly light wines from the border with Valle d'Aosta. Only 53 hectares produce the wine. The DOC was established in 1996.

Carema DOC. Red wine. Province: Torino. Village: Carema. Grape: Nebbiolo.

A wine from the borders of Piedmont and Valle d'Aosta; a relatively lightweight Nebbiolo (minimum 85%) that can gain in finesse what it loses in power. The terrain is steep and terraced; the climate cool; and prices (especially in ski resorts) can be excessive.

Colli Tortonesi DOC. Red and white wine. Province: Alessandria. Villages: Tortona, 29 others. Grapes: Barbera (100%), Freisa (maximum 15%), Bonarda, Dolcetto; Cortese, Timorasso.

A good-quality Barbera blend with ageing potential, and a very light, dry Cortese white tending to sharpness and sometimes fizzy. More serious wine is made by Martinetti using the interesting, and scarce, Timorasso grape.

Cortese DOC. White wine. Provinces: Asti, Cuneo, Alessandria. Villages: A large part of the above provinces. Grape: Cortese (85%).

An increasingly popular DOC for dry Cortese, still or sparkling, at a humbler level than that of Gavi (q.v.).

Dolcetto d'Acqui DOC. Red wine. Province: Alessandria. Villages: Acqui Terme, 24 others. Grape: Dolcetto.

A light, everyday red of good colour and certain character.

Dolcetto d'Alba DOC. Red wine. Province: Cuneo. Villages: Alba, Barolo, Barbaresco, La Morra, 30 others. Grape: Dolcetto.

As with Barbera d'Alba, Dolcetto here is not planted on the best slopes, but the skill and renown of the producers may compensate and deliver a first rate wine. The style varies from the traditional, soft, but dust-dry to something more fruity and refreshing. In most cases, youth is a virtue.

Dolcetto d'Asti DOC. Red wine. Province: Asti. Villages: Calamandrana, Canelli, Nizza Monferrato, 21 others. Grape: Dolcetto.

Less widely seen, but similar to Dolcetto d'Acqui.

Dolcetto delle Langhe Monregalesi DOC. Red wine. Province: Cuneo. Villages: Briaglia, many others. Grape: Dolcetto.

A rarely used DOC, established in 1974 for a light weight Dolcetto, said to have more aroma than most.

Dolcetto di Diano d'Alba or Diano d'Alba DOC. Red wine. Province: Cuneo. Village: Diano d'Alba. Grape: Dolcetto.

An excellent Dolcetto, generally stronger and more focused than Dolcetto d'Alba.

Dolcetto di Dogliani DOCG. Red wine. Province: Cuneo. Villages: Dogliani, Monchiero, others. Grape: Dolcetto.

Possibly the original Dolcetto; often a good one with more "grip" (or less soft) than some. Some growers are aiming for a denser, richer style aged in barriques. A group of producers working with barrique-aged wines pressed for a separate DOCG appellation for Dogliani, and succeeded in 1995.

Dolcetto di Ovada DOC. Red wine. Province: Alessandria Villages: Ovada, 21 others. Grape: Dolcetto.

The best producers make very lively wine, with as fruity an aroma as every Dolcetto and capable of developing in bottle like good *cru* Beaujolais.

Erbaluce di Caluso, Caluso DOC. White wine. Provinces: Torino and Vercelli. Villages: Caluso, 35 others. Grape: Erbaluce.

Usually available vinified dry, but excellent *passito* is also made.

Fara DOC. Red wine. Province: Novara. Villages: Fara, Briona. Grapes: Nebbiolo (30–50%), Vespolina, Bonarda Novarese (Uva Rara).

Fara, Boca, and their neighbour Sizzano, similar reds of the same quality, were all early DOCs, but are still limited in production. A mere 22 hectares produce Fara.

Favorita This dry white wine from the grape variety of the same name, grown in the Roero and Langhe hills has recently made a comeback. Best drunk young.

Freisa d'Asti DOC. Red wine. Province: Asti. Villages: 118 in the hills of Asti. Grape: Freisa.

A cheerful, fruity, sharpish red, sometimes sweet and often fizzy. It can be very appetizing, though the non-DOC Freisa d'Alba is often better made, sometimes as a full-bodied red. Also seen under the Langhe and Monferrato DOCs.

Freisa di Chieri DOC. Red wine. Province: Torino. Villages: Chieri, 11 others. Grape: Freisa.

Chieri, on the outskirts of Turin, specializes in the sweeter style of Freisa, often fizzy. Also capable of more serious reds.

Gabiano DOC. Red wine. Province: Alessandria. Villages: Gabiano, Montecestino. Grapes: Barbera (90–95%), Freisa and/or Grignolino.

From the Gabiano village north of Asti. A very long lived Barbera. Minute production.

Gattinara DOCG. Red wine. Province: Vercelli. Village: Gattinara. Grapes: Nebbiolo (Spanna), Bonarda (maximum 10%).

The best-known Spanna (Nebbiolo) of the hills north of Novara, a quite separate enclave from Barolo and the Langhe, with a broader, juicier, less austere style of wine. Few, if any, Gattinaras reach top Barolo standards, but they are both impressive and easy to like. One hundred hectares remain.

Gavi or Cortese di Gavi. DOCG. White wine. Province: Alessandria. Villages: Gavi, three others. Grape: Cortese.

Gavi does not quite reach the standards of mingled acidity and richness that say "white burgundy" does; too often its flavours are castrated by too cold fermentation. But this area can grow the Cortese grape superbly well.

Ghemme. DOCG. Red wine. Province: Novara. Villages: Ghemme, part of Romagnano Sesia. Grapes: Nebbiolo 75–100%, Vespolina, Bonarda Novarese (Uva Rara).

A very similar wine to Gattinara, generally reckoned slightly inferior, though some (like me) may prefer the rather finer, less hearty style. The best bottles at five or six years incline towards a claret like texture.

Grignolino d'Asti DOC. Red wine. Province: Asti. Villages: 35 communes in Asti. Grapes: Grignolino (100%), Freisa (maximum 10%).

Good Grignolino is refreshing and lively, slightly bitter, and pale but not pallid. Losing ground to Barbera.

Grignolino del Monferrato Casalese DOC. Red wine. Province: Alessandria. Villages: 35 communes (in the Monferrato Casalese). Grapes: Grignolino (100%), Freisa (maximum 10%).

An additional Grignolino area to the north; gained DOC status a year after Grignolino d'Asti.

Langhe DOC. Red and white wine. Province: Cuneo. Grapes: almost all grapes grown in the province of Cuneo.

Recently introduced DOC as a catchment for declassified or not yet DOC-classed Langhe wines: Langhe Bianco, L Rosso, L Nebbiolo, L Freisa, L Dolcetto, L Arneis, L Favorita, L Chardonnay.

Lessona DOC. Red wine. Province: Vercelli. Village: Lessona. Grapes: Nebbiolo (Spanna), Vespolina (maximum 25%), Bonarda.

This remarkably fine, claret-weight Nebbiolo blend is scarce, since there are only ten hectares in production. Six years is a good age for it.

Loazzolo DOC. White. Province: Asti. Village: Loazzolo. Grape: Moscato.

A Moscato *passito*, with a history. Can be a sinful, sweet dream. Rediscovered in the 1980s by Giancarlo Scaglione and Giacomo Bologna, this is produced only in minute quantities. Forteto della Luja is the best.

Malvasia di Castelnuovo Don Bosco DOC. Red wine. Province: Asti. Villages: Castelnuovo Don Bosco, five others. Grapes: Malvasia di Schierano (100%), Freisa (maximum 15%).

A light, sweet, fragrant sparkling wine, either gently bubbly or fully sparkling. Malvasia di Casorzo is very similar.

Monferrato DOC. Red, white, *rosato* wine. Provinces: Alessandria, Asti. Grapes: almost all grapes grown in this region.

DOC created in the mid-1990s to give greater respectability to many former table wines of the hills between the River Po and the Apennines: Monferrato Rosso, M. Bianco, M. Chiaretto, M. Dolcetto, M. Freisa, M. Casalese (a white from Cortese grapes).

Moscato d'Asti and Asti DOCG. White, usually sparkling (but can be still) wine. Provinces: Asti, Cuneo, Alessandria. Villages: throughout the communes.

Moscato d'Asti and Asti are basically the same, but regulations allow Moscato d'Asti to be slightly sweeter and lower in alcohol. Generally Moscato d'Asti is better than Asti, often made with great pains to be swooningly aromatic, sweet, and slightly fizzy. It must be drunk as young as you can get it. Asti itself is one of Italy's inimitable classics: sweet, buxomly fruity but girlishly giggly with its scented froth. A major industry dominated by big names in the vermouth field, normally produced in tanks, hence the moderate price.

Nebbiolo or **Nebbiolo del Piemonte** An alternative title for any Nebbiolo wine. Not classified as DOC or DOCG. Ordinary to excellent wines.

Nebbiolo d'Alba DOC. Red wine. Province: Cuneo. Villages: Alba, 16 others. Grape: Nebbiolo.

For those who can do without the stern majesty of Barolo, but love the flavours of its grape, this is the DOC to search out. Four years is usually enough to develop a delicious bouquet of fruit ranging from plums to raspberries and, with luck, truffles.

Piemonte DOC. Red, white, and rosato wines. Provinces: Alessandria, Asti, Cuneo. Grapes: Barbera, Bonarda, Grignolino, Brachetto, Cortese, Chardonnay; Moscato, Pinot Bianco, Pinot Grigio, and Pinot Nero also for sparkling ("Piemonte DOC").

A new basket-DOC for the whole region of Piedmont. Includes Piemonte Barbera, P Bonarda, P Brachetto, P Cortese, P Grignolino, P Chardonnay, P Spumante,

P Moscato. Includes DOC for *spumante*, either *metodo tradizionale* or Charmat method.

Pinerolese DOC. Red wine. Provinces: Turin, Cuneo. Villages: 32 in the area.

Deeply obscure appellation for two idiosyncratic wines. The first is Doux d'Henry, supposedly from a grape variety left by the French king in the early 1600s. The second is Ramie, grown on small terraced vineyards. Only a few thousand bottles are made.

Roero. DOCG Red wine. Province: Cuneo. Villages: 19 in the province of Cuneo. Grapes: Nebbiolo (95–98%), Arneis (2–5%).

A recently promoted DOCG for red from Nebbiolo grown in the Roero hills north of Alba, but growers may still opt to produce Nebbiolo d'Alba or Roero. This zone makes attractive red wines, far more accessible young than Barolo or Barbaresco but sometimes capable of ageing beyond five to six years.

Roero Arneis DOCG. White wine. Province: Cuneo. Villages: 19 in the province of Cuneo. Grape: Arneis.

The Arneis grape grows in the Roero hills. Soft, richly textured with a bitter-almond finish. Increasingly popular, especially the best-selling Blangè from Ceretto. For drinking young. Promoted to DOCG in 2006.

Ruchè di Castagnole Monferrato DOC. Red wine. Province: Asti. Villages: Castagnole Monferrato, six others. Grape: Ruchè (90%).

A rare red grape, sometimes spelled "Rouchet", found only in the sub-Alps above Castagnole Monferrato where it makes a tannic wine that ages to something perfumed and fine.

Sizzano DOC. Red wine. Province: Novara. Village: Sizzano. Grapes: Nebbiolo (Spanna, 40–60%), Vespolina, Bonarda Novarese (Uva Rara).

Considered by many to be one of the best of the north Piedmont Spanna (Nebbiolo) blends, and is comparable with Boca and Fara. Has potential to be a ten year wine. No newcomer, it was a wine much admired by the Italian statesman Cavour.

Spanna The alias of the Nebbiolo grape in the Novara and Vercelli hills of north Piedmont, also used as a wine name for Gattinara style wines.

Strevi DOC. White wine. Province: Alessandria. Village: Strevi. Grape: Moscato Bianco.

Created in 2005, DOC reserved for *passito* wines.

Valsusa DOC. Red wine. Province: Turin. Villages: 19 in the Valle di Susa. Grapes: Avana, Barbera, Dolcetto, Neretto (up to 60% in all), others (40%).

Fragrant mountain red, promoted to DOC in 1997.

Verduno Pelaverga DOC. Province: Cuneo. Villages: Verduno, La Morra, Roddi. Grape: Pelaverga.

It was only in the 1990s that the identity of this rare grape was definitively established, and DOC status followed swiftly in 1995. A relatively light red, for drinking young.

Leading Piedmont Producers

Anna Maria Abbona ☆☆–☆☆☆
Farigliano. 8 ha.
An ambitious producer of Dolcetto di Dogliani, the best being the subtly oaked Maioli.

Orlando Abrigo ☆☆–☆☆☆
Treiso. 15 ha. www.orlandoabrigo.it
Giovanni Abrigo makes two *cru* Barbarescos of consistent quality: Montersino and Rongallo.

Cascina Adelaide ☆☆
Barolo. 8 ha. www.cascinaadelaide.com
New modern winery with Barolos to match. Cannubi is the top wine.

Alario ☆☆
Diano d'Alba. 12 ha.
An enthusiastic grower of delicious Dolcetto, as well as fresh Barbera and concentrated Barolo Riva.

Gianfranco Alessandria ☆☆–☆☆☆
Monforte d'Alba. 6 ha.
www.gianfrancoalessandria.com
A disciple of Elio Altare (q.v.), Alessandria takes a modernist approach, favouring barrique-ageing for his top Barolo *cru*, San Giovanni, and his fine Barbera Vittoria.

Elio Altare ☆☆☆☆
La Morra. 10 ha. www.elioaltare.com
Despite the small size of this vineyard, the wines have made international impact. In 1978, Altare shocked his family and neighbours by green harvesting to reduce yields, and compounded the sin by ageing some of his wine in barriques, once remarking, "All great wines are made in barriques".

ANGELO GAJA

Angelo Gaja of Barbaresco has the highest profile of any grower in Piedmont today, aggressively taking his own line on techniques, grape varieties, style, and price. The 101 hectares of Gaja vines produce around 25,000 cases a year of Barbaresco and other Alba wines, including a Barolo, a Cabernet Sauvignon called Darmagi, two Chardonnays called Gaia and Rey, and a surprisingly long-lived Sauvignon Blanc. The wines that have always won the greatest acclaim are his single-vineyard Barbarescos such as Sorì San Lorenzo, Costa Russi, and the massively ripe and rich Sorì Tildin. So there was amazement when he announced in 2000 that he was declassifying them to Langhe Rosso.

He explained that he wanted to bring attention back to his regular Barbaresco, but admitted that the decision would allow him, should he wish, to blend in a small proportion of Barbera to these *crus*, a practice forbidden under Barbaresco DOC rules but allowed under Langhe rules.

Outside Piedmont, he has acquired the Brunello estate, Pieve di Sta Restituta in Tuscany, and created a new property on the Tuscan coast, Ca' Marcanda (q.v.), from which the first Bordeaux-style wines were released in 2002.

This most dynamic and innovative of Italian wine producers is still in his prime, untroubled by any controversy he stokes up, and as passionate as ever about his quest for the highest quality – both in his own wines and in Italy in general.

In short, he was the courageous pioneer who helped create modern-style Barolo and Barbera of superb quality.

Anselma ☆☆–☆☆☆
Barolo. 8 ha. www.anselma.it
Only Nebbiolo is grown at this estate, and the variety rises to great heights in the mighty *cru* Adasi.

Antichi Vigneti di Cantalupo ☆☆
Ghemme. 34 ha. www.cantalupovigneti.it
This domaine is one of northern Piedmont's best producers, specializing in Ghemme.

Antoniolo ☆☆–☆☆☆
Gattinara. 15 ha.
A leading name in Gattinara, which has improved in recent years after a change of generation at the helm.

Ascheri ☆☆–☆☆☆
Brà. 36 ha. www.ascherivini.it
Founded in 1880 and still family owned, this estate makes very reliable Barolo and a wide range of other wines, including a Viognier and Syrah, both called Montalupa.

Azelia ☆☆–☆☆☆
Castiglione Falletto. 12 ha. www.azelia.it
Good oaked Barbera and outstanding barrique-aged Barolo from Bricco Fiaco.

Ballarin ☆–☆☆
La Morra. 7 ha. www.cascinaballarin.com
Hit and miss in the past, but recent vintages have resulted in stylish Barolos from Bricco Ricca and Bussia.

Cascina La Barbatella ☆☆
Nizza Monferrato. 5 ha.
A dependable source for Barbera and Monferrato.

Batasiolo ☆–☆☆
La Morra. 105 ha. www.batasiolo.com
This very large winery is rapidly improving. Good Barolo and Dolcetto, even though the wines are less consistent than they should be.

Bava ☆☆–☆☆☆
Cocconato d'Asti. 57 ha. www.bava.com
A large property, with a wide range of wines. Barbera d'Asti Stradivario is rich and complex, the Chardonnay full of character, and the Barolos better than in the past.

Bel Colle ☆–☆☆
Verduno. 10 ha. www.belcolle.it
A traditional producer, with a range of wines from Barolo, Barbaresco, and Roero, always reliable, rarely thrilling.

Bera ☆☆
Neviglie. 20 ha. www.bera.it
A rising star with Moscato d'Asti and Barbera, but the company offers a wide range of wines.

Nicola Bergaglio ☆☆
Rovereto di Gavi. 15 ha.
A widely admired maker of DOC Gavi, the finest being from *cru* Minaia.

Bersano & Riccadonna ☆–☆☆
Nizza Monferrato. 240 ha. www.bersano.it
The second-largest producer in Piedmont, its 300,000 cases come from its own vineyards and from purchased grapes. Excellent Barbera, but others are humdrum. The wine museum created by the late Arturo Bersano is open five days a week.

A. Bertelli ☆☆☆
Costigliole d'Asti. 11 ha.
Bertelli produce a range of intense Barberas, and unusual, excellent wines from Merlot and the Rhône varieties.

Alfiero Boffa ☆☆☆
San Marzano Oliveto. 25 ha. www.alfieroboffa.com
Boffa is passionate about old Barbera vineyards, from which he makes a series of superb wines, mostly aged in large casks in the traditional way.

Enzo Boglietti ☆☆–☆☆☆
La Morra. 21 ha. www.enzoboglietti.com
Although the three *cru* Barolos, especially Brunate, are usually the best wines here, the wonderfully intense Barberas are almost as noteworthy.

Giacomo Borgogno & Figli ☆☆
Barolo. 14 ha. www.borgogno-wine.com
Barolo doesn't come more traditional than at Borgogno, a cellar founded in 1761 and still producing rugged, long lived wines.

Boroli ☆☆
Alba. 32 ha. www.boroli.it
Not one of the best known names in Alba, but these essentially traditional Barolos, with their red-fruits perfume and elegant structure, are immensely satisfying.

Gianfranco Bovio ☆☆–☆☆☆
La Morra 12 ha. www.boviogianfranco.com
Bovio's excellent wines are best sampled at his famous restaurant in La Morra, Belvedere.

Braida-Giacomo Bologna ☆☆☆–☆☆☆☆
Rocchetta Tanaro. 50 ha. www.braida.it
More than just a talented winemaker, the late Giacomo Bologna was a prominent figure in Italian wine. He created a new style of modern, highly concentrated, long lived Barberas, best exemplified by the estate's Bricco dell'Uccellone and Bricco della Bigotta. Ai Suma is a powerful, late-harvested Barbera made only when climatic conditions permit. Bologna died young, in 1990, but his standards are being maintained by his widow and children.

Harvesting grapes in Piedmont

Brema ☆☆–☆☆☆
Incisa Scapaccino. 18 ha.
Small quantities of outstanding Barbera.

Brezza ☆☆ ☆☆
Barolo. 16 ha. www.brezza.it
Barolo Sarmassa is grandly old-fashioned and long-lived.

Bricco Maiolica ☆☆–☆–☆☆☆
Diano d'Alba. 20 ha. www.briccomaiolica.it
Excellent range of wines: lush Dolcetto, refined Barbera, and oaky Nebbiolo.

Bricco Mondalino ☆☆
Vignale Monferrato. 13 ha. www.briccomandolino.it
Renowned for excellent Barbera d'Asti and Grignolino.

Brovia ☆☆
Castiglione Falletto. 15 ha. www.brovia.net
Highly consistent if occasionally extracted Barolo, with unusually elegant Dolcetto, too.

Buganza ☆–☆☆
Piobesi d'Alba. 10 ha. www.renatobuganza.it
Thoroughly enjoyable if uncomplicated Roero.

Burlotto ☆–☆☆
Verduno. 12 ha. www.burlotto.com
Good Barbera, often excellent Barolo, especially *cru* Gli Acclivi.

Piero Busso ☆☆☆
Neive. 8 ha. www.bussopiero.com
Consistently good single vineyard Barbarescos, aged variously in large casks and French barriques, depending on the structure of the fruit.

Ca' Bianca ☆–☆☆
Alice Bel Colle. 42 ha. www.giv.it
Good Barbera d'Asti and Gavi from a winery that is part of the huge Gruppo Italiano Vini.

Ca' d'Carussin ☆–☆☆
San Marzano Oliveto. 13 ha. www.carussin.it
Bruna Ferro makes attractive, good-value Barbera d'Asti and a rare Barbera *passito*.

Ca' Romé ☆☆–☆☆☆
Barbaresco. 7 ha. www.carome.com
Complex and essentially traditional Barbaresco, especially Maria di Brun.

Ca' Viola ☆☆–☆☆☆
Montelupo. 11 ha. www.caviola.com
The estate of respected oenologist Giuseppe Caviola, and a testing ground for his ideas. Excellent Dolcetto and Barbera-dominated Langhe Rosso Bric du Luv.

Castellari Bergaglio ☆☆
Roverato di Gavi. 12 ha. www.castellaribergaglio.it
A leading Gavi producer. Founded in 1890, this estate only produces Gavi.

Castello di Neive ☆☆
Neive. 26 ha. www.castellodineive.it

One wine stands out here: the well-balanced and stimulating Barbaresco Santo Stefano.

Cascina Castlet ☆☆–☆☆☆
Costigliole d'Asti. 18 ha. www.cascinacastlet.com
Mariuccia Borio produces delicious Moscato and a range of Barbera d'Asti, including the late-harvested Passum from semi-dried grapes.

Caudrina ☆☆☆
Castiglione Tinella. 30 ha. www.caudrina.it
The Dogliotti family is among the very best Moscato producers.

Cavallotto ☆☆–☆☆☆
Castiglione Falletto. 23 ha. www.cavallotto.com
A highly traditional producer of long lived Barolo, although some bottlings from certain vintages can be heavy handed.

Ceretto ☆☆☆
Alba. 90 ha. www.ceretto.com
The Ceretto brothers, now aided by their children, have expanded the family firm to include model estate wineries of Bricco Asili in Barbaresco, Bricco Rocche in Barolo, and the Blangè estate in Roero, where they make stylish Arneis.

They are also part owners of I Vignaioli di Santo Stefano (for Asti and Moscato d'Asti) and the new Cornarea estate. Their Barolo and Barbaresco are first-rate examples of barrique-aged Nebbiolo.

Michele Chiarlo ☆☆–☆☆☆
Calamandrana. 100 ha. www.chiarlo.it
Sound, sometimes excellent, wines, especially from Barolo and Barbaresco from an expanding portfolio of vineyards. Also a reliable source for Moscato, Gavi, and Barbera.

Chionetti ☆☆☆
Dogliani. 14 ha.
Outstanding producer of deep, rich, succulent Dolcetto di Dogliani.

Ciabot Berton ☆–☆☆
La Morra. 12 ha. www.ciabotberton.it
Barolo Roggeri is always a wine with weight and pungency, making it by far the best of the range.

Cigliuti ☆☆☆
Neive. 7 ha.
New star in Barbaresco, also making excellent Barbera d'Alba. The Barbaresco Serraboella is aged partly in casks, partly in barriques.

Clerico ☆☆☆☆
Monforte d'Alba. 21 ha.
Domenico Clerico is a forward-looking producer who, since the early 1980s, has been releasing a range of superb terroir-driven Barolos, supple Dolcetto, and a barrique-aged blend called Arte.

Cogno ☆☆
Novello. 9 ha. www.elviocogno.com
Forceful Barolo, strong Barbera, and delicious Dolcetto.

Poderi Colla ☆☆
San Rocco Seno d'Elvio. 30 ha. www.podericolla.it
Traditional producer, offering both Barolo and Barbaresco of
good quality, and a Dolcetto/Nebbiolo blend called Bricco del
Drago. The Barolo comes from Tino Colla's Dardi Le Rose
estate in Monforte and is an excellent example of traditional,
if solid, Barolo.

La Contea ☆–☆☆
Neive. 15 ha. www.la-contea.it
Admired, if occasionally stolid, Barbaresco from a leading
local restaurateur.

Aldo Conterno ☆☆☆–☆☆☆☆
Monforte d'Alba. 25 ha. www.poderialdoconterno.com
Conterno's skills as grower and winemaker, stem from five
generations of forebears, and his son Franco heads the sixth.
Conterno's Dolcetto is soft; his Barbera spicy; and his single-
vineyard Barolos also bear the Conterno signature: notably
harmonious, despite their massive chassis of tannin.

Giacomo Conterno ☆☆☆–☆☆☆☆☆
Monforte d'Alba. 14 ha.
Brother of Aldo (see above), Giovanni Conterno was the
determined upholder of Barolo's most ancient traditions.
After his death in 2004, his place was taken by his son Roberto.

The estate is particularly noted for his magnificent Barolo
Monfortino, chosen from the best vintages and aged eight
years in casks. All his wines are powerful and bold, among the
finest expressions in the region of an ultra traditional style.
But not all wine drinkers are comfortable with the wines'
uncompromising tannins.

Conterno Fantino ☆☆☆–☆☆☆☆
Monforte d'Alba. 25 ha. www.conternofantino.it
Very consistent producer of modern-style Barolo from
Ginestra and Vigna del Gris, as well as a Nebbiolo/Barbera
blend called Monprà, and aged in new oak.

Giuseppe Contratto ☆☆–☆☆☆
Canelli. 55 ha. www.contratto.it
Founded in 1867, the firm is now owned by grappa-producer
Bocchino. Excellent Asti and *metodo tradizionale* sparkling
wines as well as first-rate Barolo Cerequio.

Coppo ☆☆–☆☆☆
Canelli. 56 ha. www.coppo.it
An established *spumante* house, now becoming well-known
for its splendid, vigorous Barberas (Pomorosso is consistently
superb) intriguing barrique aged Freisa.

Cordero di Montezemolo ☆☆☆
La Morra. 32 ha. www.corderodimontezemolo.com
This property remained in the hands of the same noble family
from the 1300s onwards, and the present owners, Giovanni
and Enrico Cordero, are also descendants. They produce,
in particular, a fine if oaky Barolo, Enrico VI.

Giovanni Corino ☆☆☆
La Morra. 16 ha.
Since 1995, all the wines from this estate have been barrique
aged. The single-vineyard Barolos are magnificent, tannic yet

opulent. The Barbera Pozzo is built on the same massive scale
and is certainly not for the faint hearted.

Renato Corino ☆☆–☆☆☆☆
La Morra. 6 ha.
Renato Corino and his brother Giuliano (see Giovanni Corino
above) amicably divided the family estate in 2006, and at first
it was Giuliano who made the running. But the wines from
Renato are almost as fine, and in a similar style.

Correggia ☆☆☆
Canale. 20 ha. www.matteocorreggia.com
In 2001 a tragic accident deprived the Roero region of
its most talented young winemaker, who had rapidly
established a fine reputation for luscious Barbera and
magnificent single vineyard Roero, aged in barriques. His
widow Ornella unflinchingly maintains the standards he set.

Giuseppe Cortese ☆☆
Barbaresco. 8 ha. www.cortesegiuseppe.it
Structured and vigorous Barbaresco from Rabajà.

Deltetto ☆☆
Canale. 20 ha. www.deltetto.com
One of the most dynamic estates in the Roero, with a wide
range of wines. Lush Roero Braja, and fine Barbera and
Arneis.

Dessilani ☆–☆☆☆
Fara. 40 ha. www.dessilani.it
An excellent source for wines from little known appellations:
Fara Caramino, Ghemme, and Sizzano.

Dezzani ☆–☆☆
Cocconato. 50 ha. www.dezzani.it
This estate is a large producer of sound Barbera and Dolcetto
d'Ovada.

Einaudi ☆☆☆
Dogliani. 50 ha. www.podereinaudi.com
Founded in 1897 by Luigi Einaudi, who later became
president of Italy, the property remains in family hands. From
extensive vineyards, it produces first-rate Dolcetto di Dogliani,
rich, dense Barolo Cannubi, and a fine blend of Piedmontese
and Bordeaux varieties known as Langhe Rosso Luigi Einaudi.

Giacomo Fenocchio ☆
Monforte d'Alba. 12 ha.
www.giacomofenocchio.com
Not everyone will appreciate the stermly traditionalist style
of these Barolos, but they have solid authenticity.

Ferrando ☆☆–☆☆☆☆
Ivrea. 7 ha. www.ferrandovini.it
Quality Carema, bottled with a special black label for fine
vintages; and small amounts of sweet wines, such as his
Caluso *passito* and his barrique-aged Solativa, also from
the Caluso zone.

Fontanabianca ☆☆☆
Neive. 14 ha. www.fontanabianca.it
Aldo Pola has built a fine reputation on his barrique-aged,
velvety Barbaresco Sori Burdin.

Fontanafredda ☆–☆☆☆
Serralunga d'Alba. 90 ha. www.fontanafredda.it
The most impressive wine estate of Piedmont, founded in 1878 by Conte Emanuele Guerrieri, son of King Victor Emmanuel II, and based in a royal mansion in Serralunga.

A major producer of Barolo and Asti, but quality was patchy until 1999, when a new winemaker, Danilo Drocco, arrived and swiftly turned things around. Fine wines across the range, from powerful, single-vineyard Barolo to juicy Dolcetto and characterful sparkling wines.

Forteto della Luja ☆☆☆
Loazzolo. 8 ha. www.fortetodellaluja.it
Acclaimed sweet Moscato *passito* from Giancarlo Scaglione under the Loazzolo DOC.

Angelo Gaja ☆☆☆☆
Barbaresco. www.gajawines.com
See page 294.

Fratelli Gancia ☆
Canelli. 2,000 ha. www.gancia.it
A large family firm that pioneered the traditional (Champagne) method in Italy. Also a producer of vermouth and spirits, Gancia remains a leader in sparkling wine.

Gastaldi ☆–☆☆
Neive. 14 ha.
Best-known for Dolcetto and his impressive Langhe Rosso. Extensive use of the Langhe DOC, white and red, allows him to vary his blends.

Gatti ☆☆
Santo Stefano Belbo. 7 ha.
www.vinigatti.it
Delicious Moscato and Brachetto d'Asti.

Ettore Germano ☆☆
Serralunga. 13 ha.
www.germanoettore.com
Both opulent and tannic, these are copybook Serralunga Barolos. Sergio Gemano also has an interesting sideline in white wines.

Attilio Ghisolfi ☆☆
Monforte. 6.5 ha.
A relative newcomer to Barolo, Ghisolfi makes powerful Barolo Visette and, in complete contrast, a Pinot Nero called Pinay.

Fratelli Giacosa ☆☆–☆☆☆
Neive. 40 ha. www.giacosa.it
Very good, modern-style Barolo and Barbaresco.

Bruno Giacosa ☆☆☆–☆☆☆☆
Neive. 20 ha. www.brunogiacosa.it
Bruno Giacosa is one of Piedmont's best winemakers, admired for powerful Alba reds (especially the Red Label Riservas made only in top vintages) that age with grace, and an

excellent *tradizionale* made from Pinot Nero (though with grapes from Oltropò Pavese). His Barolo and Barbaresco are proof, if any were necessary, that great and complex Nebbiolo can be made without recourse to French oak. His best wines appear under the Falletto label. Ill health means Giacosa is less involved than in the past, but style and quality remain the same.

Gillardi ☆☆–☆☆☆
Farigliano. 7 ha. www.gillardi.it
Idiosyncratic producer, specializing in Dolcetto di Dogliani and a fine Syrah called Harys.

La Giustiniana ☆–☆☆
Rovereto di Gavi. 40 ha. www.lagiustiniana.it
Well-known producer of Gavi and Monferrato.

Cantina del Glicine ☆☆
Neive. 5 ha. www.cantinadelglicine.it
A minuscule wine house, producing consistently good-quality and structured Barbaresco.

Elio Grasso ☆☆☆
Monforte d'Alba. 14 ha.
www.eliograsso.it
Quality rarely wavers at this estate. The single-vineyard Barolos are exceptional (Chiniera made in traditional style, Runcot aged in new barriques), and the Dolcetto and Barbera are rich and satisfying, too.

Silvio Grasso ☆☆–☆☆☆☆
La Morra. 7 ha.
Grasso, who is not related to Elio (see above), makes two concentrated, persistent, single-vineyard Barolos from Ciabot Manzoni and Bricco Liuciani.

Marchesi di Gresy ☆☆
Barbaresco. 35 ha.
www.marchesidigresy.com
Founded in the last century on the site of a Roman villa: Alberto di Gresy has been producing wine here since 1973, and since 1998 with New Zealand winemaker Jeffrey Chilcott at the helm. From grapes planted in the prized Martinenga and Rabajà vineyards, di Gresy makes unusually elegant, medium bodied Barbaresco, although the Camp Gros bottling has more body and weight than the Martinenga or Gaiun.

Giacomo Grimaldi ☆☆
Barolo. 8 ha.
Ferruccio Grimaldi produces two fresh and persistent Barolos and two Barberas.

Luisin ☆☆☆
Barbaresco. 7 ha.
Splendid traditional Barbaresco from one of the zone's top sites: Rabajà, as well, as two other single vineyard bottlings. Exceptional Barberas, too.

Serralunga d'Alba castle, Serralunga

Malvirà ☆☆
Canale. 40 ha. www.malvira.com
A fine source of serious and ageworthy Roero and fresh Arneis.

Giovanni Manzone ☆☆–☆☆☆
Monforte d'Alba. 7.5 ha. www.manzonegiovanni.com
The Barolo comes from the obscure Gramolere *cru*, but is consistently good: perfumed, powerful, and long.

Marcarini ☆☆–☆☆☆
La Morra. 17 ha. www.marcarini.it
Elegant, medium-bodied Barolo, although in top vintages the Brunate rises to great heights.

Marchesi di Barolo ☆–☆☆
Barolo. 120 ha. www.marchesidibarolo.com
One of the larger Barolo houses, founded in 1861, and now producing 1.5 million bottles from all of the major Piedmontese varieties. The best wine is the Barolo Cannubi.

Marengo ☆☆
La Morra. 4 ha.
Barolo Brunate is the principal wine from this tiny estate; aged in barriques, it has plummy fruit and remarkable elegance.

Martinetti ☆☆☆
Torino.
Franco Martinetti is an advertising executive and part-time winemaker, now assisted by his son, Guido. He owns no vineyards and buys in grapes from contracted vineyards. He is best-known for a Barolo and his three Barberas, including the magnificent Sulbric, which contains some Cabernet. But his highly original full-bodied white wines, Minaia (a Cortese) and Martin (from the rare Timorasso grape), are both equally brilliant.

Bartolo Mascarello ☆☆
Barolo. 5 ha.
A tiny Barolo maker that steadfastly relies on very traditional methods to carefully produce 2,000 cases of a single wine each year. Mascarello died in 2005 but his daughter Maria Teresa continues in the same fashion.

Giuseppe Mascarello ☆☆☆
Monchiero. 12 ha. www.mascarello1881.com
Mauro Mascarello's excellent and very traditional Barolo Monprivato is austere in its youth, but develops wonderful perfume and finesse with age. Splendid Dolcetto, too.

Moccagatta ☆☆☆
Barbaresco. 11 ha.
Excellent modern-style Barbaresco from three single vineyards, and superb barrique aged Barbera.

Mauro Molino ☆☆☆–☆☆☆☆
La Morra. 12 ha.
There are two single-vineyard Barolos here. Conca, aged in 60 per cent new oak, is more highly regarded than Gancia, but both are excellent and extremely consistent. The concentrated and oaky Barbera Gattera is one of the best in the Alba region.

Mossio ☆☆–☆☆☆
Rodello. 10 ha. www.mossio.com

Delicious Dolcetto from old vines. Caramelli is the top *cru*.

Ada Nada ☆–☆☆☆
Treiso. 10 ha. www.adanada.it
An estate without pretension, yet it produces pure yet structured Barbarescos from two *crus*.

Angelo Negro ☆☆–☆☆☆
Monteu Roero. 54 ha. www.negroangelo.it
A large and dynamic estate, producing some of the best Roero in the region.

Nervi ☆☆
Gattinara. 33 ha. www.gattinara-nervi.it
The best wine is the fine, single-vineyard bottling of Gattinara from Molsino.

Fratelli Oddero ☆☆
La Morra. 35 ha. www.oddero.it
Respected family winery offering well-crafted, traditionally made, single vineyard Barolos. Vigna Rionda is almost always the best of them, but these are wines that need age to show their true complexity.

Orsolina ☆☆
San Giorgio Canavese. 20 ha. www.orsolani.it
Renowned for firm Erbaluce di Caluso and intense Caluso *passito* in tiny quantities.

Pace ☆
Canale. 19 ha.
Attractive medium-bodied Roero and Arneis, the former for medium term drinking.

Armando Parusso ☆☆☆
Monforte d'Alba. 23 ha. www.parusso.com
Marco Parusso is a modernist winemaker, excelling with his single vineyard Barolos. Yet he is no slave to dogma, and winemaking is adapted to the quality of the fruit. Fine Barbera and barrel-fermented Sauvignon Blanc, too.

Pecchenino ☆☆☆
Dogliani. 24 ha. www.pecchenino.com
Orlando Pecchenino is a single minded producer, spearheading the revival of Dolcetto di Dogliani as a serious wine. His enthusiasm for barrique-ageing and micro-oxygenation is proving controversial, but the wines are of exceptional quality.

Pelissero ☆☆☆
Treiso. 35 ha. www.pelissero.com
One of the most gifted of the new generation of open-minded, modernist winemakers, Giorgio Pelissero produces rich Barbaresco Vanotu and sumptuous barrique aged Barbera.

I Vignaioli Elvio Pertinace ☆–☆☆☆
Treiso. 70 ha. www.pertinace.it
A private cooperative producing good, if somewhat gamey, Barbaresco. Nervo is usually the best vineyard.

Cantina del Pino ☆☆–☆☆☆
Barbaresco. 7 ha. www.cantinadelpino.com
Since 1997 Renato Vacca has been producing excellent barrique-aged Barbaresco from the *cru* Ovello.

Pio Cesare ☆☆–☆☆☆☆
Alba. 52 ha. www.piocesare.it
A pillar of tradition in the Alba area, founded in 1881 by Pio Cesare, great-grandfather of Pio Boffa, who has given the winery a modern touch. Pio Cesare owns vineyards in Barolo and Barbaresco, and also selects grapes from regular suppliers to make some excellent Piedmont wines.

E Pira ☆☆☆
Barolo. 3.5 ha.
This tiny estate, run by Dr. Chiara Boschis, focuses on modern-style Barolo Cannubi, powerful and fruity despite being aged entirely in new barriques.

Produttori del Barbaresco ☆☆–☆☆☆
Barbaresco. 96 ha. www.produttoridelbarbaresco.it
This exceptional cooperative, uniting 56 growers with excellent vineyards, produces an array of single vineyard Barbarescos, made with great care in a wholly traditional style.

Prunotto ☆☆☆
Alba. 55 ha. www.prunotto.it
Founded in 1904 as a cooperative, acquired by Alfredo Prunotto in 1920, the firm has been owned since 1990 by Piero Antinori. Very careful, traditional winemaking produces benchmark Alba wines: gentle, plummy Nebbiolo, complex Barolo, and vibrant single-vineyard Barberas are first class.

Punset ☆☆–☆☆☆
Neive. 40 ha. www.punset.com
A substantial organic estate. The forceful personality of owner Marina Marcarino spills over into her wines, which have great intensity, as well as purity and a panoply of red fruits aromas, especially marked with the *cru* Barbaresco Campo Quadro.

Renato Ratti ☆☆
La Morra. 35 ha. www.renatoratti.com
The founder, the late Renato Ratti, was president of the consortium of Asti, and a respected author and local historian. His sons and nephew continue to make wines that are sound, but can be lean and lacking in weight in certain vintages.

Fratelli Revello ☆☆–☆☆☆
La Morra. 12 ha.
Impressive single vineyard Barolos, aged in a high proportion of new oak, yet elegant, too.

Roagna ☆☆
Barbaresco. 6.5 ha. www.roagna.com
Steadily improving single-vineyard Barbaresco from Luca Roagna, who only releases the wines when he considers they are ready to drink.

Rizzi ☆–☆☆
Treiso. 36 ha. www.cantinarizzi.it
Enrico Dellapiana seeks elegance more than power or overt oakiness in his Barbarescos. He is making progress.

Albino Rocca ☆–☆☆☆
Barbaresco. 15 ha. www.roccaalbino.com
Delicious Barbera Gepin here, and the single vineyard Barbarescos, once inconsistent, are now much improved.

Bruno Rocca ☆☆☆
Barbaresco. 15 ha. www.brunorocca.it
Imposing, modern style Barbaresco from *crus* Rabajà and Coparossa, and a powerful if extracted Cabernet/Nebbiolo/Barbera blend called Langhe Rabajolo. The succulent Dolcetto and Barbera are better balanced.

Rocche Costamagna ☆–☆☆
La Morra. 15 ha. www.roccchecostamagna.it
This is a traditional estate producing somewhat tough Barolos.

Rocche dei Manzoni ☆☆☆
Monforte d'Alba. 40 ha. www.roccchedeimanzoni.it
The innovative Valentino Migliorini makes splendid Barolos, plus his excellent Bricco Manzoni, a Nebbiolo/Barbera blend aged in barriques.

Gigi Rosso ☆–☆☆
Castiglione Falletto. 30 ha. www.gigirossso.com
A family firm, producing a full range of Alba wines. Reliable but rarely exceptional.

Luciano Sandrone ☆☆☆–☆☆☆☆
Barolo. 25 ha. www.sandroneluciano.com
The owner, and his brother Luca, produce top-ranked Barolo and Barbera and admired Dolcetto. Prices are high, but quality is utterly dependable, and Barolo Le Vigne is often one of the top wines of the vintage.

Saracco ☆☆
Castiglione Tinella. 35 ha. www.paolosaracco.it
A specialist in white wines. Excellent Moscato, of course, but also good Chardonnay.

Scarpa ☆☆–☆☆☆
Nizza Monferrato. 50 ha. www.scarpavini.it
An outstanding Piedmont family firm, founded in 1854. Scarpa's wines are all models of their genre. As well as good Barolo, there is fine Brachetto and Barbera, a rare and remarkable rich red Rouchet and smooth Nebbiolo.

Paolo Scavino ☆☆☆–☆☆☆☆
Castiglione Falletto. 20 ha. www.paoloscavino.com
His Barolo Bric del Fiasc is always outstanding, modern-style but not international. In some vintages it is surpassed by the bottling from Rocche dell'Annunziata, but quantities are minuscule. Enrico Scavino is also a master of Barbera and Dolcetto.

La Scolca ☆☆
Rovereto di Gavi. 50 ha. www.scolca.it
This estate is run by Giorgio Soldati, the son of its founder, whose Gavi di Gavi made the world take the Cortese grape seriously. Also a good source of sparkling wines.

Scrimaglio ☆–☆☆
Nizza Monferrato. 18 ha. www.scrimaglio.it
Dependable producer of Barbera d'Asti.

Mauro Sebaste ☆–☆☆
Alba. 18 ha. www.maurosebaste.it

Polished wines, with the focus on Arneis, Barbera, and other varieties, as well as Barolo.

Sella ☆☆
Lessona. 20 ha.
Since the late nineteenth century the Sella family has been a leading producer of the rare wines from Bramaterra and Lessona.

Sottimano ☆☆☆
Neive. 13 ha. www.sottimano.it
Andrea Sottimano produces four single vineyard Barbarescos, each with a clearly discernible character from year to year, despite a high proportion of new oak. Currà and Cottà tend to stand out.

La Spinetta-Rivetti ☆☆☆☆
Castagnole Lanze. 100 ha. www.la-spinetta.com
The Rivetti family built their reputation on Barbera d'Asti and Moscato d'Asti, and over the past decade the dynamic Giorgio Rivetti has taken the wines to a new quality level. In 2003 he built a new winery in Barolo, signalling the growing focus on Nebbiolo wines. The wines are aged in mostly new barriques, but the intensely concentrated fruit is not overpowered by the wood. The Barberas are splendid, as are the dazzling, single vineyard Barbarescos.

Terre del Barolo ☆–☆☆
Castiglione Falletto. 610 ha. www.terredelbarolo.com
A big cooperative with sound standards, thanks to immense vineyards from which to source its wines.

Terre da Vino ☆
Moriondo. 4,500 ha. www.terradavino.it
Owned by a group of cooperatives and estates in a joint venture operation. Surprisingly good-quality Barolo and Barbera for such a large company.

Travaglini ☆☆–☆☆☆☆
Gattinara. 42 ha. www.travaglinigattinara.it
Perfumed and structured Gattinara of exemplary quality.

Vajra ☆☆☆
Barolo. 25 ha. www.gdvajra.it
The modest but perfectionist Aldo Vajra makes excellent Barolo, but his other wines are equally good: single-vineyard Dolcetto and Barbera d'Alba, and a chewy, complex Freisa.

Vallana ☆–☆☆
Maggiora.
Producer of long-lived Spanna and reliable Boca.

Mauro Veglio ☆☆☆
La Morra. 11 ha. www.mauroveglio.com
Veglio produces four different Barolos. Rocche is built for the long term, while Casteletto is opulent despite very firm tannins. These wines need time to attain their majestic harmoniousness. Gorgeous Barbera d'Alba, too.

Castello di Verduno ☆☆
Verduno. 7.5 ha. www.castellodiverduno.com
Once the property of the Italian royal house, the estate is owned by the Burlotto family, who produce sound traditional Barolo and Barbaresco Rabajà, and rare Pelaverga.

Vietti ☆☆–☆☆☆☆
Castiglione Falletto. 35 ha. www.vietti.com
Luca Currado presides over a substantial estate that once seemed mired in the past, but has for some years been producing exemplary Barolos and Barberas. Currado is neither traditional nor modernist, but adapts his winemaking to the quality and style of the fruit.

Tasting panel for the DOC system

Vigna Rionda – Massolino ☆☆–☆☆☆
Serralunga d'Alba. 18 ha. www.massolino.it
A rising star, offering an impeccable range of well structured, single vineyard Barolos, and an intense Barbera d'Alba.

Virna ☆☆
Barolo. 12 ha. www.virnabarolo.it
Known until 2001 as Lodovico Borgogno, this estate is now run by Borgogno's daughter under her own name. The best of the Barolos is from Cannubi Boschis.

Gianni Voerzio ☆☆☆
La Morra. 12 ha.
After the split with more illustrious brother Roberto (q.v.), Gianni took over the family winery. As well as the fine Barolo La Serra there is a wide range of other Piedmontese varieties.

Roberto Voerzio ☆☆☆☆
La Morra. 17 ha.
Many years ago, Roberto Voerzio split from the family winery (now run by Gianni Voerzio, his brother) to open his own operation, which is now one of the best Barolo estates. Yields are very low and the top wines are aged in barriques. Quality is dazzling, and prices are high.

Valle d'Aosta

The Valle d'Aosta is France's umbilical cord to Italy (and vice versa). Its narrow confines lead to the Mont Blanc tunnel and St Bernard passes. Small vineyards perched in south-facing crannies along the valley manfully carry winemaking almost all the way from Piedmont to Savoie, with a corresponding meeting of their respective grapes.

Nebbiolo and Barbera from the south join Gamay and Petit Rouge (that tastes suspiciously like Mondeuse) from the north, with Swiss Petite Arvine, some Moscato and Malvoisie (Pinot Gris) and two indigenous grapes: Blanc de Valdigne and red Vien de Nus. Quantities are very small, but despite ample consumption by the skiers of Courmayeur and the townsfolk of Aosta, more and more of these singular wines are now being exported. In 1986, Italy's most comprehensive region-wide DOC was established. Valle d'Aosta or Vallée d'Aoste takes in 18 types of wine with their names in two languages. It takes a true enthusiast to master the differences between Torrette, Fumin, and Chambave Rouge.

Leading Valle d'Aosta Producers

Anselmet ☆☆–☆☆☆☆
Villeneuve. 5 ha. www.maisonanselmet.vievini.it
This small estate produces acclaimed oaked Chardonnay, as well as Pinot Noir, Syrah, and red blends.

Caves Coopératives de Donnas ☆
Donnas. 25 ha. www.donnasvini.com
A small cooperative specializing in Nebbiolo-dominated reds.

Cave du Vin Blanc de Morgex et de la Salle ☆–☆☆
Morgex. 20 ha. www.caveduvinblanc.com
A cooperative specializing in Blanc de Morgex and Blanc de la Salle. At up to 1,040 metres (3,400 feet) its vineyards are some of the highest in Europe. The wine is light and can be sharp. New editions are an icewine called Chaudelune and sparkling wines.

Cave des Onze Communes ☆
Aymavilles. 50 ha. www.caveonzecommunes.it
A cooperative with over 200 growers. Clean, fresh wines for early drinking.

Coopérative de l'Enfer d'Arvier ☆
Arvier. www.coenfer.it
A tiny cooperative, with 130 growers tending tiny plots. The only wine is a lightly oaked red dominated by Petit Rouge.

Les Crêtes ☆☆–☆☆☆
Aymavilles. 25 ha. www.lescretesvins.it
Costantino Charrère specializes in small quantities of wines made from obscure, low-yielding local varieties, often blended together, as well as varietal wines from Petite Arvine, Pinot Gris, and Syrah. La Sabla is the fine, unoaked red made here from Petit Rouge, Fumin, and Barbera, and the most striking white is usually the oaked Chardonnay.

La Crotta di Vegneron ☆☆
Chambave. 37 ha. www.lacrotta.it
Cooperative offering sound Fumin, Muscat, and Pinot Gris, and lush *passito* wines from Moscato and Pinot Gris.

Di Barrò ☆
Villeneuve 2.5 ha. www.dibarro.vievini.it
Clean, fresh Chardonnay and Pinot Noir, and a Moscato *passito* unflatteringly called Lo Flapì.

Grosjean ☆–☆☆
Quart. 7 ha. www.grosjean.vievini.it
The Grosjean family specializes in varietal wines from Gamay, Fumin, and Petite Arvine, and some Pinot Noir aged in barrique.

Institut Agricole Régional ☆☆–☆☆☆
Aosta. www.iaraosta.it
Experimental cellars of the regional agricultural school founded in 1969 and for many years directed by Joseph Vaudan, a priest. Some of the best wines of Aosta are produced here. There are two ranges, one for early drinking from varieties such as Müller-Thurgau, Petite Arvine, and Pinot Gris, the other more international in style and aged in barriques, including a Chardonnay; a Pinot Noir called Sang des Salasses; a Bordeaux blend called Vin du Prévôt; and a Syrah (Trésor du Caveau).

La Kiuva ☆
Arnad. 12.5 ha.
A cooperative producing a mere 3,000 cases, with both oaked and unoaked Chardonnay.

Lo Triolet ☆–☆☆
Introd. 3 ha. www.lotriolet.vievini.it
Marco Martin specializes in Pinot Gris and a Syrah-based red
called Coteau Barrage.

Albert Vevey ☆
Morgex. 1 ha.
Mario Vevey continues the family tradition, producing a single
wine: a fresh, aromatic Blanc de Morgex.

Liguria

The crescent of the Ligurian coast, linking France and Tuscany,
is scarcely regarded as a wine region and has never been an
exporter. But in the centre of the crescent lies Italy's greatest
port, and one of its most cosmopolitan cities, Genoa. Genoa
demands, and gets, much better than ordinary whites for its
fish and reds for its meat from the scattered vineyards of the
hilly coast. Far more white than red is produced.

The grape that performs wonderfully well in Liguria is
Vermentino, as much at home here as in Corsica. It is the
commonest white grape of the coast, grown particularly to the
west of Genoa. Standards vary, but it should be faintly aromatic
and dry: much the best local fish wine. DOC in Riviera di
Ponente, Colli di Luni, and in Cinqueterre blend.

DOC & Other Wines

Cinqueterre DOC. White wine. Province: La Spezia.
Villages: Riomaggiore, Vernazza, Monterosso, La Spezia.
Aged one year for Sciacchetrà. Very limited production.

The largely legendary dry white (mostly Bosco, plus
Albarola and Vermentino) of the beautiful Ligurian coast
southeast of Genoa. It should be cleanly fruity. Sciacchetrà
is the renowned specialty, made in tiny quantities from the
same grapes, shrivelled in the sun to achieve concentration,
sweetness, and a formidable 16 degrees or more of alcohol.
The vineyards are ledges on the rocky coast, sometimes only
accessible by boat. If a pruner drops his secateurs there is a
splash. How long will they survive?

Colline di Levanto DOC. Red and white wine. Province: La
Spezia. Villages: Levanto, Bonasola, Framura, Deiva Marina.
Red and white from the hills behind La Spezia.

Colli di Luni DOC. Red and white wine. Provinces: La
Spezia, Massa e Carrara. Villages: 18 communes in La Spezia
and Massa e Carrara.

Wine has been made in this area since Roman times,
but only in 1989 was it elevated to DOC status. Good reds
are made from Sangiovese based blends, whites that can
almost rival those of Riviera di Ponente predominantly
from Vermentino and a dash of Trebbiano. Leading
winemakers of the zone are investing heavily in new
equipment and expertise, and look set to demand some
respect in the future.

Golfo del Tigullio DOC. Province: La Spezia.
Vineyards around Portofino, producing all colours and
styles from Bianchetta, Ciliegiolo, Genovese, Vermentino,
and Moscato.

Pornassio DOC. Red wine. Province: Imperia.
Promoted in 2003, and exclusively for wines from the
Ormeasco grape grown in Riviera del Ponente.

Riviera Ligure di Ponente DOC. Red and white wine.
Province: Savona, Imperia. Villages: 67 communes in Imperia,
46 communes in Savona, two communes in Genoa.

The red and white wines are grown west of Genoa between
Savona and Imperia. Main red varieties are Rossese and
Ormeasco; the latter resembles Dolcetto. The whites, from
Vermentino and Pigato, are best drunk young; reds can
improve with age.

Rossese di Dolceacqua or Dolceacqua DOC. Red wine.
Province: Imperia. Villages: Dolceacqua, Ventimiglia, 13 others.
The claret of the coast near the French frontier – a country
wine from Rossese with a good balance of fruit and bite, best
after two to five years, when it can develop a real bouquet to
linger over.

Val Polcevera DOC. Red, white, *rosato* wine. Province: Genoa.
White, *rosato*, and red from a valley northwest of Genoa.

Leading Liguria Producers

Laura Aschero ☆–☆☆
Pontedassio, Imperia. 3 ha.
Signora Aschero died in 2006, but her son Marco has taken
over, so the estate continues to produce fresh ripe Vermentino
and full-bodied Pigato.

Walter de Batté ☆☆–☆☆☆
Riomaggiore, La Spezia. 1 ha.
Probably the best producer both of Cinqueterre and
Schiacchetrà, from vineyards not much larger than
handkerchiefs.

Maria Donata Bianchi ☆☆
Diano Castello, Imperia. 4.5 ha.
The Vermentino is first rate here, and there is an intriguing
red called La Mattana from Syrah and Grenache.

Bisson ☆☆
Chiavari, Genoa. 10 ha. www.bissonvini.it
Piero Lugano's estate produces enjoyable Vermentino and
Bianchetta, and a red blend called Il Musaico from Dolcetto
and Barbera. A good source for Schiacchetrà del Cinqueterre
and other *passito* wines, albeit in tiny quantities.

Lunae Bosoni ☆
Ortonovo, La Spezia.
A wide range of white and reds from Colli di Luni.

Riccardo Bruna ☆☆
Ranzo, Imperia. 6 ha.
Some of the zone's finest Pigato but sadly only produced
in small quantities.

Cane ☆☆
Dolceacqua, Imperia. 1 ha.
Small production of admired Rossese di Dolceacqua.

Cantina Cinque Terre ☆–☆☆
Riomaggiore, La Spezia. www.cantinacinqueterre.com
Co-op with 300 growers, producing
a consistently good range of dry, white DOC Cinqueterre,
with Sciacchetrà being the top wine.

Colle dei Bardellini ☆–☆☆
Sant'Agata, Imperia. 5 ha. www.colledeibardellini.it
Zesty wines from Vermentino, Pigato, and Rossese.

Durin ☆–☆☆
Ortovero, Savona. 15 ha.
www.durin.it
Among a very wide range of wines, look for the rare
Granaccia, which Antonio Basso helped to revive from near
extinction. With its sour-cherry and cranberry flavours, it
makes an ideal summer red.

Fèipu dei Massaretti ☆–☆☆
Albenga, Savona. 6 ha. www.aziendamassaretti.it
Good Pigato and Rossese, and a blend (Rossese, Sangiovese,
and Brachetto) called Russu du Fèipu.

Foresti ☆☆
Camporosso, Imperia. 20 ha.
www.forestiwine.it
The Foresti family make a range of
impressive single-vineyard Rossese di
Dolceacqua.

Forlini Capellini ☆
Manarola, La Spezia.
Family vineyard producing a good, full-
bodied Cinqueterre and Schiacchetrà.

Giuncheo ☆☆
Camporosso, Imperia. 7 ha.
www.tenutagiuncheo.it
Excellent Vermentino and Rossese di
Dolceacqua, and a herbal Syrah called
Sirius.

Enzo Guglielmi ☆
Soldano, Imperia.
www.enzoguglielmi.it
Guiglielmi's Rossese di Dolceacqua is
consistently good.

Ottaviano Lambruschi ☆☆
Castelnuovo Magra, La Spezia. 5 ha.
Reliable and aromatic Colli di Luni Vermentino.

Lupi ☆☆
Pieve di Teco, Imperia. 10 ha. www.vinilupi.it
The Lupi family, ably advised by oenologist Donato Lanati,
is among the region's top producers. Their Ormeasco, made
from grapes grown in mountain vineyards, shows uncommon
finesse and ages up to six years or more. Good Pigato and
Vermentino, too.

Cascina delle Terre Rosse ☆☆–☆☆☆
Finale Ligure, Savona. 6 ha.
Excellent Riviera Ligure di Ponente Pigato, and a red
Solitario blend from Grenache, Barbera, and Rossese.

Vecchia Cantina ☆☆
Albenga, Savona. 4 ha.
Specialist in rich Pigato and Vermentino from Riviera Ligure
di Ponente. Good passito too.

Lombardy

Lombardy has always kept a low profile in the world of wine. It
has no world famous names. Oltrepò Pavese, its productive and
profitable viticultural heart, is scarcely a name to conjure with.
Valtellina, the last Alpine valley before Switzerland, commands
more respect with its elegant Nebbiolo reds. Franciacorta too is
making a name for itself with elegant *metodo tradizionale*
sparkling wines, although some of them, however beautifully
packaged, demand a high price not always justified by the quality in the bottle. The grapes of Piedmont and the grapes of the
northeast are all grown here, and frequently blended. It is
inescapably a zone of transition, with rich possibilities but no
clear identity to bank on. The producers are not greatly trou-

bled by this, since they have a ready market
in Milan and the other cities of the north,
but there is, therefore, little incentive for
them to jack up the quality of wines such as
Oltrepò Pavese.

DOC & Other Wines

Barbera One of the commonest red
grapes of Lombardy, used both blended
and alone. In Oltrepò Pavese it can be
DOC.

Bonarda Another red grape with DOC
rights in the Oltrepò Pavese. Dark, soft,
and bitter on the finish.

Botticino DOC. Red wine. Province:
Brescia. Villages: Botticino, Brescia,
Rezzato. Grapes: Barbera, Schiava
Gentile, Marzemino, Sangiovese
(10–20%).
   A fairly powerful and sweetish red;
the local red meat wine, best with three
to four years of maturity.

Buttafuoco A forceful, concentrated red of blended Barbera,
Uva Rara, and Croatina produced near Castana (under the
umbrella DOC Oltrepò Pavese).

Capriano del Colle DOC. Red and white wine. Province:
Brescia. Villages: Capriano del Colle, Poncarale. Grapes:
Sangiovese, Marzemino, Barbera, Merlot; Trebbiano.
   A DOC for light local wines.

Harvesting grapes, LIguria

Cellatica DOC. Red wine. Province: Brescia. Villages: west of Brescia. Grapes: Schiava Gentile, Barbera, Marzemino, Incrocio Terzi No l (Barbera/Cabernet Franc).

A respectable, mild red, best within two to four years. It has been enjoyed in the area since the sixteenth century.

Curtefranca DOC. Red and white wine. Province: Brescia. Villages: 23 communes south of Lake Iseo. Grapes: Cabernet Franc, Barbera, Nebbiolo, Merlot (maximum 15%); Chardonnay and/or Pinot Bianco.

Since 1995, this has been the DOC for the former "Franciacorta", as Franciacorta DOCG is now for sparkling wines only. In 2000 the name was changed from Terre di Franciacorta.

Franciacorta DOCG. Awarded in 1995. White and *rosato* wine. Villages: as above. Grapes: Chardonnay and/or Pinot Bianco, and/or Pinot Nero, and/or Pinot Grigio.

Classic-method sparkling Franciacorta wine in white and *rosato* styles. From same province and villages as Terre di Franciacorta. A special sub-category is Satèn, a *blanc de blancs* in a *crémant* style with a maximum *dosage* of 15 grams per litre.

Garda and Garda Classico Recent DOCs for wines from the provinces of Brescia and Mantua made from local and international varieties of good quality. Too much of a catch-all to have any real identity. Shared with the Veneto.

Garda Bresciano DOC. Red and *rosato* wine. Province: Brescia. Villages: 30 communes on the western and southwestern shores of Lake Garda. Grapes: Groppello, Sangiovese, Barbera, Marzemino.

The mirror image of Valpolicella and Bardolino from the other side of the lake. Commercial qualities at least are similar, although classic Valpolicella is much deeper in flavour. The village of Moniga del Garda makes a pale Chiaretto which is lively and good when very young.

Garda Colli Mantovani DOC. Red, white, and *rosato* wine. Province: Mantova. Grapes: Garganega, Trebbiano Giallo, and/or Trebbiano Toscano, and/or Pinot Bianco; Rossanella (Molinara), Sangiovese, and Negrara.

Lightweight local wines, though with a long history; Virgil mentioned them. The white resembles Soave.

Groppello A local red grape of southwest Garda.

Grumello A subregion of Valtellina Superiore (q.v.).

Inferno A subregion of Valtellina Superiore (q.v.).

Lambrusco Mantovano DOC. Red wine. Province: Mantova. Region: zones around the River Po and the border of Emilia-Romagna. Grapes: Lambrusco Viadanese, other sub-varieties.

A DOC created in 1987 for a Lambrusco from the local Viadanese sub-variety; robust in the west, lighter towards the east of the zone. Wines are dry or more usually *frizzante*, and can hold their own with their counterparts from Emilia.

Lugana DOC. White wine. Provinces: Brescia, Verona. Region: the south end of Lake Garda between Desenzano and Peschiera. Grapes: Trebbiano di Lugano (100%), up to 10% light grapes.

Formerly a glamorous rarity to be sought out in such lovely spots as Sirmione. Now a very pleasant, light, dry, white wine, scarcely distinguishable from a good Soave.

Merlot Increasingly grown as a varietal wine in Lombardy. Very satisfactory, though not included in a DOC. Part of blend in Franciacorta and Valcalepio.

Moscato di Scanzo Passito DOC. A great rarity from Bergamo: an excellent tawny dessert Muscat from a subzone of Valcalepio.

Müller-Thurgau German grape, successfully grown in the Oltrepò Pavese, but not admitted in its DOC.

Oltrepò Pavese DOC. Red and white wine. Province: Pavia. Area: Oltrepò Pavese. Grapes: Barbera, Croatina, Uva Rara, and/or Ughetta; Pinot Grigio or Riesling Renano, up to 15% others.

The DOC for large volumes of reds and whites from the 2,000 hectares of Oltrepò Pavese. Most of the more distinctive wines of the area are either specifically named (eg. Barbacarlo, Buttafuoco) or have a specified grape variety dominant (eg. Barbera, Pinot, Chardonnay, and Sauvignon).

Oltrepò Pavese DOCG. Red and *rosato* wine. Province: Pavia. Area: Oltrepò Pavese. Grapes: Pino Nero, and/or Pinot Bianco, Chardonnay, Pinot Grigio.

Created in 2007, this DOCG applies only to *metodo classico* sparkling wine with at least 70% Pino Nero, the remainder being from Pinot Bianco, Chardonnay, or Pinot Grigio.

Pinot Pinot Nero, Grigio, and Bianco are all widely grown in Lombardy. The Oltrepò Pavese is a major supplier of base wines of Pinot for *spumante* made in Piedmont and elsewhere.

Riesling The Oltrepò DOC includes both Italian and Rhine Rieslings without distinguishing them. Both grow well here.

San Colombano al Lambro or San Colombano DOC. Red wine. Provinces: Milan, Pavia. Villages: San Colombano al Lambro, Graffignana, S Angelo Lodigiano. Grapes: Croatina, Barbera, Uva Rara; up to 15% other reds.

Hearty reds from the slopes around San Colombano. Best for drinking after two to four years.

San Martino della Battaglia DOC. White wine. Provinces: Brescia, Verona. Villages: Sirmione, Desanzano, Lonato, Pozzolengo, Peschiera. Grape: Tocai Friulano.

A distinctive character among Garda wines: dry, yellow, and tasty with something of the typical local bitterness in the finish. It is best drunk as young as possible. Also made as a fortified *liquoroso* wine.

Sangue di Giuda A fizzy, often sweet red called "Judas Blood" is the sort of wine that makes "serious" wine-lovers turn their eyes to heaven. It is usually made from local grapes Croatina and Uva Rara. It should be tried without prejudice. There are good ones.

Sassella A subregion of Valtellina Superiore (q.v.).

Sfursat or Sfurzat or Sforzato DOCG. Valtellina's equivalent of the Recioto of Valpolicella in the Veneto; a strong

(14.5 degrees) red made of semi-dried grapes, in this case, Nebbiolo. Age certainly improves it as it turns tawny, but whether the final result pleases you is a personal matter.

Valcalepio DOC. Red and white wine. Province: Bergamo. Villages: 15 in the Calepio valley. Grapes: Pinot Bianco, Chardonnay, and Pinot Grigio; Merlot, Cabernet Sauvignon.

A small production, principally red, of light wines with an ancient name but modern grape varieties. There is also a Moscato *passito* from Valcalepio.

Valgella A subregion of Valtellina Superiore (q.v.).

Valtellina (DOC) and Valtellina Superiore (DOCG). Red wine. Province: Sondrio. Sub-districts: Sassella, Grumello, Inferno, Valgella for Superiore, 12 communes for Valtellina. Grapes: Nebbiolo (called Chiavennasca, 70%), Pinot Nero, Merlot, Rossola, Brugnola, or Pignola Valtellinese. Superiore is 95% Nebbiolo. Aged for not less than two years, of which one is in wood, and four years for *riserva*.

The most successful excursion of Nebbiolo outside its home region of Piedmont. Plain Valtellina can be expected to be a fairly "hard" light red. The named Superiores develop considerable character as dry, claret-weight wines with hints of autumnal mellowness. Freshness and elegance should be the hallmarks of good Valtellina. It is hard to discern consistent differences between Sassella, Inferno, etc., but the first is generally considered the best. Switzerland (St-Moritz is just over the mountain) is a principal consumer. See also Sfursat.

Leading Lombardy Producers

Agnes ☆☆
Rovescala, Pavia. 16 ha. www.fratelliagnes.it
Bonarda is the specialty of this respected Oltrepò Pavese producer. Cresta del Ghiffi is an interesting version made from late harvested grapes, and Millennium, unlike most Bonardas, is intended to be aged.

Riccardo Albani ☆–☆☆
Casteggio, Pavia. 20 ha. www.vinialbani.it
Fresh, well-made Riesling Renano and Bonarda, and a fine red blend called Vigna della Casona from Barbera, Croatina, Uva Rara, and Pinot Noir.

Anteo ☆☆
Rocca de'Giorgi, Pavia. 26 ha. www.anteovini.it
Major producer of *tradizionale* sparkling wines from Oltrepò Pavese, notably Nature from Chardonnay and Pinot Nero.

Balgera ☆
Chiuro, Sondrio. www.vinibalgera.it
Good Valtellina, though solid rather than sophisticated.

Bellavista ☆☆☆
Erbusco, Brescia. 190 ha. www.bellavistawine.it
Vittorio Moretti's celebrated estate has, for some time, been one of the best producers of Franciacorta. These wines are stylish and very highly regarded, particularly the Gran Cuvée Brut and Rosé. The still wines are also very good, especially the Pinot Noir. This estate is Ca' del Bosco's closest competitor; prices are high.

Guido Berlucchi ☆☆
Borgonato di Cortefranca, Brescia. 580 ha. www.berlucchi.it
Since 1962, this firm has grown to be one of Italy's largest producers of classic method wines – over 400,000 cases. The Cuvée Imperiale, from Pinot Nero and Chardonnay, is usually its finest wine. Berlucchi also owns Antica Fratta, another Franciacorta estate.

Fratelli Berlucchi ☆
Borgonato di Cortefranca, Brescia. 70 ha. www.berlucchifranciacorta.it
Sound Franciacorta Brut, Satèn, and Rosé.

Tenuta Il Bosco ☆–☆☆
Zenevredo, Pavia. 152 ha. www.ilbosco.com
Large Oltrepò Pavese estate owned by Zonin, along with San Zeno at Stradella, and the base of a major *spumante* operation. Also produces still Bonarda, Barbera, and Pinot Nero.

La Brugherata ☆–☆☆
Scanzorosciate, Bergamo. 10 ha. www.labrugherata.it
Leading producer of Valcalepio, white and red. Also a good source for the rare Moscato di Scanzo.

Ca' del Bosco ☆☆☆–☆☆☆☆
Erbusco, Brescia. 146 ha. www.cadelbosco.it
Maurizio Zanella comes from a wealthy family, but he is no dilettante, and has thrown all his considerable energies into creating what is probably the outstanding estate of Lombardy. If the Pinero Pinot Noir never quite justifies its high price, the Franciacorta sparkling wines are superb, as is the Chardonnay and the Cabernet/Merlot blend rather audaciously named Maurizio Zanella. The best sparkling wine used to be the Dosage Zéro, but it has now been overtaken by the magnificent Annamaria Clementi, which spends six years on the yeasts and has tremendous depth of flavour.

Ca' dei Frati ☆☆–☆☆☆
Lugana, Brescia. 68 ha. www.cadeifrati.it
Top producer of Lugana and a lush *passito* wine made from Trebbiano and Chardonnay called Tre Filer.

Cavalleri ☆☆☆
Erbusco, Brescia. 43 ha. www.cavalleri.it
A fine source of Franciacorta, especially the Collezione Brut, and the austere Pas Dosé Brut. Also a French-style Cabernet/Merlot blend, Tajardino.

Contadi Castaldi ☆☆☆
Adro, Brescia. 100 ha. www.contadicastaldi.it
Outstanding Franciacorta producer, also owned by Vittorio Moretti of Bellavista (q.v.). The top wines include the Soul *blanc de blancs*, aged six years on the yeasts, the elegant Satèn, and the austere Brut Zero.

Cornaleto ☆–☆☆
Adro, Brescia. 18 ha. www.cornaleto.it
Luigi Lancini produces very elegant Franciacorta as well as Curtefranca.

Costaripa ☆☆–☆☆☆
Moniga del Garda, Brescia. 36 ha. www.costaripa.it
Mattia Vezzola, also the winemaker at Bellavista (q.v.), uses the new Garda Classico DOC here for a wide range of wines, some of them barrique aged. Pradamonte is from Cabernet Sauvignon, Maim a pure Groppello.

Doria ☆☆
Montalto Pavese, Pavia. 30 ha. www.vinidoria.com
Adriano Doria produces a range of wines from Oltrepò Pavese: barrique-aged Pinot Nero, the Barbera-dominated Roncorosso, and Bonarda. A D Bianco is one of the region's best Moscato *passito* wines.

Lorenzo Faccoli ☆–☆☆
Coccaglio, Brescia. 10 ha.
A sound source of sparkling wines from Franciacorta.

Sandro Fay ☆☆–☆☆☆
San Giacomo di Teglio, Sondrio. 13 ha.
Good wines, including Valgella Ca' Moreí, and barrique-aged Valgella Carteria. The Sforzato Rinco del Picchio is outstanding: raisiny and forceful, but without any clumsiness.

Ferghettina ☆☆–☆☆☆
Erbusco, Brescia. 100 ha. www.ferghettina.it
Although this house produces first-rate Franciacorta Satèn, it is also well known for its Merlot Baladello and Chardonnay Favento.

Le Fracce ☆☆
Casteggio, Pavia. 40 ha. www.le-fracce.it
Very reliable, varietal range from Oltrepò Pavese.

Frecciarossa ☆☆–☆☆☆
Casteggio, Pavia. 20 ha. www.frecciarossa.com
Good Oltrepò Pavese, especially Pinot Nero and the traditional red blend Francigeno from Merlot, Croatina, and Barbera.

Lantieri de Paratico ☆☆
Capriolo, Brescia. 17 ha. www.lantierideparatico.it
Steadily improving Franciacorta, especially the Satèn and the Brut Arcadia.

Majolini ☆☆
Ome, Brescia. 20 ha. www.majolini.it
A rising star, with increasingly ambitious Franciacorta. The Chardonnay-dominated Electo Brut is often the outstanding bottling.

Mamete Prevostini ☆☆
Mese, Sondrio. 7 ha. www.mameteprevostini.com
These are Valtellina *crus* of remarkable intensity, and the Sforzato avoids any hint of heaviness.

Mazzolino ☆☆
Corvino San Quirico, Pavia. 22 ha.
www.tenuta-mazzolino.com
A fine range of Oltrepò wines, with the emphasis on barrique-aged wines from Pinot Noir and Chardonnay.

Monsupello ☆☆
Torricello Verzate, Pavia. 50 ha. www.monsupello.it
Founded in 1893, this is a respected source of Oltrepò Pavese varietal wines, and of excellent sparkling wines from Pinot Nero. The still Pinot Nero can be rather confected.

Monte Rossa ☆☆☆
Cazzago San Martino, Brescia. 50 ha.
www.monterossa.com
The Rabotti family produces a range of excellent Franciacorta, especially the long-lived Brut Cabochon.

Montelio ☆–☆☆
Codevilla, Pavia. 27 ha.
Sound varietal wines from Oltrepò Pavese that can sometimes lack depth.

Mosnel ☆☆–☆☆☆
Camignone di Passirano, Brescia. 40 ha.
www.ilmosnel.com
Excellent Franciacorta; stylish, oak-aged Pinot Nero.

Nino Negri ☆☆☆
Chiuro, Sondrio. 36 ha. www.giv.it
Founded in 1897, but now part of the Gruppo Italiano Vini. The Valtellina region's largest cellars, benefiting from advanced technology and the direction of the experienced oenologist Casimiro Maule, it still remains a leading force. Excellent, subtle, sleek wines from all the regional *crus*, and wonderful Sfursat 5 Stelle. Production is approaching one million bottles.

Nera ☆☆
Chiuro, Sondrio. 40 ha. www.neravini.com
A sound producer of Valtellina *crus* and Sforzato.

Pasini ☆☆
Raffa di Puegnago, Brescia. 40 ha.
www.pasiniproduttori.it
Garda Classico Montezalto is a barrique-aged Cabernet Sauvignon, and the Groppello are also recommended. Refreshing Lugana, too.

Pelizzatti Perego ☆–☆☆
Sondrio, Sondrio. 12 ha.
Old-fashioned producer of delicate Valtellina *crus*.

Cascina La Pertica ☆☆–☆☆☆
Polpenazze, Brescia. 16 ha. www.cascinalapertica.it
Ruggero Brunori's top wine from this organic estate is usually the Bordeaux-style red Le Zalte, made with the advice of oenologist Franco Bernabei.

Barone Pizzini ☆☆–☆☆☆
Cortefranca, Brescia. 40 ha. www.baronepizzini.it
Respected producer of Franciacorta, especially the lush Satèn.

Aldo Rainoldi ☆☆☆
Chiuro, Sondrio. 10 ha. www.rainoldi.com
Elegant and dependable wines from all of the major Valtellina *crus*. Rainoldi has mastered the use of barriques, especially in the remarkably stylish Sfursat Fruttaio.

Ricci Curbastro ☆☆
Capriolo, Brescia. 30 ha. www.riccicurbastro.it

Rich, vintage Franciacorta Extra Brut, and an oaky, still Pinot Nero.

Conti Sertoli Salis ☆☆–☆☆☆
Tirano, Sondrio. 7 ha. www.sertolisalis.com
Ancient ruling house of the region, ambitiously revived with the '89 vintage. An excellent range of wines, using large casks and small barrels for ageing. Excellent Sforzato Canua.

Travaglino ☆–☆☆
Calvignano, Pavia. 80 ha. www.travaglino.it
A good source of Oltrepò Pavese from Riesling and Pinot Noir.

Triacca ☆☆☆
Villa di Tirano, Sondrio. 47 ha. www.triacca.com
Domenico Triacca has made enormous investments to select the best Nebbiolo clones, and to ensure they are skilfully vinified. Prestigio is a much acclaimed wine, but only for new-oak aficionados. Others may prefer the stylish *riserva*. Fine Sforzato, too.

Uberti ☆☆☆
Erbusco, Brescia. 24 ha. www.ubertivini.it
Impressive, if expensive, *cuvées* of Chardonnay-dominated Franciacorta Extra Brut Comarì and Satèn Magnificentia.

Bruno Verdi ☆☆
Canneto Pavese, Pavia. 9 ha. www.verdibruno.it
Reliable source of Oltrepò Pavese from Bonarda, Pinot Grigio, and other varieties. You'll find Sangue di Giuda Dolce here, too.

Cantina Sociale La Versa ☆–☆☆
Sta Maria della Versa, Pavia. 1,300 ha. www.laversa.it
A respected cooperative in Oltrepò Pavese, its 720 members produce six million bottles annually. It sells a fraction of the production under its own label, most notably Bonarda *frizzante* and Pinot Nero.

Virgili ☆
Mantova. 10 ha. www.cantinevirgili.com
A leading producer of DOC Lambrusco Mantovano.

Trentino-Alto Adige

The valley of the River Adige is Italy's corridor to the Germanic world and vice versa: a narrow, rock-walled but surprisingly flat-bottomed and untortuous trench among high peaks, which has carried all the traffic of millennia over the Brenner Pass, from the land of olives to the land of firs and back again.

So Germanic is its northern half, the Alto Adige, that its German-speaking inhabitants know it as the Südtirol and think of Italy as a foreign country. A large proportion of its wine production is exported for sale north of the border with the bottles labelled in German. The Trentino has a more southern culture, but even Trento feels only halfway to Italy. The region's wines are correspondingly cosmopolitan, using most of the well-known international grape varieties.

The Alto Adige has made more and more successful interpretations of the white classics. The shelter and warmth of its best slopes, counterpoised by its altitude, give excellent balance of ripeness and acidity. The 15 cooperatives are important in the region, producing 70 per cent of the wine, and some of them pursue the same high standards as the very best private estates.

Farther south in Trentino, the trend is also toward whites. But happily, local taste still maintains the survival of the native reds. The Schiava, Lagrein, and Teroldego all seem to be mountain-bred versions of the grapes of Valpolicella, although Lagrein can make wines of surprising heft and complexity. In slightly different ways they all share the smooth, inviting start and the lingering, bitter finish that you could call the *goût de terroir* of northeast Italy. A quite different local specialty is Moscato Rosa, a sublimely perfumed pink Muscat, possibly of Sicilian origin, that miraculously combines intense aroma and delicacy with high levels of natural alcohol.

The wines differ from those produced in most other Italian wine regions by being labelled varietally, with just a few exceptions that are listed below.

DOCs Shared by Alto Adige and Trentino

Caldaro or Lago di Caldaro or Kalterersee DOC. Red wine. Provinces: Bolzano, Trento. Villages: nine communes in Bolzano, eight in Trento. Grapes: Schiava (85–100%), Pinot Nero and Lagrein (15%).

The German name Kalterersee is more common than the Italian for this light and often-sweetish red, originally grown around the lake southwest of Bolzano (now designated on labels as *classico*). The lake area has an exceptional microclimate for grape-growing. Like all Schiava, it is an acquired taste, with a bitter finish that helps to make it refreshing, though some of the bottles shipped to Germany are so revoltingly sweet and mawkish that putting them in the freezer is the only way of making them drinkable.

Valdadige or Etschtaler DOC. Red and white wine. Provinces: Trento, Bolzano, Verona. Villages: 38 communes in Trento, 33 in Bolzano, four in Verona. Grapes: Schiava and/or Lambrusco (30%), Merlot, Pinot Nero, Lagrein, Teroldego and/or Negrara (maximum 70%); Pinot Bianco, Pinot Grigio, Riesling Italico or Müller-Thurgau (20%), Bianchetta Trevigiana, Trebbiano Toscano, Nosiola, Vernaccia (maximum 80%). The catch-all DOC for most of the Adige valley from Merano to Verona.

Alto Adige DOC & Other Wines

Alto Adige (Südtirol) DOC. Red, *rosato*, and white wine. Province: Bolzano. Villages: 33 communes with vineyards up to 700-metres (2,275-feet) high for red grapes and 1,000 metres (3,280 feet) for white. Grapes: 95% of any of the following: Moscato Giallo (Goldenmuskateller), Pinot Bianco (Weissburgunder), Pinot Grigio (Ruländer), Riesling Italico (Welschriesling), Müller-Thurgau, Riesling Renano (Rhein Riesling), Sylvaner, Sauvignon, Traminer Aromatico

(Gewürztraminer), Cabernet, Lagrein Rosato (L Kretzer), Lagrein Scuro (L Dunkel), Malvasia (Malvasier), Merlot, Moscato Rosa (Rosenmuskateller), Pinot Nero (Blauburgunder), Schiava (Vernatsch), Chardonnay, 5% of any other; Schiava (85%), 15% of any other.

The general DOC for a large zone, following the Adige and Isario valleys through the mountains, and including the Bolzano basin. Of the varieties allowed, the classic international grapes form the majority, several of them doing as well here as anywhere in Italy. Cabernet, Gewürztraminer, Pinot Bianco, Sauvignon Blanc, and Rhein Riesling can all be outstanding. The local characters are the Lagrein, red or *rosato*, which makes a fruity, rich, smooth, and flowing wine with a bitter twist, and the Schiava, which could be described as a jolly junior version of the same thing, refreshing at best, pallid at worst. The Traminer is also very much a local character, having its birthplace at Tramin (Termeno) just south of Bolzano. The same geographic area has several more restrictive DOCs (Santa Maddalena, or St Magdalener, for example) but they are not necessarily superior in quality.

Adige Meranese di Collina or Südtiroler Meraner Hügel DOC. Red wine. Province: Bolzano, Villages: around Merano, on both sides of the Adige river. Grape: Schiava (Vernatsch). The local light red wine of Merano, for the young and hot to drink young and cool. Meraner Hügel is part of the Südtiroler DOC.

Santa Maddalena or St Magdalener DOC. Red wine. Province: Bolzano. Villages: the hills to the north, above Bolzano (Classico is from Santa Maddalena itself). Grapes: Schiava, up to 10% Lagrein and/or Pinot Nero.

An obvious relation to Caldaro, but from better vineyards, more concentrated and stronger. Under Mussolini it was absurdly pronounced one of Italy's three greatest wines (Barolo and Barbaresco were the others). This and Lagrein Dunkel must be considered the first choice among the typical red wines of Bolzano.

Südtiroler Terlaner DOC. Was Terlano or Terlaner, but since 1993 part of the Alto Adige/Südtiroler DOC. White wine. Province: Bolzano. Villages: Terlano, Meltina, Nalles, Andriano, Appiano, Caldaro (Terlano and Nalles are classico). Grapes: 90% Chardonnay, Müller-Thurgau, Pinot Bianco, Riesling (Italico and Renano), Sauvignon, Sylvaner.

The best whites of the Alto Adige are grown in this part of the valley, particularly just west of Bolzano, where Terlano has excellent southwest slopes. Pinot Bianco, Riesling Renano, Sauvignon, and sometimes Sylvaner can all make wines of real body and balance, often in the international class. Terlano without a grape name will include at least 50% of either Pinot Bianco or Chardonnay, and may include both; it is often a good buy.

Südtiroler Eisacktaler DOC. (Was Valle Isarco or Eisacktaler; since 1993, part of Alto Adige/Südtiroler DOC). White wine. Province: Bolzano. Villages: parts of 12 communes in the Isarco Valley northeast of Bolzano to Bressanone (Brixen). Grapes: Traminer Aromatico, Pinot Grigio, Veltliner, Sylvaner or Müller-Thurgau.

The white wines of this Alpine valley are all light and delicate, in contrast to the "stiffer" wines of Terlano, to the west. Northerly location and high elevation gives some of the wines pronounced acidity, so vintage variations are common.

Trentino DOC & Other Wines

Casteller DOC. Red wine. Province: Trento. Villages: 27 communes, slopes no higher than 600 metres (1,950 feet). Grapes: Schiava (30–100%), Lambrusco (maximum 60%), Merlot, Lagrein, or Teroldego (maximum 20%).

The light, dry, everyday red of the southern half of the region from Trento to Lake Garda, but rarely seen outside.

Nosiola Trentino native white grape. The wine is fruity, dry, and (surprise!) finishes with a bitter note; it has a distinctive hazelnut perfume (*nosiola* in Trentino-dialect means "hazelnut"). It is also the base of delicious *vin santo*.

San Leonardo The most admired Cabernet/Merlot red of the Trentino. See San Leonardo (Gonzaga).

Trento DOC. White and *rosato* wine. Province: Trento. Grapes: Chardonnay, and/or Pinot Bianco, and/or Pinot Nero, and/or Pinot Meunier. Classic-method sparkling and 15 months' ageing on yeasts in bottle (36 months for *riserva*) are obligatory.

DOC for local traditional method sparkling wine. One of Trentino's most successful wines.

Teroldego Rotaliano DOC. Red wine. Province: Trento. Villages: Mezzocorona, Mezzolombardo, S Michel all'Adige. Grape: Teroldego.

Pergola-trained Teroldego vines, on the alluvial gravel deposited by the River Noce on the Campo Rotaliano, give the best of the typical smooth, well-fleshed reds of the region, with their characteristic bitter finish. The wines are attractive when young, but also have the potential to age well.

Trentino DOC. Red and white wine. Province: Trento. Villages: a long zone stretching from Mezzocorona north of Trento to 24 kilometres (15 miles) north of Verona. Grapes: Trentino DOC means 25 different wine types: Kretzer, Cabernet Franc, Cabernet Sauvignon, Chardonnay, Lagrein, Marzemino, Merlot, Moscato Giallo, Moscato Rosa, Rebo, Müller-Thurgau, Nosiola, Pinot Bianco, Pinot Grigio, Pinot Nero, Riesling Italico, Riesling Renano, Sauvignon,

The first pressing, Trentino-Alto Adige

Traminer Aromatico, Rosso, Bianco, Vin Santo, Sorni Bianco, Sorni Rosso. Trentino Rosso is a Cabernet/Merlot blend; Trentino Bianco is mostly Chardonnay and Pinot Bianco.

The southern counterpart of the DOC Alto Adige, with almost as great a range of wines, but with more emphasis on the reds. Cabernet is well-established here with excellent results; Lagrein gives some of the best examples of the regional style. Merlot is common – best when blended with Cabernet. Pinot Bianco and Traminer are the best of the dry whites, while Moscato yields a potentially excellent dessert wine.

Leading Trentino Producers

Nicola Balter ☆☆
Rovereto. 10 ha. www.balter.it
Best-known for his lush, spicy blend of Lagrein, Cabernet Sauvignon, and Merlot called Barbanico. Good Chardonnay-based sparkling wine too.

Bolognani ☆☆
Lavis, Trento. www.bolognani.com
A quality producer of white Nosiola, Müller-Thurgau, and Chardonnay. It has also won a good reputation for a medium-bodied red Bordeaux blend called Gabàn.

Castel Noarna ☆☆
Nogaredo. 7 ha. www.castelnoarna.com
Vines huddle around the base of this dramatic old castle. The strength here lies in white wines, especially the aromatic Bianco di Castelnuovo, which blends Riesling, Gewürztraminer, Chardonnay, and Sauvignon Blanc. Biodynamic since 2007.

Ca' Vit (Cantina Viticoltori Trento) ☆–☆☆☆
Ravina. 5,700 ha. www.cavit.it
Founded in 1950, this consortium of 11 cooperatives unites 4,500 growers who between them produce 65 per cent of the wine of Trento province. Only a select part is issued under the Ca'Vit label. In addition to varietal wines produced in large quantities from different subregions, there are small lots of exceptional wines, such as a *vin santo* from Nosiola, a Bordeaux blend called 4 Vicariati, and whites under the Maso Toresella label. Another good quality range to look out for is Bottega Vinai. This immense company achieves good quality at a reasonable price.

Cesconi ☆☆
Lavis. 15 ha. www.cesconi.it
A judiciously oaked Merlot, Pivier is the star turn, but some of the white wines, especially Nosiola, can be entrancing too.

Barone de Cles ☆–☆☆
Mezzolombardo. 35 ha. www.baronedecles.it
An historic estate, producing very good Teroldego Rotaliano and Lagrein.

Concilio ☆–☆☆
Volano. 500 ha. www.concilio.it
Founded in 1972, a union of three older wineries, and now making very reliable varietal wines, especially Chardonnay and Merlot.

Donati ☆☆–☆☆☆☆
Mezzocorona. 20 ha.
Marco Donati is an outstanding producer of Teroldego, especially the concentrated bottling called Sangue del Drago.

Dorigati ☆☆
Mezzocorona. 13 ha. www.dorigati.it
The Dorigati family is closely involved in running this winery, which produces excellent Teroldego and, in Methius, one of Trentino's top sparkling wines, aged up to five years on the yeasts.

Endrizzi ☆–☆☆
San Michele all'Adige, Trento. www.endrizzi.it
Good varietal wines, and interesting blends, red and white, called Masetto, as well as a barrique-aged Teroldego called Gran Masetto.

Giuseppe Fanti ☆☆–☆☆☆☆
Pressano, Lavis.
The top wines at this Trentino winery are usually the Chardonnay and the unusual white from Incrocio Manzoni (a Riesling x Pinot Blanc crossing), but Nosiola is good, too.

Ferrari ☆☆–☆☆☆☆
Trento. 120 ha. www.cantineferrari.it
A firm founded in 1902 in the heart of Trento. For many years, the leading name in Italian classic-method sparkling wines, the winery is now run by the Lunelli family. The flagship wine is the consistently outstanding Giulio Ferrari Riserva del Fondatore *blanc de blancs*, which spends ten years on the lees.

Foradori ☆☆☆
Mezzolombardo. 15 ha. www.elisabettaforadori.com
Founded in 1930, this important estate, run by Elisabetta Foradori, has long espoused the cause of Teroldego, and makes some of Trentino's best, notably the barrique-aged Granato.

Gaierhof ☆☆
Roverè della Luna. 30 ha. www.gaierhof.com
Owner Luigi Togn produces fine white wines, notably Chardonnay, and good Teroldego Rotaliano. Some wines bear the label of his other estate at Maso Poli (q.v.).

Istituto Agrario Provinciale San Michele all'Adige ☆☆
San Michele all'Adige. 50 ha. www.ismaa.it
The agricultural college built around Castel San Michele is a national leader in viticultural research. From its own vineyards, the college makes several wines both for experiment and commerce, including the excellent Castel San Michele (a Cabernet/Merlot blend) and many attractive white wines.

Letrari ☆☆
Rovereto. 23 ha. www.letrari.it
As well as sparkling wines, Letrari produce fine Marzemino, Moscato Rosa and a good Bordeaux blend called Ballistarius.

Longariva ☆☆–☆☆☆
Rovereto. 20 ha. www.longariva.it
Admirable red wines here, from low-cropped Pinot Nero (Zinzèle), Merlot (Tovi), and other varieties. Stylish barrique-aged Chardonnay, too.

Lunelli ☆☆
Ravina, 30 ha. www.cantineferrari.it
The still wine branch of Ferrari (q.v.). Good Chardonnay and Pinot Noir from single vineyard sites, and a Bordeaux blend called Maso Le Viane. The red wines are now being phased out.

Maso Furli ☆☆
Lavis. 4 ha.
Delicious whites, especially the Traminer and Chardonnay. Sadly, production is very limited.

Maso Poli ☆☆
San Michele all'Adige. 15 ha. www.masopoli.com
Owned by Luigi Togn, this is an old estate producing good Sorni Bianco from Chardonnay and Nosiola, and Pinot Nero.

MezzaCorona ☆☆
Mezzocorona. www.mezzacorona.it
This huge company now produces some 30 million bottles each year, but only a small part comes from Trentino. Sound Teroldego and sparkling wines.

Pisoni ☆☆
Lasino. 12 ha. www.pisoni.net
Rich Extra Brut sparkling wine and, especially, sumptuous Nosiola *vin santo* aged ten years in barrels.

Pojer & Sandri ☆☆☆
Faedo, Trento. www.pojeresandri.it
Mario Pojer is the oenologist, Fiorentino Sandri the viticulturist. They produce some of Trentino's most brilliant white wines, including Chardonnay, Müller-Thurgau, Nosiola, and enjoyable Pinot Nero. The wines have a delicately floral scent and fruity crispness.

Giovanni Poli ☆☆
Santa Messenza. 5 ha. www.poligiovanni.it
Better-known as grappa producers, but Poli also makes outstanding *vin santo* from Nosiola.

Pravis ☆☆–☆☆☆
Lasino. 32 hectares. www.pravis.it
A small, innovative estate producing exemplary Nosiola, a fine white blend, Stravino di Stravino, and promising Syrah.

San Leonardo ☆☆☆☆
Avio. 20 ha. www.sanleonardo.it
Owner Marchese Carlo Gonzaga uses barriques to bring finesse to Bordeaux varieties, notably his Merlot and San Leonardo, a blend that has become a Trentino classic. A recent addition to the range is Villa Gresti, a blend of Merlot and Carmenère.

Armando Simoncelli ☆☆
Rovereto. 12 ha.
A leading estate with a fine Marzemino and a Bordeaux blend called Navesèl.

De Tarczal ☆☆
Marano d'Isera. 18 ha. www.detarczal.com
An admirable range, with an exemplary Marzemino and a Bordeaux blend, only made in top vintages, called Pragiara.

Vallarom ☆–☆☆☆
Avio. 8 ha. www.vallarom.com
The Scienza family produces good Pinot Nero and Syrah, and a supple white blend called Vadum Caesaris.

La Vis ☆–☆☆☆☆
Lavis. 1,350 ha. www.la-vis.com
An important cooperative, producing 13 per cent of all Trentino DOC wine. The top ranges are Ritratti from outstanding terroirs, and the Cru collection of single vineyard wines.

Zeni ☆☆–☆☆☆☆
Grumo di San Michele all'Adige, Trento. 15 ha. www.zeni.tn.it
Roberto Zeni has run this leading estate (not to be confused with the property of the same name in the Veneto) since 1975. He is a top winemaker; his Chardonnay and Pinot Bianco are perfumed, his Teroldego harmonious. A specialty is Ororosso, a rare Teroldego *passito*.

Leading Alto Adige Producers

Abbazia di Novacella (Stiftskellerei Neustift) ☆☆
Varna. 20 ha. www.kloster-neustift.it
A lovely twelfth-century monastery producing Valle Isarco DOC, although most of the domaine's vineyards are located south of Bolzano. The top wines from Pinot Nero and other varieties are designated Praepositus.

Arunda Vivaldi ☆☆–☆☆☆☆
Meltina. No vineyards. www.arundavivaldi.it
Josef Reiterer makes exemplary *metodo classsico* sparkling wines that spend a long time on the yeast. The result is a range of wines of exceptional power and intensity.

Cantina Produttori Bolzano ☆–☆☆☆☆
Bolzano. 300 ha. www.kellereibozen.com
In 2001 the Santa Maddalena and Greis cooperatives merged. Although a wide range of Alto Adige wines is produced, the specialty here is Lagrein, which is among the region's best.

Cantina Produttori Colterenzio (Schreckbichl) ☆–☆☆☆☆
Cornaiano/Girlan. 300 ha. www.colterenzio.com
An ambitious group of 290 growers with a range of Alto Adige, Terlano, St Magdalener, and Kalterersee DOCs, with some single vineyard bottlings. The Cornell label is used for selected wines, notably Chardonnay aged in barriques, and Praedium is the label designating a wine from an outstanding site.

Cantina Cornaiano (Girlan) ☆☆
Cornaiano. 205 ha. www.girlan.it
Sound varietal wines from a good cooperative, including some serious reds under the Optimum label. The co-op has also won much praise for its Schiava.

Erste & Neue ☆–☆☆☆
Kaltern/Caldaro. 280 ha. www.erste-neue.it
Along established cooperative with over 500 members, Erste & Neue produces a good range of varietal wines, but only

the top range, called Puntay, has real personality. Excellent Gewürztraminer.

Gojer-Glögglhof ☆☆
Bolzano. 4.5 ha. www.gojer.it
Good St Magdalener and barrique-aged red Lagrein Dunkel.

Franz Haas ☆☆–☆☆☆
Montagna. 28 ha. www.franz-haas.it
A small property releasing elegant white wines including an aromatic blend called Manna, a fine Bordeaux blend called Istante, and delicious Moscato Rosa.

Haderburg ☆☆
Salorno. 11 ha. www.haderburg.it
The Ochsenreiter family produce good sparkling wines, and the still Chardonnay and Pinot Nero are increasing in quality. All wines are unoaked.

J Hofstätter ☆☆–☆☆☆
Termeno/Tramin. 50 ha. www.hofstatter.com
Founded in 1907, this family business is now managed by Martin Foradori. For decades it has offered an excellent assortment of South Tyrolean wines from different areas. The Pinot Nero red from Barthenau is outstanding, as is the Gewürztraminer Kolbenhof.

Kettmeir ☆–☆☆
Caldaro/Kaltern. www.kettmeir.com
A large long established company, sold in the 1990s to the Santa Margherita winery of the Veneto. Good white wines and *spumante*.

Alois Lageder ☆☆☆–☆☆☆☆
Magrè. 60 ha. www.aloislageder.eu
This well-known family winery supplements its own vineyards' production with purchases from over 100 more hectares. Quality is excellent at all levels, but the most dazzling wines are usually the Löwengang Chardonnay, Benefizium Pinot Grigio, and the Römigberg Cabernet Sauvignon. White and red blends are produced from Casòn Hirschprunn, an estate Lageder bought in 1991.

Lentsch ☆☆
Branzoll/Bronzolo. 14 ha. www.lentsch.it
Klaus Lentsch coaxes ripe fruit and a supple texture from Lagrein, which he ages in large casks. Good Gelbermuskateller too.

Loacker ☆☆–☆☆☆
Bolzano. 11 ha. ww.loacker.net
The Loacker family own important estates in Tuscany. This property, also known as Schwarhof, is also farmed organically. The strength here lies in red wines, notably Merlot, Cabernet Sauvignon, and Pinot Nero. The white wines mostly come from Valle Isarco.

Manincor ☆☆
Kaltern/Caldaro. 48 ha. www.manincor.com
Wine production at this noble estate only began in 1996, and since 2006 the farming has been Biodynamic. Manincor has become well-known for Mason, its barrique-aged Pinot Nero, and, in top vintages, its *prestige cuvée* Mason di Mason. Another house specialty is a delicate sweet wine, Petit Manincor, from Petit Manseng.

K Martini & Sohn ☆☆
Cornaiano/Girlan. 30 ha. www.martini-sohn.it
The Sohn is Gabriele Martini, who has raised quality to a high level. Very good Sauvignon Blanc and Chardonnay.

Klosterkellerei Muri-Gries ☆☆–☆☆☆
Bolzano. 30 ha. www.muri-gries.com
The ancient cellars of this Benedictine monastery (well worth a visit) produce a wide range of typical varietal wines under a number of Alto Adige DOCs. Lagrein, in all its guises, is the specialty. Delicious Moscato Rosa, too.

Niedermayr ☆☆☆
Cornaiano/Girlan. 15 ha. www.niedermayr.it
Josef Niedermayr supplements his estate fruit with purchased grapes, which allows him to make a huge range of wines. The Pinot Nero is supple and textured, and Euforius successfully blends Lagrein with Cabernet and Merlot. His most remarkable wine is Aureus, a *passito* from Sauvignon, Chardonnay, and Gewürztraminer, but made with a light touch.

Niedrist ☆☆–☆☆☆
Cornaiano/Girlan. 7 ha.
Mineral whites and juicy Lagrein and Pinot Nero from a small artisanal producer who sets high standards.

Schloss Rametz ☆
Merano. 10 ha. www.rametz.com
Good Chardonnay and Riesling.

Hans Rottensteiner ☆–☆☆
Bolzano. 10 ha.
www.rottensteiner-weine.com
A sound range of wines including good St Magdalener and Lagrein.

Heinrich Rottensteiner ☆
Rencio, Bolzano. 4 ha. www.obermoser.it
This is a dedicated grower making excellent St Magdalener and a spicy Cabernet/Merlot blend – unfortunately named Putz.

Schloss Sallegg ☆–☆☆☆
Caldaro/Kaltern 30 ha. www.castelsallegg.it
First-class late-harvest Moscato Rosa of exceptional power and density, and a fine range of whites wines.

Cantina Produttori San Michele Appiano ☆☆
San Michele Appiano. 370 ha. www.stmichael.it
An outstanding cooperative, offering a very good range

Cantina Produttori San Michele Appiano

of crystalline whites. Top line is Sanct Valentin from
individual vineyards.

Castel Schwanburg ☆☆
Nalles. 27 ha. www.schwanburg.com
Of Renaissance origin, this estate has developed a fine
reputation for its Cabernet Sauvignon.

Cantina Terlano ☆☆–☆☆☆
Terlano. 150 ha. www.cantina-terlano.com
Elegant if pricey white wines, in ascending order of quality:
I Classici, I Vigneti, and Le Selezioni. Tastings demonstrate
that these wines, grown on volcanic soils, can often age
20 years or more, though most people will prefer them
at a more youthful stage.

Cantina Produttori Termeno (Tramin) ☆–☆☆☆
Termeno. 230 ha. www.tramin-wine.it
Gewürztraminer is, of course, the specialty here, including a
remarkable *passito* version. Overall the white wines are better
than the reds.

Tiefenbrunner (Castel Turmhoff) ☆☆
Cortaccia/Kurtatsch. 20 ha. www.tiefenbrunner.com
Herbert and Christof Tiefenbrunner's long-established family
winery produces some of the South Tirol's most exciting
whites. The Feldmarschall (a Müller-Thurgau) comes from
vineyards 990 metres (3,250 feet) above sea level: the region's
highest. Reserve wines are called Linticlarus.

Cantina Produttori Valle Isarco (Eisacktaler) ☆
Chiusa. 90 ha. www.cantinavalleisarco.it
A respected cooperative producing reliable white wines from
Kerner and Sylvaner and other Villa Isarco specialties.

Elena Walch ☆☆☆
Termeno/Tramin. 25 ha. www.elenawalch.com
Elena Walch supplements her own vineyards by buying in
grapes from local growers. Her varietal white wines are fresh
and balanced, and she also makes outstanding Lagrein from
her Castel Ringberg estate.

Veneto

The hinterland of Venice is one-third mountain, two-thirds
plain. Its northernmost boundary is with Austria, high in the
Dolomites; in the south, it is the flat valley of the River Po.
All the important wines from the Veneto's 90,000 hectares of
vineyards are grown in the faltering Alpine foothills and
occasional hilly outcrops, in a line eastwards from Lake Garda
to Conegliano. Verona, near Lake Garda, is the wine capital,
with a greater production of DOC wine from its vineyards of
Soave, Valpolicella, and Bardolino than any other Italian region.
So important are these three in the export market that Verona
has a claim to being the international wine capital of the whole
of Italy. The nation's biggest wine fair, Vinitaly, takes place in
Verona every April. To the east, Conegliano has another claim:
to be the nation's centre of viticultural technology and research.
The Verona and Conegliano areas have strong traditions of

using grape varieties peculiar to themselves: Garganega (the
Soave grape), the Corvina of Valpolicella, and the Prosecco,
which makes admirable sparkling wine at Conegliano, are
unknown elsewhere. But less-established and self-confident
areas, such as the Berici and Euganean hills and the Piave,
prolific flatland vineyards on the borders of Friuli-Venezia
Giulia to the east, try their luck with a range of international
varieties: Pinots, Cabernets, and their kin. Merlot is the standby red of the region and is rapidly improving from acceptable
to delicious.

For many years, a titanic struggle has been underway in the
best-known regions such as Soave and Valpolicella. Here the
cooperatives are all-powerful, and keep pushing the authorities
to allow higher yields, as if they were not high enough. At the
same time, a growing band of quality-conscious producers are
trying to resist such proposals, and are also imposing on themselves ever more stringent restrictions to ensure the highest
quality. Thus these DOCs include both wines of utter drabness
and anonymity, and some of the finest wines of Italy.

DOC & Other Wines

Amarone See Valpolicella.

Arcole DOC. A new appellation, created in 2000, for vines
grown in two areas southeast of Verona: flat, alluvial soils for
blends; and higher land for varietal wines from Chardonnay,
Sauvignon, Garganega, Merlot, Cabernet Franc, Cabernet
Sauvignon, Raboso, and Corvina.

Bagnoli di Sopra DOC. Covers 15 communes in Padua.
Mostly blended wines, plus Raboso.

Bardolino DOC. Red and *rosato* wine. Province: Verona. Villages:
Bardolino, 15 others. Grapes: Corvina Veronese (35–65%),
Rondinella (10–40%), Molinara (10–20%), up to 15% others.
A pale red and even paler Chiaretto; a lighter version
of Valpolicella with the same quality (in a good example)
of liveliness. Bardolino is on glacial deposits that do not
warm up as well as the limestone of Valpolicella. It is briskest
and best in the year after the vintage. There is also a separate
DOC for wines released shortly after the harvest: Bardolino
Novello. From 2001 Bardolino Superiore (maximum yield
63 hectolitres per hectare) has been DOCG.

Bianco di Custoza DOC. White wine. Province: Verona.
Villages: south shore of Lake Garda. Grapes: Trebbiano
Toscano (35–45%), Garganega (20–40%), Tocai Friulano
(5–30%), Cortese, Riesling Italico, and Malvasia Toscano
(20–30%).
The southern neighbour of Soave and a slightly smaller
wine. Also a *spumante* (usually Charmat).

Breganze DOC. Red and white wine. Province: Vicenza.
Villages: Breganze and Maróstica, parts of 13 other
communes. Grapes: Breganze Bianco – Friulano (minimum
85%), Pinot Bianco, Pinot Grigio, Riesling Italico, Sauvignon,
Vespaiolo (maximum 15%); Breganze Rosso – Merlot, up to
15% Marzemino, Groppello, Cabernet Franc, Cabernet
Sauvignon, Pinot Nero, Freisa; plus varietal wines from

Cabernet Sauvignon, Cabernet Franc, Pinot Nero, Pinot Bianco, Pinot Grigio, Vespaiolo (minimum 85%).

Light and agreeable varietal wines from the birthplace of the great architect, Palladio. Pinot Bianco, Cabernet, and late-harvest Vespaiolo are the best (see Maculan under Producers).

Campo Fiorin An unusually serious interpretation of Valpolicella by Masi (see Producers). The wine is macerated with the skins of Recioto Amarone (q.v.) after pressing. The prototype for *ripasso* wines.

Colli Berici DOC. Red and white wine. Province: Vicenza. Villages: 28 communes south of Vicenza. Grapes: seven varieties, with limited (10–15%) mixture of other local grapes. The range is Garganega, Tocai Bianco; Sauvignon, Pinot Bianco, Merlot, Tocai Rosso (sharp, fruity young red), Cabernet.

These volcanic hills between Verona and Padua have clear potential for quality, best demonstrated by their Cabernet.

Colli di Conegliano DOC. From the slopes around Conegliano. Whites from Incrocio Manzoni, Riesling, and other varieties; reds from Cabernet Sauvignon, Merlot, and Marzemino.

Colli di Conegliano Refrontolo Passito DOC. A *passito* wine from Marzemino.

Colli di Conegliano Torchiato di Fregona DOC. White wines from Prosecco, Verdiso, and Boschera.

Colli Euganei DOC. Red and white wine. Province: Padua. Villages: 17 communes south of Padua. Grapes: Merlot (60–80%), Cabernet Franc, Cabernet Sauvignon, Barbera, Raboso Veronese (20–40%); Garganega (30–50%), Serprina (10–30%), Tocai and/or Sauvignon (20–40%), Pinella, Pinot Bianco, Riesling Italico (maximum 20%). Moscato Bianco can be still or sparkling.

Euganean wine, despite its long history, used to be rather dull, but is now being taken more seriously, as producers profit from the fine autumn climate and long growing season.

Corti Benedettine del Padovano DOC. Red and white wine. Province: Padua. Villages: between Rivers Brenta and Adige and the Adriatic. Grapes: varietal wines from Cabernet Sauvignon, Raboso, Refosco del Peduncolo Rosso; Pinot Bianco, Pinot Grigio, Chardonnay, Sauvignon, Friulano. Also sparkling Moscato and Moscato *passito*.

Gambellara DOC. White wine. Province: Vicenza. Villages: Gambellara, Montebello Vicentino, Montorso, Zermeghedo. Grapes: Garganega (80–90%), Trebbiano di Soave (maximum 20%). Also made as a Recioto di Gambellara and as Vin Santo di Gambellara.

Soave's eastern neighbour, worth trying as an alternative. Its Recioto version is sweet (and sometimes fizzy).

Garda DOC. Province: Verona.

Catch-all DOC, with very high maximum yields.

Lessini Durello DOC. White wine. Provinces: Verona, Vicenza. Villages: seven communes in Verona, 21 in Vicenza. Grapes: Durello (minimum 85%); Garganega, Trebbiano di Soave, Chardonnay, Pinot Nero (maximum 15%).

Steely, dry wines, both still and sparkling.

Lison-Pramaggiore DOC. Red and white wine. Provinces: Venice, Pordenone, Treviso. Villages: 11 communes in Venice, two in Treviso, five in Pordenone. Grapes: Chardonnay, Pinot (Bianco and Grigio), Riesling Italico, Sauvignon, Tocai Italico, Verduzzo, Cabernet (Franc and Sauvignon), Merlot, Refosco del Peduncolo Rosso.

DOC comprising the former areas that produced Tocai di Lison Cabernet and Merlot di Pramaggiore. The wine list includes 12 types; the Pinot Bianco and Riesling Italico may also be *spumante*.

Merlara DOC. Red and white wine. Provinces: Padua (six villages), Verona (three villages).

Red is a blend of Cabernet Sauvignon/Cabernet Franc, Merlot, and Marzemino. The white is from Friulano and Malvasia.

Merlot The major red grape of the eastern Veneto, included in the major DOC zones but often found as a *vino da tavola*, which may be the sign of an individualistic product of quality. Its best wines are dark and nicely fruity, often ending with an astringent note. Others are light and grassy.

Montello e Colli Asolani DOC. Red and white wine. Province: Treviso. Villages: 17 communes. Grapes: Prosecco for white; Cabernet or Merlot for red (up to 15% blending allowed).

The hills around Asolo were a resort during the Renaissance, famous for Palladio's villas. The most famous wine estate of the area is Venegazzù (q.v.).

Piave or Vini del Piave DOC. Red and white wine. Provinces: Venice, Treviso. Villages: from Conegliano to the Adriatic sea; 50 communes in Treviso, 12 in Venice. Grapes: Cabernet, Merlot, Pinot Bianco, Pinot Grigio, Pinot Nero, Raboso, Tocai, or Verduzzo.

A huge area, covering the path of the River Piave through flat country to the sea north of Venice (at Jesolo). Cabernet and Merlot both thrive well here, making rather dry wines that certainly benefit from ageing. The whites, however, need drinking young.

Pramaggiore See Lison-Pramaggiore.

Prosecco di Conegliano-Valdobbiadene DOC. White wine. Province: Treviso. Villages: Valdobbiadene, Conegliano, Vittorio Veneto, 12 other communes. Grapes: Prosecco (85–100%), Verdiso, Pinot Bianco, Pinot Grigio, Chardonnay (maximum 15%), or Verdiso (alone up to 10%). Minimum alcohol: 10.5 degrees *frizzante*, 11 degrees *spumante*.

The native Prosecco grape gives a rather austere and charmless, yellowish, dry wine but responds well to being made *frizzante* or *spumante*, whether dry or sweet. Within Valdobbiadene is a restricted 107-hectare zone where the wines have a finer texture, greater length on the palate, and the right to the title Superiore di Cartizze. Light-hearted consumers all over Italy tend to use the term "Prosecco" as a way of ordering any glass of fizz.

Raboso del Piave The local Raboso grape makes an astringent red wine, which is worth meeting, especially with four or five years' bottle age. See Piave.

Recioto See Valpolicella.

Ripasso See Valpolicella.

San Martino della Battaglia-Lugana DOC. White and fortified wine. Province: Verona, but also includes part of Brescia Province within Lombardy. Villages: small zone on southern shore of Lake Garda. Grapes: Friulano, up to 20% others. Also permitted as *liquoroso*.

Soave DOC, **Soave Superiore** DOCG, **Recioto di Soave** DOCG. White wine. Province: Verona. Villages: Soave, 12 others. Grapes: Garganega (70–90%), Chardonnay, Pinot Bianco, Trebbiano di Soave, Trebbiano Toscano (maximum 30%).

The most popular of all Italian white wines, from 5,500 hectares of vineyards. Its simple name seems to express its simple nature: smooth, light, and easy to drink. When it is well-made and, above all, fresh, it is hugely tempting. The zone is immediately east of Valpolicella, making Verona a singularly well watered city.

A central and hillier zone of Soave, with 1,700 hectares planted, is entitled to the term *classico*. Very high yields are permitted so long as 20 hl/ha are declared as IGT – ignoring the fact that the proportion declared as Soave DOC is equally dilute or mediocre. Recioto di Soave is a concentrated, semi-sweet, and rich-textured version made from dried grapes.

Tocai di Lison See Lison-Pramaggiore.

Valpolicella DOC, **Recioto/Amarone della Valpolicella** DOCG. Red wine. Province: Verona. Villages: 19 communes in the hills north of Verona, the westernmost five of which are the *classico* zone; 5,840 ha. Grapes: Corvina Veronese (40–70%), Rondinella (20–40%), Molinara (5–25%), Cabernet Sauvignon, up to 15% Merlot, Rossignola, Negrara, Barbera, Sangiovese.

Valpolicella, like Chianti, has too wide a range of qualities to be easily summed up. At its best, it is one of Italy's most tempting light reds, always reminding one of cherries, combining the smooth and the lively and ending with the bitter-almond hallmark of almost all northeast Italian reds. In commerce it can be a poor, pale, listless sort of wine. Classico is better; the pick of the villa-dotted vineyards are in the hills skirted to the south and west by the River Adige, divided by the river from Bardolino.

Much Valpolicella is made by the *ripasso* method, which means macerating the wine over the lees of Amarone. This gives the final more body and about one degree more alcohol. The results can be splendid, although some purists worry that it is a way to beef up thin wines that should have been properly made in the first place. Some producers prefer to add dried grapes rather than lees to the new wine, arguing that lees are, by definition, spent. At any Veronese gathering, the last bottle to be served is Recioto, either in its sweet form or its powerful, dry, velvety, but sometimes astringent, version known as Amarone. Recioto is made by drying selected grapes to concentrate their sugars, then giving them a long fermentation in the new year. If the fermentation is allowed to go on to the

bitter end the result is Amarone. Once marginal, Amarone is enjoying a spirited revival, and new styles have richness without astringency. Recioto is also made as a fizz.

This revival is, however, not welcomed by all. Between 2000 and 2003 the production of Amarone doubled, and by 2006 over one-third of Valpolicella grapes were being used to make this style. So Amarone has ceased to be an exceptional wine for special occasions but has evolved into an everyday, commercial product, albeit often of tremendous quality. Some critics complain that the inclusion of French varieties (as in regular Valpolicella) has robbed the wine of its typicity, as has an over-enthusiastic use of new French oak. Moreover, residual sugar, once the defining character of Recioto, is now increasingly found in Amarone too, as growers aim for ever greater richness.

Venegazzù della Casa The estate of Conte Loredan (q.v.) in the DOC Montello-Colli Asolani, but most famous for its non-DOC Cabernet/Merlot blend in the Bordeaux style, comparable perhaps to a powerful, rustic St-Emilion, and its *metodo tradizionale spumante*.

Vicenza DOC. Red and white wine. Catch-all DOC since 2000 for wines within Vicenza province.

Leading Veneto Producers

Accordini ☆☆
Pedemonte. 10 ha. www.accordinistefano.it
Stefano Accordini is a devotee of new French oak, which certainly stamps his wines, from the rich *ripasso* to the Amarone. These are dense and powerful wines that may not please traditionalists.

Adami ☆–☆☆
Colbertaldo di Vidor. 12 ha. www.adamispumante.it
Reliable producers of Prosecco and Cartizze, both *frizzante* and *spumante*.

Allegrini ☆☆☆–☆☆☆☆
Fumane di Valpolicella. 70 ha. www.allegrini.it
Franco and Marilisa Allegrini run this superb estate, which has choice plots in Valpolicella Classico. Palazzo della Torre is made by the *ripasso* method. La Grola is a barrel-aged Valpolicella without *ripasso*. La Poja comes from from a hilltop site planted solely with Corvina, and is one of Italy's most elegant red wines. Excellent Recioto and Amarone, too.

Anselmi ☆☆–☆☆☆☆
Monteforte d'Alpone. 70 ha. www.robertoanselmi.com
Roberto Anselmi was a pioneer of top quality Soave, being one of the first to use barrique-ageing (for the single-vineyard Capital Croce) and to create I Capitelli, a Recioto di Soave as rich as a Sauternes. Since 1986, he has made a fine Cabernet Sauvignon called Realdà. In 1999 Anselmi left the Consorzio, preferring to declare his wines as IGTs, even though they represent the very finest of Soave.

Bertani ☆☆–☆☆☆
Grezzana. 195 ha. www.bertani.net
Founded in 1857, this respected family firm produces a wide range of vines from districts around Verona, using its own

vineyards and purchased grapes. Its wines include model Valpolicella, the Albion Cabernet from its Villa Novare estate, and classic Amarone of exceptional balance and quality.

Bisol ✩✩
Santo Stefano di Valdobbiadene. 60 ha. www.bisol.it
A deservedly well-known producer of Cartizze and Prosecco di Valdobbiadene.

Bolla ✩–✩✩
Verona. www.bolla.it
Founded in Soave in 1883, the firm was bought by the American Brown-Formann company in 1999, and then by the major Italian GIV group in 2006. Grapes acquired from more than 400 growers are processed in ultra-modern plants in the Verona area, to make millions of cases. Bolla was one of the first companies to make single vineyard wines, which are of much higher quality than its generic bottlings. Its Amarones are impressive too.

Brigaldara ✩✩–✩✩✩
San Pietro in Cariano. 20 ha. www.brigaldara.it
Stefano Cesari is a skilled specialist in Amarone and Recioto.

Brunelli ✩✩–✩✩✩
San Pietro in Cariano. 12 ha. www.brunelliwine.com
Luigi Brunelli makes top Valpolicella, in all styles. The single-vineyard Amarone Campo del Titari, which is aged for three years in new barriques, is invariably his finest wine.

Tommaso Bussola ✩✩✩
Negrar 16 ha. www.bussolavini.com
An impeccable source for Recioto di Valpolicella – even more so than for Amarone – and the *ripasso* wines are excellent too.

Ca' La Bionda ✩✩
Valgatara di Marano 29 ha. www.calabionda.it
Less celebrated than some other Valpolicella estates, but a source of well-made wines in all styles, with well balanced Amarone.

Ca' Lustra ✩
Cinto Euganeo, Padua. www.calustra.it
A good address for varietal wines from the Colli Euganei. Reliable, medium-bodied Cabernet Sauvignon and Merlot.

Ca' Rugate ✩✩–✩✩✩
Montecchia di Crosara. 48 ha. www.carugate.it
Since 1986, the Tessaris have moved to the forefront as producers of classic Soave. Recent purchases of vineyards in Valpolicella have allowed them to expand their production of red wines, but, good though they are, they have yet to match the consistency of the Soaves.

Canevel ✩
Valdobbiadene. 25 ha. www.canevel.it
Reliable Prosecco and Cartizze, though at the sweeter end of the spectrum.

La Cappuccina ✩✩–✩✩✩
Monteforte d'Alpone. 30 ha. www.lacappuccina.it
A range of exemplary Soaves, and a real curiosity: Carmenère Campo Buri, aged in new barriques.

Case Bianche ✩
Pieve di Soligo. 32 ha. www.martinozanetti.com
Businessman Zanetti bought this estate in 1997. He uses the Case Bianche label for Prosecco, and Col Sandago for red wines, notably from the Styrian Wildbacher grape.

Castellani ✩✩–✩✩✩
Marano di Valpolicella. 63 ha. www.castellanimichele.it
Sergio Castellani produces good *ripasso* Valpolicella and a sumptuous Recioto.

Cantina del Castello ✩✩
Soave. www.cantinacastello.it
Arturo Stocchetti's Soaves are made with great care, especially the cask-aged Acini Soavi, which has a lusher texture if less finesse than the other *cuvées*.

Cavalchina ✩–✩✩
Sommacampagna. 25 ha. www.cavalchina.com
Good Bianco di Custoza and Merlot from Lake Garda.

Coffele ✩✩
Soave. 30 ha. www.coffele.it
Medium-sized producer of dependable Soave and Recioto.

Col Vetoraz ✩
Santo Stefano di Valdobbiadene. 12 ha. www.colvetoraz.it
Very reliable Prosecco and Cartizze, balancing crispness and sweetness.

Corte Sant'Alda ✩✩✩
Mezzane di Sotto. 15 ha. www.santalda.it
This estate has been run since 1978 by Marinella Camerani. She makes very good barrique aged Valpolicella, sumptuous Amarone and good Recioto. But prices are high.

Romano dal Forno ✩✩–✩✩✩✩
Illasi. 12 ha. www.dalforno.net
Since 1983, Dal Forno has established himself as one of the most dedicated producers of Valpolicella and Amarone, modelling himself on the great Quintarelli (q.v.). Production is tiny, and most of the wines are aged in new oak. With even the regular Valpolicella being made from dried bunches, it is not surprising that the wines are controversial (as well as expensive).

Those who seek out Valpolicella for freshness and charm should look elsewhere. Those who want Valpolicella or Amarone that is vin de garde will be thrilled with these wines.

Fraccaroli ✩
Peschiera del Garda. 50 ha. www.fraccarolivini.it
Good Lugana in all styles.

Le Fraghe ✩✩
Cavaion Veronese. www.fraghe.it
A small estate, producing enjoyable Bardolino and a powerful Cabernet (Sauvignon and Franc) called Quaiare.

Nino Franco ✩✩
Valdobbiadene. 2.5 ha. www.ninofranco.it
Founded in 1919, this firm produces excellent Cartizze and a sweet top Prosecco di Valdobbiadene called Primo Franco.

Gini ☆☆☆
Monteforte d'Alpone. 28 ha. www.ginivini.com
The Gini family produces a range of fresh, creamy Soaves, including Recioto, selectively harvested and aged either in tanks or in barriques. The top wine is invariably an old-vine bottling called Contrada Salvarenza, which is aged for nine months in barriques.

Guerrieri-Rizzardi ☆☆–☆☆☆
Bardolino. 82 ha. www.guerrieri-rizzardi.it
A family estate, dating back to the seventeenth century, with a small but interesting museum. Although the property is best-known for its Bardolino, it also has estates elsewhere in the Veneto from which it produces excellent Valpolicella, Amarone, and Soave. The Bardolino is admirably lively – one of the best of the pale breed.

Inama ☆☆–☆☆☆
San Bonifacio. 30 ha. www.inamaaziendaagricola.it
Stefano Inama has rapidly joined the ranks of Soave's top producers, and is equally successful with varietal Sauvignon and Chardonnay. Curiously, his top wine, Vigneto du Lot, is made from a high-yielding vineyard planted by Australian viticultural guru, Richard Smart.

The red wines come from Inama's vineyards in Colli Berici, and Bradisisimo is a chunky blend of Cabernet Sauvignon and Carmenère.

Lonardi ☆
Marano di Valpolicella. 7 ha. www.lonardivini.it
A tiny estate producing good, traditional Valpolicella and Amarone.

Maculan ☆☆☆☆
Breganze. 40 ha. www.maculan.net
Fausto Maculan must be the Veneto's most versatile winemaker. He has a sure hand with Cabernet Sauvignon (the Fratta bottling is outstanding), Crosara Merlot, and oaked Chardonnay Ferrata, but also makes impeccable varietal wines from Pinot Grigio, Pinot Nero, and the local Vespaiolo grape.

Vespaiolo is also the main variety used for his renowned barrique-aged Torcolato sweet wine, and the fully botrytized Acini Nobili. Maculan doesn't rest on his laurels, and has introduced a new *passito* wine, Madoro, from Marzemina and Cabernet Sauvignon.

Marion ☆☆
San Martino Buon Albergo. 6 ha. www.marionvini.it
Since the late 1990s Stefano Campedelli has been rising swiftly up the ranks of Valpolicella producers. He also produces IGTs from Teroldego and from Cabernet Sauvignon.

Masi ☆☆☆
Gargagnago. 160 ha. www.masi.it
The scholarly Sandro Boscaini presides over this splendid producer. For many years, Campo Fiorin has been a superb example of a *ripasso* Valpolicella, and the single-vineyard Reciotos and Amarones have always been outstanding.

Boscaini has conducted research into local, and often near-extinct, varieties and resurrected them in wines such as the Oseleta-dominated Osar and Grandarella from semi-dried Refosco and other grapes. His deep red Toar is another *ripasso*-style interpretation of Valpolicella tradition. The firm also oversees the marketing of the excellent wines from the Serego Alighieri estate, and has developed estates in Grosseto in Tuscany, and in Argentina.

Masottina ☆
Castello Roganzuolo. 44 ha. www.masottina.it
Good Prosecco and red and white blends from Colli di Conegliano. This large firm also sells wines from Friuli and Trentino.

Roberto Mazzi ☆☆
San Pietro di Negrar. 8 ha. www.robertomazzi.it
The Amarone is usually the top wine at this small estate.

Merotto ☆☆–☆☆☆
Col San Martino. 12 ha. www.merotto.it
Prosecco and Cartizze dominate production here, but there is also full-bodied Cabernet called Rossodogato.

La Montecchia ☆☆
Selvazzano Dentro. 45 ha. www.lamontecchia.it
Good wines from the Colli Euganei, and the rare Fior d'Arancio *passito* and *spumante*.

Montresor ☆–☆☆
Verona. 152 ha. www.vinimontresor.it
A large and long-established firm offering a wide range of Veneto wines, some unexceptional, others, such as the Amarone, of very high quality.

Musella ☆☆
San Martino Buon Albergo. 27 ha. www.musella.it
As well as good *ripasso* and Amarone, Musella is best-known for the Corvina/Cabernet blend, Monte del Drago.

Angelo Nicolis ☆☆
San Pietro in Cariano. 42 ha. www.vininicolis.com
A family firm steadily focused on Amarone of good quality.

Pasqua ☆–☆☆
Verona. 60 ha. www.pasqua.it
Produces 20 million bottles of Valpolicella and other wines, always reliable, rarely exceptional, although at the top level the wines have improved considerably.

Pieropan ☆☆☆–☆☆☆☆
Soave. 45 ha. www.pieropan.it
Leonildo Pieropan is unwavering in his dedication to good viticulture and scrupulous winemaking. His top Soave, La

The Serego Alighieri estate, Verona

Rocca, is as good as Soave gets, and his Calvarino is not far behind. Exquisite Recioto di Soave, and other late-harvest wines complete the range.

Piovene ☆☆
Villaga. 28 ha. www.piovene.com
A small producer of consistently flavoury red and white varietal wines from Colli Berici. This is a source for the rare Tocai Rosso variety.

Umberto Portinari ☆☆–☆☆☆
Monteforte d'Alpone. 4 ha.
Outstanding Soave, especially the single vineyard Albare.

Prà ☆☆–☆☆☆
Monteforte d'Alpone. 20 ha.
Excellent Soave, especially single vineyard Monte Grande.

Quintarelli ☆☆☆☆
Negrar. 12 ha.
No one makes more profound, subtle Recioto and Amarone than the self-effacing Giuseppe Quintarelli. The quality begins in the vineyards with grapes rich enough to absorb the drying process, followed by prolonged fermentation, and years of ageing in large casks. The most individual of his hand-crafted wines is Amarone Alzero from Cabernet Franc, but even his least starry wine has a strong personality.

Le Ragose ☆☆–☆☆☆
Arbizzano. 15 ha. www.leragose.com
Paolo and Marco Galli make impressive and highly consistent wines. They are best known for their superb Amarone, but the Valpolicella Classico is superbly balanced and enjoyable.

Castello di Roncade ☆
Roncade. 40 ha. www.castellodironcade.com
An impressive fortress producing a worthy Bordeaux called Villa Giustinian.

Ruggeri ☆☆
Valdobbiadene. 16 ha. www.ruggeri.it
The company works closely with local growers to produce about one million bottles of very good Prosecco and Cartizze.

Le Salette ☆☆
Fumane. 35 ha. www.lesalette.it
The Scamperle family has long been a reliable source of Valpolicella, Amarone, and Recioto in a lush and full-bodied style.

Le Vigne di San Pietro ☆☆
Sommacampagna. 10 ha. www.levignedisanpietro.it
Owner Carlo Nerozzi used to produce Bardolino but has stopped, turning instead to red IGT wines from the Corvina grape. However, he continues to make a very good Bianco di Custoza, and an oaky Cabernet Sauvignon: Refolà.

La Sansonina ☆☆–☆☆☆
Peschiera del Garda. 13 ha. www.sansonina.it
This is an atypical Lake Garda estate in that owner Carla Prospero, since she acquired the vineyard in 1997, has focused entirely on Merlot. The wine is meticulously made and aged in new oak that has been only lightly toasted.

Tenuta Sant' Antonio ☆☆–☆☆☆
Mezzane di Sotto. 50 ha. www.tenutasantantonio.it
The four Castagnedi brothers are rising stars in Valpolicella, with delicious Recioto, intense Cabernet Sauvignon, and a rare *passito* Chardonnay.

Santa Margherita ☆
Fossalta di Portogruaro. www.santamargherita.com
A very large company, producing wines from all over north and northeast Italy. Once a leading producer of Pinot Grigio, Santa Margherita has lost its edge. One of its more unusual wines is a fruity Malbec.

Santa Sofia ☆–☆☆
Pedemonte. 35 ha. www.santasofia.com
This estate offers a wide range of wines – Valpolicella, Soave, Bardolino – of reliable quality. Amarone can be exceptional.

Santi ☆☆
Illasi. 70 ha. www.giv.it
Founded in 1843, the winery has long been part of the Gruppo Italiano Vini complex. Good Soave and Lugana, but the star turn is the Amarone.

Sartori ☆–☆☆
Negrar. www.sartorinet.com
Despite a production of almost one million cases, the wines, most notably Amarone, can be impressive and firmly structured. The regular Valpolicellas are also much improved in recent years.

Serafini & Vidotto ☆☆–☆☆☆
Nervesa della Battaglia. 20 ha.
A leading producer in DOC Montello e Colli Asolani, best-known for the vibrant Bordeaux blend Rosso del'Abbazia.

Cantina di Soave ☆–☆☆
Soave. 3,500 ha. www.cantinasoave.it
This is unquestionably the biggest producer of Soave, yet hardly a byword for quality, although the top wines can be good. Mergers with other cooperatives have expanded the co-op's reach, and, rather surprisingly, it is a good source for serious Valpolicella. But overall the wines often lack personality.

Speri ☆☆–☆☆☆
Pedemonte. 60 ha. www.speri.com
This company, established in the nineteenth century, has continued to evolve and to refine its wines. Very good Valpolicella and first-rate Recioto and Amarone, especially from Monte Sant' Urbano.

Suavia ☆☆–☆☆☆
Soave. 12 ha. www.suavia.it
The four Tessari sisters produce consistently delicious Soave from their mature vineyards, which are planted only with Garganega and Trebbiano di Soave.

Tedeschi ☆☆☆
Pedemonte. 100 ha. www.tedeschiwines.com
Renzo Tedeschi and his family are masters of all the styles that Valpolicella can produce. His top wines contain

Corvinone as well as Corvina, setting them apart from most other expressions of Valpolicella. His *ripasso* Valpolicella, Capitel San Rocco and Corvina-based Rosso della Fabriseria are also delicious.

Tommasi ☆☆
Pedemonte. 135 ha. www.tommasiwine.it
A very large family run company, with most of its holdings in Valpolicella but also substantial vineyards in Bardolino, Soave, and other regions. Quality can be patchy, but the Valpolicella wines are reliable.

Valdo ☆
Valdobbiadene. www.valdo.com
Owned by Bolla (q.v.), this is a sound producer of Prosecco.

Venegazzù-Conte Loredan-Gasparini ☆☆
Volpago del Montello. 80 ha. www.venegazzu.com
The estate was founded in 1950 by Piero Loredan, descendant of Venetian doges, and bought by Giancarlo Palla in 1974. The fine red wines include Venegazzù della Casa and Capo di Stato, Bordeaux-style blends of great character and class, like a big, not exactly genteel, St-Emilion. After a prolonged bad patch, there are signs of revival.

Venturini ☆☆
San Floriano. 110 ha. www.viniventurini.com
Good Valpolicella and Amarone that can sometimes show signs of astringency.

Vignalta ☆☆–☆☆☆
Torreglia. 55 ha. www.vignalta.it
Excellent wines from the Colli Euganei. Particularly successful is the Merlot-dominated Gemola, and a delightful *passito* wine from Fior d'Arancio is another specialty.

Viviani ☆☆☆
Negrar. 14 ha. www.cantinaviviani.com
Small-scale production so hard to find, but excellent Recioto and Amarone. The Valpolicella is highly impressive, too.

Zenato ☆–☆☆☆
Peschiera del Garda. 70 ha. www.zenato.it
As well as extensive vineyards on the shores of Lake Garda, this well-known estate owns 20 hectares in Valpolicella, from which it produces very good *ripasso* wines and classic Amarone.

Zonin ☆–☆☆☆
Gambellara. www.zonin.it
The Zonin family firm, founded in 1821, claims to be Italy's largest private winery with 1,800 hectares of vineyards. The Veneto is the firm's base, but its estates span northern Italy, the best-known: Castello d'Albola in Chianti Classico, Ca' Bolani in the Friuli, and Feudi Principi di Butera in Sicily. One of the few producers of Recioto di Gambellara.

Friuli-Venezia Giulia

Friuli-Venezia-Giulia is unusual among Italian wine regions other than the Alto Adige since it organizes its wines according to grape varieties. The inevitable complication is that subregions within this area also lay a claim to being identified. So, with six zones and some dozen varieties, the combinations still reach a head spinning number. It helps to distinguish between them if you are clear that there is one very big DOC that embraces most of the region, two superior hill zones with Colli in their names, and three smaller and newer DOCs of less significance, in a row along the coastal plain.

The big zone is Grave del Friuli, DOC for the whole wine-growing hinterland from the Veneto border east to beyond Udine where the Alps reach down towards Trieste. The hills of Gorizia, right on the Slovenian border, are the oldest-established and best vineyards of the region. Today, this zone is generally known simply as "Collio". To the north is the separate DOC of the Colli Orientali del Friuli ("the eastern hills of Friuli") with similar growing conditions.

The coastal DOCs from west to east are Aquileia, Latisana, and Isonzo; the last, adjacent to the Gorizian hills, surely having the greatest potential for quality. These coastal vineyards tend to stress red wine, whereas the reputation of the hills is mainly based on white – whether produced from such traditional grapes as Friulano (formerly known as Tocai), Malvasia, Picolit, or Verduzzo, or more recent imports: the Pinot Bianco or Grigio, Sauvignon Blanc, and Rhine Riesling.

Together with Alto Adige, this is probably Italy's best white wine region, especially inland from the warmer coastlands. Barrique-ageing became fashionable, inevitably, in the late 1980s, but Friuli's white wines have such purity of flavour, at their best, that barrel ageing often seems superfluous. The region is also known for its delicate sweet wines, and has a growing reputation for reds based on Merlot and local varieties such as Refosco and Schioppettino. Quality is remarkably high across the board in the hillier zones, and the wines fetch good prices.

DOC & Other Wines

Friuli Aquileia DOC. Red and white wine. Province: Udine. Villages: Aquileia, 17 others. Grapes: Merlot, Cabernet, Refosco, Tocai Friulano, Pinot Bianco, Pinot Grigio, Riesling Renano, Sauvignon, Traminer Aromatico, Verduzzo.

Named after a Roman city, this DOC of around 900 hectares covers the varied production of the cooperative at Cervignano and other properties. The land is flat, the climate temperate, and efforts at quality production fairly recent. Light, fruity reds such as Cabernet and Merlot show the most promise.

Carso DOC. Red and white wine. Provinces: Trieste, Gorizia. Villages: six communes in Gorizia, six in Trieste. Grapes: Terrano (70%), up to 15% Pinot Nero and Piccola Nera; Malvasia Istriana, Vitovska, or other authorized grapes.

A tiny hill region dominated by limestone. Carso and Carso

Terrano are virtually the same, both based on the Terrano (relative of Refosco) grape.

Collio (or Collio Goriziano) DOC. Red and white wine. Province: Gorizia. Villages: west of Gorizia. Around 1,410 ha. Grapes: Riesling Italico, Sauvignon, Tocai Friulano, Traminer Aromatico, Malvasia Istriana, Merlot, Pinot Bianco, Pinot Grigio, Pinot Nero, Cabernet Franc, Cabernet Sauvignon, Chardonnay, Müller-Thurgau, Picolit, Ribolla Giall, Riesling Renano.

A DOC of such diversity of wines and styles that California comes to mind. Fruity, early developing reds of the Bordeaux varieties are less interesting than the white specialties, particularly the aromatic Friulano and Pinot Bianco and Grigio, which, at their best, balance Hungarian-style "stiffness" and strength with real delicacy. Clay and limestone soils predominate. Collio without a varietal name is a light, dry white of Ribolla and other local grapes.

Colli Orientali del Friuli DOC. Red and white wine. Province: Udine. Villages: 14 communes in the province. 2,300 ha. Grapes: Tocai Friulano, Verduzzo, Ribolla, Pinot Bianco, Pinot Grigio, Sauvignon, Riesling Renano, Picolit, Merlot, Cabernet, Pinot Nero, Refosco, Malvasia Istriana, Ramandolo (Classico); Rosato, Schiopettino.

The neighbouring DOC to Collio, with similar white wines, is perhaps slightly less prestigious except in its native Verduzzo (q.v.) and its rare dessert white, Picolit (q.v.). Merlot and Tocai are the major varieties in terms of plantings. The splendid rustic red Refosco and Cabernet are better than the Collio red wines. There are two sub-denominations; Cialla and Rosazzo.

Friuli-Annia DOC. Red, white, *rosato* wine. Villages: eight of the province of Udine on southern coast. Grapes: Cabernet Franc, Cabernet Sauvignon, Refosco, Tocai, Pinot Bianco, Pinot Grigio, Verduzzo, Traminer, Sauvignon, Chardonnay, Malvasia.

A DOC introduced in 1995. Not yet shining as brightly as Aquileia or Latisana, and will probably be best for early-drinking whites and reds.

Friuli-Grave DOC. Red and white wine. Provinces: Udine, Pordenone. Villages: Udine, Pordenone. 6,700 ha. Grapes: Merlot, Cabernet, Refosco, Tocai, Pinot Bianco, Pinot Grigio, Verduzzo, Riesling Renano, Pinot Nero, Sauvignon, Traminer Aromatico, Chardonnay.

This is the largest DOC of the region and Merlot accounts for half of its production. Grave Merlot is soft, dark, and dry with a hint of grassiness – not as good as its Cabernet Sauvignon, which has more personality and life, nor as memorable as its fruity, bitter Refosco. Grave Pinot Bianco (sometimes Chardonnay) and Tocai can be as good as the Collio equivalents.

Isonzo DOC. Red and white wine. Province: Gorizia. Villages: 20 communes around Gradisca d'Isonzo. 1,000 ha. Grapes: Tocai, Sauvignon, Malvasia Istriana, Pinot Bianco, Pinot Grigio, Verduzzo Friulano, Traminer Aromatico, Riesling Renano, Merlot, Cabernet, Chardonnay, Franconia, Pinot Nero, Refosco dal Peduncolo Rosso, plus Bianco, Rosso, Pinot *spumante*.

The DOC zone between the Collio and the Gulf of Trieste also specializes in Merlot, which can be better than that of Grave del Friuli, and Cabernet for drinking young. Its whites are light and pleasant, but they are rarely up to Collio standards, although a few estates are now working to a high level. Two sub-denominations: Rive Alte and Rive di Giare.

Friuli Latisana DOC. Red and white wine. Province: Udine. Villages: 12 communes in the province. Grapes: Merlot, Cabernet, Refosco, Tocai Friulano, Pinot Bianco, Pinot Grigio, Traminer Aromatico, Chardonnay, Verduzzo Friulano.

This DOC is dominated by Merlot, Cabernet Sauvignon, and Tocai, but Refosco is more robust and durable.

Lison-Pramaggiore DOC. Shared with the Veneto (q.v.).

Picolit. A native grape of the Colli Orientali del Friuli and its dessert wine, the Picolit is one of the almost-lost legends of the nineteenth century, along with the (really lost) Constantia

of the Cape. It yields a powerful, smooth, even dense textured wine, not necessarily very sweet, and finishing slightly bitter in the regional style. Bottles of the wine I have tasted have clearly been too young to have developed the glorious bouquet and flavour that others have reported. It is rare, extremely expensive, in part because of its very low yields, and normally overpriced.

Pignolo A tannic red variety popular in the eighteenth century and much esteemed by the growers who revived it in the 1980s.

Ramandolo DOCG. A Verduzzo produced in a subzone of Colli Orientali.

Schioppettino A native red grape of the Colli Orientali del Friuli, giving wine with some of the rasping fruitiness of a good Barbera from Piedmont.

Tazzelenghe A red grape, translatable as "cuts the tongue". Can be tart, but good examples age well.

Tocai A classic white grape of Friuli, now renamed "Friulano" to avoid confusion with wines from Hungary or even Alsace.

Verduzzo A native white grape made either into a fresh, dry white "fish" wine or a sort of Recioto from partly dried grapes – see Ramandolo, Colli Orientali. NB. Verdiso is a different white grape, mainly grown in the Veneto.

Josko Gravner winery, Collio

Leading Friuli-Venezia Giulia Producers

Angoris ☆☆
Cormòns. 130 ha. www.angoris.com
The Locatelli family produce good whites from their
seventeenth century estate, which is based in Colli Orientali
but has vineyards in various regions. The wines are much
improved in recent years, with advice from Riccardo Cotarella
and a top range called Vôs de Vigne.

Conti Attems ☆
Lucinico. 55 ha. www.attems.it
An estate dating back to medieval times, and now collaborating
with a Tuscan counterpart, namely Frescobaldi. Sound Ribolla
and Merlot, but somehow not as exciting as it could be.

Bastianich ☆–☆☆☆
Premiaracco. 28 ha. www.bastianich.com
A Colli Orientali property bought by Italian-American
restaurateur Joe Bastianich and largely replanted. Sound
varietal wines, but the outstanding bottling is the white blend
Vespa Bianco, made mostly from Sauvignon and Chardonnay,
with the wood-ageing carefully judged. A curiosity here is
Calabrone, made from partially dried Merlot and Refosco
grapes with, sometimes, jammy results.

Beltrame ☆☆
Bagnaria Arsa. 40 ha. www.tenutabeltrame.it
A leading estate in Friuli-Aquileia, with attractive reds from
Merlot and Tazzelenghe, as well as fruity whites.

Borgo Conventi ☆–☆☆
Farra d'Isonzo. 40 ha. www.borgoconventi.it
The former walled convent was developed by Gianni
Vescovo until its sale in 2002 to Tuscan wine producer
Ruffino. The vineyards are divided between Collio and
Isonzo, the latter bearing the I Fiori del Borgo label. The
white wines are dependable, and the best red wine has
long been the Merlot-based blend Braida Nuova.

Borgo Magredo ☆
Tauriano di Spilimbergo. 87 ha. www.borgomagredo.it
Part of the large agricultural Genagricola group, this
Grave estate makes a full range of accessible varietal wines
and *spumante*.

Borgo San Daniele ☆☆☆
Cormòns. 16 ha. www.borgosandaniele.it
Rich Isonzo whites, aged on the fine lees, and white and
red blends called Arbis, the red combining Cabernet and
the rare Pignolo.

Borgo del Tiglio ☆–☆☆☆
Brazzano di Cormòns. 8 ha.
Nicola Manferrari is a winemaking philosopher, much
influenced by his studies at Montpellier, which persuaded
him, rather oddly, to seek to replicate Mediterranean aromas
in his Adriatic wines. One of his ranges is called Studio,
reflecting his sense of winemaking as a continuous work
in progress. His Chardonnay and Friulano have a high
reputation, but they can be worryingly high in alcohol,
making the Tiglio wines an acquired taste.

Rosa Bosco ☆☆–☆☆☆
Moimacco. 3 ha.
Just two wines from this small Colli Orientali estate:
sumptuous barrique-aged Sauvignon Blanc and a delicious
Merlot-based Boscorosso.

Branko ☆☆–☆☆☆
Cormòns. 6 ha.
Igor Erzetic makes only 2,000 cases, including fairly oaky
Collio whites, and a Merlot helpfully called Red Branko.

Buzzinelli ☆–☆☆
Cormòns. 24 ha. www.buzzinelli.com
Good Collio whites and Isonzo reds; Friulano and Ribolla
Gialla are particularly enjoyable.

Ca' Bolani ☆
Cervignano del Friuli. 550 ha. www.cabolani.it
One of a number of Friuli estates owned by Zonin (q.v.)
of the Veneto. Ca' Bolani mainly produces stylish Aquileia
wines of fair quality.

Ca' Ronesca ☆☆
Dolegna del Collio. 52 ha. www.caronesca.it
New owner Davide Setten has maintained standards here,
producing a wide range of Collio varietal wines, and fine
Picolit.

Il Carpino ☆☆
San Floriano del Collio. 15 ha. www.ilcarpino.com
The vineyards lie along the Slovenian border in Collio,
with other parcels in Isonzo. There are two distinct styles:
Vigna Runc, unoaked, and the Carpino wines, aged judiciously
in barrels that are as likely to be Slavonian casks as French
barriques.

La Castellada ☆☆☆–☆☆☆☆
Oslavia. 7.5 ha.
Giorgio and Nicolò Bensa produce tiny quantities of fine
Collio whites, which they generously bottle-age to ensure
they are drinking well on release. As well as varietal wines,
there is a blended Bianco and a Merlot-based Rosso, both
of exceptional quality.

Castelvecchio ☆
Sagrado. 40 ha. www.castelvecchio.com
Reds are the principal wines at the Terraneo family's Carso
estate, and in certain vintages the tannins can be rather tough.

Collavini ☆–☆☆
Corno di Rosazzo. 170 ha. www.collavini.it
Manlio Collavini is the third-generation winemaker at this
large and well known estate, which draws on most of the Friuli
region for its grapes. Quality is reliable, but with the potential
to do better. The best white wine is Bianco Broy, a blend of
Chardonnay, Friulano, and Sauvignon.

Dario Coos ☆☆–☆☆☆
Ramandolo. 5 ha. www.dariocoos.it
Noted for elegant Ramandolo and Picolit.

Girolamo Dorigo ☆☆–☆☆☆☆
Buttrio. 40 ha. www.montsclapade.com

This leading Colli Orientali estate produces 18 different wines, so quality can vary. The reds – Refosco, Tazzelenghe, and above all Pignolo – are very successful: weighty and tannic without being too extracted. Gently oaked Chardonnay and lush but spicy Verduzzo are also noteworthy.

Giovanni Dri ☆☆☆–☆☆☆☆
Ramandolo. 9 ha. www.drironcat.com
With 30 vintages behind him, Dri has mastered the production of exquisite sweet wines: not only Picolit, but also the intense Ramandolo. His finest Ramandolo, Uve Decembrine, is made by cutting the stem to encourage bunch desiccation, a technique also used in Jurançon and in Australia, where it is known as "cordon-cut".

Le Due Terre ☆☆☆
Prepotto. 4 ha.
Unlike most Colli Orientali del Friuli estates, this focuses on blends, Sacrisassi red and white. The white blends Friulano and Ribolla; the red is a beautifully balanced marriage of Schioppettino and Refosco. There is also a pure Merlot, one of Friuli's best.

Fantinel ☆
Spilimbergo. 250 ha. www.fantinel.com
Founded in 1969, this property expanded rapidly and today produces an enormous range of wines of sound commercial quality.

Livio Felluga ☆☆☆
Brazzano di Cormòns. 150 ha. www.liviofelluga.it
This long-established family firm owns four different estates in Collio and Colli Orientali. Livio Felluga, the older brother of Marco, began buying vineyards in the 1950s and in 2008 was still presiding over his company in his tenth decade. The barrel aged white, Terre Alte from Friulano, Pinot Bianco, and Sauvignon Blanc, is rightly esteemed, and the Picolit are usually magnificent, though very expensive. Indeed, the entire range is of very high quality.

Marco Felluga-Russiz Superiore ☆☆
Gradisca d'Isonzo. 120 ha (Felluga), 60 ha (Russiz). www.marcofelluga.it

Marco Felluga, brother of Livio Felluga (q.v.), founded his wine house in 1956, the Russiz Superiore estate in 1967. In addition, he owns two other properties, of which the better known is the Castello di Buttrio.

The Marco Felluga label consists of the usual Collio varieties, mostly from grapes purchased from regular suppliers. Varietal wines, as well as blends such as Molamatta, dominate the range. Russiz Superiore, a model of its kind, consists of 60 hectares of terraced vines. Here, red wines such as Cabernet Franc and a Cabernet Sauvignon-dominated Riserva degli Orzoni take their place alongside the classic whites.

Conti Formentini ☆–☆☆
San Floriano del Collio. No vineyards. www.giv.it
The sixteenth-century castle and property have long belonged to the Formentini family, but since 1996, the winery has been owned by Gruppo Italiano Vini and offers a reliable range of Collio varietal wines. The castle contains an *enoteca*, restaurant, and wine museum.

Villa Frattina ☆☆
Prata di Pordenone. 60 ha. www.villafrattina.it
A leading estate in Lison Pramaggiore, with steadily improving quality. About one million bottles are produced each year.

Friulvini ☆
Zoppola. 2,200 ha. www.friulvini.it
A joint venture among five cooperatives in Friuli-Grave. Soft, easygoing wines and some barrique-aged reds.

Gravner ☆☆–☆☆☆☆
Oslavia. 18 ha.
See box below.

Isola Augusta ☆☆
Palazzolo della Stella. 42 ha. www.isolaugusta.com
Fruity Chardonnay, Cabernet, and other wines from Latisana.

Jermann ☆☆☆☆
Villanova di Farra. 130 ha. www.jermann.it
A family estate founded in 1880, it has been run for many years by Silvio Jermann. Even as a very young man, Jermann

JOSKO GRAVNER

Josko Gravner, now in his late fifties and assisted by his son Miha, has always been a trend-setter in Friuli. In the late 1980s he was pursuing low yields and was a pioneer of barrique-aged wines, although with mixed success. A decade later he was widely regarded as Collio's best winemaker. When visiting Georgia in the late 1990s he saw how wines were still being fermented and aged in clay amphorae. He adopted the idea, shipped amphorae back to Italy, and by 2001 had completely converted his winery.

Gravner ferments his white wines on the skins, leaves them there for about seven months, and ages all his wines for about five years before releasing them. As a consequence, his white wines in particular have a powerful earthiness that to his admirers speaks deeply of the soil, while his detractors deplore their undeniable oxidative character and their lack of obvious fruitiness.

He has attracted devoted acolytes in Collio and Slovenia, and his

production of Ribolla and the blended white Breg is small enough to ensure he is always sold out. He remains serenely uncompromising, insisting he relies on his instincts rather than analyses to determine such decisions as picking dates and maceration periods.

He is an avowed enemy of standardization, and while acknowledging that his wines are not for everyone, is pleased that he has a following among a loyal band worldwide who regard his wines as truly remarkable.

showed an unerring touch with white wine vinification. These are wines with ample fruit but perfect balance. His vineyards are in Collio and Isonzo, but Jermann ceased to use DOC labels many years ago, and all his wines are now IGT. As well as an impeccable range of varietal wines, there are delicious blends such as the Ribolla-dominated Vinnae and the justly celebrated Vintage Tunina (from Chardonnay, Sauvignon, Malvasia, Ribolla, Picolit) from 16 hectares of vines.

Taste Tunina if you are a sceptic about Italian whites. Jermann has always enjoyed cryptic names for some of his wines. His expensive, barrel-aged Chardonnay was called "Where the Dreams Have No End..." and is now labelled "Were Dreams, now it is just wine!" A more recent addition to the range is Capo Martino, a field blend of mostly Friulano, plus Malvasia, Ribolla, and Picolit, aged in large casks and now Jermann's most expensive white wine. Despite the larking about, Jermann's wines are serious but never ponderous.

Kante ☆☆☆
Aurisina. 6 ha.
Edi Kante's vines are planted high up on rocky limestone soils, while his cellars are tunnelled beneath them. A leading producer of the Carso region, his wines are marked by their freshness and longevity, which explains why he releases some of the wines long after they have been bottled (using litre and half-litre bottles only).

Edi Keber ☆☆☆
Cormòns. 10 ha.
Keber, now assisted by his son Kristjan, has reduced the range of wines he produces, focusing on Friulano, a complex Bianco blend, and a red-fruited Rosso that combines Merlot and Cabernet Franc.

Lis Neris ☆☆☆
San Lorenzo Isontino. 56 ha. www.lisneris.it
Alvaro Pecorari makes brilliant white wines from Pinot Grigio and Chardonnay, and a remarkable sweet wine, Confini, based on Traminer and Pinot Grigio. His top red, Lis Neris, is richly oaked, but the top white wines are aged in older barrels so as to avoid any overt oakiness. Some 2001s were still vibrantly fruit in 2008, confirming Pecorari's assertion that these are Isonzo wines that age well.

Livon ☆–☆☆☆
San Giovanni al Natisone. 200 ha. www.livon.it
This family winery has expanded considerably, and operates out of four cellars in Friuli, and also owns two properties in Tuscany. Quality varies, but at the top end, the Braide Alte blend (Chardonnay, Sauvignon, Picolit, Moscato) and the RoncAlto Ribolla are creamy and delicious.

Masut da Rive ☆☆–☆☆☆
Mariano del Friuli. 20 ha. www.masutdarive.com
An estate founded in 1995 by the Gallo brothers, this is already one of the best in Isonzo, with first rate Friulano.

Miani ☆☆☆
Buttrio. 15 ha.
A first-rate estate, run by Enzo Pontoni, with outstanding

Refosco and Merlot as well as white wines, but production is minute and prices astronomic.

Vigneti le Monde ☆–☆☆
Prata di Pordenone. 25 ha. www.vignetilemonde.com
Owned by the Pistoni Salice family, the estate produces attractive varietal wines from Grave del Friuli, and fairly tannic Cabernet Franc and Ca' Salice, a blend of Refosco and Cabernet.

Moschioni ☆☆–☆☆☆
Cividale del Friuli. 13 ha.
Local red varieties, cropped at a very low yield, give this property its individuality, making it an admirable source of barrique-aged Pignolo and Schioppettino.

Pierpaolo Pecorari ☆☆–☆☆☆
San Lorenzo Isontino. 30 ha. www.pierpaolopecorari.it
Top Isonzo wines from a low-yielding estate, with Merlot and Refosco the outstanding red wines, and Pinot Bianco the most succulent white.

Petrucco ☆
Buttrio. 25 ha. www.vinipetrucco.it.
Sound varietal white wines from a well-located Colli Orientali estate.

Pichéch ☆☆–☆☆☆
Cormòns. 7 ha. www.picech.it
Full-bodied whites, notably the Collio Bianco from Ribolla, Friulano, and Malvasia.

Pighin ☆–☆☆
Risano. 30 ha. www.pighin.com
Well-known family firm offering over a million bottles of a range of wines from Collio and Grave. More than acceptable quality across the board.

Vigneti Pittaro ☆☆
Codroipo. 85 ha. www.vignettipittaro.com
Piero Pittaro is a past president of Italy's association of oenologists. His estate produces some standard varietals, but also a range of sparkling wines and unusual specialties such as Moscato Rosa and Ramandolo.

Plozner ☆☆
Spilimbergo. 60 ha. www.plozner.it
Sound varietal wines, from Grave del Friuli, recently refreshed with more exacting winemaking and innovative packaging.

Isidoro Polencic ☆☆–☆☆☆
Cormòns. 25 ha. www.polencic.com
Impeccable and highly consistent Collio whites.

Primosic ☆☆
Madonnina di Oslavia. 26 ha. www.primosic.com
Excellent Bordeaux blend Metamorfosis sometimes outshines the reliable Collio whites, although the Chardonnay is almost always the finest wine.

Dario Princic ☆☆
Gorizia. 6 ha.
Princic has taken a leaf or two out of Gravner's book,

fermenting his Sauvignon and his white blend Trebež on the skins for over one week. A blend of Chardonnay, Sauvignon Blanc, and Pinot Grigio, it has an orange hue, a grainy texture, but no hint of oxidation. A winner with Oriental food.

Doro Princic ☆☆☆
Pradis di Cormòns. 11 ha.
This tiny Collio winery makes gorgeous Pinot Bianco and Friulano.

Puiatti ☆☆
Capriva del Friuli. 70 ha. www.puiatti.com
Giovanni Puiatti now runs the company founded by his respected father, Vittorio. The wines come from vineyards in Collio and Isonzo, and recently the range has been revamped into lines from different regions such as Ruttars. The Puiattis are passionate believers in unoaked white wines, and to prove their point, they release a range of bottle-aged, mature wines under the Archétipi label to prove that unwooded white wines can age very well – if made with the care that is characteristic of all the Puiatti ranges.

Dario Raccaro ☆☆☆
Cormòns. 5 ha.
Tiny production, so hard to find, but both the Friulano and Merlot are outstanding.

Radikon ☆–☆☆
Oslavia. 12 ha.
Like Josko Gravner, Stanko Radikon has gone through many changes of mind before finding a style of non-interventionist winemaking he is happy with. He favours high density plantings, organic farming, extended skin maceration for white wines, and ageing those wines in large casks for about three years. Bottled without sulphur dioxide, the wines have had a mixed reception.

Rocca Bernarda ☆☆–☆☆☆
Ipplis. 55 ha. www.roccabernarda.com
The Perusini family bequeathed their estate to the Knights of Malta. The property went through a number of changes in recent years but seems back on track as an outstanding estate in Colli Orientali del Friuli. Bianco Vineis is an excellent white blend, dominated by Friulano, but Rocca Bernarda continues to be best-known for its magnificent Picolit.

Rodaro ☆☆–☆☆☆
Spessa di Cividale. 45 ha.
Classic whites from Colli Orientali, and an exotic blend called Ronc (Pinot Bianco, Sauvignon, Tocai). In recent years the red wines have matched the quality of the whites.

Ronchi di Cialla ☆☆
Prepotto. 16 ha. www.ronchidicialla.com
The Rapuzzi family pioneered the production of previously obscure local varieties such as Schioppettino, Refosco dal Peduncolo Rosso, and Verduzzo. They continue to produce exemplary versions.

Ronchi di Manzano ☆☆
Manzano. 55 ha. www.ronchidimanzano.com
Roberta Borghese produces a huge number of wines at her Colli Oriental estate, but among the highlights are the Chardonnay, Pinot Grigio, and Merlot.

Ronco del Gelso ☆☆–☆☆☆
Cormòns. 25 ha. www.roncodelgelso.com
Giorgio Badin makes top Isonzo wines at his solar powered winery: outstanding white varietals, and very good Merlot. Badin is careful not to go overboard with the use of barriques, and prefers to age his top whites in either large casks or 500-litre barrels. At a comprehensive tasting in 2008, the Friulano, Pinot Grigio, and the Latimis blend from Friulano, Pinot Bianco, and late-picked Riesling stood out.

Ronco del Gnemiz ☆☆
San Giovanni al Natisone. 17 ha.
Low yields characterize Serena Palazzolo's estate in Colli Orientali del Friuli. The flagship wine is named after the property, and is a barrique-aged blend of Cabernet and Merlot, bottle-aged before release.

Ronco dei Tassi ☆☆☆
Cormòns. 12 ha. www.roncodeitassi.it
Founded in 1989, Fabio Coser's small estate has made great strides and produces utterly reliable Collio whites, especially the partly oaked blend Fosarin, from Friulano, Malvasia, and Pinot Bianco.

Roncùs ☆☆
Capriva del Friuli. 12 ha. www.roncus.it
Unusually rich Collio whites, especially the splendid and creamy Bianco Vecchie Vigne, which rather daringly puts Malvasia in the clear majority of the blend.

Russiz Superiore
See Marco Felluga.

Schiopetto ☆☆☆
Capriva del Friuli. 30 ha. www.schiopetto.it
Founded in 1965 by the late Mario Schiopetto, on a Collio property belonging to the archbishopric of Gorizia. He has been succeeded by his son, Giorgio, who has reduced the number of wines but maintained the quality.

The elegant Pinot Bianco, Pinot Grigio, and the Sauvignon are all notable, but the wine that stands out is, appropriately, named Mario Schiopetto, and is a blend of Chardonnay and Friulano, with partial barrique ageing. It has a suave opulence rarely found in Collio whites.

Scubla ☆☆–☆☆☆
Premariacco. 12 ha. www.scubla.com
Roberto Scubla has built his reputation on the first-rate Pomèdes blend of Pinot Bianco, Friulano, Chardonnay, and Riesling, matured in 50 per cent new oak.

Skerk ☆☆–☆☆☆
Prepotto. 6 ha. www.skerk.com
Splendidly mineral Carso whites from Sauvignon and Vitovska, with oak-ageing that never seems obtrusive.

Specogna ☆–☆☆
Corno di Rosazzo. 16 ha. www.specogna.it
Leonardo Specogna is a reliable source of traditionally made

Colli Orientali del Friuli wines. Note the whites are usually better than the reds, although the Pignolo is appealing.

Castello di Spessa ✩–✩✩
Capriva del Friuli. 30 ha. www.paliwines.com
This Collio estate has a good reputation but recent vintages have been less impressive, with a certain blandness creeping in.

Franco Toros ✩✩
Cormòns. 10 ha. www.vinitoros.com
White Collio wines of crispness and charm, with Pinot Bianco and Friulano sometimes showing more richness and depth.

Torre Rosazza ✩
Oleis di Manzano, Udine. 110 ha.
www.torrerosazza.com
This Colli Orientali estate became well-known when Walter Filiputti was the winemaker. Today the wines are more humdrum, although the summoning of Donato Lanati as consultant winemaker suggests the owner, Genagricola, aims to improve quality. See also Borgo Magredo.

Venica & Venica ✩✩–✩✩✩
Dolegna del Collio. 34 ha. www.venica.it
Vigorous Collio whites from the Venica brothers, and a substantial Bordeaux blend called Rosso delle Cime.

La Viarte ✩✩
Prepotto. 25 ha.
www.laviarte.it
As well as varietal wines from Colli Orientali del Friuli, the Ceschin family offer rarities such as a pure Tazzelenghe, and Siùm, a blend of Picolit and Verduzzo.

Vie di Romans ✩✩✩
Mariano del Friuli. 50 ha. www.viediromans.it
Gianfranco Gallo took over running this Isonzo estate in 1978, and has turned it into one of Friuli's finest. (Originally named after himself, Gallo had to invent the current name after a certain Californian producer instituted legal proceedings for, one assumes, effrontery at sharing its name.) The whites are very rich and the Chardonnay comes in unoaked and barrique-aged versions. Unoaked Sauvignon from 1990 and 1996 were still drinking well in 2008, although there is no reason to delay gratification for so long.

Villa Russiz ✩✩
Capriva del Friuli. 41 ha. www.villarussiz.it
Founded in 1869 by a French nobleman, Comte de la Tour, Villa Russiz has been run for some years by winemaker Gianni Menotti. An excellent range of Collio wines, with exceptionally elegant Sauvignon, Pinot Bianco, and Friulano. The oaked Chardonnay and Merlot are named De la Tour but alcohol is often high and the wines can lack finesse.

Volpe Pasini ✩✩✩
Togliano di Cividale. 52 ha.
www.volpepasini.it
Retired surgeon Emilio Rotolo bought this historic Colli Orientali estate in 1995, after four centuries in the hands of the previous owners. The top range is called Zuc di Volpe, and is dominated by lively white wines. However, the vibrant reds are of interest too: Zuc Refosco and Focus Merlot, both aged mostly in new oak.

Zamò ✩✩✩–✩✩✩✩
Manzano. 67 ha. www.levignedizamo.com
A new star in the Colli Orientali, helped to celebrity by consultant Franco Bernabei. The Zamò family don't rely on the estate for their livelihood, so they can afford to pursue perfection. Indeed, it's impossible to find a weak leak in the range.

Friulano is often the most dazzling white, but the Chardonnay-dominated Ronco delle Acacie can be as fine. Merlot, Refosco, and Pignolo lead the reds, and the Picolit is sensational but almost impossible to find.

Emilia-Romagna

It is to be expected that Italy's greediest culinary region, by all accounts, should put the emphasis on quantity rather than quality in its wine. Any ambition to produce better than simple thirst-quenchers is recent and limited to a select few. Bologna, the cooks' capital, is the hub of the region and the meeting place of its two component parts. Most of the land is the flat Po valley, following the river to the Adriatic between Ravenna and Venice.

All the wine regions of interest lie in the foothills, however tentative, of the Apennines to the south, dividing the province from Tuscany. Fizzy red Lambrusco leads, not just in Emilia but in the whole of Italy, for volume production of a distinct type of wine. It is an ingenious and profitable way of achieving notoriety in deep valley soils where more conventional quality is unlikely. Not that Lambrusco should be despised, despite its poor reputation. The best examples, often made by *metodo classico*, have richness and depth and, above all, personality.

Romagna produces nothing so exceptional. Its best-known wine is the white Albana, which has yet to distinguish itself. It is in the Colli Bolognesi and Piacentini, the hill areas nearest to Bologna and Piacenza, that progress is being made. Apart from Lambrusco, the region does have some specialties such as Gutturnio and Pagadebit that make a welcome change from the oceans of Lambrusco or Trebbiano di Romagna.

DOC & Other Wines

Albana di Romagna DOCG. White wine. Provinces: Ravenna, Forlì, Bologna. Grape: Albana. May be made in *secco* (dry), *amabile* (off-dry), *dolce* (sweet), and *passito* styles.

The standard white of Bologna and east to the coast. The Albana is a mild, not to say neutral, grape whose dry wines tend to flatness, finishing bitter to satisfy local taste. It gains more character when made *amabile* and/or *spumante*, or indeed *passito*. Inexplicably promoted to DOCG in 1987.

Barbarossa di Bertinoro A vine not found elsewhere, cultivated on a small scale at Bertinoro, the centre of the Romagna vineyards, for a good, full-flavoured red with ageing potential. See Fattoria Paradiso.

Barbera The ubiquitous red grape is popular in the area of Piacenza and in the Colli Bolognesi and Colli d'Imola.

Bianco di Scandiano DOC. White wine. Emilia. Villages: commune of Scandiano, five others southwest of Reggio. Grapes: Sauvignon (maximum 85%), Malvasia di Candia and Trebbiano Romagnolo (maximum 15%).

A white alternative to Lambrusco (q.v.) made semi-dry or distinctly sweet, sometimes fizzy and sometimes fully frothy.

Bosco Eliceo DOC. Red and white wine. Emilia. Provinces: Ferrara, Ravenna. Grapes: Trebbiano Romagnolo, Sauvignon/Malvasia di Candia, Fortana, Merlot, Sauvignon.

The Fortana is a rustic red from this DOC grown on reclaimed marshland around Ravenna.

Cagnina di Romagna DOC. Red wine. Villages: 16 communes in Forlì, five in Ravenna. Grapes: Cagnina, up to 15% other varieties.

A sweet red wine enjoyed locally as an accompaniment to roast chestnuts. Very small production.

Colli Bolognesi DOC. Red and white wine. Emilia. Provinces: Bologna, Modena. Grapes: (white) Albana (60–80%), Trebbiano Romagnolo (minimum 20%), up to 20% other whites. For named varieties: Barbera, Merlot, Riesling Italico, Pinot Bianco, Cabernet Sauvignon, Sauvignon Blanc (85%), 15% neutral grapes allowed.

An umbrella DOC for the everyday wines of Bologna. More remarkable wines are being made in the same vineyards by growers experimenting with better grapes, including Sauvignon Blanc, Cabernet Sauvignon, and Chardonnay. Growing conditions are excellent.

Colli Bolognesi Classico Pignoletto A sub-DOC for the traditional tart white grape of the region.

Colli di Faenza Hills south of Faenza. Trebbiano and Sngiovese are the principal grapes.

Colli di Imola Hills south of Imola. Bianco and Rosso, plus varietal wines from Chardonnay, Pignoletto, Trebbiano, Barbera, and Sangiovese.

Colli di Parma DOC. Red and white wine. Parma foothills. Grapes: Barbera 60–75%, with Bonarda or Croatina 25–40%, other varieties up to 15%; (Malvasia) Malvasia di Candia 85–100%, Moscato Bianco up to 15%; Sauvignon Blanc 100%.

The red resembles Oltrepò Pavese Rosso, the Malvasia may be either dry or *amabile*, usually *frizzante*; the Sauvignon Blanc usually still.

Colli Piacentini DOC. Red and white wine. The slopes south of Piacenza. Grapes: Chardinbnay, Malvasia, Pinot Grigio, Sauvignon, Trebbiano; Barbera, Bonarda, Cabernet Sauvignon, Gutturnio, Pino Nero.

The region is known for a number of blended wines, such as the white Monterosso and Trebbiano Val Trebbia, and Gutturnio: a blend of Barbera and Bonarda. A high volume zone, producing wines from innumerable varieties in every conceivable style.

Gutturnio dei Colli Piacentini See Colli Piacentini.

Lambrusco Lambrusco from Emilia was the smash hit of the Italian wine industry in the 1970s, selling like Coca-Cola (in more senses than one) in the United States.

It is simply a sweet, semi-sweet, or occasionally dry, fizzy red (or pink or occasionally white) wine, such as any winemaker could produce who had the foresight to see the demand. The common qualities are scarcely drinkable by a discerning wine-lover, but this misses the point. The market is elsewhere. More discerning palates will choose one from a named region, of which the best is Sorbara. A select few producers show true genius with this wine.

Lambrusco Grasparossa di Castelvetro DOC. Red and *rosato* wine. Emilia. Province: Modena.

Dark-coloured, tannic, rather strong, and always slightly sweet; comes from the hills southwest of Modena.

Lambrusco Reggiano DOC. Red and *rosato* wine. Emilia. Province: Reggio Emilia.

Commonest, lightest, and usually fizziest Lambrusco.

Lambrusco Salamino di Santa Croce DOC. Red wine. Emilia. Province: Modena.

Salamino di Santa Croce is a local sub-variety of the Lambrusco grape with a bunch said to resemble a little salami. Dark, soft, fruity, and at its best when dry.

Lambrusco di Sorbara DOC. Red and *rosato* wine. Emilia. Province: Modena. Grapes: Lambrusco di Sorbara (60%), Lambrusco Salamino (maximum 40%).

A good Lambrusco di Sorbara is a delight: juicy, pink wine, racy, tingling and extraordinarily drinkable – a childish wine perhaps, but marvellously thirst-quenching with rich food. In fact, the pink froth is a pleasure in itself.

Alas, off-putting chemical flavours are all too common, even in this premium Lambrusco; under no circumstances store bottles of any of them.

Pagadebit di Romagna DOC. White wine. Provinces: Forlì, Ravenna.

Pagadebit means "debt payer" thanks to generous yields. A white vine, known as Bombino in Pugliaenjoying revival and modernization around Bertinoro in Romagna. Vinified as gently dry or *amabile*. The commune of Bertinoro rates as a special sub-denomination.

Reno DOC. White wine. Province: Bologna. Grapes: Albana, Trebbiano

Grown between Imola and Modena, and around Bologna. Grapes: Montuni and Pignoletto. The wine can be dry or semi-sweet and is usually *frizzante*.

Romagna Albana Spumante DOC. White wine. Provinces: Ravenna, Bologna, Forlì. Grape: Albana. Sparkling.

Sangiovese di Romagna DOC. Red wine. Provinces:

Ravenna, Bologna, Forlì. Grape: Sangiovese di Romagna.

Romagna has its own strain of the red Sangiovese, distinct from and softer than the Tuscan one, which is the basis of Chianti. It makes pleasant, light- to medium-weight red, often with a slightly bitter aftertaste. It is produced in enormous quantities and enjoyed young, often as the Sunday wine of the region.

Sauvignon Blanc An up-and-coming white grape in this part of Italy, possibly the best of the DOC Colli Bolognesi and the major partner in the DOC Bianco di Scandiano.

Trebbiano di Romagna DOC. White wine. Provinces: Bologna, Forlì, Ravenna. Grape: Trebbiano di Romagna.

The popular, undemanding everyday white at the coastal resorts. Its style is clean-tasting and unobtrusive.

Leading Emilia-Romagna Producers

Conte Otto Barattieri ☆–☆☆☆
Vigolzone. 35 ha.
Sound Gutturnio from Colli Piacentini and a rare *vin santo* from Malvasia di Candia given almost a decade in small casks .

Francesco Bellei ☆–☆☆
Bomporto. 15 ha. www.francescobellei.it
Highly regarded Lambrusco di Sorbara and Pinot/ Chardonnay *tradizionale* from this organic estate. The Lambrusco Rifermentazione Ancestrale is released without disgorgement.

La Berta ☆–☆☆
Brisighella. 27 ha.
Sangiovese is the mainstay of this estate near Faenza, but you can also find Almante, a rare Alicante, and an oaky Cabernet Sauvignon called Ca di Berta.

Bonfiglio ☆
Monteveglio. 25 ha. www.bonfigiliovini.it
Serious Pignoletto, still and *frizzante*, from the Colli Bolognesi.

Bonzara ☆☆
Monte San Pietro, 16 ha. www.bonzara.it
A steadily improving estate, offering a good range of Colli Bolognesi wines. The Sauvignon (*passito* as well as dry) is excellent, as is Bonzarone from Cabernet Sauvignon.

Ca' Lunga ☆☆
Imola. 19 ha. www.tenutacalunga.it
With advice from consultant oenoligist Lorenzo Landi, this has become a leading producer in the Colli d'Imola.

Calonga ☆☆
Forlì. 10 ha. www.calonga.it
Very ripe Sangiovese di Romagna, Michelangiolo, and attractive herbal Pagadebit. Much improved since 2000.

Much of Emilia-Romagna's wine is café wine – drunk where it is produced

Casali ☆–☆☆
Scandiano. 10 ha. ww.casalivini.it
One of the best Lambrusco Reggianos is made at this estate. Also bottle-fermented sparkling wines and Bianco di Scandiano.

Castelluccio ☆☆☆
Modigliana. 12 ha. www.ronchidicastelluccio.it
Ronco dei Ciliegi and Ronco delle Ginestre from Sangiovese, and Ronco del Re from Sauvignon Blanc, are fashioned into some of Romagna's finest bottlings under the experienced eye of owner and wine consultant Vittorio Fiore and his son Claudio.

Cavicchioli ☆–☆☆
San Prospero. 50 ha. www.cavicchioli.it
Sandro Cavicchioli produces a million cases of very dependable Lambruscos from different DOCs. The top Sorbara is called Vigna del Cristo and takes its name from a seven hectare vineyard.

Celli ☆☆
Bertinoro. 39 ha. www.celli-vini.com
This medium-sized winery takes Albana seriously and produces it in a range of styles. Other wines include rich Chardonnay and Sangiovese.

Cesari ☆☆–☆☆☆
The backbone of this large property is Albana and Sangiovese, especially the delicious Sangiovese Reserva. Umberto Cesari is also a restless innovator, and has created Moma, which blends Sangiovese with Cabernet Sauvignon and Merlot, and Liano from Sangiovese and Cabernet, both rich and forceful barrique aged wines.

Cinti ☆☆
Sasso Marconi. 17 ha. www.collibolognesi.com
Consistently reliable varietal wines from Colli Bolognesi, including a delectable Pignoletto.

Drei Donà: Tenuta la Palazza ☆☆☆
Massa di Vecchiazzano, Forlì. 24 ha. www.dreidona.it
This is a small winery focusing on varietal wines of high quality, including a rich, barrique aged Sangiovese; concentrated Magnificat Cabernet Sauvignon; and a Chardonnay called Il Tornese. Franco Bernabei is the consultant oenologist.

Ferrucci ☆☆–☆☆☆
Castel Bolognese. 15 ha. www.stefanoferruci.it
Ilaria Ferrucci has taken over from her late father Stefano and the estate continues to make very good, sweet Albana and Sangiovese Riservas, and a sweet Malvasia called Stefano Ferrucci.

Vittorio Graziano ☆☆–☆☆☆
Castelvetro di Modena. 6 ha.
A resolutely traditional Lambrusco producer, who ages his invigorating wines for long than most. Also makes a barrique-aged red blend called Sassoscuro that combines Merlot, Syrah, and the local Malbo Gentile.

Luretta ☆☆–☆☆☆
Gazzola. 57 ha. www.luretta.com
An estate in the Colli Piacentini, producing very good Chardonnay and Cabernet Sauvignon. A fine sweet wine, Le Rane, is made from pure Malvasia.

Madonia ☆☆–☆☆☆
Bertinoro. 12 ha. www.giovannamadonia.it
A small estate producing consistently good Albana *passito*, Merlot, and Sangiovese Superiore.

Medici Ermite ☆☆
Gaida, Reggio Emilia. 60 ha. www.medici.it
Founded in the early twentieth century, the Medici family have long specialized in fine Lambrusco, sparkling and still. Their best wines, such as Concerto, have a cleansing acidity and a refreshing dry finish. Another speciality is late-harvest Malvasia that can sometimes be rather heavy.

Moro ☆☆
Santo'Ilario d'Enza. 15 ha. www.rinaldinivini.it
Paola Rinaldini produces Chardonnay and Cabernet, but is better known for her range of Lambrusco wines, including the rare house specialty: Pjcòl Ross.

Mossi ☆–☆☆
Ziano Piacentino. 60 ha. www.vinimossi.com
Luigi Mossi produces a wide range from Colli Piacentini, specializing in Gutturnio. Infernotto is an unusual blend of Barbera, Pinot Nero, Cabernet, and Bonarda.

Fattoria Paradiso ☆☆☆
Bertinoro. 60 ha. www.fattoriaparadiso.com
An estate that has been shaped into a viticultural paradise by Mario Pezzi and his descendants. Jacopo Lupo Melia makes 50,000 cases of exemplary wine, including the unique red Barbarossa (of a vine only he grows), a Cabernet, Merlot, and Syrah blend called Mito, Albana *passito*, and white semi-sweet Pagadebit. Two of Italy's best winemakers, Carlo Ferrini and Roberto Cipresso, consult for the estate.

Pasolini Dall'Onda ☆☆
Montericco Imola. 22 ha. www.pasolinidallonda
Winemakers since the sixteenth century, the Pasolini Dall' Onda family own properties in Romagna and Tuscany. Here they produce Chardonnay, Sangiovese, and a Bordeaux blend.

Poderi dal Nespoli ☆☆
Civitella di Romagna. 30 ha. www.poderidalnespoli.com
Beautiful property, producing fine Albana *passito* and a blend from Sangiovese and Cabernet: Borgo dei Guidi.

Il Poggiarello ☆☆–☆☆☆
Travo. 13 ha. www.ilpoggiarellovini.it
Fine varietal wines, including Pinot Nero from Colli Piacentini, still and sparkling. The top wine is La Barbona and is a blend of Barbera and Bonarda.

Riunite ☆
Campegine. www.riunite.it
Founded in 1950, Riunite is one of the world's largest winemaking operations. Lambrusco is the principal product,

but there is Merlot and Pinot Grigio to cater to the most modest expectations of Italian wine.

Vast quantities of mostly undistinguished Lambrusco and blush wines are shipped to the United States. Indeed, its success made the fortune of Villa Banfi, which in turn had a profound effect on Montalcino in Tuscany.

San Patrignano ☆☆☆
Coriano. 100 ha. www.sanpatrignano.org
A remarkable operation located at a drug rehabilitation centre. Quality has improved dramatically since Riccardo Cotarella was brought in as consultant winemaker in 1997. The highlights are the Sangiovese Superiore called Avi, and a dense, barrique-aged, Bordeaux-blend called Montepirolo.

San Valentino ☆☆☆
Rimini. 28 ha. www.vinisanvalentino.com
An ambitious estaste, releasing, among many other wines, a chewy Bordeaux blend called Luna Nuova, and, more impressive, a splendid if oaky Sangiovese Riserva called Terra di Covignano.

Spalletti ☆☆
Savignano sul Rubicone. 75 ha. www.spalletticolonnadadipaliano.com
This winery is housed in the ancient Castello di Ribano. It produces a full range of Romagna specialties, from Pagadebit to Albana to Sangiovese. The Rocca di Ribano Riserva and Villa Rasponi are both excellent Sangiovese di Romagna.

La Stoppa ☆☆–☆☆☆
Ancarano di Rivergaro. 30 ha. www.lastoppa.it
A leader in Colli Piacentini owned by Elena Pantaleoni. There is an attractive Cabernet Sauvignon, Barbera, Gutturnio, and sweet Malvasia. In 2002 Ageno was introduced, an amazingly opulent dry white based on Malvasia and other local varieties.

Terre Rosse ☆☆
Zola Predosa. 25 ha. www.terrerosse.it
Founded in 1965 by the late Enrico Vallania, a physician, whose genius and tenacity charted new directions in Italian viticulture. The Colli Bolognesi range includes excellent Sauvignon Blanc, Cabernet Sauvignon, Chardonnay, and Malvasia. Terre Rosse has persisted with its policy of ageing its wines in tanks only, arguably at the expense of complexity, especially of red wines.

La Tosa ☆☆–☆☆☆
Vigolzone. 16 ha. www.latosa.it
An emerging estate making very good Colli Piacentini wines from Cabernet Sauvignon (Luna Selvatica), Sauvignon Blanc, and succulent Malvasia from partly dried grapes.

Tre Monti ☆☆☆
Imola. 56 ha. www.tremonti.it
An important estate, steadily improving with the help of consultant oenologist Donato Lanati. The white wines are often the best: Albana, of course, but also Chardonnay and Trebbiano.

Trerè ☆
Faenza. 30 ha. www.trere.com
A reliable range of Romagna wines, from Albana to Sangiovese to *frizzante* Pagadebit.

Uccellina ☆☆
Russi. 10 ha. www.tenutauccellina.com
The property offers the usual range of Romagna wines, with two specialties: Ruchetto from Pinot Noir, and Burson made from the rare Longanesi variety. It also has a good reputation for Albana *passito*.

Vallona ☆☆–☆☆☆☆
Castello di Serravalle. 23 ha.
An important property in the Colli Bolognesi, producing a wide range of wines, with impressive Pignoletto and Cabernet Sauvignon.

Venturini Baldini ☆☆
Roncolo di Quattro Castella. 50 ha. www.venturinibaldini.it
Fine, full-bodied Lambrusco Reggiano, Cuvée di Pinot *tradizionale*; and Il Grinto Cabernet Sauvignon.

Fattoria Zerbina ☆☆☆
Faenza. 40 ha. www.zerbina.com
A family winery, run by Maria Cristina Geminiani, and now one of the top estates in Romagna. Her Scacco Matto is that rarity: an exceptional Albana, made only when noble rot is present. She also makes a succulent Sangiovese, Pietramora, and Marzieno, from Sangiovese with a little Cabernet Sauvignon and Merlot.

Zerioli ☆☆
Ziano Piacentino. 60 ha. www.zeriolivini.com
The Zerioli family make a wide range of Colli Piacentini DOCs plus a good *vin santo* from Malvasia.

Tuscany

To find a national identity in such a federation of disparities as Italy is not as difficult as it sounds. The answer is Tuscany. For foreigners, at least, the old Tuscan countryside of villas and cypresses, woods and valleys, where vine and olive mingle, is Italy in a nutshell.

And so is its wine. Nine out of ten people asked to name one Italian wine would say "Chianti". They would have many different ideas (if they had any at all) of what it tastes like – for if ever any wine came in all styles and qualities from the sublime to the gor-blimey it is Chianti – and this despite being the earliest of all regions, possibly in all Europe, to start trying to define and defend its wine. Certainly in modern times, the *consorzio* of its producers paved Italy's way to its DOC system.

Chianti started in the Middle Ages as a small region of constant wars and alarms between Florence and Siena. Vineyards were mostly owned by the nobility, and as recently as 50 years ago many of those farms were worked on a sharecropping system that did nothing for quality. Nor did the antiquated regulations governing wine production. After decades of wrangling a thorough research programme finally (or perhaps provisionally but convincingly) identified the best Sangiovese clones, which were then replanted, and by the end of the last century Chianti had become the biggest and most complex DOCG in Italy. There is a real unity and identity, despite its varied soils, traditions, and microclimates, because they all grow the same basic red grape, or versions of it.

Sangiovese is what holds Chianti together, but that should not imply monotony. Individual inclinations show up strongly in the balance of the blend, the type of fermentation, the use or neglect of the "governo", the method and time of ageing.

Chianti has many departments and subregions, of which the most distinguished is Chianti Classico, the region between Florence and Siena. It also has several neighbours who claim superiority for their not-dissimilar wines, most notably Brunello di Montalcino and Vino Nobile di Montepulciano. Above all, it is the firing range for the army of ambitious producers who believe that a dose of Cabernet, some new oak barrels, and a designer bottle and label add up to The Great New Italian wine. Their field marshal, Piero Antinori, has successfully demonstrated that it can. At the same time many top growers have reasserted their pride in Sangiovese, and the once chic Supertuscan, its sights aimed at the luxury international market, is no longer as prized it was in the 1990s. Today many a top estate declares its finest wine to be a pure Sangiovese.

White wine is a relative stranger here. There is no white Chianti. But several small traditional supply points are holding their own, and the most important is the popular Vernaccia di San Gimignano. Vermentino is proving popular along the Tuscan coast. Indeed, the Tuscan coast, the Maremma, with its subregions (such as Bolgheri, Montescuadaio, and Scansano), recently and rapidly became the region's most fashionable area for wine production.

Bordeaux varieties flourish here, and the path laid out by Sassicaia decades ago has been followed by numerous followers, such as Ornellaia, Guada al Tasso, and Tassinaia. No one could accuse the Tuscan wine industry of resting on its laurels.

DOC & Other Wines

Ansonica Costa dell'Argentario DOC. White wine. Province: Grosseto. Villages: coastal hills south of Grosseto near the Lazio border. Grape: Ansonica (85–100%).

A grape of obscure origin once found in many parts of southern Italy, now only encountered in Sicily and here.

Barco Reale DOC. See Carmignano.

Bianco dell'Empolese DOC. White wine. Province: Florence. Villages: Empoli, six neighbouring communes. Grapes: Trebbiano Toscano (minimum 80%), up to 20% other whites. Also *vin santo*.

Rarely seen.

Bianco Pisano di San Torpè DOC. White wine. Provinces: Livorno, Pisa. Villages: east of Pisa. Grape: Trebbiano (75–100%). Also *vin santo*.

DOC named after a (very) early martyr who was beheaded in AD68 at Pisa. A pale, dry wine with some body and a touch of bitterness.

Bianco di Pitigliano DOC. White wine. Province: Grosseto. Villages: Pitigliano and other villages north of the Lazio border. Grapes: Trebbiano (50–80%), varying proportions of Greco, Malvasia, Verdello, Grechetto, Sauvignon, Chardonnay, Pinot Bianco, Riesling Italico. Still and sparkling.

Pitigliano is in the extreme south of Tuscany near Lake Bolsena, the home of Est! Est!! Est!!! (see Latium). Its soft, dry, slightly bitter white has no particular distinction.

Bianco della Valdinievole DOC. White wine. Province: Pistoia. Villages: west and south of Pistoa. Grapes: Trebbiano (70–100%), Malvasia del Chianti, Canaiolo Bianco, Vermentino (maximum 25%), up to 5% other whites. Also *vin santo*.

A small production of plain dry, sometimes slightly fizzy, white from west of Florence.

Bianco Vergine Valdichiana DOC. See Valdichiana.

Bolgheri DOC. Red, white, *rosato* wine. Province: Livorno. Grapes: Rosso – Cabernet Sauvignon (10–80%), up to 80% Merlot, up to 70% Sangiovese, up to 30% others. Bianco – Trebbiano Toscano (10–70%), Vermentino (10–70%), Sauvignon (10–70%), up to 30% others. Also varietal Vermentino and Sauvignon Blanc.

Small region on the coast south of Livorno. Until 1994, DOC only for white and *rosato*, now covers some of Italy's most sought-after and costly reds. Around 1,300 hectares.

Brunello di Montalcino DOCG. Red wine. Province: Siena. Village: Montalcino. Grape: Brunello di Montalcino.

A big, dry red produced for many years by the Biondi-Santi family on "the Pétrus principle" – that nothing is too much trouble. But sold more in the spirit of Romanée-Conti: no price is too high. Made DOCG in 1980, the Brunello is Sangiovese, which, in the best sites here, can be disciplined in this soil to give dark, deeply concentrated wines.

The former requirement of prolonged barrel-ageing has been greatly modified, and most wines will now spend around two years in either large casks or in barriques, or a mixture of the two. Brunello still needs long bottle-age to coax a remarkable bouquet into its rich, brawny depths. Now it is made by about 200 growers, with inevitably varying standards. At its magisterial best, it is one of the great red wines of Europe.

In 2008 some of the region's most important producers were accused of blending unauthorized varieties into their Brunello. Most of them have been cleared by the authorities but the accusations provoked a debate in which the estates argued whether the monovarietal rule was too strict. Powerful voices, such as that of Angelo Gaja, argued for allowing a small proportion of other varieties to be blended in. The proposal was overwhelmingly rejected, and Brunello and Rosso di Montalcino remain pure Sangiovese. The debate also highlighted the fact that the much-expanded region includes some areas where it is difficult for Sangiovese alone to produce wines that have the density and stature of archetypical Brunello.

Candia dei Colli Apuani DOC. White wine. Province: Massa-Carrara. Villages northwest of Pisa. Grapes: Vermentino Bianco (70–80%), Trebbiano, Albarola, and/or Malvasia.

A DOC white wine rarely seen outside the marble quarry coast.

Capalbio DOC. Red, white, *rosato* wine. Province: Grosetto. Villages: south of Grosseto. Grapes: Sangiovese (minimum 50%); Trebbiano (minimum 50%).

Other permitted varieties include Vermentino and Cabernet Sauvignon.

Carmignano DOCG. Red wine. Province: Florence. Villages: Carmignano, other villages northwest of Florence. Grapes: Sangiovese (minimum 50%), Canaiolo (maximum 20%), Cabernet Franc/ Sauvignon (10–20%); up to 10% Trebbiano, Canaiolo Bianco, Malvasia; up to 10% other varieties.

Best described as Chianti (indeed the zone overlaps with Chianti Montalbano DOCG) with a just-tastable dollop of Cabernet, justified to the authorities by the fact that the Bonacossi family introduced it from Bordeaux generations ago. Carmignano is consistently well-made and justifiably self-confident. Posterity may well thank it for the inspiration to aim all quality Chianti in this direction.

A younger, easier drinking version of Carmignano is Barco Reale (DOC) – made from the same grapes from a maximum crop of 70 hl/ha (only 56 is permitted for Carmignano). There are also a Carmignano Rosato DOC and a Carmignano Vin Santo DOC; the latter can be superb.

Chianti DOCG. Red wine. Provinces: Siena, Florence, Arezzo, Pistoia, Pisa. Villages: 103 communes. Grapes: Sangiovese (75–100%), up to 10% Canaiolo; up to 10% Trebbiano, Malvasia. Maximum crop: 75 hl/ha.

There are two basic styles of Chianti: that made as fruity and fresh as possible for local drinking in its youth; and drier, more tannic, and serious wine aged in barrels or tanks and intended for bottle ageing. The traditional grape mixture is the same for both – basically Sangiovese but with variable additions of either local or international varieties .

White Trebbiano and Malvasia are added for quicker drinking Chiantis, but serious producers worked hard to eliminate the rule that required a percentage of white grapes to be included.

The *governo* is a local tradition of adding very sweet, dried, grape must (usually Colorino) to the wine after its fermentation to make it referment, boost its strength, smooth its astringency, and promote an agreeable fizz that can make young Chianti delicious. Few producers now use the *governo* for wine that is to be aged before bottling.

Fine old Chianti Riserva has marked affinities with claret, particularly in its light texture and a definite gentle astringency, which makes it feel very much alive in your mouth. Its smell and flavour are its own – sometimes reminding me faintly of mulled wine with orange and spices, faintly of chestnuts, faintly of rubber. I have also found a minty "lift" in its flavour, like young burgundy. Its mature colour is a distinct, even glowing garnet.

The future of Chianti is under constructive debate. Many producers are systematically adding a little seasoning of Cabernet or Merlot, and ageing the best wines in new, rather than often reused, oak barrels. The region as a whole continues to benefit from viticultural research aimed at improving the selections of Sangiovese planted and seeing off the overproductive clones planted decades ago. The ultimate Chianti will be made when the ultimate strain of Sangiovese has been identified (as it has in Montalcino), propagated, and its use mastered. Chianti is betting its future on the qualities of its ancestral grape variety.

The seven sub-zones include:

Chianti Colli Aretini The country to the east in the province of Arezzo; a good source of fresh, young wines.

Chianti Colli Fiorentini The zone just north of Chianti Classico around Florence, especially east along the River Arno. Several estates here are at least on a level with the best *classicos*.

Chianti Colline Pisane A detached area south of Pisa making lighter, generally less-substantial wine.

Chianti Colli Senesi A fragmented and inconsistent zone including the western flank of the *classico* area south from Poggibonsi, the southern fringes around Siena, and the separate areas of Montepulciano and Montalcino to the south. A wide range of styles and qualities.

Carmignano wine barrels

Chianti Montalbano The district west of Florence that includes the separate DOC of Carmignano. Also good Chiantis, though lesser known.

Chianti Montespertoli Created in 1997, apparently to benefit a single estate: Fattoria Sonnino.

Chianti Rufina A small area 24-kilometres (15-miles) east of Florence. Rufina is a village on the River Sieve, a tributary of the Arno. The hills behind, where the magically named Vallombrosa is hidden, contain some of the best Chianti vineyards (see Frescobaldi and Selvapiana).

Chianti Classico DOCG. Red wine. Provinces: Florence, Siena. Villages: Radda, Gaiole, Greve, San Casciano, Castelnuovo Berardenga. Grapes: Sangiovese (80-100%), up to 20% other red grapes (such as Cabernet or Merlot).

Since 1966 separated from "Chianti" and now an independent zone located between Florence and Siena. Most of its producers are members of the very active Consorzio del Marchio Storico, based near San Casciano, and seal their bottles with its badge: a black rooster.

Chianti Classico's progress during the last 15 years has been some of the most impressive in all of Italy. In 1930, when *vini tipici* were introduced, the original Chianti (which is today the *classico* region) was not able to satisfy the enormous demand for Chianti wine. So the neighbouring subzones that traditionally copied the Chianti style were officially granted the right to call their wines Chianti.

In 1963, when the DOCs were introduced, almost half of Tuscany was consequently incorporated in a huge Chianti zone. The original style was therefore blurred and huge differences in character and quality between the subregions and producers were lost.

Since 1966, Chianti Classico, with independent status, has usually been the best and most expensive wine, but very good Chiantis also come from the redefined subzones Rufina and Colli Fiorentini.

Colli dell'Etruria Centrale DOC. Red, white, *rosato* wine. Also *novello* and *vin santo*.

Vast region from Arezzo to the coast. Complex regulations but wines are based on Trebbiano and Sangiovese, plus permitted additions of local and international varieties. Essentially a catch-all DOC for reds that fail to qualify for Chianti DOCG.

Colli di Luni DOC. Red and white wine. Provinces: La Spezia, Massa e Carrara.

Northerly coastal DOC shared with Liguria. The white can be labelled as Vermentino (minimum 90%); otherwise a blend of Vermentino, Trebbiano, other local varieties. Red is Sangiovese-based, plus other local varieties. More important in Liguria than Tuscany.

Colline Lucchesi DOC. Red and white wine. Province: Lucca. Villages: Lucca, Capannori, Porcari. Grapes: Bianco – Trebbiano (45–70%), many other permitted varieties; Rosso – Sangiovese (45–70%), Canaiolo, Ciliegiolo, Merlot, others; plus varietal wines from Vermentino, Sauvignon, Sangiovese, Merlot. Also *vin santo*.

Cortona DOC. Red, white, *rosato* wine. Province: Arezzo. Grapes: varietal wines from Chardonnay, Grechetto, Pinot Bianco, Riesling Italico, Sauvignon; Sangiovese, Cabernet Sauvignon, Gamay, Merlot, Pinot Nero, Syrah. Also *vin santo*.

DOC created in 1999, and adopted with some enthusiasm by a number of important producers.

Elba DOC. Red, white, *rosato* wine. Province: Island of Elba. Grapes: Trebbiano Toscano (80–100%); Sangiovese (minimum 75%); plus Ansonica (minimum 85%), Aleatico (100%), Moscato Bianco (100%). Also *vin santo*.

The island off the south Tuscan coast, once a home for the exiled Napoléon, like a stepping stone to Corsica, has adequate dry white wines to wash down its fish, along with increasingly structured Chianti-style red wines from some highly competent

ANTINORI – CHARTING TUSCANY'S FUTURE

The Marchese Piero Antinori may well be to the twenty-first century Chianti what the Barone Ricasoli was to the Chianti of the nineteenth and twentieth – the man who wrote the recipe. Antinori is persuasive with the eloquence of an aristocrat who does not have to raise his voice.

He and his former winemaker, Giacomo Tachis, made this ancient Florentine house – based in the Palazzo Antinori, in the heart of the city – the modern pace-setter, not only for exemplary Chianti but more prophetically for Tignanello, which is Sangiovese blended with Cabernet Sauvignon and aged, Bordeaux style, in new oak barriques.

This set the trend for what became known as the Supertuscan. Since then, the Antinori family has moved on. It has expanded its vineyard holdings to over 1,800 hectares in Tuscany (Santa Cristina, Peppoli, Badia a Passignano, and Guado al Tasso in Bolgheri), Umbria (Castello della Sala), Piedmont (Prunotto), and Puglia. Extra grapes and extra wine are bought under contract.

Renzo Cotarella supervizes wine production at this growing empire. The ultramodern winery is at San Casciano (near Santa Cristina) and the Palazzo Antinori in Florence has tasting facilities. The splendid Villa Antinori, portrayed on labels of the vintage Chianti Classico, was

destroyed in World War II. The Marchese also owns an estate at Montepulciano (Siena), La Braccesca.

Nor is Antinori's vision confined to Italy. There have been substantial investments in Atlas Peak above Napa Valley, from which Antica Cabernet Sauvignon rather than Sangiovese is being produced; a daring joint venture with Château Ste Michelle in Washington to produce a luxurious Bordeaux blend called Col Solare; and estates or ventures in Hungary, Malta, and Chile. Despite the astonishing accomplishments of the house of Antinori, Piero Antinori and his children know full well that they cannot afford to rest on their laurels.

producers. The Elba specialty is the exquisite red *passito* from the Aleatico grape, and occasionally from the Ansonica variety.

Montecarlo DOC. Red and white wine. Province: Lucca. Villages: hills of Montecarlo. Grapes: Sangiovese (50–75%), varying proportions of Canaiolo, Ciliegiolo, Colorino, Malvasia Nera, Cabernet Sauvignon, Cabernet Franc, Merlot, Syrah, others; Trebbiano (40–60%), varying proportions of Sémillon, Pinot Gris, Pinot Bianco, Vermentino, Sauvignon, Roussanne, others.

A good example of the improvements possible to Tuscan wines by allowing some more aromatic grapes to elaborate the essentially neutral Trebbiano. Montecarlo's smooth, unaggressive but interesting white can develop a very pleasant bouquet with two or three years in bottle.

Montecucco DOC. Red and white wine. Province: Grosseto.

Region southwest of Montalcino, producing wines more rustic than Brunello. Red is Sangiovese (85% minimum) or Rosso is Sangiovese (60% minimum), other varieties; white is Vermentino (85% minimum) or Bianco is Trebbiano (60% minimum), other varieties.

Monteregio di Massa Marittima DOC. Red, white, *rosato* wine. Province: Grosseto. Villages: communes of Massa Marittima and Monterotondo Marittima. Grapes: Trebbiano (50%), Vermentino, Malvasia, Ansonica, other varieties; Sangiovese (80% minimum); plus Vermentino (90% minimum). Also *vin santo*.

A Maremma appellation gradually assuming importance. Chateau Lafite and Chianti producer Castellare (qq.v.) are major investors here.

Montescudaio DOC. Red and white wine. Province: Pisa. Villages: Montescudaio, six other communes. Grapes: Trebbiano (50% minimum), other varieties; Sangiovese (50% minimum), other varieties. Also varietal wines from Chardonnay, Sauvignon, Vermentino, Sangiovese, Merlot, Cabernet Sauvignon. Also *vin santo*.

Rapidly improving wines from near the coast west of Siena, although many top producers within the zone prefer to bottle their costly Cabernets and Merlots as IGTs.

Morellino di Scansano DOCG. Red wine. Province: Grosseto. Villages: Scansano, six other communes in the very south of Tuscany. Grapes: Sangiovese, up to 15% other red grapes.

DOCG since 2006 for a predominantly Sangiovese red increasingly admired. The wines at their best have body and richness but also remarkable finesse. A growing number of producers from other parts of Tuscany have joined the entrenched locals in making extremely juicy wines and ageing them in barriques. Many overdid the barrels at first; in the best Morellino their influence is scarcely perceptible.

Moscadello di Montalcino DOC. White wine. Province: Siena. Village: Montalcino. Grapes: Moscato Bianco.

This sweet Moscato has been revived as a DOC due largely to Banfi. There is also a still sweeter *liquoroso* version, though rarely seen.

Orcia DOC. Red and white wine. Province: Siena, southeast of Montalcino. Grapes: Sangiovese (60% minimum), plus other varieties; white and *vin santo* are Trebbiano (50% minimum), plus other varieties. Also *vin santo*.

Awarded DOC in 2000 to validate its extensive vineyards.

Parrina DOC. Red, white, *rosato* wine. Province: Grosseto. Village: commune of Orbetello. Grapes: Sangiovese (70% min.), other varieties; Trebbiano (30–50%), Ansonica and/or Chardonnay (30–50%), up to 20% other varieties.

Lively wines, both red and white, from near the Argentario Peninsula in south Tuscany. Parrina Bianco caught young can be a good glass with seafood.

Pietraviva DOC. Red, white, *rosato* wine. Province: Arezzo. Villages: just west of Arezzo. Grapes Chardonnay (40–80%), Malvasia, Trebbiano, others; Sangiovese (40–80%), Merlot, Cabernet Sauvignon, others. Also varietal wines from Chardonnay, Malvasia, Sangiovese, Merlot, Canaiolo, Cabernet Sauvignon, Ciliegiolo.

Pomino DOC. Red and white wine. Province: Firenze. Village: Pomino in the commune of Rufina. Grapes: Pinot Bianco and/or Chardonnay and/or Pinot Grigio (70–100%), other whites; Sangiovese (50–100%), Pinot Nero, Merlot, others. Also *vin santo*.

The move for this DOC was led by the Frescobaldis. In 1716, the zone was cited by the Grand Duchy of Tuscany as one of the best wine areas.

Rosso di Montalcino DOC. Red wine. Province: Siena. Village: Montalcino. Grape: Brunello di Montalcino. Maximum crop: 70 hl/ha.

A DOC made from Brunello grapes at Montalcino not deemed good enough to produce Brunello di Montalcino. Rosso varies greatly in quality. Some producers use the DOC as a kind of second wine; others take it seriously and set aside specific vineyards for its production. In fine vintages it can age well and offer very good value.

Rosso di Montepulciano DOC. Red wine. Province: Siena. Village: commune of Montepulciano. Grapes: Sangiovese (Prugnolo Gentile, minimum 70%), up to 20% other varieties though no more than 10% white. Maximum crop: 70 hl/ha.

DOC that is enabling producers to make Vino Nobile better by declassifying some of it to Rosso. Usually good value, especially in ripe years.

San Gimignano DOC. Red, white, *rosato* wine. Province: Siena. Villages: the communes of San Gimignano. Sangiovese (minimum 50%, *rosato* minimum 60%); plus varietal Sangiovese. Also *vin santo*.

With Vernaccia rewarded with DOCG, this DOC was created in 1996 to boost the other wines of the area.

Sant' Antimo DOC. Red and white wine. Province: Siena. Village: Montalcino. A DOC for grapes other than the region's dominant Brunello. Bianco and Rosso a varietal free-for-all with no restrictions; plus varietal Chardonnay, Sauvignon, Pinot Grigio, Cabernet Sauvignon, Merlot, Pinot Nero. Also *vin santo*.

A DOC created in 1996 to create a specific appellation for sometimes innovative and experimental wines in the shadow of the big old Brunello di Montalcino estates.

(Bolgheri) Sassicaia DOCG. A remarkable wine that has proved the most influential of all in the shaping of Tuscan wine-growing. The late Marchesi Incisa della Rocchetta grew pure Cabernet Sauvignon on the coast at Bolgheri, south of Livorno – outside any recognized wine zone. What started as a whim became a sensation. He aged it in barriques like Bordeaux and effectively made fine ripe claret with a Tuscan twist. Classified since 1994 as DOC Bolgheri, it now has its own DOCG.

Sovana DOC. Red and *rosato* wine. Province: Grosseto. Sangiovese (minimum 50%); plus varietal Aleatico (dry or sweet), Cabernet Sauvignon, Merlot, Sangiovese.

Hilly region inland from Morellino di Scansano.

Terratico di Bibbona DOC. Red, white, *rosato* wine. Province: Livorno. Sangiovese (35–65%), Merlot (30–65%), other varieties; Vermentino (minimum 50%); plus varietal Trebbiano, Vermentino, Sangiovese, Syrah, Cabernet Sauvignon, Merlot.

Large coastal and inland region south of Livorno. Created in 2006 at the instigation of Antinori.

Tignanello The firm of Antinori pioneered modern thinking about Chianti with this exceptional wine, Bordeaux-style winemaking, and ageing using barriques. Tignanello, a Sangiovese/Cabernet blend, is the obvious link between the highly individual Sassicaia and the traditional Chianti. It started the Tuscan revolution during the 1980s.

Val d'Arbia DOC. White wine. Province: Siena. Villages: 12 along the Arbia river between Radda in Chianti and Buonconvento. Grapes: Trebbiano Toscano and/or Malvasia (70–90%), Chardonnay (10–30%). Also *vin santo*.

This is a DOC for a crisp, light, typically Tuscan white made in Chianti Classico country.

Val di Cornia DOC. Red, white, *rosato* wine. Provinces: Livorno, Pisa. Villages: Campiglia Marittima, San Vincenzo, Piombino, Monteverdi Marittimo, Sassetta, Suvereto in southwestern Tuscany. Grapes: Sangiovese (maximum 50%), Cabernet Sauvignon and/or Merlot (maximum 50%), other varieties; Trebbiano (maximum 60%), Vermentino (maximum 50%), other varieties.

As in Bolgheri, Sangiovese gives only average results, and many estates are achieving remarkable results with Cabernet and Merlot. There is also a sub-appellation for Suvereto, which must be a blend of Cabernet Sauvignon and Merlot, with up to 10% other varieties.

Valdichiana DOC. Red, white, *rosato* wine. Provinces: Arezzo, Siena. Villages: 12 communes in Chiana valley south of Arezzo. Sangiovese (maximum 50%) and any combination of up to 50% Sangiovese, Cabernet Sauvignon, Merlot, or Syrah, other varieties up to 15%; Bianco Vergine is up to 80% from any combination of Chardonnay, Pinot Bianco, Pinot Grigio, or Grechetto, up to 20% Trebbiano, up to 15% others. Also

varietal Grechetto, Chardonnay, Sangiovese. Also sparkling and *vin santo*.

Bianco Vergine is a satisfactory though pretty mild, mid-dry white from eastern Tuscany, often used as an apéritif in Chianti. A slightly bitter finish gives it some character.

Vernaccia di San Gimignano DOCG. White wine. Province: Siena. Villages: communes of San Gimignano. Grape: Vernaccia di San Gimignano (90–100%).

Old-style Vernaccia was made as powerful as possible, fermented on its (golden) skins and aged in barrels for gently oxidized flavours to emerge. This was the wine Michelangelo loved. It can still be found like this, or in a modernized, pale version that can be good but can lack personality.

See also San Gimignano DOC .

Vin Santo Wine of grapes dried in the loft until Christmas or later (to shrivel and sweeten them) is found all over Italy, but most of all at every farm in Tuscany. Although it can be red or white, white is far more common. The white is from at least 70% Trebbiano or Malvasia. The red, known as Occhio di Pernice, is at least 50% Sangiovese, plus other local varieties.

The wine is fermented in very small barrels called *caratelli*, which are then sealed and placed in a loft to do their own thing for up to seven years. Inevitably, after such long ageing, some of it turns into vinegar, some into Madeira-like nectar.

Traditionally, *vin santo* is sweet, but there are some dry versions, too. It should be at least three years old. Chianti, Chianti Classico, and Montepulciano each have a *vin santo* DOC.

Vino Nobile di Montepulciano DOCG. Red wine. Province: Siena. Village: commune of Montepulciano. Grapes: Sangiovese (Prugnolo Gentile, 70–100%), Canaiolo (maximum 20%), up to 20% other varieties.

Montepulciano would like to rival Brunello di Montalcino, also in the south of the Chianti country. It is highly debatable whether it has anything as exceptional as Brunello to offer. This is essentially Chianti with a touch more body, but professional winemakers have come to the fore and the DOCG is justified by an increasing number of excellent examples.

Leading Chianti Producers

See page 343 for producers of other wines.

Castello d'Albola ☆☆–☆☆☆
Radda. 157 ha. www.albola.it
A venerable Renaissance villa that is Zonin's base in Chianti Classico. The estate also produces Le Ellere, a pure Sangiovese from a single vineyard, and an oaky blend of Sangiovese and Cabernet called Accaiolo.

Castello di Ama ☆☆☆
Lecchi, Chianti. 90 ha. www.castellodiama.com
Winemaker Dr. Marco Pallanti brought this estate into the front rank of Chianti Classico by focusing on first-rate (and very expensive) single-vineyard wines such as his Bellavista.

The estate worked hard with international varieties such as Chardonnay, Merlot (L'Apparita), and Pinot Noir

(Il Chiuso), but with mixed success, and today the focus has returned to Chianti.

Tenuta di Arceno ☆☆–☆☆☆
Castelnuovo Berardenga. 92 ha. www.tenutadiarceno.com
This is California wine tycoon Jess Jackson's outpost in Tuscany, and Pierre Seillan is the winemaker. Not surprisingly the wines are rich, oaky, and expensive. The Chiantis have typicity, but the main focus is on concentrated Bordeaux blends called Arcanum that are excellent if distinctly modern style wines.

Badia a Coltibuono ☆☆☆
Gaiole. 70 ha. www.coltibuono.com
The monks of this magical eleventh-century abbey in the woods might have been the original growers of Chianti. The buildings, cellars, and gardens (with an excellent restaurant) are perfectly preserved by the Stucchi-Prinetti family, owners since 1846.

The hills are too high here for vines; the vineyards, which have been organic since 2000, are at Monti, to the south. There are few more consistently first class Chiantis, as *riservas* back to 1958 prove. The top wine is usually Sangioveto, an uncompromising barrique-aged pure Sangiovese that needs years to shed its youthful assertiveness. When young even the Chiantis are raw and austere, and demand patience.

Fattoria di Basciano ☆☆–☆☆☆
Rufina. 35 ha. www.renzomasibasciano.it
A reliable source in the Chianti Rufina zone, with fine *riservas* and a Cabernet/Syrah blend called I Pini.

Tenuta di Bibbiano ☆☆
Castellina. 19 ha. www.tenutadibibbiano.com
A conservative estate that produces nothing but Chianti Classico. The best wine is the Montornello, which is zesty and tannic without toughness.

Borgo Scopeto ☆–☆☆
Vagliagli. 67 ha. www.borgoscopeto.com
Under the same ownership as Caparzo in Montalcino, this ancient property is also a luxury hotel. The Chiantis are all pure Sangiovese, and the best of them is Riserva Misciano, which is barrique aged. It has spiciness, complexity, and persistence.

Castello di Bossi ☆☆
Castelnuovo di Berardenga. 124 ha. www.castellodibossi.it
A big estate producing a range of robust wines from southerly vineyards. As well as fine Chianti Riserva, there is an impressive Sangiovese/Merlot blend called Cornaia that has power rather than finesse and needs time to mellow, and a sumptuous if rather hollow new-oaked Merlot called Girolamo.

Tenuta Bossi-Marchese Gondi ☆☆–☆☆☆
Pontassieve. 18 ha. www.gondi.com
The Gondis have owned this fine estate since 1592, and it is now run by Bernardo Gondi and his sister Donatella. Three different Chianti Rufinas are produced, usually with sufficient fruit to balance any astringency, and a splendid *vin santo*.

La Brancaia ☆☆☆
Radda. 25 ha. www.brancaia.it

Ancient monastic estate of La Badia a Coltibuono

Owned by the Widmer family, this 20-hectare estate produces delicious Chianti from Sangiovese with a dash of Merlot, and the Il Blu Supertuscan from Sangiovese, Merlot, and Cabernet. The wines are rich, concentrated, and sleek.

Castello di Brolio
See Ricasoli.

Castello di Cacchiano ☆–☆☆
Monti. 30 ha.
Slightly rustic, leathery Chianti Classico, but the *vin santo* is superb and rarely shows oxidation.

Villa Cafaggio ☆☆☆
Panzano. 30 ha. www.villacafaggio.it
Owned by the large firm of Casa Girelli until 2005, when Trentino winery LaVis took a controlling interest. Fine Chianti Classico Riserva; pure Sangiovese called San Martino and a pure Cabernet called Cortaccio, both of high quality.

Villa Calcinaia ☆
Greve. 30 ha. www.villacalcinaia.it
Owned by the Caponi family since 1523, the estate produces reliable Chianti Classico.

Capaccia ☆–☆☆
Radda. 3 ha. www.poderecapaccia.com
As well as good Chianti, this estate makes Querciagrande, a pure Sangiovese aged in barriques.

Caparsa ☆–☆☆
Radda. 11 ha. www.caparsa.it
The wines from this organic estate can be inconsistent, but the barrique-aged Riserva Doccio a Matteo is structured and vigorous.

La Cappella ☆–☆☆
San Donato. 8 ha. ww.poderelacappella.it
Small organic property with a bright and thoroughly typical Riserva Querciolo.

Carpineto ☆–☆☆
Dudda, Greve. 8 ha. www.carpineto.com
Partners Antonio Zaccheo and Giovanni Sacchet have built up a portolio of Tuscan estates, and here they make solid Chianti Riservas. Reliable Vino Nobile di Montepulciano Riserva, too.

Casa Emma ☆☆
Castellina. 21 ha.
Lively *riservas* with typicity and concentration.

Casaloste ☆☆–☆☆☆
Panzano. 10 ha. www.casaloste.com
Formidable Chianti Riservas from an outstanding terroir. Don Vincenzo is a pure Sangiovese from a single vineyard.

Castellare ☆☆☆
Castellina. 33 ha. www.castellare.it
Newspaper publisher Paolo Panerai has worked for decades with consultant Maurizio Castelli to fashion both excellent Chianti and a range of other wines, including a pure Cabernet (Coniale), a pure Merlot (Poggio ai Merli), and a barrique-aged Supertuscan called I Sodi di San Niccolò.

Castelli del Grevepesa ☆–☆☆
Mercatale Val di Pesa. 1,000 ha.
www.castellidigrevepesa.it
This cooperative is the largest Chianti Classico producer, with 180 members. The co-op produces a range of Chiantis, Morellino di Scansano, and Vernaccia di San Gimignano. The best wine is usually the Chianti Classico Riserva Clemente VII.

Cecchi & Villa Cerna ☆–☆☆
Castellina in Chianti. 300 ha (Cecchi), 80 ha (Villa Cerna).
www.cecchi.net
Both owned by the merchant house of Luigi Cecchi. The main focus is on Chianti Classico and excellent *riserva*, as well as a range of wines from other regions, including Scansano and San Gimignano.

Cennatoio ☆☆
Panzano. 43 ha. www.cennatoio.it
Organic estate producing Chianti Classico and a range of varietal wines.

Villa Cilnia ☆
Montoncello. 12 ha. www.villacilnia.com
Estate producing Chianti Colli Aretini and a Sangiovese/ Cabernet blend called Vocato.

Le Cinciole ☆☆
Panzano. 11 ha. www.lecinciole.it
A remote organic estate, with Chiantis from pure Sangiovese, and a weighty Cabernet-dominated IGT called Camalaione

Colognole ☆–☆☆
Rufina. 30 ha. www.colognole.it
Owned by the Contessa Spalletti, this property produces medium-bodied Chianti Rufina, all pure Sangiovese.

Il Colombaio di Cencio ☆☆
Gaiole. 23 ha. www.ilcolombaiodicencio.com
The lush, hedonistic style of these wines is well matched to the warm, southerly vineyards of the estate, which are planted to a high density. Chianti I Massi has a dollop of Merlot, while IGTs such as Il Futuro are unapologetically oaky, modern style blends.

Le Corti
San Casciano. 49 ha. www.principecorsini.com
Owned by the Corsini family since the 1420s, Le Corti benefits from the advice of Carlo Ferrini. Merlot marks the Chianti Don Tommaso, but the basic Chianti Classico is delicious. Le Corti also produces a fleshy Maremma blend called Marsiliana.

Dievole ☆☆–☆☆☆
Vagliagli. 96 ha. www.dievole.it
The Dievole vineyards line a valley north of Siena. The Chianti Classico is called Vendemmia. Unusual late-harvest Sangiovese, Novecento, and serious Sangiovese-dominated IGT called Broccato. Imaginative tours for visitors.

Fattoria di Felsina ☆☆☆☆
Castelnuovo Berardenga. 73 ha. www.felsina.it

Under manager Giuseppe Mazzocolin and winemaker Franco Bernabei, this estate is in the top ranks of Chianti producers, especially with its *riserva* Vigneto Rancia. The Sangiovese Fontalloro is first rate, as is the barrel-fermented Chardonnay I Sistri, and the *vin santo*.

Le Filigare ☆☆
Barberina Val d'Elsa. 10 ha. www.lefiligare.it
Three elegant versions of Chianti Classico in different styles and a balanced Sangiovese/Cabernet blend called Podere Le Rocce.

Castello di Fonterutoli ☆☆☆–☆☆☆☆
Castellina in Chianti. 117 ha. www.fonterutoli.it
Owned by the Mazzei family since 1435, the estate is enjoying a revival. Filippo and Francesco Mazzei, with oenologist Carlo Ferrini, deliver with remarkable consistency a deeply fruity Chianti Classico and the modern-style, Cabernet-flecked Chianti called Castello di Fonterutoli. Equally notable is Siepi, a Sangiovese/Merlot blend from a single vineyard.

Quality is outstanding. The Mazzeis have also developed a property in Scansano called Belguardo, to produce a delicious, uncomplicated Morellino.

Fontodi ☆☆☆–☆☆☆☆
Panzano. 67 ha. www.fontodi.com
The Manetti family have been tile-makers since the eighteenth century, and have owned this estate since 1969. Giovanni Manetti, assisted by oenologist Franco Bernabei, has driven Fontodi to the top ranks. The Chianti Classico is consistently good, especially the Vigna del Sorbo. The barrique-aged Flaccianello (pure Sangiovese) confirms this estate's position. Syrah and Pinot Noir show promise, but are not yet at the same level as the traditional wines.

Castello di Gabbiano ☆
Mercatale Val di Pesa. 65 ha. www.gabbiano.com
Chianti Classico estate, implausibly part of the Foster's wine group of Australia. The production of a Pinot Grigio in the hills south of Florence does the enterprise little credit.

Agricoltori del Chianti Geografico ☆–☆☆
Gaiole. 550 ha. www.chiantigeografico.it
A very large Tuscany-wide cooperative founded in 1961. The top Chianti is Riserva Montegiachi, which maintains a very high standard. Other DOC wines include Vernaccia di San Gimignano and Bianco Val d'Arbia; IGTs include a pure Merlot called Pulleraia.

Fattoria di Grignano ☆–☆☆
Pontassieve. 47 ha. www.fattoriadigrignano.com
Owned by textile manufacturers, this estate is a good source of Chianti Rufina.

Isole e Olena ☆☆☆–☆☆☆☆
Barberino Val d'Elsa. 46 ha.
On this justly admired estate-owner/winemaker Paolo de Marchi makes delicious Chianti Classico, the long-lived Sangiovese called Cepparello, and excellent *vin santo*. Under the Collezione label, de Marchi produces some non-traditional wines such as Chardonnay, Cabernet Sauvignon, and a promising Syrah.

La Leccia ☆–☆☆☆
Castellina. 20 ha. www.castellolaleccia.com
Firm, spicy Chanti Classico, especially the Riserva Bruciagna.

Lilliano ☆–☆☆
Castellina. 45 ha. www.lilliano.com
Owned by the Ruspoli family, who since 2000 have hired Lorenzo Landi as a consultant. However, the wines remain sound rather than inspired, and because of their slight rusticity, they need some bottle-age to shed their youthful tannins.

Mannucci Droandi ☆☆–☆☆☆☆
Mercatale Valdarno. 6 ha.
A small property producing wonderfully typical Chianti Ceppeto and Riserva, with sour-cherry aromas and a palate with weight and verve. The Droandis produce good Chianti from a property in the Colli Aretini.

La Massa ☆☆☆
Panzano. 23 ha.
This fine property has been owned since 1992 by Neapolitan leather producer Giampaolo Motta. The top wine is the rich fleshy Giorgio Primo, a delicious wine not always easy to identify as Chianti. From 2004 Motta has declared the wine IGT, and now half the blend is Merlot and Cabernet Sauvignon.

Castello di Meleto ☆☆
Gaiole. 140 ha. www.castellomeleto.it
A former Ricasoli castle and estate, now owned by Viticola Toscana. Consultant Stefano Chioccioli has revamped the range, but the wines, especially the Chianti Classicos, remain traditional in style despite a small amount of Merlot in the blend.

Melini ☆☆
Gaggiano di Poggibonsi. 160 ha. www.cantinemelini.it
An ancient property that now belongs to the Gruppo Italiano Vini complex. In the 1860s, Laborel Melini devised the strengthened Chianti flask, which enabled shipping the wine, and consolidated the international following for Chianti. Best-known for the excellent Chanti Classico Selvanella, Vernaccia di San Gimignano, and other wines.

Il Molino di Grace ☆☆–☆☆☆
Panzano. 36 ha. www.ilmolinodigrace.it
Chicago businessman Frank Grace bought this property in 1995; previously the grapes had been sold to local co-ops. With advice from Franco Bernabei, Grace has done a fine job, both with his Chiantis and with an IGT, Gratius, a pure Sangiovese from very old vines.

Monsanto ☆☆–☆☆☆☆
Barberino Val d'Elsa. 72 ha. www.castellodimonsanto.it
Fabrizio Bianchi's estate produces distinguished Chianti, notably the single-vineyard Il Poggio Riserva. The IGT wines are impressive, too, especially the black-fruited, pure Cabernet called Nemo, which is aged in new oak.

Monte Bernardi ☆☆
Panzano. 6 ha. www.montebernardi.com
Owned by American Michael Schmelzer since 2003 and now

farmed Biodynamically. As well as sleek Chianti Classico – regular and 100% Sangiovese Sa'etta – the estate produces a stylish Bordeaux blend called Tsingana.

Montevertine ☆☆☆
Radda. 13 ha. www.montevertine.it
Founded by Sergio Manetti in 1967, and now run by his son-in-law Klaus Reimitz. A fastidiously tended little vineyard producing Le Pergole Torte, an oak-aged, all-Sangiovese IGT of unusual quality, and Montevertine from a different vineyard and aged in large Slavonian casks. Expensive.

Nittardi ☆☆–☆☆☆
Castellina. 12 ha.
Peter Femfert, aided by oenologist Carlo Ferrini, produces ultra-reliable Chianti Classico. Despite its pretentious name, the Bordeaux blend Nectar Dei, from Maremma vineyards, is stylish and balanced.

Il Palazzino ☆☆
Monti. 18 ha. www.podereilpalazzino.it
Other than a silky *vin santo*, Chianti Classico is the primary focus of Alessandro Sderci's property. Grosso Senese is made in a muscular style, and La Pieve shows more finesse.

Fattoria di Petroio ☆☆
Quercegrossa15 ha.
www.fattoriapetroio.it
Gian Luigi Lenzi's property produces modern-style Chianti Classico that can sometimes be too overripe and toasty.

Poggio al Sole ☆☆–☆☆☆
Tavernelle Val di Pesa. 10 ha.
www.poggioalsole.com
Bought in 1990, owner/winemaker Giovanni Davaz produces excellent Chianti Classico. The best and richest Chianti is called Casasilia. Impressive Syrah, too.

Poggiopiano ☆☆–☆☆☆
San Casciano. 9 ha. www.fattoriapoggiopiano.it
Alessandro Bartoli aims high, insisting on very low yields that give his Chianti and his new-oaked Rosso di Sera exceptional concentration.

Castello di Poppiano ☆☆
Montespertoli1. 30 ha.
This immense property has been owned by the Guicciardini family since 1199. A good source of Chianti Colli Fiorentini; also produces Tricorno, a blend of Sangiovese, Cabernet, and Merlot, plus Viognier and Syrah.

Castello di Querceto ☆☆–☆☆☆
Greve. 60 ha. www.castellodiquerceto.it.
Owner/winemaker Alessandro François produces a variety of wines, either pure Sangiovese or Sangiovese-dominated blends, as well as Cignale, a Cabernet with 15% Merlot. The top Chianti Riserva, with delicious black-cherry fruit, is called Il Picchio.

Fattoria Querciabella ☆☆☆–☆☆☆☆
Greve. 61 ha. www.querciabella.com
The Castiglioni family's Biodynamic estate does produce very good Chianti, but the main focus is on the succulent Supertuscan called Camartina, and an oaked Chardonnay/Pinot Bianco blend called Batar. Quality is impeccable, but prices are very high.

Castello dei Rampolla ☆☆☆–☆☆☆☆
Panzano. 42 ha.
A beautiful and now Biodynamic property, owned for three centuries by the Di Napoli family. Very good Chianti Classico, but Rampolla's most celebrated wines are the Cabernet-dominated Sammarco, which has a longer track record of excellence than most, and Vigna di Alceo – again Cabernet, but with a dash of Petit Verdot rather than Sangiovese. The Rampolla wines seem effortlessly accomplished.

Barone Ricasoli ☆☆–☆☆☆
Gaiole. 227 ha. www.ricasoli.it
The estate has been in the Ricasoli family since 1141. The great, grim, brick-built stronghold is the site where the great, grim Bettino Ricasoli, second prime minister of Italy in the 1850s, "invented" Chianti – or at least the blend of grapes and method of production.

In 1971, the family granted control of the estate to Seagram, but this proved unsuccessful in the long-term. In 1993 Francesco Ricasoli stepped in to revive the historic estate and restore its tattered reputation, largely by throwing out thousands of bottles he deemed of insufficient quality, and by replanting most of the vineyards. He has had considerable success, especially with his top Chianti Classico named after the Castello, and a Sangiovese/Cabernet blend called Casalferro.

Riecine ☆☆
Gaiole. 30 ha. www.riecine.com
Founded in 1971 by an Englishman, John Dunkley, who died in 1999. American Gary Baumann bought the property and retained the services of winemaker Sean O'Callaghan, who has maintained quality, with very fine Chianti Classico Riserva and a Sangiovese-based IGT called La Gioia. Bauman has also planted vineyards in Montecucco DOC.

Rocca di Castagnoli ☆☆
Giaole. 100 ha. www.roccadicastagnoli.it
This large property only bottles its best wines, which include the Riserva Capraia, a Sangiovese/Cabernet blend called Stielle, and a pure Cabernet IGT, Buriano.

Rocca delle Macìe ☆–☆☆☆
Castellina. 220 ha. www.roccadellemacie.com
Founded in the 1970s, the Zingarellis' estate is one of the largest in the Chianti Classico. Their top wines are the *riserva*

Palazzo gates, village of Petrolo

Chianti Fizzano, the Cabernet/Sangiovese IGT called Roccato, and Ser Gioveto, a new-oaky Sangiovese, now plumped up with 10% each Cabernet Sauvignon and Merlot. Because of the large scale of this operation, the wines are often underestimated, but at the top level they are excellent.

Rocca di Montegrossi ☆☆
Monti. 18 ha.
A property rented by Marco Ricasoli, with two excellent wines: the Chianti Riserva San Marcellino, and the Bordeaux blend Geremia.

Ruffino ☆☆–☆☆☆
Pontassieve. 600 hectares. www.ruffino.com
The Folonaris have owned this property since 1877, but in 2000 there was a family split, and Ambrogio Folonari founded an offshoot company. Nonetheless, Ruffino retains its enormous holdings in Tuscany as well as the reputation established over many decades for its Riserva Ducale.

A Pinot Nero, Nero del Tondo, is also impressive, as is the Sangiovese/Colorino blend called Romitorio di Santedame. Ruffino also own the Greppone Mazzi estate at Montalcino (q.v.) and Borgo Conventi in Friuli. In 2004 the vast American wine group Constellation took a 40% share in the company.

San Fabiano Calcinaia ☆☆–☆☆☆
Castellina. 40 ha. www.sanfabianocalcinaia.com
Under Carlo Ferrini's advice, this beautiful estate produces very consistent wines: a rather plummy style of Chianti Classico, Cellole, and a Supertuscan, Cerviolo, aged in new barriques.

San Felice ☆☆☆
Castelnuovo Berardenga. 140 ha.
www.agricolasanfelice.it
Owned by a large insurance company, San Felice is not just a wine estate, but a beautifully restored tourist complex with classy hotel and expensive restaurant.

Winemaker Leonardo Bellacini has steadily improved the quality of its wines since he was hired in 1984. Poggio Rosso, from a single vineyard, is one of Chianti Classico's finest *riservas*, and Vigorello is a tannic, assertive Supertuscan blend of Sangiovese and Cabernet Sauvignon.

San Giusto a Rentennano ☆☆☆
Monti. 30 ha. www.fattoriasangiusto.it
Owner Francesco Martini and his brother make a very traditional Chianti from their organic vineyards, but are better-known for the costly Percarlo (strong, pure, barrique aged Sangioveto); a sumptuous Merlot called La Ricolma; and magnificent *vin santo* that is aged in cask for six years.

Selvapiana ☆☆☆
Pontassieve. 45 ha. www.selvapiana.it
Founded in 1827 by the Giuntini family of Florentine bankers, it is still owned by descendant Francesco Giuntini, now assisted by Federico Masseti. Advised by oenologist Franco Bernabei, they produce highly traditional and long lived Chianti Rufina. There are two beautifully structured, single vineyard Chiantis, Bucerchiale and Fornace, and glorious *vin santo*.

Terrabianca ☆☆
Radda. 52 ha. www.terrabianca.com
Roberto Guldener of Switzerland bought this ancient property in 1988. The top Chianti Classico is Vigna della Croce, and the estate is also known for its Campaccio (Sangiovese/Cabernet) and Cipresso (pure Sangiovese).

Vecchie Terre di Montefili ☆☆☆
Greve. 13 ha. www.vecchieterredimontefili.com
Roccaldo Acuti established this small estate in 1980. As well as fine Chianti Classico, it produces an interesting white called Vigna Regis, made from Chardonnay, Sauvignon Blanc, and Traminer. The Chianti Riserva used to be called Anfiteatro but this is now an IGT, although it remains pure Sangiovese. The Supertuscan Bruno di Rocca completes this excellent range.

Castello di Verrazzano ☆–☆☆
Greve. 42 ha. www.verrazzano.com
The vineyards surround the castle where the explorer Giovanni da Verrazzano was born in 1485. Today it is owned by Luigi Cappellini. The Chianti Classico is sound but not exceptional, but there is an excellent Sangiovese/Cabernet blend called Bottiglia Particolare.

Castello Vicchiomaggio ☆☆–☆☆☆
Greve. 33 ha. www.vicchiomaggio.it
This spectacular property has been owned by the Matta family since 1966, and is now run by John Matta. With its restaurant and accommodation in the castle, it's a popular tourist destination, but the wines have become increasingly impressive. Of the Chianti Classico wines, the most elegant is usually La Prima, barrique-aged for 19 months. There are two IGTs: Ripa delle Mandorle, a Sangiovese/Cabernet blend designed to be drunk fairly young; and Ripa delle More, a similar blend with longer barrique-ageing and more richness and power. In general, the wines are made in a plump, accessible style.

Villa Vignamaggio ☆☆☆
Greve. 52 ha. www.vignamaggio.com
The beautiful fifteenth-century villa where Mona Lisa probably lived, home of Michelangelo's biographer and one of the most prestigious Chiantis. Under guidance from oenologist Franco Bernabei, the owner, Roman lawyer Gianni Nunziante, has made substantial improvements in the vineyards and wines. The Chianti Classico, especially the Riserva, is rich and complex, and there are also IGTs such as a Cabernet Franc and Obsession, which sounds like a perfume but is in fact a new-oaked blend of Merlot, Syrah, and Cabernet Sauvignon.

Vignole ☆☆
Panzano. 12 ha.
Fine, reasonably priced Chianti Classico.

Viticcio ☆☆
Greve. 35 ha. www.fattoriaviticcio.com
Sound Chianti Classico, IGT Sangiovese called Prunaio, and impressive, new-oaked Cabernet called Monile.

Castello di Volpaia ☆☆☆
Radda. 45 ha. www.volpaia.it

The medieval castle and its hamlet were high on the list of fifteenth-century *crus*, and the village is now both a wine estate and a high-class tourist complex run by Giovanella Stianti Mascheroni. The vineyards are among the highest in Chianti Classico, so it takes special care to ensure the grapes ripen fully. The Chianti is always a refined wine that needs a few years to reach its peak, especially the Riserva Coltassala, formerly IGT but now restored to the ranks of DOCG. There is also an impressive Supertuscan, Balifico, a blend of Sangiovese and Cabernet Sauvignon.

Leading Montalcino Producers

Altesino ☆☆–☆☆☆
Montalcino. 27 ha. www.altesino.it
This highly respected small producer, which was bought in 2003 by Elisabetta Gnudi Angelini of Caparzo (q.v.), has wavered in direction, sometimes favouring Supertuscan styles over its excellent Brunello, then doing the opposite. Palazzo Altesi is barrique aged Sangiovese, to produce an almost burgundy-like suppleness and fruitiness. The top Brunello is the single vineyard Montosoli, often of exceptional quality.

Argiano ☆☆☆
Sant'Angelo in Colle. 48 ha. www.argiano.net
Since 1980 this ancient estate has been owned by a member of the Cinzano family. Under winemaker Sebastiano Rosa, quality improved greatly, and his successor Hans Vinding-Diers has maintained standards. All Brunello is vinified in the same way, then less satisfactory lots are declassified as Rosso. The wine bottled as Brunello is rich and forceful.

Vinding-Diers has also created new wines: the pure Sangiovese, Suolo, aged in new barriques and a replacement for the much admired Solengo and two lighter Supertuscans, Non Confunditur and L'O.

Castello Banfi ☆–☆☆☆
Sant'Angelo Scalo. 900 ha. www.castellobanfi
Founded in 1977 by a major American wine importer with a yearning for its ancestral land, Banfi planted immense vineyards from scratch and now produces a wide range of wines.

The top Brunello di Montalcino is Poggio alla Mura, and there are serious varietal wines from Pinot Noir (Belnero), Cabernet Sauvignon (Tavernelle), Syrah (Colvecchio), and two rich blends: "Excelsus" (a Bordeaux blend), and the new-oaked "Summus" from Sangiovese, Cabernet, and Syrah. There is also a large production of white wines, but these are mostly unremarkable. There is also a sister winery in Piedmont.

Fattoria dei Barbi ☆☆
Montalcino. 90 ha. www.fattoriadeibarbi.it
Owned for two centuries by the Colombini Cinelli family, the Barbi estate – which produces cheese, salami, and oil, as well as wine – has a long reputation.

As well as reliable Brunello di Montalcino, it produces wines for earlier consumption, such as Brusco dei Barbi, a Sangiovese made by the *governo* method. The estate has also developed vineyards in Scansano.

Biondi Santi – Il Greppo ☆☆☆
Montalcino. 19 ha. www.biondisanti.it
Founded in 1840 by Clemente Santi, whose grandson, Ferruccio Biondi Santi, is credited with creating Brunello di Montalcino. Early vintages, still alive in the bottle, are among Italy's most treasured wines. However, in the 1980s, quality slipped, and in the 1990s fungal problems affected the vineyards. Family feuding didn't help matters.

By the early 2000s, the estate was back on course, though the astonishing improvement in quality throughout the region means that Biondi Santi is no longer as pre-eminent as it used to be – except perhaps in price. The family has acquired vineyards along the Tuscan coast, from which it is producing attractive and relatively inexpensive wines such as Sassoalloro, a barrique aged Sangiovese.

Camigliano ☆☆
Montalcino. 80 ha. www.camigliano.it
The Ghezzi family produce dependable Brunello and Rosso di Montalcino, as well a pure Cabernet Sauvignon, Campo ai Mori, and a delicate Moscadello.

Campogiovanni ☆☆
Sant'Angelo in Colle. 20 ha. www.agricolasanfelice.it
Under the same ownership as San Felice (q.v.) in Chianti, and a source of suave Rosso and Brunello.

Caparzo ☆☆
Montalcino. 80 ha. www.caparzo.com
Under manager Nuccio Turone, Caparzo rose to become one of Montalcino's most consistent wineries. Fine Brunello, of course, especially the single vineyard La Casa, but also delicious Chardonnay-dominated Le Grance, and a Brunello/Cabernet blend called Ca' del Pazzo.
However, in 1999 the property was sold to Elisabetta Gnudi. She has also acquired the Borgo Scopeto estate in Castelnuovo Berardenga and Altesino in Montalcino (qq.v.). In recent years the Caparzo Brunellos seem to have lost some weight and distinction.

Casanuova delle Cerbaie ☆☆
Montalcino. 20 ha. wwww.casanuovadellacerbaie.com
This remote property in northern Montalcino also owns vineyards in the south, which together make a very harmonious Brunello. Also a Sangiovese/Merlot blend called Cerbaione.

Casanova di Neri ☆☆☆–☆☆☆☆
Montalcino. 35 ha. www.casanovadineri.com
Giacomo Neri makes regular Brunello, and two excellent single vineyard wines: Cerretalto and the sensational Tenuta Nuova. Neri doesn't apply a formula to his wines, adapting the wood-ageing to the quality and character of each vintage. There is also a pure but overpriced Cabernet, Pietradonice.

Case Basse ☆☆☆–☆☆☆☆☆
Montalcino. 8 ha. www.casebasse.it
Gianfranco Soldera defies all modern conceptions of Brunello. He ferments his wines without temperature control, like old-style Barolo, and ages them from four to six years in large casks. With their red-fruits aromas, their refined tannins, and

high acidity, they sometimes resemble Nebbiolo, too. But they are uncompromising, authentic, old-style Brunellos – from two vineyards, Case Basse and Intistieti, with different structures – that display a nobility that justifies their very high prices.

Castelgiocondo ☆☆☆
Montalcino. 235 ha. www.frescobaldi.it
This immense estate is owned by the Frescobaldi family. Production, which began with the 1975 vintage, includes Brunello and Rosso di Montalcino, as well as the robust Merlot Lamaïone.

Castiglion del Bosco ☆☆
Montalcino. 56 ha. www.castigliondelbosco.it
Owned since 2003 by the Ferragamo family, who have developed the farm as an exclusive private club. But wine production has not been neglected, and the top Brunello from here, Campo del Drago, is tannic and structured.

Cerbaiona ☆☆☆
Montalcino. 3 ha.
The laid-back Molinaris, surrounded by their 15 cats and their vines, produce tiny quantities of glorious Brunello, and a complex blend called Cerbaiona.

Ciacci Piccolomini d'Aragona ☆☆–☆☆☆
Castelnuovo dell'Abate. 40 ha.
www.ciaccipiccolomini.com
Old estate emerging with fine Brunello di Montalcino and unusually rich Rosso. Plantings of other grapes are used in the Supertuscan, Ateo, and the pure Syrah, Fabius.

Col d'Orcia ☆–☆☆☆
Sant'Angelo in Colle. 142 ha. www.coldorcia.it
A large southerly estate bought by Cinzano in 1973. Quality is high at the top of the range: the powerful Brunello, the pure Cabernet called Olmaia, and Moscadello, though larger-volume wines such as Rosso are less impressive.

Collemattoni ☆☆
Sant'Angelo in Colle. 7 ha. www.collemattoni.it
Traditionally made wines with a smoky, spicy character but no oak-derived sweetness. Riserva Fonteleotano is the top wine, but even the Rosso can be lively and full of character.

Costanti ☆☆☆
Montalcino. 10 ha. www.costanti.it
For many years, Andrea Costanti's property near the town has been an impeccable source of long-lived Brunello and Rosso di Montalcino. They are characteristic of the northern part of the region, showing elegance rather than muscle. In the 1990s, Costanti introduced a single-vineyard wine called Vermiglio, containing some Merlot and Cabernet as well as Sangiovese.

Fanti ☆–☆☆
Castelnuovo dell'Abate. 52 ha.
www.fantisanfilippo.com
Critical acclaim from the United States has helped Filippo Fanti to expand his estate rapidly. European drinkers may find the wines overripe and sweetly oaky.

La Fiorita ☆☆–☆☆☆
Castelnuovo dell'Abate. 8 ha. www.fattorialafiorita.it
Roberto Cipresso is known worldwide as a wine consultant. This is his own property. He adopts some Burgundian techniques for his winemaking, and this gives the wines an attractive lightness of touch and surprising ageability; they are aged in 500-litre barrels to avoid excessive oakiness.

Fossacolle ☆☆–☆☆☆
Tavernelle. 2.5 ha. www.fossacolle.it
Fossacolle was formerly part of the Argiano estate, and the wines are made by Argiano's cellarmaster, taking every care to avoid overripeness from these hot vineyards. The Brunello is sleek and stylish, its intrinsic power never being allowed to overwhelm the fruit.

La Fuga ☆☆
Montalcino. 10 ha. www.tenutefolinari.com
An established estate that was bought by Ambrogio and Giovanni Folinari in 2000. Quality was already good in the 1990s, and Giovanni Folinari has worked hard to improve the wines further and combat the clumsiness that can affect certain vintages.

Fuligni ☆☆☆
Montalcino. 4 ha.
A small estate with a big reputation for its thoroughly elegant wines. Roberto Guerrini ensures that quality at his family's property is impeccable, for both Rosso and Brunello.

Greppone Mazzi ☆☆–☆☆☆
Montalcino. 14 ha. www.ruffino.com
From vineyards east of the town, Ruffino produces complex Brunello given long ageing in large casks.

Lisini ☆☆–☆☆☆
Sant'Angelo in Colle. 18 ha. www.lisini.com
Consultant winemaker Franco Bernabei oversees the production of rich, reliable Brunello and delicious Rosso. The sumptuous Ugolaia is not a *riserva* but a single vineyard wine.

Mastrojanni ☆☆☆
Castelnuovo dell'Abate. 20 ha. www.mastrojanni.com
Splendid quality from this estate, which has been advised for many years by Maurizio Castelli. As well as rich Brunello (Schiena d'Asino is the outstanding single vineyard wine, bottled only in top vintages) and Rosso di Montalcino, there's a fresh Sangiovese/Cabernet IGT called San Pio. In 2008 the property was bought by Francesco Illy, of the coffee firm, and initial indications suggest the estate will be run as before.

Silvio Nardi ☆☆–☆☆☆
Montalcino. 80 ha. www.tenutenardi.com
Emilia Nardi has overseen several steps up in quality at this estate. This is particularly apparent in the Brunello Manachiara, which is aged in both large casks and barriques, but she is also moving in a new direction with a pure Merlot under the Sant'Atimo DOC.

Siro Pacenti ☆☆☆
Montalcino. 20 ha.
Powerful Rosso and Brunello di Montalcino, blending the

production of Giancarlo Pacenti's vineyards in the north and the south, but can show a heavy hand with the new barriques.

Pian del Vigne ☆☆
Montalcino. 60 ha. www.antinori.it
It would be unreasonable to expect the Antinoris to succeed at absolutely everything, but the Brunellos since the superb 1999 have been a touch disappointing.

Pieve Santa Restituta ☆☆☆
Montalcino. 16 ha.
Acquired by Angelo Gaja in 1994, the estate produces two principal Brunellos: Rennina and a single-vineyard wine called Sugarille. They are aged for two years in large casks as well as barriques, and are improving from year to year.

La Poderina ☆☆–☆☆☆
Castelnuovo dell'Abate. 23 ha. www.saiagricola.it
Owned by the SAI Agricola insurance company, this estate is making ever more stylish Brunello di Montalcino and Moscadello. See also Fattoria del Cerro.

Poggio Antico ☆☆☆
Montalcino. 33 ha. www.poggioantico.com
The Milanese banking family of Gloder bought this property in 1984 and soon began to produce Brunello to a very high standard. In addition, there is a more approachable style of Sangiovese called Altero, which can also age well.

Poggio San Polo ☆☆–☆☆☆
Montalcino. 14 ha. www.poggiosanpolo.com
The Fertonani family run this small organic estate. The barrique-aged Brunello is spicy and carries a good deal of alcohol with considerable success, and there is an impressive Sangiovese/Cabernet blend called Mezzopane.

I Poggiolo di Roberto Cosimi ☆☆☆
Montalcino. 7 ha. www.ilpoggiolomontalcino.com
Rodolfo Cosimi's boutique winery produces first-rate Brunello, especially the oaky but concentrated Beato.

Il Poggione ☆☆
Sant'Angelo in Colle. 106 ha. www.tenutailpoggione.it
The Francheschi family leave this well-known estate in the experienced hands of winemaker Fabrizio Bindocci. His Brunello di Montalcino is undeniably firm and structured, but the wine can lack the intensity and opulence of others. For those who prefer a more austere, traditional style of Brunello, Il Poggione is a good source.

Salicuti ☆☆☆
Montalcino. 3 ha. www.poderesalicutti.it
Francesco Leanza's Brunello estate is tiny, but quality is very high.

Sesta di Sopra ☆☆
Castelnuovo dell'Abate. 4 ha. www.sestadisopra.it
The first vintage here was in 1999, but the wines, both Rosso and Brunello, have plenty of zest despite the hot southerly location.

Sesti ☆☆☆
Sant'Angelo in Colle. 8 ha.

Giuseppe Maria Sesti is an astronomer and author, and observes the phases of the moon in his farming and wine-making. Adjacent to Argiano, in the castle that formerly bore the same name, this is a hot location, so Sesti strives to obtain richness and concentration without excessive alcohol. He succeeds.

Talenti ☆☆
Sant'Angelo in Colle. 20 ha. www.talentimontalcino.it
The greatly respected Pierluigi Talenti, former winemaker at Poggione, died in 1999, and his own property is now run by son Riccardo. He produces classic, slightly austere Brunello and Rosso di Montalcino.

Val di Suga ☆☆
Montalcino. 55 ha. www.tenimentiangelini.it
Owned by the Angelini family, who also own Tenuta Trerose in Montepulciano and San Leonino in Chianti Classico. Their Montalcino estate is divided between the north and south of the region, giving them a range of vineyards and grapes to work with. There are two single vineyard bottlings, both of exemplary quality: Vigna del Lago and Spuntali.

Leading Montepulciano Producers

Avignonesi ☆☆–☆☆☆☆
Montepulciano. 109 ha. www.avignonesi.it
The sixteenth-century Palazzo Avignonesi, over its thirteenth-century cellars in the heart of Montepulciano, houses the family's barrel-aged Vino Nobile. The firm was owned and run by the Falvo family until its sale in 2008 to Belgian businesswoman Virginie Saverys. The main focus is Vino Nobile, but the company produces many other wines such as DOC Cortona Desiderio Merlot and the rich, oaky, Chardonnay Marzocco. Few would dispute that Tuscany's finest vin santo is made by Avignonesi, both the regular bottling and the rare and extremely costly Occhio del Pernice. At the recently acquired Sovana estate near Pitigliano, it is also making a fine sweet Aleatico.

Le Berne ☆☆
Montepulciano. 16 ha. www.leberne.it
Since 1999 Andrea Natalini has been making steadily improving Vino Nobile, traditional in style but never lacking fruit.

Bindella ☆☆
Montepulciano. 30 ha. www.bindella.it
Founded by Swiss importer Rudolf Bindella, this estate makes fine Vino Nobile, especially the barrique-aged I Quadri and a Supertuscan blend called Vallocaia.

Boscarelli ☆☆–☆☆☆
Montepulciano. 18 ha. www.poderiboscarelli.com
Owned since 1962 by Paola de Ferrari Corradi and now run by her sons with advice from Maurizio Castelli. The estate is among the best in Montepulciano, producing Vino Nobile with depth, tone, and muscle, and a concentrated, lively Supertuscan called Boscarelli di Boscarelli.

La Braccesca ☆☆
Montepulciano. 230 ha. www.antinori.it

This large property, which extends into DOC Cortona, is owned by Antonori. These are modern style Nobiles, with Bordeaux varieties fleshing out the Sangiovese. Bramasole is the excellent Syrah based Cortona.

La Calonica ☆☆
Valiano di Montepulciano. 38 ha. www.lacalonica.com
Ferdinando Cattani's substantial estate offers ripe, fruity Vino Nobile and a savoury, Sangiovese-dominated Cortona called Girifalco.

Le Casalte ☆
Sant'Albino. 8 ha.
The Barioffi family produce dependable rather than exciting Vino Nobile.

Fattoria del Cerro ☆☆–☆☆☆
Montepulciano. 170 ha. www.saiagricola.it
Despite the size of this operation, owner SAI Agricola, an insurance company, produces first-rate Vino Nobile (the single-vineyard, barrique-aged Antica Chiusina is especially voluptuous) and a Merlot called Poggio Golo.
See also La Poderina.

Dei ☆–☆☆
Montepulciano. 38 ha.
www.cantinedei.com
Caterina Dei is a leading producer of Vino Nobile and a pure Sangiovese single-vineyard bottling called Sancta Catharina. Dry tannins can be a problem in some vintages.

Fassati ☆☆
Montepulciano. 85 ha.
www.fazibattaglia.com
Owned since 1969 by Fazi-Battaglia (see Marches). An important producer of Chianti and occasionally austere Vino Nobile di Montepulciano. Also owner of Greto delle Fate in Scansano.

Lodola Nuova ☆☆
Montepulciano. 132 ha.
www.ruffino.com
Supple, fleshy Vino Nobile with some vigour and complexity, and Syrah from Cortona. Owned by Ruffino.

Poliziano ☆☆☆
Montepulciano. 120 ha. www.carlettipoliziano.com
Owned by Federico Carletti who, with the help of Carlo Ferrini, makes juicy Chianti and Vino Nobile that is as fine as any in the region. Other impressive wines include the Cabernet based Le Stanze. The single-vineyard Asinone rises to great heights. He is also producing a delicious wine called Lhosa from vineyards in Scansano.

Romeo ☆☆
Gracciano di Montepulciano. 5 ha.
www.massimoromeo.it
A boutique winery producing rich, firmly structured, traditional Vin Nobile from organic vineyards.

Valdipiatta ☆☆–☆☆☆
Montepulciano. 30 ha. www.valdipiatta.it
The Riserva and the barrique-aged Vigna d'Afiero are the best of these succulent Vino Nobiles.

Other Tuscan Producers

Aia Vecchia ☆☆–☆☆☆
Bibbona. 38 ha.
A rapidly expanding Maremma estate owned by Filippo Pellegrini. The delicious basic wine at present is the richly oaky IGT Lagone, from Merlot, Cabernet, and Sangiovese. The Bordeaux blend called Sor Ugo, from Bolgheri fruit, is a triumph.

Fattoria Ambra ☆–☆☆
Carmignano. 18 ha. www.fattoriaambra.it
The Rigoli family produce attractive, traditional Carmignano from the property they have owned since 1870.

Ambrosini ☆☆–☆☆☆
Suvereto. 6 ha. www.ambrosinilorella.it

A small estate producing a vigorous, oaky, Sangiovese/Merlot/Syrah blend called Subertum, and an unusual Montepulciano IGT called Riflesso Antico.

Marchesi Antinori ☆☆–☆☆☆☆☆
Firenze. www.antinori.it
The present owner, Marchese Piero Antinori, is the latest in a line that began in 1385, and his daughters are poised to continue when he eventually retires. From his extensive power base in Tuscany, Antinori has expanded his holdings in regions as diverse as Umbria, Piemonte, and Puglia, not to mention the west coast of America.

Ampeleia ☆–☆☆
Roccastrada. 50 ha.
www.ampelaia.it
Elisabetta Foradori of Trentino acquired this property in Monteregio, and makes Ampeleia, a slightly austere blend of Cabernet Franc and Sangiovese, and Kepos, an unusual unoaked blend of southern French varieties.

Argentiera ☆☆
Donoratico. 60 ha. www.argentiera.eu
An ambitious joint venture between Florentine businessmen Corrado and Marcello Fratini, and Piero Antinori, with advice from Stéphane Derenoncourt. The property, the most southerly in Bolgheri, is spectacular. First releases were in 2003, so it's early days, but initial wines, Bordeaux blends, were of excellent quality.

Erik Banti ☆☆
Scansano. 30 ha. www.erikbanti.com
An excellent source of Morellino di Scansano, well established in the region for almost 30 years.

Badia a Passignano

Il Borro ☆☆
Loro Ciufenna. 40 ha. www.ilborro.it
This estate in the Colli Aretini has the resources of the
Ferragamo family behind it. The eponymous wine is a
Bordeaux blend, and Pian di Nova is mostly Syrah with
a dash of Sangiovese. Very ripe wines in an unashamedly
New World style.

Fattoria del Buonamico ☆☆
Montecarlo. 24 ha. www.buonamico.it
The Grassi family produce Montecarlo Bianco and a
Sangiovese-based Rosso, a sometimes overripe Sytah called
Fortino, and a Supertuscan blend called Cercatoja.

Bulichella ☆–☆☆
Suvereto. 12 ha. www.bulichella.it
A Japanese-owned property, farmed organically. Wines can
be hit and miss but the top bottling Coldipetrerosse, mostly
Cabernet Sauvignon, is excellent.

Ca' Marcanda ☆☆–☆☆☆
Castegneto Carducci. 65 ha.
Angelo Gaja, with a foothold in Tuscany at his Montalcino
property, extended his holdings by purchasing and planting
a vineyard in the heart of Bolgheri with Bordeaux red varieties
and Syrah. The first release was a wine called Magari: half-
Merlot, the rest Cabernet Sauvignon and Cabernet Franc.

Ca' Marcanda itself is similar, but with more Cabernet
Sauvignon. The full potential of the property has still to be
realized, good though the wines undoubedly are.

Caccia al Piano ☆☆
Castagneto Carducci, 20 ha. www.berlucchi.it
A new property founded and planted by Professor Marianno
Franzini in 1997, but then sold in 2003 to Franciacorta producer
Guido Belucchio. Its two wines are the Merlot-dominated
Levia Gravia and the Cabernet-dominated Ruit Hora. Both
wines are very concentrated but show signs of overripeness.

Caiarossa ☆
Riparbella. 12 ha. www.caiarossa.it

This remote property in DOC Montescudaio has since
2004 been under the same ownership as Château Giscours
in Margaux. The gravity-fed winery is built, for better or
worse, on feng-shui principles. The wines, which are blends
of Sangiovese with Bordeaux varieties, have so far been
inconsistent.

Campo al Mare ☆–☆☆
Bolgheri. 30 ha. www.tenutefolonari.com
This property was bought by Ambrogio and Giovanni
Folonari in 1999, and the first vintage was the difficult 2003.
The estate wine is a Bordeaux blend, and subsequent vintages
have shown spice, vigour, and persistence.

Campo alla Sughera ☆–☆☆
Bolgheri. 20 ha. www.campoallasughera.com
This property is owned by a German ceramics tycoon, and
no expense has been spared in vineyards or winery. Initial
releases were rather bland, but Arnione, a Bordeaux blend
aged in new barriques, is lush and meaty.

Campo al Sasso ☆☆–☆☆☆
Bibbona. 90 ha. www.campodisasso.it
Brothers Piero and Lodovico Antinori had always gone in
different directions, so it was a surprise, though a welcome
one, when they teamed up to establish this beautiful property
just north of Bolgheri. Vines, mostly Bordeaux varieties and
some Syrah, were first planted in 2002 so this is still a work
in progress. The mid-tier wine, Il Pino is unquestionably
delicious, but we are still waiting for the first vintage of the
grand vin Biserno.

Tenuta di Capezzana ☆☆☆
Carmignano. 100 ha. www.capezzana.it
Founded in the fifteenth century, and owned and run by the
children of Ugo Contini Bonacossi. The ex-Medici villa of the
Bonacossis may be the first place Cabernet Sauvignon was
grown in Tuscany. The excellence of its Carmignano assured
the establishment of what seemed an alien DOC in the heart
of Chianti. Other innovations include the *rosato* Vin Ruspo

THE RISE OF THE CONSULTANTS

Almost every important estate in Tuscany now comes fully equipped with a consultant oenologist, who keeps a watchful eye on every aspect of its viticultural and winemaking practices. Until the late 1960s the Tuscan wine industry was dominated by large companies, but with the wine-production boom of succeeding decades, many growers decided to become winemakers, too. At the time, although these owners may have known a great deal about grape-farming, they probably knew very little about winemaking. Other estates that were already producing wine often had

hopelessly outdated equipment. They needed advice. There were profoundly knowledgeable winemakers in the industry, but they tended to be attached to a single company: Giacomo Tachis at Antinori, and Ezio Rivella at Banfi. So a new breed of consultants arose. As the wineries they advised gained in renown, so did the consultants. Oenologists such as Maurizio Castelli, Franco Bernabei, and Vittorio Fiore could add lustre to a wine estate, and their services, however costly, were keenly sought after. More recently, a younger generation is gradually taking their place: Alberto Antonini,

Riccardo Cotarella, Attilio Pagli, Lorenzo Landi, Barbara Tamburini, Carlo Ferrini, Stefano Chioccioli, and Luca d'Attoma.

It is tempting to make fun of them, as they dash around Tuscany in their fast cars, mobile phones constantly beeping, but they have made an invaluable contribution to the success of Tuscan wines. They know about winemaking, can remedy faults, upgrade equipment – and they also know the competition and the market. Any fears that their multiplicity of clients could produce standardized wines are clearly, and most fortunately, unfounded.

and red Barco Reale, a fruity Cabernet/Merlot blend called Ghiaie della Furba, and, from 2004, a pure Syrah. Its finest wine remains the firmly structured and long-lived Carmignano, but the *vin santo* is also of the highest quality.

Chiappini ☆☆
Bolgheri. 7 ha. www.giovannichiappini.it
Giovanni Chiappini is a farmer whose land happened to be in the heart of Bolgheri. He started making wine here in 2000: the unoaked, fruity Felciaino and the rich, Cabernet/Merlot blend Guado de' Gemoli. New additions are barrique-aged Merlot and Petit Verdot.

Villa Cusona ☆☆
San Gimignano. 35 ha. www.guicciardinistrozzi.it
Owned by Girolamo Strozzi and Roberto Guicciardini, this estate dates back to the sixteenth century. It is an outstanding producer of Vernaccia di San Gimignano, and also makes Chianti dei Colli Senesi and the IGT Sangiovese, Sòdole.

Tenuta Farneta ☆☆
Sinalunga. 120 ha.
The estate is a major producer of Chianti Colli Senesi, but has built its reputation on a fine, pure Sangiovese called Bongoverno.

Marchesi de' Frescobaldi ☆☆–☆☆☆☆
Firenze. 1,000 ha. www.frescobaldi.it
The Frescobaldis rival the Antinoris as the leading aristocratic wine family of Tuscany, tracing their ancestry back to 1300, and producing wines of outstanding quality, reliability, value, and originality. All Frescobaldi wines come from their six estates throughout Tuscany. Castello di Nipozzano from Rufina is their most famous red (a superior selection is called Montesodi). Other estates are Pomino and Poggio a Remole.

Pomino Bianco is an excellent white seasoned with Chardonnay; Pomino Benefizio is almost pure Chardonnay. Frescobaldi also own Castelgiocondo (q.v.) at Montalcino, and created a joint venture with Robert Mondavi (but now under the sole control of Frescobaldi) to produce Luce, a glossy blend of Sangiovese and Merlot sourced from the Castelgiocondo vineyards. Last but not least, Frescobaldi have become the owners of Ornellaia (q.v.).

Tenuta di Ghizzano ☆☆☆
Ghizzano di Peccioli. 18 ha. www.tenutadighizzano.com
A small organic property in the hands of the Veneroso Pesciolini family since the fourteenth century. Sumptuous IGT reds: Nambrot, which is mostly Merlot, and Veneroso, a Sangiovese/Cabernet/Merlot blend.

Castello Ginori di Querceto ☆–☆☆
Ponteginori. 15 ha. www.marchesiginorilisci.it
The Ginori family own a 2,000-hectare estate based in the remote hilltop village of Querceto in Montescudaio. Wine production only began in 2002, and the top wine is the Merlot-dominated Castello Ginori.

I Giusti e Zanza ☆☆
Fauglia. 15 ha. www.igiustiezanza.it
The estate lies in northwest Tuscany, not far from the sea.

The wines – Nemorino, Belcore, Dulcamara – are named after characters in Donizetti's L'Elisir d'Amore, but they are far from frivolous. Nemorino is the simplest, Belcore is a Sangiovese/Merlot blend, and Dulcamara a Bordeaux blend. An impressive new addition is PerBruno, a pure Syrah.

Grattamacco ☆☆–☆☆☆☆
Castagneto Carducci. 10 ha. www.collemassari.it
Owner Pier Mario Meletti Cavallari built up a fine reputation for this estate in the hills behind Bolgheri. Its success was based on the Vermentino-dominated Grattamacco Bianco, aged in barriques, and the sumptuous Grattamacco Rosso, made from Cabernet, Sangiovese, and Merlot. In 2002, Cavallari leased the property to a Swiss industrialist, Claudio Tipa, for 12 years. Tipa also produces excellent wine from his Colle Massari estate in the Montecucco region. The quality of the Grattamacco wines has been maintained by Tipa.

Gualdo del Re ☆☆–☆☆☆
Suvereto. 23 ha. www.gualdodelre.it
The Rossi family began bottling in 1982, but rarely reached the quality level of their illustrious neighbours. In 2000, they hired oenologist Barbara Tamburini to improve quality, and she has been succeeding, although the wines can still be inconsistent. Pleasant white wines, but better reds, such as the fleshy Gualdo del Re Sangiovese, the Cabernet, Federico Primo, and the pure Merlot, Rennero.

Guidalberto
See Sassicaia.

Le Macchiole ☆☆☆–☆☆☆☆
Bolgheri. 22 ha. www.lemacchiole.it
After the untimely death of Eugenio Campolmi in 2002, his widow has continued to produce some of Bolgheri's finest wines, notably the Cabernet Franc, Paleo Rosso, and two scarce cult wines: Messorio (Merlot) and Scrio (Syrah). The wines are marvellous but priced accordingly.

Mantellassi ☆
Magliano in Toscana. 165 ha. www.fattoriamantellassi.it
A producer of robust Morellino di Scansano, as well as wines from Vermentino, Alicante, Ciliegiolo, and other varieties.

Mola ☆–☆☆
Porto Azzurro. 10 ha. www.tenutepavoletti.it
An excellent Elba estate, producing an oaky, Sangiovese-dominated red and a rich Aleatico. The Pavoletti family also own the Poggio alle Querce estate in Bolgheri.

Fattoria Montellori ☆☆
Fucecchio. 60 ha. www.fattoriamontellori.it
This large estate west of Florence produces a wide range of wines: among them, a pure Syrah (Tuttosole), a Cabernet/Merlot blend (Salamartino), and a pure Sauvignon. Ambition sometimes exceeds the results.

Montenidoli ☆☆
San Gimignano. 25 ha. www.montenidoli.com
Owner Elisabetta Fagiuoli produces highly drinkable Vernaccia di San Gimignano, and other wines in a wide range of styles.

Montepoloso ☆☆–☆☆☆
Suvereto. 7 ha.
Rapidly improving Swiss-owned Val di Cornia DOC property. Gabro is mostly Cabernet, Nardo an opulent Sangiovese enriched with a little Cabernet Sauvignon.

Moris ☆☆–☆☆☆
Massa Marittima. 70 ha. www.morisfarms.it
Increasingly well-known for its red wines, especially Morellino di Scansano and Avvoltore, an imposing blend of Sangiovese, Cabernet Sauvignon, and Syrah.

Ornellaia ☆☆☆☆
Bolgheri. 90 ha. www.ornellaia.com
This superb estate was developed by Lodovico Antinori, with advice from California's André Tchelitscheff and Michel Rolland. Mondavi bought a controlling interest, which passed to Frescobaldi after the sale of Mondavi. Despite all these changes, quality has remained very high. Ornellaia is a blend of Cabernet Sauvignon, Merlot, and Cabernet Franc; an astonishingly voluptuous wine with wonderful depth of flavour. Masseto is pure Merlot, and usually more massive and powerful than Ornellaia. Both are among Italy's greatest (and most expensive) red wines. Even the estate's lesser wines, La Serre Nuovo and Le Volte, are delicious.

Panizzi ☆☆
San Gimignano. 30 ha. www.panizzi.it
A fine and varied range of Vernaccia di San Gimignano as well as red San Gimignano.

La Parrina ☆☆
Albinia. 65 ha. www.parrina.it
Steadily improving wines from the coast near Orbetello. As well as the Sangiovese-based Parrina Reserva, there is an elegant Merlot called Radaia and the rare Ansonica Costa dell'Argentario.

Petra ☆–☆☆
Suvereto. 100 ha. www.petrawine.it
Created by the Moretti family, who also own Bellavista (q.v.) in Franciacorta, Petra has its base at an astonishing new winery in San Lorenzo that resembles a tilted satellite dish. Ambition, money, and early releases of rich, modern-style wines suggest that Petra is still finding its way.

Fattoria Petrolo ☆☆☆
Mercatale Valdarno. 31 ha. www.petrolo.it
Impressive wines from the Sanjust family's vineyards near Arezzo: pure Sangiovese (Torrione), and pure Merlot (Galatrona), both excellent but expensive.

Poggio Argentiera ☆☆
Banditella di Alberese. 70 ha.
www.poggioargentieria.com
A large estate that produces not only very reliable Morellino di Scansano but an unusual Alicante/Syrah blend called Finisterre, which is steeped in black fruits.

Poggio Scalette ☆☆☆
Greve. 18 ha. www.poggioscalette.it
This is consultant Vittorio Fiore's own estate, and it has made its reputation with a single wine, Il Carbonaione, a pure Sangiovese of impeccable purity. However, he has added a surprisingly mineral Merlot, Piantonaia, to the range.

Fattoria Le Pupille ☆☆☆
Magliano. 70 ha. www.elisabettageppetti.com
The leading estate in Morellino di Scansano, producing a remarkable single-vineyard bottling from Poggio Valente. Saffredi is a Bordeaux blend with, unusually, a dash of Alicante. Two specialties are *vin santo* and a sweet wine from Sauvignon and Traminer called Solalto.

La Regola ☆☆
Riparbella. 20 ha. www.laregola.com
Owned by the Nuti family, this estate produces excellent red wines as Montescudaio DOC. La Regola is mostly Cabernet Franc, aged in new oak. The second wine, Vallino delle Conche, is almost as good and excellent value.

Russo ☆☆
Suvereto. 11 ha.
A small family estate beginning to produce impressive reds: Sassobucato, an equal blend of Merlot and Cabernet Sauvignon, and the suave Barbicone, from Sangiovese and other local varieties.

Poderi San Luigi ☆☆
Piombino. 4 ha.
This tiny property produces a lovely blended wine called Fidenzio, made from Cabernet Sauvignon and Cabernet Franc.

San Michele ☆☆
San Vincenzo. 10 ha.
www.poderesanmichele.it
Small Maremma estate near Piombino, unusual in producing a pure Viognier, and a sumptuous blend of Sangiovese and Syrah called Allodio.

Santini ☆☆
Bolgheri. 13 ha.
Enrico Santini makes a delicious, supple red for early drinking (Poggio al Moro), and a richer, oakier blend of Cabernet, Merlot, and Syrah called Monte Pergoli.

Sapaio ☆☆–☆☆☆
Castagneto Carducci. 22 ha. www.sapaio.it
With advice from Carlo Ferrini, Massimo Piccin produces an excellent Cabernet-dominated Bolgheri Superiore, Sapaio, and a second wine, Volpolo, that comes close in structure and quality.

Tenuta San Guido-Sassicaia ☆☆☆☆
Bolgheri, Livorno. 90 ha. www.sassicaia.com
The late Marchese Mario Incisa della Rocchetta planted Cabernet Sauvignon on his 2,500-hectare seaside estate near Bolgheri, Tenuta San Guido, in 1944. Initially produced just for family use, Sassicaia emerged in the late 1960s as Italy's finest Cabernet. Consultant Giacomo Tachis insisted on

Petra winery, San Lorenzo

ageing the wine in good oak rather than chestnut casks, and quality improved dramatically. Since Mario Incisa's death in 1983, his son Niccolò has taken personal control of the property. Since 2000, the Marchese has worked jointly with his son-in-law, the winemaker Dr. Sebastiano Rosa, on Guidalberto, a Cabernet/Merlot blend that has come to be regarded as the second wine of Sassicaia, although the vineyards are separate.

Michele Satta ☆☆–☆☆☆
Castagneto Carducci. 25 ha. www.michelesatta.com
Unlike more fashionable Maremma producers, Satta remains true to local traditions, making creamy Viognier called Giovin Re, a pure Sangiovese called Cavaliere, as well as a Bordeaux blend called Piastraia.

Sette Ponti ☆☆☆
San Giustino. 65 ha. www.tenutasetteponti.it
Antonio Moretti's vineyards are divided: some near Arezzo, others in the Scansano district. The Sangiovese-dominated Oreno is the top wine, backed by the slightly softer and less muscular Crognolo. From Scansano comes a Morellino, a Cabernet-dominated IGT called Poggio al Lupo, and a lush Bordeaux blend called Orma. Quality is impressive but prices are high.

Castello del Terriccio ☆☆–☆☆☆☆
Castellina Marittima. 60 ha. www.terriccio.it
The handsomely named Gian Anibale Rossi di Medelana Serafini Ferri owns a large estate south of Livorno. He only began producing wine in the early 1990s, with consultant oenologists Carlo Ferrini (red) and Hans Terzer (white) giving their advice. Terriccio produces a fresh Sauvignon, Con Vento and an unoaked Chardonnay, Rondinaia. But the top wines are red: Tassinaia, a roughly equal blend of Sangiovese, Cabernet, and Merlot; the silky Cabernet-dominated Lupicaia; and the sleek, elegant Castello del Terriccio, from Syrah, supported by Petit Verdot and other varieties.

Teruzzi & Puthod ☆☆
San Gimignano. 90 ha.
Founded in 1975 by Enrico Teruzzi and Carmen Puthod, this estate was among the first to take Vernaccia di San Gimignano seriously, producing exemplary Vernaccia and also a wood-aged *riserva*, known as Terra di Tufi. In 2005 the property was bought by Campari.

Tenuta du Trinoro ☆☆☆
Sarteano. 25 ha. www.tenutaditrinoro.it
Andrea Franchetti's property lies south of Montepulciano. Very low yields and maximum new oak produce highly concentrated Bordeaux blends, the wildly expensive Trinoro itself and the more accessible second wine Cupole.

Tua Rita ☆☆☆
Suvereto. 18 ha. www.tuarita.it
The modest Besti family seem astonished by the acclaim their wines routinely receive. But they are excellent grape farmers, nurturing beautiful fruit. Giustri di Notri is their Bordeaux blend, Perlato del Bosco a pure Sangiovese, and their top wine is the marvellous Merlot Redigaffi.

Umbria

If Umbria figured on a discerning wine-buyer's shopping list in the past, it was purely for Orvieto, its golden, gently sweet, and occasionally memorable specialty. Then the limelight (such as it was) turned to Rubesco, the noble red of Torgiano near Perugia, one of the best wines and best bargains in Italy.

If Torgiano could make such good wine, so (surely) could other hills in this inland region. Indeed, Sagrantino has recently become a fashionable local variety – and with good reason. It produces rich, full-bodied, and long-lived reds, and the best examples fetch high prices. Now the Lago di Corbara region is showing that other parts of Umbria are also capable of producing excellent red wines. Sagrantino and Sangiovese are the only major varieties in the red roster, so it is understandable that in area such as Lago di Corbara international varieties are making an appearance, and with some flair.

DOC & Other Wines

Assisi DOC. Red, white, *rosato* wine. Province: Perugia. Communes: parts of Assisi, Perugia, and Spello. Grapes: Sangiovese and Merlot; Trebbiano (50–70%), Grechetto (10–30%), up to 40% others.

A recent DOC, created in 1997, as yet untested.

Colli Altotiberini DOC. Red, white, *rosato* wine. Province: Perugia. Villages: a wide sweep of country in northern Umbria, including Perugia and eight other communes. Grapes: Sangiovese (50–100%), up to 50% other varieties; Trebbiano (50–100%), up to 50% other varieties; plus varietal wines from Grechetto, Trebbiano, Merlot, Cabernet Sauvignon, Sangiovese.

DOC from the hills of the upper Tiber. Production in the area is increasing. All its wines are intended for drinking young. Limited production.

Colli Amerini DOC. Red, white, *rosato* wine. Province: Terni. Villages: Amelia, Narni, 11 others along the Tiber and Nera valleys between Orvieto and Terni. Grapes: Sangiovese (65–80%), up to 30% Montepulciano, Ciliegiolo, Canaiolo; Trebbiano Toscano (70–85%), up to 30% Grechetto, Verdello, Garganega and/or Malvasia Toscana; plus varietal Malvasia and Merlot. Also *novello*.

Production began only in 1990, and the wines have yet to establish a clear identity.

Colli Martani DOC. Red and white wine. Province: Perugia. Villages: from Bettona as far south as Spoleto. Grapes: varietal wines from Grechetto, Trebbiano, Sangiovese.

This is a fairly recent DOC, and the wines so far are promising. Of the three varietals, Grechetto seems to offer the brightest prospects.

Colli Perugini DOC. Red, white, *rosato* wine. Provinces: Perugia, Terni. Villages: six communes in Perugia, San Vananzo in Terni. Grapes: Sangiovese (minimum 50%), plus other varieties; Trebbiano (minimum 50%), plus other varieties. Also varietal Chardonnay, Trebbiano, Grechetto, Pinot Grigio, Merlot, Cabernet Sauvignon. Also *spumante*.

DOC wine from the area between Perugia and Todi.

Colli del Trasimeno DOC. Red and white wine. Province: Perugia. Villages: nine communes around Lake Trasimeno. Graoes: very complex rules but any combination of Sangiovese, Ciliegiolo, Gamay, Merlot, Cabernet Sauvignon, and Pinot Noir; any combination of Trebbiano, Grechetto, Chardonnay, Pinot Bianco, Pinot Grigio, Vermentino, Sauvignon, Riesling Italico; plus varietal Grechetto, Gamay, Merlot, Cabernet Sauvignon.

Average-quality red and white from this zone on the borders of Tuscany. Gamay and Ciliegiolo give spirit to the red, and Grechetto gives the white a slight edge of acidity essential for freshness.

Grechetto or Greco A "Greek" white grape that plays an increasingly important role. Unblended, its wine is somewhat more fruity, firm, and interesting than Trebbiano.

Lago di Corbara DOC. Red wine. Province: Terni. Villages: communes of Baschi, Orvieto. Grapes: up to 70% Cabernet Sauvignon, Merlot, Pinot Noir or Sangiovese, up to 30% other varieties; plus varietal Pinot Noir, Merlot, and Cabernet Sauvignon.

A recent DOC was created in 1998 and is proving popular and successful.

Montefalco Sagrantino and Montefalco Rosso DOC/DOCG. Red and white wine. Province: Perugia. Villages: commune of Montefalco, parts of four others.

Sagrantino di Montefalco DOCG. Grape: Sagrantino.

Montefalco Rosso DOC. Grape: Sangiovese (60–70%), Sagrantino (10–15%), up to 30% other red grapes.

Montefalco Bianco DOC. Grechetto (minimum 50%), Trebbiano Toscano (20–35%), up to 30% other white grapes.

DOC for a small area south of Assisi, where the local Sagrantino grape makes very dark red wine, tasting of blackberries. The challenge for winemakers is to control the grape's naturally high tannins, but when they succeed, the result is a rich, powerful, opulent wine of true grandeur. The true specialty is the sweet and strong *passito*, a notable dessert wine aged for a year.

Plain Montefalco red uses Sagrantino as seasoning in a less original but still smooth and agreeable wine. The white is unexceptional.

Orvieto DOC. White wine. Provinces: Orvieto, Terni. Villages: Orvieto and surrounding area, 11 communes in Terni. "Classico" is from Orvieto itself. Grapes: Trebbiano Toscano (Procanico, 40–50%), Verdello (15–25%), up to 20% Grechetto, Canaiolo Bianco, Malvasia, up to 15% other varieties.

The simple and memorable name that used to mean golden, more or less sweet wine, now suffers from the same identity crisis as many Italian whites. The taste for highly charged, then gently oxidized wines has gone. Modern vinification answers the problem with pale, clean, but almost neutered ones. Traditional Orvieto was laboriously fermented dry, was then re-sweetened with a dried-grape *passito* to be *abboccato*. If you found a good one it was memorably deep and velvety, but probably none too stable – like Frascati, a poor traveller.

Modern Orvieto is nearly all pale, but it should still have a hint of honey to be true to type. Much is dry and frankly dull, but the best producers release wines of freshness and character. In 1997, a new Orvieto Superiore was launched, requiring lower yields and a smaller proportion of Trebbiano. It is increasingly common for Chardonnay to be used as a component in the blend. There is also a small production of botrytized Orvieto, usually labelled "muffa nobile" ("noble rot").

Rosso Orvietano DOC. Red wine. Province: Terni. Villages: communes of Allerona, Baschi, Fabro, Orvieto, others. Grapes: Aleatico, Cabernet Franc, Cabernet Sauvignon, Ciliegiolo, Canaiolo, Merlot, Montepulciano, Pinot Noir, or Sangiovese (70% of blend), up to 30% Barbera, Cesanese, Colorino, Dolcetto; plus varietal versions of the principal grapes.

This is a new catch-all DOC for red wine produced around Orvieto.

Torgiano DOC. Red, white, *rosato* wine. Province: Perugia. Village: Torgiano. Grapes: Sangiovese (50–70%), Canaiolo (15–30%), others; Trebbiano (50–70%), Grechetto (15–40%), up to 15% others; plus varietal wines from Chardonnay, Pinot Grigio, Riesling Italico, Cabernet Sauvignon, Pinot Noir.

Virtually a one-man DOC; local tradition reshaped in modern terms by Dr. Giorgio Lungarotti (see Producers). This was Umbria's first DOC in 1968, its reputation built on the Lungarotti brands of Rubesco and Torre di Giano.

Torgiano Rosso Riserva became DOCG in 1990. The grapes are the same as for Rosso di Torgiano, but the maximum crop is 65 hl/ha, and the wine must be aged for three years, with an annual production of up to 8,800 cases.

Leading Umbria Producers

Adanti ☆☆–☆☆☆
Arquata di Bevagna. 32 ha. www.cantineadanti.com
This estate is best-known for its Montefalco reds (stunning *passito* wines), but it also produces good DOC Colli Martini Grechetto.

Alzatura ☆☆
Montefalco. 18 ha. www.tenutaalzatura.it
A property established by the well-known Cecchi family of Tuscany. Dense, plummy Sagrantino, and a brisker, arguably more stylish Montefalco Rosso.

Antonelli ☆☆☆
Montefalco. 40 ha. www.antonellisanmarco.it
No one makes a more elegant Sagrantino than Filippo Antonelli, whose ancestors bought the property in 1881. Well aware that the wine can have too much alcohol, he works hard in the vineyard to attain full ripeness without excessive sugar levels. First-rate Sagrantino and delicious Grechetto.

Barberani-Vallesanta ☆☆–☆☆☆
Orvieto. 50 ha. www.barberani.it

This substantial estate produces a full range of excellent Orvieto wines, including a peaches-and-cream *muffa nobile* called Calcaia. Bracing, mineral Grechetto IGT, and succulent, if oaky, bottlings of Lago di Corbara.

Paolo Bea ☆☆☆
Montefalco. 12 ha.
Giampiero Bea is a believer in non-interventionist wine-making. Both the Sagrantino and the Montefalco are given long ageing in tanks and casks. They are leaner than most wines from Montefalco, but have silky textures and a good deal of spice. Lovely *passito*, too.

Luigi Bigi ☆☆
Ponte Giulio di Orvieto. www.cantinebigi.it
Founded in 1881, and now part of the Gruppo Italiano Vini complex. This large company is best-known for its ripe, flowery, single-vineyard Orvieto, Torricella, but also produces some delicious Grechetto and serious red wines, such as the IGT Vipra from Merlot and Sangiovese.

Arnaldo Caprai ☆☆☆–☆☆☆☆
Montefalco. 135 ha. www.arnaldocaprai.it
The most sophisticated producer of the Montefalco region, with a balanced, persistent Sagrantino, Collepiano, and the exceptional bottling called 25 Anni, which has the density to survive two years in new barriques. In 2001 Caprai began the production of a wine called Outsider, a convincing and elegant Bordeaux blend.

La Carraia ☆☆–☆☆☆
Orvieto. 120 ha.
This substantial property is partly owned by consultant Riccardo Cotarella, and the wines, sourced from various parts of Umbria, are certainly well crafted. The flagship wine is Fobiano, and in complete contrast there is a more savoury Montepulciano, Giro di Vite.

Cantina dei Colli Amerini ☆☆
Fornole di Amelia. 350 ha.
www.colliamerini.it
A good source of red wines: Sangiovese, Ciliegiolo, and Merlot, and a complex but inexpensive blend called Carbio; plus Chardonnay and Grechetto.

Colpetrone ☆☆☆
Gualdo Cattaneo. 60 ha. www.saiagricola.it
Owned since 1995 by the insurance company Saiagricola, Colpetrone makes a dense, powerful style of Sagrantino, and velvety *passito*.

Decugnano dei Barbi ☆☆–☆☆☆
Orvieto. 32 ha. www.deccugnanodeibarbi.com
A good source for Orvieto and, occasionally, the botrytized version; and renowned for IL, a complex red blend, aged in barriques.

Duca della Corgna ☆–☆☆
Castiglione del Lago. 55 ha.
www.ducadellacorgna.it
A small cooperative producing a typical range of wines, red and white, from the Colli del Trasimeno DOC.

Lamborghini ☆☆–☆☆☆
Panicale. 32 ha. www.lamborghinionline.it
A property, best-known for its complex Sangiovese/Merlot blend called Campoleone.

Lungarotti ☆☆–☆☆☆
Torgiano. 250 ha. www.lungarotti.it
Giorgio Lungarotti was, until his death in 1999, the leading personality in Umbrian wine. The Torgiano DOC, which accounts for about half the production here, is an official recognition of the quality of the wines he made in this village.

Today, the estate is run by his daughters, Chiara and Teresa. The range of wines is enormous. The star is always the Rubesco Riserva Monticchio DOCG, which is aged for years in bottle before release. Torre di Giano is the white. Cabernet (in an excellent blend called San Giorgio) and Chardonnay are reliable and satisfying. Giubilante is a recent blend: a crowd-pleasing but delicious merger of Sangiovese, Cabernet Sauvignon, Montepulciano, and other varieties.

Quality overall remains high, but perhaps not as stellar as when Giorgio Lungarotti was in his prime. Perhaps too many wines are being produced. The estate includes a popular wine museum and a charming hotel, and another museum devoted to the olive and its oil.

Madonna Alta ☆☆
Montefalco. 22 ha. www.madonnalta.it
A modern winery producing red-fruited Montefalco and lush oaky Sagrantino with no trace of rusticity.

Milziade Antano ☆☆–☆☆☆
Bevagna. 10 ha.
This estate produces outstanding Montefalco reds, especially the single-vineyard Colleallodole and the voluptuous Sagrantino *passito*.

La Palazzola ☆☆–☆☆☆
Stroncone. 18 ha.
A slightly eccentric estate, offering wines such as sparkling Riesling, Uva Muffate from botrytized grapes, Merlot, and Syrah.

Palazzone ☆☆–☆☆☆
Orvieto. 27 ha. www.palazzone.com
Giovanni Dubini acquired this estate in 1969. Good Orvieto, a Viognier, a honeyed Muffa Nobilis, and a concentrated Cabernet Sauvignon/Cabernet Franc blend called Armaleo.

Perticaia ☆☆
Gualdo Cattaneo. 14 ha. www.perticaia.it
Guido Gaudigli brings a lifetime of wine-production experience to his retirement project and the results are highly satisfying: fresh, lively Montefalco and plump, accessible Sagrantino.

Castello delle Regine ☆☆–☆☆☆
Amelia. 80 ha. www.castellodelleregine.com
Franco Bernabei's advice has propelled this estate into the upper ranks within Umbria, especially for the sumptuous Merlot and a supple Sangiovese called Podernovo.

Rocca di Fabri ☆☆
Montefalco. 60 ha. www.roccadifabri.com
A modern winery set within the walls of a medieval fortress. A reliable producer of complex Montefalco reds, with rich damson and liquorice fruit and robust tannins.

Castello della Sala ☆☆–☆☆☆☆
Ficulle. 160 ha. www.antinori.it
Antinori's Umbrian castle is rightly renowned for the floral and sometimes exotic Cervaro della Sala (80% Chardonnay, 20% Grechetto) and the superb, botrytized sweet wine, Muffato della Sala. The estate's basic white wines are, of course, Orvieto, and the reliable and lemony Chardonnay. A cleverly oaked and well-balanced Pinot Nero is also produced here.

Scacciadiavoli ☆☆
Montefalco. 32 ha.
The splendidly named Dr Amilcare Pambuffetti operates the oldest winery in Montefalco. The Sagrantino is skilfully made, without heavy extraction or rusticity. The Montefalco Rosso is also at a high level, showing freshness and charm.

Spoleoducale ☆☆–☆☆☆
Petrognano di Spoleto. 350 ha. www.spoletoducale.it
A well-equipped and well-run cooperative, producing DOC Colle Martani and IGT wines plus reliable Montefalco reds. Its top Sagrantino is Casale Triocco, a selection from the top growers who accept lower yields.

Sportoletti ☆☆–☆☆☆
Spello. 20 ha. www.sportoletti.com
With advice from Riccardo Cotarella, this estate produces interesting IGT wines: a good Grechetto and Villa Fidelia, a Bordeaux blend aged in new oak.

Tabarrini ☆–☆☆
Montefalco. 11 ha. www.tabarrini.com
The enthusiastic young Giampaolo Tabarrini runs this property with great dynamism, but both his Montefalco Rosso and Sagrantino can sometimes taste overripe and overworked. But they certainly don't lack fruit.

The Marches

The central slice of the Adriatic coast, from the latitude of Florence to that of Orvieto, is probably even better-known for its dry white Verdicchio than for the beaches and fishing boats that give the wine such a perfect context. The historic cities of Urbino in the north, and Ascoli Piceno in the south of the region, draw a proportion of its visitors inland, but the eastern flanks of the Apennines hardly rival the cultural crowd-pulling quality of Tuscany. The region's red wines are less well-known than they should be. It's the Montepulciano grape that gives them muscle and complexity, and a deep fleshiness that when in balance can be very appealing. Moreover, prices, other than for the most prestigious wines, tend to be reasonable.

DOC & Other Wines

Bianchello del Metauro DOC. White wine. Province: Pesaro-Urbino. Villages: 18 commues in the valley of the River Metauro. Grapes: Biancame (Bianchello, minimum 95%), up to 5% Malvasia.

A pleasant, sharp, plain white from the north of the region, for drinking young with fish.

Colli Maceratesi DOC. Red and white wine. Provinces: Macerata, Ancona. Villages: Loreto and all of Macerata. Grapes: Sangiovese (minimum 50%), up to 50% of any combination of Cabernet Sauvignon, Cabernet Franc, Ciliegiolo, Lacrima, Merlot, Montepulciano, Malvasia Nera, up to 5% others; Maceratino (minimum 70%), up to 30% of any combination of Trebbiano, Verdicchio, Malvasia, Chardonnay, Sauvignon Blanc, Incroci Bruni 54, Pecorino, Grechetto, up to 15% others. Maceratino is a clone of Verdicchio. Also *passito*.

The Macerata region is halfway from Ancona south to Ascoli Piceno.

Colli Pesaresi DOC. Red and white wine. Province: Pesaro-Urbino. Villages: 33 communes in and around Pesaro. Grapes: Sangiovese (minimum 70%); up to 75% of any combination of Trebbiano, Verducchio, Bianchello, Pinot Grigio, Pinot Nero (off skins), or Pinot Bianco, up to 25% others. Also varietal Trebbiano, Sangiovese. Two sub-appellations – Focara Rosso must be minimum 50% of any combination of Pinot Nero, Cabernet Franc, Cabernet Sauvignon, or Merlot, up to 50% other varieties; plus a varietal Pinot Nero; Roncaglia Bianco from Trebbiano (minimum 85%), plus Pinot Nero (off skins).

Overall, needlessly complex regulations for a little used DOC of limited character.

Esino DOC. White, red, and *rosato* wine. Provinces: Ancona, Macerata. Villages: seven communes. Grapes: Sangiovese and/or Montepulciano (minimum 60%); Verdicchio (minimum 50%).

A recent DOC from 1995. The white can be dry or *frizzante*; the red can also be made in a *novello* style.

Falerio dei Colli Ascolani DOC. White wine. Provinces: Ascoli, Piceno. Villages: entire provinces. Grapes: Trebbiano Toscano (20–50%), Passerina (10–30%), Pecorino (10–30%), up to 20% others. Another of the local dry whites associated with restaurants on the beach.

Lacrima di Morro d'Alba DOC. Red wine. Province: Ancona. Villages: six south of Senigallia. Grapes: Lacrima (minimum 85%), Montepulciano/Verdicchio (maximum 15%).

A DOC from around the ancient town of Morro d'Alba. Small production but these are wines of character, although high tannins need cautious winemaking.

Montepulciano Important in the Marches as a constituent grape of the best red wines, but also made as a varietal wine.

Offida DOC in 2001; before 2001, part of Rosso Piceno. Red and white wine. Province: Ascoli, Piceno. Villages:

the hills north of Ascoli Piceno and south of River Aso. Grapes: Montepulciano (minimum 50%), Cabernet Sauvignon (minimum 30%), up to 20% other varieties; plus varietal Pecorino, Passerina. Passerina can be dry, *passito*, *vin santo*, or *spumante*.

Pergola. DOC in 2005. South of Urbino. Dry and *passito* red from 70–100% Vernaccia di Pergola (a clone of Aleatico).

Rosso Cònero DOCG Red wine. Province: Ancona. Villages: five communes in Ancona, part of two others. Grapes: Montepulciano (minimum 85%), Sangiovese (maximum 15%).

A full-strength, full-flavoured red from Monte Cònero, near the Adriatic just south of Ancona. This is one of the most flourishing DOCs of central and eastern Italy. Good Rosso Cònero has fruit to mellow and tannin to sustain it.

Rosso Piceno DOC. Red wine. Provinces: Ancona, Ascoli Piceno, Macerata. Villages: a large number in the above provinces. Grapes: Montepulciano (35–70%), Sangiovese (35–50%); up to 15% other varieties, including international varieties and Trebbiano and/or Passerina.

The standard red of the southern half of the Marches, varying widely in quality from unremarkable to hand-made and age worthy, both in barrel and bottle. At its best it has Chianti-like weight and balance.

Terreni di San Severino. DOC in 2006. Red wine. Province: Macerata. Grapes: Vernaccia (50–100%), Montepulciano or Sangiovese. Rosso Moro must have Montepulciano (60–100%), up to 40% others. Also *passito*.

Verdicchio dei Castelli di Jesi DOC. White wine. Provinces: Ancona, Macerata. Villages: 26 around the town of Jesi. Grapes: Verdicchio (minimum 85%), up to 15% Trebbiano or Malvasia.

This is the great commercial success of the Marches. Straightforward, dry, well-balanced, and clean; one of the earliest Italian whites to taste both modern and international, thanks to the skill of its promoters, initially the firm of Fazi-Battaglia (q.v.). Its marketing flair produced the distinctive, amphora-shaped bottle seen among the fishnets in practically every Italian restaurant abroad – although better quality wines are sold in normal Bordeaux style bottles. The Verdicchio is a tricky grape to grow but clearly has quality. A current trend to leave some residual sugar in the wine is not to be encouraged. There is also a *tradizionale* sparkling version.

Verdicchio di Matelica DOC. White wine. Provinces: Macerata, Ancona. Villages: Matelica, seven others. Grapes: Verdicchio (minimum 85%), up to 15% Trebbiano or Malvasia.

Verdicchio from higher ground farther inland, with a touch more acidity, but also richness and weight. Generally more highly regarded than Verdicchio dei Castelli di Jesi. Another (non-DOC) with a similar reputation is Verdicchio di Montanello.

Vernaccia di Serrapetrona DOCG. Red wine. Province: Macerata. Villages: Serrapetrona, part of Belforte del Chienti and San Severino Marche. Grapes: Vernaccia Nera (minimum 85%), Sangiovese, Montelpulciano, and/or Ciliegiolo.

A locally popular, sweet, sparkling red, which has been made since the fifteenth century.

Leading Marches Producers

Belisario ☆☆
Matelica. 300 ha. www.belsiario.it
The label used by a good cooperative specializing in Verdicchio di Matelica. Cambrugiano is partially oaked, but that can give the wine an earthy character from which the single-vineyard wines are free.

Boccadigabbia ☆☆–☆☆☆
Civitanova Marche. 35 ha.
www.boccadigabbia.com
A small, quality-focused estate specializing in expensive red IGTs from Cabernet (Akronte), Merlot (Pix), Sangiovese, and Pinot Nero. Owner Elvio Alessandria is not shy about using a great deal of new oak.

Fratelli Bucci ☆☆–☆☆☆
Ostra Vetere. 26 ha. www.villabucci.com
Concentrated, peachy Verdicchio dei Castelli di Jesi, especially the cask-aged Villa Bucci Riserva, which shows that Verdicchio can age well. And a good Rosso Piceno called Tenuta Pongelli.

Le Caniette ☆☆–☆☆☆
Ripatransone. 15 ha. www.lecaniette.it
Rich, chocolatey Rosso Piceno The top *cuvée*, Nero di Vite is only made in outstanding vintages and is aged in new oak. Many will prefer the less effortful but splendidly fruity Morellone.

Casalfarneto ☆☆
Serra de' Conti. 30 ha. www.togni.it
Apart from a small quantity of Rosso Piceno and other reds, Verdicchio dei Castelli di Jesi is the main focus here. The best bottling is usually Grancasale..

Cocci grifoni ☆☆
San Savino di Ripatransone. 80 ha.
www.tenutacoccogrifoni.it
The octogenarian Guido Cocci Grifoni is an admirable producer, whose Rosso Piceno is one of the best, and whose Falerio has few rivals. He also produces a range of Offida wines from Pecorino and Passerina.

Colonnara ☆☆
Cupramontana. 210 ha. www.colonnara.it
The Cupramontana cooperative now goes under the name Colonnara, and is making some excellent, fragrant Verdicchio, still and sparkling, as well as Lacrima di Morro.

Arringo Square, Ascoli Piceno

Coroncino ☆☆☆
Staffolo. 17 ha.
Minute production of outstanding and complex Verdicchio dei Castelli di Jesi, including a Fumé version that is aged in oak barrels.

De Angelis ☆☆–☆☆☆
Castel di Lama. 13 ha. www.tenutadeangelis.it
A cherry-scented Rosso Piceno, but the estate is best-known for its intensely fruity Montepulciano/Cabernet IGT blend Anghelos.

Fazi-Battaglia ☆☆
Castelplanio. 350 ha. www.fazibattaglia.it
Founded in 1949, this company was the first to win international recognition for Verdicchio dei Castelli di Jesi. Despite a total production of over three million bottles, standards remain very high, not just for dry Verdicchio, but also for a ripe, tobacco-scented Rosso Cònero and a botrytized Verdicchio called Arkezia.

Garofoli ☆☆☆
Loreto. 50 ha. www.garofolivini.it
Still in family hands after a century of production as both grower and negociant, Garofoli produces delightful, refreshing Verdicchio dei Castelli di Jesi to consistently high standards.

The oak-aged Serra Fioresa is perhaps an acquired taste, but the Podium bottling is impeccable. Garofoli was also a pioneer of vintage-dated sparkling Verdicchio.

Laila ☆☆
Mondavio. 40 ha. www.fattorialaila.it
It is hard to say which is better: the fine bottlings of Verdicchio dei Castelli di Jesi or the reds such as Lailum, a pure and virile Montepulciano.

Lanari ☆☆–☆☆☆
Varano. 12 ha. www.lanarivini.it
A small property producing nothing but Rosso Cònero of exceptional quality.

Mancinelli ☆☆
Morro d'Alba. 25 ha. www.mancinelli-wine.com
This estate has done much to promote the virtues of Lacrima di Morro d'Alba, experimenting with different techniques such as carbonic maceration (Sensazioni di Frutto) or the partial use of dried grapes (Terre dei Goti). There is also a delicious Lacrima *passito*.

Mancini ☆☆
Pesaro. 34 ha. www.fattoriamancini.com
An atypical property in the Colli Pesaresi but close to the Adriatic, focusing on Pinot Nero, which, Luigi Mancini claims, was first planted here in the nineteenth century by the French.

Marchetti ☆–☆☆
Ancona. 19 ha. www.marchettiwines.it
Sound Rosso Cònero and Verdicchio, but quantities are no more than 50,000 bottles.

Enzo Mecella ☆☆
Fabriano. 10 ha. www.enzomecella.com
Mecella's range is divided between Verdicchio di Matelica, and red wines such as the unusual Ciliegiolo/Merlot blend called Braccano.

La Monacesca ☆☆☆
Matelica. 20 ha. www.monacesca.it
Industrialist Casimiro Cifola revived this estate in the late 1960s, and the family continues to produce delectable Verdicchio di Matelica from old vines.

Monte Schiavo ☆☆
Maiolati Spontini. 115 ha. www.monteschiavo.it
This was originally a cooperative until acquired by the farm machinery manufacturer, Pieralisi. It produces good Verdicchio Classico as well as Rosso Cònero. Its flagship red is the pure Montepulciano Adeodata, but it veers towards overripeness.

Moroder ☆☆–☆☆☆
Montacuto. 27 ha. www.moroder-vini.it
Alessandro Moroder produces rich Rosso Cònero Dorico and (sometimes) Oro, a sweet Moscato/Trebbiano IGT from his small estate.

Oasi degli Angeli ☆☆–☆☆☆
Cupora Marittima. 1.5 ha. www.kurni.it
Tiny estate, just one wine: a legendary, Amarone-style Montepulciano called Kurni, steeped in coffee and plums. With a maximum production of 4,000 bottles, it is scarce indeed.

Saladini Pilastri ☆☆
Spinetoli. 160 ha. www.saladinipilastri.it
A large organic estate with supple, plummy Rosso Piceno.

San Lorenzo ☆☆
Montecarotto. 35 ha.
The specialty here is the Verdicchio dei Castelli di Jesi, Vigna delle Oche, which is easily capable of improving in bottle for 15 years, broadening in flavour without losing its vigour.

Santa Barbara ☆☆
Barbara. 25 ha. www.vinisantabarbara.it
Unusually powerful Verdicchio in various styles and a sound Cabernet/Merlot/Montepulciano blend called Stefano Antonucci Rosso.

Sartarelli ☆☆☆
Poggio San Marcello. 55 ha. www.sartarelli.it
Family estate that makes nothing other than highly concentrated, minerally Verdicchios, including a botrytized Verdicchio called Contrada Balciana.

Le Terrazze ☆☆–☆☆☆
Numana. 21 ha. www.fattorialeterrazze.it
Antonio Terni, who names some of his wines after Bob Dylan songs, makes good Rosso Cònero, a striking pink *tradizionale* Donna Giulia from Montepulciano grapes, and a pricey, but acclaimed red blend from Montepulciano, Merlot, and Syrah, intriguingly named Chaos.

Terre Cortesi Moncaro ☆☆
Montecarotto. 1,550 ha. www.moncaro.com
Very good cooperative producing four million bottles.
Impressive Verdicchio dei Castelli di Jesi, dry and *passito*, and
structured Rosso Cònero Riserva. Also produces varietal IGTs.

Umani Ronchi ☆☆☆
Osimo. 200 ha. www.umanironchi.it
Founded in 1960 by Gino Ronchi and now owned by the
Bernetti family. One of the best-distributed brands of the
Marches, producing over 300,000 cases of good-quality,
estate-bottled Verdicchio and Rosso Cònero. Other wines
are made from grapes that are bought in.

The winery also offers some convincing red IGTs –
Cùmaro (Montepulciano) and Pelago (Cabernet
Sauvignon/Montepulciano) – and a rare sweet Sauvignon
called Maximo. Even the simpler wines, such as Rosso
Cònero San Lorenzo, are very well made.

Velenosi ☆☆
Ascoli Piceno. 105 ha. www.velenosivini.com
A diverse range of wines from a very modern winery: powerful
Rosso Piceno, intense Chardonnay, and local varieties such as
Pecorino and Passerina.

Villa Pigna ☆☆
Offida. 130 ha. www.villapigna.com
The Rozzi family runs a model large scale estate. The Rosso
Piceno Superiore closely resembles a claret, and there is an
admirable Montepulciano IGT called Rozzano. The Rozzis
are keen to validate the new DOCs, so their Cabernasco
Cabernet, once an IGT, is now Offida DOC.

Zaccagnini ☆☆–☆☆☆
Staffolo30 ha. www.zaccagnini.it
From a range of Verdicchio dei Castelli di Jesi, the finest
is the peachy, single vineyard Salmagina.

Latium

Rome can be compared with Vienna, as a capital city with wine
so much in its veins that such artificial obstructions as bottles
and corks have traditionally been foreign to it. The winemakers' taverns of Rome are slightly farther out of town than
the Heurigen of Vienna, but are even more tempting as a summer outing, maybe to the cool of the wooded Alban Hills, or
perhaps to the Castelli Romani to the south.

Frascati, the hub of the hills and their wine, has the air of
a holiday resort. The spectacular Villa Aldobrandini and its
beautiful gardens in the heart of Frascati show that the taste
is both patrician as well as popular.

Latium, both north and south of Rome, is pock-marked with
volcanic craters which are now placid lakes. The rich volcanic
soil of the region is highly suited to the cultivation of vines.

The choice of grape varieties, which is presumably based on
the Roman taste for soft young wines, has determined that they
should remain local. The low acidity of the Malvasia, the grape
that gives character to Frascati, makes it prone to disastrous

oxidation once removed from storage in its cold damp cellar.
These were the archetypes of wines that "don't travel". Now,
with such processes as pasteurization and, more recently, cold
treatments, they are fit for the road. Even if they still taste best
in Rome. Despite the domination of white wines, there is no
shortage of ambitious growers who believe their soils are
capable of producing red wines of character, although to
achieve this they must plant international varieties and depart
from the strictures of the DOC system. Though heaven knows
there are enough DOCs to be getting on with.

DOC & Other Wines

Aleatico di Gradoli DOC. Red wine. Province: Viterbo.
Villages: Gradoli, Grotte di Castro, San Lorenzo Nuovo,
Latera (in the hills above Lake Bolsena). Grapes: Aleatico
(100%).

Very limited production of a local specialty: sweet red
wine with a faintly Muscat aroma made at both normal
strength and liquoroso (fortified to 17.5 degrees of alcohol).

Aprilia DOC. Red, white, *rosato* wine. Provinces: Latina,
Roma. Villages: Aprilia, Cisterna, Nettuno. Grapes: varietal
wines from Trebbiano, Sangiovese, Merlot.

A vineyard area established by refugees from Tunisia after
World War II. Merlot is reckoned its best product at two or
three years of age. Although one of the first DOCs, the wines
scarcely merit the dignity; however, recent experiments in
vineyards and cellars are aimed at notable improvements.
Sangiovese delivers good *rosato* here.

Atina DOC. Red wine. Province: Frosinone, southeast Lazio.
Villages: Atina, twelve others. Grapes: Cabernet Sauvignon
(minimum 50%), up to 10% Syrah, Merlot, Cabernet Franc,
up to 20% other varieties. Also varietal Cabernet from
Cabernet Franc and/or Cabernet Sauvignon.

Bianco Capena DOC. White wine. Province: Roma.
Villages: Capena, Fiano Romano, Morlupo, Castelnuovo
di Porto. Grapes: Malvasia di Candia (minimum 50%),
Trebbiano and/or Romagnolo and/or Giallo (minimum 25%);
up to 20% Bellone, Bombino.

Similar white wine to that of the Castelli Romani
(eg. Frascati) but from just north of Rome instead of south.

Castelli Romani DOC. Provinces: Roma, Latina. Grapes: red
and *rosato* from a wide range of varietals, mostly local but also
Merlot; Malvasia, Trebbiano.

Name for the verdant region, otherwise known as the
Colli Albani, where Frascati and its peers are grown. Can
be produced in a variety of styles.

Cerveteri DOC. Red and white wine. Provinces: Roma,
Viterbo. Villages: eight northwest of Rome. Grapes:
Sangiovese and Montepulciano (minimum 60%), Cesanese
Comune (25%), up to 30% others; Trebbiano (Toscano,
Romagnolo and Giallo, minimum 50%), Malvasia
(maximum 35%), up to 15% others.

Standard dry wines from the country near the coast
northwest of Rome.

Cesanese del Piglio DOCG. Red wine. Province: Frosinone, Piglio. Villages: Piglio and Serrone, Acuto, Anagni and Paliano. Grapes: varietal Cesanese.

Dry or sweet, still or sparkling red from a zone just to the left of the Autostrada del Sole, heading southeast 65 kilometres (40 miles) out of Rome.

Another two Cesanese DOCs exist: Cesanese di Olevano Romano (very scarce) and Cesanese di Affile (almost defunct, since total production in 2005 was 6,000 bottles). All three were made DOCs in an excess of bureaucratic enthusiasm in 1973, and Piglio mysteriously promoted to DOCG in 2008.

Circeo DOC. White, red, *rosato* wine. Province: Latina. Villages: Latina, Sabaudia, San Felice, Circeo, Terracina. Grapes: Merlot (minimum 85%); Malvasia Bianca, Trebbiano, and others; plus varietal Trebbiano, Sangiovese.

Colli Albani DOC. White wine. Province: Roma. Villages: Ariccia, Albano, parts of four others. Grapes: Malvasia Bianca di Candia (maximum 60%), Trebbiano Toscano, Romagnolo di Soave, and Giallo (25–50%), Malvasia del Lazio (5–45%), up to 10% others.

The local white of the Pope's summer villa at Castelgandolfo. Dry or sweet, still, or fizzy.

Colli Etruschi Viterbesi DOC. White and red wine. Province: Viterbo. Villages: 38. Grapes: Sangiovese, Montepulciano, others; Malvasia, Trebbiano, others; plus varietal Trebbiano, Grechetto, Trebbiano Giallo, Moscato Bianco, Montepulciano, Canaiolo.

Large new zone, established in 1996. Wines can be dry, sweet, or *frizzante*.

Colli Lanuvini DOC. White wine. Province: Roma. Villages: Genzano, part of Lanuvio. Grapes: Malvasia Bianca di Candia, Puntinata (maximum 70%), plus Trebbiano, others.

A lesser-known but recommended dry or lightly sweet white of the Castelli Romani.

Colli della Sabina DOC. White, red, *rosato* wine. Provinces: Rieti, Rome. Villages: 25. Grapes: Sangiovese (40–70%), Montepulciano (15–40%), others (maximum 30%); Trebbiano (minimum 40%); Malvasia (minimum 40%), others (maximum 20%).

Large inland DOC created in 1996. Wines can be dry, sweet, sparkling, or *novello*.

Cori DOC. Red and white wine. Province: Latina. Villages: Cisterna, Cori. Grapes: Montepulciano (40–60%), Nero Buono di Cori (20–40%), Cesanese (10–30%); Malvasia di Candia (maximum 70%), Trebbiano Toscano (maximum 40%), up to 10% others.

Cori is south of the Castelli Romani, where the country flattens towards the Pontine marshes. The red is soft and pleasant, but unfortunately, along with the white, it is rarely seen.

Est! Est!! Est!!! di Montefiascone DOC. White wine. Province: Viterbo. Grapes: Trebbiano Toscano (minimum 65%), Malvasia (maximum 20%), Trebbiano Giallo (maximum 15%).

Very large quantities of unpredictable wine take advantage of this, the earliest example of what is now called a fantasy name. The emphatic "It is" was the first three-star rating in history, antedating the Michelin guide by some 800 years. More recent inspectors have had less luck, but now modernization of techniques and taste is producing an acceptable, usually dry, white.

Falerno or Falernum The most famous wine of ancient Rome, from the borders of Latium and Campania to the south. Then sweet and concentrated, with affinities to Madeira, now a good, strong red of Aglianico and Barbera, and a pleasant, low-acid white. The red has a DOC in Campania.

Frascati DOC. White wine. Province: Roma. Villages: Frascati, Montecompatri, Monteporzio Catone, Colonna, Grottaferrata. Grapes: Malvasia di Candia (minimum 50%), Trebbiano or Malvasia del Lazio (10–40%), Greco, Bellone, Bombino (maximum 30%), up to 15% others.

In legend, and occasionally in fact, the most memorable Italian white wine, though possibly the one that originated the notion of wines that "do not travel", even the 30 kilometres (18 miles) to Rome.

Malvasia on volcanic soil gives a splendid sensation of whole grape ripeness, a golden glow to the wine, encouraged by fermenting it like red on its skins. The dry variety should be soft but highly charged with flavour, faintly nutty, and even faintly salty. Sweeter (*amabile*) and sweeter still (*cannellino*) versions can be honeyed, too, but I would not count on it.

The best way to learn the difference between old-style and new-style Italian whites is to go to a restaurant in Frascati and order a bottle of a good brand, and a jug of the house wine. Sadly, the luscious qualities of the latter are the ones that do not travel. Modern winemaking technology ensures that most modern Frascati is at least well-made and brisk, if not full of character.

Genazzano DOC. Red and white wine. Provinces: Rome, Frosinone. Villages: communes of Genzano, Olevano Romano, San Vito Romano, Cave, Paliano. Grapes: Sangiovese (70–90%), Cesanese (10–30%); other local red varieties (maximum 20%); Malvasia Bianca di Candia (50–70%), Bellone and/or Bombino (10–30%); up to 40% others.

This is an obscure DOC, established in 1992, that permits high yields.

Marino DOC. White wine. Province: Roma. Villages: Marino, part of Rome and Castelgandolfo. Grapes: Malvasia Bianca di Candia (maximum 60%), Trebbiano (25–55%), Malvasia del Lazio (5–45%), up to 10% others.

First cousin to Frascati. Many Romans who dine out at Marino prefer to drink it fresh and unbottled.

Montecompatri-Colonna DOC. White wine. Province: Roma. Villages: Colonna, part of Montecompatri, Zagarolo, Rocca Priora. Grapes: Malvasia (maximum 70%), Trebbiano (minimum 30%), Bellone and/or Bonvino (maximum 10%). Another alternative to Frascati in the Castelli Romani.

Nettuno. White, red, *rosato* wine. Province: Roma. Grapes: Malvasia (maximum 70%), Trebbiano (maximum 30%), up to 10% Bellone and/or Bombino.

Coastal area east of Anzio. Wines can be dry, sweet, and *frizzante*.

Tarquinia DOC. White, red, *rosato* wines. Provinces: Rome, Viterbo. Communes: 15 in Rome, 15 in Viterbo. Grapes: Sangiovese and Montepulciano (minimum 60%, with at least 25% of each), Cesanese (maximum 25%), up to 30% others; Trebbiano (minimum 50%), Malvasia (maximum 35%), up to 30% others.

A large zone, established in 1996, but permitting high yields.

Torre Ercolana The highly *recherché* specialty of one producer (see Colacicchi, next column) at Anagni. A red of Cesanese with Cabernet and Merlot, powerful in personality and maturing to outstanding quality.

Velletri DOC. White and red wine. Provinces: Latina, Roma. Villages: Velletri, Lariano, part of Cisterna di Latina. Grapes: Sangiovese (10–45%), Montepulciano (30–50%), Cesanese (minimum 10%), up to 30% other local red varieties; Malvasia (maximum 70%), Trebbiano (minimum 30%), Bellone and/or Bonvino (maximum 20%).

South of the Frascati zone of the Castelli Romani, Velletri has a DOC for both its pleasant white and its mild red.

Vignanello DOC. White and red wine. Province: Viterbo. Villages: seven communes. Grapes: Sangiovese, Ciliegiolo; Trebbiano, Malvasia; plus varietal Greco and Greco *spumante*.

Fresh wines for everyday drinking.

Zagarolo DOC. White wine. Province: Roma. Villages: Zagarolo, Gallicano. Grapes: Malvasia and Trebbiano (70–90%), Bellone and/or Bonvino (maximum 10%).

The smallest, indeed tiny, DOC of the Frascati group, with similar white wine.

Leading Latium Producers

Casale del Giglio ☆☆–☆☆☆
Le Ferriere. 150 ha. www.casaledelgiglio.it
From large coastal vineyards on former marshland comes an eclectic range of IGTs from Syrah, Cabernet Sauvignon, Petit Verdot, Petit Manseng, and Chardonnay/Viognier (Antinoo), mostly aged in oak.

Castel de Paolis ☆☆–☆☆☆
Grottaferra. 12 ha. www.casteldepaolis.it
This small property was created in 1993, and Franco Bernabei, its consultant winemaker, has brought its Frascati up to the highest standards (and prices). The floral "Vigna Adriana"

contains a proportion of Sauvignon and Viognier. The Syrah/Merlot IGT called "Quattro Mori" is one of Latium's finest barrique aged reds.

Cantina Cerveteri ☆–☆☆
Cerveteri. 2,000 ha. www.cantinacerveteri.it
This cooperative is a major producer of white and red Cerveteri and Tarquinia.

Cantina Sociale Cesanese del Piglio ☆
Piglio. 156 ha. www.cesanesedelpiglio.it
Sound Cesanese del Piglio and Passerina.

Colacicchi ☆☆–☆☆☆
Anagni. 6 ha.
A family winery, made famous by the late Luigi Colacicchi and

now owned by the Trimani family. Best-known for "Torre Ercolana", the splendid but very rare red of Cabernet, Merlot, and Cesanese: intense, long-lived, and long on the palate. Only about 700 cases are made.

Colli di Catone ☆☆
Monteporzio Catone. 10 ha.
www.collidicatone.it
Antonio Pulcini makes good Frascati Superiore under numerous labels. His two special versions of Frascati are both made from pure Malvasia; one, the single-vineyard "Colle Gaio", is made only in good years from low-yielding vines.

Falesco ☆☆☆
Montefiascone. 370 ha. www.falesco.it
The personal property of renowned oenologists Renzo and Riccardo Cotarella, producing good Est! Est!! Est!!!, specialising in new-oaked red IGTs from Merlot and Cabernet Sauvignon. The "Montiano" Merlot is remarkably complex, with undertones of cassis and cinnamon.

Some of their vineyards lie further north in Umbria, and these are the source of their excellent Cabernet Franc and Sauvignon blend called "Marciliano". This is no boutique operation: a total of around three million bottles are produced.

Fontana Candida ☆–☆☆☆
Monteporzio Catone. 97 ha. www.fontanacandida.it
Part of the Gruppa Italiano Vini complex, owning extensive vineyards, cellars, and bottling plants in the Frascati zone. The production of more than 600,000 cases includes a choice parcel of "Vigneto Santa Teresa", one of the best of all Frascatis, and a *cuvée* called "Luna Mater" that uses some rare indigenous varieties.

Gotto d'Oro ☆–☆☆
Frattocchie di Marino. 1,800 ha. www.gottodoro.it
This is the label of the Marino cooperative, whose members have 1,550 hectares of vines. As well as Frascati, it produces lightly effervescent red Castelli Romani.

Massimi Berucci ☆
Piglio. 30 ha. www.vignetimassimiberucci.it

Viterbo cathedral, Viterbo

This producer is a good source for the rare red Cesanese di Piglio, some from 50-year-old vines, and the white Passerina del Frusinato.

Paola di Mauro (Colle Picchioni) ☆☆–☆☆☆
Marino. 13 ha. www.collepicchioni.eu
This small estate is run by Paola di Mauro and son Armando, with advice from Riccardo Cotarella. They produce a remarkable traditional Marino and one of Rome's rare fine reds: a Bordeaux blend called Vigna del Vassallo.

Mazziotti ☆☆
Bolsena. 31 ha. www.mazziottiwines.com
This is an old family winery best-known for Est! Est!! Est!!! di Montefiascone, and a supple red blend called Volgente from Merlot, Sangiovese, and Montepulciano.

Sergio Mottura ☆☆–☆☆☆
Civitella d'Agliano. 45 ha. www.motturasergio.it
In northern Latium, Mottura produces IGT Grechetto in contrasting styles: oaked and unoaked. The oaked version is called Latour, which seems presumptuous, but is a simple thank-you to Louis Latour of Beaune who provides the barrels. When vintage conditions permit, Mottura also makes a fine botrytis wine called Muffo.

L'Olivella ☆☆
Frascati. 12 ha. www.racemo.it
Although located in Frascati, this organic estate is better-known for its red wines, such as Racemo IGT from Sangiovese and Cesanese, and a unique blend of Shiraz and Cesanese.

Principe Pallavicini ☆–☆☆
Colonna. 70 ha. www.vinipallaviccini.it
A noble estate that has been in family hands since 1670. It produces a good Frascati Superiore , a late-harvest Malvasia called Stillato, and an enjoyably floral Cesanese.

Palombo ☆–☆☆
Atina. 10 ha. www.vinipalombo.it
A family estate specializing in Atina DOC Cabernet Sauvignon, and a full-bodied Sauvignon Blanc called "Somiglio".

Cantina Sant' Andrea ☆☆
Borgo Vodice. 43 ha. www.cantinasantandrea.it
An organic estate specializing both in Circeo DOC and in fine sweet Moscato di Terracina.

Villa Simone ☆☆
Monteporzio Catone. 30 ha. www.pierocostantini.it
Piero Costantini makes an impressive, full-scale Frascati Superiore, including the single-vineyard Vigneto Filonardi, and a suave blend of Cesanese and Sangiovese evocatively called Ferro e Seta.

Trappolini ☆☆
Castiglione in Teverina. 20 ha.
A 20-hectare family estate producing Est! Est!! Est!!! and, more interestingly, a Sangiovese called Paterno, and a sweet, rose-scented red Aleatico called Idea.

Conte Zandotti ☆☆
Rome. 40 ha. www.cantinecontezandotti.it
Acquired by the family in 1734, this estate is now run by Enrico Massimo Zandotti. The cellars are carved into the vaults of an ancient Roman water cistern beneath the San Paolo villa. As well as good dry Frascati Superiore, there is a Malvasia IGT tasting of tropical fruit.

Abruzzo

The Apennines rise to their climax in the 2,700-metre (9,000-foot) Gran Sasso d'Italia, which towers over L'Aquila ("The Eagle"), the capital of the Abruzzo. The mountains only subside close to the sea, where Pescara is the principal town. Although it is close in proximity to Rome, the Abruzzo has long been an unsophisticated region in terms of wine production, thanks to the grip of enormous cooperatives that control over 80% production and are oriented to quantity more than quality.

Over the past decade this has certainly been changing, as growers are demonstrating the real potential of the red Montepulciano grape, especially in the hillier northern sectors of the region. White wines have lagged behind. Where the local subvariety of Trebbiano d'Abruzzo has survived (as at Valentini), it can produce surprisingly complex and long lived wines. But most of the region is planted with high-yielding clones that produce wine of scant interest. However, there is a revival of local white varieties such as Pecorino. A speciality of the Abruzzo is Cerasuolo, a *rosato* that has always had a high reputation for its vinosity.

DOC & Other Wines

Cerasuolo see Montepulciano d'Abruzzo.

Controguerra DOC. Red, white, *rosato* wine. Province: Teramo. Villages: Controguerra, four others. Grapes: Montepulciano (minimum 60%), Merlot and/or Cabernet (minimum 15%), up to 25% others; Trebbiano (minimum 80%), Passerina (minimum 15%), up to 25% others; plus varietal Chardonnay, Malvasia, Moscato Amabile, Passerina, Riesling, Ciliegiolo, Cabernet, Merlot, Pinot Nero. Also red and white *passito* wines and *spumante*.

Montepulciano d'Abruzzo DOC. Red and *rosato* wine. Provinces: Chieti, Aquilia, Pescara, Teramo. Villages: many communes in the four provinces. Grapes: Montepulciano (minimum 85%).

The production zone for this excellent red stretches along most of the coastal foothills and back into the mountains along the valley of the River Pescara, but the most complex Montepulciano comes from the Teramo hills in the north. Standards in this large area vary widely, but Montepulciano at its best is as satisfying, if not as subtle, as any Italian red: full of colour, life, and warmth. Cerasuolo is the name for its DOC *rosato*.

Montepulciano d'Abruzzo Colline Terramane DOCG.
Villges: 30 communes in the hills north of Pescara. Grapes:
Montepulciano (90%) from yields around 15% lower than for
the DOC wine.

Regarded as the heartland of Montepulciano.

Trebbiano d'Abruzzo DOC. White wine. Province:
throughout the Abruzzi region. Villages: suitable vineyards
(not exceeding 500–600 metres/1,625–1,950 feet) in the whole
region. Grapes: Trebbiano d'Abruzzo (minimum 85%), and/or
Trebbiano Toscano, up to 15% others.

A basic fruity white, except in the case of Valentini (q.v.).

Leading Abruzzi Producers

Agriverde ☆☆
Ortona. 75 ha. www.agriverde.it
A forward-looking estate offering Trebbiano and
Montepulciano in different styles. The Montepulciano
"Plateo" is barrique-aged and has admirable concentration
and persistence.

Cataldi Madonna ☆☆–☆☆☆
Ofena. 27 ha.
Luigi Cataldo Madonna's day job is teaching philosophy
at the University of Aquila. His family estate produces some
of Abruzzo's best Cerasuolo, and three Montepulcianos of
varying degrees of concentration and power.

Barone Cornacchia ☆–☆☆
Torano Nuovo. 42 ha. www.baronecornacchia.it
A leading property in the Teramo region. A new generation
has revived quality. Sound Montepulciano and Trebbiano
d'Abruzzo, and a Controguerra called Villa Torri, which
blends Montepulciano with Cabernet and Merlot.

Farnese ☆☆–☆☆☆
Ortona. 50 ha. www.farnese-vini.com
Commercially oriented winery producing wines principally
from 600 hectares of leased vineyards. Enjoyable Trebbiano
and Chardonnay, but the Montepulciano is easily the best
wine, especially from the Colline Teramane. The standard
"Casal Vecchio" range offers good value; Edizione wines are
more ambitious.

Filomusi Guelfi ☆☆
Tocca da Causaria. 10 ha.
A small estate, only founded in 1982, with Montepulciano
of power and grace.

Dino Illuminati ☆☆–☆☆☆
Controguerra. 130 ha. www.illuminativini.it
A large but highly regarded estate, founded in 1890. There
are numerous whites under the Controguerra DIC, but the
real interest here lies in the range of complex wines based on
Montepulciano. The finest is Zanna, a Colline Teramane
aged in large casks. The far more basic Riparosso is an ideal
introduction to an unpretentious but satisfying style of
unoaked Montepulciano.

Marramiero ☆☆–☆☆☆
Rosciano. 30 ha. www.marramiero.it

Although only established in 1994, this estate has risen swiftly
into the top ranks with barrique-aged Montepulciano Inferi,
good Trebbiano Altare, and an IGT from Chardonnay aged in
new oak.

Masciarelli ☆☆☆
San Martino sulla Marrucina. 327 ha. www.masciarelli.it
The ambitious Gianni Masciarelli began with three hectares
in 1981, and was still planning new ventures when he died
suddenly, and too young, in 2008. He made superb wines in
different ranges such as Marina Svetic (named after his
Croatian wife) and Villa Gemma. Like Masciarelli himself,
the wines are powerful and assertive.

Antonio e Elio Monti ☆☆
Controguerra. 13 ha. www.vinimonti.it
Elio took over from his father Antonio in 1990. Good
Montepulciano, especially the full-throttled Pignotto from
Colline Teramane, and likely to improve further now that
ubiquitous consultant Riccardo Cotarella has been hired.

Camillo Montori ☆☆
Controguerra. 50 ha. www.montorivini.it
Good Montepulciano, especially from the Colline Teramane
DOCG which the winery helped to establish, and Trebbiano
d'Abruzzo, and lively Controguerra wines, red and white.

Nicodemi ☆☆–☆☆☆
Notaresco. 30 ha. www.nicodemi.com
A new generation has been running Nicodemi, with it sleek
modern-style wines, since 2000. Nemorino from Colli
Teramane is the flagship Montepulciano, with flavours
of plum, tobacco, and Indian spices, but the Notari range
of Trebbiano and Montelpuciano arguably offer more balance
and refreshment.

Orlandi Contucci ☆☆
Roseto degli Abruzzi. 30 ha.
www.orlandicontucci.com
Although this property makes good, supple Montepulciano,
there is an atypical emphasis on varietal wines from
Chardonnay, Sauvignon, and Cabernet Sauvignon.
Donato Lanati is the consultant here.

Pasetti ☆☆
Francavilla al Mare. 40 ha.
Rich Montepulcianoand zesty Cerasuolo, and a plump,
oaky Pecorino called Testarossa. Although Pasetti is based
by the coast, their vineyards lie some distance inland at
a high elevation.

Talamonti ☆☆
Loreto Aprutino. 25 ha. www.cantinetalamonti.it
Founded in 2001, Talamonti has already developed a wide
range of products, The basic, but characterful, Montepulciano
is Moda, but Tree Saggi offers more weight, tannin, and spice.
Good Trebbiano Aternum, partially barrel aged.

Cantina Tollo ☆–☆☆
Tollo, Chieti. 3,500 ha. www.cantinatollo.it
This large cooperative, producing 16 million bottles
each year, offers outstanding value for its Montepulciano
and Trebbiano d'Abruzzo.

Torre dei Beati ☆☆–☆☆☆
Loreto Aprutino. 25 ha.
Cresated in 2000, absorbing old vineyards and planting new ones, all farmed organically. The top Montepulcianos, both barrique-aged, are Mazzomorello and Cocciapazzo, in a powerful but voluptuous style.

La Valentina ☆☆☆
Spoltore. 64 ha. www.fattorialavalentina.it
Highly concentrated wines from two different subregions. Two Montepulciano blends, aged in casks and barriques, are first-rate: Spelt and Bellovedere.

Valentini ☆☆☆
Loreto Aprutino. 65 ha.
Edoardo Valentini died in 2006, to be succeeded by his equally reclusive son Francesco. Most of their grapes are sold to cooperatives. What remains is vinified by totally artisanal methods, and as a consequence, some vintages are never released at all. The Trebbiano, from the authentic Abruzzo variety, is remarkably long-lived. The 1988 was still exotic and spicy 20 years later. The Montepulciano is perfumed, tannic, and long, the Cerasuolo properly refreshing. (Fabulous olive oil too.). Breathtaking prices.

Valle Reale ☆☆–☆☆☆
Popoli. 60 ha. www.vallereale.it
An interesting venture far inland, where the grapes ripen late and give intense fruit. Carlo Ferrini is the consultant winemaker. Three styles of Montepulciano are made, all successful within their own terms: unoaked Vigne Nuove, Valla Reale, and San Calisto, aged in new barriques.

Villa Medoro ☆☆–☆☆☆
Atri. 60 ha. www.villamedoro.it
Federica Morricone makes a delicious Trebbiano/Falanghina blend called Chimera, but the show-stoppers are the Montepulcianos, especially the wild and earthy Adrano from Colline Teramane.

Ciccio Zaccagnani ☆☆
Bolognano. 80 ha.
www.cantinazaccagnani.it
An increasingly admired estate acclaimed for fine Montepulciano San Clemente, as well as eclectic wines from Riesling, Pecorino, and *passito* Cannonau.

Campania

The region of Naples and the Sorrento Peninsula may have been cynical about tourists' tastes in the past, and left some visitors with a nasty taste in their mouths, but in many ways it is superbly adapted for wine growing. Volcanic soils, the temperate influence of the sea, and the height of its mountains give a range of excellent sites. Its own grapes have character and perform well. The red Aglianico (the name comes from "Hellenico") and white Greco both refer in their names to the Greeks who presumably imported or at least adopted them in pre-Roman times. Fiano and Falanghina are other high-quality white grapes specific to Campania. Quality wines are made at Ravello on the Sorrento peninsula, on the island of Ischia, and above all in the Irpinian Hills north of Avellino, east of Naples, where the Mastroberardino winery did more than anyone for the reputation of the region. The last decade has seen a number of wineries making the most of the superb grape varieties and the remarkable volcanic soils of Campania.

DOC & Other Wines

Aglianico del Taburno DOC. Red and *rosato* wine. Province: Benevento. Villages: 14 communes. Grapes: Aglianico (minimum 85%).

Recent DOC in an area where conditions are particularly suited to Aglianico. The wines are still rarely seen.

Asprino or Asprinio A welcome refresher; sharpish, fizzy citric white without pretensions: Naples' universal café wine. The grape, unique to the region, is unusual in often being trained up tree trunks in the manner of the ancients..

Aversa DOC. White. Provinces: Caserta, Naples. Villages: Aversa, 21 other communes. Grapes: Asprinio (minimum 85%). Can be dry or *frizzante*.

Campi Flegrei DOC. Red and white wines. Province: Naples. Villages: parts of Naples, six other communes. Grapes: Piedirosso (50–70%), Aglianico and/or Scianscisino (10–30%), up to 10% others; Falanghina (50–70%), Biancolella and/or Coda di Volpe (10–30%), up to 30% others.

This DOC, with unusual sandy and volcanic soils, also permits varietal wines from Piedirosso (dry and *passito*) and Falanghina.

Capri DOC. Red and white wine. Province: Naples. Province: the island of Capri. Grapes: Piedirosso (minimum 80%); Falanghina and Greco, plus Biancolella up to 20%.

A small supply of adequate dry white and a minute supply of light red to drink young are lucky enough to have this romantic name.

Castel San Lorenzo DOC. Red, white, *rosato* wine. Province: Salerno. Villages: Castel San Lorenzo, seven other communes. Grapes: Barbera (60–80%), Sangiovese (20–30%), up to 20% others; Trebbiano (50–60%), Malvasia Bianca (30–40%), up to 20%.

Mostly dull wines, but this DOC also permits varietal wines from Barbera and Moscato.

Cilento DOC. Red, white, *rosato* wine. Province: Salerno. Villages: Agropoli, seven other communes. Grapes: Aglianico

Mastroberardino winery, Atripalda

(60–75%), Piedirosso/Primitivo (15–20%), Barbera (10–20%), up to 10% other reds; (rosato) Sangiovese (70–80%), Aglianico (10–15%), Primitivo/Piedirosso 10–15%, up to 10% others; Fiano (60–65%), Trebbiano (20–30%), Greco/Malvasia (10–15%); up to 10% other whites; plus varietal Aglianico, with maximum 15% Primitivo/Piedirosso.

Created in 1989, this DOC is located in some outstanding terroirs and shows great promise.

Costa d'Amalfi DOC. Red, white, *rosato* wine. Province: Salerno. Villages: Amalfi, 12 other communes. Grapes: Falanghina and/or Biancolella (60%), up to 40% others; Piedirosso (minimum 40%), Aglianico and/or Scianscisino (maximum 60%), up to 40% others.

A DOC created in 1995, and including, for additional complexity, three subzones.

Falerno del Massico DOC. Red and white wine. Province: Caserta. Villages: Mondragone, four other communes. Grapes: Aglianico (60–80%), Piedirosso (20–40%), Primitivo and/or Barbera (maximum 20%); Falanghina.

These wines, show promise. Revived in their original area, they bear little similarity to their forbears but are worth watching. The rules also permit a varietal Primitivo.

Fiano di Avellino DOCG. White wine. Province: Avellino. Villages: Avellino, 14 nearby communes. Grapes: Fiano (minimum 85%), Greco, Coda di Volpe Bianco, Trebbiano (up to 15%).

One of the best white wines of the south, light-yellow and nutty in scent and flavour with liveliness and length. It is also known as Apianum, a Latin reference to bees, which apparently appreciated either its flowers or grapes – or juice.

Galluccio DOC. Red, white, *rosato* wine. Province: Caserta. Villages: Galluccio, four other communes. Grapes: Falanghina (minimum 70%); Aglianico (minimum 70%).

Greco di Tufo DOCG. White wine. Province: Avellino. Villages: Tufo, seven other communes. Grapes: Greco di Tufo (minimum 85%), Coda di Volpe (maximum 15%).

White wine of positive character, a little neutral to smell, but mouth-filling with a good "cut" in the flavour: highly satisfactory with flavoursome food. Some bouquet develops with two to three years in bottle, but only the best examples age well, as the wine is prone to oxidation. It can also be made *spumante* (rarely seen).

Guardia Sanframondi DOC. Red, white, *rosato* wine. Province: Benevento. Villages: Guardia Sanframondi, three other communes. Grapes: Sangiovese (minimum 80%); Malvasia di Candia (50–70%), Falanghina (20–30%), up to 10% others; plus varietal Falanghina (dry and *spumante*) and Aglianico.

Ipernia DOC. Red, white, *rosato* wine. Large area in east-central Campania. Grapes: Aglianico (70–100%), up to 30% others; Fiano (40–50%), Greco (40–50%), up to 20% others; plus varietal Aglianico, Piedirosso, Sciascisino; Falanghina, Fiano, Coda di Volpe, Greco. Also some *passito* and *spumante*.

Ischia DOC. Red and white wine. Province: the island of Ischia. Villages: throughout the island. Grapes: Guarnaccia (40–50%), Piedirosso (40–50%), up to 15% others; Forastera (45–70%), Biancolella (30–55%), up to 15% others; plus varietal Biancolella, Forastera, Piedirosso.

The standard red and white of this green island in the Bay of Naples are made to drink young and fresh – though newly ambitious producers are trying other ideas. The white should be sharp enough to quench thirst.

Lacrimarosa d'Irpinia A very pale, coppery *rosato* of good quality, aromatic to smell, faintly underripe to taste, made of Aglianico by Mastroberardino (q.v.).

Per'e Palummo The alternative name of the Piedirosso grape, meaning "dove's foot", applied to one of Ischia's best reds, refreshingly tannic and a shade grassy to smell.

Penisola Sorrentina DOC. Red and white wines. Province: Naples. Villages: Naples, 12 other communes. Grapes: (red: still and frizzante) Piedirosso and/or Sciascisino and/or Aglianico (minimum 60%), up to 40% others; Falanghina and/or Biancolella and/or Greco (minimum 60%).

Small DOC covering the Sorrento Peninsula in the Bay of Naples.

Ravello Red, white, *rosato* wine. Village: Ravello.

Each good of its kind, from the terraced vineyards leading up to the ravishing hilltop town of Ravello. Sea mists, I suspect, keep the wines fresh.

Sannio DOC. Red, white, *rosato* wine. Province: Benevento. Villages: all communes in the province. Grapes: Sangiovese (minimum 50%); Trebbiano (minimum 50%).

Large, catch-all DOC also permitting numerous varietal wines and classic method *spumante*.

Sant' Agata dei Goti DOC. Red, white, *rosato* wine. Province: Benevento. Village: Sant'Agata dei Goti. Grapes: Aglianico (40–60%), Piedirosso (40–60%), up to 20% others; Falanghina (40–60%), Greco (40–60%); up to 20% others; plus varietal Falanghina, Greco, Aglianico, Piedirosso.

Obscure DOC; Mustilli is the most important producer (q.v.).

Solopaca DOC. Red and white wine. Province: Benevento. Villages: Solopaca, 11 neighbouring communes. Grapes: Sangiovese (50–60%), Aglianico (20–40%), up to 30% others; Trebbiano (40–60%), Malvasia, Coda di Volpe, and/or Falanghina (maximum 60%); up to 20% others; plus varietal Falanghina, Aglianico. Spumante also permitted.

A little-known DOC zone north of Naples with decent red but rather dreary white.

Taburno DOC. Red and white wine. Province: Benevento. Grapes: Sangiovese (40–50%), Aglianico (30–40%), up to 30% others; Trebbiano (40–50%), Falanghina (30–40%), up to 30% others; (spumante) Coda di Volpe and/or Falanghina (60%), up to 40% others; plus varietal Coda di Volpe, Falanghina, Greco, Piedirosso.

See also Aglianico del Taburno DOC.

Taurasi DOCG. Red wine. Province: Avellino. Villages: Taurasi, 15 other communes in the Irpinia Hills east of Naples. Grapes: Aglianico (minimum 85%).

Among the best reds of southern Italy, made famous by Mastroberardino (q.v.). Aglianico ripens late in these lofty vineyards to make a firm wine of splendidly satisfying structure, still dark in colour even when mature at five years. It has a slightly roasted richness without being at all port-like. First-class but impossible to pin down by comparisons.

Vesuvio (Lacryma Christi) DOC. White, red, *rosato* wine. Province: Naples. Villages: villages mostly east of Naples. Grapes: Piedirosso and/or Sciascisinomin (80%), Aglianico (maximum 20%); Coda di Volpe and/or Verdeca (minimum 80%).

The designation Lacryma Christi del Vesuvio applies to four superior versions that are capable of ageing three to six years or more. The white may also be sparkling.

Leading Campania Producers

Alois ☆☆
Pontelatone. 13 ha. www.vinialois.it
Michele Alois makes fine Aglianico, but the main interest of the estate is his determination to revive local varieties such as Casavecchia and Pallagrello. Advice from Riccardo Cotarella.

D'Ambra ☆☆
Forio d'Ischia. 6 ha. www.dambravini.com
Founded in 1888 by Francesco d'Ambra, this producer of Ischia DOC is loyal to local white varieties such as Biancolella and Forestera.

Antonio Caggiano ☆☆☆
Taurasi. 20 ha. www.cantinecaggiano.it
Caggiano founded this property in 1991, and has resolutely focused on the excellent grape varieties typical of Campania. The Taurasi is magnificent, finely structured, and infused with the flavour of red fruits. The barrique-aged Fiagrè blends Fiano and Greco, as does the late-harvested, sweet Mel.

Colli di Lapio ☆☆
Lapio. 10 ha.
Clelia Romano's estate specializes in Fiano, which is full-bodied, nutty, and persistent. It also ages remarkably well.

De Conciliis ☆☆–☆☆☆
Prignano Cilento. 26 ha.
A new star in Campania. The wines are IGTs, but they are true to local traditions: powerful, barrique-aged Aglianicos called Donnaluna and Naima, suffused with cherry and plum flavours, as well as crisp Fiano.

Benito Ferrara ☆–☆☆☆
Tufo. 8 ha. www.benitoferrara.it
A tiny property producing nothing but elegant, almondy Greco from high-lying vineyards.

Feudi di San Gregorio ☆☆☆–☆☆☆☆
Sorbo Serpico. 300 ha. www.feudi.it
The great success story of Campania is the swift rise of this large property to the top ranks of south Italian producers. The whites are brilliant – Campanaro and the barrique-aged, late-harvested Privilegio (both Fiano) – and the reds unusually profound – Taurasi, of course, but also a surprisingly voluptuous Aglianico/Merlot called Serpico, and a succulent new Merlot called Pàtrimo. (The Ercolino brothers, who own the property, point out that Merlot is traditional to the region.) The company has managed to grow swiftly without any loss of quality.

Galardi ☆☆☆
San Carlo di Sessa Aurunca. 10 ha. www.terradilavoro.com
A one wine property. Terra di Lavoro, like Montevetrano (q.v.), is made by Riccardo Cotarella, but is based on local varieties Aglianico and Piedirosso.

Gran Furor ☆☆–☆☆☆
Furore. 10 ha. www.granfuror.it
An excellent range of wines from Costa d'Amalfi DOC, using only indigenous varieties.

MOLISE

Molise, a slice of central Italy stretching from the Apennines to the Adriatic, is a relative newcomer to Italy's wine map. Bottles with labels on are a novelty in a land of bulk production. The first Molise DOCs date from 1983. They are Biferno, for red and white wine from Campobasso province; and Pentro, for red and white wines from the hills around Isernia. Both specify Montepulciano for red. In Biferno it is the dominant variety, but blended with Aglianico; in Pentro it is used half-and-half with Sangiovese. Both whites are based on Trebbiano Toscano, not a formula for quality. Both allow the addition of Bombino. Varietal wines,

from international as well as local varieties, are also encountered.

One outstanding Molise winery, and one of the most modern in Italy is:

Di Majo Norante ☆☆☆
Campomarino. 85 ha. www.dimajonorante.com
An impeccably run family property, with Riccardo Cotarella as the consultant oenologist. The Montepulciano Don Luigi" is as good as the best of Abruzzo, and the mellow Aglianico Contado if often its equal. Delightful whites from Falanghina and Greco too.

Other Molise Producers

Borgo di Colloredo ☆☆–☆☆☆
Campomarino. 70 ha. www.borgodicolloredo.com
A family winery dedicated to the local grape varieties, and producing good Aglianico, Montepulciano, and Falanghina.

Fattoria di Vaira ☆☆
Petacciato. 70 ha.
An ancient property revived in 2002 and producing lean Falanghina and robust Montepulciano Monsignore.

De Lucia ☆☆
Guardia Sanframondi. 11 ha.
An excellent source of Falanghina and Aglianico from
Sannio DOC.

Luigi Maffini ☆☆☆
Castellabate. 14 ha. www.maffini-vini.com
Founded in 1996, this property uses local grapes but
releasing them as IGT. Outstanding Fiano called Kratos
when vinified in steel, Pietraincatenata when fermented
in new oak.

Mastroberardino ☆☆–☆☆☆
Atripalda. 200 ha. www.mastroberardino.com
Founded in 1878 as a continuation of a long-standing
business; now run by Piero Mastroberardino. Cellars
were renovated and expanded after being destroyed in the
earthquakes of 1980, and the subsequent installation of
ultramodern equipment signalled a new approach to the
style of their white Fiano and Greco, now made in
temperature-controlled, stainless-steel tanks.

The Mastroberardino firm split in two in 1994,
when Walter Mastroberardino departed to found his
own label Terredora (q.v.). Thereafter quality slipped for
a few years but a new generation has revitalized the firm.
The whites are as fine as ever, and the top range, Radici,
is home to exciting and structured Fiano and weighty,
meaty Taurasi.

Di Meo ☆
Salza Irpinia. 25 ha. www.dimeo.it
Sound Greco and Fiano that somehow lacks flair.

Michele Moio ☆☆–☆☆☆
Mondragone 13 ha. www.cantinemoio.it
Substantial Primitivo is released under the Falerno DOC.

Molettieri ☆☆–☆☆☆
Montemarano. 20 ha. www.salvatoremolettieri.it
A small estate, but an impeccable source of powerful Taurasi
called Cinque Querce.

Montevetrano ☆☆☆–☆☆☆☆
San Cipriano Picentino. 5 ha. www.montevetrano.it
Photographer Silvia Imparato produces, with advice from
Riccardo Cotarella, a single wine, Colli di Salerno, but it has
become a cult wine, with a price tag to match. A blend of
Cabernet, Merlot, and a dash of Aglianico, aged in new
barriques, it is not unlike a fine Bordeaux.

Mustilli ☆
Sant' Agata de' Goti. 35 ha. www.mustilli.com
Sound wines from typical Campania varieties: Aglianico,
Falanghina, and Greco.

Cantina del Taburno ☆☆–☆☆☆
Foglianise. 500 ha. www.cantinadeltaburno.it
A quality-conscious cooperative producing excellent
Aglianico, Falanghina, and other wines. The top Aglianico
bottlings here, such as the new-oaked Bue Apis, are as fine
as any in Campania.

Terredora ☆☆–☆☆☆
Montefusco. 150 ha. www.terradora.net
The spin-off Mastroberardino estate, now thoroughly
established in its own right, produces very good Taurasi
and often exceptional Fiano and Falanghina.

Vadiaperti ☆☆
Montefredane. 8 ha. www.vadiaperti.it
Crisp and classic Irpinia whites from an estate founded
in 1984.

Villa Matilde ☆☆☆
Cellole. 52 ha. www.villamatilde.com
Riccardo Cotarella advises this organic estate and helps
to produce outstanding Falerno DOC Falanghina and
Aglianico, and creamy *passito* Falanghina IGT called Eleusi,
with its aromas of dried fruits. The finest red is the rich
and concentrated Aglianico from Vigna Camarato.

Puglia

The heel and hamstrings of Italy are its most productive wine
regions. Puglia produces three times as much wine as all of
Tuscany. Their historic role has been to supply strength and
colour for more famous but frail wines in blending vats farther
north. The reds are very red indeed; very strong, and often
inclined to portiness, and the whites can suffer from flab,
although modern vinification technology has allowed cleaner
and fresher wines to be made.

The Salento Peninsula, the heel from Taranto southeast-
wards, is the hottest region. A few producers here are learning
to moderate the strength and density of their reds to make
good-quality, winter-warming wines – though a bottle still goes
a long way. Their grapes are the Primitivo (California's
Zinfandel) and the Negroamaro: "bitter black". Uva di Troia
plays a strong supporting role. North of Taranto the hills have
well-established DOCs for dry whites, originally intended as
vermouth base wines, but with modern techniques increasingly
drinkable as "fish" wines in their own right. As elsewhere in
Italy, the existence of a DOC is better evidence of tradition than
of quality. There is more interest in the fact that even in this
intemperate region successful spots have recently been found to
plant superior northern grapes – even Chardonnay.

Much the best-known DOC is Castel del Monte, and this is
largely due to the crisp *rosato* of Rivera. The list of producers
shows that things are changing; Puglian reds are no longer
ashamed of their origin. Many of Italy's top wine producers are
convinced that Puglia is capable of making outstanding wines at
moderate prices. Antinori, Pasqua, and even the Californian
Kendall-Jackson have invested heavily in the region.

DOC & Other Wines

Aleatico di Puglia DOC. Red wine. Province: the whole
of Puglia. Grapes: Aleatico (minimum 85%).

A dessert wine, approaching ruby port in its fortified
(*liquoroso*) version. Small supply, and of local interest only.

Alezio DOC. Red and *rosato* wine. Province: Lecce. Villages: Alezio, Sannicola, plus parts of Gallipoli and Tuglie. Grapes: Negroamaro (minimum 80%).

A DOC for the red and *rosato* of the tip of Italy's heel, and every inch a southern red: dark and powerful. It is moot whether to try ageing it or to take it on the chin as it is. Like many Puglian *rosatos*, the paler wine has more immediate appeal.

Brindisi DOC. Red and *rosato* wine. Province: Brindisi. Villages: Brindisi, Mesagna, just inland. Grapes: Negroamaro (minimum 70%).

The local red of Brindisi can age for five to ten years or more. Also makes a pleasant *rosato*. There is one outstanding example of Brindisi DOC: the Patrigilione from Cosimo Taurino (q.v.).

Cacc'e Mmitte di Lucera DOC. Red wine. Province: Foggia. Villages: Lucera, Troia, Biccari. Grapes: Uva di Troia (35–60%); Montepulciano, Sangiovese, and Malvasia Nera (25–35%); others (15–30%).

Scholars tell us that the dialect name refers to a local form of *governo*, in which fresh grapes are added to the fermenting must. Others say it refers to the practice of filling a goblet from the cask and down it in one. The wines are less interesting than the legends.

Castel del Monte DOC. Red, white, *rosato* wine. Province: Bari. Villages: Minervino Murge, parts of nine other communes. Grapes: Uva di Troia (maximum 65%), Sangiovese, Montepulciano, Aglianico, Pinot Nero (maximum 35% any combination of); *rosato* is similar, except that Bombino Nero is the principal grape; Pampanuto and/or Chardonnay and/or Bombino Bianco (maximum 65%), up to 35% others; plus varietal Bombino Bianco, Chardonnay, Pinot Bianco, Sauvignon, Aglianico, Bombino Nero, Pinot Nero, Uva di Troia.

Castel del Monte, the octagonal fortress of the medieval Hohenstaufens, lies 48-kilometres (30-miles) west of Bari near Minervino Murge. The leading DOC of Puglia deserves its name for an outstanding red and famous *rosato*. The red has a fat, inviting smell, considerable depth and vitality, some bite, and long, pruney finish. Rivera's "Il Falcone" is the best example (q.v.). The pale *rosato* has long been popular all over Italy for balanced force and freshness.

Copertino DOC. Red and *rosato* wine. Province: Lecce. Villages: Copertino, five other communes. Grapes: Negroamaro (minimum 70%).

A warmly recommended red made in some quantity south of Lecce on Italy's heel. The *riserva* is smooth with plenty of flavour and a bitter touch.

Five Roses A powerful, dry *rosato* from Leone de Castris (q.v.), so named by American soldiers who gave it one more rose than a famous Bourbon whiskey.

Galatina DOC. Red, white, *rosato* wine. Province: Lecce. Villages: Galatina, six other communes. Grapes: Negroamaro (minimum 65%); Chardonnay (minimum 55%); plus varietal wines from Chardonnay and Negroamaro.

Small, marginal DOC established in 1997.

Gioia del Colle DOC. Red, white, *rosato* wine. Province: Bari. Villages: Gioia del Colle, 15 neighbouring communes. Grapes: Primitivo (50–60%); Trebbiano (50–70%).

Gioia is halfway from Bari south to Taranto. The Primitivo gives a pretty brutal red in these hot hills. With age it becomes more politely overwhelming. DOC rules also permit varietal Primitivo and the possibly extinct sweet Aleatico.

Gravina DOC. White wine. Province: Bari. Village: communes of Gravina, Poggiorsini, and parts of Altamura, Spinazzola. Grapes: Malvasia Bianca (40–65%).

Dry or sweet white from around Gravina, best when containing significant amounts of Greco. A *spumante* is also permitted.

Leverano DOC. Red, white, *rosato* wine. Province: Lecce. Villages: commune of Leverano. Grapes: Negroamaro (minimum 50%), Malvasia Nera and/or Montepulciano and/or Sangiovese (maximum 40%), up to 30% others; Malvasia Bianca (minimum 50%), Bombino (maximum 40%), up to 30% others; plus varietal Malvasia Bianca, Negroamaro.

The red and the *rosato* stand with Salento's finest.

Lizzano DOC. Red, white, *rosato* wine. Province: Taranto. Villages: communes of Lizzano, Faggiano, part of Taranto. Grapes: Negroamaro (60–80%); Trebbiano Toscano (40–60%), Chardonnay and/or Pinot Bianco (minimum 30%), Sauvignon and/or Bianco di Alessano (maximum 25%), Malvasia Bianca Lugna (maximum 10%).

Salento DOC, rarely encountered.

Locorotondo DOC. White wine. Provinces: Bari, Brindisi. Villages: Locorotondo, Cisternino, part of Fasano. Grapes: Verdeca (50–65%); Bianco di Alessano (35–50%). Also *spumante*.

Locorotondo is famous for its round stone dwellings. With Martina Franca, which produces an almost identical wine, it lies east of Bari at the neck of the Salento peninsula. Serious efforts are made to keep its white wine fresh and brisk.

Martina or Martina Franca DOC. White wine. Provinces: Taranto, Bari, Brindisi. Villages: Martina Franca, parts of four other communes. Grapes: Verdeca (50–65%), Bianco di Alessano (35–50%). Also *spumante*.

Grapes and wine amount to much the same thing as Locorotondo.

Matino DOC. Red and *rosato* wine. Province: Lecce. Villages: Matino, part of seven other communes in the Murge Salentino, at the tip of Italy's heel. Grapes: Negroamaro (minimum 65%), Sangiovese, Malvasia Nera (maximum 35%).

An early (1971) DOC but still obscure.

Moscato di Trani DOC. White wine. Province: Bari. Villages: Trani, 11 other communes. Grapes: Moscato Bianco (minimum 85%). Sweet or *liquoroso*.

Sweet, golden, dessert Muscats of good quality from the north coast, west of Bari. Other Puglian Muscats, particularly those of Salento, can also be very drinkable.

Nardò DOC. Red and *rosato* wine. Province: Lecce.

Villages: Nardò, Porto Cesareo. Grapes: Negroamaro (minimum 80%), Malvasia Nera and/or Montepulciano (maximum 20%).

Recent DOC for red and *rosato* wines. The red is best after three to six years.

Orta Nova DOC. Red and *rosato* wine. Province: Foggia. Villages: Orta Nova, five other communes. Grapes: Sangiovese (minimum 60%), Uva di Troia and/or Montepulciano (30–40%). Tiny production.

Ostuni and Ottavianello di Ostuni DOC. Red and white wine. Province: Brindisi. Villages: Ostuni, six other communes, including Brindisi. Grapes: Ottavianello; Impigno (50–85%), Francavilla (15–50%).

The unusual white grapes give a very pale, mild, and dry "fish" wine. Ottavianello is a cheerful cherry-red dry wine, pleasant to drink cool and said to be related to Cinsault.

Primitivo di Manduria DOC. Red wine. Provinces: Taranto, Brindisi. Villages: Manduria, 18 other communes

Primitive harvesting methods in Apulia

along the south Salento coast. Grape: Primitivo (100%).

The Primitivo grape variety, now known to be the same as California's Zinfandel, makes black-strap reds here, some sweet and some even fortified (*liquoroso*), as though 14 degrees were not enough in the first place. You may age them or not, depending on whether you appreciate full-fruit flavour or just full flavour.

Rosato del Salento Rosatos are perhaps the best general produce of the Salento peninsula. It is not a DOC but this name is widely used.

Rosso di Barletta DOC. Red wine. Province: Bari, Foggia. Villages: Barletta, four other communes. Grapes: Uva di Troia (70%), up to 30% others. "Invecchiato" if aged for two years.

Some drink this relatively light red young and cool: others age it moderately and treat it like claret.

Rosso Canosa DOC. Red wine. Province: Bari. Village: Canosa. Grapes: Uva di Troia (minimum 65%) up to 35% others.

Canosa, between Bari and Foggia, was the Roman Canusium (an alternative name for the wine). Its wine is in a similar style to Rosso di Barletta.

Rosso di Cerignola DOC. Red wine. Province: Bari. Villages: Cerignola, three other communes. Grapes: Uva di Troia (minimum 55%), Negroamaro (15–30%), up to 15% others.

A big, dry, heady red with faint bitterness. But almost extinct.

Salice Salentino DOC. Red, white, *rosato* wine. Provinces: Brindisi, Lecce. Villages: Salice Salentino, six other communes in the centre of the Salento Peninsula. Grapes: Negroamaro (minimum 80%), Malvasia Nera (maximum 20%). (Aleatico) Aleatico (minimum 85%), *dolce* 15 degrees, *liquoroso* 18.5 degrees); Chardonnay (minimum 70%); plus varietal Pinot Bianco.

Typically big-scale southern reds that have a porty undertone accompanied by a balancing measure of astringency. I have found this to be a rather clumsy wine, but I am prepared to believe I have been unlucky; other Salento reds are often nicely balanced with an attractively clean finish. The *rosatos* can be fresh and flowery and complex with time, and are among the most distinctive of Italian rosés.

San Severo DOC. Red, white, *rosato* wine. Province: Foggia. Villages: San Severo, Torremaggiore, San Paolo Civitate, part of five other communes north of Foggia. Grapes: Montepulciano di Abruzzo (minimum 70%), Sangiovese (maximum 30%); Bombino Bianco (40–60%), Trebbiano Toscano (40–60%), Malvasia Bianca and/or Verdeca (maximum 20%)

Inoffensive wines of no special qualities but offering good value for money.

Squinzano DOC. Red and *rosato* wine. Provinces: Lecce, Brindisi. Villages: Squinzano, eight others. Grapes: Negroamaro (minimum 70%), Malvasia Nera and/or Sangiovese (maximum 30%).

Salento wines of moderate quality. The *rosato* is much less tiring to drink than the red.

Leading Puglia Producers

Antica Masseria del Sigillo ☆☆
Guagnano. 30 ha. www.vinisigillo.net
Medium-sized property that produces attractive Chardonnay and Salice Salentino, and a juicy, lively blend of Primitivo, Cabernet Sauvignon, Merlot called Terre del Guiscardo.

Al Bano Carrisi ☆☆–☆☆☆
Cellino San Marco. 65 ha. www.albanocarrisi.com
This estate offers a wide range of wines, but is best-known for its Don Carmelo Negroamaro, and has won high praise for its opulent blend of Negroamaro and Primitivo called Platone.

Michele Calò & Figli ☆☆
Tuglie. 30 ha. www.michelecalo.it
Attractive Alezio DOC *rosato*, and supple Negroamaro Mjere.

Francesco Candido ☆☆–☆☆☆
San Donaci. 160 ha. www.candidowines.com
A substantial property producing robust Salice Salentino, an impressive Negroamaro/Montepulciano blend called Duca d'Aragona, and a grandiosely named blend of Negroamaro and Cabernet Sauvignon called Immensum.

Càntele ☆☆
Lecce. 30 ha. www.cantele.it
A large winery, buying many grapes and producing rather heavy white wines, and faring better with traditional wines such as Salice Salentino and a powerful Primitivo/Negroamaro blend called Amativo.

Coppadoro ☆☆–☆☆☆
San Severo. 120 ha.
www.tenutacoppadoro.it
Coppadoro is a kind of private cooperative with 20 members, producing half a million bottles under the more than competent eye of consultant Riccardo Cotarella. Two wines always stand out: the pure Montepulciano called Radicosa, and Cotinone, a complex blend of Aglianco, Montepulciano, and Cabernet Sauvignon.

Gianfranco Fino ☆☆
Taranto. 1 ha. www.gianfrancofino.com
So small a property, producing a maximum of 10,000 bottles, seems hardly to warrant a mention, but Fino has very old vines and derisory yields, so his two wines, Es from Primitivo and Jo from Negroamaro, are incredibly concentrated, although sometimes marred by excessive alcohol.

Leone de Castris ☆☆–☆☆☆
Salice Salentino. 250 ha. www.leonedecastris.net
The estate of the Leone de Castris family is an ancient one, but the winery is ultramodern, producing 200,000 cases annually. It vinifies some of Puglia's best wine: rich and heady but not gross reds from Salice Salentino and (among others) Italy's first bottled *rosato*, Five Roses, which remains a model of the genre.

Although there are some straightforward varietal wines from Verdeca, Sauvignon, and Aleatico, the top wines are usually Donna Lisa, a pure Negroamaro, and Illemos, a voluptuous blend of Primitivo, Montepulciano, and other varieties.

Masseria Li Veli ☆☆
Cellino San Marco. 32 ha. www.liveli.it
This Salice Salentino property was bought and renovated by the Falvo family, owners until recently of Avignonesi (q.v.) in 1999. The principal wines are Pezzo Morgana, a Negroamara, and Morgana Alta, a more concentrated Negoramaro aged in new oak. The wines are lush and luxurious but also rather jammy.

Cantina del Locorotondo ☆–☆☆
Locorotondo. 1,000 ha. www.locorotondodoc.com
Founded in 1932, this cooperative focuses not only on crisp DOC Locorotondo, but on IGTs from Fiano, Pinot Nero, and various blends of local varieties.

Alberto Longo ☆–☆☆
Lucera. 35 ha. www.albertolonghi.it
If you wonder what DOC Cacc'e Mmitte actually tastes like, Longo's plummy version will give you a clue.

Mocavero ☆☆
Monteroni di Lecce. 35 ha.
www.mocaverovini.it
This medium-sized company rings the changes on Negroamaro and Primitivo. The wines are well balanced, and Puteus, a DOC Salice Salentino, is ultra-luxurious.

Racemi ☆☆–☆☆☆
Manduria1. 20 ha. www.racemi.it
Founded in 1999, and known until recently as the Accademia dei Racemi, this is a grouping of six estates primarily focused on Primitivo of the highest quality. But some of the other wines from local varieties are of great inerest, such as the Torre Guaceto from Ottavianello.

Rivera ☆☆–☆☆☆
Andria. 95 ha. www.rivera.it
Founded by the De Corato family, the estate began bottling in the early 1950s, focusing on Castel de Monte wines from family vineyards and grapes from regular suppliers.

The popularity of the lively *rosato* overshadows the quality of Il Falcone Riserva, one of Puglia's best-constructed reds. The Asti firm of Gancia has bought a share of the winery, and encouraged the production of varietal wines from Chardonnay, Sauvignon, and Primitivo. The Chardonnay Preludio No 1 has become one of Puglia's best-known wines on the export market.

Rooftops of "trullo" houses, Alberobello

Rosa del Golfo ☆☆
Alezio. 40 ha. www.rosadelgolfo.com

The Calò family has been selling wine from its estate near Gallipoli since 1938. It is best-known for its Rosa del Golfo, one of Italy's most limpid and lovely *rosatos*, and produces other wines from Verdeca and Negroamaro. A more unusual offering is a *rosato metodo classico* from Negroamaro and Chardonnay.

Rubino ☆☆–☆☆☆☆
Brindisi. 200 ha. www.tenuterubino.it

This is an expanding estate with a growing reputation for a wide range of wines, both traditional and in an international style. Torre Testa is the most intriguing wine, a pure oak-aged Susumaniello with surprising freshness for a southern wine.

Santa Lucia ☆–☆☆
Corato. 15 ha. www.vinisantalucia.com

Emerging small estate with a good range from Castel del Monte, including fruity *rosato*.

Giovanni Soloperto ☆☆
Manduria. 50 ha. www.soloperto.it

This 50-hectare estate has focused for some time on Primitivo. Good fruit and dizzyingly high alcohol. Unlike many estates that increasingly designate their wines as IGTs, Soloperto also offers DOCs such as Locotrotono and Martina Franca

Cosimo Taurino ☆☆☆
Guagnano. 150 ha. www.taurinovini.it

After Cosimo Taurino died in 1999, his son Francesco became chief winemaker. Together with oenologist Severino Garofano, he makes admirable Salice Salentino. To note especially is the famous Christmas-puddingy Patriglione, Negroamaro from ultra ripe grapes. Notarpanaro blends Negroamaro and Malvasia Nera.

Tormaresca ☆☆
Minervino Murge. 300 ha. www.tormaresca.it

The outpost in Puglia of Marchesi Antinori. Chardonnay is the major wine at present The principal red is a blend of Aglianico and Cabernet, but the range is expanding as the vineyards mature.

Torrevento ☆☆
Corato. 150 ha. www.torrevento.it

The winery buys grapes from neighbouring estates to supplement itrs own production,. The range is eclectic, with Puglian classics as well as specialities, such as Vigna Pedale, a spicy and concentrated Uva di Troia, and a Moscato *passito*.

Agricole Vallone ☆☆–☆☆☆☆
Lecce. 170 ha. www.agricolevallone.it

An estate owned by Vittoria and Maria Teresa Vallone. They produce fine Brindisi *rosato*, but the wine that has made them fampous is a splendid, perfumed Negroamaro IGT called Gratticcaia, which is fermented only after drying the grapes for a few weeks in direct sunlight.

Conti Zecca ☆☆–☆☆☆☆
Leverano. 320 ha. www.contizecca.it

The Zecca family own vineyards at four estates in various regions, from which they produce a very wide range of wines. Most of their brands, such as Santo Stefano and Donna Marzia, are for wines intended to be drunk young. Their flagship wine is Nero, a barrique-aged blend of Negroamaro and Cabernet Sauvignon.

Calabria

The vast mountainous peninsula that forms the toe of Italy has no famous wines, unless Cirò, with its athletic reputation, can be so called. Only about ten per cent of the region's 24,400 hectares of vines produce wine that is bottled locally. The rest is shipped out for blending. The local red grape is the Gaglioppo, a variety of deep colour and potentially very high alcohol, but the spots where it is grown to best effect are (with the exception of Cirò) high enough in the Calabrian Hills to cool its fiery temper. The local grape for white wines is the Greco, which is used in the extreme south at Gerace to make a very good dessert wine, which has the ability to age well, and which goes for a high price.

With little established winemaking except of the most primitive kind, Calabria, like Sicily, is modernizing in a hurry. Its DOCs, though little-known, represent wines that meet up-to-date criteria, but only account for a trifling four per cent of production. As in other regions, some of them are moribund, and profit no one but a handful of bureaucrats.

DOC & Other Wines

Bivongi DOC. Red, white, *rosato* wine. Provinces: Reggio Calabria, Catanzaro. Villages: Bivongi, eight other communes. Grapes: Gaglioppo and/or Greco Nero (30–50%), Nocera and/or Calabrese and/or Castiglione (30–50%); Greco, Mantonico, Guardavalle, Malvasia, Ansonica. Coastal DOC south of Catanzaro.

Cirò DOC. Red, white, *rosato* wine. Province: Crotone. Villages: Cirò, Cirò Marina, part of Melissa, Crucoli. Grapes: Gaglioppo (minimum 95%); Greco Bianco (minimum 90%).

Cirò is a full diet, but a soporific rather than a stimulating one. Earlier picking and new cellar techniques have reduced its tendency to oxidize, though only the *riserva* can be aged beyond three to four years. White Cirò, as modernized, is a decent standard dry white to drink young.

Donnici DOC. Red, white, *rosato* wine. Province: Cosenza. Villages: ten around and including Cosenza. Grapes: Gaglioppo (minimum 50%); Mantonico (minimum 50%), Greco and/or Pecorello and/or Malvasia Bianca (maximum 30%).

This wine is a relatively light and fruity red to drink young and fairly cool, from the central-western coastal hills of Calabria.

Greco di Bianco DOC. White wine. Province: Reggio Calabria. Villages: Bianco, part of Casignana. Grapes: Greco (minimum 95%).

A smooth, juicy, and intriguingly orange-scented sweet dessert wine made of Greco grapes at Bianco, where a few small vineyards make it their specialty. Bianco is on the south coast of the extreme toe of Italy. More vineyards are expanding production. Bianco also produces a drier, more lemony, barrel-aged dessert or apéritif white called (after its grapes) Mantonico.

Lamezia DOC. Red, white, *rosato* wine. Provinces: Catanzaro, Vibo Valentia. Villages: part of ten communes around Lamezia Terme. Grapes: Nerello Mascalese and/or Nerello Cappuccio (30–50%), Gaglioppo (known locally as Magliocco, 25–35%), Greco Nero (locally called Marsigliana, 25–35%), up to 20% others; Greco (maximum 50%), Trebbiano (maximum 40%), Malvasia (minimum 20%), up to 30% others; plus varietal Greco.

A straightforward, fairly pale, dry red from around the Gulf of St-Eufemia on the west coast. Drink it young and cool. Lametina is the name of the local non-DOC sweet or dry white.

Melissa DOC. Red, white, *rosato* wine. Province: Crotone. Villages: Melissa, 13 other communes. Grapes: Gaglioppo (75–95%), up to 25% others; Greco 75–95%, up to 20% others.

The light, yellow, dry seafood wine of the heel of the toe of Italy, around the port of Crotone. The wines resemble Cirò but don't match it for quality. Most of it is drunk locally where it represents good value.

Moscato di Saracena. Ancient wine, from Moscatello, Guarnaccia, and Malvasia Bianco, made by a combination of drying the grapes and reducing the must by boiling. Rare.

Pellaro Powerful but light red or pink wines of imported Alicante vines grown on the Pellaro Peninsula in the extreme south.

Pollino DOC. Red wine. Province: Cosenza. Villages: Castrovillari, St Basile, Sarancena, Cassano Ionio, Civita, Frascineto. Grapes: Gaglioppo (minimum 60%), up to 20% any combination of Greco Nero, Malvasia, Mantonico, Garnaccia, up to 20% others.

Monte Pollino is a 2,130-metre (6,922-foot) peak that divides northern Calabria from Basilicata. Its slopes produce a pale but powerful red that is rarely seen.

San Vito di Luzzi DOC. Red, white, *rosato* wine. Province: Cosenza. Village: San Vito. Grapes: Gaglioppo (maximum 70%); up to 30–40% any combination of Greco Nero, Nerello Cappucciom Magliocco Ganino, Sangiovese, up to 25% others; Malvasia Bianca (40–60%), Greco (20–30%), up to 30% others.

Small DOC just north of Cosenza.

Sant' Anna di Isola di Capo Rizzuto DOC. Red and *rosato* wine. Province: Crotone. Villages: Isola di Capo Rizzuto, parts of the communes of Crotone, Cutro. Grapes: Gaglioppo (40–60%).

A pale red/*rosato* to drink young and cool, from the easternmost cape (not an island) of the Calabrian coast. Almost extinct.

Savuto DOC. Red and *rosato* wine. Provinces: Cosenza, Catanzaro. Villages: 14 communes in Cosenza, six in Catanzaro. Grapes: Gaglioppo (35–45%), 30–40% any combination of Greco Nero , Nerello Cappuccio, Magliocco Ganino, Sangiovese; Malvasia Bianca and/or Pecorino (maximum 25%).

A recommended red of moderate strength and some fragrance. Odoardi the main producer (q.v.).

Scavigna DOC. Red, white, *rosato* wine. Province: Catanzaro. Villages: Nocera, Tirinese, Falerna. Grapes: Gaglioppo (maximum 60%), Nerello Cappuccio (maximum 40%), up to 5% others; Trebbiano (maximum 50%), Chardonnay (maximum 30%), Greco (maximum 20%), others.

Coastal DOC west of Catanzaro. Odoardi the main producer here, too.

Verbicaro DOC. Red, white, *rosato* wine. Province: Cosenza. Villages: Verbicaro, four other communes. Grapes: Gaglioppo and/or Greco Nero (60–80%), Malvasia, Greco Bianco, others; Greco Bianco and/or Malvasia Bianca and/or Guaranccia (70%); up to 30% others.

Northerly DOC along the coast near Campania.

Leading Calabria Producers

Caparra & Siciliani ☆☆
Cirò Marina. 213 ha. www.caparraesiciliani.it
A small cooperative, founded in 1963, and with Severino Garofano as the consultant oenologist. The winery produces a complete range of Cirò wines, white, *rosato*, and red. The whites are vinified in steel, the reds aged in traditional large casks and, for Volvito, in barriques.

Dattilo ☆☆
Marina di Strongoli. 20 ha.
A swiftly improving estate, offering a fresh Chardonnay and gutsy red Gaglioppo and Gaglioppo-based blends.

Cantine Enotria ☆
Cirò Marina1. 50 ha.
A co-op with 70 growers. A full range of Cirò wines is made, the smoky red *riserva* being a distinct notch up in quality.

Ippolito ☆–☆☆
Cirò Marina. 100 ha. www.ippolito1845.it
Founded in 1845 , this family firm produces a wide range of wines, the best being the Cirò, especially the *riserva*, which is only released after many years in bottle.

Cantine Lento ☆☆
Lamezia Terme. 82 ha. www.cantinelento.it
Fresh white wines and supple reds from organic vineyards in DOC Lamezia. The best wines are labelled Contessa Emburga (IGT) and include an exotic Sauvignon .

Librandi ☆☆☆
Cirò Marina. 230 ha. www.librandi.it
Founded in 1950 by Antonio Cataldo Librandi, and the best-known property in Calabria. Under the supervision of oenologist Donato Lanati, Librandi makes traditional Cirò

using modern techniques (the best being the plummy Riserva Duca San Felice). IGT wines include the rather leathery Gravello, made from Cabernet and Gaglioppo; a rare Magliocco; a pineappley Chardonnay called Critone; and, occasionally, a *passito* from Mantonico called Le Passule. They are not cheap.

Odoardi ☆☆
Nocera Terinese. 95 ha.
This progressive winery specializes in two DOC wines: Savuto and Scavigna red, white, and *rosato*. Indeed, they are the only significant producers of Scavigna. The white Scavigna is an aromatic blend of Chardonnay, Pinot Bianco, and Riesling, with a luxurious hint of tropical fruit on the palate.

San Francesco ☆☆
Cirò. 40 ha. www.fattoriasanfrancesco.it
The Siciliani family produce reliable wines from Cirò: red, white, and *rosato*. The spicy red Ronco dei Quattroventi has a complexity unusual for the DOC.

Santa Venere ☆☆
Cirò. 25 ha. www.santavenere.com
Gutsy red Cirò from this organic estate, and a varietal Greco that shows more vigour and finesse than the white Cirò.

Vintripodi ☆☆
Archi. 15 ha. www.vintripodi.it
This small property was founded in 1892 and is totally committed to local grape varieties, notably Nerello and Alicante. The reds are peppery and well-structured, and this is a good source of Greco di Bianco as well as Mantonico *passito*.

Luigi Viola ☆☆–☆☆☆
Saracena. 3 ha. www.cantineviola.it
We have Viola to thank for reviving the splendid Moscato di Saracena, as well as continuing to produce lush, orangey Moscato *passito*.

Basilicata

This mountainous region of the central south, almost entirely landlocked and chronically poor, would not feature on the wine list at all were it not for its romantically named Aglianico del Vulture, a close relation of Taurasi and one of the best reds of southern Italy.

DOC & Other Wines

Aglianico dei Colli Lucani A worthwhile red, from the Puglia side of Basilicata. It is worth tasting any wine made from this grape.

Aglianico del Vulture DOC. Red wine. Province: Potenza. Villages: 15 communes north of Potenza. Grape: Aglianico.

Monte Vulture, an extinct volcano, lies right in the extreme north of Basilicata, not far from the Iripinian mountains where Campania's splendid Taurasi is made. The same grapes grown at high altitudes on volcanic soil give a well-balanced red wine of firm structure, which is sometimes offered as a young, sweet sparkler, but more often as a matured red with real quality and character.

Matera DOC. Red and white wine. Province: eastern Basilicata. Grapes: Sangiovese (60–90%), Aglianico (10–40%), up to 20% others; "Moro" is Cabernet Sauvignon (60–70%), Primitivo (20–30%), Merlot (10–20%), up to 10% others; Malvasia (70–100%), up to 30% others; plus varietal Greco and Primitivo.

Established in 2005 for vineyards at over 700 metres (2,300 ft).

Terra d'Alta Val d'Agri DOC. Red wine. Southern Basilicata, near Campania. Grapes: Merlot (50–70%), Cabernet Sauvignon (30–50)%, up to 15% others.

Leading Basilicata Producers

Fratelli d'Angelo ☆☆☆
Rionero in Vulture. 50 ha. www.dangelowine.com
Founded in 1930 and run by Donato d'Angelo, this is the best-known estate in the region. Famous for their consistently good Aglianico del Vulture, they also make a barrique-aged Aglianico called Canneto, which is as good but has a touch more elegance and no obtrusive oak flavours.

Basilisco ☆☆☆
Rionero in Vulture. 10 ha.
A small property located high on the slopes of Monte Vulture, and since 1992 producing nothing but two versions of darkly fruity Aglianico del Vulture. Basilisco is the more celebrated of the two.

Basilium ☆☆
Acerenza. 350 ha. www.basilium.it
A medium-sized cooperative with a good reputation for sturdy Aglianico del Vulture.

Bisceglia ☆☆
Lavello. 55 ha. www.agricolavisceglia.com
Although this organic estate, founded in 2001, is best-known for its Aglianico, part of its production is devoted to white wines from Fiano and Falanghina

Eubea ☆☆–☆☆☆
Rionero. 15 ha.
Eugenia Sasso's organic vineyards yield two excellent Aglianicos.

Vigne di Mezzo ☆☆
Barile. 32 ha. www.feudi.it
This is the Basilicata outpost, devoted to Aglianico del Vulture, of the leading Campania estate Feudi di San Gregorio.

Cantina del Notaio ☆☆–☆☆☆
Rionero. 27 ha. www.cantinadelnotaio.com
A newcomer, having been established only in 1998, but the La Firma Aglianico has already been hailed as outstanding. It is barrique-aged, and for those who prefer a more traditional style, there is another bottling called Il Repertorio.

Paternoster ☆☆–☆☆☆
Barile. 6 ha. www.paternostervini.it
Named after the proprietors, this estate produces a few
different bottlings of Aglianico del Vulture, as well as a
Moscato called Clivus. The old-vine Don Anselmo Aglianico
usually leads the pack, although Rotondo, aged in 500-litre
barrels, is in a more modern style.

Le Querce ☆☆
Barile, Potenza. 20 ha.
An estate only founded in 1997, but already producing solid
Aglianico of very good quality.

Sicily

Of all the regions of Italy, the island of Sicily has changed most
in the past few decades. Thirty years ago it was an almost
medieval land. The marriage of dignity and squalor was visible
everywhere. Its unsurpassed Greek ruins lay apparently
forgotten. Syracuse was still a small city commanding a bay of
incredible beauty and purity where you could easily imagine the
catastrophic defeat of the Athenian fleet 2,000 years before.
Palermo was sleepy, violent, indigent but magnificent.

As far as wine was concerned, there was Marsala, a name
everyone knew but which nobody drank, and a few small aristocratic estates – the best-known on the ideal volcanic slopes of
Mount Etna, and around Syracuse, from which there was a
trickle of legendary sweet Moscato. But the general run of wine
was almost undrinkable, the best of it having been exported
northwards for blending.

An apparently well-directed regional development programme
(for which Europe has paid millions) has changed all this, and
the wine industry has become the biggest in Italy, and one of
the most modern. Enormous new vineyards supply automated
cooperatives, that churn out "correct", clean, and properly
balanced, modern wines. Three-quarters of Sicily's wine is
white, in defiance of the fact that the island's climate is overwhelmingly better suited to red. Eighty per cent of the colossal
total is made in the 50 cooperatives.

DOCs are almost irrelevant here; less than five per cent
qualifies. Until recently, this has been a table-wine industry,
based on volume rather than individuality. The palatability of
much of this ocean of wine is thanks to New World techniques
– and huge government grants. However, it has been evident
for some years that Sicily is capable of producing very good
if not great wine. A handful of red grapes shows real
distinction, and far-sighted producers from many parts of the
world have purchased vineyards in Noto or on Etna to prove
the point. In terms of volume, this quality-wine production is a
drop in the ocean, but no matter. Ancient traditions have been
revived and been shown to be of value, and Sicilian wine is coming of age. Producers such as Planeta (q.v.) have shown that
the indigenous varieties can produce wines of beauty, while
at the same time international varieties perform here with
effortless ease.

DOC & Other Wines

Alcamo or Bianco d'Alcamo DOC. White wine. Provinces:
Palermo, Trapani. Villages: around the town of Alcamo.
Grapes: Nero d'Avola (minimum 60%), up to 40% other
varieties; Catarratto Bianco Comune or Lucido, any
combination of Grecanico, Ansonica, Grillo, Chardonnay,
(maximum 40%); plus a range of varietal wines.

The white is straightforward and fairly full-bodied.

Cerasuolo di Vittoria DOCG Red wine. Provinces: Ragusa,
Caltanissetta, Catania. Villages: ten communes in southeastern
Sicily. Grapes: Nero d'Avola (50–70%), Frappato (30–50%).

An unusual pale "cherry" red of high strength, and more
serious and ageworthy than it looks. Growing in renown
and popularity.

MARSALA

An Englishman, John Woodhouse, started
the Marsala industry in 1773. Nelson
stocked his fleet with it. In a sense it is
Italy's sherry, though without sherry's
brilliant finesse or limitless ageing
capacity. Its manufacture usually involves
concentrated and/or "muted" (stopped
with alcohol) musts, known as *cotto* and
sifone – but the best, *vergine*, is made
with neither: simply by an ageing system
similar to the soleras of sherry. Fine, the
basic style, is normally sweet and rather
nasty; *superiore* can be sweet or dry, with
a strong caramel flavour; *rubino* is an
innovation, drier than fine; *vergine* is
dry, with more barrel wood flavour.

Finest, and rarest of all, is *vergine
stravecchio* or *riserva*, which must be
aged ten years or more in cask and it can
also be vintage dated: Speciali used to be
a strange aberration – Marsala blended
with eggs, or even coffee – but is now no
longer permitted under DOC regulation.
Other recent changes to the DOC are the
descriptions *oro* (gold), *ambra* (amber),
and *rubino* (ruby); the first two refer to
the wines based on white grapes, while
the latter refers to the darker varieties
less often seen.

Unfortunately, Marsala has been much
abused over the years and came to be
regarded as little more than a cooking
wine. Nor has the proliferation of barely
comprehensible rules under the DOC helped
its reputation or popularity. It took the
single-mindedness of Marco de Bartoli
(q.v.) to produce a well-aged, unfortified
style that showed much more complexity
and delicacy than most souped-up,
"traditional" Marsalas. For his pains,
his wines were denied the DOC.

Commercial Marsalas from the best
firms can nonetheless be very good,
especially in drier versions. With Marsala,
as with most other great wines, you get
what you pay for: cheap can often be
nasty, expensive can be excellent, if
not sublime.

Contea di Sclafani DOC. Red, white, *rosato* wine. Provinces: Palermo, Caltanissetta, Agrigento. Grapes: Nero d'Avola and/or Perricone (50%), up to 50% others; Catarratto and/or Insolia and/or Grecanico (50%), up to 50% others; plus varietal wines.

A large district in the centre of the island, given DOC status in 1996, and presenting a wide range of mostly varietal wines, both local and international varieties.

Contessa Entellina DOC. Red and white wine. Province Palermo. Villages: commune of Contessa Entellina. Grapes: Cabernet Sauvignon and/or Syrah (50%), up to 50% others; Ansonica (50%), up to 50% others; DOC also permits varietal wines from Catarratto, Ansonica, Grecanico, Chardonnay, Sauvignon, Cabernet Sauvignon, Merlot, Pinot Nero.

The main producer is Donnafugata (q.v.).

Delia Nivolelli DOC. White and red wine. Province: southeast of Marsala. Grapes: any combination of Nero d'Avola, Pignatello, Merlot, Cabernet Sauvignon, Syrah, and Sangiovese (65%), up to 30% others; any combination of Grecanico, Insolia, and Grillo (65%) up to 35% others; plus varietal wines.

Eloro DOC. Red and *rosato* wine. Provinces: Ragusa, Siracusa. Villages: Noto, four other communes. Grapes: Nero d'Avola, Frappato, Piganello (minimum 90%, alone or blended). There are two sub-appellations; Pachino (Nero d'Avola 80%) and Pignatello (Pignatello 80%).

Coastal region just south of Ragusa.

Erice DOC. Red and white wine. Province: east of Trapani. Grapes: Nero d'Avola (60–100%), up to 40% others; Catarratto (60–100%), up to 40% others; plus varietal wines. Also *passito* and *spumante*.

Etna DOC. Red, white, *rosato* wine. Province: Catania. Villages: Milo, 20 other communes on the lower eastern slopes of Mount Etna. Grapes: Nerello Mascalese, Nerello Cappuccio; Carricante (minimum 60%), Catarratto Bianco (maximum 40%), up to 15% others.

Suddenly fashionable, and being rescued from decline by enthusiastic and dedicated growers, excited by the quality obtained from bush vines on volcanic soils at high altitude. The reds age well to a consistency not far from claret and the whites are brisk and tasty young. A rare Bianco Superiore is made only in Milo and must contain 80% Carricante.

Faro DOC. Red wine. Province: Messina. Village: Messina. Grapes: Nerello Mascalese (45–60%), Nerello Cappuccio (15%), Nocera (5–10%), up to 15% others.

Limited production of a distinctly superior red, best aged three years or so. Undergoing a successful revival.

Malvasia delle Lipari DOC. White wine. Province: Messina. Villages: islands of Aeolian archipelago, especially Lipari. Grapes: Malvasia delle Lipari (maximum 95%), Corinto Nero (5%).

Well-known but scarcely exceptional wines (except in their lovely birthplace), made in both *passito* and *liquoroso* styles. There are many good dessert wines in Sicily; Moscato is much more interesting than Malvasia.

Mamertino di Milazzo DOC. Red and white wine. Province: southwest of Messina. Grapes: Nero d'Avola (60–90%), Nocera (10–40%), up to 30% others; Grillo and/or Ansonica and/or Inzolia (35–55%), Catarratto (45–65%), others (maximum 20%); plus varietal Nero d'Avola, Grillo-Ansonica, Grillo-Inzolia.

Marsala DOC. Provinces: Trapani, Palermo, Agrigento. Villages: throughout the provinces but above all at Marsala. Grapes: (*oro and ambra*) Catarratto and/or Grillo, Inzolia (maximum 15%); (*rubino*) Perricone, Calabrese, Nerello Mascalese, whites (maximum 30%). Minimum alcohol: 17 degrees by volume for *fine*; 18 degrees aged two years for *superiore* ; 18 degrees by volume aged five years for *vergine*.

See also box on previous page.

Menfi DOC. Red and white wine. Provinces: Agrigento, Trapani. Villages: Menfi, Sambuca, Sciacca, Castelvetrano. Grapes: any combination of Nero d'Avola, Sangiovese, Merlot, Cabernet Sauvignon, Syrah (minimum 70%); any combination of Inzolia, Catarratto, Grecanico, Chardonnay (minimum 75%); there are two sub-appellations: Feudi dei Fiori (based on 80% Chardonnay, Inzolia, Ansonica) and Bonera (based on 85% Cabernet Sauvignon, Nero d'Avola, Merlot, Sangiovese, Syrah); plus varietal wines.

This DOC neighbours Sambuca in western Sicily.

Moscato di Noto DOC. White wine. Province: Siracusa. Villages: Noto, Rosolini, Pachino, Avola. Grape: Moscato Bianco.

Little of this delicious and valued Moscato is made, but the *liquoroso* is a very good example of this sumptuous genre. The Greeks introduced the Muscat grape here 2,500 years ago. It is also made in unfortified and *spumante* styles.

Moscato and Passito di Pantelleria DOC. White wine. Province: Trapani. Province: the island of Pantelleria. Grape: Zibibbo.

The island of Pantelleria is closer to Tunisia than Sicily. The Zibibbo grape is a variant of Moscato with a singular perfume, whether made as *spumante*, *naturale*, or best of all *passito* (which can also be fortified). This has become a cult wine; production has doubled over the past decade.

Moscato di Siracusa DOC. White wine. Province: Siracusa. Village: Siracusa. Grape: Moscato Bianco.

The celebrated old Moscato vineyard of Syracuse, once the greatest city of the Greek world, home of Plato, Theocritus, and Archimedes, is apparently extinct, like the matchless beauty of its bay before Sicily began to modernize. But still made by a small handful of producers.

Salaparuta DOC. White and red wines. Province: Trapani. Inland region of 1,500 hectares, south of Alcamo. Grapes: red based on Nero d'Avola; white based on Catarratto; plus varietal wines.

DOC created in 2006.

Sambuca di Sicilia DOC. Red, white, *rosato* wine. Provinces: Agrigento, Palermo. Villages: Sambuca, seven other communes. Grapes: Nero d'Avola (20–50%), Sangiovese and/or Cabernet Sauvignon (50–80%), up to 15% others; Ansonica (50–100%), up to 50% others; plus varietal wines from local and international varieties.

Santa Margherita di Belice DOC. Red and white wine. Provinces: Agrigento, Palermo, Trapani. Villages: Santa Margherita, eight others. Grapes: Sangiovese and/or Cabernet Sauvignon (50–80%), Nero d'Avola (20–50%), up to 15% others; Ansonica, Grecanico, Catarratto, others; plus varietal Ansonica, Catarratto, Grecanico, Nero d'Avola, Sangiovese.

A small region just north of Menfi in western Sicily.

Sciacca DOC. Red, white, *rosato* wine. Province: Agrigento. Grapes: any combination of Merlot, Cabnernet Sauvignon, Nero d'Avola, Sangiovsese; any combination of Inzolia, Chardonnay, Grecanico, Catarratto. There is also a sub-appellation, Riserva Rayana: Catarratto and/or Inzolia (80%); up to 20% others; plus varietal Grecanico, Inzolia, Cabernet Sauvignon, Merlot, Nero d'Avola, Sangiovese.

Vittoria DOC. Red and white wine. Province: Ragusa. Grapes: Nero d'Avola (60–100%), Frappato (30–50%); plus varietal Ansonica, Inzolia, Nero d'Avola, Frappato.

A new DOC created in 2005 to provide softer and more accessible wines than Cerasuola di Vittoria.

Leading Sicily Producers

Abbazia Santa Anastasia ☆☆–☆☆☆
Castelbuono. 62 ha. www.abbaziasantanastasia.it
A small but ambitious organic property producing both traditional wines from Nero d'Avola and acclaimed Cabernet called Litra, and a Chardonnay called Gemelli. Some wines can show signs of overripeness, but the general style is lush and hedonistic.

Ajello ☆–☆☆
Mazara del Vallo. 68 ha. www.ajello.info
Vines were first planted on this family property in 1860. Furat is a successful blend of Nero d'Avola with French varieties. Less successful is a mock icewine called Shams from Moscato and local white varieties.

Baglio di Pianetto ☆☆–☆☆☆☆
Santa Cristina Gela. 95 ha. www.bagliodipianetto.com
A hi-tech winery established by businessman and former racing car driver Conte Paolo Marzotto, with the first vintage in 2000. The wines are skilful blends of local and international varieties, including Viognier and Petit Verdot.

Marco de Bartoli ☆☆☆
Marsala. 25 hectares. www.marcodebartoli.com
Marco de Bartoli selects grapes for a limited production of Vecchio Samperi, his unfortified expression of Marsala Vergine, in its drier versions a heady compound of walnuts

Racking wine in a Sicilian cellar

and iodine. But he so upset the authorities that his wines were denied the DOC, and he had to rebut trumped-up charges against him that nearly drove him out of business.

He stubbornly and bravely persists in producing his excellent wines, of which the most sumptuous is the almost treacley Bukkuram *passito* from Pantelleria. Red wines such as the barrique-aged Rosso di Marco from Merlot and Syrah, are something of a departure for this resolutely Sicilian producer.

Benanti ☆☆–☆☆☆
Viagrande. 44 ha. www.vincolabenanti.it
Dr Giuseppe Benanti made a careful study of the Etna soils before setting up his property. The wines are mostly blends of Nerello Mascalese and Nerello Cappuccio, but Benanti also has a property in southern Italy where he is growing Nero d'Avola. The estate produces one of Sicily's most individual whites: Pietramarina, a Carricante grown at almost 1,000 metres (3,280 feet).

Calatrasi ☆–☆☆
San Cipirello. 2,400 ha. www.calatrasi.it
A vast property with numerous labels including Terre di Ginestra and the more basic D'Istinto. The whites blend Catarratto and Chardonnay, while both Nero d'Avola and the Bordeaux varieties play their part in the reds.

Ceusi ☆–☆☆
Calatafimi. 50 ha. www.ceuso.it
The Melia family blend Nero d'Avola with international varieties to produce highly drinkable blends.

COS ☆☆
Vittoria. 25 ha. www.cosvittoria.it
The name sounds like that of a cooperative, but is in fact composed of the founders' initials. Very good, traditional wines from Cerasuolo di Vittoria DOC, and a very ripe Nero d'Avola IGT called Scyri.

Cottanera ☆☆–☆☆☆
Castiglione di Sicilia. 50 ha. www.cottanera.it
Although the Cambria family's property is extensive, production is minute, and the wines, all IGTs, are expensive and hard to find. The wines range from the fashionable varieties, such as Syrah and Merlot, to the less usual, such as Nerello and Mondeuse. All are barrique-aged.

Cusumano ☆–☆☆☆
Partinico. 450 ha. www.cusumano.it
The Cusumano brothers have constructed an excellent range of IGT wines, with perfectly satisfactory unoaked wines at one end of the range, and more sophisticated wines aged in casks of various sizes at the other. Noa, from Nero d'Avola, Cabernet, and Merlot is arguably their most successful wine. Given the scale of production, quality is high.

Donnafugata ☆☆–☆☆☆
Marsala. 260 ha. www.donnafugata.it
Owned by Giacomo Rallo and family, this is a sophisticated modern estate with vineyards in different areas. Using the Contessa Entellina DOC, they produce a wide range of blends, the toasty Nero d'Avola Mille e Una Notte, a fine Ansonica white called Vigna di Gabri, and rich, apricotty Passito di Pantelleria. The wines are consistently well-made at all levels.

Duca di Salaparuta (Corvo) ☆–☆☆☆
Casteldaccia. 140 ha. www.vinicorvo.it
The property may have been founded in 1824 by the Duca di Salaparuta, but today it is owned by the Illva Saronno group, and boasts an ultra-modern winery. For many decades, Corvo has been the most famous brand of Sicilian wine, though no more a flagship than Mouton Cadet would be for Bordeaux.

Of far more interest are the wines on which the company has always lavished care: the red Duca Enrico, an aged, pure Nero d'Avola, and Bianco di Valguarnera from Inzolia and aged in small oak barrels.

Feudo Principi di Butera ☆☆
Butera. 180 ha. www.feudobutera.it
This ambitious estate was established in 1997 by the Veneto firm of Zonin. Firmly turning its back on local traditions, it has produced standard international varietal wines – Chardonnay, Merlot, Cabernet – but to a high standard.

Firriato ☆☆–☆☆☆
Paceco. 300 ha. www.firriato.it
Despite a production of over four million bottles, this property maintains high quality standards. The wines are all IGT, and many of them blend Sicilian and international varieties. Santagostino is a spicy, blackberry-toned blend of Nero d'Avola and Syrah, Harmonium a super-rich, oak-aged Nero d'Avola, Camelot a suave Bordeaux blend.

Florio ☆☆–☆☆☆
Marsala. www.cantineflorio.com
Founded in 1883 by Vincenzo Florio, and now owned by Illva Saronno, a group that also owns Duca di Salaparuta (q.v.). Florio was known in his day as "the king of the historic Marsala"; today the company has no vines but still makes Marsala. After a lacklustre spell, the wines have improved considerably in quality. There are two vintage-dated *vergine* wines, Baglio Florio" and the unfortunately named Terre Arse. In addition, Florio has rightly won great acclaim for its lush, fortified Pantelleria called Morso di Luce.

Gulfi ☆
Chiaramonte Gulfi. 70 ha. www.gulfi.it
Sumptuous but something leathery Nero d'Avola from the variety's heartland in Ragusa.

Carlo Hauner ☆☆–☆☆☆
Salina. 40 ha.
After the death of the famous owner, Carlo Hauner, who made Malvasia delle Lipari known worldwide, his descendants continue to run the property. With its rich tones of apricot and orange, the *passito* remains a remarkable wine.

Maccari ☆☆
Noto. 50 ha. www.feudomaccari.it
In 2000, Antonio Moretti, owner of Sette Ponti in Tuscany, created this estate, at which Carlo Ferrini acts as consultant.

These are powerful oaky wines, based on a potent combination of Nero d'Avola, Cabernet Sauvignon, and Syrah.

Morgante ☆☆–☆☆☆
Grotte. 60 ha. www.morgantevini.it
With the aid of oenologist Riccardo Cotarella, the Morgante family have, since 1992, been producing excellent wines from Nero d'Avola, of which the most concentrated is "Don Antonio", with its aromas of red fruits and coffee.

Salvatore Murana ☆☆☆
Pantelleria. 8 ha. www.salvatoremurana.com
For 20 years Murana has offered a superlative range of Moscato di Pantelleria. All the wines are excellent, but the best, and most costly, is usually the intense Martingana, a *passito* with fabulously complex spice and orange zest flavours.

Palari ☆☆☆
Messina. 7 ha. www.palari.it
A boutique winery, founded in 1990, which rapidly established a high reputation for its two red blends, both Nerello-based: a Faro DOC, and the less complex Rosso del Soprano IGT.

Passopisciaro ☆☆☆
Passopisciaro. 26 ha. www.passopisciaro.com
Andrea Franchetti of Trinoro in Tuscany (q.v.) has embarked on an eccentric enterprise 1,000-metres (3280-feet) up on the slopes of Etna. Here he makes Passopisciaro from Nerello Mascalese, and a strange blend of Petit Verdot and Cesanese, aged in new oak, and named after himself. Impressive quality, and prices are high.

Carlo Pellegrino ☆☆–☆☆☆
Marsala. 300 ha. www.carlopellegrino.it
Founded in 1880, Pellegrino remains a major producer of good-quality Marsala. The property also supports a second range of wines under the Duca di Castelmonte label. The line-up is enormous, ranging from international-style Chardonnay and Cabernet to sumptuous sweet wines from Pantelleria.

Planeta ☆☆☆–☆☆☆☆
Menfi. 350 ha. www.planeta.it
Although founded as recently as 1995, the Planeta family winery has already made a huge impact, especially outside Italy. The late Carlo Corino, the winery's consultant oenologist, opted for rich, fruit-driven wines, essentially New World in style, but none the worse for that.

As well as powerful, oaky Chardonnay, Merlot, and Cabernet Sauvignon, there are also wines from southern Italian grapes such as Nero d'Avola and Fiano. Indeed, the Planetas are enthusiastic supporters of traditional wines such as Cerasuola di Vittoria. Perhaps the barriques are sometimes applied with a heavy hand, but these are impressive wines of a consistently high quality.

Rallo ☆☆
Marsala. 70 ha. www.cantinerallo.net
Rallo produces fine Marsala, the *vergine* Solera Riserva.

Today the emphasis is on table wines, from Nero d'Avola, and such varieties as Chardonnay, Syrah, and Merlot.

Rapitalà ☆☆
Camporeale. 175 ha. www.rapitala.it
This estate has been part of the GIV group since 1999. Its best-known wines are the almondy Alcamo DOC and Nuhar, a lively blend of Nero d'Avola and Pinot Nero. More recent additions to the range include the Syrah Solinero.

Settesoli ☆☆
Menfi. 6,500 ha. www.mandrarossa.it
This cooperative was founded in 1958, and is currently one of Europe's largest wineries. Its standards were established by renowned oenologist Carlo Corino. The Syrah and Nero d'Avola are among the best of the red wines and both offer outstanding value. Inycon, known in some markets as Mandrarossa, is the cooperative's best known brand.

Spadafora ☆☆–☆☆☆
Palermo. 100 ha. www.spadafora.com
Feroim this remote property, inland from Palermo, comes a fine-grained Cabernet Sauvignon IGT called Schietto. In recent years the estate has been focusing more intently on Syrah, from which it produces the excellent Sole dei Padre.

Tasca d'Almerita ☆☆☆
Sclafani Bagni. 460 ha. www.tascadalmerita.it
A family estate founded in 1830, and today owned by Conte Lucio Tasca. This has long been the source of some of Sicily's finest dry wines, including the excellent Rosso del Conte (mostly Nero d'Avola) and Nozze d'Oro (a white blend mostly from Inzolia).

If one eye is trained on tradition, the other is fixed on innovation. Cabernet Sauvignon here is one of the best of southern Italy; Chardonnay is also particularly good. The winery's principal brand name is Regaleali.

Terre di Ginestra
See Calatrasi.

Terre Nere ☆☆–☆☆☆
Randazzo. 16 ha.
Marc di Grazia made his name importing fine Italian wine into the United States, and since 2002 has had his own organic wine estate on Etna. These are intriguing single vineyard wines, one from pre-phylloxera vines, from Nerello Mascalese only. They exude red-fruits fragrance and a light smokiness, while the structure is delicate rather than powerful.

Cantina Valle dell' Acate ☆☆
Acate100 ha. www.valledellacate.com
This property, an extended family cooperative founded in 1981, upholds the tradition of Cerasuolo di Vittoria DOC, and also makes sound varietal wine from Frappato and a Chardonnay/Inzolia blend.

Zenner ☆☆
Catania. 6 ha. www.terradellesirene.com
From nothing but old vines, cultivated Biodynamically, the Zenner family make a lighter, more perfumed and elegant style of Nero d'Avola

Sardinia

Sardinia is a strange, timeless island, adrift in the centre of things and yet remote, without Sicily's innate drama, without Corsica's majestic mountains or sour social history. The modern world comes and camps on the coastline of Sardinia, the jet-set on the Costa Smeralda, the wine world on the opposite coast at Alghero, where one of Italy's most sophisticated and original wineries takes advantage of ideal natural conditions to break all the rules. Sardinia's original wines are heroically strong, designed, it seems, by and for the supermen who built the *nuraghe*, round fortress houses of colossal stones that dot the island. The most characteristic wine of the island is Cannonau, an indigenous red now known to be the same as Grenache.

The traditional practice is to prevent all the sugar from converting to alcohol: to balance strength with sweetness in something faintly reminiscent of port. The sweet red is actually best: as *liquoroso*, fortified with brandy, when it goes all the way to a port-style dessert wine. The Anghelu Ruju of Sella & Mosca is the version of Cannonau most likely to appeal to untrained tastes. Two other grapes, Girò and Monica, make similar sweet and heady reds.

Nor are old-style Sardinian white wines any easier to cope with. Nasco, Malvasia, and Vernaccia are three white grapes that all achieve formidable alcohol degrees, often tempered, like the reds, with unfermented sugar left to sweeten them. Sweet Malvasia is a serious specialty that can reach very high quality. Vernaccia, on the other hand, is usually best fermented dry and aged in the same way as sherry. (It even develops the same flor yeast that allows it to oxidize very gently to a nicely nutty maturity.) Old dry Vernaccia needs no apology. But these are specialities in decline. Whites are more likely to be made from Vermentino, which can do as well here as in Corsica, delivering full-bodied yet fresh wines that go well with the coastal seafood.

The modern movement in Sardinia consists largely of cooperatives. It was led by the Sella & Mosca winery at Alghero, and given greater credibility by the legendary Giacomo Tachis, Antinori's winemaker, who pointed out that Sardinian wine has been used to boost Tuscan for millennia. Although some of the cooperatives are well-equipped and well-managed, there is a growing number of private estates taking advantage of the island's wonderful conditions for viticulture.

DOC & Other Wines

Alghero DOC. Red, white, *rosato* wine. Province: Sassari. Villages: Alghero, seven other communes. Grapes: Torbato, Sauvignon, Chardonnay, Cabernets Sauvignon and Franc, Sangiovese, Cagnulari, Vermentino.

Since the rules for this DOC are loose, many producers have been taking advantage of it, and it now accounts for 40 per cent of all Sardinian DOC wines.

Arborea DOC. Red, white, *rosato* wine. Province: Oristano. Villages: many communes in Oristano. Grapes: varietal Trebbiano or Sangiovese.

Recent DOC with very limited production; the white also possibly *frizzante* or *amabile*.

Campidano di Terralba DOC. Red wine. Provinces: Cagliari, Oristano. Villages: Terralba, 22 communes nearby. Grapes: Bovale (minimum 80%).

A lightish dry red, pleasantly soft, best young and cool. Small production.

Cannonau di Sardegna DOC. Red and *rosato* wine. Province: whole of Sardinia. Grapes: Cannonau (minimum 90%). Can be dry, sweet, or *liquoroso*.

Cannonau (Grenache) is the basic Sardinian red grape, traditionally both strong and sweet – in fact, anything but refreshing, however rich (which it is) in flavour. The most famous old-style Cannonau is that of Oliena, near Nuoro in the eastern centre of the island, which can be called Nepente di Oliena.

Carignano del Sulcis DOC. Red and *rosato* wine. Province: Cagliari. Villages: 18 communes on the southwest coast. Grapes: Carignano (minimum 85%).

Both reasonable red and a quite smooth and fruity *rosato* are made from Carignan in this area of hilly islets and lagoons, known to the ancients as Sulcis. The red will take one to two years' ageing.

Girò di Cagliari DOC. Red wine. Provinces: Cagliari, Oristano. Villages: 72 communes. Grape: Girò.

Girò, like Cannonau, is a traditional red grape of formidable sugar content, most often seen as a sweet wine – impressive rather than attractive when it is made dry. Very limited production.

Malvasia di Bosa DOC. White wine. Provinces: Nuoro, Oristano. Villages: seven coastal communes south of Alghero. Grape: Malvasia di Sardegna.

The most highly prized of several Sardinian amber whites that can best be compared with sherry – at least in function. They go through a shorter and simpler ageing process but acquire smoothness and some depth of flavour, ending in a characteristically Italian, bitter-almond note. Dry versions, served chilled, are good apéritifs. Now rare.

Malvasia di Cagliari DOC. White wine. Provinces: Cagliari, Oristano. Villages: same 72 communes as for Girò di Cagliari. Grape: Malvasia di Sardegna.

Similar wines to the last but from less exclusively southern vineyards.

Mandrolisai DOC. Red and *rosato* wine. Provinces: Nuoro, Oristano. Villages: Sorgono and six other communes. Grapes: Bovale Sardo (minimum 35%), Cannonau (20–35%), Monica (20–35%), up to 10% others.

A new DOC for less-than-full-power Cannonau and *rosato* from modernized cooperatives.

Monica di Cagliari DOC. Provinces: Cagliari and Oristano. Villages: same 72 communes as for Girò di Cagliari. Grape: Monica. Can be dry, sweet, or *liquoroso*.

Monica di Sardegna DOC. Red wine. Province: the whole island. Grapes: Monica (minimum 85%).

A standard dry red , sometimes more enjoyable rather cool. Also frizzante.

Moscato di Cagliari DOC. White wine. Provinces: Cagliari, Oristano. Villages: same 72 communes as for Girò di Cagliari. Grape: Moscato Bianco.

The Muscat grape has a stronger tradition in Sicily than Sardinia. What is made here is sweet or *liquoroso* for local drinking.

Moscato di Sardegna DOC. White wine. Province: the whole island. Grapes: Moscato Bianco (minimum 90%).

A DOC for low-strength, sweet Muscat *spumante* – in fact the Asti of Sardinia. It can use the geographical term "Tempo Pausania" or "Tempio e Gallura" if the grapes are vinified at Gallura in the province of Sassari in the northwest.

Moscato di Sorso-Sennori DOC. White wine. Province: Sassari. Villages: Sorso, Sennori, north of Sassari. Grape: Moscato Bianco.

A near-extinct local Muscat DOC (13 hectares survive) for a strong, sweet white, reputed better than that of Cagliari in the south. Also made as *liquoroso*.

Nasco di Cagliari DOC. White wine. Provinces: Cagliari, Oristano. Villages: same 72 communes as for Girò di Cagliari. Grape: Nasco.

Another rustic, island white more appreciated sweet and strong by the locals, but in its modernized, lighter, and drier versions by visitors.

Nuragus di Cagliari DOC. White wine. Provinces: Nuoro, Cagliari. Villages: all communes in Cagliari, nine in Nuoro. Grapes: Nuragus.

A light and essentially neutral, dry white wine, the standard resort of those who have been overwhelmed by Sardinia's more characteristic products. Can be sweet or *frizzante*.

Sardegna Semidano DOC. White wine. Province: the whole island. Grape: Semidano (minimum 85%).

Semidano is believed to be an indigenous variety, and the best quality comes from the subzone of Mogoro. Can be dry, *spumante*, or *passito*.

Vermentino di Gallura DOCG. White wine. Provinces: Sassari, Nuoro. Villages: 19 communes in the north of the island. Grape: Vermentino (minimum 95%).

Can be fresh and zesty, but if you seek a more traditional style – strong and the opposite of thirst-quenching – look out for the 14 degrees *superiore*. The sole Sardinian DOCG.

Vermentino di Sardegna DOC. White wine. Province: the whole island. Grapes: Vermentino (minimum 85%).

The wine is dry white and may also be *amabile* or *spumante*. Standards are improving but remain behind Vermentino di Gallura.

Vernaccia di Oristano DOC. White wine. Province: Oristano. Villages: 16 communes in centre-west. Grape: Vernaccia di Oristano.

On first acquaintance I found this the most appealing of all Sardinian wines: a sort of natural first cousin to Spain's Montilla, or an unfortified sherry. The grapes are slightly shrivelled before fermentation, the natural strength slows down oxidation while subtle, distinct flavours develop – such as the characteristic Italian bitterness lingering in the finish.

Leading Sardinia Producers

Argiolas ☆☆☆
Serdiana. 230 ha. www.cantine-argiolas.com
Good Cannonau and Vermentino, but really outstanding IGT Turriga: a barrique-aged blend of Cannonau, Carignano, Bovale, and Malvasia, and Korem, also from local varieties. They also make a peachy sweet Nasco called Angialis.

Capichera ☆☆–☆☆☆
Arzachena. 60 ha. www.capichera.it
A source of outstanding but expensive Vermentino. Although entitled to the DOCG Vermentino di Gallura, the Ragnedda brothers, who own the property, spurned its use and bottle their wines as IGT. In some years a late-harvested but still dry version is also produced. Carignano forms the basis of their less impressive red wines, which can be meaty and overpowering.

Giovanni Cherchi ☆☆
Usini. 18 ha.
Producers of fresh, floral Vermentino di Sardegna, and a rare red Cagnulari that has freshness and charm.

Attilio Contini ☆☆–☆☆☆
Cabras. 70 ha. www.vinicontini.it
Founded in 1898. The specialty here is Vernaccia di Oristano, including Antico Gregori, an unusual and nutty version aged for many years in a solera system. There is also a cherryish Nieddera produced from this little-seen grape variety.

Dettori ☆☆
Sennori. 18 ha. www.tenutadettori.it
Extreme wines, at least when compared to most standard Sardinian whites. The Bianco is a Vermentino given long maceration on the skins, while the Cannonau has power and alcohol. Big wines that some may find too heavy.

Cantine Dolianova ☆
Dolianova. 1,200 ha. www.cantinedolianova.com
A very large co-op producing reliable and inexpensive wines from Vermentino, Cannonau, Monica, and other varieties.

Cantina Sociale di Dorgali ☆–☆☆
Dorgali. 60 ha. www.csdorgali.com
A small cooperative specializing in Cannonau di Sardegna, the variety that also dominates its IGT blends Noriolo and Fùili.

Giuseppe Gabbas ☆☆
Nuoro. 13 ha.
Small producer with vineyards on granitic soils, making good Cannonau di Sardegna Lillovè, to drink young, and very good Dule, a blend of mainly Cannonau, Cabernet, Dolcetto, and Sangiovese, aged in barriques.

Cantina Sociale Gallura ☆☆
Tempio Pausania. 360 ha. www.cantinagallura.it
A good source for Vermentino di Gallura and Moscato di Tempio Pausania. An unusual specialty here is Nebbiolo.

Alberto Loi ☆☆
Cardedu. 63 ha.
Good Cannonau and a number of blends using only local varieties. Quality is very consistent.

Mesa ☆☆–☆☆☆
Sant'Anna Arresi. 50 ha. www.cantinamesa.it
Very good and well packaged wines, from balanced unoaked varietal wines to more complex IGTs, such as Malombra, which is Carignano with a dash of Syrah. But prices are high.

Pala ☆
Serdiana. 58 ha. www.pala.it
Sound Vermentino, Cannonau, and Monica, and a somewhat astringent blend from local varieties called S'Arai.

Agricola Punica ☆☆–☆☆☆
Santadi. 30 ha.
Founded in 2002 by Tuscan winemaker Sebastiano Rosa and the Incisas of Sassicaia, with advice from Giacomo Tachis. The sole wine is Barrua, from Carignano, enlivened with Merlot and Cabernet. Expensive.

Cantina Sociale di Santadi ☆☆☆
Santadi. 600 ha. www.cantinasantadi.it
This cooperative produces wines every bit as good as those from the best private estates, thanks to input from the great Giacomo Tachis. Very good Carignano del Sulcis, of which the best are Terre Brune and Rocca Rubia, and whites from Nasco and Vermentino. A more recent development is the late-harvested Nasco called Latinia.

Sardus Pater ☆
Sant' Antioco. 300 ha. www.cantinesarduspater.com
The Sant' Antioco cooperative has had a makeover, and is firmly focused on Carignano del Sulcis, in traditional and barrique-aged versions. Attractive Vermentino, too.

Sella e Mosca ☆☆–☆☆☆
Alghero. 500 ha. www.sellaemosca.com
Founded in 1899 by the Piedmontese Emilio Sella and Edgardo Mosca, now owned by the INVEST group. This very large property produces 500,000 cases of consistently well-made wines, focusing resolutely on local varieties.

The principal lines are Vermentino, Cannonau, chocolatey Cabernet Sauvignon (Marchese di Villamarina) using the Alghero DOC, dry white Torbato, and the celebrated and port-like Anghelu Ruju, made from partly dried grapes aged for many years in casks.

Cantina del Vermentino ☆
Monti. 500 ha. www.vermentino monti.com
There is a large output from this cooperative, including DOC Vermentino di Gallura, juicy Cannonau called Tamara, and Abbaìa, a blend of indigenous varieties.

Spain

If you had asked me five years ago whether Italy or Spain was ahead in wine quality and general interest to the outsider the clear answer was Italy. It is less clear now. Italy still has it on variety; her range of grapes is unbeatable. But throughout the last decade and more, viticultural Spain has continued to reinvent itself. Old attitudes have been changing, new ideas have been accepted – sometimes, admittedly, grudgingly – but the end result is that Spain produces more better quality wines, with more regional credibility, year by year. And it is doing so without depending excessively on international grape varieties.

Part of the reason for this has been the re-establishment of real regional feelings of identity. The Franco years put Spanish winemaking into something of a state-controlled strait-jacket, from which only the most well-established – notably Rioja and sherry – managed to manifest their individuality. Once the new constitution had restored some level of self-government to the regions, Catalonia, the Basque Country, and Galicia once again displayed their nationalist aspirations, in the bottle as well as in the ballot-box, and other regions are rediscovering a heritage that had been withered under the conformity and lack of investment that characterized the Franco era.

Of course the Spanish climate is prodigiously well-suited to viticulture: poor soils in which vines can root for nutrients and moisture, blazing summers to bring the grapes to ripeness, and, in many regions, high elevations to bring welcome night-time coolness to preserve a measure of freshness and acidity in grapes and wines. In a sense it was too easy to make wine: the sunshine did most of the work. But it was hard to make good wine: tannins, sugars, and alcohol could easily run out of control. Unbalanced wines would rapidly tire after bottling, and export markets saw no reason to take an interest in them.

However, the potential clearly was enormous, and it is now being realized. Spanish winemakers are no slouches when it comes to modern winemaking techniques, and prosperous regions such as Catalonia, Rioja, and Ribera del Diero are home to some startling new wineries that combine visual beauty with the latest technology. Regions such as Toro are rich in old vines from indigenous varieties, so these well-trained winemakers have astonishing raw materials to work with. Indeed, you could argue that Spain is now the most exciting of Europe's wine countries. This is not to say that all its wines are of a high standard.

The last edition of this book listed 59 areas of Spain as having the Denominación de Origen (DO). Today there are many more, with others, now Viños de la Tierra, queueing for promotion, not to mention the relatively new Viños de Pago, a kind of superior DO for single-estate wines of individuality with a significant track record. Many of the new DOs seem political entities rather than celebrations of excellence, and the proliferation of new official regions probably confuses consumers more than it enlightens them. Nonetheless this is testimony to the ferment within the Spanish wine industry. Spain is Europe's second-biggest country (after France) and, with 1,160,000 hectares under vine, Europe's biggest vineyard. However, the hotter climate brings the need for sparser planting patterns and lower yields, so that France and Italy still make far more wine. Spain's viticultural map is dominated by the two great rivers, the Ebro and the Duero, both of which find their source in the mountainous Cordillera Cantábrica, which divides the cool, wet northwest from the continental interior. The Ebro runs southeast into the Mediterranean in the province of Tarragona, while the Duero and flows southwest, through Portugal (where it is known as the Douro) and into the Atlantic at Oporto. These two rivers, and the mountain range in which they find their origins, are responsible for most of the microclimates of northern Spain.

South of Madrid, the sun is king; wider plantations of hardier grape varieties are the norm, and water, when it comes, is gratefully received by the spongy subsoils of the most successful wine producing districts. The principal rivers in south-central Spain are the Guadiana, which waters the great central plains of La Mancha (with part of its course actually underground) and flows west then south into the Gulf of Cádiz, having formed the boundary between Spain and Portugal for its final stretch; the Tajo (or Tagus), which flows from the plateaux of Madrid west through Toledo and Extremadura into Portugal (where it is known as the Tejo) and thence into the Atlantic at Lisbon; the Júcar, which flows south and east from the mountains of Guadalajara through the winelands of the Levante, into the Mediterranean in the province of Valencia; and the Guadalquivír, which runs southwest from the central Meseta to skirt the sherry country. These rivers are the source of nearly all the irrigation seen by most of the vineyards in the south of the country, although young vines may now be drip-irrigated to help them reach adulthood.

Climatic conditions are diverse. Most regions have a Continental climate: cold winters and baking summers. But elevation and maritime influence moderate some regions. This climatic variation, and the range of indigenous grape varieties within each region, help explain how a single country can produce wines that range from racy Albariño and salt-licked Manzanilla to mighty reds from Ribera del Duero and Priorato.

The late 1990s and early 2000s saw regions previously dismissed as mediocre emerging as potentially splendid, now that the best growers are no longer content to make dreary wines. Cigales, Priorat, Bierzo, and Toro are names that spring to mind. The well-established regions, such as Rioja, are not resting on their laurels. They have listened to the complaints of their critics and the increasing indifference of the international market, and are taking measures to improve quality. Jerez has kept its nerve and continues to produce glorious fortified wines, from the raciest Manzanilla to the most profound oloroso.

Harvesting grapes, Jerez

Spanish Wine Regions

For all the inevitable complications of the system of Denominación de Origen, there is still a natural geographical logic to the different styles of wine of Spain. The entire country, mainland and offshore islands, divides into eight major wine producing regions, each of which shares a common heritage, gastronomic culture, and climate. It is these factors, of course, that determine the way wine has evolved over the years anywhere in the Old World of wine.

The Northwest

This is the slice of Spain in the top left-hand corner, above Portugal, and along the coast of the Bay of Biscay towards France. Its southern border is the Cordillera Cantábrica, which shelters the rest of Spain from the excesses of Atlantic weather. The climate is comparatively cool and wet, the landscape is lush and green, and the original culture is non-Spanish. Celtic influences dominate in Galicia; Asturias was and is a separate principality under the Spanish Crown (exactly as is Wales in the United Kingdom); and the Basque Country has one of the oldest pre-Christian cultures in Europe. Add to this the local gastronomic culture – fish, fish, and more fish – and it is not surprising that the wines produced here have evolved to be mainly light, fresh, crisp, dry, and predominantly white.

The DOs are as follows:

Region	DO	Hectares
Galicia:	Monterrei	720
	Rías Baixas	3,650
	Ribeira Sacra	1,220
	Ribeiro	2,730
	Valdeorras	1,350
Basque Country (north):		
	Chacolí de Guetaria	327
	Chacolí de Vizcaya	240

The Upper Ebro

In the shelter of the Cordillera Cantábrica the climate is more Continental, with only the very highest vineyards (Rioja Alavesa, Navarra Estella) gaining some benefit from the influences of the Bay of Biscay. Politically, the area is sandwiched between the Spanish heartland of Castile-León and the resolutely non-Spanish region of Catalonia, while some of the Rioja vineyards fall within the Basque region.

In the fifteenth and sixteenth centuries, the royal house switched capitals throughout the region as Castilian, Catalan, and Aragonés monarchs married each other and merged their kingdoms, so there were always rich and powerful people with money available for good quality wine. The main gastronomic influence here is meat – whether from herds and flocks or running wild in the forests – so it is no surprise that this is predominantly red wine country.

The final quality "burnish" was provided towards the end of the nineteenth century when phylloxera devastated the French vineyards, and a vast but discerning export market opened up for this, the region closest to the French border.

The DOs are as follows:

Region	DO	Hectares
La Rioja:	Rioja DOCa	63,500
Navarra:	Navarra	18,400
Aragón:	Calatayud	5,600
	Campo de Borja	7,400
	Cariñena	16,000
	Somontano	4,700

The Duero Valley

With one exception, this area has most of the attributes of the Upper Ebro: a Continental climate – although higher and rather cooler here – abundant food on the hoof, in the fields and forests, and a population of rich, influential people from Valladolid and Zamora, where royal courts once sat, to Salamanca, site of Spain's oldest university. So we may expect quality red wines to have been supplied to princes, bishops, and professors.

The difference in style between the Duero and the Upper Ebro is export influence. In the Upper Ebro they made wine to please the French market, as well as themselves; in the Duero they made wine to please themselves. The result, traditionally, was wines with more fruit and more alcohol, and it is still apparent today. While Rioja was still devoted to long ageing in American oak, the Duero was shipping in new French barriques.

The DOs are as follows:

Region	DO	Hectares
Castile-León:	Arlanza	410
	Arribes	750
	Bierzo	4,000
	Cigales	2,550
	Ribera del Duero	20,700
	Rueda	8,075
	Tierra de León	1,500
	Tierra del Viño de Zamora	790
	Toro	6,100

Catalonia & The Balearics

The culture here has always been a fiercely independent one. Catalonia (along with the Balearic Islands and other territories) was a Mediterranean power in the Middle Ages and, in its thinking, traditionally looks to the sea rather than inland towards Madrid. The style of cooking here is strongly Mediterranean in character – indeed, very similar to the neighbouring French region of Roussillon. Gastronomy leans heavily in favour of fish, of course, as well as very local and sophisticated versions of "surf and turf"; consequently, the wines that evolved naturally in the region were largely simple whites and *rosados* to suit the cookery.

The independent spirit of the region, however, encouraged early experimentation with non-Spanish grape varieties, and this continues today, as Catalonia is as strong on new-wave varietal wines as on its traditional styles. Most Cava – Spain's best sparkling wine – is also produced here.

The DOs are as follows:

Region	DO	Hectares
Catalonia:	Alella	315
	Catalunya	54,500
	Conca de Barberà	5,800
	Costers del Segre	4,720
	Empordà-Costa Brava	2,000
	Montsant	2,050
	Penedès	26,170
	Pla de Bages	550
	Priorato	1,725
	Tarragona	7,250
	Terra Alta	6,380
	Cava	32,300
Balearics:	Binissalem (Mallorca)	600
	Plà i Llevant (Mallorca)	335

The Levante

The export culture evident in Catalonia is even better developed in this region. The hot Mediterranean-maritime climate is ideal for the production of everyday wine. Local consumption of fish dishes (the paella was invented here) has resulted in the evolution of a plentiful supply of adequate uncomplicated whites and *rosados*, but the region's main claim to fame is its resolutely "out-to-sea" vision. Once it had acquired modern technology, the Levante became the powerhouse of Spanish exports of low-cost wines. Valencia is the country's biggest wine port, dispatching its products all over the world.

The DOs are as follows:

Region	DO	Hectares
Valencia:	Alicante	13,200
	Manchuela	4,000
	Utiel-Requena	41,400
	Valencia	15,000
Murcia:	Bullas	2,260
	Jumilla	30,000
	Yecla	7,200

The Meseta

The winemaking culture here is based on survival. There was no market for the wines of Spain's great central plateau until Madrid was founded in 1561. There was no chance of shipping them to the Levantine coast because in the south the (nominally teetotal) Moors ruled until 1492. Although food was abundant, the methods of cooking it were plain, and the climate is so searingly hot in the summer and freezing in the winter that only the hardiest of vines could survive. As a result of these factors, the wine was poor and rustic and made in the cheapest available material (earthenware jars) because there was only the local market to satisfy. Wine transport, here and in most of Spain, was in animal skins. The main contact with the outside world was the royal road from Madrid to Granada. One of the stopping-off places for official retinues was the town of Valdepeñas, and this became, and remains, a ready market for better-quality wines. This isolation and the resulting low land prices led to massive redevelopment in the 1970s and '80s, with the result that many of today's everyday wines will have a La Mancha DO.

The DOs are as follows:

Region	DO	Hectares
Madrid:	Vinos de Madrid	7,460
Castilla-La Mancha:	Almansa	7,600
	La Mancha	187,000
	Méntrida	9,050
	Mondéjar	1,100
	Ribera del Guadiana	26,000
	Uclés	1,500
	Valdepeñas	28,300

Andalucía

This is the crucible of winemaking for Spain and a good deal of Western Europe. The Greeks and other winemakers from the eastern Mediterranean settled here some 3,000 years ago, and the wines they made were in the Levantine or Greek tradition: products of a fiercely hot climate with ameliorating influences around the coast, in order to meet the demands of burgeoning export markets throughout the Mediterranean – especially during the Roman Empire – and the western European coast.

The Greek taste was for powerful sweet wines with plenty of alcohol. Centuries later it is possible to see the legacy of the Greeks in the fortified wines of Andalucía. By the time of Shakespeare, the wines of southern Spain, known then as "sack" after the Spanish word *saca*, meaning "withdrawal" (ie. from the butt), were famous. Today, the wines of this area find their being in one of the world's greatest wines – sherry.

The DOs are as follows:

Region	DO	Hectares
Andalucía:	Condado de Huelva	4,500
	Jerez/Xérès/Sherry	10,100
	Málaga	1,215
	Montilla-Moriles	7,000

The Canary Islands

In some ways a snapshot of what Spanish wine used to be like 500 years ago, when they were rediscovered and claimed for the Spanish crown. Varieties are grown here that died out on the peninsula centuries ago, production is small, and the "Canary-Sack" of Shakespearean fame is now a minority taste. Production evolved for local consumption and has developed to supply the prospering tourist trade. Tourists get some pleasant surprises.

The DOs are as follows:

Region	DO	Hectares
Canarias:	Abona (Tenerife)	1,150
	La Gomera	180
	Gran Canaria	226
	El Hierro	200
	Lanzarote	2,000
	La Palma	775
	Tacoronte-Acentejo	1,150
	Valle de Güímar	640
	Valle de la Orotava	615
	Ycoden-Daute-Isora	310

Northwest Spain

Galicia

Galicia and the north coastal vineyards of the Bay of Biscay enjoy a wetter, cooler climate than the rest of Spain, and the wines are commensurately lighter and fresher. White wines predominate, although reds and *rosados* are widely made. In the ongoing search for the definitive white wine of Spain, this area is one of the leading contenders.

Monterrei

This is a very small region of white wines from the Godello and Dona Blanca grapes. Quality is potentially good.

Rías Baixas

In the province of Pontevedra on the Atlantic coast between Santiago and the Portuguese border. The most excellent wines are whites made from the Albariño grape, but planting on steep slopes and in small parcels means they lack economy of scale and are expensive. Most whites are vinified in tanks, but some producers are seeking greater complexity by putting the wine through malolactic fermentation and, in some cases, maturation in small oak barrels.

Ribeira Sacra

A beautiful area at the confluence of two rivers, the Sil and the Miño. Much of the winemaking is on a small and simple scale, but some winemakers have invested in new technology. The wines need to show more concentration and flavour, but there is some excellent Albariño and Godello. Although most producers make red wine from a grape called the Mencía, very few do it well.

Ribeiro

An old-established area in the province of Orense, lying just east of Rías Baixas. The vineyards are concentrated in the valleys of the Miño, Avía, and Arnoya rivers. Ribeiro is famous for its light, fruity white wines. New development has provided it with some stars – mainly made from the Albariño, but also from the more widely planted (and much lower priced) Treixadura. Caiño is the most important red variety. Overall, good-value whites that can be considered the poor man's Rías Baixas.

Valdeorras

Both crisp, fresh whites and light reds are made: the whites from the excellent Godello variety, and the reds from the potentially good but usually under-achieving Mencía grape.

Basque Country

Chacolí de Guetaria (Getariako Txakolina) and Chacolí de Vizcaya (Bizkaiko Txakolina) are the two indigenous wines of the Basque Country. Most is white, made from the local Ondarribi Zuri grape. Waiters like to pour it from a height to work up some excitement. At its best it is a very crisp, grapey, thirst-quenching wine, although the quantity is so small that exports are virtually non-existent.

Leading Northwest Spain Producers

Dominio do Bibei ☆☆–☆☆☆
Manzaneda, Ribeira Sacra. www.dominiodobibei.com
An ambitious project by Javier Dominguez, who has hired Priorat veterans René Barbier and Sara Perez to make the wines: spicy, intense Lalama from Mencía, as well as a red blend and a pure Godello. They are expensive but handcrafted, from old vines grown at high elevations.

Condes de Albarei ☆–☆☆
Cambados, Rías Baixas. 170 ha. www.salnesur.com
A cooperative specializing in different styles of Albariño. Production is substantial, at around 1.5 million bottles.

Fillaboa ☆☆–☆☆☆
Salvaterra do Miño, Rías Baixas. 70 ha.
www.bodegasfillaboa.com
A pioneer of barrel-fermentation for Albariño, as well as of keeping the wine in prolonged contact with the lees. Very consistent quality. In 2000, the winery introduced a new prestige bottling called Selección Finca Monte Alto.

Galegas ☆☆–☆☆☆
Salvaterra de Miño, Rías Baixas. 40 ha.
www.galiciano.com
This relatively new winery, founded in 1995, specializes in different styles of Albariño, including the barrel-aged Veigadares and Gran Veigadares. The floral, citric Gran Veigadares, made from rigorously selected grapes, has been hailed as one of Spain's finest white wines.

Godeval ☆☆
O Barco. 17 ha. www.godeval.com
A small property located in the medieval priory of Xagoaza, and producing outstanding Godello white.

Lagar de Fornelos ☆☆–☆☆☆
O Rosal, Rías Baixas. 75 ha. www.riojalta.com
A bodega near the Portuguese border, making crisp, appley tasting wine, a pure Albariño called Lagar de Cervera. In 1988, the bodega was bought by Bodegas La Rioja Alta (q.v.), which has invested large amounts of money, which have helped to make this wine one of Galicia's best.

Martín Códax ☆
Cambados, Rías Baixas. 240 ha. www.martincodax.com
Eighty-five growers send their Albariño grapes to an up-to-date, stainless-steel winery north of Vigo. As well as good, clean, fragrant dry wines, there are two reds from the growers' vineyards in Bierzo.

Viña Mein ☆–☆☆
Leiro, Ribeiro. 16 ha. www.vinamein.com
Treixadura is the principal variety here, and Mein produces a barrel-fermented version and an unoaked wine that is wonderfully floral and delicate.

Gerardo Méndez ☆☆–☆☆☆
Meaño, Rías Baixas. www.bodegasgerardomendez.com
A boutique winery producing outstanding Albariño do Ferreiro, persistent in flavour, from extremely old vines.

Viña Nora ☆☆–☆☆☆
As Neves, Rías Baixas. 12 ha.
Pure Albariño with great intensity and creaminess, and some well handled oak.

Palacio de Fefiñanes ☆☆–☆☆☆
Cambados, Rías Baixas. www.fefinanes.com
The aristocrat of Galician wine, issuing from the small modern bodega in the palace of Fefiñanes, owned by the Marqués de Figueroa. It is 100% Albariño, but some *cuvées* are aged for up to 30 months in oak. They bear no resemblance to Vinho Verde, except in their remarkable freshness.

Rafael Palacios ☆☆–☆☆
A Rúa, Valdeorras. 14 ha. www.rafaelpalacios.com
An ambitious winery, offering As Sortes, a flamboyant barrique-aged Godello, as well as a lemony, unoaked Louro do Bolos.

Pazo de Señorans ☆☆–☆☆☆
Meis, Rías Baixas. 8 ha. www.pazodesenorans.com
As well as a standard Albariño, the estate produces a remarkable Selección de Anada, which is aged three years *sur lie* in tanks. It retains the tautness and zest of the variety, but has more weight and honeyed tones.

Rebolledo ☆–☆☆
A Rúa, Valdeorras. www.joaquinrebolledo.com
A property producing a pure Mencía red, in unoaked and oaked versions, and a successful Cabernet/Merlot, with upfront fruit that suggests it is best enjoyed young.

Vitivinícola del Ribeiro ☆–☆☆
Ribadavia, Ribeiro. 600 ha.
www.vinoribeiro.com
A quality-conscious cooperative with 800 members. The basic range is Pazo, but the more interesting wines, from Treixadura and Albariño, are under the Colección label.

Santiago Ruiz ☆☆–☆☆☆
O Rosal, Rías Baixas. 38 ha.
www.bodegasantiagoruiz.com
Small producer of high-quality white wine, commanding a high price. Unusual blend of Albariño, Loureira, and three other varieties makes an especially aromatic, floral, dry white.

A Tapada ☆☆
Rubía de Valdeorras. 11 ha.
Under the brand name Guitián, Tapada produces excellent Godello, including lush, weighty Sobra Lias, aged on the fine lees.

Terras Gaudas ☆–☆☆
O Rosal, Rías Baixas. 87 ha. www.terrasgaudas.com
Since 1990, this estate has been built up into a major player in Rías Baixas, producing a pure Albariño, and a more complex blend of this grape with Caiño and Loureira. The expensive Black Label is aged in new oak – an acquired taste.

Valdesil ☆–☆☆
Vilamartín de Valdeorras. ww.valdesil.com
An organic estate producing grassy red Mencía, and a pure Godello called Valdesil.

The Upper Ebro

Although understandably dominated by Rioja, recent developments in Navarra and, particularly, the Somontano region of Aragón, have brought the whole region forcefully to the forefront of quality winemaking in Spain.

La Rioja

As a wine region, Rioja claims a longer history than Bordeaux. Some French historians believe that the Romans may even have found the ancestor of the Cabernet in this part of Spain, and trace its ancestry back from here to Albania. Certainly the Romans followed the River Ebro up from the Mediterranean, much as they followed the Rhône, as a corridor of the climate and conditions they were accustomed to into a colder and more hostile land. High in the headwaters of the Ebro, over 600 metres up (1,950 feet), round its little tributary Río Oja, they found ideal conditions for wine of good quality.

The post-classical history of Rioja was similar to that of all the Roman wine regions. Rapid decline (accelerated in Spain by the Moorish invasion), the dominance of the Church, a slow renaissance in the sixteenth century, but no real changes until the eighteenth or early nineteenth centuries. Then it was the influence of Bordeaux that reached Rioja, the new idea of barrel-ageing the best wines as opposed to keeping them in animal hides. It was first tried in 1787, but was overruled by Luddite reaction, and finally introduced by reforming aristocratic landowners – in much the same way and at the same time as Chianti was "invented" by the Barone Ricasoli.

The first commercial bodegas of the modern age of Rioja were founded in the 1860s, by the Marqués de Riscal and the Marqués de Murrieta, with the Bordeaux château system very much in mind. Both used (and still use) grapes from their immediate districts. They sold their wine in bottle, and spread the reputation of the region at a most opportune moment. Phylloxera was invading Bordeaux, and French capital and technology were looking for a new region to develop. Before the end of the century, a dozen much bigger new bodegas had been built, drawing on grapes from a much wider area; the three regions of Rioja all con-

Adding wax capsules to bottles

tributed to their blends. The railhead at Haro formed the nucleus for this boom, and the bodegas round it remain both physically and spiritually the embodiment of late Victorian technology. The cluster of huge, rather raffish buildings almost recalls Epernay, the Champagne capital, which grew during the same lush decades.

Phylloxera reached Rioja in the early years of the twentieth century. The disruption, followed by World War I, then by the Spanish Civil War, prevented the bodegas from capitalizing on the foreign markets they had successfully opened, despite the fact that in 1926 Rioja became the first wine region of Spain to set up a Consejo Regulador to supervise its affairs. During this period, the region was making and maturing some superlative vintages (examples can still be found occasionally). Yet Rioja remained the staple of connoisseurs only in Spain and Latin America until the international wine boom of the 1970s. That decade saw the founding of a new wave of bodegas, a flurry of takeovers, and a vast increase in planting and production. It also saw modifications in winemaking techniques, which have added new styles to the already wide range produced. Today there are around 1,200 bodegas in the region.

Rioja is in fact three regions, with a total vineyard area of more than 63,500 hectares, following the valley of the Ebro from the Conchas de Haro, the rocky gorge where it bursts through the Sierra Cantábrica, to its much wider valley at Alfaro, 95 kilometres (60 miles) east and nearly 300 metres (975 feet) lower in altitude. The highest region, La Rioja Alta, has the city of Logroño as its capital, although the much smaller Haro is its vinous heart. Cenicero, Fuenmayor, and Navarrete are the other towns with bodegas. There are 20,500 hectares of vineyards. The soils are a mixture of chalky clay, iron-rich clay, and alluvial silt. The climate is cool here, and the rainfall relatively high. Rioja Alta wines have the highest acidity, but also the finest flavour and structure, finesse, and "grip" that sometimes allows them to age almost indefinitely.

The Rioja Alavesa, north of the Ebro in the Basque province of Alava, has more southern slopes and a more consistently clay soil. Its 11,500 hectares are largely Tempranillo, which here gives particularly fragrant, smooth, almost lush, light wine, tending to be pale and quick-maturing. A dozen bodegas are based in four villages: Labastida, Elciego, Laguardia, and Oyón. The Rioja Baja ("Lower Rioja"), with 18,000 hectares, has much the warmest and driest climate. Its soil is silt and iron-rich clay, its principal grape the Garnacha Tinta, and its wine stronger, broader, and less fine. Although there are few wineries here, nearly all Rioja bodegas buy some of their wine here, and several have been planting the finer grapes in the highest parts of the region. It is probably true to say that most red Riojas are blends of wines from all three regions, although the old-established bodegas draw most heavily on the areas in which they were founded, and a few in Rioja Alavesa make a particular point of the regional style of their wines.

Rioja DOCa

From the 1991 vintage, Rioja was elevated to a new "super-category" called Denominación de Origen Calificada, which translates as "Qualified Denomination of Origin". The word "qualified" in this context means a guarantee of quality, rather than its normal English interpretation of "with reservations", and is an attempt to offer an extra guarantee to the customer, exactly like the DOCG in Italy. The main consequence in the outside world is that bulk sales have been stopped, and all Rioja is now bottled in the region. The result, at least in the short-term, seems to have been that there is a lot less poor-quality wine appearing under the Rioja label. Long ageing in Bordeaux-type barrels is the hallmark of traditional Rioja. It gives the wines, whether red or white, an easily recognized fragrance and flavour related to vanilla. The best wines, with a concentrated flavour of ripe fruit, can support a surprising degree of this oaky overlay. Lesser wines become exhausted by it, losing their fruity sweetness and becoming dry and mono-tone. Spanish taste, traditionally focused on long ageing in oak, is gradually adapting. The most traditional red Riojas still have a market but it's a shrinking one, and younger people are fervent in their preference for richer, gutsier wines. Many of the traditional bodegas have modernized their wine (with earlier bottling and a faster turnover of oak barrels) on the quiet, for fear of alarming their customers, and have introduced new-style *cuvées* in an attempt to please everybody. Drink a traditional-style wine regularly and you might not notice the difference from year to year; but compare wines from ten years apart and you would. Red wines make up three-quarters of the total production of the region. The range offered by a typical Rioja bodega includes some or all of the following:

Vinos Blancos

White wines, normally very dry, principally made of the Viura grape (alias Macabeo), with or without Malvasía and/or Garnacha Blanca. They have good acidity and resist oxidation well. Made in the old way they had little grape aroma, but often very satisfying structure and balance. Better whites were formerly all aged in old oak barrels for between about three and anything up to 12 years – the best longest. Outstanding examples of these Reservas remain pale lemon-yellow and keep an astonishing freshness, roundness, and vigour beneath a great canopy of oaky fragrance. They can be compared with the best old vintages of white Graves. Sadly, this highly individual, if admittedly very old-fashioned, style has lost ground to the vogue for fresh, crisp, white wines. Few drinkers are aware how much they have lost.

Many bodegas now make all or some of their whites by long, slow fermentation followed by almost immediate bottling, the object being to capture primary grape aromas in all their freshness. The Viura makes delicious wine in this style, possibly benefiting from some bottle age. Many bodegas also make a compromise, semi-modern white, cold fermented, and briefly oak aged. Sweet white Riojas are rarely a success. Noble rot is very rare in the dry, upland atmosphere; overripe grapes are simply half-raisined. But exceptional vintages have produced beautiful, delicate, and aromatic sweet wines of apparently limitless lasting power.

Vinos Rosados

Rosé wines, made in the customary way, normally dry and pale and not oak-aged.

Vinos Tintos

Many bodegas now call all their red wines *tinto*. The former custom was to divide them into *clarete*, light-coloured red wine of fairly low strength bottled in Bordeaux bottles; and *tinto* (sometimes called "Borgoña") sold in burgundy bottles. Tinto in this sense is much darker, more fruity, fuller in body, and higher in alcohol. Both are made of a mixture of Tempranillo, the dominant red grape, with the luscious and aromatic Graciano, and the alcoholic Garnacha Tinta (the Rhône Grenache), often with some Mazuelo (or Cariñena), the Carignan of the Midi. Cabernet Sauvignon is accepted as an "experimental" variety, but is occasionally included. There are also wines from pure Tempranillo. All styles are equally made up to the level of Reservas or Gran Reservas, but Rioja's ultimate glories tend to be of the *tinto* type, which resists barrel-ageing better without growing thin and (although less fragrant) can grow marvellously velvety in the bottle.

All wines can be sold either as *joven* ("young"), which means "without oak ageing", or *con crianza*. A *vino de crianza* must spend at least 12 months in *barricas*, or 225-litre barrels. Reservas are specially selected wines at least three years old, of which one year was in *barricas*. Now, however, any of the statutory period can be substituted by twice as long in bottle. White Reservas have a minimum of six months in oak. Gran Reservas are wines of at least five years old, with at least two years in *barricas*, or twice as long in bottle. These requirements for ageing are much less than they were only a few years ago. The reason given is the change in tastes, although commercial necessity points in the same direction.

Reputable bodegas will, of course, only select wines of fine quality to mature as Reservas, and top quality as Gran Reservas – although this is only implied, not required, by the regulations. While a few of the grand bodegas have continued on their majesticway, well-made but rather washed-out wines, ideas that were once innovative have become more normal. French oak rubs shoulders with American in many bodegas, and quite often some of the barrels are new barriques. Greater care is being taken with fruit quality, too, with wines made from low-yielding vineyards and riper grapes.

Traditionalists might worry that these sumptuous, and often high-priced, new wines lack Rioja typicity, but at present there is sufficient variety of style within the region to please everybody. Another interesting development has been the revival of local varieties other than the ubiquitous Tempranillo. Graciano, Mazuelo, and Maturana can hold their own, as some bodegas are demonstrating.

Leading Rioja Producers

Finca Allende ☆☆☆
Briones. 42 ha. www.finca-allende.com
A small property run by Miguel Angel de Gregorio, who is fanatical about vineyard quality. Both Viura and Malvasía are used for the barrique aged white. The highly aromatic, red-fruit-scented Calvario comes from a single vineyard planted in 1945, and Aurus is a top blend, aged, perhaps excessively, for two years in barriques. Prices are high.

Alavesas ☆
Laguardia. 91 ha. www.solardesamaniego.com
This company makes typically pale, light, fragrant Alavesa wines, including Reservas under the name Solar de Samaniego.

Artadi ☆☆–☆☆☆
Laguardia. 70 ha. www.artadi.com
Founded in 1985 as a cooperative, Artadi is now a public company. All the wines are pure Tempranillo, and the best of them are aged in mostly French oak. They are single-vineyard wines or blends from very old vines, and have the structure to absorb the oakiness. The wines are first rate, but their toasty, chocolatey tones may seem atypical to many Rioja admirers.

Baigorri ☆☆
Samaniego. www.bodegasbaigorri.com
A modern, gravity-fed winery aiming for modern-style wines. The rather heavy white is fermented in new barriques. As for the reds, in addition to the usual Rioja hierarchy of quality, there is a wine frankly called De Garage, from old-vine Tempranillo fermented in wooden vats and aged outdoors in new barriques. The higher qualities seem rather effortful, but the Crianza is always spicy and fresh.

Baron de Ley ☆☆
Mendavia. 90 ha. www.barondeley.com
As well as the reliable standard range, there is an admirable single-vineyard Finca Monasterio, aged in new French oak, a toasty example of new wave Rioja.

Beronia ☆
Ollauri. 20 ha. www.beronia.es
Sound, easy-drinking wines, including varietal wines from Viura, Tempranillo, and Mazuelo.

Bilbaínas ☆–☆☆☆
Haro. 250 ha. www.bodegasbilbainas.com
The bodega was founded in 1901, and is now owned by the Cava company, Codorníu. The company's vineyards are planted in Haro (Rioja Alta) and Elciego, Leza, and Laguardia in Alavesa. Their aim is a wide choice of wines rather than a strong house style, but the principal wines are conservative: rather austere by modern standards. Viña Zaco is a high quality *clarete*, while Viña Pomal is its more full-bodied *tinto* complement. Pomal Reservas are the biggest and longest-lived wines, but Codorníu has introduced new barrique-aged wines, such as La Vicalanda from a ten hectare parcel, and Vicuana, which contains 25% Graciano.

Ramón Bilbao ☆☆
Haro. 50 ha. www.bodegasramonbilbao.es
Founded in 1924; a family owned company that buys in most of its wine and grapes from private vineyards. The reds are pure Tempranillo, the barrique-aged white pure Viura. Mirto is the top wine, barrique-aged and somewhat overwrought.

Bretón ☆☆
Navarrete. 160 ha. www.bodegasbreton.com
A large winery, producing good red wines under many

labels: the good-value Loriñón, Dominio de Comte, and the barrique-aged Alba de Bretón.

Marqués de Cáceres ☆–☆☆
Cenicero. www.marquesdecaceres.com
Founded in 1970 by Enrique Forner, planned with the help of Professor Emile Peynaud, and now one of the most modern of wineries. Grapes come from dozens of local growers, including the Cenicero cooperative. The wines are traditionally made but emerge less oaky than traditional Rioja, but well-balanced and fruity. The white is modern-style and unoaked, and still one of the best. Like many other Rioja wineries, Marqués de Cáceres has introduced a flagship wine called Gaudium: a rich, tannic blend of Garnacha, Graciano, and Tempranillo, and an even more exclusive, *garagiste* label, MC.

Campillo ☆–☆☆
Laguardia. 70 ha. www.bodegascampillo.com
This bodega resembles a South American presidential palace, but the interior is designed with care to ensure perfect temperature and humidity control for the ageing wines. The company forms part of the Faustino group (q.v.), and the wines, although soundly made, are fairly dull, with the exception of the ripe and silky Gran Reservas.

Campo Viejo ☆–☆☆
Logroño. www.domecqbodegas.com
One of the largest bodegas, part of the Juan Alcorta group and thus owned by Pernod Ricard. Much of the fruit is drawn from the 2,000 hectares of vines owned the group. Campo Viejo is consistently good value among the less ethereal red Riojas. Marqués de Villamagna is the bodega's top Gran Reserva, and there is a rich, barrel-fermented white from Viura.

Luis Cañas ☆☆☆
Villabuena. 90 ha. www.luiscanas.com
Luis Cañas is now in his eighties but still checks the grapes as they arrive at the winery during harvest. His descendants have successfully transformed the company into one of the best modern bodegas. The wines are excellent at all levels, from the lively redcurranty Crianza, to the Cabernet-tinged Reserva de la Familia, the old vine Amaren, and the *garagiste* Hiru 3 Racimos.

Contino ☆☆–☆☆☆☆
Laguardia. 62 ha. www.cvne.com
A single estate, with CVNE in charge of the winemaking. The aim is to produce the Viña del Olivo, which is aged for 18 months in small barrels, which contribute both a savoury quality and a silky texture. There is also a pungent and exciting varietal Graciano. When the grapes do not come up to the required standard, they are sold to CVNE for blending.

El Coto ☆–☆☆
Oyón. 150 ha. www.elcoto.com
A company producing large volumes of soft, commercial wines, but the Reserva is of above-average quality.

CVNE (Compañía Vinícola del Norte de España) ☆–☆☆☆☆
Haro. 560 ha. www.cvne.com
One of the top half-dozen Rioja houses, founded in 1879 by the Real de Asúa brothers and still owned by this family. Its own vineyards provide half of the grapes needed for red wine. Other vineyards are under contract. Reds include the excellent, vigorous Cune; the elegant, velvety Imperial (a Reservas from the Rioja Alta); and the notably full-bodied, spicy Viña Real from Alavesa, and, since 1995, the opulent old-vine Pagos de Viña Real. For white wines, CVNE used to be best-known for its traditional, oak-flavoured Viura white called Monopole, but today the wine is only lightly oaked, whereas the Viña Real white is barrel-fermented in new oak. Given that production is close to eight million bottles, quality is consistently high.

Domecq ☆–☆☆☆
Elciego. www.domecqbodegas.com
Founded in the early 1970s by the sherry house of Pedro Domecq (q.v.) and Canadian drinks giant Seagram. When the two parted company in 1974, Domecq built a modern bodega and began planting new vineyards and buying old ones in Alavesa. The company employs the Marqués de Arienzo brand, which is made as Reserva, Gran Reserva, and Reserva Especial.

Faustino ☆☆
Oyón. 650 ha. www.bodegasfaustino.com
Founded in 1860 and still family owned and run. All grapes come from around the Oyón area in Rioja Alavesa. Faustino V, the red Reserva; Faustino I, the Gran Reserva; and the aromatic, lemony white in the new style, are made largely from its own grapes from first class vineyards. The reds are given extra age in bottle rather than spending over-long in oak. A more recent addition to the range is Faustino de Autor, a new-style Reserva aged two years in French oak.

Viña Hermosa ☆–☆☆
Gimileo. 10 ha. www.santiagoijalba.com
A relative newcomer, established in 1998, and using Viña Hermosa as its main brand. In 2004 it launched a savoury new-oaked Reserva called Ogga. At present the wines are dogged rather than exciting.

Ijalba ☆☆–☆☆☆☆
Logroño. 80 ha. www.ijalba.com
The Ijalba vineyards, now mostly organic, are in Rioja Alta. The company has its own specialty: a range of wines from indigenous varieties other than Tempranillo. Maturana (white and red) and Graciano give impressive results here, giving rise to regrets that these varieties are bound to remain marginal within Rioja as a whole. Maturana is a touch rustic, but has tremendous personality, while Graciano shows consistent freshness and finesse.

LAN ☆–☆☆☆☆
Fuenmayor. 72 ha. www.bodegaslan.com
This large company, founded in 1974, changed hands in 2002, when it was acquired by Mercapita, a Madrid-based finance house. With annual production at three million bottles, LAN sources most of its fruit from contract growers. The basic ranges are of little interest, but the top wines, such

as the fruit-forward Lan a Mano, and the powerful, new-oaked Culmen, are first-rate.

Lopez de Heredia ☆☆☆–☆☆☆☆
Haro. 150 ha. www.lopezheredia.com
One of the great bastions of Rioja tradition. A family owned bodega founded by Don Raphael Lopez de Heredia y Landeta in 1877; today the winemaker is his fifth generation descendant Maria-José Lopez de Heredia. The premises, on a railway siding at Haro, are a marvel of art nouveau design, with tunnelled cellars Wagnerian in their cobwebbed splendour. (In total contrast, the new tasting room is an ultra-modern confection by architect Zaha Hadid.)

Approximately half the grapes come from its own vineyards in Rioja Alta and most of the rest from small local growers. All the wines are fermented and aged long in oak: the minimum is three years, and the Gran Reservas still spend at least nine years in cask. Indeed, the company has its own cooperage. Wines include weighty *rosado*, Tondonia (fine red and white not less than 4 *años*), Bosconia (a bigger red, at best sumptuous), Gravonia (an oaky white), and Cubillo, a red, and at 3 *años* the youngest wine. A 1947 Bosconia Gran Reserva was still intense and persistent in 2008, and the white Tondonia can age almost as long, all the while retaining its freshness.

Martínez Bujanda ☆☆–☆☆☆
Oyón. 400 ha.
www.familiamartinezbujanda.com
This old family has diverse winemaking interests, producing a wide range of wines, some of them varietal, under the Valdemar label. In 1999 it launched a resounding single-vineyard Rioja from the 80-hectare Finca Valpiedra.

Montecillo ☆☆
Fuenmayor. www.osborne.es
Part of the Osborne sherry group. Using the labels Viña Monty and Viña Cumbrero, it produces enjoyable, fruity Riojas of little complexity but great consistency.

Muga ☆☆☆
Haro. 150 ha. www.bodegasmuga.com
A small family firm founded in 1932 by Don Isaac Muga. His son, Don Isaac Muga Caño, took over on his father's death in 1969, and two years later moved to a new bodega by the famous Haro railway station. Muga remains very traditional, but their wines are consistently excellent, even the Crianza.

Much the best wine to my taste is the dark, rich Gran Reserva Prado Enea, a wine with some of the velvet pungency of burgundy. The launch of a *prestige cuvée* called Torre Muga has done much to raise the profile of the winery: it's a rich, oaky, fruity wine built for long ageing.

Marqués de Murrieta ☆☆☆–☆☆☆☆
Logroño. 300 ha. www.marquesdemurrieta.com
With Marqués de Riscal, one of the two noble houses of Rioja,

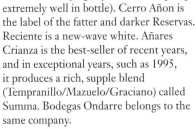

the first two bodegas to be founded, still with a special cachet, and remarkably unchanged by time. Don Luciano de Murrieta y García-Lemoine founded this, the second oldest, in 1872. In 1983, control passed to Vicente Cebrian, Count of Creixell.

Its own vineyards at Ygay near Logroño supply the majority of grapes. Wines are made by wholly traditional methods and maintain a very high standard. The small range includes the dense but magnificent white Capellanía, an elegant Reserva, and the rare and expensive Castillo Ygay – released with a decade or more of age. The Creixells have also created a micro-winery called Dalmau, dedicated to eponymous barrique aged wines, slightly jammy, but with immense concentration.

Bodegas Olarra ☆☆
Logroño. www.bodegasolarra.es
The most stylish bodega in Rioja, formed of three wings to symbolize Rioja's three regions, would look better in the Napa Valley than on an industrial estate outside Logroño. It owns no vines, but has rapidly made a name for typical and stylish wines, red and white (the white very lightly oaked and ageing extremely well in bottle). Cerro Añon is the label of the fatter and darker Reservas. Reciente is a new-wave white. Añares Crianza is the best-seller of recent years, and in exceptional years, such as 1995, it produces a rich, supple blend (Tempranillo/Mazuelo/Graciano) called Summa. Bodegas Ondarre belongs to the same company.

Ontañón
Logroño. 250 ha. www.ontanon.es
The Pérez family own lofty vineyards in Rioja Baja but age the wines in a former sweet factory in Logroño. Most of the wines are unexceptional but Arteso, from old vines, is aged, but only briefly, in new oak and shows ripe berry fruit and excellent balance.

Palacio ☆–☆☆
Laguardia. www.bodegapalacio.es
Once a Seagram property, Palacio is now part of the Antonio Barcelo group. All grapes are purchased. There are two labels: Glorioso, and the barrique-aged Cosme Palacio, developed originally by Michel Rolland. Neither wine reaches great heights, but they are soundly made and eminently drinkable.

Palacios Remondo ☆☆☆
Alfaro. 100 ha. www.vinosherenciaremondo.com
Founded by Don José Palacios Remondo in 1947 and still in the family. After Don José's death, there was a reorganization of the company, and the brilliant winemaker Alvaro Palacios took over, insisting on changes that would improve quality. Brands are Herencia Remondo, Plácet (a barrique-aged Viura white), and the elegant, concentrated La Montesa.

Federico Paternina ☆
Haro. www.paternina.com

Ysios winery, Laguardia

One of the largest bodegas, now a public company. Paternina buys in all its grapes from cooperatives and growers. Wines include Banda Azul (a variable but popular young red), Viña Vial (full and fruity Reserva), and the weightier Conde de los Andes.

Pujanza ☆☆–☆☆☆
Laguardia. www.bodegaspujanza.com
Although founded as recently as 1998, Pujanza has swiftly displayed a flair for high quality. The regular wines are rich and fruity, while the top bottling, Norte, has toastiness, freshness, and persistence.

Vinícola Real ☆☆–☆☆☆
Albelda de Iruega. www.vinicolareal.com
A new star, south of Logroño, especially for the suave 200 Monges Reserva. The property was only founded in 1989, and is a fine example of the small-scale, vineyard-focused, yet forward-looking family bodega.

Remelluri ☆☆–☆☆☆
Labastida. 105 ha. www.remelluri.com
An unusual organic estate planted at a high elevation, which gives the wines good acidic structure. After fermentation the reds are racked into large casks, and after 12 months of ageing, the maturation process continues in barriques for two years.

Yet the wines are not excessively oaky; instead, they have deep colour, voluptuous fruit, and supple tannins. Viognier and Chardonnay have been planted to produce an unorthodox barrel-fermented white that blends local and international varieties.

La Rioja Alta ☆–☆☆☆
Haro. 450 ha. www.riojalta.com
One of the group of top-quality firms round the station at Haro. Founded in 1890 and with descendants of the founders still on the board. It owns vineyards at various sites in Rioja, and also buy in grapes from local producers. The white wines here were always dull, and from 2002 they were no longer made. Viña Alberdi is the pleasant Crianza red; Viña Arana is a fine, light red; and Viña Ardanza a sumptuous, full Reserva with 20% Garnacha, worth laying down.

The top wines are the Reserva 904 and Reserva 890, selected for depth of colour and flavour to withstand, respectively, four and six years in American oak and emerge in perfect balance. It also own a Rías Baixas bodega, Lagar de Fornelos (q.v.).

Bodegas Riojanas ☆☆
Cenicero. 200 ha. www.bodegasriojanas.com
A substantial and conservative bodega in Rioja Alta, conceived in 1890 as a sort of château in Spain, by families who still own the company today. Some grapes are bought in, the rest come from its own holdings in Cenicero.

Traditional methods are used to produce the Reservas, Viña Albina, and Monte Real, a most pungent and admirable red that can age extremely well. Puerta Vieja is another brand for a crianza aged in American oak.

Marqués de Riscal ☆☆–☆☆☆
Elciego. 202 ha. www.marquesderiscal.com
The oldest existing Rioja bodega, founded in 1860 by Don Camilo Hurtado de Amezaga, Marqués de Riscal, and still owned by his descendants. The bodega was designed by a Bordeaux vigneron, and most of the wines continue to have a light, elegant, almost claret-like character – the epitome of the Rioja Alavesa. Cabernet Sauvignon has always played an important part in the blends intended for long ageing. A 1970 Reserva had 60% and an astonishing 1938, still vigorous in 1999, had 80%. The wines are aged in barrel for up to four years, then in bottle for a minimum of three, even ten. Baron de Chirel, first made in 1986, blends in some of the bodega's unique old plantations of Cabernet. White Riscal wines are not Riojas, but come from Rueda.

Riscal was one of the first large bodegas to respond to the ever-louder criticisms of falling standards within Rioja. It began reducing yields and hand-selecting the grapes; hired Paul Pontallier from Château Margaux as a consultant; and commissioned a dazzling new winery and hotel from Canadian architect Frank Gehry.

Roda ☆☆–☆☆☆
Haro. 120 ha. www.roda.es
A rare boutique winery, owned by the Rotllant family and devoted to the principal of only using fruit from vines older than 30 years. The two principal wines are Roda I and Roda II, both from 50-year-old vines, though Roda I is pure Tempranillo, aged for a longer period in mostly new oak.

Devotees of 100 per cent new oak should note the Cirsion, produced from even older vines, but only made in minute quantities. These are overall very successful modern Riojas, despite their lavish use of new French oak and their equally lavish prices.

Benjamin Romeo ☆☆☆
San Vincente de la Sonsierra. 16 ha.
Romeo is one of the few growers to espouse Biodynamism, which may explain the great power and density of his wines. Contador and La Viña de Andrés Romeo have won the highest praise but are produced in such small quantities that they are hard to find.

Viña Salceda ☆☆
Elciego. 20 ha.
A bodega making red wine only, using modern methods to make good wine with a leaning to the soft, Alavesa style. Recent expansion has enabled production to be increased. Viña Salceda is the regular quality; Conde de la Salceda the excellent Reserva.

Señorío de San Vicente ☆☆☆
San Vicente de la Sonsierra. 18 ha. www.eguren.com
A luxurious pure Tempranillo from elevated vineyards sometimes harvested as late as November. There is just one wine, and it is aged in new oak, both French and American. Despite their concentration, the wines have freshness and elegance, and a rewarding generosity of fruit. Under the same ownership as Sierra Cantabria (q.v.).

Señorío de Villarrica ☆–☆☆
Hervías. 80 ha. www.villarrica.es
A new venture incorporating a wine club and private restaurant.

The white Delicia, barrel-fermented in new oak, is elegant and piquant and carries the oak well, but the reds are jammy and extracted, more Napa than Rioja.

Sierra Cantabria ☆☆☆
San Vicente de la Sonsierra. 100 ha. www.eguren.com
The property has been owned by the Eguren family since 1870. As well as the Sierra Cantabria wines, which are reasonably priced and of very good quality, there is a spectacular new-oaked Amancio from pure Tempranillo.

Dinastía Vivanco ☆☆
Briones. 300 ha. www.dinastiavivanco.com
In 2004 Rafael Vivanco and his family created a remarkable complex around their modern bodega, including an excellent museum, restaurant, and gardens. The wines are good, too, and the varietal wines under the Colección label express perfectly the character of Graciano and Garnacha.

Navarra

Eastwards is the province of Navarra, which actually abuts Rioja and can lay claim to some of the vineyards of the Rioja Baja. Its limits are Catalonia in the east, the River Ebro in the south, and the Pyrénées to the north. The province has 18,400 hectares of vines, and utilizes the same grapes as Rioja but with more emphasis on the heavy, alcoholic Garnacha, which occupies over half the vineyards. The region used to be best-known for *rosado* wines, and then became a source of less refined and less expensive versions of Rioja. Now it is attempting to define its own identity, and placing more emphasis on varieties such as Cabernet and Merlot.

The best sites lie just south of the provincial capital, Pamplona, where the cooling influence of the Pyrénées can already be felt. The 5,200 growers are being encouraged to replant with Tempranillo, and some are also experimenting with small amounts of Cabernet Sauvignon.

Sterling work by the region's experimental laboratories at EVENA (Estación de Viticultura y Enología de Navarra) in Olite has meant Navarra has become one of the leading research establishments in Spain, and experimental plantations of all major grape varieties are under evaluation all over the region. New thinking has included barrel-fermentation of white wines such as Chardonnay, Tempranillo/Cabernet mixes, and a willingness to challenge even the mighty Rioja for quality red wines. Nonetheless, *rosado* wines still account for one-third of production. The number of cooperatives has more than halved in 20 years, but they still account for 70 per cent of production.

Leading Navarra Producers

Castillo de Monjardín ☆☆
Villamayor. 150 ha. www.monjardin.es
A substantial estate founded in 1988. Chardonnay is a specialty, both in oaked and unoaked versions. The fruity *rosado* is made from Merlot, and in addition to new-style reds blending Cabernet Sauvignon, Merlot, and Tempranillo, there is a pure Cabernet and a robust Merlot called Deyo.

Julián Chivite ☆☆–☆☆☆
Cintruénigo. 550 ha. www.bodegaschivite.com
The largest private wine company in Navarra, founded in 1860 and still family run. Its Gran Fuedo Crianza and Reserva are pleasant, full-bodied, and oaky. Wines released at affordable prices. The white Gran Fuedo is an unoaked Chardonnay.

In 1988, Chivite bought an estate near Estella called Señorío de Arinzano, and this is the source of its top range, the fine Colección 125, mostly aged in new barriques. The Colección white is Chardonnay, fermented in new oak, the reds essentially Tempranillo. The superb Vendimia Tardía, although from Moscatel, could easily be mistaken for a botrytis Semillon. In 2007 the Señorío de Arinzano estate became a Pago.

Guelbenzu ☆–☆☆☆
Cascante. 80 ha. www.guelbenzu.es
A family owned property, run by lawyer Ricardo Guelbenzu. He has taken the decision to leave the Navarra *consejo* so as to be free to blend in grapes from his vineyards in other regions. The Evo Gran Reserva is a succulent Cabernet/Tempranillo blend, aged in barriques. At the top of the range is the elegant but costly Lautus, mostly Tempranillo.

Irache ☆☆
Ayegui. 150 ha. www.irache.com
A traditional estate making a wide range of medium-bodied, fresh red and *rosado* wines from its own vineyards in Tierra Estella and also from some purchased grapes.

Racking in a Rioja bodega

Viña Magaña ☆☆
Barillas. 120 ha. www.vinamagana.com
This family owned, property has gone further than any other in Navarra in uprooting Garnacha, replacing it with Cabernet Sauvignon, Merlot, Cabernet Franc, and Syrah. Magaña wines share more than a passing similarity with good Bordeaux.

Vinícola Navarra ☆
Tiebas-Muruarte de Reta. www.domecqbodegas.com
Century-old company with French origins, and a major exporter, now owned by Allied-Domecq. No great refinement, but reliable and increasingly tasty in the better qualities. Castillo de Javieris the full-bodied Reserva, with Rioja-like oaky notes.

Nekeas ☆–☆☆
Añorbe. 230 ha. www.nekeas.com
A private cooperative founded by eight families in 1994. Chardonnay and Merlot are the principal wines, which are fruity and straightforward.

Ochoa ☆☆–☆☆☆
Olite. 143 ha. www.bodegasochoa.com
A locally popular, privately owned bodega in Olite, once the capital of the Kings of Navarra. The reds (including pure Tempranillo and barrique-aged Cabernet and Merlot) and *rosado* are soundly made, and the white Viura and the Moscatel are excellent, too. Javier Ochoa has played a major part in backing EVENA and thus has contributed a great deal to the resurgence of quality within the region.

Otazu ☆☆
Echauri. 115 ha. www.otazu.com
The most northerly estate in Navarra, founded in 1989 by Carlos Biurrun. The barrique-aged reds blend Cabernet and Merlot, with Tempranillo playing a supporting role. The white is pure unoaked Chardonnay.

Pago de Cirsus ☆☆
Ablitas. 135 ha. www.pagodecirsus.com
Other than Chardonnay, which comes in oaked and unoaked versions, the Pago wines tend to be blends of Tempranillo and Bordeaux varieties, of which the most arresting is the toasty Selección de Familia..

Palacio de la Vega ☆–☆☆
Condesa de la Vega. 30 ha. www.palaciodelavega.com
Founded in 1991, this producer is owned by Pernod-Ricard. The winery buys in most of its grapes and produces inexpensive, fruity Tempranillo, Merlot, and Cabernet.

Príncipe de Viana ☆–☆☆
Murchante. 400 ha. www.principedeviana.com
Set up in 1983 with the support of the regional government, Príncipe de Viana makes simple but well made wines. The oak-aged Reservas show more character.

Bodega de Sarría ☆☆
Puente la Reina. 210 ha. www.senoriosarria.com
A leading wine estate in Navarra, unique in the region (almost in Spain) for its château-style approach and almost Bordeaux-like results. In 1981, the ancient estate was taken over by a bank, which completely overhauled the vineyards and cellars.

In 2001 a new team was brought in to improve quality further. Tempranillo and Cabernet Sauvignon dominate the vineyards. Its best Reservas are a match for many Riojas. A new top range, Viñedo, consists of oak-aged varietal wines from individual vineyards.

Valcarlos ☆☆
Los Arcos. 180 ha.
www.bodegavalcarlos.com
A large winery established in 2000 by Faustino (q.v.) of Rioja. The medium-bodied Marqués de Valcarlos is pure Cabernet Sauvignon, aged in new American oak. The prestige range, essentially varietal and white (Chardonnay) as well as red, is Fortius, and the cherry on the cake is Elite de Fortius, a Bordeaux blend in a juicy, forward style.

Aragón

South and east of Navarra, astride the Ebro, lies the province of Aragón, whose climate tends more towards the Mediterranean. Aragón's once best known *denominación*, Cariñena, is a byword for high-strength, dark, red wine with a rustic bite, though worth oak-ageing for two years to achieve a pleasantly smooth texture. The grape here is again largely Garnacha Tinta, despite the fact that the region gave its name to the great grape of France's Midi, the Carignan.

Cariñena lies in the south of the province of Zaragoza, with 16,000 hectares of vineyard. A small DO, Campo de Borja (with 17 wineries and 7,400 hectares), lies halfway between Cariñena and the Rioja Baja. Borja (the origin of the Borgias) makes an even more rustic and alcoholic red, mostly Garnacha and more in demand for blending than drinking. Calatayud, south of Borja, makes similar wines. Most interesting, however, is probably the DO Somontano in the Pyrénées, created in 1985 and updated in 1993. Incoming winemakers discovered that the sleepy local cooperative was actually turning out some excellent wines, and that the soils and microclimates were perfect for serious viticulture.

Today, the region grows white Macabeo, Garnacha Blanca, and Chardonnay alongside the local – and splendid – Alcañón; reds are Tempranillo, Garnacha, and Cabernet Sauvignon alongside the indigenous Parreleta and Moristel (not the Monastrell in spite of many references to the contrary). The co-op has modernized, and new wineries are now experimenting with everything from Pinot Noir to Gewürztraminer.

Leading Aragón Producers

Viñedos del Alto Aragón ☆☆–☆☆☆
Salas Bajas, Somontano. 500 ha. www.enate.es
A winery founded in 1991 by the Nozaleda Arenas family, and utilizing the Enate brand name. The oaked Chardonnay is nicely lean and pungent; the reds are complex blends of Tempranillo with Cabernet and Merlot. The Cabernet/Merlot Reserva Especial is aged in new oak, as are newer wines called Merlot-Merlot, which speaks for itself, and Syrah-Shiraz, which doesn't. The wines are ambitious, and going from strength to strength. Prices, however, are quite high.

Aragonesas ☆☆
Fuendejalón, Campo de Borja. 3,500 ha.
www.bodegasaragonesas.com
A large, traditional producer, drawing on vineyards belonging
to two local cooperatives. The winery offers a good-value
range of wines under the Coto de Hayas label. Garnacha
and Tempranillo dominate here.

Alto Moncayo ☆☆–☆☆☆
Bulbuente, Campo de Borja.
A complex venture involving Bodegas Borsao, an American
importer, and Australian winemaker Chris Ringland.
Garnacha is the speciality, and these big powerful wines
have found favour with Spanish as well as the American
critics. But Barossa-meets-Spain may not please everyone.

Añadas ☆☆
Cariñena. 100 ha. www.carewines.com
Founded in 2000, the bodega produces very good wines
from international varieties, and an impressive blend
called XCLNT, which allows Garnacha to join the
Cabernet and Syrah.

Otto Bestué ☆–☆☆
Enate, Somontano. 45 ha.
www.bodega-ottobestue.com
Founded in 1999, the bodega specializes in juicy but refined
Cabernet/Tempranillo blends.

Blecua ☆☆
Barbastro, Somontano. 11 ha.
www.bodegablecua.com
A boutique winery, allied to Viñas del Vero (q.v.) and
producing, since 2000, a single wine: a deep-coloured,
black-fruited blend of Cabernet, Garnacha, and other
varieties. Very rich, very concentrated, and very expensive.

Bodegas Borsao ☆–☆☆
Borja. 2,500 ha. www.bodegasborsao.com
A Campo de Borja cooperative, offering red wines from 1,000
hectares of Cabernet Sauvignon, Garnacha, and Tempranillo.
All good value, and the Tres Picos Garnacha is unusually crisp
and engaging for a variety that is often drowned in alcohol.

Enate
See Viñedos del Alto Aragón.

Grandes Vinos y Viñedos ☆
Cariñena. 5,000 ha. www.grandesvinos.com
The largest winery in Aragón, founded in 1997 after five
cooperatives merged. The winery produces close to one
million cases from DO Cariñena.

Pirineos ☆–☆☆
Barbastro, Somontano. 2,000 ha.
www.bodega-pirineos.com
This former cooperative groups together the vineyards
of 200 growers. Pirineos, though very well equipped,
is still a custodian of tradition, using grapes such as
Moristel and Parraleta, as well as Cabernet, Merlot,
and Tempranillo. Various labels are used: Montesierra
and Señorío de Lazán.

San Alejandro ☆☆
Miedes de Aragón, Calatayud. www.san-alejandro.com
Excellent and sensibly priced wines, using the Baltasar
Gracián label and primarily Garnacha and Tempranillo,
from a former cooperative.

Viñas del Vero ☆–☆☆
Barbastro, Somontano. 870 ha. www.vinasdelvero.es
This ultra-modern, gravity-fed winery was built in 1993
and bought in 2008 by Gonzalez Byass. As is usually the
case in Somontano, the range of wines is very diverse. Some
of the wines have high acidity and benefit from some ageing
in bottle.

Virgen de la Sierra ☆–☆☆
Villarroya de la Sierra, Calatayud. 700 ha.
www.bodegavirgendelasierra.com
The oldest winery in the region remains loyal to the
local grape varieties. Good-value wines under the Cruz
de Piedra label.

Duero Valley

Castile-León

Surprisingly, it is the very heart of the high plain of Old Castile,
with some of the worst of Spain's savagely extreme climate, that
is now producing wines of a quality that seriously challenges
Rioja. Big, hot-country wines that they are, the red table wines
of the Portuguese upper Douro and the Spanish Ribera del
Duero seem to be kindred in their fine engineering. They have
the structure, the cleanness, and "cut" of a massive Bordeaux –
something not found (as far as I know) elsewhere in Spain.

Some of Spain's greatest reds, including her most expensive
by far, grow along the Duero banks, the Ribera del Duero, just
east of Valladolid towards Peñafiel. This was the discovery of
the 1980s, and it has expanded steadily through the 1990s to
total plantings of 20,700 hectares. The dominant variety is
Tempranillo, known here as Tinto Fino. Vega Sicilia, aged ten
years in cask, is the crown jewel, but excellent wines, as well as
mediocre ones, are found all over the region. Rapid expansion
means that many wines are inevitably based on young vines that
cannot always support a prolonged regime of barrel ageing,
and thus not all the wines are worth the generally high prices
demanded for them. Moreover, many recent plantings are on
flat land rather than hillsides, thus running the risk of frost
damage before harvest, as occurred in 2007 and 2008. Often the
richly fruity Crianzas offer more pleasure than tannic, over-
extracted Gran Reservas.

It is strange to find an up-and-coming white wine DO,
Rueda, only 32-kilometres (20-miles) south of Valladolid, near
the country that breeds such massive reds. Modern white-wine
technology has revolutionized Rueda. First Marqués de Riscal
from Rioja, then other investors, have seen enough potential
here to call in the best advice from France and invent a new
Rueda: a full-bodied, crisp, dry white of the kind Spain
chronically needs. Here Verdejo is the traditional grape, and

the wine must contain at least 40%. It is sometimes blended with Sauvignon Blanc, but the trend is allow Verdejo to stand on its own, which it can do perfectly successfully.

Every other wine in Old Castile is red. Toro is Rueda's nearest neighbour: a massive wine from the dusty Duero Valley, between Valladolid and Zamora. Once regarded as a source of wine for blending, it is now home to modern wineries that are pushing Toro into the elite of Spanish DOs. Its secret is an immense supply of very old bush vines, mostly Tempranillo, which is known locally as Tinta de Toro. Cigales, just north of Valladolid, is another region once known for rough *clarete*, but steadily improving in quality, with 40 wineries in operation.

León itself is the commercial centre for the province. Its vineyards lie to the west, in Bierzo, over the mountains on the borders of cool Galicia. Vilafranca del Bierzo is the centre of a region of 4,000 hectares. Bierzo wines are correspondingly the lightest of León, with good acidity and not excessively strong, but the Mencía grape gives a fragrance and structure reminiscent of fine Pinot Noir. Winemakers such as Alvaro Palacios are demonstrating the great potential of Bierzo.

Leading Ribera del Duero Producers

Aalto ☆☆☆–☆☆☆☆
Quintanilla de Arriba. 70 ha. www.aalto.es
Two powerful figures within the region teamed up in 1999 to produce Ribera del Duero from old vine vineyards. They are Mariano Garcia, the former winemaker at Vega Sicilia, and Javier Zaccagnini, the former head of the Consejo. There is no second wine, but in exceptional years a special *cuvée* called Pagos Seleccionadas is produced. Garcia's mastery is evident in the style of the wines, which is powerful and high in alcohol yet unfailingly elegant and lifted.

Abadía de Acón ☆☆
Castrillo de la Vega. 36 ha. www.abadiadeacon.com
A newcomer, dating from 2003, and with a marked preference for ageing its pure Tinto Fino wines in new oak. As well as the Acón range, there is a luxury *cuvée* called Targum.

Alión ☆☆☆
Peñafiel. 50 ha. www.bodegasalion.com
This property is a spin-off of Vega Sicilia (q.v.), producing modern-style wines entirely different in style from the mother estate. The production team is the same, headed by Vega Sicilia winemaker Xavier Ausás. The wine is pure Tinto Fino, but aged in new barriques. Quality is very high: oaky, to be sure, but with fine tannins and exceptional length of flavour. A 2007 tasting of every vintage demonstrated the wine's staying power.

Alonso del Yerro ☆☆–☆☆☆
Aranda del Duero. 26 ha. www.vay.es
Javier Alonso bought this property in 2002, and it is now farmed Biodynamically, with advice from Stéphane Derenoncourt. The top wine, Maria de Alonso del Yerro is aged in new oak, but the regular wine, which is spicy and elegant, is almost as fine.

Arzuaga ☆☆
Quintenilla de Onesimo. 150 ha.
www.arzuaganavarro.com
Founded by textile magnate Florentino Arzuaga, this estate produces a considerable number of wines, some of them *garagiste* and very expensive. Among the best are the old-vine Amaya and the ripe, airy Reserva. Under talented young winemaker Jorge Monzón, the winery is still to find its way, but may develop into one of the best.

Aster ☆–☆☆
Anguix. 95 ha. www.riojalta.com
Although founded and planted by Rioja Alta in 1990, the first vintage was only in 2000. The wines are all Tinto Fino. The wines are rich and sleek, but lack a little zest.

Dominio de Atauta ☆☆☆
Atauta. 20 ha.
In the far east of the appellation is this small estate, profiting from the many tiny pre-phylloxera vineyards around the village. Manager Bernard Sourdais, who also has a family property in Chinon, farms Biodynamically and produces wines of power and intensity. A new star.

Felix Callejo ☆–☆☆
Sotillo. 110 ha. www.bodegascallejo.com
Oaky wines from excellent, hand-picked vineyards, all Tinto Fino. The style is rather glossy and confected.

Cillar de Silos ☆☆–☆☆☆
Quintana del Pidio. 53 ha. www.cillardesilos.es
A confident family operated estate, making wines of high quality, thanks to careful sorting and the use of fine French oak. All the wines, from the *joven* to the new-oaked Flor de Silos, are worth investigating.

Condado de Haza ☆☆–☆☆☆
Roa de Duero. 200 ha. www.condadodehaza.com
Alejandro Fernández of Pesquera (q.v.) founded this property in 1993. The wines, from Tempranillo only, are aged for 15 months in American oak, and are exuberantly fruity and peppery examples of the less extracted style from Ribera del Duero. In 1995 Fernández introduce Alenza, a traditional style eschewing destemming.

Emina ☆☆
Valbuena. 450 ha. www.emina.es
An offshoot of Matarromera (q.v.), with a new winery completed in 2007 and including an educational centre. All the wines are Tinto Fino, and the most appealing is Prestigio aged in French oak.

O Fournier ☆☆–☆☆☆
Berlanga de Roa. 65 ha. www.ofournier.com
After establishing his astonishing winery in Argentina, the irrepressible José Manuel Ortega found and bought this property in 2002. The Argentine team also oversees production here, applying the same high standards.

Spiga is made from old vines and is aged in 80 per cent new barriques; in top years the best vats are selected to produce Alfa Spiga.

Fuentespina ☆☆
Fuentespina. 385 ha. www.avelinovegas.com
The Ribera del Duero outpost of the Avelino Vegas group, offering a sound range made solely from Tinto Fino. Corona de Castilla is a subsidiary label.

Hacienda Monasterio ☆☆☆
Pesquera de Duero. 70 ha. www.haciendamonasterio.com
Founded in 1992, this is a quality-oriented estate, where Peter Sisseck of Pingus (q.v.) acts as consultant winemaker. The wines are aged in varying proportions of new barriques, with older barrels bought from Château Margaux. All the wines contain, in addition to the basic Tinto Fino, a small proportion of Cabernet, Merlot, and Malbec. After some years when the wines were inconsistent, quality is now impeccable.

Matarromera ☆☆
Valbuena de Duero. 80 ha. www.matarromera.es
Belonging to a group headed by Carlos Moro, this 80-hectare property has been producing robust wines, rich in Tempranillo fruit, and very consistent from year to year. Emina (q.v.) is under the same ownership.

Emilio Moro ☆☆☆
Pesquera de Duero. 200 ha. www.emiliomoro.com
Since 1989, Moro has been producing traditional Ribera del Duero from pure Tinto Fino. The wines are splendid at all levels. In 1998, he introduced two flagship wines called Malleolus, aged, unlike his other wines, entirely in French oak.

Pago de Los Capellanes ☆☆☆
Pedrosa. 100 ha. www.pagodeloscapellanes.com
The Roderos were growers until 1996, when they established their own winery. As well as vibrant Crianza and sumptuous Reserva, Capellanes produces two single-vineyard wines of high quality, El Nogal and El Picón, the former complex and spicy, the latter overwhelmed by new oak.

Pago de Carraovejas ☆☆–☆☆☆
Peñafiel. 100 ha. www.pagodecarraovejas.com
A successful estate owned by a consortium of Madrid restaurateurs. The vineyards, planted in 1990, are well-drained and rarely affected by the spring frosts that can damage the vines of Ribera del Duero. The better qualities are aged only in French oak, and most of the wines contain some Cabernet Sauvignon. Quality was uneven at first, but is now far more consistent.

Viña Pedrosa ☆☆–☆☆☆
Pedrosa de Duero. 120 ha. www.vinapedrosa.com
The estate, founded by the Pérez Pascuas brothers, produces wines that are classic Ribera del Duero, aged mostly in older American oak, for 14–28 months. The property contains many old parcels, and 60-year-old vines are the source of the outstanding Gran Selección. These are excellent wines, rich in black fruits, but they do not come cheap.

Pesquera ☆☆–☆☆☆
Pesquera de Duero. 260 ha. www.grupopesquera.com
Fernández shot to stardom in the 1980s with Pesquera, a red wine made from Tinto Fino grapes and aged for two years in American oak. American critics are particular admirers of his dense, chewy style and powerful, tannic structure. He soon expanded his vineyards and established Condado de Haza (q.v.) in 1993. The wines are not entirely consistent, but can be magnificent at the top level. His reserve of Reserves is called Janus, and in a departure from his usual practice he produced, in 1996 and 2002 only, a parcel selection called Millenium aged in French oak.

Dominio de Pingus ☆☆☆–☆☆☆☆
Quintillana de Onesimo. 4.5 ha. www.pingus.es
Danish-born Peter Sisseck came to Ribera del Duero in 1990 to help establish Hacienda Monasterio (q.v.), for which he still acts as a consultant. He also founded what was the first *garagiste* winery in the region. He bought four hectares of very old and low-yielding Tempranillo vines, and aged the wine in new barriques for up to two years. Rave reviews from Robert Parker sent prices soaring, rather to his own amazement. The second wine, which is marginally more affordable and also of high quality, is Flor de Pingus.

Protos ☆☆
Peñafiel. 700 ha. www.bodegasprotos.com
A long-established former cooperative (founded in 1927), producing red wines well above normal co-op standards in, since 2007, a new winery designed by Norman Foster at considerable expense. Unlike most co-ops, Protos has never aimed at the lower end of the market. Although the Reserva and barrique-aged Selección have real distinction, the Crianza is a classic black-fruited Ribera del Duero that offers excellent value.

Rodero ☆☆–☆☆☆
Pedrosa de Duero. 90 ha. www.bodegasrodero.com
Since 1991, Carmelo Rodero's estate has been a rising star in Ribera del Duero. These are perfumed wines that always retain an intrinsic cherryish fruitiness; they are tannic, too, but never out of balance.

Sastre ☆☆–☆☆☆
La Horra. 45 ha. www.vinesastre.com
These organic vineyards are planted only with Tinto Fino, and over half the vines are more than 60 years old. The Crianza is excellent, but the bodega is especially proud of its special wines – Pago de Santa Cruz, Regina Vides, and the absurdly expensive Pesus – made from the oldest vines.

Señorío de Nava ☆–☆☆
Nava de Roa. 140 ha. www.senoriodenava.es
The former cooperative at Roa was taken over by VILE of León in 1986 and modernized, and the vineyards were adapted for mechanical harvesting. These are dense, chunky wines, short on finesse, but rich and chocolatey.

Valduero ☆☆
Gumiel del Mercado. 200 ha. www.valduero.com
A well-established property, all Tinto Fino, producing delicious wines that are never overwhelmed by the new, mostly American oak used to age the Reserva and Gran Reserva.

Valtravieso
Piñel de Arriba. 73 h.
www.valtravieso.com
In 2001 the Gonzalez family bought this remote property, with its conspicuously stony vineyards, and built a new winery in 2005. Pablo Gonzalez is determined to push the quality ever higher, and from 2008 only French oak is being used.

Although the standard wines are of a high quality in a modern, fruit-forward style, the most ambitious bottlings are labelled VT, and aged in new oak.

Vega Sicilia ☆☆☆☆
Valbuena de Duero.
140 ha. www.vega-sicilia.com
The most prestigious wine estate in Spain: a legend for the quality (and the price) of its wines. It was founded in 1864 on limestone hills 730-metres (2,373-feet) above sea level on the south bank of the Duero. The founder imported Bordeaux grapes (Cabernet Sauvignon, Merlot, and Malbec) to add to the local Tinto Fino, Garnacha, and Albillo. The yield is very low and the winemaking completely traditional. Only the unpressed *vin de goutte* is used, fermented for 15 days and matured in barrels of various sizes and ages for up to six years for the great Reserva Unico (Vega Sicilia itself), and three or five for its younger brother Valbuena. The result is a wine combining immense power and unmistakable "breeding". The raciness of the flavour is astonishing, and the perfume intoxicating. Vega Sicilia is one of Europe's noble eccentrics, but if proof were needed of the potential of the Ribera del Duero for fine reds of a more conventional kind, Valbuena would be evidence enough.

The estate also produces an unusual wine called Reserve Especial, which is a blend of old Unico vintages and some younger wines; it is a non-vintage wine and only 1,000 cases are produced. In 1998, long-time winemaker Mariano García left to take care of his Mauro property (q.v.), so Vega Sicilia has been going through some changes. The new winemaker is the highly capable and rigorous Xavier Ausás; Pascal Chatonnet consults. One of the main aims of the owners – the Alvarez family, since 1982 – was to eliminate the inconsistency for which the wine had been notorious. The ageing of the wine is also slightly shorter than it used to be, with greater purity and fruit intensity as a result. But, as so often in Spain, the speed of change is invisible to the naked eye.

Finca Villacreces ☆☆–☆☆☆
Quintanilla de Onésimo. 48 ha.
www.villacreces.com
The spare-time project of Peter Sisseck of Pingus (q.v.): an estate next door to Vega Sicilia producing two wines (Nebro being a pure Tinto Fino from very old vines), packed with red fruit flavours, but with sufficient stuffing to ensure good ageing potential.

Zifar ☆☆
Peñafiel. 30 ha. www.zifar.com
A new property, only founded in 2001, and aiming its lush, sleek wine at top restaurants.

Leading Toro Producers

Covitoro ☆
Toro. 1,000 ha. www.covitoro.com
An important cooperative producing highly commercial wines under the Cermeno and Baco labels. In contrast, Cañus Verus, made from 80-year-old vines and aged in mostly American oak, is a quality wine at a bargain price.

Fariña ☆–☆☆
Toro. 300 ha. www.bodegasfarina.com
It was Manuel Fariña who first put Toro on the map in the 1980s, with his rich, no-holds-barred Tempranillo reds called Gran Colegiata. Although the Fariña wines are still rich and powerful, they lack the finesse demonstrated by many other estates in the region.

Francois Lurton ☆☆–☆☆☆
Villafranca de Duero. 35 ha. www.jflurton.com
The Lurton brothers from Bordeaux were among the first outsiders to realize the potential of Toro. Together with Michel Rolland they produced the expensive and rather extracted Campo Eliseo, and under their own steam they make the delicious and fruity El Albar wines. They also make good Rueda.

Matarredonda ☆☆
Toro. 20 ha. www.mattaredonda.com
The first vintage was 2002, and all the wines are pure Tinta de Toro. In ascending order of seriousness the wines are Valdefama, Juan Rojo, and Libranza, but they are well-made, brightly packaged, and attractively priced.

Maurodos ☆☆☆
Pedrosa del Rey. 30 ha. www.bodegasmauro.com
A recent venture by Mariano Garcia of Mauro and Aalto (qq.v.). The main wine is San Román, a dense, fruit-packed, oaky wine of great stature and structure. The second wine, Prima, is more accessible and is proving highly popular.

Monte La Reina ☆–☆☆
Toro. 270 ha. www.montelareina.es
A new company, combining wine production with a hotel-restaurant, and a game reserve. Early releases were rather jammy and simple, but the owners, the Inaraja family, have the resources and will to improve.

Elías Mora ☆☆–☆☆☆
San Román. www.bodegaseliasmora.com
Founded in 2000 and run by the acclaimed winemaker Victoria Benavides. The top wines – Gran Elías Mora and 2V – have deservedly won much praise, but the simpler wines are also beautifully made and balanced.

Numanthia Thermes ☆☆☆
Valdefinjas. 28 ha.
Founded by the Eguren brothers, who also own prestigious properties in Rioja, the winery was sold in 2008 to LVMH. As well as the splendid, old-vine Numanthia, the estate produces 7,000 bottles of a *cuvée* from 120-year-old vines called Termanthia. Both have become cult wines: chewy,

full-bodied, powerful, and expensive. Yet behind the hype and fulsome praise are two impressive wines that have become the flagships for the region.

Pagos del Rey
Toro. 1,050 ha. www.pagosdelrey.com
Until 2008 this was known as Viña Bajoz, an immense cooperative until its acquisition by the Felix Solis group. New winemaker Isabel Carvajal is planning to modernize production, focusing on fruitier styles of wine, aged in a higher proportion of French oak.

Estancia Piedra ☆☆
Toro. 65 ha. www.estanciapiedra.com
A new star in Toro, belonging to Cayman Islands lawyer Grant Stein. The range of wines is extensive, and Paredinas, from centenarian vines and aged in new French oak, manages to show freshness as well as power. More surprising is the vibrancy and fruitiness of the most basic wine, Azul.

Pintia ☆☆☆
San Román. 100 ha.
www.vega-sicilia.com
Vega Sicilia owns extensive vineyards here, but as the vines are young, it buys the grapes for Pintia from growers with old vines. The first vintage was 2001 and Pintia, made with utmost attention to detail, soon became established as one of Toro's top wines, as remarkable for its purity and elegance as for its intensity of flavour.

Quinta de la Quietud ☆☆
Toro. 22 ha. www.quintaquietud.com
Owned by businessmen from Valladolid, this property lives up to its name and is run by Frenchman Jean-Francois Hébrard. Corral de Campanas is a delicious, fruit-forward young-vine Toro, and La Mula a no-holds-barred *garagiste* expression of the oldest vines. Sitting nicely between the two is the Quinta wine, which is discreetly structured and full of fruit.

Rejadorada ☆☆–☆☆☆☆
Toro. 42 ha. www.rejadorada.com
Novellum is the mid-level wine at this conscientious estate, and completely delicious, with black fruits to the fore, and tangy freshness on the finish.

Sobreño ☆☆
Toro. 80 ha. www.sobreno.com
The San Ildefonso family are based in Rioja, and apply the Rioja hierarchy to their Toro wines, which are mostly aged in good-quality American oak. The Reservas are concentrated and ambitious, but the Crianza delivers stylish, bright cherry fruit in abundance.

Vega Sauco ☆☆
Moales de Toro. 68 ha. www.vegasauco.com
Wenceslao Gil has been making wines in Toro since 1978,

and founded his own estate in 1991. His best-known wine is named after himself, Wences, a pure Tinta de Toro given extended ageing in barriques. His daughter Patricia runs a related property called Gil Luna.

Other Castile-León Producers

The wineries listed below come from a very diverse region, incuding the white-wine enclave of Rueda, the newly fashionable Bierzo, Cigales, and the wineries just outside the Ribera del Duero DO.

Abadía Retuerta ☆☆–☆☆☆
Sardón de Duero. 210 ha. www.abadia-retuerta.com
An ambitious project, established just outside the Ribera del Duero zone in 1996, with St-Emilion winemaker Pascal

Delbeck as the consultant winemaker. The million-bottle production includes a wide range of wines from Tempranillo and Cabernet Sauvignon, offering good value within their price bands. Recent additions to the range are varietal Pago wines from Tempranillo, Syrah, and Petit Verdot, all exceptional wines at very high prices.

Belondrade ☆☆
Camino del Puerto. 25 ha.
www.belondradeylurton.com
This firm was founded in 1994, and is the Rueda brainchild of Didier Belondrade and Brigitte Lurton, from the famous Bordeaux family, although divorce subsequently led to her departure. The principal wine is a barrel-fermented Verdejo from Rueda, rich in body and decidedly toasty.

Castro Ventosa ☆☆
Valtuille de Abajo. 60 ha.
www.castroventosa.com
Aromatic, dry-textured Mencía wines from Biodynamic vineyards that offer excellent value.

Frutos Villar ☆–☆☆
Cigales and Toro. 400 ha.
www.bodegasfrutosvillar.com
An important company, with vineyards in Ribera del Duero and in Toro (producing a wine labelled Muruve), as well as Cigales, where their brand is Calderona. Straightforward, modern wines from Tinto Fino.

Gótica ☆☆
Rueda. 90 ha. www.poligono10.com
Verdejo of unusual richness and of far more interest than the Sauvignon.

Lezcano-Lacalle
Triqueros del Valle, Cigales. 15 ha.
www.bodegaslezcano.es
A reliable producer of lush, fleshy, Tempranillo-based wines grown on exceptionally stony soils.

L'Ermita chapel, vineyard above Pesquera de Duero

Mauro ☆☆☆
Tudela de Duero. 35 ha. www.bodegasmauro.com
Just outside the Ribera del Duero DO, this much admired
estate is owned by Mariano Garcia, formerly of Vega Sicilia.
Yields are low, at between 25 and 40 hl/ha. The range includes
a Crianza, Vendimia Seleccionada, and the prestige bottling,
Terreus, from 100-year-old vines. See also Aalto and Pintia.

Naia ☆☆
La Seca, Rueda. 15 ha.
From very old Verdejo vines, Eulogio Calleja makes superb
white wines in differing styles.

Ossian ☆☆–☆☆☆
Nieva. 9 ha. www.ossian.es
Founded in 2005, Ossian produces a single voluptuous Rueda
from 15-year-old vines.

Pago de Vallegarcia ☆☆
Retuerta de Bullaque. 30 ha. www.vallegarcia.com
New property conceived with advice from Carlos Falco (of
Pagos de Familia Marquès de Griñon, q.v.) and viticulturalist
Richard Smart. Modern-style wines from Viognier and Syrah,
the latter at present the more successful of the two.

Palacio de Bornos ☆☆–☆☆☆
Rueda. 200 ha. www.palaciodebornos.com
Owned by Antonio Sanz, this winery is the former Bodegas
de Crianza de Castilla la Vieja. It produces barrel-fermented
Rueda from pure Verdejo, as well as racy, unoaked Sauvignon
Blanc. There is also an occasional late harvest Sauvignon.
Rather confusingly, this estate uses the Palacio de Bornos
label for its wines.

Descendientes de J Palacios ☆☆☆
Villafranca del Bierzo. 15 ha.
The famous winemaker Alvaro Palacios and his nephew
Ricardo have put the Bierzo region on the map, producing
plummy wines from very old Mencía vines, notably the
high-priced *cuvée* Corullon.

Pittacum ☆☆–☆☆☆
El Bierzo. 15 ha. www.pittacum.com
The standard Mencía is well made, but the top wine,
Aurea, comes from a single site and is aged in new oak
to give a most elegant style.

Marqués de Riscal ☆☆
Rueda. 220 ha. www.marquesderiscal.com
The pioneers of modern Rueda, still making exemplary
Verdejo and Sauvignon Blanc.

Viños Telmo Rodríguez ☆☆–☆☆☆
Logroño. www.telmorodriguez.com
Although based in Logroño, this brilliant and peripatetic
winemaker produces wine in a number of regoions.
Matallana is the main label from Ribera del Duero. He
is also producing excellent wines in Toro under a variety
of labels, including Gago (Crianza) and the complex and
highly concentrated Pago La Jara, aged in new barriques
for 17 months. In Valdeorras his label for fine Godello
is Gaba do Xil.

Dominio de Tares ☆☆–☆☆☆
**San Román de Bembibre, Bierzo. 60 ha.
www.dominiodetares.com**
Two bottlings stand out from an extensive range of Mencía
wines: Bembibre from very old vines in slate soils, and Tares
P3, with sweet oak on the nose and a bracing dry, grape skin
character.

Traslanzas ☆☆
Mucientes. 7 ha.
A boutique winery demonstrating, since 1998, the remarkable
potential of Cigales DO.

Yllera ☆☆
Rueda. www.grupoyllera.com
A large company based in Rueda but producing wines from
Ribera del Duero and Toro as well. The eponymous wine,
a Tierra de Castillo y León from pure Tempranillo, is rich
and fleshy, and the principal white is a ripe, tropical fruited
Verdejo.

Catalonia &
The Balearics

The modern Catalan is proud of the autonomy of his privileged
province. He basks in a temperate, mild-winter climate without
the extremes of most of Spain. Catalonia lies on the same
latitude as Tuscany, sheltered from the north by the Pyrénées,
facing southeast into the Mediterranean. It can be considered
as a southward extension of the best wine area of France's Côtes
du Roussillon. Both have the capacity to produce ponderous
and potent reds – and also to surprise with the quality of their
white grapes.

Catalan wines astonish with their diversity. From Priorat,
an inland enclave, come red wines of legendary colour and
strength, now rightly regarded as some of the greatest wines of
Spain. In contrast, over a century ago, the Raventós family
of Penedès realized the potential of their native white grapes,
naturally high in acid, for the Champagne treatment. Today
Penedès produces 90 per cent of Spain's sparkling wine. The
latest development, but the most significant of all, has been
the successful trial of the classic French and German grapes
in the higher parts of Penedès. The Torres family, long-
established winemakers of the region, have led the way with
a judicious mixture of these exotics and the best of the well-
tried Catalan varieties. Among the native whites, Parellada
and Xarel-lo are crisply acidic with low alcoholic degrees,
Malvasía is broadly fruity, with low acidity, and Macabeo
(the Viura of Rioja) is admirably balanced and apt for
maturing. Catalonia shares the best red grapes in Spain, above
all the Tempranillo (here often called Ull de Llebre), the
Garnacha Tinta, and the deep and tannic Monastrell. The
Cariñena (alias Carignan) is no more distinguished here than
elsewhere. Twelve zones in Catalonia now have Denominación
de Origen status and, of the Balearic islands, Mallorca now
boasts two DOs.

Catalonia

Alella

Coastal valley just north of Barcelona, now reduced to 315 hectares of vines by urban sprawl – which is a pity, since Alella has some wonderful soils for viticulture. Most of its many small growers take their grapes to the cooperative. It used to be best known for a mildly fruity, semi-sweet Xarel-lo, but little is produced today. Instead there is some good dry Chardonnay. The red is passable, but there are some experiments with Cabernet Sauvignon and Pinot Noir.

Catalunya

This is a catch-all DO, created in 1999, and many of the wineries entitled to prefer to label their wines with more local DOs. The purpose of the Catalunya DO is to allow blending of wines from different parts of Catalonia.

Conca de Barberá

This DO covers 5,800 sheltered hectares inland from the DO Tarragona, adjoining that and Costers del Segre in the northwest. Much of the grape production here is for the Cava industry, although new ideas are becoming well-established and there are large plantations of Chardonnay – indeed, this is where Miguel Torres grows the grapes for his flagship barrel-fermented Milmanda (which is then, confusingly enough, labelled Penedès). But Macabeo and Parellada are still the dominant varieties. Nonetheless, this is a region with promise, with a growing production of red wines.

Empordà-Costa Brava

The northernmost DO centred around Perelada in the province of Gerona and situated behind the cliffs and beaches of the Costa Brava and bordering Roussillon. The 2,000 hectares produce mainly Cariñena *rosado* and international varieties such as Riesling and Syrah, as well as Tempranillo and Garnacha.

Costers del Segre

This DO was ratified in 1988, really due to the influence of a single winery: Raïmat. The vineyards are in the rugged, fertile western region of Lleida (Lérida), and the region is made up of the four geographically disparate subzones of Raïmat, Artesa, Valls de Riu Corb, and Les Garrigues. Grape varieties are mainly traditional, but Cabernet Sauvignon, Merlot, and Chardonnay are also found. Most of the vineyards are cooperative-owned and devoted to producing the white wine and Cava traditional to the area, though modern methods and technological innovations are being introduced. Wines are of varying quality, with Raïmat far in the lead.

Montsant

A recent DO, only dating from 2001, and adjoining Priorato. It used to be known as the Falset subzone of Tarragona. Some sectors resemble Priorato, others are less steep. The main varieties cultivated are Cariñena, Garnacha, and Syrah.

Penedès

The biggest DO of Catalonia ranges from the coast at Sitges back into 600-metre (2,000-foot) limestone hills. Its centres are Vilafranca de Penedès, best-known for its table wine bodegas (among them Torres), and Sant Sadurní d'Anoia, 32-kilometres (20-miles) west of Barcelona, the capital of Spanish sparkling wine and headquarters of the vast firms of Codorníu and Freixenet. The table wines of Penedès have been revolutionized in the last 20 years. The reds are generally darker in colour and fruitier than traditional Riojas, but add a concentration that

---

THE TORRES FAMILY

Such has been the contribution of this Catalan family to Spanish wine that their name has become as well-known in some quarters as Spain's most famous wine-producing regions. The reasons for this are two-fold.

First, in the 1950s, with the world recovering from war, the late Miguel Torres Carbó, and his wife Doña Margarita, travelled the world selling Torres wines and promoting the Torres name in countries as disparate as Belgium and Bali. Second, their son, Miguel A Torres, studied chemistry at the University of Barcelona and went on to learn modern winemaking technology in Montpellier, before taking over the role of winemaker in 1962.

This combination of worldwide market share and new-wave winemaking skill contributed to the famous occasion in 1979 on which Torres Mas la Plana (then known as Gran Coronas Black Label) beat all-comers (including Château Latour) in a tasting of wines made principally from Cabernet Sauvignon.

Today, Miguel Torres oversees an empire which includes the Jean León property in Penedès, and his own large property in Curicó, Chile (his sister Marimar also has her own vineyards in California's Sonoma Valley), but his heart remains in his native Penedès, where he maintains a vineyard of more than 100 Catalan vine varieties as well as the classic Cabernet, Merlot, Sauvignon, and Chardonnay, which have made the family's name in international markets.

The Torres family is fully aware that is not enough to produce good wine; it is just as important to build up a loyal clientele of appreciative wine drinkers.

To that end, Miguel Torres offers winery tours, and has founded cultural centres and other ventures that inform the present generation and educate the one to follow. In 2008 a magnificent new underground bodega was inaugurated for the wines of the firm's own estates scattered across Penedès and Priorat.

Miguel Torres has retained his essential modesty, and relishes harvest time, when he can taste the new wines and offer his thoughts on blending. He is now passing the baton to his children, especially his daughter Mireia, who has already launched her own range.

Although there are other winemakers now producing costly bottles at the same level as Torres's best, no one can rival the consistent quality of his wines, from the cheapest to the most costly. That is no mean feat.

Rioja normally lacks. Exceptional wines, especially those with a proportion of Cabernet, reach the best international standards. Modern methods have brought the white wines, which still represent 80 per cent of production, under total control. There is now a benchmark dry, fruity Catalan white, which is certainly highly satisfactory if not exactly exciting. Unlike the best Rioja whites it does not (at least to my taste) take kindly to ageing in oak. Possibly less concentrated fruit, partly the result of bigger crops, is to blame.

Pla de Bages

A region some 100-kilometres (sixty-two miles) northwest of Barcelona around Manresa. Most of the production ends up as Cava, and few wineries operate here. As well as indigenous varieties, some Cabernet and Merlot are grown here.

Priorato

The long viticultural course of the River Ebro, starting near Haro in the Rioja Alta, might be said to end without shame in the western hills of Tarragona with this memorable wine. Priorato lies within the much greater denominación of Tarragona, applying to 1,725 hectares of steep, volcanic, hillside vines around the little tributary of the Ebro, the Montsant.

Its fame was derived from the almost-blackness of its red wine, traditionally a splendidly full-bodied brew of Garnacha and Cariñena that reached 16 degrees alcohol or more, with the colour of crushed blackberries and something of their flavour.

Its wine, and reputation, began to change after a handful of innovative winemakers set to work in the tiny hilltop village of Gratallops. Each acquired seven hectares, and rebuilt the terraces of their vineyards. The group collaborated but sold their wines under their own labels. Soon, half a dozen like-minded boutique wineries were making stunning wines from low-yielding Garnacha, Cabernet Sauvignon, Merlot, and even Syrah, grown in soil over the schistose bedrock. Their names were Clos Mogador, Clos de l'Obac, Clos Dofi, Clos Martinet, and the best of all, Clos l'Ermita, which has a complexity that is astonishing. In 1992, the group broke up, but most of the winemakers are still active in the region. They have been joined by a large number of new investors, who have bought up the oldest vineyards and planted new ones, and some of whom are making world class wines.

Tarragona

The table wines from this DO are normally of blending quality without the extra distinction of Priorato. Its finest products are fortified dessert wines from Garnacha and Moscatel, but the great bulk of Tarragona's exports are of a more humble nature.

Terra Alta

A DO continuing south from that of Tarragona beyond the Ebro. Mora and Gandesa are the chief centres for the 6,380 hectares of vines in the hills that rise to the mountainous province of Teruel. Many of the grapes are used for Cava, but the true potential of this region, with its fine soils and excellent drainage, is slowly being appreciated and exploited by a growing band of small, quality-oriented wineries.

Cava

While technically a DO, this is not actually a geographical region. Cava is the official term for traditional-method sparkling wine, and is produced predominantly in Penedès, though there are a few producers elsewhere in Spain. It may have been the characteristic leanness of Catalan white wine that inspired the creation of Cava. The Xarello, Parellada, and Viura (locally called Macabeo) produce high-acid musts of only slight flavour – ideal base material: the flavour of Champagne yeast comes through distinctly with its richness and softness. Wines that were stored in wooden vats (some still are) also picked up a very faint tarry taste, which added character. Chardonnay is increasingly used both in blends and in premium "varietal" Cavas. The Cavas of Penedès today range from the extremely deft and delicate, to the fat and clumsy. The best can certainly be counted among the world's best sparkling wines, and are priced accordingly. It is only in the inevitable comparison with Champagne that they lose. Where Champagne finally triumphs is in the vigour of the flavours that it assembles so harmoniously.

The Balearics

Binissalem & Plà i Llevant

The Balearic islands have a long vinous history, although Mallorca is the only one in the group that retains any vineyards at all. Binissalem, Spain's first offshore DO, was promoted in 1991, largely the result of the Ferrer (q.v.) bodega's campaign for recognition of the quality of its wines. In 1999, a new DO was created, Plà i Llevant, on the eastern side of the island. Son Bordils, founded in 1998, is another to watch. Majorcan wines are either primitive or modern.

Leading Priorat Producers

Cal Grau ☆☆☆
El Molar. 40 ha. www.grupohebe.com
All the wines are immensely rich and concentrated, but the two that are almost solely composed of traditional varieties are Les Ones and Epíleg.

Cal Pla ☆☆–☆☆☆
Porrera. 20 ha. www.cellercalpla.com
Very traditional red wines under two labels: Cal Pla and Mas d'en Compte, of which the latter is the more intense and

Rockets containing chemicals are used to disperse hailclouds

structured. The Mas white, from Garnacha, Piquepoul, and Xarel-lo, is among the very best white Priorats.

Cellers de la Cartoixa ☆☆
La Vilella Alta. www.cellerscartoixa.com
Two traditional red wines here: Montgarnatx, mostly Garnacha, and Montsalvat, mostly old vine Cariñena. They are equally good but can show too much alcohol in certain vintages.

Cims de Porrera ☆☆☆
Porrera. 54 ha.
"Cims" is Catalan for "summit", and the 150 plots that make up this former cooperative are scattered across some very high slopes. The co-op was taken over by the Pérez family of Clos Martinet in 1996 by the simple expedient of agreeing to buy the entire production. The wine is 90% Cariñena and aged in barriques. It is suffused in black fruits and liquorice, and is always beautifully balanced. The second wine is Solanes.

Clos Dominic ☆☆☆
Porrera.
A husband and wife team make two wines: Vinyes Altes, mostly Cariñena from centenarian vines, and the less flamboyant but more lush and chocolatey Vinyes Baixes, from a lower slope with a good deal of Merlot.

Clos Erasmus ☆☆☆
Gratallops. 10 ha.
This was one of the original estates of the "new" Piorat and is owned by Daphne Glorian. Most of the wine goes to the USA. It is beautifully crafted, aged in new oak, and very expensive.

Clos Figueras ☆☆–☆☆☆
Gratallops. 12 ha.
In 2000 Bordeaux wine merchant Christopher Cannan began producing wine from a site he bought in 1998 and restructured and replanted. René Barbier of Clos Mogador (q.v.) handles the winemaking. The principal wine is Clos Figueres [sic], which is aged in new oak of various sizes; the second wine is Font de la Figuera, which has more French varieties than the Clos wine. Powerful, jagged reds, and a nicely herbal white wine from Garnacha with a dash of Viognier.

Clos Mogador ☆☆☆
Gratallops. 35 ha.
René Barbier, son of the René Barbier, who ran the eponymous bodega now belonging to Freixenet, was a prime mover along with Alvaro Palacios in regenerating Priorato. His wine remains one of the very best, a blend of Cabernet, Cariñena, Garnacha, and Syrah drenched in red-fruit flavours and very long on the palate. It bears some resemblance to a top Châteauneuf-du-Pape. The peachy but not overblown white wine, Clos Nelin, is mostly Garnacha with a cocktail of southern French varieties.

Costers del Siurana ☆☆–☆☆☆
Gratallops. 50 ha. www.costersdelsiurana.com
Carles Pastrana first made the renowned Clos de l'Obac in 1989, and it remains an impressive example of new-style Priorato, blending Cabernet and Merlot with traditional varieties. Vintages in the late 1990s were a tad inconsistent. Pastrana continues the local tradition for fortified wines by producing Dolç de l'Obac, a warming blend of Garnacha, Cabernet, and Syrah.

Dits del Terra ☆☆☆
Torroja. 3.5 ha.
Brilliant South African winemaker Eben Sadie has long been fascinated by Priorat, and his intensely elegant version is among the best.

Celler de l'Encastell ☆☆
Porrera. 7 ha. www.roquers.com
Ramon Castelvlei makes the excellent Roquers de Porrera from the oldest vines of Garnacha and Cariñena, but the second wine, Marge, which includes up to 40% French varieties, is almost as concentrated and sells for a very reasonable price.

Gran Clos ☆☆–☆☆☆
Bellmunt. 32 ha.
American wine importer John Hunt bought out the previous owner, who founded the property in 1995. Cartus, from vines 80–100 years old, is the best wine, but Gran Clos runs it close.

Mas Doix ☆☆☆–☆☆☆☆☆
Poboleda. 12 ha. www.masdoix.com
Ramon Llagostera's first vintage was 1999, and in the following decade he has made his wines some of the best in Priorato. Mas Doix is half Garnacha, half Cariñena, and rich enough to obscure the high alcohol. There is also a Costes de Vinyes Velles bottling with flavours of wild berries and an extraordinary persistence on the palate.

Mas d'en Gil ☆☆–☆☆☆
Bellmunt. 45 ha. www.masdengil.com
Until 1998 this was known as Masia Barril, until renamed by its new owner, wine merchant Pere Rovira. Clos Fontà is the principal wine, aged in new oak, but the less extracted Coma Vella shows a lighter touch. The oldest vines are reserved for Gran Buig, an exceptionally lush (and expensive) wine made only in outstanding vintages.

Mas Martinet ☆☆☆
Falset. 15 ha. www.masmartinet.com
Another new style Priorato, founded by José Luis Pérez, who was one of the Gratallops pioneers. The wines are made by his daughter Sara, who is married to Rene Barbier Jr.

Mas Martinet is one of the most stylish wines from Priorat, and the second wine, Martinet Bru, is more accessible but still shows considerable concentration. From recently acquired vineyards in another sector, Pérez produces a sumptuous, and expensive, wine called Cami Pesseroles.

Melis ☆☆
**Les Fonts de Terrassa. 35 ha.
www.melispriorat.com**
Victor Gallegos's day job is running the SeaSmoke winery in southern California, but he also makes a superripe Priorato called Melis and a more balanced second wine, Elix. Both wines have a fair amount of Cabernet Sauvignon in the blend.

Alvaro Palacios ☆☆☆–☆☆☆☆
Gratallops. 27 ha. www.alvaropalacios.com
Palacios is the prime mover behind the Priorato renaissance, and the creator of its costliest wine, L'Ermita, an intense blend of mostly Garnacha with Cabernet, aged for 20 months in new barriques. Fortunately, Palacios also makes wines that are more affordable: the concentrated and persistent Finca Dofí, and the less structured but very enjoyable Les Terrasses, which is essentially Garnacha and Cariñena from purchased grapes. Low yields and rigorous grape selection are what lies behind the wines' splendour.

Rotllan Torra ☆☆
Torroja. 24 ha. www.rotllantorra.com
Jordi Rotllan makes various *cuvées* of Priorato, of which the most exciting are the barrique-aged Amadis and Tirant. Balandra, at a fraction of the price, is a bargain.

Cellers de Scala Dei ☆☆
Scala Dei. 90 ha. www.scaladei.org
Scala Dei was a great Carthusian monastery, now in ruins. The bodega, owned since 2002 by Codorníu, is in an old stone building nearby, making high-quality, oak-aged Priorato: deep, dark, and strong, but balanced with rich, soft fruit flavours.

The labels include Cartoixa Scala Dei, once dominated by Garnacha but now containing up to 40% Syrah, and the less overwhelming Negre, which is given shorter ageing in cask.

Vall-Llach ☆☆–☆☆☆
Porrera. 42 ha. www.vallllach.com
The dedicated project of Catalan singer Lluis Llach, producing remarkably powerful wines. There are three *cuvées*, all of which contain 30–50% French varieties, which contribute black-cherry fruit to the spiciness of the Spanish varieties. Vall Llach is the priciest wine, but it can be too dense and extracted, and the lesser *cuvées*, Embruix and Idus, can be more satisfying.

There are far too many wines in Priorato to list more than a selection in any detail, especially since many of them are made in very small quantities and hard to find. All the following labels are worth looking out for: Closa Batllet, GrataVinum, Gueta-Lupia, Herencia del Padri, Los Manyetes, Mas Alta, Mas d'En Just, Mas Perinet, La Perla del Priorat, Celler del Pont, Salmos (Torres), Sine Nomine, Cellers Vilella de la Cartoixa, and La Vinya del Vuit.

Leading Catalan & Balearic Producers

Abadal ☆–☆☆
Avinyò, Pla de Bages. 120 ha. www.abadal.net
Attractive, medium-bodied wines from Chardonnay and the Bordeaux varieties, all under the name of Abadal.

Albet i Noya ☆☆
Sant Pau d'Ordal, Penedès. 76 ha. www.albetinoya.com
Two brothers run this organic estate, best-known for its Cava and juicy, fresh Tempranillo, but also producing good Núria, a barrique-aged Merlot, and the Colecció range of varietal wines from Chardonnay, Cabernet, Tempranillo, and Syrah.

Alta Alella ☆☆
Tiana, Alella. 18 ha.
A company created in 2001 and producing accessible varietal wines from Chardonnay, Mataro, and Syrah.

Cavas del Ampurdán ☆
Perelada, Catalunya. www.perelada.com
The sister company of Castillo de Perelada (q.v.), making pleasant still red, white, and *rosado* from bought-in grapes. Sparkling wines are bulk-produced by the *cuve close* method. Prices are low but quality is unexceptional. This company was the defendant in a famous London court case, which took place in 1960, when the Champagne authorities succeeded in preventing it from using the term "Spanish Champagne".

Joan d'Anguera ☆☆
Darmós, Montsant. www.cellerjoandanguera.com
An old property dating from 1825 and owned by the Anguera brothers. Its calling card is the high percentage of Syrah in the wines. The new-oaked El Bugader, with 70% Syrah, is the finest of them, and Finca L'Argata can also be recommended.

An Negra ☆☆
Felanitx, Mallorca. www.annegra.com
A boutique winery producing from leased vineyards a structured wine called An, from the local red variety Callet.

René Barbier ☆–☆☆
Sant Sadurní d'Anoia, Penedès. 200 ha.
www.renebarbier.es
An old-established bodega, now owned by Freixenet (q.v.), and producing a large range of varietal wines from Catalan and international varieties. The top Selección Cabernet and Chardonnay can be impressive.

Can Rafols del Caus ☆☆
Avinyonet del Penedès. 25 ha.
A small property that has opted for mostly French varieties, and makes them well. The best are rich Merlot, and an unusually toasty Chenin Blanc called La Calma.

Celler de Capçanes ☆☆–☆☆☆
Capçanes. 300 ha. www.cellercapcanes.com
A Montsant cooperative with 80 members, and reorganized into a progressive private winery making the most of its members' old vines and excellent vineyards. Much of the crop is now sold off, leaving only the best to be aged and bottled here. Many of the wines are blends, but Mas Torto and Mas Doinis are dominated by Garnacha. Mas Collet could easily be taken for a lighter Priorato of good quality.

Castell del Remei ☆☆–☆☆☆
Lleida (Lérida), Costers del Segre. 80 ha.
www.castelldelremei.com
A long-established firm in Costers del Segre. The white and red wines, mostly blends of local and international varieties and bottled under the Gotim Bru and Oda labels, are well made, but a sweetish dimension is derived from the American oak.

Cérvoles ☆☆–☆☆☆
La Pobla de Cérvoles, Costers el Segre.
www.cervoles.com

Founded in 1997, this excellent property is under the same ownership as Castell del Remei (q.v.). It produces imposing red blends – Estrats, Muntanya – from Cabernet Sauvignon, Tempranillo, and Garnacha.

Clos Mont-Blanc ☆☆
Barberà, Conca de Barberà. 50 ha.
www.closmontblanc.com
This large modern winery produces wines to match: fresh Sauvignon, weightier Chardonnay, and creamy wines from Merlot and Syrah. Finca Carbonell is another of its labels.

Tomás Cusiné ☆☆–☆☆☆
El Vilosell, Costers del Segre. 30 ha.
www.tomascusine.com
Cusiné demonstrates the considerable potential of this region with two superb blends: Geol from mostly French varieties, and Vilosell, from mostly local ones, notably Tempranillo.

Espelt ☆–☆☆
Vilajuiga, Empordà. 200 ha.
www.espeltviticultors.com
Good-value wines from a large property dominated by Garnacha. Bright and playful packaging seems adapted to cater to the holidaymakers along the coast.

José L Ferrer ☆
Binissalem, Mallorca. 70 ha. www.vinosferrer.com
The best-known bodega of the Balearic islands, now owned by the firm Franco Roja. The vineyards are situated in the centre of the island. The local Manto Negro grape makes lively reds, and Reservas can be extremely good. There is also a dry *blanc de blancs* sparkling wine.

Cooperativa de Gandesa ☆
Gandesa, Terra Alta. www.coopgandesa.com
Old-established (1919) cooperative with 400 members. The simpler, fruitier wines are best.

Laurona ☆☆
Falset, Montsant. 25 ha. www.cellerlaurona.com
Like Clos Figueras in Priorat (q.v.) this is the brainchild of Bordeaux merchant Christophe Cannan and René Barbier. Laurona could be taken for a good Côtes du Rhône, whereas 6 Vinyes, from Cariñena and Garnacha, is closer in spirit, and flavour, to Priorato.

Jean León ☆☆–☆☆☆
Torrelavit, Penedès. 100 ha. www.jeanleon.com
In 1964, Jean León started to plant Cabernet and Chardonnay in Penedès. The wines were first-rate and excellent value. In 1993, the company was bought by Torres, which runs the estate separately to maintain its identity. The Cabernet spends two years in casks, then three years in bottle, before release. Under Torres, Merlot has been added to the range. Quality has, if anything, improved further since the Torres acquisition.

De Muller ☆☆
Reus, Tarragona. 150 ha. www.demuller.es
The great name in the classic tradition of sweet Tarragona wines. A family firm founded in 1851, the pride of the house is its altar wines, supplied to (among others) the Vatican, and its velvety, solera-aged Moscatel, Pajarete, and other dessert wines. It also produces wines in Priorato.

Naverán ☆☆
Torrelavit, Penedès. 100 ha. www.naveran.com
Medium-sized property, very much focused on red wines from Bordeaux varieties, plus Syrah. Cava is also produced.

Parxet ☆☆
Tiana, Alella. 200 ha. www.parxet.es
The leading producer in Alella, with 200 hectares of vineyards. White wines only, released under the Marqués de Alella label. The most vivacious wine is made entirely from the Pansà grape. The house also makes reliable Cava, also from indigenous varieties.

Raïmat ☆–☆☆☆
Lleida (Lérida), Costers del Segre. 2,000 ha.
www.raimat.com
The Raventós family of Codorníu has replanted the vineyards of the Castle of Raïmat, in the arid hill region of Lérida, on a grand scale, and re-opened a magnificent bodega built early in the twentieth century and subsequently abandoned. The property is run in an industrial yet sophisticated manner, with the grapes being picked at night by machine.

Cabernet Sauvignon, Merlot, and Chardonnay are blended with native grapes, but also made as varietal wines. The results have been ultra-reliable if slightly lacking in personality, but that is being rectified as special bottlings of Chardonnay and Cabernet are coming onto the market.

Pedro Rovira ☆
Móra la Nova, Tarragona.
An old family firm producing solera-aged dessert Tarragona from Pedro Ximénez, as well as everyday wines.

Jaume Serra ☆
Vilanova i la Geltrú, Penedès. 76 ha.
A low-key, but reliable producer of fresh Penedès wines, and some Cava.

Torres ☆☆–☆☆☆☆
Vilafranca del Penedès. 1,700 ha. www.torres.es
An old family company (founded 1870), which has changed the wine map of Spain over the last 30 years, and put Catalonia on a par with Rioja as a producer of top quality wines. The family vineyards are planted with Chardonnay, Gewürztraminer, Riesling, Sauvignon Blanc, Cabernet Sauvignon, Merlot, and Pinot Noir, as well as the traditional Penedès varieties, which Torres has been vigorous in preserving and propagating.

Viña Sol is a fresh Parellada white; Gran Viña Sol a blend with Chardonnay; Fransola mostly Sauvignon Blanc; Milmanda an excellent single vineyard Chardonnay, barrel fermented. Of the reds, Tres Torres is a full-bodied blend of Garnacha and Cariñena, Gran Sangre de Toro an older Reserva of the same, Coronas mostly Tempranillo, while Gran Coronas Reserva is Tempranillo with some Cabernet Sauvignon. Mas Borras is Pinot Noir, Atrium a Merlot. Mas la Plana, the top wine, is a mighty and long-lived Cabernet Sauvignon, formerly known as Black Label.

Miguel Torres is now absorbed in his mission to revive endangered Catalan varieties. The fruit of his research and hard work is the outstanding Grans Muralles from Conca de Barberá. The first vintages of this, rich, earthy, and herby, with dense soft tannins, promise real distinction with age. Total sales are around 2.5 million cases per year. (See page 395.)

Jané Ventura ☆☆–☆☆☆
El Vendrell, Penedès. www.janeventura.com
A small but definitely quality oriented estate, still loyal to Spanish varieties, white and red, although there is also a Cabernet under the Mas Vilella label. The singlevineyard wines tend to be oak-aged and have an elegant, tannic structure. Good Cava, too.

Leading Cava Producers

Castillo de Perelada ☆☆
Perelada, Empordà. www.castilloperelada.com
A celebrated Cava concern in a picturesque castle dating back to the fourteenth century, now housing a fine library, collections of glass and ceramics, a wine museum – and a casino. The best wine, Gran Claustro, is one of Catalonia's most satisfying Cavas; and a fine red, blending Bordeaux and Catalan varieties and aged in new barriques, appears under the same name. A sister company, Cavas del Ampurdán, produces the cheap and cheerful *cuve close* sparkling Perelada.

Codorníu ☆–☆☆☆
Sant Sadurní d'Anoia. 3,000 ha. www.codorniu.com
The first Spanish firm to use the classic method, and now the second biggest sparkling wine house in the world. The Raventós family have made wine in Penedès since the sixteenth century. In 1872, Don José returned from Champagne to imitate its methods. The establishment is now monumental, its vast *fin-de-siècle* buildings and 30 kilometres (18 miles) of cellars lie in a green park with splendid cedars. They include a considerable wine museum and attract enormous numbers of visitors. Codorníu is also the owner of other estates in Spain (Raïmat, Masía Bach), Mexico, Argentina, and California.

The wines range from simple and fruity (Anna de Codorníu) to highly refined. The Non Plus Ultra occupies the middle range, and the top bottling is the vinous Jaume Codorníu, with 50% Chardonnay giving it greater elegance.

Conde de Caralt ☆–☆☆
Sant Sadurní d'Anoia. www.condedecaralt.com
A famous old sparkling wine bodega, now part of the Freixenet group (q.v.). The name now appears on a range of fairly simple still wines.

Freixenet ☆☆
Sant Sadurní d'Anoia. 1,000 ha. www.freixenet.com
The biggest Spanish Cava house, and now the biggest sparkling wine producer in the world, overtaking the giant Codorníu with an annual production of 200 million bottles. The top Freixenet wines are special releases such as Reserva Real; Brut Nature is the best standard line; the lightly sweet Cordón Negro is the best seller. Carta Nevada is a cheaper brand, and a Brut Rosé is also made. Freixenet also owns Castellblanch, a reliable brand.

Gramona ☆–☆☆☆
Sant Sadurní d'Anoia. 100 ha. www.gramona.com
Founded in 1921, this is a family owned Cava house that has recently started producing a range of unusual table wines, such as barrique-aged Sauvignon Blanc, a Pinot Noir rosé, and an Icewine. Its vintage Cavas are of exceptional quality: the Celler Batlle and III Lustros, both traditional Xarel-lo and Macabeo *cuvées* and given long ageing on the yeasts.

Cavas Hill ☆
Moja. 50 ha. www.cavashill.com
The English Hill family arrived in Penedès in 1660. In 1884, Don José Hill Ros established this commercial bodega, which produces both Cava and still wines. Labels include the very dry Brut de Brut. The top red is the Gran Reserva.

Juvé y Camps ☆☆
Sant Sadurní d'Anoia. 470 ha. www.juveycamps.com
Sizeable family firm making superior and expensive Cava from its own vineyards and from grapes bought in from carefully selected growers. Top *cuvées* are the vintage Cava and Gran Juvé y Camps. The grandly named Reserva de la Familia is a fruity Cava, made in substantial quantities. The Rosado Brut is pure Pinot Noir. Some still wines are also produced.

Antonio Mascaró ☆
Vilafranca del Penedès. 40 ha. www.mascaro.es
An old family bodega, respected for its Cava wines and fine brandy, and also making simple varietal wines such as Sauvignon Blanc.

Marqués de Monistrol ☆
Sant Sadurní d'Anoia. www.arcobu.com
This is a long-established and reliable Cava house, now owned by the Arco group (that owns Berberana in Rioja). It also produces good Penedès still wines from French grape varieties.

Segura Viudas ☆–☆☆
Sant Sadurní d'Anoia. 50 ha. www.seguraviudas.com
The three Cava companies owned by Freixenet (q.v.) all shelter in the same cellars. Segura Viudas is the *prestige marque*. Its best wine is the Reserva Heredad, made solely from Catalan varieties and offered in a vulgar bottle with its own built-in coaster.

The Levante & Meseta

By far the greatest concentration of vineyards in Spain lies south and southeast of Madrid, in a great block that reaches the Mediterranean at Valencia in the north and Alicante in the south. This central band, with scattered outposts farther west towards Portugal in Extremadura, contained no great names, no lordly estates, no pockets of perfectionism. Its wines combined various degrees of strength with various degrees of dullness – but in the main, a generous helping of body.

The last 15 years have seen changes. Spain's membership of

the EU has exposed the traditional cooperative producers of the region to the realities of competition. Modern market forces have prompted producers to invest in modern technology. Central Spain, like California's Central Valley, has a climate of extremes, but predictable extremes. This allows oenologists to "design" wines by regulating picking dates and controlling fermentation.

While large-scale cooperatives still make much of the wine, estates and smaller bodegas are emerging. Experimental plantings are introducing French grapes; unsuspected flavours are being coaxed by skilled winemakers from local varieties. Central Spain has a long road ahead of it, but it is no longer an unrelieved ocean of mediocrity.

The DO Ribera del Guadiana, with 26,000 hectares of vines, shows particular promise, especially within the subzone known as Tierra de Barros. White grapes used to dominate here, but producers are confirming that the soils and climate are far better suited to reds, although growers must be on their guard against over-ripeness.

Toledo province, southwest of Madrid, contains the DO of Méntrida, a 9,000-hectare spread of mostly Garnacha vines supplying strong red wine. Until the 1980s, the minimum alcohol for its red wines had to be 14 degrees, and some offenders reached 18. Today the wines are more balanced, but there is still some way to go.

By far the biggest wine region in the whole of Spain, demarcated or not, is La Mancha, the dreary plain of Don Quixote. It has 187,000 hectares under vine, mostly planted with an essentially flavourless white variety called Airén, but recent vineyards are more likely to be planted with the more promising Verdejo. The one superior enclave of La Mancha is DO Valdepeñas, 160-kilometres (100-miles) south of Madrid. The old winemaking method here was fermentation in the tall clay *tinajas*, obviously descended from Roman or earlier vessels. Modern methods have shown clearly how much better the wine can be. Such producers as Los Llanos and Felix Solin now cool-ferment and oak-age their wines, and the results are enjoyable while lacking the grandeur of the best from Rioja or Ribera del Duero.

The sorry tale continues with the DO of Manchuela, east of La Mancha, and making both white and red wine on its 4,000 hectares. The smaller DO of Almansa around Albacete concludes the toll of the Castilian plain. Its 7,600 hectares are planted with dark grapes, mostly Garnacha and Monastrell.

The term "Levante" embraces six DOs of only very moderate interest at present, but some considerable potential as modern methods creep in. To the north, on the coast, is Valencia (and what was formerly called Cheste), liberal producers of alcoholic white wine and, to a lesser degree, red, although a handful of estates are demonstrating the true potential of the region for flavoury reds from good varieties.

Inland from Valencia lies Utiel-Requena, a hill region of black grapes (the principal one, the Bobal, as black as night)

used formerly for colouring wine. The local technique was to ferment each batch of wine with a double ration of skins to extract the maximum colour and tannin: a brew called *vino de doble pasta*. Its by-product, the lightly crushed juice with barely any skin contact or colour, surplus to the double brew, makes the second specialty of the region: a racy, pale *rosado* more to the modern taste. But some producers are demonstrating that Bobal, if handled correctly, can make interesting red wine.

The DO Alicante covers both coastal vineyards, producing sweet Moscatel, and hill vineyards for red wines, *vino de doble pasta* and *rosados*. A little local white wine is (relatively) highly prized. Behind Alicante in the province of Murcia there are three *denominaciónes*: Bullas (much *rosado*), Yecla, and Jumilla, whose respective cooperatives are struggling to teach their inky material modern manners. So far, Jumilla seems to be marginally the most advanced of the three, with some wines showing surprising potential to age in bottle.

The striking achievements of the Marqués de Griñón in Castilla-La Mancha stumped the DO authorities, who solved the problem by granting him his own appellation (see Dominio de Valdepuesa) in 2002.

Leading Levante & Meseta Producers

Altolandon ☆☆
Landete, Manchula. 55 ha. www.altolandon.com
One of the best Manchuela producers, active since 2000, with vineyards at over 1000 metres. Ir specializes in blends from international varieties.

Arrayán ☆☆
Santa Cruz del Retamar, Méntrida. 26 ha. www.arrayan.es
A leading bodega in Méntrida, its vineyards were planted with advice from the Australian viticulturalist Dr Richard Smart. The wines are Bordeaux varieties and Syrah, and Premium, which blends them all with great conviction.

Ayuso ☆
Villarrobleda, La Mancha. 350 ha. www.bodegasayuso.es
A family concern since 1947. These La Mancha wines, released under the Estola label, used to be thin and faded, but have been gaining in body and fruit.

Rafael Cambra ☆☆
Onteniente, Valencia.
A quirky property, with interesting wines: Uno is pure Monastrell, Dos a blend of Cabernets Franc and Sauvignon, and Minimum a blend of Monastrell and Cabernet Franc. They have weight and freshness and modern sophistication.

Casa de la Viña ☆
Alhambra, Valdepeñas. 1,000 ha.
www.domecqbodegas.com

Castile La Mancha, Campo de Criptana

A major producer of agreeable, medium-bodied Valdepeñas. The property is part of the Bodegas y Bebidas group, and thus owned by Allied-Domecq.

Casa Castillo ☆☆–☆☆☆
Jumilla. 174 ha. www.casacastillo.es
This traditional estate was restructured in the 1990s and new varieties planted, primarily Monastrell but also Cabernet Sauvignon and Syrah. The Pie Franco Monastrell shows the full potential of the variety, and the other red wines are also of a very high standard.

Castaño ☆☆
Yecla. 400 ha. www.bodegascastano.com
A leading 350-hectare domaine in Yecla, well-equipped and producing a wide range of wines, mostly pure Monastrell, but also blends with Syrah and Cabernet. Most of the wines are unoaked; some are given a dose of American oak. They all offer excellent value.

Vinícola de Castilla ☆☆
Manzanares, La Mancha. www.vinicoladecastilla.com
This is a large, hi-tech, million-case winery that used to belong to Rumasa. The simple young wines are more enjoyable on the whole than the Gran Reservas, which can lack fruit. Pleasant Cabernet Sauvignon and other de Guadineja label.

Centro-Españolas ☆
Tomelloso, La Mancha. 240 ha.
www.allozo.com
A modern and well equipped winery, working almost exclusively with the local varieties and bottling its wines under the Allozo label.

Dehesa del Carrizal ☆☆
Retuerta del Bullaque, La Mancha. 28 ha.
www.dehesadelcarrizal.com
A small property promoted to Pago status in 2006. International varieties form the base of all the wines.

Gandía ☆–☆☆
Chiva, Valencia. 200 ha. www.vicentegandia.com
This vast business has been making serious efforts to improve quality ever since it bought the Hoya de Cadenas property in 1992. The best value wines are released under the Castillo de Líria label, and there is a fine Tempranillo/Cabernet blend called Ceremonia, bottled under the Utiel Requena DO.

Juan Gil ☆☆–☆☆☆
Jumilla. 200 ha. www.juangil.es
Monastrell is the best wine from this progressive and well marketed property, although the Petit Verdot is good too, with plummy fruit and assertive tannins.

Gutiérrez de la Vega ☆☆
Parcent, Alicante. www.castadiva.es
A small family property, founded in 1978, showing the excellent quality that can be achieved using indigenous grapes such as Monastrell and Moscatel, all released under the Casta Diva brand.

Bodegas Huertas ☆
Jumilla. 80 ha. www.bodegashuertas.es
Clean, well-made reds and *rosado* from Monastrell grapes, proving that Jumilla is not necessarily a bruiser of a wine.

Jesús del Perdón ☆
Manzanares, La Mancha. 3,600 ha. www.yuntero.com
A large cooperative known particularly for its dry white, but the red has improved considerably in recent years. The brand name is Yuntero, plus Mundo de Yuntero for organically grown Airén and Tempranillo.

Jiménez-Landri ☆☆
Méntrida. 27 ha. www.bodegasjimenezlandi.com
A long established property, producing modern style wines, notably Piélago, a structured and stylish blend of Garnacha and Syrah.

Los Llanos ☆☆
Valdepeñas. 350 ha. www.gbvinartis.com
The first house in Valdepeñas to bottle its own wines. The oak-aged Reservas and Gran Reservas set new standards for the region. Señorío de Los Llanos Gran Reserva is a fine, aromatic, and silky wine, and the Pata Negra Gran Reserva, made only in top years, is even finer. In 2004 the bodega was acquired by a venture capital company, and now forms part of the Vinartis group.

Finca Luzón ☆☆
Jumilla. 600 ha. www.bodegasluzon.com
Modern-style wines from a new venture in Jumilla, which has grown rapidly to a production of one million bottles per year. Most of the reds are from Monastrell, Tempranillo, Syrah, and Cabernet Sauvignon, although some of the varietal wines, especially Syrah, show promise.

Manuel Manzaneque ☆☆
El Bonillo, Albacete, DO Finca Elez. 35 ha.
www.manuelmanzaneque.com
A small property in the Meseta at 1,000 metres: these are some of the highest vineyards in Spain. The reds blend Cabernet and Tempranillo in varying proportions, and the best white is a full-bodied, oak-aged Chardonnay. The property has been promoted to a Vino de Pago.

Enríque Mendoza ☆☆–☆☆☆
Alfás del Pí, Alicante. www.bodegasmendoza.com
A medium-sized estate, thoroughly international in its approach to reds, producing full-bodied Cabernet, Merlot, Shiraz, Petit Verdot, and French-style blends. Plus Moscatel, of course.

Mustiguillo ☆☆–☆☆☆
La Cuevas de Utiel, Valencia.
www.bodegamustiguillo.com
Bobal is the variety that dominates these wines, which are released as Viños de la Tierra. These are rich, plummy wines with no trace of rusticity.

Cooperativa Nuestra Señora del Rosario ☆
Bullas. www.bodegasdelrosario.es
This very large cooperative is well-equipped and makes

consistently fruity white (Macabeo), also *rosado* and red, both from Monastrell. Almost all Bullas wine that is exported comes from here.

Piqueras ☆
Almansa. 45 ha. www.bodegaspiqueras.es
A large producer, and just about the only one in Almansa with aspirations to quality. A new winery was built in 2002. The reds are easily the best wines, and combine Monastrell, Tempranillo, and Syrah. The pure Syrah, Valcanto, is rather jammy.

Salvador Poveda ☆☆–☆☆☆
Monóvar, Alicante. www.salvadorpoveda.com
An outstanding Alicante bodega, known especially for its rich dessert Fondillón, a fortified Monastrell given long cask ageing.

Bodegas La Purísima ☆–☆☆
Yecla. 3,325 ha. www.bodegaslapurisima.com
This immense cooperative produces more half the wine from Yecla. The quality of the wines, mostly from Monastrell, has improved considerably over recent years. Trapío, from low-yielding old vines, is the best of them.

Bodegas Real ☆–☆☆
Valdepeñas. 350 ha. www.bodegas-real.com
A large company, producing good-value Chardonnay and Tempranillo. The prestige brand is Palacio de Ibor, a more structured wine for short term ageing.

El Regajal ☆☆
Aranjuez, Viños de Madrid. 12 ha.
A boutique winery that produces a single wine that blends Tempranillo, Cabernet Sauvignon, Merlot, and Syrah. The result is lush, and too oaky for some.

Agapito Rico ☆–☆☆
Jumilla. 100 ha.
This property has moved away from the traditional brawny style of Jumilla to produce fruity, straightforward red wines, mostly unoaked, from varieties such as Merlot and Syrah.

Bodegas San Isidro ☆
Jumilla. www.bsi.es
The region's largest cooperative, processing the production from thousands of hectares, much of which is sold in bulk. But wines bottled under the Sabatcha label can be of good quality.

Sandoval ☆☆–☆☆☆
Ledaña, Manchuela. 11 ha.
Founded in 2001, this property, owned by Spanish journalist Victor de la Serna, successfully blends the local Bobal with Syrah and other varieties, and ages them in French oak.

Sierra Salinas ☆☆–☆☆☆
Yecla, Alicante. 50 ha. www.sierrasalinas.com
Founded in 2000, the bodega remains loyal to local varieties such as Garnacha and Monastrell, although Cabernet Sauvignon gives some backbone to most of the blends. Excellent wines, though sometimes of alarming strength.

Félix Solís ☆☆
Valdepeñas. 1,000 ha. www.felixsolis.com
This family owned winery owns extensive vineyards, but also buys in grapes and must. It is a large-scale maker of reds and *rosados* with a reputation for oak aged reds, especially Viña Albali Reserva. The company is very dynamic and has formed a new division, Pagos del Rey, which has acquired bodegas in Rioja, Rueda, Toro, and Ribera del Duero.

Dominio de Valdepusa ☆☆☆
Malpica de Tajo, Toledo. 42 ha. www.pagosdefamilia.com
The Marqués de Griñón founded this property in 1989, planting Bordeaux varieties and Syrah. The wines have been of exceptional quality and made in an avowedly French style, though they have their own personality, with more power than most Bordeaux or Rhône wines. Today the property is part of the Arco group (see Berberana), but the Marqués remains fully involved.

Vegalfaro ☆☆
El Derramador-Requena, Utiel-Requena.
www.vegalfaro.com
Founded in 1999, this bodega produces dark, lush wines from Tempranillo and the French varieties, all at fair prices.

El Vínculo ☆☆
Campo de Criptana, La Mancha. 30 ha.
www.elvinculo.com
Alejandro Fernández of Pesquera (q.v.) has boldly ventured into La Mancha, creating this new property in 1999, just to prove his hunch that the region was capable of producing fine wine. The wine is very much in the Pesquera style: rich, tannic, and given long ageing in American oak.

Andalucía

The great fame and success of sherry were achieved to some degree at the expense of the other regions of Andalucía. From their long-established trading base, the sherry makers were able to buy the best from their neighbours to add to their own stock. Sherry may be the best *vino generoso* of Andalucía, but it is not the only one. Montilla can compete, with very similar wines, and Málaga with alternatives at the sweeter end of the range.

Málaga

Málaga, on the Costa del Sol, is strictly an *entrepôt* rather than a vineyard centre. The grapes that make its sweet (occasionally dry) brown wines are grown either in the hills 40 kilometres (25 miles) to the east or the same distance to the north. In the nineteenth century their wines were famous as "Mountain".

East are the coastal vineyards of Axarquía, where the grape is the Moscatel. North around Mollina (in fact towards Montilla) it is the Pedro Ximénez (or PX). Rules require that all the grapes are brought to Málaga to mature in bodegas. Various methods are used to sweeten and concentrate the wines, from sunning the grapes, to boiling down the must to *arrope*, as in Jerez.

The styles of the finished wine range from a dry white of Pedro Ximénez, not unlike a Montilla amontillado, to the common dark and sticky *dulce* color, thickly laced with *arrope* (reduced grape juice used to make sweetening). The finest quality, comparable in its origins to the Essencia of Tokaj, is the *lágrima*, the "tears" of uncrushed grapes. The difference is that noble rot concentrates Tokaj, in Málaga it is the sun. Other Málagas are *pajarete*, a dark, semi-sweet apéritif style; the paler *semi-dulce*; and the richly aromatic Moscatel. The finer wines are made in a solera system like sherry, with younger wine refreshing older. A great rarity, a century-old vintage Málaga from the Duke of Wellington's estate, bottled in 1875, was a superlative, delicate, aromatic, and still sweet dessert wine in 1995.

But Málaga is in decline. The large commercial wineries live on, but the the specialists such as Scholtz Hermanos, with their magnificent old soleras, have been forced by declining fashion and sales to shut their doors for good. Hope comes from such newcomers as Telmo Rodríguez who has revived an ancient Moscatel vineyard to make "Mountain wine" again, with wonderful results.

Montilla-Moriles

Montilla's wines are close enough to sherry to be easily confused with (or passed off as) its rivals. The soil is the same albariza, but the climate is harsher and hotter, and the Pedro Ximénez, grown here in preference to the Palomino, yields smaller crops, producing wines of a higher alcoholic degree and slightly lower acidity. The finest wines are often fermented in tall clay *tinajas*, like giant *amphoras*, and rapidly develop the same flor yeast as sherry. They fall into the same classifications: fino, oloroso, or palo cortado – the finos being from the first light pressing. With age, fino becomes amontillado, "in the style of Montilla". Unfortunately, however, the sherry shippers have laid legal claim in Britain (the biggest export market for Montilla) to the classic terms. Instead of a Montilla fino, amontillado, or oloroso, a true and fair description, the label must use "dry", "medium" or "cream". Montilla has much to recommend it as an alternative to sherry. Its finos in particular have a distinctive dry softness of style, with less "attack" but no less freshness. A cool bottle of Montilla disappears with gratifying speed.

Last of the Andalusian *denominaciónes*, and most deeply in the shadow of Jerez, is the coastal region of Huelva, near the Portuguese border. Condado de Huelva (known in Chaucer's time as "Lepe") has exported its strong white wines from the Zalema variety for 1,000 years. The commercial power of Jerez has effectively kept it in obscurity. Until the 1960s, its wine was blended and shipped as sherry, but fewer of the old soleras are being maintained. Now that it has to compete with its old paymaster, times are not easy, and the region is increasingly making light white wines.

Leading Andalucía Producers

Alvear ☆☆–☆☆☆
Montilla. 200 ha. www.alvear.es
An independent firm, founded by the Alvear family in 1729. Today it is still owned and managed by family members.

Fermentation in *tinajas* and ageing through the solera system are carried out according to the traditions of Montilla, producing wines of high quality. Fino CB is its biggest seller. CB is a slightly fuller fino, and other names and styles include Carlos VII amontillado, Asunción oloroso, and a wide range of superb wines from Pedro Ximénez, which differs from the Jerez version since it is not fortified.

Cobos ☆
Montilla. www.navisa.es
Wines of variable quality, but the Pompeyo fino and Tres Pasa PX are reliable.

Gracia Hermanos ☆☆
Montilla. www.bodegasgracia.com
A bodega with high standards, owned by Pérez Barquero (q.v.). Its best wines are released under the Taromaquia label and range from fruity fino to lavish Pedro Ximénez.

Málaga Virgen ☆–☆☆
Málaga. 250 ha. www.bodegasmalagavirgen.com
This is now the leading Málaga bodega, having absorbed the old firm of López Hermanos. Trajinero is probably the best dry Málaga; Cartojal is a "pale-cream" *pálido*; and the flagship is the straight Málaga Virgen, aged two years in cask without topping up.

Jorge Ordóñez ☆☆☆
Málaga.
A new firm, founded in 2003, that is reviving magnificent Málagas from Moscatel grapes.

Bodegas Pérez Barquero ☆–☆☆☆
Montilla. www.perezbarquero.com
A well-equipped winery producing a reliable range of different styles under the brand name Gran Barquero. Top of the range is the magnificent 30-year-old Pedro Ximénez called La Cañada.

Viños Telmo Rodríguez ☆☆☆
Logroño. www.telmorodriguez.com
The ubiquitous Spanish winemaker has sought out steep vineyards within Málaga to produce what he calls "mountain wine", a style popular centuries ago in Britain. It is an unctuous Moscatel, given greater suppleness with long barrel-ageing and susceptible, I suspect, to years of development in the bottle.

Toro Albala ☆☆–☆☆☆
Aguilar de la Frontera, Montilla. 70 ha. www.toroalbala.com.
Remarkable wines , of which easily the best are the ancient soleras producing amontillado and very sweet PX styles of great concentration and swagger.

Bodegas Privilegio del Condado ☆
Bollullos del Condado. 1,600 ha. www.vinicoladelcondado.com
The main cooperative of Huelva, responsible for large quantities of brandy, some table wines, and some good, solera-aged, sherry-style *generosos*.

Sherry

Sherry, like many Mediterranean wines, was first appreciated in and shipped to the countries of northern Europe for its strength, its sweetness, and its durability – all qualities that made it a radically different commodity from medieval claret. By Shakespeare's day, while spirits were still unknown, "sack" (as it was then called) was hugely popular as the strongest drink available. The warming effect of a "cup of sack", at perhaps 17 degrees alcohol, was the addiction not just of Sir John Falstaff, but of every tavern-goer. Sack came from Málaga, the Canary Islands, and even from Greece and Cyprus. But the prince of sacks was "sherris", named after the Andalucían town of Jerez de la Frontera.

Jerez has had an international trading community since the Middle Ages. Until the rise of Rioja it was unique in Spain for its huge bodegas full of stock worth millions. The refinement of its wine from a coarse product, shipped without ageing, to the modern elaborate range of styles began in the eighteenth century. Like Champagne, (which it resembles in more ways than one) it flowered with the wealth and technology of the nineteenth century. What its makers have done is to push the natural adaptability of a strong but not otherwise extraordinary, indeed rather flat and neutral, white wine to the limit. They have exploited its potential for barrel-ageing in contact with oxygen – the potentially disastrous oxidation – to produce flavours as different in their way as a lemon and a date. And they have perfected the art of blending from the wide spectrum in their paintbox to produce every conceivable nuance in between – and to produce it unchanging year after year.

The making of sherry today, folklore apart, differs little from the making of any white wine. A fairly light wine is rapidly pressed and fermented. Eventually it reaches a natural strength of between 12 and 16 degrees. At this point it is fortified with spirit to adjust the strength to 15 or 18 degrees, depending on its quality and characteristics. This is where sherry's unique ageing process begins.

It is the wayward nature of sherry that different barrels (500-litre "butts") of wine, even from the same vineyard, can develop in different ways. The essential distinction is between those that develop a vigorous growth of floating yeast, called flor, and those that do not. All the young wines are kept in the "nursery" in butts filled four-fifths full. The finest and most delicate wines, only slightly fortified to maintain their finesse, rapidly develop a creamy scum on the surface, which thickens in spring to a layer several inches deep.

This singular yeast has the property of protecting the wine from oxidation, and at the same time reacting with it to impart subtle hints of maturity. These finest wines, or finos, are ready to drink sooner than heavier sherries. They remain pale because oxygen is excluded by the floating yeast. They can be perfect at about five years old. But their precise age is irrelevant because, like all sherries, they are blended for continuity in a solera (see box below).

Young wines of a heavier, clumsier, and more pungent style grow less flor, or none at all. A stronger dose of fortifying spirit

discourages any flor that may appear. This second broad category of sherry is known, if it shows potential quality, as oloroso. These wines are barrel-aged without benefit of flor, in full contact with the air. Their maturation is therefore an oxidative process, darkening their colour and intensifying their flavour. A third, eccentric, class of sherry is also found in this early classifying of the crop – one that combines the breadth and depth of a first-class oloroso with the fragrance, finesse, and "edge" of a fino. This rarity is known as a palo cortado.

These three are the raw materials of the bodega – naturally different from birth. It is the bodega's business to rear them so as to accentuate these differences, and to use them in combinations to produce a far wider range of styles. A fino which is matured beyond the life span of its flor usually begins to deepen in colour and broaden in flavour, shading from straw to amber to (at great age) a rich, blackish-brown. Every bodega has one or more solera of old finos, which have been allowed to move through the scale from a fresh fino, to a richer, more concentrated fino-amontillado, to an intensely nutty and powerful old amontillado.

Commercially, however, such true and unblended amontillados are very rare. In general usage the term has been more or less bastardized to mean any "medium" sherry, between dry fino and creamy old oloroso in style, but rarely with the quality of either. All sherries in their natural state, maturing in their soleras, are bone dry. Unlike port, sherry is never fortified until fermentation is over – all sugar used up. Straight, unblended sherry is therefore an ascetic, austere taste: a rarity in commerce. The only exception is *dulce*: concentrated wine used for sweetening blends.

As the sherry ages in the bodega, evaporation increases both the alcohol content and the proportion of flavouring elements. Very old sherries still in wood often become literally undrinkable in their own right – but priceless in the depth of flavour they can add to a blend. Classic sherry-blending is very much the art of the shipper, but anyone can try it for himself by acquiring, say, a bottle of a very old dry sherry such as Domecq's Río Viejo or González Byass Duque, and simply adding one small glassful of it to a carafe of an ordinary medium sherry. The immediate extra dimension of flavour in the everyday wine is a revelation.

Each shipper in Jerez will create and promote its own brands. The best of these will be the produce of a single, prized solera, usually slightly sweetened with *arrope*. A touch of near-black but almost tasteless *vino de color* may be needed to adjust the colour. Possibly a little younger wine in the same style will be added to give it freshness. A common commercial blend, on the other hand, will consist largely of low-value, minimally aged *rayas* or *entre finos* (the term for second-grade wine in the fino style). A small proportion of wine from a good solera will be added to improve the flavour, then a good deal of sweetening wine to mask the faults of the base material. It is, unfortunately, wines made to this sort of specification that have given sherry the image of a dowdy drink of no style.

The sad result is that the truly great wines of Jerez, wines that can stand comparison in their class with great white burgundy or Champagne, are absurdly undervalued. In recent years, many of the major shippers have released new wines in order to stimulate fresh interest in sherry as a whole. Thus vintage-dated or age-dated sherries, and minute bottlings from the most ancient soleras, have been introduced onto the market, and in 2000 aged-dated sherries became an officially recognized category for the first time. For connoisseurs they are a true delight, but have had little impact on the overall sales and consumption of sherry, which continues to suffer from its stuffy image.

The Sherry Region

Jerez lies 16-kilometres (10-miles) inland from the Bay of Cádiz in southwest Spain. Its vineyards surround it on all sides, but all the best of them are on outcrops of chalky soil in a series of dune-like waves to the north and west, between the rivers Guadalete and Guadalquivír.

The Guadalquivír, famous as the river of Seville, from which Columbus set out to discover America, Magellan to circum-navigate, and Pizarro to conquer Peru, forms the northern boundary of the sherry region. Its port, Sanlúcar de Barrameda, Jerez, and Puerto are the three sherry towns. The land between them is the zone known as Jerez Superior, the heart of the best sherry country.

There are three soil types in the sherry region, but only the intensely white albariza, a clay consisting of up to 80 per cent pure chalk, makes the best wine. It has high water-retaining properties that resist summer drought and the desiccating wind, the Levante, that blows from Africa. It also reflects sunlight up into the low-trained bush vines so that the grapes bask in a slow oven as they ripen. Barro, a brown, chalky clay, is more fertile but produces heavier, coarser wine. Arena, or sand, is little used now for vineyards at all. Each distinct, low, vineyard hill has a name: Carrascal, Macharnudo, Añina, and Balbaina are the most famous of the *pagos*, as they are called, surrounding Jerez in an arc of albariza to the north and west. A separate outbreak of excellent soil gives rise to the *pagos* south and east of Sanlúcar, 22 kilometres (14 miles) from Jerez, of which the best-known name is Miraflores.

Since the export market went into decline in 1979, there has been a massive reconversion in the sherry industry, with cash incentives to grub up excess vineyard land, and a spate of takeovers and mergers in the business. Sherry had boomed – give or take the odd war – from the Middle Ages until 1979, and planting reflected everyone's expectation that it would continue to do so. By 1997, the job was completed, and the vineyards today occupy 10,100 hectares.

Sampling sherry in a bodega

Leading Sherry Producers

Antonio Barbadillo ☆☆–☆☆☆☆
Sanlúcar de Barrameda. 500 ha. www.barbadillo.com
The biggest bodega in Sanlúcar, with a big stake in the Manzanilla business and some wonderful old wines. It was founded in 1821 by Don Benigno Barbadillo. Five generations later, the company is still family owned, although Harvey's has a shareholding. Offices (in the former bishops' palace) and the original bodegas are in the town centre.

In the surrounding albariza areas of Cádiz, Balbaina, San Julian, Carrascal, and Gibaldin, its vineyards produce a wide range of Manzanillas and other sherries. Barbadillo was a pioneer of dry white Palomino (Castillo de San Diego) that has enjoyed phenomenal success on the domestic market. In the late 1990s, it launched Manzanilla En Rama, drawn directly from cask and bottled with only the lightest filtration, and Reliquias, a stunning range of extremely old, rare, and costly sherries from ancient soleras.

John William Burdon ☆☆
Puerto de Santa María. www.caballero.es
Formerly an English-owned bodega, and one of the largest bodegas of the mid- to late nineteenth century. It has long been owned by Luis Caballero (q.v.). Wines are Burdon Fino, a Puerto-style fino, Don Luís Amontillado, and Heavenly Cream.

Luis Caballero ☆
Puerto de Santa María. 33 ha. www.caballero.es
Founded in the 1830s with a stock of wine from the dukes of Medina, this has been in the Caballero family since 1932, and is now run by Don Luis Caballero. All wines are supplied from own vineyards; major brands include fino Pavón and amontillado Don Luis. Fino is the specialty, as Don Luis has his own formula, made by adding some very young wine to the wine drawn from solera. Don Luis is also the owner of Burdon and Lustau (qq.v.).

Croft ☆–☆☆
Jerez de la Frontera. 370 ha.
The port shipper (founded 1768) gave its name to the sherry division of International Distillers and Vintners in 1970. In 2001, the company was acquired by González Byass (q.v.). Rancho Croft on the edge of town is a huge complex of traditional-style buildings housing the most modern plant and 70,000 butts. Market research led the company to launch the first pale cream sherry, Croft Original. Croft Particular is a pale amontillado, classic medium-dry, and Delicado a true fino.

Delgado Zuleta ☆☆–☆☆☆
Sanlúcar de Barrameda. www.delgadozuleta.com
Family firm founded in 1744 and still independent. The best-known wine is La Goya, a Manzanilla pasada. Other wines include the Zuleta Amontillado .

Pedro Domecq ☆☆–☆☆☆
Jerez de la Frontera. 1,050 ha. www.domecq.es
The oldest, largest, and one of the most respected shipping houses, founded in 1730 by Irish and French families and including in its history (as English agent) John Ruskin's father. Today it is part of the Diageo empire. The late head of the firm, Don José Ignacio Domecq, was recognized worldwide both literally and figuratively as "the nose" of sherry. The finest wines are the gentle Fino La Ina; Sibarita, an old palo cortado of which fewer than 400 cases are released each year; and Rio Viejo, a dark, rich but dry oloroso. Tiny quantities of very old wines are released each year, under labels such as Amontillado 51-1A (average age: 50 years) and Venerable PX.

Garvey ☆☆
Jerez de la Frontera. 500 ha. www.bodegasgarvey.com
One of the great bodegas, founded in 1780 by Irishman William Garvey, who built what for many years remained the grandest bodega in Spain: 170 metres (558 feet) long. It is owned by the Ruiz-Mateos family. A new winery and bodegas have been built on the outskirts of Jerez. San Patricio (named after the patron saint of Ireland), a full-flavoured fino, is its best-known sherry. Others include Tío Guillermo Amontillado, Ochavico Dry Oloroso, and La Lidia Manzanilla.

González Byass ☆☆–☆☆☆☆
Jerez de la Frontera. 820 ha. www.gonzalezbyass.es
One of the greatest sherry houses, founded in 1835 by Don Antonio González y Rodriguez, whose London agent, Robert Blake Byass, became a partner in 1863. The company is still directed almost entirely by the González family. Its best-known sherry is the world's biggest selling fino, Tío Pepe, which is of outstanding quality. La Concha Amontillado, San Domingo Pale Cream, and Nectar Cream are exported throughout the world. There is a range of glorious old sherries, including Amontillado del Duque and Apóstoles dry oloroso. This was the first shipper to release vintage-dated sherries, beginning with 1963. It also makes one of the greatest of all dessert sherries, Matúsalem, and an astonishing PX called Noë. Other interests include Croft sherry (q.v.).

Harvey's ☆–☆☆
Jerez de la Frontera. 400 ha. www.domecq.es
The famous Bristol shipper was founded in 1796. In 1822 the first John Harvey joined the firm. It is now part of Allied-Domecq, and today Harvey works closely with its Jerez partner, Pedro Domecq (q.v.). The firm became famous as blenders of "Bristol" sweet sherries, above all Bristol Cream, now the world's biggest selling brand, and a huge export business.

Hidalgo ☆☆☆
Sanlúcar de Barrameda. 200 ha. www.lagitana.es
Small bodega, founded in 1792 and is still owned and run by the Hidalgo family. The principal brands include: the yeasty vibrant La Gitana Manzanilla, Jerez Cortado (a palo cortado), Napoleon dry amontillado, and the outstanding Manzanilla Pasada Pastrana.

Emilio Lustau ☆☆–☆☆☆☆
Jerez de la Frontera. 170 ha. www.emilio-lustau.com
Founded in 1896, and since 1990 owned by Luis Caballero (q.v.), the company makes good-quality sherries under the

Solera Reserve label. They include the rare amontillado Escuadrilla and the dry oloroso Don Nuno. All wines from Caballero's own bodega are now released under the Lustau label. But the glory of the house is the range of rare almacenista sherries from small private stockholders. These stocks were built up by local professional families who sold the wines in bulk to the shippers.

As shippers developed their own vineyards, the role of almacenistas diminished, so it was a bright idea on the part of Lustau in 1981 to bottle and market a selection of these excellent, hand crafted wines. They come in all styles, from the most delicate Manzanillas to a range of Landed Age Rare Sherries of which the Rare Dry Oloroso and the Amoroso are particularly fine.

Marqués de Real Tesoro ☆☆
Jerez de la Frontera. www.grupoestevez.es
A somnolent company reinvigorated with new investment in the 1990s. The new owner, who is also the proprietor of Valdespino (q.v), has acquired the brand name Tío Mateo from Harveys and developed it into a first class fino. Clearly a bodega to watch.

Osborne ☆☆–☆☆☆
Puerto de Santa Maria. 500 ha. www.osborne.es
A large and expanding family owned bodega, which was founded in 1772 by Thomas Osborne Mann from Devon. The family today is totally Spanish and the title of Conde de Osborne was created by Pope Pius IX. In 1872, Osborne took over Duff-Gordon and still uses that name in certain markets.

Among its sherry brands are Quinta Fino, Coquinero Fino Amontillado, and 10RF Oloroso. The finest sherries are limited solera bottlings under the Rare label, and their high cost reflects their very limited production. The Osbornes are major brandy producers, too.

Rainera Pérez Marín ☆☆
Sanlúcar de Barrameda.
A small company, with first class Manzanilla, La Guita, which is the first sherry in this style to print its bottling date on the back label, a vital piece of information for consumers seeking the freshest wine.

Sanchez Romate ☆☆
Jerez de la Frontera. 60 ha. www.romate.com
A respected small bodega, founded in 1781 and still an independent company. Brands include Marizmeño Fino; NPU (Non Plus Ultra) Amontillado; and Cardenal Cisneros PX.

Sandeman ☆☆–☆☆☆
Jerez de la Frontera. 360 ha.
www.sandeman.com
One of the great port and sherry shippers, founded in London in 1790 by George Sandeman, a Scot from Perth. It now belongs to Sogrape, but a descendant, David Sandeman, is chairman. The traditional methods used produce some fine sherries, and the company maintains old soleras for its top wines, such as the superb palo cortado Royal Ambrosante, and the ultra-rich Royal Corregidor and Imperial Corregidor dessert sherries.

Terry ☆
Puerto de Santa María. www.domecq.es
A once famous name, now belonging to Harvey and thus Allied-Domecq. Terry still produces a range of standard sherries but today is better known for its brandies.

Valdespino ☆☆☆–☆☆☆☆
Jerez de la Frontera. www.grupoestevez.es
Many sherry fanciers have long regarded this ultra-traditional house as the finest sherry producer of them all. The wines were uncompromising, especially the rich, dry palo cortado (El Cardinal) and amontillado (Tío Diego) styles. Coliseo was the aficionado's amontillado: mouth-puckeringly dry, but explosive and intense in flavour.

However, in 1999, the company was sold to the Estevez Group. No changes have been made to the production team or style, and one can only hope it stays that way.

Valdivia ☆☆–☆☆☆
Jerez de la Frontera. 250 ha. www.bodegasvaldivia.com
Founded in 2003 by a cement tycoon, the company was sold on in 2008 to Jose Maria Ruiz-Mateos. The sherries, especially the Sacramento Oloroso, are of high quality.

Williams & Humbert ☆☆–☆☆☆
Jerez de la Frontera. www.williams-humbert.com
Founded in 1877 by Alexander Williams and his brother-in-law, Arthur Humbert. Today the company is part of the Medina group. Vineyards on albariza soils in Carrascal, Balbaina, and Los Tercios produce good wines. The best-known is Dry Sack, which is a light oloroso in style and, despite its name, not dry. Other brands are Canasta Cream, Walnut Brown, A Winter's Tale, and the impressive palo cortado, Dos Cortados. In the early 2000s, the company began to release rare and expensive vintage dated wines.

Wisdom & Warter ☆☆
Jerez de la Frontera. www.wisdomwarter.es
Wisdom and Warter, although apparently a short-cut recipe for bargain sherry, are the names of the two Englishmen who founded the company in 1854. It has long been a subsidiary of González Byass, but is run independently. The main brands are Olivar Fino, Royal Palace Amontillado, and the Tizon Palo Cortado.

The Canary Islands

Wine production varies from a cottage industry turning out tiny quantities of excellent wine made from museum varieties, which long ago died out on the peninsula, to quite large-scale wineries with real ambitions in the export department. However, even the largest winery in the largest DO (Bodegas Insulares in Tacoronte-Acentejo) admits that the lack of economy of scale on the islands, the eternal thirst of the tourist trade, and the sheer cost of shipping wine to mainland Europe are stacking the odds against them at the moment. But the same used to be said of Australia and New Zealand, and there have been big developments there. There are seven main islands, and DO wine is produced on four of them, with country wines on some of the others. Three of the DOs are island-wide.

Abona (Tenerife) DO zone in the southwestern quarter of the island, planted in Listán Blanco and Listán Negro, and Bastardo Negro. Light wines in all three colours of no export significance.

El Hierro The first vines on this island were planted by an Englishman, John Hill, in 1526. Today there are three subzones with vines planted on steep slopes up to 610 metres (2,000 feet) in altitude. As well as the staples Listán, Negramoll, Pedro Ximénez and Verdello, they also grow the rare Bujariego, Bremajuelo, Gual, Baboso, and Mulata. Some wines of exemplary quality, especially sweet wines and *rancios*, but the quantity is too small to be significant.

La Gomera The most recent of the DOs, recognized in 2003 and uniting 12 bodegas. The main white grape is the individual Forastera, which dominates the vineyards. Its wines have potential, with good acidity. They are rarely seen, since the total production is around 30,000 bottles.

El Monte (Gran Canaria) The DO covers the entire island, with production concentrated in the northeast sector. Listán Negro is the most important variety, though a wide range of others is also grown. Gran Canaria is best-known for its "mountain red" wine from Listán.

Lanzarote Beguiling black volcanic soils are the hallmark of this island, with vines planted in hollows scooped out of the ground to protect them from the prevailing winds. Most of the cultivation is of Malvasía and the sweet, semi-fortified style is a descendant of the original "Canary-Sack", which was famed in Shakespeare's day. There are dry wines made from the same grape, as well as a growing production of dry white from Listán Blanco and Diego, and a tiny amount of red and *rosado*.

La Palma The "Isla Bonita" is as famous for its banana plantations as for its wine, but there are three subzones, making anything from rustic, artisanal wines in the north to some respectable examples in the south. Grapes are Malvasía, Listán, Bujariego, Gual, Verdello, Bastardo, Sabro, and Negramoll, and wines come in all three colours. A handful are aged in French oak.

Tacoronte-Acentejo (Tenerife) The Canary Islands' first and largest DO covers the northwest of Tenerife and, of all of them, has the best chance of achieving export markets. There are 30 bodegas in the area making good reds from Listán Negro and a few pleasant whites mainly from Listán Blanco and Malvasía. Production has been steadily increasing since the DO was granted.

Valle de Güímar (Tenerife) This is almost a continuation of the vineyards of Abona, running up the southeastern coast of the island, with mainly Listán Blanco for mostly white wines of good, everyday quality. There is some small amount of *rosado* made from Listán Negro, and sweet Moscatel.

Valle de la Orotava (Tenerife) On the northwest coast between Tacoronte in the north and Ycod in the south, in a valley running down from the volcano to the sea. Pleasant, light white and red wines are made here in roughly similar quantities, with a small amount of *rosado*. Grape varieties: Listán Blanco and Negro.

Ycoden-Daute-Isora (Tenerife) This DO covers the extreme western part of the island and takes its name from the town of Icod de los Vinos, site of the famous 1,000-year-old "dragon tree". Mainly Listán Blanco and Negro. About two-thirds of production is white of good, clean, crisp style. There is also some light red and *rosado*.

Leading Canary Islands Producers

El Grifo ☆☆
San Bartolomé, Lanzarote. 30 ha. www.elgrifo.com
The oldest bodega on the island – founded in 1775, and re-established in 1980. Wines are mainly white – including an excellent sweet Malvasía.

Viña Frontera ☆
Frontera. www.cooperativafrontera.com
A well-equipped winery producing fruity whites from Verijadiego and red from Listán Negro.

Bodegas Insulares Tenerife ☆☆
Tacoronte. www.bodegasinsularestenerife.es
A bodega with all the latest kit and plenty of built-in room for expansion. The best wines are Viña Norte Tinto Maceración, made from Listán Negro and Negramoll by carbonic maceration, and Viña Norte Tinto Madera made from the same grapes but aged for four months in oak. A quality leader in the islands.

Cueva del Rey ☆☆
Icod de los Vinos.
Fascinating boutique winery run by Fernando González, an English teacher with a passion for white wines. He has a tiny bodega fitted with fibreglass tanks, and regales visitors with excellent tapas and a look round his museum. His wines, both white and red, are currently among the best of the Ycoden DO.

Monje ☆☆
El Sauzal. 17 ha. www.bodegasmonje.com
A small but admired bodega in Tacoronte-Acentejo. The wines range from Hollera Monje, made by carbonic maceration, to the oak-aged Monje d'Autor.

Portugal

Portugal, the most conservative wine country in Europe, has moved decisively into the new wine world – happily without abandoning her highly original style or her sheaf of indigenous vines. Portugal doesn't do Chardonnay and Cabernet. You may well not be able to pronounce what she offers, but there is more reason every year to investigate. Where you used to be confronted with leathery tannins and would struggle to find fruit, young winemakers with modern ideas offer full and original grape flavours in robust, splendidly structured wines. Grape varieties are one difference from Spain; another is the Atlantic. The Portuguese climate feels the ocean alongside.

Conservative as she is, Portugal was the first country in modern times (and also in ancient, when you consider port) to invent a new style of wine for export, and to get it so spectacularly right that it became one of the biggest-selling brands on earth. The wine, if you remember, was Mateus Rosé. With its competitors, it still accounts for a fair part of Portugal's wine exports.

It is the measure of Portuguese conservatism that neither the Mateus style, nor for that matter port, has ever caught on in a big way in their home country. With the rapid development of an urban middle class and a supermarket society outside Lisbon and Oporto, the Portuguese people are gradually being weaned onto more international styles of wine. Yet this is no little backwater. Its production is large enough to place it at tenth in the league of wine-producing nations, although less wine is now consumed in the home market. Conservative they may be, but the Portuguese were the first to establish the equivalent of a national system of *appellation contrôlée*: the first delimited area being the Douro in 1756. Then came a wave of demarcations, starting in 1908 with Vinho Verde. Portugal had legally defined boundary, grapes, techniques, and standards, for all of what were then her better wines. For many years, unfortunately, these sat heavily on progress, leading to a distorted picture of where the best wines were really being grown. Happily, much of the confusion over regional boundaries was resolved with the introduction of new legislation, more or less coinciding with Portugal's entry to the European Union.

The country now has a four-tier appellation system, which parallels that of France. The best wines qualify for DOC (Denominação de Origem Controlada) status, of which there are currently 30. Next are the four IPRs (Indicações de Proveniência Regulamentada), which are regions on a five-year probation for DOC status. In 1992, eight broader Vinhos Regionais were introduced. The fourth distinction is Vinhos de Mesa (table wines), which covers the rest. During the long period while the regional system was out of date, many of Portugal's better wine companies took to using brand names that gave no indication of their origin. Regulations now insist, however, that all wines must have their region of origin indicated on the label, unless they are bottled as *vinho de mesa*, without a vintage date.

Another Portuguese peculiarity was the ascendancy of merchant companies over primary producers. This situation has now been reversed; encouraged by the availability of EU grants, individual estates are very much the rising stars. The last 25 years have seen the rise of single *quintas* (estates): individual properties growing their own grapes and making their own wine.

Although there used to be relatively few big wine estates outside the Douro, ever larger domaines are being created, especially in southern regions such as Palmela, the Alentejo, and Ribatejo. Esporão is one property with 650 hectares of vineyards. Nonetheless, Portugal is still a land of smallholdings, with about half their production taken to the country's numerous cooperative cellars. Most of the rest who have wine to spare after supplying their families and friends, sell it to merchants. Many of the bigger and better merchants buy and bottle wine from each of the major areas; there is little regionality at this level, either.

Traditionally, the Portuguese practice was to divide all wines into two categories: *verde* or *maduro*, and these names are still used on the wine lists of many restaurants. Vinho Verde is unaged wine, and the use of the term is now legally limited to the northern province, the Minho; sparkling rosés would, however, logically fit into this category. Maduro means "mature". It implies long ageing in barrel (or in cement vat) and bottle. But the *verde/maduro* division is becoming blurred as more young wines, red and white, are now reaching the market. The very real virtue of Portuguese wine made in the time-honoured way is its structure; it is engineered to last for decades, evolving from what could be gum-withering astringency to a most satisfying texture, when firmness is rounded out to velvety smoothness without losing the feel of the iron fist within. Its vice is lack of flavour, and often only the shyest fragrance for such a potent wine. Such wines remain popular on the domestic market, but most go-ahead *quintas* and merchants are opting for a more modern style: drinkable young, but also capable of bottle age.

A peculiar piece of terminology is used for selected, long aged wines. The word Garrafeira has much of the meaning of Reserva, but with the added implication that it is the merchant's "private" best wine, aged for some years in barrel and subsequently in bottle, to be ready for immediate drinking when sold. What is admirable about the Portuguese wine scene is that the best producers and cooperatives have embraced modern wine-making techniques to ensure the wines can compete with the best from elsewhere in Europe, while staunchly remaining faithful to the 500 indigenous grape varieties. This gives the wines tremendous personality. On the other hand, the combination of obscure regions of origin and obscure grape varieties has made life difficult for the modern non-Portuguese wine drinker, who, having grappled with some success with similar systems found in France and Italy, has a limited appetite for a further struggle with Portuguese names and regions. This has hindered the development and popularity of the wines on international markets.

Transporting port down the Douro by traditional flat-bottomed boat

Portuguese Wine Regions & Styles

The wines of Portugal (excluding port) are described below, progressing geographically, as nearly as possible, from north to south. The headings are the names of the officially recognized regions or DOCs. For port, see pages 419–25.

Vinho Verde & the Minho

This northerly region extends up from Oporto and almost as far east as Vila Real. Its name is synonymous with the wines it produces: probably Portugal's most original and successful contribution to the world's wine cellar. What is "green" about Vinho Verde is not its colour (55 per cent is red and the white is like lemon-stained water). It is its salad-days freshness, which seems to spring straight from the verdant pergolas where it grows in promiscuous polyculture with maize and vegetables.

Traditionally, the vines hang in garlands from tree to tree, or are trained on pergolas of granite post and chestnut lintel. Growing the grapes so high above the ground has several advantages. It slows their ripening and produces the desired sugar/acid balance; it counteracts the tendency to fungal diseases in a cool and rainy climate; it also allows for other cultivation below and between. However, modern vineyards are being trained on lower systems (some of the best come from single vineyard properties), making the operation easier to mechanize as well as producing wines with greater ripeness, and thus greater commercial appeal abroad .

The traditional method of making Vinho Verde is to encourage an active malolactic fermentation. The cool climate, the grapes cultivated, and their elevated training result in very high levels of malic acid. The natural bacterial conversion of malic to lactic acid takes the rasp out of the acidity, and adds the tingle of its by-product, CO_2. In some country inns the jug wine from barrels is not unlike very dry, fizzy, and rather cloudy cider.

Nowadays, however, only a few jug wines are made in the traditional way, and almost no Vinho Verde undergoes malolactic fermentation in bottle, as this creates a sediment. The vast majority of commercial wineries finish the wine to complete bacterial stability, and then bottle it with an injection of CO_2 to arrive at approximately the same result. The last method also gives the winemaker the option of sweetening his wine (with unfermented must) without the danger of its refermenting.

The total dryness and distinct sharpness of "real" Vinho Verde is not to everyone's taste, so many bottlings that are exported are considerably sweetened. In the red version, fermented with stalks and all, it contrives with high tannin to make an alarmingly astringent drink, which foreigners rarely brave a second time. The merchants' brands of Vinho Verde do not normally specify which part of the wide region they come from. Of the nine subregions, Amarante and Peñafiel, just inland from Oporto, produce the most white wine. Braga, the centre of the Minho, has good-quality, fresh red and white.

Lima, along the river of the same name north of Braga, specializes in slightly more full-bodied reds. Melgaço and Monção, along the River Minho on the Spanish border in the north, are most famous for their single variety white: Alvarinho, much the most expensive (and most alcoholic) wine of the region, but only by courtesy, if at all, a Vinho Verde. Alvarinho is smooth and still, sometimes aged in wood and softly fragrant of apricots or freesias, rather than brisk and tinglingly fruity. It is mostly bottled young but, unlike ordinary Vinho Verde, it can be aged for two to three years in bottle.

Transmontano

Northeastern Portugal, from Vila Real to Bragança, is largely an elevated plateau, much of which is too cold for viticulture to thrive. Nonetheless wines here are produced under the Trás-os-Montes DOC. The red grapes are mostly those found in the Douro; white wine is in the minority. Production is dominated by cooperatives in Valpaços and Chaves, and the wines are rarely seen outside Portugal.

The Douro

The mythology of the Douro reports that it was its terrible table wine that forced merchants to lace it with brandy and create port. It may have been so, but since 1991 the region has made great strides and today produces admirable table wines, which are indisputably among Portugal's very best. The improvement began to happen when growers realized that good table wines needed the pick of their grapes, rather than the rejects from port they had made them from before. The Douro also provides a number of well-known merchants' Garrafeiras (private reserve), and, in the shape of Barca Velha, an old-fashioned red wine of international stature to put beside Spain's Vega Sicilia, from 160 kilometres (100 miles) farther up the same river.

Beiras (Dão & Bairrada)

The Beiras is too large a region to have any cohesive character. On the other hand, it contains two DOCs that are among the country's best-known wines: Dão and Bairrada.

The region of Dão, centred on the old cathedral city of Viseu, 80-kilometres (50-miles) south of the Douro, is set among pine-forested country along the valleys of three rivers: the Alva, the Mondego, and the Dão, where they cut through hills of granite boulders and sandy soil. The vast majority of its 20,000 hectares of vineyard is planted with black grapes (several of which it has in common with the Douro).

The profile of a red Dão remains, despite the care and skill of several of the merchants who mature it, a rather dry, hard wine, strangely lacking in bouquet or lingering sweetness. With the region's cool nights, it is not always easy for the grapes to reach full maturity, so tannins can be quite tough. But growers and winemakers are coming to grips with these difficulties, and better site selection and grape selection is already yielding impressive results. The main reason for the Dão's poor image is that, until 1990, the ten local cooperatives had a near-monopoly on production. The EU put a stop to that. There was, for many years, only one estate-grown Dão on the market – Conde de Santar. It no longer enjoys supremacy, though, as a number of single *quintas* now make very good wine.

Once the cooperatives had lost their monopoly, a number of producers were encouraged to buy in grapes and make their own wines. Sogrape is probably in the strongest position, having invested about four million pounds in a new winery at Quinta dos Carvalhas. Its wines have steadily improved. The replacement of varieties such as Tinta Roriz and Baga with better suited ones such as Touriga Nacional and Alfrocheiro has also done much to improve quality. In the past, Dão was a blended wine, but today one of its components, Touriga Nacional, is increasingly being bottled as a varietal wine. Very impressive it can be, too.

Although it remained undemarcated until 1979, some 70 years after the Dão region, Bairrada is a real rival in the quality of its wines. The name applies to an area between Dão and the Atlantic, north of Coimbra, and south of Oporto, with the towns of Mealhada and Anadia as its main centres. Its low, heavy-soiled, lime-rich hills have about the same vineyard area as Dão, and the same preponderance of red grapes (90 per cent) over white. But its climate is more temperate, its grape varieties different, and its *adegas* more individual.

Two local grapes not found elsewhere have outstanding qualities. The red Baga is a late-ripening variety, high in tannin and acid, which give real authority and "cut" to a blend. As the dominant variety it needs 15–20 years' ageing, but can eventually achieve the fragrance of fine claret. The aromatic local white grape is the Bical, which seems to have an exceptional balance of acidity and extract, aromatic of apricots, brisk and long-flavoured. Another grape, the more neutral Maria Gomes, forms the basis of Bairrada's sparkling wine industry, which now has some very palatable products.

Baga can be an excellent grape – but not everywhere in Bairrada. Since 2003 the DOC rules have been changed to allow other varieties to be planted and employed in the wines. The same is true of white wines, which may now contain international varieties, too. The consequence of these changes is that quality overall has improved but at the expense of regional identity. Consumers need to know where to go to find good Baga-based Bairrada.

One other DOC of interest is the Lafões region in the wetter west of the Beira Alta. It has only recently been regulated and produces a wine that is similar in style to Vinho Verde.

Estremadura

The biggest Lisbon area, immediately north of the city, is the Estremadura, which, among its 32,000 hectares, includes three of the four historic wine regions. Carcavelos is nearest to extinction, with just one remaining but dwindling vineyard: Quinta dos Pesos, which now sells its grapes to a local priest who doubles as a winemaker. It is a light, amber, velvety, not oversweet, slightly fortified dessert or apéritif wine like a soft, nutty, and buttery Verdelho or Bual Madeira.

More is heard of Bucelas, whose 200 hectares of white wine vineyards lie 16-kilometres (10-miles) due north of Lisbon.

Despite its proximity to the capital, the region is enjoying a new lease of life, producing a handful of crisp, fragrant, dry white wines from the aromatic Arinto grape.

Still more is heard of Colares, not because there is any quantity but because it is a true original. Its vineyards are an unplottable sprawl in the sand dunes of the Atlantic coast west of Lisbon, between Sintra and the sea. They grow the Ramisco: a tiny, bloomy, dark-blue bullet of a grape whose thick skin would tan an ox-hide. Grown in pure sand (the plants have to be planted at the bottom of deep pits, which are then progressively filled in) it makes wine of quite unreasonable inkiness and astringency. There is also a white Colares based on Malvasia. Grafting is unnecessary – phylloxera is baffled by sand. Production is dwindling.

The Estremadura is home to some giant cooperatives, such as Arruda and São Mamede de Ventosa, as well as smaller, quality producers, including Quinta de Abrigada and Quinta de Pancas near Alenquer. Indeed, Alenquer is the subregion currently showing the most potential. Obidos is best known for its sparkling wines. There is a likelihood that the name of the region will be changed to Lisboa.

Ribatejo

The area northeast of Lisbon, where Wellington held the famous battle lines of Torres Vedras, is now a large DOC. From here, eastwards to the far banks of the Tagus beyond Santarém, Ribatejo used to be bulk wine country. For all that, it is a good source of wine, and has attracted the interest of a new generation of young winemakers. It is also one of the few regions in Portugal to grow commercial quantities of international grapes, including Cabernet Sauvignon, Merlot, and Chardonnay.

Terras do Sado

Across the Tagus, between the bridge and Setúbal on the far side of the Arrabida peninsula, lies a region with nearly 20,000 hectares of vineyards, divided between good, plain red wine and the sumptuously aromatic Muscat of Setúbal – a fortified wine with a minimum of 17 degrees of alcohol. It was apparently the creation of the firm of José Maria da Fonseca (q.v.) of Azeitão, who originally had a quasi-monopoly in the area (there are now other producers among whom J P Vinhos is leader).

Setúbal in this form is akin to a *vin doux naturel*, its fermentation stopped by the addition of spirit, in which the skins of more Muscat grapes, themselves highly aromatic, are steeped and macerated to give it the precise fragrance of a ripe dessert grape. The wine is barrel-aged and drunk without further ageing in bottle (though this does no harm), either at six years (when it is still amazingly fresh and grapey) or at 25 or more (when it has taken on more piquant notes of fragrance – I have noted geranium leaves – and developed the tobacco hue and satin texture of a fine tawny port).

DOC Setúbal more or less overlaps with DIC Palmela, which mostly produces red wine from the Castelão grape, and some white from Fernão Pires. The Vinho Regional allows more flexibility and many international varieties are making an appearance.

Alentejo

The vast area south of the Tagus was "discovered" in wine terms as recently as the beginning of the 1990s. Its brown hills are covered with the dark cork oaks that serve to furnish the world with its best quality corks. The Alentejo region as a whole has seen quite a dramatic improvement over the past decade in the quality of its wines, while certain subareas are now recognized for making the best wines, notably Reguengos (home to Esporão and José da Sousa), Redondo, Evora (Cartuxa is the leader), and Borba towards Elvas (of preserved-plums fame). Borba has a good cooperative and the Quinta do Carmo within its boundaries.

Herdade do Mouchão and Tapada do Chaves at Portalegre are making wines that can be outstanding. Traditional varieties such as Aragonez and Trincadeira are prized here, and most of the good wines are red: summers here are baking. Alentejo's potential has not been lost on the big merchants, either. Caves Aliança has invested at Borba and Sogrape in Vidigueira. These regions are virtually neighbours of the Spanish Extremadura, and, as a result, their wines are correspondingly high in alcohol.

Algarve

The wines of the demarcated Algarve on the south coast are likewise high in alcohol, but that is the only characteristic this region shares with the Alentejo. Cooperatives used to dominate, but only one remains in business. The handful of private estates are proving more successful at catering to the tastes of the region's golfers and holidaymakers. There are, surprisingly, four DOCs, but they are mostly moribund. In the early 2000s, the singer Cliff Richard sought to bestow much needed lustre on the Algarve by making a wine called Vida Nova from his estate there.

Portuguese Rosé

The fabulous success of Mateus and subsequent Portuguese semi-sweet, semi-sparkling rosés was achieved by applying the idea (not the traditional technique) of Vinho Verde to red grapes from a region where the wine had no particular reputation: the hills north of the Douro round the town of Vila Real. It did not matter that this was not a demarcated region; rather the reverse. It meant that when the local grapes ran out, supplies could be found in other areas. Today, rosés are made of grapes from almost anywhere in Portugal. The principal rosé winemaking areas are Bairrada and the Setúbal peninsula south of Lisbon. It is a process, then, and not a regional identity that characterizes these wines. They are made with a very short period of skin contact after crushing to extract the required pink tinge, then fermented like white wine; the fermentation is stopped while about 18 grams per litre of original grape sugar remain intact, then bottled with the addition of CO_2 under pressure.

Leading Minho Producers

Quinta da Ameal ☆☆
Ponte de Lima. 12 ha. www.quintadoameal.pt
A scrupulously run organic estate making excellent wines, oaked and unoaked, from the Loureiro grape. And full-bodied Arinto.

Quinta da Aveleda ☆–☆☆☆
Penafiel. 160 ha. www.aveleda.pt
Each year this estate produces one million cases of the most famous brands of Vinho Verde: Casal Garcia and Aveleda, both of which are medium dry. Quinta da Aveleda is a more traditional, bone dry wine. There are also successful wines from Touriga Nacional, which appear under the Aveleda label even though the grapes come from the owners' estate in Bairrada.

Adega Cooperativa Regional de Monção ☆☆
Mazedo. 1,000 ha. www.adegademoncao.com
A large cooperative that nonetheless maintains high standards. It is known for the pure Alvarinho Deu La Deu, which is made in two versions, with or without oak.

Quinta de Covela ☆☆
São Tomé de Covelas. 30 ha. www.covela.pt
Nuno Araújo's Biodynamic estate does not produce Vinho Verde, but instead focuses on intriguing white lends from Avesso and Chardonnay, and reds that blend Touriga Nacional with Bordeaux varieties.

Paço de Teixeiró ☆
Teixeiró. 12 ha. www.pacodeteixeiro.pt
Miguel Champalimaud of Quinta do Côtto also owns this small property that produces a reliable white wine from Avesso and Loureiro.

Quinta de Soalheiro ☆☆☆
Melgaço. 10 ha. www.soalheiro.com
A small but outstanding producer of a single Vinho Verde from the Alvarinho grape.

Leading Transmontano Producers

Casal de Valle Pradinhos ☆☆
Macedo de Cavaleiros. 30 ha.
The top wine here is Valle Pradinhos, which blends traditional Douro varieties with Cabernet Sauvignon to give a rich, deep, tannic wine.

Quinta do Sobreiró de Cima ☆
Valpaços. 40 ha. www.q-sobreirodecima.com
Production only began here in 2001. The white wine is mostly Verdelho, while the reds are built around Touriga Nacional and other varieties.

Leading Douro Producers

Domingos Alves e Sousa ☆☆–☆☆☆
Santa Marta de Penagulão. 110 ha.
www.alvesdesousa.com
Small Bordeaux-trained producer with five properties in the Baixo Corgo subregion of the Douro, which is now making some top red wines from local (port) grapes. The oak-aged Quinta da Gaivosa is rich and concentrated for keeping; Quinta da Vale de Raposa produces a range of single variety wines, as well as a new-oaked Grande Escolha in top vintages. The quality here is the result of both scrupulous winemaking and rich resources in the form of very old vines.

Chryseia ☆☆☆
Régua. www.chryseia.com
A triumphant joint venture between Bruno Prats, former owner of Château Cos d'Estournel and the Symington family. The first vintage was in 2000, and the wine was made entirely from traditional Douro varieties. Elegantly balanced strength. The second label is Post Scriptum.

Quinta do Côtto ☆☆–☆☆☆
Cidadelha. 60 ha. www.quinta-do-cotto.pt
Based in a magnificent eighteenth-century manor house, this estate was specializing in table wines from the Douro before it became fashionable to do so. Miguel Champalimaud, the owner, also produces port (q.v.), but it is less consistent than his red wine. The top *cuvée* is Grande Escolha.

Quinta do Crasto ☆☆–☆☆☆
Sabrosa. 70 ha. www.quintadocrasto.pt
Well-situated, family owned property in the Douro, making some inspiring non-fortified Douro wines as well as port. It has managed to tame the hard tannins that mar so many Douro red wines, and its success is noticeable in a fruity young wine and also a full, fleshy Reserva. Recent additions to the range include a Touriga Nacional, the tremendous new-oaked Vinha Maria Teresa, and Xisto, a less extracted wine made jointly with Jean-Michel Cazes of Château Lynch-Bages.

A A Ferreira ☆☆
Vila Nova de Gaia. www.sogrape.pt
Barca Velha, launched by port producer Ferreira in the 1950s, quickly established itself as Portugal's most prestigious red wine. Grapes, mainly Tinta Roriz, were grown at Quinta do Vale do Meão (q.v.) and trodden in big stone lagares, yielding about 4,000 cases a year.

Barca Velha was only released in the best vintages, while lesser vintages were declassified to Ferreirinha Reserva Especial. However, in 1999, the quinta was sold, depriving Ferreira of its best grapes. Quinta de Leda is now the principal source. Owned by Sogrape (q.v.) since 1987.

Niepoort ☆☆☆–☆☆☆☆
Oporto. 43 ha. www.niepoort-vinhos.com
Of Dutch origin, this family owned port shipper has gone from strength to strength under Dirk Niepoort. Redoma is the name given both to his monumental Douro red, and to a powerful, oaky white from old vines. In 1999, Niepoort added Batuta, an equally intense red from very low-yielding vines, and aged mostly in new oak.

These are now among the most impressive dry wines of Portugal. With restless energy Niepoort continues to acquire small estates and parcels from which he produces an expanding portfolio of table wines of remarkable character and individuality, and usually steering clear of the massive, oaky styles that are coming to dominate the region.

Pintas ☆☆☆
Pinhão. 2 ha.
A husband-and-wife team of distinguished Douro winemakers have since 2001 made superb, plummy, powerful wine from the Vale de Mendiz vineyard. In 2004 they added an equally remarkable white wine, from local varieties such as Viosinho, called Guru.

Quinta do Portal ☆☆
Sabrosa. 100 ha. www.quintadoportal.pt
A large company producing both ports and table wines from a number of estates in the Douro. The Reserva and Grande Reserva can be excellent, and the white Frontaria, from Gouveio and Malvasia, is both inexpensive and individual, with lively apricot fruit.

Ramos Pinto ☆☆–☆☆☆
Vila Nova da Gaia. 210 ha. www.ramospinto.pt
Under João Nicolai d'Almeida, Ramos Pinto was one of the first port houses to launch table wines, here under the Duas Quintas label. Blended from two *quintas*, Bom Retiro and Ervamoira, the wines (especially the Reservas) are solid and appealing.

A wine from a single estate, Quinta dos Bons Ares, combines the local grape, Touriga Nacional, and Cabernet in an 80/20 blend. The property is now owned by Champagne Louis Roederer, but the family continues to manage it.

Quinta de Roriz ☆☆–☆☆☆
Pinhão. 42 ha. www.quintaderoriz.com
A venerable port estate, now in partnership with the Symington family. As well as port, the property now makes first-class table wines from the local grapes.

Quinta de la Rosa ☆☆
Pinhão. 55 ha. www.quintadelarosa.com
The Bergqvist family have owned this property for over a century, and remain very much in charge. The property produces a good range of estate-bottled ports and Douro wines, with the best wines under the estate name, and a second range, Vale de Clara, from purchased fruit.

Quinta do Vale Dona Maria ☆☆☆
Ervedosa do Douro. 21 ha. www.quintavaledonamaria.com
Cristiano van Zeller is one of the most dynamic and versatile of Douro producers, and after he sold Quinta da Noval in 1993, he revitalized an estate belonging to his wife's family. There are good ports, of course, but the table wine is splendid, a richly oaky and powerful blend of Douro varieties. Some single vineyard wines, such as Casa de Casal de Loivos, are being added to the range, but in very small quantities.

Barrels of port, Niepoort wine lodge, Vila Nova de Gaia

Quinta do Vale Meão ☆☆☆–☆☆☆☆
Vila Nova de Foz Côa. 87 ha.
This historic estate was part of the Ferreira vineyards until its sale in 1999 to a former president of the company, Francisco Olazabal. The grapes for Ferreira's legendary Barca Velha were grown here, but now they are used for the Quinta's own red wine, a new-oaked superstar of the Douro.

Other properties include: Brunheda (Tua), Quinta do Fojo (Sabrosa), Lavradores do Feitoria (Sabrosa), Poeira (Pinhão), and Quinta do Vallado (Peso da Regua).

Leading Beiras Producers

Boas Quintas ☆☆
Mortágua. 10 ha. www.boasquintas.com
Although founded in 1991, Boas Quintas takes a traditional approach, working only with local varieties. The best wines are bottled under the Quinta da Fonte de Ouro label.

Palace Hotel do Buçaco ☆–☆☆
Mata do Bussaco. 3 ha. www.almeidahotels.com
Within the cellars of this extravagant hotel matures one of Europe's most unusual wines. The hotel's vineyards are near Curia in the Bairrada region, and grow its typical grapes. The red is trodden in stone lagares, while the white has become more modern in style, being fermented in new barriques.

The wines, which are only available at the Almeida group of hotels, are offered in vintages decades old. The best vintages (eg. white: '85, '84, '66, '65, '56; red: '82, '78, '70, '63, '60, '58, '53) have an exquisite hand made quality, but some vintages are oxidized.

Dão Sul ☆☆
Carregal do Sal. 90 ha. www.daosul.com
A company that, while based in the Dão, works closely with growers in other regions too. Consequently the range is extremely varied, but the winemaking is expert, resulting in eminently drinkable, modern, balanced wines. Labels include Quinta de Cabriz, and Quinta do Encontro in Bairrada.

Quinta da Foz de Arouce ☆☆–☆☆☆
Foz de Arouce. 15 ha. www.fozdearouce.com
Owner João Osório is fortunate that his daughter married the expert winemaker João Portugal Ramos (q.v.), who makes his wines. Although not in the Bairrada itself, the estate's principal grape is Baga, which gives a dense and profound wine.

Filipa Pato ☆☆
Amoreira da Gândara. www.filipapato.net
The daughter of Luis Pato (q.v.), Filipa Pato gained international experience before returning to her native region. She specializes in intriguing blends from Portuguese varieties only, sourced from the Bairrada and Dão regions, as well as single-vineyard wines under the Lokal range.

Luis Pato ☆☆☆
Amoreira da Gândara. 65 ha. www.luispato.com
Luis Pato began making his own wines in 1980, and has subsequently established himself as one of the leading independent producers in Portugal. He relies heavily on the local Baga grape, continually monitoring its performance in a variety of different soils. This has resulted in two excellent single vineyard wines: Vinha Pan and Vinha Barrosa, the latter made from very old, low-yielding vines. All his top red wines are aged in French oak. Their high tannin and acidity makes them candidates for long ageing.

Pato has spent many years experimenting in the vineyard and the winery, with the result that there has been considerable variation in style from one vintage to the next. In 1994, he launched the remarkable Quinta de Ribeirinho Pé Franco, a limited-production red made from incredibly low-yielding ungrafted Baga vines. Pato also makes attractive, dry white wines from the local Arinto, Cerceal, and Cercealinho varieties. There is also a single-variety white from Bical called Vinha Formal. He also has a small amount of Cabernet Sauvignon and Touriga Nacional in his vineyards, which he usually blends with Baga grapes.

In 2001, Pato formally left the Bairrada DOC to free himself from bureaucratic restrictions.

Quinta de Pellada.
See Quinta de Sães.

Quinta dos Roques ☆☆–☆☆☆
Abrunhosa do Mato. 75 ha.
A family owned estate that focuses firmly on local varieties, with Rui Reguinga, a celebrated consultant, to advise on vinification since 2002. Serious reds from Touriga Nacional and Jaen have seriously set the pace for the future of the Dão region. In 1997 the family bought a second property, bottled separately, called Quinta das Maias.

Quinta de Sães ☆☆–☆☆☆
Seia. 45 ha.
Small property in the Dão region, owned by Alvaro de Castro. Red and white wines from mostly local grapes are refined and sophisticated. The top bottling is Carrocel, which is aged in barriques for up to 18 months. Castro also owns another Dão property, Quinta de Pellada (q.v.).

Casa de Saima ☆☆–☆☆☆
Sangalhos. 18 ha,
A traditional property in Bairrada, with winemaker Rui Moura Alves making outstanding red and white wines, mainly from the local Baga and Bical respectively. Their red Garrafeiras, foot-trodden in *lagares*, are classic Baga wines that age well.

Caves São João ☆☆
Avelás de Caminho. 25 ha. www.cavessojoao.pt
Family owned producer in the heart of the Bairrada region, sourcing gapes from local growers as well as from its own vineyards. Two brothers, Alberto and Luis Costa, age, blend, and bottle some of the most impressive red wines from Bairrada and the neighbouring Dão region.

Bottled respectively under the Frei João and Porta dos Cavaleiros labels, the Reservas, sporting a cork label, have great depth and ageing potential. The company has recently launched a Cabernet-based wine called Quinta do Poço do Lobo from its own vineyard. And for good measure, its white Bairradas are among the best in the region.

Leading Estremadura Producers

Fundação Oriente ☆–☆☆
Colares. 9 ha.
A charitable foundation that has taken on the brave venture of reviving the wines of Colares, white as well as red. The first vintage was 2004.

Quinta do Monte d'Oiro ☆☆–☆☆☆
Freixial de Cima, Alenquer. 15 ha. www.quintadomontedoiro.com
José Bento dos Santos doesn't believe in formulae, and his vineyards contain Rhône varieties as well as local ones. The wines combine the intensity of the northern Rhône with the broader shoulders of the southern Rhône.

Quinta de Pancas ☆☆–☆☆☆
Porto de Luz, Alenquer. 50 ha. www.quintadepancas.pt
Splendid sixteenth-century *quinta* north of Lisbon. Some of Portugal's first Cabernet Sauvignon was planted and vinified here. The white wines include a delightful wine made from the Arinto grape (Quinta de Dom Carlos), and a soft, toasty Chardonnay. The top red wines are high-priced varietal wines from Cabernet Sauvignon, Tinta Roriz, and Touriga Nacional.

Casa Santos Lima ☆–☆☆
Aldeia Galega da Merceana. 180 ha. www.casasantoslima.com
The estate is within the Alenquer DOC, but the wines bear a regional appellation. With almost all the production exported, quality and style vary to suit individual importers. The top wine is Touriz, easily decoded as a blend of the Touriga and Roriz varieties.

Caves Velhas ☆–☆☆
Bucelas. 10 ha. www.cavesvelhas.pt
This estate keeps alive the flame of Bucelas, offering wine in various manifestations, including new-oaked Quinta da Boição.

Leading Ribatejo Producers

Quinta de Alorna ☆–☆☆
Almeirim. 200 ha. www.alorna.pt
This large estates works mostly with local varieties, although Cabernet Sauvignon also gets a look in. Most of the vineyards are machine-picked and the wines are frankly commercial, well made but rarely reaching great heights.

Quinta do Casal Branco ☆☆
Almeirim. 140 ha. www.casalbranco.com
The first bottled vintage here was 1990, and in 2003 the winery was modernized. There are numerous ranges, such as Cork Grove and Capucho, the latter consisting of red Bordeaux varietals. The best red and white wines appear under the Falcoaria label.

Falua ☆☆
Almeirim. 65 ha. www.falua.net
Since 2000 Falua has been the Ribatejo base of Alentejo producer João Portugal Ramos, in conjunction with his brother-in-law Luis de Castro. Grapes are sourced from their own vineyards as well as from those of contract growers, and the wines, from Portuguese as well as French varieties, are fresh and impeccably made. The main range is Tagus Creek, and there is a prestige label called Conde de Vimioso.

Quinta da Lagoalva de Cima ☆☆
Alpiarça. 45 ha. www.lagoalva.pt
The grandfather of the Campilho brothers, who own this grand estate in the Ribatejo, was once ambassador to London. It was at Lagoalva that Portugal's first Syrah was produced, though most of the wines are made from local varieties such as Castelão, Touriga Nacional, and the white Arinto. Quality is sound, and the wines have a welcome elegance.

Leading Terras do Sado Producers

Adega Cooperativa de Palmela ☆
Palmela. 1,300 ha. www.acpalmela.pt
A large cooperative that dominates the Palmela region. The range is enormous, but the best Palmela red is bottled under the Villa Palma label.

José María da Fonseca ☆☆☆
Azeitão. 700 ha. www.jmf.pt
Founded in 1834, this is one of Portugal's leading wine companies, run by two brothers, António and Domingos Soares Franco, descendants of the founder. Fonseca is famous for its superlative fortified Setúbal, but the quantity produced is minute compared to its range of red wines.

Periquita is the best-known, made from a blend of local grapes of the same name (now known throughout Portugal as Castelão); Quinta da Camarate is a ripe, blackcurranty blend of Castelão, Cabernet, and Touriga Nacional; and the José da Sousa Reserva from the Alentejo is a good, peppery blend of local grapes fermented in large clay amphorae. It also owns a winery in Dão, which bottles the Terras Altas brand.

Other wines include Garrafeiras, coded by letters (such as RA or TE) to indicate origin or grape blend, and a range of international varieties such as Sauvignon Blanc and Syrah under the Colleccion Privada label.

Leading Alentejo Producers

Azamor ☆
Ciladas. 27 ha. www.azamor.com
A Portuguese husband and English wife own this estate, where the first vintage was 2003, and employ a Barossa winemaker, Tim Smith, as their consultant. The initial releases were somewhat jammy, but these are early days.

Adega Cooperativa de Borba ☆–☆☆
Borba. 2,200 ha. www.adegaborba.pt
One of Portugal's most go-ahead cooperatives is to be found on the edge of the little town of Borba. As well as using local varieties such as Aragonez and Alicante Bouschet, the winery is happy to employ non-regional varieties such as Touriga Nacional and Syrah in its blends. The wines are all well made, especially given the scale of the operation.

Quinta do Carmo ☆☆
Borba. 150 ha. www.quintadocarmo.pt
This Alentejo estate, once the property of the Bastos family, is now owned by the Rothschilds of Château Lafite-Rothschild and Portuguese tycoon José Berardo. The vineyards used to be dominated by Alicante Bouschet, which resulted in very long lived wines, but the new owners have reduced the proportion to produce a wine that may be more elegant, yet lacks the solidity of vintages of yesteryear. Of the famous Alentejo growths, this shows the least typicity. See also Dona Maria.

Dona Maria ☆☆–☆☆☆
Estremoz. 72 ha. www.donamaria.pt
Júlio Bastos's ancestral property, Quinta do Carmo, was sold by him to the Lafite-Rothschild group in 1988, but after various transactions, he has been able to return in triumph to his house and build a new winery there. Because the Carmo brand no longer belongs to him, he has chosen a different name for his wines, which include traditional blends under the Dona Maria label, and a blend of French varieties called Amantis. There is also a Garrafeira, an act of homage to the great wines of Carmo's past.

Fundação Eugenio de Almeida – Herdade de Cartuxa ☆–☆☆☆
Evora. 200 ha. www.cartuxa.pt
This immense Alentejo property, managed as a charitable trust, lies close to the city of Evora. Fairly rigorous selection means the foundation's main label, Cartuxa, is a silky red, but the best Trincadeira and Aragonez grapes are held back for Pêra Manca, which has quickly established itself as one of Portugal's leading wines, only released in outstanding years. Reds are rather more successful than the whites, although the white Pêra Manca can also be magnificent. The remainder of the estate's production is bottled as *vinho regional*, or sold off to a local cooperative.

Cortes de Cima ☆☆–☆☆☆
Vidigueira. 105 ha. www.cortesdecima.pt
The first vintage from this estate was 1996, and it made its name by releasing an unauthorized Syrah called, appropriately, Incognito. This remains its best known wine, but the Reserva, and the varietal Aragonez are equally rich and stylish.

Herdade do Esporão ☆–☆☆☆
Reguengos de Monsaraz. 650 ha. www.esporao.com
The huge Esporão estate near Reguengos de Monsaraz in the Alentejo is owned by a company called Finagra. Planted in the 1970s, the vineyards are supplemented by a further 500 hectares belonging to contract growers. Esporão suffered a chequered start to life, but under the shrewd ownership and management of financier José Roquette, the investment is now paying dividends. Esporão is the principal label, but Monte Velho is a hugely successful brand within Portugal itself. The varietal bottlings, Reservas, and Private Selection are the most exciting wines. Much of the credit for Esporão's success is due to Australian winemaker David Baverstock.

Herdade dos Grous ☆☆
Beja. 70 ha. www.herdadedosgrous.com
A German-owned property producing very stylish red wines from Portuguese varieties and a dash of Syrah.

Herdade do Mouchão ☆☆☆–☆☆☆☆
Sousel. 38 ha.
A highly unusual estate, in that its huge red wines rely heavily on low-yielding Alicante Bouschet grapes for colour and structure. When Mouchão is on form, it is the Alentejo at its very best: chunky, long-lived wines, with a long, spicy finish. In exceptional vintages a prestige bottling is released called Tonel 3–4, which is even more imposing than the already weighty regular Mouchão.

João Portugal Ramos ☆☆–☆☆☆
Estremoz. 140 ha. www.jportugalramos.com

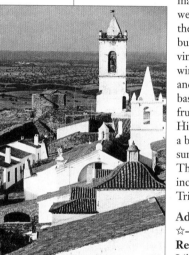

This dynamic winemaker made his name as a consultant for many of the top estates in Portugal, as well as for cooperatives keen to improve the quality of their wines. In 1999, he built a modern winery in which to vinify his own expanding range of wines from both his own vineyards and those he buys from on a contract basis. His wines are marked by vibrant fruit, delicate oak, and impeccable balance. His most appealing wines are Vila Santa, a blend from local varieties, and the sumptuous Marqués de Borba Reserva. There are also spicy varietal wines, including a splendid Syrah and Trincadeira. See also Falua.

Adega Cooperativa de Redondo ☆–☆☆☆
Redondo. 3,000 ha. www.acr.com.pt
Like some other Alentejo co-ops, that at Redondo is well equipped and makes some excellent wines, including its Anta da Serra blends and some lush varietal reds from Cabernet Sauvignon as well as Portuguese varieties.

Quinta do Zambujeiro ☆☆–☆☆☆
Borba. 30 ha. www.zambujeiro.com
Bought in 1998 by a Swiss businessman, Zambujeiro is one of the few boutique wineries in the Alentejo. Yields are low and levels of concentration are high – and so are the prices. However, the wine is first rate: opulent and sleek, with only the merest hint of alcohol.

Leading Portuguese Producers

Caves Aliança ☆–☆☆☆
Sangalhos. 400 ha. www.caves-alianca.pt
One of Portugal's principal still and sparkling wine producers. Founded in 1927, it used to be owned by a consortium of partners, but today the majority owner is José Berardo.

Rooftops and chapel, Estremoz

A public company controlled by the Neves family, based in the Bairrada, but offering Vinho Verde (the dry Casal Mendes), Dão, and Douro rosé as well as its admirable Bairrada red, Aliança Tinto Velho, and very passable *méthode traditionnelle* sparkling wine. The company has also acquired over 100 hectares in the Alentejo. With the assistance of French oenologist Pascal Chatonnet, Aliança has launched a sophisticated range of wines from individual properties, such as Quinta da Terrugem in the Alentejo.

Bacalhôa Vinhos de Portugal ☆–☆☆☆
Azeitao. 400 ha. www.bacalhoa.com
This enormous company was known as J P Vinhos until 2005, when the name was changed. Under the former winemaker Peter Bright, who was Australian, the wines became very well known and widely distributed on export markets. New World influence is evident in the Cova da Ursa, a barrel-fermented Chardonnay, and the Cabernet-dominated Quinta da Bacalhôa. There are also robust wines from Portuguese varieties, including a Touriga Nacional called Só, and Tinto da Anfora, a warming, spicy red from the Alentejo. And it is gratifying to find a wide and excellent range of Moscatels from Setúbal.

D F J Vinhos ☆
Valada. 300 ha. www.dfjvinhos.com
This enterprising company is almost entirely focused on the export market. Although based in Ribatejo, it produces wines from all over Portugal, except for the Alentejo. D F J's main asset is its winemaker, José Neiva, a controversial figure who aims for rich, jammy, high-tech wines with a good dose of alcohol. The top range is called Grand' Arte.

Caves Messias ☆
Mealhada. 260 ha. www.cavesmessias.pt
A merchant house founded in 1926. Based in Bairrada, where it owns 130 hectares at Quinta do Valdoeiro, it also owns estates in Dão and the Douro. The latter is the Quinta do Cachão, from which it produces a full, spicy Douro red. Also producer of the Santola brand of Vinho Verde, robust Bairradas, red and white, and a range of sparkling wines.

Sogrape ☆–☆☆☆
Avintes. 800 ha. www.sogrape.pt
Portugal's biggest winemaker, and the producer of Mateus Rosé. The other wines are of impressive quality across the board. The Guedes family, which founded Sogrape in 1942, still control the firm, and also own Ferreira and Offley port (see pages 422–23).

They have made a big investment in Dão, at Quinta dos Carvalhais, and at Herdade do Peso in the Alentejo. Other wines include Grão Vasco, a good Dão made at the company's own winery near Viseu; the reliable Vinha do Monte from Alentejo; Vila Regia, a ripe Douro red; and Terra Franca, a soft, fruity Bairrada. New ventures include Touriga Nacional from Dão, and varietal wines from the Alentejo. Sogrape is also active in Argentina.

Port

What the English have long known as port, and the Portuguese and other nations as Porto, belongs with Champagne and sherry in the original trinity of great "processed" wines. Each is an elaboration on the natural produce of its region to enhance its latent quality. Being capital intensive, requiring the holding of large stocks for long periods, their trade has become concentrated in the hands of shippers. Single vineyard ports, and even single vintage ports, are still the exceptions in an industry, which lives day to day on long-established and consistent blends.

Unlike Champagne and sherry, port was the child of political pressure. In the late seventeenth century the British were obliged by their government to find alternatives to the French red wines they preferred. They turned to Portugal, an old and useful ally, for a convenient substitute for claret. Finding nothing to their liking in the existing vineyards (which is surprising; Lisbon had good wine, if Oporto did not) the enterprising traders pushed inland from Oporto up the valley of the Douro into the rugged hinterland. What they tasted there that made them persevere is hard to imagine. They could hardly have chosen a more difficult and inaccessible place, with a more extreme climate, to develop as a major new wine area. They started around Regua, about 96-kilometres (60-miles – or three mule-days) upstream from Oporto where the River Corgo joins the main stream. Gradually, finding that the higher they went the better the wine became, they built terraces up the steep-sloped mountains surrounding the Douro and its tributaries: the Távora, the Torto, the Pinhão, and the Tua. They dotted the mountainsides with white walled *quintas*, or farms, and demonstrated that once cultivated, the thin, arid soil of granite and schist became extraordinarily fertile. Today, not just the grapes, but the nuts, oranges, almonds, and even the vegetables of the Douro Valley are famous.

The first port was apparently a strong, dry, red wine, made even stronger with "a bucket or two" of brandy to stabilize it for shipping. It got a very cold reception from British claret-lovers, who complained bitterly. The shippers tried harder, and at some time in the eighteenth century hit on the idea of stopping the fermentation with brandy while the wine was still sweet and fruity. History is unclear on when this became the standard practice, since as late as the 1840s, the most influential British port shipper of all time, James Forrester (who was created a Portuguese baron for his services), was urging a return to unfortified (therefore dry) wines. Modern ideas provide surprising justification for Forrester's notions: today, the Douro is providing some of Portugal's best dry red table wine. Sweet or dry port was the most-drunk wine in Britain from the early eighteenth century to the early twentieth .

Today, port is one of the most strictly controlled of all wines. A series of statutory authorities regulate and oversee every stage of its making. All 26,000 hectares of vineyards are classified for quality on an eight-point scale by the register of each property (there are tens of thousands of growers), taking into account its situation, altitude, soil, inclination, grape varieties, standard of cultivation, fertility, and the age of its vines. It is then given an annual quota. Only 40 per cent, on average, of the total Douro crop may be turned into port; the rest is just made into red wine. The maximum yield, allowed for vineyards classified as "A" on the eight-point scale, is 700 litres per 1,000 vines.

In the past, innumerable local varieties were planted together in the vineyards, and it took considerable research in the 1970s, mostly conducted by Ramos Pinto, to isolate the most important varieties: Touriga Nacional, Touriga Francesa, Tinta Roriz, Tinta Barroca, Tinta Cão, plus Tinta Amarela, and Sousão. Today they are planted separately, and later blended.

At harvest time, late September in the Douro, bureaucracy seems remote enough. The grinding labour of picking and carrying the crop from the steep terraces to the press-houses is carried on with amazingly cheerful, even tuneful, energy by gangs of villagers. On remote little farms, and with the best-quality grapes at some of the largest *quintas*, the crop is still trodden barefoot at night in open granite *lagares*, and then fermented in the *lagares* until it is ready to be "stopped" with brandy. In the case of most port shippers, however, much the greater proportion of the crop is machine-crushed and fermented in stainless-steel autovinifiers which, as the name might suggest, keep the juice automatically pumping over the grape skins. These autovinifiers were the great step forward of the 1980s; more recently the shippers have come to appreciate again the virtues of foot-treading in *lagares*. But labour is harder to get these days, and a fascinating technical development has been the invention in the 1990s of "robotic *lagares*", in which machines mimic the operation of foot-treading, while allowing weary harvesters to get an early night instead of treading monotonously into the early hours of the morning. With any of these methods, the moment comes when about half the grape sugar is fermented into alcohol. This is when the half-made wine is run off into barrels one-quarter full of brandy. Fermentation stops instantly.

The great majority of the port is moved, after its first racking off its gross lees, to the shippers' lodges to mature. These lodges are huddled together across the River Douro from Oporto, in Vila Nova de Gaia. In the past, the casks, known as pipes, were transported down-river on the beautiful Viking-style *rabelos*. But once the river was dammed for hydroelectric power, that was no longer feasible. It used to be obligatory for port to be shipped through Vila Nova da Gaia, but not any more. One important shipper, Noval, now moves its stock for maturation to air-conditioned warehouses upstream; while Sandeman and Cockburn keep substantial amounts of their port in the Douro. The newer single-estate boutique producers also keep their stock in the Douro; and now the local authority in Vila Nova de Gaia is encouraging the shippers to move again, out of the crowded, narrow streets of Gaia and into more spacious premises away from the centre.

Once in the shipper's lodge, port, like sherry, is classified by tasting and its destiny decided by its quality and potential for improvement. Most ports join a sort of perpetual blending system whose object is an unchanging product. Simple, fruity, and rather light wines without great concentration are destined to become ruby port, aged for up to about two years in wood and bottled while their bright-red colour and full sweetness show no sign of maturity. This is the cheapest category.

Young wines with more aggressive characters and greater concentration – some outstandingly good, some of only moderate quality – are set aside to develop into tawnies, so-called from their faded colour after many years in wood. Tawnies include some of the greatest of all ports, kept for up to 40 years in cask, then (usually) refreshed with a little younger wine of the highest quality. Tawnies also include some very ordinary mixtures with scarcely any of the character of barrel age, made by blending young red and white ports (very popular in France as an apéritif). Their price varies accordingly. The best tawnies have an indication of age on the label; 20 years is old enough for most of them – the high premium for a 30- or 40-year-old wine is seldom worth it. Styles among top tawnies vary from the intensely luscious (eg. Ferreira's Duque de Bragança) to refinement and a dry finish (eg. Taylor's 20-year-old). There is no legal requirement for all the wine in a 10-year-old, for example, to be at least that age; instead, the wine is required to match the tasting profile for that style, as determined by an expert tasting panel. Although the system is open to abuse, the top shippers maintain a high standard, as they wish to preserve their reputations. The great majority of port falls into one or other of the above categories, which together are known as "wood ports"; their whole maturing process takes place in wood.

Vintage port, by contrast, is the product of one of the three or four vintages in a decade that come close to the shipper's idea of perfection, which have so much flavour and individuality that to make them anonymous, as part of a continuing blend, would be a waste of their potential. Whether or not a shipper "declares" a vintage is entirely his own decision. It is very rare that all do so in the same year. The Douro is too varied in its topography and conditions.

Vintage ports are blended in the particular style the shipper has developed over many years, using the best lots of wine from his regular suppliers – including, invariably, his own best vineyards. They are matured for a minimum of 22 and a maximum of 31 months in cask for their components to "marry", then bottled as infants. Very young vintage port can actually be delicious at this stage; but within a couple of years the wines close up and become undrinkably tannic, aggressive, and concentrated in flavour. (Lately a fashion has developed in the USA for drinking vintge port very young, and some new, lighter blends have been released to cater to this taste.) Almost all their maturing therefore happens in the airless, "reductive" conditions of a black-glass bottle with a long cork, designed to protect the wine for decades, while it slowly feeds on itself. Its tannins and pigments react to form a heavy, skin-like crust that sticks to the side of the bottle. Its colour slowly fades and its flavour evolves from violently sweet and harsh to gently sweet, perfumed and mellow. Yet, however mellow, vintage port is designed to have "grip": a vital ingredient in wine, which should never lose its final bite even in old age.

Between the clear-cut extremes of wood port and vintage port come a number of compromises intended to offer something closer to vintage port without the increasingly awkward need to cellar the wine for between 10 and 30 years. Vintage character (or vintage reserve) is effectively top-quality ruby port whose ingredient wines were almost up to true vintage standards, but kept for four or five years in cask. These potent and tasty wines are "ready" when bottled, but will continue to develop, and may even form a slight "crust" in bottle if they are kept too long. The term "crusted" or "crusting" port is sometimes used for the same style (though not officially recognized in Portugal). Late-bottled vintage (or LBV) is similar, but is made of the wine of one "vintage" year, kept twice as long as vintage port in barrel: ie. from 3.5 to six years. The label "LBV" carries both the date of the vintage and the bottling, and the wine is much lighter in colour and flavour than vintage port, but should have some of its firmness. It may or may not form a deposit in bottle according to its maturity on bottling, and the degree to which the shipper has chilled and filtered it for stability. Late-bottled vintage port that forms a deposit is usually labelled "traditional". LBVs from Warre and Smith Woodhouse are usually unfiltered.

A rare but sometimes succulent style of port is known as *colheita*. After decades in wood these wines acquire a fine intensity and elegance, but care must be taken to avoid oxidation. Except from masters of the style, such as Cálem, Burmester, Andresen, and Niepoort, they are a risky purchase, as lesser examples can taste tired and astringent.

White port is made in the same way as red port, but of white grapes, usually fermented further towards dryness before being fortified with brandy. It is intended as an apéritif rather than a dessert wine, but never achieves the quality or finesse of, say, a fino sherry. Its underlying heaviness needs to be enlivened, and it can be far more enjoyable as a long drink with tonic water, ice, and a slice of lemon.

An increasingly popular compromise is to declare a single-*quinta* vintage port. Some properties, themselves single *quintas*, in contrast to shippers buying from a range of sources, are declaring this category almost every year. (They usually also make table wine; see previous pages. Because they don't have the years of stocks of the big shippers, single-*quinta* vintage and table wines are their specialties.) Quinta de la Rosa is probably the best-known example.

But for some time, the major shippers have also declared single-*quinta* wines in lesser vintages, when no vintage wine under their own name is declared. Leading examples include Taylor's Quinta de Vargellas and Croft's Quinta da Roeda. They can do this because in lesser years, their top *quintas* may still produce outstanding wine that would, in top years, be a major contributor to the vintage wine. Single-*quinta* ports will mature sooner than classic vintages, but often have distinct and charming character. Being bottle-matured, these wines will of course form a crust, and will need decanting.

The number of single-quinta wines is growing from vintage to vintage. This means that the dominance of the market by the famous British shippers is diminishing, even if only slightly. Properties such as Quinta do Crasto and Quinta de Roriz, which once supplied the major shippers, are now nurturing and bottling their own vintage ports. Although there are some very fine examples, they can lack the consistency and reliability of the renowned names.

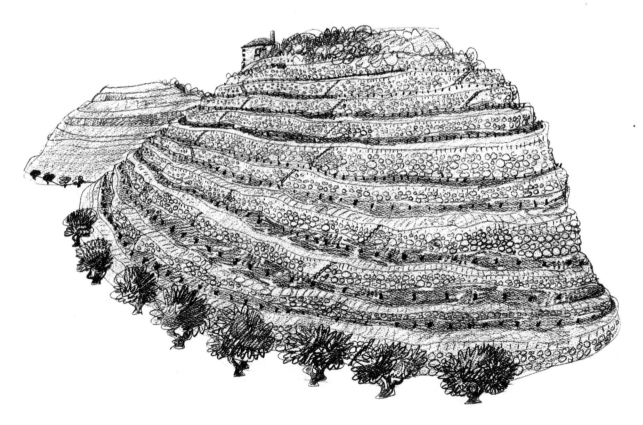

Terraced port vineyards in the Upper Douro

Leading Port Producers

Cálem ☆☆
Vila Nova de Gaia. Vintages: 1935, '48, '55, '58, '60, '63, '66, '70, '75, '77, '80, '82, '83, '85, '91, '94, '97, 2000, '03.
Founded in 1859 by a family already long-established in the port trade, Cálem was sold in 1989 to the Sogevinus group. The family retained the excellent Quinta da Foz at Pinhão, so the new owners will not be able to make use of the firm's best grapes. However, the company will be producing single-*quinta* ports from Quinta do Arnozelo. Cálem had a fine reputation for its *colheita* wines, but its vintage ports could lack consistency.

Churchill ☆☆–☆☆☆
Vila Nova de Gaia. Vintages: 1982, '85, '91, '94, '97, 2000, '03. www.churchills-port.com
Founded in 1981 by John Graham and named after his wife, this is the first independent port shipper to be set up in the last 50 years. It has gone from strength to strength, making some splendidly concentrated wines, originally from a number of well-situated *quintas* belonging to the Borges de Sousa family.

A new generation of that family has reclaimed its quintas, but Graham has bought other estates to remain supplied with good grapes. Quinta da Gricha is bottled by Churchill as a single-quinta port. Churchill also makes fine LBV, and an excellent dry white port which has been aged for around ten years in wood, and is one of the few shippers to have good stocks of delicious, mature, crusted port. A table wine called Churchill Estates was first produced in 2002.

Cockburn ☆☆
Vila Nova de Gaia. Vintages: 1900, '04, '08, '12, '27, '35, '45, '47, '50, '55, '60, '63, '67, '70, '75, '77, '83, '85, '91, '94, '97, 2000, '03.
Founded in 1815, Cockburn is one of the greatest names in port, owned since 2006 by the Symington family. Its properties are the Quintas do Tua (30 hectares), da Santa Maria near Regua (18 hectares), do Val do Coelho, and do Atayde near Tua, and, since 1989, the 300-hectare Quinta dos Canais in the Upper Douro, which is the source of its single-*quinta* wine. Cockburn's wines have a distinctive dry finish, or "grip", and the vintage ports can lack succulence.

Quinta do Côtto ☆
Cidadelha. www.quinta-do-cotto.pt
The Champalimaud family, who have owned their estate near Regua since the seventeenth century, are now the best-known of the new breed of grower-bottlers: their single-*quinta* vintage is made and matured in the Douro, and not moved down to Vila Nova de Gaia for bottling. Recent vintages have been less sweet than one would normally expect from a vintage style. They make one of the Douro's best red table wines (see previous pages).

Croft ☆☆–☆☆☆
Vila Nova de Gaia. Vintages: Croft – 1900, '04, '08, '12, '17, '20, '22, '24, '27, '35, '42, '45, '50, '55, '60, '63, '66, '70, '75, '77, '82, '85, '91, '94, 2000, '03. Quinta da Roêda – 1967, '70, '78, '80, '83, '87, '95, '97, '05. www.croftport.com

Perhaps the oldest port firm, founded in 1678 and originally known as Phayre and Bradley, Croft was bought in 2001 by the Fladgate group, which includes Taylor's and Fonseca, and which has reinstated *lagares* and generally improved quality.

The jewel in its crown is the superb Quinta da Roêda with 63 hectares at Pinhão. Grapes from this *quinta* are responsible for the distinctive floweriness of Croft's vintage wines, which are again now among the finest of all vintage ports, early maturing and well-balanced in style. Purists were dismayed when in 2006 the firm launched a pink port, the first of its kind. Croft is also well known as a sherry producer (q.v.) though now under separate ownership.

Delaforce ☆☆
Vila Nova de Gaia. Vintages: 1908, '17, '20, '21, '22, '27, '35, '45, '47, '50, '55, '58, '60, '63, '66, '70, '75, '77, '82, '85, '94, , 2000, '03. Quinta da Corte – '78, '80, '84, '87, '92, '94, '95, '97.
Founded in 1868, this firm is still run by the Delaforces, although in 2001 (like Croft, q.v.) it was bought by the Fladgate group. The firm's finest wines, which have great freshness and elegance and are slightly drier than the Croft ports, come from the contracted Quinta da Corte vineyard in the Rio Torto valley. The tawny ports are of excellent quality, as are the rare *colheitas*.

Dow ☆☆☆☆
Vila Nova de Gaia. Vintages: 1904, '08, '12, '20, '24, '27, '34, ('42 & '44), '45, '47, '50, '55, '60, '63, '66, '70, '72, '75, '77, '80, '83, '85, '91, '94, '97, 2000, '03. www.dows-port.com
Since 1961, this venerable brand has been run by the ubiquitous Symington family. The firm's 76-hectare Quinta do Bomfim at Pinhão, sometimes released as a single-*quinta* port, is one of the finest on the Douro. Supported by Quinta da Senhora da Ribeira, Bomfim gives mightily tannic and concentrated vintage port, recognizable by its dry finish in maturity. Dow also sells a full range of ruby, tawny, and white ports.

A. A. Ferreira ☆☆–☆☆☆
Vila Nova de Gaia. Vintages: 1945, '47, '50, '58, '60, '63, '66, '70, '75, '77, '78, '80, '82, '83, '85, '91, '94, '95, '97, 2000, '03. www.sogrape.pt
An historic Portuguese house, Ferreira in the mid-nineteenth century was the richest in the Douro, ruled over by the famous Dona Antónia, who built the magnificent Quintas do Vesuvio and do Vale de Meão, colossal establishments in the remotest high Douro. The family members still own many vineyards, although the company was sold in 1987 to Sogrape (q.v.).

Today, Ferreira sells more bottled port in Portugal than any other house. Its vintage wines are usually fairly light in style, and are outclassed by its superb tawny ports: Superior, Dona Antónia, and above all the superlative 20-year-old Duque de Bragança. Ferreira was also a pioneer of table wines from the Douro, notably the legendary Barca Velha.

Fonseca Guimaraens ☆☆☆☆
Vila Nova de Gaia. Vintages: 1904, '08, '12, '20, '22, '27, '34, '45, '48, '55, '60, '63, '66, '70, '75, '77, '80, '83, '85, '92, '94, '97, 2000, '03. www.fonseca.pt

Despite its name, Fonseca has been an English family business for over a century, and has been linked to Taylors since the 1940s. The firm started in the eighteenth century as Fonseca, and was bought by Manuel Pedro Guimaraens in 1822. Its vineyards of Quinta Cruizeiro (65 hectares) and Quinta Santo António (40 hectares), both in the Val de Mendiz near Alijo, are splendidly sited. All its best wines are still made by treading. Fonseca is regularly one of the finest and richest vintage ports, and lighter vintages are bottled under the Guimaraens label. Its Bin No 27 is an admirable premium ruby. It has an LBV and the single-quinta Quinta do Panascal, and since 2002, an organic port called Terra Prima.

Gould Campbell
See Smith Woodhouse.

W & J Graham ☆☆☆☆
Vila Nova de Gaia. Vintages: 1904, '08, '12, '17, '20, '24, '27, '35, '42, '45, '48, '55, '60, '63, '66, '70, '75, '77, '80, '83, '85, '91, '94, '97, 2000, '03. www.grahams-port.com
Graham, now part of the empire of the Symington family (with Warre, Dow, etc.), is renowned for some of the richest and sweetest vintage ports. Graham's Quinta dos Malvedos on the Douro, near Tua, provides exceptionally ripe fruit for vintage port of great colour, body, and guts, which mellows to a singularly sumptuous wine. Part of the crop is still trodden. Malvedos used to be the company's second wine, but now it is also issued as a single-*quinta* wine. Tawny and LBV follow the full bodied, luscious style. Particularly good is the Six Grapes premium ruby port.

Kopke ☆
Vila Nova de Gaia. Vintages: 1934, '35, '42, '45, '52, '55, '58, '60, '63, '66, '70, '74, '75, '77, '78, '79, '80, '82, '83, '85, '87, '91, '92, '95, 2000, '03. www.kopkeports.com
In name at least, the oldest of all the port firms, Kopke was founded by a German in 1638 and owns 60 hectares of vines. It now belongs to the Sogevinus group. The vintage port is reliable, but Kopke is best known, and rightly so, for its splendid old *colheitas*.

Niepoort ☆☆☆
Porto. Vintages: 1927, '45, '55, '60, '63, '66, '70, '75, '77, '78, '80, '82, '83, '85, '87, '91, '92, '94, '97, 2000, '03, '05. www.niepoort-vinhos.com
A small, Dutch, family owned company, founded in 1842, is currently being run by the fifth generation of Niepoorts. Tawnies are the house specialty, including *colheitas* and a Garrafeiras. These are tawnies given further ageing in glass demijohns. But the Niepoort vintage ports should not be underestimated; they have been going from strength to strength for some time, as have his table wines, see also previous pages.

Quinta do Noval ☆☆☆☆
Vila Nova de Gaia. Vintages: 1904, '08, '12, '17, '20, '24, '27, '31, '34, ('41 & '42), '45, '50, '55, '58, '60, '63, '66, '67, '70, '78, '80, '82, '83, '85, '87, '91, '94, '95, '97, 2000, '03, '04. www.quintadonoval.com
Perhaps the most famous, and one of the most beautiful

quintas on the Douro, perched high above Pinhão. It belonged to the van Zeller family until 1993, when it was sold to AXA-Millésimes. A tragic fire in 1982 destroyed the historic records of the company and part of the stock. Old Noval vintages were some of the most magnificent of all ports. The '31 is legendary and the '27 was even better. Some rows of ungrafted vines still make an astoundingly concentrated Nacional vintage port.

The new owners have, if anything, improved quality even further, and in 1995 introduced robotic lagares. Quinta do Silval is another property, which is the main source for the second label, Silval Vintage.

Offley ☆
Vila Nova de Gaia. Vintages: 1945, '50, '54, '60, '62, '63, '66, '67, '70, '72, '75, '77, '80, '82, '83, '85, '87, '94, '95, '97, 2000, '03. www.sogrape.pt
This firm was founded in 1737 by William Offley, and joined by James Forrester in 1803. His nephew, Baron Joseph James Forrester, was famous for mapping the Upper Douro, and saving the vineyards from a fungal disease in the 1850s. The company, formally known as Forrester & Co., was sold in 1929 and again in 1983 to Martini & Rossi – which has since sold to Sogrape. The vintage is rarely exceptional and the best wine is Baron Forrester Tawny. The style is generally considered to be early drinking, fat, and well rounded.

Poças ☆
Vila Nova de Gaia. Vintages: 1960, '63, '70, '75, '85, '91, '94, '95, '97, 2000, '03, '04, '05. www.pocas.pt
An independent family company founded in 1918, owning two Douro properties: the Quintas das Quartas and Santa Barbara, run on traditional lines. It is, relatively speaking, a newcomer to vintage ports, having made its first declaration in 1960. These are sound, medium bodied wines.

Quarles Harris ☆☆
Vila Nova de Gaia. Vintages: 1908, '12, '20, '27, '34, '45, '47, '50, '55, '58, '60, '63, '66, '70, '75, '77, '80, '83, '85, '91, '94, '97, 2000, '03.
Together with Warre, Graham, Dow, etc. (qq.v), Quarles Harris is now part of the remarkable stable of the Symington family. There are no vineyards, but long-standing contracts with good growers along the Rio Torto maintain a style of very intense, full vintage port with a powerful bouquet. Harris (not Quarles) is the brand for tawnies, ruby, and white ports.

Ramos Pinto ☆☆–☆☆☆
Vila Nova de Gaia. Vintages: 1924, '27, '35, '45, '50, '52, '55, '60, '61, '70, '75, '80, '82, '83, '85, '91, '94, '95, '97, 2000, '03, '04. www.ramospinto.pt
Founded in 1880, and one of the most distinguished houses, now owned by Champagne Louis Roederer. Its properties include the famous Quinta Bom Retiro, with 50 hectares in the Rio Torto valley, the Quinta da Bons Ares, and Quinta da Ervamoira, the source of many of its fine tawnies.

Tawnies are its specialties, but the company also produces two highly successful white ports as well as a reliable vintage. It also release excellent table wines, see also previous pages.

Royal Oporto ☆
Vila Nova de Gaia. Vintages: 1908, '41, '43, '44, '45, '47, '54, '55, '58, '60, '62, '63, '67, '70, '77, '78, '79, '80, '85, '87, '95, '97, 2000. www.realcompanhiavelha.pt
Royal Oporto is the famous brand of the Real Companhia Velha, which was founded in 1756 by the Marquis de Pombal to control the port trade. The company is now part-owned by the Casa do Douro (set up as the controlling body for the port trade), the result of a now infamous business deal. Its interests are now half in port and half in other wines. Quality was unremarkable for many years, but since the late 1990s there have been significant signs of improvement.

Sandeman ☆☆
**Vila Nova de Gaia. Vintages: 1904, '08, '11, '12, '17, '20, '27, '34, '35, '42, '45, '47, '50, '55, '60, '63, '66, '67, '70, '75, '77, '80, '82, '85, '94, '97, 2000, '03.
www.sandeman.com**
Founded in 1790, Sandeman is among the biggest shippers of both port and sherry. The firm – renowned for its logo of "the don" – was bought by Seagram in 1980, and then sold to Sogrape in 2001. But it is still chaired by George Sandeman, a direct descendant of the founder. The firm's vineyards are the Quintas de Confradeiro and Casal at Celeirós (48 hectares on the Pinhão River). Quinta Laranjeira (214 hectares at Moncorvo) is a big new development in the highest Douro near Spain. Sandeman's vintage wines are fruity though not especially rich, and they seem intended for medium term drinking.

Single-*quinta* port is produced from Quinta do Vao, near Pinhão, and this is explicitly intended to be drunk young, as has become fashionable in the United States. Their tawnies are attractively nutty, and the company offers a range from 10- to 40-years-old.

Smith Woodhouse ☆☆–☆☆☆
**Vila Nova de Gaia. Vintages: 1904, '08, '12, '17, '20, '24, '27, '35, '45, '47, '50, '55, '60, '63, '66, '70, '75, '77, '80, '83, '85, '91, '94, '97, 2000, '03.
www.smithwoodhouse.com**
Together with Graham, Warre, etc. (qq.v.), now part of the Symington family property. Smith Woodhouse also ships Gould Campbell vintage ports. Both come largely from the Rio Torto. Gould Campbell vintages are big, dark, powerful, and very long lasting wines; the Smith Woodhouse style is more fragrant and fruity and its tawnies notably so. Less expensive than the flagship labels of the Symington empire, they can be excellent value.

Taylor, Fladgate & Yeatman ☆☆☆–☆☆☆☆
Vila Nova de Gaia. Vintages: 1904, '06, '08, '12, '17, '20, '24, '27, '35, '38, '40, '42, '45, '48, '55, '60, '63, '66, '70, '75, '77, '80, '83, '85, '92, '94, '97, 2000, '03. www.taylor.pt
Founded in 1692, Taylor is one of the oldest and best shippers, still owned by descendants of the Yeatman family. The style of the tremendous vintage wines, of unrivalled ripeness, depth, and every other dimension, is largely derived from the famous Quinta de Vargellas (220 hectares), high on the Upper Douro above São João de Pesqueira.

In 1973, it bought the Quinta de Terra Feita (100 hectares) at Celeiros up the Pinhão valley, and in 1998 bought two more properties near Pinhão. The vintage ports are still trodden by foot or by so-called robotic *lagares*. Both Vargellas and Terra Feita are sometimes released as single-*quinta* vintages, and very occasionally there is a release of the expensive Vargellas Vinha Velha. Fonseca (q.v.) is an associate company. Taylor's LBV is the biggest-selling one on the market. Its tawnies (particularly the 20-year-olds) are also exceptional.

THE SYMINGTON FAMILY

With a mixture of brilliant winemaking skill, good communication abilities, and commercial acumen, the Symington family have evolved into the most powerful family in the Douro. Andrew James Symington sailed from Glasgow to Porto in 1882, and in time became a partner in Warre's. Compared with the other British families already established in the Douro, Symington was a relative newcomer. His family also became involved with Dow's, but it was only in 1961 that the Symingtons began to accumulate shippers and the *quintas* that supported each one. Warre was taken over in 1961, Graham's and Smith Woodhouse in 1970. Winemaker Peter Symington maintained impeccable standards while keeping the style of each house distinct. Gould Campbell and Quarles Harris are the bargain brands in the Symington group. It was an inspired move to acquire Quinta do Vesúvio in 1989 and to run this great property separately to produce a distinguished single-*quinta* port. At about the same time the family expanded its empire by become partners in, and subsequently owners of, the Madeira Wine Company, giving them control of Blandy's, Cossart, Leacock, and Rutherford & Miles. More recently, they acquired Cockburn's in 2006. The British shippers were slow to begin making remarkable table wines in the Douro, but when the Symingtons took the plunge they astutely did so in partnership with the former owner of Cos d'Estournel, Bruno Prats, and in Chryseia created one of the region's finest wines.

Members of the family perform the following roles:
Peter (born 1944): winemaker (semi-retired)
Paul (1953): marketing director
Dominic (1956): Madeira
John (1960): European sales director
Rupert (1964): North American sales director
Charles (1969): vineyards and winemaking

Quinta do Vesuvio ☆☆☆
Vila Nova de Gaia. Vintages: 1990, '91, '92, '94, '95, '96, '97, '98, '99, 2000, '01, '03, '04, '05.
www.quintadovesuvio.com
This magnificent Upper Douro estate used to be owned by A A Ferreira, but was acquired by the Symington family in 1989. Although technically a single-quinta port, it is made entirely in lagares and given the same care as all the other Symington vintage ports. Vesuvio aims to release a vintage every year, except when conditions are so dire, as in 1993, as to make this impossible.

Warre ☆☆☆☆
Vila Nova de Gaia. Vintages: 1904, '08, '12, '20, '22, '24, '27, '34, ('42), '45, '47, '50, '55, '58, '60, '63, '66, '70, '75, '77, '80, '83, '85, '91, '94, '97, 2000, '03.
www.warre.com
Dating from 1670, and the oldest English port firm, Warre is now one of the largest firms in the Symington group. The vintage wines are based on the 40-hectare Quinta da Cavadinha near Pinhão, from which a single-*quinta* wine has also been produced since the 1970s. The vintage style is extremely fruity with a fresh, almost herbal bouquet, and a firm "grip" at the finish. Recent vintages have been beautifully balanced and lingering. Warrior is a good vintage-character wine and the revamped tawny range under the Otima"label is well-packaged and of fine quality. The Bottle-Matured LBV, which is unfiltered, is one of the very best wines in this style.

Other Port Producers
Boutique estates that produce some port but more table wine can be found listed under "Douro Producers".

Andresen ☆☆–☆☆☆
Vila Nova. www.jhandresen.com
João Henrique Andresen left his native Denmark for Portugal as a teenager, and was still only 19 when he founded the port house that still bears his name. Since 1942 it has been owned by the Santos company. It specializes in very old tawnies as well as vintage ports, *colheitas* going as far back as 1900, and an unusual white port aged up to ten years in cask.

Barros Almeida ☆
Vila Nova de Gaia. www.porto-barros.pt
This is a substantial shipper of medium quality ports, founded in 1913, and now owned by the Sogevinus group which has also acquired Cálem (q.v.) and also owns Kopke, Burmester, and Cálem (qq.v.). The *colheitas* can be remarkable.

J W Burmester ☆☆–☆☆☆
Porto. www.burmesterporto.com
A Portuguese house, originally of English and German foundation in 1750, and in family hands until, sold in 1999 to Amorim, and then to Sogevinus. Grapes from its own vineyards and well-chosen wines from around Pinhão go to make its superb tawnies and ancient *colheitas*.

Martinez ☆☆
Vila Nova de Gaia. www.martinez.pt
An old firm founded in 1790 and bought by Harvey's in 1961. Now part of the Symington group. The best wines are fine tawnies, and there's an attractive single-*quinta* port from Quinta da Eira Velha.

Rebello Valente ☆
Vila Nova de Gaia. Vintages: 1945, '47, '55, '63, '66, '67, '70, '72, '75, '77, '80, '83, '85.
Now a subsidiary of Sandeman (q.v.), the firm of Robertson Bros. is the shipper of Rebello Valente vintage ports. The wines are of average quality.

Quinta de la Rosa ☆☆
Pinhão. www.quintadelarosa.com
This charming property near Pinhão produces a small quantity of elegant vintage port ideal for medium term drinking. All the top ports are foot trodden. Unlike most shippers, La Rosa aims to release a vintage wine every year, although 1993 proved impossible.

Rozès ☆
Vila Nova de Gaia. www.rozes.pt
A shipper, owned since 1999 by Champagne house Vranken and selling mostly to France. Modest quality, although top-of-the-range tawnies can be good.

Flat-bottomed boats on the Douro, Porto

Madeira

The very existence of Madeira has been touch and go for a century and a half. No other famous wine region has suffered so much the combined onslaught of pests, diseases, disillusioned growers, and public neglect.

What has kept Madeira alive is the unique quality its old wines have of getting better and better over decades or even centuries. The remaining bottles of Madeira from before its troubles began are proof that the island can make the longest-lived wines in the world. At a century old, their flavours are concentrated into a pungency that would be overwhelming were it not so fresh. They leave the mouth so cleanly and gracefully as you swallow, that water could not be more reviving. Harmony between sweetness and acidity can go no further. (The other wine that can pull off the same trick is Tokaj).

Madeira is the largest of a cluster of islands 643-kilometres (400-miles) west of the coast of Morocco. In the fifteenth century, the Portuguese, who landed on the island, set fire to the dense woodland that covered its slopes. The fire burned for years, the ashes from an entire forest enriching the already fertile volcanic soils.

Madeira flourished as a Portuguese colony. Prince Henry the Navigator ordered the sweet Malvasia grapes of Greece to be planted, as well as sugar cane from Sicily. Later, with the discovery of the West Indies, bananas became an important part of the island's harvest. The crops were, and still are, grown in a garden-like mixture on steep terraces that rise halfway up the 1,829-metre (6,000-foot) island-mountain. As in northern Portugal, the vines are trained on pergolas to allow other crops beneath. With its warm climate, Madeira was a natural producer of "sack", like Jerez and the Canaries. English legislation of 1665 settled its destiny by forbidding the export of European wines to British colonies except through British ports and in British ships. Madeira was presumably deemed to be in Africa, and so became the regular supplier for American vessels heading west. By the end of the seventeenth century, the American and West Indian British colonists used Madeira as their only wine.

Far from being spoilt by the long, hot voyage across the mid-Atlantic, the wine seemed to improve. Later, with growing British interests in the Far East, it was discovered to benefit even more from a voyage to India. So fine was their sea-matured Madeira that casks were shipped as ballast to India and back to give connoisseurs in Europe an even finer wine. It was during the eighteenth century that brandy was added, as it was to port, to sweeten and stabilize it.

In America, the appreciation of old Madeira became a cult – southern gentlemen would meet to dine simply on terrapin and canvas-back duck, before "discussing" several decanters of ancient wine, named sometimes for their grapes, or for the ship that carried them, or the families in whose cellars they had rested and become heirlooms. Thus a Bual might be followed by a Constitution, and that by a Francis, a Butler, or a Burd. A popular pale blend, still sometimes seen, is known as Rainwater – because, apparently, of a similarity of taste. Almost the same reverence was paid to its qualities in England – and still is, by the few who have tasted such wines. Quantities became far too great to transport through the tropics as a matter of course. In the 1790s, Napoléon's navy also put difficulties in the way of merchant seamen.

A practical substitute was found in warming the wines in hot stores (Portuguese *estufas*) for several months, depending on quality. The least good wine was heated the most, for the shortest period of time; the better for longer periods at more moderate temperatures. (The very finest wines received no artificial heat: rather, three to five years in cask in a sun-baked loft). The rules today stipulate 45°C (113°F) as the minimum temperature to which the wines must be heated. The outcome is a stabilization of the wine that renders it almost indestructible.

Four principal grape varieties and three or four others were grown for different styles of wine. The original, the Malvasia or Malmsey, made the richest; the Bual a less rich, more elegant but equally fragrant wine; Verdelho a soft, much drier wine with a faintly bitter finish; the Sercial (the same grape as the Esgana Cão of the Portuguese mainland) a fine, light wine with a distinct acid "cut". Tinta Negra Mole was planted to make the red wine once known as "Tent". Bastardo, Terrantez, and Moscatel were also grown in smaller quantities.

Madeira was at the peak of its prosperity when a double disaster struck. In the 1850s came *oidium*, the powdery mildew. In 1873, phylloxera arrived; 2,400 hectares of vineyard were destroyed, and only 1,200 replaced with true Madeira vines. To save grafting, the remainder was replanted (if at all) with French-American hybrids, whose wine may not be used for Madeira, nor exported from the island. Since then, Madeira has lived on its reputation, kept alive by memories, by a meagre trickle of high quality wines, and by the convenient French convention of sauce *madère*, which is easily enough satisfied with any wine that has been cooked. Half the wine from the island today is destined for sauce-making with no questions asked. Unfortunately, even the replanting of the original European vines, the four classics, was neglected in favour of the obliging Tinta Negra Mole.

Today, over 85 per cent of the crop (hybrids apart) is Tinta Negra Mole. Until EU regulations put a stop to the practice in 1993, many wines labelled with the classic Madeira varieties were in fact from Tinta, which had been manipulated until a semblance of the chosen style had been achieved. Current regulations require 85 per cent of a wine to be of the grape variety named. "Malmsey" can no longer be simply a style; it has to be genuine Malvasia. The age of the wine can also appear on the label: 3, 5, 10, or 15 years. Three and 5 are often disappointing, as they are not varietal wines but described with stylistic definitions on the label, such as "Finest Medium Rich" or "Finest Dry". It is invariably better to pay the small premium for 10 or 15 years.

Taking note of the EU regulations, the island's 2,000 growers have been busy regrafting vines to the classic varieties. It is their only hope. They cannot thrive on cheapness and low quality. They have no cash crop of "instant" wine; it all needs ageing. The *estufas* are expensive to run. With the reputation of Madeira and its wines in steady decline, the authorities took the radical decision to ban all exports of bulk wines from 2002.

The maintaining of dated solera (as in Jerez) used to be standard practice, but is no longer permitted. Old solera bottlings still turn up at auction and can be outstanding value. The Madeira shippers still occasionally declare a vintage – always a rarer occurrence with Madeira than with port, and taking place not immediately after the vintage but some 30 years later.

Vintage Madeira is kept in cask for a minimum of 20 years, then may spend a further period in glass 20-litre demijohns before bottling – when it is deemed ready to drink. In reality it is still only a young wine at this stage; it needs another 20–50 years in bottle to achieve sublimity.

In the early 2000s, the shippers introduced a new style of wine: the vintage dated *colheita*. Blandy took the initiative with a 1994 single harvest Malmsey, and Henriques & Henriques and Justino Henriques soon followed suit with wines from 1995. The late Noël Cossart, the fifth generation of the old firm of Madeira shippers Cossart Gordon, counselled, "Never to buy a cheap Sercial or Malmsey; these grapes are shy growers and must consequently be expensive; whereas Bual and Verdelho are prolific and develop faster and may be both cheaper and good."

Vintages

The most famous Madeira vintages up to 1900, bottles of which are still occasionally found, were 1789, 1795 (esp. Terrantez), 1806, 1808 (Malmsey), 1815 (esp. Bual), 1822, 1836, 1844, 1846 (esp. Terrantez and Verdelho), 1851, 1862, 1865, 1868, 1870 (Sercial), 1880 (esp. Malmsey).

Since 1900 over two dozen vintages have been shipped: 1900 (the last year Moscatel was made), 1902 (esp. Verdelho and Bual), 1905 (esp. Sercial), 1906 (esp. Malmsey), 1907 (esp. Verdelho and Bual), 1910, 1914 (Bual), 1915 (Bual, Sercial), 1916, 1920, 1926 (esp. Bual), 1934 (Verdelho), 1940, 1941 (esp. Bual), 1950, 1954 (esp. Bual), 1956, 1957, 1958, 1960 (Bual, Terrantez), 1965 (Bual), 1966 (Bual, Sercial), 1968 (Verdelho), 1969 (Terrantez), 1971, 1972 (Malmsey, Verdelho), 1973 (Verdelho), and 1974 (Terrantez), 1976 (Bual, Terrantez), 1977 (Bual, Verdelho), 1978 (Terrantez), 1981 (Verdelho).

Leading Madeira Shippers

Barbeito ☆☆
Funchal. www.vinhosbarbeito.com
This producer is 52 per cent owned by a Japanese trading company. An impressive range of vintages is kept in stock, some of which were purchased after the founding of the company. A house specialty is a 50/50 blend of Verdelho and Bual. The firm has also accepted the new "single harvest" style with enthusiasm.

Artur de Barros e Sousa ☆☆
Funchal.
A tiny producer, known until 1922 as Lomelino, and nineteenth-century vintage wines under that name still appear at auction. The finest wines are called Reserva and are blends of unspecified older wines, including Bastardo and Terrantez.

H M Borges ☆–☆☆
Funchal. www.hmborges.com
A firm in the hands of the same family since the 1870s. Good 10- and 15-year-olds and the occasional single-harvest or *colheita* wine.

Justino Henriques ☆–☆☆
Caniço. www.justinosmadeira.com
The house was founded in 1870 and now belongs to the French La Martiniquaise company. So it is not surprising that Henriques is a major supplier of innocuous cooking Madeira. But it also nurtures some traditional styles, made in *estufas*, from Tinta Negra Mole as well as from the noble varieties.

Henriques & Henriques ☆☆☆
Câmara de Lobos. www.henriqueshenriques.pt
The only shipper to own vineyards (the largest on the island), the firm is owned by a consortium of different families and was managed, until his untimely death in 2008, by John Cossart. The cellars are the most technically well-equipped on the island. Produces a wide range of well-structured, rich, toothsome wines including very fine old Reserves and vintages.

Madeira Wine Company ☆☆☆
Funchal. www.madeirawinecompany.com
In 1913, a number of shippers in the beleaguered trade formed the Madeira Wine Association to pool their resources and share facilities. Reconstituted in 1981 as the Madeira Wine Company, the group (owned since 1989 by port shippers Symington) controls 26 companies and accounts for around 60 per cent of Madeira sales.

The main winery is in an old army barracks – blends corresponding to its 120 different labels are made up in the company's lotting rooms. One of its old lodges, next to the tourist office in Funchal, is open for visits and tasting. Here you can buy vintage wines dating back to the nineteenth century. The wines are cellared together, but preserve their house styles.

The top labels include:
• Blandy's the main range is named after various British dukes and consists of 3-year wines from Tinta Negra Mole. The 5-year wines are varietals, as are the older blends. An innovation, launched in 2000, is a 1994 Harvest Malmsey, a kind of early vintage declaration. There are also glorious old vintages, mostly seen at auctions.
• Cossart Gordon established in 1745, and once the leading Madeira shipper. Wines slightly less rich than Blandy's.
• Leacock's and Miles (ex-Rutherford & Miles) other brands, midway in sweetness between Cossart Gordon and Blandy.

Pereira D'Oliveira ☆☆–☆☆☆☆
Funchal.
The family firm owns some vineyards near Funchal, but purchases most of its grapes to produce a full range of traditional wines.

Switzerland

So rare are Swiss wines outside their own country that it is easy to assume that they fall short of international standards and remain the special taste of a blinkered culture. If this was once true, it is a misleading picture today. Many Swiss are critical and wine-conscious, and most have money to spare – which is a good thing, for Swiss wines are expensive by almost any standards. Land prices and the cost of culture of their cliff-hanging vineyards are startlingly high. To justify inevitably high prices, there should, in principle, be every pressure on growers to concentrate on high quality. In practice, growers were, until very recently, cushioned against market forces by subsidies and protectionist measures.

Now, however, the chill winds of competition are blowing through the vineyards, and white wine import quotas have been relaxed. The imported wines often undercut the home grown version. Greater exports might deliver expanding markets that would help producers to survive, but their excessively high prices render the wines uncompetitive. Only one per cent of Swiss wine leaves the country. For the moment, strong domestic demand, and tourists' consumption of house wines in hotels and restaurants – albeit usually an indifferent Fendant or Dôle that scarcely enhances the image of Swiss wine – helps the Swiss industry to survive. The Swiss vineyards are divided into six major regions, with around three-quarters of them located within the French-speaking Suisse Romande. The Valais (5,113 ha) is the most important, followed by the Vaud canton (3,838 ha), the Swiss-German part (2,593 ha), the Geneva area (1,297 ha), the Italian-speaking Ticino (1,065 ha), and the region of the Trois Lacs including Neuchâtel, Lac de Bienne, Vully and Jura (940 ha). In the Swiss German area the main cantons are Zurich (613 ha), Schaffhausen (473 ha), Graubünden (419 ha) and Aargau (393 ha).

The emphasis was on red wines 150 years ago, the best of which came from Graubünden in the German speaking east. The best whites came from the north shore of Lake Geneva between Lausanne and Montreux in the Vaud canton, where the steep south slopes ripened the local Chasselas to perfection. Further up the Rhône valley, in the mountainous Valais, there was a largely part-time wine-growing tradition. Vineyards were irregularly planted with obscure grapes chosen for their dazzling sweetness and strength in the dry and sunny Alpine climate.

The modern industry began to take shape when the Chasselas spread up the Rhône valley, when pressure for the sunny lake slopes of Lake Geneva as building land drove half the wines out of the Vaud, and when selected forms of the Pinot Noir and Gamay began to penetrate from France, via Geneva and then eastwards. Meanwhile, Müller-Thurgau, bred by the eponymous Swiss scientist a century ago at Geisenheim, began to invade the eastern cantons. Nowadays in Switzerland this wine is often found under the name Riesling-Sylvaner.) In 1945, the Italian-speaking Ticino (or Tessin) adopted the Merlot of Bordeaux as its main red grape variety, after it was successfully planted by the scientist Alderige Fantuzzi, who was charged with replanting the Ticino after phylloxera had destroyed the vineyards. Although in the last 100 years the overall vineyard area has diminished considerably, selected areas such as German speaking Switzerland, the Valais, Vaud, and Geneva have increased their hectarage. Plantings of red varieties are also increasing and now account for 52 per cent of plantings. Nevertheless, Switzerland remains a minnow in the grand scheme of wine, with only 14,846 hectares of vineyards accounting for just 0.2 per cent of global production. Plantings of red varieties are increasing and now account for 58 per cent of all plantings. Pinot Noir accounts for 30 per cent of all plantings with 4,450 hectares, followed by Gamay (1,584 ha), Merlot (1,006 ha), the two local crossings Gamaret (351 ha) and Garanoir (189 ha), and then Syrah (177 ha). Chasselas is the main white variety (4,152 ha), followed by Müller-Thurgau (502 ha), Chardonnay (314 ha), Sylvaner (235 ha), and Pinot Gris (208 ha).

   The essential information given on the often rather taciturn, though frequently highly decorative, Swiss wine label is laid down by the federal government. Generally speaking, for white wines, if there is no other indication of grape variety, assume Chasselas. Red wines will, in the main, be Pinot Noir and/or Gamay. Some German-Swiss labels use terms with no international validity – but then they not only never travel abroad, they seldom leave the confines of the canton in which they were grown. Italian-Swiss wine labels are simplicity itself as there are essentially only two types of wine: Merlot and the hardly cultivated Nostrano, made from a clutch of hybrid grapes. The maker's name seems to be considered of little importance to the consumer and is often tucked away down at the bottom in small print. Pride of place may be given to a brand-

Château s'Aigle, Chablais district, the Vaud

name (Les Murailles), estate name (Château d'Allaman), or village name (St Saphorin). It is not always easy to tell which is which. Although *chaptalization* is permitted, and quite commonly practised at the lower quality levels, all Swiss wines can be assumed to be dry unless a specific caution is included on the label: *mi-flétri* or *flétri* (literally "shrivelled") in the French-speaking cantons, Spätlese where German is the *lingua franca*. There has been a growth in late-harvest and emphatically *flétri* wines over recent years, and many of these are of exceptional quality. Since 1996 the richest of them have been entitled, if they meet certain criteria (which include a minimum Oechsle level of 130 and a mandatory ageing period in oak), to be labelled as Grains Nobles. The Swiss also make wide use of screwcaps instead of corks for wines designed to be drunk young – which includes most Chasselas.

The French-Speaking Cantons

All the principal vineyards of the French-speaking cantons (Suisse Romande) lie along the south-facing right bank of the Rhône, from its emergence into the Valais (a suntrap sheltered on both sides by towering Alps), round the shores of Lake Geneva – simply a widening of the Rhône – to its departure through the gently rolling farmlands of Geneva canton into France. Also included in this group are the three lakes of Neuchâtel, Biel/Bienne, and Morat, each of which enjoys good, south-facing, lake-shore conditions. Three-quarters of all Swiss wine is grown in Suisse Romande, much of it is white.

The Valais (Wallis)

The Valais (which begins, geographically, at the Grimselpass and ends at St Maurice on the right bank, and St Gingolph on the left) has Switzerland's driest and sunniest climate. On its steeper vineyards, terraced on arid mountain slopes, irrigation by means of wooden channels known as *bisses* used to be common practice. Nowadays, irrigation is limited to periods of severe drought, and then only during the growing season .

Wine-growing starts in earnest somewhere between Visp and Sierre, reaches a crescendo around Sion, the heart (and capital) of the Valais, and begins to wind gradually down after the Rhône has executed its sharp right turn at Martigny. At its upper extremes, the village of Visperterminen above Visp has what are reported to be Europe's highest vineyards at up to 1,100 metres (3,600 feet) above sea level. In the upper Valais, the principal wine-growing villages are Salquenen/Salgesch, Sierre, and St Léonard; and in the lower Valais, Vétroz, Ardon, Leytron, Chamoson, Saillon, and Fully are the most important centres. Action has finally been taken in the Valais in response to an awareness of the urgent need for some notion of *crus*. For too long, Fendant (ie. Chasselas), which accounts for the largest quantity of wine produced in the Valais, was sold without mention of village or vineyard name. Since many were of poor quality (and the consumer had no way of differentiating), the

result was that all Fendants, whether good, bad, or indifferent, tended to be tarred with the same bottom-of-the-market brush. Nowadays there will often be a village or vineyard name appended; the appellation Fendant may even be omitted. Sylvaner, known here as Johannisberg (sometimes Rhin, either Petit or Gros), makes aromatic, fuller-bodied yet dry wines; when late-harvested, they can be impressive indeed.

Lakes of Chasselas are one thing; the so-called white "specialties" of the Valais, generally considered to be the great undiscovered potential of Swiss wines, are quite another. First comes the incomparable Petite Arvine, its name said to come from the Latin meaning "pale yellow". Distinguished by its fine nose and characteristic salty finish, it is usually vinified dry; some growers harvest a small proportion of the crop late to make a *mi-flétri* or *flétri*. Humagne Blanche ("vigorous vine" in Latin) is a nervy, stimulating wine once prescribed as a post-partum tonic to young mothers. It requires the best sites, performs rather irregularly, and ripens late – all of which had contributed to a gradual decline over the years, but that decline is happily now in reverse.

Amigne, whose favoured sites are concentrated in and around Vétroz, is made in extremely limited quantities (since only 40 hectares remain) into a rich, velvety white wine, almost always with some residual sugar but sufficient acidity and backbone to give it good keeping qualities.

Rarer still are a clutch of very old, quaintly named varieties, found mainly in the upper Valais around Visp. In centuries past they were harvested early to give quite sharp, thirst-quenching wines designed for vineyard quaffing after a hard day's work. Of these, the finest is Heida (or Païen), thought to be the same as, or a relation either of Savagnin (the same grape as used in *vin jaune*), or of Traminer. Himbertscha, whose name sounds vaguely raspberry-related, apparently means "trellis-grown" in the upper Valais dialect, referring to the traditional method of training this particular grape, while Lafnetscha turns out to be the Blanchier of Savoie. Both give clean-tasting, rather acidic wines that need plenty of time to mature. Finally comes Gwäss (Gouais Blanc), another native of the Jura, sharply reminiscent of cider when young.

Of the non-indigenous but well-established varieties, the Marsanne grape thrives here under the name of Ermitage, giving (especially around Fully) a full-bodied wine with a striking nose and an elusively smoky flavour. Malvoisie (alias Pinot Gris) may be vinified dry (in which case it is often labelled Pinot Gris), or harvested late and made into a sweet wine – and often labelled Malvoisie. Muscat has been grown in the Valais since the sixteenth century, and is made here with all residual sugar fermented out, closer in style to a Muscat d'Alsace than to any other. Tiny quantities of Gewürztraminer, Riesling, Aligoté, Chardonnay, Chenin, and Pinot Blanc are also to be found.

Over half of Valais wine is red, and two-thirds of this is Pinot Noir, which acquits itself with some distinction, particularly around Sierre. The better growers are experimenting with Burgundy clones and varying proportions of new oak. Pinot Noir is also blended with Gamay and called Dôle, at its lower levels a good lunchtime wine quaffed throughout Switzerland in multiples of the decilitre to accompany uncomplicated meals. To qualify for the appellation, a Dôle must contain at least

51 per cent Pinot Noir and reach a certain minimum Oechsle level prescribed by the cantonal wine commission; if it misses the mark it is labelled Goron. Gamay is also vinified alone, especially from the villages around Martigny.

Of antique red grapes, there is Humagne Rouge (no relation of the white Humagne Blanche but reckoned by some to be Oriou, from the Valle d'Aosta). It makes robust, pleasantly tannic, and appetizing country wine. Cornalin (alias Landroter or Rouge du Pays) is a once rare variety that has won some deserved popularity and now occupies over 90 hectares. Its irregular yield and uneven performance make it a tricky commercial proposition for most wine growers. Its deep colour, good tannins, and superb fruit, however, make it an extremely interesting proposition for interested wine drinkers. Finally, in the upper Valais, Eyholzer Roter (the Mondeuse of Haute-Savoie) is to be found, which gives a tawny-reddish, rather rough country wine. Syrah, a fairly recent import, deserves special mention, particularly from around Chamoson; some Nebbiolo is also being grown.

Leading Valais Producers

Charles Bonvin ☆–☆☆☆
Sion. Owner: Bonvin family. 30 ha. www.charlesbonvin.ch
Founded in 1858, Bonvin has some of its best vineyards at up to 700 metres (2,275 feet), on slate and chalk soils. There are three Chasselas wines on offer. Its barrel-fermented white wine is an attractive blend of Pinot Blanc, Chardonnay, and Petite Arvine. When climatic conditions are favourable, Bonvin makes a remarkable sweet wine from Amigne and other varieties called Cuvée d'Or, which is aged for two years in barriques.

Oskar Chanton ☆☆–☆☆☆
Visp. Owner: Josef-Marie Chanton. 9 ha. www.chanton.ch
Over 20 wines can be tasted in the venerable old Chanton cellar in Visp, including rarities from the upper Valais like Heida, Himbertscha, Lafnetscha, and Gwäss, rescued from oblivion by Josef-Marie Chanton. The Arvine is superb, as are the late-harvested Malvoisie and Gewürztraminer. More innovations have come from his son Mario, in the form of sweet wines from Heida and Hibou.

Marie-Thérèse Chappaz ☆☆–☆☆☆
Fully. Owner: Marie-Thérèse Chappaz. 8 ha. www.chappaz.ch
Mme. Chappaz is best known for her late-harvest wines, of which the finest are probably her peppery Petite Arvine Grains Nobles.

Fernand Cina ☆☆
Salgesch/Salquenen. Owner: Manfred and Damian Cina. 10 ha. www.fernand-cina.ch
The 50-year-old firm has a penchant for barrique-aged wines, although such varieties as Cornalin and Humagne do well enough without. The range of Pinot Noirs is particularly impressive. Cabernet Franc is also doing well.

Gérald Clavien ☆–☆☆
Miège/Sierre. Owner: Gérald Clavien. 5.4 ha. www.clavien.ch
The wines of this young, dynamic grower (who was a chef before taking over his father's vineyards) feature on the lists of all the top restaurants in Switzerland. Sierre is the hub of red wine-growing in the Valais; Clavien's straight Pinot Noir and Tête de Cuvée are notable, also the Dôle Blanche (a rosé from Pinot Noir). Some full-bodied Humagne Blanc is also made.

Fabienne Cottagnoud ☆☆
Vétroz. Owner: Fabienne and Marc-Henri Cottagnoud. 3.5 ha. www.fabiennecottagnoud.ch
A wide range of wines from this small property: spicy, pungent Humagne Rouge, smoky Pinot Noirs, and splendid Amigne Grains Nobles.

Benoît Dorsaz ☆☆
Fully. Owner: Benoît Dorsaz. 4 ha. www.benoit-dorsaz.ch
The bread-and-butter wines here are Fendant and Gamay, but far more rewarding is the barrique-aged Quintessence line from Humagne, Syrah, and Cornalin. Floral Viognier, too.

René Favre ☆–☆☆
St Pierre-de-Clages. Owner: Mike Favre. 12 ha. www.petite-arvine.com
It's a mystery that a 12-ha estate can produce almost every conceivable Valais style, but Favre does it. Some wines are over-oaked, but the Petite Arvine and Pinot Noirs are stars.

Germanier-Balavaud ☆–☆☆☆
Vétroz. Owner: Germanier family. 30 ha. www.jrgermanier.ch
Germanier is a producer of a wide range of wines of good concentration and length. As well as the standard Valais wines, there are some fascinating Reserves: delicious Amigne, a gamey, oaky, yet elegant Syrah called Cayas, and the superb Mitis, a late-harvest Amigne fermented in new oak. Today the wines are made by the Germaniers' nephew Gilles Besse, and his newest wine is a pure Cornalin called Champmarais.

Labuthe ☆☆
Vétroz. Owner: Philippe Labuthe. 5 ha. www.vins-labuthe.ch
Amigne finds two expressions here: dry, austere, and powerful; and off-dry, with aromas of dried apricots.

Adrian Mathier ☆☆–☆☆☆
Salgesch/Salquenen. Owner: Diego Mathier. 25 ha. www.nouveau-salquenen.ch
Interesting wines with personality, including sophisticated and concentrated Pinot Noirs, lush Marsanne, and a fine, late harvest Amigne.

Simon Maye & Fils ☆☆–☆☆☆
St Pierre-de-Clages. Owner: Maye family. 11 ha. www.simonmaye.ch
A small, top-quality grower making three highly prized Fendants (Le Fauconnier, Trémazière, and La Mouette), Johannisberg, Dôle, Pinot Noir, Humagne Rouge, plus some Chardonnay, Malvoisie, and dry and lightly sweet Petite Arvine. His richly spicy Syrahs are among the country's finest.

Denis Mercier ☆☆☆
Sierre. Owner: Denis Mercier. 6.3 ha.
Mercier has cult status in Switzerland and his wines seem to

justify it, with perfectly balanced Fendants; intense and herbal Païen; spicy, lively Cornalin; creamy, honeyed Ermitage *flétri*.

Domaine du Mont d'Or ☆–☆☆☆
Pont de la Morge. Owner: Simon Lambiel. 21 ha. www.montdor-wine.ch
The most famous property of Sion, established in 1847 on a steep, dry, sheltered hill by a soldier from the Vaud, who installed the irrigation system by *bisses* which is still in operation. The vines are terraced with 15 kilometres (24 miles) of dry stone walls. The domaine is best known for its Johannisbergs, both dry and late harvested. Also produced are a musky, weighty Malvoisie, a rather jammy Syrah, a magnificent honeyed Petite Arvine, and strong, tannic, and alcoholic Dôle.

Caves Orsat ☆–☆☆☆
Martigny. Owner: Rouvinez. 30 ha. www.cavesorsat.ch
A large winery founded in 1874 and owned since 1998 by the important firm of Rouvinez. Fendant and Dôle are sound, but the top range is called Primus Classicus, and includes a full-bodied, apricot-tinged Marsanne and a splendid damsony Cornalin.

Provins Valais ☆–☆☆☆
Sion. 1,200 ha. www.provins.ch
Highly regarded central cooperative of the Valais producing some 23 per cent of all Valais wines and thus 10 per cent of all Swiss-bottled wines. Its vast range includes well-known brand names like Pierrafeu Fendant, Johannisberg Rhonegold, Pinot

Noir St Guérin, and the barrique-agd Maître de Chais bottlings. To the usual vast Valaisan spectrum of grapes it adds Pinot Blanc, Chardonnay, Sauvignon Blanc, and Syrah. Its Chasselas de St Léonard, made (exceptionally for Switzerland) without malolactic fermentation, is reserved for top restaurants. More recently it has made some outstanding sweet wines, such as the Marsanne Grains de Malice.

Other wines to watch out for, and all made by winemaker Madeleine Gay, are Domaine Evêché (Diolinoir), Domaine Tournelette (Pinot Noir), and Domaine du Chapitre (Petite Arvine, Amigne, and Humagne Blanche).

Gérard Raymond ☆–☆☆
Saillon. Owner: Gérard. 5 ha. www.gerardraymond.ch
Tiny family business producing top Fendant, Johannisberg, Arvine (the pride of the house), Muscat, Malvoisie, and Dôle Blanche. Its reds are also notable, particularly Dôle and Pinot Noir. Raymond is one of the few Valaisan growers to make Nebbiolo.

Cave Rodeline ☆☆
Fully. Owner: Yvon and Claudine Roduit. 6 5 ha.
A small family business, run by an uncle and nephew, making the full range of Valais wines on some prime terraced sites . Of especial note are its Ermitage and Petite Arvine (vinified dry and *flétri*), Cornalin, Pinot Noir (of which a proportion is oak-aged), and Syrah.

Serge Roh, Caves Les Ruinettes ☆☆
Vétroz. Owner: Serge Roh. 10 ha. www.vins-roh.com
This solid producer offers a substantial range of wines from the simple Fendant de Vétroz to an outstanding Syrah de Vétroz.

Bernard Rouvinez ☆☆
Sierre. Owner: Jean-Bernard and Dominique Rouvinez. 82 ha. www.rouvinez.ch
These brothers' estate lies next to a nunnery; they are the only men permitted to enter the nunnery grounds to tend the vines. On their own property, two-thirds of the grapes are red, predominantly Pinot Noir. They vinify excellent varietal Pinot Noir and Chasselas. However, their most notable creations are Le Tourmentin, a Pinot Noir/ Syrah/Cornalin/ Humagne Rouge blend, and Le Trémaille (Chardonnay and Petite Arvine). These elegant, attractively presented wines indicate fresh thinking and a willingness to innovate – a hopeful sign in a sometimes overly tradition bound region. They also own the estate of Château Lichten.

St Jodernkellerei ☆–☆☆
Visperterminen. Cooperative. 50 ha. www.jodernkellerei.ch
The best place, other than Oskar Chanton (q.v.), to experience the rare specialties of Visp, such as Heida in three different versions.

Varone ☆–☆☆
Sion. Owner: Jean-Pierre and Philippe Varone. 12 ha. www.varone.ch
A traditional producer that supplements its own fruit with purchases from other growers. Its best Chasselas comes from the Uvrier vineyard.

Traditional Swiss signs

Maurice Zufferey ☆☆
Muraz sure Sierre. Owner: Maurice Zufferey. 8.5 ha.
www.maurice-zufferey-vins.ch
Sierre is red wine country and Zufferey's are particularly
notable (though he also produces many other specialties). Two
Pinot Noirs are made (one oak-aged), Dôle, Syrah, a deeply
coloured Humagne Rouge, and the tricky but infinitely
rewarding Cornalin which Zufferey was among the first to
revive in the Valais.

Other Valais Producers

Philippoz Frères
Leytron. www.philippoz-freres.ch

Les Fils Maye
Riddes. www.maye.ch

Caveau de Salquenen
Salgesc. www.gregor-kuonen.ch

Cave du Rhodan
Salgesc. www.rhodan.ch

Madeleine & Jean-Yves Mabillard-Fuchs &
Cave de la Madeleine
Vétroz & Venthône. www.fontannaz.ch

Didier Joris
Chamoson. www.didierjoris.ch

The Vaud

The canton of Vaud includes all the vineyards of the north
shore of Lake Geneva and the Rhône, as high upstream as the
border with the Valais at Bex: an 80-kilometre (50-mile) arc of
southern slopes. It is divided into three main zones: Chablais,
the right bank of the Rhône between Ollon and the lake;
Lavaux, the central section between Montreux and Lausanne;
and La Côte, from Lausanne round to Nyon at the border with
Geneva. Further north, just short of Lake Neuchâtel, are the
little enclaves of Côtes de l'Orbe and Bonvillars; half the
villages in the Vully vineyard on Lake Morat also belong to
Vaud. The canton has its own appellation systems, which
control origin, grape varieties, and Oechsle levels.

The appellations of Chablais include the villages of
Villeneuve, Yvorne, Aigle, Ollon, and Bex, all with good southwest slopes above the Rhône. Yvorne, with its minerally,
gunflint character, real vigour, ripeness and length is generally
considered to be the greatest of all Chablais wines. At its very
best it is undoubtedly a match for (though subtly different
from) the top wines from Lavaux.

Lavaux is certainly Switzerland's most scenic vineyard, piled
high in toppling terraces above the lakeside villages. The view
from among the vines is superb: the mountains of Savoie a great
dark, jagged-topped bulk against the sun opposite, the lake
surface below gleaming grey, wrinkled by white paddle-steamers
gliding from village pier to village pier. Erosion is a serious
problem: a brown stain in the lake after a night's heavy rain is
bad news for a wine grower. Lavaux boasts the *crus* of Dézaley
(for centuries considered to be the high point of Swiss white

wine) and nearby Calamin, as well as six of Vaud's 26 appellations. Chasselas from the upper slopes takes on a liveliness and
an almost aromatic quality that distinguishes it from the more
austere dryness of the lower vineyards. Each village, however,
has its committed supporters and the names of Epesses, St
Saphorin, Rivaz, Cully, Villette, Lutry, Chardonne, and others
are writ correspondingly large on the label.

La Côte, situated between Lausanne and Nyon, has 12 appellations. The best-known of these are Féchy, Perroy, Mont-
sur-Rolle, Tartegnin, Vinzel, and Luins. This is a more gentle,
often southeasterly sloping vineyard whose wines rarely have
the vigour or flavour of those of Lavaux or Chablais, but do
make deliciously floral pre-prandial quaffing wines. For some
unknown reason the term *grand cru* can be applied to any
wine that comes from a *clos* or walled vineyard, regardless of
its quality.

Chasselas dominates the Vaud vineyards, although a very
small part is also made over to Pinot Gris, Pinot Blanc, and
Riesling/Sylvaner. About a quarter of the vineyards are planted
with red grapes, so Pinot Noir and Gamay are also found here,
either vinified singly, or blended and designated Salvagnin (a
so-called "label of quality" that has fallen somewhat into disre-
pute over the years). Overproduction in this area has been a
serious problem here for some time, with average yields
frequently surpassing 100 hectolitres per hectare, for red as
well as white wines. The wines – especially those made from
Chasselas – enjoy an enthusiastic local following that can
baffle those more used to the forthright flavours of Alsace
or Australia.

Leading Vaud Producers

Henri Badoux ☆☆
Aigle. Owner: Henri Olivier Badoux. 55 ha.
www.badoux.com
A substantial, second-generation, family owned business with
vineyards in Yvorne, Aigle, Ollon, Villeneuve, St Saphorin,
Féchy, Vinzel, and Mont-sur-Rolle. The two leading wines
are the famous Aigle les Murailles (with the classic lizard
label) and Yvorne Petit Vignoble. Badoux's Aigle Pourpre
Monseigneur, a Pinot Noir/Gamay blend from the Chablais
district, benefits from some ageing.

Louis Bovard ☆☆
Lavaux. Owner: Louis Bovard. 17 ha.
www.domaineboverard.com
A forward-looking estate, producing not only Chasselas from
top sites in Epesses, St Saphorin, and Dézaley, but also good
Sauvignon Blanc, Syrah, and Merlot. About one-third of the
vineyards are cultivated Biodynamically.

Jean-Michel Conne, Cave Champ de Clos ☆☆
Chexbres. Owner: Jean-Michel Conne. 12 ha.
www.conne.ch
By dint of wise buying of vineyards outside Lavaux, and by
inheritance of the family vineyards, a considerable holding
of good sites around Lake Geneva has been built up.
Especially famous is the Dézaley Plan Perdu, St Saphorin
Le Sémillant (a sur lie bottling), and Ollon L'Oisement.

Several Pinot Noirs (of which the oak-aged is labelled Cartige) are also produced.

Dubois Fils Vins ☆☆
Epesses. Owner: Jean-Daniel Dubois. 9 ha. www.dubois.ch
The Dubois are believers in allowing Chasselas to go through malolactic fermentation. They offer a wide range of *crus*, including Epesses, St Saphorin, and Dézaley, all of which are capable of ageing for 20 years, after which they acquire a slight honeyed tone.

Hammel ☆–☆☆
Rolle. Director: Martin Federer. 70 ha. www.hammel.ch
This is a leading domaine and merchant house of La Côte, producing Chasselas from various Vaudois vineyards: Domaine Les Pierrailles and La Bigaire (La Côte), Domaine de Riencourt (Bougy), Clos du Chatelard (Villeneuve), and Clos de la George (Yvorne).

Obrist ☆–☆☆
Vevey. Owners: Schenk group (q.v.). 65 ha. www.obrist.ch
One of the largest growers of Vaudois white, with a particular reputation for its Yvornes: Clos du Rocher, Clos des Rennauds, and Près-Roc. Also famous is its Cure d'Attalens and Salvagnin Domaine du Manoir.

Gérard Pinget ☆☆
Rivaz. Administrator: C Pinget. 10 ha.
A traditional estate whose top wines include the steely Dézaley Renard (its label sports a fox), St Saphorin, and Soleil de Lavaux.

Schenk ☆–☆☆
Rolle. Owner: Schenk family. 37 ha. www.schenk.ch
This, the largest Swiss wine firm, was founded and based at Rolle since 1893. Its principal estates are in Yvorne, Mont-sur-Rolle, Vinzel, and Féchy. Its subsidiary companies in Switzerland include Obrist (q.v.), Maurice Gay, and the Cave St Pierre in the Valais.

J & P Testuz ☆☆
Treytorrens-Cully. Owner: Jean-Pierre Testuz. 60 ha. www.testuz.ch
The Testuz family trace their wine-growing roots back to Dézaley in 1538. In 1865, they sold the first bottled wine in Switzerland. Their Dézaley, L'Arbalète, is one of the finest of the area. Other Lavaux wines include the fine St Saphorin Roche Ronde and Epesses. Chablais wines include Aigle Les Cigales and Yvorne Haute-Combe.

Other Vaud Producers

Domaine Henri Cruchon
Echichens. www.henricruchon.com

Domaine La Colombe
Féchy. www.lacolombe.ch

Domaine de Maison Blanche
Mont-sur-Roll. www.domainemaisonblanche.ch

Cave Expérimentale Agroscope Changins-Wädenswil
Nyon. www.acw.admin.ch

Domaine Jean-François Neyroud-Fonjallaz
Chardonne. www.neyroud.ch

Geneva

The canton is divided into three districts: the biggest – Mandement – to the north on the right bank of the Rhône, includes Dardagny, Russin, and above all, Satigny. South of the river (and of the city) is Arve-et-Rhône, centred around Lully-Bernex. The area that sets off around the other side of the lake is called Arve-et-Lac. Since the slopes are gentle and the vines well-spaced out, mechanical harvesting is a possibility, which gives the wines a useful price advantage.

The area has increased its vineyards steadily and, with 1,297 hectares under vine, is now third in importance after the Valais and the Vaud. Chasselas (often, but not inevitably, known here as Perlan) is no longer the principal variety, that place having been taken by Gamay. Chasselas is often bottled with a slight prickle to make up for the character it frequently lacks. Riesling/Sylvaner, Pinot Gris, Pinot Blanc, and Gewürztraminer are also to be found; impressive results are being achieved with Aligoté and Chardonnay, as well as with the red crossing Gamaret.

Leading Geneva Producers

Domaine du Centaure ☆–☆☆
Dardagny. Owner: Claude Ramu. 18 ha. www.domaine-du-centaure.ch
A range of mythologically named wines is produced in the district of Le Mandement, west of Geneva. Although Gamay is important here, the emphasis is on atypical varieties such as Kerner, Muscat, Scheurebe, Pinot Blanc, and a blend of Cabernet/Merlot.

Domaine des Curiades ☆–☆☆
Lully. Owner: Jacques and Christophe Dupraz. 12.5 ha. www.curiades.ch
The domaine offers about 20 wines, varietal and blended, with some Sauvignon Blanc and Pinot Noir aged in barriques.

Charles Novelle & Fils ☆–☆☆
Satigny. Owner: Jean-Michel Novelle. 7 ha.
When Jean-Michel Novelle took over running the domaine in the 1980s, he replaced most of the Chasselas with 17 other varieties, many of them international rather than Swiss. Always experimenting, Novelle has made sweet wines from artificially dried Sauvignon and Petit Manseng grapes.

Bernard Rochaix ☆–☆☆
Peissy. Owner: Bernard Rochaix. 48 ha. www.lesperrieres.ch
Two-thirds of production is of white wines. As well as a fragrant Chasselas and lively Aligoté, Rochaix produces an attractive unoaked Chardonnay, often more enjoyable than his barrel fermented version. Neither Pinot Noir nor Cabernet Sauvignon is really successful here.

Other Geneva Producers

Domaines Les Hutins
Dardagny.

Domaine des Balisiers
Satigny. www.balisiers.ch

Domaine du Paradis
Satigny. www.domaine-du-paradis.ch

Lakes Neuchâtel, Biel, & Morat

Vines grow all along the northern shores of all three lakes, sheltered by the Jura chain, which forms the backbone of the route from Geneva up to Basle. The best-known villages on Lake Neuchâtel are Cortaillod, Auvernier, Boudry, and St Blaise; on Lake Biel, the names of Schafis and Twann are famous; while on Lake Morat, the Fribourg villages of Praz, Nant, and Môtier enjoy a certain renown.

Chasselas reigns here once more, to give wines that are light, dry, and given to a natural prickle ("l'étoile") – a result of their being mainly bottled *sur lie*. There is no Gamay north of Geneva; Pinot Noir is the only permitted red variety. The limestone hills to the north and west of Lake Neuchâtel and the temperate climate seem to bring out some of the elusive finesse of the Pinot Noir grape.

Neuchâtel Pinots from reputable growers may be expected to have some distinction; in a good year they may be considered the best Pinots Switzerland can produce. The pale rosé, Oeil-de-Perdrix ("partridge eye") – an appellation native to Neuchâtel, now widely used all over Switzerland – is an appealing Pinot Noir rosé.

Leading Neuchâtel Producers

Château d'Auvernier ☆☆
Auvernier. Owner: Thierry Grosjean. 60 ha.
www.chateau-auvernier.ch
One of the oldest established houses, having been in the same family since 1603, making nervy Neuchâtel *blanc*, Oeil-de-Perdrix, Pinot Noir d'Auvernier, barrique-aged Pinot Gris, and a small amount of Chardonnay. High quality winemaking.

Caves de la Béroche ☆☆
St-Aubin-Sauges. Owner: Albert Porret. 51 ha.
www.caves-beroche.ch
This is the family's fourth generation, making Chasselas, Chardonnay, Viognier, an Oeil-de-Perdrix, and a little Pinot Gris. The estate also vinifies the organic wines from the Domaine des Coccinelles.

Châtenay-Bouvier ☆–☆☆
Boudry. Director: Janine Schaer. 30 ha.
www.chatenay.ch
There are large quantities of white, rosé, and red wines made by this estate, the best of which include Chasselas and Pinot Noir from the 17-hectare Domaine de Château Vaumarcus. The Bouvier Frères label is used for its sparkling wines, which were the first ever produced in Switzerland.

Other Neuchâtel Producers:

Grillette Domaine de Cressier
Cressier. www.grillette.ch

Charles Steiner
Ligerz. www.schernelz-village.ch

The German-Speaking Cantons

Because the German-speaking cantons favour the same grape varieties and use broadly the same vinification techniques, they tend to be grouped together and called, for some obscure reason, eastern Switzerland. There are the usual concentrations around lakes (Constance, Zürich) and along rivers (Rhine, Aare, Limmat), with the odd microclimate thrown in (notably the four villages in Graubünden known as the Bündner Herrschaft). Wine is grown in eight of the Swiss-German cantons: Graubunden, St Gallen, Thurgau, Schaffhausen, Zürich, Aargau, Basselland, and Bern. The most productive cantons today are Zürich (scattered between Wädenswil, home of the Federal School of Oenology and Viticulture; Winterthur; and the villages along the north shore of the lake); and Schaffhausen, where the Hallau vineyard is the largest in eastern Switzerland. Consumption of Swiss-German-produced wines is almost exclusively local.

Up here north of the Alps, the colour balance changes and red begins to predominate in the shape of Pinot Noir (alias Blauburgunder, or Clevner on Lake Zürich). Riesling/Sylvaner is the main white variety, which performs well in the right (ie. secateur-wielding) hands to give surprisingly aromatic, lively wines – frequently of more interest than run-of-the-mill Chasselas from further south. Pinot Noir excels in the Bündner Herrschaft, whose warm autumn climate ripens it to real substance, with colour and a velvet touch. Elsewhere, the Swiss Germans exhibit a mystifying fondness for pale, slightly fizzy Blauburgunders, a penchant not inevitably shared by others.

Besides these two (plus a little Gewürztraminer, Pinot Blanc, and Pinot Gris) there are some specialties confined to the Swiss German cantons. Completer is an extremely rare, late-ripening, late-harvested specialty found in Graubünden, where it is long-matured and liquorous, and on the lakeshore of Zürich, where it is more austere. Its name is linked to the evening office of Compline, after which the monks were said gratefully to quaff a glass or two. Räuschling is an old-established Zürich variety, which makes elegant, crisp white wines. Freisamer is a potentially promising cross between Sylvaner and Pinot Gris.

Leading Swiss German Producers

Adank ☆☆
Fläsch. Owner: Hansruedi Adank. 5.5 ha.
www.adank-weine.ch
Although Adank is known for his Sauvignon Blanc and Pinot

Gris, it is the Pinot Noirs that command the most attention. There is also a small quantity of Syrah, a rarity in this region.

Schlossgut Bachtobel ☆☆–☆☆☆
Ottoberg. Owner: Hans-Ulrich Kesselring. 5.8 ha.
www.bachtobel.ch
Schlossgut Bachtobel, which farms its vineyard without fertilizers or herbicides, produces mostly Pinot Noir, plus Riesling/Sylvaner and tiny amounts of Pinot Gris and Riesling. There are three Pinot Noirs, each *cuvée* with a different number. Hans-Ulrich Kesselring died in 2008.

Donatsch ☆☆–☆☆☆
Malans. Owner: Thomas Donatsch. 4.5 ha.
www.donatsch-malans.ch
The beautiful, old, wood-panelled restaurant Zum Ochsen /\in the patrician village of Malans has belonged to the family for over 150 years. This is the best place to sample Thomas Donatsch's superb Pinot Noirs and finely structured Chardonnays, although they are also found on the wine lists of most top Swiss restaurants. Both his Pinot Noir and Chardonnay are aged in barriques. Also produced are Pinot Blanc, Pinot Gris, and he has also tried his hand at Cabernet Sauvignon, which he planted in 1983.

Daniel Gantenbein ☆☆☆
Fläsch. Owner: Daniel Gantenbein. 4 ha.
Gantenbein is Switzerland's most famous Pinot Noir producer, the clones he planted having come from the Domaine de la Romanée-Conti. Unique, too, is his Riesling (clones from Dr. Loosen), that all agree is the most "Germanic" Riesling Switzerland has to offer. The Chardonnay and the sweet wines are also noteworthy.

Andrea Lauber ☆☆
Malans. Owner: Andrea Lauber. 3 ha.
www.lauber-weine.ch
The lovely, onion-domed Gut Plandaditsch is a Malanser landmark. Especially notable is the Laubers' deep-ruby Pinot Noir, powerfully aromatic Pinot Blanc, late-harvested Freisamer, and oak-aged Completer. The mouth-filling Chardonnay, produced in tiny quantities, spends up to seven months in new oak.

Nussbaumer ☆–☆☆
Aesch. Owner: Nicolas Dolder. 7 ha.
www.domainenussbaumer.ch
A small firm, acquired by the Dolder family in 2004, producing Riesling/Sylvaner, Chasselas, Pinot Gris, Gewürztraminer, Räuschling, and Pinot Noir in its Aesch and Arlesheim vineyards, just a stone's throw from the border with Alsace. House specialties include Chrachmost, a classic-method sparkling Chasselas, and a straw wine made from the Garanoir grape.

Weinkellerei Rahm ☆–☆☆
Hallau. Owner: Peter Rahm. 16 ha. www.rimuss.ch
Rahm is the largest wine firm in Schaffhausen, with an output of 1.5 million bottles. Many of the wines are commercial, such as the range of *frizzantes*, but at the top level the Pinot Noir can be very good.

Hermann Schwarzenbach ☆–☆☆
Meilen. Owner: Hermann Schwarzenbach. 7 ha.
www.reblaube.ch
Small, old-established house with a range of 23 wines, including Riesling/Sylvaner (some late harvested as Beerenauslese), Freisamer, Sémillon, Räuschling, Chardonnay, Pinot Gris, and – the only grower still to make it on Lake Zurich – Completer. Pinot Noir is produced both straight and late harvested, fermented in oak vats and recommended as a keeper.

Other Swiss German Producers

Buess Weinbau
Sissach. www.buessins.ch

Davaz Weine
Fläsch. www.davaz-wein.ch

Weingut Thomas Marugg
Fläsch. www.marugg-weine.ch

Weingut Eichholz, Jenins, Fromm Weine
Malans. www.fromm-weine.ch

Weinbau Toni Ottiger
Kastanienbaum. www.weingut-rosenau.ch

Baumann Weingut
Oberhallau. www.baumannweingut.ch

Weingut Pircher
Eglisau. www.weingut-pircher.ch

Schloss Salenegg
Maienfeld. www.schloss-salenegg.ch

The Italian-Speaking Cantons

The Ticino or Tessin divides into four main areas: north and south of Monte Céneri (Sopraceneri and Sottoceneri respectively), the shores of Lake Lugano (Luganese), and the districts of Mendrisiotto. There are just over 1,000 hectares of vines under cultivation. It is a delightfully uncomplicated area, producing mainly red wines, where Merlot, with 82 per cent of the surface, holds sway over a bunch of miscellaneous black grapes (Bondola, Freisa, Barbera) blended into everyday table wine labelled Nostrano. The VITI "label of quality" is awarded by a commission of experts to Merlot wines of one year's bottle age that pass chemical analysis and taste tests. A few growers are successfully ageing some Merlots in new oak (often calling the result "Riserva"). It gives them distinct character, no longer the typical, soft, one-dimensional Merlot del Ticino.

There is little white wine grown in Ticino: the soils are all wrong and the climate far too benevolent, though there is some Chardonnay and a few other varieties to be found. The foxy *Vitis labrusca* hybrid Americano is vinified less and less; what remains is usually made into grappa.

Leading Ticino Producers

Angelo Delea ☆–☆☆
Losone. Owner: Angelo Delea. 11 ha.
www.delea.ch
Restaurateur-turned-wine-grower, Angelo Delea produces some long-macerated, powerful Merlots in the Sopraceneri region. Each year he buys in 40 per cent new barrels, into which goes his best Merlot (labelled Riserva); the remainder is aged in used *pièces*. Delea also produces a Chardonnay, Pinot Blanc and – for old times' sake – white, rosé, and red Americano.

Werner Stucky ☆☆–☆☆☆
Rivera. Owner: Werner and Lilo Stucky. 3 ha.
One of the young Swiss German pioneers of the region, Werner Stucky produces tiny quantities of Merlot, straight and oak-aged, both of them sold out by year's end. His other specialty is Conte di Luna, a blend of Merlot and Cabernet Sauvignon. These are tannic wines that gain in opulence from being bottle aged.

Eredi Carlo Tamborini ☆☆–☆☆☆
Lamone. Owner: Claudio Tamborini. 32 ha.
www.tamborini-vini.ch
An important Ticino house with steadily improving Merlot. Vigna Vecchia is its best, oak-aged from vines

between 30 and 60 years old. The Comano Vigneto ai Brughi and Castello di Morcote are also excellent.

Fratelli Valsangiacomo ☆☆
Mendrisio. Owner: Uberto Valsangiacomo.
16 ha. www.valsangiacomo.ch
Uberto Valsangiacomo is the sixth generation of this distinguished old Ticino house, and produces some of the most respected bottles of the regions: Roncobello and L'Ariete, among a host of other unoaked and barrique-aged Merlots (all Merlots), Cagliostro (a Merlot rosé), and two Merlot bubblies. A swashbuckling brigand adorns the label of Valsangiacomo's fruity blend of Chardonnay, Sémillon, and Sauvignon: Il Mattirolo.

Vinattieri Ticinesi ☆–☆☆
Ligornetto. Owner: Luigi Zanini.
50 ha. www.zanini.ch
Members of the Zanini family have invested heavily in vineyard and cellar. Bottles of their best Merlots bear vineyard names (sometimes complete with beautifully contoured sketch maps): Ligornetto, the old-vine Vinattieri Rosso, Roncaia; all are oak-aged to some degree or other and bottled without filtration. His other red wines include Syrah and Pinot Noir.

Christian Zündel ☆☆
Beride. Owner: Christian Zündel. 4 ha
Zündel only produces about 7,000 bottles per year, but he has attained a fine reputation for his rich Orizzonte, which is Merlot with a dash of Cabernet Sauvignon.

Other Ticino Producers:

Daniel Huber
Monteggio. www.hubervini.ch

Adriano Kaufmann, Beride,
Casa Vinicola Gialdi
Mendrisio. www.gialdi.ch

Ivini di Guido Brivio
Mendrisio. www.brivio.ch

Austria

Austria's wine history goes back at least two millennia – until shortly after the Romans conquered the Danubian provinces in 16BC. It is an interesting question why modern wine culture arrived here far later than elsewhere in Western Europe. Even during the 1920s and '30s only the very finest Austrian wines were sold in bottle. Still today, a significant proportion of Austrian wine is sold in wine inns run by growers (called Heurigen or Buschenschenken). The 1985 diethyleneglycol scandal put an end for some years to the industry's commercial success with off-dry and sweet white wines in the German mould (regulated by a German-style wine law introduced in 1972). Diethylene glycol was added to such wines by many large commercial bottlers to simulate the sweet wines much in favour with the important German market. Whilst there is no evidence of anyone's health having been damaged by this illegal practice – in contrast to the Italian methanol scandal of the following year – enormous damage was done to the good name of Austrian wine.

The Austrian authorities responded by rushing through legislation to control the wine industry further. The 1985 law (amended the following year) is complemented by a system of controls and monitoring that make the nation's wine industry the most strictly controlled in the world. The scandal also had entirely unexpected consequences. Instead of turning domestic consumers off their nation's wines, they switched from mass-produced wines to hand-crafted ones made by family run estates. This coincided with a boom for dry white wines. The result was a renaissance for regions such as the Wachau and Kamptal whose growers had previously made and sold good-quality dry white wines to loyal private customers in relative obscurity. In Styria, an entire new wine culture was born during the 1980s as a number of producers switched from wines for everyday drinking in two-litre bottles (*doppler*) to quality varietals.

In the early 1990s, this was followed by a red wine revolution during which dozens of younger Austrian producers, particularly in Burgenland, mastered the making of international-style red wines. Much of their inspiration came from across the Alps in Italy. Although France was the prime source of new grape varieties (Cabernet Sauvignon, Merlot, and to a lesser extent Syrah), these are usually blended with indigenous grapes to create sophisticated *cuvées*, an adopted word in the vocabulary of many young Austrian winemakers. Unlike the majority of fine Austrian wines, which are sold under vineyard (or *ried*) names, they tend to be sold under fantasy names such as Comondor, Bella Rex, or Perwolff in the mould of Italian wines such as Sassicaia or Darmagi. In the 1990s many of these red wines were heavily oaked, but by the early 2000s the emphasis was on clarity of fruit and elegance rather than pounding the palate with oak.

Austria remains primarily a white wine producer, and in this respect most wine-growers are true to their nation's winemaking traditions. Its wine industry is founded on light- to full-bodied dry whites from the indigenous Grüner Veltliner grape. It accounts for 36 per cent of Austria's 51,000 hectares of vineyards, and gives wines with a distinctive aroma of white pepper, lentils, and other vegetal notes, but at high levels of ripeness they are replaced by smokey and even exotic fruit aromas. The grape's flexibility – it will yield dry wines with anything from 10–15 degrees natural alcohol, and impressive dessert wines – is its greatest strength. In international blind tastings, setting Grüner Veltliner against some of the world's great Chardonnays, the Austrian grape has performed very well.

Nonetheless, the white wines that have attracted most international praise have been the Rieslings. The noble white grape of Germany appears to have arrived in Austria towards the end of the nineteenth century, and there are still only 1,300 hectares planted with it in Austria. However, on the primary rock soils of the Wachau, the beautiful rocky gorge through which the River Danube flows between Melk and Krems, it yields great dry wines that can match the finest of Alsace and Germany. Such is the strength of domestic demand for the top Wachau Rieslings that importers from other countries must beg for every bottle from the top producers. Names such as Franz Hirtzberger, Emmerich Knoll, F X Pichler, and Franz Prager (qq.v.) are mentioned by Austrian wine-lovers in tones of awe. Similarly, fine, dry Rieslings come from parts of other regions in Lower Austria, most importantly Senftenberg and Stein in the Kremstal, and Langenlois-Zöbing in the Kamptal. A comparable discrepancy between supply and demand exists with the best Sauvignons and Morillons from Styria (a synonym for Chardonnay, which arrived in the region during the nineteenth century) where producers such as Polz and Tement (qq.v.) are almost perpetually sold out.

Harvesting in the Danube Valley

Although it was almost exclusively dessert wines that were affected by the 1985 scandal, in this field, too, recent years have seen dramatic developments. The Neusiedler See-Hügelland region in the state of Burgenland has a recorded history of systematic dessert wine production, which goes back to 1617. For much of its history it was part of Hungary. This tradition is centred upon the town of Rust on the eastern bank of the shallow Neusiedlersee lake, the source of autumnal mists that promote the development of noble rot. However, during the 1990s, it has been the wines from Illmitz on the opposite bank of the lake that have attracted attention. The names of Illmitz winemakers Alois Kracher and Willi Opitz are now known around the world. Most of Austria's dessert wines are sold under the Trockenbeerenauslese and Beerenauslese names borrowed from the Germans during the 1960s. Today some are vinified in new oak casks like top Sauternes. Rust has its own tradition: a sweet wine midway in weight between a BA and TBA, and vinified to a higher alcoholic degree (and hence a lower level of residual sugar) than comparable wines from Illmitz. However, in recent years, top Rust growers have followed the stylistic norms set by Kracher for wines of great intensity and sweetness. Thus, in practice, a modern Ruster Ausbruch is hard to distinguish from an Illmitz TBA – but is none the worse for that.

Sadly, the worldwide fashion for Chardonnay has not left Austria untouched. Although a handful of winemakers produce powerful wines in the international style (most prominently Velich and Kollwentz (qq.v.) in the Burgenland), most results lag behind those achieved with traditional grapes such as Weissburgunder (Pinot Blanc), Grauburgunder (Pinot Gris), or aromatic grapes such as Muskateller and Traminer. The majority of Austria's fine dry white and dessert wines continue to be made from varieties such as these. Thankfully, the pendulum is beginning to swing back in the direction of tradition. Even the style-conscious yuppies of Vienna enjoy an evening in a Heurige drinking unpretentious local wine out of a glass mug (known as a viertel because it contains a quarter-litre) while listening to Schrammelmusik: Viennese folk music. The quality revolution of the late 1980s and 1990s has brought better and more diverse wines, and the top growers of Vienna are reviving an ancient tradition, the Gemischter Satz, whereby vineyards were planted in a field blend of numerous varieties, which are then harvested and vinified together.

The wine regions of Austria are usually divided into four principal areas. Vienna (with 680 hectares within the city limits), the Burgenland (14,650 hectares), Steiermark (ie. Styria, with 3,270 hectares), and Lower Austria (33,000 hectares). The Burgenland is divided into four subregions: Neusiedlersee (8,310 hectares), which takes in all the vineyards north and east of the lake; Neusiedlersee-Hügelland (3,910 hectares) west of the lake, with Rust and Eisenstadt its principal towns; Mittelburgenland (1,880 hectares), and Südburgenland (450 hectares), red wine regions south of the lake and along the Hungarian border.

Styria is divided into three subregions, of which the most important is the Südsteiermark (1,740 hectares), plus the Süd-Oststeiermark (1,100 hectares) and the Weststeiermark (430 hectares). Styria is best-known as a white wine region, but Weststeiermark has a tradition of producing Schilcher, a markedly acidic rosé that has an ardent following within Austria itself. Lower Austria is the most complicated region. Over half the production comes from the Weinviertel (16,000 hectares) to the north of Vienna, which used to be undistinguished, but today a growing number of producers is striving for better quality. Far more important in terms of quality are the three subregions close to the Danube west of Vienna: the Wachau (1,390 hectares), Kremstal (2,175 hectares), and Kamptal (3,870 hectares), the source of Austria's finest white wines. Separating these regions from Vienna are the less significant Traisenthal (680 hectares) and Wagram (2,730 hectares), which until 2008 was known as Donauland. Immediately southeast of Vienna is Carnuntum (890 hectares), which can produce excellent red wines, while south of the capital is the Thermenregion (2,330 hectares), which includes the once famous heavy white wines from Gumpoldskirchen.

The estates below are divided into the four main regions, with subregions indicated within each producer entry.

Leading Lower Austria Producers

Leo Alzinger ☆☆☆–☆☆☆☆
Unterloiben, Wachau. 9 ha. www.alzinger.at
With both Riesling and Grüner Veltliner in top sites in Dürnstein and Unterloiben, the largely self-taught Alzinger makes sleek, elegant wines, with a fine acidic structure, lean but fruity, racy but never harsh. Invariably repay keeping. The Smaragd wines from 2007 are of 4-star quality.

Bründlmayer ☆☆☆–☆☆☆☆
Langenlois, Kamptal. 75 ha. www.bruendlmayer.at
The diffident, thoughtful Willi Bründlmayer runs one of the largest and most modern wine estates in Austria. Although he is admired for his barrel-fermented Chardonnay and burgundy inspired Pinot Noir, most of his production is traditional-style dry whites.

Right across the impressive range the quality is excellent, the sublime Rieslings from old vines in the Heiligenstein site and magisterial Grüner Veltliner from the Lamm and Käferberg vineyards rank among Austria's greatest wines. The Sekt, too, with three years on the yeasts, is one of the country's finest.

Domäne Wachau ☆☆–☆☆☆
Dürnstein, Wachau. 420 ha.
www.domaene-wachau.at
Long one of Europe's finest winemaking cooperatives, quality took a leap forward with the appointment of Fritz Miesbauer and Willi Klinger as co-directors in 1995. After their departure in the early 2000s, quality took a nose-dive, but recent vintages have been back on form.

In 2007 the name was changed from Freie Weingärtner Wachau. Excellent Rieslings from the first-class Achleiten of Weissenkirchen and Singerriedel of Spitz, and Grüner Veltliners from the Kellerberg of Dümstein are the stars of the wide range produced. However, even the simpler wines, such as the Terrrassen Thal Wachau blend, are well-made and full of character.

Schloss Gobelsburg ☆☆–☆☆☆
Gobelsburg, Kamptal. 35 ha. www.gobelsburg.at
A monastic estate, this was leased by Willi Bründlmayer (q.v.) and Michael Moosbrugger in 1996, and they cultivate the vineyards organically. There is good Riesling from Heiligenstein and Gaisberg, and the once bewilderingly alcoholic Grüner Veltliners from Ried Lamm and Ried Grub are now more restrained. Moosbrugger is also making some serious red wines from St-Laurent and Pinot Noir.

Franz Hirtzberger ☆☆☆☆
Spitz, Wachau. 17 ha. www.hirtzberger.at
Franz Hirtzberger's natural optimism and talent for winning over opponents are mainly responsible for the success of the Vinea Wachau wine-growers' association that created the styles and regulations for the region. The Hirtzberger Rieslings from the great Singerriedel and Hochrain vineyards and his Grüner Veltliner from the first-class Honivogl site are among Austria's finest and most sought-after wines.

Josef Högl ☆☆–☆☆☆
Spitz, Wachau. 7.5 ha. www.weingut-hoegl.at
Modest, shy Josef Högl learnt quickly while he worked for the Prager and F X Pichler estates (qq.v.). Since going solo he has joined the first rank of Wachau producers with dry whites that combine power with clarity and polish.

Josef Jamek ☆☆–☆☆☆
Joching, Wachau. 25 ha. www.weingut-jamek.at
Josef Jamek pioneered dry, *unchaptalized* wines in the Wachau in the 1950s and remained one of the region's leading producers in the 1980s. His eponymous restaurant brought gastronomic culture to the region and became an institution.

In 1996, his son-in-law, Hans Altmann, and daughter Jutta took over, and a new era began. The best wines are the famous Rieslings from the first-class Klaus vineyard of Weissenkirchen and the dry Weissburgunder. Elegance, rather than power, has always been the Jamek hallmark. After a period when the wines lacked grip and minerality, quality had clearly recovered by the late 1990s.

Emmerich Knoll ☆☆☆☆
Unterloiben, Wachau. 15 ha.
Four generations of the Knoll family, all called Emmerich, are responsible for making this estate's unique wines. Extremely long lived, they need years of bottle-ageing for their full, minerally character to emerge. The dry Rieslings from the Schütt, Loibenberg, and Kellerberg sites are among Austria's finest white wines. In vintages such as 2007 when botrytis affects the vineyards, Knoll also produces sumptuous sweet wines.

Malat ☆☆–☆☆☆
Palt, Kremstal. 48 ha. www.malat.at
Best-known for powerful, dry white wines, but Cabernet and Pinot Noir also show promise. He bottles his best Veltliner and Riesling under the confident label Das Beste.

Mantlerhof ☆☆
Brunn im Felde, Kremstal. 14 ha. www.mantlerhof.com
Josef Mantler is best known for the rare white Roter Veltliner grape, from which he makes rich, supple, dry wines. His Grüner Veltliners are also great and long-lived.

Markowitsch ☆☆☆
Göttlesbrunn, Carnuntum. 30 ha. www.markowitsch.at
Gerhard Markowitsch is the most dynamic of the Carnuntum growers, equally adept with white and red wines. His Chardonnay is toasty and powerful, and his best red is the Cuvée Rosenberg: an intense and deeply structured blend of Zweigelt, Merlot, and Cabernet Sauvignon. Markowitsch is also making progress with Pinot Noir.

Sepp Moser ☆☆
Rohrendorf, Kremstal. 50 ha. www.sepp-moser.at
The roots of this estate go back to 1848, but in its present form it dates from the split-up of the erstwhile Lenz Moser company in 1986. With the help of son Nikolaus, Sepp Moser rapidly made it one of the nation's leading white wine producers.

In 2000, Nikolaus Moser was given full responsibility for the winemaking, and by 2006 had converted the estate to Biodynamism. The barrel-fermented Chardonnay is among Austria's best, but it is the lush, complex, dry Riesling from the first-class Gebling site that is the real star. Increasingly good Burgenland reds, too, from his Apetlon estate.

Nigl ☆☆☆
Senftenberg, Kremstal. 25 ha. www.weingutnigl.at
Martin Nigl's sleek, minerally, dry Rieslings and Grüner Veltliners have made the estate a leader in the Kremstal region. Top are the magnificent Rieslings from the first-class Kremsleiten and Piri sites Nigl usual labels his best wines as Privat.

Nikolaihof ☆☆☆
Mautern, Wachau and Kremstal. 18 ha. www.nikolaiho.at
The recorded history of the Saahs family's Biodynamic estate goes back more than a millennium, and the magnificent buildings stand on Roman foundations.

The best dry Rieslings are superb and intensely mineral, both the Kremstal wines from the stony Steiner Hund site in Krems, and the Wachau wines from Mautern. These are wines that improve greatly with ageing. The excellent Weinstube is the perfect place to experience them.

F X Pichler ☆☆☆☆
Oberloiben, Wachau. 14 ha. www.fx-pichler.at
Regarded as Austria's number one winemaker, Franz Xavier Pichler – frequently referred to simply as "F X" – is a fanatical perfectionist. His great dry white wines are as concentrated as they are individual. The most spectacular Rieslings and Grüner Veltliners come from the great Kellerberg vineyard of Dürnstein. Some of the richest wines are rather grandiosely labelled "M" (for "Monumental") or "U" (for "Unendlich"), referring to the prolonged finish. These wines can seem too massive for their own good, combining high alcohol and extract with some residual sugar. But their intrinsic quality and complexity are undeniable. The next generation is gradually taking over.

Rudi Pichler ☆☆☆
Wösendorf, Wachau. 12 ha. www.rudipichler.at
Rudi Pichler Jr. has been going from strength to strength as one of the Wachau's rising stars with lush, powerful, and aromatic dry Rieslings from Achleiten and Kirchweg, and minerally Grüner Veltliner from Hochrain. The magnificent 2007s may be his finest ever vintage.

Franz Prager ☆☆☆–☆☆☆☆
Weissenkirchen, Wachau. 15 ha. www.weingutprager.at
Since marrying Ilse Prager, Toni Bodenstein has consolidated the reputation of this excellent domaine, which has owned outstanding sites (Achleiten, Klaus, Steinriegl) for over three centuries. This he has done with a meticulous attention to detail. The dry Rieslings marry seductive, ripe fruit with minerally depth, and Grüner Veltliners share their elegance.

Reinisch ☆☆–☆☆☆☆
Tattendorf. 40 ha. www.j-rat.at
In the early 1980s Reinisch was already making red wines, but they were feeble. Current vintages are in total contrast, with intense and stylish Pinot Noir and St-Laurent. The Grand Reserves are the most concentrated wines, but the regular reserves come close.

Other Lower Austria Producers

Angerer ☆–☆☆
Lengenfeld, Kamptal. 33 ha. www.kurt-angerer.at
Kurt Angerer names many of his white wines after the soils on which they are grown rather than by single vineyard names. The Grüner Veltliner Loam is particularly fine. In recent years Angerer has been taking more interest in red wine production.

Peter Dolle ☆–☆☆
Strass, Kamptal. 32 ha. www.dolle.at
A dynamic property, producing a wide range of white wines, notably the Rieslings from Gaisberg and Heiligenstein.

Johann Donabaum ☆–☆☆
Spitz, Wachau. 5 ha. www.weingut-donabaum.at
A small property but with excellent terraced vineyards. The white wines are full of fruit but with a tendency to overripeness.

Ludwig Ehn ☆☆
Langenlois, Kamptal. 15 ha. www.ehnwein.at
Ehn specializes in exotic, dry Riesling from the great Heiligenstein vineyard and rich Ried Panzaun from a mixed planting of ancient vines.

Christian Fischer ☆☆
Sooss, Thermenregion. 17 ha. www.weingut-fischer.at
A red wine specialist in the Thermenregion, raising Merlot to unaccustomed heights. Gradenthal is an imposing blend of Zweigelt, Cabernet, and Merlot, aged in a high proportion of new oak.

Forstreiter ☆☆
Krems, Kremstal. 26 ha. www.forstreiter.at
Meinhard Forstreiter cultivates a range of varieties, but his best wines are the racy Grüner Veltliner, notably the Alte Reben, Exclusive, and, from centenarian vines, Tabor. Charming Gelber Muskateller, too.

Fritsch ☆☆
Oberstockstall, Wagram. 19 ha. www.fritsch.cc
A leading producer of vibrant, dry Grüner Veltliner and a plummy red blend called Foggathal, packed with blackberry fruit.

Walter Glatzer ☆–☆☆
Göttlesbrunn, Carnuntum. 24 ha. www.weingutglatzer.at
A leading property east of Vienna. He remains faithful to Austrian red varieties. His best Zweigelt is called Dornenvogel, and there is a fine, Zweigelt-dominated blend called Cuvée Gotinsprun, aged mostly in new barriques.

Graf Hardegg ☆☆
Seefeld-Kadolz, Weinviertel. 43 ha. www.grafhardegg.at
Proximity to the Czech border may explain the name of the top-selling wine, the racy Grüner Veltliner called Veltlinsky. Also noteworthy are the Pinot Noir and the exotic Viognier. Occasionally, brilliant Riesling Eiswein is produced.

Hiedler ☆☆–☆☆☆
Langenlois, Kamptal. 26 ha. www.hiedler.at
Hiedler's white wines are made for long age rather than instant gratification. His dry Riesling from the great Heiligenstein site, the powerful Veltliner Maximum, and Chardonnay are among the region's finest.

Hirsch ☆–☆☆
Kammern, Kamptal. 25 ha. www.weingut-hirsch.at
Johannes Hirsch can excel with Riesling from the Heiligenstein. His other wines are always sound but rarely thrill.

Markus Huber ☆☆
Reichersdorf, Traisental. 20 ha. www.weingut-huber.at
Young Huber is a rising star, already with a chestful of awards. The best wines are the Riesling and Grüner Veltliner from the Berg vineyard.

Jurtschitsch ☆–☆☆☆
Langenlois, Kamptal. 74 ha. www.jurtschitsch.com
Reliable producer of super-clean, modern whites from around Langenlois. Good Chardonnay and a red blend called Rotspon, but the Rieslings and Grüner Veltliner are the stars.

Stift Klosterneuburg ☆☆
Klosterneuburg, Wagram. 108 ha.
www.stift-klosterneuburg.at
Augustine monks of Klosterneuburg have made wine for nearly nine centuries, but the operation is now a commercial company owned by the monastery. Grapes from the vineyards, from Tattendorf south of Vienna to within the city limits of the capital itself, are supplemented by small producers in Burgenland and Niederösterreich. The top wines are from single vineyards. A good reputation for white wines, such as Weissburgunder, and more recently for some formidable reds, such as the barrique aged St-Laurent. The four-level cellars have three million bottles, including the Austrian State Wine Archive.

Krug ☆–☆☆
Gumpoldskirchen. 28 ha. www.krug.at
Known for sweetly oaky Cabernet Sauvignon, Krug also
remains loyal to the traditions of the village, with sound,
sometimes, stolid Rotgipfler and Zierfandler.

Lagler ☆–☆☆
Spitz. 13 ha. www.weingut-lagler.at
Karl Lagler, father and son, like to pick late at their palette
of vineyards, and the results are full-bodied Smaragd wines,
without excessive alcohol, for medium-term drinking.

Leth ☆☆
Fels am Wagram, Wagram. 38 ha. www.weingut-leth.at
Racy whites, including an exuberant Roter Veltliner. Red vines
are in a minority here, but the Gigama Zweigelt is juicy and
nicely supported by oak.

Loimer ☆☆☆
Langenlois, Kamptal. 28 ha. www.loimer.at
Dynamic Fred Loimer produces a range of whites from
traditional grapes. His finest wines are the old-vine Grüner
Veltliner from the Spiegel site, and Riesling from Steinmassl.

Ludwig Neumayer ☆☆–☆☆☆
Inzersdorf, Traisental. 8 ha. www.weinvomstein.at

The wines that put this region on the map include Neumayer's
sophisticated dry Rieslings, Weissburgunders, and Grüner
Veltliners from the Traisental. Top range is labelled Der Wein
vom Stein.

Bernhard Ott ☆☆
Feuersbrunn, Wagram. 28 ha. www.ott.at
The Falstaffian Ott offers a plethora of Grüner Veltliners,
all spicy and vigorous.

Pfaffl ☆☆–☆☆☆
Stetten, Weinviertel. 55 ha. www.pfaffl.at
Roman Pfaffl's dry Grüner Veltliner, Sauvignon Blanc,
Chardonnay, and Riesling from just northeast of Vienna are
arguably the Weinviertel's finest.

Pitnauer ☆–☆☆
Göttlesbrunn, Carnuntum. 11 ha. www.pitnauer.com
These wines come from vineyards close to the Slovak border.
The powerful Franz Josef blend of Zweigelt and Cabernet is
best, and there is a rich Pinot Blanc.

Proidl ☆☆
Senftenberg, Kremstal. 20 ha. www.proidl.com
Exemplary Rieslings from steep vineyards, racy, tight,
and elegant. Grüner Veltliner comes a close second.

The Baroque monastery of Klosterneuburg

Robert Schlumberger ☆
Bad Vöslau, Thermenregion. 10 ha. www.schlumberger.at
Robert Schlumberger, son of a branch of the Alsace family, made Austria's first *méthode traditionnelle* Sekt in 1842. The Sekt side of the business is now based in Vienna, while the family firm has focused its attention on Bordeaux style reds.

Schmelz ☆☆–☆☆☆
Joching, Wachau. 8 ha. www.schmelzweine.at
Reliable and improving producer of juicy, substantial, dry Riesling and Grüner Veltliner.

Schmidl ☆☆–☆☆☆
Dürnstein, Wachau. 9 ha. www.weingut-schmidl.at
Franz Schmidl, who is also the local baker, has half his vineyards in the renowned Kellerberg, and makes underrated Riesling and Grüner Veltliner from this site.

Stadlmann ☆–☆☆
Traiskirchen, Thermenregion. 15 ha. www.stadlmann-wein.at
Some of the best wines of the Thermenregion from vineyards south of Gumpoldskirchen. Best are the dry Weissburgunder and Zierfandler (occasionally Zierfandler TBA).

Stadt Krems ☆☆
Krems, Kremstal. 31 ha. www.weingutstadtkrems.at
After he left the Freie Weingärtner, the town estate of Krems snapped up Fritz Miesbauer in 2003 and gave him a free hand as winemaker. Improvements were swift, with Grüner Veltliner from the Weinzielberg often outstanding.

Hofkellerei Fürst Liechtenstein ☆
Wilfersdorf, Weinviertel. 38 ha. www.hofkellerei.at
This is a princely estate, producing sound wines from Grüner Veltliner and Zweigelt. Wines include the barrrique-aged Zweigelt Profundo.

Weingut Salomon/Undhof ☆☆–☆☆☆
Stein, Kremstal. 25 ha. www.salomonwines.com
Some of the best wines from the first-class vineyard of Krems' beautiful Gothic and Renaissance suburb, Stein. The soils of these are almost identical to those of the neighbouring Wachau. Most of the production is dry Riesling and Grüner Veltliner, and the Gelber Traminer is almost as fine.

Uibel ☆–☆☆
Ziersdorf, Weinviertel. 6 ha. www.uibel.at
A small estate, but in good vintages the Grüner Veltliners have zip and flair. Rarer but excellent Fruhroter Veltliner, too.

Petra Unger ☆☆
Furth, Kremstal. 10 ha. www.ungerwein.at
From 2006 Petra Unger has separated herself, and her vines, from the family estate, and now strikes out on her own with, initially, good results, especially with Grüner Veltliner.

Weinrieder ☆☆
Kleinhadersdorf, Weinviertel. 20 ha. www.weinrieder.at
Extremely reliable Grüner Veltliner, but the estate is best known for its exquisitely balanced Icewines from a range of varieties.

Leading Burgenland Producers

Feiler-Artinger ☆☆☆
Rust, Neusiedlersee-Hügelland. 26 ha. www.feiler-artinger.at
Superlative Ruster Ausbruch; the finest is the intense Essenz. In contrast are the flavoury red blends, both from Cabernet and Merlot, and Cuvée Solitaire from Austrian varieties.

Gesellmann ☆☆–☆☆☆
Deutschkreutz, Mittelburgenland. 25 ha. www.gesellmann.at
Albert Gesellmann has been taking an already admired estate to new levels, building on the reputation for red wines established by his father. Two powerful blends, Opus Eximium (Blaufränkisch, St-Laurent, and Blauburgunder) and "Bella Rex" (Cabernet and Merlot) are most impressive.

Martin Haider ☆–☆☆☆
Illmitz, Neusiedlersee. 12 ha. www.weinguthaider.at
Modest Martin Haider specializes in botrytis wines from a range of varieties. TBAs from a range of white varieties can be exceptional. Dry wines are less successful.

Gernot Heinrich ☆☆☆
Gols, Neusiedlersee. 35 ha. www.heinrich.at
Gernot Heinrich has long been one of the Burgenland's top producers of rich, structured red wines. He shows a remarkable fidelity to Austrian varieties, although one of his best known wines, the black fruited Gabarinza, has some Merlot in the blend. His Pannobile, a Zweigelt-dominated blend using a name shared by a number of growers who are members of the Pannobile association, is almost as good.

Juris (G Stiegelmar) ☆☆☆
Gols, Neusiedlersee. 18 ha. www.juris.at
This estate is run by the untiring Stiegelmar family. Georg, more or less retired now, is the traditionalist, attached to the ancient Hungarian traditions of the Burgenland, but he has not stood in the way of his California trained son, Axel. The best wines are the reds – St-Laurent, Ina'mera (Blaufränkisch with Cabernet and Merlot), and St Georg (St-Laurent and Pinot Noir). The pure Cabernet is surprisingly plummy, and the Pinot Noir has more fruit than finesse.

Unlike many Burgenland producers, the Stiegelmars do not pack their wines with more tannin than the wine's fruit structure can absorb, and they handle barrique-ageing with rare mastery. Delicious TBAs, too, and one of the pioneers of straw wine in the Burgenland.

Kerschbaum ☆☆–☆☆☆
Horitschon, Mittelburgenland. 30 ha. www.kerschbaum.at
Paul Kerschbaum is a master of Blaufränkisch, and the exceptionally pure Ried Hochäcker is often preferable to the Ried Dürrau, which can be overwhelmed by new oak. The splendid Cuvée Impresario blends Blaufränkisch with Zweigelt and Cabernet, and has exceptional elegance.

Kollwentz ☆☆☆
Grosshöflein, Neusiedlersee-Hügelland. 20 ha.
www. kollwentz.at
Andi Kollwentz is one of Austria's most talented young winemakers, following his father Anton as a prime mover in creating Burgenland wines that can compete with the best. He has played an important role in the recent red wine revolution. The dry whites are clean and crisp, but less exceptional than the reds. To such admirable reds as Eichkogel, an enjoyable blend of Blaufränkisch and Zweigelt, and Steinzeiler, a similar blend but with a dash of Cabernet Sauvignon, Kollwentz has added a fine Pinot Noir and two exalted barrel-fermented Chardonnays, Tatschler and Gloria. If that weren't enough, the TBAs are at the same superb level of quality.

Alois Kracher ☆☆☆☆
Illmitz, Neusiedlersee. 25 ha. www.kracher.at
When Alois Kracher died far too young in 2007, the president of Austria attended his funeral. Quite right too, as Kracher restored the reputation on Austrian wines after the blight of the 1985 scandal. He was a perfectionist with a cosmopolitan perspective who remained true to his roots in the sandy soil of Illmitz. In recent years his superbly crafted dessert wines picked up almost every conceivable accolade. They combined honeyed richness with perfect balance. The Zwischen den Seen wines were traditionally made in tanks or old casks, the Nouvelle Vague wines in new oak, like Sauternes. Grand Cuvée is the designation Kracher gives given to the best, but not necessarily the richest, wine in any vintage. Kracher's son Gerhard, who worked by his side, has taken his place.

Krutzler ☆☆☆
Deutsch-Schützen, Südburgenland. 11 ha.
www.krutzler.at
Reinhold Krutzler's silky reds are Südburgenland's finest and most elegant wines. Blaufränkisch is the dominant grape variety, and it attains unusual purity of blackberry and cherry fruit. Top of the range is the seductive Perwolff, given more structure by the inclusion of some Cabernet.

Helmut Lang ☆☆☆
Illmitz, Neusiedlersee. 14 ha.
Lang is another master of sophisticated sweet wines from the Burgenland. Chardonnay, Sauvignon, and Welschriesling seem to give the best results, though Lang is greatly admired for his Scheurebe. Lang is keen on Pinot Noir, made in a dense, oaky style, remote from burgundy, but impressive on its own terms.

Hans & Anita Nittnaus ☆☆
Gols, Neusiedlersee. 33 ha. www.nittnaus.at
The ever more sophisticated reds which Hans Nittnaus has made since the late '80s epitomize the red wine revolution occurring in Burgenland. Rich, powerful Comondor, made principally from Zweigelt and Blaufränkisch, and his pure old-vine Blaufränkisch are masterly expressions of Burgenland fruit.

Josef Pöckl ☆☆☆
Mönchhof, Neusiedlersee. 28 ha. www.poeckl.com
René Pöckl is a Zweigelt enthusiast, which dominates his superb and consistent Admiral blend. Rêve de Jeunesse is quite different, blending Syrah and Cabernet with Zweigelt to give a rich, slightly confected wine. Pöckl is equally skilled with TBAs, but seems increasingly committed to his red wines.

Engelbert Prieler ☆☆–☆☆☆
Schützen, Neusiedlersee-Hügelland. 20 ha.
www.prieler.at
The Prielers make some of the best wines of the Hügelland. The unoaked Pinot Blanc has more zest and individuality than the international-style, oaked Chardonnay. Blaufränkisch is delicious here, especially from Ried Goldberg. Prieler also makes tiny quantities of Cabernet Sauvignon with a slight herbaceous tone. Daughter Silvia is developing her own line of wines, notably a rich, rather tannic Pinot Noir.

Heidi Schröck ☆☆–☆☆☆
Rust, Neusiedlersee-Hügelland. 10 ha.
www.heidi-schroeck.com
An enthusiast for the local traditions of Rust, Schröck makes exemplary Ausbruch. She has helped to revive Furmint in Rust, although the dry wine is very austere and it works better as Ausbruch Turner, a pure Furmint from a single vineyard. Best red wine is the Blaufränkisch Kulm.

Ernst Triebaumer ☆☆☆
Rust, Neusiedlersee-Hügelland. 20 ha.
www.triebaumer.com
Ernst Triebaumer has single-handedly demonstrated that the Blaufränkisch grape can produce great red wines if planted in the right place. His dark, rich, tannic Blaufränkisch Mariental is one of Austria's most sought after reds. The Ausbruch wines are also impressive, matching richness with harmony. And in complete contrast, his Chardonnay and Sauvignon Blanc are among Austria's best.

Hans Tschida – Angerhof ☆☆☆
Illmitz, Neusiedlersee. 18 ha. www.angerhof-tschida.at
A specialist in richly botrytized wines, Tschida maintains their purity and intensity by ageing them, with the exception of Chardonnay TBA, in stainless steel. He also produces Schilfwein but it lacks the complexity of the botrytis wines.

Umathum ☆☆☆
Frauenkirchen, Neusiedlersee. 25 ha. www.umathum.at
It would be easy to mistake Josef Umathum's reds for French wines, although he works almost exclusively with traditional Austrian grapes. The most impressive is the red *cuvée* from the Hallebühl vineyard, a powerful, tannic Zweigelt-dominated blend. The *cuvée* from Haideboden (blending Zweigelt, Blaufränkisch and Cabernet Sauvignon) is equally rich but more supple.

Velich ☆☆
Apetlon, Neusiedlersee. 10 ha. www.velich.at
This estate has the reputation of one of Austria's leading white wine producers. Impressive as the entire range is, the seductively rich, barrel-fermented Tiglat and Darscho Chardonnays have to be singled out as outstanding, though to some palates they seem excessively weighty. Excellent TBAs.

Other Burgenland Producers

Paul Achs ☆☆
Gols, Neusiedlersee. 25 ha. www.paul-achs.at
Richly fruity, modern-style reds good Pinot Noir and
Blaufränkisch.

Braunstein ☆
Purbach, Neusiedlersee-Hügelland. 22 ha.
www.braunstein.at
Birgit Braunstein selects the best wines of any vintage to be
oak-aged and labelled as Oxhoft. The Chardonnay can be
overblown, but both the St-Laurent and the Cuvée Oxhoft
can be powerful, almost meaty wines.

Schlossweingut Esterházy ☆
Eisenstadt, Neusiedlersee-Hügelland. 65 ha.
www.esterhazy.at
The ancient princely family of Esterházy, patrons of Haydn
and tamers of the Turks, own vineyards spread around Rust,
St Georgen, St Margaretten, Grosshöflein, and Eisenstadt.

Beneath the castle, 140 great casks line the cellars.
Unfortunately, until the early 2000s, the wines were
mediocre. But a new winery was built in 2006 and the
range was restructured: Klassik wines for every day drinking,
Estoras for international blends with an Austrian character,
single vineyard wines (usually barrique aged), and Tesoro
for a top new-oaked Bordeaux blend. Sweet wines provide
the icing on the cake.

Gager ☆☆–☆☆☆
Deutschkreuz, Mittelburgenland. 35 ha.
www.weingut-gager.at
Josef Gager's punchy, richly oaked red blends, Cablot in a
Bordeaux style, Quattro from Austrian varieties, Tycoon a bit
of everything, aren't exactly subtle, but they are well-crafted
and concentrated.

Schloss Halbturn ☆–☆☆
Halbturn, Neusiedlersee. 65 ha. www.schlosshalbturn.com
A noble estate and a byword for mediocrity until 2002,
when a new director arrived and began turning things around.
Imperial, red and white, is the label for barrique-aged blends,
while the Grand Vin is a TBA. The wines are greatly
improved, but the marketing strategy, with the use of French
and English terms, seems confused and confusing.

Hans Igler ☆
Deutschkreuz, Mittelburgenland. 33 ha.
www.weingut-igler.at
Hans Igler was a pioneer of serious, oak aged reds. Since his
death in 1994, his daughter and son-in-law continue his work.
Best-known is the subtle, medium-bodied Blaufränkisch/
Cabernet Sauvignon Cuvée Volcano. In 1999, they launched
Ab Ericio, a Merlot-dominated blend, in an attempt to return
the Igler estate to the esteem it enjoyed a decade ago.

Münzenrieder ☆–☆☆
Apetlon, Neusiedlersee. 22 ha. www.muenzenrieder.at
This estate, which only began bottling in 1991, has acquired a
reputation for rich, full-bodied TBAs.

Gerhard Nekowitsch ☆☆
Illmitz, Neusiedlersee. 4 ha. www.nekowitsch.at
This tiny property has carved a niche for itself as a producer
of Schilfwein, made from bunches left to dry on reeds from
the Neusiedler See. The peachy Tradition version is generally
preferable to the somewhat cloying red grape version called
The Red One.

Willi Opitz ☆–☆☆☆
Illmitz, Neusiedlersee. 17 ha. www.willi-opitz.at
Self-publicist Willi Opitz makes some remarkable and
original dessert wines, but dry wines lack flair.

Pittnauer ☆☆
Gols, Neusiedlersee. 18 ha. www.pittnauer.com
As a member of the Pannobile group, Gerhard Pittnauer
makes a rich Zweigelt-led blend under this name. But his
superb St-Laurent Alte Reben, with its unusual peppery
tone reminiscent of Syrah, is of comparable quality.

AUSTRIAN WINE CLASSIFICATION

TafelWein / Landwein Minimum 13° KMW
(63° Oechsle). A *tafelwein* must come
from a single wine area, maximum
alcohol 11.5%, maximum residual
sugar 6g/l.

Qualitätswein From a single wine area,
minimum 15° KMW (73° Oechsle)
enriched up to maximum 19° KMW
(94° Oechsle).

Kabinett Minimum 17° KMW (83.5°
Oechsle), maximum 19° KMW (94°
Oechsle), maximum residual sugar
9g/l, no *chaptalization*.

Prädikatswein Qualitätswein "of
exceptional maturity or vintage":
no *chaptalization*. The grades are:
Spätlese late-picked grapes with
minimum 19° KMW (94° Oechsle).

Auslese Selected late-picked grapes with
minimum 21° KMW (105° Oechsle).

Eiswein Made from frozen grapes with
minimum 25° KMW (127° Oechsle).

Beerenauslese Selected late-picked
overripe grapes with noble rot, minimum
25° KMW (127° Oechsle).

Ausbruch Overripe, nobly rotten grapes
that have dried naturally. Minimum 27°
KMW (138° Oechsle).

Trockenbeerenauslese Nobly-rotten,
raisin-like grapes, minimum 30° KMW
(150° Oechsle).

The Wachau has its own set of
categories. The basic wine is Steinfeder,
essentially an *unchaptalized*
Qualitätswein up to 10.7%. The next step
up is Federspiel, essentially a dry
Kabinett with a maximum alcohol of
11.9%. The ripest wines are called
Smaragd, and are the equivalent of a
Spätlese or indeed Auslese Trocken
elsewhere in Austria.

Peter Schandl ☆☆
Rust, Neusiedlersee-Hügelland. 15 ha.
www.schandlwein.com
Best-known for rich, traditional Ausbruch. But Schandl's white wines from Chardonnay, Gelber Muskateller, and Pinot Blanc are very enjoyable.

Tinhof ☆–☆☆
Eisenstadt. Neusiedlersee-Hügelland. 11 ha.
www.tinhof.at
French-trained Erwin Tinhof makes a good range of dry wines, red and white, less oaky than in the past.

Wenzel ☆☆
Rust, Neusiedlersee-Hügelland. 11 ha.
Robert Wenzel was an ultra-traditionalist, but his son Michael has freshened the style, and introduced modern, dry wines, including an Alsace-style Pinot Gris aged in Austrian oak, and a dense, tannic Pinot Noir. Intense Ausbruch, too.

Zantho ☆
Andau, Neusiedlersee. 70 ha. www.zantho.com
Unusual joint venture between Josef Umathum (q.v.) and the Andau co-op, to produce sizeable volumes of traditional Austrian reds, principally Zweigelt. The Reserve is delicious, but the venture will rise or fall on its Zweigelt Classic.

Leading Wien (Vienna) Producers

Christ ☆☆
Jedlersdorf. 15 ha. www.weingut-christ.at
An enterprising collection of wines, strong on Grüner Veltliner, but also including a Weissburgunder Vollmondschein (picked at the full moon), and Mephisto, a convincing red blend of Zweigelt, Cabernet, and Merlot.

Cobenzl ☆☆
Am Cobenzl. 35 ha. www.weingutcobenzl.at
This large property is owned by the city of Vienna, and the wines are steadily improving, especially the Weissburgunder. Other Viennese wineries complain that subsidies from the city administration give Cobenzl an unfair commercial advantage.

Edlmoser ☆☆
Mauer. 9 ha. www.edlmoser.at
Michael Edlmoser worked in California with Paul Draper at Ridge, and seems to have returned with a sense of balance that infuses all his wines: delicious Chardonnay, Riesling, Gelber Muskateller, and Gemischter Satz.

Mayer am Pfarrplatz ☆☆
Heiligenstadt. 26 ha. www.mayer.pfarrplatz.at
Franz Mayer is the largest grower in Vienna and runs a popular and authentic Heurige. His modern, well-run cellar produces a range of wines, of which the best are Riesling from the Nussberg and a zesty Grüner Veltliner. Under the same ownership as Rotes Haus, a five-hectare property on the Nussberg.

Schlumberger ☆
Bad Voslau. www.schlumberger.at
The best of the Viennese sparkling wine houses, offering a particularly fruity *blanc de noirs* underpinned by good acidity.

Wieninger ☆☆–☆☆☆
Stammersdorf. 35 ha. www.wieninger.at
Vienna's leading estate makes everything from traditional, dry Riesling to barrel-fermented Chardonnay and deeply coloured Cabernet/Merlot from vines on outstanding sites such as the Nussberg and Bisamberg. The Nussberg Alte

Gabled cellar entrances, Falkenstein district

Reben Gemischter Satz (a compound of great site, old vines, and typical Viennese style) is irresistible.

Other Vienna Producers

The proliferation of Heurigen in all the wine villages of Vienna means that a very wide range of wine is made. Most of it is consumed by thirsty customers and tourists, but the best Heurigen also bottle their wines. They can be of high quality and are usually sensibly priced. A selection of the best Vienna Heurigen estates should include: Hengl-Haselbrunner (Döbling), Reinprecht (Grinzing), Zahel (Mauer), Fuhrgassl-Huber (Neustift), and Schilling (Strebersdorf).

Leading Styria Producers

Gross ☆☆–☆☆☆
Ratsch, Südsteiermark. 36 ha. www.gross.at
Alois Gross is one of the most consistent winemakers of the Steiermark, making elegant, aromatic wines from a wide range of grapes. Best are his single vineyard Sauvignon, Gewürztraminer, and Grauburgunder.

Erich & Walter Polz ☆☆☆
Spielfeld, Südsteiermark. 70 ha. www.polz.co.at
The Polz brothers are leading figures in the wine revolution that began in Styria during the mid-1980s. They were pioneers in the move away from sweet wines and mass production in favour of quality dry wines.

They produce two styles of wine: the lighter, very fresh Klassik wines; and the richer, slower maturing, vineyard designated wines. Best of the latter are the Weissburgunder, Morillon, and Sauvignon Blanc from the first-class Hochgrassnitzberg vineyard direct on the Austrian-Slovenian border.

Sattlerhof ☆☆☆
Gamlitz, Südsteiermark. 32 ha. www.sattlerhof.at
Wilhelm Sattler was a leader of the dry wine movement in Styria, and made some wonderfully rich whites. Today it is run by his son Willi, who continues to produce long lived Sauvignon, Chardonnay, and Grauburgunder.

E & M Tement ☆☆☆
Berghausen, Südsteiermark. 65 ha. www.tement.at
The interior of Manfred Tement's cellar may look rather like a Heath Robinson cartoon, but the dry white wines that come out of it are frequently some of Styria's finest.

No other Austrian winemaker makes such judicious use of new-oak casks for fermenting and maturing white wines. His Sauvignon Blanc and Morillon from the first-class Zieregg vineyard are masterpieces of this style: at once rich and refined. In contrast, the Klassik varietal wines are vividly fruity, very clean, and crisp.

Other Styria Producers

Erwin Sabathi ☆☆–☆☆☆
Leutschach, Südsteiermark. 19 ha. www.sabathi.com
A rising star, with excellent steep sites such as the Pössnitzberg. Delicious Sauvignon and creamy Chardonnay with striking finesse.

Lackner-Tinnacher ☆☆
Gamlitz, Südsteiermark. 18 ha. www.tinnacher.at
This husband-and-wife-team make beautifully crafted traditional-style Steiermark whites, including a particularly superb, dry Gelber Muskateller and rich Grauburgunder, but other wines are all good.

Domäne Müller ☆–☆☆
Gross St Florian, Sudsteiermark. 36 ha. www.mueller-wein.at
The domaine unites two properties, one at Ehrenhausen, the other ar Deutschlandsberg in Weststeiermark. The range is varied and patchy, and the best wine seems to be the Deutsche Weingärten Sauvignon Blanc.

Skoff ☆☆
Gamlitz. 56 ha. www.skoff.com
Walter Skoff follows the usual Styrian hierarchy of Klassik, wines aged in large casks, and a barrique-aged line called Royal. Barriques rarely suit the sharp fruitiness of Styrian whites, and here the best wines are the single-vineyard Sauvignon and Chardonnay that retain their raciness and purity.

Winkler-Hamarden ☆☆
Kapfenstein, Süd-Oststeiermark. 34 ha. www.winkler-hamarden.at
A delightful property located (with a hotel and restaurant) in an old castle. The vineyards are on volcanic slopes, and although the majority of production is of traditionally made white wines, the estate is also well-known for its Olivin, Styria's best Zweigelt.

Wohlmuth ☆☆
Fresing. 65 ha. www.wohlmuth.at
This expanding estate has been making a splash in Austrian wine circles. The range of complex, but it's the Klassik and the partly oaked Summus wines that impress the most. Gerhard Wohlmuth also tries his hand at barrique-aged reds.

Central & Eastern Europe

The end of Communism in Eastern Europe had, and is still having, profound effects on wine industries that had been centrally directed for decades. Their markets had been almost exclusively the undemanding Soviet bloc. Existing sales channels disappeared almost literally overnight in 1989. For most of them (Bulgaria being the exception) trading links with western markets had eroded. A fresh start was necessary.

Hungary

Hungary, always the closest to the west, was the first to call in western aid and profit by flying winemaker technology. But in any context, historical or cultural, Hungary is incontestably the regional leader. Indeed, in all of Europe, only France and Germany have older and more evolved traditions of quality winemaking than Hungary's most famous vineyards. Whether the Hungarians can recapture their former standing in the world of wine depends in part on whether the world continues to prize the "international" grape varieties above all others, or whether, as in Italy, there is a real place for authentic ethnic traditions. By the late 2000s, Hungary's table wine production was focused resolutely on branded varietal wines – goodbye Szürkebarát, hello "Pinot Grigio" – aimed at supermarkets and their customers. Many of these wines were well-made and very attractively priced, but they bore little relation to traditional Hungarian wines. Admittedly, tradition in Communist times could often be equated with oxidation, but perhaps the pendulum has swung too energetically in the opposite direction.

The Hungarian words of appreciation for the country's traditional wines sum up their character and appeal. Hungarians call a good white wine "fiery" and "stiff" – masculine terms that promise a proper partner for the paprika in their cooking.

Such wines can still be found in the historical sites of Hungarian viticulture, the hill regions that dot the country from the southwest northwards, skirt the long Lake Balaton, then run up the Slovak border from near Budapest to Tokaj.

Despite the grubbing-up of old vines and massive plantings of international varieties in the 1960s and early '70s, and in spite of the current popularity of international varieties and styles, Hungary remains rich in indigenous grapes of character that have the potential to contribute splendid wines to the world scene – grapes that often simply do not succeed elsewhere. The most notable of all is the vigorous Furmint, the dominant grape of Tokaj, which not only rots nobly but in its dry form, yields strongly sappy and high-flavoured wine. The Hárslevelű or "linden leaf", is scarcely less notable: an excellent dry-climate late-ripener with abundant crops and good acid levels, as well as resistance to fungal diseases.

Szürkebarát, or "grey friar", is more familiar than it sounds. It is a form of Pinot Gris grown to splendid effect on the volcanic Mount Badacsonyi. The Kéknyelű ("blue-stalk") of the same vineyards north of Lake Balaton is a modest producer of concentrated and complex golden-green wines for the fish course. More widespread are three other white Hungarians: Ezerjó ("thousand blessings"), which is a good bulk-producer on the Great Plain, making fine wine only at Mór in the north; Leányka ("little girl") whose delicate, dry white is probably the best wine of Eger, again in the northern hills; and Mézesfehér ("white honey"), an archetypal description of the national view of a good glass of wine. The last is, regrettably, less grown now. Most widespread of all is the Olaszrizling (same as the Austrian Welschriesling). The Great Plain makes most of its white from it, and on Mount Badacsonyi it rises to its maximum flavour and concentration.

The great Hungarian red grape is the Kadarka, which flourishes equally on the Great Plain producing a firm wine with a slight but convincing "cut", and at Eger, Kunság, and Szekszárd, producing a big, stiff, spicy red for ageing. Unfortunately, it is a late and unreliably ripening variety and its low yield has meant that the rather lighter Kékfrankos (the same as the Austrian Blaufränkisch or German Lemberger) has been planted more and more as a substitute. The Austrian Zweigelt, on the other hand, is a newcomer with different virtues of softness, darkness, and a pleasantly sweet scent. There is also a long tradition of growing Pinot Noir in southern Hungary around Villány, and Merlot around Eger in the north.

Added to these are many grapes whose identification causes no problems: Szilváni, Cabernet (Sauvignon and Franc), Sauvignon Blanc, Pinot Blanc, Rajnairizling, Tramini, Muskat Ottonel or Muskotály. Each of Hungary's notable wines is called by a simple combination of place and grape name. The place name has the suffix "i". Thus Ezerjó from Mor is Mori Ezerjó.

Hungary has around 69,000 hectares of vines. Even under the former regime, even in Tokaj, the most important and famous area of all, many smallholders still owned land (a maximum of ten hectares) although their grapes had to be sold to the state farms for vinification. Today, although some vineyards remain in state ownership, the majority have now been wholly or partly privatized; substantial areas are owned by either major producers or cooperatives, but a very significant proportion is in the hands of small growers who, often with the assistance of foreign capital or partners, have invested in their own vinification and bottling facilities.

Currently there are 22 designated wine regions (although much very acceptable wine is produced outside them). There are vineyards and regions in all parts of the country with the exception of the large area west of the border with Romania.

The Great Plain

The Danube divides Hungary almost down the middle. East of the river in southern Hungary lies the sandy Pannonian or Great Plain (Alföld): a vast expanse of steppe-like country that has a long tradition of wine growing because vines help to bind the soil.

The Csongrád wine region embraces 2,840 hectares, producing wines almost entirely for the domestic market. The most common varieties grown here are Rajnairizling, Zöldveltelini (Grüner Veltliner), and Kékfrankos. The warm Hajós-Baja region, with more loess than sand, includes just over 2,000 hectares, which give higher quality wines. Principal grapes are Chardonnay, Cabernet Sauvignon, Zweigelt, and Kadarka. Hajósi Cabernet has a particularly good name.

By far the largest region of the Great Plain is Kunság, which totals 28,000 hectares. Soil quality and water-table levels vary, the summers are dry, precipitation is low, and winters frosty. A quarter of Hungary's total wine production comes from this region. Seventy per cent of it is white, everyday wine, only some of which is bound for western Europe. Both still and sparkling wines, the latter mainly reflecting the domestic market's preference for sweeter wines, are made from indigenous and international grapes, including Kadarka, Kövidinka, Ezerjó, Olaszrizling, Kékoporto, Kékfrankos, Cabernets Sauvignon and Franc, Zweigelt, Zöldveltelini, and Ottonel Muskotály.

THE CLASSES OF THE TRADITIONAL WINES OF TOKAJ

The following are the classic categories for Tokaj wines, although some, especially Szamorodni, are now being replaced by less specific "late harvest" styles.

Tokaji Szamorodni This is Tokaji "as it comes" – ie. the lesser wines, sweet (édes) or dry (száraz) according to the quantity of aszú grapes used.

Tokaji Aszú Like Tokaji Szamorodni, Aszú wines can only be made in years when there are sufficient high-quality aszú grapes – ie. grapes infected with noble rot (Botrytis cinerea). Destalked, hand-picked aszú grapes are stored six to eight days, then kneaded to a pulp that is added to a base Tokaji wine, or to must, by the puttony (a hod of 20–25 kilos). The eventual sweetness depends on the number of puttonyos added to the 136–140-litre barrels (called gönci) of either one-year-old base wine or unfermented or fermenting must – usually 4, 5, or 6 puttonyos; 6 is for the finest wines. (The puttony system describes a ratio of paste to wine, as no one today uses these specific measures.) Thereafter the wine is macerated and stirred for up to 48 hours, settled and racked, fermented, and then aged in small oak barrels for not less than two years plus one more year in bottle. Bottles used to be stored upright in the exceedingly humid cellars of the region, but today they are more likely to be laid on their sides.

Tokaji Aszú Esszencia The harvesting and vinification is the same as or Tokaji Aszú, but for this wine the sugar content is higher than for 6 puttonyos. Fermentation can takes years to complete, and the finished wine is aged for at least three years in oak and for two more in bottle.

Tokaji Esszencia While aszú grapes are being stored before being mashed, the pressure of their own weight produces a minute amount of highly concentrated juice at the bottom of the tub (one puttony yields only 142 mm of this Esszencia). The juice is then allowed to ferment extremely slowly for many years in oak casks. In practice, it scarcely ferments at all, and the alcohol level rarely exceeds three degrees; the sugar content is too high.

Northern Transdanubia

This great area includes much of the traditional wine-growing districts on the slopes of the old volcanic hills, which run up from Lake Balaton to the Danube/Slovakian border, but it also embraces newer wine districts.

The 1,820-hectare Aszár-Neszmély region is dominated by Hilltop Neszmély, a refurbished winery devoted exclusively to the export market. The moderate climate and good soils produce white wines that are fragrant, rich in acids, full-bodied, and keep well. Principal grape varieties of the region include Olaszrizling, Rizlingszilváni (alias Muller-Thürgau), Leányka, Sauvignon Blanc, Chardonnay, the Muscat-like Irsai Olivér, and Tramini.

Similar in size is the Badacsony region, a series of south-facing volcanic hills on the north shore of the 80-kilometre (50-mile) long Lake Balaton. After Tokaj, this region is second-dearest to Hungarians and its basalt soils produce warming – sometimes fiery – full-flavoured and fruity white wines. The grapes are grown by cooperatives as well as by small individual producers and the wines sold largely on the domestic market.

There is a growing number of wine cellars opening their doors to the many tourists who visit the lake. Badacsony's best are reckoned to come from the Olaszrizling, Szürkebarát (Pinot Gris), and dryish Kéknyelű grapes, but Rizlingszilváni and Ottonel Muskotály are also widely planted. The best producer is Huba Szeremley.

Farther east along the northern lake shore lies the Balatonfüred-Csopak region, some 2,270 hectares of red sand soils, less hilly than Badacsony, but likewise farmed by co-ops and smaller individual producers. A slightly warmer microclimate gives wines with more roundness, less "nerve". Overall, the style is softer than the Badacsony wines. Here the Olaszrizling makes notable wines, but Rizlingszilváni, Rajnairizling, Chardonnay, Sauvignon Blanc, Tramini, and Ottonel Muskotály are also widespread.

Almost behind the Badacsony region, on a second line of hills north of the lake, is the smaller (1,510 hectares) Balatonfelvidék region. Here, too, the vines are on south-facing volcanic slopes, but lack the benefit of the sun's rays being reflected from the lake's surface. Mainly small growers make excellent Olaszrizling, Chardonnay, Pinot Gris, and Rizlingszilváni, especially for the home market.

Thirty-two-kilometres (20-miles) west of Budapest is the 2,000-hectare Etyek-Buda region. A century ago the potential of its climate and loess and sand soils caught the eye of Champagne-trained József Törley for growing Chardonnay to produce sparkling wines. Törley's successor in the region today is Hungarovin (now owned by the huge German company Henkell & Söhnlein), joined by some small producers, growing Sauvignon Blanc, Zenit, Rajnairizling, Pinot Blanc, and Zengő, among other varieties. Smaller still is the Mór region, an 890-hectare stretch known principally for its robustly distinctive Móri Ezerjó wines, one of the country's best dry whites, although its quartz-rich soils over limestone also produce Sauvignon, Tramini, and a Rajnairizling which have acidity and "fire".

Further north and closer to the Austrian border is the 750-hectare Pannonhalma-Sokoróalja region, lying at the foot of the Bakony hills south of Györ. Virtually all of its production is consumed in the domestic market. The main grapes of the region are Olaszrizling, Rajnairizling, Chardonnay, Ottonel Muskotály, Rizlingszilváni, and Tramini.

Hungary's smallest region is Somló, 690 hectares on the slopes of a single volcanic plug. Wine-growing is largely in the hands of small producers, some with as little as one hectare of vines, selling almost entirely to the domestic market. Characterful wines are made from Olaszrizling, Furmint, Tramini, Hárslevelű, and Chardonnay, and, most interesting of all, the sharp, bracing Juhfark. Béla Fekete and István Inhauser are among the best growers here.

The last of Northern Transdanubia's regions is Sopron, 1,880 hectares that run up to the border with Austria's Burgenland. A milder climate than most of Hungary and diverse soils are more favourable to red wine production. Here Kékfrankos is the principal grape, although Zweigelt, Merlot, and Cabernet are also grown. The best bear comparison with Austria's from over the border. There are whites, too, made from Tramini, Leányka, Zöldveltelini, and some Chardonnay.

Southern Transdanubia

The area south of Lake Balaton and west of the Danube houses four of Hungary's best-known wine regions. Balatonmelléke lies just west of the lake, and its 1,170 hectares only became a recognized wine region in 1998; white varieties dominate. More important is Balatonboglár, 2,880 hectares of brown forest soils and sandy loess with a sub-Mediterranean climate, which means the springs are early, summers long and warm, and frosts rare, although rain (and frequently hail) is plentiful. Red and mostly white wines are produced, from Olaszrizling, Chardonnay, Sauvignon Blanc, Királylánky, Kékfrankos, Merlot, and Cabernet Sauvignon. Most of the vineyard area is under the control of the Balatonboglár Winery (owner of the "Chapel Hill" export brand and itself owned by Henkell & Söhnlein), the rest is in the hands of small growers.

To the south, around the town of Pécs, is the Mecsekalja, a region of 940 hectares. It is the warmest of Hungary's wine regions and the wine produced here is almost all white, from local and imported varieties, including very respectable off-dry Olaszrizling, good Pinot Blanc, Furmint, Cirfandli (a specialty), Chardonnay, and Sauvignon.

One of Hungary's oldest and most renowned wine regions is Szekszárd in the south-central part of the country, with

Church and vineyard, Lake Balaton

2,300 hectares under vine. It produces some of Hungary's best reds on gentle slopes of sandy loess, which follow the course of the Danube. It is the only region other than Eger permitted to produce Bikavér (Bull's Blood). It built its reputation for reds (likened to Bordeaux) on the Kadarka grape, but Szekszárd now depends mainly on the international varieties of Merlot and the two Cabernets, and the native Kékfrankos. White wines are made from Chardonnay and Olaszrizling. Foreign investors have shown some interest in the region. The best-known producers are Vesztergombi, Dúszi, Vida, and Takler. Just north of Szekszárd is the large (3,150 hectares) but diffuse Tolna region, which was only given its own identity in 1998. A full panoply of varieties is grown here.

Villány-Siklós (1,890 hectares) is the combined name for two historic wine regions named after their principal towns. Red wines predominate in the Villány half where, on hills of stiff loess, the Kadarka has given way to the Kékoportó (probably the Blauer Portugieser), which takes full advantage of the mild winters and long, hot summers to produce some full-bodied wines that can take readily to oak. The two Cabernets, Merlot, Pinot Noir (producing some unmistakably Burgundian wines), Zweigelt, and the native Kékfrankos are also grown in the Villány half. There seems little doubt that this is Hungary's best region for serious, Bordeaux style wines. In the Siklós part of the region, small producers concentrate predominantly on white grapes, notably Olaszrizling, Tramini, Chardonnay, and Hárslevelű. The best red wine producers, and thus among the best in all Hungary, are Bock, Attila Gere, Tamás Gere, Vylyan, and Tiffan.

Northern Hungary

The lower slopes of the Bükk hills and the sheltering Mátra mountains north of the vineyards produce some of Hungary's best known wines. Between Eger and the industrial city of Miskolc, the 1,590 hectares of the Bükkalja (-*alja* means "foothills") region benefit from a good microclimate and soils underlaid by tufa – perfect for vines. Cabernet Sauvignon, Leányka, Olaszrizling, Zweigelt, and Kékfrankos are the principal grapes. Most of the production is vinified by large wineries in Eger or Budapest.

To the south of the baroque city of Eger is the 5,160-hectare Eger wine region itself. Eger is famous for its Egri Bikavér (Bull's Blood) on which its reputation as a potent red wine producer was built. Bikavér is in fact a style of wine, not a brand, made from a blend of Kékfrankos, Merlot, Cabernets Sauvignon and Franc, and Kékoporto. Kadarka is no longer the principal native grape in the blend. In fact, today there is a range of Bikavérs as individual producers determine the exact blending proportions and amount of ageing that suits their vineyards best. After a long spell in cellar, some extraordinarily powerful wines can emerge, although inevitably, perhaps, some export versions are all too variable.

In addition to Bikavér, Eger produces some fine, fresh, white wines, too, best of all from Leányka, a specialty of the region, but also using Chardonnay, Riesling, Olaszrizling, Tramini, and some Ottonel Muskotály. The underlying tufa may be the secret of Egri quality. The biggest producer, Egervin, privatized in

1993 but under Hungarian ownership, now owns the impressive tufa-quarried cellars in the city, which are lined with vast red-hooped casks. The best producers in Eger, with an ever-expanding palette of grape varieties and blends, are GIA (Tibor Gál), Thummerer, and Béla Vincze.

Farther west, around the town of Gyöngyös, is the Mátraalja region, an almost exclusively white wine region of some 7,000 hectares. Today the region's biggest producers are two co-ops, Nagyréde and Danubiana. Nagyréde sells some of its wines under the export labels Cool Ridge and Matra Mountain. Under new German owners, in the 1990s, Danubiana bought and re-equipped the huge Gyöngyös winery, and brought in Hungary's first flying winemaker, Hugh Ryman. French and Australian investment has followed. Half of the region's total output is exported. Principal grape varieties include Olaszrizling, Pinots Gris and Blanc, Rizlingszilváni, Zöldveltelini, Leányka, Tramini, Hárslevelű (most famously from the town of Debrő), Chardonnay, Sauvignon Blanc, and the fragrant Ottonel Muskotály, which produces the region's dry Muscat specialty.

The final region is the 5,860-hectare Tokajhegyalja, usually shortened to Tokaj, in the far northeast of Hungary, adjoining the Slovakian border. Tokaji Aszú is often thought to be the only wine of Tokaj (see below). There are in fact several table wines made from one or other of the four grape varieties permitted in the "great" Tokaji wines: Furmint, Hárslevelű, Sargamuskotály (Yellow Muscat or Muscat Lunel), and Oremus, a hybrid cross between Furmint and the Bouvier grapes, which was only admitted to the Tokaji canon in 1994, and may also be called Zéta. A little Chardonnay also features.

Tokaji

Tokaji stands head and shoulders above the other wine regions of central and eastern Europe as the producer of their one undisputed wine of luxury and legend. Late-harvested, unctuously rich Tokaji (Tokay is the western spelling of the name) was the choice of Russian tsars, the kings of Poland, and emperors of Austria – even of Louis XIV of France. It was almost certainly the first wine to be made purposely of botrytis shrivelled grapes. The mid-seventeenth century is given as its known origin, at least a century before similar sweet wines were first made on the Rhine. Sweet Sauternes is also more recent in origin, though its start date is obscure.

By the early 1700s, the wines of Tokaj were so important that their overlord, the prince of Transylvania (of the Rakoczi family) created the first recorded vineyard classification, grading the Tokaj vineyards into "primae", "secundae" and "tertiae" plots.

In some respects the Tokajhegyalya (Tokaj hills) compares with Burgundy's Côte d'Or. The vines occupy a similar area on the lower and mid-slopes, though of much higher hills. The best sites tend to be on the lower middle slopes, some on pure volcanic soil, some on warm, light loess. Moreover the first-, second-, and third-class growths correspond, up to a point, to the *grands* and *premiers crus* and villages wines of Burgundy.

Like the Côte d'Or, too, Tokaj has excellent cellars, but here they are narrow tunnels driven into the volcanic tufa, sometimes wandering for a kilometre or more, deeply lined with damp, black fungus and sheltering single or double rows of little 136-litre casks, or *gönci*, usually black with age. Vintage time is very late, delayed – ideally – until the hot sun, alternating with misty nights (the Rivers Bodrog and Tisza skirt the hills), has induced a heavy infestation of botrytis. But unlike Sauternes, or any other wine, Tokaji Aszú is made in two stages: first a fully fermented "base" wine; then the collection of dry (*aszú*) grapes, shrivelled either by botrytis or simple raisining, which are macerated with the base wine or must and re-fermented to absorb their sweetness and highly concentrated aromas. (See box on page 450.)

Such wines, with their intense sweetness and concentrated, dried-fruit flavours, balanced by swingeing acidity, can be alarmingly penetrating when they are young, leaving the mouth with a whistle-clean sharpness despite their sugar content. With age they mellow to magical complexity and roundness, without losing their clean, fresh finish. The richest wines from the best vintages can easily age for a century or more. Eventually, even more important than the degree of sweetness, though, will be the singular quality of the vineyard. A handful of great sites have been celebrated for centuries, and single-vineyard wines from them are now being released. Two sites in the commune of Tarcal have historically been regarded as the greatest of all: Szarvas (the property of the state) and Mezés Mály.

But Tokaji Aszús can no more be the only product of the region than can Auslesen in Germany. The regular drinking is dry, largely Furmint, table wine, which can be admirably lively and fiery. The less luxurious aperitif or dessert wine is Tokaji Szamorodni – literally "as it comes"; which means the whole vineyard is harvested without any selection of *aszú* grapes. Dry Szamorodni can be similar to sherry with its own distinctive "cut". There is another style of wine that is made by a few producers: Forditas. This is made by pressing the *marc* again after the *aszú* mixture has been pressed, and then adding dry wine for a further fermentation. The rather unsatisfactory outcome is a wine midway in style between Szamorodni and Aszú.

For those for whom the best is not good enough there remains a category richer even than a 6-putt wine: Tokaji Aszú Esszencia (or Essencia). Such sweet intensity is overwhelming; years of maturity are needed to tame it. The legendary Tokaji "Essence" goes even further. Its sugar content is so high (up to 800 grams per litre) that yeasts can make no impression on it; an interminable snail's pace fermentation was traditionally ended by the discreet addition of a little brandy. Esszencia is the free-run juice of a pile of *aszú* bunches, pressed by their own weight alone to produce eggcup quantities. Since an eggcup of the elixir was reputedly enough to convert an imperial deathbed into something much more lively, Esszencia has for centuries been the most highly prized of all wines – and virtually unobtainable.

The renaissance of the Tokaj region is now well under way, with over a dozen companies, including several major foreign investors, involved. There is still some debate about the "authentic" style of Tokaji Aszú wines. During the Communist era, the wines were often pasteurized and sometimes lightly fortified: processes that (together with the inevitable attitudes of a command economy) tended to oxidize the wines prema-

turely. Modern practices, including regular topping-up of barrels, the replacing of *gönci* by larger barrique-type barrels of up to 500 litres, refermenting with must instead of base wine, and earlier bottling result in fresher wines with less of the marked Tokaj cellar character. The debate and the changes have been good for the region, and there will always be room for different interpretations of tradition. Great Aszús, like great Sauternes, are wines to lay down for 20 years or more, so the jury will still be out for at least another decade.

However, investors and winemakers have now learnt that to produce nothing but Aszú wine is not commercially viable, as there are some vintages when conditions make it all but impossible. Hence the resurgence in dry Furmint to make good use of healthy grapes not suitable for Aszú production, and the creation of new, and controversial, late harvest wines. These are not legally defined, but tend to be sweet wines made from over-ripe but not botrytized grapes; they also differ from Aszú wines in being mostly unoaked. Some critics, and producers, consider such wines a deviation and distraction; others say they are a necessary extension of the product range and, moreover, have proved popular with consumers.

Leading Tokaji Producers

János Arvay ☆–☆☆☆
Tokaj. Owner: János Arvay and Christian Sauska. 81 ha. www.arvaybor.hu
The former winemaker at Disznókő (q.v.) set up a joint venture in 2000 with a Hungarian now resident in the United States. The Aszú wines, which have a minimum of 5 *puttyonos*, are marketed under the Hétfürtös label. Arvay also produces a wide range of other wines, dry, semi-sweet, and sweet, but the Aszú wines are the best by a long way.

Grof Degenfeld ☆–☆☆☆
Tarcal. Owner: Degenfeld family. 100 ha. www.grofdegenfeld.com
The noble Degenfeld family lived in Romania in poverty in the 1950s, then migrated to Germany, where their fortunes revived. In their native Tokaj they bought and largely replanted vineyards, some of them first-class sites, and bought back the family mansion. The Aszú wines, initially oxidative, are now fresher and more opulent. These wines are supplemented by a full range of other styles, including a barrel aged Furmint.

Zoltán Demeter ☆☆
Tokaj. Owner: Zoltán Demeter. 5 ha.
With a decade of experience at Hetszoló, Degenfeld, and Királyudvar, this talented winemaker also produces under his own label small quantities of barrique-fermented dry Furmint and sweet wines from the Lapis vineyard.

Chateau Dereszla ☆–☆☆
Bodrogkeresztúr. Owner: Edonia Group. 60 ha. www.dereszla.com.
The d'Aulan family, who also own Château Sansonnet in St-Emilion and Alta Vista in Argentina, created this property in 2000. They favour a good proportion of Hárslevelű in the

Aszú wines, and do not favour long barrel ageing. Initial releases of Aszú were of middling quality, and the winery seems to place equal emphasis on late-harvest and dry styles, which are well-made.

Disznók ☆☆☆
Tokaj. Owner: AXA Millésimes. 100 ha.
www.disznoko.hu
One of the great old Tokaji estates, bought at privatization (1992) by the French insurance group AXA and directed initially by Jean-Michel Cazes of Bordeaux, and since 2001 by Christian Seely. AXA undertook a major investment in the splendid volcanic clay vineyards and a new winery. Under current winemaker Lászlo Mészáros, a full range of Szamorodni and Aszú wines is produced in a zesty, modern style. The AXA team has been meticulous in its research into the vinification of Tokaji, and the results have been shared with other producers. Both French and Hungarian oak is used to age its wines, and if there are still a few who criticize the Disznókő wines as too similar to Sauternes, others hail them as among the region's very best. Bottle age reinforces their true Tokaji character.

Dobogó ☆☆
Tokaj. Owner: Zwack family. 6 ha.
www.dobogo.hu
There cannot be a Hungarian who does not recognize the name of Zwack, as the family who created the highly popular Unicum, an astonishingly bitter digestif. Here in Tokaj, Isabella Zwack runs a small property that has, since 1997, produced fine 6-Puttyonos Aszú and dry Furmint with flair.

Gundel ☆☆–☆☆☆
Mád. Owner: Ronald Lauder and George Lang. 26 ha.
www.gundel.hu
The most famous restaurant in Budapest, lovingly restored in the 1990s, also produces its own wines here (as well as in Eger). High quality, especially for its Aszú wines.

Hétszol ☆☆
Tokaj. Owner: Grands Millésimes de France, Suntory, and other investors. 50 ha. www.tokaj-hetszolo.hu
A major foreign investment, with extensive vineyards replanted on the steep southern slope of the Tokaj mountain. Sadly the wines have never fulfilled their high potential, and the future is uncertain.

Királyudvar ☆☆–☆☆☆
Tarcal. Owner: Anthony Hwang. 75 ha.
ww.kiralyudvar.com
After Chinese-American businessman Anthony Hwang tasted a wine made by István Szepsy (q.v.), he dashed to Tokaj to talk to him and persuaded him to oversee a new venture. Hwang has bought many top vineyards here, and restored a former seventeenth-century winery in Tarcal. Szepsy is no longer closely involved with the project, and the very capable Zoltán Demeter is now in charge of wine production. The usual range of typical Tokaj wines, of which the finest is the single-vineyard Lapis Aszú, is supplemented since 2005 by a fine (and pricey) dry Furmint, and by a range of late harvest wines.

Châteaux Megyer & Pajzos ☆–☆☆
Sárospatak. Owner: Jean-Louis Laborde. 140 ha.
Major joint venture, initially between GAN (French insurance company) and a French-led consortium, but purchased in 1998 by Jean-Louis Laborde, owner of Château Clinet in Pomerol. The two properties are distinct, but used as a single source of grapes. In general, Megyer is the lighter, more commercial wine, with Pajzos focusing on higher quality levels.

Quality has been variable, though some fine Aszú wines have appeared under the Pajzos label. In addition there is dry Muscat and Furmint, Chardonnay (Megyer), and late-harvest, single-varietal wines.

Oremus ☆☆–☆☆☆
Tolcsva. Owner: Bodegas Vega Sicilia. 115 ha.
www.tokajoremus.com
The name of the original 1630 Tokaj Aszú was bought at privatization by Vega Sicilia of Spain in 1993. Originally based in Sarospatak, it built a new winery in Tolcsva in 1999. Aszús were at first made in an oxidative style, but it wasn't long before the wines became more intense and vigorous. A good, dry Furmint called Mandolás and late-harvest varietal wines supplement production. András Bacsó is the experienced manager and winemaker.

Patricius ☆☆
Tokaj. Owner: Dezső Kékessy. 80 ha. www.patricius.hu.
Rooted in the region for many centuries, the Kékessy family established the property in 1999 and built a gravity fed winery, where they produce a full range of wines, from dry Furmint, to late harvest wines, to Aszú.

Pendits ☆☆☆
Abaújszantó. Owner: Márta Wille-Baumkauff. 10 ha.
www.pendits.de
In the 1970s, Mrs Wille-Baumkauff left Hungary to marry a German, and returned here in 1991 to develop her property in Mád. At first the label was the anonymous MWB, but has been changed in honour of her best first growth vineyard. Since 2005 her estate has been farmed organically. Since 1999 quality has been first rate.

Royal Tokaji Wine Company
Mád. Owner: private investors. 106 ha.
www.royal-tokaji.com
Ambitious Anglo-Danish-Hungarian joint venture founded in 1989 (the first of the "Tokaji Renaissance") to specialize in Aszú wines. Parcels in one second-class and four first-class sites in Mád and Tarcal produce single vineyard Betsek, Birsalmás, Nyulászó, Szt Tamás, and Mezés Mály. Blue Label (in the USA Red Label) is a vintage-dated 5-Puttonyos Aszú; Gold Label a 6-Puttonyos blend. The aim is the maximum intensity of vineyard and cellar character, with lower alcohol than some Aszús from other producers, and higher sweetness levels matched with corresponding acidity. In 2002 a late harvest Cuvée Ats (named for the cellar master Karoly Ats) and in 2003 the first Royal dry barrel-fermented Furmint was produced. (Quality is not rated here because of Hugh Johnson's participation in the venture.)

István Szepsy ☆☆☆–☆☆☆☆
Mád. Owner: István Szepsy. 46 ha. www.szepsy.hu

The Szepsys have been making Tokaji Aszú from Mád and Tarcal since the sixteenth century. There is a legend that his ancestor, Maté Szepsy, invented the Aszú method, but the modest István Szepsy says that this is not so, although Maté did play a part in its creation.

In the 1980s, he came to realize that the mass-produced Tokajis from the state farm were a travesty of the real thing, and quietly continued producing authentic Aszú from his family's vineyards. He was the first manager of Royal Tokaji (q.v.), and made his own first vintage in 1993.

From the first his wines have attracted much outside attention: so far production cannot meet the demand. To keep up with it, Szepsy introduced "late-harvest" wines bottled without the customary barrel ageing. Szepsy accounts for the quality by his vineyard practice: low trained vines, hard pruning, green harvesting, and rigorous selection of berries only at the peak of botrytis. Base wine added to the *aszú* grapes is must from the same vineyard. The wine is aged for as long as he deems necessary in Hungarian oak barrels. At first the Aszú wines were invariably 6-Puttonyos, but since 1998 he has produced a single Aszú wine, without specifying the *puttonyos* level but with up to 230 grams of residual sugar.

Samuel Tinon ☆☆–☆☆☆
Olaszliszka. Owner: Samuel Tinon. 5 ha. www.samueltinon.com

Tinon came to Tokaj from his native Bordeaux in the early 1990s, but it was only in 2000 that he launched his own range of wines, including luxurious Aszú Eszencia.

Tokaj Kereskedöház/Tokaj Trading House Co ☆–☆☆
Sátoraljaújhely. 80 ha. www.crownestates-tokaji.hu

Former state-owned property with vineyard holdings much reduced from its heyday of 1,600 hectares, although the firm retains the first-class Szarvas vineyard and still purchases grapes from 200 growers who farm 1,000 hectares. It makes dry and sweet wines (Furmint, Hárslevelű, Yellow Muscat, Szamorodni, Aszú, and "museum" wines aged for decades before release).

The company makes its top Aszú wines in a style that has not changed greatly since the Communist years, but which its finest old Aszús show to have been consistent for a century. In Britain, the wines are released under the not entirely accurate Crown Estates label, with dry wines bottled under the Castle Island brand.

Uri Borok ☆☆☆
Mád. Owner: Vince Gergely. 13 ha.

Although Gergely's wines across the board are among Tokaj's

finest, he has made a speciality of outstanding Muskotály, sourced from very old vines in the fine Szent Tamás vineyard.

Other producers to note include:
Bene, Bodnàr Dusóczky, Evinor, Monyók, Tokaj Classic, and Tolcsva-Bor.

Other Hungarian Producers

Joszef Bock ☆–☆☆
Villány. 50 ha. www.bock.hu

Beginning with just over one hectare in 1991, Bock has built up an estate of 50 hectares and produces a huge range of wines. But his specialties are barrique aged reds, including a rare Hungarian Syrah, and Capella Cuvée, from the two Cabernets.

Bela Fekete ☆☆–☆☆☆
Somló.

One of the best Somló producers, with fresh, fiery Juhfark and assertive Hárslevelű.

Attila Gere ☆☆–☆☆☆
Villány. www.gere.hu

Attila Gere started life as a forester, but by the late 1970s well understood the potential of Villány for fine red wines and first bottled his own in 1986. Today he is equally adept at elegant Kekfránkos and Bordeaux style reds, especially the splendid if oaky Kopar Cuvée, made only in top vintages.

Tibor Gál ☆–☆☆
Eger. www.galtibor.com

Gál spent years working for Lodovico Antinori in Tuscany, before returning to Hungary in 1993 and setting up his own winery and planting over 50 hectares of vineyards. As well as producing Cabernets and Egri Bikaver, he focused on Pinot Noir, releasing three rather tannic single-vineyard wines aged in new oak. Although Gál died in a car accident in 2005, his international partners have maintained the business.

Pannonhalmi Apátsági ☆☆
Pannonhalma. www.bences.hu

Vines were apparently cultivated at this Benedictine monastery in the tenth century. The tradition was revived a few years ago, and the first new wine was in 2003. The range includes extremely well-made Sauvignon, Gewürztraminer, white blends, and Pinot Noir. The wines have a sophistication not often encountered in Hungary, even today.

Sandahl ☆☆
Badacsony. www.villasandahl.com

A Swedish couple have installed themselves here to produce nothing but dry Riesling. The 2006 vintage showed crispness, extract, and concentration.

Wrought iron gate with grapevine motif, Tokaj

Szerelmey ☆☆–☆☆☆
Badacsony.
White wines are the strength at this large private estate, founded by an *émigré* who made his fortune in Nigeria before returning to Hungary. The volcanic soils on which the grapes are rooted give the wines considerable spice and vigour.

Thummerer ☆–☆☆
Eger. www.thummerer.hu
Former flower-grower Vilmos Thummerer has since 1985 built up one of Eger's largest and most important wineries, well-known for Bikaver, for Vili Papa, an oaked Bordeaux blend, and for wine tourism.

Vesztergombi ☆☆
Szekszard.
Brothers Ferenc and Joszef are foremost producers of Bikaver and of the rarer Kadarka, continuing a family tradition that goes back to the eighteenth century.

Weninger ☆☆
Sopron. www.weninger.com
In 1997 Franz Weninger, who has an estate in the Burgenland, developed vineyards, now Biodynamic, across the border in the town of Balf. His best wine is Kékfrankos, especially from the Spern Steiner vineyard, with its gneiss and schist soils.

Wunderlich ☆☆
Villany. www.wunderlich.hu
Thanks to the confidence and purse of new investors, Alajos Wunderlich has been able to construct a lavish new winery to house his up-to-date equipment and his mostly Hungarian oak barrels, in which his red wines are mostly aged. From a wide range, Cabernet Franc stands out.

The Czech & Slovak Republics

Unlike Hungary, the quality of whose top wines was world-famous in the past, these two republics have traditionally grown wine for their own use, rather than for export. Even with the advent of less repressive political regimes, they still do.

The former capital of both countries, Prague, may account for much of the consumption, but the wine-production capitals are Bratislava in Slovakia, and Mikulov and Znojmo in Moravia. Bratislava lies on the River Danube virtually on the Austro-Hungarian border; the Moravian towns look across the border onto Austria's Weinviertel.

Slovakia is the chief producer of the two republics, with some 12,900 hectares, a sharp decrease on a decade earlier. The principal white varieties are Rhine Riesling, Pinot Blanc, Gewürztraminer, Sauvignon Blanc, Pinot Gris, and Muscat Ottonel; supporting roles are taken by Welschriesling, Grüner Veltliner, and Müller-Thurgau. Only 20 per cent is red, with Frankovka (Austrian Blaufränkisch, Hungarian Kékfrankos) and Svatovavrinecké (St-Laurent) the leading grapes. There

are some 600 hectares of Cabernet Sauvignon and a few rare plantings of Pinot Noir on the hills between Bratislava and Pezinok. The big, old, state bottling companies of Raca (in the outskirts of Bratislava), Pezinok, some 19 kilometres (12 miles) to the north-east, and Nitra, another 64 kilometres (40 miles) farther on used to account for the vast majority of the entire state production.

Modra, just north of Pezinok, has its own viticultural and oenology school. Nenince to the east along the Slovak-Hungarian border probably has a head start on quality production in the country. Kosice, far to the east, is also surrounded by vineyard land. Names of breakaway cellars, which ought to have become well-known but have remained somewhat obscure include Topolcany, Hurbanovo, Gbelce, Hlohovec, and Trnava, all of which have some fine vineyards to draw on. Although private cellars did develop throughout the 1990s, they have had limited impact outside the zones of production. At European wine fairs, the wines of Slovakia remain conspicuous by their absence.

Slovakia's other special pride is in possessing a small corner of the Tokaji vineyard on the Hungarian border, growing 65% Furmint, 25% Hárslevelű, and 10% Muscat de Frontignan to produce her own Tokaji. Sadly, the wines are a pale shadow of the real thing, so it is just as well that Slovakia owns no more than ten per cent of the region's vineyards.

Moravia's 17,841 hectares of vineyards lie between Brno and the Austrian border, and many of the grapes are similar to those of its neighbour. The industry is centred in the towns of Znojmo, Blatnice, Mikulov, and Velké Pavlovice, which make both still and sparkling wines. Many growers have expanded their hitherto family production to offer bottled wines of fair quality for commercial distribution. White wines, such as Grüner Veltliners, Pinots Blanc and Gris, and Rieslings, are often lively and highly drinkable, the first choice in the *vinarnas*, the wine-bars of Prague, but the standard of red wines from St-Laurent, Zweigelt, and even Cabernet is gradually improving. Moravia's wines score in terms of both value and variety.

Bohemia, the western province with Prague at its heart, has a mere 713 hectares, including some Riesling of fair quality and some intriguing Pinot Noir based reds. But full ripeness does not come easily here, and Moravian or Slovakian wine is the people's choice. The return, since 1989, of some noble families to their hereditary estates (and vineyards) is giving a boost to the home industry, but at present the quality sector remains small.

In Slovakia the only estate with any international recognition is Kastiel Béla, close to the Danube and owned by the family of the wife of Egon Müller of Scharzhof in Germany's Saar. With Müller supervising wine production, it is not surprising that the property's dry Rieslings are of high quality. Most Czech wineries are very small and cater to local demand. Larger commercial wineries include Bzenec, with an annual output of almost one million cases, but the wines are commercial, lack personality, and often rather sweet. Much the same is true of Templárské, the republic's largest winery, with 1,000 hectares at its disposal, and the vast Bohemia Sekt sparkling wine company.

The Former Yugoslavia

Most of the countries that once made up Yugoslavia are in the wine business, some more traditionally and interestingly than others. Only land-locked and mountainous Bosnia-Herzegovina's production is negligible. Few of these countries' wines have made much of an impression outside the Balkans. Promotional budgets are slender, and the best wines easily find a local market. However, wines from Slovenia and Croatia are now beginning to make their mark, aided by the fact that the best wines are now of very good quality.

The former Yugoslavia came tenth among the world's wine-producing countries and tenth among exporters: a respectable position for a country that had to build its wine industry almost from scratch after World War II. The industry roots are as old as Italy's, but long occupation by the Turks in the easterly regions of the country removed the sense of continuity.

The postwar reconstitution of the industry combined the Austro-Hungarian traditions of the north, the Italian influence down the coast, and some truly Balkan traditions in the east and south. In particular, Croatia's Dalmatian coast, and Macedonia likewise, have good indigenous grape varieties, whose origins can be traced back to ancient times, although these are threatened by the general trend in all these countries to adopt the tried and trusted international varieties as part of the concerted effort to regain a slice of the export market.

The old wine industry was state-controlled, but always consisted almost half-and-half of small, independent growers and state owned farms. The small growers (the law allowed them to own up to ten hectares of land) took their crops to the local, giant sized cooperatives. These in turn supplied the larger regional organizations, which acted as négociants, blenders, and distributors. The 1990s saw a burgeoning of small private estates and a privatization of larger enterprises that could benefit from efficiencies of scale to broach export markets.

Slovenia

Slovenia, tucked into the Italian-Austrian-Hungarian northwest corner of the country, makes the best and most expensive wines of the countries that formerly made up Yugoslavia. The 24,600 hectares of vineyards are divided by a no-man's land strip, empty of vines, from the alpine border, past the capital, Ljubljana, down to the border with Croatia. There are three principal regions: Primorska between Italy and Croatia along the coast; Podravje, with around 10,000 hectares just south of the borders with Austria and Hungary; and, east of Ljubljana,

Posavje, an almost exclusively white wine area. The most attractive of the northerly Germano-Austrian style wines come from around Maribor, Ptuj, Ljutomer (or Lutomer), and Ormož, between the valleys of the Mura (which forms in places the border with Austria and Hungary), the Sava, and the Drava tributaries to the Danube. The most exciting dry whites and reds produced in the Italian tradition come from the north of the Istrian peninsula and up into the mountains alongside the Friuli border region.

These days, Slovenia is taking a lot of care in the grading of her wines. By 2007 about half the country's wine production was still in the hands of cooperatives, but the private sector is growing, is cooperating to promote its wines, and is very mindful of the need to maintain high quality. Slovenia is also rapidly becoming a very pleasant, civilized country for the tourist to visit.

The combined influences of the Adriatic, the Alps, and the Hungarian plain make the climate moderate, while limestone subsoils favour white wine. The Adriatic influence gives more

ripening potential for solid, dry wines and the better reds; the long, cool autumns of the alpine Maribor region and the only slightly warmer hillsides south of Hungary give lighter, more aromatic and grapey styles, the best of which are often sold under the Slovenian equivalent of the familiar Kabinett, Spätlese, Auslese, Beerenauslese, and TBA hierarchy.

The hills between Ljutomer and Ormož, only 80 kilometres (50 miles) from the west end of Lake Balaton, bear a vineyard almost as famous as Mount Badacsonyi, known by the name of Jeruzalem from its crusader connections. The majority of the exports from this admirable region used to be of Laski Rizling, which is fortunately being increasingly displaced by flavoury Pinots Blanc and Gris, Gewürztraminer, Sylvaner, and Rhine Riesling. It seems a pity to waste a first-rate vineyard on what is essentially a second-rate grape, however satisfactory its performance – and some of the late-picked wines here are more than satisfactory.

South of the Drava, the Haloze Hills produce a similar range of white wines. South again, the Sava valley, continuing into Croatia and on to its capital, Zagreb, makes light red Cvicek of local grapes. At the western end of Slovenia, on the Italian border, four small viticultural regions known collectively as Primorska have a mild Mediterranean climate. Their best-known wine is a vigorous, crisp, and tangy red called Kraski Teran. Teran is the Italian Refosco, and Kraski signifies that it is grown on the rugged limestone karst that stretches up the coast. Merlot, both Cabernets, and Barbera can be found, but tend to be used to produce relatively high-acid, Italian styles, which crave the company of oily foods. However, the weight and quality of the best of the dry whites, from Sauvignon Blanc, Pinot Blanc, and Pinot Gris to the earthy, slightly creamy, yellow Ribolla or Rebula, another Italian export, deserve real international acclaim.

The gates of St Vitus Cathedral, Prague

At this end of the country, names such as Vipava, especially for fresh, delicate young whites; Brda, which has some extraordinary private vineyards; and Koper, south of Trieste, hold promise for the future. Tastings in 2008 confirm that there are a growing number of small estates clearly aiming for high quality in a wide range of styles, even if in many cases, quality was equated with a high degree of alcohol and long periods of ageing in mostly new oak barrels.

Leading Slovenian Producers

Batič ☆☆
Sempas, Vipava Valley.
Miha Batič is firmly in the Slovenian avant-garde, farming organically, favouring high density plantings, and producing white blends after long macerations of the grapes, a technique revived by Gravner across the border in Friuli. The white wines are more successful than the reds, although the Cabernet Franc has personality.

Cotar ☆–☆☆
Gorjansko, Kras region.
Brnako Cotar only has seven hectares, planted on red soils, but makes a wide range of wines, mostly red. The red wines can sometimes be herbaceous, but the Malvasia, Chardonnay, and Sauvignon are admirable.

Dveri-Pax ☆–☆☆
Jarenina. www.dveri-pax.com
Owned by a Benedictine monastery, the firm owns 68 hectares in three different wine regions. The range of wines is broad and whites from Sauvignon and Gewürztraminer seem particularly successful.

Vinska Klet Goriška Brda ☆
Dobrovo, Goriška Brda. www.klet-brda.com
This, a 600-member cooperative in western Slovenia, is the country's largest winery. The best wines are released under the Bagueri label and receive some oak-ageing, but more visible is the Quercus range developed jointly with a British wine consultant. The result is a line of lightly oaked, slightly bland wines. But all the wines are well-made, although there is some greenness evident in some Bordeaux red varieties.

Jeruzalem Ormož ☆
Ormož. www.jeruzalem-ormoz.si
The third largest winery in Slovenia, producing exclusively white wines. The best wines are bottled under as Gold Label, with rich Chardonnay and Sauvignon Blanc leading the range, but the other wines tend to be bland. There's Furmint here, too.

Joannes ☆☆
Malečnik, Podravje. www.joannes.si
A fine source of white wines, such as a lovely appley Pinot Blanc/Chardonnay blend and an exciting Sauvignon Blanc.

Miro ☆☆
Jeruzalem.
A joint venture between Miro Munda and the Polz brothers from Styria. Ten hectares of vines produce only white wines, with some generous oaked blends and exceptionally bright unoaked Pinot Blanc and Sauvignon.

Movia ☆☆–☆☆☆
Dobrovo, Goriška Brda. www.movia.si
Aleš Kristančič has a strong following for the wines he produces from his 18 hectares of Biodynamically farmed vines. Only the white wines are aged in barriques; he prefers traditional large Slovenian casks for his reds. The whites can be earthy, but also have power, extract, and personality, especially the Sauvignon and Rebula.

Edi Simčič ☆☆–☆☆☆
Dobrovo, Goriška Brda.
Edi Simčicic and his son Aleks aim for a more international style, relying heavily on small French oak. Whether such treatment is ideal for Slovenian Sauvignon Blanc or Pinot Gris is up for debate, but the oak-ageing works well with Rebula and with his Bordeaux blend called Duet.

Sutor ☆☆
Vipava Valley. www.sutor.si
The Lavrenčič family have been in the Vipava region for over 500 years. Since 1991 brothers Primož and Mitja have run this small property. The decomposed slate soils seem to give intensity and purity to their fine white wines, of which the most curious is Burja, a blend of Malvasia, Rebula, and Welschriesling.

Vinakoper ☆–☆☆☆
Koper. www.vinakoper.si
This former cooperative owns hundreds of hectares, mostly along the Istrian coast. The principal range is called Capris, but the top wines are bottled under the Capo d'Istria label. The dry unoaked Malvazija is a triumph, as is the plummy Refošk, but the Capo Cabernet can be slightly herbaceous.

Vipava ☆–☆☆
Vipava. www.vipava1894.si
This large private company produces substantial quantities of wine: the Ventus range is essentially varietal and mostly unoaked, Lanthieri seems more cask aged, and the Storia blends are aimed at top local restaurants. The white Zenen is from a local variety, but is a touch sweet for most tastes. But the Malvazija is creamy and lush, and the red Storia is a dense, if rather extracted, Cabernet based blend. So you need to pick and choose.

Serbia & Montenegro

The republic of Serbia was formerly the whole of the eastern landlocked third of Yugoslavia from Hungary to Macedonia. Now its northern section, north of the River Danube, comprises the region of Vojvodina. It used to include two now independent enclaves to the south: Montenegro on the south-eastern coast and Kosovo, squeezed into a circle of mountains between Albania, Macedonia, and Serbia. It has, though, lost a significant southern slice adjacent to Albania, cut away to become Macedonia. The industry is dominated by the Navip company, which has access to 1,700 hectares and numerous wineries; it produces a complete range of wines as well as other drinks. Serbia has been relatively conservative in its grape varieties, with the dark Prokupac as its chief red grape and Smederevka (Smederevo is near Belgrade) as its rarely exciting white, often made in an off-dry style.

Its oldest and most famous vineyard is Zupa, 129-kilometres (80-miles) south of the capital between Svetozarevo and Kruabzevac. Zupsko Crno ("Zupa red") is a blend of Prokupac with the lighter Plovdina. Prokupac is also widely used for rosé (*ruzica*). More and more Sauvignon Blanc, Chardonnay, Cabernet, Merlot, and Gamay is now being planted.

Vojvodina has a history of red winemaking (Carlowitz was once a famous example). Today a wide range of mainly white grapes makes nicely aromatic and balanced wines, the best of them in the Fruska Gora Hills by the Danube north of Belgrade. Gewürztraminer and Sauvignon Blanc can be particularly tasty, though I fear they are less widely planted than Laski Rizling. Further north and east, Subotica and Banat are the areas bordering on Hungary and Romania, both with sandy Great Plain soils and light wines; Subotica growing the Hungarian red Kadarka and white Ezerjó. As for Kosovo, its wine industry was in crisis on account of war and the period of instability that followed. Now that it is precariously independent, there is at least a possibility of some fresh investment.

The hearty, red, Vranac-based wines of Montenegro used to disappear to the Russian market. Since 1990, there have been some haphazard attempts to interest the West in them. They deserve to succeed, as the wines can be balanced, ripe, and quite intense, and appear to take well to wood ageing. There is also an indigenous white called Krsta that gives a rather grassy wine. Most Montenegro wineries have no international presence, other than the state-owned Plantaže, which produces a range of Vranac reds in different styles, as well as some robust barrique-aged blends with a good dose of Syrah.

This southerly end of the country, along the Bosnian coast, counts an unusually good unknown white variety among its potential surprises. I have found a touch of the apricot smell of the Zilavka grape, which makes me wonder whether its lightness is a clever piece of blending.

Tastings in 2008 revealed a panoply of somewhat coarse Serbian wines, of which the best tended to be unpretentious whites from Welschriesling, Sauvignon Blanc, or Chardonnay. Among the more active wineries are Aleksandrovič, Jelič, Kovačevič, Navip, and a new venture called World of Wine in Palič that produces three million bottles of uninspired wine.

Croatia

The 52,000 hectares of Croatia's vineyards are more or less equally divided between two distinct and very different parts: Slavonia, the continental north between Slovenia and Serbia, between the Drava and the Sava rivers; and the coast, from the Istrian peninsula in the north all the way south to Bosnia-Herzegovina, including the Dalmatian coast and its lovely islands.

Slavonia has half the grape hectarage, but its wines have neither the appeal of Slovenia's whites, close though they are,

nor of some of the new wines of Vojvodina to the east. Grapes such as Traminer, Riesling, Welschriesling, and Austria's Zweigelt are grown here.

Croatia's best wines come from the regions of Istria and Dalmatia. Istria grows the same grapes as western Slovenia: Merlot, Cabernet, Pinot Noir, and Teran for reds – the Merlot is particularly good. The white wines include rich Muscats and Malvasias, and Pinot Blanc, the base of the local sparkling wine.

Dalmatia has Yugoslavia's richest array of original characters – mainly red. Plavac Mali (the genetic godfather of California's Zinfandel) is the principal grape, supported by Plavina, Vranac, Babi, Cabernet, Merlot, and Modra Frankija (Blaufränkisch).

Plavac Mali is the most important and interesting of these varieties; rich in tannin, colour, and alcohol, it also has a capacity to age in the medium term. Regular bottlings are the most satisfactory reds to buy on the coast, and it has its moments of glory. One is Postup, a concentrated, sweet red, aged for years in oak, produced on the Pelješac peninsula north of Dubrovnik. A 15-year-old Postup is still bright red, a strange sort of half-port-style with more than a hint of retsina, a big (over 14 degrees), well-balanced and structured wine that would appeal to those who like Recioto from Valpolicella. Dingač, also made from partly dried grapes, is very similar, although these days both wines are more likely to be dry than sweet. Another is Faros from the island of Hvar, a degree lighter than Postup, and softly dry rather than sweet: a full-bodied, warmly satisfying wine without coarseness. The regular quality of coastal red is simply called Plavac. Some find Babič, when aged three or four years, a better wine. It grows only in tiny stone-walled plots close to the sea at Primosten in northern Dalmatia, and this viticultural oddity is protected by enjoying World Heritage status. This lithe red has Burgundian nuances. The dry rosé of the coast, made from several grapes, is called Opol.

White Dalmatian wines are in a minority, but in greater variety than red. The Marastina is the most widespread white variety and has its own appellation at Cara Smokvica. Grk is the oxidized, sherry-like specialty of the island of Korcula. Pošip (which some equate with Furmint) makes heavy but not flat wine. Like the local Malvasia, it often works best as an unoaked wine. Bogdanusa, especially on the islands of Hvar and Brac, can be surprisingly light, crisp, and aromatic. Vugava, grown on the remote island of Vis, is similar. Sometimes they are presented as separate varieties, sometimes in blends. It is hard to discover, in fact, whether some are different names for the same grape. Dalmatia's dessert wines, whether of red or white grapes or both, are known as Prošek. The best tends to be a family matter, nursed in a little cask and given to guests in a thick tumbler with absolutely appropriate pride.

Leading Croatian Producers

Badel 1862 ☆–☆☆
Zagreb. www.badel1862.hr
This is Croatia's largest wine and spirits producer, with an interest in ten dispersed wineries, of which it owns three. Many of the wines, such as the Graševina (with and without oak), are merely competent, but among the highlights are Plavac Mali from Hvar, and very meaty, concentrated Dingač.

Degrassi ☆
Basanija.
Moreno Degrassi owns 15 hectares in the Buje region, from which he produces plump Malvazija, zesty Chardonnay, earthy Refošk, and rather light Cabernet Sauvignon.

Enjingi ☆
Kutjevo.
Graševina may be the mainstay of this 47-hectare estate, but far more interesting is the barrique-aged white blend called Venje, from Graševina, Pinot Gris, Riesling, and other varieties.

Grgic Vina ☆☆
Trstenik, Pelješac.
Although Mike Grgić became famous as a Napa winemaker, he has always been intensely proud of his Croatian roots, and has focused here on indigenous varieties such as Plavac Mali and the white Pošip. But the Californian influence shows through in a generous use of oak.

Katunar ☆–☆☆
Krk. www.katunar.com
Zlahtina is a white variety found only on the island of Krk, and Katunar's version is intensely herbal and nicely concentrated. The best red is the rather leathery but characterful barrique-aged Nigra Riserva, made from three local varieties with a dash of Grenache.

Krauthaker ☆☆
Kutjevo. www.krauthaker.hr
Vlado Krauthaker is one of Croatia's best known winemakers, with 70 hectares at his disposal. Although renowned for his Graševina, the Sauvignon, the single-vineyard Rosenberg Chardonnay, and the delicate white, apricotty Zelenac have far more interest. In exceptional years Krauthaker produces a TBA style wine.

Kutjevo ☆
Kutjevo. www.kutjevo.com
The former cooperative, privatized in 2004, is the region's largest company. A tasting of its white wines from 2006 failed to reveal many wines that rise above the ordinary.

Zlatan Otok ☆☆
Hvar. www.zlatanotok.hr
Zlatan Plenkovi was named Croatian winemaker for the year in 2007, and is best-known for his powerful Plavac Mali. He has also planted a wide range of native white varieties on his 75 hectares of vineyards, and these are the basis for his white blends.

Macedonia

22,400 hectares of mostly red grapes, with the deeply coloured Vranac in centre stage, set the scene. The reds are often spiced up with Cabernet and Merlot, which have come on well here. There seem to be one or two good whites in among the plethora of Smederevka, whose only salvation lies in the soda water so ubiquitously added to it. Some leafy but quite balanced and intense Chardonnay has appeared, and Zilavka can produce a strong dry wine cut with refreshing acidity. Flourishing wineries include Bovin in the Tikves region, Popovs Kula near Skopje, and the renovated Skovin in Skopje.

Romania

The long-established quality and individuality of Romanian wine suffered badly in the socialist era. The country speaks a Latin-based tongue and has both cultural and climatic affinities with France. Once the wines of Moldavia were drunk in Paris. Much of the white wine from the western part of the country, especially the hilly enclave of Transylvania, needed German terms on the labels to serve the needs of Romania's largest Western market. This hardly helped the development or understanding of this still unnecessarily poor and secretive country. And yet Romania has 180,000 hectares of vines, which, since privatization, have been split into smallholdings; this in turn has made it difficult for ambitious investors to purchase substantial vineyards and cultivate them by modern means.

Since 1990, companies such as the British importer Halewood International and the German Reh-Kendermann winery have invested and upgraded existing wineries. There are some French joint ventures as well, equally geared to the export market. Foreign winemakers have been taken on as consultants. The upshot has been the creation of bland, characterless brands, except where private estates with a historic reputation were returned to their pre-Communist owners and developed by their heirs with a view to producing finer wines. Quality is now improving as new plantings and restructured vineyards come on stream. However, exports are still bedeviled by the popular assumption that Romanian wine is extremely cheap. Inexpensive brands produced for European supermarkets may be a profitable path for investors, but they do not moderate the image of Romania as a source of bargain basement wines.

Romania's wine-growing regions surround the central Carpathian mountains. The main centres are Târnave, at 488 metres (1,600 feet) on the Transylvanian plateau to the north; Cotnari to the northeast in Moldavia; Vrancea (including the once-famous Panciu, Odobeşti, Coteşti, and Nicoreşti) to the east; Dealul Mare to the southeast; Murfatlar in the extreme southeast by the Black Sea; and in the south Stefâneşti, Drăgăşani, and Segarcea. In the west, part of the sandy Banat plain to the west of Timişoara (where the 1989 freedom movement began) carries on the viticultural region and traditions of the Great Hungarian Plain. Around Miniş, east of Arad, and Recaş, east of Timişoara, some good red international grapes can be found, including Pinot Noir.

The remainder of the vineyards are stocked with a mixture of international varieties (Merlot and Sauvignon Blanc predominate) and Romania's own white grapes, the Fetească Albă Regală and Tămaîoşă and the red Băbeasca and and Fetească Neagră. Strangely, there is very little Chardonnay. Such as there is can be found mostly in Murfatlar, where it has superb but rarely realized potential.

Cotnari produces the most individual wine, although it has become quite rare. Despite its very northerly position near the Ukraine/Moldovan borders, long, fine, misty autumn conditions permit white grapes to overripen, shrivel, even develop noble rot in some years. Native grapes, Tămaîosă, Românescă Grasă (akin to Furmint and probably the better of the two), Fetească Albă and Francusa are used to produce dessert wines aged in old oak casks.

Târnave produces a reasonable white blend called Perla de Tîrnave and "varietal" Fetească and "Riesling" (regrettably mostly Italian/Welsch/Laski rather than Rhein). Undoubtedly the best whites here are made from the rarer Pinot Gris and Gewürztraminer. Muscat Ottonel produces short-lived but highly scented styles, which may be sweetened. Among a sea of very dull whites and some often good (but make sure it is the less-usual (brut) sparkling wine from Panciu, Vrancea's most notable wine is the pale, acidic, brisk red Băbaescă of Nicoreşti.

The outstanding 64-kilometre (40-mile) stretch of south-facing hill-slopes of the Dealul Mare overlooking the Bucharest plain specializes in Merlot, Cabernet Sauvignon, and the scarcer but potentially fine Pinot Noir. Urlat, Tohani, and Săhăteni are among other names behind which lie some great potential. British investors have created the Prahova winery here, which dominates the export market.

Murfatlar, just inland from Constanta on the Black Sea, is traditionally a white and dessert wine area. Yields are low, fruit quality is intense but, all too often, good white grapes are left to overripen and produce a clumsy, sweetish, dessert-style wine from the likes of Chardonnay and Pinot Gris. There are, in fact, also excellent-quality red grapes in this area.

In the southern vineyards along the Danube tributaries such as the Olt, flowing down from the Carpathians to the river, Stefăneşti and Drăgăsani are better-known for whites, including Sauvignon Blanc; and Segarcea and Sadova for reds including Cabernet Sauvignon. The vineyards of Sâmbureşti are among the best-managed and produce all the classics other than Chardonnay. Entry into the European Union has facilitated an injection of subsidies aimed at modernizing vineyards and wineries, but it has also put a halt to extensive new plantings. The challenge for Romania's wine industry is whether to aim for the cheap international market, or to focus more on its indigenous varieties and historic individuality. Perhaps both can be accomplished simultaneously?

Leading Romanian Producers

Cotnari ☆–☆☆
Cotnari. www.cotnari.ro
Founded in 1948, the company was privatized in 2000 and controls 1,100 hectares. It still specializes in sweet and semi-sweet wines and maintains stocks of older wines for sale.

Davino ☆☆
Ceptura. www.davino.ro
Dan Balaban created this 50-hectare domaine in 1992 and although he has some international varieties such as Sauvignon Blanc, the primary emphasis is on excellent blends, red and white, featuring local varieties such as the Fetească family. The top wine, produced only in outstanding vintages, is grandly called Flamboyant, and blends Fetească Neagră with Cabernet and Merlot; it maintains the delicacy that marks the more refined Romanian reds.

Murfatlar ☆–☆☆
Basarabi. www.murfatlar.com
This immense cooperative, with 3,000 hectares, was privatized in 2001 and controls a large share of the domestic market. The use of French and British consultants has improved quality at the top end, with the best wines labelled Trei Hectare. This range includes a creamy, lively, barrel-fermented Chardonnay and a vibrant Fetească Neagră, with pronounced sour-cherry flavours.

Prahova Valley ☆
Prahova, Dealu Mare. www.prahova-wine.com
The principal brand of Halewood International, the British company that has been involved in Romanian wine production for many years. The firm, which owns 400 vineyards in various regions, focuses on international varietal brands such as Prahova Valley and Cherry Tree Hill.

Recaş ☆
Recaş. www.recaswine.ro
In 1998 Briton Philip Cox founded this substantial property in western Romania, building new underground cellars in 2003. Its labels include La Putere and Castle Rock, but Cox is keenly interested in new clones of Pinot Noir, which may provide wines of greater character.

Carl Reh ☆–☆☆
Oprisor. www.carlreh.ro
The wine-centered Reh family from Germany have been active in Romania for some time, and now own 400 hectares of which about 100 are organically farmed. Their brands include River Route, Val Duna, and La Cetate, the latter made solely from estate grown fruit. The Cetate wines are lightly oaked and have varietal typicity.

Serve ☆–☆☆
Ceptura, Dealu Mare. www.serve.ro
Wine producer Comte Guy Tyrel de Poix, who owns Comte Peraldi in his native Corsica, founded this company in 1994, though he only got into his stride in the early 2000s after a new winery was completed. Terra Romana is the principal range, featuring both native and international varieties. Quality is steady, and production now exceeds one million bottles.

Prince Stirbey ☆☆
Drăgăsani. www.stirbey.com
Ileana Kripp is the grand-daughter of the last Prince Stirbey and has reclaimed the estate that has been in the family since the eighteenth century. The family also owned the country's largest nurseries, thus conserving many indigenous varieties, in which the property now specializes. With only 25 hectares of vineyards, the Kripps can maintain control of the whole wine producing process, which may explain why quality is well above average.

Vinarte ☆☆
Bucharest. www.vinarte.com
With 450 hectares in three different wine regions, Tuscan producer Fabio Abisetti, who founded Vinarte in 1998, can offer a wide range of varieties. Most of the wines are red, although the barrique-aged Cabernet and Merlot can show both herbaceousness and earthiness. Stylistic issues apart, the standard of winemaking is high, but Fetească Neagră takes a back seat to international varieties.

Bulgaria

Of all the countries in Central and Eastern Europe, Bulgaria was the most adept at reprogramming its wine industry to earn Western currency. In the late 1970s, Bulgarian wine had become standard fare in several Western markets, since up to 85 per cent of production was exported. The industry succeeded by offering, with the help of generous government subsidies, excellent value for money in familiar flavours – above all in rich Merlot and well-hyped Cabernet Sauvignon, which satisfied palates brought up on red Bordeaux. Post-Communist privatization put an end to that, and frequent changes of government (and policy direction), and the collapse of the country's banking system, led to a decline in the wine industry.

Wine is a major preoccupation of the whole country. Over 150,000 hectares are planted with vineyards, about 60 per cent of them with red vines, but some 35,000 hectares have been abandoned and are no longer suitable for wine production. After Bulgaria's integration into the European Union in 2007, the vineyard area was capped at 153,000 hectares. Both Cabernet Sauvignon (19,500 hectares) and Merlot (19,000 hectares) have been present in Bulgaria for well over a century and their plantings are expanding. The rest is the insipid Pamid and such other traditional varieties as Gamza (the Hungarian Kadarka), Melnik, and Mavrud, and a little Pinot Noir and Gamay.

The white vineyard caters much more for everyday local drinking and distillation – almost half is the lightly peachy Georgian grape, Rkatsiteli, backed up by Ugni Blanc, Rizling (here confusingly often referred to as Riesling), Red Misket, Dimiat (or Smederevka), and Muscat Ottonel, and growing plantings of Chardonnay, Rhein Riesling, Sauvignon Blanc, and Aligoté alongside small areas of Tamianka and Gewürztraminer. Of late, progress in the control of the vinification process has conclusively demonstrated that the better white varieties are as much at home here as their red counterparts. Chardonnay is beginning to show its natural superiority, with and without the use of new oak casks.

There are five main wine regions. The three major ones are grouped around the mountain range of the Stara Planina, which forms the central backbone of the country from Serbia to the Black Sea. The fourth is perched in the high central valleys. Fifth is a small region tucked away around Melnik, on the southwest border. Conditions are cooler in the northern region, but both north and south can produce good, ripe, raw material. The European Union is in the process of recognizing some 51 appellations, but only two subregions have thus far won official approval. Consequently, the labelling and appellation system for Bulgarian wines is still a work in progress.

A long-term consequence of privatization has been a breakdown of the tidy system of grape delivery, which existed when vineyards were tied to a specific winery. There is now something of a free-for-all on the grape market each autumn. A great number of vineyards are falling out of production altogether. Many wineries, where they could afford it, have had to subsidize growers throughout the year in order to try to ensure that they would have a right to buy the resultant crop.

Many of the new Bulgarian wine producers are revamped cooperatives or large investments aimed at churning out inexpensive varietal wines or blends with little national character. However, at the same time there is a growing handful of serious-minded producers starting boutique wineries and planting organic or Biodynamic vineyards. That is not to say their wines are as good as their aspirations, but at least it gives the world a reason to take Bulgarian wines seriously.

Eastern Region

This cool region, between the mountains and the Black Sea, specializes in white wines, sparkling wines, and brandy. Subregions include Varna, Shumen, Preslav, Khan Krum, and Targovishte. It includes many noted subregions, notably Varna, Shumen, Targovishte, and Razgad. The main grapes are Riesling, Rkatziteli, Aligoté, Chardonnay, Misket, Muscat Ottonel, Ugni Blanc, Dimiat, and Fetiaska.

Northern Region

The northern region has the River Danube as its northern boundary. It is known for its quality red wines – the main varieties being Gamza (the Kadarka of Hungary), Cabernet Sauvignon, and Merlot.

The former state winery of Russe (now merged with Boyar) on the Danube's banks controls a lot of potentially good red grapes from all over the region. Subregions include Suhindol, best-known for its Merlot and other reds, and Lyaskovets, which shows promise for Chardonnay.

Southern Region

The southern region grows Cabernet and some Pinot Noir and Merlot, but also makes some well-known traditional wines such as Mavrud, Bulgaria's pride: a substantial, dark, Rhône-like wine that often needs long ageing. The region around Plovdiv has the best reputation for this variety. Another traditional grape variety, Pamid, makes a rather pallid everyday wine. Whichever way you look at it, however, the region's greatest potential lies more in the richly ripe Merlots of Stambolovo, Liubimetz, and in the Sakar mountain region.

Southwest Region

This is a very small and distinct region on the Yugoslav border across the Rhodope mountains in the southwest of the country. Best-known is the Melnik wine from Harsovo. Bulgarians have the greatest respect for Melnik; its red wine, they say, is so concentrated that you can carry it in a handkerchief. It needs five years' ageing and will last for 15.

Sub-Balkan Region

This is the narrow strip south of the Balkan range, which includes the famous Sungurlare valley where the Red Misket is grown, and the Valley of Roses (the source of attar of roses), which specializes in Muscats. A fair proportion of Rkatsiteli is also grown in this region where it can produce cool, delicate, white peach aromas.

Leading Bulgarian Producers

Belvedere ☆
Sofia. www.belvedere.bg
This French-owned company owns a number of brands, including Menada Trinity, Oriahovitza, Sakar, and Domaine Katarynza. The wines can be well-made but lack some character.

Boyar Estates ☆–☆☆
Sofia. www.domaineboyar.com
This important company has been through many transformations over the years, absorbing existing wineries and creating new ones. The range is inevitably a complex one, but Boyar has become best-known for creating the Blueridge brand, although the wines are far from impressive. Some Reserve wines, however, including the Domaine Boyar Merlot, have been lush and peppery.

Damianitza ☆☆
Struma Valley. www.dimianitza.bg
Philip Harmandjiev, a force for progress in Bulgaria, owns a winery that was privatized in 1997 and handles fruit mostly from the Melnik region. No Man's Land is the basic range, recalling the vacant strips of land that once separated Bulgaria from its southern neighbours. ReDark is a Cabernet-based blend that spends ten months in small oak barrels. Perhaps the most interesting wines are those under the Uniqato label, which features only local grapes aged in Bulgarian oak. Current production is around two million bottles.

Enira ☆☆
Plovdiv. www.bessavalley.com
The brainchild of St-Emilion proprietor Stephan von Neipperg, who became convinced of the potential of this area

for good quality wines at a moderate price. Together with manager Marc Dworkin, he planted vineyards from 2001 onwards, and the first vintage was 2004. The wines are Merlot based, but Neipperg does not go overboard with new oak.

Initial vintages have been packed with fruit, almost to excess, but rather high in alcohol. Nonetheless they are modern-style wines a world away from the vapid offerings of 20 years ago.

Maxxima ☆☆
Bessa Valley.
A boutique winery with a growing reputation for sophisticated Chardonnay, Merlot, Cabernet Sauvignon, and Gamza.

Edoardo Miroglio ☆
Elenovo. www.emiroglio-wine.com
A Piedmontese textile magnate founded this winery in 2002 and now owns 250 hectares. The basic range is Sant'Illia, and the better wines carry the owner's initials, E M. Releases from 2006 and 2007 were heavy-handed, but these are early days.

Santa Sarah ☆–☆☆
Nova Zagora.
A thoroughly modern winery in central-southern Bulgaria founded by German-based wine importer Ivo Genowski. The 40 hectares of vineyards are being converted to Biodynamism, and Genowski is winning a good reputation for his Cabernet, Merlot, and Mavrud.

Svishtov ☆
Svishtov. www.svishtov-winery.com
A privatized cooperative, Svishtov's claim to fame is that about half its 430 hectares of vineyards are planted with Cabernet Sauvignon. Unfortunately the red wine is herbaceous, while the Cabernet Rosé, a big seller, is extremely simple. But Chardonnay can be good.

Telish ☆–☆☆
Sofia. www.telishwinecellars.com
Privatized in 1996, this old winery has succeeded in hiring Michel Rolland as its consultant. It controls some 550 hectares, and the best wines are Bordeaux varietals coming from its vineyards in the south, which are bottled under the Castra Rubra label. Concentrated and succulent wines with good potential, justifying Rolland's interest in the property.

Terra Tangra ☆–☆☆
Sakar. www.terratangra.com
Modern style wines, based mostly on French varieties grown near the Turkish border, with a generous use of barrique ageing for the top ranges such as Grand Reserva.

Pulden winery, Perushtitsa

Former Russian Empire

The former Soviet Union was the world's third-largest wine producer, although it also imported large quantities of inexpensive wines from eastern Europe. But there have been a number of hiccups in its progress. The first came under Gorbachev, who in a drive against alcohol uprooted half the nation's vineyards, and ended up instead with millions of vodka-drinking alcoholics. Then with the post-communist break-up of the Soviet Union, former wine-producing republics such as Moldova, Armenia, and Georgia broke away.

A glimpse of past glories appeared in London in 1990 at an auction by Sotheby's of dessert wines from the private estates of the tsar's and other great families in the Crimea. The Muscat wines of the imperial Massandra estate were outstanding among a variety of very well-made old "ports", "sherries", "Madeiras" and even "Cahorski". A 1966 White Muscat was still sumptuous and fresh in 2008.

Under Vladimir Putin's rule, the rapidly expanding Russian middle classes (not to mention the super-rich oligarchs and their hangers-on) showed more interest in fashionable imported wines than in Russian wines, which were mostly of mediocre quality. The thirst for French, Italian, and American wines was so considerable that when in 2006 Putin banned all imports of Georgian and Moldovan wines – allegedly on sanitary grounds – the Russian drinking public was unfazed.

Nonetheless there is a sluggish but growing interest in domestic wines. With the loss of the wines from former republics already mentioned, and those from the surprisingly large vineyards of the former Central Asian republics, Russian investors have looked instead to promising growing regions such as Krasnodar and Rostov, where French varieties are being planted to supplement the obscure indigenous vines. Labels such as Château Le Grand Vostock and Vina Vedernikoff may be worth looking out for in the future.

Moldova

President Brezhnev would come to Moldova to while away a weekend among not only the long-lived local Cabernet Sauvignons, but also some of the finest Bordeaux captured from the Germans during the last war. One look at the dark-soiled, rolling vineyards over fine limestone subsoils, and one taste of the immature wines, are enough to show that this could be a first class producer.

The climate, moderated by the nearby Black Sea, provides close to ideal growing conditions in the 147,000 hectares of vineyards. (However, by 2008 only 102,000 hectares were still in production, and about 15 per cent of them were planted with undesirable hybrids.) Bottles of the fragrant Cabernet blend, "Negru de Purkar", leave no one in doubt of Moldova's potential. Native grape varieties are similar to those of Romania, and there are substantial plantings of Aligoté, Rkatsiteli, Sauvignon Blanc, Chardonnay, Merlot, Cabernet Sauvignon, and Pinot Noir. White wine represents approximately 70 per cent of production.

Given the poverty of the region, its wine industry is surprisingly energetic. But Moldova was dealt a crippling blow when in 2006 the Russians vindictively banned imports of its wines. Overnight 75 per cent of Moldava's production, admittedly at the sweeter end of the spectrum, lost its traditional home. The Moldovans have responded by seeing this as an incentive to step up their efforts to export their wines, but that remains an uphill struggle, despite a vigorous and intelligent marketing association.

Leading Moldovan Producers

Acorex ☆
Cahul. www.acorex.net
Founded in 1999, this company controls 3,000 hectares and releases wines under a number of export labels, such as Albastrela and Legenda. Its most promising, and well-packaged, line is an inexpensive varietal range called Taking Root.

Bostavan ☆
Chisinau. www.bostavan.md
Bostavan takes pride in its semi-sweet barrique-aged red called Black Doctor, a blend of Cabernet, Merlot, and Saperavi, and tastier and better balanced than one might expect from this style.

Dionysus Mereni ☆
Merenii-Noi. www.dionysis-mereni.com
The best wines, from French grapes as well as local varieties such as Rara Neagra, are bottled under the Rariret label. Quality is patchy, with some stewed wines. Riesling Icewine and a botrytis Riesling have attracted attention.

Lion Gri ☆
Chisinau. www.lion-gri.com
Founded in 1997, this company's wines, all 16 million bottles per annum, are aimed entirely at the export market.

Purcari ☆–☆☆
Purcari. www.purcari.md
Founded in 1827, this venerable company was purchased in 2003 by Victor Bostan, the owner of Bostavan (q.v.). Its 300 hectares are planted on gentle terraced slopes, which are best suited to red wines. Barrrique-aged Chardonnay and Cabernet can be good, but Purcari is best known for fragrant Negru de Purcari, a traditional blend of Cabernet, Rara Neagra, and Saperavi, aged in oak casks of varying sizes.

Chateau Vartely ☆
Orhei. www.vartely.md
New owners took over in 2004 and have consolidated an impressive range of mostly varietal wines. Quality is satisfactory rather than exciting, with occasional exceptions such as the lush Muscat Ottonel Icewine made in 2006.

Armenia

In Soviet times there were 37,000 hectares planted here, with at least 200 grape varieties, many of them indigenous. Of these the most esteemed was probably Areni, which grows near the village of that name. A number of older vintages tasted in the mid-2000s were either nondescript or tired, with the exception of some fortified wines in the style of French *vins doux naturels*. Armenia was, and probably is, still better known for its excellent brandies than for its wines.

Georgia

Though tiny in relation to Russia, Georgia has a far more ancient and original wine culture, with at least 500 indigenous vine varieties. Its most famous wine region is Kakhetia, east of Tbilisi, where the climate is at its most continental. The princely estate of Tsinandali was developed in the nineteenth century to make the finest Kakhetian wines, famous for fragrance and bite – and preferred by the poet Pushkin to burgundy.

Today the area under vine is 61,500 hectares, which sounds impressive but is in fact half the area of 20 years ago. Three-quarters of these vineyards are within Kakhetia, but Imeretia, with a more humid climate closer to the Black Sea coast, also has important and venerable winemaking traditions, with scores of indigenous grape varieties.

Throughout Georgia private farmers can still be found using methods of pre-classical antiquity. The *kvevri*, a clay fermenting jar buried in the ground, is still found in many properties. Its strongly tannic produce is not for fine palates. Georgia is also the home of a flourishing sparkling wine industry. Most of the wine is sweet, which is the preferred national taste.

The early years of independence were not a good time for the wine industry, although brandy production flourished. Under the Soviet system all bottlings had been done outside the republic. Thus Georgia was left with some excellent vineyards but very limited production facilities. Attempts at joint ventures foundered as investors gave up, deterred by incompetent management and corruption. Russia supplied many willing consumers, despite the fact that some Georgian wines, when analysed in the early 2000s, were found to be fraudulent. Then in 2006 Russia imposed a ban on imports of Georgian wines, dealing a heavy blow to the industry.

In spite of these obstacles the industry continues to modernize itself, with help from large outside investors such as Pernod-Ricard. Special labels are created for western markets, which has led to bewildering profusion of brands, many of them produced by the same company. Some excellent wines are made by Teliani Valley, Telavi (including a remarkable clay-fermented, barrique-aged Saperavi), Old Tbilisi and Tamada (both labels of the Georgian Wine and Spirits Company), Kindzmarauli, Orovela, and Tblivino.

Mediterranean

The warm summers and mild winters of the eastern Mediterranean climate make it an ideal region for viticulture, which has been practiced for centuries in various countries. But cultural factors have also come into play, such as Islamic cultures that may have tolerated but did not actively encourage wine consumption. This is why Greece, for example, has its indigenous grape varieties and wine styles, whereas those of North Africa were for the most part imposed by French colonial masters.

Greece

Greece as a producer of serious, varied, good-by-exacting-standards, lovely-to-drink-not only-when-you're-there, wines takes a bow in this edition of the *Companion*. Her wine-list today is unrecognizable to occasional visitors who have never got past retsina before.

The ancient Greeks were responsible for colonizing the Mediterranean and the Black Sea with the vine, exporting their wines in exchange for Egyptian grain, Spanish silver, and Caucasian timber. In the Middle Ages, the Peloponnese and Crete were valued sources of Malmsey sack for northern Europe. Her wine industry, though, was almost shut down by the occupying Turks for so long that not much remained when Greece was liberated in the nineteenth century – except a full hand of interesting grape varieties.

The largely alkaline (in places, volcanic) soils and multifarious microclimates of Greece make her a natural country of the vine. With about 130,000 hectares of grapes (not all for wine) she is a major producer. After Greece entered the EU, new systems of regulation came into effect and had a positive influence on wine quality. So did generous Brussels grants. Under the earlier primitive conditions, with hot fermentations, the best qualities that could be produced were all sweet wines. The Greek taste remained faithful to what appears to be an ancient tradition of adding pine resin during fermentation to make retsina. It goes too well with Greek cooking to be ignored, but today demand for this wine is falling, except among tourists, as the national palate turns increasingly to the fine Greek wines,

mostly from indigenous varieties, of which there are 300. A handful of producers attempt to make a high quality retsina, in order to show that such a wine can exist.

At present, Greek wine can usefully be divided into national brands (usually blends); retsina, and other traditional and country wines for uncritical first-year drinking; and wines from defined areas now controlled by an appellation system in accordance with EU law. There are 28 such areas. The industry has been dominated by cooperatives and by large companies such as Boutari and Tsantali, but since the 1990s there has been a growth of small, high-quality estates run by owners and winemakers with international experience. All this is positive, but producers, large and small alike, have to contend with declining domestic consumption. The Peloponnese has more than half of Greece's vineyards and produces more than a third of her wine.

Patras, at the mouth of the Gulf of Corinth, is the main wine centre, with four appellations: Muscat, Muscat of Rio, Mavrodaphne, and plain Patras. Mavrodaphne can be the most notable of these: a sweet, dark red wine of up to 16 degrees of alcohol, something in the style of Recioto of Valpolicella, much improved by long maturing. (The excellent bottling from Spiliopoulos called Nyx has a strong resemblance to old tawny port.) Plain Patras white is for drinking young. Two other appellations of the Peloponnese are interesting: the region of Nemea for strong red with real ageing potential made from the Agiorgitiko (St George) grape, and Mantinia for a delicate, spicy white.

The vineyards of northern Greece, from Thrace in the east through Macedonia to Epirus, appear to have most potential for quality. Its most important appellations are: Naoussa (west of Thessaloniki) for potent though balanced and nicely tannic red; Amynteio, at 610 metres (2,000 feet) in the mountains of Macedonia, producing lighter red; and Zitsa (near Joannina in Epirus) for a light mountain white from the Debina grape. The most important recent development was the planting of the Sithonian peninsula, the middle one of the three fingers of Halkidiki, with Cabernet and other grapes, by the firm of Carras (q.v.). The island of Crete is second to the Peloponnese in hectarage, but only third in production (Attica has far more productive vineyards). Crete has four local appellations, all for dark and more or less heavy and sweet reds: Daphnes, Arhanes, Sitia, and Peza – Peza being the seat of the island's biggest producer, its cooperative. The grapes are all indigenous: Kotsifali, Mandelaria, and Liatiko.

Attica (including mainland Boetia and the island of Euboea) is Greece's most productive wine area, overwhelmingly for retsina, but there are now an increasing number of high quality estates – Hatzimichelalis, Evharis, Semeli, and Strofilia among them. Savatiano is the principal grape from which retsina is made, but other important varieties grown in the Attica region include Assyrtiko, Cabernet Sauvignon, and Syrah.

Next in importance for hectarage and quality comes Cephalonia, which, with the other Ionian (western) islands musters around 10,000 hectares. Cephalonia is known for its dry white Robola, its red Mavrodaphne, and its Muscat. Zakinthos to the south makes a white Verdea. The central mainland region of Thessaly also has 10,000 hectares of vineyards, but only one important appellation: Rapsani, a middleweight red from Mount Olympus, plus those of Messenikola and Anhialos.

The wines of the Aegean islands, the Dodecanese and the Cyclades, have more renown, notably the pale-gold Muscat of Samos, the luscious *vin santo* and fresh, vigorous, dry white of the volcanic Santorini, from Europe's most punishing vineyards, the Muscat of Lemnos, and the sweet Malvasia and Muscat of Rhodes. Malvasia is grown on many islands and is often their best product. Other island wines with esoteric reputations are the very dark red Páros and the Santa Mavra of Levkas, whose grape, the Vertzani, is unknown elsewhere. Greek wine is advancing so fast that visitors should take every opportunity to try the latest bottlings.

A scene at a Greek taverna

Leading Greek Producers

Achaia-Clauss ☆

Patras.

Once one of the the biggest and most famous Greek wine houses, but it is now experiencing fierce competition from other expanding producers. Demestica is the best known wine. Otherwise it produces a large variety of dry and sweet wines from vineyards in the Peloponnese and Crete, and Mavrodaphne.

Alpha ☆☆–☆☆☆

Amyndeon, Macedonia. 33 ha. www.alpha-estate.gr

The vineyards are 600-metres (1,950-feet) up in the hills, and planted with a range of Greek and international varieties. Alpha One is a very concentrated if tannic blend of Montepulciano and Mavrodaphne, while the estate blend is from Syrah, Xinomavro, and Merlot, a mix that works surprisingly well. Alpha made a stab at Pinot Noir in 2005 and produced a good spicy wine that nonetheless lacked varietal character.

Antonopoulos ☆☆–☆☆☆

Patras. 23 ha. www.antonopoulos-vineyards.com

Established by Constantine Antonopoulos, who died in a car crash in 1994, this up-and-coming estate is now run by his cousins. The production from its own vineyards is supplemented by grapes purchased from a further 50 hectares that are farmed by the Antonopoulous team. Elegant white wines from Chardonnay and local varieties such as Moschofilero. The winery also excels at oaked Cabernet Sauvignon.

Biblia Hora ☆☆–☆☆☆

Kavala, Macedonia. 35 ha.

A venture founded in 2001 by two of Greece's top winemakers: Vassilis Tasktsarlis and Evanghelos Gerovassilou. The range is eclectic: delicious Assyrtiko white, as well as a blend of Assyrtiko and Sauvignon; a pure Agiorgitiko, aged in oak, and a new-oaked blend of Cabernet and Merlot, an opulent pure Merlot, and a new oaked Cabernet Sauvignon. A convincing offering, with the reds marginally more successful than the whites.

J Boutari & Son ☆–☆☆☆

Naoussa, Thessaloniki. www.boutari.gr

Long-established producer that has grown rapidly in recent years, covering several appellations with new wineries at each locality. The main winery is in Naoussa specializing in Naoussa wines and obtaining good results from Xinomavro.

There are five other wineries, including facilities on Santorini and Crete. The range is enormous, with 40 different wines, and in addition to the well-known top Grande Reserve red from Naoussa, there are excellent wines from Santorini, including a gorgeous vin santo, and varietal wines from indigenous varieties.

Cambas ☆☆

Kantza, near Athens.

Another long-established producer, founded in 1882, with wineries in Kantza and Mantinia. It produces a wide range of table and sparkling wines, as well as ouzo and brandy. Since 1992, Cambas has been owned by Boutari, but it is run independently. The flowery Mantinia is excellent, but the Nemea Réserve may be a touch too tannic for some modern tastes.

Domaine Carras ☆☆

Halkidiki, Macedonia. 475 ha. www.portocarraswines.gr

Developed primarily in the 1960s, this major organic estate was created by John Carras with advice from Professor Emile Peynaud of Bordeaux. The well-known Château Carrasis a blend of Cabernets Sauvignon and Franc with Merlot and Limnio, matured in French oak. There are also some varietal wines from Limnio and Syrah.

In the 1990s, this huge estate and tourist complex ran into financial difficulties, and was sold in 1999. Quality has declined since the family relinquished control.

Driopi ☆☆

Koutsi, Nemea. 9 ha.

Under the same ownership as Tselepos (q.v.), the first vintage here was in 2003. Rich Agiorgitiko reds, and a Reserve aged in new French oak, which obscures the fleshy fruitiness of the regular version.

Gaia ☆☆☆

Nemea. 7 ha. www.gaia-wines.gr

Founded in 1994, this estate has acquired a high reputation for its Thalassitis, a Santorini white from very old vines, which comes in oaked and (preferable) unoaked versions. The Agiorgitiko rosé is wonderfully fruity, and there is a superb Nemea called Gaia Estate, which needs time to shed its youthful tannins. A new addition to the range, since 2006, is S, an elegant and lively blend of Agiorgitiko and Syrah.

Gentilini ☆☆

Minies, Cephalonia. www.gentilini.gr

A small family estate, the pioneer of quality on the island, owned by Marianna Cosmetatos, producing fine wines from the indigenous Robola. A cask-aged Sauvignon/Chardonnay (Gentilini Fumé) is also produced, and the top red wine is blend of Agiorgitiko and Syrah.

Gerovassiliou ☆☆☆

Epanomi, Macedonia. 40 ha. www.gerovassiliou.gr

The former oenologist at Carras has his own estate making outstanding whites from Malagousia, Viognier, and Chardonnay. The reds are steadily improving, with various blends employing Syrah, as well as a pure Syrah.

Hatzidakis ☆☆–☆☆☆

Pyrgos, Santorini. www.hatzidakiswines.gr

A small winery that produces wonderfully racy Assyrtiko from Santorini, as well as *vin santo* and a rare red wine from the island's Mavrotragano grape.

Hatzimichalis ☆☆

Atlantes, Athens-Lamia. 180 ha. www.hatzimichalis.gr

An 80-hectare private estate owned by Dimitri Hatzimichalis, which produces a range of wines from indigenous and international varieties. Using purchased grapes as well as his own vineyards, Hatzimichalis now produces around one million bottles. Overall, the reds are better than the whites, but Laas, from Athiri, Robola, and Assyrtiko, has crispness, vigour, and length.

Kir-Yanni ☆☆–☆☆☆☆
Naoussa. 50 ha. www.kiryanni.gr
After Yannis Boutari left his family winery in 1997, he brought his skills to this estate, working with grapes such as Xynomavro and Merlot. The blackberry-scented Syrah is a touch austere, but the Xynomavro is a fine tannic, leathery wine with more than a passing resemblance to Nebbiolo. Particularly successful is Dyo Elies, which blends Syrah, Merlot, and Xinomavro into a bracing but harmonious whole.

Kourtakis ☆–☆☆
Markopoulo, Attica. No vineyards. www.kourtakis.com
A family merchant house using the brand names of Kouros and Calligas, and producing three million cases. As well as a successful Mavrodaphne of Patras, they also produce large quantities of the international best-selling retsina from the Savatiano grape of Attica. Given the volumes produced, quality is sound.

Domaine Costa Lazaridi ☆☆–☆☆☆☆
Drama, Macedonia. 200 ha. www.domaine-lazaridi.gr
Main label is Amethystos, red, white, and rosé. The red has a savoury, herbal character that is very individual. There is also a range of varietal wines, Greek and international, under the Château Julia label. Michel Rolland has been a consultant for the estate since 2004.

Mercouri ☆–☆☆☆☆
Koralahori, west Peloponnese. 18 ha. www.mercouri.gr
An old private family estate with an interesting wine museum. The main production is outstanding reds made from Mavrodaphne and from the Refosco grape, taken from Friuli in 1870. Good white Roditis, too, and a rather heavy Viognier.

Oenoforos ☆☆
Selinous, near Corinth. www.oenoforos.gr
A small, recently developed estate, now partly owned by Kourtakis (q.v.), with a gravity-fed winery, producing fresh, long-lived whites (especially the Roditis called Asprolithi) from very high vineyards overlooking the Gulf of Corinth. Very different in style is the rich, oaky Chardonnay.

Pavlidis ☆☆
Drama. 60ha. www.ktima-pavlidis.gr
Founded in 1998, Pavlidis is best-known for its Thema range (a good Syrah/Agiorgitoko red, and a tangy Sauvignon/Assyrtiko white), as well as varietal wines from Chardonnay, Assyrtiko, and, unusually, Tempranillo.

Samos Cooperative ☆☆–☆☆☆☆
Malagari, Samos. www.samoswine.gr
With two wineries, this union of about 300 growers produces remarkable Muscat wines that are either naturally sweet or fortified, and exported widely. Top of the range, the Samos Nectar, made from sun-dried grapes, is rich and golden, maturing continuously and darkening in bottle.

Semeli ☆☆
Stamata, Attica. 28 ha. ww.semeliwines.com
This small estate northeast of Athens has its vineyards at a height of 450 metres above the plains of Attica. Decent Savatiano and Roditis whites, and fine, tobacco-scented reds from Agiorgitiko and Cabernet Sauvignon. The flagship wine, Château Semeli, is a Bordeaux blend.

Sigalas ☆☆☆
Santorini. 23 ha. www.sigalas-wine.gr
Delicious, biting Assyrtiko from old vines, but the barrique-aged version neutralizes the fruit. Sigalas also produce the island's red specialty, Mavrotragano, as well as a magnificent wine from sun-dried Mandilaria grapes and a sumptuous and highly concentrated *vin santo*.

Skouras ☆☆☆
Ghymno, Nemea. www.skouras.gr
Owned by George Skouras, a highly imaginative and talented French-trained winemaker producing magnificent Agiorgitiko and Nemea, but also experimenting successfully with Cabernet, Chardonnay, and Viognier. His top red is usually Megas Oenos, which is a blend of Agiorgitiko with Cabernet: a cherryish wine with a distinct oak influence.

Strofilia ☆☆
Anavissos, Attica.
Exciting red, white, and rosé from an estate near to Cape Sounion. The three proprietors, all engineers, also run an excellent wine bar, Strofilia, near the centre of Athens. In recent years, production has expanded greatly, and, with three wineries in different regions, Strofilia is no longer a boutique winery. But quality remains high.

Tsantali ☆☆
Aghios Pavlos, Halkidiki. 200 ha. www.tsantali.gr
Second-generation Macedonian merchant house, which made its name with Olympic ouzo. Various appellation areas supply a wide range of wines, such as the fine Rapsani and Agiorgitiko from Nemea. Acceptable versions of international varieties (Chardonnay, Merlot, Syrah) are also being made.

Tselepos ☆☆–☆☆☆☆
Riza Tegeas, Arcadia. 35 ha. www.tselepos.gr
Founded in 1989, the vineyards are planted at over 750 metres (2,440 feet). This suits varieties such as Chardonnay and Gewürztraminer well, and, surprisingly, Merlot and Cabernet can also be brought to ripeness with impressive results in the bottle. But the Mantinia Moschofilero is a useful reminder of how excellent white wines from indigenous varieties can be.

Vaeni Naoussa Cooperative ☆–☆☆
Naoussa. www.vaeni-naoussa.gr
Large cooperative in western Macedonia vinifying 50 per cent of Naoussa production; mainly strong, above-average red wines from the Xynomavro grape. Once rather coarse, the wines have in recent years become softer and more mellow.

Cyprus

Wine culture in Cyprus, most easterly of the Mediterranean islands, has had seismic changes in fortune over the centuries. Cypriot wines were famed throughout classical, Byzantine, and early medieval times. In a bizarre international tasting known as the "Battle of Wines" at the French court, Cyprus was the outright winner. Then came three centuries of Islamic rule, and production went into dramatic decline. British government from 1878 brought stability – and a market. In more recent times it focused on the lower end of the market, selling vast quantities to the Soviet bloc and selling grape concentrate to the British. These markets are all but extinct, so Cyprus's wine industry has had to smarten up.

Modern Cyprus has no great range of wines to offer, but what she does she does well, producing low-cost sherry imitations, both dry and sweet, modelled on the Spanish (the term "Cyprus sherry" can no longer appear on the labels of wines for sale in the EU); smooth, dry, red and white table wines; and her own extremely luscious liqueur wine, Commandaria, the modern successor to the classical wine Nama, made of grapes dried on the vine, which was so highly prized over 2,500 years ago. Commandaria is to Cyprus what Constantia is to South Africa, or Tokaji is to Hungary.

Cyprus has, until very recently, been intensely conservative about grape varieties. Having never been afflicted with phylloxera, and intending to stay untainted, she spurned new-fangled introductions and planted only three grapes: Mavro the black, Xynisteri the white (which accounts for the vast majority of planting), and Muscat of Alexandria. Today there is a small but increasing volume of varietal wine made from international grapes, and wines from specific regions of the island. In 1990, after some 30 years of strictly controlled trials with non-native grapes, 12 were made available for commercial cultivation. Among them Grenache, Carignan, Syrah, Merlot, Cabernet Franc, and Cabernet Sauvignon now produce varietal wines; Malvasia Grossa and Palomino (of Jerez) are usually used in blends with the indigenous white varieties. The quest for better wine has renewed interest in the island's less-planted native varieties, the black Maratheftico and the less interesting Ophtalmo: the former is difficult to cultivate but can produce outstanding wines. The traditional varieties can also produce good wines; Mavro particularly from high altitude sites, provided its yield is restricted. Xynisteri has to be harvested most carefully, as the grapes are prone to oxidization.

All the island's vineyards lie on the south, mainly limestone, slopes of the Troodos Mountains, between 240 and nearly 1,500 metres (800–5,000 feet), the best located above 990 metres (3,250 feet), some on soils of igneous origin. Since 1990, total grape hectarage has decreased from a peak of over 50,000 hectares to 15,000 as the industry comes to terms with overproduction and a declining export market for its fortified and basic table wines.

Most Cyprus wine is still made by a handful of very large wineries in the coastal towns of Limassol and Paphos (convenient for export), but, as part of the quality drive, the Cypriot government has supported the building of small, modern wineries within the vineyard areas themselves.

The island's most distinctive wine, Commandaria, was given full legal protection of origin and production in 1993. Its delimited region comprises 14 of the higher-altitude wine-producing villages on the Troodos slopes. The most famous are Kalokhorio, Zoopiyi, and Yerasa. The best Commandaria is made from pure Xynisteri – a light-brown wine of considerable finesse, which can be drunk young.

Other commercially more important wines blend Xynisteri with Mavro to make a dark-tawny wine that can be superb after five or more years in barrel. The grapes are simply sun-dried for at least a week in the vineyard, then pressed and fermented. Long before all the grape sugars are turned into alcohol, fermentation stops naturally, giving a wine of at least 10 degrees alcohol. Once fermentation is complete, the wine is fortified – usually to 15 degrees, although the legal limit is 20 degrees. Maturation takes place in oak casks in Limassol and Paphos for a minimum of two years. Alas, prices – and hence quality – remain low.

Four concerns dominate the Cyprus trade. KEO produces the smooth red Othello and Commandaria St John, as well as one of the best dry Cyprus "sherries", Keo Fino, and light table wines using the Laona label. Its slightly fizzy Bellapais is a refreshing white. ETKO makes the Emva range of fortified wines, as well as a good white from Xynisteri called Nefeli and possibly the island's finest red, INO: a single-estate Cabernet, produced in tiny quantities. Loel has a sound red Hermes, Commandaria Alasia, and a dry white made from the Palomino grape. Some of the best Cyprus brandies are also distilled by Loel. The cooperative SODAP, which has 10,000 members, has as its flagship wine the red Afames. It also makes dry white under the Arsinoe brand and Commandaria St Barnabas. Even in 2008, these four companies accounted for 80 per cent of production.

These are essentially products of the past, and the major wine companies know they must change their approach if they are to survive and prosper in international markets. KEO created the Mallia project, which has preserved and revived indigenous varieties such as Maratheftiko. At the same time, the company is working more closely with its contracted growers, for without good grapes there can be no good wines. As a cooperative, SODAP is moving more slowly into the modern era, but has created a successful export range under the Island Vines label, and the other two companies will be introducing new ranges that will, they hope, have broader appeal.

Small, quality-conscious producers such as Vouni Panayia are beginning to provide strong competition to the big four, but only, as yet, on the domestic market. Other names to keep an eye on include Aes Ambelis, Kalamos, Kyperounda (with vineyards at 1,140 metres/3,075 feet, the island's highest), Nicolaides, Tsiakkas, Vardalis, Vasa, and Vlassides.

Turkey

If Noah's vineyard on the slopes of Mount Ararat was really the first, Turkey can claim to be the original home of wine. (Awkward researchers ask where Noah took the cuttings). Hittite art of 4000BC is possibly better evidence that Anatolia (central Turkey) used wine in highly cultivated ways. In relation to such a time span, the long night of Islam has been scarcely more of an interruption than Prohibition was in the United States. Since the 1920s, Turkey has again been making good wines: much better than her lack of a reputation leads us to expect. One of the most surprising bottles of fine wine I have ever drunk was a 1929 Turkish red – at a friend's house in Bordeaux. I took it for a Bordeaux of that famous vintage.

Turkey has 600,000 hectares of vineyards, but only three per cent is made into wine – the rest being table grapes. Kemal Atatürk founded the twentieth-century wine industry in his drive to modernize the country, although it is held back by lack of a domestic market: 99 per cent of the population is Muslim. Many Turks who do drink prefer beer or *raki* to wine; others are deterred by the high taxes imposed by the government.

The state monopoly, Tekel, is by far the biggest producer, with six wineries handling wines from all regions and dominating exports, particularly with popular bulk wines to Scandinavia. There are also 25 private wineries, two at least with very high standards. Wine production has been steadily increasing over the past decade, and in 2008 it stood at 275 million litres.

The main wine regions are Trakya, the Thrace–Marmara region on the European side of the Bosphorus, the Aegean coast around Izmir, central Anatolia around Ankara, and eastern Anatolia, towards Mount Ararat. The majority of the grapes are local varieties (of which there are over 1,000) whose names are unknown in the West, except in Trakya, where Cinsault, Gamay, and Sémillon (supported by Clairette) make the best-known red and white.

The Doluca company only began importing cuttings of Chardonnay and Cabernet Sauvignon in the early 1990s. A Gamay red called Hosbag (from Tekel) is not remarkable, but Trakya Kirmisi, made of the Turkish Papazharasi and Adakarasi varieties, is a good, vigorous wine. Kirmisi is Turkish for "red" and Beyaz for "white"; Sarap for "wine". Trakya Beyaz (a dry Sémillon) is a popular export.

Of the private firms, Doluca and Kavaklidere are the leaders. Doluca, at Mürefte on the Sea of Marmara, founded in 1926, has well made reds: Villa Doluca of Cinsault and Karasakiz. Doluca also makes Riesling and Muscat, but most of the wines are blends from different grapes and regions. Kavaklidere, the largest independent firm, is based in Ankara but sources grapes from as far apart as Thrace and eastern Anatolia. It concentrates on Anatolia's indigenous grapes, producing Yakut and Dikmen, red blends of Bogazkere, Kalecik Karese, and Oküzgözü (though the best-selling Yakut also contains some southern French varieties), and both sweet and dry whites from Narince, Emire, Sultanine (with a very fresh Primeur), and Cankaya.

Eastern Anatolia is also the home of the best-known of Turkish reds, the heavy and powerful Buzbag, made of Bogazkere near Elazig. This is the produce of Tekel, the state enterprise, and remains Turkey's most original and striking wine. Turasan winery is based in Cappadocia, and mainly produces blends, dry and sweet.

The Aegean region counts Cabernet and Merlot (known, I believe, as "Bordo") among its reds, along with Carignan and Calkarasi. Most of the white is made of Sultanye, the seedless table grape with no real winemaking potential. Some Sémillon and Muscat is grown – the Muscat probably the best.

A third century winery, Kizilcalar valley, Cappadocia

The Levant

Lebanon

What wine might be in the Levant, were it not for the followers of the Prophet, is a tantalizing topic. In 1840, Cyrus Redding had heard tell (he certainly had not been there), that "Syria makes red and white wine of the quality of Bordeaux". But there is current evidence that the eastern Mediterranean can make great wine. Land of Canaan, now the Bekaa Valley, emerged in the 1970s as a producer that compares with Bordeaux, just as Redding had reported.

In the early nineteenth century its reputation was for dry, white "vin d'or". In 1857 Jesuits founded a vast underground winery at Ksara, northeast of Beirut, with over a mile of barrel-filled natural tunnels. It is still the largest (and oldest) Lebanese winery, producing a very good fresh white. But the estate that fluttered the dovecots of the wine trade is Chateau Musar, at Ghazir, 26-kilometres (16-miles) north of Beirut. It was founded in the 1930s by Gaston Hochar, with vineyards in the Bekaa Valley. In 1959, his son Serge, after training in Bordeaux, became winemaker. Bottles started appearing in London. In 1982, he showed a range of vintages going back to the 1940s, which proved beyond doubt that the region can make extraordinarily fine and long-lived reds based on Cabernet Sauvignon with some Cinsault and Carignan, aged in barriques – not at all unlike big Bordeaux of ripe vintages. Whites include an oaked version from the indigenous Obaideh grape, similar to Chardonnay, which is surprisingly capable of ageing a decade and more. During the civil war of the 1980s, Hochar, stoically carrying on making fine wine with Syrian tanks in his vineyards, became a figure of legend in the wine world. Some recent vintages, however, suggest that commercial success is stretching the supply.

The other well-established Bekaa Valley producer is Château Kefraya. The end of the civil war in Lebanon persuaded some brave entrepreneurs to create new wine estates. One of the most ambitious is Massaya, founded in 1998 by architect Sami Ghosn. Domaine Wardy followed in 2000. The total area under vine in Lebanon is around 2,000 hectares, so it remains small in terms of its production. However, the country, with 120 producers, now has a future as an expanding source of good wine, which was hardly the case in the past.

Leading Lebanese Producers

Clos St Thomas ☆–☆☆
Chtaura, Bekaa Valley. 65 ha. www.closstthomas.com
Said Thoma, an arak producer, bought the property in 1990, but the first vintage was only in 1998. The grapes are farmed without irrigation and picked by hand. Les Gourmets is a surprisingly spicy blend of Sauvignon, Chardonnay, and a little Muscat. The best red, Château St Thomas, blends Cabernet, Merlot, and Syrah, and ages the wine in new oak. Big and brawny, it has more power than finesse.

Château Ka ☆–☆☆
Chtaura, Bekaa Valley. 100 ha. www.chateauka.com
Although founded in 1974, this company, which produces fruit juice as well as wine, closed during the civil war and only reopened in 2005. The château wine is a Cabernet-based blend of considerable sophistication; Source de Rouge its more quaffable little brother, with a dash of Syrah.

Château Kefraya ☆☆
Kefraya, Bekaa Valley. 300 ha.
www.chateaukefraya.com
Owner Michel de Boustros works with a French winemaker to produce a good range. Blanc de Blancs is not a sparkling wine, but a convincing blend of Sauvignon, Chardonnay, and Viognier. The top red is the Comte de M blend from Cabernet and Syrah, aged in new oak. Quality has improved since 2000.

Cave Kouroum ☆☆
Kefraya, Bekaa Valley. 180 ha.
www.cavekouroum.com
Until a few years ago this property used to sell grapes, which explains the many varieties planted. The Syrah and Syrah/Cabernet are impressive: powerful wines with concentration and length.

Château Ksara ☆–☆☆
Bekaa Valley. 334 ha.
Jesuits made the wine here from 1857–1973, but over the past decade they have employed a winemaker who formerly worked at Prieuré-Lichine in Margaux. Cabernet Sauvignon plays a large part in the blends, which sometimes show a slight herbaceousness. Production is close to two million bottles.

Massaya ☆☆–☆☆☆
Chtaura, Bekaa Valley. 50 ha.
Founded in 1998 by the Ghosn family, with advice from Dominique Hébrard from St-Emilion and Daniel Brunier of Châteauneuf-du-Pape. The wines, polished and well-made, are ranged in three tiers: Classic, Silver, and a single Gold blend from Cabernet and Mourvèdre, aged in new French oak.

Château Musar ☆☆–☆☆☆
Ghazir, Bekaa Valley. 180 ha.
www.chateaumusar.com.lb
Serge Hochar is now handing over to his son Gaston, but the style of the wines remains unchanged. The reds are meaty and long-lived, and the white wine, though made from obscure local grapes, can, mysteriously, age for 20 years. Although not the most refined of wines, Musar exudes character.

Domaine Wardy ☆–☆☆
Zahlé, Bekaa Valley. 45 ha.
www.domaine-wardy.com
A rapidly expanding winery that made its mark with Sauvignon Blanc and Chardonnay, and reds from Merlot and Cabernet Sauvignon.

Israel

Winemaking in Israel dates back to ancient times, although the modern industry was established at the end of the nineteenth century with a gift to the state from Baron Edmond de Rothschild: the founding of wineries at Rishon le Zion, south of Tel Aviv, and Zichron Ya'acov, south of Haifa. These two wineries, which remain the largest in Israel, sell their wines under the Carmel brand.

Israel now has 4,000 hectares of vineyards. The first to be planted were concentrated in the hot coastal regions of Samson and Shomron (which is still the largest wine growing region) with predominantly Carignan, Grenache, and Sémillon grapes to make sweet sacramental wine. Interest was primarily kosher. In the mid-1970s, the principal of the University of California at Davis, Cornelius Ough, identified the cool-climate Golan Heights as an ideal location for wine grapes. The improvement in quality was considerable. There are now vineyards up to 1,100 metres (3,600 feet), on a range of volcanic-basaltic soils in the Golan Heights and the Upper Galilee, producing the grapes for Israel's best wines.

The introduction of classic varieties, first Cabernet Sauvignon, then Merlot and Chardonnay in the 1980s heralded the beginning of a quality-wine industry and a move to producing dry table and sparkling wines that could compete internationally. By 2000, 80 per cent of all Israeli wines were dry. Although the large companies still dominate production, there has been an explosion of boutique wineries, many of which began as hobby operations. Some of them produce rustic wines, others are of high quality. These small wineries are mostly clustered in the hills around Jerusalem, and benefit from the elevation. There is also a small group of traditional kosher wineries, which also vary in quality. A recent trend has been the increase in kosher-wine production, even though the winery owners may well be secular Jews. The reason is that the major export market is the United States, where Orthodox Jews require kosher wines but seek international-style wines of good quality.

The Golan Heights Winery, in the small town of Katzrin high up in the Golan, led the way, making oak-aged Chardonnay and Cabernet (Yarden is the premier label), classic-method sparkling wines, and complex Merlot. Barkan, Israel's third-biggest winery, makes Sauvignon Blanc and Cabernet Sauvignon of acceptable quality. Its production is now around 4.5 million bottles annually, and it has also set up a joint venture with a kibbutz to create another Golan winery, called Galil Mountain, with the emphasis on international varieties.

Among the newcomers are Dalton near the Lebanese border, which is establishing a reputation for barrique-aged Cabernet, Merlot, and Chardonnay; Tishbi, which is the renamed and revamped Baron winery; Recanati in Emek Hefer, and Cfar Tabor in Lower Galilee; and Domaine du Castel. This last winery is the most ambitious of all, ageing its red wines for two years in new French oak. The drawback is price, but its second wine, Petit Castel, is almost as good and less overtly oaky.

Leading Israel Producers

Barkan ☆–☆☆☆
Kibbutz Hulda. 300 ha. www.barkan-winery.com
This large winery, producing six million bottles each year, has been through various incarnations and is now owned by an Israeli brewery. Its vineyards are located throughout the country. The Reserve wines are ripe and accessible, and there is a fascinating label called Altitude, displaying three Cabernets grown at different elevations.

Binyamina ☆–☆☆
Zichron Ya'acov. No vineyards. www.binyaminawines.com
Israel's fourth largest winery, renamed after its sale in 1992 to two Hollywood producers, who invested in modern winery equipment. The Special Reserve range is of sound quality, but the wines overall do not rise to great heights. Kosher.

Carmel ☆–☆☆☆
Rishon le Zion. 1400 ha. www.carmelwines.co.il
The Carmel cooperative used to be a byword for mediocrity, but in the late 1990s it went through a revolution. Its vineyards were all in hot coastal regions, so it began planting in cooler hillside locations and a built a new winery in the Upper Galilee. Fruit selection became more rigorous, and quality soon began to improve. The less expensive, simpler ranges are Vineyards Selected and Private Collection, but the best wines appear under the Appellation and single vineyard labels. Of particular interest are the Petite Sirah and Carignan, showing that these much abused varieties – at least in Israel – can produce succulent wines.

Domaine du Castel ☆☆☆
Ramat Raziel. 15 ha. www.castel.co.il
Eli Ben-Zaken, a former restaurateur, was the first grower to demonstrate, in 1992, that Israel could produce classic wines from Chardonnay and Cabernet that could compete with the best from the New World. All wines are aged in French oak and show excellent balance. The Grand Vin, a Bordeaux blend dominated by Cabernet, ages well. The second label is Petit Castel, which is less oaky. Kosher.

Chillag ☆☆
Yehud. 3 ha.
Owner/winemaker Orna Chillag worked for Antinori, and it rubbed off, as she uses Italian terminology on the labels. The top range is Primo, with very ripe, intense Cabernet and Merlot.

Clos de Gat ☆☆–☆☆☆
Kibbutz Harel. 14 ha. www.closdegat.com
A highly regarded winery, with an Australian-trained winemaker. Barrel-fermented Chardonnay is rich and weighty, and the estate blend is a Bordeaux-style wine aged in new barriques.

Dalton ☆–☆☆
Ranat Gan. 70 ha. www.dalton-winery.com
A rapidly expanding and well-equipped winery that now offers a wide range of products. The best wines are the Reserves, with expressive versions of Sauvignon, Syrah, Merlot, and Cabernet. Kosher.

Ella Valley Vineyards ☆☆
Beit Shemesh. 80 ha. www.ellavalley.com
Named after the Judean Hills valley where David fought
Goliath, Ella Valley makes sophisticated wines, avoiding an
excessive use of new oak. Chardonnay is reliable here, and
Cabernet Franc a blend of Cabernet Sauvignon and Syrah
show promise.

Flam ☆☆
Ya'ar Ha'kdoshim. 12 ha. www.flamwinery.com
From vineyards in Galilee and the Judean Hills, Golan Flam,
who worked in Italian and Australia, fashions rich, high-
alcohol wines from the Bordeaux varieties as well as Syrah
and Chardonnay. As is often the case in Israel, the Merlots
show less herbaceousness than the Cabernets.

Galil Mountain Winery ☆☆
Kibbutz Yiron. 100 ha. www.galilmountain.co.il
This offshoot of the Golan Heights winery (q.v.) is partly
owned by the northern Galilee kibbutz on which it is located.
The first vintage was 2000. In 2006, during the war with
Lebanon, the army took over the winery, but left in time for
the harvest to be completed. The flagship wine is Yiron, an
excellent and structured Cabernet/Merlot blend that ages well.
Chardonnay and Viognier show promise, Pinot Noir less so.

Golan Heights Winery ☆☆☆
Katzrin. 640 ha. www.golanwines.co.il
Californian know-how and winemakers yielded good results
here from the outset, in 1982, and since 1991 another American,
Victor Schoenfeld, has maintained very high standards. Golan
Heights sets the pace for other Israeli wineries to follow. Golan
is the simplest range, Gamla the mid-range, and Yarden the
very reliable top range. Now the vineyards are 30 years old,
it has been possible to make a few single-vineyard wines
of exceptional quality. Merlot and Syrah show the greatest
promise, but all the wines are well made and in balance. Kosher.

Hevron Heights ☆–☆☆
Kiryat Arba.
French-owned, the winery was founded in 2000.

From grapes grown in the Judean Hills come some rather
burly, oaky wines from Merlot, Cabernet, and Syrah. Kosher.

Margalit ☆☆
Hadera. www.margalit-winery.com
An organic estate that was Israel's first boutique winery,
founded in 1989 and producing only Bordeaux varieties
and Chardonnay. Production remains tiny at 20,000 bottles,
so the wines are hard to find.

Recanati ☆☆
Emek Hefer. No vineyards. www.recanati-winery.com
The medium-sized Recanati winery sources its grapes
from vineyards in the Upper Galilee and the Judean Hills.
The best wines are in the Reserve range, from a lush
Sauvignon Blanc to stylish Syrah and a compact, spicy
Petite Sirah/Zinfandel blend.

Sea Horse ☆☆
Moshav Var-Giyora. 1 ha. www.seahorsewines.com
Ze'v Dunie is a well known film-maker, who became
interested in wine after making a documentary on the subject.
He buys in most of the grapes he needs, and simply produces
the wines he himself likes. The dry Chenin Blanc is splendid,
and the Cabernet, Syrah, and Petite Sirah are all sturdy and
concentrated.

Segal ☆–☆☆
Kibbutz Hulda, Sorek. 50 ha. www.segalwines.co.il
This long-established winery was bought by Barkan (q.v.),
but is run independently. The inexpensive Segal Red is a
best-seller within Israel, but the best wines are released under
the Merom Galil label: rather oaky reds, a stylish Chardonnay,
and a silky, sweet Muscat.

Tanya ☆–☆☆
Ofra. 3 ha. www.tanyawinery.co.il
The first vintage here was 2002, and the main focus is on the
red Bordeaux varieties, solo and blended. Quality fluctuates
but the Reserve Cabernet and Red Blend Reserve are ripe
and complex. Kosher.

KOSHER WINES

Much Israeli wine is kosher. This means
it is produced under strict rabbinical
supervision that can be a constraining
factor as well as an additional cost.

The process begins in the vineyard,
which is supposed to be left fallow every
seventh year, though in practice it is
usually sold to a non-Jew for that one year
period only. Sabbath observance is strictly
maintained. In the winery, only Orthodox
Jews may come into direct contact with
the wine, by handling pumps and other
equipment. Certain products commonly
used in winemaking are forbidden, such

as isinglass, a fining substance made
from non-kosher sturgeon. Some rabbis
insist on *maaser*, a ceremony derived
from the *tithe* paid to the temple in
Jerusalem in Biblical days. Those who
follow this precept must destroy one per
cent of their annual production. An ultra-
rigorous form of kosher wine is known as
meshuval, which requires the wine to be
flash-pasteurized, following an obscure
rabbinical dictate that apparently makes
it mandatory if a wine is to be poured by
a non-Orthodox Jew without losing its
kosher status. Few wineries produce

meshuval wines, and those that do
usually have kosher catering companies
as their clients.

Such regulations must be irksome
to producers, since they have nothing to
do with the quality of the wine. However,
there is a growing demand for kosher
wines from Orthodox families who wish
to drink excellent wines without
compromising their adherence to Jewish
law. This explains why estates such as
Domaine du Castel, never kosher in the
past, changed its mind, and its practices,
in 2003.

Tishbi ☆–☆☆

Zichron Ya'acov. 100 ha. ww.tishbi.com

The Tishbis are a well-known Israeli winemaking family; their winery was originally known as Baron, but the name was changed in 2000. They farm vineyards in various regions, so the range is wide. Quality in unexceptional, but there are occasional surprises, such as a vibrant Cabernet Franc from the Jerusalem Hills.

Tulip ☆☆

Kfar Tikva. 5 ha. www.tulip-winery.co.il

Kfar Tikva is a community for the disabled, many of whom work in the winery, which was created in 2003. Cabernet Sauvignon, Cabernet Franc, and Shiraz are the main varieties; the wines are intense and oaky, if somewhat one-dimensional.

Vitkin ☆☆

Kfar Vitkin, Netanya. 5 ha. www.vitkin-winery.co.il

Doron Belogolovsky is intrigued by varieties rarely seen in Israel, such as Barbera, Sangiovese, and Tempranillo. The quality of the wines is hit and miss, but the Riesling is dry and spicy, and the Petite Sirah and Carignan, both from old vines, are dramatic and concentrated.

Yatir ☆☆

Beit Yatir. 30 ha. www.yatir.net

The leading winery in the Negev region, Yatir forms part of the Carmel group but is run independently. The eponymous wine is a blend of Cabernet, Syrah, and Merlot, made in a lush quasi-Australian style. Kosher.

North Africa

Nearly half a century ago, North Africa's wine-producing countries, Tunisia, Algeria, and Morocco, accounted for no less than two-thirds of the entire international wine trade. Algeria was by far the biggest producer of the three, with most of the vast quantity being exported to Europe (mainly to France) as blending wine. Independence from France resulted in an immediate decline, for there was practically no domestic market; political instability and religious fervour inhibited investment in badly needed renovation of vineyards and wineries, and the trend has been either to pull up or neglect the vineyards. The current drive, however, is towards improving wine quality from the best sites for export.

Tunisia

The institution of an Office du Vin in 1970 marked the start of Tunisia's coordinated plan to make wines for export. Her vineyard area devoted to wine production has been reduced from 50,000 hectares in its heyday to some 15,000 hectares, all in the vicinity of Tunis (and ancient Carthage) on the north coast. Muscats are the most characteristic wines here, as they are of the Sicilian islands lying not far off-shore. Reds, rosés, and whites are made of French Midi-type grapes, in many cases using modern methods. As in Algeria, the pale rosés are often the most attractive wines and constitute about two-thirds of production. Tunisia has adopted the French AC system, and appellations include: Mornag (the largest), Grand Cru Mornag, Coteaux d'Ultique (near the sea north of Tunis), Tébourba, Sidi Salem, and Kelibia.

The biggest producer is the Union des Caves Coopératives Viticoles (UCCV at Djebel Djelloud; also known as Vignerons de Carthage), which makes 65 per cent of Tunisian wine. The Union makes an unusual dry white Muscat, Muscat de Kelibia, from vineyards at the tip of Cap Bon to the northeast. It is highly aromatic, not over-strong, but nonetheless difficult to enjoy with a meal. The UCCV's best-quality red is Magon, from Tébourba in the valley of the Oued (River) Medjerdah, west of Tunis. The Cinsault and Mourvèdre in this wine give it both roundness and greater personality than the standard Coteaux de Carthage. Other union wines include Château Mornag (red and rosé) from the Mornag hills east of Tunis; a pale, dry Gris d'Hammamet, a blend of Cinsault, Grenache, and Carignan; and a dry, Muscat-scented rosé called Sidi Rais.

The most notable wines of the state-owned Office des Terres Domaniales are the earthy reds from Domaine Thibar, from the hills 137-kilometres (85-miles) west of Tunis up the Medjerdah valley, and Sidi Selem from Kanguet, near Mornag. Other note-worthy producers include the Société Lamblot for its red Domaine Karim from the Coteaux d'Ultique; Domaine Magon, now benefiting from German investment; Château Feriani, which makes one of Tunisia's tastiest red wines from the same area; Héritiers René Lavau for its Koudiat, another strong red from Tébourba. Better than these are the strong, sweet, dessert Muscats, under the appellation Vin Muscat de Tunisie.

The German firm of Langguth has produced and exported wine here under the Sidi Saad label since the 1960s, and more recently the Sicilian Calatrasi company has invested in 200 hectares of vineyards south of Tunis. Under the Selian label, Calatrasi produces gutsy, fruit-forward Carignan and Syrah. Such ventures should give the Tunisian wine industry a much-needed boost. A more recent venture is Domaine Atlas, founded in 2003, with 160 hectares of Carignan, Syrah, and Cabernet Sauvignon; its top wine is Ifrikia, a spicy but rather confected Carignan/Cabernet blend. Ceptunes, which is Swiss-owned, produces the Didona brand (notably a crisp Chardonnay) from a winery completed in 2002. Chardonnay is also the best white wine from the French-owned Kurubis in Korba, and the spicy red Kurubis is a blend of Syrah and Mourvèdre.

Algeria

The biggest and most intensely planted of France's former North African colonies has seen a reduction in her wine grape vineyard from 365,000 hectares, its total of the 1960s, when Algeria was the world's sixth-largest wine producer, to around 35,000 today – and her productivity has gone down by an even greater proportion to a mere one per cent of pre-1962 levels. Wineries have closed their doors by the thousands, often under violent threats, their number shrinking from 3,000 over just 40 years to 50. Many of the older vineyards on the fertile plains, which could never have produced good wine, have been converted to cereals, and viticulture has retreated to the hill vineyards, which produced superior wine in French days. A dozen *crus* were indeed given VDQS status before independence.

Of these, seven were recognized by the ONCV (Office Nationale de Commercialization des Produits Viticoles) as quality zones. They are all located in the hills about 80-kilometres (50-miles) inland in the two western provinces of Oran and Alger. Of the two, Oran has always been the bulk producer, with three-quarters of Algeria's vines. The ONCV, which is responsible for the bulk of Algerian wine production, has standard labels that reveal nothing about the origin of the wine except its region – and in the case of its prestige brand, Cuvée du Président, not even that. Le Président is a matured, faintly claret-like wine which, when last tasted, I did not find as good as the best regional offerings. The western quality zone, the Coteaux de Tlemcen, lies close to the Moroccan border, covering north-facing sandstone hills at 760 metres (2,500 feet). Red, rosé, and white wines are well-made: strong, very dry but soft in the style the Algerians have mastered. The rosés and whites in particular have improved enormously with cool fermentation.

The Monts du Tessalah at Sidi-bel-Abbès to the northeast seem rather less distinguished; certainly less so than the 3,000-hectare Coteaux de Mascara, whose red wines in colonial days were frequently passed off as burgundy. Mascara reds are powerful and dark with real body, richness of texture, and, wood-aged as they are sold today, a considerable aroma of oak and spice. A certain crudeness marks the finish. This I have not found in the Mascara white; dry though it is, it would be creditable in the south of France: pleasantly fruity, not aromatic but smooth and individual – perhaps as good as any white wine made in North Africa.

At Dahra the hills approach the sea. The former French VDQS *crus* of Robert, Rabelais, and Rénault (now known as Tanghrite, Aïn Merane, and Mazouna) make smooth, dark, and full-bodied reds and a remarkable rosé with a fresh almost cherry-like smell, light and refreshing to drink – a skilful piece of winemaking. Further east and further inland, in the province of Al-Jazair (Algiers), the capital, the Coteaux du Zaccar makes slightly lighter, less fruity wines. Again, the rosé, though less fruity than the Dahra, is well-made. South of Zaccar and higher, at 1,220 metres (4,000 feet), the Médéa hills are cooler, and finer varieties are grown along with the standard Cinsault, Carignan, and Grenache. Cabernet and Pinot Noir go into Médéa blends, which have less flesh and more finesse than Dahra or Mascara. Easternmost of the quality zones is Aïn Bessem-Bouira, making relatively light reds and what some consider Algeria's best rosés.

Morocco

The vineyards of Morocco devoted to wine production now cover only 11,000 hectares: a sharp decline since independence in 1956, when there were 50,000 planted. It has the tightest organization and the highest standards of the three North African wine countries. The few wines that are AOG (Appellation d'Origine Garantie) have similar controls to French appellation wines, strictly applied. They are produced by a central organization, SODEVI, and the important cooperative, Les Celliers de Meknès, which dominates the domestic market. Quality here has improved in recent years, with some appealing Cabernet/Syrah and Cabernet/Merlot blends.

Four regions of Morocco produce fair wines, but by far the best and biggest is the Meknès/Fès area at 460–610 metres (1,500–2,000 feet) in the northern foothills of the middle Atlas Mountains, where the regions of Saiss, Beni Sadden, Zerkhoune, Beni M'Tir, and Guerrouane are designated. The last two have achieved remarkable reds of Cinsaut, Carignan, and Grenache, respectively sold abroad as Tarik and Chantebled (and in Morocco as Les Trois Domaines). Tarik is the bigger and more supple of the two, but both are smooth, long, and impressive. The 2,400-hectare Guerrouane also specializes in an AOG *vin gris*: a very pale, dry rosé of Cinsault and Carignan, which substitutes for the white wines Morocco lacked until recently. Now a tolerable Sauvignon Blanc presages better things.

A little wine, but none of consequence, is made in the Berkane/Oujda area to the east near the Algerian border. The other principal areas are around Rabat, on the coastal plain, in the regions of Gharb, Chellah, Zemmour, and Zaër. The brand names Dar Bel Amri, Roumi, and Sidi Larbi, formerly used for pleasant, soft reds from these zones, have been abandoned in favour of the regional and varietal names.

Further south down the coast, the Casablanca region has three wine zones: Zenata, Sahel, and Doukkala. The first produces a solid red marketed as Ourika. South of Casablanca the firm of Sincomar makes the standard drinking of every thirsty visitor: the Gris de Boulaouane. Boulaouane is the archetypal North African refresher: very pale, slightly orange, dry, faintly fruity, extremely clean, and altogether suited to steamy Casablanca nights.

Other labels that may be encountered are Castel Fréres' Atlas Vineyards, with 1,000 hectares of vines and a brand called Halana; Domaine Ain Amhajir, the French-owned Domaines Delorme, and Domaine de Sahari, the last owned by Bordeaux négociant Williams Pitters. After he sold William Pitters, Bernard Magrez established a property called Kahina near Meknès and makes a boutique wine from Grenache and Syrah. Tandem is the joint venture of Rhône producer Alain Graillot and Jacques Poulain; the first vintage was 2005 and the wine is based on old Syrah vines from Rommani and Benslimane.

Other Countries

Egypt By 2008 Egypt was producing 8.5 million bottles of wine, distinguished by such names as Cru Cleopatra, primarily for consumption by undiscriminating tourists.

Ethiopia The French firm of Castel has planted 125 hectares of noble French varieties south of Addis Adaba.

Asia

The wine grape has been grown in the East for centuries. Chinese gardeners in the second century knew how to make wine, so did the Arabs, until they renounced alcohol in the eighth century – at least in theory. Afghan vineyards supplied the Indian Moghul court in the sixteenth century. But wine never became part of daily life in these countries, unlike the West. The reason, perhaps, is the nature of their cuisine. Strongly seasoned dishes are best washed down by a simple, refreshing liquid – even if each course is regaled by the local spirit. For all that, there are the beginnings of a modern industry in several Asian nations.

Wines from Japan, India, and China reach Western markets but Thailand, South Korea, Vietnam, and Indonesia now have nascent industries, principally for local consumption. Even Nepal has two hectares of vinifera – the world's highest vineyard – while the tiny Himalayan kingdom of Bhutan has ventured into winemaking under the patronage of its royal family.

China

Vines were growing in China 200 years before they reached France. Wine, often sweet and fortified, has been consumed at Chinese banquets for centuries and is also used for medicinal purposes, infused with plants, herbs and, more unusually, animal organs, rodents, and reptiles.

Viticulture spread over the centuries throughout central and northwest China. The Autonomous Region of Xinjiang, in the far northwest, accounts for almost a quarter of the 70,000 wine-producing hectares of vines in China. The major wine-producing regions are in the northeast – in Shandong and Hebei (16,000 hectares) and Jiangsu provinces, and around Beijing and Tianjin.

The modern industry is largely the product of foreign intervention. Under its "Four Modernizations" programme, beginning in the late 1970s, the Chinese government actively courted foreign interest in the modernization of its wine industry. The first to participate was Rémy Martin. In 1980, Rémy teamed up with a provincial farm bureau to establish a large-scale modern winery in Tianjin. Its Dynasty label quickly rivalled the longer established Great Wall, now also with a foreign joint venture partner. It has subsequently become the market leader among the Western-style domestic wines, with sales of 13 million bottles annually.

In the mid-1980s, two further foreign joint ventures established large-scale plantings of premium European varieties. The Huadong (East China) winery at Qingdao' on the northeast seaboard in Shandong Province was set up by Hong Kong based investors. Allied-Domecq used to be but is no longer the foreign partner, and the wines can be of surprisingly good quality. Dragon Seal Wines began as a joint venture with Pernod-Ricard, which is no longer involved. It produces creditable Chardonnay and Cabernet Sauvignon. Both Huadong and Dragon Seal are now leading brands. The leading compa-

nies, with a combined domestic market share of 52 per cent, are Great Wall, Chang Yu, and Dynasty; the Weilong winery is in hot pursuit. By 2008 China was claiming to be the world's sixth largest wine producer, although all statistics relating to wine production in China are unreliable. Its 450 wineries, some of them very small, are spread over 26 provinces. A few large, long-established wineries dominate the market. The Changu Yu Winery at Yantai in Shandong is the largest, bottling its wines under various labels including Noble Dragon, a joint venture with Austrian producer Lenz Moser. Its most eccentric product is a Vidal Icewine that is surprisingly good. The other leading wineries – Beijing Yeguangbei, Lianyungang (Jiangsu), Dynasty, Great Wall, and Tong Hua (Jilin) – make about the same volume combined. Some now import bulk wine for blending or for bottling locally.

More recent ventures include Lou Lan, a 400,000-case winery in the Gobi Desert run by Frenchman Gregory Michel and backed by investors from Hong Kong. Imported cuttings were planted in 1998: Cabernet, Merlot, Syrah, Chenin, Riesling, and other varieties. The top range of varietal wines is being released under the Turpan Basin label. In 2002, the Maotai Changli winery released wines from Cabernet Franc and other varieties. The Austrian Swarovski family, owners of Norton in Argentina, have invested in Shang-Li, where 300 hectares are being planted at Bodega Langes, mostly with Merlot and Cabernet.

Catái is a joint venture in Shandong with the Sardinian firm Sella & Mosca, with Chardonnay, Merlot, and Cabernet Sauvignon in the range. The Grace winery has been doing well with Chardonnay and Merlot and with its top Merlot/Cabernet blend called Chairman's Reserve. Feng Huang is a label created by the Taillan group from Bordeaux and the Chinese ministry of agriculture; the first vintage was 1999. Native grape varieties are used to make most of China's wine. Best-known is the Dragon's Eye, the grape used to make Great Wall. Beichun, a hybrid of the *Vitis amurensis* species native to north China, is suited to the harsh climate of its border region. Other varieties are being tried, especially Rkatziteli, Muscat Hamburg (the backbone of the Dynasty operation), and Italian Riesling. Most impressive of all are the wines being made from the more recently introduced classic varieties: Chardonnay, Riesling, Pinots Noir and Meunier, Cabernet Sauvignon, and Gamay. Legally, wine in China need contain only 70 per cent fermented grape juice, but it is virtually certain that such questionable "wines" will be reserved for the domestic market.

India

India's first modern winemaking concern, the Andhra Winery and Distillery, was established in 1966 at Malkajgiri, Hyderabad, in the state of Andhra Pradesh. The problem with most Indian wines is that they are made from table grapes, although in the 1990s the planting of international varieties became more common. It is estimated that there are about 13,000 hectares in production.

The first wine to cause a stir was the launch in 1985 by Chateau Indage, which started off as a joint venture with Piper-

Heidsieck, of Omar Khayyám, a sparkling wine based on Chardonnay, made near Poona in the Maharashtra Hills, southeast of Bombay. A sweeter Marquise de Pompadour followed for the domestic market, and there is a vintage *méthode traditionelle* called Celèbre. The estate's dry red is made from the local Arkawati grape, the white from Ugni and Chardonnay. With 400 hectares of vineyards, Indage has a lot of grapes to use. Under the smartly packaged Ivy range, it offers blends of Sauvignon Blanc, Sémillon, and Chardonnay, a Viognier, and Malbec and Shiraz. The wines from the 150-hectare Grover Vineyards at the base of the Nandi Hills near Bangalore are widely available in India. Since 1995, Michel Rolland has acted as their consultant, and has assembled a Cabernet/Shiraz blend called La Réserve as its flagship wine. Vineyards (Sauvignon, Chenin Blanc, and a blush Zinfandel) were planted in the late 1990s on 15 hectares at the Sula Estate near Nasik, 193-kilometres (120-miles) north-east of Bombay, by American-educated Rajiv Samant. By 2008 he had 650 hectares under vine and three wineries in operation, producing, among other wines, Sauvignon Blanc, Chenin, Shiraz, and Zinfandel. The first vintage was 2000, and current production is around three million bottles.

Indonesia

The solitary enterprise in Indonesia, Hatten Wines, was founded in 1994 and is located on Bali. It relies on black Isabella (*Vitis labrusca*) grapes grown in vineyards a few kilometres from the city of Singaraja in the north, where the slopes provide some respite from the tropical heat and humidity. A full range of wines is produced, white, rosé, red, and sparkling, and even a local attempt at a Pineau de Charentes.

Japan

The Daizenji Temple at Katsunuma, in the central Honshu prefecture of Yamanashi west of Tokyo, is the spiritual home of Japan's wine industry. Legend has it that the first vines were planted here in the eighth century by a holy man, although early interest in the grape was probably more for the medicinal value of the fruit.

Winemaking came later, in the nineteenth century, although Yamanashi remained at the centre, and is home to the most of the modern 30-odd serious winemaking enterprises. Other wine grape producing regions are Nagano, an adjacent prefecture to the west; Yamagata, further to the north on Honshu island; and Hokkaido, the large island at Japan's northern extremity.

Growers must contend with unsuitable growing conditions – monsoonal weather patterns (central and southern regions); a long, severe winter (the north); drainage problems and acid soils – and high costs. The main focus of Japanese viticulture is on the growing of grapes for the table, rather than on providing top-grade raw materials for winemaking. This is reflected in the varieties and in viticultural practices. *Vitis labrusca* varieties and hybrids, introduced over the course of the nineteenth century from North America, account for almost 80 per cent of Japan's total of some 25,000 hectares under vine. Kôshû, the local white and the *Vitis vinifera* descendant of the original vines planted at Katsunuma in the eighth century, provides the backbone of the industry's winemaking identity, if not the bulk of the wine produced. It is a heavy-bearing vine, producing big, round, pink-tinged berries, with which winemakers habitually do battle to extract colour, flavour, and body. European varieties have been trialled since the 1960s.

Seibel, a variety that looked promising in the experiments, was successfully crossed with the native vine to create a new variety called Kiyomi. It produces a conventional, though strongly acidic, wine with a resemblance to Pinot Noir. In more recent experimentation, Kiyomi has been crossed back to the native vine to produce a new commercial hybrid, Kiyomai, which will not need to be buried in soil for protection during the severe winter, as is the case with other varieties, Kiyomi included. The northern European varieties such as Müller-Thurgau and Zweigelt may well prove to be suited to the harsh winter conditions in Hokkaido.

The surprise is that there are some premium local wines (Semillon, Chardonnay, Cabernet, Merlot, and Kôshû) now being made in an attempt to keep pace with imports. Five huge, diversified beverage conglomerates, which together account for three-quarters of total output, dominate the industry. The brewer Suntory produces an acclaimed red blend called Tomi. It vies for top position with soft-drinks giant Sanraku, which sells particularly good Chardonnay, Merlot, and Cabernet under the Mercian label. Manns Wine is emphasizing the local varieties Kôshû, Dragon's Eye, and local-Euro crosses, which are adapted to Japan's rainy climate, as well as Chardonnay, Merlot, and a French-oaked Cabernet. Another brewer, Sapporo (Grand Polaire label) and Asahi Breweries (Ste Neige label) are other big players. Smaller, family owned wineries are likewise concentrated in Yamanashi, among them Marufuji (Rubaiyat label), Shirayuri (L'Orient label), Maruki, and the quality-conscious Château Lumière. Such quality wines are, and are likely to remain, the exceptions; most wine labelled as "Japanese" is blended with imports from South America and Eastern Europe.

Chung Tai Chan monastery and vineyard, Taiwan

South Korea

With about 600 hectares of vineyards, South Korea has a wine industry of sorts. Majuang is the generic name for all local wine, mostly made from low-quality, imported bulk wine with some locally grown Seibel and Muscat Hamburg grapes added for "authenticity". Producers include Comfe, Grand Coteau, and Chateau Mani.

Thailand

The growing market for wine in Thailand has spawned some local winemaking ventures. Château de Loei is a 100-hectare vineyard and winery at Phurua, in the cooler Loei River district in northern Thailand. Château de Loei settled on Chenin Blanc as the base for its first commercial wine, released in 1995.

Small quantities of red wine, made mainly from Shiraz, were available from the second vintage in 1996. Prohibitive taxes and duties on imported wine provide a big incentive to meeting the challenge of growing wine grapes in this part of the tropics. The Siam Winery produces a wide range of wines, mostly of them slightly sweet, under the Monsoon Valley label.

Vietnam

Rice wine is more important than grape wine in Vietnam, but the Dalat company began wine production in 1999. It sources grapes from Phan Rang, the country's main table grape region, and Cardinal is the main variety used. A full range of the wines, tasted in 2008, did not inspire much enthusiasm. Snake wine looks more intriguing, and the product from the Van Tranh company has an added bonus: a scorpion clutched in the jaws of the snake.

United States

It would be hard to guess from the current level of enthusiasm and connoisseurship in the US that until the late 1960s, wine-growing was an exotic activity that had only succeeded in gaining footholds on the fringes of North America. The distribution of all American wine was regulated by the Bureau of Alcohol, Tobacco, and Firearms as though it were an ignitable, if not explosive, substance. That bureau has now been replaced by the Alcohol & Tobacco Tax and Trade Bureau (TTB), but its regulatory powers are much the same. Wine-drinking was an infrequent, low-profile, even faintly suspect activity. Prohibition had almost snuffed out the promise of healthy Americans, free of neuroses, freely accepting the happy legacy of Mediterranean culture.

During the past 40 years, both the production and consumption of wine have vastly increased. In the world league of wine producers, the USA remains fourth, making over half as much wine as France or Italy, the two giants of the wine world. Imports have soared. The per capita consumption now stands at nine litres a year.

The figure is still modest, and the neurosis has not entirely departed, but wine has finally permeated America's soul as an essential part of the good life. Almost every state has aspiring wine-growers; a couple of dozen have a wine industry. But it is the emphasis put on wine in restaurants and hotels, in publications and publicity, which proves that a great change has taken place. America has at last developed its own wine culture, with its own references, a budding appellation system, rating systems, and indigenous ideas about the use of wine with food. What is more, it is successfully exporting aspects of this new thinking to the rest of the world.

California

It now seems so natural to include California in the shortlist of the world's top winelands that it bears repetition that this status is relatively new. Although Napa Valley in particular had established a fine reputation for its wines during the late nineteenth century, the 1970s was the decade when California decisively took up her position in the world of wine. Until this time an adolescent America had not been ready for what she (and wine in general) had to offer. But the generation of winemakers that followed the repeal of Prohibition had done indispensable groundwork for an industry that appeared to be remarkably friendless. Hardly anyone was prepared for the impact when, in the late 1960s, Americans started to change their habits, to look outwards for new ideas, to start thinking about their environment, their diet, and their health, and to discover that they had a well of the world's most satisfactory beverage in their own backyard.

From the early 1970s on, growth has been astonishingly rapid. In 1970, there were 240 bonded wineries (ie. licensed premises for wine production). By 2000 their number had grown to 1,450, and by 2007 to a bewildering 2,687 (with an additional 3,200 in other states). By 2006 wine grape vineyards were holding steady at around 193,000 hectares, up from 136,000 in 1990. But beneath these figures, impressive as they are, everything was in ferment: grapes, men, priorities, areas, tanks, and philosophy. They still are.

Predictably, the other drink businesses – brewers, distillers and soft-drink manufacturers – have moved in to control what they can of the mass-market production, although with varying degrees of success. The enduring domination of that market by Gallo may be attributable to the fact that the company is still run personally by the families of the brothers who started it.

At the other extreme, in what rapidly and rather unkindly became known as boutique wineries, fashion has rocketed about from one winery to another, as drinkers even newer to wine than the winemakers tried to make up their minds what they liked, at the same time as discovering who made it – or if he made it again the following year. The cult of the winemaker is nowhere more developed than in California. A handful of them, and many are women, carry such kudos that any winery hiring them can charge enormous sums for their wines. This is not to cast doubts on the skills of those winemakers, but merely to remark that the prestige of the consultant winemaker counts for more in determining the commercial success of a winery than such elusive factors as vineyards and terroir.

There are more shifting sands than enduring landmarks. Essentially, this is an industry with no structure and very few rules. There are four approaches to finding what you want in California, and you need them all. There is no escaping the dominance of the brand or winery name. The grape variety is the only firm information available about what is in the bottle. The area of production is sometimes a good clue to the style of the wine, but not, in many cases, its quality. And the vintage date at least tells you how old it is – and often considerably more.

Access to the essentials in this chapter is therefore organized into three alphabetical directories: of wineries and brands, of grapes (and wine types), and of areas. How good are the wines, and where do they fit into an international comparison?

In the last 20-odd years, the top-class of handmade wines have proved that they can outshine in blind tastings the very European wines they emulate. The reason they do this with almost monotonous predictability is inherent in their nature. It is the fully ripe grape that makes California wines comparable with the great vintages and the best vineyards of Europe. There are also, however, the rate of ripening and the question of soil to consider. Both of these have more bearing on the long-term quality of wine than California is at present inclined to allow. The concomitant disadvantage of the superripe grape is the relentless force of flavour that it gives. Heartiness suits Americans – at least today's Americans. It suits many wine-drinkers everywhere. The mood might waver, but only briefly. Not long ago, the terms of highest praise were "impressive fruit", "awesome", "heaps of varietal character", "distinct notes of French oak". There followed a time when "delicacy", "balance", "harmony", and "elegance" became the bywords for quality. That moment turned out to be ephemeral. Within a very few years, "heaps" and "impressive" returned to fashion with greater vigour than before.

The American wine press has a disproportionately large role to play in deciding the fluctuating fortunes of any winery. Only in Bordeaux is the wine writer's verdict so eagerly awaited. With hundreds of wineries producing expensive Cabernets from Napa and Sonoma, the poor consumer needs help in making a choice. They can be forgiven for concluding that the wine with the highest score in the wine press is "the best" or "the hottest". The press tends to reward richness and power over finesse. Understated wines, such as those once produced by Mondavi, win relatively low scores because they are less rich (but often more elegant) than those of their rivals.

The proprietors of a great many California wineries are keen on their wines making a splash in society. Being, in the main, first-generation men and women in wine, these entrepreneurs and their winemakers must respond to the latest sales reports, rather than the voices of their fathers, or the voices of their often new vineyards. If society wants size, size it shall have, and California wine of late has become more top-heavy, and more alcoholic, than ever, with unabashed wines priced to appeal to princes. Even Pinot Noir sometimes weighs in at over 16% alcohol.

VARIETALS & VARIETIES

The useful if ungrammatical word "varietal" was coined in California as shorthand for a wine that is either made entirely from, or derives its character from, one named grape variety. Up to 1983, the law required that the named variety be a mere 51 per cent of the total. From 1983, the requirement is 75 per cent. Most high-quality varietals have long been closer to 100 per cent, but there is nothing in the rules to prevent a producer blending, for example, 20 per cent of Syrah into a Pinot Noir without declaring the blend on the label.

Yet, there is a growing band of producers, often small-scale, that have worked a vintage or two in Gevrey-Chambertin or St-Julien, and who are trying to fashion wines with elegance as well as the hallmark lushness of California grapes. But it's not easy. California grape-growers might talk of "cool-climate" regions, but California's climate is more Mediterranean than Bordelais or Burgundian.

Personal taste is the final arbiter – as I was reminded when I rashly asked a gathering in New York if they would really like all red Bordeaux to have the character of the great champion of modern vintages, 1961. "Of course," they said. What a fool I must be, not to want the most concentrated, the most over-whelmingly full-flavoured (but the least refreshing) of all wines with every meal. Perhaps they had a point. After all, the 1961 clarets are shy little things in the face of California's most outsized efforts.

The Climate

Since Prohibition ended or, more precisely, since the University of California at Davis became eminent in research, California has looked more to sun than soil for guidance as to where to plant which varieties. Between 1940 and 1960, scientists at the university developed a system of five climate regions that governed planting in California for several decades, but is now substantially out of use. It was based on cumulative heat during an April 1 to October 31 growing season. The measure is "degree days" (a day's average temperature minus 50).

The regions approximate roughly to: Burgundy (Region I, up to 2,500 degree days); Bordeaux (Region II, 2,500–3,000 degree days); the Rhône (Region III, 3,000–3,500 degree days); Sherry (Region IV, 3,500–4,000 degree days); and North Africa/Middle East (Region V, over 4,000 degree days).

The system worked well enough to steer growers to Monterey and the Santa Maria Valley in Santa Barbara in the 1970s, but mounting experience with climate regions has shown as many shortcomings as virtues. Chardonnay prospers in several locales where heat says it should not, and Cabernet refuses to ripen at sites where heat says it should. That is because the system cannot take into account important factors such as hours of daylight, susceptibility to fog and/or wind, soil fertility, and elevation.

The Soils

While, in California, the notion of climate regions rules, soil was thought to play a role only in so far as it drained well or poorly. Though a smattering of growers have begun to suspect a great role for it, soil has yet to be treasured in anything like the way it is in Europe. Progress, to give the devil his due, will be slow. In the coastal counties where fine points matter most, soils are erratic, because California's geologically young Coastal Ranges are endlessly changing. Two examples may suffice.

At the grandest scale, the San Andreas fault marks two separate pieces of the North American tectonic plate. Soils on opposite sides of California's most famous manufacturer of earthquakes can be completely unrelated within a distance of mere inches – most strikingly so in the Santa Cruz Mountains.

On a far smaller level, what is now called the Russian River drained through the Napa Valley into San Francisco Bay, until geological activity caused Mount St Helena to rise, blocking its course, at which point it turned westwards to flow into the Pacific Ocean, leaving the Alexander and Napa Valleys to evolve in different ways.

It must also be remembered that the growers of St-Emilion, of Meursault, of Chianti, have had centuries to work out, essentially by trial and error, which grape varieties are best adapted to which soils. In those corners of California that have been growing grapes for a century or more, it is also possible to point to the best terroirs. But to say that Rutherford is the source of magnificent Cabernet is not the same as to explain why that should be the case. In Europe wine estates usually grow the grapes they require. In California grape farmers dominate the industry, and the "estate-grown" wine is the exception rather than the rule. For farmers the temptation is to plant the variety that will fetch the best price rather than the one best adapted to a particular terroir.

Terroir, in California as elsewhere, is an infinitely subtle hodgepodge of factors, bundling together climate, soil, subsoil, drainage, wind strength, luminosity, clonal material, and many others. What is remarkable is how much California has achieved with so little understanding of its vineyards. When, in decades to come, that understanding has evolved, and been absorbed into the production of wine, the results could be even more spectacular.

American Viticultural Areas (AVAs)

As climate was losing ground and soil was failing to gain it, American grape-growers, led by Californians, persuaded the US federal government to establish a rudimentary system of appellations of origin, beginning in the early 1970s. The regulations do nothing more than draw boundaries around more or less homogeneous areas. They imply no degree of quality. They impose no limitations on varieties, nor planting practices, nor yields. Indeed, they permit a wine to carry the area name when up to 15 per cent of it comes from grapes grown elsewhere.

In spite of all that, the more than 100 California AVAs are proving useful, at least up to a point. They are forcing growers to look at which varieties grow better than others, and to plant them. Carneros and Chardonnay are one case in point, the Russian River Valley and Pinot Noir another. As a result, the viticultural areas are the most useful framework for any *tour d'horizon* of contemporary California. Names with a black dot preceding them indicate an important AVA. The principal sub-AVAs are then indented below the heading.

North Coast AVA This encompasses most of Lake County, Mendocino, Napa, Sonoma, and Marin, the major wine-growing counties north of San Francisco Bay.

• **Napa County/Napa Valley AVA** The most concentrated and prestigious region with 14,800 hectares and some 400 wineries. The cooler southern tip (Carneros) of a 40-kilometre- (25-mile-) long valley, opens out onto San Francisco Bay. The warmer northern end (Calistoga) is sheltered by landmark Mount St Helena.

The towns between, south to north, are Napa, Yountville, Oakville, Rutherford, and St Helena. Diverse soils and climates make it versatile, but history, old and new, favours Cabernet Sauvignon above all other varieties. Recent figures in hectares include: Cabernet Sauvignon (7,589), Merlot (2,775), Pinot Noir (1,100), Cabernet Franc (1,340), Syrah (1,400), Zinfandel (1,670), Chardonnay (9,850), and Sauvignon Blanc (4,000).

Atlas Peak AVA Upland valley AVA east of Stags Leap, developed with Sangiovese foremost in mind (but not necessarily best).

Carneros AVA At the southern end of the valley, and shared with Sonoma County. Designed for Pinot Noir but Chardonnay is the gem, and Merlot and Syrah are coming up. Sparkling wine is a particular strength.

Yountville AVA Valley floor of southern Napa Valley. Lean, elegant Cabernet and excellent Chardonnay.

Howell Mountain AVA In the hills east of St Helena; historic home of Zinfandel, now more planted with Cabernet.

Napa Valley vineyards

Mount Veeder AVA In hills west of Napa and Yountville; mostly Cabernet.

Rutherford AVA The heart of the valley, where Cabernet has grown longest, and some would say, best.

Oakville AVA Adjoins Rutherford on the south and extends Cabernet zone, but grows every grape variety from Chardonnay to Zinfandel surprisingly well. No white better than Sauvignon Blanc.

St Helena AVA Adjoins Rutherford on the north; planted mainly with Cabernet Sauvignon.

Spring Mountain AVA The hills west of St Helena grow Cabernet and Chardonnay, and a dash of fine Riesling.

Diamond Mountain AVA In the hills west of Calistoga. Exceptional for robust Cabernet.

Stags Leap District AVA In the southeast quarter of the

GRAPES & GENERIC WINE NAMES

Alicante Bouschet A red, jug-wine standby, giving density and colour, but a few wineries produce single-varietal versions. 450 hectares.

Barbera High-acid variety planted mostly in hotter San Joaquin Valley for blending. Shows considerable promise in Sierra Foothills. 3,450 hectares.

Cabernet Franc Plantings steady, especially in North Coast and Santa Barbara; mostly for blending with Cabernet Sauvignon and Merlot, but increasingly for varietals. 1,410 hectares.

Cabernet Sauvignon Makes California's best red: fruity, fragrant, tannic, full-bodied. Needs maturing in oak, and from Napa at least four years in bottle. The best comes from the central Napa Valley, parts of Sonoma, and the Santa Cruz Mountains. 30,740 hectares.

Carignane Some old vines survive in field blends in Sonoma and Mendocino, and lesser-quality vineyards in the San Joaquin Valley. Gradually declining. 1,625 hectares.

Carnelian A red crossing introduced in 1973, it added colour but not flavour to blends, and is now in decline. 390 hectares.

Charbono Red grape of mysterious origins, giving inky, thick-textured wines. Has detractors as well as fans, but with only 30 hectares, hard to find.

Chardonnay California's most successful white grape, capable of great wines in the Burgundian tradition with barrel fermentation and lees stirring. Good judgement is needed not to produce over-intense, ponderous wines (especially in Napa). Parts of Sonoma and the Central Coast (Monterey, Santa Barbara) tend to have a lighter touch. At its pinnacle in

Carneros, Anderson Valley; excels in Russian River Valley, and (in a quirkier way) Edna Valley. Surprisingly good in Ukiah, even Lodi. Huge plantings have made it California's most-planted variety at 38,200 hectares.

Chenin Blanc A surprisingly popular, usually rather dull white grape, appreciated for its high crop, good acidity levels, and clean, adaptable flavour. Pleasant when semi-sweet (although best dry); good in blends not needing age. Plantings peaked at 12,500 hectares in 1990; now dropped to 4,600 hectares.

Dolcetto This Piedmontese grape is being attempted by a dozen wineries, but results so far bear little resemblance to the toothsome original. A mere 37 hectares.

French Colombard High-acid, white, blending variety mostly planted in hotter regions of San Joaquin Valley, where very high yields made it popular. Plantings have dwindled from a peak of 25,000 hectares down to 11,700.

Fumé Blanc See Sauvignon Blanc.

Gamay Beaujolais Not the Beaujolais grape, but a form of Pinot Noir. In the process of being phased out. 56 hectares.

Gewurztraminer After a hesitant start, a success in California, where its wine is oddly softer and less spicy than in Alsace. Most successful in Anderson Valley, nearly as good in Russian River Valley, and parts of Salinas Valley. 560 hectares.

Grenache A source of flavourful red or rosé in warmer Monterey areas. Most plantings in San Joaquin, often for port style wines. Being taken more seriously as part of the Rhône variety revival. 3,000 hectares.

Johannisberg Riesling (or White Riesling) Despite impressive results in both dry and late-harvest styles in Anderson Valley, Spring Mountain, and parts of Sonoma, California Riesling has failed to match the success of the variety in Oregon and Washington. 800 hectares.

Malbec Mostly used in California for blending in Meritage styles. Arrowood (q.v.) produces the best single-varietal version. Currently 450 hectares.

Malvasia Bianca The common Italian grape, recommended for dessert wines in hotter regions such as southern Monterey but capable of pleasant, soft, table wine in cooler areas. 730 hectares.

Marsanne From Mendocino to Santa Barbara, winemakers are trying their hand at Marsanne. No version has yet risen to great heights. 28 hectares.

Meritage Term concocted, after a competition in 1988, to describe Bordeaux blends from California. By no means universally adopted on labels.

Merlot The Pomerol grape became a runaway success as a varietal, especially when made bland and priced moderately. Now being elbowed aside by Pinot Noir. 21,700 hectares.

Mission The coarse old local grape of the Franciscan missionaries. Some 240 hectares are left in the hottest regions and the Sierra Foothills.

Mourvèdre/Mataro No examples of this grape from its Provençal heartland of Bandol can match the centenarian vineyards of Contra Costa County for longevity. The few producers with access to these vineyards make splendid wines. 350 hectares.

valley floor, devoted almost entirely to Cabernet Sauvignon, more supple here than elsewhere in Napa.

Oak Knoll District AVA South of Yountville, so a cool area, known for Cabernet, Merlot, and Chardonnay.

Chiles Valley AVA East of Howell Mountain, best for Cabernet and Zinfandel.

Wild Horse Valley AVA East of Carneros, a relatively cool upland valley. Only 40 hectares planted.

Other AVAs are pending, notably Calistoga and Pope Valley (due north of Chiles, extending to the Lake County line, splendid for Sauvignon Blanc).

• **Sonoma County** Napa's nearest rival both physically and in terms of prestige. Sonoma sits between the Pacific and Napa. It is much larger in area than Napa, and more diverse, geologically and topographically. There is no blanket AVA

Muscat or Moscato The best is Muscat de Frontignan or Moscato di Canelli, recommended for white table wines in cooler regions; for dessert wines in hotter areas. Its best production is a sweet, low-alcohol wine so unstable that it must be kept refrigerated. 390 hectares planted. Muscat of Alexandria is a hot-climate grape grown mainly for eating.

Napa Gamay To avoid confusion with Gamay Beaujolais (q.v.), this variety, which may have some distant kinship with Gamay itself, has been renamed Valdiguié. 215 hectares.

Nebbiolo Piedmont's noble grape, now up to 74 hectares in California. Fog is the very thing it likes best. Few convincing results as yet.

Petit Verdot Gaining popularity as a prized component in Bordeaux blends. 524 hectares.

Petite Sirah California's name for a robust and tannic French grape, Durif, and other equally obscure varieties. Can be intriguing, especially from Sonoma, Napa, and Mendocino, but mostly useful for giving colour and tannin to Rhône-style blends. 2,480 hectares.

Pinot Blanc Similar to a low-key Chardonnay, whether actually the Muscadet grape Melon (most of the total) or true Pinot Blanc. 195 hectares.

Pinot Gris Increasingly popular in both Alsace and (mostly) Italian styles, but so far, Oregon has proved far more successful with this grape than California. 2,945 hectares.

Pinot Noir Burgundy's red grape is widely regarded as the last great hurdle for California's winemakers – early results were overstrong, heavy, and dull. Recent years have seen increasing popularity and success, especially in Anderson Valley, Russian River Valley, Santa Barbara, Carneros, Arroyo Grande, and Santa Lucia Highlands. Also used to make classic-method sparkling wines. 11,850 hectares.

Port A "generic" name taken from the Old World for sweet dessert wine, which rarely resembles the Portuguese original – although it may well have qualities of its own. Most are made from Zinfandel or Petite Sirah, a handful from the Douro varieties used for genuine port.

Roussanne There were blushes all around when it turned out that some delicious Roussannes from the later 1990s were, in fact, made from mislabelled Viognier vines. Authentic Roussanne grows in San Luis Obispo, with excellent results. 72 hectares.

Ruby Cabernet Bred by H P Olmo at Davis to give balanced, Cabernet-like wines from warmest climates, it proved a useful blending component in San Joaquin Valley. 2,720 hectares.

Sangiovese A new hope in the late 1980s, Tuscany's great red thus far has shown greatest promise in Amador, performing almost as well in Mendocino (Ukiah-Hopland), Sonoma (Alexander Valley), and Napa (Atlas Peak). But its popularity is waning. 900 hectares.

Sauvignon Blanc Mondavi invented the term Fumé Blanc for oaked Sauvignon, the style that remained most popular until recent years, when a preference emerged for fresher versions, often unoaked and vinified without aspirations to producing a poor man's Chardonnay. A clonal varation called Sauvignon Musqué gives a more tropical rendering of the grape's aromas and flavours, and is favoured by some growers and winemakers. 6,250 hectares.

Sémillon Bordeaux's sweet-wine and Australia's dry wine grape, little exploited as yet in California, where it is generally too productive. 465 hectares.

Sherry California "sherry" has never achieved the standard of imitation of the Spanish original found in, for example, South Africa. Usually heated to mimic the oxidative character of genuine sherry.

Syrah In 1986, there were only 50 hectares planted across the state; today there are 7,620. Syrah flourishes just about everywhere: in Napa, the Sierra Foothills, Paso Robles, and Santa Barbara. Delivers rich, peppery wines of a quality that's improving from year to year.

Thompson Seedless A neutral white table, dessert, and distilling wine grape. Never mentioned on the label, but often present in many jug whites and Charmat sparklers. Its 90,000 hectares are grown mostly for raisins; about one-third of its crop is crushed for wine such as "sherry".

Valdiguié Hard-to-pronounce new name for Napa Gamay (q.v.).

Viognier Rhône Rangers couldn't resist trying their hand at this tricky grape. A handful succeed, but many California Viogniers are either too oaky or too alcoholic. 900 hectares.

Zinfandel California's own red grape, of Croatian origin, and identical to the Italian Primitivo. Immensely successful and popular for all levels of wine, from cheap blends to fresh, light versions, and to galumphing, sticky blackstrap. The best have excellent balance, a lively raspberry flavour and ample backbone. "White" (blush) Zinfandel is a commercial smash hit. 21,000 hectares.

covering its 14,600 hectares of vines and 200-plus wineries. Nor is it synonymous with one grape variety. The major players in hectares are: Cabernet Sauvignon (5,120), Merlot (3,050), Pinot Noir (4,470), Syrah (740), Zinfandel (2,440), Chardonnay (6,500), Sauvignon Blanc (1,100).

Alexander Valley AVA Reaches north from Healdsburg to Mendocino County line; a warm valley, at its best with Cabernet Sauvignon and Zinfandel.

Bennett Valley AVA Created in 2003, a 260-hectare region south of Santa Rosa and dominated by the Matanzas Creek estate.

Carneros AVA Sonoma has more than half of the surface area in this, which is shared with Napa, but less than half of the vineyards. See Napa.

Dry Creek Valley AVA Ever warmer as it runs northwest from Healdsburg, superbly suited to Zinfandel, and showing promise with both red and white Rhône varieties.

Rockpile AVA Approved in 2002, 65 hectares in hot coastal hills of northwest Sonoma.

Knights Valley AVA Due north of Calistoga in Napa; mostly Cabernet, most of which goes to wineries outside this sparsely populated region.

Russian River Valley AVA Fog-cooled, broad expanse ranging from Healdsburg, south to Santa Rosa, southwest to Forestville and Sebastopol; shows best with Pinot Noir and Chardonnay for both still and sparkling, yet does well with Zinfandel, too. Green Valley (Chardonnay, sparkling wine) is the cooler sub-AVA of Russian River Valley; Chalk Hill (Chardonnay, Sauvignon) the warmer one. The valley remains best-known for its rich, spicy, and elegant Pinot Noirs, produced with consistent success for over 20 years

Sonoma Valley AVA Stretches from Santa Rosa south through Kenwood and Glen Ellen to Sonoma town, where it opens to San Francisco Bay, without declaring a particular variety as premier. Cabernet-dominated Sonoma Mountain is a sub-AVA to Sonoma Valley; also, Sonoma Valley overlaps Sonoma's portion of Carneros.

Northern Sonoma AVA Covers all of the Russian River drainage. Sonoma Coast AVA is another catch-all, but includes some vineyards high in the coastal range that are proving excellent for Chardonnay and Pinot Noir. Growers in the coastal range are petitioning for their own AVA, cumbersomely named Fort Ross/Seaview.

• **Mendocino County/Mendocino AVA** Directly north of Sonoma County, Mendocino – and the Mendocino AVA – are splendidly schizophrenic. The region from Redwood Valley south through Ukiah and Hopland is warmer and drier than any part of Sonoma, but over a markedly shorter season. There are 56 wineries in the county. The coastward Anderson Valley is as cool and rainy as California grape-growing areas can be. The county has about 40 wineries and 6,800 hectares under vine. Principal varieties are: Cabernet Sauvignon (1,060 hectares), Chardonnay (1,750), Pinot Noir (770). Despite being rather thinly planted, Gewurztraminer and Riesling are important in Anderson Valley.

Anderson Valley AVA Anchored on Boonville on the cool west side of the county, the valley has made some of California's most extraordinary dry Gewurztraminer, elegant Riesling, long-lived Chardonnay, and Champagne-like sparkling wines, since its revival in the late 1960s.

McDowell Valley AVA A tiny, essentially one-winery area in the southeast corner of the county, which does well with Rhône varieties, red and white.

Potter Valley AVA A sparsely settled, upland valley northeast of Ukiah, which sends most of its grapes elsewhere. Chardonnay currently appears to lead.

Redwood Valley AVA Warm, inland area north of Ukiah, best for Cabernet and Petite Sirah.

Mendocino Ridge AVA Between Anderson Valley and the Pacific, limited to vineyards high in the coastal mountains.

Other minor Mendocino AVAs are Cole Ranch, Dos Rios, and Yorkville Highlands.

• **Lake County AVA** North of Napa, east of Mendocino, Lake County is the warmest and driest grape-growing region

---

ANDRÉ TCHELISTCHEFF & THE CONSULTANTS

Long before his death, aged 92, in 1994, the California wine world had silently and unanimously bestowed the title of its "dean" on André Tchelistcheff. Born in Russia and trained in France, his career spanned the whole history of the industry, from Prohibition to the current decade; for 36 years (1937–73) at Beaulieu and thereafter, as consultant to many of the best wineries all over California and beyond. He threw out, or revamped, outdated winery equipment, introduced cold fermentation for white wines and malolactic for reds, and in the early 1940s introduced the idea of ageing red wine in small oak barrels. His Reserve Cabernet from top Rutherford vineyards, named after his employer Georges de Latour, has served as a model for California winemakers ever since. Among the many winemakers who were at least partly trained by him, are the late Joe Heitz, Mike Grgich of Grgich Hills, and Warren Winiarski of Stag's Leap.

Today, there is a new band of consultant oenologists whose usually well-publicized contribution confers instant cachet on any wine they help to produce. They tend to be experts in viticulture as well as winemaking, and are often no slouches when it comes to marketing either. At present, some of the names to conjure with are: Helen Turley, Heidi Peterson Barrett, Philippe Melka, Andrew Erickson, and Marco diGiulio.

on the North Coast. Primary plantings in its 3,500 hectares of vineyard are: Cabernet Sauvignon (1,340) and, most brilliant to date, Sauvignon Blanc (730). There are only 14 wineries, but many large wineries throughout the state buy grapes from here. Lake County AVAs are Clear Lake (where Sauvignon Blanc excels), Red Hills, Benmore Valley, Guenov Valley, and High Valley.

• **Central Coast** Where the North Coast is a compact though woozy 2:1 rectangle, the Central Coast is a scaled-down imitation of Chile, a 560-kilometre- (350-mile-) long snake-thin strip, running from southern San Francisco Bay all the way to Santa Barbara County. The principal wine-growing counties it includes are, north to south, Monterey, San Luis Obispo, and Santa Barbara, with Alameda and San Benito counties in supporting roles.

• **Santa Barbara County** Significant viticulture has only been established here since the early 1970s, yet in this short career, Santa Barbara has begun to emerge as a distinctive region in its own right. It now has around 100 wineries, and 8,540 hectares of vines, with Chardonnay (2,900) and Pinot Noir (1,300) primary among them. The county also shows great promise for Syrah and Merlot.

Santa Maria Valley AVA Sea-fog-cooled, true east-to-west valley, running inland from the town of Santa Maria. Memorable, above all, for Pinot Noir.

Santa Ynez Valley AVA Pinot Noir excels in a fog-cooled stretch from Lompoc to Buellton; Cabernet Sauvignon, Sauvignon Blanc, and (unaccountably) Riesling, prevail in a sunnier and much warmer zone inland of Buellton, around Solvang and Los Olivos County.

Santa Rita Hills AVA Approved in 2001, this cool area lies at the western end of Santa Ynez Valley and has developed its own style of full-bodied Pinot Noir.

• **San Luis Obispo County** The county has a long history, mostly with Zinfandel, a durable presence in hills west of Paso Robles. Diversity arrived with the wine boom of the 1970s in the form of both more varieties and more growing regions, especially down on the cool plain stretching south from San Luis Obispo town. The county has 110 wineries, and more than 11,200 hectares of vines. Cabernet Sauvignon (3,500 hectares) and Merlot (1,700) dominate red plantings, although the region is becoming better known for Syrah and Zinfandel. Other than the AVAs listed below, there is a minor hill region called York Mountain.

Arroyo Grande AVA Based in the eponymous town at the southernmost corner of the county, Arroyo Grande was planted for sparkling wine, but still Pinot Noir and Chardonnay are now dominant.

Edna Valley AVA Lies between the towns of San Luis Obispo and Arroyo Grande; planted almost entirely with Chardonnay.

Paso Robles AVA Mountain-sheltered, relentlessly sunny, high inland valley; the hills west of Paso Robles town continue to produce heady Zinfandel and splendid Rhône-style reds; the rolling plain east of that town is newly famous for soft Cabernet.

• **Monterey County/Monterey AVA** Monterey blossomed in the late 1960s as an easy answer to urban pressures on old vineyards in Alameda and Santa Clara counties, and then exploded in plantings in the early 1970s to a peak of 15,000 hectares. Today the total has risen slightly to 16,200. Most of the vines are in the Salinas Valley from Gonzales down through Soledad and Greenfield to King City. Major local wineries are thin on the ground, so most of the grapes go elsewhere as the basis of "Coastal" commodity wines. Leading grape varieties are Chardonnay and Cabernet Sauvignon. Also Merlot, Pinot Noir, Syrah and Sauvignon Blanc.

Arroyo Seco AVA The floor of the Salinas Valley between Soledad and Greenfield grows whites well, especially lightsome Chardonnay.

Carmel Valley AVA Monterey's only ocean-facing district, with sheltered vineyards that grow some dark, intriguing Cabernet on high ground, where sea fog seldom reaches.

Chalone AVA High in the Gavilan Mountains above the east side of the Salinas Valley at Soledad is a virtual monopoly of Chalone Vineyards (q.v.).

Santa Lucia Highlands AVA The west hills of the Salinas Valley, from Gonzales down to Greenfield, recently planted, yet already producing some lush Pinot Noir and Syrah.

Other minor AVAs are Hames Valley, San Bernabe, and San Lucas.

• **Alameda County** Urban expansion has made the historic Livermore Valley virtually the last redoubt of grapes in the county. Livermore is the main wine town, Pleasanton its satellite. Leading varieties among a total 1,000 hectares are Chardonnay, Cabernet Sauvignon, Merlot, and Sauvignon Blanc.

San Francisco Bay AVA is a catch-all for Alameda County and the area south of San Francisco.

Livermore Valley AVA East of San Francisco Bay, anchored on the town of Livermore, Sauvignon Blanc, and Semillon make inimitable wines in an historic district, but do not reign because Chardonnay rules the market.

• **Santa Clara/Santa Cruz Counties** In the nineteenth century, when Almaden and Paul Masson were powers, Santa Clara rivalled Napa, but those palmy times long since have given way to silicon in chips. Little remains, but what does falls mostly within the well-regarded Santa Cruz Mountains AVA.

Santa Cruz Mountains AVA Encompasses parts of, from north to south, San Mateo, Santa Clara, and Santa Cruz counties. Acreage here, although modest, is gradually increasing and now stands at 450 hectares, tended by 60 producers.

Other minor AVAs: Santa Clara Valley; San Ysidro, to the east of Gilroy; and Ben Lomond.

• **San Benito County** In its heyday, Almaden planted vines on several thousands of acres in San Benito, and successfully lobbied for some new AVAs to encompass them before abandoning them and the region. Most of the AVAs (and some of the vineyards) have fallen into disuse. Currently, only one AVA flourishes: Mount Harlan. The others are Cienega Valley, Lime Kiln Valley, Pacheco Pass, and Paicines. Mount Harlan AVA High in the Gavilan Mountains and the fiefdom of Calera Winery (q.v.), Mount Harlan almost backs onto the similar fiefdom of Chalone (q.v.).

• **South Coast AVA** Covers the subtropical to desertous counties south of the Techachapi Mountains, most notably Riverside, where Temecula's 520 hectares dominate the region. Scattered small plantings are in Los Angeles, Orange, and San Diego counties, larger ones in San Bernardino (where historic Cucamonga, with 400 hectares and three wineries remaining, is fading towards extinction as a growing area, due to urban pressure from Los Angeles).

San Pasqual AVA A one-vineyard AVA east of San Diego, too often beset with Pierce's disease to have declared itself.

Temecula AVA In the southwest corner of Riverside County, along San Diego County's north boundary. Pioneered in the late 1960s, versatile in a modest way, with several of its 20 producers beginning to look beyond Chardonnay and Sauvignon to Rhône and/or Italian red varieties for a new lift. Pierce's disease has destroyed many vineyards since the '90s.

• **The Interior** The huge San Joaquin Valley – modestly supplemented by the minnow Sacramento Valley – is California's Midi. Huge volume is generally the watchword in, from north to south, San Joaquin, Stanislaus, Madera, Fresno, and Kern counties. A few particular areas give definition; quickly sketched, they are:

Lodi AVA A low-lying, rich-soiled, reliably sunny part of San Joaquin County, at the mouth of the San Joaquin Valley. Long famous for Zinfandel, and more recently, a source of large volumes of reliable Chardonnay, Cabernet Sauvignon, and Merlot for, in particular, blending into commodity wines.

Clarksburg AVA In many ways a westward extension of Lodi into the Sacramento river delta. It grows a Chenin Blanc of more character than most in California, but plantings have turned towards Chardonnay in answer to a booming market.

Dunnigan Hills AVA Success by the pioneer R H Phillips winery is drawing other growers into a nascent region, just in the lee of the Coastal Ranges, near the Sacramento County town of Woodside. Chardonnay is important by hectarage, Sauvignon Blanc by result.

• **Sierra Foothills AVA** The AVA covers nearly all of the vineyards in four counties: Amador, Calaveras, El Dorado, and Yuba. Amador, at the centre, has unbroken history going back to the Gold Rush. Area under vine is modest (2,300 hectares) with Zinfandel dominant. Vineyards range in elevation from 300–900 metres (1000–3000 feet). Small wineries rule.

El Dorado AVA Covers all of the vineyards in the eponymous county. One centre is in the hills north and east of Placerville. Rhône and Italian varieties have replaced Bordeaux in the hearts of many growers. Most of the other plantings in the region circling around Somerset are virtual extensions of Amador's Shenandoah Valley.

Shenandoah Valley-California AVA The historic heart of Gold Country wine growing stretches eastward from Plymouth to Fiddletown. It has made its fame with heady Zinfandels, often from centenarian vines. Here, too, Syrah and Sangiovese are quickly becoming the new challengers.

Fiddletown AVA Anchored on the village of Fiddletown, is an eastward, more elevated extension of the Shenandoah Valley.

Leading Napa Valley Producers

It is a dull (and unusual) week in California when another new winery does not announce itself. All it takes is a hectare or two of vines, some leased "custom crush" facilities, a label, a salesman, and a good review in the American wine press.

Specifically, each entry below states (if the information was available) the location of the winery, its ownership, vineyards owned (if any), website, and a brief description and assessment. Inevitably, there are omissions, but the following entries include all the major players, the top-quality producers, and a selection of smaller, but quirky or interesting estates or labels.

Acacia Winery ☆☆
Napa. Owner: Constellation. 60 ha.
www.acaciawinery.com
Acacia Pinot Noir has exciting qualities of freshness, the berry smell and soft texture of burgundy – clear indication, since reinforced, that the Carneros district suits the variety. In 1999, Acacia revived vineyard-designated Pinots, a practice abandoned some years earlier in favour of blends. Quality is less distinctive now that Acacia is under corporate ownership.

Araujo ☆☆☆☆
Calistoga. Owner: Bart Araujo. 16 ha.
www.araujoestatewines.com
In the early 1990s, Bart Araujo bought one of the Napa's most famous vineyards, Eisele, and began producing the wine under his own label with advice from Michel Rolland. The Cabernet remains a Napa classic, and there is splendid Syrah, too. Biodynamic since 2000.

Artesa ☆☆
Napa. Owner: Codorníu S.A. 162 ha.
www.artesawinery.com
The second major sparkling wine producer, established in Carneros by a Spanish Cava house, Codorníu Napa is bold in architecture (glasshouse modern) but cautious in style. In the late 1990s, it changed its name from Codorníu, at the same time that it decreased sparkling wine production in favour of still wines from Chardonnay, Pinot Noir, and Merlot.

Vineyards holdings have expanded into Alexander Valley and the Sonoma Coast, and the range of wines has expanded correspondingly.

Atlas Peak Vineyards ☆–☆☆
Napa. Owner: Fortune Brands. 200 ha.
www.atlaspeak.com
The first serious effort to make Napa Valley into Sangiovese as well as Cabernet country was spearheaded by Piero Antinori and his co-investors. Antinori selected the Sangiovese strain from Montalcino, yet it took many years for high-quality wines to emerge, and then only in the case of the Reserves. Consenso is a Sangiovese/Cabernet blend, and there is also a series of Cabernets from other Napa "mountain" AVAs.

Baldacci Vineyards ☆–☆☆
Stags Leap. Owner: Tom Baldacci. 15 ha.
www.baldaccivineyards.com
An ambitious, perhaps over-ambitious, range of wines, of which the best are the luscious Cabernets from the estate vineyard.

Beaulieu Vineyards ☆–☆☆☆
Rutherford. Owner: Diageo. 500 ha. www.bvwines.com
Founded by a French family, the de Latours, B V (as it is familiarly known) set the pace in the Napa Valley throughout the 1940s, 1950s, and 1960s under a winemaker of genius, the late Russian-born André Tchelistcheff. At Beaulieu, he pioneered small-barrel ageing and malolactic fermentation for reds, cold fermentations for whites, and was one of the first to discover the virtues of the Carneros region for cool-climate varieties. After the founding family sold to Heublein in 1969, and Tchelistcheff retired in 1973, Beaulieu went into a long period of drift. But by the late 1990s, there were signs of revival. There are many different ranges of wines.

At the top are the Reserves (including Carneros Chardonnay, the Tapestry Bordeaux blend, and Tchelistcheff's legacy, the Georges de Latour Private Reserve Cabernet Sauvignon). Also of interest is the Signet Collection of limited production wines, often from Rhône or Italian varieties. In the middle an extensive grouping of Napa Valley varietals is led by a vibrant Sauvignon Blanc. At the low end of the price scale is Coastal line.

The Rhine House at the Beringer/Los Hermanos winery

Benessere ☆–☆☆
St Helena. Owner: John Benish. 20 ha.
www.benesserevineyards.com
Small quirky property with (for Napa) an atypical penchant for Sangiovese and Zinfandel.

Beringer Vineyards ☆☆–☆☆☆
St Helena. Owner: Foster's Wine Estates. 1,100 ha.
www.beringer.com
One of the great old stone-built wineries of Napa, with coolie-cut tunnels into the hills as its original cellars. Under the Beringers it declined, was bought in 1969 by Nestlé, which fixed it on an upward course. The late winemaker, Myron Nightingale, set a quiet, even reserved style after 1969. His speciality was a sweet Sauvignon made from grapes artificially botrytized, which is still occasionally produced.

His successor, Ed Sbragia, who directed winemaking here from 1984 to 2008, favoured bold wines. It was Sbragia who introduced the excellent barrique-aged Private Reserves from Cabernet, Chardonnay, and Merlot. The next ranges down are the varietal wines from Napa and Knights Valleys, while the more basic Founder's Estate consists of varietal wines with the California appellation. Quality is remarkably consistent at all levels.

Biale ☆☆☆
Napa. Owner: Biale family and partners. 3 ha.
www.robertbialevineyards.com
This small winery bottles up to nine Zinfandels, one from its own Aldo's Vineyard (planted 1937), the others from outstanding old vineyards in Napa and Sonoma. Highly consistent.

Blankiet ☆☆☆
Yountville. Owner: Claude Blankiet. 6 ha.
www.blankiet.com
Cult winery employing a string of top consultants who formerly fashioned estate-grown Merlot and Cabernet, but since 2006 have focused on a sumptuous, and exceedingly expensive, proprietary red.

Bond ☆☆☆
Oakville. Owner: Bill Harlan. www.bondestates.com
A clever concept dreamt up by the owner of Harlan Estate (q.v.), whereby he works jointly with the owners of a handful of hillside vineyards and markets the wines, produced by the Harlan winemaking team, under the collective and beautifully designed Bond label. Lavishly oaked Cabernets offered at a very high price.

Bouchaine ☆
Napa. Owner: Gerret Copeland. 35 ha.
www.bouchaine.com
Although the main focus here is on Pinot Noir, Bouchaine's wines are sourced from many parts of the North Coast, thus diluting its identity.

Bryant Family Vineyard ☆☆☆
Calistoga. Owner: Don Bryant. 4 ha.
One of Napa's cult Cabernets, immensely sweet and rich, selling for astonishingly high prices. Recent changes of winemaker have not altered its style.

Burgess Cellars ☆☆–☆☆☆
St Helena. Owner: Tom Burgess. 40 ha.
www.burgesscellars.com
This often underrated winery became known for its robust Cabernet Sauvignon and vibrant Zinfandel. The latter is no more: the vines were grafted over to Cabernet in 2003.

Cain Cellars ☆☆☆
St Helena. Owner: Meadlock family. 34 ha.
www.cainfive.com
"Cain Five" is an ambitious and solidly structured Bordeaux-style blend using estate and neighbouring Spring Mountain grapes. "Cain Cuvée" is its declassified, value sibling. Exotic Sauvignon is from Monterey plantings of the Musqué strain.

Cakebread Cellars ☆☆–☆☆☆
Oakville. Owner: Cakebread family. 138 ha.
www.cakebread.com
The Cakebreads gained a good reputation for their weighty, dry Sauvignon Blanc. But the Cabernets are of much greater interest, especially those made from selected parcels: Rutherford Reserve, Three Sisters, and Benchland Select. Fine quality, but expensive. Other wines are sourced from vineyards throughout the North Coast.

Cardinale ☆☆☆
Oakville. Owner: Jess Jackson. 85 ha.
www.cardinale.com
A Jackson label, drawing on mountain vineyards in Napa and Sonoma. Very rich, and expensive, Cabernet/Merlot blends.

Caymus Vineyards ☆–☆☆☆
Rutherford. Owner: Chuck Wagner. 61 ha.
www.caymus.com
Caymus used to produce a wide range of wines, but by 2000, Wagner was focusing almost exclusively on Cabernet, especially the sleek and highly acclaimed Special Selection. The successful white blend, Conundrum, is now being produced at a different facility in Monterey. See Mer Soleil.

Chappellet ☆☆☆
St Helena. Owner: Donn Chappellet. 48 ha.
www.chappellet.com
Donn Chappellet was the second man, behind Robert Mondavi, to build a new winery in the Napa. He has long been renowned for his deep-flavoured, austere, built-to-last Cabernet Sauvignon, from the uppermost slopes of his amphitheatrical vineyards. In recent years, there have been two Cabernets. One, subtitled Pritchard Hill, is approachable early. The other, Donn Chappellet Signature, upholds the original premise and fulfils the original promise.

Chappellet is also one of the few reliable sources for dry, firm, long-flavoured Chenin Blanc as well as an extraordinary *moelleux* – sadly, quantities have diminished. A remarkable range includes Chardonnay, which ages admirably and big, easy, and charming Cabernet Franc.

Chateau Montelena ☆☆–☆☆☆☆
Calistoga. Owner: Michel Reybier. 33 ha.
www.montelena.com
Old stone winery, north of Calistoga, at the foot of Mount

St Helena, which has a 30-year record of some of the best California Chardonnays and Cabernets from the estate vineyard. Two distinguished winemakers set the style here: Mike Grgich up to 1974, followed by Jerry Luper up to 1981. Since 1981, Bo Barrett has maintained the highest quality. The Chardonnay, lean with very little new oak, is atypical of most from Napa, and much fresher. The Napa Cabernet is a much cheaper alternative to the costly Estate Cabernet. In 2008 the property was sold to the owner of Château Cos d'Estournel.

Chateau Potelle ☆–☆☆
Mt Veeder. Owner: Fourmeaux family. 120 ha.
www.chateaupotelle.com
Jean-Noël and Marketta Fourmeaux du Sartel came to California as agents of the French government, to measure California's wine industry. They liked what they saw enough to join up, beginning as négociants, and eventually buying vineyards and a winery high on Mount Veeder. They also buy in fruit from Paso Robles. Quality is inconsistent, but the best wines appear under the cryptic VGS label.

Chimney Rock ☆☆–☆☆☆
Stags Leap Owner: Terlato Wine Group. 48 ha.
www.chimneyrock.com
Winemaker Doug Fletcher's silky Cabernet epitomizes its region of origin, and new owners have focused exclusively on Bordeaux varieties, white and red. The Cape Dutch design of the winery makes a pleasing, if anomalous, contribution to the Silverado Trail that runs through the eastern side of the valley.

Clos du Val ☆☆–☆☆☆
Stags Leap. Owner: John Goelet. 134 ha.
www.closduval.com
Winemaker Bernard Portet was brought up at Château Lafite, where his father was manager. As in Bordeaux, he blends Merlot with Cabernet. His wines are reckoned supple by Napa standards, but they are still deep-coloured, juicy, and long on the palate. They can age beautifully. Pinot Noir and Chardonnay, both from Carneros, tend to be less assured. Taltarni in Victoria, Australia, has the same owner.

Clos Pegase ☆☆
Calistoga. Owner: Jan Shrem. 185 ha.
www.clospegase.com
A major architectural competition was won by the American architect Michael Graves. The resulting winery is Napa's most striking post-modernist building to date, and it is also home to Shrem's imposing modern art collection. It produces steadily improving Chardonnay, Merlot, Pinot Noir, and Cabernet, often in a gently herbaceous style.

Colgin ☆☆–☆☆☆
Oakville. Owner: Ann Colgin. 11 ha.
www.colgincellars.com
Renowned for extremely expensive, new-oaked Cabernet Sauvignons and Syrah. They epitomize the fashionable Napa style, with very high alcohol (close to 16 degrees).

Corison ☆☆☆
St Helena. Owner: Cathy Corison. 3 ha. www.corison.com
As winemaker at Chappellet from 1980–1989, Corison helped to solidify Chappellet Vineyard's reputation before launching out on her own. She makes nothing but Cabernet Sauvignon (apart from a little Anderson Valley Gewurztraminer), in a rich but elegant style. A vertical tasting held in 2007 of every vintage revealed admirable consistency.

Cosentino ☆
Yountville. Owner: Mitch Cosentino. 51 ha.
www.cosentinowinery.com
Cosentino buys in grapes from all over the North Coast and offers the countless visitors to his tasting room a wide range of wines. Many are excellent, but they tend to be hit and miss.

Robert Craig Wine Cellars ☆☆–☆☆☆
Napa. Owner: Robert Craig. 16 ha.
www.robertcraigwine.com
Craig specializes in rich, Cabernet-dominated blends from the mountains around Napa Valley.

Cuvaison ☆☆
Calistoga. Owner: Schmidheiny family. 182 ha.
www.cuvaison.com
The winery took on its present form in 1979, when the Swiss Schmidheiny family bought the business and developed a large vineyard property in Carneros. Chardonnay remains the star turn, especially the Reserve bottlings, but Cuvaison also produces very good Merlot and Pinot Noir.

Dalla Valle ☆☆☆–☆☆☆☆
Napa. Owner: Naoko Dalla Valle. 10 ha.
www.dallavallevineyards.com
Despite their reputation as Napa blockbusters, these Cabernet Sauvignon and Cabernet Franc wines from hillside vineyards have remarkable intensity and elegance. Recent replantings have severely reduced production, but by 2010 the estate will be back on track. In 2006 Michel Rolland became consultant.

Darioush ☆☆–☆☆☆
Napa. Owner: Darioush Khaledi. 40 ha.
www.darioush.com www.darioushwinery.com
A flamboyant property, built in homage to Persepolis, with a luxurious visitors' centre. The wines – most Napa Cabernet and Viognier, and Russian River Valley Chardonnay and Pinot Noir – are sumptuous yet rarely overblown.

Diamond Creek Vineyards ☆☆☆
Calistoga. Owner: Boots Brounstein. 9 ha.
www.diamondcreekvineyards.com
The Cabernet from these four small vineyards – Volcanic Hill, Red Rock Terrace, Gravelly Meadow, and Lake – reflects four different soils and situations, a subject little enough studied in California. They are all big, tough, wildly expensive wines, designed for long ageing, and repaying it. Cabernet Franc, Malbec, and Merlot are added to the predominant Cabernet Sauvignon. The creator of this beautifully landscaped property, Al Brounstein, died in 2006, but his widow maintains the high standards he set.

Domaine Carneros ☆☆
Carneros. Owner: Taittinger and Kobrand. 80 ha.
www.domaine.com

The winery, a pastiche of Taittinger's French château, makes a startling intrusion into the Carneros landscape; the wines, however, are a more graceful hybrid of Taittinger style and Carneros grapes. Still wines, especially Pinot Noir, are growing in volume at the expense of sparkling wines.

Domaine Chandon ☆☆
Yountville. Owner: LVMH. 445 ha.
www.domainechandon.com
The spearhead of France's invasion of California, a characteristically stylish and successful outpost of Moët in Champagne. A wine factory and an entertainment at the same time, with a first-class fashionable restaurant. All of the wines are excellent: the Reserve *cuvées* are the show stoppers; Etoile is an intriguing blend of older vintages. Out of context in Europe, the sheer fruitiness of the Napa grapes makes the wines taste rather sweet, even though they are substantially drier than most *brut* Champagnes. There is also a growing range of still wines.

Dominus ☆☆☆
Yountville. Owner: Christian Moueix.
42 ha. www.dominusestate.com
The then maker of Pétrus found his ideal Napa vineyard (ex-Inglenook) in the early 1980s. Applying Bordeaux techniques made his wines massive but unfriendly at first. Since 1991, Dominus has relaxed enough to rank just below Napa's very best Cabernets, and fine tuning continues.

Duckhorn Vineyards ☆☆–☆☆☆☆
St Helena. Owner: GI Partners. 75 ha.
www.duckhornvineyards.com
Duckhorn is best-known for his splendid Merlots, which he was producing long before the variety became so fashionable. The Cabernet is excellent too, as is the spicy Zinfandel/Cabernet/Merlot blend called Paraduxx. Duckhorn has also developed a Pinot Noir estate in Mendocino called Goldeneye (q.v.). In 2006 a private equity company took a controlling interest in the brand.

Dunn Vineyards ☆☆☆–☆☆☆☆☆
Howell Mountain. Owner: Randall Dunn. 14 ha.
Since 1979, this ex-Caymus winemaker has been making small lots of dark, stern Cabernet, both from his own Howell Mountain vineyards, and from purchased fruit. The wines are intense but restrained in style, and age exceedingly well, as Dunn intends.

Etude
Napa. Owner: Foster's Wine Estates. No vineyards.
www.etudewines.com
Consulting winemaker Soter started making wines under the Etude label, almost as much to showcase his technical ability to potential clients as for commercial reasons. The most esteemed wines were Pinot Noirs from Carneros, using varied clonal material. The company was sold in 2001 and Soter moved to Oregon to develop his own vineyards.

Far Niente ☆☆☆
Oakville. Owner: Nickel family. 100 ha.
www.farniente.com
A famous pre-Prohibition name, reborn in its original stone building, with its old vineyard replanted and now bearing fruit. From 1983 winemaker Dirk Hampson established the style here: extravagant, toasty Chardonnays; sumptuous, oaky Cabernets; and Dolce, a sweet wine, modelled, ambitiously, on Yquem. The current winemaker is Stephanie Putnam.

Flora Springs ☆☆–☆☆☆☆
St Helena. Owner: Komes and Garvey families.
264 ha. www.florasprings.com

After some years courting delicacy, especially in the Sauvignons, Flora Springs has turned gutsy in every wine on the list, especially in the Reserve Cabernets from Rutherford, and the Bordeaux blend called Trilogy. The latest projects are a Supertuscan-style wine called Poggio del Papa and various single vineyard Cabernets.

Folie à Deux ☆
St Helena. Owner: Trinchero family.
15 ha. www.folieadeux.com
From the 1990s Folie à Deux had a bipolar existence: inexpensive blends on the one hand, and some serious Napa Cabernet and Amador County Zinfandels on the other. In 2004 the property was bought by the Trinchero family, who have developed the range of commercial three-variety blends called Ménage à Trois, while preserving some of the more serious bottlings.

Forman ☆☆☆
St Helena. Owner: Ric Forman. 34 ha.
www.formanvineyard.net
The former Sterling winemaker, Ric Forman uses grapes from his own hill vineyards, and others down at Rutherford, to make classic French-style Chardonnay and Cabernet.

Franciscan ☆☆–☆☆☆☆
Rutherford. Owner: Constellation. 105 ha.
www.franciscan.com
With magnificently located vineyards in Rutherford and Carneros, it's hardly surprising that the winery is often at its peak with reds, most especially Cabernet Sauvignon and a Bordeaux blend called Magnificat. Franciscan also has a fine reputation for Cuvée Sauvage Chardonnay, fermented with natural yeasts. New corporate ownership has left the general approach of the winery unaltered.

Freemark Abbey ☆☆–☆☆☆
St Helena. Owner: Jackson Family Estates. 120 ha.
www.freemarkabbey.com
This famous winery was established in an abandoned nineteenth century stone winery, just north of St Helena, by a group of leading Napa grape growers. One partner

The Robert Mondavi winery, Oakville

(Brad Webb) had made history by pioneering small barrels at Hanzell (q.v.) in the late 1950s. The partners soon built up an excellent reputation for Chardonnay, and for rich Cabernets, none more so than an outstandingly concentrated and balanced wine from a Rutherford grower called Bosché (and so labelled).

In 1973, they pioneered sweet, botrytized Riesling, labelled Edelwein. In 2001, the ageing partners sold the property. After a financially turbulent period, the property was bought by Jess Jackson.

Frog's Leap ☆☆☆
Rutherford. Owner: John Williams. 80 ha.
www.frogsleap.com
Originally a partnership located on the site of the one-time frog farm that led to the name, it is now solely owned, and has moved to drier land at Rutherford. But the wines, especially the Cabernet and Zinfandel, remain everything they were when the winery was earning its reputation.

John Williams remains untainted by Napa glitz, and his wines, from organic, dry farmed vineyards, are balanced and immensely pleasurable. Perhaps it helps that Williams has one of the best senses of humour in Napa. Evidence: a white blend called Leapfrögmilch, now supplemented by the luscious Frögenbeerenauslese.

Green and Red Vineyard ☆☆–☆☆☆
St Helena. Owner: Jay Heminway. 13 ha.
www.greenandred.com
Tiny Chiles Valley winery that specializes in intense Zinfandel and Syrah, grown at high elevations.

Grgich Hills Cellars ☆☆–☆☆☆
Rutherford. Owner: Austin Hills and Mike Grgich.
150 ha. www.grgich.com
Croatian by birth, Grgich has been making wine in Napa Valley since the early 1960s, notably at Beaulieu and Chateau Montelena. His forte is Chardonnay, but the Cabernet and Zinfandel are consistently good. Biodynamic since 2006. The octogenarian Grgich is also leading a wine revival in his Croatian homeland.

Hagafen Cellars ☆
Napa. Owner: Ernie Weir. 8 ha.
www.hagafen.com
The original and still one of the leading producers of kosher wines from classic vinifera varieties.

Harlan Estate ☆☆☆☆
Oakville. Owner: Bill Harlan. 16 ha.
www.harlanestate.com
Property developer Bill Harlan founded the Merryvale winery, and established his own organic property in 1987. The top wine is a new-oaked Cabernet of impeccable balance and cult following. See also Bond.

Hartwell Vineyards ☆☆☆
Stags Leap. Owner: Bob Hartwell. 8 ha.
www.hartwellvineyards.com
Hartwell's Stags Leap vineyards yield exceptional Merlot and Cabernet Sauvignon.

Heitz ☆–☆☆☆
St Helena. Owner: Heitz family. 140 ha.
www.heitzcellar.com
Until his death in 2000, Joe Heitz was known worldwide for his Cabernet, more locally for his Chardonnay and specialties such as Grignolino "port". Yet they all reflected the man, a sometimes gruff original. Most of the grapes are bought from friends, one of whom, Martha May, has already passed into legend as the name on Martha's Vineyard, Heitz's flagship Cabernet: a dense and gutsy wine of spicy, cedary and gumtree flavours. Bella Oaks Vineyard is often of similar stature. Bacterial infections in the winery led to many disappointing bottles from the 1990s, but the problems were eventually sorted out, and recent vintages have been back on form.

Hess ☆☆–☆☆☆
Napa. Owner: Donald Hess. 320 ha.
www.hesscollection.com
Swiss businessman and art collector, Hess (the winery is in fact a museum) aims high with wines from estate vineyards on Mount Veeder, Howell Mountain, and near San Pablo Bay. The Hess Appellation wines, bearing the California appellation, have replaced the Hess Select range.

Hundred Acre ☆☆☆
St Helena. Owner: Jayson Woodbridge. 11 ha.
www.hundredacre.com
Canadian Woodbridge gave up the law in 1999 to purchase and develop vineyards in Napa. His opulent Cabernets, cleverly marketed, sell for very high prices. More recently, Woodbridge has been producing Shiraz from Barossa Valley, too.

Judd's Hill ☆☆–☆☆☆
St Helena. Owner: Art Finkelstein. 6 ha. www.juddshill.com
Finkelstein was one of the owners of the successful Whitehall Lane (q.v.), but sold up in 1988 and built up his own property in the eastern hills. Exceptional Estate Cabernet. Additions to the range include old-vine Zinfandel and Petite Sirah from Lodi.

Robert Keenan ☆
St Helena. Owner: Robert H Keenan. 20 ha.
www.keenanwinery.com
High, cool vineyards on Spring Mountain Road produce Chardonnay and Cabernet Sauvignon, which is blended with Napa Merlot and oak-aged. Even the Merlot, for which Keenan is now celebrated, can be tannic and astringent. The Zinfandel introduced in 1999 is considerably more ingratiating.

Charles Krug ☆☆
St Helena. Owner: Peter Mondavi and family. 345 ha.
www.charleskrug.com
C Mondavi & Sons is the company name at the oldest of Napa's historic wineries, now run by Cesare Mondavi's son, Peter. The other son was Robert, who left in 1966 to start his own winery, with spectacular success.

Krug, often underrated, produces a sound range of varietals at, for Napa, low prices; the Reserve bottlings are especially good value. Chardonnays from Carneros vineyards and a Pinot

Noir add depth to the range. The top wine is the excellent Vintage Selection Cabernet, produced only in top years. There is also a range of inexpensive wines under the CK Mondavi label, made from purchased fruit.

Kuleto ☆☆–☆☆☆
St Helena. Owner: Pat Kuleto. 50 ha.
www.kuletoestate.com
Restaurateur Pat Kuleto developed his wine estate in rugged canyon country near Pritchard Hill, and the first vintage was 2001. High elevation and cool nights gives the wines their freshness and zest.

Laird Family Estates ☆☆
Napa. Owner: Laird family. 810 ha.
www.lairdfamilyestate.com
The Lairds own vast vineyards throughout Napa, and until recently they sold the fruit to other wineries. From 1999 they started producing their own wines, drawing on their best parcels of Chardonnay, Cabernet, and Syrah.

Cliff Lede ☆☆–☆☆☆
Yountville. Owner: Cliff Lede. 22 ha.
www.cliffledevineyards.com
This Canadian building tycoon moved swiftly from 2003 onwards to create a new winery, tasting room, hotel, and art gallery. The top wine is Poetry, a Cabernet-based blend. Winemaker Michelle Edwards has been successful across the board. Even the silky, aromatic Sauvignon is irresistible.

Lewis Cellars ☆☆☆
Napa. Owner: Randy Lewis. No vineyards.
www.lewiscellars.com
Lewis buys in Napa Cabernet, Syrah, and Merlot, and Chardonnay from Russian River. The latter can be rather heavy, but the red Reserves are superb.

Livingston-Moffett ☆☆☆
St Helena. Owner: John Livingston. 4 ha.
www.livingstonwines.com
Long-lived Cabernet from the estate vineyards, as well as bought-in Cabernet, called Stanley's Selection.

Luna ☆☆
Napa. Owner: Mike Moone and partners. 9 ha.
www.lunavineyards.com
As well as Napa standards such as Cabernet and Merlot, Luna has focused on Italian varieties such as Pinot Grigio, Sangiovese, and Tocai Friulano. Well-made, but marked by high alcohol.

Markham Vineyards ☆
St Helena. Owner: Mercian. 140 ha.
www.markhamvineyards.com
One of the first Napa wineries to take Merlot seriously. Markham, although sold to a Japanese company in 1988, continues to turn out a range of well-made varietal wines, which is dependable if not especially exciting.

Louis M Martini ☆–☆☆
St Helena. Owner: E & J Gallo. 240 ha.
www.louismartini.com
Gallo bought this historical company in 2002. Three generations of Martinis have their name on the shortlist of California's great individual winemakers. Martini Cabernets of the 1960s rank alongside Beaulieu in quality, but in a different and leaner style: more reminiscent of claret. The business was bought by E & J Gallo in 2002, but the best wines, from the Monte Rosso Vineyard, have been retained.

Mayacamas ☆☆–☆☆☆
Napa. Owner: Robert Travers. 20 ha.
www.mayacamas.com
Mayacamas is the name of the mountains between Napa and Sonoma Counties. The Travers' predecessors, the Taylors, planted Chardonnay and Cabernet during the 1940s, in a spectacular natural amphitheatre 610 metres (2,000 feet) up. The sun, the fogs, the winds, the cold, and the rocks of the hills conspire to concentrate grape flavour into something you can chew.

Travers' Cabernets are awe-inspiring in colour and bite for the first five years at least. Those weaned on thick, fleshy, valley-floor Cabernets find the Mayacamas style unacceptably austere, but to other tasters they are an authentic reminder of the way Napa Cabernets used to taste. The Chardonnay is individual, too: lean and flinty.

Merryvale ☆☆☆
St Helena. Owner: Jack Slatter and partners. 30 ha.
www.merryvale.com
Two of California's best winemakers, Bob Levy and Steve Test, kept Merryvale at a high standard since the late 1980s, and Australian winemaker Larry Cherubino is maintaining high standards. Most of the wines appear under the sensibly priced Starmont label, but the top wines are meticulously crafted bottlings such as Silhouette Chardonnay, the Bordeaux blend, Profile, and remarkable Rutherford Cabernet.

Miner Family Vineyards ☆☆–☆☆☆
Oakville. Owner: Miner family. 35 ha.
www.minerwines.com
A glitzy new winery on the Silverado Trail is the showroom for this new property, underwritten by a computer software fortune. Opulent, oaky wines, the best being Cabernets from Napa and Pinot Noirs from Santa Lucia Highlands.

Robert Mondavi ☆☆–☆☆☆☆
Oakville. Owner: Robert Mondavi and family. 386 ha in Napa. www.robertmondavi.com
Mondavi's energy and enquiring mind took less than ten years to produce the most important development in the Napa Valley since Prohibition. He fitted the standard definition of a genius better than anyone I know. He aimed to achieve top quality but on an industrial scale. Inspiration and perspiration took him there (see box right).

The winery is (in the local jargon) state of the art. The "art" includes not only advanced analysis and every shiny gadget, but a personal knowledge of every French barrel-maker worth a hoop. In 2001, he built an even more splendid winery, equipped with wooden fermentation vats, in emulation of many a top Bordeaux château. Since the acquisition of the winery by the Constellation group, standards at the top end have been maintained by chief winemaker Genevieve Janssens.

Its best wine is the Cabernet Sauvignon Reserve; a gentle titan you can drink after dinner with relish, but would do well to keep for 20 years.

The regular Cabernet is a model of balance between berries and barrels, and there are excellent, if high-priced, regional Cabernet bottlings from Oakville and Stags Leap, the latter being more graceful. Each vintage the Pinot Noir Reserve grows more velvety and satisfying. Among whites, it is best known for Fumé Blanc, a Sauvignon/ Semillon blend with the body and structure (and barrel-age) of first class Chardonnay. The Chardonnay (notably the Reserve) can be a touch too opulent. See also Opus One.

Monticello Vineyards ☆–☆☆
Napa. Owner: Jay Corley. 59 ha.
www.corleyfamilynapavalley.com
Monticello is the label for the basic production; Corley goes on Reserve bottlings. The reds used to be rather lean, but recent vintages have shown more flesh and weight.

Mount Veeder ☆☆☆
Mt Veeder, Napa. Owner: Constellation. 25 ha.
www.franciscan.com
Rocky vineyard known for concentrated, earthy, tannic Cabernets.

Mumm ☆–☆☆
Rutherford. Owner: Pernod Ricard. 45 ha.
www.mummnapa.com
For many years part of the Seagram empire, Mumm's focus on sparkling wines of ebullient fruitiness has made them popular California originals in both Europe and on their home turf. Blanc de Noirs is the archetype; luxury *cuvée* DVX reaches for the other end of the stylistic pole. But the ever reliable Cuvée Napa is the best-seller that has made the domaine's reputation.

Newton ☆☆☆
St Helena. Owner: LVMH. 42 ha.
www.newtonvineyard.com
Eglishman Peter Newton founded Sterling Vineyards (q.v.) in 1964, and after its sale to Coca-Cola founded, with his wife Su Hua, a magnificent and exotic vineyard high on Spring Mountain. They were pioneers of excellent Graves-style Sauvignon Blanc, which was phased out, and of Napa Merlot.

Today the emphasis is on Cabernet and on Chardonnay from purchased grapes. Luxury goods group LVMH took a controlling interest in 2001, but the Newtons continued to run the property until Peter's death in 2008.

Niebaum-Coppola ☆☆–☆☆☆
See Rubicon.

Opus One ☆☆☆☆
Oakville. Owner: Constellation and Philippine de Rothschild. 42 ha. www.opusonewinery.com
Founded in 1979 as a 50-50 deal between the late Philippe de Rothschild and Robert Mondavi. Cabernet-based red, originally a sort of Mondavi "Reserve of Reserves", now has its own architecturally wondrous home, at the centre of an estate vineyard planted at Bordeaux densities. In theory, styled to be Franco-American, but ripe, rich Napa grapes rule.

Pahlmeyer ☆☆☆
Napa. Owner: Jayson Pahlmeyer. 45 ha.
www.pahlmeyer.com
Pahlmeyer has hired a succession of well-known consultant winemakers (most recently Michel Rolland in 2003) to satisfy his taste for very rich, alcoholic wines that have a devoted following. Recently he has been acquiring more vineyards in Atlas Peak and the Sonoma Coast, allowing him to add Pinot Noir to his range. But the best-known, and most consistent wine, is the Proprietary Red.

ROBERT MONDAVI

Only the brothers Gallo have rivalled Robert Mondavi as a force in California winemaking, and they could not match Mondavi when it came to innovation.

When he left his family's Charles Krug winery to start his own company in 1966, he created the first new Napa winery of modern times. It was often forgotten what courage this took, and Mondavi came close to financial disaster, until a lawsuit decided in his favour, and this allowed him to put his fledgling winery on a more secure footing. Mondavi immediately established himself as a relentless experimenter on all fronts, and resolute champion of the Napa Valley as the New World's greatest wine region. The mock-Franciscan mission winery buildings at

still house endless experiments. Of the daunting quantities of Napa wine for sale under the Robert Mondavi name, the Cabernet Sauvignons (and now the Pinot Noirs, too) trumpeted his successes loudest, none more so than his gentle-but-gigantic Reserves. Fumé Blanc (his globally accepted coinage for oaked Sauvignon Blanc) is a Californian style single-handedly created by Mondavi.

In 1979 he brought the prestige of a Bordeaux First Growth to Napa, when Baron Philippe de Rothschild became his partner in Opus One. In 1995, in a reverse gesture, he joined his own name with that of the Frescobaldis in Tuscany. In between, he turned Mondavi-Woodbridge into a formidable player

in the low-priced field; acquired more than 400 hectares of vineyard and the Byron Winery in Santa Barbara County; turned his company from private to a publicly owned corporation; became a partner in a Chilean winery; and acquired a number of other wineries.

However, family squabbles and the sale of Mondavi to the giant Constellation group led to the withdrawal of the family from the running of the company that bears their name. Nonetheless, when Robert died in 2008 at the age of 94, the entire wine world united in praise of the man who, more than any other, was responsible for the revival of the fortunes and esteem of Californian wines in the modern era.

Joseph Phelps ☆☆–☆☆☆☆
St Helena. Owner: Joseph Phelps. 264 ha.
www.jpwines.com
An ex-builder with an unerring sense of style, Phelps built his beautiful redwood barn in the choppy foothills east of St Helena. In the 1980s he was offering not only superb Napa Cabernet but unusual (for California) German-style nobly sweet wines. Under former winemaker Craig Williams, Rhône variety wines were added, but in the early 2000s the decision was taken to focus the range more narrowly on its luxury Bordeaux-style blend Insignia, Cabernet Sauvignon, and Pinot Noir from a recently developed vineyard on the Sonoma Coast.

Pine Ridge Winery ☆☆–☆☆☆
Napa. Owner: Leucadia. 92 ha. www.pineridgewinery.com
Separately bottled Rutherford, Howell Mountain, and Stags Leap Cabernets teach delicious lessons about internal divisions of climate and soil in Napa. The white wines can be rather heavy, but Malbec and a Tannat-based blend add spice to the range.

Plumpjack ☆☆☆
Napa. Owner: Gordon Getty and partners. 21 ha.
www.plumpjack.com
Founded in 1996, Plumpjack has rapidly established a reputation for rich, oaky Cabernet, especially the Reserve bottling. The estate caused a sensation by releasing some of the 1997 wine with a screwcap closure. The Plumpjack empire has expanded to include restaurants in San Francisco (where one of the partners happens to be mayor), a luxury hotel in Carneros, and another vineyard on Howell Mountain that produces wines under the name of Cade.

Pride Mountain ☆☆☆–☆☆☆☆
St Helena. Owner: Pride family. 32 ha.
www.pridewines.com
The vineyards are high on Spring Mountain, and the results are very intense wines from Chardonnay, Cabernet, Merlot, Syrah, and Viognier.

Provenance ☆☆
Rutherford. Owner: Constellation. 18 ha.
www.provenancevineyards.com
Established in the late 1990s. The best wines are Rutherford Cabernet Sauvignon and Merlot sourced from leading grower Andy Beckstoffer's vineyards.

Quintessa ☆☆☆
Napa. Owner: Augustin Huneeus. 68 ha.
www.quintessa.com
After the sale of Franciscan (q.v.), Huneeus retained the isolated hillside Quintessa vineyard as his personal property, opening a new winery in 2003. The only wine is a polished and expensive Bordeaux blend.

Raymond Vineyards ☆–☆☆
St Helena. Owner: Raymond family and Japanese brewers, Kirin. 260 ha. www.raymondwine.com
The Napa Valley Reserve line is high-quality, typically oaky – and taken one step further by the Raymond Generations range. Long-time residents of Napa, the Raymonds are pioneer growers of Chardonnay in Jameson Ridge (at the extreme southern end of Napa), and venturing into Monterey for the less expensive R Collection range.

Regusci ☆☆–☆☆☆
Napa. Owner: Jim Regusci. 26 ha. www.regusciwinery.com

Newton vineyard, Spring Mountain

Grower Regusci turned wine producer in 1996, taking advantage of a fine old stone winery, Full-bodied spicy Cabernet and Bordeaux blends in an energetic if slightly rustic style.

Rocca ☆☆–☆☆☆
Yountville. Owner: Mary Fran Rocca. 9 ha.
www.roccawines.com
Although the first vintage was in 1999, winemaker Celia Masyczek was soon making the most of some excellent Cabernet and Syrah grapes. Ripe and generous wines that avoid jamminess and excessive weight.

Rombauer Vineyards ☆
St Helena. Owner: Rombauer family.
www.rombauervineyards.com
The Rombauers own vineyards but sell the entire crop to other wineries, obliging them to buy in fruit for their own range of classic varietals. A magnet for tourists, with wines to match.

Round Hill Cellars ☆
St Helena. Owner: Marko Zaninovitch. 15 ha.
www.roundhillwines.com
Developed by the Van Asperen family, Round Hill supplies a wider market with sunstantial volumes of good-value versions of distinct variety-plus-region character, notably Napa Cabernet and Merlot under the Round Hill and Rutherford Ranch labels.

Rubicon ☆☆–☆☆☆
Rutherford. Owner: Francis Ford Coppola. 100 ha.
www.rubicon-estate.com
Movie man Coppola and his winery have become a major force in the Napa Valley. He bought the hidden half of the historic Inglenook property in 1979, the showcase half in 1995, and 22 hectares close by in 2002. The entire property is farmed organically. With the winemaking tuned up, Cabernet-based Rubicon at last begins to impress, now that it is no longer incurably tannic. Cask Cabernet is the second wine, more accessible than Rubicon. The less expensive ranges, usually made from purchased fruit, are hit-and-miss, so the Estate wines (Merlot, Viognier) are the ones to go for.

Rudd ☆☆☆
Oakville. Owner: Leslie Rudd. 18 ha.
www.ruddwines.com
The former Girard estate was bought by delicatessen-king Rudd in 1996. Celebrated winemaker David Ramey fashioned the initial releases of Carneros Chardonnay and Napa reds, and has since been replaced by Charles Thomas. Recent Cabernets have been very rich but somewhat extracted.

Rutherford Hill Winery ☆
St Helena. Owner: Terlato Wine Group. 80 ha.
www.rutherfordhill.com
Founded in 1976 by the partners of Freemark Abbey (q.v.), the winery's initially high reputation slipped in the 1980s, and in 1996 it was bought by its present owners. Quality has yet to return to its original high level, but the whites are attractive.

St Clement Vineyards ☆☆–☆☆☆
St Helena. Owner: Foster's Wine Estates. 8 ha.
www.stclement.com
Winemaker Danielle Cyrot continues her predecessors' strategy of producing excellent Chardonnay and Merlot from Carneros, Mount Veeder Syrah, and an impressive range of Napa Cabernets.

St Supéry ☆☆
Rutherford. Owner: Robert Skalli. 217 ha.
www.stsupery.com
Sensibly priced Cabernet and Sauvignon Blanc from Dollarhide Ranch show what Napa's easterly, upland Chiles Valley can do with Bordeaux varieties, red and white. There's an excellent visitors' centre, too.

Saintsbury ☆☆☆
Napa. Owner: Richard Ward and David Graves. 22 ha.
www.saintsbury.com
Burgundian inspiration here – Chardonnay and Pinot Noir are the only wines. The Pinot is exceptional, notably the Reserve, but the Brown Ranch bottlings can be atypically overwrought. Recent vintages have seen an intriguing expansion into more single vineyard Pinots.

V Sattui ☆
St Helena. Owner: Daryl Sattui. 120 ha.
www.vsattui.com
Good Cabernet, Zinfandel, and Riesling, as well as a bewildering range of less prestigious wines, draw thousands of customers to this hospitable tasting room, to which a deli and a picnic ground are attached.

Schramsberg ☆☆–☆☆☆
Calistoga. Owner: Hugh Davies. 26 ha.
www.schramsberg.com
Robert Louis Stevenson drank "bottled poetry" at Schram's ornate white, verandahed house, built by founder Jacob Schram in the 1860s. So have I, many times, under the Davies regime. Refounded in 1966, Jack Davies produced sparkling wines only, of a very high standard, none more so than his luxury *cuvée*, J Schram (1989), which instantly set new standards for California.

In 1998, Jack Davies died and Duckhorn (q.v.) took a minority share. Vicious family infighting marred the last years of Jamie Davies's life, and she died in 2008. Hugh Davies has added J Davies, a fine, understated Cabernet blend, to the line.

Screaming Eagle ☆☆☆☆
Oakville. Owner: Charles Banks and Stanley Kroenke. 23 ha. www.screamingeagle.com
Napa's most costly trophy Cabernet, a dense, sweet wine of soaring and tenacious flavours, initially made by Heidi Peterson Barrett, but now made by Andrew Erickson. The wine is full-bodied, rich, and oaky but unlike some cult Napa Cabernets, it has a remarkable purity and finesse. The 1995 is the most seductive vintage, with 1994 and 1998 close behind. In 2006 the property was sold to two financiers for an astonishing $50 million.

Sequoia Grove ☆☆–☆☆☆
Napa. Owner: Allen family. 10 ha. www.sequoiagrove.com
Cabernet Sauvignon is easily the best wine here, especially the Reserve.

Shafer ☆☆☆–☆☆☆☆
Napa. Owner: John Shafer. 80 ha.
www.shafervineyards.com
Since 1978, John Shafer, and now his son, Doug, have produced immaculate Stags Leap Cabernet and Merlot, with Elias Fernandez responsible for winemaking since 1984. The top wine is the new-oaked Hillside Select Cabernet, and the Syrah is also good, but the Sangiovese is no longer made. The Carneros Chardonnay can be overblown.

Signorello ☆☆–☆☆☆
Napa. Owner: Signorello family. 40 ha.
www.signorellovineyards.com
The Signorellos are grape farmers turned wine producers, offering luxurious and heavily toasted whites and reds. The top wine is usually the opulent and powerful Bordeaux blend Padrone.

Silver Oak Cellars ☆☆
Oakville. Owner: Raymond Duncan. 136 ha.
www.silveroak.com
Silver Oak – founded by the late Justin Meyer, who began adult life in the priesthood – only makes Cabernet Sauvignon, in separate Napa and Alexander Valley bottlings. They differ in structure (the Napa is more tannic) but not in style, as both are aged exclusively in American oak, creating wines that can be drunk with pleasure on release.

Silverado Vineyards ☆☆–☆☆☆
Napa. Owner: Disney family. 162 ha.
www.silveradovineyards.com
Silverado's estate-grown Chardonnay, Sauvignon Blanc, and Cabernet Sauvignon are all ripe, supple, and sophisticated, with a growing reputation. The most intriguing wine is Solo from its original Cabernet vineyard, since replanted, in Stags Leap.

Sinskey ☆☆
Napa. Owner: Rob Sinskey. 70 ha. www.robertsinskey.com
Unlike most Napa wineries, Sinskey places enormous weight on organic viticulture, as practiced in its Stags Leap and Carneros vineyards. Certainly the wines have a fine brightness of fruit. Alsace-style whites are delicious, as is the range of Pinot Noir and the reliable Cabernet Franc.

Smith-Madrone ☆–☆☆
St Helena. Owner: Stuart and Charles Smith. 14 ha.
www.smithmadrone.com.

Schramsberg, near Calistoga

Vineyards at 520 metres (1,700 feet) up on Spring Mountain yield remarkable wines in a simple cellar. Sweet or dry lemony Riesling is easy to love, young or old. The Cabernet is lean and long lived.

Spottswoode ☆☆☆
St Helena. Owner: Mary Novak. 15 ha.
www.spottswoode.com
One of the most elegant and balanced Cabernets in California comes from Spottswoode, right in the town of St Helena. Wonderfully consistent wine that ages well, but is drinkable young. Intriguingly pure Sauvignon Blanc, too. Undemonstrably organic since 1985.

Staglin ☆☆☆
Rutherford. Owner: Staglin family. 20 ha.
www.staglinfamily.com
Blessed with magnificent vineyards in Rutherford, the Staglins produce fine, structured Cabernet and very good Sangiovese. Michel Rolland came on board as a consultant in 1999, and ever since the wines have been stronger and more alcoholic, and, some would say, less refined.

Stag's Leap Wine Cellars ☆☆–☆☆☆☆
Napa. Owner: Marchese Antinori and Ste Michelle Wine Estates. 91 ha. www.cask23.com
Founder Warren Winiarski is a political science professor turned winemaker. His Cabernets have startled the French with their resemblance to great Bordeaux. My notes are full of "harmony, elegance, feminine, finesse".

Cask 23 is a riper Reserve Cabernet, and the Fay Vineyard bottling can be almost as fine. The two Chardonnays, made in contrasting styles, are good, too, although my favourite remains the Cabernet. The wine world was taken aback when in 2007 this wonderful property was sold, but all agree that it remains in very good hands.

Stags' Leap Winery ☆☆
Napa. Owner: Foster's Wine Estates. 36 ha.
www.stagsleap.com.
Unusually among Napa wineries, this has acquired a high reputation for its Petite Sirah.

Sterling ☆☆
Calistoga. Owner: Diageo. 485 ha.
www.sterlingvineyards.com
The long, white building, like a Greek monastery, hugs the top of a lump in the valley floor big enough to need cable cars to get up it. British money built it in the 1960s; Coca-Cola bought it in 1978; and Seagram took over in 1983. The Sterling mainstay is well-made if unremarkable Napa wine, but the best wines are from single vineyards, notably a Merlot from Three Palms Vineyard, Cabernet from Diamond Mountain, Chardonnay and Pinot Noir from Winery Lake.

Stony Hill ☆☆
St Helena. Owner: Peter McCrea. 16 ha.
www.stonyhillvineyard.com
Fred McCrea was the first of the flood of men from busy offices who realized that the Napa Valley offered something better. He planted white grapes in the 1940s and made 25 vintages of his own understated style of wine. Neither the variety nor the maturation grab your attention; the point seems to be boundless vigour and depth without an obvious handle. Eleanor McCrea continued her husband's total integrity of purpose after his death. When she died, son Peter took up the reins with no compromise. The style, given the paucity of new oak, remains unfashionable, but is valid on its own terms. As are the delicate Riesling and Gewurztraminer.

Storybook Mountain Vineyards ☆☆–☆☆☆☆
Calistoga. Owner: Dr. Jerry Seps. 17 ha.
www.storybookwines.com
Jerry Seps revels in Zinfandel and makes nothing else. There are five different blends, and they all tend to be splendid.

Sutter Home ☆
St Helena. Owner: Trinchero family. 2,430 ha.
www.sutterhome.com
A family operation (named after another pre-Prohibition family) that once specialized in small lots of red Zinfandel; later in huge volumes of White Zinfandel, sustained by enormous vineyards in inland areas. The winery now offers the usual varietals, most bearing California as an appellation, all at modest prices. See also Trinchero.

Swanson Vineyards ☆☆–☆☆☆
Rutherford. Owner: W Clarke Swanson. 56 ha.
www.swansonvineyards.com
The estate vineyards are located in Oakville, yet the style still leans as heavily on new-oak barrels as terroir. Some of the finest wines are from Sangiovese and Syrah. Frozen-dinner tycoon Clarke Swanson also owns Avery's of Bristol.

Terra Valentine ☆☆
St Helena. Owner: Angus Wurtele. 27 ha.
www.terravalentine.com
Retired businessman Wurtele bought an old winery and property, now largely replanted, in 1995, and focuses on intense Spring Mountain Cabernet. Other wines are sourced from Russian River Valley.

Philip Togni ☆☆☆
St Helena. Owner: Philip Togni. 10 ha.
www.philiptognivineyard.com

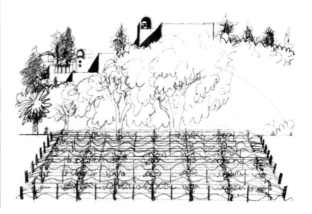

Sterling vineyard, Calistoga

From high on Spring Mountain, veteran British-born but Bordeaux-trained Togni makes sumptuous, long-lived Cabernet, and tiny quantities of an exquisite sweet wine from Black Hamburg, Ca' Togni.

Trefethen ☆☆–☆☆☆
Napa. Owner: Trefethen family. 260 ha.
www.trefethenwines.com
The Trefethens bought the former Eshcol vineyards near Napa, in 1968, and ever since the vineyard has supplied all their needs. This is a cool site, well-suited to varieties such as Riesling and Cabernet Franc. However, in recent years the Cabernet Sauvignon has reached great heights and an elegance rarely encountered in Napa Valley.

Trinchero ☆–☆☆
St Helena. Owner: Trinchero family. 376 ha.
www.trincherowinery.com
With the Sutter Home White Zinfandel a riproaring success, the Trincheros set about making the most of their 80 hectares of Napa Valley vineyards with this new label featuring their own name. They also offer a second tier of wines made from their vineyards in Lake and Santa Barbara counties.

Turley ☆☆
St Helena. Owner: Larry Turley. 6 ha.
www.turleywinecellars.com
The former partner of John Williams of Frog's Leap (q.v.), Larry Turley went his own way in 1994, specializing in Zinfandel and Petite Sirah from ancient vineyards. The wines are ultra-ripe and very alcoholic, which has made them controversial and, in the eyes of some, hard to swallow.

Turnbull ☆☆–☆☆☆
Oakville. Owner: Patrick O'Dell. 75 ha.
www.turnbullwines.com
After purchasing the winery from its founders in 1993, O'Dell expanded the vineyard holdings and showed a willingness to think new thoughts, but thus far, the Cabernet continues to out-mint, out-spice even Martha's Vineyard. Among the other offerings are Syrah, Viognier, and a Rhône blend called Old Bull Red.

Twomey ☆☆
Calistoga. Owner: Ray Duncan. 20 ha.
www.twomeycellars.com
Since 1999, under the same ownership as Silver Oak (q.v.). The specialty here is fleshy, savoury Merlot, but some Sauvignon Blanc and Pinot are also produced.

Viader ☆☆☆
St Helena. Owner: Delia Viader. 9 ha.
www.viader.com
Argentinian-born Delia Viader at first made just one wine from her organic hillside vineyards: a seductive blend of Cabernet Franc and Cabernet Sauvignon. This has been supplemented by a Syrah, V (a Bordeaux blend dominated by Petit Verdot), and, since 2003, some single-vineyard Cabernet Sauvignon, Cabernet Franc, and Tempranillo from Napa Valley under the DARE label. Viader is married to Robert Mondavi's son Tim.

Vine Cliff ☆☆☆
Napa. Owner: Charles Sweeney. 16 ha. www.vinecliff.com
A major winery in the 1880s, this was revived in 1984, when terraced organic vineyards were planted. First releases were in 1993, and established an opulent style of high quality.

Whitehall Lane Winery ☆☆
St Helena. Owner: Thomas Leonardini. 45 ha.
www.whitehalllane.com
Merlot is the top wine here. Its wines have won extravagant praise, but some vintages can be a touch jammy.

ZD Wines ☆
Napa. Owner: De Leuze family. 16 ha. www.zdwines.com
Carneros Chardonnay, aged in American oak, is the principal wine here, but there is also Pinot Noir and Cabernet Sauvignon. Sound, if often one-dimensional, wines.

Leading Sonoma County Producers

Alderbrook Vineyards ☆–☆☆
Healdsburg. Owner: Terlato Wine Group. 26 ha.
www.alderbrook.com
Frequent changes of owner and winemaker have occasioned numerous changes in style. In general, Alderbrook offers crisp whites and medium-bodied reds. The Zinfandels can be admirable.

Alexander Valley Vineyards ☆
Healdsburg. Owner: Hank Wetzel. 60 ha.
www.avvwine.com
The dry, Burgundian-style Chardonnay is the estate's best known wine, but there is also plump Cabernet Sauvignon and charming Cabernet Franc and Syrah, all produced from Alexander Valley fruit.

Armida ☆–☆☆
Healdsburg. Owner: Steve and Bruce Cousins.
No vineyards. www.armida.com
Russian River Valley is the main source of fruit for Armida, which is enjoying a new lease of life in recent years. Pinot Noir and Zinfandel are the strongest suits.

Arrowood ☆☆☆
Glen Ellen. Owner: Jackson Family Estates. 12 ha.
www.arrowoodvineyards.com
Long-time Château St Jean winemaker Richard Arrowood set up on his own in the late 1980s. He buys in grapes from outstanding Sonoma vineyards. As well as the standard varietals, there is superb Viognier (sometimes late harvest) and Malbec. In 2000, Mondavi bought the label, which was sold to Jess Jackson in 2006, but Arrowood remains at the helm.

Benziger ☆☆–☆☆☆
Glen Ellen. Owner: Benziger family. 35 ha.
www.benziger.com
The late Bruno Benziger (d. 1989) and five sons started out to build a small, Sonoma based winery. Within a decade they found themselves selling well more than one million cases a year of mass-market wine, mostly under the Glen Ellen label. In 1994 the Benzigers sold the brand, and returned to their

original idea, this time producing wines under the family name. Bruno's son Mike became intrigued by Biodynamism, and by 2001 the estate was converted. Only small quantities of estate wine are produced, but the Bordeaux blend and the Sauvignon Blanc shine out. The range is amplified with some purchased Sonoma County wines, Pinot Noir from new vineyards near the coast, and with some unusual varieties produced for the Imagery Series, sold from a separate tasting room in Sonoma Valley.

Buena Vista ☆–☆☆
Sonoma. Owner: Ascentia Wine Estates. 400 ha.
www.buenavistacarneros.com
Historically important as the winery of Agoston Haraszthy, "the father of California wine". Restarted in 1943 by Frank Bartholomew, then sold to German owner Racke in 1979, and sold again in 2001, 2005, 2007, and 2008. Most grapes come from Carneros, and Chardonnay dominates. The best wines are usually Pinot Noir and Shiraz from its Ramal Road estate.

Chalk Hill ☆–☆☆
Healdsburg. Owner: Fred Furth. 142 ha.
www.chalkhill.com
Despite being an estate winery, it has been a medium in search of a message, or vice versa, for most of its career, changing names from Donna Maria to Chalk Hill in 1982, and changing styles to suit a succession of winemakers. The vineyards seem most suited to Sauvignon Blanc and Chardonnay.

Chateau Souverain ☆☆–☆☆☆
Geyserville. Owner: Foster's Wine Estates. 132 ha.
www.souverain.com

Souverain grows its own red grapes in Alexander Valley, but it's too hot here for Chardonnay, which is bought in, usually from Russian River Valley. The whites can be quite plump, but the reds are opulent and extremely drinkable. All wines, even Reserves, sensibly priced. In 2006 the winery itself was bought by Francis Ford Coppola, who has developed a resort complex here, while the Souverain wines are now produced at another facility owned by Foster's.

Chateau St Jean ☆☆–☆☆☆
Kenwood. Owner: Foster's Wine Estates. 100 ha.
www.chateaustjean.com
A showplace winery specializing in white wines of the sort of subtropical ripeness more often associated with the Napa Valley. In the 1970s and early 1980s, Richard Arrowood (q.v.) dazzled the wine world with his numerous single-vineyard white wines, both Sauvignon and Chardonnay.

After Arrowood's departure in 1990, the range was trimmed down, and some excellent red wines joined the list, none finer than the blend called Cinq Cépages. Arrowood was also a master of formidable, sweet, late-harvest Rieslings and Gewurztraminers, but they are no longer produced.

Cline ☆–☆☆☆
Sonoma. Owner: Cline family. 60 ha.
www.clinecellars.com
The Clines own fabulous old vineyards in Contra Costa County that produce intense Zinfandel and Mourvèdre. In southern Sonoma they have planted Rhône varieties. The best wines are full of character and fire, but those bottled under the California appellation are of far less interest.

Buena Vista winery, Sonoma

Clos du Bois ☆–☆☆☆
Geyserville. Owner: Constellation. 365 ha.
www.closdubois.com
Clos du Bois wines were well-established before there was a winery. The best are the proprietary wines, such as Marlstone Alexander Valley (Merlot-based blend), Briarcrest Alexander Valley Cabernet Sauvignon, and Calcaire Alexander Valley Chardonnay.

Cobb ☆☆–☆☆☆
Occidental. Owner: David Cobb. 6 ha. www.cobbines.com
From late-ripening chilly coastal vineyards, the Cobbs produce Pinot Noir of the greatest refinement.

B R Cohn ☆☆
Glen Ellen. Owner: Bruce Cohn. 26 ha. www.brcohn.com.
Bruce Cohn made the transition from rock group manager to grape farmer with relative ease, and today his winery specializes in Merlot and Cabernet Sauvignon. The Olive Hill Cabernet is the wine that makes Cohn noteworthy.

La Crema ☆☆
Windsor. Owner: Jackson Family Estates. No vineyards.
www.lacrema.com
This outpost of the Jess Jackson empire specializes in Chardonnay and Pinot Noir from cool coastal vineyards, from Anderson Valley to the Sonoma Coast. The wines are consistently good and attractively priced.

Dashe ☆☆–☆☆☆
Alameda. Owner: Mike Dashe. No vineyards.
www.dashecellars.com
Dashe trained at Lafite and Cloudy Bay, then spent a decade as assistant winemaker at Ridge. No wonder he makes wines, mostly Dry Creek and Alexander Valley Zinfandel, with flair and conviction.

Dehlinger ☆☆☆
Sebastopol. Owner: Tom Dehlinger. 18 ha.
www.dehlingerwinery.com
Dehlinger is devoted to Pinot Noir, and produces a number of different bottlings from different parcels of his vineyards. A rich style, highly regarded. There are also small amounts of Chardonnay, Syrah, and other varieties. Sold mostly through a mailing list, and thus hard to find.

DeLoach ☆☆–☆☆☆
Santa Rosa. Owner: Boisset. 7 ha. www.deloachvineyards.com
From tiny beginnings, Cecil DeLoach built a substantial business by making wines that taste first and foremost of grape variety and vineyard. But expansion proved too rapid, and the ailing estate was bought by the Burgundian négociant Boisset in 2003. The expert Greg La Folette was hired as winemaker, and many wines were sourced from outstanding organic or Biodynamic vineyards. Very good Zinfandel and Pinot Noir. Top blends bear the mysterious designation "OFS", but often the single-vineyard wines are more characterful.

Dry Creek Vineyard ☆☆–☆☆☆
Healdsburg. Owner: David Stare. 80 ha.
www.drycreekvineyard.com
Maker of one of California's best dry Sauvignon Blancs (Fumé Blanc), with other whites in the same old-fashioned, balanced, vital, but not-too-emphatic, dry style. Reserve Chardonnays are barrel-fermented and aged *sur lie*; while the Chenin Blanc, which is totally unoaked, is equally delicious. Very good Zinfandel and Petite Sirah head the range of reds.

Dutton Estate ☆☆
Sebastopol. Owner: Joe and Tracy Dutton. 400 ha.
www.duttonestate.com
The Dutton family own some of the most substantial vineyards in Russian River Valley, and use some of them to produce their own wines. Both Chardonnay and Pinot Noir, in various bottlings, succeed best.

Dutton Goldfield ☆☆–☆☆☆
Sebastopol. Owner: Steve Dutton and Dan Goldfield.
400 ha. www.duttongoldfield.com

LABELS

Two pieces of information included on the label of many good Californian wines give a helpful indication of what to expect in the bottle.

Alcohol content is measured in degrees or percentage by volume (the two are the same). Traditional wines vary between about 11.5 and 14 degrees, enough to make a substantial difference to taste and effect, with some fashionable Zinfandels attaining a natural but absurd level of 16.5%. But the law allows the labeller a remarkable latitude of 1.5 degrees from the truth. As a practical tip, if you find a he-man Napa Chardonnay, for example, too powerful for you at 14.5 degrees, there is no law against adding a drop of water. Perrier refreshes clumsy wines beautifully.

Residual sugar is most commonly reported on labels of Riesling and Gewurztraminer. It is the unfermented sugar left (or kept) in the wine at bottling. Below 0.5% by weight, sugar is rarely detectable and the wine should taste fully dry. Above about 1.5% it would be described as "off-dry, above 3% as "sweet" and above 6% as "very sweet". A "selected bunch late-harvest" (roughly equivalent to a German BA) might have 14% and a "selected berry late-harvest" (roughly equivalent to a German TBA) as much as 28%. Measurement in grams per 100 millilitres is the same as measurement in percentages.

The Not the Whole Truth factor. If a grape variety is specified on the label, only 75% of the wine needs to be made from that variety. If a county name, such as Sonoma, is cited, only 75% of the grapes need come from that county. If a specific AVA, such as Howell Mountain, is cited on the label, only 85% of the wine need come from that region. If a single vineyard is identified on the label, 95% of the wine must come from that site. If a vintage is specified, 95% of the wine must come from that year. The widely used term "Reserve" has no legal definition and can be employed at the whim of the producer.

Another and separate Dutton family venture, with Steve Dutton farming the vineyards, mostly in Green Valley, and Dan Goldfield making the wines. Numerous single-vineyard bottlings of excellent Chardonnay, Pinot Noir, Syrah, and Zinfandel.

Duxoup Wine Works ☆
Healdsburg. Owner: Andrew Cutter. No vineyards.
www.duxoupwineworks.com
Marx-inspired name (Groucho), but vibrantly fruity red wines, including a Syrah that has pleased local tasters, and a wild Charbono. All grapes come from Dry Creek Valley vineyards.

Merry Edwards ☆☆–☆☆☆
Sebastopol. Owner: Merry Edwards. 14 ha.
www.merryedwards.com
This veteran winemaker has now focused her activities on Sauvignon Blanc and Pinot Noir, from her own vines and from purchased fruit. Despite being aged in a substantial proportion of new French oak, the Pinots are perfumed and balanced.

Failla ☆☆–☆☆☆
Calistoga. Owner: Ehren Jordan. 4 ha.
www.faillawines.com
Jordan's day job is winemaker at Turley (q.v.), but the wines he produces from his own organic property and from neighbouring vineyards in the Sonoma Coast hills could hardly be more different: intense Pinot Noir and Syrah of real pungency and vigour.

Gary Farrell ☆☆☆
Healdsburg. Owner: Ascentia Wine Estates. 20 ha.
www.garyfarrell.com
For many years the former winemaker for Davis Bynum made his own wines at that company's winery. Finally in 2000 he acquired a splendid new winery in Russian River Valley, only to see the business sold in 2005. Farrell, a master of Pinot Noir, stayed on until 2007, but is no longer associated with the winery that bears his name. Current releases of Chardonnay and Pinot Noir are well-crafted but expensive.

Ferrari-Carano ☆☆–☆☆☆
Healdsburg. Owner: Donald and Rhonda Carano. 490 ha. www.ferrari-carano.com
The Dry Creek winery and gardens are dramatic; so is the winemaking style. Reserves exceed even Texas-sized expectations, and overripeness can mar the wines' purity. Reds are improving every year, especially the Supertuscan-style Siena and the Bordeaux blend, Trésor.

Gloria Ferrer ☆☆–☆☆☆
Sonoma. Owner: Freixenet. 136 ha. www.gloriaferrer.com
Catalonia rather than Champagne is the parent of this sparkling wine house, named after the wife of the president of Freixenet. A capacious winery and substantial vineyards spell serious intent. Thus far, the vintage-dated Royal Cuvée exceeds the rest of the range for depth and riches; the Carneros Cuvée is even toastier after seven years on the yeasts. As nationwide sparkling wine sales have slumped, Gloria Ferrer has made up the slack with a range of fairly light table wines, too.

Fisher ☆☆
Santa Rosa. Owner: Fred Fisher. 25 ha.
www.fishervineyards.com
Rich, bold wines from both Napa and Sonoma that can veer towards portiness. The top red is usually the high-priced Wedding Vineyard Cabernet.

Flowers ☆☆☆
Cazadero. Owner: Walt and Joan Flowers. 30 ha.
www.flowerswinery.com
This is the leading winery based in the highlands along the Sonoma Coast. The microclimate is cool but luminosity is high, so the wines, Chardonnay and Pinot Noir, show purity and intensity.

Foppiano ☆
Healdsburg. Owner: Louis J Foppiano. 80 ha.
www.foppiano.com
One of the oldest family owned wineries, maintaining its already respectable standards. Foppiano is the standard label; Riverside by Foppiano is a second label.

Fritz ☆–☆☆
Cloverdale. Owner: Donald Fritz. 36 ha.
www.fritzwinery.com
Much Chardonnay here, some of it rather blowzy. Quality is not always consistent, but Zinfandel can be impressive, especially the Rogers Reserve Zinfandel from Dry Creek.

Gallo Family Vineyards ☆–☆☆
Healdsburg. Owner: Gallo family. 900 ha.
www.gallosonoma.com
In the late 1990s the Gallos, formerly entrenched in the Central Valley, began acquiring vineyards in Sonoma, rather to the alarm of other growers there. This was not just a winemaking and commercial exercise, but a makeover for the Gallo image. The campaign has been successful, and since 1991 the Sonoma estates have turned out a series of single-vineyard varietal wines that can be of good quality.

Geyser Peak Winery ☆☆
Geyserville. Owner: Ascentia Wine Estates. 485 ha.
www.geyserpeakwinery.com
An old winery-turned-vinegar-works became a winery once again in 1972. Its wines soared in popularity during the reign of sure-handed Aussie winemaker Daryl Groom, but repeated changes in ownership from 1997 onwards resulted in his departure.

At present the Geyser Peak portfolio remains much as it was in his day. Sauvignon Blanc and Shiraz are the stars in a wide range of forward, fruity wines, and Cuvée Alexandre is a powerful Bordeaux blend. The second label is Canyon Road.

Gundlach-Bundschu ☆☆
Sonoma. Owner: Jeff Bundschu. 122 ha.
www.gunbun.com
A famous San Francisco wine business, destroyed by the 1906 earthquake. Grapes from the old vineyards were sold until 1973, when the winery reopened. The range is excellent, especially Cabernet and Merlot, and a Gewurztraminer, crisp and refreshing like an Alsace wine. Chardonnay and Riesling

are also admirable. Varied elevations and microclimates at the southern end of Sonoma Valley encourage this versatility.

Hanna ☆☆
Santa Rosa. Owner: Dr Elias Hanna. 183 ha.
www.hannawinery.com
After a hesitant start, the winery began hitting its stride in the 1990s, especially with its whites. The excellent winemaker, Jeff Hinchcliffe, was hired in 2000, so quality should improve further. Hanna has a fine reputation for its Sauvignon Blanc, and for sturdy reds from the high-elevation Bismark Ranch in the Mayacamas Mountains.

Hanzell ☆☆–☆☆☆
Sonoma. Owner: Alex de Brye. 17 ha. www.hanzell.com
Scene of revolutionary winemaking in the late 1950s, when James D Zellerbach set out to make burgundy-style wines in small French oak barrels. The steep, south-facing vineyard gives high alcohol, but the concentration and balance of both the Chardonnay and the Pinot Noir (though occasionally funky) still makes them among California's most impressive, demanding long maturation.

The winery is (vaguely) a miniature Château du Clos de Vougeot. Bob Sessions made the wines here from 1973 until his retirement in 2001. The thoughtful Michael Terrien has taken his place.

Hartford Court ☆☆☆
Forestville. Owner: Jackson Family Estates. 20 ha.
www.hartfordwines.com
Don Hartford, a son-in-law of Jess Jackson, has overseen the production of increasingly remarkable wines: single vineyard Pinot Noirs, many from ultra-cool Sonoma coastal sites, and old-vine Zinfandel from a number of different sites in Russian River Valley.

Hirsch ☆☆☆
Cazadero. Owner: David Hirsch. 30 ha.
www.hirschvineyards.com
Sonoma's top Pinot winemakers fight to get their hands on Hirsch's fruit, grown since 1980 in the coastal highlands. Since 2002, when Hirsch set up his own winery, there is even less of it to go around.

Paul Hobbs ☆☆–☆☆☆
Sebastopol. Owner: Paul Hobbs. 8 ha.
www.paulhobbs.com
Consultant winemaker Hobbs has his own label, producing Chardonnay, Cabernet Sauvignon, and Syrah mostly from fruit purchased from leading vineyards in Sonoma and Napa. The style favours richness of texture and power.

Iron Horse ☆☆–☆☆☆
Sebastopol. Owner: Sterling family. 65 ha.
www.ironhorsevineyards.com
I took an instant liking to Iron Horse Cabernet, tannic to start, ripely sweet to finish, like good claret. That was maybe 30 years ago. Since then, perfumed Pinot Noir, vibrant Chardonnay, and even more lively sparkling Iron Horse (one of California's best bubblies) have stolen the limelight.

Jordan Vineyard and Winery ☆☆
Healdsburg. Owner: Thomas Jordan. 112 ha.
www.jwine.com
When built in 1972, this was the most extravagant tycoon's château in California. Today it is a Bordeaux-style mansion and winery, deliberately set on producing claret like the Médoc, in a setting of dark oaks and golden grassland, beautiful even by Sonoma standards. Both Cabernet and Chardonnay are still stylish wines, but can lack personality. An affiliated company, J, produces one of California's most appealing classic method bruts.

Keller ☆☆–☆☆☆
Petaluma. Owner: Arturo Keller. 35 ha.
www.kellerestate.com
The Mexican owner planted vines in the cool Petaluma Gap region and, after many years of selling grapes to other wineries, began his own production of spicy, concentrated Pinot Noir and flamboyant Syrah in 2001.

Kenwood ☆☆
Kenwood. Owner: Gary Heck. 400 ha.
www.kenwoodvineyards.com
Wide range of varietals from Sonoma grapes, including Jack London Vineyard and Artist's Series Cabernet Sauvignons. Reds are increasingly stylish, and the unfussy Sauvignon Blanc is very good.

Kistler ☆☆–☆☆☆☆
Sebastopol. Owner: Stephen Kistler and Mark Bixler.
50 ha. www.kistlervineyards.com
Hilltop vineyards on the Napa/Sonoma watershed and new sites close to the Pacific shore, plus grapes purchased from Sonoma's top sites, deliver Chardonnay grapes for artisan-method wines. The reclusive Kistler practises non-interventionist winemaking, and routinely produces some of California's greatest Chardonnays. Recent vintages show him just as adept at magnificent Pinot Noir.

Korbel ☆
Guerneville. Owner: Gary Heck. 800 ha owned or leased.
www.korbel.com
Until Domaine Chandon came on the scene, this was the first choice in widely available California sparkling wine, though then innocent of any Chardonnay or Pinot Noir. It is still a reliable bargain, especially the extremely dry Natural. The flagship wine is the barrel-fermented Le Premier Reserve. Korbel is also a major producer of American brandy.

Kosta Browne ☆☆
Kewnwod. Owner: Dan Kosta and Michael Browne.
No vineyards. www.kostabrowne.com
Founded in 1997 by two sommeliers who now specialize in single-vineyard Pinot Noir from Russian River and the Sonoma Coast. Critics are divided in their response: some consider them among California's finest, others find their richness and high alcohol excessive.

Kunde ☆–☆☆☆
Kenwood. Owner: Kunde family. 325 ha. www.kunde.com
Long-time growers in the Sonoma Valley, the Kundes turned

to winemaking in 1990. The wines are well-crafted and accessible. The range is enormous, and there is some remarkable old-vine Zinfandel.

Lancaster Estate ☆☆–☆☆☆
Healdsburg. Owner: Ted Simpkins. 22 ha.
www.lancaster-estate.com
Little-known but high-quality estate in southern Alexander Valley, producing structured if expensive wines from the Bordeaux varieties.

Landmark ☆☆
Kenwood. Owner: Damaris Ethridge. 8 ha.
www.landmarkwine.com
Highly regarded in California, but often exaggerates the toasty-buttery school, particularly noticeable in the Damaris Reserve bottling, least in the Overlook blend. Still finding its way with Pinot Noir, the best coming from the Kastania Vineyard.

Laurel Glen ☆☆☆
Glen Ellen. Owner: Patrick Campbell. 15 ha.
www.laurelglen.com
Campbell studied philosophy at Harvard, then farmed vineyards for a Zen monastery before setting up his own small Sonoma Mountain winery in 1981. Very solid Cabernet Sauvignon, built to last. The second label, Counterpoint, can be good value.

Limerick Lane ☆☆
Healdsburg. Owner: Michael Collins. 14 ha.
www.limericklanewines.com
Best-known for splendid Zinfandel, but the unique selling point here is Dry Furmint and a wine modelled on Tokaji Aszú.

Littorai ☆☆☆
St Helena. Owner: Ted Lemon. 5 ha. www.littorai.com
Ted Lemon was the first Californian to be hired to make wines at a famous Burgundy estate: Roulot in Meursault. He has

applied his Burgundian skills to the grapes from various sites in Sonoma and Mendocino. The results are highly impressive: elegant and almost ethereal Chardonnay and Pinot Noir. And for fun, an astonishing, viscous late-harvest Chardonnay in 2006.

Lynmar ☆☆
Sebastopol. Owner: Fritz family. 19 ha.
www.lynmarwinery.com
This Russian River Valley winery is going from strength to strength. Particularly admirable are the understated and elegant estate-grown Pinot Noirs called Quail Hill.

Marcassin ☆☆
Calistoga. Owner: Helen Turley and John Wetlaufer. 4 ha.
America's most celebrated winemaker and her husband own a small vineyard on the coastal highlands and produce Chardonnay and Pinot Noir in the full-blown style that has won such acclaim in some circles and puzzlement in others.

Marimar Estate ☆☆☆
Sebastopol. Owner: Marimar Torres. 32 ha.
www.marimarestate.com
The emphatically individualistic Torres does all in her power to subdue California fruitiness in favour of finesse, in her Chardonnay as well as her Pinot Noir. The results can be stunning. Marimar is the sister of the renowned Miguel Torres of Spain (q.v.).

Martinelli ☆–☆☆☆
Windsor. Owner: Lee Martinelli. 122 ha.
www.martinelliwinery.com
The Martinelli family, farmers in Russian River Valley since the 1870s, turned to grapes a century later. Today they produce a wide range of mostly single vineyard wines, crafted under the eye of consultant winemaker Helen Turley.

Matanzas Creek Winery ☆☆
Santa Rosa. Owner: Jackson Family Estates. 33 ha.
www.matanzascreek.com
Greedy pricing in the late 1990s, based on the estate's reputation for Merlot and Chardonnay, was not matched by quality, and in 2000 Jess Jackson bought this leading Bennett Valley property. The varietal focus, including reliable

Franciscan mission, Sonoma

Sauvignon Blanc, remains unchanged but the wines are being fine-tuned by a team of French winemakers.

Mauritson ☆☆–☆☆☆
Healdsburg. Owner: Clay Mauritson. 122 ha.
www.mauritsonwines.com
This grower-turned-winemaker specializes in spicy Dry Creek Zinfandel and powerful Rockpile Syrah, Petite Sirah, and Zinfandel.

Peter Michael ☆☆☆–☆☆☆☆☆
Calistoga. Owner: Sir Peter Michael. 52 ha.
www.petermichaelwinery.com
British media tycoon Peter Michael has, at vast expense, developed superb vineyards high above Knights Valley. The results are spectacular: some of California's best Chardonnay, Sauvignon, and, increasingly, red wines, too. Very expensive.

Michel-Schlumberger ☆–☆☆
Healdsburg. Owner: Jacques Schlumberger. 40 ha.
www.michelschlumberger.com
Organic since 2006, this beautiful property performs patchily, but Chardonnay, Pinot Blanc, and Cabernet Sauvignon often succeed.

Mill Creek ☆
Healdsburg. Owner: Bill Kreck. 30 ha.
www.mcvonline.com
Soft and agreeable rather than competition wines, but the Cabernet and Merlot can be good.

Murphy-Goode ☆–☆☆
Geyserville. Owner: Jackson Family Estates. 142 ha.
www.murphygoodewinery.com
This estate used to produce three versions of Sauvignon Blanc, in ascending order of richness. After Jess Jackson bought the estate in 2006 the range was pared down to simple varietal offerings.

Nalle ☆☆–☆☆☆
Healdsburg. Owner: Doug Nalle. No vineyards.
www.nallewinery.com
One of too few in California who pays more than lip-service to terroir, Nalle produces a single old-vine Zinfandel, which makes it immediately obvious why Dry Creek Valley should be planted to more of the variety. The wines, beautifully balanced, are the perfect riposte to those who think Zinfandel has to have 16 degrees of alcohol to be drinkable.

Pax Wine Cellars ☆☆
Santa Rosa. Owner: Joe Donelan. No vineyards.
www.paxwines.com
Pax was established in the early 2000s as a négociant winery specializing in single-vineyard hillside Syrahs made by partner Pax Mahle. Up to 15 bottlings each year did show the specificity of individual sites, but alcohol levels could be excessive. Mahle left the winery in 2008: its future is uncertain.

Peay ☆–☆☆☆
Annapolis. Owner: Nick and Andy Peay. 20 ha.
www.peayvineyards.com.

From their vineyards in the highlands of the Sonoma Coast, Nick Peay's wife Vanessa Wong fashions exemplary Pinot Noir and Syrah, mostly to top restaurants.

J Pedroncelli Winery ☆–☆☆
Geyserville. Owner: Pedroncelli family. 42 ha.
www.pedroncelli.com
An old-reliable for local country jug wines, now making Dry Creek Zinfandel, Gewurztraminer, Chardonnay, and Cabernet Sauvignon to a higher and stylish standard, and at very reasonable prices.

Preston ☆☆
Healdsburg. Owner: Lou Preston. 40 ha.
www.prestondrycreek.com
Organic grower first, vintner second, Lou Preston appropriately dotes on estate Sauvignon and Zinfandel from Dry Creek Valley – and has turned increasingly towards Rhône and Italian varieties. Preston wearied of marketing a large volume of wine, so reduced production so he can return to the good life as a farmer.

Quivira ☆☆
Healdsburg. Owner: Henry Wendt. 40 ha.
www.quivirawine.com
Exemplary Zinfandel from Dry Creek Valley, and juicy Sauvignon Blanc from Biodynamic vineyards. New owners since 2006 have maintained the status quo.

Radio Coteau ☆☆–☆☆☆
Graton. Owner: Eric Sussman. No vineyards.
www.radiocoteau.com
With considerable experience in Burgundy, Eric Sussman set up his small négociant winery in 2002, buying fruit principally from organic vineyards in Sonoma and Anderson Valley. His Pinot Noir satisfyingly combines Californian muscularity with Burgundian refinement.

A Rafanelli ☆☆☆
Healdsburg. Owner: David Rafanelli. 20 ha.
arafanelliwinery.com
A rustic Dry Creek winery, but there's nothing rustic about these delicious Zinfandels and Cabernets.

Ravenswood ☆☆–☆☆☆
Sonoma. Owner: Constellation. 5 ha.
www.ravenswood-wine.com
Joel Peterson first expressed his passion for Zinfandel and other red wines in an anonymous shed. Buying small lots of grapes from ancient vineyards, before the practice became fashionable, he made some remarkable wines.

In the 1990s, the business expanded a hundred-fold, but the top wines remained as good as before. In 2001, Peterson sold the winery. The Ravenswood motto is: "No Wimpy Wines", which doesn't do justice to some of California's most brilliant and drinkable Zinfandels.

J Rochioli ☆☆–☆☆☆
Healdsburg. Owner: Rochioli family. 52 ha.
Sonoma Pinot Noir producers queue up to buy Rochioli's grapes. These days there are even fewer to go around, as Tom

Rochioli is now making wine himself. Expensive and hard to find, except on top restaurant wine lists.

Roshambo ☆–☆☆
Healdsburg. Owner: Naomi Brilliant. 47 ha.
www.roshambowinery.com
Zany winery with a populist agenda and youthful appeal, founded in 1999 by the granddaughter of the late Frank Johnson, whose celebrated vineyard supplies the winery. The wines can be hit-and-miss but convey a welcome message.

St Francis ☆☆–☆☆☆
Kenwood. Owner: Kobrand. 212 ha.
www.stfranciswine.com
Merlot used to be the best wine, but the earthy, single-vineyard Cabernets, Syrahs, and Zinfandels can be equally impressive.

Sausal Winery ☆
Healdsburg. Owner: Demostene family. 60 ha.
www.sausalwinery.com
One of the Sausal Zinfandel vineyards was planted in 1877, and is the source of the winery's Century Zinfandel. Other bottlings are from vines almost, if not quite, as venerable.

Sbragia Family Vineyards ☆☆–☆☆☆
Geyserville. Owner: Sbragia family. 18 ha.
www.sbragia.com
Recently retired Beringer winemaker Sbragia has set up his own winery, where the varietal wines show the same generosity and ebullience as his Reserves for Beringer.

Scherrer ☆☆–☆☆☆
Sebastopol. Owner: Fred Scherrer. 20 ha.
www.scherrerwinery.com.
Fred Scherrer is an intellectual among winemakers, adapting his harvesting and winemaking to the particularity of each vintage. The results are refined wines from his own ancient Zinfandel vineyards as well as newer plantings on the Sonoma Coast.

Schug ☆☆
Sonoma. Owner: Walter Schug. 17 ha.
www.schugwinery.com
German-born Walter Schug made his name as the winemaker for Phelps (q.v.). Since 1990, with his own winery, he focuses on understated yet indelible Chardonnay and Pinot Noir, sourced from vineyards throughout Sonoma County. The style is elegant.

Sebastiani ☆–☆☆
Sonoma. Owner: William Foley. 121 ha.
www.sebastiani.com
A name intimately connected with the historic little city of Sonoma. Sebastiani moved from being a bulk producer to high quality with smooth speed, but family feuds in the Sebastiani family resulted in a sale of most of its best-known brands in 2000 and the sale to William Foley in 2008. The winery, diminished in scale, now focuses on straightforward Sonoma County bottlings and a few exceptional wines, such as its Cherryblock Cabernet.

Seghesio ☆☆☆
Healdsburg. Owner: Seghesio family. 162 ha.
www.seghesio.com
A long-established concern that only began to bottle its own wines in 1983. Zinfandel has been the signature, and there are usually five different wines to choose from. Sangiovese bottlings from the family's venerable vineyard and from newer plantings are among California's best.

Simi ☆☆–☆☆☆
Healdsburg. Owner: Constellation. 244 ha.
www.simiwinery.com
Repeated changes in ownership have not helped the historic Simi winery to maintain a consistent image or quality. At their best, Simi's Alexander Valley Cabernet and barrel-fermented Chardonnay Reserve are first rate.

Sonoma-Cutrer ☆☆
Windsor. Owner: Brown-Forman. 445 ha.
www.sonomacutrer.com
For years, Brice Jones's winery reigned as California's all-Chardonnay specialist, offering a range from named vineyards: Les Pierres, Cutrer, and Russian River Ranches. Les Pierres was usually the best. In 1994, Jones broke Chardonnay's hegemony, adding Pinot Noir. Quality remained steady, but other Sonoma Chardonnays eventually came to match or even surpass those from Sonoma-Cutrer. Jones has not been involved with the property since 2001.

Stonestreet ☆☆☆
Healdsburg. Owner: Jackson Family Estates. 400 ha.
www.stonestreetwines.com
Stonestreet can draw on Jackson's huge vineyard holdings in Alexander Valley. Quality is excellent: very good Chardonnay, and even better, the Bordeaux blend called Legacy, and Christopher's Vineyard Cabernet.

Rodney Strong ☆
Healdsburg. Owner: Klein Foods. 365 ha.
www.rodneystrong.com
The late Rodney Strong, a veteran Sonoma producer, had already ceased long ago to be linked with the winery that bears his name, though winemaker Rick Sayre maintained continuity. Wines lack excitement, except Alexander's Crown Cabernet.

Stryker Sonoma ☆
Geyserville. Owner: Craig MacDonald. 11 ha.
www.strykersonoma.com
Drawing fruit from all over Sonoma, this stylish modern winery produces a wide range of varietals. The whites are often disappointing, but the Cabernet and Zinfandel are solid.

Stuhlmuller ☆☆
Healdsburg. Owner: Fritz Stuhlmuller. 61 ha.
The Stuhlmullers are well-established growers who in 1996 began to produce small volumes of Chardonnay, Cabernet, and Zinfandel, all of good quality.

Joseph Swan ☆–☆☆
Forestville. Owner: Rod Berglund. 5 ha.
www.swanwinery.com

The late Joseph Swan pioneered Dry Creek Zinfandel, and his son-in-law follows in his footsteps, though the Pinot Noirs can be as varied as the Zinfandels, and quality is erratic.

Tandem ☆☆–☆☆
Sebastopol. Owner: Greg LaFollette. No vineyards. www.tandemwinery.com.
DeLoach winemaker LaFollette created his own négociant label in 2001 and produces beautifully crafted if high-priced Chardonnay and Pinot from top Sonoma vineyards.

Trentadue ☆☆
Geyserville. Owner: Trentadue family. 100 ha. www.trentadue.com
The Trentadues sell grapes to Ridge and others, but also make their own powerful reds from Zinfandel and Petite Sirah.

Unti ☆☆–☆☆☆
Healdsburg. Owner: Unti family. 24 ha. www.untivineyards.com
Zinfandel and Syrah are the star turns here, but Grenache and Barbera are equally vibrant.

Vérité ☆☆–☆☆☆
Healdsburg. Owner: Jess Jackson. www.veritewines.com
A concept winery, permitting winemaker Pierre Seillan to draw on the top Sonoma vineyards of Jess Jackson to produce high-priced re-interpretations of St-Emilion (Le Désir), Pomerol (La Muse), and Pauillac (La Joie). Rich and very concentrated wines.

Viansa ☆–☆☆
Sonoma. Owner: 360 Global Wine Company. 36 ha. www.viansa.com
Sam Sebastiani left his family winery to set up on his own in 1986. He created a wide range of Italian style wines. The less ambitious wines, such as the clean Arneis and Pinot Grigio, often succeed better than the more ambitious blends. Sebastiani sold the company, and its bustling Italian marketplace and tasting room, in 2005.

Williams & Selyem ☆☆–☆☆☆
Healdsburg. Owner: John Dyson. 21 ha. www,williamsselyem.com
Artisanal to an extreme but never rustic, Burt Williams and Ed Selyem made Russian River and Sonoma Coast Pinot Noir for all it is worth, having taken Domaine de la Romanée-Conti as their philosophical model. Selyem retired in 1998 with back problems, and the label was sold to viticulturist Dyson, and Bob Cabral makes the wines. The Pinots are excellent, but other varieties can be over-alcoholic.

Leading Mendocino Producers

Claudia Springs ☆☆
Philo. Owner: Bob Klindt. 10 ha. www.claudiasprings.com
A low-key operation, but the wines, especially the Viognier and Zinfandel, are highly enjoyable.

Edmeades ☆☆–☆☆☆☆
Philo. Owner: Jackson Family Estates. 25 ha. www.kj.com

The Mendocino cog in Kendall-Jackson's Family Estates wheel specializes in named vineyard wines, especially Pinot Noir, Zinfandel, and Petite Sirah. The wines are big and intense.

Esterlina ☆
Philo. Owner: Sterling family. 54 ha. www.esterlinavineyards.com
The Sterlings own the sole vineyards within the Cole Ranch AVA, and supplement those holdings with vines in the Anderson and Alexander Valleys. Pinot Noir from Anderson Valley shows well; Bordeaux varieties from Cole Ranch less so.

Fetzer ☆☆–☆☆☆
Hopland. Owner: Brown-Forman. 800 ha. www.fetzer.com
Fetzer, operating from Mendocino County but reaching far beyond it, was among the first wineries in California to make good to outright excellent wines on a large scale. It was also a pioneer in operating at several different price levels by labelling wines clearly. In its case, Reserve is at the top, Barrel Select in the middle (and the most striking in value), while proprietary names such as Sundial Chardonnay and Eagle Peak Merlot mark the lower tier. The Bonterra brand is California's leading range of organic wines.

Goldeneye ☆☆–☆☆☆
Philo. Owner: GI Partners. 61 ha. www.goldeneyewinery.com
Created by Napa's Dan Duckhorn in 1997 as a Pinot Noir outpost. The project has proved very successful, with very ripe, fiery wines that help set new standards for Anderson Valley.

Greenwood Ridge ☆☆–☆☆☆
Philo. Owner: Allan Green. 6 ha. www.greenwoodridge.com
Green's best wines come from vineyards high on the Mendocino Ridges, which supply his Riesling, Merlot, and Cabernet. These are supplemented by Chardonnay and Sauvignon from other Mendocino sites. The robust Zinfandel is bought from Sonoma.

Handley Cellars ☆☆
Philo. Owner: Milla Handley. 20 ha. www.handleycellars.com
Ex-Château St Jean winemaker Handley has won praise for Chardonnay, Gewurztraminer, Pinot Noir, and classic method sparklers.

Husch ☆
Philo. Owner: Zac Robinson. 100 ha. www.huschvineyards.com
Vineyards in Anderson Valley and Ukiah provide grapes for a full range of wines, of which the best are the Pinot Noir, Gewurztraminer, and Chardonnay. Quality lurches from sound to rustic.

Lazy Creek ☆☆
Philo. Owner: Josh Chandler. 8 ha.
The Gewurztraminer from this tiny Anderson Valley property is one of Mendocino's best, and Chardonnay and Pinot Noir are not far behind.

Lolonis ☆–☆☆
Redwood Valley. Owner: Lolonis family. 73 ha.
www.lolonis.com

The proudly Greek-American Lolonis family supply many wineries with their organic grapes and started producing their own wines in the 1990s. Initially rustic, the wines are now improving.

McDowell Valley Vineyards ☆☆☆
Hopland. Owner: William Crawford. 135 ha.
www.mcdowellsyrah.com

This estate remains true to a cause, making a statement about the tiny, once-forgotten McDowell Valley in south Mendocino as a source of wines from Rhône varieties, most especially Syrah from vines planted in 1948 and 1959. Plus splendid Viognier and invigorating Grenache rosé.

Monte Volpe ☆☆
Redwood Valley. Owner: Greg Graziano. 8 ha.
www.domainesaintgregory.com

Old Mendocino-hand Graziano is doing intelligent work with Italian varieties, especially Barbera. Another label, Enotria, is dedicated specifically to Piedmontese varieties. Red wines from the Pinot family are labelled as Domaine Saint Gregory.

Navarro ☆☆☆
Philo. Owner: Edward T. Bennett and Deborah Cahn. 35 ha. ww.navarrowine.com

Ted Bennett takes advantage of a relatively foggy area to make uncommonly long lived wines, notably Chardonnay, Riesling, and Gewurztraminer, in an Alsace style, sweet as well as dry. Robust Pinot Noir, too.

Parducci ☆
Ukiah. Owner: Mendocino Wine Group. 100 ha.
www.parducci.com

The oldest winery in Mendocino, it had a troubled history until it was bought in 2004 by its current owners, a consortium of local growers and winemaker Paul Dolan. They have already transformed Parducci into America's first "carbon neutral" winery.

Roederer Estate ☆☆☆
Philo. Owner: Champagne Roederer. 142 ha.
www.roedererestate.net

A large-scale venture with vineyards in the cool Anderson Valley. Impressive from the first vintage onwards. The vintage *cuvée* is L'Ermitage, but the standard *cuvée*, Estate Brut, sometimes rivals it in quality.

Scharffenberger
Philo. Owner: Champagne Roederer. 50 ha.

John Scharffenberger was a pioneer of sparkling wine production in Anderson Valley. In 1989 Pommery became a majority shareholder, and in 1998 the name was changed to Pacific Echo. But in 2005 Roederer bought the property, the name reverted to Scharffenberger, and the bearer of that name set up a chocolate business. The wines were earthy in the past but are certain to improve under new ownership.

Leading San Francisco Bay Producers

Ahlgren ☆☆
Boulder Creek. Owner: Dexter Ahlgren. 10 ha.
www.ahlgrenvineyard.com

Ahlgren's outstanding Cabernet comes from Santa Cruz Mountains fruit, but his other wines are sourced from various parts of the Central Coast.

Bargetto ☆
Soquel. Owner: Bargetto family 16 ha. www.bargetto.com
The most serious wines (Chardonnay, Merlot, Cabernet) come from the Santa Cruz Mountains, and the Italian varieties, to which Barghetto is increasingly turning, from the Central Coast. Quality is variable.

Bonny Doon ☆–☆☆☆
Santa Cruz. Owner: Randall Grahm. 56 ha.
www.bonnydoonvineyard.com

Randall Grahm, the most sharp-witted man in the California wine business, became the foremost of the "Rhône Rangers" while operating from a modest barn in the Santa Cruz Mountains. Since then he has reinvented himself, and his business, repeatedly. He continues to pursue Rhône-like wines (a Mourvèdre called Old Telegram; a Grenache called Clos de Gilroy; a red Châteauneuf-style blend called Le Cigare Volant; and a delicious Marsanne/Roussanne named Le Sophiste), but in 2006 he sold his Big House and Cardinal Zin brands, and is severely reducing his output. At the same time he has launched a new Riesling venture in Washington State called Pacific Rim (q.v.). His future is happily unpredictable.

David Bruce ☆–☆☆
Los Gatos. Owner: David Bruce. 10 ha.
www.davidbrucewinery.com

A bottle of Richebourg converted dermatologist David Bruce to wine, and he set up shop high in the Santa Cruz Mountains. There he made brilliant Pinot Noir and Chardonnay, but

---

CORO MENDOCINO

Ten Mendocino wineries have joined forces in order to create an upmarket blended red wine that would be a kind of flagship for the region and help consolidate its identity. Each winery can compose the blend as it sees fit, but must follow a certain protocol. Thus, at least 40 per cent but no more than 70 per cent of the blend must be Zinfandel, with a range of Rhône and Italian varieties playing second (or third) fiddle. The wine must be aged for at least 12 months in oak barrels, of which 25 per cent to 75 per cent must be new, and a further 12 in bottle. Numerous group tastings monitor quality as the wine ages. The wines carry a high price tag but have mostly been well received.

disease in the vineyards and TCA problems sadly damaged his reputation. Today, the range, supplemented by purchased fruit from top vineyards in the Central Coast, is more diverse. Dr Bruce has now retired and winemaking is in the hands of Mitri Faravashi and his assistants.

Cinnabar ☆☆
Saratoga. Owner: Tom Mudd. 13 ha.
www.cinnabarwine.com
Lofty vineyards produce classic Santa Cruz Mountains wines, while more commercial ranges are made from purchased Central Coast fruit.

Clos La Chance ☆☆
San Martin. Owner: Bill Murphy. 60 ha.
www.closlachance.com
An eclectic range that includes fresh Chardonnay from Napa and Santa Cruz Mountains, and graceful Cabernet Franc and Cabernet Sauvignon. Production has expanded but quality remains dependable, especially for the estate grown range.

Concannon ☆–☆☆
Livermore. Owner: Wente family. 80 ha.
www.concannonvineyard.com
Founded by Col. Joseph Concannon to make altar wine, in the same year as the other great Livermore Valley winery, Wente Vineyard, it has been owned since 1991 by members of the Wente family, but run separately. There is renewed focus on estate Petite Sirah, Sauvignon Blanc, and Assemblage, the proprietary name for red and white Bordeaux blends. Grapes for Chardonnay and other varietals are largely bought-in from Central Coast sources.

Thomas Fogarty ☆☆–☆☆☆
Portola Valley. Owner: Dr.
Thomas Fogarty. 10 ha.
www.fogartywinery.com
Gewurztraminer from Monterey is often stunning, as are the Pinot Noir, Chardonnay, and red Bordeaux varieties from the Santa Cruz Mountains.

Kalin Cellars ☆☆
Novato. Owner: Terrance
Leighton. No vineyards.
www.kalincellars.com
A scientist-winemaker based in, of all unlikely places, Marin County, produces oaky Chardonnays and Pinot Noir from Livermore and Sonoma fruit, released for sale only when Leighton thinks they are ready to drink.

Kathryn Kennedy ☆☆☆
Saratoga. Owner: Kathryn Kennedy.
3 ha. www.kathrynkennedywinery.com
Kennedy, and her son Marty Mathis, do mainly one thing, and do it well: rich, oaky Cabernet. Plus Santa Cruz Mountains Syrah and a Merlot-dominated blend. Extravagant prices.

Mount Eden ☆☆☆
Saratoga. Owner: Jeff and Eleanor Patterson. 16 ha.
www.mounteden.com
This renowned property was founded by Martin Ray, a great pioneer but a difficult character who lost control of the winery in the 1970s. The vines are old and still produce tiny quantities of prodigious Chardonnay, Pinot Noir, and Cabernet Sauvignon; but the bulk of production is an Edna Valley Chardonnay.

Ridge ☆☆☆☆
Cupertino. Owner: Otsuka Co. 210 ha.
www.ridgewine.com
One of California's accepted First Growths, Ridge's Montebello vineyard is isolated on a mountain top, south of San Francisco, near an atmospheric old stone winery that is cooled by a natural spring. Cabernet is the outstanding wine from Montebello, but the Ridge vineyards also produce an elegant Chardonnay.

The Cabernet has a reputation for darkness and intensity without too much beef, and usually benefits from long ageing. For Montebello, 20 years is not old; the Médoc is the natural point of reference. Almost as renowned are the estate's superb Zinfandels, from Napa Valley, Paso Robles, and, above all, Geyserville and Lytton Springs in Sonoma.

Paul Draper has been the winemaker here for over 30 years, and, unlike many California winemakers, he adapts his vinification techniques to the nature of the fruit harvested.

Again atypically, he favours American oak over French barriques. For consistency as well as quality, Ridge is hard to beat.

Santa Cruz Mountain Vineyard ☆☆
Santa Cruz. Owner. Jeff Emery. 6 ha.
www.santacruzmountainsvineyard.com
Restaurateur Ken Burnap founded this excellent little property in the mid-1970s, specializing in powerful Pinot Noir and Cabernet, which sometimes suffer from too much alcohol. In 2004 he sold the business to his natural successor, winemaker Jeff Emery.

Savannah-Chanelle ☆☆
Saratoga. Owner: Mike Ballard. 6 ha.
www.savannahchanelle.com
Since 1996, when the present owner bought the property, it has increasingly focused on Pinot Noir, both from its estate vineyard and from various sources in Sonoma. Good Cabernet Franc, too.

Wente ☆☆
Livermore. Owner: Wente family.
1,215 ha. www.wentevineyards.com
One of the great wine dynasties of America. The founder, Carl, started with Charles Krug in the Napa Valley, and moved to the stony Livermore Valley in 1883 because land was cheaper. White wines made the Wente name. In the early 1960s its Sauvignon Blanc was my favourite; bold, sappy, old-

Oakville Vineyards, Villa Mt Eden

Bordeaux style. Since then, Riesling and Chardonnay have done brilliant turns as well, and reds have become firmly ensconced in a broad, sound range, mostly sourced from the family's extensive vineyards in Monterey as well as Livermore. The sparkling wine is serious, and spends five years on the yeast.

Leading Sierra Foothills Producers

Amador Foothill Winery ☆
Plymouth. Owner: Ben Zeitman and Katie Quinn. 4 ha.
www.amadorfoothill.com
This small, Shenandoah Valley vineyard, and the neighbouring ones from which it buys grapes, produce rugged, tannic Zinfandel, and juicy Sangiovese.

Boeger Winery ☆–☆☆
Placerville. Owner: Greg Boeger. 38 ha.
www.boegerwinery.com
From vineyards at up to 915 metres (3,000 feet), Boeger produces innumerable wines, so quality is variable. The most reliable, and they can be excellent, are the Zinfandel, Barbera, Viognier, and blended reds.

Ironstone ☆–☆☆
Murphys. Owner: Kautz family. 1,780 ha.
www.ironstonevineyards.com
The Kautzes own only 28 hectares in the Foothills, but thousands more in Lodi and the San Joaquin Valley. From these sites they produce a range of simple varietal wines that are clean, fresh, and inexpensive. The Cabernet Franc is a specialty. More serious wines are released as Reserves or under the Christine Andrew label. The winery is the most spectacular in the Foothills, and has much in common with a theme park, made all the more engrossing as the theme in question is gold.

Karly ☆
Plymouth. Owner: Buck Cobb. 8 ha. www.karlywines.com
Big, jammy Zinfandels are the Karly benchmarks, but there is delicious Orange Muscat and a sound range of Rhône varieties, too.

Lava Cap Winery ☆☆
Placerville. Owner: David Jones family. 24 ha.
www.lavacap.com
One of the most consistently stylish of the Sierra Foothills producers. The top range is called Stromberg and comes from vineyards planted at 975 metres (3,200 feet).

Madroña ☆☆
Camino. Owner: Dick Bush. 14 ha.
www.madrona-wines.com
Bush started planting his vineyards at 915 metres (3,000 feet) in 1973. In some years the grapes don't fully ripen, but when they do, he produces a fine range of wines, white and red.

Monteviña ☆
Plymouth. Owner: Trinchero family. 160 ha.
www.montevina.com
In 1988, the Trinchero family of Sutter Home bought Monteviña and began planting many Italian varieties. Despite a complete commitment to such wines, quality has rarely risen above the respectable, though there have been a few excellent wines under the Terra d'Oro label.

Renaissance ☆☆
Oregon House. Owner: Fellowship of Friends.
150 ha. www.renaissancewinery.com
A remarkable site producing remarkable wines: earthy, tannic, long-lived Cabernet and Zinfandel, as well as supple Sauvignon, a growing range of Rhône varieties, and exceptional late harvest wines.

Renwood ☆–☆☆☆
Plymouth. Owner: Robert Smerling. 80 ha.
www.renwood.com
Since 1992, Smerling has set out to make Amador Zinfandel more famous by making it to a still-more heroic scale than previously, and raising the prices in proportion. There are up to seven different old-vine bottlings; the wines are remarkably sophisticated for Amador, and so are the Barberas. Production has soared with the development of the cheaper Red Label range.

Shenandoah Vineyards ☆–☆☆
Plymouth. Owner: Leon Sobon. 20 ha.
www.sobonwine.com
Under the same ownership as Sobon (q.v.), Shenandoah offers a wide range of wines, though only the Special Reserve wines rival Sobon in quality. Excellent fortified wines.

Sierra Vista ☆☆–☆☆☆☆
Placerville. Owner: John MacReady. 13 ha.
www.sierravistawinery.com
MacReady makes some of the best Syrah in the Foothills, especially from Red Rock Ridge. Fine Viognier, too, and a Tavel-style rosé called Belle Rose. The Cabernet and Zinfandel are on the burly side of the spectrum.

Sobon ☆☆
Plymouth. Owner: Leon Sobon. 34 ha.
www.sobonwine.com
Under the same ownership as Shenandoah Vinbeyards (q.v.), Sobon focuses more precisely on powerful single vineyard Zinfandels, many from ancient vines.

Domaine de la Terre Rouge ☆☆–☆☆☆☆
Fiddletown. Owner: William Easton. 28 ha.
www.terrerougewines.com
Since 1987 William Easton has shown a sure touch not only with Zinfandel but with Syrah and Barbera. The Cabernet Sauvignons, however, can be too evidently overripe. Some wines are bottled under the Easton name. Quality can be exceptional, for whites as well as reds, except when oak overwhelms the fruit.

Villa Toscano ☆
Plymouth. Owner: Jerry Wright. 42 ha.
www.villatoscano.com
A tourist destination as much as winery, with pastiche Tuscan architecture and gardens. The wines are brightly varietal, with Tempranillo and Rhône-styles alongside the Italian standards.

Leading Monterey Producers

Bernardus ☆☆–☆☆☆
Carmel Valley. Owner: Bernardus Pon. 20 ha.
www.bernardus.com
This well-funded winery, owned by a Dutch wine distributor, has maintained a high reputation for classy, well-made, varietal wines, from Burgundian and Bordeaux grapes, and for a splendid Bordeaux blend called Marinus.

Chalone ☆☆–☆☆☆
Soledad. Owner: Diageo. 120 ha.
www.chalonevineyard.com
For 50 years a lonely outpost of viticulture on a limestone hilltop near the Pinnacles National Monument, where all water had to be brought up by truck. Then Dick Graff (who has since died) stunned California with surprisingly Burgundian Pinot Noir and Chardonnay.

Pinot Blanc also does well on this elevated site, and the old-vine Chenin Blanc is one of California's best. Viognier and Syrah were later additions to the range. Quality slipped in the 1990s, and bacterial problems crept into many of the wines, but the problem has been resolved. Recent changes in ownership and winemaker led to some loss of individuality, although the wines are still of fine quality.

Heller Estate ☆☆
Carmel Valley. Owner: Gilbert Heller. 50 ha.
www.hellerestate.com
Carmel's first vineyard, now organic, on steep slopes not far from the ocean. The Cabernet is ripe, deep, and impressive, the Merlot more accessible and opulent, and the easy-to-like Chenin Blanc a not-quite convincing disciple of Vouvray. Over recent years the range has been expanded to include Malbec, Cabernet Franc, and Meritage blends.

Jekel Vineyards ☆
Greenfield. Owner: Brown-Forman. 135 ha. www.jekel.com
The whites (especially Riesling and Gravelstone Chardonnay) produced by Jekel are ripe but not heavy, but the reds are less convincing. But quality has slipped in recent years, and in 2004 the winery was closed, with production taking place at Fetzer (q.v.).

Joullian ☆☆
Carmel Valley. Owner: Sias and Joullian families. 16 ha.
www.joullian.com
For many years, Ridge Watson has run this estate on behalf of its Oklahoman proprietors. The estate vineyards produce fine Semillon, Cabernet Sauvignon, and Syrah, but other varieties are made from fruit purchased from other Monterey growers.

J Lohr ☆☆
San Jose. Owner: Jerry Lohr. 800 ha. www.jlohr.com
If only there were more California wineries such as this one, focusing on sensibly priced varietal wines that are well-crafted and full of fruit. Most of the grapes come from Monterey and Paso Robles.

Meador Estate Wines ☆☆
Monterey. Owner: Doug Meador. 120 ha.
www.meadorestates.com
Meador, the idiosyncratic grower and owner of Ventana Vineyards (q.v.), releases some of his most individualistic wines, fluctuating from vintage to vintage, under his family name.

Mer Soleil ☆–☆☆
Soledad. Owner: Charles Wagner. 158 ha.
www.mersoleilvineyard.com
Wagner of Caymus (q.v.) began planting in the Santa Lucia highlands in 1988 and has developed this brand of exotic Chardonnay, considered magnificent by some, overblown by others. Recent additions to the range are Silver, a crisper unoaked Chardonnay, and Late, a botrytized Viognier.

Mirassou ☆
San Jose. Owner: E & J Gallo. 400 ha. www.mirassou.com
Despite the sale of this Monterey pioneer, the sixth generation of the Mirassou family is still involved. The wines on offer are straightforward, easy-drinking varietals of dwindling quality.

Monterra
See Delicato.

Morgan ☆☆–☆☆☆
Salinas. Owner: Dan Lee. 26 ha. www.morganwinery.com
Founded in 1992, Morgan produces sound Chardonnay and Pinot Noir, both estate grown, and thus organic, and from purchased Monterey fruit. Pure red fruits characterize the best bottlings of Pinot Noir, which is probably its finest wine.

Paraiso Vineyards ☆–☆☆
Soledad. Owner: Rich Smith. 730 ha.
www.paraisovineyards.com.
Rich Smith sells grapes to other wineries, but takes his pick for his own label. These are charming rather than structured wines, perfect for summer drinking. Chardonnay, Syrah, and Pinot Noir have performed best so far.

Roar ☆☆–☆☆☆
Soledad. Owner: Adam Franscioni and Gary Pisoni. 57 ha. www.roarwines.com.
In 2001 two of the Santa Lucia Highlands' top growers joined forces to produce small batches of their own Pinot Noir, made in an exuberant style by Adam Lee of Siduri (q.v.).

Talbott ☆☆
Gonzalez. Owner: Talbott family. 325 ha.
www.talbottvineyards.com
The Talbott fortune derives from neckties. They sell most of their grapes, and the Chardonnay from Sleepy Hollow Vineyard is much sought after. Their own Chardonnays are lush and oaky, with a marked tropical fruit character.

Ventana Vineyard ☆☆–☆☆☆
Soledad. Owner: Douglas Meador. 120 ha.
www.meadorestates.com
Doug Meador is an iconoclastic viticulturist, who believes he can attain high yields without compromising quality. His Sauvignon and Gewurztraminer grapes are sold to wineries across the state. His own winery releases standard varietal wines, but the top bottlings are sold under the Meador Estate label (q.v.). Syrah and Riesling are often the best wines.

Leading San Luis Obispo County Producers

Adelaida ☆☆–☆☆☆
Paso Robles. Owner: Van Steenwyck family. 37 ha.
www.adelaida.com
This quirky winery, tucked into the hills, produces Pinot Noir from venerable 45-year-old vines. Cabernet Sauvignon can be excellent, as Syrah and other Rhône varieties, from recently planted vineyards, are now coming onstream. After an unsettled patch Adelaida is again a winery to watch.

Alban ☆☆☆–☆☆☆☆
Arroyo Grande. Owner: John Alban. 30 ha.
www.albanvineyards.com
John Alban had a conversion experience in Condrieu, and in 1990 started planting the first American vineyard devoted exclusively to Rhône varieties. His experience and skill ensure that these are some of the best Rhône-style wines in California, powerful but balanced.

Domaine Alfred ☆☆–☆☆☆
San Luis Obispo. Owner: Terry Speizer. 34 ha.
www.domainealfred.com
Terry Speizer bought this Edna Valley vineyard in 1994, revitalized it, and converted it to Biodynamism. He specializes in rich, toasty Pinot Noir, as well as Chardonnay and Syrah.

L'Aventure ☆☆☆
Paso Robles. Owner: Stéphan Asséo. 24 ha.
www.aventurewine.com
Asséo left his native St-Emilion as he wanted to blend grape varieties. After much wandering, he settled on the rugged west side of Paso Robles and planted Cabernet Sauvignon and Rhône varieties on disparate soil types. From these he blends very powerful yet elegant wines that teeter on the edge of overripeness without ever tumbling over.

Baileyana ☆☆–☆☆☆
San Luis Obispo. Owner: Niven family. 77 ha.
www.baileyana.com
The Nivens are leading growers in Edna Valley and use the grapes from their new-clone Firepeak Vineyard to supply their own label. Pinot Noir is the most rewarding wine, with red-fruits aromas and a good deal of spice.

Claiborne & Churchill ☆
San Luis Obispo. Owner: Clay Thompson and Fredericka Churchill. No vineyards. www.claibornechurchill.com
Unusually, this winery, buying in all its requirements, specializes in Alsace style wines, as well as exotic Chardonnay from Edna Valley.

Eberle ☆☆
Paso Robles. Owner: Gary Eberle. 16 ha.
www.eberlewinery.com
An intense loyalist to Paso Robles, particularly dedicated to Cabernet Sauvignon and Syrah, Eberle was the first to plant Syrah in the region, but the vineyard later succumbed to phylloxera. Many of Paso Robles' top winemakers worked here, and learned their craft from Eberle.

Edna Valley Vineyard ☆–☆☆☆
San Luis Obispo. Owner: Diageo. 440 ha.
www.ednavalleyvineyard.com
This is a joint venture between the huge Diageo group and the family that owns the Paragon Vineyards, which occupy half the Edna Valley AVA. Mostly Chardonnay, powerful and barrel aged, and smaller quantities of Pinot Noir, Syrah, Viognier, and, when the climate permits, late harvest Riesling.

EOS ☆
Paso Robles. Owner: Arciero family. 255 ha.
www.eosvintagecom
A large operation on the plateau east of Paso Robles. The wines are sound but never exciting.

Garretson ☆–☆☆
Paso Robles. Owner: Mat Garretson. No vineyards.
www.garretsonwines.com
So ardent an enthusiast for Rhône-style wines is Mat Garretson that he used to be known as Mr Viognier. He was also a founder of the splendid Hospices du Rhône festival held each year in Paso Robles. His own wines are patchy, but can be very good, despite their unpronounceable Gaelic names.

Robert Hall ☆–☆☆
Paso Robles. Owner: Robert Hall. 100 ha.
www.roberthallwinery.com
Grape-farmer Hall turned wine producer in 1999, built a handsome winery, and turns out well-made if unspectacular Rhône- and Bordeaux-style wines.

Austin Hope ☆☆–☆☆☆
Paso Robles. Owner: Austin Hope. 57 ha.
www.austinhope.com
An experienced grower and winemaker. Hope founded his own label in 2000, focusing exclusively on Rhône varietals and blends. Powerful in style, the wines are nonetheless balanced and invigorating.

Justin ☆☆☆
Paso Robles. Owner: Justin Baldwin. 34 ha.
www.justinwine.com
Retired banker Justin Baldwin and his wife Deborah came to this remote mountain location in 1982, and founded what has become one of the top Central Coast estates. All the wines under the Justin label are first rate: lively Sauvignon; balanced Chardonnay and Viognier; superb Bordeaux varietals; and a blend called Isosceles. Unswerving quality, especially for reds.

Laetitia ☆–☆☆
Arroyo Grande. Owner: Selim Zilkha. 250 ha.
www.laetitiawine.com
The vineyard was originally planted by a Champagne house to produce sparkling wine; in 2001 the property was sold. The new owner supplemented the range of sparkling wines with sound Chardonnay, Syrah, and Pinot varieties, white and red.

Linne Calodo ☆☆–☆☆☆
Paso Robles. Owner: Matt Trevisan. 7 ha.

Trevisan named his winery after a local soil type. Using mostly purchased fruit, he produces a range of Rhône-style blends under such names as Sticks & Stones, Slacker, and Rising Tides. But there is nothing whimsical about these powerful, intense reds that have acquired a cult following.

Meridian ☆–☆☆
Paso Robles. Owner: Foster's Wine Estates. 2,835 ha.
www.meridianvineyards.com
A very large wine company, producing a wide range of extremely well-made and moderately priced wines. Nor are the often excellent Reserve bottlings overpriced. Much of the fruit comes from Santa Barbara vineyards as well as from Paso Robles.

Peachy Canyon ☆–☆☆
Paso Robles. Owner: Doug Beckett. 50 ha.
www.peachycanyon.com
In the 1990s the Becketts produced a splendid set of Zinfandels from various vineyards, but quality has slipped over the past decade.

Saxum ☆☆☆
Paso Robles. Owner: Justin Smith. 8 ha.
www.saxumvineyards.com
This young grower produces superb Syrah from his family's James Berry Vineyard, with its complex soils of shale and limestone.

Tablas Creek ☆☆
Paso Robles. Owner: Perrin and Haas families. 50 ha.
www.tablascreek.com
The Perrin brothers, owners of Beaucastel in Châteauneuf-du-Pape, teamed up with importer Robert Haas to import and plant much-needed authentic plant material, which they farm organically. As well as supplying vines to other estates, they have also begun producing white and red Rhône blends, as well as some unusual wines such as Picpoul and Counoise.

Talley ☆☆☆
Arroyo Grande. Owner: Brian Talley. 66 ha.
www.talleyvineyards.com
Cabernet, the Talleys discovered, doesn't ripen here, but Burgundian varieties certainly do. The upshot is a range of impeccable and elegant Chardonnays and Pinot Noirs.

VinaRobles ☆–☆☆
Paso Robles. Owner: Hans Nef. 77 ha.
www.vinarobles.com
A Swiss restaurateur planted the vineyard in 1996 and the first vintage was 1999. The range is considerable: Cabernet, Syrah, rosé, and exceptional Petite Sirah.

Windward ☆☆
Paso Robles. Owner: Marc Goldberg. 6 ha.
www.windwardvineyard.com
Nothing but estate-grown Pinot Noir here, made in a delicate, scented style that is distinctly Burgundian.

Leading Santa Barbara County Producers

Alma Rosa ☆☆
Buellton. Owner: Richard Sanford. 42 ha.
www.almarosawinery.com
After Sanford left his eponymous winery in 2005, he founded this new property, sourcing fruit from the organic vineyards that remained in his possession. Early days, but so far the Pinot Noir, unsurprisingly, is the most exciting wine.

Au Bon Climat ☆☆–☆☆☆☆
Santa Maria. Owner: Jim Clendenen. 36 ha.
www.aubonclimat.com
Few have done better than irrepressible Jim Clendenen at realizing the potential of the fog-shrouded Santa Maria Valley to produce intense and long-lived Chardonnay and Pinot Noir. While Clendenen's single-vineyard Pinots from the Santa Maria and Santa Ynez Valleys are often superb, the whimsically named La Bauge au-Dessus, Knox Alexander, and Isabelle bottlings sometimes stir the soul more deeply.

Clendenen is a Burgundian at heart, and strives for balance and elegance. Perhaps for that reason he is more admired in Europe than in his native land.

Babcock ☆☆–☆☆☆
Lompoc. Owner: Bryan Babcock. 35 ha.
www.babcockwinery.com
Babcock made its name with its consistent Sauvignon Blanc, but red wines have grown in renown, especially the Black Label Syrah, the Bordeaux blend called Fathom, and Pinot Noir from the Santa Rita Hills.

Beckmen ☆☆–☆☆☆
Los Olivos. Owner: Tom Beckmen. 70 ha.
www.beckmenvineyards.com
Beckmen follows the growing Santa Barbara trend towards Rhône varieties, both selling grapes and producing a growing volume of his own wines. The Syrah, with its freshness and vibrancy, can be exceptional.

Brander ☆–☆☆
Los Olivos. Owner: Frederic Brander. 17 ha.
www.brander.com
Fred Brander makes outstanding Sauvignon Blancs, as well as Chardonnay, Syrah, and Merlot.

Brewer Clifton ☆☆
Lompoc. Owner: Greg Brewer and Steve Clifton.
No vineyards. www.brewerclifton.com
Two young winemakers teamed up in 1996 to produce single-vineyard Pinot Noir and Chardonnay from top sites in Santa Barbara. The winemaking is identical for each; only the vineyard differs. Although much admired, the wines can suffer from excessive alcohol.

Byron Santa Maria
Santa Maria. Owner: Jackson Family Estates. 260 ha.
www.byronwines.com
Pioneer Santa Barbara winemaker Ken Brown sold the winery he founded to Robert Mondavi in 1990, but after

various changes in ownership it was acquired by Jess Jackson in 2007, so its future direction is uncertain.

Cambria ☆☆–☆☆☆
Santa Maria. Owner: Jackson Family Estates. 565 ha.
www.cambriawines.com
Jess Jackson bought much of the vast Tepusquet Vineyard in 1987, and uses it as the principal source for this Santa Barbara label. The reserve Chardonnay can be heavy-handed, and the simple bottlings are sometimes preferable. Charming Pinot Noir and sound Syrah, too.

Curtis ☆☆
Buellton. Owner: Kate Firestone. 26 ha.
www.curtiswinery.com
Curtis specializes in Rhône varieties, and the Heritage Cuvée proves it's possible to make highly drinkable Southern Rhône-style blends at a sensible price.

Fiddlehead ☆☆
Lompoc. Owner: Kathy Joseph. 40 ha.
www.fiddleheadcellars.com
Kathy Joseph only makes wines she enjoys: Santa Barbara Sauvignon Blanc, and Pinot Noir from Santa Rita Hills and Oregon. Quality has climbed a notch since her own Fiddlestix Vineyard has come on stream.

Firestone Los Olivos.
Owner: William Foley. 216 ha.
www.firestonewine.com
Firestone (of tyre fame) pioneered the climatically quirky part of the Santa Ynez Valley around Los Olivos. The family produced good, sometimes excellent, varietal wines at moderate prices. In 2007 the property was sold, and the new owner expanded the operation by opening a second Firestone winery in Paso Robles. Whether the Firestone style will alter, and for better or worse, it is too early to say.

Foley ☆☆
Solvang. Owner: William Foley. 80 ha.
www.foleywines.com
Known as Carey Cellars until bought by Foley in 1997. Changes in winemaker have led to stylistic fluctuation, but current wine-maker Kris Curran, who developed the successful SeaSmoke winery (q.v.), is likely to focus on rich, full-bodied Pinot Noir and Syrah. Under the same ownership is LinCourt Vineyards.

Foxen ☆–☆☆☆
Santa Maria. Owner: Richard Doré and Bill Wathen.
4 ha. www.foxenvineyard.com
Since 1987, this small winery has improved from year to year. Titanic yet silky Pinots and richly flavoured Chardonnays from single vineyard sites.

Jaffurs ☆☆
Santa Barbara. Owner: Craig Jaffurs. No vineyards.
www.jaffurswine.com

Jaffurs buys in fruit from top vineyards to craft his exceptional Syrahs and other wines. The style can be on the lush side, with its emphasis on sweet American oak.

Koehler ☆☆
Los Olivos. Owner: Kory Koehler. 27 ha.
www.koehlerwinery.com
Good, concentrated wines from a wide range of varieties: Pinot Noir and Syrah show the most promise.

Richard Longoria ☆☆
Los Olivos. Owner: Richard Longoria. 3 ha.
www.longoriawine.com
A veteran Santa Barbara winemaker, Longoria makes a wide range of wines under his own name, emphasizing fruit rather than oak.

Melville ☆☆
Lompoc. Owner: Ron Melville. 56 ha.
www.melvillewinery.com

Greg Brewer of Brewer-Clifton (q.v.) makes the wines: rich tannic Pinot, bright Syrah, and crisp unoaked Chardonnay.

Andrew Murray ☆☆–☆☆☆
Los Olivos. Owner: Andrew Murray.
No vineyards.
www.andrewmurrayvineyards.com
James Murray planted Rhône varieties on beautiful hillside vineyards from 1990 onwards, and his son, Andrew, turned them into gorgeously opulent wines, white as well as red. Then in 2006 James Murray sold the property, leaving Andrew with no estate vineyard. Fortunately, good connections allow Andrew to buy fruit from other Santa Barbara vineyards and continue his skilful work.

Fess Parker ☆☆
Los Olivos. Owner: Fess Parker.
285 ha. www.fessparker.com
Elderly readers may recall Parker in his most famous screen role as Davy Crockett. Today he, and his son Eli, produce wine. The basic range carries the California appellation, but there are also estate wines. The style is full-bodied and oaky, and clearly finds favour with the countless visitors who flock to the winery and its restaurant.

Qupé ☆☆☆
Santa Maria. Owner: Bob Lindquist. 5 ha.
www.qupe.com
Lindquist was one of the first winemakers to specialize in Rhône varieties, and his Syrah, Roussanne, and Viognier remain among the finest in California.

Sanford ☆☆
Buellton. Owner: Terlato Wine Group. 145 ha.
Richard Sanford was one of the first to recognize the potential of what is today the Santa Rita Hills for Pinot Noir and Chardonnay. He planted his vineyards from 1971, but had

Wine press, Fess Parker winery, Los Olivios

to enter into various partnerships to sustain his winery. In 2005 he had a falling out with the Terlato family, who were unhappy about his costly commitment to organic farming, and he left the winery that bears his name to reclaim his independence at Alma Rosa (q.v.).

SeaSmoke Cellars ☆☆–☆☆☆
Lompoc. Owner: Bob David. 40 ha.
www.seasmokecellars.com
Burgundy enthusiast Bob David wanted to produce only Pinot Noir, and planted a splendid undulating site in the Santa Rita Hills. Under winemaker Kris Curran, now of Foley (q.v.), and her successor Victor Gallegos the style has been unashamedly big and brawny.

Stolpman ☆☆–☆☆☆
Lompoc. Owner: Tom Stolpman. 61 ha.
www.stolpmanvineyards.com
Lawyer Tom Stolpman planted his impeccably maintained vineyards in 1991 in order to sell fruit, but a few years later was producing wine. Rhône varieties dominate, but winemaker Sashi Moorman also shows a sure touch with a Bordeaux blend called Angeli, and with Italian varieties too.

Lane Tanner ☆☆–☆☆☆
Santa Maria. Owner: Lane Tanner. No vineyards.
www.lanetanner.com
A gifted interpreter of Santa Barbara Pinot Noir and Syrah, whether blended or from named vineyards.

Kenneth Volk ☆☆
Santa Maria. Owner: Kenneth Volk. 2 ha.
www.volkwines.com
Ken Volk made the reputation for Wild Horse in San Luis Obispo, but left after a corporate takeover made it unlikely that he could develop his penchant for unusual grape varieties. He has now set up his own winery, so wines such as Negrette are back on the menu.

Zaca Mesa ☆☆–☆☆☆
Los Olivos. Owner: John Cushman. 99 ha.
www.zacamesa.com
Along with Firestone (q.v.), one of the first to plant in the Santa Ynez Valley, with vineyards on a 457-metre (1,500-foot) flat-topped "mesa". Since the mid-1990s it has shifted its focus to Rhône varieties. Syrah is the flagship, Viognier shows a typicity rare in California. Cuvée Z is a blend of estate-grown Rhône varieties.

Other California Producers

Arcadian ☆☆☆
Santa Ynez. Owner: Joseph Davis. No vineyards.
www.arcadianwinery.com
Joe Davis trained in Burgundy, and it shows in his wines, which are made from vines he leases and farms himself. Yields are very low, and the wines, both Chardonnay and Pinot Noir, are finely poised and concentrated. Their modest alcohol levels discourage high ratings from some American critics, but the wines age well.

Blackstone ☆–☆☆
Gonzalez. Owner: Pacific Wine Partners. No vineyards.
www.blackstonewinery.com
Million-case négociant winery with facilities in Monterey and Sonoma. Tasted blind over many years, these wines show well, with admirable typicity.

Bogle ☆–☆☆
Clarksburg. Owner: Warren V Bogle. 500 ha.
www.boglewinery.com
A standard range of varietal wines, almost always under the California appellation which permits inter-regional blending. Excellent Petite Sirah.

Calera ☆–☆☆☆
Hollister. Owner: Josh Jensen. 34 ha.
www.calerawine.com
For Josh Jensen, burgundy is the Holy Grail, and limestone vineyards the path to it. So he found one of the few limestone areas in California and planted it with Pinot Noir. Rather funky wines from individual sites, plus less costly regional blends. Terrific Viognier.

Callaway ☆
Temecula. Owner: Patricia Lin. 28 ha.
www.callawaywinery.com
For most of the 1980s, Callaway specialized in unoaked Chardonnay and Chenin Blanc. In the 1990s, Pierce's Disease attacked many vineyards, so the company began purchasing grapes from California to supply its needs. New owners from 2005.

Delicato ☆–☆☆
Manteca. Owner: Delicato family. 3,650 ha.
www.delicato.com
The Delicatos own the colossal San Bernabe Vineyard in southern Monterey. It recently began producing its own wines: the excellent Monterra range delivers beautiful fruit at bargain prices.

Ficklin Vineyards ☆☆–☆☆☆
Madera. Owner: Ficklin family. 14 ha. www.ficklin.com
California's most respected specialist in port style wine, made by a solera system. It is neither vintage nor tawny in character, but it does age indefinitely like vintage. It needs careful, often early, decanting. Recently, Ficklin has revived the issue of vintage dated wines.

E & J Gallo ☆–☆☆☆
Modesto. Owner: Gallo families. 2,450 ha. www.gallo.com
See page 517.

Kendall-Jackson ☆☆–☆☆☆
Santa Rosa. Owner: Jackson Family Estates. 5,100 ha.
www.kj.com
Since the early 1990s, Kendall-Jackson expanded from a medium-sized company based in Lake County to one of the biggest players in California, and thus the world. The company structure is very complex, with varying ownership of vineyards, subsidiary wineries, and estates purchased over the years. Kendall-Jackson prides itself on using only "coastal"

fruit, broadly defined as anything other than grapes from the torrid San Joaquin Valley. Its Vintners' Reserve range of fruit-driven varietals has proved a huge success. The K J vineyards are analyzed as "flavour domaines": in other words, blending components for the major brands.

The more fascinating part of the story occurred more recently when Jackson scooped up nearly a dozen existing small properties, and then invented a couple more, for his Jackson Family Wines division. These included Cambria, La Crema, Edmeades, Hartford Court, Pepi, Lokoya, Matanzas Creek, and Stonestreet (qq.v.). Recently created labels for small-production wines in specific styles (and at high prices) include Cardinale (q.v.), Verité, Atalon, and Carmel Road.

Langtry Estate ☆
Middletown. Owner: Magoon family. 150 ha.
www.langtryestate.com
A huge property straddling the Lake-Napa County line, where Lillie Langtry first planted vines in the nineteenth century. In 2003, the estate, formerly known as Guenoc, was named after her. Quality is inconsistent.

Lucas ☆☆
Lodi. Owner/winemaker: David Lucas. 8 ha.
www.lucaswinery.com
Lodi's top producer of Zinfandels, the best of which is made from 80-year-old vines.

Moraga ☆☆☆
Los Angeles. Owner: Tom Jones. 6 ha.
Hidden away in the canyons of star-studded Bel Air is this small vineyard, with a microclimate exceptional enough to allow it to produce sumptuous and expensive Cabernet Sauvignon.

Ojai ☆☆–☆☆☆
Oak View. Owner: Adam Tolmach. No vineyards.
www.ojaivineyard.com
Pierce's Disease has done for the Ojai vineyard, but Tolmach buys fruit from top estates in Santa Barbara and Ventura counties. Syrah has overtaken Pinot Noir as the best wine, made in an opulent and concentrated style.

Orfila ☆–☆☆
Escondido. Owner: Alejandro Orfila. 25 ha.
www.orfila.com
Owned by an Argentinian diplomat since 1994, this is the leading winery in San Pasquale Valley near San Diego, with striking Gewurztraminer and Merlot. Some wines are sourced from other counties.

Patz & Hall ☆☆–☆☆☆
Sonoma. Owner: Donald Patz, James Hall, and Ann Moses. No vineyards. www.patzhall.com
An acclaimed négociant winery, specializing in Pinot Noir and Chardonnay from top-quality North Coast vineyards.

THE GALLO FAMILY

Ernest and the late Julio Gallo have done more to determine the direction and rate of growth of wine drinking in the USA than anybody else in history. By far the biggest wine producers in America, and probably the world, E & J Gallo is still privately owned and directed by the second and third generations.

The sons of an Italian immigrant grape farmer, they were brought up in Modesto in the Central Valley. They started making wine in 1933, when Ernest was 24, and Julio 23. Julio made the wine and Ernest sold it.

They built their first winery in 1935, where the present vast plant now stands, and in 1940 started planting vineyards to experiment with better grapes. They realized the limitations of Central Valley grapes and bought from growers in Napa and Sonoma. They were prepared to outbid rivals.

In the 1950s, the Gallos started a craze for flavoured "pop" wines with the fortified Thunderbird, to be followed by a series of such enormously advertized and vastly popular gimmicks as fizzy Ripple

and Boone's Farm apple wine. In 1964 they launched Hearty Burgundy which, with Chablis Blanc, set a new standard for Californian jug wines.

The Gallos have been moving slowly but steadily upmarket, taking America with them. In 1974, they introduced their first varietal wines, and in the mid-1980s bought and developed thousands of hectares in Sonoma, which formed the basis of Gallo Sonoma. This bold enterprise proved they were capable of producing first-rate varietal wines from a range of individual Sonoma vineyards. This helped alter the image of Gallo from purveyors of jug wines to serious wine producers. Starting to export was part of their strategy. This campaign was spearheaded by third-generation Gallos such as Gina and Matthew, who took charge of the Sonoma operations.

Impressive though this achievement has been, Gallo remains a Californian phenomenon, a business that single-handedly produces as much wine as all of Australia.

The wines are sumptuous: a lot of (indeed, sometimes too much) new oak and alcohol.

R H Phillips ☆
Esparto. Owner: Constellation. 530 ha.
www.rhphillips.com
This once-lonely pioneer grower in Dunnigan Hills, northwest of Sacramento, now has company there. Consistently agreeable reds and whites from Rhône varieties enticed the rivals.

Quady ☆☆
Madera. Owner: Andrew Quady. 6 ha.
www.quadywinery.com
Quady makes good Amador County port style from Zinfandel, but his star turn has always been his stylish and beautifully packaged Muscats. The celebrated Essensia is from Orange Muscat; Elysium is a red version from Black Muscat.

Ramey ☆☆☆
Healdsburg. Owner: David Ramey. No vineyards.
www.rameywine.com
David Ramey, former winemaker for Matanzas Creek, Dominus, and Rudd, began to produce wines, mostly Chardonnay, under his own name from 1996 onwards. The Cabernets, mostly sourced from northern Napa, can be equally polished.

Rosenblum ☆☆–☆☆☆
Alameda. Owner: Diageo. 14 ha.
www.rosenblumcellars.com
Kent Rosenblum is passionate about Zinfandel, and sources small parcels of grapes from throughout the estate, releasing up to ten versions each year. He favours heft over elegance, but this can sometimes be a winning formula with Zinfandel. In 2008 he sold the brand.

Rosenthal ☆–☆☆
Malibu. Owner: George Rosenthal. 10 ha.
www.rosenthalestatewines.com
In 1987 Rosenthal began planting vines high in the hills behind Malibu. Results remain mixed, with some faulty wines alongside some undoubted successes. There is crisp Chardonnay as well as robust red.

Siduri ☆☆–☆☆☆
Santa Rosa. Owner: Adam Lee. No vineyards.
www.siduri.com
Lee buys Pinot Noir grapes from Oregon as well as California, keeping a close eye on the up-to-20 vineyards he buys from. These are very ripe but stylish wines, despite a sometimes lavish use of new oak.

Sine Qua Non ☆☆–☆☆☆
Ventura. Owner: Manfred Krankl. No vineyards.
An Austrian restaurateur runs this eccentric operation, producing small lots of exotic wines sold mostly to collectors on his mailing list. He has collaborated with the late Austrian sweet wine supremo, Alois Kracher (q.v.), on a range of dessert wines. The flamboyant wines, such as overpowerful Pinot Noir and Syrah, do not always justify the high prices demanded for them.

Steele ☆☆
Kelseyville. Owner: Jed Steele. 26 ha.
www.steelewines.com
Jed Steele worked for Kendall-Jackson until a spectacular falling-out took place. He buys in most grapes for his own label, and retains a fondness for Lake County and Mendocino fruit. Fleshy wines accessible young, as a whole. Shooting Star is the second label.

Testarossa ☆☆☆
Los Gatos. Owner: Rob and Diana Jensen. No vineyards.
www.testarossa.com
Using grapes from top vineyards in Monterey and Santa Barbara, the Jensens produce a range of oaky but elegant wines that invariably show their vineyard origins clearly. Mostly Chardonnay and Pinot Noir, but some Syrah is now coming on stream.

Sean Thackrey ☆☆–☆☆☆
Bolinas. Owner: Sean Thackrey. No vineyards.
www.winemaker.net
Art dealer and winemaker, Thackrey has made some extraordinary Syrah and Rhône-style blends over the past two decades. Unfortunately, as soon as he makes a vineyard famous, it ups its prices or sells to a rich buyer, so consistency of supply is a problem. Occasionally funky wines; never dull.

The Pacific Northwest

If, in the early 1970s, America was waking up to superlative quality from Napa and Sonoma, by the end of the decade the avant-garde were heralding the Pacific Northwest as the up-and-coming wine region, with strong hints that the new area would produce something that was closer to the European model: wines less overbearing than the California champions. Much of this expected potential has now been fulfilled.

In the early 1960s, a young man from Salt Lake City, Utah, enrolled in a viticulture programme at the University of California at Davis. That man was David Lett. He became enamoured of Pinot Noir, but felt that, in most cases, California wasn't getting it right. He began studying climatological data from Oregon's Willamette Valley, and became convinced that the valley was the best place outside Burgundy to grow Pinot Noir grapes. In 1965, he moved to Oregon and began planting a vineyard. His Eyrie Vineyards made its first wine in 1970, and it was still drinking well in 2008.

About the same time, a group of professors from the University of Washington began a winemaking project as a hobby, in a garage in Seattle. By 1967, they had made several very tasty wines from grapes grown in the Yakima Valley of central Washington. When the late André Tchelistcheff, then winemaker at Beaulieu Vineyards in Napa Valley, tasted their wines, he encouraged the men to produce more. Thus, Associated Vintners (now Columbia Winery) was born.

As early as 1979, Oregon Pinot Noir gained international accolades, when David Lett's 1975 Pinot Noir was placed second in a competitive blind tasting in Paris, organized by Robert Drouhin of Beaune; Drouhin's own 1959 Chambolle-Musigny won first place. Drouhin was so impressed that he visited Oregon several times, eventually establishing a vineyard and winery near Lett's in 1988.

In less than 30 years, the Pacific Northwest wine industry has burgeoned. Vineyards have expanded enormously. In Washington, there are now 550 wineries, farming 12,545 hectares. In Oregon, there are 370 wineries and over 7,000 hectares of vineyards, of which just under half are planted with Pinot Noir. The two industries are as distinct as the geography that separates them. North of the California border, in western Oregon, the Coastal Range acts as a very effective rain-catcher and offers shelter to the Umpqua Valley to the south, then further north, to the Willamette Valley, where 70 per cent of Oregon's vineyards are located. Umpqua is drier and warmer than Willamette; Cabernet will usually ripen there, but not further north.

Oregon's annual rainfall is a reasonable 75–100 centimetres (30–40 inches), and the latitude the same as that of Bordeaux. For the most part, this is a gentle, maritime climate, best-suited to cool-climate grape varieties. Although the star, to date, has been Pinot Noir, recent years have seen increased plantings of Pinot Gris, Chardonnay, and Pinot Blanc. The quality of Gewurztraminer is generally high, and the area also produces some good sparkling wines. Riesling, mostly made in a dry style, is enjoying an unexpected but welcome revival. Oregon's occasional problems derive from unwelcome rainfall in autumn, often just before or during harvest. This leads to considerable vintage variation. However, viticultural practices, aided by global warming, have manipulated vines into maturing earlier than before, and in practice that often means before the autumnal rains begin to fall.

Oregon takes pride in the fact that its appellation rules are the strictest in the USA. If a region or subregion is named on the label, then the wine must contain at least 95 per cent of grapes from that area. Any varietally labelled wine must consist of at least 90 per cent of that variety (with the sole exception of Cabernet Sauvignon, which is rarely produced here).

In complete contrast to Oregon, the vineyards of Washington have been planted two ranges back from the Pacific Ocean, east of the much higher Cascade Mountains, in an area with a mere 20 centimetres (eight inches) of rain a year: the Columbia River Basin, and within it, the more grape-specific Yakima Valley. The region's deep, sandy soil, long, summer daylight hours, and hot sunshine, have proved ideal for wine grapes.

The latitude – 160 kilometres (100 miles) further north than Willamette – and the continental extremes of temperature (very cold in winter and surprisingly chilly even on a summer night) have proved particularly suited to the Bordeaux varieties: Semillon, Sauvignon Blanc, Cabernet Sauvignon, Cabernet Franc, Merlot, and, especially, Syrah. Chardonnay and Riesling also fare extremely well in eastern Washington. Grapes ripen well while keeping remarkably high acidity, with a consequent intensity of flavour.

AVAs have proliferated in Oregon in recent years. Willamette Valley (160 kilometres/100 miles) from Portland south to Eugene is the main northern Oregon AVA. Within it are numerous subregions, all AVAs: Chehalem Mountains, Dundee Hills, Eola-Amity Hills, McMinnville, Ribbon Ridge, and Yamhill-Carlton. There are topographical and soil differences between them, but most consumers will have difficulty distinguishing them in terms of their flavour profiles.

The southern AVAs are the blanket appellation of Southern Oregon; Umpqua Valley (AVA: Douglas County, centred on Roseburg, another 80 kilometres/50 miles south); Rogue Valley (Jackson and Josephine counties, centred on Grant's Pass, 80 kilometres/50 miles south again); and Applegate (a subzone of Rogue Valley). Further AVAs have been created along the Columbia River that separates Oregon from Washington: Columbia Gorge, Columbia Valley, and Walla Walla Valley (which is shared with Washington).

Washington's vineyards are concentrated in the Yakima Valley, but its established wineries are centred around Seattle in suburbs such as Woodinville, which is still the stronghold for many of Washington's largest and most prestigious wineries. In this state too AVAs have mushroomed as growers seek to pin an identity on their subregions. They are Puget Sound (mostly planted with hybrids), Columbia Valley and Columbia Gorge, Yakima Valley, Walla Walla Valley, Horse Heaven Hills, Rattlesnake Hills, Wahluke Slope, and Red Mountain. In the past, the grapes were often transported the 240 kilometres

(150 miles) over the Cascades to Seattle, but several companies have now built wineries near the vineyards. In the 1980s, Washington, with a climate promoting high acidity, was thought better for white grapes than for red. By the mid-1990s it was apparent that Washington was capable of producing rich but elegant reds, although a further swing in fashion has seen a return to popularity not only of Chardonnay but of Riesling. Among the red grapes, Merlot and Cabernet Sauvignon are level-pegging at about 2,400 hectares each, while Syrah has been mounting a strong challenge with 1,150. Neighbouring Idaho, whose vineyards are east of Oregon along the Snake River, has 490 hectares under vine and 32 wineries. Chardonnay shows considerable promise.

Oregon

Leading Willamette Valley Producers

A to Z Wineworks ☆☆
Dundee. Owner: Bill and Debra Hatcher and partners. No vineyards.
www.atozwineworks.com
In 2002 some well-known winemakers joined forces to create what has become a successful negociant business, with good packaging and a catchy slogan ("Aristocratic wines at democratic prices"). Night & Day is a splendid Bordeaux blend at an irresistible price.

Adelsheim ☆☆–☆☆☆☆
Newberg. Owner: David Adelsheim. 80 ha.
www.adelsheim.com.
David Adelsheim, the pioneer who pressed most strongly for Oregon's strict appellation rules, is still going strong. The focus remains on fine Pinot Noir from its own and neighbouring vineyards. Also produced are Chardonnay, Pinot Gris, Auxerrois, and Syrah.

Amity Vineyards ☆–☆☆
Amity. Owner: Myron Redford. 6 ha.
www.amityvineyards.com
Amity, established in 1976, produces long-lived Pinot Noir of variable quality, and more Gewurztraminer than any other Oregon winery. Pinot Blanc and Riesling are made with equal devotion.

Anam Cara ☆☆
Newberg. Owner: Nick and Sheila Nicholas. 12 ha. www.anamcaracellars.com
The first vintage here was 2004: poised, delicate, almost ethereal Pinot Noir, and Rieslings with bite.

Anna Amie ☆–☆☆
Carlton. Owner: Dr. Robert Pamplin. 48 ha.
www.anneamie.com
Formerly known as Chateau Benoit. In 1999 the property changed hands, vineyards were replanted, and a new winemaker hired in 2007. The winery is still finding its way, but current releases are fresh and appealing.

Archery Summit ☆☆–☆☆☆
Dayton. Owner: Leucadia. 45 ha.
www.archerysummit.com
Founded at great expense in 1992 by Napa winemaker Gary Andrus, Archery Summit was sold in 2003. The focus is exclusively on numerous bottlings of high-priced and oaky Pinot Noir.

Argyle ☆☆☆
Dundee. Owner: Lion Nathan. 130 ha.
www.argylewinery.com
The winery was founded in 1987 by a partnership including Brian Croser and Bollinger, with a view to making *méthode traditionnelle* sparkling wines. They include notable bargains. It also produces very good Chardonnay, Pinot Noir (notably Nuthouse and Spirithouse bottlings), and a delicious dry Riesling.

Beaux Frères ☆☆☆
Newberg. Owner: Michael Etzel and Robert M Parker. 10 ha. www.beauxfreres.com
Beaux Frères began as a much lauded producer of small quantities of intense, oaky, and expensive Pinot Noirs. Co-owner Parker is the famous wine critic, winemaker Etzel his brother-in-law. Initial releases packed too much of a punch, but in the 2000s Etzel backed away from that style, reducing the proportion of new oak and converting the vineyards to Bioynamism. As a consequence, current releases show more stylishness.

Bergstrom ☆☆☆
Newberg. Owner: Josh Bergstrom. 18 ha.
www.bergstromwines.com
Burgundy-trained Bergstrom has refined his Pinot Noirs since his first releases in 1999, and now produces some of the most complex and rewarding Pinots in the valley. The vineyards are Biodynamic, and the winemaking varies according to the quality of the fruit. Outstanding Chardonnay and Riesling, too. But the wines don't come cheap.

Bethel Heights ☆☆–☆☆☆☆
Salem. Owner: Casteel family. 20 ha.
www.bethelheights.com
Since 1984, Bethel Heights has been one of Oregon's most consistent Pinot Noir producers, known for its excellent vineyard in the Eola Hills and a roster of fine wines, which also includes unoaked Chardonnay, Pinot Gris, and Pinot Blanc. Twins Ted and Terry Casteel have now handed over production to the next generation, who have maintained quality.

Brick House ☆☆
Newberg. Owner: Doug Tunnell. 11 ha.
www.brickhousewines.com
Doug Tunnell exchanged the life of a foreign correspondent for that of a vigneron, and produces small quantities of powerful Pinot Noir from Biodynamic vineyards. The other house specialty is delicious Gamay.

Broadley ☆☆☆
Monroe. Owner: Broadley family. 12 ha.
www.broadleyvineyards.com

The Broadleys specialize in powerful, new oaked, unfiltered Pinot Noir that is often of exceptional quality. Skilful winemaking from first-rate fruit ensures the wines, despite their intensity and toastiness, are finely balanced.

Brooks ☆–☆☆
Amity. Owner: Pascal Brooks. No vineyards.
www.brookswine.com.
Founded in 1998 by winemaker Jimi Brooks, who died aged 38 in 2005, making his son Pascal (born 1996) the world's youngest winery owner. The family only buys from organic and Biodynamic vineyards and specializes in Riesling as well as Pinot Noir.

Chehalem ☆☆
Newberg. Owner: Harry Peterson-Nedry. 106 ha.
www.chehalemwines.com
From its first commercial crush in 1990, Chehalem has become known for deep, intense, estate-grown Pinot Noirs. More than any other Oregon grower, Peterson-Nedry is committed to Riesling, which he produces in various styles. Bracing unoaked Chardonnay, too.

Cristom ☆☆–☆☆☆
Salem. Owner: Paul Gerrie. 27 ha.
www.cristomwines.com
The Gerries bought this winery in 1992, and hired one of California's brightest and best – Steve Doerner, formerly of Calera – as their winemaker. Cristom annually produces 7,000 cases of delicious Pinot Noir, Viognier, and Syrah.

Dobbes ☆–☆☆☆
Dundee. Owner: Joe Dobbes. 87 ha.
www.dobbesfamilyestate.com
Dobbes supplements his estate-grown Pinot Noirs, some of which are exceptional, with Viognier and Syrah from Rogue Valley. The freshness and sleek textures of the Pinots probably reflects Dobbes's spells with top Burgundian growers such as Roumier. He also produces a cheap and cheerful range called Wine by Joe.

Domaine Drouhin ☆☆☆
Dundee. Owner: Maison Drouhin. 41 ha.
www.domainedrouhin.com
The unique outpost of Burgundy in the northwest, founded by Robert Drouhin in 1987. Drouhin's daughter Veronique has produced consistently fine wines. Her regular bottling is of a high standard, but two barrel selections, Laurène and Louise, are even better. Not surprisingly, this is the most Burgundian of Oregon estates. Partly oaked Chardonnay was added to the range in 1997.

Elk Cove ☆☆–☆☆☆☆
Gaston. Owner: Campbell family. 77 ha.
www.elkcove.com
Elk Cove was one of the pioneers, founded in 1977. A range

of single-vineyard Pinot Noirs takes centre change, flanked by Alsace-style white wines. Adam Campbell took over in 1997, banished Chardonnay, and has presided over a considerable improvement in quality.

Erath ☆☆–☆☆☆
Dundee. Owner: Ste Michelle Wine Estates. 32 ha.
www.erath.com
The second oldest Oregon winery, founded in 1968, was bought by the giant Washington state winery in 2006. The Pinots, other than the basic Oregon Pinot Noir, remain of good quality, but the whites from Pinot Blanc and Pinot Gris are uninspired as yet.

Evesham Wood ☆☆
Salem. Owner: Russell Raney. 5 ha.
Small estate winery established in 1986, now producing approximately 4,000 cases of organically grown wine, including two perfumed, understated Pinot Noirs, and two Chardonnays, one of which is unoaked.

Eyrie Vineyards ☆–☆☆☆
Dundee. Owner: Jason Lett. 22 ha.
www.eyrievineyards.com
Delicate, pretty Pinot Noirs, oaky Chardonnays, and deliciously fruity Pinot Gris are this Oregon pioneer's stock in trade. Since his first vintage in 1970, David Lett was a maverick; he sticks to his style, even though the industry around him changed. Some of his wines have proven remarkably and deliciously age-worthy. Also produces rather drab Pinot Meunier. A vertical tasting held in 2008 from 1970 to the present day showed many Pinots from the 1970s still drinking well, while more recent decades held many dry and disappointing wines. In the early 2000s David's son Jason took over as winemaker, and some weeks after that vertical tasting, David Lett died.

Four Graces ☆☆–☆☆☆
Dundee. Owner: Steve Black. 38 ha.
www.thefourgraces.com
The Four Graces is touchingly named after Black's four daughters. Although the property was only created in 2003, it has already made an impact with some impressive Reserve Pinots.

Patricia Green ☆☆
Newberg. Owner: Patricia Green. 21 ha.
www.patriciagreencellars.com
The exuberant Patsy Green, an experienced Oregon winemaker, specializes in up to 15 single-vineyard Pinot Noirs each vintage, from her own and other vineyards. Stylistically, they vary considerably, as indeed they should.

King Estate ☆☆
Eugene. Owner: King family. 190 ha. www.kingestate.com
This huge, new, well-financed operation, managed by Ed King III, supplements its own organic vineyard production by

Argyle winery, Dundee

buying grapes from other growers. The château-style winery focuses on Pinot Gris, Pinot Noir, and Chardonnay, and the estate-grown Domaine wines can be excellent. King Estate has become as well-known for its Pinot Gris as for its Pinot Noirs.

Lemelson ☆☆
Carlton. Owner: Eric Lemelson. 61 ha.
www.lemelsonvineyards.com
Eric Lemelson's father Jerome invented the bar code; Eric himself is an environmental lawyer, so the estate, divided among a number of distinctive vineyards, is run on organic principles. The ultra-modern winery is gravity fed, and produces a range of lush, bold Pinot Noirs, and attractive Riesling and Pinot Gris.

Maysara ☆☆
McMinnville. Owner: Moe and Flora Momtazi. 91 ha.
www.maysara.com
This large Biodynamic vineyard was planted in the late 1990s and the first vintage was 2001. The Pinots are quite tannic but have vigour and flair.

Montinore ☆–☆☆
Forest Grove. Owner: Rudy Marchesi. 93 ha.
www.montinore.com
A magnificent estate, planted in the early 1980s with a dozen different vine varieties. Now Biodynamic and half devoted to Pinot Noir, which is often less interesting than the Pinot Gris.

Panther Creek ☆☆–☆☆☆
McMinnville. Owner: Liz Chambers. No vineyards.
www.panthercreekcellars.com
Ken Wright (q.v.) used to make the wines here, but now has his own label. The present winemaker is Michael Stevenson, who buys in grapes from top vineyards and produces attractive and harmonious Pinot Noir and some unoaked Chardonnay.

Scott Paul ☆☆–☆☆☆
Carlton. Owner: Scott Paul Wright. 7 ha.
www.scottpaul.com
This former Los Angeles record producer and burgundy fanatic came to Oregon in 2001 and produces artisanal blends of Pinot Noir, of which the finest are Audrey and La Paulée.

Ponzi ☆☆
Beaverton. Owner: Ponzi family. Winemaker: Luisa Ponzi. 49 ha. www.ponziwines.com
Pioneer Oregon winery passed on to the second generation, although the founder Dick and Nancy Ponzi are still very much present. The three Ponzi children control operations, and Luisa makes the wine. Still highly regarded for its unctuous Chardonnay and Pinot Gris, suave Pinot Noir, and courageous Arneis.

Rex Hill ☆☆–☆☆☆
Newberg. Owner: Bill and Debra Hatcher. 53 ha.
www.rexhill.com
A long-established winery that was in the doldrums in the early 2000s, until the new owners came in like a hurricane, invested heavily in the winery, and revitalized the vineyards, which are being converted to Biodynamism. The numerous

Pinot Noirs are much improved, though the unoaked Chardonnay remains innocuous. See also A to Z Wineworks.

St Innocent ☆–☆☆
Salem. Owner: Mark Vlossak. No vineyards.
www.stinnocentwine.com
This producer was established in 1988 Vlossak purchases grapes from various vineyards, and processes them in a new winery built in 2007. Quality is variable.

Domaine Serene ☆☆☆–☆☆☆☆
Dayton. Owner: Ken Evenstad. 62 ha.
www.domaineserene.com
These have always been impressive Pinot Noirs; a new winery, opened in 2001, and a greater use of Dijon clones, has raised quality even further. The Chardonnays are among Oregon's most sophisticated and elegant.

Sokol Blosser ☆☆
Dundee. Owner: Alex and Alison Sokol Blosser. 35 ha.
www.sokolblosser.com
One of Oregon's larger and more mature wineries, Sokol Blosser flagged in the late 1980s with changes in winemaker and general confusion. Today a new generation is at the helm and it is back on its feet with Russ Rosner producing very good Pinot Noirs. Rather to the surprise of the family, two zanily packaged and inexpensive multi-varietal blends, Evolution (white) and Meditrina (red) have proved to be well deserved hits.

Soter ☆☆☆
Yamhill. Owner: Tony Soter. 12 ha.
www.sotervineyards.com
Tony Soter was one of Napa's most respected consultant winemakers, but in 1997 he planted vineyards in his native Oregon, to which he has now returned full-time. True to his style, his Pinot Noirs are graceful and stylish, and he also makes some delicious sparkling wines.

Stoller ☆–☆☆
Dayton. Owner: Bill Stoller. 72 ha.
www.stollervineyards.com
The Stollers' ancestral turkey farm is now a flourishing vineyard, and in 2006 they built a solar-powered, gravity-flow winery. Good but unexceptional Chardonnay and Pinot Noir has yet to establish a clear signature.

R Stuart & Co ☆–☆☆
McMinnville. Owner: Rob Stuart. No vineyards.
www.rstuartandco.com.
Former Erath winemaker Stuart has set up his own negociant winery. The 2006 range of Pinot Noirs was supple and juicy, but the character of each site did not shine through.

Tunkalilla
Salem. Owner: Brian Croser. 3 ha.
Croser helped establish what is now the Argyle winery, and is now planting once again. A 2008 Riesling will be the first release, with Pinot Noir to follow.

Torii Mor ☆☆–☆☆☆
Dundee. Owner: Don Olson. 4 ha.
www.toriimorwinery.com

The first commercial wines were made in 1993 from Olson's Dundee Hills vineyard. Torii Mor doesn't lack ambition: prices for single-vineyard bottlings of Pinot Noir climb to $100, although many of these are made in pitifully small quantities.

Westrey ☆☆–☆☆☆
Dundee. Owners: Amy Wesselman and David Autrey. 9 ha. www.estrey.com
Winemaking experience in Burgundy moulded this partnership. Their first vintage was 1993, and since 1998 they have assembled a band of single-vineyard Pinots that share a perfumed red-fruits character and a welcome lightness of touch. Flowery Pinot Gris too.

WillaKenzie Estate ☆☆–☆☆☆
Yamhill. Owner: Bernard Lacroute. 51 ha. www.willakenzie.com
Since 1995, computer tycoon Lacroute, who grew up in the Mâconnais, has invested a fortune in this fine estate and modern winery. From the outset this French winemakers have produced Pinot Noirs of different structure and character, depending on the vineyard block from which they come. The Pinot Gris is exotic and spicy, as it should be.

Willamette Valley Vineyards ☆–☆☆
Turner. Owner: Jim Bernau. 20 ha. www.wvv.com
One of Oregon's biggest producers. Most of the wines are unremarkable, but the top end of the range is first rate, with sumptuous single-vineyard Pinot Noirs .

Ken Wright ☆☆☆–☆☆☆☆☆
Carlton. Owner: Ken Wright. No vineyards. www.kenwrightcellars.com
Wright produces as many as 12 separate bottlings of Pinot Noir each vintage from parcels of vines he manages, but does not own. A passionate believer in terroir, Wright was foremost in pushing for the recognition of the Willamette's new AVAs. These are wines of great finesse and concentration, securing his reputation as one of Oregon's most experienced and gifted winemakers.

Leading Rogue Valley Producers

Abacela ☆☆
Roseburg. Owner: Earl Jones. 24 ha. www.abacela.com
Intriguing property, planting Spanish and Italian varieties as well as classic Bordeaux and Rhône grapes. Remarkably tangy Albariño.

Bridgeview ☆
Cave Junction. Owner: Robert Kerivan. 83 ha. www.bridgeviewwine.com
By Oregon standards a large commercial winery, Bridgeview has developed a following for its Blue Moon range, especially the good value Riesling.

Foris ☆☆
Cave Junction. Owner: Ted Gerber. 102 ha. www.foriswine.com
The Gerbers began producing wine commercially in 1987. Winemaker Bryan Wilson has pushed Foris to the top of the league in Rogue Valley, with a fine range of varietal wines, notably Riesling and Cabernet Franc.

Valley View ☆
Jacksonville. Owner: Wisnovsky family. 12 ha. www.valleyviewwinery.com
Valley View has recently made great strides with a wide range of varieties, but some wines have been marred by off-aromas. Pioneer Peter Britt planted 200 varieties in experimental vineyards here in the 1850s.

Leading Umpqua Valley Producers

Henry Estate ☆
Umpqua. Owner: Scott Henry. 18 ha. www.henryestate.com
Scott Henry is best-known as the inventor of a trellising system that has been adopted throughout the world. His estate, on the fertile valley floor, specializes in easy-to-drink Chardonnay, Gewurztraminer, Pinot Gris, and Pinot Noir. The Barrel Fermented and Select wines have pronounced American oak flavours.

SUSTAINABILITY

This much abused term applies to vineyard practices that are sensitive to the environment and to the health of the workers. However, in Oregon, the concept is taken very seriously indeed, and it's estimated that about 30 per cent of all vineyards maintain varying degrees of certified sustainability.

"Salmon Safe" is a programme that ensures nothing is done that could conceivably harm another of the state's great industries: salmon fishing and consumption. "LIVE" stands for Low Input Viticulture and Enology, and is step just below organic and Biodynamic viticulture. All these systems share an attempt to maintain and promote biodiversity, with woodland, roamed by local fauna, separating individual vineyards.

Whereas in other parts of Europe such devotion to eliminating chemicals and artificial fertilizers from the vineyards is regarded as a form of eccentricity, in Oregon it is fast becoming the norm, to the benefit of the environment, those who tend the vines, and, inevitably, those who consume the wines.

Leading Columbia Valley Producers

Cathedral Ridge ☆–☆☆☆
Hood River. Owner: Robb Bell. No vineyards.
www.cathedralridgewinery.com
This tourism-oriented winery nonetheless producers splendid full-bodied reds from Bordeaux varieties, Syrah, and Zinfandel. Rock Star Red is a convincing blend of Cabernet and Syrah.

Mount Defiance ☆
Hood River. Owner: Robert Morus. 12 ha.
www.mtdefiancewines.com
The wine names say it all: Hellfire for the Gewurztraminer/Pinot Gris/Chardonnay blend; Brimstone for the Syrah/Cabernet/Merlot red. No finesse here, but Brimstone is an admirable quaffing wine. Phelps Creek winery is under the same ownership.

Rockblock ☆☆☆
Dayton. Owner: Ken Evenstad. No vineyards.
www.rockblocksyrah.com
The Columbia Valley outpost of Domaine Serene (q.v.) produces stunning Syrahs from Walla Walla and from Rogue Valley.

Washington

Leading Washington Producers

Barnard Griffin ☆☆
Richland. Owner: Deborah Barnard and Rob Griffin. No vineyards. www.barnardgriffin.com
Rob Griffin used to work at the Hogue Cellars (q.v.) but as he always had a hankering for his own small winery and more experimental wines, setting up on his own in 1991 came as a great opportunity. He makes a wide range of wines in a supple, fruity style, of which the best are inevitably the Reserves.

Betz Family Winery ☆☆☆
Redmond. Owner: Betz family. No vineyards.
www.betzfamilywinery.com
After many years at Chateau Ste Michelle, Bob Betz MW knew as much as anybody about who grew the best grapes in Washington. So in 1997 he set up his own winery, sourcing fruit from outstanding growers to produce intense, full-bodied Syrah and Bordeaux blends.

Canoe Ridge ☆☆–☆☆☆
Walla Walla. Owner: Diageo. 58 ha.
www.canoeridgevineyard.com
The vineyard was planted from 1989 onwards along the Columbia River, confusingly next to Chateau Ste Michelle's (q.v.) Canoe Ridge Estate, but the winery is 80-kilometres (50-miles) away in downtown Walla Walla. John Tantalizing Merlot, Cabernet, and Chardonnay remain the winery's focus.

Cayuse ☆☆–☆☆☆
Walla Walla. Owner: Christophe Baron. 20 ha.
www.cayusevineyards.com
A Frenchman who worked in Australia as a flying winemaker, Baron has been making a fine reputation for himself here since 1997, having discovered stony soils here that reminded him of Châteauneuf-du-Pape. The Syrahs are brilliant, and the Tempranillo and flab-free Viognier are wines to watch.

Chateau Ste Michelle ☆☆–☆☆☆
Woodinville. Owner: Ch Ste Michelle Wine Estates. 1,420 ha. www.ste-michelle.com
Much the biggest concern in the northwest (1.7 million cases annually), and with its top wines among the best. The large showpiece winery at Woodinville, 24-kilometres (15-miles) northeast of Seattle, was outgrown in 1983, when a new facility, three times as big, was built on the Columbia River near Paterson. The wines produced cover the full spectrum: Riesling, Chardonnay, Sauvignon Blanc, Gewurztraminer, Chenin Blanc, Semillon, Merlot, Cabernet Sauvignon, and port styles – all notably well-made, the whites being especially successful in the local market.

Special emphasis in recent vintages has been laid on the winery's vineyard-designated Chardonnays, Cabernet Sauvignons, and Merlots, which rank among the northwest's finest. The dry Riesling offers brilliant value. In the late 1990s, the company undertook some interesting joint ventures: with Antinori to produce a high-priced red blend from Horse Heaven Vineyard called Col Solare (q.v.); and with Ernst Loosen in Germany to produce sensational Eroica Rieslings, including America's finest TBA style wine. Ste Michelle, by virtue of its size, its technical professionalism, and its marketing ability, is a worthy flagship for the whole winemaking industry in the northwest.

Col Solare ☆☆☆
Benton City. Owner: Antinori and Ste Michelle Wine Estates. 12 ha. www.colsolare.com
After some years of dependence on Chateau Ste Michelle's vineyard and winemaking resources, this joint venture, producing a single Cabernet-based blend, now has its own vineyards on Red Mountain and, from 2007, its own winery. This is a fine but international-style wine, sold at a high price.

Columbia Winery ☆☆–☆☆☆
Woodinville. Owner: Ascentia Wine Estates. 150 ha.
www.columbiawinery.com
One of the pioneers of the northwest, founded in 1962 by a group of professors at the University of Washington, and still one of the best. From 1976 to 2006 it was directed by David Lake, a British master of wine. Now making a wide variety of excellent wines including Gewurztraminer, Cabernet Sauvignon, Syrah, Merlot, Semillon, Chardonnay, and Riesling, drawing on long-established contracts with some of the best grape growers, particularly Otis Vineyards and Red Willow and Wyckoff in the Yakima Valley.

Columbia Crest ☆–☆☆☆
Paterson. Owner: Ste Michelle Wine Estates. 1,000 ha.
www.columbia-crest.com

For 25 years, Columbia Crest has focused on good-value wines, from the basic but well-crafted Two Vines range to the more serious Reserve and Grand Estates wines. The reds, from Cabernet Sauvignon, Merlot, and Syrah, are especially successful.

Covey Run ☆
Zillah. Owner: Ascentia Wine Estates. 100 ha.
www.coveyrun.com
A well run winery, focusing on range of varietal wines at attractive prices, especially Riesling.

DeLille Cellars ☆☆☆
Woodinville. Owner: Lill family and partners. 8 ha.
www.delillecellars.com
The first vintage here was in 1992, and the winery's reputation was swiftly made. Winemaker Chris Upchurch focused from the start on ultra-premium, Bordeaux-style red and white wine blends sourced from eastern Washington vineyards.

Chaleur Estate is a complex and heady blend, selected from the best barrels. The white is a Graves-style blend. Doyenne is Rhône-inspired, and Grand Ciel is, since 2004, a Cabernet Sauvignon sourced from DeLille's own vineyard in Red Mountain.

DiStefano ☆☆
Woodinville. Owner: Mark Newton.
No vineyards. www.distefanowinery.com
Originally established to produce sparkling wine, Newton switched the emphasis to rich Cabernet Franc, Cabernet Sauvignon, Merlot, and, more recently, Syrah and Viognier. They veer in style from the opulent to the over-extracted.

Dunham ☆☆
Walla Walla. Owner: Eric Dunham.
37 ha. www.dunhamcellars.com
Dunham used to be a winemaker at L'Ecole 41 (q.v.), and began his own label in 1995, making a range of powerful, oaky wines, mostly Cabernet Sauvignon and Syrah.

L'Ecole 41 ☆☆–☆☆☆
Lowden. Owner: Marty Clubb. 20 ha.
www.lecole.com
Using, for the most part, purchased grapes from Walla Walla, this winery, founded in 1983 and based in a former schoolhouse, goes all out for opulent, showy wines, such as Merlot, Cabernet, and a powerful, barrel-fermented Semillon. A Bordeaux blend called Apogee and the Seven Hills Syrah have lifted quality to an even higher level.

Forgeron ☆–☆☆
Walla Walla. Owner: Marie-Eve Gilla and partners.
No vineyards. www.forgeroncellars.com
Gilla is French and Dijon-trained, which explains her wish to retain the typicity of the well-known vineyards from which she sources fruit. The style is soft and lush, with Merlot and Syrah showing some elegance.

Gordon Brothers ☆–☆☆☆
Pasco. Owner: Gordon family. 40 ha.
www.gordonwines.com
Since 1985 the Gordons have made sound varietal wines from their vineyards overlooking the Snake River. Syrah has been the most exciting wine in the winery's roster.

Hedges Cellars ☆☆☆
Benton City. Owner: Tom and Anne-Marie Hedges.
33 ha. www.hedgescellars.com
Founded in 1990 by a potato farmer with vision, Hedges now occupies an imposing château-style winery close to its vineyards on Red Mountain. For some years the Hedges wines have demonstrated the exceptional quality of Red Mountain fruit. The Cabernet/Syrah blend is juicy and good value, but the top wines are the Three Vineyards, and the rare single-vineyard blends. powerfully structured Red Mountain Reserve.

Hightower ☆☆–☆☆☆
Benton City. Owner: Tim and Kelly Hightower.
4 ha. www.hightowercellars.com
Splendid Cabernet Sauvignon and Merlot, opulent but never overblown, from top Columbia Valley sites, including Red Mountain.

Hogue Cellars ☆–☆☆
Prosser. Owner: Constellation. No vineyards.
www.hoguecellars.com

This winery, founded by a long-established farming family, struck a chord from its earliest vintages. Since Vincor and then Constellation acquired the business, the range has been simplified: basic varietal wines, Genesis (a label reserved for more distinctive varietal wines), and Reserve Chardonnay, Merlot, and Cabernet Sauvignon. At all levels, the wines stress value for money.

Isenhower ☆☆–☆☆☆
Walla Walla. Owner: Brett Isenhower.
1 ha. www.isenhowercellars.com
Former pharmacist Isenhower buys fruit from seven vineyards and specializes in hand-crafted Syrahs, sumptuous and powerful, and exotic Roussanne/Viognier. Bordeaux blends and Cabernet Franc are recent additions to the range.

K Vintners ☆☆–☆☆☆
Walla Walla. Owner: Charles Smith. 2 ha.
www.kvintners.com
This former rock band manager is a self-taught winemaker. That might not sound like a winning formula, but his single-vineyard Syrahs are concentrated and convincing, although at the gamey end of the spectrum.

Kiona ☆☆
Benton City. Owner: Williams family. 18 ha.
www.kionawine.com
This laid-back winery, a pioneer of Red Mountain fruit,

Walla Walla vintners

now specializes in deep, dark Cabernet Sauvignon, Merlot, and Syrah, and delicious late-harvest Riesling and Gewurztraminer. Unusual Lemberger is worth looking out for.

Leonetti ☆☆☆
Walla Walla. Owner: Gary Figgins. 20 ha.
www.leonetticellar.com
Figgins has a legendary reputation, based on the splendid, dark-red wines he made in the 1980s, some of which are still going strong. Selected grapes from many vineyards and ample new oak make for expensive but very worthwhile Merlot and Cabernet. The wines are sold through a (full) mailing list, so are all but unobtainable.

Long Shadows ☆☆–☆☆☆
Walla Walla. Owner: Allen Shoup. No vineyards.
www.longshadows.com
In 2002 the former boss of Stimson Lane had the fine idea of persuading international winemakers of the highest calibre to work with resident winemaker Gilles Nicault on Washington wines from outstanding vineyards. Among the outsiders involved are Randy Dunn from Napa, John Duval from Barossa, Michel Rolland from Pomerol, Armin Diel from the Nahe, and Giovanni Folonari from Tuscany.

McCrea ☆☆–☆☆☆
Rainier. Owner: Doug McCrea. No vineyards.
www.mccreacellars.com
The first Washington Viognier was produced here, and McCrea maintains his devotion to a range of Rhône varieties, including Mourvedre and Counoise as well as Syrah and Grenache sourced from some of the state's best vineyards.

Northstar ☆☆
Walla Walla. Owner: Stimson Lane. No vineyards.
www.northstarmerlot.com
Merlot and nothing but was the rule here, and the opening of a dedicated winery in 2002 confirmed Stimson Lane's confidence in the project. However, other Bordeaux varieties, including Petit Verdot, have been added to the range.

Pepper Bridge ☆☆–☆☆☆
Walla Walla. Owner: Norm McKibben and partners.
162 ha. www.pepperbridge.com
McKibben developed some of Walla Walla's outstanding vineyards, and his winery draws on two of them: Pepper Bridge and Seven Hills. Rugged yet stylish Cabernet Sauvignon is the star here, with Merlot hot on its heels.

Quilceda Creek ☆☆☆–☆☆☆☆☆
Snohomish. Owner: Alex Golitzin. No vineyards.
www.quilcedacreek.com
Winery established in 1979. Quilceda's winemaker Paul Golitzin has set the standard in Washington for new-oaked Cabernet and Merlot in the Médoc tradition. Quantities are small and prices high, but Columbia Valley Cabernet doesn't get any better than this.

Seven Hills ☆☆–☆☆☆
Walla Walla. Owner: Casey McClellan. 8 ha.
www.sevenhillswinery.com
McClellan draws on blocks of the celebrated Seven Hills Vineyard, but also uses fruit from Red Mountain and Oregon. There is a wide range of varietal wines, but the most serious wines are Cabernet Sauvignon, Merlot, and the Walla Walla blend called Pentad.

Tamarack ☆–☆☆
Walla Walla. Owner: Ron Coleman. No vineyards.
www.tamarackcellars.com
Elegant easygoing wines from Chardonnay, Cabernet Sauvignon, Merlot, Sangiovese, and Syrah. A good dose of new oak gives some polish and sophistication.

Terra Blanca ☆–☆☆
Benton City. Owner: Keith Pilgrim. 33 ha.
www.terrablanca.com
The best Cabernet Sauvignon, Merlot, and Syrah come from Red Mountain, but other varieties are bought in from Yakima Valley vineyards. Sound wines, aged only in French oak. One of the specialties is a range of late-harvest and Icewines.

Waterbrook
Walla Walla. Owner: Precept Brands. No vineyards.
Eric Rindal developed a range of moderately priced wines with clean, varietal flavours tempered with American oak. In late 2006 the winery was bought by a Seattle company, and its future direction is uncertain.

Andrew Will ☆☆☆–☆☆☆☆☆
Vashon. Owner: Chris Camarda. 18 ha.
This small winery made its reputation offering single-vineyard Merlots, subsequently supplemented by some Cabernet Sauvignon and Sangiovese. Then in the early 2000s the self-taught Chris Camarda had a change of heart, and decided to focus instead on blends from the principal vineyards he buys from. These are consistently profound and satisfying wines.

Woodward Canyon ☆☆–☆☆☆
Lowden. Owner: Rick Small. 17 ha.
www.woodwardcanyon.com
The first wines were made here in 1981, making Rick Small something of a Walla Walla pioneer. Woodward Canyon is noted for its toasty Cabernet and Merlot, especially its Old Vines Cabernet.

Idaho

Leading Idaho Producers

Indian Creek Winery ☆–☆☆
Kuna. Owner: Bill Stowe and partners. 6 ha.
www.indiancreekwinery.com
One of the half-dozen wineries grouped in the Caldwell area, southwest of Boise, and one of the state's most interesting properties. Bill Stowe produces a better-than-average Pinot Noir, including a stylish, dry white Pinot Noir, with smaller quantities of Riesling and Chardonnay. The winery's first vintage was in 1987.

Ste Chapelle ☆☆
Caldwell. Owner: Ascentia Wine Estates. 150 ha.
www.stechapelle.com
Founded in 1970, Ste Chapelle soon established a fine track
record with Riesling, Chardonnay, Gewurztraminer, and
sparkling wines made from Riesling, Chardonnay, and Pinot
Noir. Ste Chapelle is by far the largest of Idaho's 32 wineries,
controlling almost half of the state's 490 hectares of vineyards,
and producing 150,000 cases. It also buys in Washington
grapes. The style is for crisp, elegant, and slightly floral wines,
dictated largely by the climate, which does not reliably ripen
the grapes.

Other Idaho Producers

Camas Winery ☆
Moscow. www.camasprairiewinery.com
One of Northern Idaho's oldest premium wineries, offering
a few vinifera wines as well as numerous sweet fruit wines.

Cana Vineyards ☆–☆☆
Wilder.
Established in 1990 on the site of the former Lou Facelli
winery. Mostly Cabernet and Merlot.

Carmela Vineyards ☆–☆☆
Glenns Ferry. www.carmelavineyards.com
Some 12 hectares in the Hagerman viticultural area.
Best-known for Cabernet Franc.

Hell's Canyon Winery ☆–☆☆
Caldwell. www.hellscanyonwinery.org
Planted in 1981, these are the oldest wine-grape vineyards
in Idaho, producing some 3,000 cases of Bordeaux varieties,
Syrah, and Chardonnay from 15 hectares.

Parma Ridge ☆–☆☆
Parma. www.parmaridge.com
Four hectares planted in 1998, producing Gewurztraminer,
Viognier, Merlot, and other varieties.

Sawtooth ☆
Nampa. www.sawtoothwinery.com
The six hectares are planted with Cabernet Sauvignon,
Chardonnay, and various Rhône varieties, which are able
to ripen in one of the state's warmer regions.

Vickers Vineyard ☆–☆☆
Caldwell.
Kirby Vickers in the Snake River Valley produces small
quantities of good Chardonnay.

Other Regions of the USA

For centuries the true wine vine, *Vitis vinifera*, could not be
successfully grown in the climate of most of North America.
The problems are extremes of cold in the north and centre, and
of heat and humidity in the south. The cold simply kills the
vines in winter. Humidity brings rampant mildew; the heat of
southern summers, a general malfunction of the vine (instead of
respiring at night and building up sugar, the plant continues to
grow; the sugar is used in excessive foliage and the grapes,
despite months of broiling heat, are scarcely ripe).

Two regions, the northeast (led by New York State) and the
southeast (led by Virginia), have strong wine traditions of their
own, and are now enjoying a great revival. Michigan, too, is
beginning to produce wines of genuine interest and quality.
Until very recently, their wine industry was based on native
grapes, adapted to the local climate, but most wineries today
concentrate on vinifera. In the south, the grape is the
Muscadine, or Scuppernong, a plant very different from the
classic wine vine (its berries are like clusters of marbles with
tough skins that slip off the flesh). The powerful flavour of its
sweet wine was once immensely popular in America in a famous
brand called Virginia Dare. Scuppernong still flourishes, but
bears no relation to the wines of the rest of the world. But now,
almost every state of the union outside these areas has hopeful
winemakers – hopeful of seeing their industry, fledgling or a
century old as some of them are, establish itself as part of the
American wine boom. Only Alaska, North Dakota, and
Wyoming are still winery free.

A number of long-established wineries have distinct local
markets. In the past, these tended to be a disincentive to experimenting with new grapes. When it was assumed for so long that
Vitis vinifera could not be grown, it was a brave winemaker who
did more than dip a toe in the water with a hectare or two of
experimental planting. With modern knowledge, more and
more dippers are reporting success. There are certainly quite
large areas where the microclimate appears to make vinifera a
practicable proposition after all. There are also new hybrid
vines, crosses between vinifera and American natives, which
show the hardiness of the natives without their peculiar
flavours, but their overall importance in the eastern market has
been overshadowed by recent successes with vinifera.

The wine boom is being led from the metropolitan areas of
America, which have latched on to the varietal names of
California. Riesling, Chardonnay, Cabernet Sauvignon are now
household words. The best hybrids (Seyval Blanc, Vidal Blanc,
Chambourcin) still have a long way to go. At present, in fact,
wine-growers in the eastern and central states are looking three
ways at once: at the old American varieties of *Vitis labrusca*, the
exciting but risky viniferas, and the hybrids between the two. In
the east, hybrids and labrusca will probably always play a role,
but the majority of wine-growers are now betting on vinifera.

New York State

The New York State wine industry, long established around the Finger Lakes, south of Lake Ontario, was once considered a maverick backwater by most wine lovers. Originally based on varieties and chance hybrids of the native vine, *Vitis labrusca*, its wines were characterized by the peculiar scent of labrusca known as "foxiness". Most also had high acidity, usually masked by considerable sweetness. In the 1960s non-foxy French-American hybrids replaced labrusca in all but the most conservative wineries. Although it is usually acceptable and occasionally very good, little of the wine is exciting by European or Californian standards. Some companies in New York, as elsewhere in the east, still see labrusca as reliable and well-adapted to the stresses of the eastern climate but they are in a shrinking minority. Most labrusca grapes are today used for jam and fruit juice. Since the mid-1950s, a vocal minority, first led by Dr. Konstantin Frank, was dedicated to proving that vinifera vines could successfully be grown in the Finger Lake areas. Their successes, at least with white wines, convinced many. Most of the original vineyards have now planted at least some vinifera, and promising new vineyards are growing vinifera almost exclusively.

America's wine boom started to affect New York in the mid-1970s. In the late '80s, there were shifts in the industry that would influence the direction of New York wine growing. First Seagram and then Coca-Cola decided that the industry could be expanded. Seagram bought Gold Seal, and Coca-Cola bought Taylor's and Great Western, the largest and most important wineries in the region. All three wineries have since closed, and Seagram and Coca-Cola have decided to get out of the Finger Lakes wine business altogether. Today, a new generation of wine producers (many of them descendants of the original growers who supplied Taylor's) is concentrating on the types of vinifera that do well in cool climates, especially Riesling, Chardonnay, and Pinot Noir.

In 1976, the state law was changed to encourage "farm wineries", lowering the licence fee for firms producing fewer than 21,000 cases a year, and easing restrictions on their sales. The result was the rapid start-up of exactly the small, open-minded enterprises New York needed to improve its image. Dozens of small wineries were born or reborn, mainly in the Finger Lakes but also in the Hudson River Valley above New York City – which has a long history of nearly being a wine region – and on Long Island, where the maritime climate is kinder than upstate. It also gives the wines an elegant acidic structure, so that they have a very different personality than those from, say, Napa Valley. Of the state's six wine regions, it is Long Island that is booming, its wineries benefiting from three AVAs: the Hamptons, North Fork, and Long Island itself. From small

beginnings in 1973, when the Hargraves planted vines on North Fork, 28 wineries now dot the map. Chardonnay and Merlot seem to be the consumers' preferred choice, but growers are also trying Riesling, Gewurztraminer, Chenin Blanc, and Cabernet Franc.

The other New York wine regions are Lake Eyrie/Chautauqua (immense, with 8,000 hectares planted but 90 per cent labrusca); Hudson River Valley (over 30 wineries); Central New York and Lake Ontario (no AVAs) and Niagara Escarpment (AVA since 2005). By 2007 there were 240 wineries in New York State, and 12,600 hectares of vineyards.

Leading New York State Producers

Finger Lakes
Anthony Road ☆–☆☆
Dresden. Owner: John Martini. 30 ha.
www.anthonyroadwine.com
Martini planted nothing but hybrids in 1973, but only Vignoles remains. Today the focus is on Riesling, unoaked Chardonnay, and Pinot Grigio.

Fox Run Vineyards ☆☆–☆☆☆
Penn Yan. Owner: Scott Osborne and Michael Lally. 22 ha. www.foxrunvineyards.com
The owners, who bought Fox Run in 1990, have done well with Riesling, Chardonnay, and Merlot. Pinot Noir, Cabernets Sauvignon and Franc are coming along, and the company is also trying the little-known Lemberger grape.

Glenora Wine Cellars ☆–☆☆
Dundee. Owner: Gene Pierce and Scott Welliver. 6 ha. www.glenora.com
One of the best-regarded smaller wineries of the Finger Lakes, specializing in sparkling wines. In addition, there is Chardonnay, very good Riesling, and Bordeaux reds.

Dr. Konstantin Frank's Vinifera Wine Cellars ☆☆
Hammondsport. Owner: Willy Frank. 33 ha. www.drfrankwines.com
Founded by Dr. Konstantin Frank in 1962, and now run by his grandson Frederick. Vinifera Wine Cellars has produced good, fine, and sometimes brilliant white wine, including Rkatsiteli and selected late-harvest Riesling; and reds from Merlot and Pinot Noir are much improved. Sparkling wines are released under the Chateau Frank label, but are less noteworthy than the still wines. The second label is Salmon Run.

Knapp Vineyards ☆
Romulus. Owner: Gene Pierce and Scott Welliver. 40 ha. www.knappwine.com
In 2000 this well-established property came under the same

Lenz winery, Cutchogue

ownership as Glenora (q.v.). Riesling and sparkling wine can be good, but wines from hybrids can be pallid and soupy.

Lamoreaux Landing ☆☆
Lodi. Owner: Mark Wagner. 48 ha.
www.lamoreauxwine.com
One of the best of the Seneca Lakes wineries. Hybrids have been phased out, and production now focuses on Chardonnay, Gewurztraminer, Cabernet Franc, Pinot Noir, and Cabernet Sauvignon.

Sheldrake Point ☆☆–☆☆☆
Ovid. Owner: Chuck Tauck, Bob Madill, and others.
17 ha. www.sheldrakepoint.com
Founded in 1998, and with vineyards that are still young, Sheldrake Point already shines as a producer of delicious Cabernet Franc, fine Rieslings, and intense Icewine.

Standing Stone Vineyards ☆
Hector. Owner: Tom Macinski. 16 ha.
www.standingstonewines.com
Dry, well-balanced Riesling, Gewurztraminer, and Vidal Icewine are the particular strengths here, but the future of the Cabernet Franc and Merlot is also looking good.

Hermann J Wiemer Vineyard ☆–☆☆
Dundee. Owner: Fred Merwarth. 70 ha. www.wiemer.com
The Bernkastel-born ex-winemaker has had striking success with Riesling in various styles, and also produces creditable Chardonnay, Merlot, and sparkling wines. In 2007 Wiemer sold the property to his winemaker.

Hudson River

Benmarl Wine Company ☆
Marlboro. Owner: Mark Miller. 15 ha. www.benmarl.com
An historic vineyard in the Hudson River Valley, where the hybrid Dutchess was raised in the nineteenth century, this has been restored by Mark Miller, who runs it as a cooperative of some 1,000 wine-lovers, the Société des Vignerons. They help finance, pick, and drink Frontenac and Baco Noir, and, more recently, Merlot, Syrah, Pinot Noir, and Zinfandel.

Millbrook ☆☆
Millbrook. Owner: John Dyson. 12 ha.
www.millbrookwine.com
These days John Dyson is better known as the owner of Williams Selyem (q.v.) in Sonoma, but he has been here since the mid-1980s. He dabbles in varieties such as Tocai Friulano and Zinfandel, but his best wines come from Chardonnay, Cabernet Franc, and Pinot Noir.

Long Island

Bedell ☆☆
Cutchogue. Owner: Michael Lynne. 32 ha.
www.bedellcellars.com
Founded in 1980 by Kip Bedell, the property was sold in 2000, although Bedell stays on as winemaker. Behind the jazzy labels of the wines are complex and intriguing blends, red and white, as well as some standard varietals. The sister winery is Corey Creek.

Castello di Borghese ☆☆
Cutchogue. Owner: Marco and Anne Marie Borghese.
34 ha. www.castellodiborghese.com
The pioneering Hargrave family found ideal conditions for vinifera vines on the North Fork of Long Island, 113-kilometres (70-miles) east of New York City, with the ocean close by on three sides. Their Chardonnay, Sauvignon Blanc, and Pinot Noir competed convincingly with top-rank California or Oregon wines. In 1999, they sold the property, and the new owners have created a Meritage and plan to add some Italian varieties to the vineyards.

Channing Daughters ☆☆
Bridgehampton. Owner: Walter Channing and partners.
11 ha. www.channingdaughters.com
The Channing vineyards teem with varieties such as Teroldego, Dornfelder, Lagrein, Malvasia, Merlot, and Cabernet Sauvignon, most of which are used in unusual blends. Some white varieties are co-planted and co-fermented in a kind of homage to Jean-Michel Deiss of Alsace. Intriguing wines, well-crafted and packaged.

Lenz Winery ☆☆
Peconic, Long Island. Owner: Eric Fry. 28 ha.
www.lenzwine.com
Scrupulous viticulture and winemaking result in very good estate-bottled Merlot and Cabernet, aged only in French oak.

Macari ☆
Mattituck. Owner: Joseph T Macari Jr. 74 ha.
www.macariwines.com
Founded in 1995, Macari produces a bewildering variety of wines, with patchy results. The whites have the edge, especially Chardonnay and Sauvignon Blanc.

Palmer ☆☆
Aquebogue. Owner: Robert Palmer. 36 ha.
www.palmervineyards.com
An estate founded in 1986 that pioneered what one could call the classic Long Island style: clean, vibrant fruit, especially Chardonnay, and a Loire-style Cabernet Franc.

Raphael ☆☆
Peconic. Owner: John Petrocelli. 20 ha.
www.raphaelwine.com.
Founded in 1996 with the aim of producing exceptional Merlot, supplemented by small lots of Sauvignon, Chardonnay, and Cabernet Franc. Initial releases of Merlot were robust and sumptuous. Paul Pontallier of Château Margaux acts as the consultant here.

Wölffer ☆–☆☆☆
Sagaponack. Owner: Christian Wölffer. 21 ha.
www.wolffer.com
Wölffer, like his winemaker Roman Roth, is from Germany and has invested heavily in this property. Chardonnay and Merlot are the principal wines, and Wölffer enjoys the dubious distinction of producing the first Long Island wine (the new-oaked Premier Cru Merlot) with a price tag of over $100.

New England

Winemaking in New England is still on a very small and experimental scale. During the early years of the wine industry in the northeast, it was believed that the regional character should be asserted by developing only the best of the hybrids. While opinion about the relative merits of hybrid and vinifera vines has mostly shifted towards vinifera in recent years, hybrids will probably always play at least a minor role in New England, because of the difficult growing conditions.

There are 16 wineries in Massachusetts, but even some of the better known, such as Chicama on Martha's Vineyard, supplement their own production with grapes or wine brought in from California. The state of Rhode Island, which is deeply invaded by ocean inlets, has around half a dozen small vineyards; the biggest, Sakonnet, growing mostly vinifera vines. Sakonnet's Chardonnay, Gewurztraminer, Cabernet Franc, and Vidal have not only a very loyal local following, but are also becoming known in other parts of the east, and even in California. Connecticut's first winery, Haight Vineyards, founded in 1975 at Litchfield, west of Hartford, managed to grow vinifera (Chardonnay and Riesling), and the hybrid Seyval. Several other wineries have followed. The most promising are Chamard and Stonington Vineyards, both along the coast. Chamard grows only vinifera (Chardonnay, Cabernet Sauvignon, Pinot Noir, and Merlot) on its eight-hectare vineyard, and is best known for its Chardonnay, as is Stonington, which was founded in 1987.

The Mid-Atlantic

There is growing conviction that Virginia may become the most promising wine-growing state in the east. The other mid-Atlantic states of Maryland, southern Pennsylvania, and perhaps a belt stretching inland into West Virginia, Kentucky, and Tennessee might have as much potential. It is a well-publicized fact that Thomas Jefferson had no luck, but modern vines, sprays, and know-how have started to change the situation. And so has foreign investment which has taken a thoroughly optimistic view of the region's potential – Virginia in particular.

Maryland & Pennsylvania

In the 1940s, Philip Wagner made history at Boordy Vineyards, near Ryderwood in Maryland, by planting the first French-American hybrids in America. These vines had been bred by the French to bring phylloxera-resistance to France, but ironically it was to be America that appreciated their virtues of hardiness and vigour. Boordy then added Chardonnay (classic method sparkling) and some major international varieties to the list, while retaining some Seyval Blanc and Vidal. By 2009 there were 34 wineries in the state, employing both hybrids and vinifera. Basignani Winery has Cabernet, Chardonnay, and Riesling along with Vidal and Seyval. Elk Run Vineyards has

mostly vinifera vines including some Sangiovese, and also makes sparkling and dessert wines.

The southeast corner of Pennsylvania, a state with over 100 wineries in production, although many of them are hobby wineries, apparently has much in common with Maryland. Soils and climates are very variable; there are certainly good vineyard sites among them. Mazza Vineyards is happy with its south Pennsylvania Chardonnay and Riesling, and even happier with white hybrids. Twin Brook, east of Philadelphia, on the other hand, has done quite well with Pinot Grigio.

Eric Miller of neighbouring Chaddsford Winery makes excellent Chardonnay and Chambourcin, and a Bordeaux-style blend called Merican. Crossing Vineyards in Bucks County shows a sure touch with white vinifera wines. Allegro Vineyards in York Country makes a reliable Bordeaux blend called Cadenza.

Virginia

Lying between the cold weather extreme of the northeast, and the intense heat and humidity of the south (where the deadly vine ailment Pierce's Disease thrives), Virginia is the rising star in the east. The state now has 135 wineries, a remarkable number considering that the first successful vinifera grape wines were made here just over 20 years ago. In 2008 there were over 1,000 hectares under vine. Contributing to this success is an unusually supportive legislation, plus the affluent and educated customers in Washington DC, who bolster the local wine industry.

Foreign investors were the first to show confidence. As long ago as 1976 the Italian wine giant Zonin planted 50 hectares in Barboursville, and the Belgian Patrick Duffeler followed in 1985. Today Chardonnay is the most widely planted variety, and among red vinifera, Cabernet Sauvignon and Cabernet Franc. Grape growing is not always easy here, and diseases such as mildew are common. Moreover, many estates have yet to find winemakers who can fully exploit the fruit quality. Nevertheless, few states in America have made such swift progress in quality as Virginia.

Leading Virginia Producers

Barboursville ☆–☆☆
Barboursville. Owner: Gianni Zonin. 50 ha.
www.barboursvillewine.com
The Italian-owned estate has yet to succeed with Nebbiolo, despite the presence of a Piedmontese winemaker, but wines such as Pinot Grigio and the Merlot-dominated Bordeaux blend Octagon are winners.

Boxwood ☆☆
Middleburg. Owner: John Kent Cooke. 6.5 ha.
www.boxwoodwinery.com
The model here is Bordeaux, the two top wines being Boxwood, a Médoc-style blend, and Topiary, which is an interpretation of St-Emilion. In 2006 French consultant Stéphane Derenoncourt was taken on.

Breaux ☆
Purcellville. Owner: Paul Breaux. 35 ha.
www.breauxvineyards.com
Eighteen varieties grow in the Breaux vineyards, but wines recently tasted, such as Cabernet and Viognier, have been rather herbaceous.

Horton ☆–☆☆
Gordonsville. Owner: Dennis Horton. 30 ha.
www.hvwine.com
Denis Horton makes over 30 wines from Bordeaux, Rhône, and Portuguese varieties, and he is best-known for his Viognier.

Jefferson ☆☆
Charlottesville. Owner: Stanley Woodward. 8 ha.
www.jeffersonvineyards.com.
For the past 20 years, Jefferson has focused on Bordeaux-style wines and produces an excellent Meritage as well as varietal wines.

Kluge ☆☆
Charlottesville. Owner: Patricia Kluge. 77 ha.
www.klugeestate.com
Founded in 1999, businesswoman Patricia Kluge's estate doesn't lack resources or ambition. As well as classic-method sparkling wines, she produces Bordeaux-style wines with advice from Michel Rolland.

Linden ☆☆
Linden. Owner: Jim Law. 12 ha.
www.lindenvineyards.com
The vineyards are all on hillsides, and produce wines that can age well. Chardonnay is the house specialty, and in some vintages Law produces four of them. Piquant, lively Cabernet Franc, too.

Oasis ☆–☆☆
Hume. Owner: Dirgham Salahi. 40 ha.
www.oasiswines.net
Classic-method sparkling wine is the specialty here, with some *cuvées* aged between five and 15 years on the yeasts.

Pearmund ☆☆–☆☆☆
Broad Run. Owner: Christ Pearmund. 10 ha.
www.pearmundcellars.com
Chardonnay vines were planted here in 1976, although the winery was not established until 2003. Opulent, buttery Chardonnay and some stylish Bordeaux-style reds, including a spicy Petit Verdot.

Williamsburg Winery ☆☆
Williamsburg. Owner: Patrick Duffeler. 20 ha.
www.williamsburgwinery.com
Owned by a Belgian, this winery and resort produces about one quarter of all Virginia wine. The barrel-fermented Acte 12 Chardonnay is deservedly popular, and the Bordeaux blend called Gabriel Archer Reserve ages well.

The Midwest

Lake Michigan and Lake Erie provide the heat storage to make life bearable for vines in the Midwest states of Ohio and Michigan. These large, relatively shallow bodies of water moderate temperatures to allow numerous families of grapes to be grown, including some of the more hardy vinifera varieties, as well as hybrids. The Lake Erie Islands (known locally as the "Wine Islands"), lying in the shallow western basin of Lake Erie, are especially significant. For a dozen years a few hundred hectares of wine grapes, including Chardonnay, the two Cabernets, Riesling, Pinot Noir, and Gewurztraminer have produced successfully on the lime-rich soils. Most of these grapes are used by Ohio's largest winery, Firelands, located on the mainland at Sundusky; and by the almost equally large Meier's Wine Cellars.

Lake Erie's central basin, just east of Cleveland, also provides important microclimates that are hospitable to wine grapes. Chalet Debonné Vineyards of Madison make wines from both vinifera, native American, and hybrid grapes. In contrast, towards the Pennsylvania border, Markko Vineyards in Conneaut makes high-quality Chardonnay, a Mosel-style Riesling, and a Cabernet. Ferrante and Harpersfield wineries, near Geneva, have also successfully focused on Chardonnay and Riesling. Many of Michigan's best wineries lie on the jagged peninsulas to the north of Traverse City, on the eastern shore of Lake Michigan. There are almost 6,000 hectares of grapes in the state, but only 730 are devoted to wine grapes. The industry is expanding fast, with around 100 wineries in operation by 2008. Michigan's vineyards and wineries are close to Chicago at the lake's southeastern corner. Notable ones include Black Star, Fenn Valley Vineyards, Peninsula Cellars, Shady Lane, and, biggest by far, St Julian. Château Grand Traverse in particular has a fine reputation for its stylistically varied Rieslings.

There are wineries in the other northern Midwest states – in Indiana, Illinois, Wisconsin, even Minnesota, where small vineyards and dedicated growers often face sub-zero temperatures and other adverse growing conditions. Much of the production of Indiana and southern Ohio is located in the Ohio River Valley AVA, which borders the river from West Virginia to its junction with the Mississippi.

Missouri and Arkansas would seem improbable places to plant vines, but both states have long-established vineyards. Missouri, indeed, enjoyed the distinction of having the first official appellation granted to a viticultural area in the United States, in 1980, when the Bureau of Alcohol, Tobacco and Firearms declared Augusta, just west of St Louis, a designated region. Its first vines were planted in hills above the Missouri River in the 1830s. Both states have strong research programmes at state-funded universities. It is far too cold here for most vinifera vines, but wineries including Stone Hill and Mount Pleasant at Augusta grow excellent hybrids such as Seyval and Vidal for full-bodied white wines, and produce sturdy if often rustic or medicinal Norton reds.

Arkansas, to the south, has one unexpected outcrop of vinifera growing in the peculiar microclimate of a mountain plateau called Altus, settled in the 1870s by Swiss, Austrian, and Bavarian immigrants who understood mountains. According to Al Wiederkehr, whose Swiss family founded its winery in 1880, thermal inversion currents produce a very tolerable climate in which Riesling, Chardonnay, Sauvignon Blanc, Muscat Ottonel, Cabernet, Pinot Noir, and Gamay feel pretty much at home. Most of his hectarage is planted with these grapes, although he is not burning his boats with hybrids.

The Southwest

Much of the southwest is too humid and subject, like the Deep South, to Pierce's Disease, to make it a viable region for vines, although growing grapes and making wine began here before the business took hold in California. Southern New Mexico and west Texas have the oldest commercial wine-growing regions in America. Catholic priests founded a mission with vineyards in El Paso on the Rio Grande in Texas around 1600, producing sacramental wine from the Mission grape. Nevertheless, only over the past three decades has there been a serious move towards establishing a modern wine industry of some quality.

Of the southwest wine-producing states, Texas is the clear leader, with over 100 wineries and 1,380 hectares of vineyards. (New Mexico has 26 wineries, Colorado 50, Arizona 13, Oklahoma 30, Utah five, and Nevada three.) The Texas vineyards are widely spread out across the vast state, whose total area is larger than France. The wineries range in size from boutique to fairly large. The cool, dry climate of the high plateau area around Lubbock was the site of some of the first successful vineyards in Texas. Attention was drawn to the area by the premium wines from the Llano Estacado ranch, where the McPherson family and their partners pioneered vinifera vines. New Mexico now has 22 wineries, including La Chiripada Winery, north of Santa Fe, where the Johnson family produce award-winning wines mostly from vinifera. Gruet represents the French influence in New Mexico (the winery is on the outskirts of Albuquerque; the vineyards are in southern New Mexico at 4,200 feet), with 80,000 cases annual of sparkling wines from Chardonnay and Pinot Noir. Very good Chardonnay is also made at La Viña, New Mexico's oldest wineries, in the south of the state.

Colorado's production capacity continues to rise. Of its 265 hectares, 85 per cent are of *Vitis vinifera* and predominantly Chardonnay and Merlot, although Cabernet, Pinot Noir, Riesling, and Sauvignon are doing well, and one producer, Grande River Vineyards, well-known for its red and white Meritages, is trying Viognier. Plum Creek Winery has added Sangiovese to its roster of French varieties. Arizona's Callaghan Vineyards has widened the range to include some red wines from Californian grapes, but the Bordeaux blend called Buena Suerte draws plaudits. Nevada's principal winery, Pahrump Valley Vineyards near Las Vegas, produces Merlot and Chardonnay, as well as light-hearted wines aimed at the substantial tourist market.

Leading Texas Producers

Becker ☆☆–☆☆☆
Stonewall. Owner: Dr. Richard Becker. 20 ha.
www.beckervineyards.com
Thirty-five thousand cases of serious Hill Country Chardonnay, Viognier, and Cabernet, the latter aged in American oak and gently herbaceous.

Fall Creek ☆☆
Tow. Owner: Ed Auler. 22 ha. www.fcv.com
Frost and Pierce's Disease have played havoc with the Aulers' vineyards, so much fruit is bought in. There is fresh Chardonnay and Chenin Blanc, but the best wine is the Cabernet-based Meritus.

Flat Creek ☆
Marble Falls. Owner: Rick Naber. 8 ha.
www.flatcreekestate.com
Australian winemaker Craig Parker injected some originality at this Hill Country estate by producing Primitivo and Sangiovese, but since his departure in 2006 the list is more disparate until the new winemaker, Charlie Kidd, can make his mark.

Llano Estacado ☆–☆☆
Lubbock. Owner: 38 shareholders. 41 ha.
www.llanowine.com
Founded in 1976 on a grand scale, and met with initial success. The winery has been through various transformations, of both ownership and winemaking, but makes sound varietal wines, sometimes from fruit from other states, and a top Supertuscan-style blend called Viviano.

McPherson ☆
Lubbock. Owner: Kim McPherson. No vineyards.
McPherson was the original winemaker at Llano Estacado, and set up his own label in 2000. Interesting wines from Rhône and Italian varieties in a light, drinkable style.

Stonehouse ☆
Spicewood. Owner: Howard and Angela Moench. 2 ha.
www.stonehousevineyard.com
Radiologist Moench grows and produces Norton as a table wine and a fortified style. To justify their tasting room, Angela Moench imports a range of wines called The Lyre from her native Barossa.

Canada

Canada was discovered, in fine wine terms, in the 1970s, when old fears and prejudices about which vines could survive here were tossed aside. The formidable know-how that had been accumulating in new wine districts around the world provided answers to problems that had seemed insuperable.

A massive grubbing-up programme in 1988 in the two leading provinces, Ontario and British Columbia, encouraged growers to pull out their hybrids in favour of vinifera. Canada now has some 10,000 hectares planted with wine grapes, of which about 80 per cent are in Ontario. Much of Canada's domestic market is controlled by monopolistic "liquor boards", thus limiting the choice of wines available to consumers. This anachronistic system had its roots in a wish to maintain tight control over the availability of alcoholic drinks, especially spirits.

In the twenty-first century it seems totally out of place, and although reform and in some cases abolition is under way, the process is painfully slow. Some of these boards can be unscrupulous or worse in their labelling practices. "Canadian' for example may mean no more than bottled in Canada (and grown in, eg., South America).

Ontario

Ontario took its place at the high table of the world's cool-climate wine regions in the 1980s. In the south of the province, the Niagara Peninsula, lake-locked and escarpment-sheltered, is Canada's natural vineyard, lying on the same latitude as northern Oregon. It is one of the designated viticultural areas in the Vintner's Quality Alliance (VQA), which sets standards to which all the leading estates adhere. Bitterly cold winters here produce conditions ideal for making one of the world's great Icewines.

Once a rarity, Icewine now accounts for five per cent of all Ontario wine production. Indeed, Canada as a whole is now the world's largest producer of the style. As well as this luscious specialty, Niagara produces Chardonnay, Riesling, Pinot Noir, and some wines from hybrids. The 2000s are seeing Niagara fine-tune its style, identify its most privileged sites, and build a world class reputation. There are currently 140 wineries in Ontario as a whole.

Leading Ontario Producers

Cave Spring Cellars ☆☆–☆☆☆
Jordan. Owner: Leonard Pennachetti. 70 ha.
www.cavespringcellars.com
Vinifera varieties were planted here in 1978, and the winery opened its doors in 1986. Best-known for its white wines, and winemaker Angelo Pavan has released some exceptional Riesling and Chardonnay, as well as dessert and Icewines.

Château des Charmes ☆☆
St. David's. Owner: Paul Bosc. 110 ha.
www.chateaudescharmes.com
Paul-Michel Bosc is a fifth-generation wine-grower who emigrated to Canada in the 1960s, and became the first to plant a wholly vinifera vineyard. Award-winning VQA estate wines include Icewine, late-harvest, an impressive range of white and red varietals, as well as *méthode traditionnelle* sparkling wines. True to his roots, Bosc has more recently planted unusual varieties such as Auxerrois and Savagnin.

Clos Jordanne ☆☆☆
Niagara Peninsula. Owner: Constellation and Boisset. 55 ha. www.leclosjordanne.com
A dazzling new venture, or it will be if the winery commissioned from renowned architect Frank Gehry ever gets built. Initial releases of the estate's Pinot Noir, especially the top bottling Le Grand Clos, seem to justify the hype, as the chorus of approval has been deafening.

Creekside Estate ☆☆
Jordan Station. Owner: Peter Jensen. 40 ha.
www.creeksideestate.com
A property in the Annapolis Valley that is also developing the Paragon Estate on Niagara Peninsula. Creekside has a fine reputation for Sauvignon Blanc, and also produces good Pinot Noir, Bordeaux-style blends, and Vidal Icewine.

Henry of Pelham Family Estate ☆–☆☆☆
St Catharines. Owner: Speck family. 70 ha.
www.henryofpelham.com
This estate was planted on land owned by the descendants of Henry Smith, who was awarded Crown land after the American Revolutionary War for being an Empire loyalist. For some years, winemaker Ron Giesbrecht has produced impressive varietal wines from vineyards on the Niagara Bench. The Cabernet/Merlot is among the best, and there is a remarkably fine Baco Noir. The flagship dessert wine is Riesling Icewine.

Hillebrand Estates ☆☆
Niagara-on-the-Lake. Owner: Peller Estates. 40 ha.
www.hillebrand.com
Hillebrand's top wines are released as Showcase wines, and the Trius range, including a Bordeaux-style red blend, is also of fine quality. Icewines, from both Vidal and Riesling, are first rate.

Inniskillin ☆☆–☆☆☆
Niagara-on-the-Lake. Owner: Constellation. 52 ha.
www.inniskillin.com
Founders Donald Ziraldo and Karl Kaiser, who both retired in 2006, spearheaded the birth of the modern wine industry in Ontario. Since its establishment, Inniskillin has concentrated on varietal wines from Niagara-grown grapes. The winery is now housed in a 1920s barn, possibly designed by Frank Lloyd Wright, on the Brae Burn Estate. All Inniskillin wines have earned strong national and international recognition, especially the übersweet Icewine and late-harvest Vidal. In 1999, Inniskillin released no fewer than five single vineyard

Chardonnays. The most bizarre offering is the the high-priced Sparkling Vidal Icewine. There is a four-tier hierarchy of quality: Varietal series, Reserves, Single Vineyard, and Founders', which is only produced in top vintages. See also Inniskillin Okanagan (British Columbia).

Magnotta ☆–☆☆

Vaughan. Owner: Gabe and Rossana Magnotta. 73 ha.
www.magnotta.com

Ontario's third largest winery. Icewine specialist, producing it not only from Riesling and Vidal, but also from Cabernet Franc. Like Inniskillin, it also makes a sparkling Icewine. Quality has been erratic.

Malivoire ☆☆–☆☆☆

Beamsville. Owner: Martin Malivoire. 26 ha.
www.malivoirewineco.com

Malivoire produces rich and high-priced Moira Vineyard Chardonnay and Gewurztraminer here, and an excellent old-vine Maréchal Foch.

Pelee Island Winery ☆–☆☆

Kingsville. Owner: Walter Schmoranz. 220 ha.
www.peleeisland.com

Many of the wines from this enormous winery are simple and unpretentious, but some, such as the Barrique Chardonnay and Vidal Icewine, rise above the average.

Pillitteri Estates ☆☆

Niagara-on-the-Lake. Owner: Pillitteri family. 21 ha.
www.pillitteri.com

Some of the vineyards here are 50 years old. The Bordeaux red varieties do well here, but the specialty is Icewines from Riesling and Vidal, and, surprisingly, Cabernet Franc and Cabernet Sauvignon.

Thirty Bench Wines ☆☆

Beamsville. Owner: Andres Wines. 28 ha.
www.thirtybench.com

A boutique winery, making its reputation by slashing yields to very low levels and by harvesting as late as the climate will allow. The result is very concentrated wines, perhaps exaggeratedly so. New ownership since 2005 has stabilized quality. Riesling and Bordeaux blends are the most exciting wines.

Vineland Estates ☆☆

Vineland. Owner: Allan Schmidt. 30 ha.
www.vineland.com

Hermann Weis from the Mosel planted vinifera and hybrid vines on the slopes of the Niagara Escarpment in 1979. The first bottling was in 1984. Vineland claims to have the best location for growing Riesling, but produces a wide range of red and white wines, dry, semi-dry, and sweet.

British Columbia

There are two distinct wine-growing regions in "BC": the Okanagan and Similkameen valleys in the central-southern part of the province, and the coastal areas of the Fraser Valley and Vancouver Island. Almost all production comes from the 160-kilometre (100-mile) long Okanagan Valley, which has 2,700 hectares of vinifera benefiting from its immense lake. The whole of the Okanagan is arid; its south end predominantly planted with classic red wine grapes (Pinot Noir, Merlot, and Cabernet Sauvignon); and the less arid north favouring white grape varieties (Riesling, Chardonnay, Pinot Blanc, Pinot Gris, Gewurztraminer, and Semillon). It would appear that global warming has been advantageous here, with fewer wines trembling on the edge of ripeness. The province currently has 120 wineries.

Leading British Columbia Producers

Blue Mountain ☆☆

Okanagan Falls. Owner: Ian Mavety. 31 ha.
www.bluemountainwinery.com

Growers from the early 1970s, the Mavetys began producing their own wines, all estate grown, in 1991. Sparkling wine has been a specialty, but recent vintages of Pinot Noir have been impressive.

Burrowing Owl ☆☆

Oliver. Owner: Jim Wyse. 46 ha.
www.bovwine.com

A gravity-fed winery was built here in the southern Okanagan in 1997, and initial releases were of Chardonnay, Pinot Gris, Merlot, and Cabernet, but Syrah and Pinot Noir have been added. The Bordeaux reds are the outstanding wines at present.

Calona ☆–☆☆

Kelowna. Owner: Andres. No vineyards.
www.calonavineyards.com.

The Okanagan's oldest winery, which was established here under a different name in 1932. Howard Soon has been making the wines since 1980. The medium-bodied wines have been rather lacklustre, but a change of ownership in 2005 is likely to see the range spruced up.

CedarCreek ☆☆

Kelowna. Owner: Gordon Fitzpatrick. 60 ha.
www.cedarcreek.bc.ca.

Founded in 1987, CedarCreek has won recognition not only for its refined Riesling and Gewurztraminer, but for fine reds, especially Pinot Noir, in its top Platinum Reserve range.

Gray Monk Estate ☆–☆☆

Okanagan Centre. Owner: Heiss family. 20 ha.
www.graymonk.com

Gray Monk is a long-established family run winery overlooking Okanagan Lake. Winemaker George Heiss Jr. concentrates on varietals only. The focus is on white wines, the Pinot Gris and Gewurztraminer being especially good.

Inniskillin Okanagan ☆☆
Oliver. Owner: Constellation. 9 ha. www.inniskillin.com
The pioneers of Inniskillin Ontario (q.v.) continue the
tradition in Okanagan. Vineyards are located in the south
of the valley, just north of the US border, in an area known
as the Golden Mile. The hierarchy of wines is similar to that
of Inniskillin Ontario, except that instead of Founders', there
is a series called Discovery devoted to varieties new to the
Okanagan such as Marsanne, Chenin, and Malbec. Inniskillin,
unlike many other Okanagan wineries, has done well with
Cabernet Sauvignon, too.

Jackson-Triggs ☆☆–☆☆☆
Oliver. Owner: Constellation. 173 ha.
www.jacksontriggswinery.com
Founded in 1993, this winery has vineyards in Niagara as well
as the Okanagan. Given that this is one of Canada's largest
wineries, the standard of its wines, from simple Sauvignon to
dazzling Icewine, is remarkable.

Mission Hill ☆☆–☆☆☆
Westbank. Owner: Anthony von Mandl. 360 ha.
www.misssionhillwinery.com
A huge and extravagant winery in one of the loveliest settings
in the province. John Simes was formerly winemaker at
Montana Winery (q.v. New Zealand), who increased the use
of barrel fermentation and oak ageing. The Icewines can be
exceptional, but there are also some excellent wines in the
SLC range (Select Lot Collection), including a delicious
Syrah, and a Merlot-dominated blend called Oculus.

Osoyoos Larose ☆☆–☆☆☆
Oliver. Owner: Taillan and Constellation. 24 ha.
An ambitious venture, uniting Okanagan vineyards and
expertise from a major Bordeaux negociant, who also own
Château Gruaud-Larose. The Grand Vin is a Bordeaux blend,
Merlot-dominated and marked by a good deal of new oak.
It's a sumptuous wine but has an invigorating herbaceous edge.

Quails' Gate ☆☆
Kelowna. Owner: Ben and Tony Stewart. 50 ha.
www.quailsgate.com
One of the oldest producing vineyard sites in the Okanagan.
In 1961 the Stewarts were the first to plant Chasselas, which
they still produce. As well Icewines, the top wines here are
the Family Reserves. Winemaker Grant Stanley believes
the potential for fine Pinot Noir is considerable.

Sumac Ridge ☆☆
Summerland. Owner: McWatters family and
Constellation. 50 ha. www.sumacridge.com
Sumac Ridge Estate produced its first vintage in 1980,
supplementing its own grapes with fruit from other vineyards
in the Okanagan and Similkameen valleys. The winery was
one of the first to develop Icewine and Meritage-style wines,
white as well as red, in the region.

Tinhorn Creek ☆
Oliver. Owner: Kenn Oldfield. 52 ha. www.tinhorn.com
Fruit-forward wines, with whites such as Pinot Gris and
Chardonnay generally stronger than the reds.

Central & South America

Despite the economic problems that beset many Central and South American countries in the early twenty-first century, their wine industries continue to flourish. Chile remains a still inconsistent source of good-value wines, and the tremendous potential of Argentina is now being realized, with a growing number of properties producing first rate wines. Uruguay too has been learning to master its best known, if often angular, grape variety, Tannat, although other countries, such as Mexico, Brazil, and Peru have yet to make much impact on the crucial international markets. Nonetheless, South America remains a continent of enormous promise that is certain to keep surprising us in the years to come.

Chile

After a fumbled start as an exporter in the 1980s Chile came of age as a wine-producing country in the 1990s. New regions were planted, adding to the diversity of Chilean wines, and scores of well-trained winemakers, many with international experience, took their places at the helm of the many new wineries. There was never any doubt about the quality of Chilean fruit, but for a long time, an uncritical domestic market and a rather naive approach to modern winemaking prevented flavours getting from the vineyard into the bottle. Now, however, Chile is firmly on the international scene.

Wine has been made in Chile since the missionaries introduced vines in the mid-sixteenth century, but the first real quality developments only began when the copper-rich landowners of the nineteenth century paraded their wealth with vineyards. French vine cuttings were shipped to Chile in 1851, just before phylloxera hit Europe, thus ensuring a store of un-plagued rootstock and a unique marketing edge for future

generations. The big leap came in the 1980s, when – prompted by the efforts of winemakers such as Miguel Torres – there was widespread investment in modern winemaking equipment.

The quality wine growing region, in which 117,000 hectares are planted, is spread across three main zones: the Aconcagua and Casablanca valleys; the Central Valley; and the southern region. Aconcagua incorporates the main east-west valley to the north of Santiago, but enjoys less coastal influence than Casablanca, the source of some of Chile's best white wines. The Central Valley, where most wineries are based, is divided (moving north to south) into the four valleys of Maipo, Rapel, Curicó, and Maule, each irrigated by rivers flowing off the Andes, although channel irrigation is often being replaced by more controllable drip irrigation.

These are all immense regions, so generalizations are tricky, but Maipo and Rapel are generally warmer than the other two. As Chilean growers learn more about their terroirs, subregions are being delineated. Two of the most exciting are Colchagua, and Apalta within Rapel.

In recent years wineries have become much more adventurous in choosing where to plant new vineyards. The cool San

Antonio and Leyda valleys, west of Santiago and a few miles from the ocean, are now the source of some unusually refined wines. The more northerly Limarí valley, also coastal, is well suited to fine Chardonnay.

The Chilean climate is perfect – almost too perfect, in that vines rarely have to struggle. Although rainfall increases as you move south, there is little difference between average temperatures in Maipo and Maule. The biggest variances are west to east, according to position relative to the Andean and Coastal ranges; it is easier to find wine style differences within valleys. Regions south of Maule, such as Bío-Bío and Triaguén, are attracting interest, especially for Chardonnay, but heavy rainfall can mar the crop.

The flow of knowledge, ideas, and technology into this 4,000-kilometre- (2,500-mile-) long nation has facilitated the harnessing of its viticultural resources. The briefly fashionable belief that wine of international standards is made simply with stainless steel and new oak has switched to a philosophy of "vineyard first, winery second", bringing issues such as canopy management, irrigation, and soil study to the top of the agenda. Viticulturists are planting well-exposed slopes in preference to valley-floor sites on overrich soils and many growers are not content supplying the big bodegas, but are going it alone.

Among red varieties, Merlot, planted in 15 per cent of Chile's vineyards, now shares as much of the limelight as easy-drinking Cabernet Sauvignon, which has traditionally been the most successful Chilean signature in export markets. A very few producers have managed to tame Pinot Noir, and Malbec shows potential, but is unlikely to surpass that from Argentina. In whites, Chardonnay and Sauvignon Blanc are the dominant pair, especially from Casablanca. In the 1990s, it became apparent that much of what was thought to be Merlot was in fact Carmenère, which is now enjoying some celebrity as Chile's unique grape variety (see box on page 538). Among other varieties, Syrah and Viognier show considerable promise.

Despite all this most wines on the domestic market are sold in the same packaging as milk cartons, and at low prices. By the mid-2000s most wineries were losing money; many were either part of larger agricultural corporations or owned by rich individuals. Consolidation seems inevitable, and more than ever the large companies must focus relentlessly on exports shipped in large volumes. It is scarcely possible for a Chilean winery to survive with a production of less than 100,000 cases, which is the main difference between its wine industry and that of other New World countries. At the same time an encouraging counter-development is the emergence of a growing number of what might be dismissed as boutique wineries. In practice, however, these wineries, by adopting a perfectionist rather than a solely commercial approach, have set new standards for Chilean fine wine at a reasonable price.

Leading Chile Producers

Almaviva ☆☆☆–☆☆☆☆
Maipo. Owner: Concha y Toro and Baroness Philippine de Rothschild. 70 ha. www.bpdr.com
This fascinating joint venture produces a single wine, the Cabernet Sauvignon dominated Almaviva. It effortlessly demonstrates the potential of the best Maipo vineyards – these were planted 30 years ago – but it can be argued that the wine is closer in style to Bordeaux than what we expect of Chile. Nonetheless, it has been of excellent quality since the first vintage in 1996, and those first vintages have stood the test of time. However, the high price demanded for the wine from the outset has raised some eyebrows.

Anakena ☆☆
Cachapoal. Owner: Jorge Gutierrez and Felipe Ibanez. 400 ha. www.anakenawines.cl
This venture, founded in 1998, has never played safe, producing, as well as some standard varietals, experimental blends that do not always pay off. Vineyards in various regions, including Leyda, allow a wide range of styles. Riesling, Pinot Noir, and Syrah have been impressive.

Aquitania ☆☆–☆☆☆
Maipo. Owner: Paul Pontallier and Bruno Prats. 16 ha. www.aquitania.cl
Chile seems to have no problem enticing highly qualified investors from France. This starry pair from the Médoc came across an exciting site in 1990, and launched their joint venture. The red wines are aged in 300-litre French oak barrels. The principal label was Domaine Bruno, but it was never as exciting as one might have hoped. 2000 was the last vintage, and it has been replaced by wines such as Lazuli, a pure Cabernet Sauvignon. An associated label is SoldeSol, a thrillingly austere Chardonnay from the cool, wet Traiguén region.

Araucano ☆–☆☆☆
Colchagua. Owner: François Lurton. 20 ha. www.jflurton.com
The basic wines from the Chilean outpost of the Lurton family are not that distinguished, but bottlings such as the superripe Carmenère called Alka, and the Carmenère/Cabernet blend called Clos de Lolol are lush and spicy.

Bisquertt ☆☆
Colchagua. Owner: Bisquertt family. 700 ha. www.bisquertt.cl
Bulk wine producers for many years, Bisquertt re-equipped its winery in 1993, switching attention to premium, bottled wine under the Casa La Joya label. The basic ranges are disappointing, but the Casa La Joya Gran Reserva Cabernet and Carmenère are fleshy and rich.

Chateau Los Boldos ☆
Requinoa. Owner: Sogrape. 285 ha. www.chateauboldos.com
Of nineteenth-century origin, this estate was bought in 1990 by an Alsace family, then sold in 2008 to the major Portuguese company Sogrape, which should herald much needed improvements in quality.

Caliterra ☆–☆☆
Colchagua. Owner: Viña Errazuriz (q.v.). 250 ha. www.caliterra.com
In 1995 California's Mondavi became an equal partner in this dynamic winery, but its share was sold to Errazuriz in 2004.

The winery has developed a large Colchagua estate (and label) called Arboleda. The Sauvignon Blanc and Chardonnay are reliable if not outstanding, but the reds from Arboleda are show more distinction, both the spicy, plummy Carmenère and the opulent Syrah.

Viña Canepa ☆☆–☆☆☆
Colchagua. Owner: Canepa family. 550 ha. www.canepawines.cl

I imported my first Chilean Cabernet from the Canepas in 1970, when their fruit-growing fortune (and friendship with the Gallos of California) made them Chile's first modern winemakers. The Canepa vineyards were split up in 1996 (see TerraMater) but the descendants of José Canepa still have substantial holdings, which are boosted by vineyards leased on long-term contracts. The Reserve wines can be excellent: sleek, juicy Syrah; velvety Malbec; vigorous, toasty Casablanca Chardonnay. The top wines are the elegant Maipo Cabernet called Finisimo, and the sumptuous, ultra-ripe Magnificum, which blends Cabernet, Merlot, Malbec, and Carmenère perfectly. Syrah and Carmenère show promise.

Carmen ☆☆–☆☆☆
Maipo. Owner: Claro group. 525 ha. www.carmen.com

The oldest winery brand in Chile, but now boasts a state-of-the art winery in the Maipo valley. It may be next door to its sister (Santa Rita), but in terms of technology and winemaking philosophy, the two are distant cousins.

Former winemaker Alvaro Espinoza was a pioneer of organic wine production, and one of the first to recognize the potential merits of Carmenère. Since 2002, his place has been taken by María del Pilár González. The organic Nativa Chardonnay is the best of the whites, and the red blends and Syrah released under the Winemaker's Reserve label are tannic and structured. The top wine is the voluptuous and mighty Gold Reserve Cabernet Sauvignon.

Casablanca ☆–☆☆
Casablanca. Owner: Santa Carolina (q.v.). 280 ha. www.casablancawinery.com

The winery, which, since 1992, has put the cool-climate Casablanca valley firmly on the map. Inaugural winemaker Ignacio Recabarren used the pungent Sauvignon Blanc and citric Chardonnay as his ticket to international acclaim. The Cefiro series uses fruit sourced from various regions, but the whites from Casablanca are the winners, and the Merlot can also be exceptional. Nimbus is a new range of estate wines, but recent releases have been disappointing. Look out, too, for the opulent El Bosque Carmenère. The oaky Cabernet/Carmenère blend called Neblus is the "icon" wine, but can be rather grassy.

Concha y Toro ☆–☆☆☆
Santiago. Owner: Larraín and Giulisasti families. 4,700 ha. www.conchaytoro.com

Founded in 1883, this has long been Chile's biggest winery, producing round 20 per cent of all Chilean wine. Including its own vineyards, Concha y Toro now controls around 18,000 hectares. Not surprisingly, the range of wines is enormous, ranging from the unoaked Sunrise label to more complex brands such as the innovative Terrunyo single vineyard wines, both overseen by Ignacio Recabarren.

For many years the Castillero del Diablo range of seven varietals has offered excellent value. The flagship wine is Don Melchor, from lush Maipo Cabernet fruit. In addition to these various brands, Concha y Toro also owns subsidiary wineries, which are listed under their own names.

Cono Sur ☆☆–☆☆☆
Chimbarongo. Owner: Concha y Toro (q.v.). 940 ha. www.conosur.com

Who would have thought a Chilean winery could forge its reputation on Pinot Noir? Winemaker Adolfo Hurtado Cono Sur delivers this varietal (from Casablanca and Bío-Bío grapes) in four different guises: unoaked, Reserve, Visíon, 20 Barrels Limited Edition and, using Casablanca fruit only, Ocio.

The Vision range also includes a fine Riesling from Bío-Bío and what may well be Chile's best Viognier. Since 2003 an organic Cabernet/Carmenère from Colchagua has been added to the range.

Cousiño Macul ☆☆
Santiago. Owner: Cousiño family. 420 ha. www.cousinomacul.cl

Precariously close to the suburbs and smog of Santiago, Cousiño Macul is one of Chile's oldest and most beautiful wine

CARMENÈRE

The obscure Bordeaux variety Carmenère, virtually wiped out by phylloxera in its native land, thrived in Chile, where the louse was unknown. Carmenère, a very vigorous variety, grows differently from Merlot, and doesn't taste much like Merlot, yet for decades it was believed that Carmenère was in fact Merlot. And it was sold as such. Only in 1993 did eagle-eyed ampelographers from Montpellier spot the difference.

Some wineries pretended not to notice, but others, notably Carmen, proudly bottled Carmenère as a varietal wine.

Carmenère is very vigorous and ripens three weeks later than Merlot. Its yields need to be reduced to ensure that by the time it is harvested it is fully ripe. Unfortunately, unripe examples of Carmenère are quite common, and can be spotted from their characteristic aroma of green peppers. But when fully ripe, Carmenère can be a lush, cherry-toned wine, with overtones of coffee and chocolate. Until recently little more than a curiosity, Carmenère is now being taken seriously by many producers, and powerful (sometimes too powerful) and structured wines are now widely available. So far, the most promising regions for the variety are Isla da Maipo and Apalta.

estates. But urban pressures have led to the gradual selling-off of the vineyards, and new vineyards in Buin, south of the city, are being planted. A new Cabernet blend, Finis Terrae, reveals a more modern and spicy style of red, aged in new oak, in contrast to the renowned, if old-fashioned Antiguas Reservas, which has the ability to age many decades.

Aligning itself with other leading estates, Cousiño Macul introduced in 2004 an "icon" wine, a Cabernet/Merlot blend, aged in new barriques, called Lota. Except at the very top level, the wines have been humdrum for many years.

De Martino ☆☆–☆☆☆
Isla de Maipo. Owner: De Martino family. 300 ha. www.demartino.cl
This traditional estate has been organically cultivated since 2002. The style is rich, oaky, and powerful: a far cry from some of the bland ranges offered by other Chilean wineries. The top wine is the structured Gran Familia Cabernet Sauvignon, but more individual are the single vineyard wines first produced in 2003; the Syrah, Carmenère, and some blends from old bush vines are outstanding. Simpler wines carry the Santa Inés label.

Echeverría ☆☆–☆☆☆
Curicó. Owner: Echeverría family. 80 ha. www.echewine.com
Since diverting attention from bulk-wine production to a premium range of varietals, Echeverría has been one of the leading boutique wineries, small enough to hand-craft its best wines, large enough to have some marketing muscle. Cabernet Sauvignon is outstanding, particularly the Family Reserve and the luxurious new Limited Edition. The Sauvignon Blanc is stylish, the Chardonnay Family Reserve distinctly buttery. The overall style is delicate, rather than opulent, offering wines designed to be drunk with food, as Echeverría has focused its marketing on restaurants worldwide.

Luís Felipé Edwards ☆–☆☆☆
Colchagua. Owner: Luís Felipé Edwards. 600 ha. www.lfewines.com
Founded in 1976, this beautiful estate, another of the emerging stars of the Colchagua valley, only began bottling its own wines in 1994. The estate varietals are uninspired, although the new Syrah shows promise, but the Reserves are rich and ripe. The flagship wine is Doña Bernarda, a Cabernet Sauvignon marked by new oak. In recent years there has been a keen interest in vineyard development, with terraced hillsides sites in Colchagua and new plantings in Leyda that will come on stream in 2010.

Emiliana ☆☆–☆☆☆
Colchagua. Owner: Concha y Toro (q.v.). 595 ha. www.emiliana.cl
Since the late 1990s Emiliana has been the leading large-scale organic winery in Chile, sourcing fruit from vineyards in Casablanca, Maipo, and Colchagua, all under the supervision of top winemaker Alvaro Espinoza. Novas is the principal range, but the top wines are the highly concentrated red blend Coyam, and G, supposedly the country's first Biodynamic wine.

Errázuriz ☆☆–☆☆☆
Aconcagua. Owner: Eduardo Chadwick. 595 ha. www.errazuriz.com
Out on its own, to the north of Santiago, Errázuriz is best-known for the powerful and distinctive Don Maximiano Cabernet Sauvignon. Winemaker Francisco Baettig, following on from his predecessor Ed Flaherty, is pursuing projects such as Wild Ferment wines using wild yeasts to express a local character.

Vineyards in Casablanca and the Central Valley provide Chardonnay, Sauvignon Blanc, and Merlot grapes for the range. Most of the wines are soft and forward, but there are single-vineyard wines with far more character. In 1999, Eduardo Chadwick created a high-priced wine bearing his name, drawing on fruit from a vineyard in Maipo, close to Almaviva. It is made in a richer, spicier, more opulently oaky style than Don Maximiano. A more recent venture is Kai, a full-bodied Carmenère from its Aconcagua vineyards, and the Cumbre Shiraz is in much the same powerful style. See also Seña.

Fournier ☆☆
Maule. Owner: Jose Manuel Ortega. 50 ha. www.ofournier.com
Following on the success of his spectacular estate in Mendoza, former banker José Manuel Ortega created a property in Chile in 2007, with old vineyards in Maule and new plantings in San Antonio. As in Mendoza, the top wine will be called Alpha, followed by the dense but not overblown red blend, Centauri.

Gracia ☆☆
Cachapoal. Owner: Córpora Group. 1,000 ha. www.gracia.cl
Founded in 1993, this winery buys in fruit from regions as varied as Aconcagua in the north, to Bío-Bío in the south. The best wines emerge from the Reserva Superior range, with fleshy Merlot, medium-bodied stylish Cabernet, and very well-balanced Chardonnay from Bío-Bío, although the Pinot Noir from the same region has yet to attain comparable quality. The recently launched flagship wine is Caminante from Aconcagua: a dense, smoky blend of Cabernet, Merlot, and Carmenère. The Córpora Group also owns Viña Porta, which produces excellent Merlot, as well as other wines.

Haras de Pirque ☆☆☆
Pirque. Owner: Eduardo Matte. 145 ha. www.harasdepirque.com
Eduardo Matte owns a successful stud farm, and decided to

Viña Tarapacá, Isla de Maipo

plant vineyards – appropriately in the shape of a horseshoe – on the slopes around his Maipo property. A dazzling new winery, also horseshoe-shaped and reminiscent of Opus One in Napa, was ready for the first vintage in 2000.

The basic range, Equus, is at a far higher quality level than most Chilean equivalents, and the very concentrated Character and Elegance ranges are already among the most serious wines in the country. A new addition is the Cabernet/Carmenère blend called Albis, blended with advice from Italian consultant Renzo Cotarella.

Casa Lapostolle ☆☆–☆☆☆☆
Colchagua. Owner: Marnier-Lapostolle family. 350 ha. www.casalapostolle.com

With advice from oenologist Michel Rolland, this Rapel valley winery received acclaim from its first vintage in 1994, and quality has remained at the same high level thereafter. Originally a joint venture with the wealthy Rabat family, this has been solely owned by the Marnier-Lapostolles since 2003.

As you would expect from Rolland, his signature wine is a Merlot (Cuvée Alexandre), which is macerated for 30 days and aged in new oak for 16 months. It is now joined by a very elegant Cuvée Alexandre Cabernet.

Profiting from very old vines in Apalta, Lapostolle has more recently released a rich, tannic, and expensive blend called Clos Apalta. Other red blends, from different regions, are Tanao and Borobo, which have yet to displace the other premium wines in quality. In general, these wines have a Bordeaux-style elegance that is rare in Chile.

Viña Leyda ☆☆
Leyda. Owner: Viña Tabali. 217 ha. www.leyda.cl

The Fernandez family released their first vintage from this cool region in 2001, but six years later sold the property to another winery. The main focus is Pinot Noir, in numerous guises, of which the most persuasive thus far are the intensely red-fruited single-vineyard Las Brisas and Cahuil bottlings.

Loma Larga ☆☆
Casablanca. Owner: Diaz family. 35 ha. www.lomalarga.com

With the first vintage in 2004, these are early days for this boutique winery. The labelling is hopelessly confusing and is set to be reformed, but quality is invigorating, with good Pinot Noir and completely convincing Cabernet Franc.

Los Maquis ☆☆–☆☆☆
Colchagua. Owner: Ricardo Rivadeneira. 124 ha. www.maquis.cl

Bulk wine brings in the cash, allowing the owner/winemaker to concentrate since 2003 on a distinctive red blend: Lien. Bordeaux varieties (other than Cabernet Sauvignon) and Syrah are the components, and the result in 2005 supple, discreetly tannic, and delicious. A second wine, Calcu, is made from purchased fruit, and is almost as fine.

Casa Marin ☆☆–☆☆☆
San Antonio. Owner: Maria Luz Marin. 40 ha. www.casamarin.cl

A brave venture in San Antonio, with the first plantings in 2000. Brave because the climate is not always ideal, and

botrytis and frost and have played havoc with crop levels. Nonetheless the Sauvignon is among Chile's most refined, and the Pinot Noirs are full-bodied but by no means heavy handed.

Matetic ☆☆–☆☆☆
San Antonio. Owner: Jorge Matetic. 90 ha. www.mateticvineyards.com

Jorge Matetic, as well as Maria Luz Marin, are justifying the expectations made of the San Antonio valley. Founded in 1999 and organic since 2004, Matetic's best wines, under the EQ label, have just the poise and intensity of fruit that are so often lacking in Chile's more standard wines. Sauvignon Blanc and Chardonnay are crisp and tangy, with a dash of maritime spray, and Pinot Noir's initial promise is being challenged by some excellent Syrah.

Maycas de Limarí ☆☆
Limarí. Owner: Concha y Toro. 320 ha. www.conchaytoro.com

In 2005 Concha y Toro bought the existing Francisco de Aguirre winery to provide a base for its new Limarí label under the direction of top winemaker Marcelo Papa. Initial releases, from Chardonnay and Syrah, have been highly promising, thanks to their bracing natural acidity.

Misiones de Rengo ☆☆
Rengo. Owner: Compania Chilena da Fosforos. 120 ha. www.misionesderengo.cl

Under the same ownership as Viña Tarapacá (q.v.), this new winery has achieved rapid success with its well crafted, sensibly priced wines, of which the best appear under the Cuvée designation, although certain Reservas, such as the Carmenère, are also at a high level.

Montes ☆☆–☆☆☆☆
Curicó. Owner: Aurelio Montes and partners. 550 ha. www.monteswines.com

Aurelio Montes is one of Chile's most talented winemakers, now drawing much of his finest fruit from extensive vineyards in the Apalta region. For many years, his Montes Alpha Chardonnay and Cabernet Sauvignon (and more recently Syrah) have been outstanding. Montes has not rested on those laurels, and has launched a superb red blend called Alpha M, and what is certainly Chile's richest and most powerful Syrah: the high-priced Folly from Apalta, now matched by an equally grandiose Carmenère, Purple Angel.

Mont Gras ☆–☆☆
Colchagua. Owner: Gras family. 423 ha. www.montgras.cl

The standard varietals and Reservas here are not that different from those from a dozen other large wineries in Chile, although the Casablanca Chardonnay and the Merlot Reserve do stand out.

Mont Gras's pride and joy is the unique vineyard called Ninquén, 90 hectares planted across the undulating slopes of a hilltop plateau. This is the source of its top wines, Cabernet Sauvignon and Syrah made in a plump, rounded style. A recent innovation is Soleus, a range of organically farmed wines from Maip.

Morandé ☆☆
Casablanca. Owner: Pablo Morandé. 360 ha.
www.morande.cl
While at Concha y Toro (q.v.), Pablo Morandé was the first winemaker to realize the potential of the Casablanca valley. Today, his own winery is in Rapel, although half his vineyards are in Casablanca. The wines, mostly white, made from Casablanca fruit, are characteristically pure and elegant, and there are some impressive Gran Reservas, mostly reds, from Maipo grapes. His top wines are the House of Morandé Cabernet Sauvignon; and the sumptuous Golden Harvest Sauvignon Blanc, from botrytis affected grapes. Yet in recent years quality seems to have become less exciting, despite a conscious revamping of the business.

Odjfell ☆☆
Maipo. Owner: Dan Odjfell. 100 ha.
www.odjfellvineyards.com
Norwegian shipping tycoon Dan Odjfell spent a fortune building a gravity-fed winery in the late 1990s. After a few years when brettanomyces infected the wines, quality has been steady in recent years, especially among the red wines within the two top ranges, Armador and Orzada.

Pérez Cruz ☆☆☆
Maipo. Owner: Pérez Cruz family. 140 ha.
www.perezcruz.com
Tucked against the foothills of the Andes is one of South America's most spectacular wineries, sinuously shaped like an upended boat. Only red wines are produced, in a bold, full-throttled style. Cabernet Sauvignon, Malbec, Syrah, and Carmenère are the principal reds, and there are two impressive blends: Petit Verdot-dominated Quelen and Syrah-dominated Liguai.

Punto Alto ☆
Casablanca. Owner: Michel Laroche. 55 ha.
www.larochewines.com
This began as a joint venture between Chablis maestro Laroche and Jorge Coderch of Valdivieso, but in 2004 Laroche became sole owner. So far the varietal wines have been correct rather than exciting.

La Rosa ☆–☆☆
Cachapoal, Rapel. Owner: Ossa family. 864 ha.
www.larosa.cl
One of the oldest wineries in Chile, La Rosa draws fruit from extensive vineyards in the Cachapoal valley. Some of the best red wines come from the 145 hectares planted at the Palmeria estate, a unique plantation of over 1,000 Chilean palms as well as vines.

San Pedro ☆–☆☆
Curicó. Owner: Compania Cervecerias Unidas. 2,500 ha.
www.sanpedro.cl
Since 1994, San Pedro has belonged to Chile's biggest brewer, leading to substantial investment in a state-of-the-art winery. The surrounding 1,200 hectares of vineyards make up one of the largest single estates in the Central Valley. In the early 2000s, San Pedro embarked on an ambitious expansion programme, purchasing Finca La Celia in Argentina and creating Tabalí in Limarí. Ironically, the achievements by its subsidiaries have often outshone those of the parent company, despite the unquestionable gifts of its chief winemaker Irene Paiva. Despite the industrial size of the winery, the flagship wine, an old-vine Cabernet Sauvignon called Cabo de Hornos, is made in an old-fashioned way that allows it to age very well, developing a savoury complexity in time.

Santa Carolina ☆–☆☆
Santiago. Owner: Empresas Watts company. 650 ha.
www.santacarolina.com
This is one of the easiest wineries for the traveller to visit, as the handsome old buildings are close to Santiago, although the home vineyards are now replaced by housing. However, Santa Carolina has planted extensively throughout all the main valleys, gaining a wide spectrum of fruit sources. Chardonnay, Malbec, and Cabernet Sauvignon come from close to the Cordillera in Maipo. Excellent Merlot is grown in extensive vineyards near San Fernando, and Chardonnay has been planted in Casablanca.

For some reason quality became lacklustre in the 2000s, and a new team was brought in to renovate the vineyards and improve the winemaking and cooperage. These efforts seem to be paying off and wines such as the old-vine Barrica Selection Carmenère can be exceptional.

Santa Helena ☆–☆☆
Colchagua. Owner: Compañía Cervecerias Unidas. 1,100 ha. www.santahelena.cl
Under the same ownership as San Pedro (q.v.), this large Colchagua winery was given its autonomy in 2001, which encouraged further expansion. The top range is Selección del Directorio, offering wines of a sound but unexceptional quality, but the recently introduced "icon" blend, DON, a Cabernet-based blend, does show the distinction of Colchagua fruit.

Santa Inés
See De Martino.

Santa Rita, Viña ☆–☆☆☆
Buin, Maipo. Owner: Claro Group. 2,200 ha.
www.santarita.cl
Erratic quality saw this long-established giant slip from the top, but expansion of its Buin estate and an extensive winery upgrade are rapidly turning things around. The whites mostly still lack appeal, but there are persuasively fruity reds under the Medalla Real label, and some excellent wines in the Floresta range, but they are made in small quantities.

The flagship wine is the sleek, voluptuous Cabernet called Casa Real, but the new Triple C from Cabernet Sauvignon, Cabernet Franc, and Carmenère, is even more complex. New plantings in cooler regions such as Limarí should lead to wines that will refresh the range.

Seña ☆☆☆
Aconcagua. Owner: Eduardo Chadwick. 42 ha.
Two leading Pacific coast families, on different continents, joined forces in 1995 to produce an elegant, eucalyptus-tinged Cabernet Sauvignon from a vineyard at the cooler end of the

Aconcagua valley. After the sale of Mondavi, Chadwick continued on his own and began converting the estate to Biodynamism. Ed Flaherty, the Errázuriz winemaker, oversees production, and results have been consistently impressive.

Casa Silva ☆☆–☆☆☆
Colchagua. Owner: Mario Silva. 800 ha. www.casasilva.cl
The Silva family has produced bulk wines from its varied vineyards since 1977, but in 1997 began producing its own wine. Results were impressive from the start. Casa Silva may well be the only property in Chile to bottle a Sauvignon Gris: a richer, juicier grape than Sauvignon Blanc.

The top reds are the supple Quinta Generación (Cabernet/Carmenère) and the very refined Cabernet/Carmenère/Merlot blend called Altura. Detailed vineyard studies have been undertaken, and when those lessons have been absorbed, Casa Silva may increase even further in stature.

Tabalí ☆☆–☆☆☆
Limari. Owner: Guillermo Luksic and Viña San Pedro. 180 ha. www.tabali.com
This energetic enterprise was founded in 2003, but draws on vineyards planted in the mid-1990s by consultant Jacques Lurton. The Chardonnay and Carmenère Reserves were among the most impressive of the first releases, but quality is excellent across the board.

Viña Tarapacá ☆–☆☆
Isla de Maipo. Owner: Compania Chilena da Fosforos. 600 ha. www.tarapaca.cl
In 1996, this ancient winery switched its activity from the western side of the Maipo valley to the Isla del Maipo, renovating the winery and acquiring vineyards in Casablanca. The Maipo vineyards are very diverse in soil structure and microclimate, and are the source of a range of six wines called Terroir that have yet to live up to the ambition of their billing. Overall, quality is sound but unremarkable.

TerraMater ☆–☆☆
Maipo. Owner: Cánepa sisters. 700 ha. www.terramater.cl
After the splitting up of the original Cánepa estate (q.v.) in 1996, three sisters retained the Maipo vineyards, and there are other sites in Curicó and Maule. They are proud of their Zinfandels, a curiosity in Chile, but they can hardly compete with the better Californian examples. The best of their wines appear under the Altum label. The other wines are lush and supple, but lack personality.

Terranoble ☆☆–☆☆☆
Talca. Owner: Mario Geisse, Patricio de Solminihac, and other investors. 150 ha. www.terranoble.cl
This small Maule winery was founded in 1994 and has

impressed with its richly concentrated Gran Reserva Cabernet and Merlot. New vineyard sources in Casablanca and Colchagua will expand the range.

Torreón de Paredes ☆☆
Rengo. Owner: Paredes family. 150 ha. www.torreondeparedes.cl
A family run estate, with vineyards in the Cachapoal valley. The reds (Merlot and Cabernet Sauvignon) are more impressive than the range of whites, although there is a good oaked Sauvignon Blanc. Alvaro Paredes lavishes passionate care and attention on improving the viticulture, with increasingly impressive results. The flagship wine is Don Amado, named in honour of the founder.

Miguel Torres ☆☆☆
Curicó. Owner: Torres family. 436 ha. www.migueltorres.cl
When Miguel Torres set up his winery two decades ago, he ushered in a new era for the Chilean wine industry. The introduction of modern winemaking equipment – including stainless-steel fermentation tanks – allowed the white wines to be cold-fermented, while imported oak barrels replaced old *rauli* casks.

His innovations shocked the Chileans into realizing the true potential of their vineyards. Nor have the Torres team rested on their laurels; they are continuously on the lookout for outstanding vineyard sites (such as the slatey Empedrado vineyard in Maule) that will set their wines apart from the often standardized models that dominate the Chilean industry. The range is considerable, and even the more modest wines are well made. Among the top bottlings are the barrel-fermented Maqueha Chardonnay; the robust and ageworthy Manso de Velasco Cabernet from very old vines; and a Carignan-dominated blend called Cordillera.

Undurraga ☆☆
Talagante. Owner: Piccioto family and José Yuraszeck. 1,000 ha. www.undurraga.cl
This highly traditional and long-established winery was undergoing something of a renaissance, until in 2006 a row led to the founding family pulling out of the business. The vineyards are split between Maipo and Colchagua – growing Sauvignon Blanc, Chardonnay, Merlot, Cabernet Sauvignon, and Pinot Noir. The whites are disappointing, but the Reserve reds have been richly fruity, and oak is used with discretion. The top wines are the Founder's Collection Cabernet and Altazor, an old-vine Cabernet aged in new oak, but there are sure to be changes now that the Undurragas are no longer involved.

Valdivieso ☆☆
Curicó. Owner: Mitjans Group. 140 ha. www.valdiviesovineyard.com
Originally the biggest Chilean sparkling wine producer,

Undurraga winery and vineyard, Talagante

Valdivieso today is better-known for its still wines. The company has its own vineyards but also sources grapes from unirrigated vineyards close to the coastal mountains. Ever since the arrival in late 2001 of talented New Zealand winemaker Brett Jackson quality has been pushed up a few notches. The premium blend, Caballo Loco, is made by a solera system and thus carries no vintage date; it usually contains about 50 per cent of the previous year's blend. A recent addition to the top tier is the leather-scented Eclat, based on old-vine Carignan from Maule.

Los Vascos ☆☆
Colchagua. Owner: Domaines Barons de Rothschild (Lafite) and the Claro group. 580 ha.
www.vinalosvascos.com
Los Vascos is a French-Chilean collaboration, which has attempted to squeeze Chilean fruit into a Bordeaux mould. Yet the wines have yet to reach the level that this sort of potential suggests. However, the top bottling, Le Dix, sourced from old Cabernet vines, has shown considerable improvement over recent vintages, thanks to fine-tuning by new winemaker Marco Puyo (who moved to San Pedro in 2006).

Ventisquero ☆–☆☆☆
Rancagua. Owner: Agrosuper group. 1,600 ha.
www.ventisquero.com
With amazing rapidity, Chile's largest chicken producer has developed vineyards and a series of ranges of wines targeted at different markets, under diverse labels such as Yali, Grey, and Southern Wind. Aurelio Montes has been a consultant to the enterprise, and in 2006 former Grange winemaker John Duval also helped to craft the winery's superb top Syrah, Pangea. Initial releases in 2001 were no more than sound and fruity, but Ventisquero has made great strides in recent years, even with its best Pinot Noir, Queulat.

Veramonte ☆☆
Casablanca. Owner: Constellation. 400 ha.
www.veramonte.cl
Launched in 1996 by Augustín Huneeus (who remains a shareholder), at the warm end of the Casablanca valley, Veramonte even grows Cabernet and Merlot, though it also buys red grapes from Maipo. The whites are fresh and citric, and the reds are much improved, especially the Merlots and the top red blend Primus, which is spicy and lively.

Viu Manent ☆☆–☆☆☆
Colchagua. Owner: Viu family. 374 ha.
www.viumanent.cl
The red wines at this visitor-friendly estate are all sound, but special mention must be made of the Malbecs. No other Chilean estate produces a range of four Malbecs. Two are outstanding: the full-bodied, spicy Special Selection, and the intense, new-oaked Viu One.

The Viu family is developing new vineyards that are potentially superb, so this is an estate to watch, especially now that a new winemaker, New Zealander Grant Phelps, is in place and expanding the range with white wines from Casablanca and a Viognier.

Argentina

Is the soul of Argentina Spanish or Italian? Neither, of course, but its wine in the old days certainly had Italian blood. Argentina is the only country outside Europe with a natural wine culture, the fifth biggest producer and consumer of wine in the world. Through all Argentina's political travails over the past 50 years, the domestic market for wine was so enthusiastic (an annual 90-odd litres a head, more recently falling, as elsewhere, to about one-third that level) that exports were negligible. The local taste was for wines in the Italian style (often sold in *fiaschi* as Chianti then was) or "Reserva" wines kept far too long in cask. In the 1990s, that began to change. The government policy of pegging the peso to the US dollar gave the country a new era of stability. Foreign investors began to buy large vineyards and construct wineries with an eye on the export market. By 2000, there were 1,200 wineries, most of them in the Mendoza region. Yet exports never managed to rise above seven per cent overall. Then, in late 2001, the economy collapsed, and the peso was devalued. Many poorer Argentinians suffered as a consequence, but the new investors, both local and foreign, did not lose heart and remained convinced of both the quality and commercial potential of Argentinian wines. Indeed, fresh investors continue to buy land and construct wineries.

Of the 212,000 hectares under vine, about 140,000 are in Mendoza, which also accounts for over 70 per cent of production. Argentina's other principal grape-growing regions are (from north to south) Salta, San Rafael, and Patagonia, which is divided into two regions, Neuquén and Río Negro. The vineyards of Salta reach as high as 2,000 metres (6,500 feet) in the Andean foothills (the Colomé vineyard is even higher, at 3,100 metres). The most important region within Salta is the Cafayate valley, which produces some notably aromatic white wines and stylish reds. Mendoza City lies only a short distance from Santiago de Chile, but with the highest point of the Andes, Mount Aconcagua, in between. Its surrounding vineyards vary from the very warm plain of Guaymallén to the east, through the central, long-established Luján de Cuyo region just south of the city where the principal bodegas are, up to a height of 1,200–1,500 metres (3,900–4,041 feet) in the Uco Valley to the southwest, where cool conditions are making their impact. Uco is divided into three subregions: San Carlos, Tunuyán, and Tupungato.

Still in the province of Mendoza, but far south over the desert, the vineyards of San Rafael are irrigated by the Atuel and Diamante rivers. Further south in Patagonia, on the 39th parallel and equivalent to Hawke's Bay in New Zealand, is the Río Negro, where wine has, until recently, taken second place to fruit production, but recent releases show great promise. Near the town of Neuquén, also in Patagonia, irrigation has allowed a completely new region to be developed since the late 1990s.

Rainfall is rare in all these regions. The arid air cuts mildew and insect problems to a minimum. Hail, on the other hand, is a frequent scourge. Flood irrigation from the comprehensive canal network has been the rule. Intelligently used, it produces perfect grapes (it also rules out phylloxera), although many growers are now installing drip systems for greater control. Some vineyards are still trained on a pergola system (known here as "parral"), which, when properly managed, can give good results. Zuccardi in Mendoza is an ardent enthusiast for the system – it rarely succumbs to frost damage, but the great majority of growers prefer trellised vines.

Red wines are what Argentina does best – so far. Among the whites, Argentina's unique contribution is the Torrontés, an extremely aromatic variety, related to Muscat, usually vinified dry and thus an ideal apéritif wine. The high valleys of Salta suit it best. Argentina has large tracts of Italian table-wine grapes, among them Bonarda, Barbera, Sangiovese, and some Nebbiolo, but the grapes that will make Argentina's name are Cabernet, Syrah, Merlot, and, most of all, Malbec. Just why Malbec, relegated from Bordeaux in favour of the Cabernets during the nineteenth century, makes such satisfying, juicy-textured wines here, no one is sure. One explanation may be that Malbec was brought here in the 1850s before phylloxera in France, so the plant selection may well be superior to that now in France. In France, Malbec sometimes ripens with difficulty, but in Argentina, ripeness is not a problem, so Malbec rarely has harsh tannins, and, depending on its handling in the winery, can exhibit flavours ranging from blueberry to mocha, from damsons to chocolate.

Argentinian viticulturalists have been enthralled by the influence of high altitude on vine growth – and wine character. The higher the altitude, the lower the average temperature, but the greater the difference between daytime and night-time temperatures. The outcome is much slower ripening, which, it's thought, may result in more intense aromas and flavours. Higher elevations also give thicker grape skins, higher polyphenols, and other benefits. The less welcome news is that some varieties, such as Cabernet Sauvignon, simply won't ripen properly at very high altitudes. Wineries such as Catena have embarked on controlled experiments to compare the results of Malbec planted at varying altitudes, and the future should yield some precise conclusions, rather than the enlightened hunches relied on today.

Argentina's strength lies in its ability to produce well-made and attractively priced commercial wines for the competitive export market, as well as a growing band of powerful, deep-flavoured, structured wines all aiming, with varying success, for status as "icon" wines. The best quality/price ratio lies somewhere in between these two extremes. At its best, Argentinian wine can probably surpass all but the best of Chile for vibrancy and character. Nonetheless, there are still too many dreary, even faulty wines that make it out of the country, usually heavily disguised as new "brands" for markets determined to purchase at the lowest possible price regardless of quality. Caveat emptor.

Leading Argentinian Producers

Achaval Ferrer ☆☆☆
Luján de Cuyo, Mendoza. Owner: Manuel Ferrer and Santiago Achaval. 36 ha. www.achaval-ferrer.com
Achaval Ferrer produces only estate grown wines, from some

of Mendoza's oldest vines. Roberto Cipresso (from Montalcino) makes the wines, and has won a strong following for his highly concentrated and expensive reds, especially his Malbecs from Finca Altamira.

Alta Vista ☆☆☆
Luján de Cuyo, Mendoza. Owner: Aulan family. 175 ha. www.altavistawines.com
Excellent Malbecs at all levels from this French owned property. Alto is one of the top wines of Argentina: 80% Malbec, 20% Cabernet Sauvignon, from 60-year-old vines, and aged in new barriques. Expensive but superb.

Altos Las Hormigas ☆–☆☆
Mendoza. Owner: Antonio Morescalchi. 40 ha. www.altolashormigas.com
A relatively small all-Malbec producer, offering delicious wines, especially the blueberry-tinged Reserva. The winery takes its name from the ants that ate the vineyards one year.

Andeluna ☆☆–☆☆☆
Tupungato, Mendoza. Owner: Ward Lay. 70 ha. www.andeluna.com
An American potato-crisp fortune is behind this property in Uco Valley. Michel Rolland acts as the consultant, so the wines are rich and fleshy, but the Malbecs have elegance, too. The top wine is a Bordeaux blend, aged in new barriques, called Pasionado.

Valentín Bianchi ☆–☆☆
San Rafael, Mendoza. Owner: Bianchi family. 330 ha. www.vbianchi.com
An important and very large producer employing a number of labels, including Genesis, Particular Famiglia Bianchi. The top wines include the Stradivarius Cabernet Sauvignon, but Famiglia Bianchi offers the best value.

Luigi Bosca ☆☆
Luján de Cuyo. Owner: Arizú family. 618 ha. www.luigibosca.com.ar
An outstanding grape grower, with vineyards that are close to organic and now flirting with Biodynamism. The cheapest range is La Linda, but the best wines appear under the Gala and Finca Los Nobles labels. But the wildly expensive Icono, a Malbec/Cabernet blend, is a fruit bomb that lacks finesse.

Walter Bressia ☆☆–☆☆☆
Luján de Cuyo. Owner: Walter Bressia. No vineyards. www.bressiabodega.com
This well-connected winemaking consultant established his own label in 2001. Conjuro, a Bordeaux blend, is his most expensive bottling, but its smaller brother Profundo, despite the pretension of its name, runs it close.

Humberto Canale, ☆
Río Negro, Patagonia. Owner: Giulio Canale. 150 ha. www.bodegahcanale.com
Founded in 1909, Canale is a leading Río Negro winery, exporting mostly under its Black River label. Although the wines are reliable and consistent, they lack personality.

Catena Zapata ☆☆☆
Agrelo, Mendoza. Owner: Dr. Nicolás Catena. 425 ha.
www.catenawines.com
Founded in 1902, Catena became Argentina's largest bulk wine producer. Dr. Nicolás Catena, while an economics professor at Berkeley, got to know the best wines of California and immediately began improving his own wines. Catena has been a pioneer of viticultural research, identifying the best clones of Malbec, and experimenting with high-density and high-altitude plantings.

Catena began exporting in 1991 and was soon regarded as the leading producer of high-quality Argentinian wines, although in recent years some other wineries have achieved similar levels of quality and consistency. There are three bodegas. At the striking, Mayan-style winery in Agrelo, Catena produces the wines sold under the Alamos (excellent value Chardonnay), Catena, and Catena Alta labels. At Bodegas Esmeralda, it produces its largest brand, Argento. At La Rural it produces brands for the domestic and American market, such as Rutini and Trumpeter. The two flagship wines are Nicolás Catena, a magnificent and sumptuous, oaky, Napa-style Cabernet, and Caro, a joint venture with Château Lafite, first made in 2000 and more sleek and structured than the Nicolás Catena. Future projects include a range of single vineyard Malbecs.

Finca La Celia ☆☆
San Carlos, Mendoza. Owner: San Pedro (Chile).
600 ha. www.fancalacelia.com.ar
A new winery for this growing brand opened in 2002. Rich, juicy Reserve Malbec and Malbec blends from Uco Valley, which is also the source of La Celia's top wine, Supremo, a Bordeaux blend with a dash of Syrah.

Chacra ☆☆
Río Negro, Patagonia. Owner: Piero Incisa della Rocchetta. 12 ha. www.bodegachacra.com
Hans Vinding-Diers of Noemía (q.v.) alerted his Italian friend to the existence of a very old Pinot Noir vineyard in Río Negro, which now forms the basis for Chacra, although a new Pinot vineyard has also been planted nearby. The wine is very concentrated and spicy, but, given its very high price, essentially a curiosity.

Chakana ☆☆
Agrelo, Mendoza. Owner: Juan Pelizzatti. 100 ha.
www.chakanawines.com.ar
Well-made commercial wines from a former marketing man, who bought the property in 2003. Both Malbec and Cabernet Sauvignon have been impressive.

Cheval des Andes ☆☆☆
Perdriel, Mendoza. Owner: LVMH. 38 ha.
www.terrazasdelosandes.com

In 1999 Pierre Lurton, director of Château Cheval Blanc in St-Emilion, selected a parcel of old ungrafted vines belonging to Terrazas, and this forms the basis of a luxurious new-oaked blend, with slightly more Cabernet than Malbec. The aim from the outset was to combine New World character with Old World balance, and in this the venture has been successful.

Clos de la Siete ☆☆–☆☆☆
Tunuyán, Mendoza. Owner: consortium of mostly French investors. 400 ha. www.clos7.com.ar
Michel Rolland conceived this remarkable project, based on highly promising terroir in the Uco Valley. Individual investors produce their own wines, and there is a joint wine, Clos de la Siete, composed of around 80 per cent of the total crop. The wine is around 50 per cent Malbec, and made in the rich, powerful style that is Rolland's hallmark.

Colomé ☆☆–☆☆☆
Molinos, Salta. Owner: Donald Hess (California). 30 ha.
www.bodegacolome.com
From very old vineyards high in the Calchaquies Valley in the Cafayate area, Hess has, since 2001, been making a rich, complex blend of Malbec, Cabernet, and Tannat. The second wine is Amalaya.

Dominio del Plata ☆☆–☆☆☆
Agrelo, Mendoza. Owner: Pedro Marchevsky and Susana Balbo. 130 ha. www.dominiodelplata.com.ar.
A good-quality range of wines created by a husband-and-wife team, who are among Argentina's best and most experienced winemakers. Under the Anubis umbrella, Balbo has her own wine, while Marchevsky uses the BenMarco label. Balbo's Cabernet-dominated wine is called Brioso and combines power and stylishness. BenMarco is an unusual and somewhat gamey blend of mostly Malbec, plus Bonarda, Syrah, Cabernet, and Tannat. The basic range, Crios, offers excellent value, especially the perfumed Torrontés.

Eral Bravo ☆☆–☆☆☆
Agrelo, Mendoza. Owner: Matias Sánchez Nieto.
155 ha. www.eralbravo.com
The Sánchez Nieto are a long-established Mendoza family, and this new venture can draw on some of their excellent vineyards in Luján de Cuyo and Uco. The top wine is called YBS, which sounds more like a bank than a bottle, but the standard Cabernet and Malbec varietals are almost as good.

Etchart ☆
Cafayate, Salta, and Luján de Cuyo, Mendoza.
Owner: Pernod Ricard. 450 ha.
This venerable property was founded in 1850. In more recent times, it pioneered drip irrigation in Argentina. The basic ranges are the unoaked Río de Plata line, plus the lightly

Catena Zapata winery, Agrelo

oaked Privado wines. In recent years Etchart seems to be losing ground to more dynamic competitors.

Fabre Montmayou ☆☆–☆☆☆
Vistalba, Mendoza. Owner: Hervé Joyaux. 87 ha. www.domainevistalba.com
Joyaux is a former Bordeaux négociant, so the French influence is strong here. Excellent Malbec, and spicy, oaky Grand Vin from centenarian vines. The company also has vineyards in Río Negro, where it produces some increasingly impressive wines from Merlot and Malbec/Syrah under the Infinitus label.

Bodega del Fin del Mundo ☆☆
Neuquén, Patagonia. Owner: Julio Viola and Grupo La Inversora. 850 ha. www.bodegadelfindelmundo.com
It was Julio Viola who created the irrigated slopes that made possible viticulture in the desert on the outskirts of Neuquén. His was the first of the wineries here, and was completed in 2003. Malbec Reserva is usually the best wine, being better balanced than the expensive and extracted Special Blend. The cheaper Postales and Ventus ranges offer good value, but the winery has yet to make a success of Pinot Noir.

Flechas de los Andes ☆☆–☆☆☆
Tunuyán, Mendoza. Owner: Laurent Dassault and Benjamin de Rothschild. 115 ha.
One of the developments within the Clos de la Siete (q.v.). Gran Corte is a blend of Malbec, Merlot, and Syrah; Gran Malbec, as its name suggests, a pure Malbec. Both are made in a very powerful, no-holds-barred style that is certainly impressive, if somewhat overwhelming on the dinner table.

Finca Flichman ☆–☆☆☆
Maipú, Mendoza. Owner: Sogrape (Portugal) (q.v.). 300 ha. www.flichman.com.ar
Since the Portuguese Sogrape company bought this old estate in 1997, the winemakers have supplemented the rather anodyne Reserva bottlings with some more prestigious *cuvées*.

Dedicado, a Cabernet/Syrah blend, is now an ungainly wine, as are two wines that pay homage to their principal vineyards areas: Paisajes de Barrancas and Paisajes de Tupungato. However, the new Espresiones range shows precisely the vibrancy of fruit at which Mendoza excels.

O Fournier ☆☆☆
La Consulta, Mendoza. Owner: José Manuel Ortega. 94 ha. www.ofournier.com
The Fournier winery hovers like a UFO over the Uco Valley, making it one of the most remarkable modern wineries to be found anywhere. Ortega was a banker, who has thrown his fortune into estates in Chile and Spain as well as here, but so far Argentina is producing the most exciting wines. Unlike other Mendoza wineries, Fournier uses a good deal of Tempranillo in his top blend, Alfa Crux, although the A Crux Malbec, from purchased old vines, is equally exciting. Urban is an inexpensive range explicitly aimed at younger consumers.

Santiago Graffigna ☆☆
San Juan. Owner: Pernod Ricard. 200 ha. www.graffignawines.com
Based in the Tulum Valley since 1870, this large winery focuses on Cabernet Sauvignon and Syrah. Certainly the plump, weighty reds, especially the eponymous Santiago Graffigna blends, are of more interest than the Torrontés or Pinot Grigio.

Infinitus
See Fabre Montmayou.

Kaiken ☆☆–☆☆☆
Luján de Cuyo. Owner: Aurelio Montes. 95 ha. www.kaikenwines.com
When one of Chile's top winemakers turned his hand to Mendoza fruit in 2002, expectations were high, and by and large they have been fulfilled. Both the Reserva and Ultra ranges offer Malbec and Cabernet Sauvignon of complexity and elegance.

Lagarde ☆–☆☆
Luján de Cuyo, Mendoza. Owner: Pescarmona family. 227 ha. www.lagarde.com.ar
Decent commercial Merlot and Malbec, and promising Viognier, a variety first planted by this century old estate. A top Malbec blend called Guarda has lifted overall quality.

Lavaque ☆
Cafayate, Salta. Owner: Lavaque family. 464 ha. www.lavaque.com
Growers for many decades, the Lavaques opened their own winery in 2003. The emphasis is on inexpensive wines, with oak staves often used in place of barrels, under a variety of labels, such as Inca and Finca de Altura; the Nanni wines are made from organic grapes.

Bodega Lurton ☆☆
Tunuyán, Mendoza. Owner: Francois Lurton. 250 ha. www.jflurton.com.
Bordelais brothers Jacques and François Lurton were among the first outsiders to recognize the true potential of Mendoza, although today the company is run by François alone. The ranges are complex, being directed at a variety of different markets, but the best wines are often Piedra Negra, from Uco Malbec aged in new barriques, the Cabernet-based blend Gran Lurton, and the old-vine Malbec blend called Chacayes.

Masi Tupungato ☆☆
Tupungato, Mendoza. Owner: Masi (Italy). 70 ha.
Masi is a master of Corvina and Rondinella in its native Valpolicella, and has duplicated the experience in the very different terroir of the Uco Valley. Both Corbec and Passo Doble are blends of Veneto varieties and Malbec, with the latter wine made by the *ripasso* method for which Masi is known back home. The wines are good, but an aura of eccentricity hangs over the venture.

Mendel ☆☆☆
Luján de Cuyo. Owner: Roberto de la Mota and Santiago Mayorga. 17 ha. www.mendel-wines.com
As former winemaker for Terrazas (q.v.), Roberto de la Mota is among Mendoza's most skilled and experienced practitioners. At his own winery he draws from 80-year-old

vines to create a wonderfully spicy, floral Malbec, and a dense, more structured Cabernet/Malbec blend called Unus.

Monteviejo ☆☆–☆☆☆
Tunuyán, Mendoza. Owner: Catherine Péré-Vergé. 300 ha. www.monteviejo.com
Michel Rolland's Clos de la Siete is filling up with impressive wineries, but none can match the scale of Monteviejo, in complete contrast to the more modest structures at the owner's Pomerol properties. The wines are made on a similarly grandiose scale: a pure Malbec and a Chardonnay under the Lindaflor label, and an opaque, superripe Malbec-based blend under the Monteviejo label. Not for the faint hearted.

Las Moras ☆
Tulum Valley, San Juan. Owner: Penaflor group. 120 ha. www.fincalasmoras.com
Australian consultants have helped since 2001 to focus this fruit-driven brand as it attacks, with much success, the competitive export market. Best-known is the inexpensive Andean brand, and an opulent Malbec/Bonarda blend called Mora Negra.

Nieto Senetiner ☆☆–☆☆☆
Luján de Cuyo, Mendoza. Owner: Perez Companc (energy company). 352 ha. www.nietosenetiner.com
Good-quality wines at all price levels. The top Malbec is called Cadus, and another top wine, the Bordeaux blend Don Nicanor, is ripe, stylish, and balanced.

Noemía ☆☆☆
Río Negro, Patagonia. Owner: Noemí Marone Cinzano. 13 ha. www.bodeganoemia.com
The owner is better known as the proprietor of Castello di Argiano in Montalcino. Her winemaker, Hans Vinding-Diers, worked in Patagonia in the late 1990s, and with his encouragement she bought small vineyards dating from the 1930s and 1950s. The first vintage was 2001. Quantities are small, so Vinding-Diers can adopt a perfectionist and no-expense-spared approach. The wine is beautifully balanced and long, and those on tighter budgets can opt instead for the second wine, J Alberto, which is almost as fine.

Norton ☆☆–☆☆☆
Luján de Cuyo, Mendoza. Owner: Gernot Langes-Swarovski. 680 ha. www.norton.com.ar
A classic Mendoza bodega acquired in 1989 by Austrian owners. The basic varietal range is humdrum, but the oaky Reservas are very reliable, especially the vibrant, plummy Malbec. The top red blends are Privada, excellent for medium-term drinking, and a very oaky, Merlot-dominated blend, Perdriel. These are among Mendoza's most consistent wines.

Bodega NQN ☆☆
Neuquén, Patagonia. Owner: Lucas Nemesio. 160 ha. www.bodeganqn.com.ar
NQN is a highly sophisticated new winery outside Neuquén, with production and marketing conducted like military campaigns. Yet the wines are sound, with very ripe basic wines under the Picada label, and more concentrated bottlings under the Malma label. Only the Pinot Noir disappoints.

Poesía ☆☆☆
Luján de Cuyo. Owner: Hélène Garcin-Lévêque. 13 ha. www.bodegapoesia.com
The Garcins own properties in Pessac-Léognan, St-Emilion, and Pomerol, but have a special fondness for their parcel of old Cabernet and Malbec in Mendoza. The wine is sumptuous yet lively, and the second wine, Clos des Andes, runs it close.

Pulenta ☆☆–☆☆☆
Agrelo, Mendoza. Owner: Pulenta family. 135 ha. www.pulentaestate.com
Until 2002 the Pulenta brothers sold their fruit to Trapiche, but now they have their own label and a highly modern winery. The varietal wines are beautifully made, and the Cabernet Franc has great charm. The top wine is a complex blend called Gran Corte, a selection of the finest barrels of the vintage.

Carlos Pulenta/Vistalba ☆☆–☆☆☆
Luján de Cuyo. Owner: Carlos Pulenta. 58 ha. www.carlospulentawines.com
Carlos Pulenta used to be president of Trapiche (q.v.) and then helped set up Salentein (q.v.), before establishing his own winery on the family estate. Pulenta has an artistic touch, evident from the beauty of the winery itself and the stylishness of the adjoining restaurant, one of Mendoza's finest. The wines, complex red blends with at least 40% Malbec, are ranged in descending order of quality as Corte A, B, and C. Wines produced from Uco Valley fruit are bottled under the Tomero label, a range that includes an outstanding Petit Verdot.

La Riojana ☆–☆☆
La Rioja, Salta. 4,000 ha. www.lariojana.com.ar
An enormous cooperative with 600 members, but with the help of consultant oenologists it has acquired a good reputation for its wines, especially for aromatic Torrontés. The full range of wines is bewildering, but includes a number from organic vineyards; the top bottlings are called Raza.

La Rural
See Catena Zapata.

Salentein ☆☆–☆☆☆
Tupungato, Mendoza. Owner: Mijndert Pons. 885 ha Torrontés. www.bodegasalentein.com
This ambitious modern winery and estate was founded in 1998 by a Dutch agricultural entrepreneur. Progress has been swift, with the construction of a magnificent winery, cultural centre, and restaurant, and, from 2004, a separate winery for the second range of wine called El Portillo. The range offers a good selection of varietals, and the best wines are bottled under the Primus label. Of particular interest are the Pinot Noir vineyards, planted at 1,500 metres (4,040 feet). In style these are restrained and elegant wines, showing clearly the benefits of high-altitude viticulture in the Uco Valley.

Santa Julia
See Zuccardi.

Saurus ☆☆
Neuquén, Patagonia. Owner: Schroeder family. 125 ha. www.familiaschroeder.com.

Saurus is one of a group of wineries sharing a slope with Fin del Mundo and NQN, and the first vintage was 2003. The best wines are bottled as Patagonia Select, and here Cabernet and Malbec are particularly successful, with Pinot Noir meriting an honourable mention.

Finca Sophenia ☆–☆☆☆
Tupungato, Mendoza. Owner: Roberto Luka. 130 ha. www.sophenia.com.ar
This winery, sourcing its fruit from vineyards at 1,200 metres (3,936 feet) in Uco Valley, got off to a poor start in 2002, but quality has improved dramatically. Altosur is the basic range, and delivers good value. The wines under the Sophenia label show more concentration, and the Cabernet and Malbec are both excellent. The top wines, including an outstanding red blend, are called Synthesis.

Terrazas ☆☆–☆☆☆
Perdriel, Mendoza. Owner: LVMH. 1000 ha. www.terrazasdelosandes.com
From vineyards at an altitude varying from 750–1,200 metres (2,460–3,936 feet), the Terrazas team, led since 2006 by Pablo Rodriguez, produces wines of excellent quality. Terrazas is the basic range, but the Reserve and top Afincado lines, aged mostly in French oak, are worth the extra cost. Terrazas also has a joint venture with Château Cheval Blanc called Cheval des Andes (q.v.).

Michel Torino ☆–☆☆
Cafayate, Salta. Owner: Peñaflor. 420 ha. www.micheltorino.com.ar
Torino has benefited from enormous investments made by a succession of recent owners, culminating in Peñaflor's (q.v.) acquisition in 1999. Since 2006 the vineyards have been certified as organic. Although Cafayate has a good reputation for its Torrontés, Torino's red wines are now distinctly better than the whites. The uninspired basic range is called Collección; the top wines are bottled as Don David and include an unusually zesty, spicy Malbec. Altimus is a super-premium export label, based on Malbec with additions of Syrah and Cabernet.

Pascual Toso ☆☆
Guaymallén, Mendoza. Owner: J Llorenta y Cía. 400 ha. www.bodegastoso.com.
The ebullient Enrique Toso remains at the helm of a concern best-known for fine Cabernets, made from very old vines, and for a substantial production of sparkling wines, some of which are made by the classic method. The top wine is the Merlot-dominated Maddalena, made with advice from Californian consultant Paul Hobbs.

Trapiche ☆–☆☆☆
Maipú, Mendoza. Owner: Peñaflor group. 1,075 ha. www.trapiche.com.ar

Argentinians in traditional dress at local festival

Although Trapiche produces almost three million cases each year, it maintains high standards. Former winemaker Angel Mendoza set the standard, which has been admirably maintained by his successor Daniel Pi. Among the best wines are the broad, plummy Broquel Malbec, and the pricey Iscay Malbec/Merlot blend, originally developed by former consultant oenologist, Michel Rolland. In 2003 Trapiche launched a limited series of fascinating single vineyard Malbecs.

Trivento ☆–☆☆
Maipú, Mendoza. Owner: Concha y Toro (Chile) (q.v.). 460 ha. www.trivento.com
Trivento's wines follow a Chilean model, in that there is a clear hierarchy of styles and qualities. Despite the resources behind them, the wines lack some personality. However, the Golden Reserve Malbec, from very old vines, has concentration and weight, and there are occasional surprises such as the exotic Chardonnay and the lively Viognier.

Domaine de Vistalba
See Fabre Montmayou.

Weinert ☆–☆☆
Luján de Cuyo, Mendoza. Owner: Weinert family. 40 ha. www.bodegaweinert.com
A medium-sized winery, producing extremely old-fashioned reds, aged for years in old casks. They seem to inspire admiration and bafflement in equal degrees.

Yacochuya ☆☆
Cafayate, Salta. Owner: Michel Rolland and Arnaldo Etchart. 14 ha. www.sanpedrodeyacochuya.com
Pomerol owner and consultant Michel Rolland, a long-time devotee of Argentinian wines, is particularly excited about this vineyard, set at 2,035 metres (6,633 feet), from which he produces a predominantly Malbec wine, aged in new barriques for 12 months. It is dense and extracted, with daunting levels of alcohol in some vintages.

Zuccardi ☆☆
Maipú, Mendoza. Owner: Zuccardi family. 650 ha. www.familiazuccardi.net
This estate, founded by Alberto Zuccardi, was established in the 1960s, and a new winery was constructed in 1998. One-third of the property is now organically cultivated. The winery is technically innovative, having experimented successfully with techniques such as micro-oxygenation and mechanical punching down.

The range of wines is broad, as production feeds a variety of export markets (Santa Julia is best-known in Britain, Santa Rosa elsewhere), and the top wines are smartly packaged under the Q label. These are well-made, commercial wines, rarely disappointing, rarely thrilling. Tempranillo is a house specialty, and to their credit the Zuccardis have launched a range called Innovación, featuring unusual grape varieties such as Verdelho, Marselan, and Tannat.

Mexico

Given the world-class produce of its northerly neighbour, it would be surprising if Mexico were not producing very creditable wines. The oldest American wine industry is being revived with investment from abroad, and technical advice from the University of California at Davis. At present, the country produces 1.6 million cases of wine. Vineyards have been part of the northern Baja California landscape since the 1880s, when Bodegas de Santo Tomás first opened its doors. The industry is far older, having its roots in the Parras Valley, where a mission winery was established in 1597. Today it continues to function under the name Casa Madero.

But it's Baja California, with some 20 wineries operating by 2008, that is the main focus of attention. The Guadalupe Valley, north of Ensenada, and San Vicente to its south, now have extensive vineyards, with fashionable European varieties ousting both the indigenous Mission grape, and other widely grown but less favoured grapes such as Chenin Blanc and Grenache. Most of the wine is exported, since there is little domestic demand, the wine-loving *bourgeoisie* of the cities preferring prestigious imported bottles. However, some wine routes are being established, encouraging visitors from across the border that lies just 13 km (70 miles) to the north to tour the region.

Wente Vineyards of California and the historic Santo Tomás bodega have joined forces to produce a Cabernet Sauvignon, with equal amounts of wine from either side of the border used to make Duetto, a Bordeaux blend aimed at export markets. Another pioneer of the modern wine industry is LA Cetto (with almost 3,000 hectares of vineyards in two separate regions), making successful wines with Chardonnay, Nebbiolo (Cetto was a native of Piedmont), and Cabernet. Best of all is a superlative Private Reserve Petite Sirah.

But it was the investment of Pedro Domecq from Spain that set Mexican wine on a new course. Domecq now has vast vineyards in the Guadalupe Valley. Its premium wine, Château Domecq, is a Nebbiolo/Merlot blend, its white counterpart a Sauvignon Blanc. Freixenet is the other principal Spanish interest, with vineyards in the high-altitude Querétaro region and a predictable focus on sparkling wines. Two new notable wineries in the Guadalupe Valley are the ambitious Monte Xanic, founded in 1988, which has full-bodied Cabernet and Merlot, and rich, barrel-fermented Chardonnays; and Château Camou, which first produced wines in 1995 and is turning out prize-winning Fumé Blanc and Chardonnay. Other rewarding wineries in Mexico are the Swiss-owned Mogor Badan, with a tannic Bordeaux blend; Cavas Valmar, a quality-driven family operation established on the outskirts of Ensenada in 1985 and making good Cabernet Sauvignon; and Casa de Pietra, which succeeds in selling its Cabernet Sauvignon and Tempranillo on the American futures market.

Down south near Mexico City, Domecq and Freixenet have joined the pioneer, Caves de San Juan, in the mountains of Querétaro. Undoubtedly, Mexico has great potential, even if the local taste lags far behind the aspirations of her modern vineyards and wineries.

Brazil

The immense domestic market of South America's largest country, with a population of over 180 million, has led some of the biggest names in drinks – Cinzano, Domecq, Heublein, Martini & Rossi, Moët & Chandon, Suntory, and National Distillers – to invest in Brazil.

By far the biggest and most important of Brazil's wine-growing regions is the Vale dos Vinhedos just west of Bento Gonçalves. At 215-metres (698-feet) above sea level, this sub-tropical region was settled by north Italians in the nineteenth century. Each family planted a small plot of vineyard on the steep slopes of land granted by the Brazilian government. Smallholdings remain important, with at least 16,000 owners cultivating their vines. The other major region is in São Francisco Valley in northeastern Brazil. Here the tropical climate means that talk of traditional growing seasons is irrelevant, so vintages can be staggered. The ViniBrasil project here plans for five vintages each year! Ample sunshine and low rainfall allow grapes of reasonable quality to be produced, and the vineyards are controlled by investors from Portugal as well as Brazil.

Total production is around 400 million bottles per year, but about 80 per cent of the 60,000 hectares of vines are non-vinifera varieties (with better disease resistance) for wines for the domestic market. The best producers are now making acceptable wines from classic varieties, notably Chardonnay, Cabernet, and Merlot, and are experimenting with better clones and trellising systems. Other producers are content with excessively high yields, with predictably uninteresting results. The generally hot and sunny climate suits the vine, although rainfall is often in the form of torrential downpours. Early picking to avoid the risk of disease under these conditions often results in wine that is light in body, and rather high in acidity.

The Brazilian wine industry is dominated by Vinicola Aurora, a huge cooperative in Bento Gonçalves, which draws on 1,300 growers with 1,350 hectares. Sparkling wine has proved surprisingly successful, with Salton, De Lantier (owned by Martini & Rossi), and Chandon do Brasil all producing quaffable bottles. Lidio Carraro produces good Tempranillo, Tannat, and Bordeaux blends in the Vale do Vinhedos. Pizzato follows a similar strategy, but without the Tempranillo. The firm of Miolo has constructed a thoroughly modern new winery, from which it produces sparkling wine, a blend of Portuguese varieties called Quinta da Seival, and a range of wines from São Francisco called Terranova. Although best known for Charmat-method sparkling wine, Salton is making strides with table wines, including some perfectly acceptable Sauvignon Blanc, Teroldego, Merlot, and Malbec.

Peru

One would be forgiven for not knowing that a Peruvian wine industry existed at all, yet wine was being produced close to Cuzco as long ago as 1560. Vines were introduced here by the Spanish conquistador Marquis Francisco de Caravantes. Geographically (only ten degrees from the equator) and socio-economically (political turmoil coupled with hyperinflation of the past), conditions in Peru would not seem conducive to the hedonistic world of grape-growing and winemaking.

Most of the country's 11,000 hectares of grapes go for distillation into the ubiquitous Pisco, to make the Pisco Sour that heals away the heat and dust of the day (despite its proximity to the equator the wine region is arid). The parched lunar landscape results from being on the wrong side of the Andes, and vines need irrigation to thrive.

Two hundred and ninety-kilometres (180-miles) south of Lima along the Pan American Highway, lies the town of Ica, at the heart of Peru's wine region. Viña Tacama is by far the biggest, best, and most important winery in Peru. Founded in the 1540s, it has been solely owned since 1889 by the Olaechea family whose French winemaker, Robert Niederman, ran the property for many decades, producing good Chenin Blanc, Sauvignon, Malbec, and even sparkling wine. Professor Emile Peynaud used to act as consultant here, and Tacama still takes advice from the current generation of Bordeaux academic oenologists. Other quality-focused wineries include Ocucaje, Tabernero, and Vista Alegre.

Uruguay

Uruguay is often called the Belgium of South America: small, flat, and with a population of just three million, it is dominated by its giant neighbours, Brazil and Argentina, both physically and oenologically. Its wine industry is supported by a thirsty local population, almost as avid wine drinkers as the neighbouring Argentinians. The per capita consumption is round 32 litres annually, although only a small proportion of this would be considered fine wine.

Uruguay has been making wine since the 1700s, variously influenced by France, Spain, Germany, and Italy. Basque influence is of particular importance, and the Tannat variety of southwestern France was brought here by a Basque immigrant in 1874. Its Mediterranean-type climate suggests that it is eminently suited to producing quality wine grapes. At present, French grapes predominate, and Merlot and Tannat show particular promise. The country is principally divided into five wine zones which are simply called the Southern, South Western, Central, North Western, and Northern zones. The one showing most potential for quality is also the oldest and largest: the Southern zone, south of the capital Montevideo.

Today Uruguay is active on the export market, where its robust reds and fruit forward whites, all reasonably priced, are attracting increasing attention. Since this small country cannot compete with Argentina and Chile at the cheaper end of the spectrum, it has shifted its focus to fine wine, made without pretension but with considerable sophistication.

Leading Uruguayan Producers

Ariano ☆–☆☆
Las Piedras. Owner: Elizabeth Ariano. 110 ha.
www.arianohermanos
The Ariano vineyards are on two regions, and the focus of the winery is on easy-to-drink, mostly unoaked wines. In top years Ariano produces Don Adelio Tannat, which is aged in American oak.

Bouza ☆☆–☆☆☆
Melilla. Owner: Juan Luis Bouza. 23 ha.
www.boegabouza.com
The Bouzas made their money in the pasta industry and bought this property in 2001 and aimed from the outset at high quality. The Chardonnays, both oaked and unoaked, are stylish, but the various Tannat bottlings are the great success here, combining power and concentration with a welcome vigour and lift.

Castillo Viejo ☆☆
Las Piedras. Owner: Etcheverry family. 130 ha.
www.castilloviejo.com
Once a bulk wine producer, Castillo Viejo has sharpened its act in recent years. The whites see no oak, allowing the fruit of Viognier and Sauvignon Blanc to shine out. But 70 per cent of production is of red wine, the best bottled as The Reserve of the Family. Cabernet Franc as well as Tannat are the most successful wines.

Filgueira ☆–☆☆
Canelones. Owner: Dr. Martha Chiossoni. 45 ha.
www.bodegafilgueira.com
All wines are estate grown, with vineyards that date from the 1920s but were completely restructured and planted to higher densities in the 1990s. The top range is called Premium: the whites are Sauvignon Blanc and Sauvignon Gris, but the reds, from Tannat and Merlot, are considerably more characterful.

Juanicó ☆–☆☆
Canelones. Owner: Deicas family. 240 ha. www.juanico.com
Juanicó is the country's second largest winery, and until the 1970s the vineyards were designed for brandy production. As it continues to move into the fine wine sector, it has hired as consultant the Australian Peter Bright and Michel Rolland from France. Bernard Magrez from Bordeaux is involved with Juanicó in a joint venture, Casa Magrez. The top range, a red blend called Preludio produced only in top years, is now made to a high standard.

Marichal ☆–☆☆
Canelones. Owner: Marichal family. 50 ha.
ww.marichalwines.com
A family winery, very much focused on Tannat, which has drive and concentration, and on Pinot Noir, which can be rustic.

Pisano ☆☆–☆☆☆☆
Progreso. Owner: Pisano family. 30 ha.
www.pisanowines.com
The most dynamic of Uruguayan wineries, with three brothers dividing the work between them. All the wines are made to a high standard, though some of the most prestigious bottlings, such as the new-oaked blend Arretxea, can be rather overwhelming in their fruit and power.

The RPF (Reserve of the Pisano Family) is the most consistent range, but the less ambitious but very attractive Rio de Los Pajaros range is intended to be drunk young. The winemaker, Gustavo Pisano, amuses himself by producing oddities such as Etxe Oneko, a fortified wine from 60-year-old Tannat vines.

Pizzorno ☆–☆☆
Canelón Chico. Owner: Carlos Pizzorno. 20 ha.
www.pizzornowines.com
Founded in 1910, the winery has been moving steadily in recent years into the fine wine sector. Tannat Reserva and the red blend called Pizzorno are the most consistent and successful wines.

Toscanini ☆–☆☆
Canelón Chico. Owner: Toscanini family. 110 ha.
www.toscaniniwines.com
Toscanini produces a substantial range of modern, oaky wines, featuring Tannat, Syrah, and Bordeaux varieties in various combinations.

Australia

Oh, the surprise when modern Australian wine first appeared in Europe. The lush flavours, the full-bodied fruit – the utter drinkability of these wines. Chardonnays that tasted of pineapple and cream, Cabernets full of blackcurrant: no wonder we loved them. That was back in the mid-1980s; and looking back, we shouldn't have been surprised.

Australian wine swept into favour around the world in the mid-1980s, with a suddenness that surprised almost everyone. The world was unprepared for such intensely fruity Chardonnay and Cabernet, lavishly seasoned with oak, at prices far below those for such wines from France or California. But then the world had resolutely ignored the quality of Australian wine for generations. The world had long underestimated the importance of wine in the life of the country, where it is a common pastime to visit cellar doors, or winery retail outlets, to taste, discuss, and, usually, buy. Europeans have rarely acknowledged how knowledgeable and critical many Australians are; how many wineries, wine regions, and "styles" (the favourite Australian wine word) this country, with a relatively small population, can profitably support.

By the early 1980s, open-minded critics overseas were acknowledging that Australia's best wines are excellent: different in flavour from California's but not a jot inferior, and presenting a far wider range of styles. In Australia, Shiraz (the Syrah of the Rhône), Semillon (no é), and Riesling have been excellently grown for decades. First-class Chardonnay and Cabernet joined them in the 1970s. The 1990s saw Australian winemakers make progress with Pinot Noir, and a surge of interest in Rhône-style wines based on Grenache, Shiraz, and Mourvèdre (sometimes called Mataro in Australia). And by the 2000s many growers, especially in Victoria, were trying their hand, often with remarkable success, at Italian varieties.

Growers were innovative but the industry in which they participated was often chaotic. Family vineyards and wineries proliferated, but it was not always easy for them to survive in an increasingly crowded market. The Australian wine industry is volatile, and in the 1990s many successful medium-sized wineries were being taken over by the handful of very large companies that dominated production: Penfolds, Hardys, Orlando Wyndham. Before long some of the very large companies themselves, such as Rosemount, disappeared into the giant maw of what is now Foster's. Where those large companies excelled was in the creation of brands. Australia long ago lost any inhibitions (rarely an Australian failing) about blending wines from different grapes and different regions – even as much as 1,600 kilometres (1,000 miles) apart. And within these regions, until the recent boom, Australia's four main wine-growing states had only half-a-dozen quality areas of any importance. New South Wales had the (then almost moribund) Hunter Valley, to the north of Sydney; Victoria had Rutherglen and its neighbourhood in the northeast, and Great Western in the west. South Australia, throughout the twentieth century much the greatest producer, had the Barossa Valley, Southern Vales, and Clare grouped round Adelaide, and Coonawarra in the remote south. Western Australia had the Swan Valley at Perth. The Murray River, flowing between the three eastern states, irrigated large areas for low-quality wine, most of which was distilled.

The large companies became skilled at mixing and matching, drawing on fruit from different regions and even different states to compose stylistically consistent blends that were perfectly matched to consumers' expectations. Not only in Australia itself, but in export markets, wine buyers soon came to know what to expect from a Rosemount Show Reserve or a Penfold Bin 707. This proved an enormous strength to the industry. No need to worry unduly about the nuances of vintage and appellation: the brand told you all you needed to know. The development of the industry was greatly aided by the Australian show system, in which every region had one or more wine competitions judged, overwhelmingly, by winemakers. The medals handed out by judges were of course useful marketing tools, but many wineries submitted their wines because they genuinely wanted to know whether they were of a high standard. A Bendigo winery might be popular with the locals, but if it wished to expand or export, it was important to know whether the wines were likely to appeal outside the immediate neighbourhood. The judgment of the professionals provided useful guidelines and often identified winemaking flaws. Some criticize the wine shows either as mere money-making exercises or as attempts by judges, who are usually drawn from the big companies, to impose standardized styles that will inhibit the development of more individual winemaking talents. There may be some truth in both these allegations, but overall the show system has so far done more good than harm.

In the 1990s new regions were developed, such as Tasmania, Orange, and Margaret River. In addition, an increasingly knowledgeable public was able to see the merit of regionality. The modern Australian wine lover (and his counterparts abroad) can now argue passionately about, for example, the best areas in which to grew Pinot Noir. With this new interest in regionality came the first stages in the formulation of an appellation system for Australia (the two being intimately related, of course). Some of these attempts to create formal appellations (known rather clumsily as Geographical Indications) have become bogged down in acrimonious law suits, as growers jostle for position, demanding to be included in a prestigious new appellation rather than left just beyond its boundaries.

Despite the enormous appeal of the wines, the Australian wine industry has become increasingly troubled in the current century. Markets once solidly faithful to their wines, such as Britain, have also been flirting with wines from other areas such as Chile and South Africa that offer the same approach to brands as the Australians. One can trust the resourceful Australians to solve pure marketing problems. What is proving more intractable is Mother Nature. Drought is nothing new in parts of Australia, but the shortage of water has become a vexed political issue. Vineyards dependent on generous irrigation are finding that their water supply is either sharply diminished or in danger of vanishing altogether. This affects both the quantity of wine and often the quality of what remains to be harvested. Grape growers are not just in competition with other grape growers; farmers of all kinds are queuing up, often cheque books in hand, for ever decreasing resources. Destructive bush fires can also damage wines. By 2008 experienced winemakers were talking of "smoke taint" as a new flaw being detected in wines from vineyards, such as many of those in Yarra in 2007 and again in 2009, that had been wrapped in smoke from bush fires. (However, only the most sensitive of Australian palates can as yet detect this taint.)

Australians are nothing if not resilient and optimistic, so it is likely that these problems will be resolved. If the global image of Australian wine is still too influenced by brands, visitors to the country will be aware of the astonishing diversity and energy of its wineries and winemakers. Now the industry must find ways to revive international interest in the excellence of the wines.

Australia's Wine Regions

New South Wales

Canberra 350-hectare region of about 35 small wineries clustered around the Australian Capital Territory (ACT), many of them in decidedly cool spots at relatively high altitude.

Hunter Valley Australia's oldest wine region. The Lower Hunter, around Pokolbin, some 160-kilometres (100-miles) north of Sydney, is a long-established producer of serious Shiraz and age worthy Semillon. Cloud cover mitigates the extreme summer heat, but rain often dampens the vintage. Chardonnay and Cabernet have been fairly successful in the past 20 years. The Upper Hunter, developed since the 1960s, is mostly a white wine area, well-suited to Chardonnay.

Mudgee Small, long-established area 160-kilometres (100-miles) west of the Hunter Valley and 365 metres (1,200 feet) higher, with a sunnier, later season. Wines from Mudgee are usually full flavoured, with Chardonnay often the best wine.

Orange 2,750-kilometres (1,709-miles) west of Sydney, this region, which has volcanic soils, was planted in the 1980s at elevations above 365 metres (1,200 feet). Ripeness is problematic at the highest elevations. The region is best-known for Shiraz, Chardonnay, and Riesling. About 1,400 hectares.

Riverina Fertile, flat, fruit-growing land around Griffith, 480-kilometres (300-miles) west of Sydney. Known predominantly for unexciting bulk wines until the mid-'80s, when extraordinary botrytis-affected Semillon emerged as the area's speciality. More sophisticated methods of irrigation are upgrading the table wines, too, although water shortages have put the brakes on expansion.

Other Areas There are a handful of exciting new wine regions that have emerged across New South Wales in the last 20 years, including the warm Hastings Valley in the north, and the cool regions of Cowra and Hilltops in the centre of the state. Southwest of Canberra, Tumbarumba is proving to be a good region for Chardonnay and other grapes destined for sparkling wines.

Victoria

Central Victoria This is a diffuse region, spreading from around the old gold-mining towns of Bendigo and Ballarat, and encompassing the area of Heathcote. All wineries are relatively new, and some excellent wines are produced, with the especially minty, intense, powerful Shiraz styles.

Geelong This cool area southwest of Melbourne was, in the last century, one of Victoria's most promising. It fell victim to phylloxera, but was re-established in the 1960s. Pinot Noir is very successful, Shiraz less so.

Goulburn Valley Important small, historic area 160-kilometres (100-miles) north of Melbourne. Marsanne is a regional speciality.

Grampians Region 225-kilometres (140-miles) west of Melbourne, with fairly new wineries jostling with some very old ones at places like Great Western. The Shiraz is rich and flavoursome.

Macedon Ranges Small, cool, hilly region north of Melbourne, with a growing handful of wineries. Sparkling wine and Burgundian varieties very good indeed. Sunbury to the south, slightly warmer and possibly more suited to red wines.

PRINCIPAL GRAPE VARIETIES

Chardonnay Far and away Australia's most popular white grape variety, planted almost everywhere, and produced in a variety of styles, from green-tinged, unwooded wines that are light and crisp, to deep-yellow, barrel-fermented wines that are rich, creamy, and sweet. Destined to be hugely popular until the end of time.

Shiraz The quintessential Australian red grape, currently enjoying massive interest both at home and overseas. Styles: rich, deep, chocolatey wines in warmer climates such as the Barossa Valley and McLaren Vale; through smooth, soft, and relatively delicate ones in the Hunter Valley; to dusty, peppery, elegant examples in cooler areas such as southern Victoria and Western Australia. Shiraz/ Viognier blends, based, sometimes a little heavy handedly, on the Côte-Rôtie model, are currently ultra-fashionable, but can result in a silky blandness.

Cabernet Sauvignon Like Chardonnay, planted right across Australia, and relatively successful in most areas. At its best in fashionable regions such as Margaret River, Coonawarra, and the Yarra Valley, usually when it is blended with varying proportions of Merlot and Cabernet Franc to produce "Bordeaux blends" that bear little resemblance to Bordeaux.

Pinot Noir After years of promise and occasional brilliance, Pinot Noir producers finally began consistently to crack it in the early 1990s. Styles vary, inevitably, but some exciting, and occasionally world-class, wines are emerging from regions such as Victoria and Tasmania.

Semillon At its best, in the Lower Hunter, Semillon is a total (and thoroughly undervalued) triumph: a light, dry white wine, Chablis-green when young and lively, ageing superbly for up to 20 years. Also promisingly grassy in Margaret River, but many examples in the Barossa or Clare are masked by heavy-handed oak maturation. Also widely used for cheaper sparkling wines, and often blended with Chardonnay.

Riesling Some of Australia's best white wines – excitingly perfumed, crisply dry, and full of the ability to age superbly – and also some of the best value. Outstanding in Clare and Eden Valley.

Mornington Peninsula Cool, fashionable, maritime-influenced region south of Melbourne, with a surprisingly large number of small wineries.

Northeast Victoria Illustrious area, between Milawa and Rutherglen on the New South Wales border, famous for superb dessert wines, especially Muscat. Recent developments include large new vineyards in the King Valley, and smaller ones in the Ovens Valley, Beechworth, and the Victorian Alps.

Northwest Victoria Long-established, mainly irrigated area along the Murray River, stretching from the huge vineyards at Mildura and Robinvale, through Swan Hill and down to Echuca. Source of much of Australia's good-value bulk wine.

Pyrenees Hilly region around the town of Avoca, 193-kilometres (120-miles) northwest of Melbourne. A handful of wineries turn out solid, rather earthy wines.

Strathbogie Ranges About 1,500 hectares planted at elevations of around 365 metres (1,200 feet) on stony granite soils. Good for Riesling and Chardonnay, has potential for Pinot Noir.

Yarra Valley This region has been a vine-growing region since the nineteenth century; 48-kilometres (30-miles) east of Melbourne, it is now re-established and realizing its full potential. Small wineries rub shoulders with some of the state's largest ones to produce exceptional, cool-climate wines – among Australia's best. Fine sparkling wines, too.

Other Areas Whether it is the scattered, disparate wineries of Gippsland, southeast of Melbourne, or the wineries strung along the Great Dividing Range that cuts a swathe through central Victoria and up into New South Wales, there are numerous other regions that add to the state's viticultural colour.

South Australia

Adelaide Hills Still one of Australia's most talked-about "cool-climate" regions, around the Mount Lofty Ranges southeast of Adelaide. Some remarkable Sauvignon Blanc, Pinot Noir, and Chardonnay are produced.

Adelaide Plains Formerly important vine-growing area, including recently restored Penfolds' Magill estate, now largely swallowed by the city suburbs.

Barossa Valley Oldest and most important region, 56-kilometres (35-miles) northeast of Adelaide, settled by Germans in the 1840s. Good all-round producer and home to many of Australia's largest wineries. Renowned for powerful, sometimes too powerful, Shiraz.

Clare Smaller area, 64-kilometres (40-miles) north of Barossa, with as long a history as the Barossa. 396-metre (1,300-foot) hills give it a cooler season in which Riesling does especially well, though Semillon, Shiraz, and Cabernet can also be fine.

SECONDARY GRAPE VARIETIES

Cabernet Franc Initially planted and mostly used to blend with Cabernet Sauvignon, but occasionally crops up as a brightly flavoured, purple varietal.

Chenin Blanc Mainly used as a blending grape, but also occasionally appears on its own as a fresh white wine.

Durif A Shiraz-like grape used occasionally in northeast Victoria for interesting dark wine. Often better than its reputation.

Gewurztraminer Mostly used to produce cheap, sweet, grapey white wine, blended with Riesling, but some makers treat it seriously and with great success.

Grenache Overshadowed by Shiraz, but dry-farmed old vines in Barossa and McLaren Vale yield powerful, succulent Rhône-style reds.

Marsanne Once almost solely confined to the vineyards of Tahbilk, producing remarkably long-lived, aromatic whites, now another beneficiary of the interest in Rhône-style wines, and cropping up in all sorts of places.

Merlot On the verge of creeping onto the list of principal varieties, this red grape started life in Australia as a blender. Plantings have shot up since 1998, but exciting monovarietal versions are thin on the ground.

Mourvèdre Yet another Rhône-style rediscovery, Mourvèdre (or **Mataro**, as it used to be known in its less trendy days) is often found in blends with Shiraz and Grenache.

Muscadelle Occasionally used in dry white blends, but most impressive in its dark, luscious dessert form (known as Tokay) in northeast Victoria.

Muscat Brown Muscat used in northeast Victoria for superbly luscious dessert wines; lesser variety, Muscat Gordo Blanco, or Lexia, used to make a fruity, sweet white in the irrigated areas.

Pinot Gris Some increased plantings in the cooler areas, but it has yet to take off and capture public enthusiasm.

Pinot Meunier Important variety for sparkling winemakers, but not exactly widely planted.

Sauvignon Blanc Nowhere near as successful as in New Zealand, but in certain places such as the Adelaide Hills, central Victoria, Margaret River, and Coonawarra, produces pungent, racy wines.

Verdelho Surprisingly good, gently aromatic white variety encountered in the Hunter and in Western Australia. Often overlooked but can be delicious.

Other Varieties Currently produced on a very small scale (either by one or just a handful of winemakers) but nevertheless providing exciting glimpses of the future include: Barbera, Dolcetto, Nebbiolo, Malbec, Tempranillo, Roussanne, Petit Verdot, Sangiovese, Viognier, Fiano, Arneis, Albariño, Vermentino, and Zinfandel.

Coonawarra Remote area 400-kilometres (250-miles) south-east of Adelaide, on an eccentric flat carpet of red earth over limestone with a high water table. Its latitude makes it relatively cool; its soil is absurdly fertile. The result is some of the best wines in Australia, though in some vintages, Cabernet Sauvignon struggles to ripen. In good vintages the Cabernet can be remarkably long-lived.

Eden Valley Cooler region to the south of the Barossa, home to a handful of high-quality wineries, and a useful source of premium grapes for others. Riesling excels.

Langhorne Creek Tiny historic area, 75-kilometres (47-miles) southeast of Adelaide on rich, alluvial soil. Red wines are soft and wonderfully generous.

McLaren Vale Warm region immediately south of Adelaide. A combination of old, traditional wineries and younger, more modern wineries, most producing particularly good red wines with richness and power.

Riverland The Murray continues its way across the border from Victoria, and the region becomes known as the Riverland. The majority of Australia's bulk production comes from these huge vineyards and wineries, as do some good-value bottled wines.

Other Areas Coonawarra is not the only area suited to the vine in the vast tracts of land south of Adelaide. Neighbouring Wrattonbully has similar soils, and Padthaway has for a long time been an important source of good, cooler climate grapes. Now joined by huge new vineyards in places such as Koppamurra, north of Coonawarra, and Mount Benson, over on the South Australian Limestone Coast.

Western Australia

Geographe New name for the long coastal plain between Perth and Margaret River, home to a handful of diverse wineries.

Great Southern This is a sprawling region of diverse topography and soil, and includes the regions of Mount Barker and Frankland River. There are a growing number of wineries that are attracted to the cool, slow-ripening conditions here.

Margaret River Western Australia's top-quality wine region, 322-kilometres (200-miles) south of Perth, on a promontory with markedly oceanic climate. It does well with a variety of wines, especially sensational Cabernet and Chardonnay.

Chateau Tahbilk was established 1860

Pemberton New, much-hyped region with great potential. The cool-climate has provided some exceptional Pinot Noir and Chardonnay, and fruit from the region is already sought after by wineries in the eastern states.

Swan Valley Old, hot, vine-growing area on the outskirts of Perth, traditionally known for jammy reds, dessert wines, and the famous Houghton "White Burgundy".

Queensland

Minor wine producing state. Most vines are grown in the Granite Belt region just across the border with New South Wales. Although Queensland well deserves its name as the "Sunshine State", the best wineries here are at high altitude and a little cooler.

Tasmania

Following the search for a cooler climate to its logical conclusion, a number of wineries have consequently sprung up in Tasmania, near Launceston in the north of the island and Hobart in the south. Sparkling wines from this region (as you would expect from the relatively chilly conditions) are extremely good, as are Pinot Noir Riesling and Chardonnay.

Northern Territory

The proud possessor of a single winery, Château Hornsby, at Alice Springs, obstinately irrigating in the fierce heat, and producing passable wines, too.

Leading New South Wales Producers

Vineyard holdings are somewhat misleading, since it is very common for estates to supplement their own estate-grown grapes with fruit bought in from neighbouring properties, or even from other regions entirely. Moreover, with a spate of recent mergers and acquisitions, vineyard holdings are often, sometimes rather confusingly, shared among various wineries within the group.

APERA AND TOPAQUE

Quite what sort of committee came up with these names is not clear, but these are what Australian "sherry" and Tokay are now called. Fortified wines were the foundation of the Australian wine industry, and even though fashion has moved in other directions, they can still be sensational. Tokays, in particular, dark, treacly and made from the Muscadelle grape, often come from the same producers as liqueur Muscats and are of equally stellar quality. But the EU doesn't care for these names – "sherry" because sherry comes only from Spain, and Tokay because of Hungarian Tokaji. As part of a deal with the EU, Australia will use the name Apera for its sherry-style fortifieds from 2010, and the name Tokay will be phased out over ten years. Perhaps the names won't seem so comical by then.

Canberra

Clonakilla ☆☆
Murrambateman. Owner: Tim Kirk. 8 ha.
www.clonakilla.com.au
One of the first, and one of the best, producers in the Canberra district. Excellent Riesling and Viognier, but the property is best-known as a pioneer of the Shiraz/Viognier style, first made here in 1992. Clonakilla's remains one of the best.

Lark Hill ☆☆–☆☆☆
Bungendore. Owner: David Carpenter. 10 ha.
www.larkhillwine.com.au
The highest, and one of the best, wineries in the Canberra region. Winemaker Sue Carpenter's wines include Chardonnay, Cabernet/Merlot, delicate Germanic Riesling, and often remarkable Pinot Noir. Biodynamic from 2008.

Hunter Valley

Arrowfield ☆
Jerrys Plain. Owner: Hokuriku. 60 ha.
www.arrowfieldwines.com.au
The Upper Hunter firm has established a reputation for very good value. Now merged with the Red Hill estate in Mornington Peninsula, it has obscured whatever stylistic signature it once had, and most of its wines are now sourced from many regions and states.

Bimbadgen ☆–☆☆
Pokolbin. 40 ha. www.bimbadgen.com.au
The estate wines have a good reputation, but the whites in particular are decidedly sweet. The Shiraz and Botrytis Semillon, however, have lushness and intensity.

Brokenwood ☆☆☆
Pokolbin. Owner: Iain Riggs and partners. 15 ha.
www.brokenwood.com.au
Originally set up by a partnership of Sydney wine-lovers that included wine author James Halliday, Brokenwood is now guided by the phlegmatic Iain Riggs. Multi-regional blends are produced here, but it is the estate wines – in particular superb, limey ILR Reserve Semillon and (atypically sturdy for the region) Graveyard Vineyard Shiraz – that impress most. Its most popular wine by far is the ripe, gently oaky Cricket Pitch Sauvignon/Semillon.

Drayton's Family Wines ☆–☆☆
Cessnock. Owner: Drayton family 55 ha.
www.draytonswines.com.au
This old family company has been making wine since the 1850s. Traditional Hunter styles predominate, with the William Pokolbin Shiraz held back for five or more years to be released at its peak .

Hope Estate ☆☆
Broke. Owner: Michael Hope. 100 ha.
www.hopeestate.com.au
Standard Hunter varietals, plus Merlot. Fresh wines, not too extracted. The winery has moved into the former Rothbury facilities, and Hope has also acquired vineyards in W. A.

Hungerford Hill ☆☆
Pokolbin. Owner: James Kirby. No vineyards.
www.hungerfordhill.com.au
Part of Southcorp for many years, the winery was sold to
a businessman in 2002 and given a new lease of life. Under
winemaker Phillip John's direction, Hungerford Hill offers
smartly packaged wines produced only from fruit grown
in newish wine areas in central and south New South Wales,
such as Hilltops, Cowra, and Tumbarumba. Successes
include Tumbarumba Sauvignon, Clare Riesling, and
Hilltops Cabernet.

Lake's Folly ☆☆☆
Pokolbin. Owner: Peter Fogarty. 12 ha.
www.lakesfolly.com.au
First the hobby, then the passion of a distinguished surgeon
from Sydney, Max Lake. He started the first new Hunter
winery in 40 years, ignoring tradition, to prove that
Cabernet can be the same splendid thing under Hunter
skies as elsewhere. Then he did the same with Chardonnay.
In 2000, the property was sold to a Perth businessman.
Quality remains high, and production small.

McGuigan Simeon ☆–☆☆
**Pokolbin. Owner: A public company. 5,200 ha (managed
and controlled). www.mcguiganwines.com.au**
After selling Wyndham Estate (q.v.) to Orlando, the
McGuigan brothers set up on their own winery in 1992,
and started to build another empire. Production expanded
considerably when Brian McGuigan bought Simeon winery
in Mildura and Miranda, and now tops one million cases.
A vast range of wines is produced, with little clear stylistic
thumbprint. Some Hunter wines are released under the
Personal Reserve label.

McWilliam's ☆☆–☆☆☆☆
Pokolbin. Owner: McWilliam family. 70 ha.
www.mcwilliams.com.au
Although the main winemaking facilities are now at Hanwood
in Riverina, the Lower Hunter remains the life and soul of the
company. The flagship wines such as the extraordinary, long-
lived Elizabeth and Lovedale Semillons and some excellent
Shirazes are made at the legendary Mount Pleasant winery
in the Hunter Valley.

Larger-volume wines are made at Hanwood, and a new
vineyard at Barwang in the Hilltops area is producing
encouragingly flavoursome, cooler-climate style wines.
The company has also bought out other wineries in recent
years: Evans & Tate in Western Australia and Brand's Laira
in Coonawarra. The old fortified sherry-style wines are less
well-known but worth looking out for.

Meerea Park ☆☆
Pokolbin. Owner: Rhys Eather. No vineyards.
www.meereapark.com.au
The Eathers were grape farmers who sold their vineyards in
order to finance their winery. Winemaker Rhys Eather buys
grapes mainly from Hunter Valley and Orange. Among the
white wines there is fresh, clean Verdelho, concentrated
Semillon, and apricotty Viognier. Shiraz is the best red:

Terracotta, which is co-fermented with Viognier, and
Munro, from old vines, which is bottle-aged before release.
These are unusually rich and damsony for Hunter Shiraz.

Petersons ☆–☆☆
Mount View. Owner: Colin Peterson. 100 ha.
www.petersonswines.com.au
An accomplished small winery whose first releases were in
1981. The range includes an exceptional Shiraz, Chardonnay,
a good Semillon, and Cabernet. Many of the grapes are
sourced from the Peterson vineyards in Mudgee.

Poole's Rock ☆☆
Pokolbin. Owner: David Clarke. 92 ha.
www.poolesrock.com.au
Although based in the Lower Hunter, Poole's Rock, like
so many other wineries, draws fruit from other regions, too.
The Poole's Rock label is reserved for wines from the Hunter
vineyards, while Cockfighter's Ghost uses grapes from South
Australia and Tasmania. Quality is patchy but can, as in the
case of the Tasmania Pinot Noir, be high.

Rosemount Estate ☆–☆☆☆
Denman. Owner: Foster's Wine Group. 1,500 ha.
www.rosemountestate.com
Once one of the country's most confident wineries, with some
of Australia's most popular wines in export markets. From
the winery in the Upper Hunter (where the famous Roxburgh
Chardonnay vineyard is situated), winemaker Philip Shaw
drew fruit from across the country to produce a staggering
array of good wines. In 2001 Southcorp acquired Rosemount,
but the marriage was to end in tears.

Today the range has far less coherence than in the past.
Some of the standard ranges, such as the crowd-pleasing
Diamond varietals and Show Reserve wines (now including
a Marlborough Sauvignon Blanc), remain in place, as do
the flagship Roxburgh Chardonnay and Balmoral Shiraz.

Rothbury Estate ☆–☆☆
Pokolbin. Owner: Foster's Wine Group.
www.fosters.com.au
Long-lived Semillon, in the true old Hunter style, made the
reputation of this impressive winery when it belonged to Len
Evans and partners; Syrah backed it up. Changes in ownership
began in 1995, and today Rothbury is just one more brand in
the Foster's portfolio, although it still produces some good
Hunter wines.

Saddler's Creek ☆–☆☆
Pokolbin. Owner: John Johnstone. 12 ha.
www.saddlerscreekwines.com.au
Horse-breeder Johnstone owns this property, with most
wines made from purchased fruit from Langhorne Creek
and McLaren Vale as well as the Hunter. The best-known
brand is Bluegrass Shiraz and Cabernet Sauvignon Their
oaky sweetness makes the wines accessible young. They are
commercial yet sophisticated, but the reds can be tiring.

Scarborough ☆☆
Pokolbin. Owner: Scarborough family. 40 ha.
www.scarboroughwine.com.au

Unusually for this area, the main focus here is Chardonnay, although the Semillon is good, too. The Scarboroughs have acquired and replanted the former Lindemans Sunshine Vineyard, which should prove an exciting source of fruit.

Tempus Two ☆–☆☆☆
Pokolbin. Owner: McGuigan Family.
www.tempustwowinery.com.au
A subsidiary label for McGuigan (q.v.), with its own imposing new winery. As a négociant business, it sources wine from all parts of Australia. Quality varies but the Copper range is made to a high standard.

Tower ☆☆☆
Pokolbin. Owner: Evans family and partners.
No vineyards. www.towerestatewines.com.au
The late Len Evans founded Tower in 1999, and he selected small parcels of outstanding fruit from the Hunter, Clare, the Adelaide Hills, Tasmania, and other regions, the idea being to produce exceedingly good wine in maximum lots of 1,000 cases each. The project has continued since Evans's death, with the emphasis on wines of perfume and elegance. Tower is also the most stylish hotel in the Hunter Valley.

Tyrrell's ☆☆–☆☆☆☆☆
Pokolbin. Owner: Bruce Tyrrell. 370 ha.
www.tyrrells.com.au
Murray Tyrrell was one of the main architects of the Hunter revival of the 1970s, building on a traditional Semillon and Shiraz base, but startling Australia with his well-calculated Vat 47 Chardonnay, the wine that really led the way for the variety in Australia. Despite success with long-lived Vat 9 Pinot Noir, Tyrrell's strength now lies in Shiraz (Vat 9); individual vineyard wines such as Semillons from the Stevens and Belford vineyards, and the dependable Old Winery range. The purchase of vineyards in Heathcote, McLaren Vale, and the Limestone Coast have fuelled an expansion of the business.

Wyndham Estate ☆–☆☆
Dalwood. Owner: Orlando Wyndham. 150 ha.
www.wyndhamestate.com.au
This is one of Australia's oldest wineries and part of the huge Orlando Wyndham group. Consequently, the original Hunter winery is no longer the centre of the operation. Quality is reliable but hardly ever remarkable. The Bin series offers excellent value, but the Show Reserves often show more flair.

Mudgee

Botobolar ☆–☆☆
Mudgee. Owner: Kevin and Trina Karstrom. 22 ha.
www.botobolar.com
The winery sticks to organic principles, and produces some of Mudgee's most engaging wines, especially Shiraz.

Huntington Estate ☆☆–☆☆☆
Mudgee. Owner: Tim Stevens. 40 ha.
www.huntingtonestate.com.au
One of Mudgee's most serious quality wineries. It was sold in 2006, but continues to produce refined but substantial Cabernet blends and Shiraz.

Miramar ☆
Mudgee. Owner: Ian MacRae. 35 ha.
www.miramarwines.com.au
One of the most competent wineries in Mudgee, bringing out powerful characteristics in each variety, especially Chardonnay/Semillon, Cabernet, and Shiraz.

Orange

Bloodwood Estate ☆☆
Orange. Owner: Stephen Doyle. 8 ha.
www.bloodwood.com.au
Stephen and Rhonda Doyle were pioneers in the high region of Orange. Toasty Chardonnay, exotic Riesling, spicy Cabernet, and a ludicrously juicy Malbec rosé called Big Men in Tights.

Brangayne ☆–☆☆
Orange. Owner: Don Hoskins. 25 ha.
www.brangayne.com
The Hoskins family own this small property, with vineyards high up in Orange. Rather heavy, toasty Chardonnay (Isolde), but elegant medium-bodied Pinot Noir and Cabernet/Shiraz blend (Tristan), made under contract by Simon Gilbert.

Cumulus ☆☆
Cudal. Owner: Assetinsure. 509 ha.
www.cumuluswines.com.au
Former Rosemount winemaker Philip Shaw and his partners run the former Reynolds estate, giving them overnight an extensive range of varieties. There are two ranges: Rolling (from Central Ranges fruit), and Climbing (from estate vine-yards planted at over 600 metres/1,950 feet). The Climbing range shows varietal typicity but not, as yet, great character.

Logan ☆
Apple Tree Flat. Owner: Peter Logan. 14 ha.
www.loganwines.com.au
Since 1997, this winery has specialized in wines from Orange, although other ranges such as Weemala also use Mudgee fruit.

Riverina

Casella ☆–☆☆
Yenda. Owner: Casella family. www.casellawines.com.au
Casella is one of the great success stories of the Australian wine industry, thanks to its creation of the hugely popular Yellowtail brand, which has taken the United States by storm.

The wines are frankly commercial, but that is not to say they are mediocre. Some show excessive if crowd-pleasing residual sugar; others have shown well in blind tastings. The company now produces some 12 million cases.

Nugan ☆–☆☆☆
Griffith. Owner: Nugan Group. 600 ha.
www.nuganestate.com.au
Not all the fruit from its extensive vineyards are used for the Nugan wines – many are sold off to bulk wineries. Riesling comes from King Valley, Shiraz from McLaren Vale, some Cabernet from Coonawarra. Although expansion has been rapid, the company does produce some very good wines, with Shiraz and Durif performing exceptionally well.

Other Areas

Cassegrain ☆–☆☆

Port Macquarie. Owner: Simon Gilbert. 154 ha.
www.cassegrainwines.com.au
A fascinating development in the warm region of the Hastings Valley, in the north of the state. In 2005 the property was sold to Simon Gilbert, although Gerard Cassegrain remains involved in the winemaking. Part of the vineyard is being run on Biodynamic principles, and grapes are also sourced from vineyards in various regions. Wines can be very impressive – especially a softly spicy, generous Merlot, and an unusual, vibrant, purple-coloured Chambourcin.

Trentham Estate ☆–☆☆

Trentham Cliffs. Mildura. Owner: Anthony and Patrick Murphy. 60 ha. www.trenthamestate.com.au
A minnow compared to the very big vineyards just across the river in Victoria, but a popular and reliable producer, nonetheless. Whites are clean and tasty, and reds – particularly good Merlot and Shiraz – are characterized by soft, approachable, sweet fruit. La Famiglia is a range devoted to Italian varieties, and includes a richly juicy Vermentino.

Leading Victoria Producers

Because of the plethora of regions within Victoria, producer entries have been organized as follows:
Central: Ballarat, Bendigo, Goulburn Valley, Heathcote, Strathbogie Ranges, Upper Goulburn
Northeast: Alpine Valleys, Beechworth, Glenrowan, King Valley, Rutherglen
Northwest: Murray Darling, Swan Hill
South: Geelong, Mornington Peninsula
West: Grampians, Henty, Pyrenees
Melbourne: Macedon Ranges, Sunbury, Yarra

Central Victoria

Balgownie ☆☆–☆☆☆

Maiden Gully. Owner: Forrester family. 42 ha.
www.balgownieestate.com.au
Mildara bought this Bendigo property in 1986, and in 2001 it was sold again. Its founder, Stuart Anderson, built one of the best names in Australia for Cabernet Sauvignon. In 2002 the company bought vineyards in Yarra Valley to supply it with Chardonnay and Pinot Noir. After a dull patch, the wines have improved greatly since the early 2000s, although the Yarra wines have yet to match the Bendigo Shiraz and Cabernet at their best.

BlackJack ☆☆☆

Harcourt. Owner: McKenzie and Pollock families. 6 ha.
www.blackjackwines.net.au
Planted in 1988, this Bendigo vineyard has become a source of lush, damsony Shiraz that is never overblown.

Delatite ☆–☆☆☆

Mansfield. Owner: Ritchie family. 25 ha.
www.delatitewinery.com.au
Ros Ritchie produces very remarkable white wines and characteristically minty reds from these very cool Upper Goulburn vineyards. Riesling and Gewurztraminer are among the best. His other wines include Sauvignon Blanc, Pinot Gris, and Tempranillo.

Heathcote Estate ☆☆

Heathcote. Owner: Bialkower and Kirby families. 30 ha.
www.heathcoteestate.com
A new venture employing Larry McKenna from New Zealand as a consultant. One of the owners is also proprietor of Yabby Lake (q.v.), and that estate's winemaker, Tom Carson, is also producing the wines here. The vines are young, but there is no doubting that those involved in the property have the will to succeed.

Heathcote Winery ☆☆

Heathcote. Owner: Stephen Wilkins and partners.
18 ha. www.heathcotewinery.com.au
Shiraz, especially the flagship Curagee bottling, is everything one hopes for from Heathcote: elegant as well as full-bodied.

Jasper Hill ☆☆☆☆

Heathcote. Owner: Ron Laughton. 24 ha.
www.jasperhill.com.au
Remarkable wines from a Biodynamically run vineyard in central Victoria. Laughton bought the property in 1979 because he wanted to make Shiraz from ungrafted, dry-farmed vines, and this is where he found the soils to allow him to do so – triumphantly.

Riesling is as fragrant as you could wish for; reds (Georgia's Paddock, a straight Shiraz; Emily's Paddock a Shiraz/Cabernet Franc blend) are massively structured but also gorgeously approachable. Demand far outstrips supply.

Mitchelton ☆☆

Mitchellstown, Nagambie. Owner: Lion Nathan. 150 ha.
www.mitchelton.com.au
An extraordinary edifice, looking like a 1970s monastery, on the banks of the lovely Goulburn River. A lookout tower, aviary, and restaurant were built to attract tourists. But the wines are another matter entirely. The Mitchelton label is used for estate wines: peachy Marsanne, aged in cask and distinctly aromatic for this grape; well-made Riesling; hefty Chardonnay; and excellent Print Shiraz. Other labels include Blackwood Park and Preece.

Sutton Grange ☆☆–☆☆☆

Sutton Grange. Owner: Peter Sidwell. 13 ha.
www.suttongrangewinery.com
A rising star in the Bendigo region. French winemaker Gilles Lapalus has converted the vineyards to Biodynamic farming, and seeks balanced vines that do not produce too much sugar and alcohol. The results are excellent Viognier, a convincing Fiano, and surprisingly floral Shiraz.

Tahbilk ☆☆–☆☆☆

Tahbilk. Owner: Purbrick family. 200 ha.
www.tahbilk.com.au
Victoria's most historic and attractive winery, and one of Australia's best. The old farm, with massive trees, stands by the Goulburn River in lovely country, its barns and cellars

like a film set of early Australia. Dry, white Marsanne starts life light, but ages to subtle roundness; Riesling is crisp but full of flavour and also ages well. The Shiraz is consistently one of the best-value in Australia, and 1860 Vine Shiraz (from the remaining rows of original vineyard) remarkably Old World in style. The Cabernet Sauvignon is more earthy, but also long lived.

Northeast Victoria

All Saints ☆–☆☆☆
Wahgunyah. Owner: Brown family. 65 ha. www.allsaintswine.com.au
Traditional old Rutherglen winery (established 1864), producing a full range of table, fortified, and sparkling wines. Bought in 1991 by Brown Brothers (q.v.) and lavishly renovated. In 1998, Peter Brown became sole owner, but died in 2005. Fabulous Museum releases from ancient soleras of Muscat and Tokay. The other wines are rarely more than adequate.

Bailey's ☆☆–☆☆☆
Glenrowan. Owner: Foster's Wine Group. 143 ha. www.baileysofglenrowan.com.au
The famous makers of heroic Shiraz, a caricature Aussie wine with a black and red label rather like a danger signal. A thickly fruity wine, which ages 20 years to improb-able subtlety. Even better (and amazing value, too) are the dessert Muscats and Tokays, profoundly fruity, intensely sweet and velvety. Ten years ago it seemed likely that the fabulous old stocks of dessert wines would atrophy, but great efforts have been made to refresh them, and they are now up with the best from Rutherglen.

Brown Brothers ☆☆
Milawa. Owner: Brown family. 400 ha. www.brown-brothers.com.au
This old family winery, with vineyards scattered across northern Victoria, seems to be continually expanding and innovating. As well as a wide, reliable range of conventional wines and deservedly popular Orange Muscats, Brown Brothers also experiments with new varieties and styles (mostly sold cellar-door only), such as excellent, ultra-cool-climate Sauvignon Blanc and Italian varietals. The top wines are named Patricia after the family matriarch, who died in 2004.

Bullers ☆–☆☆☆
Rutherglen. Owner: Andrew Buller. 50 ha. www.buller.com.au
Old family firm producing superb fortified Muscat and Tokay at Rutherglen, and some enormously flavoursome – and highly alcoholic – red wines such as Durif at Beverford.

Campbells of Rutherglen ☆☆–☆☆☆
Rutherglen. Owner: Colin Campbell. 64 ha. www.campbellswines.com.au
Under Colin Campbell, this traditional Rutherglen winery

has smartened up its image and modernized its approach. Superlative Muscat and Tokay (especially Merchant Prince and Isabella labels) are still the backbone, but wonderfully spicy Bobbie Burns Shiraz and a stout, impressive Durif called The Barkly Durif are also very good.

Castagna ☆☆☆
Beechworth. Owner: Julian Castagna. 4 ha. ww.castagna.com.au
Biodynamic farming and non-interventionist winemaking result in complex Genesis Syrah (Castagna deliberately uses the French name) and a savoury Sangiovese/Syrah blend called Un Segreto. These have become cult wines.

Chambers Rosewood ☆–☆☆☆☆
Rutherglen. Owner: Chambers family. 50 ha. www.chambersrosewood.com.au
Bill Chambers is a veteran winemaker, eccentric but hugely respected for his old Liqueur Muscat and Tokay, the best of which are of remarkable antiquity. The Rare range contains wines up to 90 years old. The dry wines are truly bizarre, but worth a punt at the cellar door.

Giaconda ☆☆☆–☆☆☆☆
Beechworth. Owner: Rick Kinzbrunner. 12 ha. www.giaconda.com.au
Does any Australian vineyard produce finer Chardonnay than Giaconda? It has a minerality rarely found outside Burgundy, as well as great depth of flavour and longevity. The perfectionist Kinzbrunner also makes savoury, tangy Shiraz, good Pinot Noir, and a pure Roussanne called Aeolia. Quantities are tiny and sold to mailing-list devotees and top restaurants.

Morris Wines ☆☆☆☆
Rutherglen. Owner: Orlando Wyndham. 80 ha. www.morriswines.com
Dave Morris's Liqueur Muscat is Australia's secret weapon: an aromatic, silky treacle that draws gasps from sceptics. The old tin winery building is a treasure-house of ancient casks of Muscats and Tokays, so concentrated by evaporation that they need freshening with young wine before bottling. Magnificent though many other Rutherglen fortified wines are, the Morris Old Premium wines somehow end up winning buckets full of gold medals at Australia's wine shows.

Pfeiffer ☆–☆☆
Wahgunyah. Owner: Chris Pfeiffer. 32 ha. www.pfeifferwines,com.au
Pfeiffer's energies are divided between nurturing his stocks of old fortified Rutherglen Tokay and Muscat, and producing table wines such as Riesling, Marsanne, and Shiraz. The former are more successful.

Tahbilk winery, Goulbourn

Stanton & Killeen ☆☆–☆☆☆
Rutherglen. Owner: Chris Killeen. 45 ha.
www.stantonandkilleen.com.au
A small, old, family winery that has been gradually expanding its range and volumes. Its Cabernet, Shiraz, and Durif are among the best in northeast Victoria. Muscats, Tokays, and vintage "ports" are not as treacly and luscious as some, but are balanced and elegant.

Northwest Victoria

Lindemans ☆–☆☆☆
Karadoc. Owner: Foster's Wine Group. Vineyards in Hunter Valley, Sunraysia, Coonawarra, and Padthaway.
www.lindemans.com.au
Once one of Australia's great wine companies, now part of Fosters. Started in 1870 in the Hunter Valley and celebrated for special "Bin" wines in the 1960s and 1970s that, in many cases, are still drinking well today, Lindemans has now become another mega-brand, producing wines from a variety of sources. The Hunter Valley winery has been run down, and most production is based here in Victoria. At the base of the pyramid is Bin 65 Chardonnay, one of the world's most easily recognized white wines. Other wines include a solid range from Padthaway, and the Coonawarra reds Limestone Ridge (Shiraz/Cabernet), St George Cabernet, and the Pyrus blend.

Southern Victoria

Bannockburn ☆☆☆
Bannockburn. Owner: Hooper family. 27 ha.
www.bannockburnvineyards.com
This Geelong property has had a rough few years. Stuart Hooper died in 2001, and long-term winemaker Gary Farr left in 2005 to found By Farr (q.v.). But his replacement, Michael Glover, has maintained, perhaps even improved quality, fashioning intense Chardonnay and Pinot Noir, all from estate grown fruit. But they don't come cheap.

By Farr ☆☆☆
Bannockburn. Owner: Gary Farr. 17 ha.
www.byfarr.com.au
Gary Farr, former winemaker for Bannockburn Vineyards (q.v.) has, since 1999, had his own label. A stubborn individualist, Farr has mellowed slightly with age, perhaps thanks to the presence of his son Nick at the Geelong winery. Production is very limited, but the Chardonnay, Pinot Noir, and Viognier are all excellent.

Del Rios ☆☆
Anakie. Owner: Del Rio family. 15 ha. www.delrios.com.au
A small Geelong estate, releasing its wines since 2000. Plump, honeyed Marsanne, creamy Chardonnay, and ripe, fleshy Pinot Noir.

Dromana Estate ☆–☆☆☆
Dromana. Owner: public company. 23 ha.
www.dromanaestate.com.au
Glorious Pinot Noir and Chardonnay are made at this Mornington Peninsula property by Duncan Buchanan. Dromana made its name under Garry Crittenden, who was a pioneer of Italian varieties in Australia, but he is no longer involved in the company.

Elgee Park ☆☆
Merricks North. Owner: Baillieu Myer. 5 ha.
www.elgeeparkwines.com.au
The oldest vineyard in the Mornington Peninsula, producing extremely good wines in frustratingly minute quantities.

Kooyong ☆–☆☆☆
Red Hill South. Owner: Giorgio Gjergja. 34 ha. www.kooyong.com
A Mornington Peninsula winery that made its first wines in 2001. Elegant Pinot Noir is the goal of winemaker Sandro Mosele, and of the numerous single vineyard bottlings, the finest is usually Haven.

Lethbridge ☆☆–☆☆☆
Lethbridge. Owner: Ray Nadeson and partners. 10 ha.
www.lethbridgewines.com
Excellent results from this organic Geelong vineyard: a citric toasty Alegra Chardonnay and the sumptuous Indra Shiraz.

Paringa Estate ☆☆☆
Red Hill South. Owner: Lindsay McCall. 22 ha.
www.paringaestate.com.au
The reputation and success of this tiny Mornington Peninsula winery is completely out of proportion to its size. Perfectly sited, trellised vineyards produce exceptional fruit. Chardonnay is intense and lingering; Pinot is wild and spicy; Shiraz dusty and peppery. Nonetheless, in some vintages overripeness results in alarmingly high alcohol, especially in the Pinot Noir.

Scotchmans Hill ☆☆–☆☆☆
Drysdale. Owner: David Browne. 75 ha.
www.scotchmanshill.com.au
This winery is the leading light on the Bellarine Peninsula, south of Geelong. The intense fruit flavours of the Chardonnay and Pinot Noir, made by Robin Brockett, have ensured them a quick rise to the top. Lesser wines are released under the Swan Bay label.

Stonier ☆☆–☆☆☆
Merricks. Owner: Lion Nathan. 20 ha.
www.stoniers.com.au
A consistently successful winery, despite frequent changes of winemaker. Stonier produces complex, extremely well-made Chardonnay, and silky and raspberry-packed Pinot. Not surprisingly, the Reserve range is substantially superior to the standard wines, which, nonetheless, are still good.

Lindemans winery, Karadoc

T'Gallant ☆☆–☆☆☆
Main Ridge. Owner: Foster's Wine Group. 25 ha.
www.tgallant.com.au
Kevin McCarthy created this innovative winery, releasing unusual, quirkily packaged wines, such as hugely ripe and spicy Pinot Gris; yeasty, gently bronzed, white Pinot Noir; crisp, unwooded Chardonnay; and Holystone: a good, dry rosé. Under corporate ownership since 2003, the winery is now focusing on Pinot Noir and Pinot Gris in various forms.

Western Victoria

Best's Wines ☆☆–☆☆☆
Great Western. Owner: Thomson family. 50 ha.
www.bestswines.com
A famous old name in Victoria, highly picturesque in its original buildings at Great Western in the Grampians. Bin O Shiraz is reliably good and surprisingly silky and elegant; Thomson Family Shiraz (exclusively from 130 year old vines) is a much more serious affair: dark, chewy, and glorious.

Blue Pyreenes ☆–☆☆
Avoca. Owner: John Ellis and partners 177 ha.
www.bluepyrenees.com.au
Under new ownership since 2002, this estate continues to offer a wide range of varietal wines and also Reserves. Sparkling wines (especially Midnight Cuvée, a *blanc de blancs* made from grapes that are picked by hand under spotlights at night) have improved considerably. The Richardson Cabernet Sauvignon is usually the best wine, from old vines grown at almost 600 metres (1,950 feet).

Crawford River ☆☆–☆☆☆
Condah. Owner: John Thomson. 21 ha.
www.crawfordriverwines.com
A remarkable little property in the Henty region, first planted in 1975, and for decades the source of brilliant Riesling that can develop well over 20 years. The Cabernet Sauvignon is less successful, and can show a green streak.

Dalwhinnie ☆☆–☆☆☆☆
Moonambel. Owner: David Jones. 18 ha.
www.dalwhinnie.com.au
Possibly the best producer in the Pyrenees region, with powerful Chardonnay (sensibly balanced by savoury, toasty oak); chunky, ripe, black Cabernet; and vibrant, resinous, lingering Shiraz. In 2000, an elegant Pinot Noir was added to this impressive range but was discontinued after 2007.

Mount Langi Ghiran ☆☆–☆☆☆
Buangor. Owner: Rathbone family. 95 ha. www.langi.com.au
Organic Grampians estate, and one of Australia's foremost exponents of rich, peppery, Rhône-like Shiraz, also producing discreet Chardonnay, Pinot Gris, and Riesling. In 2002 the property was acquired by the owners of Yering Station in Yarra Valley, and quality remains impeccable.

Seppelt Great Western ☆☆–☆☆☆
Great Western. Owner: Foster's Wine Group.
www.seppelt.com.au
Under Southcorp and now Foster's, sparkling wine remains the old winery's *raison d'être*. The old cellars at Great Western are now also home to a vast new development that handles sparkling wine production for Southcorp. Seppelt sparklings are still very much the focus here, especially the love-them-or-loathe-them sparkling Shirazes. A revamped range of Seppelt table wines, all from Victorian fruit, have also brightened this winery's image. See also Seppeltsfield (Barossa).

Taltarni ☆☆–☆☆☆
Moonambel. Owner: John Goelet. 132 ha.
www.taltarni.com.au
The brother winery to Clos du Val (q.v.) in the Napa Valley: extremely modern and well-equipped. The original winemaker Dominique Portet made brawny Cabernet Sauvignon and Shiraz in a powerful, tannic style, and the wines aged well.

More Merlot and Cabernet Franc have been added to recent vintages, bringing extra subtlety, and a Heathcote Shiraz, from Taltarni's own vineyards, has been added to the range. Whites are less sure-footed, but Sauvignon Blanc is excellent. Despite the departure of Portet in 2000 to set up his own winery (q.v.), the style remains formidable and tannic. See also Clover Hill (Tasmania).

Melbourne

Bindi ☆☆☆
Gisborne. Owner: Dhillon family. 6 ha.
Macedon Ranges estate producing tiny quantities of greatly sought-after Chardonnay and Pinot Noir. Yields are kept low to maximize the fruit concentration, yet the wines, despite prolonged oak-ageing, are rarely heavy or excessively dense. Two special bottlings, Block 5 and Original Vineyard, seem just about equal in quality.

Coldstream Hills ☆☆–☆☆☆
Coldstream. Owner: Foster's Wine Group. 180 ha.
www.coldstreamhills.com.au
Founded by the country's leading wine critic, James Halliday, the Yarra estate succumbed to a takeover in 1996 from Southcorp (now Foster's). Production has been greatly expanded and Sauvignon and Merlot were introduced. Yet, Coldstream Hills still makes some of Australia's most stylish Pinot Noir and Chardonnay, as well as elegant Cabernet Sauvignon and Merlot. Andrew Fleming makes the wines, with James Halliday as consultant.

Cope-Williams ☆☆
Romsey. Owner: Cope-Williams family. 20 ha.
www.cope-williams.com.au
In a setting that feels remarkably like a country garden in Sussex, the Cope-Williams family (originally from the old country) produce full-bodied sparkling wines from the Macedon Ranges.

Craiglee ☆☆☆
Sunbury. Owner: Carmody family. 10 ha.
www.craiglee.com.au
The self-effacing manner of Pat Carmody hides a skilful grape-grower and winemaker. His Chardonnay is tight and gently toasty, but it is the supremely elegant, enticingly peppery Shiraz that really shines from this historic winery.

De Bortoli (Yarra Valley) ☆–☆☆☆
Dixons Creek. Owner: De Bortoli family. 300 ha.
www.debortoli.com.au
The dynamic Victorian arm of the successful New South Wales wine family. Wines made from fruit grown across Victoria appear under the good-value Windy Peak and Gulf Station labels. Wines from the Yarra Valley vineyards are better quality, especially the citrus-tangy Chardonnay and the dark berry fruited Cabernet.

The range of wines is simply enormous, and complicated by the fact that the family has more vineyards and a winery in Riverina. Since 1982 this has been the source of the heavyweight but delicious botrytis Semillon called Noble One, and other wines under the Sacred Hill label.

Diamond Valley ☆☆☆
Croydon Hills. Owner: Graeme Rathbone. 4 ha
Despite a recent change in proprietor, former owner David Lance continues to produce outstanding Yarra Pinot Noir, as well as Chardonnay and Cabernet. Lance has rightly won acclaim for his powerful and complex Close-Planted Pinot Noir, with its earthy aromas and rich, plummy flavours. Wines from purchased fruit are released under the Blue Label.

Domaine Chandon ☆☆☆
Coldstream. Owner: LVMH. 100 ha.
www.domainechandon.com.au
Exciting Yarra Valley investment, established in 1986 with the foreign expertise of Moët and the local knowledge of Tony Jordan, one of Australia's foremost wine consultants. Wines are made from both estate and bought-in fruit, and aged two years on the yeast. The first commercial classic-method sparkler was released in 1989, and quickly rose to the top of Australia's competitive sparkling wine hierarchy.

Smaller production of *blanc de blancs*, *blanc de noirs*, and a *cuvée prestige* (aged six years and vintage dated) represent exceptional quality. Under the Green Point label, Chandon is making great progress with still Chardonnay, Sauvignon, and Pinot Noir.

Giant Steps ☆☆–☆☆☆
Healesville. Owner: Phil Sexton. 35 ha.
www.innocentbystander.com.au
After Phil Sexton sold Devil's Lair winery to Southcorp, he established this new property in the Yarra Valley. Fruit from local growers' vineyards supplies the Innocent Bystander range, while estate fruit from Tarraford Vineyard has rapidly gained a reputation for serious Pinot Noir and robust Chardonnay.

Hanging Rock ☆☆
Newham. Owner: Ellis family. 6 ha.
www.hangingrock.com.au
Reliable wines from the Macedon Ranges and other parts of Victoria under the (cheap) Rock label, but exceptional quality to be found in wines made from estate fruit. Jim Jim Sauvignon Blanc can be almost searing in its grassy intensity; and Heathcote Shiraz is a powerfully oaky expression of the grape.

Mount Mary ☆☆☆
Lilydale. Owner: Dr. David Middleton. 13 ha.
www.mountmary.com.au
A near-fanatical doctor's pastime that became very serious indeed. John Middleton's Quintet Cabernet blend is like a classic Bordeaux: mid-weight, complex, and intensely fruity. The Chardonnays are strong, rich, and golden; new-oak fermented and, like the Cabernets, easily ten year wines. Exceptional Pinot Noir is also made, but not every year.

Dr. Middleton was impervious to fashion or criticism, and there are many who find the wines too lean and herbaceous, yet there is no shortage of demand for his very expensive wines. Dr. Middleton died in 2006, and this Yarra property is now owned by his son.

Oakridge Estate ☆☆☆
Coldstream. Owner: David Bicknell and partners.
10 ha. www.oakridgewines.com.au
Although this Yarra Valley winery produces good Shiraz, Merlot, and Chardonnay, its financial problems led to various changes in ownership. Today it is partly owned by the skilful winemaker David Bicknell, who has raised quality to new heights. His Chardonnay is especially successful, and Bicknell deliberately avoids any winemaking formulae, adapting to the demands of each vintage.

Dominique Portet ☆☆
Coldstream. Owner: Dominique Portet. 1.5 ha.
www.dominiqueportet.com
After retiring from Taltarni (q.v.), Portet took time off before setting up shop in the Yarra Valley. Current successes include the crisp Sauvignon Blanc and a succulent Heathcote Shiraz.

St Huberts ☆☆
Coldstream. Owner: Foster's Wine Group. 35 ha.
www.fosters.com.au
The modern re-incarnation of one of the Yarra's nineteenth century showpieces. Since Foster's acquired the property, quality has remained good, even though production has increased threefold. Good if tight Cabernet, which is rare in Yarra.

Seville Estate ☆☆☆
Seville. Owner: Graham van der Meulen. 8 ha.
www.sevilleestate.com.au
Tiny vineyard and winery in the southern Yarra Valley. In 1997, it was bought by Brokenwood of Hunter Valley and in 2005 by the present proprietor. Particularly elegant wines, with juicy Cabernet, spicy Shiraz, and low-key, deeply flavoured Chardonnay.

Tarrawarra ☆☆☆
Yarra Glen. Owner: Besen family. 29 ha.
www.tarrawarra.com.au
Single-mindedly striving to produce the region's best Chardonnay and Pinot Noir from a very impressive, expensive winery, and occasionally coming close to achieving that aim. Winemaker Clare Halloran has been careful to

avoid excessive extraction and the wines are poised and stylish, with the Pinot Noir showing remarkable complexity. Tin Cows is the more affordable second label.

Wantirna Estate ☆☆
Wantirna South. Owner: Reg Egan. 4 ha.
www.wantirnaestate.com.au
A tiny estate located in the suburbs of Melbourne, where Egan produces an extremely good Pinot Noir, a most suave, gentlemanly Cabernet/Merlot blend, and tiny quantities of other very well-made wines from Yarra Valley fruit.

Yabby Lake ☆☆
Tuerong. Owner: Kirby Group. 45 ha.
www.yabbylake.com
Under the same ownership as Heathcote Estate and Escarpment in New Zealand, Yabby Lake in Mornington Peninsula has lured one of the country's best winemakers, Tom Carson, away from Yering Station (q.v.). Pinot Noir especially shows enormous promise.

Yarra Burn ☆☆–☆☆☆
Yarra Junction. Owner: Constellation. 10 ha.
www.yarraburn.com.au
Good Yarra producer used by BRL Hardy as a production base for its steep, cool-climate Yarra vineyard, Hoddles Creek – a vineyard so steep that it has inspired a new range of wines rather amusingly called Bastard Hill. The Bastard Hill Chardonnay is first-rate: toasty yet vigorous. Fine Pinot Noir, too.

Yarra Ridge ☆
Yarra Glen. Owner: Foster's Wine Group. 80 ha.
www.fosters.com.au
Now under Foster's ownership, these are medium-bodied wines, well-made but for early drinking and explicitly aimed at the "youth" market.

Yarra Yarra ☆☆–☆☆☆
Steels Creek. Owner: Ian Maclean. 9 ha.
www.yarayarravineyard.com.au
So good they named it twice? A small property, focusing on Sauvignon/Semillon blends that age surprisingly well, a Syrah/Viognier, and a Cabernet Franc and Cabernet Sauvignon blend called Cabernets, aged in French oak. It is medium-bodied, elegant, understated.

Yarra Yering ☆☆☆
Coldstream. Owner: Carrodus family. 36 ha.
www.yarrayering.com
Dr. Bailey Carrodus, who died in 2008, was an individualist who initiated the wine revival of the Yarra Valley, with an unirrigated vineyard producing small yields of high quality fruit. He was not keen on varietal labelling; a Bordeaux-type blend is called Dry Red No 1, a Rhône-type, Dry Red No 2. Both wines are wonderfully forthright, and inescapably Australian in their abundance of fruit. More recently he added Pinot Noir, Viognier, Sangiovese, and a "port"-style wine to his range. All his wines were characterized by their vibrancy and aromatic pungency. The future of this highly individual property is uncertain.

Yeringberg ☆☆–☆☆☆
Coldstream. Owner: Guillaume de Pury. 20 ha.
www.yeringberg.com
The remnant of a wonderful old country estate near Melbourne, making some excellent wines, still in the hands of its Swiss founding family. Pinot Noir, Marsanne/Roussanne, Chardonnay, Cabernet, and Merlot are delicate and charming. The potential of the old estate shows, though production is tiny.

Yering Station ☆☆–☆☆☆
Yarra Glen. Owner: Rathbone family. 115 ha.
www.yering.com
This historic old winery, now completely modernized, was one of Victoria's first, and its renaissance in the mid-1990s was exciting, while wine quality was not always so. It has been expanded by the Rathbones, and a joint venture with Champagne Devaux has resulted in a sparkling wine called Yarrabank. All the wines are well-made and balanced, but it's the Reserves that stand out as exceptional.

Other Areas

Bass Phillip ☆☆☆
Leongatha South. Owner: Phillip Jones. 15 ha.
This tiny Gippsland winery closely resembles a small domaine in Burgundy – in size, approach, passion, and much more than occasionally in the glass. Few other Australian wineries even come close to making Pinot Noir as well as Phillip Jones.

The three grades of quality are always eagerly sought-after, even though the wines sometimes fall short of the purely technical perfection prized by most Australian winemakers.

Leading South Australia Producers

Adelaide Hills and Plains

Ashton Hills ☆
Ashton. Owner: Stephen George. 3.5 ha.
This is the oldest Pinot Noir vineyard in the Adelaide Hills, and the first vintage was 1987. However, the wines are less exceptional than their pedigree.

Bird in Hand ☆☆
Woodside. Owner: Nugent family. 100 ha.
www.birdinhand.com.au
Since 1999, the Nugents have produced stylish reds from the Adelaide Hills, and excellent Clare Valley Riesling and Shiraz.

Chain of Ponds ☆☆
Gumeracha. Owner: Honi Dolling. 220 ha.
Most of the fruit from these vineyards is sold to other wineries, but Chain of Ponds has established a good reputation for an eclectic range of wines under its own label.

The Lane ☆☆
Hahndorf. Owner: John Edwards. 63 ha.
www.thelane.com.au
Edwards used to supply grapes to Hardys, but since 2003 has released wines under his own label from his well-equipped winery. Bright Viognier and Pinot Gris, and bold, peppery Cabernet Sauvignon.

Leabrook ✩✩–✩✩✩
Leabrook. Owner: Colin Best. 3 ha.
www.leabrookestate.com
High-density plantings deliver wines of uncommon intensity
from Pinot Noir, Cabernet Franc, and Merlot.

Longview ✩–✩✩✩
Macclesfield. Owner: Duncan MacGillivray. 80 ha.
www.longviewvineyard.com.au
Since the first vintage, 2001, Longview, has released a diverse
range of wines of very varied quality. The Yakka Shiraz has
been the most consistent.

Nepenthe ✩✩–✩✩✩
Lenswood. Owner: McGuigan Simeon. 110 ha.
www.nepenthe.com.au
Peter Lenske, a winemaker with considerable experience in
Burgundy, brought this estate to the top ranks since the mid-
1990s, but is no longer involved. In 2007 this fine winery was
bought, improbably, by industry giant McGuigan Simeon.

The crisp Riesling and Sauvignon Blanc are the stars among
the white wines, their red counterparts being from the top
Pinnacle range: the leafy Pinot Noir and a Cabernet/Merlot
blend called The Fugue. The style of the wines is tight and
elegant, so they benefit from some bottle ageing.

Petaluma ✩✩✩–✩✩✩✩
**Piccadilly. Owner: Lion Nathan. 500 ha, in the Adelaide
Hills, Coonawarra, and Clare. www.petaluma.com.au**
Despite the takeover of this wonderful property by the New
Zealand brewer, Petaluma remains one of Australia's leading
wineries. All the wines bear the stamp of its brilliant and
dedicated winemaker, Brian Croser, who stayed on after the
sale of the business but finally left in 2005 to set up Tapanappa
(q.v.). The current winemaker is Andrew Hardy. The range
consists of the gloriously limey Riesling from Clare, and the
long-lived Chardonnay from the Piccadilly valley, which
continues to shine. Coonawarra, a Cabernet blend, is clean,
tight, and slow to develop. Recent additions are the Viognier
and Shiraz and the very complex (and expensive) single-
vineyard Tiers Chardonnay. The second label, Bridgewater
Mill, provides more immediate, approachable wines.

Primo Estate ✩✩–✩✩✩
Virginia. Owner: Joe Grilli. 40 ha.
www.primoestate.com.au
Joe Grilli is deceptively softly spoken but a true innovator:
his wines simply shout their flavours and quality. Deliciously
fruity Colombard, silky Shiraz, brave Nebbiolo, and
Sparkling Red with its dry finish, share the limelight
with serious, Amarone-style Cabernet. Based on the hot
Adelaide Plains, Grilli has also been sourcing fruit from
more prestigious regions.

Shaw & Smith ✩✩✩
**Balhannah. Owner: Martin Shaw and Michael Hill-Smith.
80 ha. www.shawandsmith.com**
The fortuitous pairing of winemaker Martin Shaw with
restaurateur, master of wine, and cousin, Michael Hill-Smith
has resulted in one of the best wineries in the Adelaide Hills.

Unwooded Chardonnay is one of the best in the country:
all crisp, apple fruit. M3 Chardonnay is at the other end
of the spectrum, with powerful, creamy, oak treatment;
and Sauvignon Blanc often rivals the best of Marlborough
with its mouth-watering fruitiness. As for the red wines,
Shiraz is proving exceptional.

Geoff Weaver ✩✩✩
Lenswood. Owner: Geoff Weaver. 11 ha.
www.geoffweaver.com.au
Former Hardy's chief winemaker, Geoff Weaver, presides
over his own Adelaide Hills winery, and is producing some
wonderful, classy wines. Sauvignon can be pungently fruity;
Chardonnay invariably brilliant; Riesling floral and limey;
and Pinot Noir uncommonly elegant. Without exception,
these are wines of impeccable balance and clarity.

Barossa and Eden Valleys

Barossa Valley Estates ✩✩–✩✩✩
**Marananga. Owner: Hardys. Vineyards: 65 growers across
the Barossa Valley. www.bve.com.au**
This cooperative, mostly owned by Hardys, is renowned
for its extremely powerful wines under the E & E label.
Typical Barossa Shiraz: jammy, sweet flavours, enhanced
by American oak. The top wines are the E & E Black
Pepper and Ebenezer Shirazes.

Basedow ✩
Tanunda. Owner: James Estate. No vineyards.
www.basedow.com.au
A sometimes excellent Barossa winery, buying in all its grapes,
since the vineyards were sold off in 1982. In the late 1970s,
its Shiraz reached real heights of richness and complexity.
Today the wines are mostly run-of-the-mill.

Bethany ✩✩
Tanunda. Owner: Schrapel family. 46 ha.
www.bethany.com.au
Traditional growers and winemakers with an understated
style that manages to avoid clumsy portiness for the red wines.
There is good Riesling from Eden Valley, intense Reserve
Shiraz, and stylish old-vine Grenache that acquires cherry
fruit and a whiff of tobacco as it ages.

Rolf Binder ✩✩–✩✩✩
Tanunda. Owner: Rolf Binder. 28 ha.
www.rolfbinder.com
Known as Veritas until 2004, Binder's winery changed its name
in 2004 to avoid confusion with an American brand. Rolf
Binder's Austrian and Hungarian origins are reflected in the
names of his wines. In every other respect they are typical
Barossa, hewing fine Grenache and Shiraz from vineyards
he considers outstanding. A zest for experimentation means
that most of the wines are available only in tiny quantities,
which has helped some of them achieve cult status in the
United States.

Wolf Blass ✩–✩✩✩
Nuriootpa. Owner: Foster's Wine Group. 140 ha.
www.wolfblass.com.au

The ebullient Wolf Blass arrived in Australia 30 years ago, and immediately put his skills as a blender and marketer to good use, gradually building up one of Australia's most widely recognized wine empires. If anyone was a pioneer of what have become known as "fruit-driven wines", it was surely Wolf Blass. A series of takeovers and mergers led to Blass's incorporation within the Foster's group.

A heavy reliance on American oak and excessive fruit sweetness led to a period when Wolf Blass wines seemed to have become caricatures of Australian styles. But a new winemaking team under Chris Hatcher has maintained the lush accessibility of the wines, while giving them more finesse and precision. He excels with Riesling and Shiraz.

Grant Burge ☆☆–☆☆☆
Tanunda. Owner: Grant Burge. 440 ha.
www.grantburgewines.com.au
After his Krondorf winery was snapped up by Mildara in 1986, Burge set up on his own. His own vineyards are substantial, but he also buys in fruit. The Riesling and Chardonnay come from Eden Valley, but he is best-known for the excellent Holy Trinity, first made in 1995, a blend of Grenache, Shiraz, and Mourvèdre. Its sleek texture and vibrant fruit are oddly reminiscent of a medium-bodied Zinfandel. His blockbuster Meshach Shiraz, a Grange pretender, is also worth seeking out, as is the Shadrach Cabernet, a blend of fruit from Coonawarra and Barossa.

Burge Family Winemakers ☆☆–☆☆☆
Lyndoch. Owner: Rick Burge. 10 ha.
www.burgefamily.com.au
Rick Burge likes Rhône wines, and his best wines are the peppery Old Vine Grenache and Shiraz, both of which pack a punch.

Leo Buring ☆☆☆
Nuriootpa. Owner: Foster's Wine Group.
www.leoburing.com.au
Although the original Leo Buring winery in the Barossa Valley has now been transformed into Richmond Grove (q.v.), wines under the Leo Buring label continue to be produced at Penfolds, around the corner. Buring himself crafted stunning Rieslings, principally from Eden Valley, and they remain the brand's specialty today, but the Rieslings are sourced from many parts of Australia.

Colonial Estate ☆–☆☆☆
Lights Pass. Owner: Jonathan Maltus. 45 ha.
www.colonialwine.com.au
Not content with creating an ambitious but successful collection of St-Emilion estates, Maltus has, since 2002, founded a flurry of labels at this new estate, based on parcels of old vines he has bought or leased. Primarily Shiraz, these wines are aimed at the export market, and do not fight shy of oak and alcohol.

Dutschke ☆–☆☆
Lyndoch. Owner: Wayne Dutschke. 18 ha.
www.dutschkewines.com
Strictly for fans of porty, oaky Barossa Shiraz.

John Duval ☆☆☆
Tanunda. Owner: John Duval. No vineyards.
www.johnduvalwines.com
The chief winemaker of Penfolds (and hence Grange) for three decades, Duval on retirement launched his own label, since he knew where to find the best fruit in the Barossa. His wines are exceptionally refined and stylish.

Elderton ☆☆
Nuriootpa. Owner: Ashmead family. 60 ha.
www.eldertonwines.com.au
Traditionally huge, chocolatey, alcoholic reds have amassed a clutch of awards at shows, among them the infamous Jimmy Watson trophy for a particularly liquorous Cabernet. Command Shiraz is made from vines planted between 1895 and 1905, and this American-oaked wine is as rich and jammy as one would expect.

Glaetzer ☆☆–☆☆☆
Tanunda. Owner: Glaetzer family.
www.glaetzer.com
Ben Glaetzer has no vineyards of his own, but buys in fruit from good Barossa sites and makes some sturdy Shiraz. Amon-Ra is the top wine, but some will prefer the less flamboyant, and less expensive, Godolphin.

Greenock Creek ☆☆–☆☆☆
Seppeltsfield. Owner: Michael and Annabelle Waugh. 22 ha.
Rave reviews for its Shiraz from the American press has given cult status to this winery. The vineyards are dry-farmed and low yielding, so the wines have all the concentration and power one could wish for. Numerous *cuvées* of Shiraz and Cabernet are produced. Tasted side by side with other Greenock Creek Shirazes, the 7 Acre seems the most complete.

Haan ☆☆
Nuriootpa. Owner: Hans Haan. 36 ha.
www.haanwines.com.au
Ambitious Barossa producer, with bright, jammy Merlot Prestige and a Bordeaux blend called Wilhelmus that has concentration and swagger.

Henschke ☆☆☆–☆☆☆☆
Keyneton. Owner: Henschke family. 110 ha.
www.henschke.com.au
A fifth generation family firm, with two justly famous brands of Shiraz: Hill of Grace (deep wine from ancient vines) and Mount Edelstone (easier, more elegant red). Other wines include a crisp, dry, and delicate Riesling; and elegant blends such as Keyneton Estate from Shiraz, Cabernet, and Malbec; and Johann's Garden from Grenache, Mourvèdre, and Shiraz.

The intense Cyril Henschke Cabernet comes not from Barossa but from Eden Valley. The top reds are easily capable of ageing and improving for 15 years or more. The dream team of winemaker Stephen Henschke and viticulturist Prue Henschke hit their stride ten years ago and have not faltered. The estate has been organic for some years, and Biodynamic trials are underway.

Kaesler ☆☆

Nuriootpa. Owner: Reid Bosward. 37 ha.
www.kaesler.com.au

High-powered Shiraz, the best being designated Old Vine. The most impressive wine is the Old Bastard Shiraz from vines planted in 1893. Winemaker Reid Bosward keeps the tannins nicely under control, and the red wines acquire a leathery warmth with age.

Langmeil ☆☆–☆☆☆

Tanunda. Owner: Lindner and Bitter families. 20 ha.
www.langmeilwinery.com.au

No other property in the Barossa can match Langmeil for the antiquity of its vines: 1.5 hectares of Shiraz planted in 1843. From this parcel Paul Lindner produces the glorious and far from overblown Freedom Shiraz. Other Shiraz bottlings are also of a very high standard, but the whites are disappointing.

Peter Lehmann ☆☆–☆☆☆

Tanunda. Owner: Hess Group. 50 ha.
www.peterlehmannwines.com.au

Peter Lehmann is one of the great showmen and pillars of Barossa, founding his winery when the market for grapes dried up in 1978. Since 2003 the company has been owned by Swiss tycoon Donald Hess, but the Lehmann family remain closely involved. The wines, mostly sourced from over a hundred local growers, bask in their sense of place. Eden Valley Rieslings can be wonderful, and Cabernet and Shiraz can be as rich and full as you'd wish. The top wines – The Mentor (a Cabernet blend), Stonewell, and a host other delicious Shirazes – are worthy newcomers to the pantheon of Barossa legends.

Charles Melton ☆☆☆

Tanunda. Owner: Charlie Melton. 20 ha.
www.charlesmeltonwines.com.au

One of the nicest men in the Barossa, Charlie Melton produces some of the region's best wines. Cabernet and Shiraz stuffed with ripe fruit; Rosé of Virginia, an intriguing cross between a heavy rosé and a light red; and a deep-flavoured Shiraz/Grenache/Mataro blend called Nine Popes, the catalyst for the revival in interest in Rhône styles.

Mountadam ☆☆–☆☆☆

High Eden Ridge. Owner: David Brown. 80 ha.
www.mountadam.com.au

Adam Wynn trained in Bordeaux and established this high-altitude winery with the help of his father, David. After David Wynn died in 1995, Mountadam changed hands twice, and is now owned by an Adelaide businessman, who has installed former Petaluma winemaker Con Moshos to run the property. Chardonnay and Shiraz are the best of the new regime's wines, with a very austere Riesling close behind. The grapes grown here go into the Mountadam range of first class varietals.

Murray Street ☆☆–☆☆☆

Greenock. Owner: Andrew Seppelt. 46 ha.
www.murraystreet.com.au

Founded in 2001, this boutique winery has not been slow to impress. The Greenock Shiraz has splendid blackberry fruit. The flagship wine, Benno, is a Shiraz/Mataro blend that can be rather jammy.

Orlando ☆–☆☆☆

Rowland Flat. Owner: Pernod Ricard.
www.jacobscreek.com

One of the biggest wine companies in Australia, and known worldwide for the phenomenally successful Jacob's Creek, produced by winemaker Philip Laffer and his team. Often maligned, the Jacob's Creek range, especially at Reserve level, can deliver good if not great wines at fair prices. But there is more to the range than this one brand.

PENFOLDS

Few wine companies anywhere else in the world could lay claim to being the undisputed number one in their particular country, but Penfolds undoubtedly occupies that enviable position in Australia.

Since 1844, when Christopher Rawson Penfold and his wife, Mary, established a vineyard at Magill, on the outskirts of Adelaide, the Penfold name has been synonymous with consistency and quality. Initially, of course, and until the middle of the twentieth century, after Penfolds had moved to its current huge winery in the Barossa Valley, most of that wine was fortified.

But from the 1950s on, when winemaker Max Schubert began to release his Grange Hermitage onto an unsuspecting market, the Penfolds banner was held aloft by rich, oaky, quintessentially South Australian reds. More recently, the white wines in the portfolio have begun to show the same kind of consistent quality, but it is still the reds that most wine-lovers associate with the name.

The cornerstone of Penfolds' success is the extraordinary range of choice vineyards – often old and low-yielding – that the company has amassed over the years. These vineyard resources allow almost unlimited flexibility when it comes to blending (the soul of Penfolds – indeed Australian – winemaking), and ensure remarkable consistency of style year after year. This consistency is enhanced by the characteristic Penfolds' trademark: lavish, unrestrained use of new American oak for some, but by no means all, of the top wines.

Not surprisingly, Penfolds has been through a succession of owners over the years, moving from a family empire, through the hands of a couple of major brewers, and finally ending up as the flagship of the enormous Foster's Wine Group. John Duval (q.v.) retired as chief winemaker in 2002, and his successor is the engaging Peter Gago. Penfolds has the confidence, and track record, to publish every five years a book entirely devoted to its own wines, with independent tasting notes.

The Gramp's wines are packed with succulent fruit; Steingarten Riesling, from an individual, rocky vineyard is beautifully steely and tight; and Coonawarra Cabernets such as St Hugo and Jacaranda Ridge, while very oaky, can be very enjoyable. Morris of Rutherglen, Richmond Grove, and Wyndham Estate (qq.v.) in the Hunter, are also part of the empire.

Penfolds ☆☆–☆☆☆☆
Nuriootpa. Owner: Foster's Wine Group. 8,000 ha.
www.penfolds.com
While Grange may no longer be the only true first-growth of the Southern Hemisphere (arguably, Henschke's Hill of Grace has swelled the number to two), Penfolds remains Australia's most esteemed red wine company (see page opposite). Classic Penfolds wines include Kalimna Shiraz, Magill Estate, RWT Barossa Shiraz, and Bin 707 Cabernet Sauvignon. "Port"-style fortifieds are excellent, with Grandfather a legend, and white wines are improving. Its flagship white, the tight, citric Yattarna Chardonnay, has won praise, but few believe it justifies its high price.

Richmond Grove ☆☆–☆☆☆
Tanunda. Owner: Orlando Wyndham.
www.richmondgrovewines.com
Richmond Grove now has its home in the heart of the Barossa, in the old Château Leonay winery established by Leo Buring at the end of the nineteenth century. Fittingly, John Vickery, the winemaker who made some remarkable, seemingly immortal Rieslings under the Leo Buring label during the 1960s, '70s, and '80s, is back here, in a consultant capacity. The best wine is usually the mouthwatering Watervale Riesling, but there is also some delicious Pinot Gris and Pinot Noir from the Adelaide Hills.

Rockford ☆☆☆
Tanunda. Owner: Robert O'Callaghan. No vineyards.
www.rockfordwines.com.au
Small Barossa winery with one of the region's true characters, the reticent Rocky O'Callaghan, at the helm. Styles are particularly regional and thoroughly traditional: big, brawny Grenache and Basket Press Shiraz are totally seductive, as is the exceedingly rare but worth searching for Sparkling Black Shiraz, which has achieved an almost cult following.

St Hallett ☆☆–☆☆☆
Tanunda. Owner: Lion Nathan. 40 ha.
www.sthallett.com.au
Across the board, the wide variety of styles made here by winemaker Stuart Blackwell are good, but the Old Block Shiraz (one of the first wines to exploit the marketing potential of the Barossa's ancient viticultural heritage) is consistently top of the tree. Good Eden Valley Riesling too, and a bargain white Poacher's Blend.

Saltram ☆☆–☆☆☆
Angaston. Owner: Foster's Wine Group. 120 ha.
www.saltramwines.com.au.
For a while, in the 1960s and '70s, when Peter Lehmann was winemaker, Saltram produced classic red wines such as Mamre Brook Cabernet and Metala Shiraz/Cabernet. During the '80s, under the ownership of Seagram, quality was reliable but sluggish. After the takeover by what is now Foster's, there were fears for Saltram's future, but winemaker Nigel Dolan has steered Saltram back to its former exalted position, especially for Shiraz. The second label, Pepperjack, offers excellent value.

Seppeltsfield ☆☆–☆☆☆☆
Nuriootpa. Owner: Holmes à Court family and Kevin Mitchell.
The fate of this magnificent winery, with its fabulous stocks of old fortified wines, was in doubt for some time, until it found new owners with the resources and commitment to maintain the complex. As well as fine Tokay and Muscat, the range includes superb old tawny "port"-styles, such as the century-old and seemingly immortal Para.

Spinifex ☆☆
Nuriootpa. Owner: Peter Schell and Magali Gely. No vineyards.
www.spinifex.com.au
Schell seeks out numerous small vineyards in the Barossa and Eden Valleys, as building blocks for his blends. The winemaking is artisanal, and the results, if sometimes quirky, full of personality.

Historic wine press, Rutherglen

Thorn-Clarke ☆–☆☆☆
Angaston. Owner: Clarke family. 270 ha.
www.thornclarkewines.com
A sleek and well-run winery that only began production in 2002. The basic Sandpiper offers good value, while the best fruit is reserved for the Shotfire Ridge range and the mighty William Randell Shiraz. The winemaking exudes competence.

Torbreck ☆☆☆
Tanunda. Owner: David Powell. 36 ha.
www.torbreck.com
Torbreck has, since 1995, specialized in small quantities of wines that feature various blends of Shiraz and Viognier, with the exception of The Steading, which blends Grenache and Mourvèdre. The Factor is the most expensive *cuvée*, but Run Rig, from 120-year-old Shiraz vines, is as good. These wines are plummy and tannic, as old-vine Shiraz should be, but they are rarely overblown, and the oak handling is masterly. In 2002, marital problems led to the estate going into receivership, but Powell regained control in 2008.

Turkey Flat ☆☆☆
Tanunda. Owner: Peter Schulz. 55 ha.
www.turkeyflat.com.au
Schulz is the custodian of a magnificent Shiraz vineyard from 1847, and some of the Grenache is a mere 90 years old. These as well as younger vineyards are the sources for exemplary Shiraz and a fine Grenache/Mataro/Shiraz blend under the alarming name of Butchers Block.

Veritas
See Rolf Binder.

Yalumba ☆☆☆
Angaston. Owner: Hill-Smith family. Vineyards: plantings at Coonawarra, Koppamurra, and at Oxford Landing on the Murray River. Also three other estate vineyards: Heggies, Pewsey Vale, and Hill-Smith Estate, all in Eden Valley. www.yalumba.com
The sixth generation of the Hill-Smith family is active in this distinctively upper-crust winery that has an air of the turf about it. Its finest wines in the past were "ports", but the fortifieds were sold to Mildara Blass some years ago; since the planting of higher and cooler land in the 1960s, dry whites have been very good and hugely popular.

Yalumba wines range from the bargain bubbly Angas Brut, through reliable stalwarts such as elegant Coonawarra Cabernet The Menzies to The Signature from Cabernet and Shiraz, and the flagship Shiraz, Octavius (aged in 90-litre American barrels called octaves).

Wines from the Hill-Smiths' cooler vineyard estates are also very good. Hill-Smith Sauvignon Blanc is crisp and grassy; Pewsey Vale Riesling is a classic wine, honeyed and long lived; and chief winemaker Louisa Rose has proved herself to be Australia's leading vinifier of Viognier.

Clare

Tim Adams ☆☆
Clare. Owner: Tim Adams. 25 ha.
www.timadamswines.com.au
All wines made by this talented winemaker display solid regional character. Riesling is crisp and limey; Semillon, lemony and balanced with good oak; Aberfeldy Shiraz, full of big, jammy, red fruit flavours; and The Fergus (85% Grenache), suitably heroic. Estate-grown Tempranillo is the latest addition to the range.

Jim Barry ☆☆–☆☆☆
Clare. Owner: Barry family. 247 ha.
www.jmbarry.com
One of the largest wineries in Clare, where Mark Barry produces a wide range. Whites include Chardonnay, Sauvignon, and both dry and sweet Rieslings, of which the finest is La Florita from Watervale. Among the reds are a fine McCrae Wood Cabernet, and a remarkable single-vineyard Shiraz called The Armagh, thick with prune and cherry and spice.

Grosset ☆☆☆–☆☆☆☆☆
Auburn. Owner: Jeffrey Grosset. 22 ha.
www.grosset.com.au

One of Australia's best small wineries. Jeffrey Grosset is a fastidious but open-minded winemaker, producing quite delicious Riesling (Watervale for drinking young, Polish Hill for the long haul), and a Cabernet blend called Gaia, as well as smaller quantities of intense Chardonnay and gamey Pinot from vineyards in the Adelaide Hills.

Stephen John ☆☆
Watervale. Owner: John family. 6 ha.
www.stephenjohnwines.com
Good wines, mostly from Clare, with succulent Riesling and Merlot.

Kilikanoon ☆☆–☆☆☆
Penwortham. Owner: Kevin Mitchell. 300 ha.
www.kilikanoon.com.au
The energetic Kevin Mitchell makes over 20 wines from vineyards in various parts of South Australia, and has recently become part-owner of Seppeltsfield (q.v.). The style is big and burly, and some wines have excessive alcohol, but the excellent Mort's Reserve Riesling shows that Mitchell can show a lighter touch when he wants to.

Knappstein Wines ☆☆–☆☆☆
Clare. Owner: Lion Nathan. 115 ha.
www.knappsteinwines.com.au
This well-known Clare winery, like its parent company Petaluma (q.v.), is now owned by Lion Nathan. The top white is the Ackland Vineyard Riesling, but the winery has always been equally adept with hefty red wines, especially under the Enterprise label.

Leasingham ☆☆–☆☆☆
Clare. Owner: Hardys. 260 ha.
www.leasingham-wines.com.au
New ownership meant a revamp for this famous old winery. Old labels such as the Bin 56 Cabernet/Malbec and Bin 7 Riesling were reintroduced, and a premium range, Classic Clare, added. Riesling is excellent, so are the Cabernet and Shiraz – especially the resinous, thickly textured Classic Clare.

Mitchell ☆☆–☆☆☆
Sevenhill. Owner: Andrew Mitchell. 75 ha.
www.mitchellwines.com.au
A very reliable Clare producer, known for memorable lime-scented Watervale Riesling, plus good Semillon, and vigorous Peppertree Shiraz and Cabernet. All are among Clare's best.

Mount Horrocks ☆☆–☆☆☆
Auburn. Owner: Stephanie Toole. 10 ha.
www.mounthorrocks.com
This vivacious winemaker, one of Clare's best international ambassadors, produces impeccable dry Riesling, and a fascinat-ing sweet Cordon Cut Riesling, made by snipping the stems and leaving the cut bunches on the vine to desiccate. Red wines are increasingly fine, too, especially the plump, berry-stashed Cabernet/Merlot. Stephanie and her partner Jeffrey Grosset share winery premises for their quite distinct labels.

Neagles Rock ☆☆–☆☆☆
Clare. Owner: Steven Wiblin and Jane Willson. 26 ha.
www.neaglesrock.com
The couple began production in 1997 but soon established
a very high level of quality with the classic Clare varieties,
and a convincing Sangiovese to boot.

Pikes ☆☆
Sevenhill. Owner: Pike family. 60 ha.
www.pikeswines.com.au
Andrew Pike was the top viticulturalist for Penfolds, so he
understands vineyards, both his own and those he buys from.
Very good Rieslings lead the range, and most of the red wines
are blends.

Sevenhill Cellars ☆☆
Sevenhill. Owner: Manresa Society. 70 ha.
www.sevenhillcellars.com.au
This old Jesuit church and winery is one of the most
attractive places in Clare, and the wines produced by the
fathers are somewhat old-fashioned, but nonetheless among
the region's best. Monumental in stature, with abundant
fruit and spice, the red St Ignatius, based on Shiraz,
Cabernet, Malbec, and Grenache, is surprisingly drinkable
when young, but also capable of ageing for long periods.
The fragrant Rieslings and the plummy Inigo Shiraz are
also good.

Skillogalee ☆☆
Sevenhill. Owner: David Palmer. 60 ha.
www.skillogalee.com
A fine Clare property benefiting from vineyards that were
planted in 1970 to give concentrated Riesling and a rich
Cabernet blend.

Taylors ☆–☆☆☆
Auburn. Owner: Taylor family. 600 ha.
www.taylorwines.com.au
An extremely large vineyard, with a similarly large
winery, located in a region where such facilities are rare.
The Taylors produce substantial quantities of middle-of-the-
road wines, although the Riesling can often be exceptional.

Since 1999, the best wines have been bottled under the
St Andrews label, with Cabernet and Shiraz clearly the
most exciting wines. There is a sharp upward curve in
quality with the St Andrews range. In some markets,
the wines are sold as "Wakefield" (to avoid any conflict
with a well-known port house).

Wendouree ☆☆☆–☆☆☆☆☆
Clare. Owner: Tony Brady. 12 ha.
This small, old vineyard has produced some of Australia's
most powerful, concentrated red wines for decades.
Thankfully, it seems that nothing is set to change, as Tony
Brady sees himself merely as the guardian of a great tradition,
preferring to interfere as little as possible during the fruit's
passage from vineyard to bottle. An ardent Australian
following means these wines are almost impossible to find.

Coonawarra

Balnaves ☆☆☆–☆☆☆☆☆
Coonawarra. Owner: Doug Balnaves. 52 ha.
www.balnaves.com.au
The Cabernet Sauvignons here, coaxed by winemaker Pete
Bisell from excellent vineyards, are among Coonawarra's best,
especially the top selection The Tally. The peppery Shiraz,
aged in French oak, is also very fine.

Bowen Estate ☆☆–☆☆☆
Coonawarra. Owner: Doug Bowen. 33 ha.
www.bowenestate.com
An ex-Lindemans winemaker, Doug Bowen offers a sleek
Coonawarra Cabernet that can age well. The Ampelon
Shiraz is an uncommonly opulent example from this area,
but only made in top vintages. Emma Bowen now works
at her father's side.

Brand's ☆☆
Coonawarra. Owner: McWilliams family. 300 ha.
www.mcwilliams.com.au
Brand's is now wholly owned by McWilliams, and has become
a reliable source of creamy, plump reds. The Stentiford Shiraz
comes from some of Coonawarra's oldest vines.

Hollick ☆☆
Coonawarra. Owner: Ian and Wendy Hollick. 150 ha.
www.hollick.com
Expanding producer making a successful range of varietals,
and an unusual, for Coonawarra, blend of Sangiovese and
Cabernet called, with a nod to Tuscany, Hollaia. Ravenswood
is the flagship Cabernet.

Katnook Estate ☆☆–☆☆☆
Coonawarra. Owner: Freixenet. 330 ha.
www.katnookestate.com.au
Katnook Estate is one of Coonawarra's most unusual wineries,
in that some of its best wines are often not red but white.
Sauvignon Blanc and Chardonnay are invariably juicy and
measured. The reds are very sound, although the top Odyssey
Cabernet and Prodigy Shiraz can be too jammy for some
tastes. The second label, Founders Block, offers less extracted
wines at a fair price.

Leconfield ☆☆
Coonawarra. Owner: Hamilton family. 44 ha.
www.leconfieldwines.com
The label of the 1980 Cabernet reveals that the grapes were
"picked by experienced girls". This amuses winemaker Paul
Gordon, who shows a similar light-heartedness in his wines,
which are never heavy or extracted. The Cabernet Sauvignon
is invariably the most arresting wine.

Majella ☆☆
Coonawarra. Owner: Lynn family. 60 ha.
www.majellawines.com.au
This highly rated winery offers an oaky but stylish
Shiraz/Cabernet blend called Mallea, and a more restrained
blackcurrant Cabernet Sauvignon.

Parker Estate ☆☆☆
Coonawarra. Owner: Rathbone family. 20 ha.
www.parkercoonawarraestate.com.au.
The Parker family were nothing if not ambitious, and designated their biggest, ripest Cabernet Sauvignon a "First Growth". Fortunately, quality was consistently high, and the winery also produced a Merlot with more individuality than most. In 2004 the property was sold and is now in the safe hands of the owners of Yering Station and Mount Langi Ghiran (qq.v.).

Penley Estate ☆☆–☆☆☆
Coonawarra. Owner: Kym Tolley. 90 ha. www.penley.com.au
Born into a wine family so with wine in his blood, Kym Tolley did his apprenticeship at Penfolds (q.v.), before setting up on his own. He now produces some seriously good wines in Coonawarra, especially a dark, dense, multi-layered Cabernet.

Reschke ☆–☆☆
Coonawarra. Owner: Burke Reschke. 145 ha. www.reschke.com.au
The Reschkes have been farmers in Coonawarra for over a century, but wine production only began in 1998. The range is quite eclectic and includes a delicate Sauvignon Blanc and a piquant Vitulus CS.

Rymill ☆–☆☆
Coonawarra. Owner: Peter and Judy Rymill. 100 ha. www.rymill.com.au
From excellent and extensive vineyards, winemaker Sandrine Gimon manages to fashion very good Cabernet for comparatively low prices. Showpiece winery building and elegant packaging complete the picture.

Wynns ☆☆–☆☆☆
Coonawarra. Owner: Foster's Wine Group. 900 ha. www.wynns.com.au
The Wynns were an important Melbourne wine family making their greatest impact in South Australia. They took over the old Riddoch winery in Coonawarra, and promptly carved a name for the region with some spectacular Shiraz and long-lived Cabernet. Both remain reliably brilliant (with the former excellent value), and have been joined by Chardonnay, Riesling, and a Cabernet/Merlot/Shiraz blend.

Two flagship wines, John Riddoch Cabernet and Michael Shiraz – hugely-structured, massively ripe, opulent wines – crown the range. Given the scale of production here (around 250,000 cases), quality remains gratifyingly high.

Zema Estate ☆☆–☆☆☆
Coonawarra. Owner: Zema family. 65 ha. www.zema.com.au
The personable Zema family and their experienced winemaker Greg Clayfield produce full-bodied, structured, and tannic Shiraz and Cabernet, the Family Selection being the finest

but only made in top vintages. Tastings in 2007 confirm that these wines can develop over two decades.

Langhorne Creek

Bleasdale Vineyard ☆☆
Langhorne Creek. Owner: Michael Potts. 64 ha. www.bleasdale.com.au
The fifth generation of the pioneering Potts family operates this working slice of Australian history (it still has the huge, old, red-gum beam press). In this arid area the vineyards are irrigated by flooding through sluices from the Bremer River. The wines are supple and consistently good value, with the Frank Potts Cabernet Sauvignon often showing some distinction.

Bremerton ☆☆
Langhorne Creek. Owner: Willson family. 120 ha. www.bremerton.com.au
Founded in 1985 by Craig Willson, Bremerton's winemaking has now been placed in the capable hands of his daughter, Rebecca. The best wines, not surprisingly, are red: the delicate Bordeaux blend called Tamblyn, and a jammy Shiraz called Old Adam.

Gotham
Mona Vale ☆☆–☆☆☆
Owner: Bruce Clugston. No vineyards.
Minute production of first rate Shiraz.

Lake Breeze ☆☆–☆☆☆
Langhorne Creek. Owner: Greg Follett. 75 ha. www.lakebreeze.com.au
The Follett family have been growing grapes for 70 years, but only making wine for the past 20. Their Cabernet Sauvignons, made with a light touch but with abundant fruit and discreet oak, are worth seeking out.

McLaren Vale

Anvers ☆☆
Kangarilla. Owner: Wayne Keoghan. 16 ha. www.anvers.com.au
The first vintage at this Adelaide Hills winery was 1998, using estate grapes and a good deal of fruit from other regions. Plump, rich Cabernet and Shiraz.

Battle of Bosworth ☆
Willunga. Owner: Joch Bosworth. 75 ha. www.battleofbosworth.com.au
This organic property grows good Cabernet and Shiraz, but the finished wines often show considerable sweetness.

Chapel Hill ☆☆
McLaren Vale. Owner: Schmidheiny family. 44 ha. ww.chapelhillwine.com.au
In 2000, this well-known property was sold to the Swiss owner of Cuvaison in Napa Valley (q.v.). In 2004 Michael Fragos became the winemaker, and like his predecessor Pat Dunsford

Old red-gum lever press, Bleasdale Winery

is making very attractive and accessible wines. Riesling and Albariño are good, Chardonnay (wooded and unwooded) very good, but the reds, especially the soft, concentrated Shiraz wines, are often exceptional.

Clarendon Hills ☆☆–☆☆☆
Blewitt Springs. Owner: Roman Bratasiuk.
Pharmacist Roman Bratasiuk sources fruit from old, dry-grown, low-yielding vineyards in McLaren Vale, and uses traditional techniques such as natural yeasts and minimal sulphur additions to produce huge, concentrated wines. Mighty Shiraz, Grenache, and Merlot, winning great applause in the USA but little-known within Australia itself.

Coriole ☆☆☆
McLaren Vale. Owner: Lloyd family. 33 ha.
www.coriole.com
Wonderfully ripe Shiraz is the main focus here, but Semillon and Chenin Blanc can be refreshingly grassy, and Sangiovese shows promise. The top Shiraz is the sumptuous, minty Lloyd Reserve, with all the power and concentration that anyone could desire from a McLaren Vale red.

D'Arenberg ☆☆–☆☆☆
McLaren Vale. Owner: Osborn family. 160 ha.
www.darenberg.com.au
With the eccentric but often inspired Chester Osborn at the helm, the family company has become more innovative, with interesting white and red blends, mostly from Rhône varieties.

Highlights include the mighty Dead Arm Shiraz and Laughing Magpie Shiraz/Viognier, and in some vintages, Osborn produces an amazingly raisiny Noble Riesling. With so many wines, there is inevitably some inconsistency, but a D'Arenberg wine is always worth trying.

Dowie Doole ☆☆
McLaren Vale. Owner: three vineyard owners. 37 ha. www.dowiedoole.com
Three partners combined to form this McLaren Vale winery. So far the Shiraz has been their best wine.

Foster's Wine Group
The renowned brewery group has absorbed Southcorp and Beringer Blass and now has an extraordinary portfolio of wineries, large and small. The wineries and brands include: Lindemans, Beringer, Penfolds, Rosemount, Wynn, Seppelt, Devils Lair, Coldstream Hills, St Huberts, Buring, Tollana, Yarra Ridge, T'Gallant, Baileys, Annie's Lane, Rothbury, Maglieri, Saltram, Wolf Blass, Pepperjack, Mamre Brook, Mildara, and Jamiesons Run. This list may shrink if, as has been expected, Foster's decides to shed some of them.

Fox Creek ☆–☆☆
Willunga. Owner: Watts family. 60 ha.
www.foxcreekwines.com
A relative newcomer, with first releases in 1995, Fox Creek has swiftly gained a good reputation for rich and bold Reserve bottlings of Shiraz and Cabernet. The whites are simpler.

Gemtree ☆–☆☆☆
McLaren Vale. Owner: Buttery family. 138 ha.
www.gemtreevineyards.com.au
A very experienced team of viticulturalists and winemakers runs this important property. They produce a wide range of wines, of which the best are the Shirazes. The first vintage was 1998 and the company has yet to show a clear focus.

Hardys ☆–☆☆☆
Reynella. Owner: Constellation. 1,200 ha.
www.brlhardy.com.au
One of the great old Adelaide wine dynasties, now part of the worlds's largest wine group. The family's origins were in McLaren Vale, where rich and fruity reds are still made – including top-of-the-range labels such as Eileen Hardy Shiraz and Thomas Hardy Cabernet – but pioneering vineyard moves into Padthaway and other new South Australian regions have resulted in fruit for a wide range of other well-known wines, such as the Nottage Hill and Banrock Station varietals, the Starvedog Lane range, and the Stamp Series.

Quality is increasingly encouraging. Hardys has also absorbed many important wineries, such as Houghton, Leasingham, Yarra Burn, and Chateau Reynella (qq.v.).

Geoff Merrill Wines ☆☆–☆☆☆
Woodcroft. Owner: Geoff Merrill. 60 ha.
geoffmerrillwines.com
Geoff Merrill is one of Australia's highest-profile winemaking characters, a former enfant terrible who remains as energetic and dynamic as in his youth. Serious, surprisingly understated, and elegant wines are released under his eponymous label, while much more approachable, fruity wines come out as Mount Hurtle. Shiraz has become the house specialty, with powerful yet refined Reserves. At the top of the range is the high-priced Henley Shiraz.

Mitolo ☆☆–☆☆☆
Virginia. Owner: Frank Mitolo.
www.mitolowines.com.au
Farmer Frank Mitolo had the foresight to hire Ben Glaetzer to make his wines, and the result is a fine collection of Shiraz and Cabernet bottlings, all of which show concentration and flair.

S C Pannell ☆☆–☆☆☆
Wayville. Owner: Stephen Pannell. No vineyards.
Steve Pannell was largely responsible for the top wines at Hardys over many years, and has now set up his own, more artisanal winemaking company, specializing in small quantities of beautifully crafted varietal wines from McLaren Vale and the Adelaide Hills.

Penny's Hill ☆–☆☆
McLaren Vale. Owner: Tony Parkinson. 44 ha.
www.pennyshill.com.au
A sound range of varietal wines, with somewhat jammy fruit, and inclined to be slack in structure.

Pertaringa ☆–☆☆
McLaren Vale. Owner: Geoff Hardy and Ian Leask. 32 ha. www.pertaringa.com.au
A joint venture between a well-known winemaker and

viticulturalist, Geoff Hardy and viticulturist Ian Leask. The Shiraz is a bit of a bruiser, but there is also Cabernet, Grenache, Sauvignon, and Semillon on offer.

Pirramimma ☆–☆☆
McLaren Vale. Owner: Johnston family. 180 ha. www.pirramimma.com.au
This long-established wine estate is still making bulk wine, but it is also using its own label for clean, blackberryish Cabernet, dense Shiraz, and a vibrant, chocolatey Petit Verdot.

Chateau Reynella ☆☆☆
Reynella. Owner: Hardys. 180 ha. www.hardys.com.au.
Chateau Reynella, with its historic cellar and vineyard just south of Adelaide, was bought by Thomas Hardy in 1982. Steve Pannell (q.v.) revived the reputation of the wines, of which the best are magnificent Cabernet and Shiraz under the Basket Pressed range.

Serafino ☆☆
McLaren Vale. Owner: Steve Maglieri. 125 ha. www.mclarensonthelake.com
High quality Shiraz, never overblown, from a property that has been steadily revamped, for tourism as well as wine production, since it was acquired in 1998.

Shingleback ☆☆–☆☆☆
McLaren Vale. Owner: John Davey. 128 ha. www.shingleback.com.au
Shiraz, which dominates the vineyards, is the clear star at the family winery, founded in 1998.

Tatachilla ☆–☆☆
McLaren Vale. Owner: Lion Nathan. www.tatachillawinery.com.au
Quality was impressive under winemaker Michael Fragos, but since he left to join Chapel Hill in 2004, quality has become patchy, although the top Shiraz wines are rich and shapely.

Wirra Wirra ☆☆☆
McLaren Vale. Owner: Roger Trott. 25 ha. www.wirrawirra.com
The resurrection (in 1969) of a fine old ironstone winery has resulted in the production of essentially more graceful wines than the macho style that more usually emanates from McLaren Vale. Under winemaker Samantha Connew, Wirra Wirra has attained a fine reputation for its reds.

Church Block is a Cabernet/Merlot/Shiraz blend. RSW Shiraz is dark and resinous, and The Angelus blends Cabernet from Coonawarra and McLaren Vale to achieve remarkably harmonious results, with the former's berry fruit and the latter's chocolatey density.

Woodstock ☆–☆☆
McLaren Flat. Owner: Scott Collett. 32 ha. www.woodstockwine.com.au
Woodstock began producing wines in 1982. It now makes a wide range of varietals, including Cabernet, Shiraz, and Chardonnay, as well as an excellent sweet botrytis Semillon and tawny "port".

Other South Australia Producers

Angove's ☆
Renmark. Owner: Angove family. 480 ha. www.angoves.com.au
A conservative old family company, within the Riverland irrigated area, well-known for producing good-value lines from a multiplicity of varieties, as well as sherry-style wines.

Henry's Drive ☆
Padthaway. Owner: Brian Longbottom. 300 ha. www.henrysdrive.com
First vintage here was 1998, with American-oaked Shiraz the leading wine. Production has grown rapidly to 100,000 cases.

Hewitson ☆☆–☆☆☆
Mile End. Owner: Dean Hewitson. No vineyards. www.hewitson.com.au
Dean Hewitson was a winemaker at Petaluma before starting his own négociant business close to Adelaide. Access to outstanding South Australian vineyards is reflected in the quality of the wide range of wines.

Stonehaven ☆☆–☆☆☆
Padthaway. Owner: Hardys. 900 ha. www.stonehavenvineyards.com.au
Founded in 1998, this ambitious Padthaway winery draws on the immense vineyard resources of its parent company, to produce excellent Chardonnay, Cabernet, and Shiraz under the Stepping Stone and Hidden Sea labels.

Tapanappa ☆☆☆
Wrattonbully. Owner: Brian Croser, Jean-Michel Cazes, and Maison Bollinger. 11 ha. www.tapanappawines.com.au
This joint venture of an exalted trio of proprietors gives Brian Croser, since he left Petaluma, the freedom to pursue his ultra-refined style of winemaking. Vineyards are limited at present, but include a section of the Tiers Vineyard in the Adelaide Hills, which Croser made famous for its Chardonnay. Quality so far has been as high as hoped for, but these are early days. In 2007 came the first Foggy Hill Pinot Noir from Fleurieu near the coast south of Adelaide – a wine of lovely purity. There is much more to come.

Two Hands ☆☆–☆☆☆
Marananga. Owner: Michael Twelftree and Richard Montz. No vineyards. www.twohandswines.com
Since 2000, the lush, jammy style of these Shirazes, sourced from many areas in South Australia, has won acclaim, especially in the USA. Scarcity and high prices has helped to whip up the enthusiasm.

Leading Western Australia Producers
Great Southern

Alkoomi ☆☆–☆☆☆
Frankland. Owner: Mervyn and Judith Lange. 102 ha. www.alkoomiwines.com.au
This well-established estate is a pace-setter for the new Frankland area, best enjoyed as clean, tannic Shiraz and crisp, intense Riesling and Sauvignon Blanc.

Castle Rock ☆☆
Porongurup. Owner: Diletti family. 40 ha.
www.castlerockestate.com.au
Well-tended vineyards and a gravity-fed winery help to
produce elegant wines from Sauvignon Blanc and Riesling,
and an often outstanding, silky Pinot Noir.

Ferngrove Vineyards ☆
Frankland. Owner: Murray Burton. 415 ha.
www.ferngrove.com.au
Murray Burton has established vineyards in different parts
of Great Southern, and has also built a new winery and tourist
attraction in 2000, which was also the date of the first vintage.
Cabernet Sauvignon and Shiraz/Viognier are polished, and
the whites juicy. But the range lacks consistency.

Forest Hill ☆☆☆
Denmark. Owner: Tim Lyons. 25 ha.
www.foresthillwines.com.au
Planted from 1965, these are the oldest vines in Western
Australia, and still form the basis for production from
this boutique winery. Former Houghton winemaker Larry
Cherubino is the consultant here. The top bottlings are
from individual blocks of Chardonnay, Riesling, Cabernet,
and Shiraz.

Frankland Estate ☆☆
**Frankland. Owners: Judi Cullam and Barrie Smith.
30 ha. www.franklandestate.com.au**
Frankland Estate has, for many years, backed the cause
of Riesling in Western Australia, and its Isolation Ridge
Riesling is one of the best: lemony with mineral undertones.
Olmo's Reward (a Bordeaux blend) is initially tight and
intriguingly austere.

Goundrey ☆–☆☆
Mount Barker. Owner: Vincor. 185 ha.
www.goundreywines.com.au
Goundrey is one of the Great Southern region's most
dramatically ambitious wineries. Huge investment and
rigorous winemaking resulted in some good wines, especially
the brooding Reserve Shiraz. The wines can lack character,
but there are some pleasant surprises such as the vigorous
Cabernet/Tempranillo.

Howard Park ☆☆–☆☆☆
Denmark. Owner: Jeff and Amy Burch. 230 ha.
www.howardparkwines.com.au
Howard Park draws on its own vineyards, and those of
contracted growers, to make blends incorporating the best
properties of various Western Australian regions. It produces
fragrant, sometimes austere Riesling and Chardonnay, intense
Shiraz, and tight, long-lived Cabernet. Vintage variation is
important here, and acidity levels can be very high in certain
years. Madfish is the label used for simpler wines.

Plantagenet Wines ☆☆–☆☆☆
Mount Barker. Owner: Lionel Samson and Co. 125 ha.
www.plantagenetwines.com
The senior winery at Mount Barker, with John Durham,
formerly of Cape Mentelle, in charge of winemaking since
2007. Chardonnay (either the excellent unwooded Omrah
or spicy, wooded Plantagenet) and perfumed Riesling are
the white wine successes here, and Shiraz, with dusty, edgy
flavours, is remarkably Rhône like. The Cabernet Sauvignon
is tight, even austere, in its youth, but blossoms with eight
years in bottle. Intense, raspberry-scented Pinot Noir, too.

West Cape Howe ☆☆
**Denmark. Owner: Gavin Berry and Rob Quenby.
80 ha. www.westcapehowe.com.au**
A good range of varietal wines, red as well as white, are made
here from the Great Southern vineyards.

Wignalls ☆–☆☆
Albany. Owner: Wignall family. 16 ha.
www.wignallswines.com.au
This vineyard is stuck out on its own near the remote town
of Albany, but has forged an impressive reputation with
some of the state's best Pinot Noir. Shiraz shows promise.

Geographe

Capel Vale ☆☆–☆☆☆
Capel. Owner: Dr. Peter Pratten. 220 ha.
www.capelvale.com
Successful winery, sourcing fruit from all of Western
Australia's principal regions. Dr. Pratten, a former radiologist,
says he wants to make Old World wines from New World
fruit. The ranges have proliferated over the years. The
easy-drinking Debut range does what it intends to do, but
the more distinguished wines are the regional wines (notably
the Margaret River Cabernet and Mount Barker Shiraz)
and from single vineyards, under the Whispering Hills label.

Peel Estate ☆☆
Baldivis. Owner: Will Nairn and partners. 16 ha.
www.peelwine.com.au
Strong California influence shows in this blossoming estate,
which was founded in 1979. Chenin Blanc aged in oak is
modelled on the lovely Chappellet Napa wine. Zinfandel is
clean and aromatic, while Shiraz with 15 months in French
and American oak seems to be a wine for long ageing.

Willow Bridge ☆☆
Dardanup. Owner: Dewar family. 70 ha.
www.willowbridgeestate.com
Founded in 1997, this winery swiftly established a good
reputation for its supple reds, primarily Shiraz, and intensely
fruity whites from Sauvignon and Semillon.

Margaret River

Amberley Estate ☆☆
Yallingup. Owner: Vincor. 32 ha.
This medium-sized company has established a good name
for itself with clean, reliable, sometimes very good wines,
including fruity, fresh, off-dry Chenin Blanc, lively Shiraz,
and medium-bodied, juicy Cabernet blends.

Ashbrook Estate ☆☆☆
Willyabrup. Owner: Brian and Tony Devitt. 12 ha.
Remote family run winery in the middle of a red-gum forest.

Excellent and much sought-after white wines are produced, including tropical-fruit Riesling, rich Semillon, crisp Sauvignon Blanc, and rich, intense Chardonnay. The wines are sold mostly through a mailing list, so are hard to find.

Brookland Valley ☆☆–☆☆☆
Willyabrup. Owner: Hardys. 16 ha.
www.brooklandvalley.com.au
One of Margaret River's newer success stories, Brookland Valley combines a popular approach to wine tourism at his Flutes restaurant, with some downright delicious wines.

The unoaked Sauvignon/Semillon is particularly good, with intense grass and pea flavours. The Cabernet/Merlot and Reserve Cabernet are often outstanding: spicy and beautifully structured. As well as the estate wines, there is a less expensive range called Verse 1, first made in 1998.

Cape Mentelle ☆☆☆
Margaret River. Owner: LVMH. 200 ha.
www.capementelle.com.au
One of the great success stories of the Margaret River. David Hohnen, Cape Mentelle's founder and original winemaker, trained in California and maintained the highest standards here until his departure in 2003. Cape Mentelle popularized the Semillon/Sauvignon blend in this area, and produces excellent Chardonnay, elegant, spicy Shiraz, and chunky, thoroughly idiosyncratic Zinfandel. Hohnen also established the remarkable Cloudy Bay in New Zealand, and more recently the McHenry-Hohnen estate (q.v.).

Clairault ☆☆
Willyabrup. Owner: Bill Martin. 50 ha.
www.clairaultwines.com.au
Clairault's wines include excellent Cabernet Sauvignon and Semillon/Sauvignon, a style increasingly identified as particularly suited to this region. In the past some vintages of the Cabernets have shown herbaceous characters, but this seems less apparent now.

Cullen ☆☆☆–☆☆☆☆
Cowaramup. Owner: Cullen family. 30 ha.
www.cullenwines.com.au
Cabernet/Merlot made the Cullens' reputation, especially the brilliant Diana Madeline Reserve, but this Biodynamic estate, one of Margaret River's first, is also producing quite excellent and incredibly flavoursome Chardonnay and oak-aged Sauvignon/Semillon, under the shrewd eye of winemaker Vanya Cullen. A recent addition to the range is the delicious, perky Mangan: an unusual blend of Petit Verdot and Malbec. There is an excellent small restaurant.

Devil's Lair ☆☆–☆☆☆
Margaret River. Owner: Foster's Wine Group. 87 ha.
www.devils-lair.com.
These skilfully packaged wines are quite excellent, with zesty, citric Chardonnay and generously flavoured, oaky Cabernet leading the way. Despite the acquisition by the vast Southcorp company (and subsequently Foster's), quality has remained very high, while production has grown considerably. The second label, Fifth Leg, offers good value.

Edwards Vineyard ☆☆–☆☆☆
Cowaramup. Owner: Edwards family. 48 ha.
www.edwardsvineyard.com.au
This family run estate is offering the styles that are becoming Margaret River classics: a citric Semillon/Sauvignon blend, an elegant Shiraz, and a robust, black fruits Cabernet Sauvignon.

Evans & Tate ☆–☆☆
Wilyabrup. Owner: McWilliams Wines. 85 ha.
www.evansandtate.com.au
Evans & Tate began as a boutique winery, and grew to become the largest estate in Western Australia. Thereafter further expansion and mergers led to the company's collapse, and its purchase in 2007 by McWilliams.

Before the bankruptcy Evans & Tate managed to keep up the standards of its wines, but it is unclear in which direction McWilliams will take its acquisition. Certainly the 2007 Reserve Shiraz is an outstanding wine.

Leeuwin Estate ☆☆–☆☆☆☆
Margaret River. Owner: Horgan family. 130 ha.
www.leeuwinestate.com.au
A substantial modern winery (built with advice from California's Robert Mondavi) in the green hills and woods of the Margaret River – although the ocean is only a jog away. The Chardonnays are sensational, with aromas, liveliness, richness, and grip to out-do anything else in Australia and most in California. Rieslings have varied from excitingly steely to melon-rich. Cabernets are rich but not overripe.

After a period of some uncertainty, Leeuwin's star is again shining as bright as ever. A new Sauvignon/Semillon blend oozing class was launched in 2008. The second label, Prelude, is no shelter for mediocre wines, and can be of high quality. A fine restaurant and art gallery and summer outdoor concerts make Leeuwin an important destination.

Lenton Brae ☆☆–☆☆☆
Wilyabrup. Owner: Tomlinson family. 15 ha.
www.lentonbrae.com
A small winery, founded in 1982, producing stunning Chardonnay and stylish Cabernet and Cabernet/Merlot.

McHenry Hohnen ☆☆–☆☆☆
Margaret River. Owner: Hohnen and McHenry families. 120 ha. www.mchv.com.au
The owners' vineyards, in four districts, gives David Hohnen and his daughter Freya a wide range of varieties to work with, which explains the eclectic nature of the range: Rhône-style whites, a southern Rhône blend called 3 Amigos, and, harking back to Hohnen's days at Cape Mentelle, a Zinfandel. The style is Margaret River at its most elegant.

Moss Wood ☆☆☆
Wilyabrup. Owner: Keith Mugford. 18 ha.
www.mosswood.com.au
The winery that put the Margaret River among Australia's top-quality areas. Moss Wood Cabernet seems to define the style of the region: sweetly clean, faintly grassy, intensely deep, and compact – almost thick, in fact, but without the clumsiness that implies. Definitely for very long ageing. Good, citric

Chardonnay and a rather neutral Pinot Noir are also made. The Cabernet, including the separately bottled Glenmore Cabernet, is head and shoulders above the other wines.

Pierro ☆☆–☆☆☆
Margaret River. Owner: Dr. Michael Peterkin. 18 ha. www.pierro.com.au
Pierro is a high-quality winery producing small quantities of well-received wine, including one of Margaret River's best barrel fermented Chardonnays. The Sauvignon/Semillon, which Peterkin was the first to produce here, can be herbaceous. The best red wine is the cedary Cabernet/Merlot.

Rosily ☆☆
Wilyabrup. Owner: Scott and Allan families. 12 ha. www.rosily.com.au
Planted in 1995, Rosily initially sold grapes to other wineries but now produces delicate and understated wines from Cabernet and Shiraz as well as white varieties.

Stellabella ☆☆–☆☆☆
Margaret River. Owner: Janice McDonald, Stuart Pym, and partners. 95 ha. www.stellabella,com.au
A venture with a sense of humour, founded in 1997, and run by two leading winemakers: Janice McDonald and Stuart Pym. Three ranges of wine focus primarily on different interpretations of the Margaret River classics: an elegant, oaky Semillon/Sauvignon, and an intense Cabernet Sauvignon.

With its quirky packaging and astute marketing, Stellabella, Suckfizzle, and Skuttlebutt have been a great success and production has expanded.

Vasse Felix ☆☆–☆☆☆
Cowaramup. Owner: Holmes à Court family. 170 ha. www.vassefelix.com.au
One of the Margaret River pioneers, and still up there with the best. The basic and good-value range is called Classic Dry White and Red. The Chardonnay, especially the top Heytesbury bottling, can be a touch over-oaked. The Cabernet/Merlot is quite a substantial wine, but cannot match the pure Cabernets, with their voluptuous taste of blackberries and slight mintiness.

Voyager ☆☆☆–☆☆☆☆
Margaret River. Owner: Michael Wright. 110 ha. www.voyagerestate.com.au
Cliff Royle makes outstanding Chardonnay that is toasty, but always backed by good acidity. The Shiraz is more Rhône than Barossa in style, and the Cabernet/Merlot is an opulent wine with cassis aromas and a long, earthy finish. The top cuvée is a barrel-selection called Tom Price, the white being a Graves-style blend rather than a Chardonnay. These are wines that try hard to impress, and usually do.

Xanadu ☆☆
Margaret River. Owner: Rathbone Group. 130 ha. www.xanaduwines.com.au
The winery (its name, not surprisingly, inspired by Coleridge's poem) fared well in the 1990s, but ambition and over-expansion led to it foundering in the years that followed. In 2005 it was acquired by Rathbone, which also owns Yering Station, Mount Langi Ghiran, and other wineries. The Xanadu wines are sound, and the second range, Dragon, offers good value.

Pemberton

Picardy ☆☆–☆☆☆
Pemberton. Owner: Pannell family. 7 ha. www.picardy.com.au
The Pannells were the founders of Moss Wood (q.v.), and this is their retirement project, the goal being to produce intense, Burgundian-style Chardonnay and Pinot Noir, although their Shiraz can be splendid, too. First releases were in 1997. The finest wines are labelled Tête de Cuvée, but are only made in minute quantities.

Smithbrook ☆☆
Pemberton. Owner: Lion Nathan. 60 ha. www.smithbrook.com.au
Yilgarn, a Bordeaux-style blend of Cabernet, Merlot, and Petit Verdot is the flagship wine here.

Swan Valley

Paul Conti ☆–☆☆
Woodvale. Owner: Conti family. 17 ha. www.paulcontiwines.com.au
A (stylistically) leading Swan Valley producer, with well-placed coastal vineyards at Marginiup and Yanchep. Elegant Shiraz, and clean, balanced Chardonnay.

Houghton ☆☆–☆☆☆
Middle Swan. Owner: Hardys. 500 ha. www.houghton-wines.com.au
The most famous name in Western Australia, the wines at this Swan Valley winery were, for 50 vintages, made by the legendary Jack Mann. Now, benefiting from newer vineyards in cooler parts of the state such as Margaret River, Pemberton, and Frankland, Houghton's lustre has revived.

Moondah Brook is a basic range from Great Southern vineyards; Crofters is a range from cool climate vineyards. In 1999, Houghton introduced regional wines, such the bright, elegant Frankland River Shiraz, the lush, concentrated Margaret River Cabernet, and a milk-chocolatey Gladstones Shiraz. Jack Mann, a blend of Cabernet and Malbec, remains the top wine: opaque and damsony.

Yet for many Houghton is associated with the blended White Classic, first made in 1937 and for many years Australia's best-selling "White Burgundy". A vertical tasting in 2008 showed that this modest wine ages rewardingly for up to a decade.

Vasse Felix vineyard, Cowaramup

Sandalford ☆☆
Caversham. Owner: Prendiville family. 144 ha.
www.sandalford.com
This old-established winery on the Swan River now relies
almost entirely on fruit from its more southerly vineyards, and
is producing some excellent wines. Chardonnay and Verdelho
are the best of the whites, and a spicy, elegant Shiraz and tight,
earthy Cabernet Sauvignon share the honours as the best of the
reds. The cheaper range, called Element, provides good value.
Sandalera is a splendid, long-aged dessert wine in the Iberian
style. After a bad patch in the 1990s, winemaker Paul Boulden,
appointed in 2001, has made good progress in improving quality.

Leading Queensland Producer

Ballandean Estate ☆
Ballandean. Owner: Angelo and Mary Puglisi. 18 ha.
www.ballandeanestate.com
Angelo Puglisi is known as the godfather of winemaking
in Queensland, and Ballandean Estate, while the first, is still
one of the best in the Granite Belt area. The eclectic range
includes Shiraz and Merlot, fortified wines, and an unusual
sweet white from the rare (in Australia) Silvaner variety.

Leading Tasmania Producers

Domaine A ☆☆
Campania. Owner: Peter Althaus. 20 ha.
www.domaine-a.com.au
Swiss engineer Peter Althaus is passionate about Bordeaux,
and despite an unfavourable climate for Bordeaux varieties,
makes an intense, oaky Cabernet by keeping yields extremely
low. In complete contrast, he also produces a zesty, unoaked
Sauvignon and an improved Pinot Noir. The second label
here is Stoney Vineyard.

Bay of Fires ☆☆
Pipers River. Owner: Hardys.
www.bayoffireswines.com.au
Although the Pinot Noir can be good, the specialty here
is sparkling wine. Arras is aged four years on the yeasts
and is one of Tasmania's finest classic method wines.

Clover Hill ☆☆
Lebrina. Owner: Taltarni Wines. 66 ha.
www.taltarni.com.au
Founded in 1986, the label is devoted to sparkling wines.
The standard vintage blend has always been very good but
it is the more recent vintage *blanc de blancs* that shows real
class and distinction.

Dalrymple ☆
Pipers Brook. Owner: Yalumba Wines. 12 ha.
www.dalrymplevineyards.com.au
Quality here has long been patchy, but the property's sale
in 2007 to Yalumba suggests that improvements are likely.

Freycinet ☆☆–☆☆☆
Tasman Highway. Owner: Bull family. 10 ha.
www.freycinetvineyard.com.au
One of Tasmania's top wineries, located near the ocean
on the East Coast, and producing refreshing Riesling and
Chardonnay, as well as superb, complex, beetroot-and-spice
Pinot Noir.

Frogmore Creek ☆☆
Richmond. Owner: Jack Kidwiler and Tony Scherer.
18 ha. www.frogmorecreek.com.au
This is a complex operation, founded and then sold by
Andrew Hood, who makes the wines at countless boutique
wineries in Tasmania, and run by French winemaker Alain
Rousseau. Riesling in different styles are the best wines,
and 40 Degrees South is the good-value second label.

Stefano Lubiana ☆☆
Granton. Owner: Steve Lubiana. 18 ha.
www.slw.com.au
From relatively small vineyards, Lubiana makes a wide
range of wines, from sparkling traditional method brut
to Pinot Noir, Riesling, and Pinot Grigio. All the wines
are well-made, yet can lack personality.

Moorilla Estate ☆☆–☆☆☆
Berriedale. Owner: David Walsh. 20 ha.
www.moorilla.com.au
One of the first bold souls to look for quality in Tasmania
back in 1958, and in a cool corner at that. Frost, birds,
and underripeness were problems, until better vineyards
were planted near the Tamar River. David Walsh is
transforming the property into a tourist destination,
with an art museum and restaurant. The wines have
become very stylish, with labels that have shocked the
primmer citizens of Hobart. Riesling, Chardonnay,
and Pinot Noir are all delicious; Syrah has a way to go.

Piper's Brook ☆☆
Piper's Brook. Owner: Kreglinger. 200 ha.
www.kreglingerwineestates.com
This bold enterprise was created by an eclectic mind
in search of ideal conditions: cool but not too cool.
Dr. Andrew Pirie planted hilltop vineyards within sight
of the island's north coast (and reach of sea winds) and
from these he made superb dry Riesling and austere
Chardonnay, very characteristic Pinot Noir, Cabernet
with lively and intense flavours, and one of Australia's
most complex sparkling wines.
    Ninth Island is the second label: wines with less
intensity, but no less attractive. The property was sold
in 2001, and Pirie left to take on new projects. Quality
remains good, if without the flair and excitement that
marked the Pirie days.

Pirie ☆☆–☆☆☆
Launceston. Owner: Dr Andrew Pirie. No vineyards.
www.andrewpirie.com
Pirie brings the same care, expertise, and impeccable taste
to his own winery, from which the first vintage was 2004.
However, the ambitious Tamar Ridge project (q.v.) took
on Pirie as chief winemaker in 2005, so the future of his
own label is uncertain.

Spring Vale ☆☆
Cranbrook, East Coast. Owner: Lyne family. 7 ha.
www.springvalewines.com
One of the wineries to confirm the east coast of Tasmania as a great place to grow Pinot Noir. The Pinot Noir is round, earthy, and deliciously spicy, and the Gewurztraminer delightfully floral.

Tamar Ridge ☆–☆☆
Kayena. Owner: Gunns Ltd. 140 ha.
www.tamarridge.com.au
On an island where many vineyards are garden sized, Piper's Brook and now Tamar Ridge are the large scale exceptions. Owned by a timber company, the plantings have been ambitious, overseen by Dr. Richard Smart, while the wine-making is overseen by Dr. Andrew Pirie. Not surprisingly, progress has been swift, although at present the wines are reliable and balanced rather than thrilling.

Boutique wineries have proliferated in Tasmania, but most of them have such limited production that most of their wines never reach the mainland, let alone other countries.

The following, nonetheless, are names to keep an eye on: Bass Fine Wine, Bream Creek, Chromy, Derwent, Meadowbank, Morningside, Pressing Matters, Roslyn, Silk Hill, and Winstead.

Leading Northern Territory Producer

Château Hornsby ☆
Alice Springs. Owner: Denis and Miranda Hornsby.
3 ha.
Maverick, tourist-oriented winery, with heavily irrigated vines, in the searing heat of the outback. Harvesting takes place before dawn, to protect the pickers as well as the grapes. Reds are full and clean flavoured.

New Zealand

The transformation of New Zealand wine in the last few decades has been astonishing. Indeed, it hasn't been so much of a transformation as an invention. And it has given us some of the most vivid flavours ever to appear in a wine bottle.

While almost every Australian settler, it seems, planted vines for wine, the new New Zealanders did much less to exploit the temperate climate and fertile soils of their islands. No real wine industry, beyond isolated missions and private estates, existed until Dalmatian Kauri gum workers and Lebanese immigrants in the Auckland area started to provide for their own needs, early in the twentieth century. Their products were crude, from poor vines unsuited to the warm humidity of Auckland. Phylloxera forced them to plant hybrids. Most of the wine was fortified and probably deserved its unflattering title of "Dally plonk". And the small, strait-laced Anglo-Saxon community, frequently muttering about Prohibition, hardly provided an encouraging marketplace. Until 1961, it was illegal to drink wine in restaurants and there were other irksome restrictions on consumption.

Matters began to change quite briskly in the late 1960s, as New Zealanders developed both a tentative export market to Australia and Great Britain – and also a taste for wine themselves. In 1960, almost half of the total 390 hectares of vines was in the Auckland area, and most of the rest in Hawke's Bay on the central-east coast of the North Island. The 1960s saw a trebling of the Auckland hectarage and the development of Waikato, 65 kilometres (40 miles) south; the Hawke's Bay vineyards doubled in size and an important new area sprung up at Poverty Bay near Gisborne, north of Hawke's Bay.

Results were encouraging, even if the first mass plantings were decidedly unambitious. The market's chief interest was in cheap fortified wines – made all the cheaper by the illegal addition of water. For table wines, Müller-Thurgau was widely considered to be as high a mark as New Zealand could profitably reach. Early planters mistakenly took German advice that their climate was closer to that of Germany than of France. Experiments with Sauvignon Blanc and then with Chardonnay in the 1970s proved, however, that the climate of the main fruit growing region, the east coast of North Island, was not so much German as central French. These east-coast areas flourished in the 1970s, quintupling their vineyards, while Auckland's actually shrank slightly. But the 1970s also saw the vine move to the South Island of New Zealand: by 1980, Marlborough had nearly 800 hectares, and trial planting had moved as far south as Canterbury and Central Otago.

New Zealand's true potential as a producer of fine wine burst upon the world in the mid-1980s: to be precise, in February 1985, when British wine critics, buyers, and journalists attended a tasting held at New Zealand House in London. Those present are unlikely to forget the excitement of that morning, as it became apparent that a dozen different wineries had produced a number of white wines of a racy vitality and tingling fruitiness that are only met with on rare occasions elsewhere in the world. The best Sauvignon Blancs were the most memorable, giving an extra dimension to this essentially second-league variety. The verdict was unanimous: New Zealand had jumped into the first division of the world's white wine producers.

Subsequent tastings confirmed the fact, adding Chardonnays of extremely sound quality, a few Rieslings, Chenin Blancs, and Gewurztraminers of fine quality by any standards, and some promising red wines. Any shortcomings in the early quality of the reds were more due to inexperience than to the quality of the grapes. Significant developments, especially with Pinot Noir, which benefits from the cool climate from Martinborough southwards, and advances in vinification techniques have proved their worth. Cabernet

Sauvignon/Merlot blends, especially from Hawke's Bay, have improved out of recognition, again with better vinification techniques, better viticulture, and the discovery of some exceptional sites and soils. In general, there has been a considerable widening of the range of grape varieties planted. Several wineries now produce very good Syrah, and Zinfandel is out of quarantine. Pinot Gris is also showing great promise.

An enormous growth in vineyards has changed the picture. Existing wineries have planted furiously and there has been an explosive increase in the number of winemaking facilities. New viticultural areas are being essayed, with isolated wineries appearing in unexpected places. Such expansion also brings danger: as some outlying valleys in Marlborough and Hawke's Bay, for example, are proving awkwardly susceptible to frost.

By the late 1990s, the best winemakers had learned to temper the sometimes over-herbaceous or vegetal character of their wines, especially in the Cabernets and Merlots, as well as finding warmer areas to plant these varieties. It had also become apparent that the international eye-catcher, among red wines, was going to be Pinot Noir, especially from Martinborough and Central Otago. (By 2007, there were 4,400 hectares planted, 42 per cent of them in Central Otago). For the present, however, it is still with white wines that New Zealand conquers. If international taste should begin to tire of the powerfully flavoured Marlborough Sauvignons (Sauvignon Blanc now accounts for over half of all New Zealand's vineyards) there is no shortage of superb Rieslings and Chardonnays.

New Zealand's natural gift is what the winemakers of Australia and California are striving for: the conditions that give slowly ripened, highly aromatic fruit. The wines are developing the strength, structure, and occasionally even the elusive delicacy of those from (for example) the Loire, Alsace, possibly the Médoc, possibly Champagne – with a freshness and vigour that are New Zealand's own.

The potential for sparkling wines has been nurtured, using classic methods and nearly always with Pinot Noir and Chardonnay grapes. And visitors to the country can attest to the splendid quality of its best botrytis Rieslings and Semillons.

North Island Wine Regions

Auckland

500 hectares. Until the 1970s this was New Zealand's largest grape growing region, but its almost subtropical climate, with considerable cloud cover and frequent autumn rain, was never suited to the vine. It is now eclipsed as a wine region (both in terms of quantity and quality) by Gisborne, Hawke's Bay, and Marlborough to the south. Urban sprawl has turned vineyards into shopping malls, but many important wine companies are still based here. Just north of the city is the small Matakana subregion, where a few wineries huddle behind the beaches. See also Waiheke Island.

Wineries include: Awa Valley, Babich, Coopers Creek, Delegat's, Kumeu River, Lincoln Vineyards, Matua Valley, Nobilo, Soljans, Villa Maria, and West Brook.

Gisborne

1,190 hectares. This sunny and fertile area on the east coast of the North Island is well-suited to white grape varieties, notably Chardonnay, although it suffers from autumn rains that force the harvest forward, and from active phylloxera, which has resulted in almost total replanting. Wineries are few, as most grapes are sent for blending to the major producers in Auckland.

Wineries include: Bushmere, Millton, and T W Wines.

Hawke's Bay

4,340 hectares. One of the established regions with the greatest promise, situated on the east coast south of Gisborne, and in the rain shadow of the island's volcanic mountain centre. Its sunshine and its glorious mixture of soils – silt, shingle, and clay – provide enormous potential for red and white grapes and the number of wineries is growing. Together with Waiheke Island, this is one of the few spots where Bordeaux varieties usually ripen fully and Syrah has already proved itself. Growers are now identifying the best subregions, such as Gimblett Gravels and the Ngatarawa Triangle.

Wineries include: Alpha Domus, Brookfields, Craggy Range, Kim Crawford, Esk Valley, Kemblefield, Matariki, Mission, Church Road, Ngatarawa, C J Pask, Sacred Hill, Sileni, Te Mata, Trinity Hill, and Vidal.

Northland

This rainy, humid region in the extreme north of the island was the site of New Zealand's first vineyard in 1819, but it is ill-suited to grape growing. A growing number of wineries are trying to prove its suitability, however, especially in the Matakana valley. Chardonnay, Pinot Gris, and Syrah can do well here. Now, there are also a couple of isolated wineries even further north, Longview at Whangarei and Okahu Estate at Kaitaia.

Wineries include: Ake Ake, Karikari, and Marsden.

Waikato Bay of Plenty

150 hectares. A small, rainy region, spreading eastwards from Waikato, about 72-kilometres (45-miles) south of Auckland, to the Bay of Plenty. Most of the larger wineries, such as Morton Estate, source their grapes from Hawke's Bay, Gisborne, or elsewhere in New Zealand.

Wineries include: Mills Reef, Morton, and Vilagrad.

Wairarapa

770 hectares. This is the region at the southern end of the North Island, northeast of Wellington, with the small town of Martinborough at its centre. Wairarapa's combination of good soil, low rainfall, and autumn sunshine first prompted the planting of vineyards in 1978. Four wineries had their first vintage in 1984 and three of them, Martinborough Vineyards, Dry River, and Ata Rangi, have since established a firm reputa-

tion for Pinot Noir from low yielding vines.

Since 2000 there have been substantial plantings in Te Muna, a few miles from Martinborough. Sauvignon and Chardonnay are good, too, but the record with red Bordeaux varieties and Syrah is more patchy.

Wineries include: Alana, Ata Rangi, Dry River, Escarpment, Gladstone, Martinborough Vineyard, Palliser, and Te Kairanga.

Waiheke Island

216 hectares. A small island in the Hauraki Gulf a short ferry ride from Auckland with a far drier climate than the capital (30 per cent less rainfall) and better soil (lighter and freer-draining). Vines were first planted by the Goldwaters in 1978, then by Stephen White at Stonyridge. Others followed suit, mainly planting Bordeaux varieties.

Wineries include: Cable Bay, Goldwater Estate, Miro, Mudbrick, Stonyridge, and Te Wau.

South Island Wine Regions

Canterbury

925 hectares. One of several newer wine regions in the South Island, around Christchurch on the mid-east coast. Its coldish climate and low rainfall lured an increasing number of small wineries into the area during the 1980s, and resulted in some impressive Riesling and Pinot Noir. The plains around Christchurch, however, tend to be very prone to frost, which causes problems.

Wineries include: Larcomb, St Helena, and Tressilian.

Central Otago

1,250 hectares. The southernmost vineyards in the world, on the 45th parallel, with dramatic scenery in the Gibbston Valley, close to Queenstown; other vineyards overlook the shores of Lake Wanaka and cower beneath schist outcrops around the town of Alexandra. Otago is currently the fastest-growing vineyard area in New Zealand, especially around Cromwell. There has been a corresponding explosion of boutique wineries.

The climate in this region is more continental than the other regions, and vintages can vary quite considerably. This is proving an outstanding region for rich, savoury Pinot Noir, and good Chardonnays and Rieslings are made here, too.

Wineries include: Akarua, Black Ridge, Carrick, Chard Farm, Felton Road, Gibbston Valley, Mount Difficulty, Mount Edward, Peregrine, Quartz Reef, Rippon, and Waitiri Creek.

Marlborough

11,500 hectares. Sunny, stony-soiled Marlborough, the region around the town of Blenheim at the northeastern tip of the South Island, has proved the making of New Zealand's wine industry. Since it was pioneered by Montana in 1973, it has produced some of the world's best Sauvignon Blanc, and is easily the country's largest grape growing region.

Marlborough's excellent soil, low rainfall (irrigation is essential here, at least for young vines) and cool autumns, combined with its position in New Zealand's sunniest corner, make it ideal for growing well-flavoured fruit, especially for white wines: Sauvignon Blanc, Chardonnay, and Riesling have all proved successful, and there is some delicious Pinot Noir. Wind, and in some valleys, frost, are the only serious problems for Marlborough growers. Some recently planted valleys are particularly susceptible to frost.

Wineries include: Cloudy Bay, Forrest, Framingham, Fromm, Herzog, Highfield, Huia, Hunter's, Isabel, Jackson Estate, Lawson's Dry Hills, Montana, Mount Riley, Nautilus, Saint Clair, Allan Scott, Seresin, Wairau River, and Wither Hills.

Nelson

700 hectares. Small, somewhat inaccessible region to the west of Marlborough, which shares some of that region's beneficial conditions, but suffers from autumn rainfall. The vineyards are mostly undulating, and most of the growing number of wineries are boutique, rather than large concerns. The quality of the wines is excellent.

Wineries include: Greenhough, Neudorf, Seifried Estate, and Te Mania.

Waipara

1,200 hectares. The considerable potential of the geographically small region of Waipara, north of Christchurch, is now being realized and plantings are expanding. Compared to Canterbury, the climate is distinctly warmer and the soil limestone-based, proving suitable for Pinot Noir and Chardonnay, and resulting in a growing number of wineries .

Wineries include Daniel Schuster, Mud House, Pegasus Bay, and Waipara Springs.

Harvest-time, New Zealand

Leading North Island Producers

Hawke's Bay

Alpha Domus ☆☆
Hastings. Owner: Ham family. 35 ha.
www.alphadomus.co.nz
Serious if extracted reds from Hawke's Bay: Bordeaux blends under the Aviator and Navigator labels. Quality is variable but the Semillon is a success.

Brookfields ☆☆
Taradale. Owner: Peter Robertson. 24 ha.
www.brookfieldsvineyards.co.nz
The emphasis is on reds that will age in bottle: a pure Cabernet, a Cabernet/Merlot blend, and an outstanding Syrah. The hefty, oaky Marshall Bank Chardonnay is fermented and aged in barriques.

Craggy Range ☆☆☆
Havelock North. Owner: Terry Peabody. 272 ha.
www.craggyrange.co.nz
The shrewd investment of Brisbane businessman Peabody and the viticultural and winemaking skills of Steve Smith MW have fused to launch a lavish new winery, with extremely impressive releases right from the outset. Numerous bottlings of Sauvignon, Chardonnay, Riesling, and Merlot reflect different vineyard sites, in Te Muna near Martinborough as well as Hawke's Bay. Initial releases of Syrah and Cabernet Sauvignon in 2001 showed remarkable concentration and focus. In 2007 a Pinot Noir from Central Otago was added to the already impressive range.

Kim Crawford ☆☆
Hastings. Owner: Constellation.
www.kimcrawfordwines.co.nz
Crawford was the winemaker at Coopers Creek until he founded his own label in 1996. It proved a great success and was bought by Vincor in 2003, and is now part of the Constellation group. In 2008 Crawford left the company that bears his name. Wines were sourced from various regions, and as well as the standard varietals, the range included Viognier and Arneis.

Esk Valley ☆☆–☆☆☆☆
Napier. Owner: Villa Maria (q.v.). Shares vineyards with Villa Maria. www.eskvalley.co.nz
Formerly a large family firm, Esk Valley produces some of the country's best reds under winemaker Gordon Russell. All the wines are made from Hawke's Bay fruit. It offers a wide range of wines, the basic range being Black Label; the superior bottlings being the Reserves; and the remarkable The Terraces: a scarce red Bordeaux blend produced only in outstanding vintages.

Kemblefield ☆☆
Hastings. Owner: John Kemble and Kaar Field. 90 ha.
www.kemblefield.co.nz
John Kemble, once closely involved with Ravenswood in Sonoma Valley (q.v.), takes credit for introducing Zinfandel to New Zealand. The best wines are grandly known as The Distinction, and there are also Reserves produced only in top vintages. The white wines are very good, but the red wines, with the occasional exception of the Reserve Cabernet, lack depth.

Matariki ☆☆☆
Hastings. Owner: John O'Connor. 68 ha.
www.matarikiwines.co.nz
Matariki is located in the heart of the Gimblett Gravels region, where O'Connor has most of his vines. Until 1997, he produced bulk wines, and since then has overseen a rapidly improving range of rich and full-flavoured varietals. The zesty Chardonnay is sometimes preferable to the hefty, oaky Reserve, but Reserve bottlings of Merlot and Syrah are excellent, and a new Sangiovese shows promise. The house specialty is the Bordeaux blend, Quintology: concentrated and vibrant. Stony Bay is the second label: delicious Chardonnay.

Mission ☆☆
Napier. Owner: Catholic Society of Mary. 50 ha.
www.missionestate.co.nz
Founded in 1851, this is the oldest winery in Hawke's Bay, located in a beautiful spot at the foot of grassy hills. The reserve range is very reliable, and the top range appears under the Jewelstone label: Chardonnay, Cabernet/Merlot, and a youthful Syrah.

Ngatarawa ☆–☆☆☆
Hastings . Owner: Alwyn and Brian Corban. 25 ha.
www.ngatarawa.co.nz
The Corbans have been making wine in New Zealand for over a century, although the winery that bears their name now belongs to Montana. Ngatarawa is housed in an attractive winery building, around old racing stables. Top of the range is the Alwyn Reserve: high-priced Chardonnay, Cabernet, and Botrytis Riesling made only in top vintages. Also of high quality is the Glazebrook label, which consists of wines from different regions. The Stables range is more accessible in style.

C J Pask ☆☆
Hastings. Owner: Chris Pask, John Benton, and Kate Radburnd (also winemaker). 90 ha.
www.cjpaskwinery.co.nz
Chris Pask, pilot-turned-viticulturist, was the first person to plant on what is now the highly rated Gimblett Road area – with silt over shingle in old river bed vineyards. He concentrates on Bordeaux varieties, plus Chardonnay and Syrah. The flagship wines are called Declaration, and include a Bordeaux blend, Chardonnay, Malbec, Merlot, and Syrah. Quality is not always as consistent as one would hope for.

Sacred Hill ☆☆☆
Napier. Owner: Mason family. 125 ha.
www.sacredhill.com
From a range of vineyards in Hawke's Bay and Marlborough (having bought the former Cairnbrae estate there), winemaker Tony Bish makes a variety of impressive wines under the Special Selection label. These include the very stylish Sauvage

Sauvignon (barrique-fermented with indigenous yeasts); the toasty, peachy Rifleman's Chardonnay; the powerful but harmonious Bordeaux blend called Helmsman's; Deer Stalker's Syrah and the smoky, opulent Brokenstone Merlot.

Sileni ☆☆
Hastings. Owner: Graeme Avery and partners. 106 ha. www.sileni.co.nz
Together with Craggy Range (q.v.), this is the most stunning winery complex in Hawke's Bay. But vast expenditure and a succession of serious frosts in the vineyards have proved troublesome. The wines are cleanly made and balanced, and there is an unusual focus on Semillon, both dry and sweet.

Stonecroft ☆☆
Hastings. Owner: Dr Alan Limmer. 10 ha. www.stonecroft.co.nz
Alan Limmer pioneered Syrah in New Zealand. His first vintage, 1987, was released in 1990, and he has repeated its success in subsequent years. Limmer is very keen on trying different grape varieties, especially from the Rhône, and has also taken some Zinfandel from Kemblefield (q.v.). Gewurztraminer can be excellent, too.

Te Mata ☆☆☆–☆☆☆☆
Havelock North. Owner: John Buck, Michael Morris, and partners. 120 ha. www.temata.co.nz
One of the oldest wineries in New Zealand, recently restored and renowned for its Coleraine, one of the country's best Cabernet/Merlot blends. (The restorations have resulted in an attractive winery complex, with a barrel cellar that would not be out of place in the Médoc).

Winemaker Peter Cowley aims to make long-lived wines with plenty of acid backbone. The whole range is reliable, but the best bottles tend to be the Cape Crest Sauvignon, Coleraine Cabernet/Merlot, the lighter but more accessible Awatea Cabernet/Merlot, Bullnose Syrah, and Elston Chardonnay. Since 1996, other wines have been emerging from Te Mata's expanding new estate, also in Hawke's Bay, called Woodthorpe. Few wineries in New Zealand have a track record to match Te Mata's.

Trinity Hill ☆☆–☆☆☆
Hastings. Owner: John Hancock and partners. 40 ha. www.trinityhill.com
John Hancock built his reputation as the winemaker for Morton Estate (q.v.) before setting up his own winery in 1993. Most of the best wines come from vineyards in the Gimblett Road area, and Hancock has a fondness for obscure (by New Zealand standards) varieties, such as Arneis and Alvarinho, Montepulciano and Tempranillo. The outstanding wines are the very expensive Homage range: Chardonnay, Syrah, and The Gimblett Merlot/Cabernet.

Vidal ☆☆–☆☆☆
Hastings. Owner: Villa Maria (q.v.). 45 ha. www.vidal.co.nz
One of the oldest wineries in Hawke's Bay, dating from 1905, Vidal is part of the Villa Maria group, offering stylish whites, but the best wines are the full-bodied reds from Cabernet Sauvignon and Syrah from organic vineyards on the Gimblett Gravels.

Wairarapa

Alana ☆–☆☆
Martinborough. Owner: Ian Smart. 17 ha. www.alana.co.nz
Smart's first vintage was 1997. The whites, both Sauvignon and Chardonnay, are fresh and mouthwatering, and the Pinot Noir, while light, has great charm.

Ata Rangi ☆☆☆
Martinborough. Owner: Clive and Alison Paton, and Oliver Masters. 40 ha. www.atarangi.co.nz
Outstanding Pinot Noir from Martinborough, with a silky texture, complexity, and intensity. They produce Chardonnay from Hawke's Bay as well as Martinborough, and Celebre, a Cabernet/Merlot/Syrah blend in varying proportions, depending on the vintage. Syrah, first made in 2001, has been discontinued, but the Pinot Gris and Botrytis Riesling are fine additions to the range.

Burnt Spur ☆☆
Martinborough. Owner: Martinborough Vineyard. 32 ha. www.burntspur.co.nz
Under the same ownership as Martinborough Vineyard, but the vineyards are located eight-kilometres (five-miles) south of the town. The moderately priced Pinot Noir is ripe and fleshy, and the Sauvignon Blanc and Pinot Gris are attractive.

Dry River ☆☆☆–☆☆☆☆
Martinborough. Owner: Julian Robertson and Reg Oliver. 18 ha. www.dryriver.co.nz
Small estate with finely crafted and magisterial wines, made for former research chemist Neil McCallum. He sold the winery in 2002 to its present American owners, but remains as winemaker. Complex Pinot Noir, made by blending different techniques and barrels, lush Pinot Gris, and lovely Riesling and Gewurztraminer. These are among the most sought-after wines in New Zealand, and this acute demand is reflected in the wines' very high prices.

Escarpment ☆☆–☆☆☆
Martinborough. Owner: Kirby Group. 24 ha. www.escarpment.co.nz
Larry McKenna left Martinborough Vineyards (q.v.) in 2001 to set up his own winery in conjunction with an Australian group from Victoria. The vineyards are in the Te Muna district. The first estate wines are from the 2002 vintage. In 2006 McKenna added a trio of single vineyard Pinot Noirs. The style overall is rich and weighty.

Gladstone ☆☆
Carteton, Wairarapa. Owner: Christine and David Kernohan. 14 ha. www.gladstone.co.nz
White wines are the focus here, especially racy Sauvignon and crisp Pinot Gris. Recent vintages have seen a marked improvement in their toasty but fresh Pinot Noir.

Martinborough Vineyard ☆☆☆
**Martinborough. Owner: Duncan and Derek Milne.
22 ha. www.martinborough-vineyard.co.nz**
One of Martinborough's founding wineries, with plantings
that began in 1980. Winemaker Larry McKenna spent time
in Burgundy and produced elegant, Burgundian-style wines
with intensity and delicacy. After his departure to set up his
own winery, Escarpment (q.v.), his place was taken by Claire
Mulholland and then by Paul Mason.

The winery's reputation for Pinot Noir (although some
vintages have aged less well than predicted) means that its
excellent Chardonnay, Riesling, and rich, barrel-fermented
Pinot Gris are sometimes overlooked. In 2003 it released
a Reserve Pinot Noir called Marie Zelie, which at the time
was the country's top priced Pinot.

Matawihi ☆☆
**Masterton. Owner: Alastair Scott. 75 ha.
www.matawihi.co.nz**
The first vintage here was 2004, but from the outset the
Pinot Noirs have been fresh and vibrant. Sauvignon Blanc
is also produced.

Murdoch James ☆–☆☆
**Martinborough. Owner: Roger Fraser. 20 ha.
www.murdochjames.co.nz**
Wines were first made here in 1986 during the earliest
era for this region. Pinot Noir is the main focus, but Pinot
Gris and Sauvignon Blanc are just as good, with attractive
tropical fruit tones.

Palliser ☆☆–☆☆☆
**Martinborough. Owner: public unlisted company.
85 ha. www.palliser.co.nz**
One of the leading Martinborough wineries, and a source
of delicious Riesling and savoury Pinot Noir that have
attracted a number of prestigious awards.

Te Kairanga ☆☆–☆☆☆
**Martinborough. Owner: numerous shareholders.
100 ha. www.tekairanga.co.nz**
As well as the range of varietals and Reserves, the rapidly
expanding Te Kairanga makes inexpensive wines under the
Runholder label. Te Kairanga established its reputation under
Australian winemaker Chris Buring, who has been replaced by
Wendy Potts. Quality here is impressive, especially for Pinot
Noir, of which there are several *cuvées*.

Other North Island Producers

Babich ☆☆–☆☆☆
**Henderson, Auckland. Owner: Babich family. 225 ha.
www.babichwines.co.nz**
A large, old Auckland family winery, highly respected for
consistent quality and value. It has developed vineyards in
various regions so as to get the best quality from each variety.
The Babich reputation is largely based on Chardonnay,
notably the Irongate Vineyard.

There is also an Irongate Cabernet/Merlot blend, and two
wines in the flagship Patriarch range: Cabernet Sauvignon
and Chardonnay. Other varieties, such as Sauvignon Blanc,
Pinot Noir, Syrah and Pinotage, are bottled under the
Winemaker's Reserve label.

Cable Bay ☆–☆☆
**Waiheke Island. Owner: Neill Culley. 26 ha.
www.cablebayvineyards.co.nz**
Neill Culley was the wine maker at Babich (q.v.) before
founding his own winery in 1996. As with other producers
based on Waiheke Island, Cable Bay also owns vineyards in
Marlborough to supply Pinot Noir, Sauvignon Blanc, and
Riesling. The best wine is usually the silky Waiheke
Chardonnay.

Coopers Creek ☆☆
**Huapai, Auckland. Owner: Andrew and Cynthia Hendry.
www.cooperscreek.co.nz**
The company, founded in 1980, has expanded considerably
since then, and now sources grapes from its own vineyards
in Gisborne and from other contracted vineyards in
Marlborough and Hawke's Bay. This allows winemaker Simon
Nunns to offer a huge range of wines, which, at the top end,
are of very good quality.

Delegat's ☆☆
**Henderson, Auckland. Owner: Jim and Rosemari Delegat.
1,200 ha. www.delegatwines.com**
Streamlining of production in the mid-1980s and good
winemaking skills (from Brent Marris and now from Michael
Ivicevich) led to a significant improvement. This is a family
winery, and the only brother-and-sister team in New Zealand.
The best wines are the Reserves from Hawke's Bay, and the
Marlborough wines, which are sold under the hugely
successful Oyster Bay label.

Goldwater Estate ☆☆
**Waiheke Island. Owner: New Zealand Wine Fund.
52 ha. www.goldwater.co.nz**
The Goldwaters planted the first vines on Waiheke back
in 1978, on an island vineyard which benefits from a warm,
dry microclimate. They concentrated on fragrant, delicate
Bordeaux blends, and on Sauvignon and Chardonnay.

The Sauvignon, and some of the Chardonnay, comes from
Marlborough, and these wines represent the great majority
of the production. In 2006 the estate merged with Vavasour
in Marlborough.

Heron's Flight ☆☆
**Matakana. Owner: David Hoskins and Mary Evans.
6 ha. www.heronsflight.co.nz**
David Hoskins has done much to counter the view that
Northland is too wet for vines. He used to make a
Cabernet/Merlot blend and Chardonnay, but but now
focuses exclusively on Italian varieties such as Sangiovese
and Dolcetto.

Kumeu River ☆☆☆
**Kumeu, Auckland. Owner: Brajkovich family. 25 ha.
www.kumeuriver.co.nz**
Kumeu River specializes in serious Chardonnay, with
the Maté Vineyard given the full Burgundian treatment.

Winemaker Michael Brajkovich MW is also skilled with lesser varieties such as Pinot Gris and Pinot Blanc, and there are some stylish Bordeaux blends such as Melba, from Merlot and Malbec. Michael is a fervent exponent of the Auckland area for grape growing, despite controversy. Brajkovich has added two new single-vineyard Chardonnays to keep Maté company: Coddington and Hunting Hill.

Lincoln Vineyards ☆–☆☆
Henderson, Auckland. Owner: Peter Fredatovich. No vineyards. www.lincolnwines.co.nz
With no vineyards of its own, Lincoln buys in fruit from Auckland, Marlborough, and Gisborne. The Heritage Collection ranges are aged in American oak, Reserves in French oak. Lincoln used to be known for its fortified wines, and its venerable Archive "ports" are splendid, but declining stocks make them an endangered species.

Matawhero ☆–☆☆
Gisborne. Owner: Denis Irwin. 30 ha.
A highly individual, small-scale family operation whose hand-made wines have won acclaim, notably the dry, aromatic Gewurztraminer, a discreet Chardonnay, and Bordeaux blends. Performance can be erratic.

Matua Valley ☆–☆☆☆
Waimauku, Auckland. Owner: Foster's Wine Group. 148 ha. www.matua.co.nz
California-style winery just north of Auckland, founded in 1974 by Ross and Bill Spence. It was Ross who isolated and propagated the single clone of Sauvignon that has been planted in New Zealand for the past 20 years.

Ararimu is the top label for Chardonnay and Merlot, and there are some excellent wines under the Matheson Vineyard label from Hawke's Bay. Marlborough wines are sold under the Shingle Peak label. The Innovator series is reserved for special lots of Viognier, Pinot Noir, and Syrah.

Mills Reef ☆☆–☆☆☆
Tauranga, Bay of Plenty. Owner: Preston family. 34 ha. www.millsreef.co.nz
Excellent wines under the top Elspeth label, especially lush Syrah, fleshy Merlot and Malbec, and an impressive Cabernet/Merlot blend, suggesting plums and blackberries.

Millton ☆☆☆
Manutuke, Gisborne. Owner: James and Annie Millton. 30 ha. www.millton.co.nz
It takes a brave person indeed to establish an organic and partly Biodynamic estate in Gisborne, but James Millton has studied the approach thoroughly and has no doubts about its effectiveness. He produces an interesting range of styles on vineyards protected by steep slopes, which includes a fresh Viognier, luscious oaked Chenin, and fine, botrytized Riesling. Fine Chardonnay and Pinot Noir justify the Milltons' faith.

Montana Wines ☆–☆☆☆
Auckland. Owner: Pernod Ricard. 3,000 ha. www.montanawines.com
For many years New Zealand's biggest wine company, it grew even larger by acquiring Cooks and Corbans. It played a major role in the 1970s, when it pioneered the new Marlborough region, where there is a showcase winery and visitors' centre. There are other wineries at Auckland, Gisborne, and Hawke's Bay. The Marlborough wines include a very dry Sauvignon Blanc, slightly spicy Riesling, and an excellent Chardonnay. Montana's Church Road Estate in Hawke's Bay focuses on Chardonnay and red varieties, especially Bordeaux blends.

Montana has for some years had a joint venture with Champagne Deutz to produce Deutz Cuvée Marlborough, which is at a higher level than its well-known Lindauer sparkling wine. Wines appear under the guise of numerous brands, the best-known being Brancott, Church Road, Longridge, andStoneleigh. Some single-vineyard wines appear in the Terroir series. Given the immense scale of the operation, quality can be surprisingly high.

Morton Estate ☆–☆☆☆
Katikati, Bay of Plenty. Owner: John Coney. 420 ha. www.mortonestatewines.co.nz
This winery (its façade in an attractive Cape Dutch style) benefited in the 1990s from the talents of John Hancock, one of the country's best winemakers (now running Trinity Hill, q.v.). Morton's reputation stands on Chardonnay, with the Black Label and (since 1998) Coniglio bottlings the top of the range, followed by a Bordeaux blend called The Regent, Reserves, and the White Label.

Mudbrick ☆☆–☆☆☆
Waiheke Island. Owner: Nick Jones. 10 ha. www.mudbrick.co.nz
Many of the grapes are bought from Marlborough, but the reds come mostly from estate vineyards on the island. The Syrah is intense and peppery, and the Shepherds Point Cabernet/Merlot is supple, oaky, and concentrated.

Nobilo ☆☆
Kumeu, Auckland. Owner: Constellation. 670 ha. www.nobilo.co.nz
The Nobilos originally came from Dalmatia, and worked hard on the red varieties that ripen well in the warm, damp Auckland climate. Since its takeover by Australian wine giant Hardy and its parent company Constellation, Nobilo has grown to become New Zealand's third-largest wine company.

The range is very broad, and so is quality. Some of the best wines come from Nobilo's sister wineries, Drylands, in Marlborough, and Selak's.

Selak's
Now owned by Nobilo (q.v.).

Stonyridge ☆☆☆
Waiheke Island. Owner: Stephen White. 6 ha. www.stonyridge.co.nz
Stonyridge focuses on Bordeaux varieties, and its finest wine is the excellent and high-priced Cabernet blend called Larose. Fallen Angel is a range made from non-Waiheke grapes. Serious, perfectionist winemaking can be found here, with intense attention to detail and passionate commitment to quality.

Te Whau ☆☆☆
**Waiheke Island. Owner: Tony and Moira Forsyth.
3 ha. www.tewhau.co.nz**
A tiny winery with a destination restaurant on a cliff above the
Hauraki Gulf. Herb Friedli, the winemaker, learnt his craft
with John Middleton, the awkward perfectionist of the Yarra
Valley. It shows, in a Bordeaux blend called The Point, tense
Chardonnay and savoury Syrah. (Whau is pronounced Fow.)

Villa Maria ☆☆☆
**Mangere, Auckland. Owner: George Fistonich. 1,150 ha.
www.villamaria.co.nz**
Villa Maria is New Zealand's largest privately owned winery.
In decreasing order of quality and volume,
the ranges here are Reserve, then Cellar
Selection, and then Private Bin. Gisborne,
Hawke's Bay (for good reds), and
Marlborough are the main grape sources.

Given the large volumes, quality is
astonishingly high, especially at Cellar
Selection and Reserve levels, and the
wines are sensibly priced. Sauvignon
Blanc, Riesling, Chardonnay, Pinot
Noir, and Botrytis Riesling are often
outstanding. Pinot Noir is consistently
excellent at all levels.

A new winery and visitors' centre
opened near Auckland airport in 2004,
and there is a second impressive winery in
Marlborough. Esk Valley and Vidal (q.v.)
are also part of the group.

West Brook ☆
**Waimauku, Auckland. Owner: Anthony
Ivicevich. 8 ha. www.westbrook.co.nz**
With Auckland's vineyards in irreversible decline,
Ivicevich has to bring fruit in from Marlborough and
Hawke's Bay. The result is a wide range of wines, to
enjoy young.

Leading Marlborough Producers

Churton ☆☆–☆☆☆
**Renwick. Owner: Sam Weaver. 12 ha. www.churton-
wines.co.nz**
Favouring organic and Biodynamic practices wherever
feasible, former wine merchant Weaver makes serious
and structured Pinot Noir and good Sauvignon Blanc from his
own vineyard and from other sources, working carefully with
individual growers.

Clos Henri ☆☆
**Blenheim. Owner: Jean-Marie Bourgeois. 36 ha.
www.clos-henri.com**
That one of Sancerre's top producers chose to develop a
vineyard here must be taken as a vote of confidence in
Marlborough. The first vintage was in 2003,
and initial releases of Sauvignon Blanc and
Pinot Noir have been impressive.

Cloudy Bay ☆☆☆
**Blenheim . Owner: LVMH. 700 ha.
www.cloudybay.co.nz**
Founded in 1985 by the Australian David Hohnen, whose
Western Australian winery Cape Mentelle had already
received great acclaim, Cloudy Bay rapidly became the
spearhead of New Zealand's assault on the international wine
market in the late 1980s. Its pungent, nettle-sharp Sauvignon
Blanc, made from vines grown in Marlborough's stony soil
and near-ideal climate for white wines, has been one of the
benchmarks for the finest expression of this grape's varietal
character to be found anywhere, and sells out all around the
world within weeks of its release – it includes some Semillon
and a small amount of oak.

Winemaker Kevin Judd, who left in
2009, gradually introduced a barrel-
fermented Sauvignon (Te Koko), an
excellent, oaky Chardonnay, Pinot Noir,
and lush Gewurztraminer. Other
successful extensions to the range include
Pelorus classic-method sparkling wine,
and first-rate Late Harvest Riesling.

Dog Point ☆☆☆
**Renwick. Owner: Sutherland
and Healy families. 80 ha.
www.dogpoint.co.nz**
James Healy and Ivan Sutherland
made their reputations as, respectively,
winemaker and viticulturalist at Cloudy
Bay until they left to set up their own
company in 2002. They focus on
Sauvignon, Chardonnay, and Pinot Noir,
all made to the highest standards. Not
everyone likes oaked Marlborough Sauvignon, but the Section
94 Sauvignon, which is fermented and aged in older barrels,
has enjoyed widespread acclaim.

Fairhall Downs ☆☆
**Blenheim. Owner: Ken Small. 32 ha.
www.fairhalldowns.co.nz**
From vineyards in Brancott valley, Small and his son-in-law,
Stuart Smith, produce both good Sauvignon Blanc and
appealing Pinot Gris. The dark-fruited Pinot Noir is
also very reliable.

Forrest ☆☆
**Renwick. Owner: Dr. John Forrest.
130 ha. www.forrest.co.nz.**
A deservedly respected source of typical Marlborough
Riesling, Gewurztraminer, and Sauvignon, and, since 2000,
of Pinot Noir, too. More recently Arneis and botrytized
Riesling and Chenin have joined the roster.

Framingham ☆–☆☆
Renwick. Owner: Sogrape. 30 ha. www.framingham.co.nz
This winery has the oldest Riesling vines in Marlborough,
and consequently it produces some of the finest expressions
of this variety in New Zealand. The Dry is dry, the Classic
off-dry; both exemplary. The other white wines and the

Highfield winery, Blenheim

Pinot Noir, can lack concentration, however.

The Montepulciano – how did this grape end up in Marlborough? – is juicy and attractive. In 2007 the Portuguese company Sogrape bought the property.

Fromm ☆☆–☆☆☆
Blenheim. Owner: Pol Lenzinger and George Walliser. 21 ha. www.frommwineries.com
Unusually for a Marlborough winery, Fromm has specialized in Pinot Noir since 1992, and the Clayvin Vineyard bottling can be outstanding. The wines are supple and elegant and also age well. The Chardonnay Reserve, however, shows heavy-handed oak influence, but the Riesling is plump and vigorous.

Fromm has returned to his Swiss vineyards and the organic property is now owned by friends of his, also from Switzerland. Long-term winemaker Hätsch Kalberer remains in place.

Grove Mill ☆–☆☆☆
Renwick. Owner: local investors. 185 ha (mostly leased). www.grovemill.co.nz
From small beginnings, Grove Mill has grown to be a substantial operation, with a brand new winery. The Pinot Noir can be dour, but both the Sauvignon and the Reserve Riesling are exemplary. Cheaper, attractively priced ranges are bottled under the Sanctuary and Frog Haven labels.

Hans Herzog ☆☆–☆☆☆
Blenheim. Owner: Hans Herzog. 11 ha. www.herzog.co.nz
Swiss restaurateur Hans Herzog came to Marlborough in the mid-1990s. His luxurious restaurant and his winery run side by side. Unlike most wineries here, Herzog offers a wide range of varieties, including Montepulciano, Nebbiolo, and Viognier.

Highfield ☆–☆☆
Blenheim. Owner: Tom Tenuwera and Shin Yokoi. 2 ha. www.highfield.co.nz
Good, straightforward varietal wines, notably Chardonnay. The Elstree Brut is a rich, toasty, traditional-method sparkling wine, one of New Zealand's best. Almost all the grapes are purchased.

Huia ☆☆–☆☆☆
Blenheim. Owner: Claire and Mike Allan. 16 ha. www.huia.net.nz
Founded in 1996, Huia is a quality-conscious estate, using an unusually high proportion of natural yeast fermentation. All the wines are beautifully crafted and impeccably balanced. A very dependable source of Sauvignon Blanc and Pinot Noir.

Hunter's ☆☆–☆☆☆
Blenheim. Owner: Jane Hunter. 37 ha. www.hunters.co.nz
After the death of pioneering Ernie Hunter in 1987, his widow Jane has maintained this family winery as one of the South Island's best. The varietal range includes good barrel-fermented Chardonnay and ripe and fruity Sauvignon Blanc, as well as Riesling and oaky Pinot Noir. The excellent Miru Miru sparkling wine is produced exclusively for export.

Isabel Estate ☆☆☆
Renwick. Owner: Michael and Robyn Tiller. 54 ha. www.isabelestate.com
The Isabel vineyards are planted at an unusually high density – far higher than that commonly encountered in New Zealand. Winemaker Patricia Miranda uses indigenous yeasts whenever possible. The resulting wines are zesty and concentrated, the stars being Chardonnay, and spicy, complex Pinot Noir.

Jackson Estate ☆☆–☆☆☆
Blenheim. Owner: John Stichbury. 100 ha. www.jacksonestate.co.nz
Jackson is best-known for its pungent Sauvignon Blanc, citric, spicy Chardonnay, and graceful Riesling, both in dry and botrytized styles. In the late 1990s, the Stichburys planted new clones of Pinot Noir, which are now producing refined and charming wines.

Lake Chalice ☆☆
Renwick. Owner: Phil Binnie. 70 ha. www.lakechalice.com
Fiery Sauvignon and delicate, unoaked Chardonnay, and steadily improving Pinot Noir, all given native yeast fermentations. The best wines in outstanding years, usually from single vineyards, are bottled under the Platinum label.

Lawson's Dry Hills ☆☆–☆☆☆
Blenheim, Marlborough. Owner: Barbara Lawson. 44 ha. www.lawsonsdryhills.co.nz
The late Ross Lawson and his wife Barbara began by supplying grapes to other wineries and began producing their own wines in 1992, and now release about 50,000 cases. The white wines used to be best: lush Gewurztraminer, benchmark Sauvignon, and appley Chardonnay. However, the 2007 Pinot Noir is outstanding.

Mount Riley ☆☆
Blenheim. Owner: Buchanan family. 120 ha. www.mountriley.co.nz
First releases date from 1996, and the wines are consistently fresh and even elegant. The top wines are the 17 Valley Chardonnay and Pinot Noir, both well-balanced and extremely enjoyable.

Nautilus ☆☆–☆☆☆
Renwick. Owner: Yalumba. 80 ha. www.nautilusestate.com
This Marlborough property is expanding fast. Chardonnay, Sauvignon, and Pinot Noir have been steadily improving, and now are among the best from the region.

The Ned ☆☆
Brancott. Owner: Brent Marris. www.thened.co.nz
After he sold Wither Hills (q.v.) in 2002, Brent Marris could have retired for life. Instead he acquired a large property in the Wairau valley and developed it. He now produces very good Sauvignon, Pinot Gris, and Pinot Noir.

No 1 Family Estate ☆☆
Renwick. Owner: Daniel Le Brun. www.no1familyestate.com
After Le Brun, who was raised in the Champagne region,

sold his eponymous business in 1997, he established a new winery for the production of *méthode traditionelle* sparkling wine. He produces various numbered *cuvées* from Chardonnay and Pinot Noir.

Saint Clair ☆☆–☆☆☆
Blenheim. Owner: Neal Ibbotson. 200 ha. www.saintclair.co.nz
This ambitious winery produces three tiers of wine: basic Marlborough bottlings, single vineyard wines, and Reserves. The single-vineyard wines show clearly the differing character of the increasingly dispersed Marlborough vineyards.

All the wines are well-made (since 1996 by Matt Thomson) and the best include the Fairhall Riesling, the Wairau Reserve Sauvignon, the Omaka Reserve Chardonnay and individual-block bottlings of Pinot Noir and other varieties.

Allan Scott ☆☆–☆☆☆
Blenheim. Owner: Allan Scott. 80 ha. www.allanscott.com
Scott is an experienced viticulturist who set up his own winery in 1990. It has grown to become one of the largest privately owned estates in the region, and now offers single-vineyard wines as well as its classic range. The wines are consistently well-made and stylish: exemplary expressions of Marlborough fruit with its refreshing acidity. The Sauvignon Blanc is always impeccable.

Seresin ☆☆☆
Blenheim Owner: Michael Seresin. 111 ha. www.seresin.co.nz
Seresin is a film maker based in London, and runs his estate to high ideals: organic farming, Biodynamic by 2011, and a reliance, whenever possible, on indigenous yeasts. The white wines are delicious: racy Riesling and Sauvignon, elegant, dry Pinot Gris, and Chardonnay in unoaked and oaked styles.

The sparkling wine, Moana, spends three years on the yeasts. The Pinot Noir is rich but lacks finesse. The commitment to quality at Seresin is commendably rigorous.

Staete Landt ☆☆
Blenheim. Owner: Ruud Maasdam and Dorien Vermaas. 21 ha. www.staetelandt.co.nz
This enthusiastic Dutch couple are aiming for perfection in their wines, conducting rigorous soil analysis and selection during harvest. The Sauvignon Blanc is made in a rounded style, the Pinot Gris has freshness as well as weight, and the Pinot Noir shows unusual precision.

Wairau River ☆☆
Blenheim. Owner: Chris and Phil Rose. 200 ha. www.wairauriverwines.com
Phil Rose is a farmer-turned-grape-grower, initially for Montana. The main focus is on ultra-typical Marlborough Sauvignon and Chardonnay, and is adding Riesling, Pinot Noir, and Pinot Gris to the range. The estate-grown wines are bottled under the Home Block range.

Winegrowers of Ara ☆–☆☆
Renwick. Owner: Dr. Damian Martin and partners. 385 ha. www.winegrowersofara.co.nz

An immensely ambitious project that hopes to plant some 1,600 hectares. The first crop was in 2005. The top range is called Resolute; the tier beneath is called Composite.

Initial releases of Sauvignon and Pinot Noir did not live up to the hype that accompanied the founding of the estate, but these are early days.

Wither Hills ☆☆
Blenheim. Owner: Lion Nathan. 300 ha. www.witherhills.co.nz
In 2002 the brewery group Lion Nathan paid a fortune for the estate Brent Marris and his father, John Marris, had developed in only eight years. Nobody begrudged the Marrises their success, as they had built up one of New Zealand's top estates with skill and hard work, especially in the vineyard. The formula was simple: varietal wines (Sauvignon, Chardonnay, Pinot Noir) of exemplary purity and balance. Winemaker Ben Glover has maintained that style, if not quite the flair of the Marris era.

Leading Nelson Producers

Greenhough ☆☆–☆☆☆
Hope, Nelson. Owner: Andrew Greenhough and Jennifer Wheeler. 11 ha. www.greenhough.co.nz
A rising star from Nelson, with good Chardonnay, and often dramatic and spicy Pinot Noir.

Neudorf ☆☆☆
Upper Moutere. Owner: Tim and Judy Finn. 23 ha. www.neudorf.co.nz
One of Nelson's leading wineries, owned by a friendly husband-and-wife team. A 100-old clapboard building houses the winery. The new-oaked Chardonnay is often the best wine, showing considerable complexity, and many consider it New Zealand's finest. The Riesling and Sauvignon are good, too, and the Pinot Noir, especially from the Moutere vineyard, improving all the time.

Seifried Estate ☆☆
Appleby. Owner: Hermann and Agnes Seifried. 195 ha. www.seifried.co.nz
A fast-growing and ambitious enterprise; the Seifrieds have built a new winery, not to mention restaurant and conference centre. The Seifrieds' son, Chris, is now responsible for the winemaking. Basic wines are sold under the Old Coach Road label, while the best wines appear under the Winemaker's Collection label.

Some good dry and late-harvest Riesling; also good Chardonnay, Gewürztraminer, and Pinot Noir. A new vineyard has been planted on exceptionally stony soil at Brightwater, which, it's hoped, will eventually deliver red wines of exceptional quality.

Te Mania ☆–☆☆☆
Richmond. Owner: Jon Harrey. 8 ha. www.temaniawines.co.nz
This is a small winery with a wide range of wines. Chardonnay is tangy and citric, and the Pinot Noir Reserve is surprisingly rich and concentrated.

Leading Central Otago Producers

Akarua ☆☆–☆☆☆
Bannockburn. Owner: Sir Clifford Skeggs. 47 ha.
www.akarua.com
Akarua's main interest is in Pinot Noir. Low yields and careful winemaking result in wines that are gaining in body and complexity as the vines age.

Amisfield ☆–☆☆☆
Lake Hayes. Owner: John Darby and partners. 60 ha. www.amisfield.co.nz
Claire Mulholland was for many years the winemaker at Martinborough Vineyard, so it is no surprise that the Pinot Noirs she now makes at Amisfield are first rate. The Pinot Gris is made in an off-dry style, but the dry Riesling is better balanced.

Black Ridge ☆☆
Alexandra. Owner: Sue Edwards and Verdun Burgess. 7 ha.
www.blackridge.co.nz
Burgess was a pioneer in an extremely tough region of schist cliffs and thin soils. He has focused on firm, dry, and age-worthy Rieslings, fresh Chardonnay, and somewhat earthy Pinot Noir.

Carrick ☆☆
Bannockburn. Owner: Steven Green. 25 ha. www.carrick.co.nz
Established in 2000, producing zesty, high-acidity whites, and gently oaky Pinot Noir.

Chard Farm ☆☆
Gibbston. Owner: Rob Hay. 27 ha.
www.chardfarm.co.nz
Named after the Chard family who came out from the eponymous Somerset village. Riesling and Pinot Noir are the specialties here, the former limey and zesty, the latter very perfumed and supple. Two single vineyard Pinots, The Tiger and The Viper, have been added to the range.

Felton Road ☆☆☆
Bannockburn. Owner: Nigel Greening. 30 ha.
www.feltonroad.com
Although Felton Road bottlings are among the most sought-after wines in New Zealand, the first releases were as recent as 1997. Blair Walter has been the winemaker from the outset. He produces two Rieslings (one dry, the other less so); two Chardonnays (unoaked and barrique fermented); and a range of superb Pinot Noirs made in a non-interventionist style.

The most sought-after Pinots are the acclaimed Block 3 and Block 5 bottlings, but the regular wine is almost as good at a fraction of the price. Nigel Greeening has remarked, "The French have terroir and Richebourg. We have dirt and Block 3." Both Walter and Greening are ardent practitioners of Biodynamism.

Gibbston Valley ☆☆–☆☆☆
Gibbston. Owner: Mike Stone. 60 ha. www.gvwines.co.nz
Alan Brady, originally from Ulster, pioneered grape-growing in Central Otago in 1981, but sold this successful winery in 1997 to set up his own handcrafted operation at Mount Edwards (q.v.). Riesling can be delicious and Chardonnay impressive, but Pinot Noir is the best wine, especially the Burgundian-style Reserve, which is aged in new oak. Winemaker Christopher Keys has added some single-vineyard wines to the range – not just Pinot Noir Le Maître, but Riesling and Pinot Gris, too.

Hawkshead ☆☆
Gibbston. Owner: Denis Marshall and Ulrike Kurenbach. 5 ha.
www.hawksheadwine.com
Former politician Marshall only began planting in 2001, and the first vintage here was in 2005. However, the Pinot Noir is already remarkably perfumed and sleek.

Kawarau ☆☆–☆☆☆
Cromwell. Owner: Charles Finny and Wendy Hinton. 15 ha.
www.karawauestate.co.nz
This organic vineyard has for some years has been producing superb Pinot Noir with impeccable balance, especially the Reserves. The winery also produces two good Chardonnays.

Mount Difficulty ☆☆☆
Bannockburn. Four vineyard owners. 40 ha.
www.mtdifficulty.co.nz
Since the first vintage in 1998, Matt Dicey has turned out some delicious wines from Chardonnay and Pinot Noir: both big wines with a lot of swagger and style.

As the vineyards have matured, he has been able to produce single-vineyard wines of great subtlety, such as the elegant Long Gully Vineyard Pinot. The second label is Roaring Meg, although there is nothing feeble or second-rate about the wines bearing it.

Mount Edward ☆☆–☆☆☆
Gibbston. Owner: Alan Brady and partners. 14 ha.
www.mountedward.co.nz
Alan Brady, the founder of Gibbston Valley (q.v.), sold the winery when it grew too large for his comfort, and in its place he set up this boutique winery, where he could control the entire process. Using minimal equipment and intervention, Brady produces sleek and concentrated Pinot Noir, from his organic vineyards and those belonging to contracted growers.

Olssens ☆☆
Bannockburn. Owner: John Olssen. 10 ha.
www.olssens.co.nz
Fresh, supple, well-balanced wines from Chardonnay and Pinot Noir. The Reserve Pinot is called Slapjack Creek, which has considerable concentration and weight.

Gibbston Valley winery and vineyard, Gibbston

Peregrine ☆☆–☆☆☆
Queenstown. Owner: Greg Hay. 50 ha.
www.peregrinewines.co.nz
A large operation by local standards, offering a wide range that includes Gewurztraminer and Sauvignon Blanc. The core wines nonetheless are the weighty Pinot Gris, spicy, cherry-tinged Pinot Noir, and powerful, vibrant, dry Riesling.

Pisa Range ☆☆–☆☆☆
Cromwell. Owner: Warwick and Jenny Hawker. 33 ha.
www.pisarangeestate.co.nz
Austrian Rudi Bauer has made some of the best wines to emerge from Central Otago, and is responsible for the excellent Pinot Noir here, especially the Poplar Block bottling, which has remarkable charm and complexity.

Quartz Reef ☆☆–☆☆☆
Cromwell. Owner: Rudi Bauer and partners. 15 ha.
www.quartzreef.co.nz
Austrian winemaker Rudi Bauer has spent 20 years in New Zealand, and is now installed at Quartz Reef, which opened its doors in 1998. As well as good Pinot Gris and Pinot Noir, Bauer produces delicious Chauvet sparkling wine in a joint venture with the Champagne house of that name. You can taste the connection.

Rippon ☆☆☆
Wanaka. Owner: Lois Mills. 15 ha. www.rippon.co.nz
Rolfe Mills planted the first vines in the region (apart from the nineteenth century settlers) in 1976, choosing an exquisite site on the shores of Lake Wanaka. The best wines here are Pinot Noir and Riesling. Young Pinot vines are bottled under the Jeunesse label; the top Pinot Noir is delicate yet long-lived. The same is true of the powerfully dry Riesling.

After the death of Rolfe Mills, his son Nick, who honed his winemaking skills at Burgundy's top estates, returned in 2002 to take control. The vineyards are now Biodynamic.

Valli ☆☆☆
Gibbston. Owner: Grant Taylor. 6 ha.
Grant Taylor, the winemaker at Gibbston Valley (q.v.), releases three Pinot Noirs from single vineyards. Handcrafted and delicious.

Waitiri Creek ☆☆
Gibbston. Owner: Paula Ramage and Alistair Ward. 8 ha. www.waitiricreek.co.nz
Contract winemaker Matt Connell produces good Pinot Noir and Pinot Gris from two vineyards.

Wild Earth ☆☆
Bannockburn. Owner: Quintin Quider. 35 ha.
www.wildearthwines.co.nz
This substantial property has two very different vineyards: one early ripening, the other not, giving consultant winemaker Grant Taylor contrasting material to work with. The first vintage was 2004 and the silky Pinot Noir has met with great acclaim.

Other South Island Producers

Giesen ☆☆
Sockburn, Christchurch. Owner: Marcel, Alex, and Theo Giesen. 200 ha. www.giesen.co.nz
The Giesen brothers came originally from the Palatinate, where their father had just one hectare of vines as a hobby, and developed the largest winery in Canterbury, although most of their vineyards are in Marlborough. Indeed, by 2006 theirs was the sixth-largest winery in the country.

They make stylish, dry Riesling, which develops with bottle age, and in the right years, some lovely late-harvest wines. They have a fine track record with Sauvignon and Chardonnay, and are also working hard on their Pinot Noir and sparkling wine.

Mud House ☆☆
Waipara. Owner: New Zealand Vineyard Estates. 212 ha. www.mudhouse.co.nz
Although based in Waipara, the company has extensive vineyards in Marlborough and Central Otago, too. Good quality across the range, especially in the top Swan range, which, ironically contains no wines from Waipara itself.

Pegasus Bay ☆☆–☆☆☆
Amberley, Waipara. Owner: Donaldson family. 40 ha. www.pegasusbay.com
Winemakers Matt Donaldson and Lynette Hudson have worked wonders for this Waipara winery, the first in the area, started by his parents. Their white wines, even the Sauvignon Blanc, are unusually lush and creamy, and there are exceptional late-harvest wines both from Riesling and Chardonnay as well as a keen dry Riesling.

Perhaps their best-known wine is the top Pinot Noir called Prima Donna. Wines made from fruit not grown in Waipara are bottled under the Main Divide label.

Pyramid Valley ☆☆
Waipara. Owners: Mike and Claudia Weersing. 19 ha (owned and leased). www.pyramidvalley.co.nz
A small property planted with high-density Chardonnay and Pinot Noir in 2000, and farmed Biodynamically. There is fine Riesling and other varieties in its Growers Collection, from purchased grapes, to keep it occupied until its first estate vintage in 2006.

Waipara Springs ☆☆
Waipara. Owner: Moore and Grant families. 26 ha.
www.waiparasprings.co.nz
Waipara Springs is one of the pioneers of the area, concentrating on Pinot Noir, Merlot, Chardonnay, and Gewurztraminer. Premo is the top range.

South Africa

South Africa joined the wine world under its Dutch colonists in the 1600s. In the 1800s it became known for one of the world's best sweet wines. In the twentieth century it was a popular resource for "sherries" and bargain white wines. In the 1970s it started playing catch-up to Australia and California. But it really came to life at the end of apartheid.

The reasons for the backwardness of the country in viticulture were largely self-imposed. The government purposely limited both the supply of good grape-vines and the land to grow them on. Nor could the welcome establishment of the Wine of Origin system in 1973 make much headway, given the isolation of South Africa during the apartheid era. International sanctions inhibited the importation of good quality vines and cuttings, and South African winemakers, however skilled, could not stay fully in touch with the viticultural and other developments in the rest of the wine world. But now that South Africa is no longer a pariah among nations, the full potential of its vineyards is slowly being realized.

There are those who argue that the natural conditions of the Cape for the vine are as good as any on earth, and a growing number of wines since 1998 are showing this to be the case. The essential grape varieties are now at last being planted, and some spectacular wines are emerging from the lovely estates of Stellenbosch and Franschhoek, and from the remoter regions of Robertson and Swartland. Cooler regions such as Walker Bay and Elgin are also beginning to show their potential. The natural advantages of the coastal region of the Cape are impressive. Ideal slopes can be found facing every point of the compass. There is an eight-month growth period; never any frost, never any hail, autumn rain is rare, and there are very few of the diseases that plague other vineyards.

An important quality factor is the wide range of temperatures: cool nights between hot days, the Cape pattern, reduce night-time respiration from the vine leaves. The plant, unable to consume sugars accumulated during the day, stores more of them. None of these conditions is a guarantee of good wine, but taken together, with intelligent handling, they encourage optimism.

On the downside, while most coastal-region vineyards need soil pH adjustment, the major problems facing South Africa's growers in the past two decades have related to the quality of planting material. It was only in the mid-1980s that the authorities liberalized regulations governing the importation of vines. This followed the "Chardonnay scandal", in which it became clear that the draconian agricultural legislation left the avant-garde farming community with no alternative but to smuggle in premium varieties unavailable from the nurseries. Moreover, the vineyards established – particularly of Cabernet – were severely virus infected, often inhibiting ripening and leading to harshly tannic wines. More recent plantings are all on virus-free material, but only in recent years have nurseries been able to cope with the demand from growers.

Many grape farmers were not wine drinkers. South Africa has long been a brandy, rather than a wine, culture. Non-white

Cape Dutch architecture distinctive of many estates

Prohibition ended in 1962; grocers could only sell wine from 1979. Government regulation encouraged the planting of vines for eventual distillation, or for the production of cheap fortified wines. So when South Africa finally emerged from the nightmare of apartheid, its vineyards were dominated by grapes – notably Chenin Blanc and Colombard – not associated with fine wine production. These grapes are still dominant, but hot on their heels are varieties with greater commercial appeal such as Sauvignon Blanc and Chardonnay.

Given this background, it is astonishing how swiftly South Africa has progressed. There is growing domestic demand, and the swift replacement of poor-quality vineyards with plantings of good modern clones in carefully selected sites. That bastion of conservatism and protectionism, the KWV – an organization founded in 1918 to protect grape farmers from low wine prices, by fixing a minimum price and distilling the surplus – has had its powers curtailed throughout the 1990s. This has left the industry free to develop in ways more attuned to the requirements of an increasingly international market. Successful brands have been created to provide inexpensive wine of sound quality, and at the opposite end of the spectrum, new estates have sprouted like mushrooms.

By 2002, a new cellar was opening its doors every eight days – even if many of them were the tiniest of boutique wineries. At the same time, "empowerment" projects are burgeoning, as landowners find ways not only to provide good working and living conditions for their (mostly black) farm workers, but also to involve them more actively in the business.

The old staple grape of South Africa was Steen, the local name for Chenin Blanc, which was used for everything from thirst-quenchers (it was saved by its relatively high acidity and could be very pleasant) to "sherry"-style fortifieds – which were the country's biggest international success. If there was a red equivalent, it was Pinotage, an odd cross between Pinot Noir and Cinsault peculiar to the Cape, making a dark, scented wine not to everybody's taste. It plays a pivotal role in the so-called "Cape Blend", an officially recognized style that combines Pinotage with Bordeaux varieties. Some winemakers see this as a style unique to South Africa; others regard it as an underhand way to give Pinotage more prestige than it deserves. Now Sauvignon Blanc has proved a hit, with strong demand on domestic and export markets and Chardonnay (absent from

the Cape until the 1970s) is steadily improving, while there are successful attempts to revive wines from Chenin and Semillon, which can be excellent if yields are kept low, from the few old vineyards that have not been grubbed up. Cabernet and Shiraz are now the mainstays of red wine production, but there is increasingly elegant Pinot Noir from Walker Bay and lush Merlot from Stellenbosch.

Dozens of young winemakers, still in their twenties, have worked vintages in regions as diverse as Priorat and Burgundy, and have brought their knowledge and experience back to South Africa. If the actual achievement is not quite as stellar as the South Africans themselves would have us believe, there is no doubt that the potential for great wines is beginning to be realized.

Regions of Origin

The Wine of Origin system was introduced in 1973, dividing wine-producing areas into four major regions (Breede River Valley, Coast, Olifants River, and Little Karoo), and a considerable number of "districts" and "wards", a system that only the most determined consumer can hope to understand. Regardless of the official category to which they belong, the following are the most important wine regions.

Breede River Valley An immense region that includes the important districts of Worcester (q.v.), Robertson (q.v.), and Swellendam. Almost 13,000 hectares are planted but much of the production is used for distillation into brandy.

Cape Point A very cool, one-winery designated area on the other side of the mountains from Constantia. Sauvignon and Sémillon are the best grapes here.

Coastal Region A catch-all appellation that may be given to wines made from grapes grown in all of the following regions: the Stellenbosch, Durbanville, Swartland, Paarl, Constantia, and Tulbagh districts.

Constantia Once the world's most famous Muscat wine, from the Cape. The ward in which it was produced is now a highly regarded cool-climate area. There are few estates, many of them hemmed in by suburban development, but all maintain high quality.

Darling Region northwest of Cape Town, best-known for Sauvignon Blanc, although other varieties, red as well as white, are beginning to prove themselves.

Durbanville A small, hilly district just north of Cape Town. Durbanville Hills is by far the most important producer based in this distinctly cool area. Sauvignon and Merlot perform best.

Elgin A cool area, east of Cape Town, with shale and clay soils. Although long championed by Neil Ellis, Paul Cluver used to be the only winery here. There are now a few others, and some Stellenbosch wineries source grapes from here.

Elim A tiny region east of Walker Bay, and the most southerly in the country, but with a growing reputation for Sauvignon and other cool climate wines.

SOUTH AFRICA IN ROUND FIGURES

South Africa, with 102,000 hectares of vineyards, is the world's ninth largest wine producer, with three per cent of total world production. Fifty-six per cent of the grapes are white. Chenin Blanc, although in decline, still represents almost 19 per cent of plantings, with Colombard at around 18 per cent; Cabernet Sauvignon, with 13 per cent, is the leading red grape, with Shiraz in second place with ten per cent.

Fortified wines represent about seven per cent of the domestic market. There are 59 cooperatives and 481 estate wineries and private cellars. Domestic consumption of South African wine remains steady at around 7.5 litres per capita.

Franschhoek A beautiful and narrow valley east of Stellenbosch, and named after the Huguenots who settled here. It is now the self-proclaimed gastronomic centre of South Africa, and home to many high-quality and ambitious estates.

Klein (Little) Karoo The easternmost Wine of Origin district. Very little rainfall and all irrigated vineyards. Best for dessert wine and brandy, though some good Chenin Blanc is also produced. A vast and elongated area.

Olifants River Northerly Wine of Origin district, with a hot, dry climate. Once known mostly for wine for distilling from irrigated vineyards, Olifants River is now producing a growing range of value-for-money wines.

Paarl A region of growing importance, 80-kilometres (50-miles) northeast of Cape Town. It boasts some of the country's best vineyards, both red and white. Includes the wards of Franschhoek (q.v.) and Wellington, the latter of which tends to be warmer than the rest of Paarl.

Robertson A Wine of Origin district inland and east of Cape Town. Irrigated vineyards with alluvial and calcareous soils along the Kogmanskloof and Breede rivers provide some high-quality white, especially Chardonnay, and much-improved red table wines, as well as fine sparkling wines.

Stellenbosch The beautiful old Cape Dutch town and its demarcated region 50-kilometres (30-miles) east of Cape Town, extending south to the ocean at False Bay. Most of South Africa's best estates, especially for red wine, are in the mountain foothills of the region. Includes the wards of Bottelary, Devon Valley, Jonkershoek Valley, Papegaaiberg, and Simonsberg.

Swartland A warm Wine of Origin district around Malmesbury, between Tulbagh and the west coast. Most of the growers here supply cooperatives, but the excellent conditions that exist for Mediterranean varietals are now encouraging new estates to establish themselves in their own right. Swartland's old-vine Chenin Blanc is increasingly prized.

CAPE WINEMAKER'S GUILD

This loose grouping of 37 ambitious winemakers was founded in 1983. Membership is by invitation only, and now represents a who's who of top South African winemakers. In 1985 the CWG launched its annual auction, at which members offered very small quantities of their finest wines (often no more than a single barrel) for sale. There was a danger that the wines selected, on the basis of the CWG's own blind tastings, were simply the ripest and biggest wines, but that trend has been corrected, and auction offerings are now testing-grounds for more elegant styles or original blends.

These special bottlings have often shown the full potential of Cape wines, setting new standards for quality and style. The equally well-known Nederburg auction is only open to buyers from the wine trade; the Guild auctions are open to all.

Tulbagh A district sheltered in the hills north of Paarl, and formerly best-known for white wines, although some stunning Rhône-style wines and other reds are altering that perception.

Walker Bay Southeast of Cape Town and close to the coastal town of Hermanus (including the Hemel-en-Aarde valley) is this region that has already won a high reputation for Burgundian varieties.

Worcester Enormous wine region around the Breede and Hex river valleys, bordering Robertson to the east. Rainfall is usually high enough for good table wine; southeast to Swellendam irrigation is necessary. Its vineyards produce 22 per cent of all South Africa's wine.

Leading Stellenbosch Producers

Alto ☆☆
Owner: Distell and Lusan Premium Wines. 76 ha. www.alto.co.za
A superbly sited vineyard, running straight up a granite mountainside near the sea for a mile and a half (in which it rises nearly 300 metres/975 feet) yielding long-lived Cabernet and a red blend called Alto Rouge.

L'Avenir ☆☆–☆☆☆
Owner: Michel Laroche. 60 ha.
L'Avenir began as an extremely unlikely joint venture, created in 1992, between urbane Mauritius sugar broker Marc Wiehe and enthusiastic winemaker François Naudé. They built a reputation for Chardonnay, velvety Pinotage, and cassis-infused Cabernet Sauvignon. In 2005 the property was sold to Chablis producer Laroche and Naudé retired. Much of the vineyard has been replanted.

Beyerskloof ☆☆–☆☆☆
Owner: Beyers Truter and Simon Halliday. 70 ha. www.beyerskloof.co.za
Beyers Truter was the respected winemaker at Kanonkop (q.v.), but this is essentially his own label, specializing in tannic, structured Bordeaux blends and lush Pinotage. In 2001, Truter introduced a Cape blend called Synergy.

Le Bonheur ☆☆
Owner: Distell and Lusan Premium Wines. 54 ha. www.lebonheur.co.za
Le Bonheur's vineyards, on the generally north-facing slopes of the Klapmutskop mountain, have been extensively replanted over the last 20 years. This estate produces a fine Cabernet; a Bordeaux blend called Prima; and good, unwooded Sauvignon Blanc.

J P Bredell ☆–☆☆☆
Owner: Anton Bredell. 95 ha. www.bredellwines.co.za
Since 1991, some of the Cape's best "ports" have been produced here, and red wines are growing in quality.

Clos Malverne ☆☆
Owner: Seymour Pritchard. 27 ha.
www.closmalverne.co.za
Attractive Sauvignon and Pinotage, and a brambly Cape blend called Auret.

Cordoba ☆☆
Owner: Jannie Jooste. 36 ha. www.cordobawines.co.za
A boutique winery on the Helderberg specializing in a burly, oaky Cabernet Franc/Merlot blend called Crescendo. Production was temporarily halted while the vineyards were being replanted.

Dalla Cia ☆☆–☆☆☆
Owner: Giorgio Dalla Cia. No vineyards.
www.dallacia.com
On retiring as Meerlust's winemaker, the irrepressible Dalla Cia continued to make wine under his own name: a spicy, oaky Cabernet, and a Bordeaux blend named, naturally, after himself – Giorgio.

Delaire
Owner: Laurence Graff. 22 ha. www.delairewinery.co.za
This ailing estate was acquired by jeweller Laurence Graff, who has spent on a fortune renovating the estate and adding a restaurant and hotel. A new winemaker, Chris Kelly, is also in place, and there is no reason why Delaire should not begin to produce exceptional wines.

Delheim ☆☆
Simonsberg. Owner: Sperling family. 150 ha.
www.delheim.com
Delheim has long produced traditional Cape style reds, tannic and short on fruit, as well as off-dry white wines from Riesling and Gewurztraminer. Recent vintages have shown greater ripeness, especially the plummy Vera Cruz Shiraz and botrytized Riesling.

De Toren ☆☆☆
Owner: Emil den Dulk. 20 ha. www.de-toren.com
A new star, De Toren's sole wine is a dense, voluptuous Bordeaux blend called Fusion V, first produced in 1999. This exceptional wine is made by Albie Koch, who, despite his tender years, has had extensive winemaking experience in California and France.

De Trafford ☆☆☆
Owner: David Trafford. 5 ha. www.detrafford.co.za
Former architect David Trafford makes most of his wines from purchased fruit, employing natural yeast fermentation. As well as rich, powerful Cabernet, Merlot, and Shiraz, he produces luscious Chenin Blanc with complex aromas of cooked apples. His apricotty "straw wine" is also made from Chenin.

De Waal ☆–☆☆
Owner: de Waal family. 120 ha. www.uiterwyk.co.za
A beautiful estate (one of the less flamboyant), bottling a small quantity of its best wines in a traditional cellar. Previously known as Uiterwyk, the name was changed in 2001. Consistently good Pinotage, especially the old-vine bottling called Top of the Hill.

Distell
www.distell.co.za
A vast company, formed by the amalgamation of the Distillers and Stellenbosch Farmers groups. Principal estates are Alto, Le Bonheur, Uitkyk, Neethlingshof, and Stellenzicht, but other ventures include Nederburg, Plaisir de Merle, Zonnebloem, Fleur du Cap, Le Roux, and Durbanville Hills. All told, Distell, in 2002, controlled about 30 per cent of all Cape wine production.

Eikendal ☆–☆☆
Owner: Substantia company. 65 ha. www.eikendal.com
The wines at this Swiss-owned estate have long been sound, if not always exciting, but quality is improving with new investments in the winery. Lush Chardonnay and Semillon.

Neil Ellis ☆☆☆
Owner: Neil Ellis and Hans Pieter Schroeder.
www.neilellis.com
Since 1988, Neil Ellis has set himself up as a leading winemaker/négociant at the top-end of the Cape wine market. He sources grapes from vastly different microclimates to produce a range of wines, each with striking individuality. The Premium wines are very reliable, and the Vineyard Selection range is often outstanding, if pricey. Several Sauvignon Blanc *cuvées*, some of them emphatically grassy, as well as some top Cabernets have confirmed his reputation.

Ernie Els ☆☆–☆☆☆
Owner: Ernie Els and Jean Engelbrecht. 72 ha.
www.ernieelswines.com
Although this grotesquely expensive Bordeaux blend bears the famous golfer's name, the fruit comes mostly from Rust-en-Vrede (q.v.), where the wine is also made. The result: an international-style red, sleek and oaky. The winery also produces Cirrus, a Syrah made in collaboration with Napa's Silver Oak winery; like all Silver Oak Cabernets, it is aged in rather sweet American oak.

Ken Forrester ☆☆☆
Owner: Ken Forrester. 33 ha.
www.kenforresterwines.com
Former restaurateur Forrester is an ardent champion of unfashionable varietals, in his case Chenin Blanc and Grenache. The consultant winemaker is Martin Meinert (q.v.), and the dry Chenins are among the Cape's finest, as is his botrytized version called T: a glorious confection of apricot and cream. Also noteworthy are the delicate Sauvignon Blanc, and the fresh and spicy Grenache/Syrah blend.

The Foundry ☆☆☆
Owner: Chris Williams and James Reid. No vineyards.
www.thefoundry.co.za
Opulent yet refined Syrah and Viognier are the focus of this boutique winery, founded by Meerlust winemaker Chris Williams.

Glenelly ☆☆
Owner: May-Eliane de Lencquesaing. 57 ha.
In her mid-seventies, the then owner of Château Pichon-Lalande decided to develop this property near Rustenberg and

the first vintage was 2003, blending Shiraz with the Bordeaux varieties. The wine is well-balanced and should gain weight as the vines age. With such a perfectionist owner great things can be anticipated.

Grangehurst ☆☆–☆☆☆
Owner: Jeremy Walker. 14 ha. www.grangehurst.co.za
The gifted Walker originally focused on two wines: an elegant Pinotage, and a fine Cabernet/Merlot blend. Since the late 1990s he has added Nikela, a concentrated yet vigorous Cape blend, and an impressive pure Cabernet.

Hartenberg ☆☆
Owner: Hartenberg Holdings. 95 ha. www.hartenbergestate.com
A substantial investment programme has contributed to noteworthy improvement in the estate's formerly rustic wines. The various Shiraz bottlings, notably The Stork, are particularly impressive, but Chardonnay and Merlot are lush and inviting too.

Hidden Valley ☆–☆☆
Owner: David Hidden. 44 ha. www.hiddenvalleywines.com
Exuberant former oilman Hidden bought this property in 1998 and built a winery into the rock. In 2008 he persuaded Warwick winemaker Louis Nel to lead the team, and the range is still being developed. There are two Sauvignons, one from this estate, the other from Elim fruit. You can compare the two at the estate restaurant.

Ingwe ☆☆
Owner: Alain Moueix. 24 ha. www.ingwewines.co.za
Alain Moueix owns various properties in St-Emilion and Pomerol, so Bordeaux rules at his Helderberg outpost. The basic wines are not of great interest, but the Ingwe Bordeaux blend is stylish and oaky.

Jordan ☆☆☆
Owner: Gary and Kathy Jordan. 105 ha. www.jordanwines.com
After successful careers, Kathy (an economist) and Gary (a geologist) Jordan returned to the family farm, and immediately established it as a quality avant-garde producer. Healthy, virus-free vineyards and meticulous cellar practices have contributed to their success. Their top wine is the concentrated and chocolatey Cobbler's Hill Reserve: a Cabernet-dominated blend aged in new oak, but quality is high throughout the range. The Nine Yards Chardonnay shows perfectly integrated oak, and the Syrah is bright and lively.

Kanonkop ☆☆☆
Owner: Krige family. 100 ha. www.kanoncop.co.za
Winemaker Beyers Truter is devoted to Pinotage, and regularly produced one of the Cape's richest and best. Equally remarkable was his long-lived Bordeaux blend, Paul Sauer: rustic in the best sense, since it never lacks fruit despite its rude vigour. Long-established vineyards and traditional vinification techniques, such as fermentation in shallow troughs, ensured consistent quality. Truter is now taking a back seat and concentrating on Beyerskloof (q.v.), and the new winemaker is the very talented Abrie Beeslaar.

Kanu ☆☆
Owner: Hydro Holdings. 40 ha. www.kanu.co.za
The first vintage here was 1998, made by Chenin maestro Teddy Hall, who left in 2003. The most important wine here, unusually, is the crisp Chenin, which retains lively acidity, as does its honeyed late harvest version. Sauvignon and Chardonnay are equally good. There is a sound Bordeaux blend called Keystone.

Kleine Zalze ☆☆
Owner: Kobus Basson. 55 ha. www.kleinezalze.co.za
A tourist complex as well as a winery, from which emerges a four tiered range, in ascending order of quality: Foot of Africa, Cellar Selection, Vineyard Selection, and Family Reserve. The wines are commercially driven but very well made. The Sauvignon Blanc can be outstanding.

Longridge ☆☆
Owner: Aldo van der Laan. 40 ha. www.longridge.co.za
This former négociant winery is enjoying an new incarnation with robust, powerful, varietal wines.

Meerlust ☆☆☆
Owner: Hannes Myburgh. 160 ha. www.meerlust.co.za
Hannes Myburgh occupies the same exquisite manor house that his ancestors called home in 1756. Giorgio Della Cia, who made the wines from 1978, retired some years ago, and has been replaced by the equally able Chris Williams. Cabernet Sauvignon had already been planted here in the 1960s, followed by Merlot, Cabernet Franc, and Pinot Noir following in the 1970s.

Meerlust's top wine is the Bordeaux blend called Rubicon, but the Merlot and idiosyncratic Pinot Noir are almost as fine. It took Dalla Cia 11 years to be satisfied with his Chardonnay, first released in 1995, and, unexpectedly, a dead ringer for Meursault. All the wines, Chardonnay included, benefit from five years of bottle age. Rubicon, in its youth, can have assertive tannins and dour pickle tones, but with patience, the wine becomes cedary and harmonious.

Meinert Wines ☆☆–☆☆☆
Owner: Martin Meinert. 13 ha. www.meinertwines.com
Martin Meinert established the reputation of Vergelegen (q.v.). Since the late 1990s, he has focused on his own label. His Cabernet blend, Devon Crest, and Merlot are rich and profound, and it's arguable whether his top red blend, Synchronicity, is superior.

Middelvlei ☆–☆☆
Owner: Momberg family. 130 ha. www.middelvlei.co.za
An estate with a long-established reputation for Pinotage, and recently for Cabernet Sauvignon and Shiraz.

Morgenhof ☆–☆☆
Simonsberg. Owner: Anne Cointreau-Huchon. 72 ha. www.morgenhof.com
The Morgenhof wines are extremely reliable and good-value,

especially the lush Bordeaux blend once called Première Sélection but renamed Morgenhof Estate.

Morgenster ☆☆

Somerset West. Owner: Giulio Bertrand. 40 ha. www.morgenster.co.za
Piedmontese industrialist, Bertrand, bought the run-down property in 1993 in order to develop olive groves. Inevitably vineyards followed, the aim being to produce a St-Emilion-style wine with the help of Cheval Blanc winemaker Pierre Lurton. The first vintage was 2000: ripe, oaky, and stylish. The second wine is the lighter, cherry-tinged Lourens River Valley. Bertrand has not been able to resist adding a Nebbiolo to the range, and it is remarkably good, even if lacking in varietal character.

Mulderbosch ☆☆☆

Owner: Hydro Holdings. 27 ha. www.mulderbosch.co.za
Mulderbosch has the reputation of being the Cape's answer to New Zealand's Cloudy Bay: several highly successful Sauvignon Blanc vintages together with some excellent Chardonnay have contributed to this image, though winemaker Mike Dobrovic is too eclectic a personality to fit easily into so simplistic a comparison. The Sauvignon is surely the most mouth-watering of all those the Cape can offer.

A plummy Merlot/Cabernet blend sold under the Faithful Hound label, and a lush late-harvest Sauvignon complete an impressive range.

Neethlingshof ☆–☆☆

Owner: Distell and Lusan Premium Wines. 93 ha. www.neethlingshof.co.za
Hans-Joachim Schreiber, a retired German banker, bought Neethlingshof in 1985. He invested heavily in the property, and established its reputation for sound Chardonnay and Shiraz, and for outstanding botrytized Riesling. It is now part of the Distell group.

Overgaauw ☆☆

Owner: van Velden family. 75 ha. www.overgaauwco.za
Long-established, family owned property, producing one of the best Cape "ports" as well as the Cape's only Sylvaner. Merlot and Cabernet are increasingly impressive, as is the Bordeaux blend Tria Corda.

Rudera ☆☆

Owner: Riana Hall. 18 ha. www.rudera.co.za
This was the private label of the winemaker at Kanu (q.v.), vinifying grapes sourced mostly from leased vineyards, and producing delicious Chenin Blanc in both dry and nobly sweet styles. In 2008 a divorce led to Hall's departure, but the winery continues under his ex-wife's direction.

Rust-en-Vrede ☆☆–☆☆☆

Owner: Engelbrecht family. 50 ha. www.rustenvrede.com
Until the late 1990s, this historic estate produced highly

regarded, Cape-style reds that were tannic and often astringent in their youth. Since 1998, Jannie Engelbrecht's son, Jean, has been in charge, and he adopted a fleshier, more accessible style. The elegant Estate blend is a far cry from the earthier vintages of a decade ago, and varietal wines from Cabernet and Shiraz are in the same mould. Englebrecht also works closely with golfer Ernie Els on the latter's own label and on a more experimental range they call Guardian Peak.

Rustenberg ☆☆☆–☆☆☆☆

Owner: Simon Barlow. 150 ha. www.rustenberg.co.za
Perhaps the most beautiful estate in the Cape: low white Dutch buildings shaded by enormous trees, and with extensive vineyards on south-facing slopes. Recent replanting, substantial cellar investment, and a change of winemaker (Adi Badenhorst, succeeded by Randolph Christians) have all confirmed Rustenberg's place in the front rank of South Africa's producers. The flagship red is the superb Peter Barlow Cabernet blend; the top white, the Five Soldiers Chardonnay. Brampton is the second label, and the excellent John X Merriman Bordeaux blend occupies the space between.

Saxenburg ☆☆–☆☆☆

Owner: Adrian Bührer. 85 ha. www.saxenburg.co.za
Saxenburg is widely regarded for its red wines, particularly those sold under the Private Collection (Reserve) label. The Shiraz and Cabernet have been particularly successful. Winemaker Nico van der Merwe is exceptionally skilled, but some of the wines are too expensive for the quality.

Simonsig ☆☆–☆☆☆

Owner: Malan family. 215 ha. www.simonsig.co.za
Frans Malan and his three sons had runaway successes with blended, wood matured whites, and were the first in the Cape to make a true *méthode traditionnelle* sparkling wine. Simonsig's reputation for red wines is based firmly on Pinotage, but new wines have been added to the range: Frans Malan Cape blend, the single-vineyard Merindol Syrah, and the charming and cedary Bordeaux blend called Tiara. Chenin, oaked and unoaked, remains immensely and deservedly popular on the domestic market.

Stark-Condé ☆☆☆

Owner: José Condé. 40 ha. www.stark-conde.co.za
A new star in Stellenbosch, Condé is an American who, since 1998, has been producing small quantities of sumptuous, concentrated, polished Cabernet Sauvignon and Syrah.

Stellenzicht ☆☆

Owner: Distell and Lusan Premium Wines. 77 ha. www.stellenzicht.co.za
Stellenzicht achieved international recognition in the 1990s

Neethlingshof, Stellenbosch

for its Shiraz. Since 1998, Guy Webber has been the winemaker, and the estate is now part of the Distell group, but the emphasis remains on Pinotage and Shiraz. The principal range of varietal wines is Golden Triangle, but the Stellenzicht Vineyards wines (Syrah, an estate blend, and Semillon) can be exceptional.

Sterhuis ☆☆–☆☆☆
Bottelary. Owner: Kruger family. 48 ha
Johan Kruger used to make the wines for Jordan (q.v.). Unusually for Stellenbosch, there is a greater focus on white wines than red, since the estate includes many old Chenin bush vines. Astra White is a top white blend, and the Barrel Selection Chardonnay is almost as fine. Nor does Kruger fail when it comes to red wines: Astra Red is a polished and persistent Bordeaux blend.

Thelema ☆☆☆
Owner: Webb and McLean families. 95 ha.
www.thelema.co.za
This beautiful estate lies high up in the hills. Although the soils are relatively fertile, the skills of winemaker Gyles Webb have won Thelema a worldwide reputation for its finely structured Cabernet Sauvignon, Merlot, Sauvignon Blanc, and Chardonnay. The range is remarkable for its consistency from year to year, and the Merlot reserve, a wondrous confection of black fruits, oak, and chocolatey nuances, is one of the Cape's finest. Grape supply has been augmented by the acquisition of vineyards in Elgin.

Tokara ☆☆
Owner: G T Ferreira. 110 ha. www.tokara.com
This venture had a lavish new winery and restaurant to show by late 2002, but no wines. Now vineyards in Stellenbosch, Walker Bay, and Elgin give winemaker Miles Mossop plenty to work with. The result is a range of great purity, blends as well as varietal wines, and good-value second wines under the Zondernaam label.

Uva Mira ☆☆–☆☆☆
Owner: Denise Weedon. 30 ha.
www.uvamira.co.za
High in the hills lies this fine property, overseen by young winemaker Matthew van Heerden. Elevation gives the Sauvignon, Chardonnay, and Uva Mira Bordeaux blend a cool-climate elegance with just a touch of delicate herbaceousness. The first vintage was 2004.

Vergelegen ☆☆–☆☆☆☆
Somerset West. Owner: Anglo American Farms. 120 ha.
www.vergelegen.co.za
Vergelegen is one of the Cape's oldest properties (dating back to around 1700), a mansion and glorious gardens rich in history and full of treasure. It has been extensively renovated since being purchased by Anglo American Farms in 1987, and a new hilltop winery was built. Winemaker Martin Meinert put Vergelegen on the map, and since 1997, Andre van Rensburg has consolidated its reputation. Although best-known for Sauvignon and Chardonnay, the red wines – Cabernet, Merlot, and the superb Estate blend – are increasingly rich and complex. Bordeaux remains Van Rensberg's model, although he knows full well the climate and terroir are different.

Vergenoegd ☆☆
Owner: Faure family. 90 ha. www.vergenoegd.co.za
This 300-year-old estate once supplied bulk grapes to wholesalers, such as the KWV. Today it bottles all its own wine, and since the late 1990s, quality has increased dramatically, with firm, tannic Cabernet and age-worthy Merlot, as well as good Cape style "port".

Villiera ☆☆
Owner: Grier family. 210 ha. www.villiera.com
Until 2002 this estate was considered to be within Paarl; with a stroke of the pen it became part of Stellenbosch. It is cooler than average and strongly focused on value-for-money, high-quality wines. Villiera has been particularly successful with Merlot and Merlot/Cabernet blends, and a complete range of classic-method sparkling wines.

Vriesenhof/Talana Hill/Paradyskloof ☆☆–☆☆☆
Owner: Jan Boland Coetzee and partners. 37 ha.
www.vriesenhof.co.za
On the Helderberg side of Stellenbosch, Vriesenhof's mountain slopes are cooled by the breeze coming off False Bay. The estate has a good reputation for Cabernet and Cabernet-based blends, sold either under the premium Talana Hill label, or as Vriesenhof. The Bordeaux blend called Kallista can be rather tough, but there is fine Chardonnay and Pinotage, and a growing enthusiasm on winemaker Coetzee's part for Pinot Noir.

Warwick Estate ☆☆–☆☆☆
Simonsberg. Owner: Ratcliffe family. 55 ha.
ww.warwickwine.com
Very much a family business, this leading property was run with both energy and charm by Norma Ratcliffe and she has now handed the reins to her equally accomplished son Mike.

For some years, its top wine has been the successful Bordeaux blend Trilogy, but recent additions to the range are a Chardonnay, the Cape blend, Three Cape Ladies, and, most recently, a Bordeaux blend called The First Lady, in honour of Norma Ratcliffe. Warwick also has a good reputation for its blueberry-scented Cabernet Franc.

Waterford ☆☆–☆☆☆
Owner: Jeremy Ord. 50 ha. www.waterfordestate.co.za
After Ord bought this hillside farm in 1998, he constructed a charming Tuscan-style cloistered winery, and hired Kevin Arnold, formerly of Rust-en-Vrede (q.v.), to make the wines. From the outset Arnold made some effortlessly balanced Cabernet and Shiraz, and less convincing white wines, but caused some controversy when he released a multi-varietal blend called The Jem: the wine is concentrated and opulent yet fresh, but the price is stratospheric.

Zevenwacht ☆–☆☆
Owner: Harold Johnson. 200 ha. www.zevenwacht.co.za
Zevenwacht's vineyards are cooled by breezes off False Bay. They yield easy-drinking red wines with flavour rather than weight, and lush, spicy Gewurztraminer.

Zorgvliet ☆☆
Owner: Mac van de Merwe. 50 ha. www.zorgvliet.com
A change in ownership and a new winemaker in Neil Moorhouse have worked wonders at Zorgvliet. The Cabernet and Petit Verdot are sumptuous and oaky, and there is a fine Bordeaux blend called Richelle.

Leading Constantia Producers

Buitenverwachting ☆☆–☆☆☆
Owner: Richard Mueller and Lars Maack. 120 ha. www.buitenverwachting.com
Part of Van der Stel's original Constantia farm and a consistently good Cape producer. The wines are nurtured by winemaker Hermann Kirschbaum, who has been here since 1993. Buiten Blanc is its crowd-pleasing white blend, but more impressive wines include rich Sauvignon Blanc and Chardonnay, a leafy Cabernet Franc, and the excellent Cabernet/Merlot blend called Christine.

Constantia Glen
Owner: Gus Allen. 30 ha. www.constantiaglen.com
The Allen family planted vines from the mid-1990s on their cattle ranch, first made wine here in 2005, and built a winery in 2007. The first releases, Sauvignon Blanc, show attractive lime and melon characters, and a red Bordeaux blend is due to follow.

Constantia Uitsig ☆☆
Owner: David McKay and partners. 31 ha. www.constantia-uitsig.com
Bought in 1988 as a run-down property, Constantia Uitsig has been entirely replanted with mostly white grapes. Some of the wines are made in both a wooded and unwooded style. Although the Merlot-dominated red blend is very enjoyable, the strength here lies with white varietals such as Sauvignon, Semillon, and Chardonnay.

Groot Constantia ☆–☆☆
Owner: Groot Constantia Trust. 90 ha. www.grootconstantia.co.za
The original farm, founded by the Cape's first governor, Simon van der Stel, in 1685, and the source of the legendary Constantia dessert wine of the eighteenth and nineteenth centuries. An extensive replanting programme and renovation of the cellar have contributed to an improvement in the wines, but direction by committee allows little initiative on the part of the winemakers. The best wine has always been the red Gouverneurs' Blend, aged in new oak; biscuity Chardonnay and Semillon are also released under the Gouverneurs label.

Klein Constantia ☆☆–☆☆☆
Owner: Jooste family. 82 ha. www.kleinconstantia.com
An historic property, which was part of Van der Stel's original Constantia farm. The Joostes bought the estate in 1980 and renovated it, and in 1984 hired Ross Gower as winemaker, although he left in 2004. Cool vineyards, state-of-the-art viticulture, and a well-managed cellar ensure a high overall quality for all the estate wines. Sauvignon (especially the excellent Perdeblokke bottling), Semillon, and Chardonnay

are attractive and vigorous, but the red wines can sometimes be lean, although recent vintages have been fleshier. Lowell Jooste and Ross Gower revived the famous sweet wine of Constantia, which they sell as Vin de Constance. It is made from unfortified late-picked Muscat à Petits Grains, replanted here in 1982, and has flavours of dried apricot and, sometimes, marmalade. Nobody knows how close it comes to its legendary forebear, but it is a very clean, intense wine which will undoubtedly mature for many years.

Steenberg ☆☆
Constantia. Owner: Graham Beck. 64 ha. www.steenberg-vineyards.co.za
This is a relative newcomer to this historic region, although the original Steenberg farm was planted in 1682. In the 1990s, the estate was revived as a tourist-and-leisure complex, and a winery was added in 1996. It has enjoyed great success with its melony Semillon, as well as aromatic Sauvignon. In addition, there are some attractive reds, a discreet Cabernet/Merlot blend called Catharina, and a brave stab at Nebbiolo.

Leading Paarl and Wellington Producers

Backsberg ☆–☆☆
Paarl. Owner: Michael Back. 130 ha. www.backsberg.co.za
Backsberg was established by the late Sydney Back, one of the Cape's pioneering estate wine producers, and has an enviable reputation for high-quality, value-for-money wines. The emphasis is on well-crafted wines that are enjoyable on release.

Diemersfontein ☆–☆☆
Wellington. Owner: David and Susan Sonnenberg. 48 ha. www.diemersfontein.co.za
The Sonnenbergs, who founded Woolworth's in South Africa, bought this farm in 1942, and in the 1990s converted it into a luxury hotel and wine estate. Most of the wine appears under the Diemersfontein label, but top selections bear the Carpe Diem label. The focus is on Pinotage, Merlot, and Shiraz, and the style is reminiscent of some Australian wines, with a surfeit of upfront, jammy, oaky fruit. But they enjoy huge commercial success.

Fairview ☆☆–☆☆☆
Paarl. Owner: Charles Back. 300 ha. www.fairview.co.za
No one has his finger more firmly on the pulse of the international market for Cape wines than Charles Back, who has enjoyed great success with Shiraz above all.

The Goats Do Roam range (his take on Côtes du Rhône) has combined a fun-loving image with good-quality wines. He delights in adding unexpected wines to his range, such as a Swartland Carignan, a Grenache-dominated blend called Caldera, and a Petite Sirah. Back himself admits that he barely understands the structure of his own company, since it is constantly evolving. He is also the sole proprietor of the former joint venture, Spice Route (q.v.).

Glen Carlou ☆☆–☆☆☆
Paarl. Owner: Hess group. 85 ha. www.glencarlou.co.za
Under winemaker David Finlayson, Glen Carlou rose to the top ranks within Paarl. The stalwarts of the range include

rich Chardonnays, polished Cabernets, and the fine Bordeaux blend, Grande Classique. In 2001 the property was bought by Donald Hess to add to his portfolio of wineries in Napa Valley and Argentina.

KWV ☆–☆☆

Paarl. www.kwv.co.za
The national wine cooperative was established in 1918, with statutory powers to govern the wine industry. Initially it was founded to protect grape-growers in their price negotiations with wholesale merchants, but its role changed into that of policeman for the entire wine industry.

Embroiled in politics and numerous conflicts of interest, it has had to be entirely restructured in the 1990s and early 2000s. As a wine producer, it has churned out large volumes of bland varietal wines under the KWV and Roodeberg labels, the Chenin Blanc always good value. Quality improved with the introduction of the new-oaked Cathedral Cellars range, led by the Bordeaux blend called Triptych.

In 1996, KWV launched Perold, a dense Shiraz of good quality and an outrageous price. Since then the company has launched KWV Lifestyle, KWV Mentors, and a Reserve range. See also Laborie.

Laborie ☆–☆☆

Paarl. Owner: KWV. 40 ha. www.laboriewines.com
A very attractive estate on the slopes of the Paarl Mountain, owned by the KWV, and used as a guesthouse. The wines are easygoing and well-made, if not especially concentrated.

Mischa ☆–☆☆

Wellington. Owner: Barns family. 120 ha. www.mischaestate.com
The Barns family are nurserymen and understand their land and their dry-farmed vineyards, which will soon be organic. They make fresh and balanced Shiraz and Viognier, and softer wines under the Eventide label.

Mont du Toit ☆☆

Wellington. Owner: Stephan du Toit and Bernd Philippi. 28 ha. www.montdutoit.co.za
Founded in 1997, this South African/German venture first made its mark with a powerful 1998 Syrah/Cabernet/Merlot blend. Rheingau producer Bernhard Breuer was also involved until his untimely death in 2004.

Nabygelegen ☆☆–☆☆☆

Wellington. Owner: James McKenzie. 17 ha. www.nabygelegen.co.za
An old property revived in 2002. The top wine is 1712, the date of the farm's creation; it's a Bordeaux blend with supple tannins and fine length. A curiosity here is the late-harvest Harslevelú.

Nederburg ☆–☆☆☆

Paarl. Owner: Distell. No vineyards. www.nederburg.co.za
Although most of the wines from this large estate are thoroughly commercial, Nederburg has become renowned

for its annual auction, featuring both its own top wines and special bottlings from throughout the Cape. Nederburg has a well-deserved reputation for its rich, sweet wines made from botrytized Chenin Blanc. Since 2005 there has been a determined effort to improve quality, especially with two idiosyncratic blends appropriately called Igenuity.

Rupert & Rothschild ☆☆–☆☆☆

Paarl. Owner: Benjamin de Rothschild and Rupert families. 90 ha. www.rupert-rothschildvignerons.com
When two multi-millionaires teamed up to establish this new venture, it was done on a lavish scale. Yet first releases in 1997 were unsatisfactory. The range was revamped and quality soon improved. Despite the untimely death of co-founder Anthonij Rupert in 2001, the estate he helped to create goes from strength to strength, especially with the voluptuous Baron Edmond bottling. Baroness Nadine is the second wine.

Scali ☆☆

Voor Paarderberg. Owner: Willie de Waal. 70 ha. www.scali.co.za
The de Waals have been farming here for generations, selling grapes to other producers, but since 1999 Willie de Waal has retained about a tenth of the crop for his own exacting Mediterranean-style wines made with artisanal care. Good Syrah and a full-bodied white blend from Chenin and Chardonnay.

Veenwouden ☆☆

Paarl. Owner: van der Walt family. 15 ha. www.veenwouden.com
Veenwouden, owned by South Africa's most celebrated tenor, made a remarkable debut in 1993. Deon van der Walt and his winemaker brother Marcel planted their vineyard with a view to producing Pomerol-style wines. Although tragedy struck when Deon was murdered by his own father, Marcel has maintained production and quality.

Veenwouden's Merlot and Cabernet/Merlot Classic blend might not be easily mistaken for Right Bank Bordeaux, but they are wonderful wines, nonetheless: rich and concentrated, but showing far more elegance than most Cape wines in this style. A small quantity of Chardonnay has been added to the range.

Vilafonté ☆☆☆

Paarl. Owner: Mike Ratcliffe, Zelma Long, and Phil Freese. 17 ha. www.vilafonte.com
Mike Ratcliffe represents South African commercial acumen,

A goat house, on Fairview estate, Paarl

Zelma Long Californian winemaking, Phil Freese avant-garde viticulture. This formidable team has developed a vineyard, planting only Bordeaux varieties. Series C is the top wine, Cabernet based, and Series M the blend – both seamless wines of very high quality.

Vondeling ☆☆
Voor Paardeberg. Owner: Julian Johnsen and partners. 40 ha. www.vondelingwines.co.za
Farm manager Johnsen has revived this fine old property, favouring organic farming and minimal intervention in the winemaking. The wine range is eclectic, so Vondeling has yet to establish its identity. But quality, white and red, is very good.

Welbedacht ☆–☆☆☆
Wellington. Owner: Schalk Burger. 120 ha. www.welbedacht.co.za
Springbok rugby player Schalk bought the property in 1997, but local opposition to a private estate in an area dominated by cooperatives meant the first vintage was only in 2005.

The wines are too numerous to list, but the basic range is called Meerkat, after a local rodent, and has proved very popular. The top wine is Number Six, a multi-varietal blend consciously styled as an "icon" wine; despite that, it is sumptuous and balanced.

Welgemeend ☆☆
Paarl. Owner: consortium of investors. 11 ha. www.welgemeend.co.za
In the 1970s Billy Hofmeyr was a pioneer of Bordeaux blends and ageing in new barriques, and his daughter Louise followed the same principles until 2006, when she sold the property. Much of the Hofmeyr team remains in place, so for the moment quality is unimpaired. At the same time the estate is being transformed into a tourist and convention centre.

Leading Franschhoek Producers

Boekenhoutskloof ☆☆–☆☆☆☆
Owner: Boekenhoutskloof Winery Ltd. 20 ha. www.boekenhoutskloof.co.za
Since 1996, when this property was founded, Marc Kent has been its winemaker and was rewarded for his brilliance by being offered a share of the business. He is a non-interventionist winemaker, using mostly natural yeasts and ageing the wines in barrel with minimal racking. Much of the fruit is sourced from outside the Franschhoek region.

His barrique-fermented Semillon resembles an opulent and waxy white Graves, and ages well. His Syrah is equally remarkable, and often more complex than the very concentrated Cabernet Sauvignon. These wines are only made in small quantities. Larger-volume bottlings that are still of excellent quality are released under the Porcupine Ridge label.

Boschendal ☆–☆☆
Franschhoek. Owner: Douglas Green Bellingham. 200 ha. www.boschendalwines.com
One of the Cape's largest single estates, perched on the boundary between Franschhoek, Paarl, and Stellenbosch, with coolish vineyards stretching along the Simonsberg. It has changed hands twice in three years so the future direction of the reliable but unremarkable wine range is uncertain.

Cabrière ☆–☆☆☆
Owner: Achim von Arnim. 30 ha. www.cabriere.co.za
The flamboyant Achim von Arnim has long been recognized as one of the Cape's leading producers of *méthode traditionnelle* sparkling wines under the Pierre Jourdan label. Although the sparkling wines can be very good, Cabrière's reputation for Pinot Noir is perhaps less easily understood.

Cape Chamonix ☆☆–☆☆☆☆
Owner: Chris Hellinger. 50 ha. www.chamonix.co.za
A former fruit farm, Chamonix has been producing wines since 1993, and in 2001 the energetic Gottfried Mocke became the winemaker. The vineyards are high and the elevations helps to explain the quality of the Chardonnay and Pinot Noir, especially the Reserves. However, Troika, the Bordeaux blend, is fresh, concentrated, and persistent, too.

Grande Provence ☆–☆☆
Owner: Alex van Heeren. 22 ha. www.grandeprovence.co.za
This is one of the latest luxury tourist complexes in the region, but its all red vineyards, supplemented by purchased white grapes, produce a range of expensive wines. The style of the Cabernet and Shiraz, and the Grande Provence Bordeaux blend, is superripe, lush, and oaky – rather strenuously ambitious.

Môreson ☆☆
Owner: Richard Friedman. 20 ha. www.moreson.co.za
The estate has a reputation for sparkling wine, but the reds seem more successful. The Pinotage is in a ripe, plummy style and the Merlot is rich in sweet red fruits.

La Motte ☆☆
Owner: Hanneli Koegelenberg. 108 ha. www.la-motte.com
La Motte traces its origins back to the Huguenots. Under its present owner, the daughter of Dr. Anton Rupert, the property has been fully restored. In the 2000s the whole vineyard was being progressively replanted and is now farmed organically. The top range is called Pierneef, and includes a concentrated Sauvignon Blanc and a broad, silky Shiraz/Viognier. La Motte is also well known for a medium-bodied, harmonious Cabernet/Merlot blend called Millennium.

L'Ormarins ☆☆–☆☆☆☆
Owner: Johann Rupert. 210 ha. www.lormarins.co.za
The Rupert fortune has been put to work here, with the entire 50-hectare estate being replanted on slopes at a higher density. In addition a new gravity-fed winery of the utmost technical sophistication has been built. The wine range is being revamped, with the top label being Anthonij Rupert, in honour of Johann's late brother. The first release was the chewy, oaky 2005 Cabernet. As well as standard varietals, often sourced from other vineyards in Darling and Swartland, there is a supple Sangiovese and a Bordeaux blend called Optima.

Plaisir de Merle ☆☆
Owner: Distell. 400 ha. www.plaisirdemerle.co.za
Once a supply farm for Nederburg (q.v.), Plaisir de Merle subsequently made an effort to improve rather dull quality by hiring as a consultant, Paul Pontallier – director of Château Margaux. The Cabernet and Merlot are often excellent, and a new Cabernet Franc is stylish if oaky.

Leading Producers from Other Regions

Allesverloren ☆☆
Riebeek-West, Swartland. Owner: Danie Malan. 180 ha. www.allesverloren.co.za
Although this estate produces good Cabernet and Shiraz, it is best-known for its reliable and succulent vintage "ports". Touriga Nacional and Tinta Barocca are also made as table wines, but lack the intensity of the Portuguese originals.

Altydgedacht/Tygerberg ☆–☆☆
Durbanville. Owner: Parker family. 170 ha. www.altydgedacht.co.za
A large property owned by the Parkers for five generations. Most of the grapes are sold off but their own Sauvignons are delicious. Tygerberg is the export label.

Beaumont ☆☆
Walker Bay. Owner: Sebastian Beaumont. 34 ha. www.beaumont.co.za
Since 1993, a reliable source of flavoury Pinotage, Shiraz, Mourvèdre, and Chenin Blanc.

Graham Beck ☆☆–☆☆☆
Robertson. Owner: Graham Beck. 180 ha. www.grahambeckwines.co.za
Beck's property is divided between two sites: the major part is in Robertson, and the remainder, which vinifies grapes from cooler coastal sites, is based at a separate winery in Franschhoek. Although Beck is well-known for its excellent sparkling wines, its table wines are becoming increasingly impressive, especially the single-vineyard Ridge Shiraz, Old Road Pinotage, and intense, tannic Coffeestone Cabernet Sauvignon. Lower down the scale are extensive ranges of well-made varietal wines.

Boplaas ☆☆
Calitzdorp, Klein Karoo. Owner: Carel Nel. 65 ha. www.boplaas.co.za
One of the Cape's leading "port"-type wine producers, and a good source for Pinotage, Shiraz, and fortified Muscadel.

Bouchard Finlayson ☆☆☆
Walker Bay. Owner: Peter Finlayson and partners. 16 ha. www.bouchardfinlayson.co.za
Winemaker Peter Finlayson, formerly with Hamilton Russell Vineyards (q.v.), has been involved since 1990 in a joint venture with Paul Bouchard, formerly of Bouchard Aîné. Some grapes are bought in, but increasing volumes of their own plantings are gradually coming into production. These are extremely distinctive, cool-climate wines, and the rather citric Kaaimansgat Chardonnay, from vineyards at 700 metres

(2,296 feet), together with the Galpin Peak Pinot Noir, are among the Cape's finest expressions of these varieties.

Cape Point ☆☆
Noordhoek, Cape Point. Owner: Sybrand van der Spuy. 31 ha. www.capepointvineyards.co.za
A remarkable patchwork of vineyards, along the very cool coastline south of Cape Town. Initial releases of Sauvignon and Chardonnay were impressively minerally, though over-oaked. A Graves-style white blend, Isliedh, shows fine potential, and it will be fascinating to see the results of winemaker Duncan Savage's experiments with fermentation in amphorae once those wines are on the market.

Paul Cluver ☆☆–☆☆☆
Grabouw, Elgin. Owner: Dr. Paul Cluver. 90 ha. www.cluver.com
Until 1997, the grapes from what is now Elgin's leading property were sold to Nederburg (q.v.). Winemaker Andries Burger is Cluver's son-in-law, and has worked at Château Margaux. The appley Chardonnay and silky Pinot Noir are impressive, but Cabernet Sauvignon can be austere. Pinot Noir is increasingly restrained and elegant.

Darling Cellars ☆☆
Darling. Owner: consortium of shareholders. 1,300 ha. www.darlingcellars.co.za
Winemaker Abé Beukes produces two ranges of wine from the company's extensive vineyards: the single-vineyard DC wines, and the top Onyx line. Cabernet and Shiraz are the stars of both ranges.

De Grendel ☆☆
Durbanville. Owner: Sir David Graaff. 104 ha. www.degrendel.co.za
The Graafs bought this property in 1896 as a stud farm, then began farming here. Vines were only planted in 2000, and the wines are made by the experienced Charles Hopkins. This is a cool, windy site, and Sauvignon Blanc does exceptionally well. But Merlot and Shiraz are good, too. The flagship wine, an understated Bordeaux blend called Rubaiyat, is made from Stellenbosch fruit.

De Wetshof ☆☆–☆☆☆
Robertson. Owner: Danie de Wet. 180 ha. www.dewetshof.com
Danie de Wet was trained in Germany, and brought back boundless enthusiasm for white wines of styles not then found in South Africa. His experimental work with Riesling, Sauvignon Blanc, and Chardonnay, and with his noble-rot sweet wine, Edeloes, shook old ideas about the Robertson area, and about South African whites in general.

He is one of the leading producers of Chardonnay in the Robertson region, with several different *cuvées*, ranging from Finesse (lightly wooded) to Chardonnay d'Honneur and Bateleur (both barrel fermented). These Chardonnays are remarkable for their citric freshness and lack of heaviness. Twelve hectares of Pinot Noir are now beginning to produce some fragrant, raspberry-scented wines of undoubted potential.

Durbanville Hills ☆–☆☆☆
Durbanville. Owner: Distell. 770 ha.
www.durbanvillehills.co.za
An ambitious joint venture between majority shareholder Distell and a group of leading local growers. Large new cellars were built in time for the 1999 vintage, and veteran winemaker Martin Moore (formerly of Groot Konstantia, q.v.) was hired to supervise production. There are three ranges: basic varietals; the mostly new-oaked Rhinofields wines; and single vineyard wines, aged in new French oak. The standard varietal wines are for early drinking, and the Sauvignon Blanc can be vegetal. The single-vineyard Caapmans Cabernet/ Merlot, and Luipardsberg Merlot are rich and fleshy.

Flagstone ☆☆
Somerset West. Owner: Constellation. No vineyards.
www.flagstonewines.com
Bruce Jack buys in fruit from dozens of vineyards through the country to make a wide range of wines with flair, including characterful, grassy Sauvignon Blanc from Elim, Pinotage, and a complex red blend called Longitude. In 2007 Flagstone was bought by giant drinks company Constellation, but Jack insists his role, and freedom, remain unchanged. Long may that continue.

Groote Post ☆☆
Darling. Owner: Nick Pentz. 117 ha.
www.grootepost.com
This historic property includes a dairy farm, nature reserve, and good restaurant. But the wines are no afterthought, and both Sauvignon and Merlot are highly enjoyable. Only the Pinot Noir disappoints. Relatively cool vineyards yield fine Sauvignon, Chardonnay, and Merlot.

Hamilton Russell Vineyards ☆☆–☆☆☆
Walker Bay. Owner: Anthony Hamilton Russell. 52 ha. www.hamiltonrussellvineyards.com
The first of the new generation of cool-climate producers focused on Pinot Noir and Chardonnay. By 1998, mediocre clones had been replaced, and recent vintages have consolidated Hamilton Russell's position in the front rank of producers working with these varieties. These are arguably the most Burgundian of Cape Pinots – great purity and length of flavour.

Havana Hills ☆☆–☆☆☆
Philadelphia. Owner: Kobus du Plessis. 65 ha.
www.havanahills.co.za
A fairly remote property yet only a few miles from the ocean, giving considerable maritime influence. A new star in the Cape, especially for the Du Plessis Reserve range: red wines that show elegance and restrained use of oak.

Hermanuspietersfontein ☆☆
Walker Bay. Owner: Pretorius family. 57 ha.
www.hpf1855.co.za
Sauvignon Blanc, in various guises, is the main focus here, but red wines such as the Cabernet Franc and the Bordeaux blend, Die Arnoldus, are spicy and precise. The first vintage here was 2005, and so long as customers can pronounce the name on the label, this is an estate to follow.

Iona ☆☆
Grabouw, Elgin. Owner: Andrew Gunn. 35 ha.
www.iona.co.za
Lean, grassy Sauvignon is Iona's calling card, and now Chardonnay and piquant Shiraz have been added to the range.

Kloovenburg ☆☆
Riebeek-Kasteel. Owner: Pieter du Toit. 130 ha.
www.kloovenburg.com
The vineyards, on the slopes of Kasteel Mountain, are refreshed by constant breezes, which give the wines their freshness. Much of the fruit is sold to other wineries, but the Merlot, Cabernet, and Shiraz are all bright and accessible, if not especially profound. A red blend, not made every year, is Eight Feet, a reference to the four Du Toit children and their penchant for a little foot treading.

Lammershoek ☆☆☆
Malmesbury, Swartland. Owner: Stephan and Kretzel families. 130 ha. www.lammershoek.co.za
The appeal of this property to Paul Kretzel was the abundance of old bush vines. Much of the fruit is sold off, but since 2000 small quantities of Rhône-style red wines and idiosyncratic whites have been produced. The excellent blends are called Roulette, and the white, from Chenin and Chardonnay, is both mineral and weighty. The barrel-fermented Chenin is like a barrel of quinces.

Land's End ☆☆
Moddervlei, Elim. Owner: Dave Hidden. 20 ha.
A label created for wines made from grapes sourced from the handful of growers who planted in ultra-cool Elim in 1997. Initial releases showed great promise: exotic Sauvignon and zesty Semillon. In 2005 the property was bought by the owner of Hidden Valley (q.v.).

Meerendal ☆–☆☆
Durbanville. Owner: consortium of businessmen. 100 ha. www.meerendal.co.za
This historic property is now enjoying a revival under new owners. Excellent Sauvignon and oaky single vineyard Pinotage.

Newton Johnson ☆☆–☆☆☆
Hemel en Aarde. Owner: Dave and Felicity Johnson. 15 ha. www.newtonjohnson.com
High hillside vineyards and a new winery make some of Walker Bay's best Pinot Noir and Chardonnay.

Nitida ☆☆
Durbanville. Owner: Bernhard Veller. 16 ha.
www.nitida.co.za
The first vintage here was 1996, and Nitida soon established a well-deserved reputation for its Sauvignon Blanc. The flagship wine is the Merlot/Cabernet blend called Calligraphy, which can be somewhat hard and austere in some vintages. The opulent white Graves style Coronota shows greater promise.

Rijk's Private Cellar ☆☆
Tulbagh. Owner: Neville Dorrington. 34 ha. www.rijks.co.nz
Restrained, fruit forward wines, aimed at the restaurant

market since the first vintage in 2000. Dorrington has also created a Shiraz-only property next door, called, rather confusingly, Rijk's Estate.

Sadie Family Wines ☆☆☆
Malmesbury, Swartland. Owner: Eben Sadie and family. 10 ha.
The youthful Sadie was the much-lauded winemaker at Spice Route (q.v.), but in 2002 devoted himself full-time to his own venture. His principal wine, Columella, is made in small quantities from vineyards leased and controlled by Sadie. Sadie is passionate about the potential of old-vine Shiraz from the Swartland valleys, and Columella is predominantly Shiraz with a slight addition of Mourvèdre.

Its white equivalent is Palladius, blending Chenin with Rhône varieties. Yields are exceptionally low and vinification both non-interventionist and meticulous. The second label is Sequillo. Sadie's experience in Priorat, where he has another property, has taught him to keep potentially runaway alcohol under control.

Saronsberg ☆☆–☆☆☆
Tulbagh. Owner: Nick van Huyssteen. 40 ha. www.saronberg,com
An ambitious new winery, which also encloses the owner's art collection. The Sauvignon is bought from other regions, and the best estate wines are red, with two superb blends aged in new barriques: Full Circle, which is Shiraz-dominated, and Seismic, which is Cabernet-dominated.

Spice Route ☆☆–☆☆☆
Malmesbury, Swartland. Owner: Charles Back. 200 ha. ww.spiceroutewines.com
In the late 1990s the marketing genius of Charles Back of Fairview (q.v.) and the winemaking brilliance of Eben Sadie created the new Spice Route brand, which swiftly established a reputation for rich, full-flavoured, slightly gamey wines from Mediterranean varieties, with a preference for dry-farmed bush vines. In 2002, Charl [sic] du Plessis took over from Sadie, expanded the range with white wines from Darling.

Springfield ☆☆☆
Robertson. Owner: Abrie Bruwer. 150 ha. www.springfieldestate.com
Springfield sold its production to bulk-wine producers until 1995. Since then, Bruwer has gone from strength to strength, focusing on quality to such an extent that production has dropped by two-thirds. The winemaking is artisanal, with the exception of the racy Sauvignons. All other wines are made from uncrushed berries fermented with natural yeasts, and are bottled without filtration.

His most remarkable wines are called Méthode Ancienne, the red being pure Cabernet, minty and peppery; the white, a rich Chardonnay. But the minerally Life from Stone Sauvignon remains the wine that put Springfield on the map.

Swartland Winery ☆
Malmesbiury, Swartland. Owner: 60 growers, previously in the cooperative. 3,200 ha. www.swwines.co.za

The cooperative became a private company in 2005, but the vineyard structure remained essentially the same. Growers, following fashion, had once planted Chardonnay, but have replaced it with more suitable varieties such as Shiraz, Pinotage, and Chenin.

The top Indalo range is essentially the same as the Reserve line (known as Eagle Crest in export markets), but with more oak ageing. Quality is still lacklustre, but is likely to improve.

Tulbagh Mountain Vineyards ☆☆☆
Tulbagh. Owner: Jason Scott and George Austin. 16 ha. www.tmv.co.za
Chris Mullineux made the reputation of this organic property, and his successor Callie Louw remains faithful to his style. Theta is a pure Shiraz, Viktoria a Rhône style blend. The white blend components change from year to year, but the wine is Chenin dominated. There is also a fascinating Chenin straw wine made by a solera system.

Zandvliet ☆–☆☆
Robertson. Owner: Paul de Wet family. 155 ha. www.zandvliet.co.za
The Shiraz was a pioneering red from Robertson, and today the winery produces at least three bottlings.

Zimbabwe

Zimbabwe lies on the same line of latitude as much of Bolivia and southern Brazil, and climate conditions are by no means perfectly conducive to growing quality grapes for making wine (heat and sunshine in abundance, but also frost during the growing season, and summer rains that affect the harvest). An industry of sorts began in 1965. The first wines were of poor quality and dubious grapes – Jacques, Issor, and Farrazza – which have since been replaced by the planting of noble varieties, imported from South Africa. The vineyards are mainly located some 1,200-metres (4,000-feet) above sea level, north of Harare.

Since the early 1980s, tremendous progress has been made. The use of irrigation, cold fermentation, modern equipment, winemakers trained in Germany, Australia, and South Africa, together with the consultation of flying winemakers brought about an upsurge in quality.

The political unrest and violence that marred Zimbabwe in the early years of the twenty-first century have inevitably complicated life for the handful of functioning estates, and it is unlikely that the estates that once flourished are still active. They remain cited here as an act of faith, in the hope that when the country eventually emerges from its present chaos, they will flourish again. They include Worringham, where wines were first made in the 1960s, but which no longer appears to exist; and Mukuyu at Marondera, 60 kilometres (37 miles) from the capital African Distillers (Stapleford Wines) was based in Gweru, north of Harare, and produced substantial volumes of Sauvignon Blanc, Muscat, a Cabernet/Merlot blend, and a very exciting Pinotage from 180 hectares of vineyards in Bulawayo, Gweru, and Odzi.

England & Wales

England and Wales are at the farthest northern limit of the zone that grapes will ripen in the open – a fact that has not discouraged some 350 landowners from planting vineyards, great and small. They were indulged as eccentrics until the 1990s. Then with the turn of the century they suddenly became a talking point. Could it really be that they were onto something? The revival of English winegrowing (it was probably introduced by the Romans, and was widespread in the Middle Ages) started slowly in the 1950s, and accelerated rapidly in the 1970s. The excellent summer of 1976 encouraged many to think that winegrowing could be more than a hobby. In spite of a succession of dismal harvests in the late '70s, with vintage rain a regular occurrence, the industry has consolidated its position, helped by global warming in the '90s. In total, about 1,900 hectares are in production, across southern England and Wales, with concentrations in the traditional fruit-growing areas of Kent and Sussex, Essex and Suffolk, along the south coast through Hampshire as far as Cornwall, and north through Berkshire, Wiltshire, and Somerset as far as Hereford and Worcester. Total annual production in 2007 was 2.1 million bottles, almost all of it white.

It is too early to say that any regional styles have emerged. English wine is a light, refreshing, often slightly tart summer drink. Its best qualities are floweriness, delicate fruitiness, and crisp, clean freshness. Its acidity should be noticeable and matched with fragrant, fruity flavours, whether dry or semi-sweet. Most observers agree that the style of English wine with the greatest potential is sparkling wine, a conviction bolstered by global warming – though still undermined by the climatic perils of the English summer. Indeed, the best bottles can hold their own against some of the mightiest brands of Champagne. The last few years have seen some large-scale investment in English vineyards by new owners, often from outside the industry, with deep pockets and big ambitions to make top sparkling wines. These quality-oriented projects offer English wine its best chance yet of making its mark.

The best bottle-fermented sparkling wines develop good lees character from two to three years' ageing. Still wines aged in oak also look convincing. More complex flavours are evolving as the vines age and the winemakers grow more skilful. Good English wines clearly benefit from bottle age; several years is often not too much. Indeed, they need it, particularly in vintages of high acidity.

In this cool climate, with uncertain weather, early ripening and resistance to rot are two major factors governing the choice of grapes. But some growers, especially the larger ones, are moving away from grapes such as Müller-Thurgau and Schönburger, bred for early ripening, and from varietal wines, in favour of blends. New German varieties designed to ripen well in cool weather, and the (excellent) hybrid Seyval Blanc, are still prominent, although classic French varieties are increasingly used. The confidence to plant Pinot Noir and Chardonnay only came recently, but it has given the industry a dimension it lacked before. There are also some serious dessert wines being made, mainly from botrytis-infected Bacchus and Huxelrebe.

If English sparkling wines have yet to make a wide impact on the international wine scene it may be that their price is simply too high. Good equivalent bottles from California or New Zealand are half the price, if not less, than the best from England. Much the same is true of the leading still wines. It is all too common at tastings to come across a truly excellent English wine, perhaps a Pinot Blanc, and then note that it is priced considerably higher than the principal competition, in this case Alsace.

If English wine is to cease to be a niche product and enjoy more international presence, then it needs to be more competitive. On the other hand, the costs of land, and thus of production, are very high. It will be fascinating to see if the undeniable increase in quality is matched in future by more astute marketing and sales.

Leading England & Wales Producers

A'Beckett's ☆
Devizes, Wiltshire. Owner: Langham family. 2.5 ha.
www.abecketts.co.uk
From vineyards planted in 2001, the Langhams produce a full range of wines, including supple Pinot Noir and a rather bland Estate Blend.

Bookers Vineyard ☆–☆☆
Bolney, West Sussex. Owner: Rodney and Janet Pratt. 10 ha. www.bookersvineyard.co.uk
The Pratts' daughter Samantha Linter makes the wines, and about half the production is of Pinot Noir.

Breaky Bottom ☆–☆☆
Lewes, East Sussex. Owner: Peter Hall. 2 ha.
www.breakybottom.co.uk
Seyval Blanc and Müller-Thurgau are planted on chalk downland. Wines made in a non-interventionist style by Peter Hall have attracted a loyal following. Since 1994, a very good classic-method sparkling has been made from Seyval Blanc. These are lean wines that definitely benefit from bottle age.

Camel Valley ☆☆
Bodmin, Cornwall. Owner: Lindo family. 7 ha.
www.camelvalley.com
Winemaker Sam Lindo is no amateur, and worked in

Vineyards have become a familiar site in rural England

New Zealand before taking over at Camel Valley. The estate has scooped up a number of awards for its Brut, and for its Pinot Noir rosé.

Carr Taylor ☆
Westfield, East Sussex. Owner: Carr-Taylor family. 14 ha. www.carr-taylor.co.uk
Founded in 1971, this is now run by the second generation of the family, and the best bottles are the bottle-fermented sparkling wines.

Chapel Down Winery ☆☆
Tenterden, Kent. Owner: Chapel Down Wines Ltd. 10 ha. www.chapeldownwines.co.uk
One of the largest wineries in the UK, handling grapes from all over the southeast and since 1995 the owner of Tenterden. The sparkling wine is of good quality, and grapes such as Pinot Blanc and Pinot Noir are producing wines of greater interest than those from hybrids and crossings.

Chilford Hall ☆
Linton, Cambridgeshire. Owner: Alper family. 7 ha. www.childfordhall.co.uk
Long-established vineyard, with many early ripening German grapes, giving light-bodied but fragrant wines.

Davenport ☆☆
Crowborough, East Sussex. Owner: Will Davenport. 5 ha. www.davenportvineyards.co.uk
This acclaimed organic estate produces dry white blends and sparkling wine under the Limney label, and, in rare vintages when conditions permit, a delicate Pinot Noir.

Denbies ☆☆
Dorking, Surrey. Owner: Adrian White. 106 ha. www.denbiesvineyard.co.uk
The UK's largest vineyard, coating south-facing slopes of the North Downs. The winery is one of the most modern in Britain. A comprehensive range of wines, with some award-winning ones, especially Bacchus and the Greenfields sparkling wine from Burgundian varieties. A blend of Dornfelder and Pinot Noir makes a plump, attractive red.

Dunkery ☆
Wootton Courtenay, Somerset. Owner: Derek Pritchard.
An estate within the Exmoor National Park. The specialties are Pinot Noir and sparkling wines. All wines are fully dry.

Gifford's Hall ☆
Hartest, Suffolk. 5 ha. www.giffordshall.co.uk
This small property has developed a reputation for its dry white from the Madeleine Angevine variety.

Halfpenny Green ☆
Halfpenny Green, Staffordshire. Owner: Martin Vickers. 10 ha. ww.halfpenny-green-vineyards.co.uk
These are northerly vineyards, but benefit from south-facing slopes. Almost all the varieties planted are early ripening, and the wines are essentially simple, for early drinking.

Hidden Spring ☆
Horam, East Sussex. Owner: Graham and Sue Mosey. 3 ha. www.hiddenspring.co.uk
The range of wines has been simplified to a Pinot Noir and an off-dry white. Cider is also produced.

Hush Heath ☆☆–☆☆☆
Cranbrook, Kent. Owner: Richard Balfour-Lynn. www.hushheath.com
Hotelier Balfour-Lynn has one aim: to produce outstanding rosé sparkling wine, and to that end constructed in 2008 a modern winery. Vintages since 2004 have certainly met with great acclaim.

Llanerch ☆
Pendoylan, Vale of Glamorgan, Wales. Owner: Peter and Diana Andrews. 3 ha. www.llanerch-vineyard.co.uk
The largest vineyard in Wales, with vines on south-facing slopes in the Ely valley. The estate wines are released under the Cariad label, including dry and off-dry whites, and an off-dry sparkling wine.

New Hall ☆
Purleigh, Essex. 67 ha. www.newhallwines.co.uk
A large vineyard that also sells grapes to other wineries. Bacchus and sparkling wines are regular award winners. In 2007 a Chardonnay was added to the range.

Northbrook Springs ☆
Bishop's Waltham, Hampshire. Owner: Brian Cable. 5 ha.
This chalky downland location near Southampton looks to be very promising. The wines, made with advice from consultant John Worontschak, are good and improving, with occasional excellent late-harvest wines, and a Fumé-style Reichensteiner and Bacchus blend.

Nyetimber ☆☆–☆☆☆
Pulborough, West Sussex. Owner: Eric Heerema. 104 ha. www.nyetimber.com
The estate that, since 1992, has proved that England can make sparkling wines from traditional Champenoise varieties. Stuart and Sandra Moss were the owners behind this success story, but sold the property in 2006 to its present owner, who plans to increase production considerably by planting an additional 90 hectares. Nyetimber wines have won innumerable awards.

Penshurst ☆
Penshurst, Kent. Owner: David Westphal. 5 ha.
Well-established since 1971, with modern winery. Most of the wines are off-dry.

Ridgeview ☆☆–☆☆☆
Ditchling, East Sussex. Owner: Mike Roberts. 18 ha. www.ridgeview.co.uk
Ridgeview has followed the lead of Nyetimber by planting only Chardonnay and Pinots Noir and Meunier, and producing traditional-method sparkling wines. The first vintage was 1997 and quality since has been consistently high and rewarded with critical acclaim. This is the English wine closest to Champagne in flavour.

Sandhurst ☆
Sandhurst, Kent. Owner: Anne Nicholas. 10 ha.
www.sandhurstvineyards.co.uk
Well-run vineyard on a mixed farm. Good, oak-aged Bacchus
and Seyval Blanc sparkling.

Sharpham ☆–☆☆
Totnes, Devon. Owner: Mark Sharpham. 4 ha.
www.sharpham.com
This winery produces red wines from Dornfelder, Pinot
Noir, and others, including a Madeleine Angevine fermented
in new oak.

Stanlake Park ☆
Twyford, Berkshire. Owner: Peter Dart. 10 ha.
www.stanlakepark.com
This is the former Thames valley estate, renamed when after
changed ownership in 2005. Unlike many English wineries,
it offers a range of varietal wines, including Bacchus,
Gewurztraminer, and Pinot Noir.

Tenterden
See Chapel Down.

Three Choirs ☆
Newent, Gloucestershire. Owner: limited company.
30 ha. www.three-choirs-vineyard.co.uk
The largest producer in the west of England, but the wines,
especially the reds, can be inconsistent in quality. The range
includes vintage sparkling, white Siegerrebe, rosé, red, and
dessert wines.

Wickham ☆
Shedfield, Hampshire. Owner: Angela Baart and
Gordon Channon. 7 ha. www.wickhamvineyard.com
Under new ownership since 2000, Wickham produces
a full range of styles, including a rosé sparkling wine from
Dornfelder. Under John Charnley, Wickham acquired a good
reputation for sparkling rosé, a Pinot Noir/Triomphe blend,
and for an oaked white, supplied to the House of Commons.
In 2000, Wickham was sold to its present owners.

Wyken ☆
Bury St Edmunds, Suffolk. Owner: Carla Carlisle.
2 ha. www.wykenvineyards.co.uk
Small vineyard that makes a prize-winning Bacchus and
a creditable red.

World Wine Regions

The following maps show the major wine-producing regions of the world. Words in serif type on the maps indicate names and places connected with wine; sans serif type indicates other information of interest. Please also refer to the individual keys on the maps.

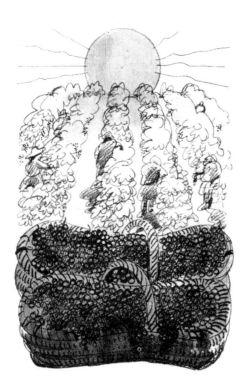

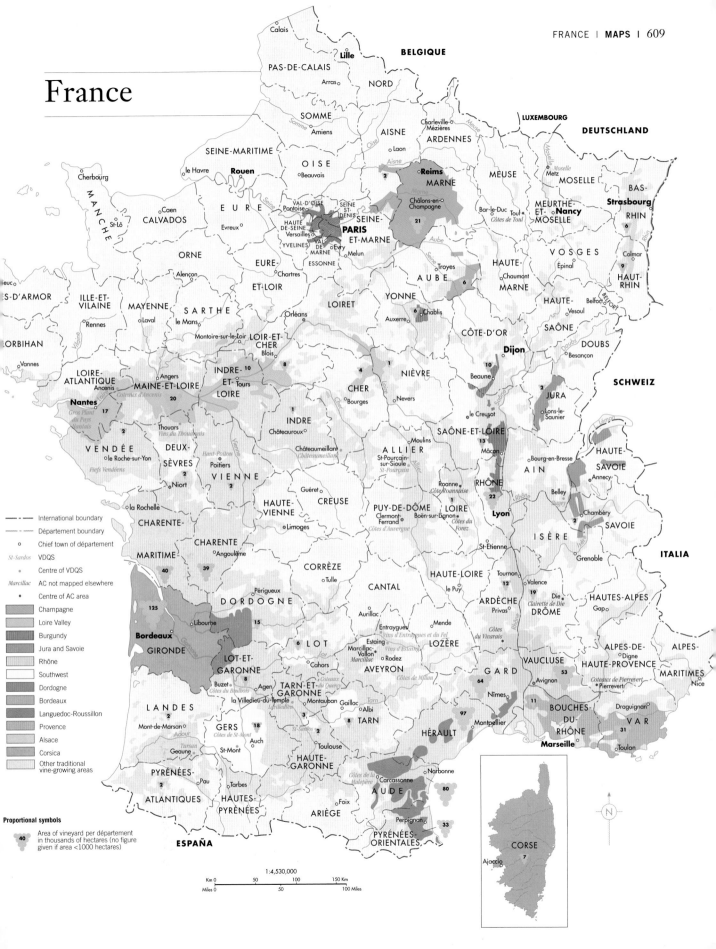

Bordeaux

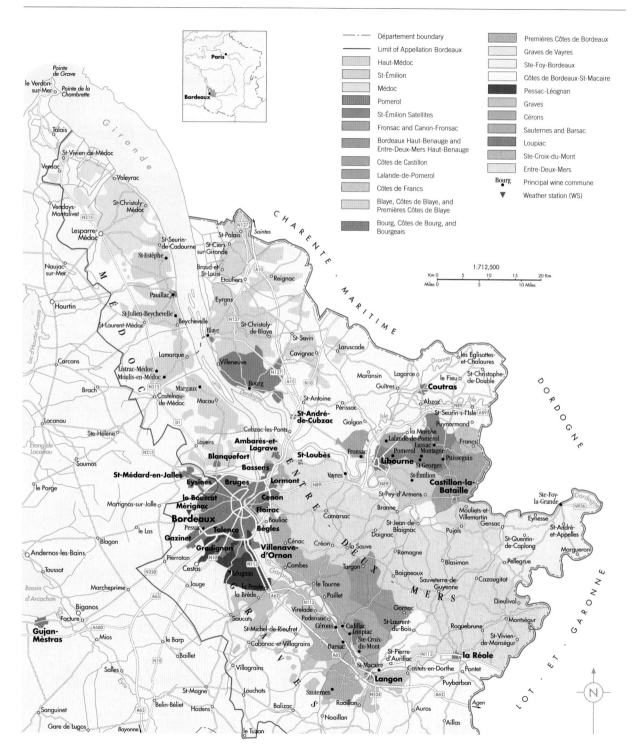

Paris

Bordeaux

– ·· – ·· –	Département boundary
———	Limit of Appellation Bordeaux
	Haut-Médoc
	St-Émilion
	Médoc
	Pomerol
	St-Émilion Satellites
	Fronsac and Canon-Fronsac
	Bordeaux Haut-Benauge and Entre-Deux-Mers Haut-Benauge
	Côtes de Castillon
	Lalande-de-Pomerol
	Côtes de Francs
	Blaye, Côtes de Blaye, and Premières Côtes de Blaye
	Bourg, Côtes de Bourg, and Bourgeais
	Premières Côtes de Bordeaux
	Graves de Vayres
	Ste-Foy-Bordeaux
	Côtes de Bordeaux-St-Macaire
	Pessac-Léognan
	Graves
	Cérons
	Sauternes and Barsac
	Loupiac
	Ste-Croix-du-Mont
	Entre-Deux-Mers
Bourg	Principal wine commune
▼	Weather station (WS)

1:712,500

Km 0   5   10   15   20 Km
Miles 0   5   10 Miles

Burgundy

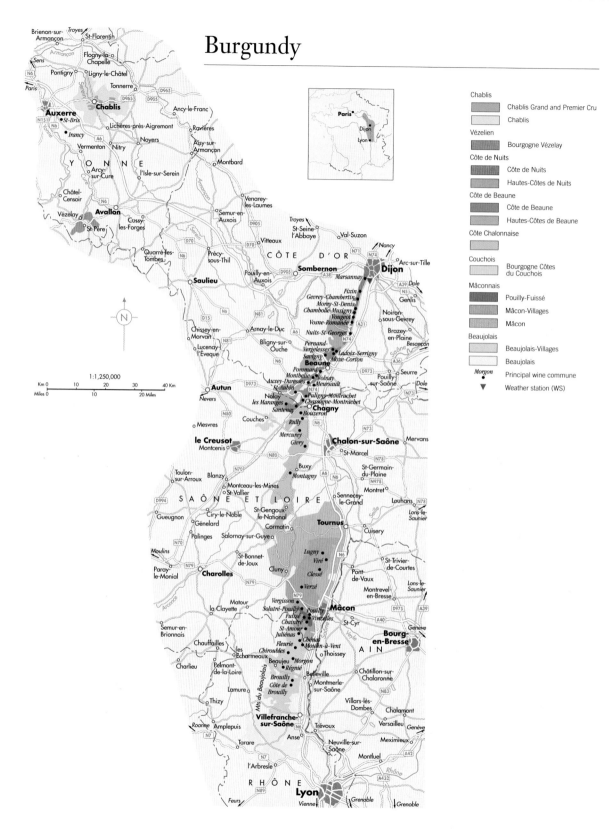

Brienon-sur-Armançon
Troyes
St-Florentin
Sens
Paris
N6
Armançon
Pontigny
Flogny-la-Chapelle
Ligny-le-Châtel
Tonnerre
D965
D905
Ancy-le-Franc
Auxerre
Chablis
St-Bris
N151
N6
Lichères-près-Aigremont
Ravières
Irancy
A6
Noyers
Alsy-sur-Armançon
Vermenton
Nitry
Y O N N E
Montbard
Arcy-sur-Cure
l'Isle-sur-Serein
Châtel-Censoir
Vézelay
Avallon
St-Père
Quarré-les-Tombes
Précy-sous-Thil
Semur-en-Auxois
D905
Venarey-les-Laumes
Troyes
St-Seine l'Abbaye
Val-Suzon
Nancy
Arc-sur-Tille
Saulieu
Chissey-en-Morvan
Vitteaux
D70
C Ô T E   D ' O R
Sombernon
A38
Marsannay
N71
N74
Dijon
Dole
Pouilly-en-Auxois
D905
A39
N5
Genlis
Fixin
Gevrey-Chambertin
Morey-St-Denis
Chambolle-Musigny
Vougeot
Vosne-Romanée
Noiron-sous-Gevrey
Brazey-en-Plaine
Besançon
Nuits-St-Georges
N74
A31
Côte
A36
N81
Arnay-le-Duc
A6
Bligny-sur-Ouche
Pernand-Vergelesses
Savigny
Ladoix-Serrigny
Aloxe-Corton
D15
N81
Lucenay-l'Eveque
Beaune
Pommard
Montbellard
Volnay
Pouilly-sur-Saône
Dole
Autun
Auxey-Duresses
Meursault
St-Aubin
N74
Seurre
D973
Nolay
Puligny-Montrachet
Chassagne-Montrachet
les Maranges
Santenay
Chagny
Bouzeron
Nevers
N80
Couches
Rully
N6
N73
le Creusot
Montcenis
Mercurey
Givry
Chalon-sur-Saône
Mervans
St-Marcel
Mesvres
Toulon-sur-Arroux
Blanzy
Buxy
Montagny
St-Germain-du-Plaine
N978
N70
Montceau-les-Mines
St-Vallier
A6
Montret
Louhans
N78
D994
S A Ô N E   E T   L O I R E
St-Gengoux-le-National
Sennecey-le-Grand
Selle
Lons-le-Saunier
N78
Gueugnon
Ciry-le-Noble
Génelard
Salornay-sur-Guye
Cormatin
Tournus
Cuisery
Moulins
N70
St-Bonnet-de-Joux
Lugny
Viré
N6
St-Trivier-de-Courtes
Paray-le-Monial
N79
Charolles
Cluny
Clessé
Pont-de-Vaux
Montrevel-en-Bresse
Lons-le-Saunier
N79
Verzé
la Clayette
Matour
Vergisson
Solutré-Pouilly
Pouilly
Mâcon
Fuissé
Vinzelles
St-Cyr
A40
Geneve
Bourg-en-Bresse
Chaintré
St-Amour
Juliénas
Chénas
A6
A39
A40
A975
Semur-en-Brionnais
Chauffailles
les Echarmeaux
Fleurie
Moulin-à-Vent
Thoissey
A I N
Chiroubles
Charlieu
Pelmont-de-la-Loire
Beaujeu
Morgon
Régnié
Châtillon-sur-Chalaronne
N83
Lamure
Brouilly
Côte de Brouilly
Belleville
Montmerle-sur-Saône
Villars-lès-Dombes
Chalamont
Thizy
Mts du Beaujolais
Chamont
Versailleu
Geneve
Roanne
Amplepuis
Villefranche-sur-Saône
Trévoux
Meximieux
N7
Tarare
Anse
Neuville-sur-Saône
Montluel
A42
N7
l'Arbresle
Montluel
A432
R H Ô N E
N89
Lyon
Grenoble
Feurs
Vienne
Grenoble
Rhône

Paris
Dijon
Lyon

Chablis
Chablis Grand and Premier Cru
Chablis

Vézelien
Bourgogne Vézelay

Côte de Nuits
Côte de Nuits
Hautes-Côtes de Nuits

Côte de Beaune
Côte de Beaune
Hautes-Côtes de Beaune

Côte Chalonnaise

Couchois
Bourgogne Côtes du Couchois

Mâconnais
Pouilly-Fuissé
Mâcon-Villages
Mâcon

Beaujolais
Beaujolais-Villages
Beaujolais

Morgon   Principal wine commune
▼   Weather station (WS)

1:1,250,000

Km 0   10   20   30   40 Km
Miles 0   10   20 Miles

N

The Loire Valley

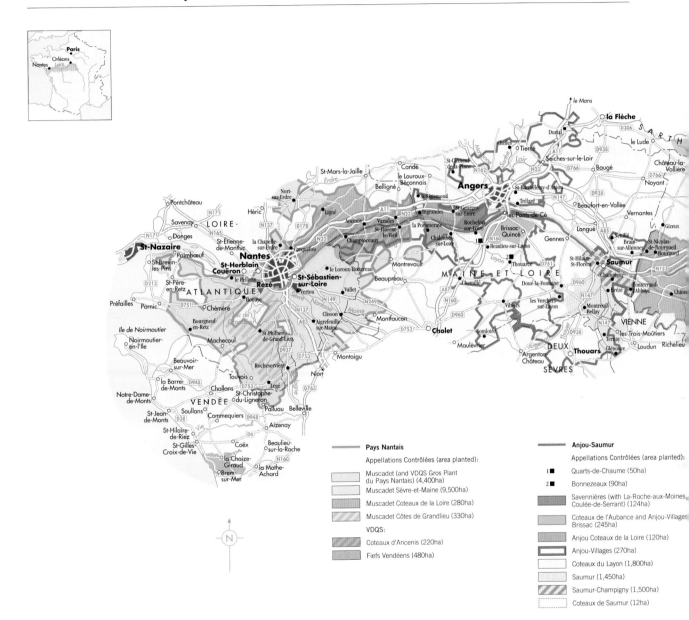

Pays Nantais

Appellations Contrôlées (area planted):

Muscadet (and VDQS Gros Plant du Pays Nantais) (4,400ha)

Muscadet Sèvre-et-Maine (9,500ha)

Muscadet Coteaux de la Loire (280ha)

Muscadet Côtes de Grandlieu (330ha)

VDQS:

Coteaux d'Ancenis (220ha)

Fiefs Vendéens (480ha)

Anjou-Saumur

Appellations Contrôlées (area planted):

1 ■ Quarts-de-Chaume (50ha)

2 ■ Bonnezeaux (90ha)

Savennières (with La-Roche-aux-Moines, Coulée-de-Serrant) (124ha)

Coteaux de l'Aubance and Anjou-Villages Brissac (245ha)

Anjou Coteaux de la Loire (120ha)

Anjou-Villages (270ha)

Coteaux du Layon (1,800ha)

Saumur (1,450ha)

Saumur-Champigny (1,500ha)

Coteaux de Saumur (12ha)

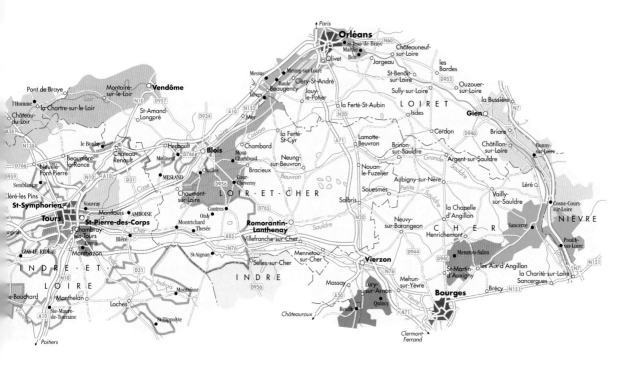

1:1,250,000

Km 0   10   20   30   40 Km

Miles 0   10   20 Miles

	Touraine
	Upper Loire

Appellations Contrôlées (area planted):

Bourgueil, St-Nicolas-de-Bourgueil, and Chinon (4,450ha)

Vouvray and Montlouis-sur-Loire (2,350ha)

Touraine Noble-Joué (20ha)

AMBOISE   Name that can be added to the AC Touraine

Appellations Contrôlées (area planted):

Coteaux du Loir and Jasnières (140ha)

Coteaux du Vendômois (150ha)

Cheverny and Cour-Cheverny (660ha)

Reuilly and Quincy (320ha)

Sancerre, Pouilly-sur-Loire, and Pouilly-Fumé (3,650ha)

Menetou-Salon (450ha)

Coteaux du Giennois (150ha)

VDQS:

Valençay (135ha)

Orléans (100ha)

Orléans-Cléry (40ha)

— · — · —   Département boundary

● Brézé   Major wine-growing commune

▼   Weather station (WS)

Champagne

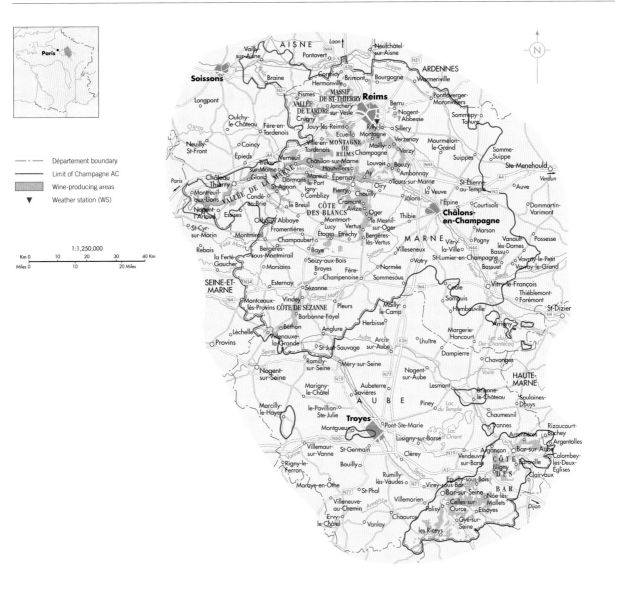

Paris

Département boundary
Limit of Champagne AC
Wine-producing areas
▼ Weather station (WS)

1:1,250,000

Km 0   10   20   30   40 Km
Miles 0   10   20 Miles

Alsace

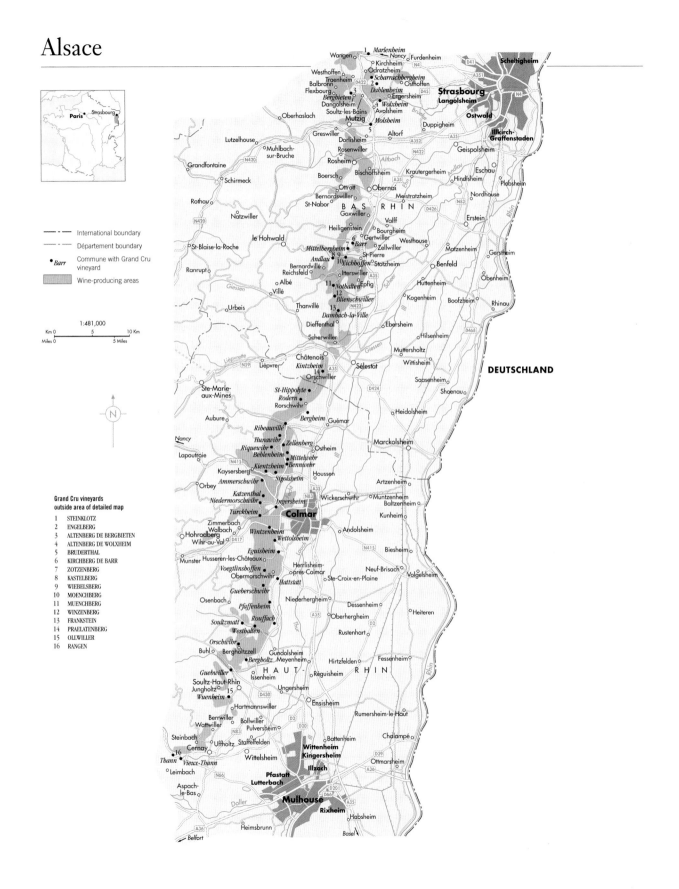

International boundary

Département boundary

• *Barr* Commune with Grand Cru vineyard

Wine-producing areas

1:481,000

Km 0   5   10 Km

Miles 0   5 Miles

**Grand Cru vineyards
outside area of detailed map**

1   STEINKLOTZ
2   ENGELBERG
3   ALTENBERG DE BERGBIETEN
4   ALTENBERG DE WOLXHEIM
5   BRUDERTHAL
6   KIRCHBERG DE BARR
7   ZOTZENBERG
8   KASTELBERG
9   WIEBELSBERG
10   MOENCHBERG
11   MUENCHBERG
12   WINZENBERG
13   FRANKSTEIN
14   PRAELATENBERG
15   OLLWILLER
16   RANGEN

Northern Rhône

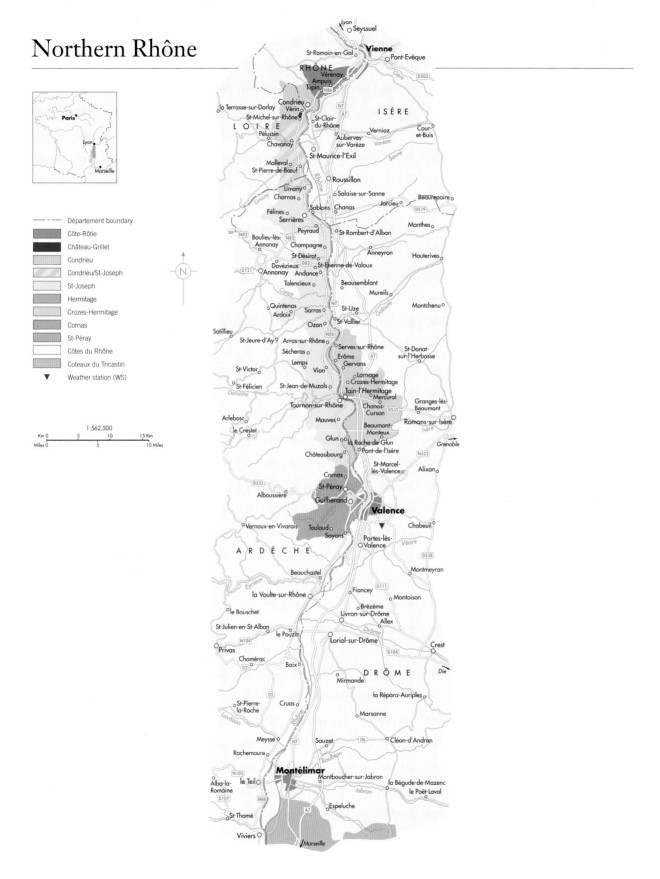

Paris•

Lyon

Marseille•

— - — Département boundary

Côte-Rôtie

Château-Grillet

Condrieu

Condrieu/St-Joseph

St-Joseph

Hermitage

Crozes-Hermitage

Cornas

St-Péray

Côtes du Rhône

Coteaux du Tricastin

▼ Weather station (WS)

N

1:562,500

Km 0   5   10   15 Km

Miles 0   5   10 Miles

Southern Rhône

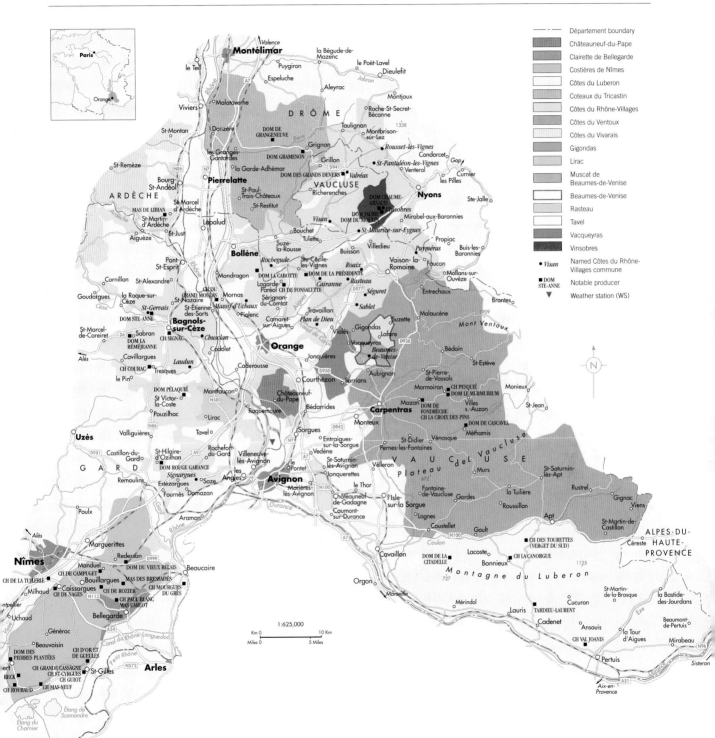

Legend:
- Département boundary
- Châteauneuf-du-Pape
- Clairette de Bellegarde
- Costières de Nîmes
- Côtes du Luberon
- Coteaux du Tricastin
- Côtes du Rhône-Villages
- Côtes du Ventoux
- Côtes du Vivarais
- Gigondas
- Lirac
- Muscat de Beaumes-de-Venise
- Beaumes-de-Venise
- Rasteau
- Tavel
- Vacqueyras
- Vinsobres
- • *Visan* — Named Côtes du Rhône-Villages commune
- ■ DOM STE-ANNE — Notable producer
- ▼ Weather station (WS)

Paris

Orange

Valence
Montélimar
le Teil
Puygiron
le Poët-Laval
Dieulefit
la Bégude-de-Mazenc
Espeluche
Aleyrac
Montjoux
Viviers
Malataverne
DRÔME
Roche-St-Secret-Béconne
St-Montan
Donzère
DOM DE GRANGENEUVE
Taulignan
Montbrison-sur-Lez
1338
les Granges-Gontardes
Grignan
DOM GRAMENON
Rousset-les-Vignes
Condorcet
Gap
St-Rémèze
la Garde-Adhémar
Grillon
DOM DES GRANDS DEVERS
St-Pantaléon-les-Vignes
Curnier
Bourg-St-Andéol
Pierrelatte
St-Paul-Trois-Châteaux
VAUCLUSE
Valréas
Venterol
les Pilles
ARDÈCHE
MAS DE LIBIAN
St-Marcel-d'Ardèche
St-Restitut
Richerenches
DOM CHAUME-ARNAUD
Nyons
Ste-Jalle
St-Martin-d'Ardèche
Lapalud
DOM JAUME
Vinsobres
Mirabel-aux-Baronnies
St-Just
Visan
DOM DU MOULIN
Aiguèze
Bouchet
St-Maurice-sur-Eygues
Propiac
Buis-les-Baronnies
Pont-St-Esprit
Suze-la-Rousse
Tulette
Villedieu
Puyméras
Cornillon
Bollène
Rochegude
Ste-Cécile-les-Vignes
Roaix
Vaison-la-Romaine
Faucon
Mollans-sur-Ouvèze
Goudargues
la Roque-sur-Cèze
St-Alexandre
Mondragon
DOM LA CABOTTE
DOM DE LA PRÉSIDENTE
Cairanne
Rasteau
Séguret
Entrechaux
Brantes
St-Gervais
DOM STE-ANNE
GRAND MOULIN
Mornas
Lagarde-Paréol CH DE FONSALETTE
Sérignan-du-Comtat
Sablet
Suzette
Malaucène
1909
St-Marcel-de-Careiret
Sabran
CLOU
St-Nazaire
Massif d'Uchaux
Travaillan
Violès
Gigondas
Lafare
Mont Ventoux
DOM LA RÉMÉJEANNE
CH SIGNAC
Chusclan
St-Étienne-des-Sorts
Piolenc
Plan de Dieu
Beaumes-de-Venise
Bédoin
Cavillargues
Codolet
Camaret-sur-Aigues
Vacqueyras
St-Estève
Laudun
Bagnols-sur-Cèze
Orange
Jonquières
Aubignan
St-Pierre-de-Vassols
St-Estève
Alès
CH COURAC
Tresques
Sarrians
Carpentras
Monieux
le Pin
DOM PÉLAQUIÉ
Caderousse
Courthézon
Mazan
CH PESQUIÉ
St-Jean
Montfaucon
St-Victor-la-Coste
Châteauneuf-du-Pape
Mormoiron
DOM LE MURMURIUM
Pouzilhac
N580
Bédarrides
DOM DE FONDRÈCHE CH LA CROIX DES PINS
Villes s.-Auzon
Roquemaure
Lirac
Monteux
Carpentras
DOM DE CASCAVEL
Uzès
Valliguières
Tavel
Sorgues
D942
St-Didier
Vénasque
Méthamis
Castillon-du-Gard
St-Hilaire-d'Ozilhan
Rochefort-du-Gard
Entraigues-sur-la-Sorgue
Pernes-les-Fontaines
VAUCLUSE
GARD
DOM ROUGE GARANCE
Villeneuve-lès-Avignon
Vedène
St-Saturnin-lès-Avignon
Velleron
Plateau
de
St-Saturnin-lès-Apt
Signargues
les Angles
le Pontet
Jonquerettes
672
Rustrel
Remoulins
Estézargues
Saze
Avignon
le Thor
l'Isle-sur-la-Sorgue
Murs
Fontaine-de-Vaucluse
Gordes
la Tuilière
Gignac
Viens
Fournès
Domazan
Morières-lès-Avignon
Châteauneuf-de-Gadagne
Lagnes
Roussillon
St-Martin-de-Castillon
Poulx
Aramon
Durance
Caumont-sur-Durance
Coustellet
Goult
Apt
ALPES-DU-HAUTE-PROVENCE
Céreste
CH DES TOURETTES (VERGET DU SUD)
Marguerittes
Cavaillon
Lacoste
Bonnieux
1125
la Bastide-des-Jourdans
Nîmes
Redessan
DOM DE LA CITADELLE
CH LA CANORGUE
St-Martin-de-la-Brasque
CH DE LA TUILERIE
Manduel
CH DE CAMPUGET
Bouillargues
Beaucaire
Montagne du Luberon
727
Caissargues
MAS DES BRESSADES
CH DE ROZIER
CH MOURGUES DU GRÈS
Orgon
DOM DE LA CITADELLE
Beaumont-de-Pertuis
Milhaud
CH DE NAGES
CH PAUL BLANC MAS CARLOT
N113
Bellegarde
Mérindol
Cucuron
TARDIEU-LAURENT
Beaumont-de-Pertuis
Montpellier
Uchaud
Marseille
Lauris
Ansouis
la Tour d'Aigues
Mirabeau
Générac
Cadenet
N96
Sisteron
Beauvoisin
CH D'OR ET DE GUEULES
CH VAL JOANIS
A34
Canal du Rhône à Languedoc
DOM DES PIERRES PLANTÉES
CH GRANDE CASSAGNE
CH ST-CYRGUES
CH GUIOT
St-Gilles
Arles
Pertuis
BECK
CH ROUBAUD
CH MAS-NEUF
Aix-en-Provence
A51
Étang de Scamandre
Étang du Charnier

1:625,000
Km 0   10 Km
Miles 0   5 Miles

N

Provence

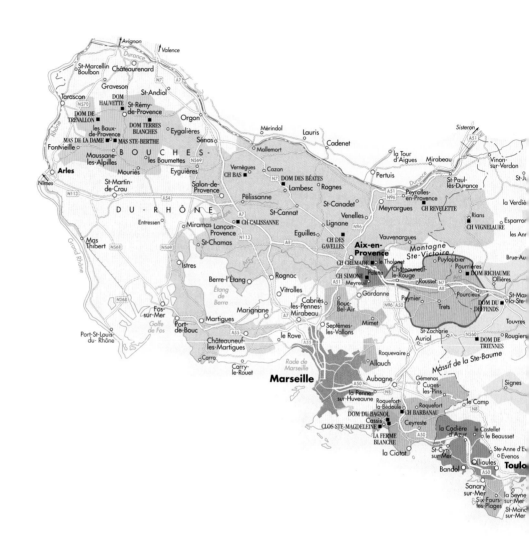

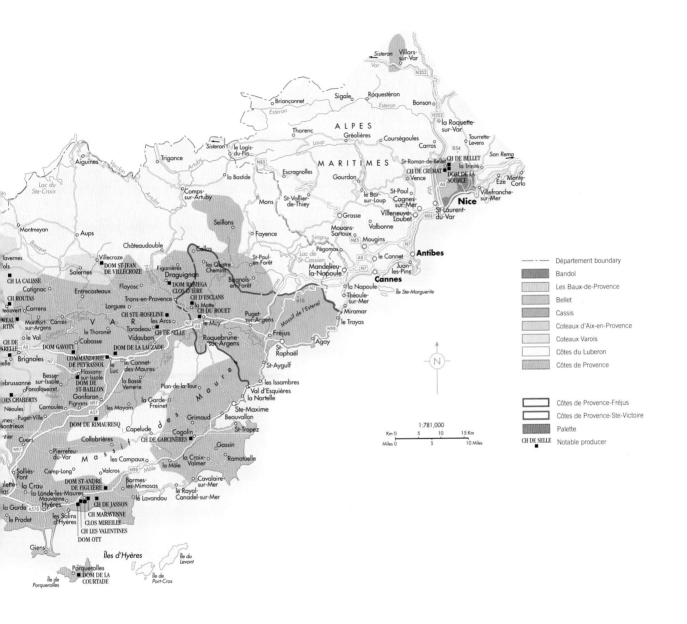

Western Languedoc

--- ---	Département boundary
■ CH HAUT GLÉON	Notable producer
	Cabardès
	Corbières
	Corbières-Boutenac
ALARIC	Corbières subregion
	Languedoc
LA CLAPE	Languedoc subregional appellation
Quatourze	Languedoc terroir
	Malepère
	Fitou

	Limoux
	Minervois
	Minervois-La Livinière
CLAMOUX	Minervois subregion
	Muscat de St-Jean de Minervois
	Rivesaltes
	St-Chinian
BERLOU	St-Chinian subregional appellation
▼	Weather station (WS)

1:509,000

Km 0   5   10 Km
Miles 0   5 Miles

Eastern Languedoc

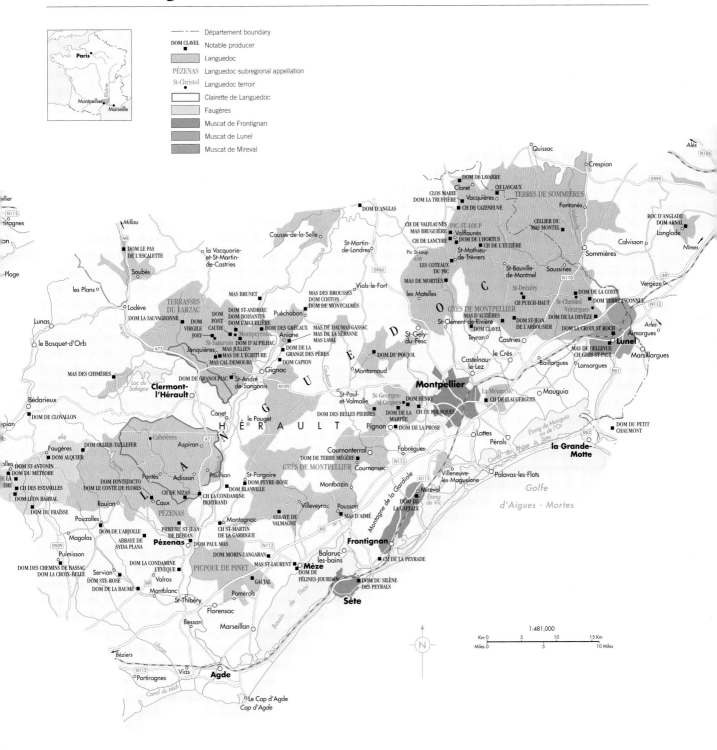

Département boundary
DOM CLAVEL ■ Notable producer
Languedoc
PÉZENAS Languedoc subregional appellation
St-Christol Languedoc terroir
Clairette de Languedoc
Faugères
Muscat de Frontignan
Muscat de Lunel
Muscat de Mireval

Paris

Montpellier
Marseille

Rhône

Alès
N106

Quissac
Crespian
DOM DE LAVABRE
D999
Claret CH LASCAUX
CLOS MARIE Vacquières
DOM LA TRUFFIÈRE
CH DE CAZENEUVE TERRES DE SOMMIÈRES
Fontanès
ROC D'ANGLADE
DOM D'ANGLAS CELLIER DU DOM ARNAL
CH DE VALFLAUNÈS MAS MONTEL Langlade
Causse-de-la-Selle MAS BRUGUIÈRE PIC-ST-LOUP Calvisson
CH DE LANCYRE Valflaunès Sommières Nîmes
St-Martin- DOM DE L'HORTUS
de-Londres Pic St-Loup CH DE L'EUZIÈRE
658 St-Mathieu- N110
de-Tréviers Saussines A9
LES COTEAUX St-Bauville- Vergèze
DU PIC de-Montmel
MAS DE MORTIÈS St-Drézéry DOM DE LA COSTE
CH PUECH-HAUT St-Christol
les Matelles GRÈS DE MONTPELLIER Vérargues DOM TERRE INCONNUE
St-Clément-de-Rivière MAS D'AUZIÈRES N113
DOM ST-JEAN DOM LA DEVÈZE
DE L'ARBOUSIER Arles
DOM CLAVEL DOM LA CROIX ST ROCH
Teyran Castries Lunel
le Crès MAS DE BELLEVUE
Castelnau- CH GRÈS ST-PAUL Marsillargues
le-Lez Baillargues
Montpellier Lansargues
La Méjanelle Mauguio D61
Montarnaud Étang de Mauguio
ou de l'Or
St-Gély- CH DE FLAUGERGUES
du-Fesc

MILLAU
N9
DOM LE PAS
DE L'ESCALETTE
la Vacquerie-
et-St-Martin-
de-Castries
Soubès
les Plans
Lodève
Lunas
le Bosquet-d'Orb
TERRASSES
DU LARZAC
DOM LA SAUVAGEONNE
MAS BRUNET
DOM FONT
CAUDE DOM ST-ANDRIEU
DOM VIRGILE DOM BOISANTIN
JOLY DOM D'AIGUELIÈRE
DOM DES GRÉCAUX
Montpeyroux Aniane
DOM SATURNIN DOM D'AUPILHAC
MAS JULLIEN MAS DE LA SÉRANNE
Jonquières MAS DE L'ÉCRITURE MAS DE DAUMAS GASSAC
MAS CAL DEMOURA MAS LAVAL
DOM DE LA
GRANGE DES PÈRES
DOM CAPION
Gignac
MAS DES CHIMÈRES
DOM DE GRANOUPIAC St-André-
de-Sangonis
Bédarieux
DOM DE CLOVALLON
498
DOM OLLIER-TAILLEFER
Cabrières
Faugères Aspiran
DOM ALQUIER A75
DOM ST-ANTONIN
DOM DU MÉTÉORE FAUGÈRES Fontès Adissan
CH DES ESTANILLES DOM FONTEDICTO DOM LE CONTE DE FLORIS
DOM LÉON BARRAL CH DE NIZAS
DOM DU FRAÏSSE Caux CH LA CONDAMINE
Roujan BERTRAND
Pouzolles PÉZENAS
Magalas DOM DE L'ARJOLLE
Puimisson PRIEURÉ ST-JEAN
ABBAYE DE DE BÉBIAN
DOM DES CHEMINS DE BASSAC SYLVA PLANA
DOM LA CROIX-BELLE Pézenas DOM PAUL MAS
DOM LA CONDAMINE DOM MORIN-LANGARAN
Servian L'ÉVÊQUE
N9 Valros PICPOUL DE PINET
DOM STE-ROSE
DOM DE LA BAUME Montblanc
St-Thibéry
Bessan
Marseillan
Béziers
N112 Vias
Portiragnes Agde
Canal du Midi
Le Cap d'Agde
Cap d'Agde

HÉRAULT
Hérault
Canet
le Pouget
A75
Paulhan
St-Pargoire
DOM PEYRE-ROSE
DOM BLANVILLE
Montbazin
GRÈS DE MONTPELLIER
DOM DE TERRE MÉGÈRE
Cournonterral
Cournonsec
N113
Montagnac
CH ST-MARTIN
DE LA GARRIGUE
A9
ABBAYE DE
VALMAGNE
Villeveyrac
Poussan
MAS D'AIMÉ
Balaruc-
les-bains
Mèze
DOM DE
FÉLINES-JOURDAN
N113
MAS ST-LAURENT
GAUJAL
Pomérols
Florensac
Sète
DOM DU SILÈNE
DES PEYRALS

LANGUEDOC
Coulazou
St-Paul-
et-Valmalle
Pignan
DOM DES BELLES PIERRES
St-Georges-
d'Orques
DOM DE LA
MARFÉE
DOM DE LA PROSE
Fabrègues
Lattes
Pérols
Montagne de la Gardiole
Mireval
DOM DE
LA CAPELLE
Étang
de Vic
Villeneuve-
lès-Maguelone
Palavas-les-Flots
la Grande-
Motte
D62
DOM DU PETIT
CHAUMONT
Golfe
d'Aigues - Mortes

DOM HENRY
CH DE FOURQUES
Frontignan
CH DE LA PEYRADE

Viols-le-Fort
MAS DES BROUSSES
DOM COSTON
DOM DE MONTCALMÈS
DOM DU POUJOL

N

1:481,000
Km 0   5   10   15 Km
Miles 0   5   10 Miles

Germany

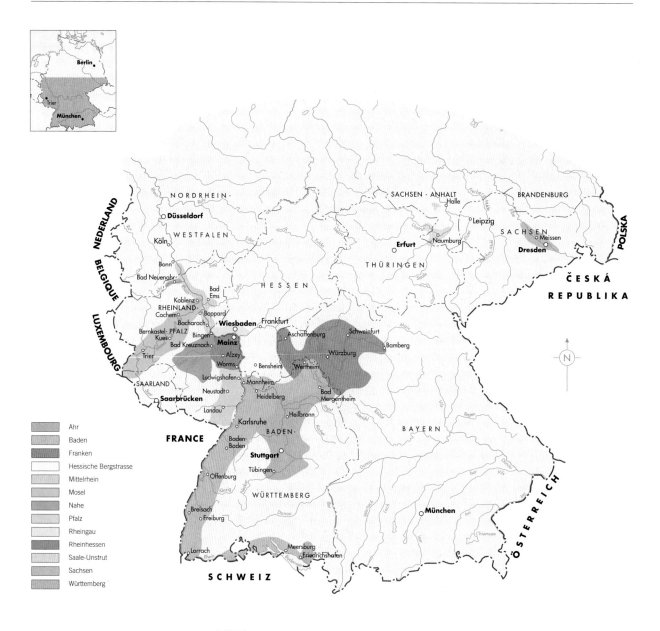

Ahr
Baden
Franken
Hessische Bergstrasse
Mittelrhein
Mosel
Nahe
Pfalz
Rheingau
Rheinhessen
Saale-Unstrut
Sachsen
Württemberg

1:4,500,000

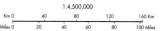

Km 0   40   80   120   160 Km
Miles 0   20   40   60   80   100 Miles

Italy

ÖSTERREICH

SCHWEIZ

Bolzano

TRENTINO-
ALTO ADIGE

FRIULI-
VENEZIA
GIULIA

Udine

Gorizia

SLOVENIJA

Trieste

VALLE
D'AOSTA

Lago
Maggiore

Sondrio

Lago di
Como

Trento

Gattinara

Como

Bergamo

VENETO

Novara

LOMBARDIA

Vicenza

Treviso

Vercelli

Brescia

Lago di
Garda

Verona

Torino

Milano

Pavia

Cremona

Mantova

Padova

Venezia

PIEMONTE

Alessandria

Piacenza

Parma

Ferrara

Adige

FRANCE

Alba

Cuneo

LIGURIA

Savona

Genova

Reggio
nell'Emilia

Modena

EMILIA-

Bologna

ROMAGNA

Ravenna

La Spezia

Forlì

SAN
MARINO

Pistoia

Firenze

Pesaro

Pisa

Lucca

MARCHE

Ancona

Livorno

TOSCANA

Siena

Arezzo

Macerata

Isola d'Elba

Montepulciano

Perugia

Ascoli
Piceno

Grosseto

UMBRIA

Teramo

Terni

ABRUZZO

Pescara

Corse

Viterbo

L'Aquila

LAZIO

Roma

MOLISE

Latina

Foggia

CAMPANIA

Benevento

Bari

Volturno

PUGLIA

Sassari

Napoli

Salerno

Isola d'Ischia

BASILICATA

Taranto

SARDEGNA

Isola di Capri

Agri

Sinni

Cagliari

N

Is. Eolie o Lipari

CALABRIA

Messina

Reggio di
Calabria

Trapani

Palermo

Catania

SICILIA

Siracusa

---- International boundary
—·— Regione boundary
▨ Wine-producing area
▨ Land above 600 metres

1:7,500,000

Km 0   100   200 Km
Miles 0   50   100 Miles

Piedmont

DOCG Barbaresco

DOC Barbera d'Alba

DOC Barbera d'Asti

DOCG Barolo

DOCG Brachetto d'Acqui

DOC Dolcetto d'Alba

DOC Dolcetto d'Asti

DOC Dolcetto di Diano d'Alba

DOCG Dolcetto di Dogliani

DOC Grignolino d'Asti

DOC Grignolino del Monferrato Casalese

DOC Langhe

DOCG Asti and Moscato d'Asti

DOC Nebbiolo d'Alba

DOCG Roero and Roero Arneis

- - - - Provincia boundary

Vineyards

Woods

—500— Contour interval 100 metres

1:456,000

Km 0   5   10 Km

Miles 0   5   10 Miles

N

Tuscany

COLLI LUCCHESI
○ Lucca
MONTECARLO
○ Pisa
○ Pistoia
Livorno
CHIANTI
MONTALBANO
Pontedera
CARMIGNANO
Prato
○ Borgo San Lorenzo
CHIANTI COLLI
FLORENTINI
CHIANTI
COLLINE
PISANE
○ Cecina
CHIANTI
MONTESPERTOLI
Firenze
CHIANTI
RUFINA
Vernaccia
di San
Gimignano
Poggibonsi
Figline
Valdarno
POMINO
MONTESCUDAIO
Volterra
BOLGHERI
CHIANTI
CLASSICO
SASSICAIA
CHIANTI
COLLI SENESI
CHIANTI
VAL DI CORNIA
Piombino
Portoferraio
Isola d'Elba
ELBA
TOSCANA
Massa
Marittima
Val d'Arbia
Siena
CHIANTI
COLLI ARETINI
Arezzo
Sansepolcro
SAN MARINO
COLLI PESARESI
Urbino
Pesaro
Fano
Bianchello
del Metauro
Falerio dei
Colli Ascolani
LACRIMA DI
MORRO D'ALBA
MONTEREGIO DI
MASSA MARITTIMA
BRUNELLO DI
MONTALCINO
MONTECUCCO
SANT'ANTIMO
VALDICHIANA
Cortona
CORTONA
Città di Castello
Metauro
Umbertide
Gubbio
Verdicchio dei
Castelli di Jesi
Jesi
Senigallia
Ancona
CONERO
Fabriano
ROSSO
CONERO
Grosseto
Moscadello di
Montalcino
Montalcino
Montepulciano
VINO NOBILE
DI MONTEPULCIANO
VIN SANTO DI
MONTEPULCIANO
Lago
Trasimeno
COLLI DEL
TRASIMENO
Perugia
TORGIANO
TORGIANA RISERVA
Verdicchio
di Matelica
MARCHE
Macerata
ROSSO PICENO
Scansano
MORELLINO
DI SCANSANO
Bianco di
Pitigliano
COLLI
PERUGINI
UMBRIA
Assisi
ASSISI
Ansonica Costa
dell'Argentario
Isola del Giglio
PARRINA
SOVANA
Orvieto
MONTEFALCO
SAGRANTINO
Foligno
VERNACCIA DI
SERRAPETRONA
COLLI MACERATESI
Fermo
Argentario
Porto
Ercole
Orbetello
Orvieto
Orvieto
Classico
Lago di
Bolsena
COLLI
MARTANI
Spoleto
Norcia
Ascoli
Piceno
Est! Est!! Est!!!
LAGO DI
CORBARA
Orvieto
Montefiascone
Tuscania
COLLI
AMERINI
Narni
Terni
ROSSO PICENO
SUPERIORE
Viterbo
Teramo
MONTEPULCIANO
D'ABRUZZO COLLINE
TERAMANE
Civitavecchia
Civita
Castellana
Rieti
MONTEPULCIANO
D'ABRUZZO
CERVETERI
Bracciano
Lago di
Bracciano
LAZIO
L'Aquila
Trebbiano
d'Abruzzo
Pescara
Roma
Tivoli
Loreto
Aprutino
Chieti
Marino
Frascati
Subiaco
CESANESE
DI AFFILE
Avezzano
Celano
Trebbiano
d'Abruzzo
Colli Albani
Colli Lanuvini
Aprilia
VELLETRI
Fiuggi
CESANESE
DEL PIGLIO
Trebbiano
d'Abruzzo
Sulmona
ABRUZZO
Lanciano
CASTELLI
ROMANI
Anzio
Latina
Frosinone
Sora
MONTEPULCIANO
D'ABRUZZO
Vasto
Priverno
Terracina
Pontecorvo
Cassino
PENTRO DI ISERNIA
Isernia
BIFERNO
Formia
Gaeta
MOLISE

EMILIA-ROMAGNA
COLLI
BOLOGNESI
Imola
Lugo
Albana
di Romagna
Faenza
Ravenna
Forlì
SANGIOVESE DI
ROMAGNA
Trebbiano di
Romagna
Cervia
Cesena
Cesenatico
Pagadebit
di Romagna
Rimini
Cattolica

Legend

International boundary

Regione boundary

BIFERNO Red wine

TORGIANO Red and white wine

Zagarolo White wine

DOCG/DOC boundaries are distinguished
by coloured lines

Land above 600 metres

1:1,875,000

Km 0 — 20 — 40 Km
Miles 0 — 10 — 20 — 30 Miles

Roma

Spain

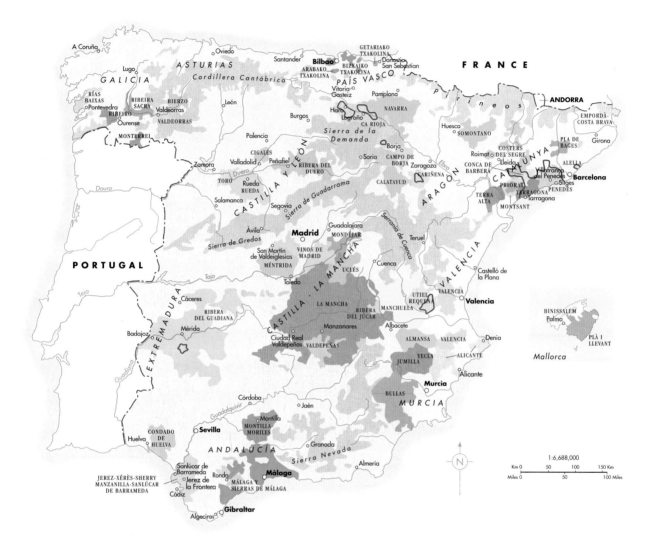

A Coruña
Oviedo
Santander
ASTURIAS
Cordillera Cantábrica
Lugo
GALICIA
RÍAS
BAIXAS
Pontevedra
RIBEIRA
SACRA
RIBEIRO
Ourense
BIERZO
VALDEORRAS
Valdeorras
MONTERREI
León
GETARIAKO
TXAKOLINA
Bilbao
Donostia
San Sebastián
BIZKAIKO
TXAKOLINA
ARABAKO
TXAKOLINA
PAÍS VASCO
Vitoria-
Gasteiz
Pamplona
NAVARRA
Haro
Logroño
CA RIOJA
Sierra de la
Demanda
FRANCE
ANDORRA
P i r i n e o s
EMPORDÀ-
COSTA BRAVA
PLA DE
BAGES
Girona
Huesca
SOMONTANO
Burgos
Palencia
Zamora
Valladolid
Peñafiel
CIGALES
RIBERA DEL
DUERO
Soria
CAMPO DE
BORJA
Borja
Zaragoza
Ebro
ARAGÓN
CARIÑENA
CALATAYUD
Raimat
COSTERS
DEL SEGRE
Lleida
CONCA DE
BARBERÀ
CATALUNYA
Villafranca
del Penedès
ALELLA
PLA DE
BAGES
PENEDÈS
Sitges
Barcelona
TERRA
ALTA
PRIORAT
MONTSANT
TARRAGONA
Tarragona
Douro
TORO
Rueda
RUEDA
CASTILLA Y LEÓN
Salamanca
Segovia
Sierra de Guadarrama
Ávila
Sierra de Gredos
Madrid
Guadalajara
MONDÉJAR
San Martín
de Valdeiglesias
VINOS DE
MADRID
MÉNTRIDA
Serranía de Cuenca
Teruel
VALENCIA
Toledo
Tajo
UCLÉS
CASTILLA-LA MANCHA
Cuenca
Castelló de
la Plana
PORTUGAL
Tejo
EXTREMADURA
Cáceres
RIBERA
DEL GUADIANA
Mérida
Badajoz
Guadiana
LA MANCHA
RIBERA
DEL JÚCAR
Manzanares
Ciudad Real
Valdepeñas
VALDEPEÑAS
Albacete
MANCHUELA
UTIEL
REQUENA
VALENCIA
Valencia
Denia
ALMANSA
VALENCIA
YECLA
JUMILLA
ALICANTE
Alicante
Murcia
BULLAS
MURCIA
BINISSALEM
Palma
PLÀ I
LLEVANT
Mallorca
Córdoba
Jaén
Guadalquivir
Sevilla
CONDADO
DE
HUELVA
Huelva
MONTILLA-
MORILES
Montilla
ANDALUCÍA
Granada
Sierra Nevada
Almería
JEREZ-XÉRÈS-SHERRY
MANZANILLA-SANLÚCAR
DE BARRAMEDA
Sanlúcar de
Barrameda
Jerez de
la Frontera
Ronda
Cádiz
MÁLAGA Y
SIERRAS DE MÁLAGA
Málaga
Algeciras
Gibraltar

1:6,688,000
Km 0   50   100   150 Km
Miles 0   50   100 Miles

N

- - - International boundary
TORO   Denominación de Origen (DO)
⬜   Cava DO
▨   Land above 1000 metres

Portugal

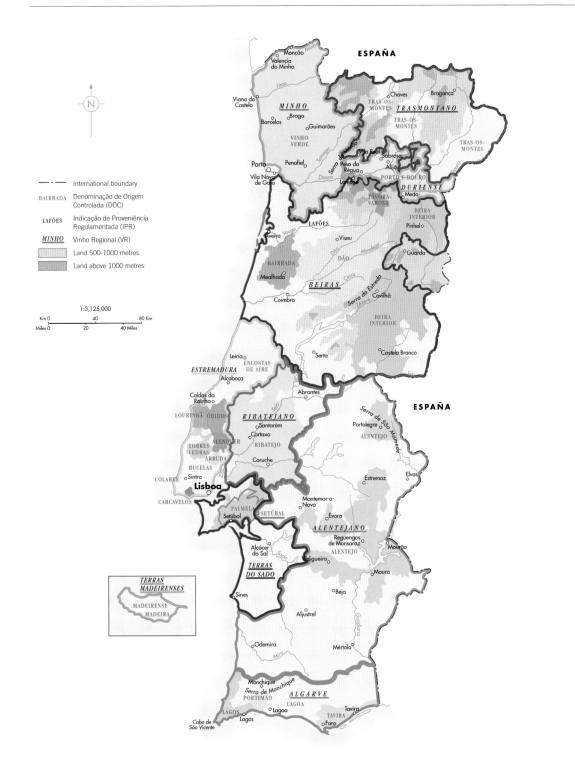

International boundary

BAIRRADA   Denominação de Origem
            Controlada (DOC)

LAFÕES   Indicação de Proveniência
            Regulamentada (IPR)

MINHO   Vinho Regional (VR)

            Land 500-1000 metres

            Land above 1000 metres

1:3,125,000

Km 0   40   80 Km
Miles 0   20   40 Miles

ESPAÑA

Monção
Valência
do Minho

Viana do
Castelo

MINHO

Barcelos
Braga
Guimarães

VINHO
VERDE

Porto
Penafiel
Vila Nova
de Gaia

Chaves
Bragança

TRAS-OS-
MONTES
TRASMONTANO

TRAS-OS-
MONTES

TRAS-OS-
MONTES

Vila Real
Sabrosa
Peso da
Régua
Alijó

Lamego

PORTO E DOURO

DURIENSE

TÁVORA-
VAROSA

Meda

BEIRA
INTERIOR

LAFÕES

Pinhel

Aveiro

Viseu

Guarda

DÃO

BAIRRADA

Mealhada

BEIRAS

Serra da Estrela
Covilhã

Coimbra

BEIRA
INTERIOR

Leiria

ENCOSTAS
DE AIRE

Serta

Castelo Branco

ESTREMADURA

Alcobaça

Caldas da
Rainha

Abrantes

ESPAÑA

LOURINHÃ ÓBIDOS

RIBATEJANO

Santarém
Cartaxo

RIBATEJO

Serra de São Mamede

Portalegre

ALENTEJO

TORRES
VEDRAS
ARRUDA

ALENQUER

BUCELAS

COLARES   Sintra

Coruche

Lisboa

CARCAVELOS

PALMELA

SETÚBAL
Setúbal

Montemor-o-
Novo

Évora

Estremoz

Elvas

ALENTEJANO

Reguengos
de Monsaraz

Mourão

Alcácer
do Sal

*TERRAS
DO SADO*

Vidigueira

ALENTEJO

Moura

Sines

Beja

TERRAS
MADEIRENSES

MADEIRENSE
MADEIRA

Aljustrel

Odemira

Mértola

Monchique
Serra de Monchique
PORTIMÃO

ALGARVE

LAGOA

Tavira
TAVIRA

LAGOS

Cabo de
São Vicente

Lagoa

Lagos

Faro

Switzerland

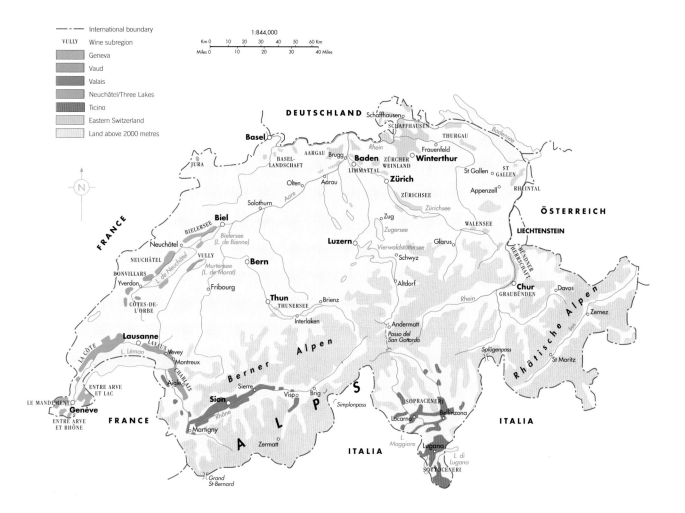

International boundary

VULLY Wine subregion

Geneva

Vaud

Valais

Neuchâtel/Three Lakes

Ticino

Eastern Switzerland

Land above 2000 metres

1:844,000

Km 0 10 20 30 40 50 60 Km

Miles 0 10 20 30 40 Miles

N

DEUTSCHLAND

Schaffhausen
SCHAFFHAUSEN

Basel

THURGAU

Frauenfeld

Bodensee

AARGAU Brugg

Baden

ZÜRCHER
WEINLAND

Winterthur

BASEL-
LANDSCHAFT

Rhein

LIMMATTAL

St Gallen

ST
GALLEN

JURA

Olten

Aarau

Zürich

ZÜRICHSEE

Appenzell

RHEINTAL

Aare

Solothurn

Zürichsee

ÖSTERREICH

Zug

FRANCE

BIELERSEE

Biel

Zugersee

WALENSEE

LIECHTENSTEIN

Neuchâtel

Bielersee
(L. de Bienne)

Luzern

Vierwaldstättersee

Glarus

NEUCHÂTEL

VULLY

Schwyz

BÜNDNER
HERRSCHAFT

BONVILLARS

Murtensee
(L. de Morat)

Bern

Chur

Davos

Yverdon

L. de Neuchâtel

Fribourg

Altdorf

Rhein

GRAUBÜNDEN

CÔTES-DE-
L'ORBE

Thun

THUNERSEE

Brienz

Zernez

Inn

Interlaken

Andermatt

Berner

Alpen

Splügenpass

Rhätische Alpen

LA CÔTE

Lausanne

LAVAUX

Vevey

Passo del
San Gottardo

St Moritz

L. Léman

Montreux

ENTRE ARVE
ET LAC

CHABLAIS

Aigle

Sierre

Visp

Brig

Simplonpass

SOPRACENERI

LE MANDEMENT

Genève

Sion

A L P E N

Locarno

Bellinzona

ITALIA

ENTRE ARVE
ET RHÔNE

FRANCE

Rhône

Martigny

Zermatt

ITALIA

L.
Maggiore

Lugano

L di
Lugano

SOTTOCENERI

Grand
St-Bernard

Austria

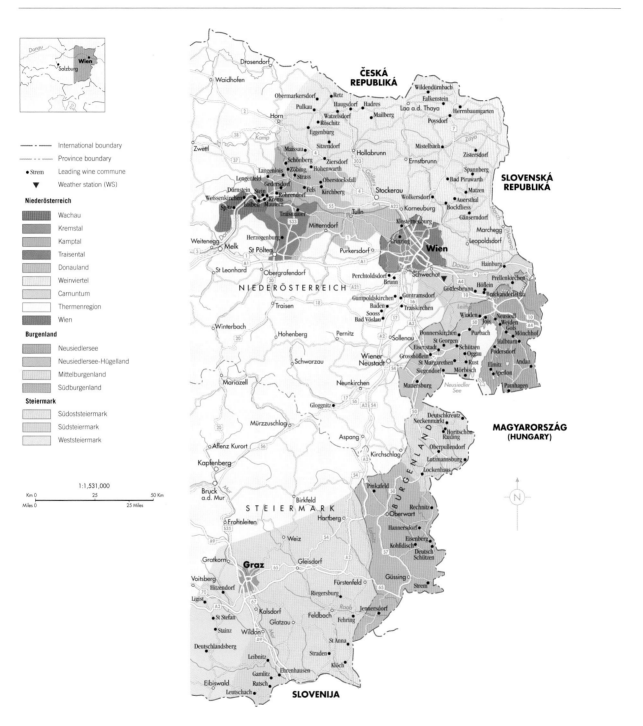

International boundary
Province boundary
● Strem Leading wine commune
▼ Weather station (WS)

Niederösterreich
Wachau
Kremstal
Kamptal
Traisental
Donauland
Weinviertel
Carnuntum
Thermenregion
Wien

Burgenland
Neusiedlersee
Neusiedlersee-Hügelland
Mittelburgenland
Südburgenland

Steiermark
Südoststeiermark
Südsteiermark
Weststeiermark

1:1,531,000

Km 0   25   50 Km
Miles 0   25 Miles

Hungary

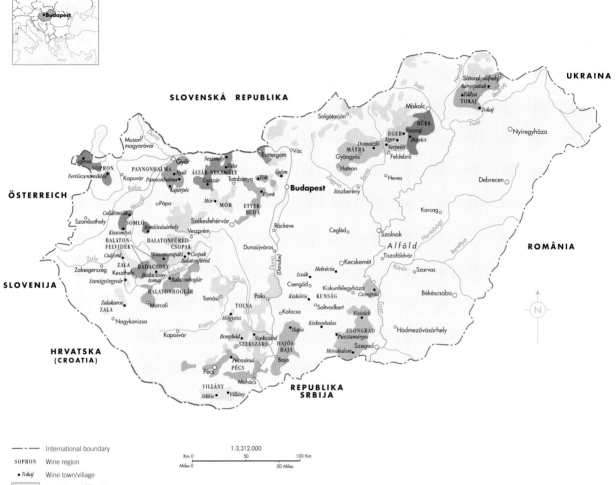

International boundary

SOPRON   Wine region

• *Tokaj*   Wine town/village

Land above 400 metres

1:3,312,000

Km 0   50   100 Km

Miles 0   50 Miles

Greece

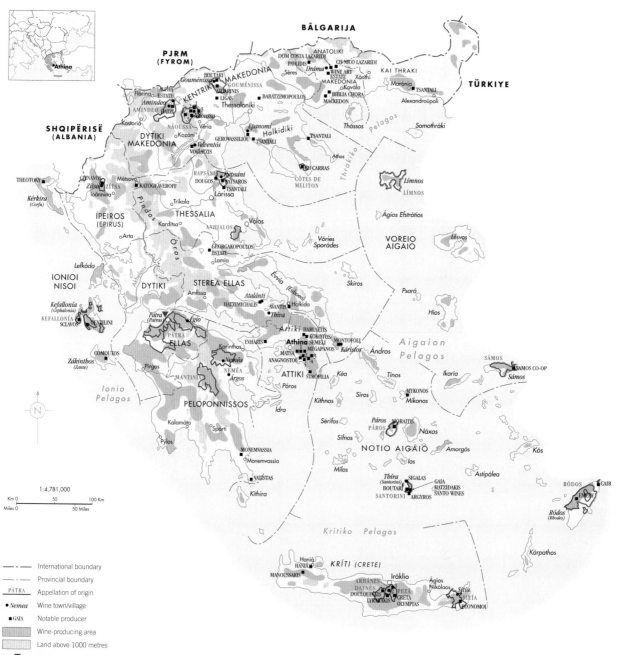

BÂLGARIJA

PJRM
(FYROM)

ANATOLIKI
DOM COSTA LAZARIDI
PAVLIDIS   CH NICO LAZARIDI   KAI THRAKI
KENTRIKI   Dráma   Xánthi
MAKEDONIA   WINE ART   Maróni
Gouménissa   ESTATE   TSANTALI
BOUTARI   MAKEDONIA   Kavála
GOUMÉNISSA   Séres   BIBLIA CHORA
ALPHA   ALARINIS   MACKEDON
Florina   ESTATE   LIGAS   Thessaloníki
ESTATE   HATZI   Alexandroúpoli
Amindeo   Náoussa   Samothráki
AMINDEO   Véria   Epanomí   Thássos
HATZI   NÁOUSSA   Halkidiki
Kastoria   Kozáni   GEROVASSILIOU
                  Velventós TSANTALI
DYTIKI   VOGIATZIS
MAKEDONIA   Athos
                                      CH CARRAS
SHQIPËRISË   CÔTES DE
(ALBANIA)   RAPSÁNI   MELITON
                  Rapsáni
THEOTOKY GLINAVOS DOUGOS MATSAROS
          Métsovo   TSANTALI
Kérkira   Zítsa ZITSA Lárissa
(Corfu)   Ioánnina
          KATOGI AVEROFF
          Trikala   Límnos
                             LÍMNOS
IPEIROS   Karditsa
(EPIRUS) THESSALIA   Ágios Efstrátios
Arta   ANHIALOS
          Vólos
          Vóries
          Sporádes   Lésvos
Lefkáda   GEORGAKOPOULOS   VOREIO
          ESTATE   AIGAIO
IONIOI   Lamía
NISOI
          DYTIKI   STEREA ELLAS Skíros Psará
          Amfissa
Kefallonía HATZIMICHALIS Atalánti Híos
(Cephalonia)   AVANTIS Halkida
KEFALLONIA Pátra   Thíva   Evvia
SCLAVOS   (Patras)   (Euboea)
           Égio   Athína HARLAFTIS
COMOUTOS   PÁTRA   Attikí KOKOTOS
Zákinthos ELLAS   EVHARIS SEMELI MONTOFOLI
(Zante)   Korinthos MEGAPANOS Káristos
DENTILINI Neméa   MATSA Ándros
           NEMÉA   ANAGNOSTOU
           Pirgos   ATTIKI STROFILIA Kéa
           MANTINIA Póros   Síros
Ionio   Argos   Kíthnos
Pelagos   PELOPONNISSOS   Ídra Sérifos Tínos MYKONOS
           Kalamáta   Míkonos
           Spárti   Ikaria SÁMOS
           Pýlos   SAMOS CO-OP
                       Sífnos   Páros   Sámos
           MONEMVASSIA   PÁROS MORAITIS
           Monemvassia Míli   SIGALAS Náxos
           VATZÉSTAS   NOTIO AIGÁIO Ios Amorgós Kós
           Kithira   Thíra
                                (Santorini) GAIA RÓDOS
                                BOUTARI HATZIDAKIS CAIR
                                SANTORINI SANTO WINES EMERY
                                ARGYROS
                                              Astipálea Ródos
                                                         (Rhodes)
           Kritiko Pelagos   Kárpathos

                   Haniá
                   HANIÁ KRÍTI (CRETE)
           MANOUSSAKIS Iráklio
                   ARHÁNES Ágios
                   DAFNÉS Nikólaos Sitía
                   DOULOUFAKIS PEZA SITÍA
                   LYRARAKIS CRETA ECONOMOU
                           OLYMPIAS

1:4,781,000

Km 0   50   100 Km
Miles 0   50 Miles

—·—·— International boundary
———   Provincial boundary
PÁTRA Appellation of origin
● Nemea Wine town/village
■ GAIA   Notable producer
         Wine-producing area
         Land above 1000 metres
▼   Weather station (WS)

California

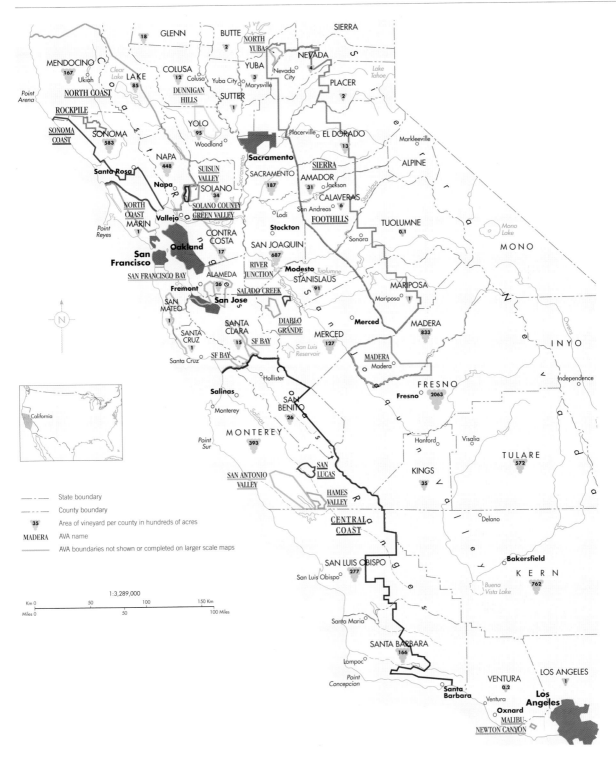

GLENN
18
BUTTE
2
SIERRA

MENDOCINO
167
Ukiah
Clear
Lake
LAKE
85
COLUSA
12
Colusa
NORTH
YUBA
YUBA
3
Yuba City
Marysville
NEVADA
4
Nevada
City
PLACER
2
Lake
Tahoe

Point
Arena
NORTH COAST
DUNNIGAN
HILLS
SUTTER
1
Placerville
EL DORADO
13
Markleeville

ROCKPILE
YOLO
95
Woodland

SONOMA
COAST
SONOMA
583
NAPA
448
Sacramento
SACRAMENTO
SACRAMENTO
187
SIERRA
AMADOR
31
Jackson
ALPINE

Santa Rosa
Napa
SUISUN
VALLEY
SOLANO
34
SOLANO
CALAVERAS
6
San Andreas

NORTH
COAST
MARIN
1
Vallejo
SOLANO COUNTY
GREEN VALLEY
Lodi
FOOTHILLS
TUOLUMNE
0.1
Sonora
MONO
Mono
Lake

Point
Reyes
CONTRA
COSTA
17
Stockton
SAN JOAQUIN
687

Oakland
San
Francisco
SAN FRANCISCO BAY
ALAMEDA
26
RIVER
JUNCTION
Modesto
STANISLAUS
91
Tuolumne
MARIPOSA

Fremont
SALADO CREEK
Mariposa
1
INYO

San Mateo
SAN
MATEO
1
San Jose
SF BAY

SANTA
CRUZ
1
SANTA
CLARA
15
SF BAY
DIABLO
GRANDE
MERCED
127
Merced
MADERA
833

Santa Cruz
SF BAY
San Luis
Reservoir
MADERA
Madera
Independence

Hollister
FRESNO
Fresno
2063

Salinas
SAN
BENITO
26
Hanford
Visalia

Monterey
KINGS
35
TULARE
572

Point
Sur
MONTEREY
393

SAN
LUCAS
Delano

SAN ANTONIO
VALLEY
HAMES
VALLEY
California

CENTRAL
COAST
Bakersfield
KERN
762

SAN LUIS OBISPO
277
San Luis Obispo
Buena
Vista Lake

Santa Maria

SANTA BARBARA
166
VENTURA
0.2
LOS ANGELES
1

Lompoc
Los
Angeles

Point
Concepcion
Santa
Barbara
Ventura
Oxnard
MALIBU-
NEWTON CANYON

---- State boundary
-·-· County boundary
35 Area of vineyard per county in hundreds of acres
MADERA AVA name
—— AVA boundaries not shown or completed on larger scale maps

1:3,289,000
Km 0   50   100   150 Km
Miles 0   50   100 Miles

Pacific Northwest

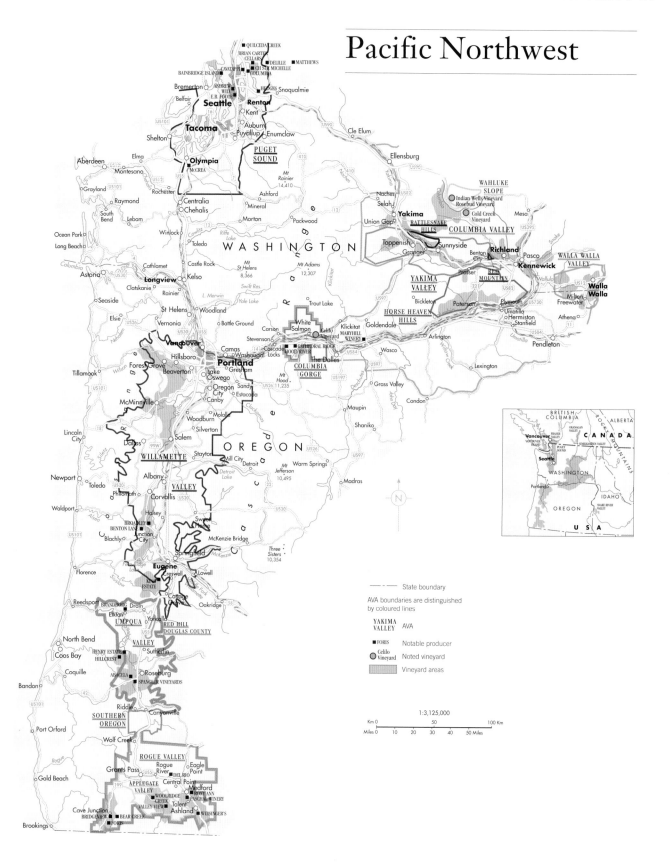

QUILCEDA CREEK
BRIAN CARTER CELLARS
DELILLE ■ MATTHEWS
BAINBRIDGE ISLAND
CAVATAPPA ■ CH. STE MICHELLE COLUMBIA
Bremerton ANDREW WILL
Belfair E.B. FOOTE HEDGES ■ Snoqualmie
Seattle **Renton**
Kent
Tacoma Auburn
Shelton Puyallup Enumclaw Cle Elum
Ellensburg
Aberdeen Elma **PUGET SOUND**
Montesano Olympia McCREA
Grayland Mt Rainier 14,410
Raymond Rochester Ashford
Centralia WAHLUKE SLOPE
South Bend Chehalis Mineral Naches Indian Wells Vineyard
Lebam Selah Rosebud Vineyard
Ocean Park Morton Packwood Yakima Cold Creek Vineyard
Long Beach Toledo RATTLESNAKE HILLS COLUMBIA VALLEY
Winlock WASHINGTON Union Gap Mesa
Cathlamet Castle Rock Toppenish Sunnyside Benton City Richland Pasco
Astoria Longview Kelso Mt St Helens 8,366 Granger YAKIMA VALLEY RED MOUNTAIN Kennewick WALLA WALLA VALLEY
Clatskanie Mt Adams 12,307 Prosser
Seaside Rainier Brosser Walla Walla
Elsie St Helens Woodland Bickleton Milton Freewater
Vernonia Battle Ground Trout Lake Paterson Plymouth Athena
Tillamook Vancouver Carson HORSE HEAVEN HILLS Umatilla Hermiston Stanfield
Forest Grove Hillsboro White Salmon Klickitat MARYHILL WINERY Arlington Pendleton
Beaverton Camas Celilo Vineyard Goldendale Wasco
Portland Washougal CATHEDRAL RIDGE The Dalles Grass Valley
Lake Oswego Cascade Locks HOOD RIVER COLUMBIA GORGE Lexington
Gresham Mt Hood 11,235 Condon
Oregon City Sandy Maupin
McMinnville Canby Estacada
Woodburn Molalla
Lincoln City Silverton Shaniko
Dallas Salem
OREGON
Newport Stayton Warm Springs
Albany Mill City Detroit Madras
Toledo WILLAMETTE Mt Jefferson 10,495
Philomath VALLEY Corvallis
Waldport Halsey Sweet Home
BROADLEY McKenzie Bridge
BENTON LANE Junction City Three Sisters 10,354
Blachly Springfield
Florence Eugene Lowell
KING ESTATE Creswell
Reedsport Cottage Oakridge
BRANDBORG Drain
Elkton Yoncalla RED HILL DOUGLAS COUNTY
UMPQUA
North Bend VALLEY
Coos Bay HENRY ESTATE Sutherlin
HILLCREST
Coquille ABACELA Roseburg
SPANGLER VINEYARDS
Bandon
Riddle
SOUTHERN Canyonville
OREGON
Port Orford Wolf Creek
ROGUE VALLEY
Grants Pass Rogue River Eagle Point
Gold Beach DEL RIO
APPLEGATE Central Point Medford
VALLEY ROXMANN WINERY
WOOLRIDGE CREEK PASCHAL WINERY
Cave Junction VALLEY VIEW Talent Ashland
BRIDGEVIEW BEAR CREEK WEISINGER'S
Brookings FORIS

BRITISH COLUMBIA ALBERTA
Vancouver OKANAGAN VALLEY CANADA
VANCOUVER ISLAND FRASER VALLEY SIMILKAMEEN VALLEY
PUGET SOUND
Seattle
WASHINGTON
Portland IDAHO
OREGON SNAKE RIVER VALLEY
USA

——— State boundary

AVA boundaries are distinguished by coloured lines

YAKIMA VALLEY AVA

■ FORIS Notable producer

○ Celilo Vineyard Noted vineyard

Vineyard areas

1:3,125,000

Km 0 — 50 — 100 Km
Miles 0 — 10 — 20 — 30 — 40 — 50 Miles

South America

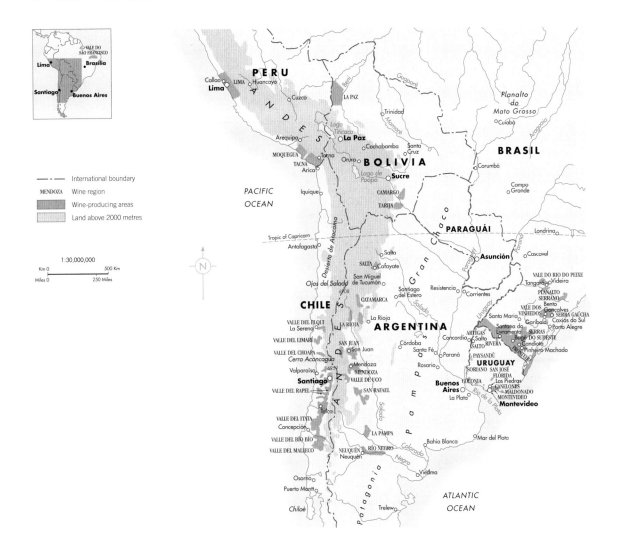

Legend:

- – · – · International boundary
- MENDOZA Wine region
- Wine-producing areas
- Land above 2000 metres

1:30,000,000

Km 0 ——— 500 Km
Miles 0 ——— 250 Miles

Map labels:

VALE DO SÃO FRANCISCO

Lima • Brasília
Santiago • • Buenos Aires

PERU

PACIFIC OCEAN

Callao
LIMA · Huancayo
Lima
Cuzco
LA PAZ
Trinidad

Arequipa
Lago Titicaca
La Paz
Cochabamba
Santa Cruz
MOQUEGUA
TACNA · Tacna
Oruro
Arica
BOLIVIA
Corumbá

Iquique
Lago de Poopó
Sucre
CAMARGO
TARIJA

Tropic of Capricorn
Antofagasta

Beni
Mamoré
Guaporé

Planalto do Mato Grosso
Cuiabá

BRASIL

Campo Grande

PARAGUÁI
Londrina

Ojos del Salado 6908
Salta
SALTA · Cafayate
San Miguel de Tucumán
CATAMARCA

CHILE

Desierto de Atacama

VALLE DEL ELQUI
La Serena
VALLE DEL LIMARÍ
VALLE DEL CHOAPA
Cerro Aconcagua 6958
Valparaíso
Santiago
VALLE DE UCO
SAN RAFAEL

VALLE DEL RAPEL

VALLE DEL ITATA
Concepción
VALLE DEL BÍO BÍO
VALLE DEL MALLECO
NEUQUÉN · RÍO NEGRO
Neuquén

Osorno
Puerto Montt

Chiloé

LA RIOJA
La Rioja
SAN JUAN
San Juan
Mendoza
MENDOZA

ARGENTINA

Santiago del Estero
Córdoba
Santa Fé
Rosario
Paraná

Resistencia
Corrientes

Gran Chaco
Porcomayo

Asunción
Cascavel

VALE DO RIO DO PEIXE
Tangará · Videira
PLANALTO SERRANO
VALE DOS VINHEDOS
Bento Gonçalves
Santa Maria
Garibaldi
SERRA GAÚCHA
Caxias do Sul
Porto Alegre
ARTIGAS
Santana do Livramento
Salto
SERRAS
BAGÉ DO SUDESTE
RIVERA
Candiota
Pinheiro Machado
PAYSANDÚ
Concordia
SORIANO SAN JOSÉ
FLORIDA
Uruguay
Buenos Aires
COLONIA
Las Piedras
CANELONES
MALDONADO
MONTEVIDEO
La Plata
Río de la Plata
Montevideo

LA PAMPA
Bahía Blanca
Mar del Plata

RÍO NEGRO
Viedma

Patagonia
Colorado
Negro
Salado

Pampas

Trelew

Paraná
Uruguay

ATLANTIC OCEAN

N

New Zealand

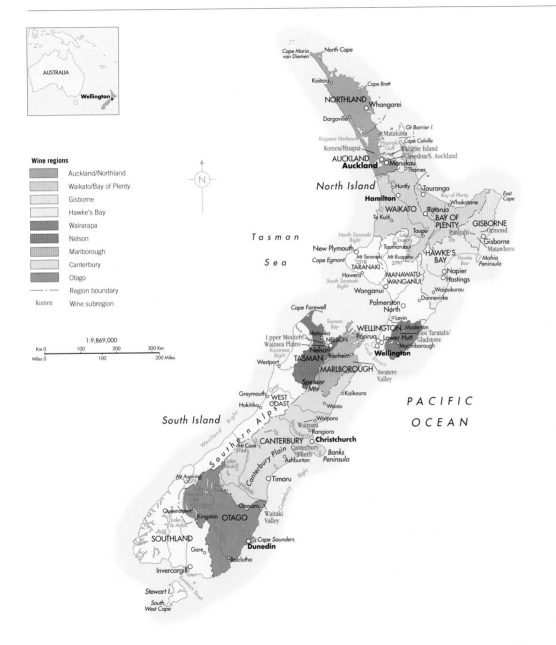

Wine regions

- Auckland/Northland
- Waikato/Bay of Plenty
- Gisborne
- Hawke's Bay
- Wairarapa
- Nelson
- Marlborough
- Canterbury
- Otago
- — · — Region boundary
- Kumeu Wine subregion

1:9,869,000

Km 0   100   200   300 Km
Miles 0   100   200 Miles

AUSTRALIA

Wellington

Cape Maria
van Diemen
North Cape

Kaitaia
Cape Brett

NORTHLAND
Whangarei

Dargaville
Gt Barrier I.

Matakana
Kaipara Harbour   Cape Colville
Hauraki   Waiheke Island
Kumeu/Huapai   Gulf
Clevedon/S. Auckland
AUCKLAND
Auckland   Manukau
Thames

North Island   Huntly   Tauranga
Bay of Plenty   East
Cape
Hamilton   Whakatane
WAIKATO   Rotorua
Te Kuiti   BAY OF   GISBORNE
PLENTY
Taupo   Ormond
North Taranaki   Lake   Patutahi
Bight   Taupo   Gisborne
New Plymouth   Taumarunui   Matawhero
Cape Egmont   Mt Taranaki   Mt Ruapehu   HAWKE'S   Mahia
2518   2797   BAY   Hawke   Peninsula
TARANAKI   Bay
Hawera   Napier
South Taranaki   MANAWATU-   Hastings
Bight   WANGANUI   Waipukurau

Tasman   Wanganui   Dannevirke

Sea   Palmerston
North
Levin

Cape Farewell   WELLINGTON   Masterton
Porirua   East Taratahi/
Tasman   Gladstone
Bay   Upper Moutere   Motueka   Lower Hutt   Martinborough
Waimea Plains   NELSON   **Wellington**
Karamea   Nelson   Blenheim
Bight   TASMAN   Cook Strait
Westport   MARLBOROUGH   Awatere
Valley
Spenser
Mts   Kaikoura

Greymouth   WEST
COAST   Waiau   PACIFIC
Hokitika
Waipara   OCEAN

South Island   Southern Alps   Waipara
Rangiora
Westland Bight   Waimakariri   CANTERBURY   **Christchurch**
Mt Cook   Canterbury   Banks
3764   Plains   Peninsula
Lake   Ashburton
Wanaka   Canterbury
Lake   Plain
Pukaki
Mt Aspiring   Timaru
3077

Queenstown   Oamaru
Kingston   OTAGO   Waitaki
Lake   Valley
Te Anau   Canterbury
SOUTHLAND   Bight
Cape Saunders
Gore   **Dunedin**
Balclutha
Invercargill
Foveaux Strait
Stewart I.
South
West Cape

Western Australia

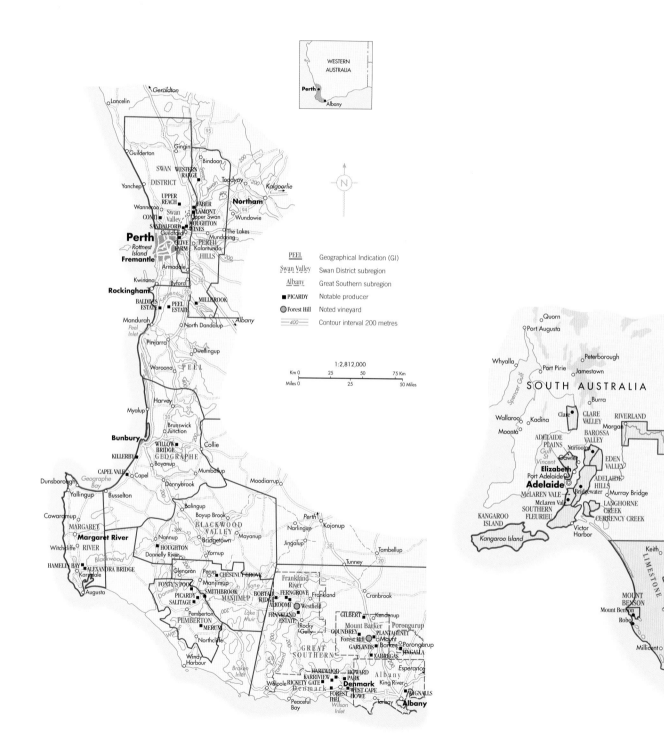

WESTERN
AUSTRALIA

Perth •
      Albany

Geraldton
Lancelin

Guilderton
Gingin
SWAN WESTERN
DISTRICT RANGE   Bindoon
Yanchep   Toodyay   Kalgoorlie
       UPPER   Avon
       REACH FABER   Wundowie
Wanneroo FABER LAMONT **Northam**
CONTI Swan Upper Swan
       Valley HOUGHTON
SANDALFORD VINES
       Guildford
Perth ■ OLIVE PERTH The Lakes
Rottnest FARM HILLS   Mundaring
Island Kalamunda
Fremantle   Armadale

Kwinana   Byford
Rockingham   MILLBROOK
       BALDIVIS PEEL
       ESTATE ESTATE   _Albany_
Mandurah   North Dandalup
Peel
Inlet Pinjarra
       Dwellingup

Waroona   P E E L

Harvey

Myalup
       Brunswick
       Junction
Bunbury
       WILLOW Collie
KILLERBY BRIDGE
       GEOGRAPHE
       Boyanup
CAPEL VALE   Mumballup
Dunsborough Capel
       Geographe
       Bay   Donnybrook   Moodiarrup
Yallingup   Busselton
                     Perth
Cowaramup   Balingup   Narlingup
MARGARET   Boyup Brook   Kojonup
Margaret River BLACKWOOD Mayanup
Witchcliffe **RIVER** Nannup VALLEY Jingalup
       Blackwood Bridgetown
HAMELIN BAY   Yornup   Tunney
ALEXANDRA BRIDGE Glenaran Perup CHESTNUT GROVE
       Karridale   FONTY'S POOL Frankland
       Augusta   Manjimup   River   Cranbrook
       PICARDY SMITHBROOK FERNGROVE Frankland
       SALITAGE MANJIMUP BOBTAIL ALKOOMI Westfield
       Pemberton RIDGE FRANKLAND GILBERT Kendenup
       PEMBERTON MERUM ESTATE   Mount Barker Porongurup
       Northcliffe   Rocky GOUNDREY PLANTAGENET
              Gully   Forest Hill Mount Porongurup
                     GARLANDS Barker JINGALLA
       Windy   GREAT   KABRIGAS
       Harbour   SOUTHERN   Esperance
              HAREWOOD HOWARD Albany
       Walpole KARRIVIEW PARK King River
       RICKETY GATE **Denmark**
              FOREST WEST CAPE
       Peaceful HILL HOWE SWIGNALLS
       Bay   Denmark   **Albany**
              Wilson Torbay
              Inlet

Legend

PEEL   Geographical Indication (GI)
Swan Valley Swan District subregion
Albany   Great Southern subregion
■ PICARDY   Notable producer
◉ Forest Hill Noted vineyard
—400—   Contour interval 200 metres

1:2,812,000

Km 0   25   50   75 Km
Miles 0   25   50 Miles

South Australia

Quorn
Port Augusta
Peterborough
Whyalla Port Pirie Jamestown
S O U T H   A U S T R A L I A
Wallaroo Kadina Burra
Moonta Clare CLARE RIVERLAND
       VALLEY
       BAROSSA
       VALLEY Morgan Ren
ADELAIDE Nuriootpa Berr
PLAINS EDEN
Gulf Cawler VALLEY
St
Vincent **Elizabeth**
       Port Adelaide ADELAIDE
Adelaide HILLS
       Bridgewater
McLAREN VALE Murray Bridge
KANGAROO McLaren Vale LANGHORNE
ISLAND SOUTHERN CREEK
       FLEURIEU CURRENCY CREEK
Kangaroo Island Victor
       Harbor
              Keith
              LIMESTONE
              COAST
MOUNT
BENSON Na
Mount Benson
       Robe
              Penola
       Millicent

South and Southeast Australia

State boundary
● Penola   Notable wine town
HUNTER   Geographical Indication (GI)
Land 500-1000 metres
Land above 1000 metres

1:6,625,000

Km 0   50   100   150 Km
Miles 0   50   100 Miles

N

QUEENSLAND

SOUTH BURNETT
Murgon
Chinchilla
Nanango
Gympie
Cooroy
Caloundra
Dalby
Warwick
Toowoomba
◎ **Brisbane**
Ipswich
Murwillumbah
GRANITE BELT
Stanthorpe
Casino
Lismore
Tenterfield
Ballina
Inverell
Glen Innes
Grafton
Bingara
New England Range
Coffs Harbour
Armidale
Macleay
Gunnedah
Kempsey
Tamworth
Port Macquarie
Coonabarabran
HASTINGS RIVER
Liverpool Range
Taree
Dubbo
Macquarie
Denman
Muswellbrook
Mudgee
Gulgong
HUNTER
Wellington
MUDGEE
Hunter
Pokolbin
Maitland
Rylstone
Cessnock
Newcastle
Condobolin
ORANGE
Turon
Parkes
Orange
Forbes
Bathurst
RANGE
Lake Cargelligo
Hillston
COWRA
Lithgow
Katoomba
Penrith
Blayney
Cowra
Liverpool
Parramatta
NEW   SOUTH   WALES
Lachlan
Booligal
West Wyalong
RIVERINA
HILLTOPS
Camden
◎ **Sydney**
Wentworth
Mildura
Hay
Murrumbidgee
Griffith
Temora
Young
SOUTHERN HIGHLANDS
Port Kembla
Wollongong
Karadoc
Leeton
Cootamundra
Shellharbour
MURRAY DARLING
Balranald
Narrandera
Junee
CANBERRA DISTRICT
Yass
Goulburn
SHOALHAVEN COAST
Robinvale
Murrumbateman
Nowra
Ouyen
Nyah
Moulamein
Wagga Wagga
RANGE
Braidwood
SWAN HILL
Swan Hill
Deniliquin
AUSTRALIAN CAPITAL TERRITORY
◎ **Canberra**
Murray
PERICOOTA
RUTHERGLEN
Tumbarumba
Strathmerton
Corowa
Albury
TUMBARUMBA
Cooma
VICTORIA
NAGAMBIE LAKES
Echuca
GLEN ROWAN
Wangaratta
BEECHWORTH
Australian Alps
PYRENEES
Bridgewater
GOULBURN VALLEY
Shepparton
Glenrowan
Myrtleford
DIVIDING
Bendigo
Benalla
KING VALLEY
ALPINE VALLEYS
Horsham
Nagambie
STRATHBOGIE RANGES
Whitfield
Omeo
ULLY
Moonambel
Maryborough
HEATHCOTE
Heathcote
Seymour
UPPER GOULBURN
Snowy
Stawell
Avoca
Castlemaine
Kyneton
MACEDON RANGES
Alexandra
Tambo
Orbost
Ararat
GRAMPIANS
Woodend
Hanbury
GREAT
Cape Howe
milton
Ballarat
Sunbury
Yarra Glen
Healesville
GIPPSLAND
HENTY
SUNBURY
YARRA VALLEY
Heywood
Bannockburn
Bairnsdale
Lakes Entrance
Portland
GEELONG
Geelong
Port Phillip Bay
◎ **Melbourne** ⊙
Sale
Yallourn
Warrnambool
Colac
Hastings
Traralgon
Leongatha
Cape Otway
MORNINGTON PENINSULA
Wonthaggi
Foster
Wilsons Promontory

South Africa

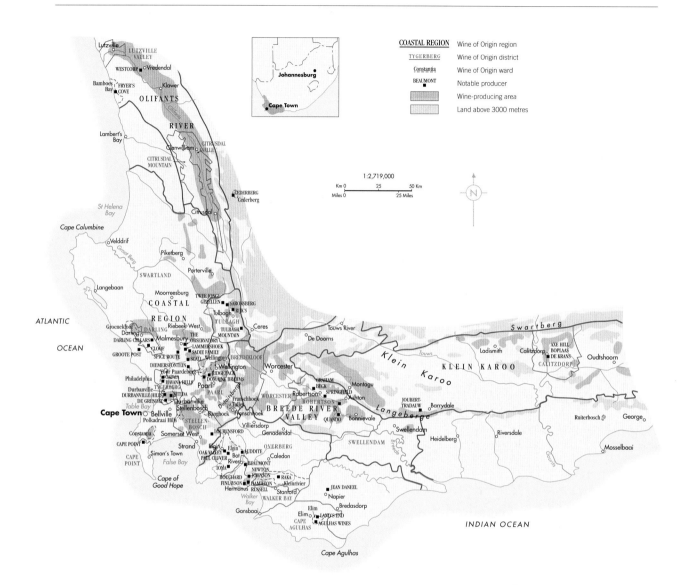

COASTAL REGION — Wine of Origin region
TYGERBERG — Wine of Origin district
Constantia — Wine of Origin ward
BEAUMONT ■ — Notable producer
— Wine-producing area
— Land above 3000 metres

1:2,719,000

Km 0   25   50 Km
Miles 0   25 Miles

Johannesburg

Cape Town

Lutzville
LUTZVILLE VALLEY
WESTCORP ■ Vredendal
Bamboes Bay ■ FRYER'S COVE
OLIFANTS Klawer
RIVER
Lambert's Bay
CITRUSDAL VALLEY
Clanwilliam
CITRUSDAL MOUNTAIN
St Helena Bay
Cape Columbine
CEDERBERG ■ Cederberg
Citrusdal
Velddrif
Piketberg
SWARTLAND
Langebaan
Moorreesburg
COASTAL
REGION
TWEE JONGE GEZELLEN ■ SAROSNBERG ■
RIJK'S ■
Tulbagh
TULBAGH
TULBAGH MOUNTAIN
Ceres
Touws River
De Doorns
Swartberg
ATLANTIC
OCEAN
Groenekloof
Darling
DARLING
DARLING CELLARS ■
GROOTE POST ■
Malmesbury
Riebeek-West
THE OBSERVATORY ■
LAMMERSHOEK ■
SADIE FAMILY ■
SCALI ■
SPICE ROUTE ■
Wellington
BREEDEKLOOF
Worcester
Klein Karoo
KLEIN KAROO
Ladismith
Calitzdorp
AXE HILL
BOPLAAS ■
DE KRANS ■
CALITZDORP
Oudtshoorn
DIEMERSFONTEIN ■
Voor Paardeberg
CAPA ■
HAVANA HILLS ■
NITIDA ■
TYGERBERG
GRAHAM ■
BECK ■
SPRINGFIELD ■
Montagu
Philadelphia
Durbanville
DURBANVILLE HILLS ■
DE GRENDEL ■
Durbanville
RIDGEBACK ■
DOMAINE BRAHMS ■
Paarl
Ashton
Robertson
ROBERTSON
Barrydale
JOUBERT-TRADAUW ■
Ruiterbosch
George
Table Bay
Cape Town
Bellville
Polkadraai Hills
STELLENBOSCH
Stellenbosch
Banghoek
Franschhoek
Franschhoek
Worcester
BREEDE RIVER VALLEY
QUANDO ■
Bonnievale
Langeberge
Swellendam
Mosselbaai
Riversdale
Constantia
Somerset West
LOURENSFORD ■
Villiersdorp
Genadendal
SWELLENDAM
CAPE POINT ■
Strand
Elgin
OAK VALLEY ■
ELGIN
Elgin
OVERBERG
Heidelberg
Simon's Town
False Bay
IONA ■
PAUL CLUVER ■
Bot River
LUDDITE ■
BEAUMONT ■
Caledon
CAPE POINT
Cape of Good Hope
HOUGHARD ■
FINLAYSON ■
NEWTON ■
JOHNSON ■
HAMILTON ■
RUSSELL ■
RAKA ■
Kleinrivier
Hermanus
Stanford
JEAN DANEEL ■
Napier
Bredasdorp
Walker Bay
WALKER BAY
Gansbaai
Elim
Elim ■
LAND'S END ■
AGULHAS WINES ■
CAPE AGULHAS
INDIAN OCEAN
Cape Agulhas

Enjoying Wine

It is the inquisitive who enjoy wine most. The essence of the game is variety; you could taste a different wine every day of your life and yet not learn it all. Each wine evolves with time. There will always be new wines to taste, and new combinations of wine with food to try. There will also always be more to learn about yourself, your palate, and its reactions.

No single attitude or set of rules can apply to a commodity that can be either a simple foodstuff as basic as bread and cheese, or one of the most *recherché* of luxuries, or anywhere in between. There are enamel-mug wines and Baccarat-crystal wines, and there is no point in pretending that one is the other.

This chapter is concerned with choosing, buying, storing, serving, and appreciating wine that is above the *ordinaire* or jug level. Once a wine has a named origin (as opposed to being an anonymous blend) it reflects a particular soil, climate, culture, and tradition. For better or worse, the wine then has some character. The mastery of wine consists in recognizing, bringing out, and making the most of that character. I cannot improve on the late André Simon's definition of a connoisseur: "One who knows good wine from bad, and appreciates the distinctive merits of different wines." Thank heaven all white wines are not Sauvignon Blancs, however fresh, flowery, and fragrant, or all reds great thumping Cabernets. It is a crucial (but also a common) misunderstanding of the nature and variety of wine to say that a Barolo, for example, is better than a Rioja, or a Pauillac than a Napa Cabernet. The secret is to learn to understand and enjoy each of them for what they are.

There is only one essential I would press on you, if you are going to spend more than a bare minimum and buy wines above the jug level: and that is to make a conscious act of tasting. Become aware of the messages your nose and mouth are sending you – not just about wine, but about all food and drink. Seek out new tastes and think about them.

By far the greater part of all fine wine, and even – perhaps especially – of the best, is thrown away by being used as a mere drink. A great bottle of wine is certainly wasted if nobody talks about it, or at least tries to pinpoint in his or her own consciousness the wonderful will-o'-the-wisp of fragrance and flavour.

Buying Wine

To buy wine and get exactly what you expect is the exception rather than the rule. Wine is a moving target: a kaleidoscope of growers and vintages that never stands still. If this bothers you, there is a solution – stick to a brand, since the whole point of a brand is to deliver unvarying flavour and style. But you will be sacrificing the great fascination of wine, its infinite variety, not to mention the fun of the chase: the satisfaction of finding a winner (and the chagrin of backing a dud).

There are few cardinal rules in such an open field, where one day you may be buying from the corner store, the next by mail order, and the third direct from the producer. But it is certainly better to think carefully about what you want to buy before you buy it. Sometimes, of course, you will just want a decent bottle to accompany a dish you are preparing for guests that very day, but whenever possible, buy ahead of your needs.

Nobody can take in all the offerings of a well-stocked store at a glance. Do your wine buying when you are in the mood and have time to browse, to compare prices, to make calculations, to use reference books. By far the best place to do this is at home, by comparing the price lists of alternative suppliers. Given time you can make an order that qualifies for a discount. Buying by the case, even the mixed case, is invariably cheaper than buying by the bottle. Keep an eye out for "bin-end sales", usually held in January, when all the top merchants send out lists of discounted wines, either because they are overstocked or because they are moving on to a new vintage. Although you should take care not to buy a tired wine that's in decline, such lists often contain wonderful mature German wines or vintage ports from lesser known shippers, and many other bargains.

A fine wine needs time to rest. Although many modern white and light red wines are so stable that you could play skittles with them and do them no harm, all mature red wines need a settling period of at least several days after being moved. Your chances of serving a wine at its best are far greater if you can prepare it calmly at home.

In the past, wine-buyers had to rely on either their own knowledge and experience or those of their wine merchant. Today there are many more ways to acquire information. This edition of the *Wine Companion* includes the website addresses of all producers who have them. These sites vary in quality, but most give detailed information about the range and styles of wines produced, and provide email addresses so that, should you wish, you can obtain further information from that producer. Moreover, there are many websites and blogs that specialize in providing information to consumers in the form of tasting notes, vintage notes, news about changes in the industry, and so forth. These sites may or may not be linked to sites selling wine. Some of the more rarefied and detailed wine websites are pay sites; many others are free.

An Investment in Pleasure

An investment in future pleasure is often one of the most profitable of all. Inflation aside, when you come to drink the wine, now better than when you bought it, the expenditure will be a thing of the past; the pleasure will seem a gift from the gods. In fact, very little money is needed to convert you from a bottle-by-bottle buyer to the proud possessor of a "cellar". Calculate what you spend on wine in three months, or two months, or at a pinch only one month – and spend it all at once in a planned spree. Put the wine away. Then continue to buy the same quantity as before but use it to replenish your stock, instead of for instant drinking. All you have done is to borrow

three, two, or one month's wine money and the interest on that is your only extra expenditure. Your reward is wine you have chosen carefully and kept well, ready when you want it, not when you can get to the shops.

Make an effort to be clear-headed about what you really need. Do not spend more than you can comfortably afford. Think twice before buying unknown wines as part of a package. Do not buy a quantity of wine you have never tasted and might not like. Consider whether home delivery is really practicable: will there be someone at home to answer the door? Can you easily lift a full case of wine, especially one that comes in a wooden box?

One of the wiliest ways of broadening your buying scope is to join with a small group of like-minded people to form a syndicate. A syndicate can save money by buying bigger lots of wine, thus bringing within reach extraordinary bottles at prices that would make you, on your own, feel guilty for months. Three or four friends who have never tasted Château Latour or Romanée-Conti will enjoy them more if they buy and open them together, sharing their opinions (and their guilt). While there may be laws that prevent an unlicensed citizen from selling wine, even to a friend, there is nothing to stop them sharing its cost.

The Wine Trade

The structure of the wine trade has changed radically in recent years from a fairly rigid pattern of brokers, shippers, agents, wholesalers, and retailers to an intricate but fluid mixture of ingredients, some old and some new. It is not surprising that such a pleasant vocation has more volunteers than the army. The great growth areas have been in "experts", writers and consultants, and in ingenious methods of selling with or without a shop.

In America the period has seen wine change from being a minority – even a faintly suspect minority – interest to a national pastime. The wine trade has recruited regiments of specialists at every level. Locally, the retailers are the most prominent, nationally, the marketing men. But what remains sovereign (and to the foreigner most bizarre) is the changing legislation from state to state. Scarcely two are alike. New York, California, Texas, Florida, and a few more states are relatively free to benefit from all the rich possibilities; the remainder are more or less inhibited by local legislation, especially laws that prohibit the dispatching of wine across certain state lines. This denies consumers the freedom to buy and ship wine directly while protecting the interests of local retailers. Even individual counties can stick their oar in and say what you may and may not drink. However, in recent years, the grip exercised by local retailers on interstate shipments has relaxed slightly, or been prised open by determined legislators, and unless neo-Prohibition rears its ugly head, it should, in the future, be easier rather than more difficult for wine-lovers to buy the bottles they want from the source of their choice.

In Britain, the wine-drinking consumer is relatively fortunate. Changes started in the 1960s with the ponderous tread of the brewers, fearful that a growing taste for wine would erode their sales of beer, buying scores of traditional local wine shops and replacing them with chains tied to national brand-marketing

ideas. Unfortunately, many of these new shops were dismal, and the rising generation of vocational wine merchants – as opposed to accountants – wanted nothing to do with them. They found it easy to reinvent the old individualistic wine trade for the new generation of better-travelled and more knowledgeable (if less wealthy) wine lovers. Today there is a specialist for almost every area of the wine-growing world, as well as well-stocked independent merchants in city and countryside alike.

Traditional wine merchants offer the old virtues of personal service, storage or delivery to your door, and credit (at a price). Personal service consists largely of word-of-mouth recommendations based on a regular customer's known tastes and resources. Some firms offer cellar plans, recommending wines for laying down, storing them, and advising when they are becoming ready to drink. There are some specialist companies that will store your wine for you in secure conditions and then, should you wish, sell part of your stock should its value increase to an irresistible level.

Many merchants offer wines *en primeur* (or, as Americans know it, as "futures"), that is, many months in advance of bottling and shipping. The supposed advantage is a more favourable price and the opportunity to secure wines from the most sought-after properties. For the purchaser, the disadvantage is having to part with your cash well in advance of delivery for a wine you yourself have had no opportunity to taste and assess. Such firms are skilful at offering the best wines of a new vintage early, while they are still in their makers' cellars and long before they are even bottled, at "opening" prices that usually rise once the wines come on the general market. Buying futures should be avoided in times of economic uncertainty. Should the merchant from whom you have ordered the wine go out of business, you may well find you have no title to the wine you bought, which may still be resting in its barrels in Bordeaux or Napa. You will have bought your "cases" of wine many months before the wine is bottled and stacked in real cases.

At the opposite extreme, making wine available and tempting to every shopper, are the supermarkets. Most of them, and the high-street retailers and chains that are their rivals, offer a rather simple and limited range, sometimes under their own brand names. Others, such as the best French supermarkets and British chains, such as Majestic, will have a fine-wine section that can match many a quality-conscious independent merchant's list. For European wine-drinkers, the supermarkets and national chains are now the primary source for their purchases. Some supermarkets and chains select with care to build a constantly evolving range of interest and value; the majority buy primarily on price, and quality can be dismal.

A further source of wine is the wine club, often linked to national newspapers or periodicals; some of them, such as The Wine Society in Britain, offer a more extensive range of services, including storage.

In wine-producing regions it is common to buy direct from the producer. Just about every wine-drinking household in Tours or Stuttgart or Vienna will have its favourite producers, visited on a regular basis for a congenial hour in the cellars while the latest vintage is loaded into the car. In regions where the vine struggles to grow, or is not even planted, it is more practical to buy from merchants or via the internet.

A display of modern Italian wines. Bottles to be kept for longer than ten weeks should be stored in a cool, quiet place (see page 647).

Buying wine over the ether is practical and easy. Often the range of wines on offer is good and varied, and special offers and discounts are constantly being dangled before the consumer and can be good value. The drawbacks are those common to most forms of e-commerce: credit card security (or lack thereof) and a lack of recourse when something goes wrong. Should a delivery arrive very late, or should the wines delivered not correspond to what you ordered, or should some of the bottles be smashed, you might well be able to obtain refunds or other redress, but the process can be laborious. On the other hand, many buyers, especially in remote areas far from a good wine merchant, find the advantages far outweigh the drawbacks.

The Marketing Man Cometh

Remember that, for many large wine companies, wine is not the supreme drink but a mere product. Produced in enormous volumes, it needs to be marketed and sold as aggressively as possible. Supermarkets and national retailers usually lack qualified staff, and recommendations take the form of cards quoting favourable reviews from wine writers – which may or may not be reliable indications of quality and value.

Many wines are discounted or offered as part of special promotions; nothing wrong with that, except that such offers form part of a trade war between the largest companies, battling each other for shelf space. Few consumers are aware that wines given window space or other prominent display are there because their producers have paid lavishly for the privilege. The assumption that such favoured treatment is a reflection of the wine buyer's personal enthusiasm is entirely wrong.

Packaging is an essential part of the armoury of marketing. Stylish labelling is always welcome, but is hardly the most important component of a bottle of wine. Be on your guard whenever you see "original" bottles, such as those coated with a simulacrum of dust, or those with laddish labels along the lines of "Sad Old Git" or "Miserable Bastard". With so much energy going into subsidiary matters such as packaging, the wine inside the bottle is unlikely to be memorable.

Learn While You Drink

Mention has already been made of websites as good sources of information, as indeed is the welcome proliferation of books on every conceivable subject and wine region. There are other, more personal ways of expanding one's knowledge and purchasing skills. Wine clubs and some leading merchants often offer a great deal of information about the wines they sell, and some of them organize periodic tastings, which feed the urge to learn while you drink. Such tastings are often tutored by the best experts in the field, who will give participants the opportunity to question and talk to notable authorities on wine. Some merchants, individual wine experts, and auction houses, such as Christie's, offer wine education courses that are often run by genuine experts in the field.

Many wine fairs are restricted to wine professionals. Some others, however, are specifically designed to appeal to the general public. They are often organized either by major retailers or by wine magazines. For a modest fee, they can give you access to an enormous number of fine wines which are usually poured by those who either make the wine or own the property, again giving those present the opportunity to quiz the experts directly. Such consumer wine fairs are increasingly common and popular events on both sides of the Atlantic. These events are often linked to "winemaker dinners" or masterclasses, at which some of the most prestigious figures in the wine world pour and discuss their wines. These can be expensive, but often give you a rare opportunity to taste rare older vintages in the company of the producer.

If the one-day wine fair merely whets the appetite, then you might consider a wine tour. These have become popular in England, and can be an extremely effective way to learn about wine. They tend to be package tours for small groups, led by experts in the region being visited. It is as close as the enthusiastic amateur will get to the life of the professional: walking the vineyards, tasting from the barrel in the cellar, questioning the winemakers, and, twice a day, enjoying Rabelaisian meals with excellent wines.

Wine Auctions

In the past 20 years or so, auctions have come to epitomize both the scholarship and the showmanship of wine. At first, it was Michael Broadbent at Christie's; then a succession of auctioneers at Sotheby's and elsewhere, became wine's ringmasters and at the same time the repositories of esoteric vinous knowledge. Auctions are now regularly used in the USA, Germany, South Africa, and many countries besides Britain to sell and publicize at the same time. But the London auction houses have another role: simply to turn over private cellars, surplus stocks, and awkward small amounts of wine that complicate a wine merchant's life. There is a steady flow of mature wine, young wine, and sometimes good but unfashionable wine at absurdly low prices. Anyone can buy, but the bargains are often in lots larger than an individual may want. It is common practice to form syndicates to buy and divide such lots.

But bear in mind that much wine is consigned to auction for a good reason: a restaurant or private collector may be offloading stock surplus to requirements. On the other hand, a collector may also have found the wine disappointing and decided to get rid of it. Beware especially of the 11-bottle case, often a sure sign that bottle number 12 has already been drunk – without pleasure. There is always an element of risk in buying wine at auction (the wine may be splendid, but it may also have been stored in abysmal conditions), but they can provide you with genuine bargains. Before bidding it is crucial to become familiar with current prices for top growths; tables are often found in leading wine magazines. Read the terms and conditions: the hammer price may be considerably augmented by additional costs such as taxes and the "premium" – the latter being nothing other than a private tax imposed by the auction house.

Speculating in Blue Chips

The auction houses established a flourishing market in old wines. In their wake, a new class of, so to speak, second-hand wine merchants or brokers has sprung up, led by Farr Vintners in London. Their business can be compared with antiquarian booksellers: finding rare wines on behalf of collectors – for collectors there certainly are today, as there never were in the spacious days when a gentleman filled his cellars with First Growth claret as a matter of course.

Those who buy such blue-chip wines in quantity these days are more likely to be engaged in the less gentlemanly game of speculation. Wine is a commodity susceptible to buying cheap and selling dear – but happily, with no certainty of success.

The more expensive the wine, the greater the chance of its appreciation. But other factors come into it, too: the vintage and its reputation (which will shift, not always predictably, as time goes on); the general financial climate; the popularity of the château or grower in question; perhaps most of all the proven ability of the wine to age.

It is the classed growths of Bordeaux and vintage port that are known or presumed to have the longest potential life span – therefore the biggest spread of opportunity for reselling at a profit. Modern burgundies and German wines, even Champagne, are considered relatively poor risks, with or without justification. The only exceptions would be the most prestigious of all Burgundies, those from the Domaine de la Romanée-Conti or growers such as the late Henri Jayer. The very best Italian, Australian, and Californian wines, and such rarities as Tokaji Eszencia, also have a certain following.

Who Do You Believe?

In the past, most wine writers were historians, connoisseurs, or dilettantes. Today there is a new breed: the wine critic, whose primary role is to assess individual wines for the benefit of the consumer. Robert Parker was the first to introduce the now widely adopted system of marking wines on a 100-point scale. There are obvious flaws to such a system, the principal one being that it gives the impression that a tasting note is a definitive assessment rather than a snapshot taken of a living product in a constant state of evolution and transformation. Such a system affects certainty where there can be no such thing.

Yet there can be no doubt that many, perhaps most, wine-drinkers find such scoring systems positive and useful, assisting them in their choices. Scores are usually accompanied by some kind of commentary on the flavour or style of the wine in question, which may be more useful than the score itself. Most wine-drinkers lack the opportunities to taste dozens, even hundreds, of wines each week, and are grateful to the tasting professionals who are willing to submit to the endurance test.

Scores are only as reliable as the critic making the score. If you find your own judgment concurring with one critic more than another – or with one newspaper columnist more than another – then you have grounds for trusting his or her judgment. The wine score may be a blunt and flawed instrument, but it serves a useful purpose. Just don't expect infallibility.

Choosing Wine

Buying a bottle of wine is as easy, or as complicated, as one chooses to make it. Most of the time one's choice, whether in a shop, a restaurant, or one's own cellar, has already been edited down and the only decisions to be made are whether one feels more like Chinon or Conchagua, South African Sauvignon or Austrian Grüner Veltliner. It's a question of mood, weather, occasion: one makes the decision instinctively.

If one happens to be visiting a wine-producing country, then one will probably want a local wine: perhaps something one knows, perhaps something one has never heard of. If the latter one will probably ask advice, and hope one's advisor shares one's tastes: the wine world today is divided between those who favour blockbuster wines and those who prefer elegance and balance. One of the skills we all develop is that of deciphering tasting notes on wine lists: we look for clues as to which camp a wine falls into. "Massive" is a giveaway; "sweet fruit" more subtle; "delicate" or "linear" green lights, if you fall into the elegance camp.

In a restaurant, or indeed if you're buying to drink with dinner at home, your choice of food comes into play. This is where the complications really begin, if you let them. But choosing wine to go with food is in reality no more complicated than choosing vegetables to go with meat or fish: the factors that make you decide whether to have broccoli with garlic or green peas with mint are flavour, texture, weight, and seasonality. Wine is not very different. In the end there is only one reason for selecting a particular wine: because you like it. There is no more sense in buying a wine that somebody else admires but you don't than there is in buying a picture or a chair for that reason. Wine is about enjoyment: it's not an exam.

Matching Wine To Food

Because most of us, most of the time, base our drinking decisions on what we are planning to eat, that's the angle we should look at first. Our starting point, most days, is what is in the fridge, or what is on the menu. And then the old rules come into play, do they not? Red wine with red meat, white wine with white meat or fish. Well, they do and they don't. The traditional rules evolved in the days of simpler, more predictable food, when roast beef came with Yorkshire pudding, chicken was roast or fried, and fish was in a cream sauce, or grilled and served with lemon juice.

Yes, that's an oversimplification of what our grandparents and great-grandparents ate, but their range of flavours and ingredients was certainly less than ours. For us, chicken might mean Thai, or Szechuan, or Indian; a recipe for lamb might come straight from Morocco or Spain; we might feast on tapas or sushi. Applying those rules of what to drink with what might make you beware of Barossa Shiraz with raw fish, and to that extent they're worth remembering; but after that it's your palate you should listen to, not your grandmother.

But it's not just food that has changed; wine has changed just as much. The tannins that made big reds suitable only for hunks of meat have been tamed: they are now often so silky that they can be trusted to behave themselves with vegetable dishes, or Indian food, or Korean. Fruit flavours are much more to the fore than they were 25 years ago; whites are more aromatic. Alcohol levels are in general higher than they were even ten years ago, and acidity is often lower than it was in the past. Wines can, in addition, be drunk younger than used to be the case. Ageing a wine in bottle is much more likely now to be a matter of choice than necessity.

So how should we apply these different circumstances? Simply by thinking of wine as another ingredient in the whole. If you're serving lamb, a delicately flavoured meat, how are you cooking it? With haricot beans and pesto? With roasted vegetables? With pommes dauphinoise? With garlic and rosemary? With black olives? With cumin and mint? Or with lemon juice, in the Greek fashion? All will flatter the lamb, and all will flatter wine, but instinctively we think of a bigger, richer red with pommes dauphinoise, or with haricot beans. Why? Because those starchy textures coat the mouth. They demand more tannin, more acidity.

Black olives are good at dealing with young, tannic reds; roasted vegetables like tomatoes and aubergines suit rich, solid, slightly sweetish reds. Cumin and mint might suggest earthy flavours; garlic and rosemary will go with pretty much anything. The Greek habit of putting lemon juice on meat requires wine with more acidity. (Matching acidity with acidity is a key rule.) So one might put a fairly hefty Portugese with the haricot beans; perhaps a Zinfandel with the roasted vegetables; an Australian Cabernet with the pommes dauphinoise; a classic red Bordeaux with the garlic and rosemary; a northern Rhône with the black olives; a Spanish Garnacha with the cumin and mint; a Chianti or a Greek red with the lemon juice.

These are not instructions, just ideas. You can use ingredients to bridge the gap between the food of your choice and the wine you want to drink: Dover sole will go with light red if you serve it with roasted root vegetables (though beware of tannin with fish: they clash), with rich white (perhaps mature white burgundy) if you put it with a creamy sauce, and with crisp Chablis if you grill it and squeeze lemon juice over it. The first option feels wintry and comforting; the second formal and traditional, the third light and summery. It's about mood and occasion, and the wine is simply part of the whole dish.

The points to bear in mind are weight, texture, and flavour. If you want to serve a powerful, weighty red with a light dish, add some substantial, strongly flavoured, mouth-coating accompaniments. Conversely, sharply acidic ingredients – tomatoes, lemons, perhaps preserved lemons in a tagine, with lots of fresh herbs – can help make a bridge between a substantial dish and a white wine, albeit a weighty white.

White wine is extremely versatile with modern food. The sort of complicated dishes that some chefs delight in, with otherwise unrelated ingredients brought together in unexpected ways, are often easier to match with white than with red. The protein aspect of the dish may play only a secondary part to these other flavours, and mature vintage Champagne, for example, can adapt with ease to Thai or Indian flavours as well as anything loosely described as fusion. Alsace is a good bet with Indian food, and Sauvignon Blanc with Thai – it matches well

with the lemon grass and lime leaves. Riesling can handle spices, especially ginger – but a big, dry, weighty Grosses Gewächs Riesling from the Pfalz will go with wild boar or venison as well, providing that something fruity and sweet – redcurrant jelly, cranberry sauce – is added to make the bridge.

Which brings us to the question of texture. This might sound like a refinement too far, but any cook instinctively thinks of texture when putting a meal together. In Chinese food texture is as important as flavour; and so it should be when matching food with wine. The silky, slippery textures of Chinese food require silkiness, even unctuousness, in wine: fine, mature red Bordeaux can work if the spices are used with a light hand; Pinot Noir likewise, which at its best has that same silkiness. But think too of sweet wines: the unctuousness of Sauternes or Tokaji can be perfect with Szechuan food, where the sweetness of the wine meets the heat of the chilli at a point of harmony. (Chilli needs something to temper it before it can go with wine. Sweetness in the wine is the easiest weapon, but the unctuousness of dessert wines is a problem with Indian dishes. A slightly sweetish rosé can be a good solution here, or an unoaked Chilean Merlot.)

Likewise, at a truffle dinner in Provence good local reds proved a good match because their silky tannins sat well with the rich textures – the egg-based sauces, the cream, the softness of slow-cooked meat – that were the vehicles for the truffles. You wouldn't normally think of putting Provençal reds with truffles, but similar textures enabled the two to meet. It's texture that enables modern reds to go with many more foods that were the case in the past. Uruguayan Tannat, light, blackberryish and silky, might have been just as successful; so might unoaked Argentine Malbec.

Bubbles are texture, too. I've mentioned the joys of mature Champagne with all sorts of unexpectedly spicy dishes: it's the bubbles that lighten the match. In the same way Asti or Moscato Spumante will enliven Christmas pudding where Sauternes would be wearying, even though the sweetness levels of both would appear to make Sauternes appropriate. Mature Champagne will go with meringue, which one certainly wouldn't expect; with the light texture of hot, fresh foie gras, too, it is the only choice, even though Sauternes or the equivalent is a must with the more solid cold version. It is simply a matter of texture.

Sweetness in wine is useful when matching with food. Some foods demand a touch of sweetness: scallops, sweetbreads, crab, pâté, for example. The traditional matches – Mosel Riesling, or *demi-sec* Vouvray, or perhaps a light Alsace – are still unrivalled here. But the roundness of mature dry white can work just as well: a Chablis with some bottle age, for instance. But putting sweet wines with desserts is not as easy as at looks: many desserts are simply too sweet. Fruit-based ones are best, if you want a harmonious match: a fruit tart, perhaps, or wild strawberries (oddly enough, these are excellent with red Bordeaux – it's a classic Bordelais combination). Citrus fruit can be difficult with dessert wines: an intense, pungent tarte au citron is usually too sweet and too acidic for even the sweetest and most acidic sweet wine, though you could try it with a five- or six-puttonyos Tokaji, which can have the punchiness to cope. Chocolate, if it's sufficiently dark and bitter, can work with red Bordeaux, though not a very tannic one; with a light, sweet chocolate mousse you might be better off with Asti.

The one food that people tend to think of as being utterly wine-friendly is often the most difficult to match with wine. Most cheese is not very nice with red, though try telling that to people who have been brought up on the idea that red wine is what you drink with cheese. White is generally much, much nicer. The exceptions are hard cheeses like mature cheddar, which do go with reds; but soft cheeses and blue cheeses don't. Stilton and port go together because of the sweetness of the port, not its redness; and in that other classic combination, Rocquefort and Sauternes, it's partly the sweetness and intensity of the wine and partly its lusciousness, its rich mouthfeel, that bring the two together.

Modern wines do, however, bring their own problems with them. Overextraction and overoaking are the dangers: wines that are unnecessarily solid and chewy are not food friendly. So-called "icon" wines can be far more difficult to match with food than their lighter, cheaper siblings; more difficult to drink on their own, too. So what are they for, one might ask? Well, usually they're for showing-off. And show-off wines are as tedious at the table as show-off food, or show-off people.

Before you choose a wine, decide whether it is going to spend even a moment in the limelight – and who, beside yourself, will be drinking it. Test yourself with your reaction to the reported behaviour of Voltaire, who habitually gave his guests Beaujolais while he drank the finest burgundies himself. Whether you give priority to the food or the wine is the next question. Ideally they should share the stage as harmonious equals – no more rivals than a hero and heroine. But having talked about food as a starting point, what do you do when the wine is the starting point?

Wine Divided Into Ten Basic Styles

I have risked a rather arbitrary division of the infinite variety of wine into ten categories, and associated each category with a selection of dishes, as a guide to where to start to look, whether your starting point is the wine or the food. No such generalization can be defended in every particular case, but it is true to say that certain criteria of flavour, age, and quality can be applied across the board. Some wines could appear equally in two different categories, but for the sake of clarity I have put them firmly where, in my judgement, they most often belong.

Unoaked dry white wines of neutral, simply "winey" flavour. These wines are better with simple food, especially with strong-flavoured or highly seasoned dishes, eg. *hors d'oeuvres* (*antipasti*), aïoli or fish stew, mussels, herrings and mackerel (which need a rather acid wine to cut their oil), salads, red mullet, grilled sardines, terrines, and sausages. All should be served very well chilled (about 8°C/46°F).

Examples are: simple Bordeaux Blanc, Gaillac, Muscadet, Swiss whites, such as Fendant; most standard Italian whites (including Soave, Verdicchio, Orvieto Secco, Frascati, Gavi, Pinot Bianco, and Pinot Grigio); most unoaked Spanish and Portuguese whites; simple Austrian Grüner Veltliner, many Greek whites.

Light, fresh, grapey white wine with fruity and sometimes flowery aromas. The very aromatic, German-style grapes are nearly always in this or the sweet white wine category. All these wines make excellent apéritifs or refreshing between-meal or evening drinks, most of all in summer. Those with relatively high acidity are also good with many first courses, but are dominated by seriously savoury dishes and lack the substance to be satisfying throughout a meal. Suitable dishes to accompany them include: poached trout, crab salad, cold chicken. They need slightly less chilling than the previous category.

Wines include: German Qualitätswein, most Kabinetts and some traditionally fruity Spätlesen; light French Sauvignons from Bordeaux, Bergerac, and Touraine; Savoie whites (Crépy, Apremont); Portuguese Vinho Verde and Spanish Albariño; certain California and most South African Chenin Blancs; simple Australian Rieslings; some New Zealand Sauvignons and English Müller-Thurgaus and Seyval Blancs; Viognier, Petit or Gros Manseng from southwest France, Italian Arneis, light, dry Muscats from anywhere; Argentine Torrontés.

White wines with body and character, aromatic from certain grapes or with the bouquet of maturity. Fine French dry whites all come into this category. High flavour often makes them taste rich even when fully dry. Without food, these wines can be too assertive; they are best matched with a savoury dish that is also rich in flavour and pale in colour, eg. oysters, clams, lobsters and prawns, smoked fish, frogs' legs, snails, onion or leek tart, ballotines, prosciutto, salmon, turbot, and other rich fish in butter, hollandaise or other rich sauces, scallops, poultry, sweetbreads, hard Swiss cheeses. Wines should only be lightly chilled (10°–13°C/50°–55°F).

Examples are: all good mature Chardonnays (eg. white burgundies after two or more years depending on their quality); their equivalents from California and Australia; Alsace Riesling, Gewurztraminer, and Pinot Gris; Sancerre, Pouilly Fumé, and Savennières from the Loire; fine white Graves; mature white Rhône wines (eg. Hermitage Blanc) and young Condrieu; top Italian whites (the best examples of Frascati, Soave Classico, Verdicchio, Cortese di Gavi, Pomino, or Chardonnay); best-quality mature Rioja, Rueda, and Penedès whites from Spain; Manzanilla sherry or fino; Hungarian Szürkebarát (Pinot Gris) or Furmint; Austrian Rotgipfler and top Grüner Veltliner or Riesling; Ruländer (Pinot Gris) from Baden; Grosses Gewächs Riesling from the Pfalz or Rheingau, Silvaner from Württemberg, Assyrtiko from Santorini, top New Zealand Sauvignons, Australian Semillons and dry Clare and Eden Rieslings with three or four years in bottle.

Many popular branded whites also come into this category, if one ignores the requirement of character: these wines tend to have plenty of flavour, some of which may be derived from oak, or oak chips, and they might have some residual sugar.

Sweet white wines. Varying from delicately fruity and lightly sweet to overwhelmingly luscious, these wines are to be sipped slowly by themselves and are rarely improved by food. Very rich and highly flavoured desserts, however delicious, tend to fight sweet wines. Chocolate and coffee ones can be fatal. If you want anything at all, the best choice is a dessert such as French apple or raspberry tart, crème brûlée, plain sponge cake, or such fruit as peaches or apples. Sweet white wines are usually drunk after meals, but in France often as apéritifs, too. They are normally served very well chilled.

The finest natural sweet wines are produced by the action of noble rot. These include Sauternes and Barsac and the best qualities of Ste-Croix-du-Mont and Monbazillac, which are the most potent, Vouvray and Anjou whites of certain years, late-gathered wines of Alsace and Austria, and the rare and expensive very late-harvested wines of Germany, Beerenauslesen, and Trockenbeerenauslesen and wines of similar style from Australia, New Zealand, and California. Traditionally fruity German wines offer every gradation between the light flowery whites and the intensely sweet ones with the same delicately acid flavour. None of them is really a mealtime wine. Tokaji Aszú, on the other hand, finds matches at both the start of a banquet (with foie gras) and with fruity and/or creamy desserts at the end.

Sweet Muscats are found in most wine countries. They range from the feather light, such as those from Asti in northern Italy, where the very low-strength base wine for *spumante* is delicious; to the richer fortified *vins doux naturels* made in the south of France at Beaumes-de-Venise. Heavier Muscats are made in Languedoc and Roussillon (Rivesaltes), southern Italy (especially Sicily), on the east coast of Spain, at Setúbal in Portugal, in Greece and Russia, and (best of all) in northeast Victoria, Australia.

Rosé wines. The current and enormous fashionability of rosé has produced a general rise in quality, with more and more rosés being made for their own sake, rather than as a mere by-product of red. They can be made by fermenting the juice of red grapes very briefly with the skins, then separating it and making it like white wine, or by bleeding the red vats before too much colour has been obtained. The great exception is pink Champagne, which can be a blend of white wine with a little red. Few things are more delicious.

Rosés divide broadly into two camps: white wine rosés, pale and delicate in colour though often quite intense in flavour, and red wine rosés, darker and heavier. Provence rosé comes into the first category, along with the paler Spanish *rosados*; most South American *rosados* and the darker Spanish ones come into the second. Most rosés are dry or only slightly off-dry: the exceptions are Portuguese carbonated fizzy rosés and Californian "blush" wines.

Rosés are no longer just summer picnic wines, they are now popular all year round, and are useful with such dishes as artichokes, crudités, salami, or taramasalata, but also with more substantial vegetarian dishes and with some Indian food – do not despise sweeter rosés here.

Grapey young reds with individuality, not intended to mature. Beaujolais is the archetype of a light red wine: made to be drunk young while it is still lively with fresh grape flavour. Beaujolais-Villages is a better, stronger, and tastier selection. Simple young Bordeaux, burgundy, and Rhône reds, Cabernet from the Loire, simple young Malbec from Argentina, Tannat from Uruguay, and Mondeuse from Savoie should have the same appeal. Similar wines can be found in the Midi (Corbières, Minervois, Roussillon, St-Chinian), made by the Beaujolais technique of carbonic maceration: light wines to drink young.

Italy's Valpolicella and Bardolino, light Barbera and Dolcetto, and even Chianti, can be freshly fruity if they are caught young enough. Fizzy red Lambrusco is a sort of caricature of the style. Spain provides some examples from La Mancha. Portugal's red Vinho Verde is an extreme example not to everyone's taste. The heat of the vineyards of California, Australia, South Africa, and South America have proved inimical to this style of wine. Light Zinfandels and Gamays from California sometimes achieve it.

This class of wine has tended to fall victim to the fashion for weighty, oaky reds, but in its liveliness and vigour it is perhaps the safest and best all-round bet for mealtimes, appetizing with anything from pâté to fruit and often better than a more serious or older wine with strong cheese, in mouthfuls rather than sips. For the same reason it is the easiest red wine to drink without food. It is usually best served cool. Ideal dishes include: pâtés and terrines (including those made from vegetables), quiches, salads, hamburgers, liver, ham, grilled meats, many cheeses, and soft fruits such as raspberries, plums, peaches, or nectarines.

Soft, fruity everyday or "jug" reds. Most inexpensive branded reds come into this category, in which country or region of origin counts less than a reliably juicy, ripe flavour. They are produced in large quantities to a set standard, and are often found discounted in supermarkets. They might be a little jammy in style, and are often seasoned with oak – or more probably oak chips. They are probably as often drunk without food as with it, and may be comfortingly low in acidity.

Mature reds of light to medium strength and body. This category includes most of the world's finest red wines, epitomized by claret (red Bordeaux) and most of the typical wines of Burgundy and the Rhône, although some of the greatest fall into the next class, depending on the ripeness of the vintage. These wines need more care in serving than any others since they often throw a deposit in maturing.

They are wines for meat and game dishes with the best ingredients and moderate seasoning. Lamb, beef, veal (also sweetbreads and tongue), chicken, duck, partridge, grouse, pheasant are all ideal, although very gamey birds may need wines from the next category. Only mild cheeses should be served with these relatively delicate wines. They need to be served at a temperature of between 15°C and 18°C (60°F and 65°F) to bring out their flavour.

Wines in this category (apart from French) include the best of Rioja and Penedès from Spain; Chianti Riservas, Tuscans such as Tignanello, Carmignano, and Venegazzú; Southern Italians from such grapes as Nerello Mascalese, Nero d'Avola, and Aglianico; Portuguese reds, especially from Dão, Alentejo, and Bairrada; top California, Oregon, and Washington Cabernets and Pinot Noirs with the exception of a few mentioned in the next category; Coonawarra, Western Australian, and some Hunter Valley reds; top South African estates; Argentinian Malbec; Chilean Cabernet; Uruguayan Tannat, Chateau Musar from the Lebanon; top Greek reds; and Bordeaux blends from New Zealand.

Exceptionally concentrated, full-flavoured, and powerful reds, usually but not always needing to mature. In Europe this category depends more on the vintage than the producer. Wines that achieve this status fairly regularly include Pétrus in Pomerol, Chambertin and Corton in Burgundy, Hermitage and Châteauneuf-du-Pape (Côte-Rôtie is more often in the previous category), exceptional Roussillons (not for maturing); Barolo and Barbaresco, Brunello di Montalcino, Recioto and Recioto Amarone from Valpolicella; Spanish Vega Sicilia, Pesquera, and Priorato; Portuguese Barca Velha and other Douro reds; Dalmatian Posip and Postup. Occasional vintages produce many such wines: 1961 in Bordeaux, 1971 in Burgundy, and more recently 1990 for both.

California, Australia, and South Africa find it hard not to make such big reds. Most of their best wines are carefully restrained in ripeness, but in California a number of wines, especially Zinfandel, are made to be larger than life. Australia makes many such wines, especially in Victoria and Barossa and the Southern Vales in South Australia. Top Shiraz such as Penfold's Grange and Henschke's Hill of Grace are the supreme examples.

Well-hung game and strong-flavoured cheeses are the obvious choice for these wines, although those in the appropriate price bracket are also excellent with barbecues and on picnics – when someone else is driving.

Fortified wines. Wines whose natural strength is augmented with added alcohol, either during the fermentation to preserve the natural sweetness (as in port) or after they have fermented to dryness, as a preservative (as in sherry). Since the role of these wines is largely determined by their sweetness, which is at their makers' discretion, all that can usefully be said is that dry versions (whether of port, sherry, Madeira, or their regional equivalents) are intended as apéritifs, while sweet ones are used either before or after meals according to local taste and custom.

The French, for example, prefer sweet apéritifs, the Italians bitter ones, and the British, who divide everything along class lines, some sweet and some dry. In all cases, smaller glasses are needed because the alcoholic strength is higher than that of table wine. They also have their uses with certain foods. Dry sherry is always drunk in Spain with tapas, which are infinitely various savoury snacks. It is one of the best wines for smoked eel and cuts the silky sweetness of fine Iberian ham. Old oloroso sherry, whether dry or with added sweetness, is very good with cake, nuts, and raisins. Port, both vintage and tawny, is often drunk with cheese. Madeira has a soft, spicy cake especially designed for it. (The cake known in Britain as Madeira cake is, on the island of Madeira, called "English cake".)

Other wines in this category include Spanish Málaga and Tarragona, Sicilian Marsala, Cypriot Commandaria, French *vins doux naturels* (eg. Banyuls), the Australian fortified Muscats and Tokays, the latter now renamed Topaques, Australian "sherry", now renamed Apera, and a host of other wines, now gradually being stripped of their borrowed names, in the New World.

Storing Wine

The greatest revolution in the history of wine was the discovery that if air could be excluded from wine, its life span was increased enormously. And, even better, that it could take on an undreamed-of range of flavours and a different, less grapey, and infinitely more subtle and interesting smell.

The invention that made airtight storage possible was the cork, which came into use some time in the seventeenth century. It is possible that the ancient Greeks knew the secret, but all through the Middle Ages and up to the seventeenth century, the premium was on new wine, not old. The latest vintage often sold for twice as much as the remnants of the previous one, which stood a good chance of having become vinegar. The only exceptions were the class of high-strength and possibly sweet wines generally known as "sack", products of hot sunshine in the eastern Mediterranean, southern Spain, and later, the Canary Islands. Their constitution allowed them to age in barrels in contact with air and take on the nuttiness and warmth of flavour we associate with sherry.

Ageing in bottles under cork is a totally different process. Instead of oxidizing, or taking in oxygen, the wine is in a state of "reduction" – in other words, what little oxygen it contains (absorbed in the cellars, while being "racked" from one cask to another, and in being bottled) is being used up (reduced) by the life processes within it. So long as it lives (and wine is a living substance with a remarkable life span), it is the battleground of bacteria, the playground of pigments, tannins, enzymes: a host of jostling wildlife preying on each other. No air gets through a good cork as long as it is kept wet, in contact with the wine, so that there is no risk of the vinegar process starting.

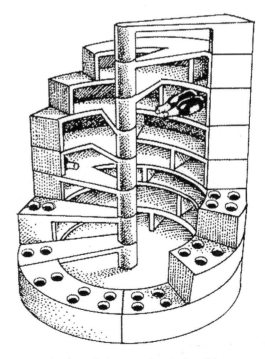

A customized under-stair storage system such as this can accommodate a surprising amount of bottles.

Whether the reduction process is beneficial, and for how long, is the determining factor in deciding when a bottled wine will be at its best.

Today, an increasing number of wines are being sealed with screwcaps. Most of them are intended for rapid consumption, but others, such as Australian Rieslings, can be kept for up to ten years. The wines, if properly stored, will age well, but retain more freshness than a corked version of a similar style. This has become an immensely controversial topic. Cork companies have been lobbying furiously to ensure their survival, and, to be fair to them, investing considerably in research to eliminate cork taint. Cork taint produces a complex chemical called TCA that affects a bottled wine in varying degrees: from a perceptible flatness of aroma and taste, to a slight mustiness, to a thoroughly disagreeable whiff of burnt residue and decay.

Alternative closures have been developed, such as the plastic cork (hard to extract, impossible to re-insert), the glass stopper (costly and with a seal that may yet prove imperfect), reconstituted cork, and the screwcap. Screwcaps do have their critics, but most agree that they have the merit of being simple, inexpensive, and effective.

Which Wines to Store

The great majority of wines are made with the intention of being ready to drink as soon as possible. This is true of all bulk wines, most white wines except very sweet and particularly full-bodied ones, nearly all rosés, and the whole class of red wines that can be compared with Beaujolais – whose character and charm lie in a direct flavour of the grape. Reduction spoils their simple fruitiness. The only table wines that benefit from storage are a minority of sweet or very concentrated, intensely flavoury whites and those reds specifically made, by long vatting with their skins and pips, to take up pigments and tannins as preservatives – which includes, of course, all the world's best.

Precisely how much of these elements combine with the juice and how well they act as preservatives is only partly in the hands of the winemaker. The overriding decisive factor is the vintage. And no two vintages are exactly alike. The analysis of the grapes at harvest time may be similar, but each crop has stood out in the fields through a hundred different days since the vine flowers opened. The number and size of the grapes, the formation of the bunches, the thickness of the skins, and the yeasts they gathered will always be subtly different. No two vintages develop in the same way or at precisely the same speed. But the better wines of each vintage will always last longer and mature further, to more delicious flavours, than the less good.

Thus laying down wines for maturing is always an exploratory business. Experts will give their opinion that the 2000 Bordeaux need from five to 15 years to reach their best, depending on their quality. Such a margin will be safe enough, although it is scarcely a very helpful guide.

It is worth bearing in mind that later harvesting at higher ripeness levels – not just in Bordeaux but throughout the wine world – is giving richer, more supple wines with softer tannins. There is no reason to doubt that such wines will age as well as the best wines of the 1960s and '70s, but they are also accessible at a younger age. In the past, many red wines needed long ageing in bottle because they contained a measure of unripe tannins that made the wine unpalatable when young, while whites wines were dosed in sulphur dioxide that also made the wine disagreeable in its youth. The wines of today are far more approachable, and whether you like a fine burgundy or Bordeaux or Shiraz in its dazzling youth or in its mellow, subtle, old age is finally a matter of taste. Always remember that a bottle drunk just before it reaches its peak of complexity and flavour will be more rewarding that a bottle consumed after it has reached that peak and begun its descent into a tired old age.

Wine Merchants & Brokers

In the past, only the grandest producers were capable of maturing and bottling their wine satisfactorily; marketing was an idea that was entirely unknown to them. The key to what the

---

BOTTLE SIZE, SHAPE, & CAPACITY

Each European wine region has a long-established traditional bottle shape that helps to preserve an identity in the public mind. In most cases the New World wines based on the same grape varieties are also sold in the appropriately shaped bottles to help identify the style of the wines.

Colour of glass is as important as shape. All Rhine wines are bottled in brown glass, all Mosels in green. White Bordeaux is in clear glass, red Bordeaux is in green. For table wines whose origin is not important the Cubitainer, Tetrapak, or bag-in-box are plausible inventions, although in practice, no wine is well-served by such a device.

Champagne is one wine which comes with a range of bottle sizes – but the various sizes that are available are for purely celebratory reasons. Bottles of red Bordeaux also come in several sizes (right). The bigger the bottle the longer the wine keeps, the slower it matures, and the better it will become.

consumer wanted was held by the merchants, who blended wine to the customers' tastes. Today, buying wine direct from the maker has largely changed the shape of the wine trade.

It is the broker's job to know his region in the finest detail, to be a sort of family doctor to the small grower's wine, to advise him on its condition, choose samples with him, and take them to the right merchant. To the merchant, the broker is a valued talent-spotter who can gather and submit the right samples. The merchant's traditional function is to finance the wine while it is maturing, to make sure it suits the customers' tastes, then to bottle and ship it. In many cases he and his agents create both the wine and the market. His agents provide the link with the wholesalers, who are stockholders for retailers. The possible permutations of the system are endless. Its advantages are that each aspect of the chain from grower to table has its highly experienced expert, whether in knowing the right time to bottle or the turnover of a nightclub's refrigerator.

Is it Time to Try?

Happily, there are always plenty of other people opening bottles of every vintage and adding to a general pool of information about it, transmitted through wine books and magazines and catalogues. You will never have to look very far for an indication of whether it is time to try the wine you are storing. You can even tell a certain amount about the maturity of red wine without opening the bottle, by holding its neck up to a strong light; the depth and quality of colour are quite readable through the glass.

The more difficult decision, assuming you intend to lay down some wine, is how much of which vintages to buy. It is probably a mistake to plump too heavily for one vintage – you never know whether the next one will be better. It is more sensible to buy regularly as good vintages turn up, which, with global warming, is with growing frequency. Since there is rarely enough space (and never enough money) it is worth making a calculation of how much dinner-party wine you are likely to use, which in turn depends on how many of your friends share your passion. Let us suppose that you give an average of one dinner party a month for eight people, and each time use four bottles of mature wine (in addition to such current items as young white wines and possibly Champagne). Your annual consumption will be about 48 bottles. Perhaps you use another bottle a week on family occasions (or alone). That makes about eight dozens a year. The theoretically ideal stock is arrived at by multiplying the annual consumption by the number of years it stays in the cellar. Since this number varies from perhaps two, for fine white wines, to ten or more for the best reds, a finer calculation is needed. Let us say that two of the eight dozens are two-year wines, four are five-year wines, and two are ten-year wines. The total is 2x2 + 4x5 + 2x10 = 44 cases.

Besides table wines, two other kinds of wine are worth laying down: Champagne and vintage port. Champagne is a relatively short term proposition. Vintage Champagne almost invariably gains a noticeable extra depth of flavour over two or three years. Lovers of old Champagne will want to keep it far longer, up to ten or even 20 years, until its colour deepens and its bubbles quieten. This is very much a British taste. Champagne

drinkers in Germany, for example, prize freshness more than maturity. In Britain, it is worth keeping non-vintage Champagne for a year or two as well, but I have found that in America it is usually mature (sometimes overmature) by the time it reaches the customer. Vintage port is an entirely different matter. The way the wine goes through almost its whole life cycle in the bottle is explained in the section on port. It needs cellaring longer than any other wine – except the almost unobtainable vintage Madeira. All good vintages need 20 years or more to reach their hour of glory.

The practical arrangements for storing wine are a challenge to most householders. The ideal underground cellar is even more remote than its ideal contents. But the storage conditions that make an underground cellar ideal are relatively easy to reproduce upstairs (at least in temperate climates) if the space is available. If money is no object and you have sufficient space, there are various temperature- and humidity-controlled storage systems that can be installed in your house or buried in your garden.

The conditions required are darkness, freedom from vibration, fairly high humidity, and a reasonably even temperature. Darkness is needed because ultraviolet light penetrates even green glass bottles and hastens ageing prematurely. Vibration is presumed to be bad (on what evidence I am not sure; it would have to be pretty violent to keep any normal sediment in suspension). Humidity helps the corks to stay airtight, but much more important is that the wine remains in contact with the corks inside the bottle. It is essential to store all wine horizontally, even if you only expect to keep it for a month or two. Excess humidity is a serious nuisance; it rapidly rots cardboard boxes and soon makes labels unreadable. My own answer to the label problem is to give each one a squirt of scentless hair lacquer before storing it away.

Temperature & Time

Temperature is the most worrisome of these two conditions. The ideal is anything between a steady 7°C and 18°C (45°F and 65°F). A 10°C (50°F) cellar is best of all, because the white wines in it are permanently at or near the perfect drinking temperature. It is highly probable that wines in a cold cellar mature more slowly and keep longer than wines in a relatively warm one.

Chemists point out that chemical reaction rates double with each 10°C (18°F) increase in temperature. If the maturing of wine were simply a chemical reaction this would mean that a wine stored in a cellar at 19°C (68°F) would mature twice as fast as one in a 10°C (50°F) cellar. But it is not so simple; wine is alive. Its ageing is not just chemical but a whole life process.

One should not exaggerate the effects of fluctuation, either. My own (underground) cellar moves gradually from a winter temperature of about 8°C (48°F) to a summer one of over 15°C (60°F) without the wine suffering in any detectable way. The most common difficulty arises in finding a steadily cool place in a house or flat heated to 21°C (70°F) or more in winter, when outside temperature can range from 15°C (60°F) to below freezing. The answer must be in insulating a small room or large cupboard near an outside wall. In practice, fine wines are successfully stored in blocked-up fireplaces, in cupboards under the stairs, in the bottoms of wardrobes… ingenuity can always find somewhere satisfactory. The same applies to racks and bins. A bin is a large, open shelf (or space on the floor) where a quantity of one wine is laid, bottle on bottle. In the days when households bought very few wines, but bought them a barrel at a time, the bin was ideal. For collections of relatively small quantities of many different wines, racks are essential. They can either be divided into single-bottle apertures (either one or two bottles deep) or formed into a diamond pattern of apertures that are large enough to take several bottles – a half-dozen or a dozen depending on the quantities you usually buy. I find it convenient to have both single-bottle and dozen-bottle racks.

A much more complex problem, as a collection grows, is keeping track of the bottles. It is difficult not to waste space if you deplete your stock in blocks. Where space is limited you want to be able to use every slot as it becomes vacant. This is the advantage of the random storage system. But its efficaciousness depends entirely on dedicated book-keeping. If this is not your line you are likely to mislay bottles just when you want them. Very fine wines – most classed as growth Bordeaux, for instance – are shipped in wooden packing cases that are perfect storage while the wine matures. If you do buy such wines by the complete case, there is no point in unpacking it until you have reason to think the wine will be nearing maturity.

If possible, make allowance in your storage arrangements for bigger-than-normal bottles. The standard 75-centilitre bottle has been accepted by generations as the most convenient regular size – though whether it was originally conceived as being a portion for one person or two is hard to say. But bigger bottles keep wine even better. Length of life, speed of maturity, and level of ultimate quality are all in direct proportion to bottle size. Half-bottles are occasionally convenient, particularly for such powerful and expensive sweet wines as great Sauternes or Beerenauslese, where a little goes a long way. Otherwise, bottles are better, and magnums better still. Double magnums begin to be difficult to handle (and how often can you assemble enough like-minded friends to do justice to one?). The counsel of perfection is to lay down six magnums to every 12 bottles of each wine on which you pin really high hopes.

It is not necessarily only expensive wines that are worth laying down. Many Australian reds, for example, will evolve from a muscle-bound youth into a most satisfying maturity. One of my greatest successes was a barrel of a three-year-old Chilean Cabernet, which I bottled in my amateurish way in my own cellar. It reached its delectable peak 10 years later.

TYPES OF GLASSES

You can argue that there is only one perfect wine glass, equally ideal for all table wines but there is also a case for enjoying the traditional, sometimes fanciful, shapes adopted by different regions to promote the identity of their products.

A "tulip" glass has the rim turned in to concentrate the bouquet. This is the classic Bordeaux model, excellent for all red wines and most white.

Burgundy glasses can be large enough to hold half a bottle comfortably. The popularity of glasses with an out-turned lip waxes and wanes.

Experiment, therefore, with powerful, deep-coloured, and tannic reds from whatever source. Be much more circumspect with white wines. Most of those that have proved that cellaring improves them beyond a year or two are expensive already: the better white burgundies, the best Chardonnays, Sauternes of the best châteaux, and outstanding German Auslesen – which probably provide the best value for money today. The neglected areas to add to these are fine Chenins from the Loire (both sweet and dry), top-quality Alsace wines, and what was once considered the longest-lived of all white wines, the rare white Hermitage of the Rhône.

Glasses

Each wine region has its own ideas about the perfect wine glass. Most are based on sound gastronomic principles that make them just as suitable for the wines of other regions, too. Perhaps the most graceful and universally appropriate is the shape used in Bordeaux. A few are flamboyantly folkloric – amusing to use in their context but as subtle as a dirndl at a

dinner party. The traditional *römer* of the Rhine, for instance, has a thick trunk of a stem in brown glass ornamented with ridges and excrescences. It dates from the days when Rhine wine was preferred old and oxidized, the colour of the glass, and presumably when Rhinelanders wanted something pretty substantial to thump the table with. The Mosel, by contrast, serves its wine in a pretty, shallow-bowled glass with a diamond-cut pattern that seems designed to stress the wine's lightness and grace. Alsace glasses have very tall, green stems that reflect a faint green hue into the wine. Glasses like these are pleasant facets of a visit to the wine region, adding to the sense of place and occasion, but you do not need them at home.

The International Standards Organization (ISO) has pre-empted further discussion by producing specifications for the perfect winetasting glass. Its narrowing-at-the-top shape is designed as a funnel to maximize the smell of the wine for the taster's nose. However the wine trade has largely abandoned this glass in favour of the Chianti glass by Riedl, which is a similar shape but is larger and more expansive, and seems to flatter the wine more. (The Austrian glassware designer Georg Riedel has devised countless models, each intended to complement a particular style of wine. The Chianti glass is generally

TYPES OF GLASSES

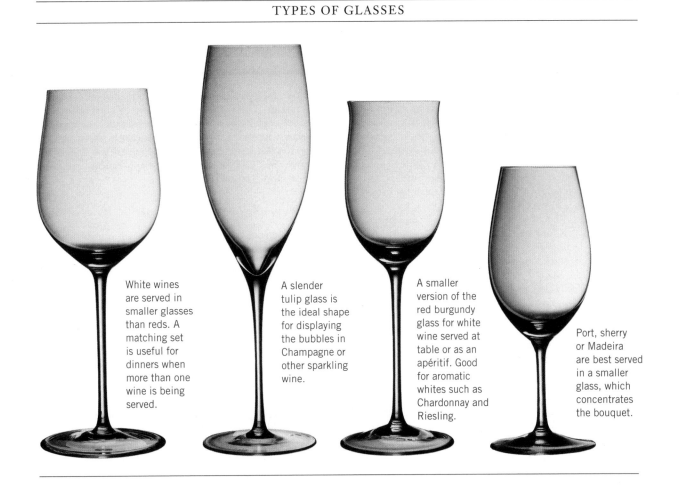

White wines are served in smaller glasses than reds. A matching set is useful for dinners when more than one wine is being served.

A slender tulip glass is the ideal shape for displaying the bubbles in Champagne or other sparkling wine.

A smaller version of the red burgundy glass for white wine served at table or as an apéritif. Good for aromatic whites such as Chardonnay and Riesling.

Port, sherry or Madeira are best served in a smaller glass, which concentrates the bouquet.

reckoned to be the best all-purpose wine glass, however.) For ordinary table use Riedl glasses may be expensive – expensive to break, at any rate – but other good glassmakers have followed with designs that are not dissimilar. All should have the crucial characteristics of any good wine glass: they should be clear, unornamented, of rather thin glass, with a stem long enough for an easy grip and an adequate capacity. Capacity is important. A table-wine glass should never be filled more than half full. A size that is filled to only one-third by a normal portion (about 11 cl/4 fl.oz or an eighth of a bottle) is best of all. Anything larger is merely ostentatious – and more likely to get knocked over. "Correct" glassware has become something of a fetish in some circles. But how many of us want a dozen or more styles of glass in our crowded cabinets? The styles illustrated on the previous page are more than sufficient to make the most of each type of wine.

Displaying the Bubbles

Sparkling wines are best served in a slightly smaller but relatively taller glass filled to about three-quarters of its capacity, giving the bubbles a good way to climb – one of the prettiest sights wine has to offer. They should never under any circumstances be served in the shallow *coupes*, now very rarely seen. Dessert wines, being stronger, are served in smaller portions in smaller glasses, usually filled to between a half and two-thirds of their capacity. Their scents are more pungent than table wines; to plunge your nose into a wide bowl of port fumes would be almost overpowering.

When several wines are being served at the same meal it saves confusion if each has a slightly differing glass. In any case, guests should be told that the order of pouring is from left to right (ie. the first wine is poured into the left-hand glass and so on in order). I imagine this tradition is for the practical reason that a right-handed drinker is less likely to knock over this first glass in reaching for his second. As a further precaution against confusion (if two or more similar wines are being poured) it is a simple matter to slip a little rubber band around the stem of one of the glasses.

Wine glasses should be as clean as you can possibly make them – which is, unfortunately, beyond the capacity of any dishwasher. Detergents leave a coating, which may or may not have a taste or smell, but is always detectable to the touch. It even affects the fizz of Champagne. There is only one way to achieve a perfectly clean, polished, brilliant glass. After washing with soap or detergent to remove grease, it should be thoroughly rinsed in clean hot water, then not drained but filled with hot water and only emptied immediately before it is dried. A clean linen or cotton cloth polishes a warm, wet glass perfectly (and very quickly) whereas it leaves smears and fluff on a cold one.

The best place to keep glasses is in a closed cupboard, standing right way up. On an open shelf they collect dust. Upside down on a shelf they pick up odours of wood or paint. An alternative to a closed cupboard is a rack where they hang upside down, but dust on the outside of a glass is no better than dust on the inside.

Serving Wine

The no-nonsense approach to serving wine takes up very little space or time. The cork is out before discussion starts. There are times, and wine, for this can-of-beans attack, which it would be pretentious to deny. But here I put the case for taking trouble to make the most of every bottle. On the basis that anticipation is a part of every great pleasure, I argue that you should enjoy reading the label, be aroused by handling the bottle, relish removing the capsule, feel stirred by plunging in the corkscrew. Sensuous enjoyment is the entire purpose of wine. The art of appreciating it is to maximize the pleasure of every manoeuvre, from choosing to swallowing. The art of serving wine is to make sure that it reaches the drinker with all its qualities at their peak. No single factor is as important to success or failure as temperature. The characteristic scent and flavour of wine consists of infinitely subtle volatile compounds of different molecular weights, progressively heavier from light white wines to heavy reds. It is the temperature that controls their volatility: the point at which they vaporize and come to meet your sense of smell.

Each grape variety seems to behave differently in this respect. The Riesling scent is highly volatile; a Mosel sends out its flowery message even when it is too cold to drink with pleasure. Champagne's powerful fragrance of grapes and yeasts can hardly be suppressed by cold (although I have known people who seem to try). The Sauvignon Blanc is almost as redolent as the Riesling; the Chardonnay much less so – less so, in fact, than the Gamay; Beaujolais is highly volatile at low temperatures. The Pinot Noir vaporizes its ethereal sapidity even in a cool Burgundian cellar, whereas the Cabernets of Bordeaux hold back their aromas, particularly when they are young. In a Bordeaux *chai* it tends to be the oak you smell more than the wine. California and other warm-climate Cabernets are often more forthcoming.

Are Aromas Everything?

It will be seen that these observations tally more or less with the generally accepted norms of serving temperatures shown on page 656. Not that aromas are everything. We expect white wines to be refreshingly cool; we expect red wines to awaken our palates with other qualities of vigour and completeness. It is fascinating to test how much your appreciation is affected by temperature. Taste, for instance, a good mature Meursault and a Volnay of the same quality (they are the white and red wines of neighbouring vineyards, made of grapes with much in common) at precisely the same fairly cool temperature and with your eyes shut. You will find they are almost interchangeable.

It is time to forget the misleading term "room temperature" to describe the ideal environment for enjoying red wines. Whatever the temperature of dining rooms in the days when it was coined (and it must have varied from frigid to a fire-and-candle-heated fug), the chances of arriving at the right temperature by simply standing the bottle in the room where it is to be drunk are slight. An American dining room at 21°C

(70°F) plus is much too warm for wine. At that temperature the alcohol becomes unpleasantly heady. Mine, at 15°C (60°F), is good for burgundy but too cold for Bordeaux.

Everybody has, in his refrigerator, a cold place at a constant temperature that can be used for cooling white wine. Nobody I have met has a 16°C (63°F) oven. On the other hand, since an ice bucket is a perfectly acceptable (in fact, by far the most efficient) way of chilling wine, why not a warm-water bucket for red? Water at 21°C (70°F) will raise the temperature of a bottle from 15°C to 18°C (55°F to 65°F) in about eight minutes, which is the same time as it would take to lower the temperature of a bottle of white wine from 18°C to 13°C (65°F to 55°F) in a bucket of icy water. (Ice without water is much less efficient in cooling.) In a fridge, incidentally, where air rather than water is the cooling medium, the same lowering of temperature would take about one hour.

Bear in mind that the prevailing temperature affects the wine not only before it is poured out but while it is in your glass as well. Serve white wine on a hot day considerably colder than you want to drink it. Never leave a bottle or glass in the sun; improvise shade with a parasol, the menu, a book, under your chair… anywhere. At one sumptuous outdoor buffet in South Africa, the white wine was admirably cold but the red wine was left on the table in the sun. Not only was it ruined beyond recognition but I nearly burned my tongue on it. There are circumstances where the red wine needs an ice bucket, too.

Cooling Vessels

Failing the ideal arrangement of storing white wine permanently at the perfect drinking temperature – that of a cool cellar – the most efficient way to chill it rapidly is by immersing the entire bottle in ice cold water. A refrigerator takes up to ten times as long as an ice-bath to achieve the same effect. The perfect ice bucket is deep enough to immerse the whole bottle, neck and all: otherwise you have to put the bottle in upside down to start with to cool the neck. Insulated cooler sleeves, which are kept in the freezer and placed around the bottle when needed, are also effective. There is also a sort of open-ended Thermos flask that keeps an already chilled bottle cool by maintaining a wall of cold air around it.

Do You Decant?

Wine-lovers seem to find a consensus on most things to do with their subject, but decanting is a divisive issue. There is one school of thought, the traditional, that holds that wine needs to "breathe" for anything from a few minutes to a few hours, or even days, to reach its best. Its opponents, armed with scientific evidence, proclaim that it makes no difference or (a third view) that it is deleterious. Each is right about certain wines, and about its own taste. But they are mistaken to be dogmatic.

There are three reasons for decanting. The most important is to clean the wine of sediment. A secondary one is the attraction of the plump, glittering, glowing-red decanter on the table. The third is to allow the wine to breathe. Nobody argues with the first two. The debate revolves around when the operation should take place.

The eminent Professor Peynaud, whose contribution to gastronomy in general and Bordeaux in particular should make us listen carefully, wrote (in *Le Goût du Vin*), "If it is necessary to decant [at all], one should always do it at the last possible moment, just before moving to the table or just before serving [the wine]; never in advance." The only justification Peynaud sees for aeration, or letting the wine breathe, is to rid it of certain superficial faults that sometimes arise. Otherwise, he says, decanting in advance does nothing but harm; it softens the wine and dulls the brilliance of its carefully acquired bouquet.

Scientifically minded Americans have come to much the same conclusions, although their consensus seems to be that decanting makes no difference that can in any way be reliably detected. My own experience is that almost all wines change perceptibly in a decanter, but whether that change is for the better or worse depends partly on the wine and partly on personal taste. There are wine-lovers who prefer their wine softened and dulled; vintage port in particular is often decanted early to soothe its fiery temper; its full "attack" is too much for them. They equate mellowness with quality. Tradition in Spain equates the taste of oak (as in Rioja) with quality. Who can say they are wrong about their own taste?

The English have always had strong ideas about how their wines should taste. One hundred years ago they added Rhône or Spanish wine to claret; it was altogether too faint for them without it. There are surely some people who preferred the burgundies of the days before the strict application of the appellation laws to the authentic, straight-from-the-grower burgundy we drink today. The Californians, too, have their own taste. They love direct, strong-flavoured wines that often seem as though the transition from fruit juice was never completed. Not surprisingly, ideas about decanting differ.

There are certain wines that seem to curl up when you open the bottle – like woodlice when you turn over a log. The deeply tannic Barolo of Piedmont shows nothing but its carapace for an hour or sometimes several. If you drink it during that time you will have nothing to remember but an assault on your tongue and cheeks. But in due course, hints of a bouquet start to emerge, growing stronger until eventually you are enveloped in raspberries and violets and truffles and autumn leaves.

The standard French restaurant practice is not to decant burgundy. If it is true that the Pinot Noir is more volatile than the Cabernet, the practice makes sense – the contact with the air when pouring from bottle to carafe wakes the Bordeaux up; the burgundy does not need it.

Those who believe in decanting would give several hours' airing to a young wine, one or two to a mature wine (these terms being relative to the expected maturing time), and treat an old wine as an invalid who should be kept out of draughts. Yet, strange to say it is an often repeated experience of those who have tasted very old and very great wines (Château Lafite 1803 was a case in point) that they can add layer upon layer of bouquet and flavour hour after hour – even, in some cases, tasting better than ever the following day. I regularly finish the bottles the evening after opening them. The only general rule I have found is that the better the wine, taking both origin and vintage into account, the more it benefits from prolonged contact with the air.

OPENING AND DECANTING WINE

There is much debate about whether and when to decant wine; whether breathing is a good thing or not. Modern scientific opinion tends to be against it. Certainly its effects are hard to predict, but if a rule of thumb is called for, I suggest the following:

Vigorous young ("young" in this context relates to the vintage – a great vintage is young at ten years, a poor one up to four or five) red Bordeaux, Cabernets, Rhône reds, Barolo and Barbaresco, heavy Zinfandels, Australian Shiraz, Portuguese reds, and other similar tannic wines: decant at least one hour before drinking, and experiment with periods of up to six hours.

"Young" red burgundy, Pinot Noirs, and traditional Spanish wines: decant just before serving.

A foil-cutter is a useful device for neatly removing the top disc of a capsule. When I am decanting I cut off the rest with a knife as well. Sometimes it seems a shame.

The corkscrew being used here is the Leverpull, which grips the bottle and uses powerful leverage to pull the cork in one movement. A reverse movement of the handle then removes the cork from the screw.

This is a good cork; 14 years old and stained by wine only on the bottom. The degree of seepage round the cork, if any, is easy to read. The less seepage the better the chance of a perfect bottle.

I hold the bottle neck over a candle or a bright torch as I pour, and position my head so that the light shines through the wine in the neck. It is a beautiful sight.

When you see sediment moving into the neck of the bottle, stop pouring. In fine wines sediment sometimes sticks to the glass (the dark patch visible here). This is usually a positive sign.

The first sniff. Some fine mature wines have a glorious moment of revelation on decanting, which it would be a pity to miss. Others need time in your glass to open up and show that full beauty.

Sometimes a wine that is a distinct disappointment on opening changes its nature entirely. More than once I have had a bottle with a poor, hard, loose-fitting cork and, on first tasting, a miserable, timid smell and very little flavour at all (although the colour might be good). Twenty-four hours later it seemed to have recharged its batteries; it opened up into the full-blooded, high-flavoured wine I had expected. The moral must be to experiment and keep an open mind. The same is true of decanting white wine. The aesthetic appeal of a golden wine shimmering in the decanter is genuine enough, but some would argue that certain wines – young *premier cru* burgundy, or austere whites, such as Savennières – benefit from aeration. As with the reds, there are no hard and fast rules, but it is worth experimenting and seeing for yourself whether you prefer the decanted wine.

The pros and cons of decanting are much more long-winded than the process itself. The aim is simply to pour the wine, but not its sediment, into another receptacle (which can be a decanter, plain or fancy, or another bottle that has been well-rinsed). If there is enough advance warning, take the bottle gently from its rack at least two days before you need it and stand it upright. Two days (or one at a pinch) should be long enough for the sediment to slide to the bottom. If you must decant from a bottle that has been horizontal until the last minute you need a basket or cradle to hold the bottle as near its original position as possible, but with the wine just below cork level. Cut the capsule right away. Remove the cork gently with a counter-pressure corkscrew. Then, holding the decanter in the left hand, pour in the wine slowly in one smooth movement until you see the sediment advancing as a dark arrow towards the neck of the bottle. When the sediment reaches the shoulder, stop pouring.

It makes it easier to see where the sediment is if you hold the neck of the bottle over a candle flame or a torch, or (I find best) a sheet of white paper or a napkin with a fairly strong light on it. Vintage port bottles are made of very dark glass (and moreover are usually dirty), which makes it harder to see the sediment. If the port has been lying in one place for years, its sediment is so thick and coherent that you can hardly go wrong. If it has been moved recently it can be troublesome, and might even need filtering. Clean, damp muslin is the best material; I have found that coffee filter papers can give wine a detectable and disagreeable taste.

Opening Sparkling Wine

Sparkling wines should be spur of the moment, celebratory drinks. When opening expensive bottles, it is a good idea to have a stopper that will keep the fizz intact if the celebration should be short lived. Five easy steps to opening a bottle of sparkling wine are as follows:
1. Tear off the foil hiding the wire "muzzle" to uncover the "ring". Tilt the bottle and untwist the ring, being careful not to point the bottle at anyone.
2. Remove the muzzle. Tilt the bottle, holding the cork down firmly with your thumb. Ease the cork sideways and upwards with the other thumb.
3. When the cork feels loose, grasp it firmly and twist, keeping the bottle tilted, with a glass beside you to take the first foam.

4. Specially made pliers are sometimes used when a Champagne cork is very stiff, or when opening a number of bottles.
5. Butlers in the great Champagne houses pour Champagne by holding the bottle with a thumb in the indentation known as the "punt".

Opening Vintage Port

Bottles of vintage port older than about 20 years often present a special problem – the cork becomes soft and crumbly and disintegrates in the grip of a corkscrew. Spongy corks are almost impossible to remove. The answer is to cut the top off the bottle, which can be done in either of two ways.

Port tongs are specially made for the job. Heat them until red hot over an open flame, then clamp the tongs around the upper neck of the bottle for a minute. Wipe quickly around the hot neck with a wet rag – it will crack cleanly all round and the top with the cork will come away easily.

An equally effective and more spectacular way of opening an old bottle of port is to grasp it firmly in one hand and take a heavy carving knife in the other. Run the back of the knife blade up the neck of the bottle to give a really sharp blow to the "collar". The neck will crack cleanly. Practise before making your début at a dinner party. Confidence is all.

If a port cork crumbles into the bottle, it is possible to filter the wine through a clean, muslin-lined glass or plastic funnel, or to use one of the handsome old-fashioned silver funnels, which has a built-in strainer.

Corks & Corkscrews

The first corks must have been like stoppers: driven only halfway home. There is no known illustration of a corkscrew until 100 years after corks came into use. Although screwcaps, crown closures and synthetic corks now offer cheaper and simpler ways of keeping the wine in and the air out, cork remains the way most fine wine is still sealed. What makes cork so ideal as a wine plug? Certainly its lightness, its cleanness, and the simple fact that it is available in vast quantities. It is almost impermeable. It is smooth, yet it stays put in the neck of the bottle. It is unaffected by temperature. It very rarely rots. It is extremely hard to burn. Most important of all it is uniquely elastic, returning, after compression, to almost exactly its original form. Corking machines are based on this simple principle: you can squeeze a cork enough to slip it easily into the neck of a bottle and it will immediately spring out to fill the neck without a cranny to spare.

As for its life span, it very slowly goes brittle and crumbly, over a period of between 20 and 50 years. Immaculately run cellars (some of the great Bordeaux châteaux, for example) re-cork their stocks of old vintages approximately every 25 years, and one or two send experts to recork the château's old wines in customers' cellars. But many corks stay sound for half a century. The only thing that occasionally goes wrong with a cork is a musty smell that develops. Corks are carefully sterilized in manufacture, but sometimes one or two of the

THE TEMPERATURE FOR SERVING WINE

Nothing makes or mars any wine so much as its temperature.

The following chart serves to show the ideal temperatures for each category of wine. It is wrong, however, to be too dogmatic. Some people enjoy red wines several degrees warmer than the refreshing temperature I suggest for them here, and some like their white wines considerably colder than the moderate chill I advocate for the best appreciation of scent and flavour.

It is also worth remembering that on a hot day, "room temperature" may be considerably higher than that listed below, so red wines may need to be immersed briefly in an ice bucket.

DOMESTIC FRIDGE TEMP.		CELLAR TEMPERATURE ▼ THE IDEAL CELLAR		ROOM TEMP. ►
SWEET WHITES	DRY WHITES	LIGHT REDS		FULL-SCALE REDS

C°4 5 6 7 8 9 10 11 12 13 14 15 16 17 18

Temp (°C)	Wine
6–8	MUSCADET
8–9	CHABLIS
9–11	MACON
8–9	BORDEAUX BLANC
11–12	CHINON
13	BEST WHITE BURGUNDIES & GRAVES
15–16	RED BURGUNDY
5–7	SAUTERNES
9–10	BEAUJOLAIS NOUVEAU
12–13	BEAUJOLAIS CRU
6–7	GEWURZTRAMINER
12–13	COTES DU RHONE (RED)
15–16	TOP RED RHONE
6–7	SANCERRE/POUILLY
16–17	VINTAGE PORT
4–5	GROS PLANT
7–9	ALSACE/RIESLING
13	MIDI REDS CORBIERES, ETC.
4–5	MUSCATS
6–7	SYLVANER
15	ORDINARY RED BORDEAUX
4–5	ALIGOTE
8–9	FINO SHERRY
11–12	TAWNY PORT
13	CREAM SHERRY
5	TOKAJI
11–12	AMONTILLADO
13	MADEIRA
15	CAHORS
16–17	FINE RED BORDEAUX
6–7	NON VINTAGE CHAMPAGNE
11	MONTILLA
15	MADIRAN
11	VIN JAUNE
16	BANDOL
5–6	SPARKLING WINE SEKT, CAVA, ETC.
8–9	BEST CHAMPAGNE
5–6	EISWEIN
8–9	GOOD GERMAN & AUSTRIAN WINES
11	BEST DRY GERMAN WINES
13	BEST SWEET GERMAN WINES
5–6	LIEBFRAUMILCH
4–6	SWEET LOIRE CHENIN BLANCS
6–7	FRASCATI
11	VALPOLICELLA
6–7	ORVIETO
13	FIASCO CHIANTI
8–9	SOAVE
13	SICILIAN REDS
8	VERDICCHIO
13	"BULLS" BLOOD
10–11	TOP TOKAJI ASZUS
5–6	VINHO VERDE
13	BARBERA
7–8	FENDANT
11	VALDEPENAS
11	DOLE
13	LIGHT ZINFANDELS
4–5	RETSINA
7	LAMBRUSCO
7	YUGOSLAV RIESLING
15–16	CALIFORNIA/AUSTRALIAN/OREGON PINOT NOIR
7	SOUTH AFRICAN CHENIN BLANC
4–5	LIGHT MUSCATS
7–8	CHARDONNAY
10	TOP CALIFORNIA/AUSTRALIAN CHARDONNAYS
16	BEST CALIFORNIA CABERNETS & ZINFANDALS
7	NZ SAUVIGNON
6–7	JOHANNISBERG RIESLING
9	CALIFORNIA
7	BAROSSA RIESLING
8–9	SAUVIGNON BLANC
13	OLD HUNTER VALLEY WHITES
10	LIQUEUR MUSCATS
17	TOP AUSTRALIAN CABERNET/SHIRAZ
8–9	VIN ROSE

F°39 41 43 45 46 48 50 52 54 55 57 59 61 63 64

many cells that make up the cork (there are 20–30 in a square millimetre) are infected with fungus. When these cells are in contact with wine, the wine picks up the smell and becomes "corky" or "corked". If the taint is minimal, only someone already familiar with the wine in perfect condition will detect it; if it is flagrant, it will be obvious to all. Any taint between these two extremes will diminish one's pleasure from the wine, without the cause of that disappointment being immediately traceable. In such cases we are more likely to blame the wine rather than the real culprit, the cork, for our dismay.

Sometimes an old or poor-quality cork might simply be pushed into the wine by the corkscrew. A gadget made of three parallel lengths of thick wire with a wooden handle is made for fishing for lost corks. It is reasonably effective, but a simpler answer is to leave the cork in and pour the wine out, holding the cork down with a knife or a skewer until it floats clear of the neck. Synthetic corks can also provide a challenge for many corkscrews; brute force may be the only solution, but might result in a broken corkscrew, lost in the cause of opening a mediocre wine. The quality of the corkscrew is extremely important. The simple screw-with-a-handle has long since been improved on by designs that use counter-pressure against the bottle. The straight pull is strictly for the young and fit; it can take the equivalent of lifting 80 pounds to get a cork out.

Various dodges are used to provide leverage, but the most important factor of all is the blade – the screw – that pierces and grips the cork. At all costs avoid narrow gimlets on the one hand and open spirals of bent wire on the other. The gimlet will merely pull out the centre of a well-installed cork; the bent wire will simply straighten if it meets with resistance. A good corkscrew blade is a spiral open enough to leave a distinct chimney up the middle, and made like a flattened blade with a sharp point and two cutting edges on its horizontal sides.

Types of Corkscrew

Endless ingenuity has been applied to the mechanical problem of grasping a cork in a bottle and pulling it out without exertion. A straight pull with the bottle between your knees is neither dignified nor necessary; all you need is some sort of leverage against the rim of the bottle. A foil cutter (shown on page 654) cleanly removes the top of the foil capsule before the corkscrew is inserted into the exposed cork.

The Unfinished Bottle

A wine, once exposed to air, will gradually, or even swiftly, deteriorate. Nonetheless, leftover wine can be conserved for enjoyment the next day. Devices such as the Vacuvin, which employs a simple pump to extract the oxygen from the bottle, which is at the same time sealed with a rubber "cork", are imperfect but useful nonetheless. It is worth keeping a small supply of clean half-bottles into which small volumes of left-overs can be poured, thus reducing the amount of oxygen to be pumped out. Another device is a spray of nitrogen gas, which acts as a barrier between the remaining wine and the oxygen above it.

Opened bottles seem to keep better when refrigerated, and this applies to red wines as much as white. The ability of an opened bottle to survive depends not only on the storage conditions, however, but also on the style of the wine. Big, oaky Chardonnays seem more prone to swift oxidation than an intense, reductive Riesling. Saying this, though, there are no tested formulae. Champagne bottles need to be re-sealed with a special stopper, which is available from most wine merchants. The bizarre method of placing an upended spoon in an opened Champagne bottle is unreliable. Leftover wines are often best dedicated to the stew or the sauce, and even corked wines can be used for cooking without imparting their musty flavours to the dish.

Tasting Wine

There are winetastings on every level of earnestness and levity, but to taste wine thoroughly, to be in a position to give a considered opinion, demands wholehearted concentration. A winetaster, properly speaking, is one who has gone through a professional apprenticeship and learned to do much more than simply enjoy what he tastes. He is trained to examine every wine methodically and analytically until it becomes second nature.

Although I am by no means a qualified professional taster, I often find myself, ridiculously, putting a glass of tap water through its paces as though I were judging it for condition and value. If I do not actually hold it up to the light, I certainly sniff it and hold it in my mouth for a moment while I see how it measures up to some notional yardstick of a good glass of water. Then naturally I spit it out. Whether or not you have any desire to train your palate (it has its disadvantages, too; it makes you less tolerant of faulty or boring wines) it makes no sense to pay the premium for wines of character and then simply swallow them. It is one of the commonest misunderstandings about wine that if it is "better", it will automatically give more plea-sure. To appreciate degrees of quality you need conscious, deliberate awareness. You need to know what sort of quality you are looking for. And you need a method to set about finding it.

Pierre Poupon, one of the most eloquent of Burgundians, has written, "When you taste, don't look at the bottle, nor the label, nor your surroundings, but look directly inwards to yourself, to observe sensations at their birth and develop impressions to remember." He even suggests shutting your eyes to concentrate on the messages of your nose and mouth.

Before dinner parties become like prayer meetings, let me say that there is a time and place for this sort of concentration. But if you apply it at appropriate moments it will provide you with points of reference for a more sociable approach. What, to start with, are you tasting for? A very basic winetasting for beginners might consist of five wines to show the enormous variety that exists: a dry white and a sweet one; a light young red and a fine mature one, and a glass of sherry or port.

The point here is that the wines have nothing in common at all. Another very effective elementary tasting is to compare typical examples of the half-dozen grape varieties that have very marked and easily recognized characters. Most tastings are intended to compare wines with an important common factor, either of origin, age, or grape variety.

A tasting of Rieslings from a dozen different countries is an excellent way of learning to identify the common strand, the Riesling taste, and judge its relative success in widely different soils and climates. A variant of this, more closely focused, would be to take Rieslings of the same category of quality (Kabinett or Spätlese) from the principal wine regions of Germany.

Vertical & Horizontal Tastings

Tastings of the same wine from different vintages are known in the jargon as "vertical"; those of different wines (of the same type) in a single vintage are known as "horizontal". Professional tastings concerned with buying are nearly always horizontal. The important thing here is that they should be comparing like with like. It is of no professional interest to compare Bordeaux with burgundy, or even Chablis with Meursault; if the Chablis

---

LEGS

An ideal tasting glass, to the specifications of the International Standards Organization, is about 6-in (152-mm) high and would hold 7 fl oz (215 ml). For tasting purposes it is usually only filled to about one-fifth of capacity. The tall funnel shape is designed to capture the aroma, or bouquet, for the taster's nose. It needs a long enough stem to keep the hand away from the bowl. (Professional tasters often hold their glass by its foot.) The thinner the glass, within reason, the better. Wine is tasted more vividly from thin glass.

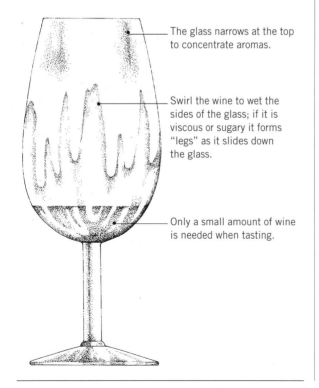

The glass narrows at the top to concentrate aromas.

Swirl the wine to wet the sides of the glass; if it is viscous or sugary it forms "legs" as it slides down the glass.

Only a small amount of wine is needed when tasting.

---

is a good Meursault it is a bad (because atypical) Chablis.

A Médoc that tasted like a Napa Valley wine would be a poor Médoc – although it might be hard to convince a Napa grower that the converse was true. Most of us, of course, drink most of our wine with meals. We judge it, therefore, partly by how well it goes with the sort of food we like. Professional and competitive tasters always judge wine either by itself or in company with other wines, which gives them a different, and clearer, point of view. It is clearest of all when you are hungry and not tired; the end of the morning is the time most professionals prefer to attend a tasting. The ideal conditions, in fact, are rather unattractively clinical: a clean, well-lit place without the suggestive power of atmosphere, without the pervasive smell of wine barrels, without the distraction of friendly chatter – and above all without the chunks of cheese, the grilled sausages, and homemade bread that have sold most of the world's second-rate wine since time immemorial.

Whether you should know what you are tasting, or taste "blind" and find out afterwards, is a topic for endless debate. The power of suggestion is strong. It is very difficult to be entirely honest with yourself if you have seen the label; your impressions are likely to reflect, consciously or otherwise, what you think you should find rather than simply what your senses tell you – like a child's picture of both sides of a house at once.

If I am given the choice, I like to taste everything blind first. It is the surest method of summoning up concentration, forcing you to ask yourself the right questions, to be analytical and clear minded. I write a note of my opinion, then ask what the wine is or look at the label. If I have guessed it right, I am delighted; I know that my mental image of the wine (or memory, if I have tasted it before) was pretty close to reality. If (which is much more frequent) I guess wrong, or simply do not know, this is my chance to get to know the wine, to taste it again carefully and try to understand why that grape, in that vineyard, in that year, produced that result. This is the time to share impressions with other tasters. It is always interesting to find out how much common ground there is among several people tasting the same wine. So little is measurable, and nothing is reproducible, about the senses of smell and taste. Language serves them only lamely, leaning on simile and metaphor for almost everything illuminating that can be said.

The convenient answer, normally used at competitive tastings, is the law of averages. Ask a group of tasters to quantify their enjoyment, and reduce their judgement to scores, and the wine with the highest average score must be the "best". The disadvantage of averaging is that it hides the points of disagreement, the high and low scores given to the same wine by different tasters who appreciate or dislike its individual style, or one of whom, indeed, is a better judge than another. At a well-conducted tasting the chairman will therefore consider an appeal against an averaged score and encourage a verbal consensus as well, especially where gold medals hang on the result.

This is as close to a final judgement on wine quality as fallible beings can get. But at best it represents the rating by one group of one bottle among the wines they tasted that day. It takes no account of other wines that were not tasted on the same occasion. All one can say about medal winners is that they are good of their sort. For competitive tastings, taster against taster, "blindness" is the whole point of the exercise. The individual (or team) with the widest experience and the best memory for tastes should win. For competitive tastings, wine against wine, it is the only fair method. But it can nonetheless produce misleading results. It tends to favour impact at the expense of less obvious but ultimately more important qualities. When California Cabernets are matched against red Bordeaux of similar age, the Californians almost always dominate. They are like tennis players who win by serving ace after ace.

The Grand Tour

The act of tasting has been anatomized by many specialists. To me there are five aspects of wine that convey information and help me gauge its quality: origin, age, the grape varieties involved, and how long it will keep (and whether it will improve). They constitute the grand tour of its pleasures, the uplift excepted. To take them in order they are its appearance, smell, the first impression the wine makes in your mouth, its total flavour as you hold it there, and the taste it leaves behind. I take each of these into account, note each separately (writing a note is not only an *aide-mémoire*; it forces you to make up your mind) and then draw a general conclusion. Tasting is a demanding discipline, quite distinct from the mere act of drinking. It sometimes has to be a quick and private little ceremony at a party where wine is not an accepted priority. Yet to contract the habit and apply a method of one kind or another is the only way to get full value out of your wine. There is more to appearance than simply colour. Fine wine is brilliantly clear. Decanting should make sure that even old wine with sediment has the clarity of a jewel, capturing and reflecting light with an intensity that is a pleasure in itself.

Wine is more or less viscous, at one extreme forming heavy, slow-moving "legs" on the walls of the glass, at the other instantly finding its own level like water. The more dense it is, the more flavour-giving "extract" and/or sugar it contains – which, of course, is neither good nor bad in itself; it must be appropriate to the kind of wine. On the other hand a deposit of crystals in white wine does not imply poor quality; it is a perfectly natural precipitation and certainly not, under any circumstances, a fault. "Colour [I quote Professor Peynaud] is like a wine's face. From it you can tell age, and something of character." That is, you can if you have certain other information about the wine, which the smell will soon provide.

The best way to see its colour clearly is to hold the glass against a white surface – a piece of paper will do – and to tip it slightly away from yourself so that you are looking through the rim of the liquid. Shallow silver tasting-cups are common in parts of France – particularly Burgundy – where wine is kept in dark cellars. It is easier to judge the colour of red wine in a shallow layer over the brightly reflecting silver than in a glass, where it is in a greater mass. The *tastevin* worn on a ribbon around the neck has become the ceremonial symbol of Burgundy.

White wines grow darker as they age; reds go through a slow fading process from purplish through red to a brickish reddy brown (that can be seen even through the green glass of the bottle by looking at the neck against a light). In young wines, the colour in the glass is almost uniform from edge to edge. In older wines the rim is usually decidedly paler. A browning rim is a sure sign of maturity in red wines.

Sheer redness is an indicator of quality rather than a virtue in its own right. The famous 1961 Bordeaux vintage can often be recognized from right across the room by its extraordinary glowing darkness – even in maturity a colour of pregnancy and promise. Red burgundy rarely has the same deep tints, and never precisely the same hue as Bordeaux. Much the same is true of Barolo. Traditional Rioja is generally rather pale, but this is because it has been aged for so long in cask; modern Rioja is darker in colour, while Beaujolais is light-coloured in a different way; it has more the translucent purple of grape juice.

In general, hot-country wines of good grape varieties, the Cabernets and Syrahs, for example, from Australia, California, and South Africa, have more intensity of colour than their cool-country equivalents. Vintage port is deep purple-red, ruby port a much lighter, more watery colour, and tawny port, aged in wood for many years, can be anything from the brown-red of old claret to a clear, light-amber when it is very old – the most extreme example of a red wine fading.

White wine has scarcely less variety than red. Chablis has a green light in its pale gold, which is uncommon in other white burgundies. Mosels also have a touch of green, with less of the gold, while Rhine wines tend to a straw colour, deepening almost to orange in old sweet examples. Sherry is coloured by oxidation: young finos only very slightly, old olorosos to a mahogany brown. When great sweet Sauternes ages, it goes through all the tints of gold to arrive at a deep, golden brown.

Hold Your Nose

You have only to hold your nose while you sip to realize that it is the organ that does most of the serious work of tasting. Unfortunately, our sense of smell is our least cooperative, least stable faculty. While taste, like hearing and sight, is constantly awake, the sense of smell rapidly wearies. This is apparent if you sniff more than half a dozen times in rapid succession at the same glass (or the same rose); its message becomes dimmed. Your nose needs a different stimulus.

For this reason, winetasters place a great deal of faith in their first impression. They swirl the wine once or twice to wet the sides of the glass and volatize as much of the smell as possible. Then they exclude all other thoughts and sniff.

The nerves of smell have instant access to the memory (their immediate neighbour in the brain). The first sniff should trigger recognition: possibly the memory of the identical wine tasted before. If the smell is unfamiliar it will at least transmit this piece of negative information, and suggest where in the memory-bank partially similar smells are to be found.

The smell will also be the first warning sign if there is something wrong with the wine: perhaps a slight taint of vinegar, the burning sensation of too much sulphur, or a mouldy smell from an unsound cork or an unclean barrel. Most wines have a more or less agreeable but simple compound smell of grapes and fermentation, and in some cases barrel wood: the smell we recognize as "winey". At its simplest, the better the wine, the more distinctive and characteristic this smell, and the more it attracts you to sniff again. At this stage, certain grape varieties declare themselves. The eight "classics" all set a recognizable stamp on the smell of their wine. Age transmutes it from the primary smell tasters call the "aroma" to a more complex, less definable, and more rewarding smell. This scent of maturity is known, by analogy with the mixed scents of a posy of flowers, as the "bouquet".

The essence of a fine bouquet is that you can never put your finger on it. It seems to shift, perhaps from cedar to wax to honey to wildflowers to mushrooms. Mature Riesling, for example, can smell like lemons and petrol, Gewürztraminer like grapefruit, Chardonnay like butter – or rather, they can fleetingly remind you of these among many other things.

By the time the glass reaches your lips, then, you have already had answers, or at least clues, to most of the questions about the wine: its overall quality, its age, perhaps its grape (and by deduction, possibly its origin).If all is well, the taste will confirm the smell like the orchestra repeating the theme introduced by a soloist, adding the body of sound, the tonal colours that were missing. Only at this stage can you judge the balance of sweetness and acidity, the strength of the alcohol, and whether it is counterpoised by the intensity of fruity flavours, and the quantity and quality of tannin. Each wine has an appropriate combination of these elements; its quality is judged on whether they harmonize in a way that is both pleasant in itself and typical of its class. In fact, typical comes before pleasant. A young red wine might be disagreeably tannic and astringent; the taster's job is to judge it for the latent fruitiness that in time will combine with the tannins.

Different parts of your mouth pick up different facets of flavour. It is the tip of your tongue that recognizes sweetness, so sweetness is the first taste you become aware of. Acidity and

---

HOW TO TASTE WINE

The secret of getting the maximum pleasure out of wine is to remember that we smell tastes: it is our noses and the nerves high in the brain behind the nasal cavity that distinguish nuances of flavour – not our tongues, lips, or palates. The mouth detects what is sweet, sour, salt, bitter, burning, smooth, oily, astringent. But the colour and character of a flavour lie in its volatile compounds, which need the nose to apprehend them. Thus the procedure for tasting wine pivots around the moment of inhalation: the first sniff is crucial, since the sense of smell rapidly wearies.

First look carefully at the precise colour, clarity, and visual texture of the wine. Using a piece of white paper can help.

Swirl the wine to volatize its aroma while you concentrate. The glass should only be filled to about a fifth of its capacity.

Try to exclude all other thoughts and sniff. First impressions are crucial and should trigger recognition.

Take a generous sip, a third of a mouthful, and "chew" it so that reaches all parts of your mouth.

The final judgement comes when the volatile compounds rise into the upper nasal cavity from the back of your mouth.

At a professional tasting you must spit out all the wine: it is essential to keep a clear head.

saltiness are perceived by taste-buds along the sides of your tongue and palate, bitterness by the soft back part of your tongue. The tastes switch off in the same order: sugar after a mere two seconds or so; salt and acid after rather longer. Bitterness, which you notice last, lingers – a quality the Italians appreciate; many of their red wines (Valpolicella is an example) have a slightly bitter aftertaste.

Science can measure many (not all) of the chemical constituents that provide these sensations. It has identified more than 400 in wine up to now. But our perception of them is entirely personal. A few tasters, like a few musicians, might have "perfect pitch", but most people probably have slight blind spots. Someone who takes three spoonfuls of sugar in coffee must have a high threshold of perception for sweetness. If you need to smother your food with salt you will hardly pick up the subtle touches of saltiness in wine.

Sweet, sour, salt, and bitter in any case hardly start to express the variety of sensations that evolve in your mouth between sipping and swallowing. The moment of maximum flavour is when the wine reaches the soft palate and you start to swallow. Its vapour mounts directly to the olfactory nerves through the channels that link mouth and nose. At a serious tasting, where it is essential to spit the wine out to keep a clear head and stay the course, this moment can be maximized by holding a small quantity in the very back of the mouth and breathing in through slightly parted lips. The grimace and the gurgling are a small price to pay for the redoubled concentration of flavour achieved.

Red wines contain more or less tannin, the substance that turns hide to leather. Very tannic wine is so astringent (like walnut or broad bean skins) that your mouth can begin to feel leathery and further tasting can be difficult. Tannin varies in taste and quality, too, from fully ripe, agreeable astringency, or the mouth-drying astringency of oak, to unripe, green harshness. Acids vary from harsh to delicately stimulating – not just in their concentration, or their power (measured in units of pH), but in their flavours. Of the wine acids, malic is green-appley, citric is fresh and lemony, tartaric is harsh. Acetic is vinegary, lactic is mild, and succinic is a chemical cousin of glutamic acid. We owe much of the lip-smacking, appetizing taste of wine to tiny traces of succinic acid generated as a by-product of fermentation.

As for the alcohol itself, in low concentrations it merely has a faintly sweet taste, but at about 11% by volume it begins to give the mouth the characteristic feeling of winey warmth known as "vinosity". (Lighter wines, such as many German ones at 8–9%, lack this feeling.) Add the ability of your tongue to differentiate between (more or less) fluid or viscous, to pronounce one liquid feels like satin, and another like velvet, and the permutations begin to be impressive. Finally, add the all-important element of persistence – how long the final flavour lasts. Really great wines have more to offer at the beginning, in the beauty of the bouquet, and at the end, in the way they haunt your breath for minutes after they have gone. Logical in all things, French scholars have even invented a measure of persistence; one second of flavour after swallowing is known as a caudalie. According to one theory, the hierarchy of the wines of Burgundy is in direct proportion to their caudalie-count.

When participating in a blind-tasting, or offered a glass by a host who asks for your opinion, do remember that the primary goal of tasting wine is not to identify it with precision. Some tasters have a remarkable aroma/taste memory and a knack for identifying wines; others can analyze the wine with great brilliance yet be incapable of pinning down its identity. Tasting, and then drinking, a wine is an act of hedonism; the performance of a dazzling party trick is not compulsory.

Order of Tasting

In tasting wine, as in serving it at a dinner party, take care to organize a crescendo of flavour. Powerful, strong-flavoured wines followed by lighter ones, however good, make the latter appear as pygmies. The conventions are to follow younger with older, lighter with heavier, drier with sweeter, and to put red after white. Bordeaux professionals, however, will often taste red before white. It is worth trying both methods.

Tasting: Further Reading

In recent years, a number of excellent books tackle this subject in great detail. *Michael Broadbent's Winetasting* is both concise and authoritative; Len Evans's *How to Taste Wine* distils the experience of one of the greatest tasters, and Michael Schuster's *Essential Winetasting* is probably the best of a large number of how-to books on this topic.

Glossary

Cross-references are in **bold**.

Abboccato (Ital) Slightly sweet (*eg.* Orvieto).

Abfüllung (Ger) Bottling (see **Erzeugerabfüllung**).

Amabile (Ital) A little sweeter than *abboccato*.

Amaro (Ital) Bitter.

Amarone (Ital) Strong red wine made from dried grapes in Valpolicella.

Amtliche Prüfung (Ger) Certification of standard quality by chemical analysis and tasting. Compulsory since 1971 for all **QbA** and **QmP** wines. Each wine is given an AP number which must be displayed on the label.

Anbaugebiet (Ger) The broadest category of wine region, of which there are 13 (*eg.* Mosel, Baden).

Annata (Ital) The year of the vintage.

Assemblage (Fr) The blending of the final wine from its components.

Assemblaggio (Ital) See **assemblage**.

Auslese (Ger) Literally "selected": the third category of **QmP** wines, made only in ripe vintages and usually naturally sweet. Auslesen often have a slight degree of noble rot, which adds subtlety to their fruity sweetness. With bottle age their primary sweetness mellows to more adult flavours.

Azienda Agricola (on a wine label) (Ital) A wine estate.

Barrique (Fr) The standard Bordeaux barrel for ageing the wine, holds 225 litres.

Beerenauslese (Ger) Literally "selected berries": the category of **QmP** wine beyond **Auslese** in sweetness and price. Only very overripe or nobly rotten grapes are used to make intensely sweet wines, which age admirably.

Bereich (Ger) One of 34 districts or subregions (*eg.* Bereich Bernkastel) within the 13 **Gebieten**. Bereich names are commonly used for middling to lower quality wines (they are legal for **QbA** as well as **QmP**) blended from the less-distinguished vineyards of the district.

Bianco (Ital) White.

Blanc de Blancs (Fr) Wine made from white grapes alone; often applied to all-Chardonnay Champagnes.

Blanc de Noirs (Fr) White wine made from red grapes alone; often applied to all-Pinot Champagnes.

Blush (US) Pale pink wine, usually quite sweet, made from Zinfandel or other red grapes.

Bodega (Sp) Winery or cellar.

Botte (Ital) Cask or barrel.

Botrytized (Pronounced with the accent on the first syllable.) Grapes or wine infected, naturally or artificially, with *Botrytis cinerea*, the noble rot of Sauternes: hence normally very sweet.

Bottiglia (Ital) Bottle.

Bric (or **Bricco**) (Ital) Hilltop; commonly encountered on labels of single-vineyard wines from Piedmont.

Brix (US) The American measure of sugar content in grapes, also known as Balling, approximately equal to double the potential alcohol of the wine, if all the sugar is fermented. 19.3 Brix is equivalent to 10 degrees of alcohol by volume.

Cantina (Ital) Wine cellar.

Cantina sociale or **cooperativa** (Ital) A growers' cooperative cellar.

Casa vinicola (Ital) A wine firm, usually making wine from purchased grapes. See also **tenementi**.

Cascina (Ital) Northern term for a farm or estate.

Cava (Sp) Sparkling wine (made by the traditional method, if DO), mostly in northeast Spain.

Cépage (Fr) Grape variety.

Cerasuolo (Ital) Rosé wine, especially from Abruzzo.

Chai (Fr) Cellar or custom-made structure for ageing wine in barrels.

Charta (Ger) An organization founded in 1983 by leading growers in the Rheingau. It laid down stylistic criteria for drier styles of Rieslings, but became increasingly anachronistic after the creation of the **Erstes Gewächs** system. These days its goals have been absorbed into the guidelines of the **VDP** estates.

Chef de culture (Fr) Vineyard manager.

Chiaretto (Ital) "Claret" – usually meaning very light red, but it can also refer to rosé.

Clairet (Fr) Dark pink wine, originally from Bordeaux.

Classico (Ital) The "classic" heart of a DOC zone, by implication (and usually) the best part.

Cold stabilization A near-universal winery practice for preventing the formation of (harmless) tartaric acid crystals in the bottle. The offending tartaric acid is removed by storing wine near freezing point for about 15 days.

Colheita (Port) A single-vintage tawny port, aged seven years or more in wood.

Collage (Fr) Fining; clarification of the wine, traditionally with beaten egg white.

Consorzio (Ital) A consortium of producers of a certain wine area who join forces to control and promote it.

Côte/coteaux (Fr) Hillside or slope.

Coulure (Fr) Failure of the vine flowers to set.

Crémant (Fr) French sparkling wine produced by the traditional method outside the Champagne region.

Crianza (Sp) Wine aged in oak, though for a shorter period than **Reserva** or **Gran Reserva.**

Cru (Fr) Growth, as in *cru classé* (classified growth) or *cru bourgeois* in Bordeaux; also a term for vineyard classification in Burgundy and other régions, as in *premier* or *grand cru*.

Crush (US) A Californian term for the vintage; also the quantity of grapes crushed, measured in tons per acre.

Cuvaison (Fr) The time the new wine spends in the vat during the fermentation and maceration process.

Cuve (Fr) Vat, used for fermentation or storage.

Dolce (Ital) Fully sweet (technically, with between five per cent and ten per cent residual sugar).

Dosage (Fr) The amount of sugar added to a sparkling wine during disgorgement.

Edelfäule (Ger) Botrytis.

Einzellage (Ger) An individual vineyard site. There are some 2,600 Einzellagen in Germany. Officially, the minimum size for an Einzellage is five hectares, although there are a number much smaller than this. A **Grosslage** is a unit of several Einzellagen supposedly of the same quality and character. The Einzellage or Grosslage name follows the village (**Gemeinde**) name on the label.

Eiswein (Ger) Wine made by pressing grapes that have been left hanging on the vine into mid-winter (sometimes January), and are gathered and pressed in early morning, while frozen solid. Since it is the water content of the grape that freezes, the juice, separated from the ice, is concentrated sugar, acidity, and flavour. The result is extraordinarily sweet and piquant wines with almost limitless ageing capacity, less rich but more penetrating than BA or TBA, often fetching spectacular prices.

Encépagement (Fr) Choice of grape varieties in a vineyard.

Engrais (Fr) Fertilizer.

Enologo (Ital) Oenologist or winemaking consultant.

Enoteca (Ital) "Wine library" – Italy has many establishments with wide national or regional reference collections of wine. Also a wine shop.

Erstes Gewächs (Ger) See **Grosses Gewächs** below.

Erzeugerabfüllung (Ger) Estate-bottled.

Etichetta (Ital) Label.

Fass (Ger) A barrel. "Holzfässen" are large oak barrels, the traditional containers in German cellars.

Fattoria (Ital) Tuscan term for a farm or wine estate.

Feinherb (Ger) An ill-defined term used by some growers as an alternative to the contradictory **halbtrocken**. Usually denotes Halbtrocken in style or slightly sweeter.

Field-grafting (US) A method much used for converting established vines from one variety to another. The old vine top is cut off near the ground and a bud of the new variety grafted on.

Finca (Sp) Estate.

Flor (Sp) Layer of yeast that prevents a young sherry from oxidation and gives a fino its distinctive flavour. Also found in wines such as Vin Jaune from the Jura.

Flurbereinigung (Ger) The term for the government-sponsored consolidation of vineyard holdings by remodelling the landscape, a process that has revolutionized the old system of terracing in most parts of Germany, making the land workable by tractors and rationalizing scattered holdings.

Fouloir-égrappoir (Fr) Rotary machine for tearing the grapes off their stalks and crushing them. *Foulage* is crushing, *éraflage* removing the stalks.

Free-run juice The juice that flows from the crushed grapes "freely" before pressing. By implication, superior. Normally mixed with pressed juice.

Frizzante (Ital) Slightly fizzy, but with much less pressure than sparkling wine.

Füder (Ger) The Mosel barrel, an oak oval holding 1,000 litres or about 111 cases.

Futures (US) *See* **en primeur.**

Gas chromatograph An expensive gadget for analyzing a compound (*eg.* wine) into its chemical constituents.

Gebiet (Ger) Region.

Gemeinde (Ger) Village or commune. The village name always comes before the vineyard on German labels.

Gérant (Fr) General manager of a large property.

Gondola (US) A massive hopper for carrying grapes from vineyard to crusher, behind a tractor or on a truck.

Grand cru (Fr) Legally defined term, usually the best vineyards in an area (Burgundy, Alsace, Bordeaux). Can be better than **premier cru** (Burgundy) or not (Bordeaux).

Grand vin (Fr) Unregulated term generally used to mean the top wine of property, in contrast to the second or other wines.

Grosses Gewächs (Ger) "First Growth" vineyard, as established by the VDP classification.

Grosslage (Ger) A "collective vineyard", consisting of a number of **Einzellagen** of similar quality. Unfortunately, the wine law does not permit the label to distinguish between a Grosslage and an Einzellage name. Grosslage names are normally used for **QbA** wines, but also sometimes for such wines as **TBA**, when a single Einzellage cannot produce enough grapes to fill even a small barrel.

Halbtrocken (Ger) "Semi-dry" (*halb* = half) – wine with no more than 18 grams of unfermented sugar per litre. Although the concept is unsatisfactory, this style of wine can be more satisfying than **trocken** in vintages when acidity is very high.

Icewine Wine made from frozen grapes, a technique traditional (as **Eiswein**) to Germany.

Imbottigliato (or **messo in bottiglia**) **nel'origine** (or **del produttore all'origine**) (Ital) Estate-bottled.

Jahrgang (Ger) Vintage (year).

Jóven (Sp) A style of young, fresh wine, usually without oak ageing.

Jug wines (US) Originally, wines collected from the winery in a jug for immediate use – therefore of ordinary quality. Now standard wines sold in large bottles.

Kabinett (Ger) The first category of natural, unsugared, Qualitätswein mit Prädikat (**QmP**). Fine Kabinett wines have qualities of lightness and delicacy which make them ideal refreshment, not inferior in the right context to heavier (and more expensive) **Spätlese** or **Auslese** wines.

Kellerei (Ger) Wine cellar; by inference a merchant's rather than a grower's establishment (which would be called a **Weingut**).

Landwein (Ger) A category of **trocken** or **halbtrocken** tafelwein introduced in 1982.

Legno (Ital) Wood (as in barrel).

Liebfraumilch (Ger) A much-abused name for a "wine of pleasant character" with between 18 and 40 grams of residual sugar, officially originating in the Pfalz, Rheinhessen, Rheingau, or the Nahe. It must be in the QbA category and should be mainly of Riesling, Silvaner, or Müller-Thurgau grapes. Since neither its character nor quality is remotely consistent, its popularity, now dwindling, can only be ascribed to its simple and memorable name.

Liquoroso (Ital) Strong, usually fortified, wine, whether sweet or not.

Maître de chai (Fr) The cellarmaster in charge of all winemaking operations.

Marc (Fr) The solid matter – skins, pips, and stems – left after pressing.

Meritage (US) Term for red or white blends made from Bordeaux varieties.

Méthode traditionelle/classique (Fr) Now the mandatory term for sparkling wines made using the Champagne method. Applied to wines from outside the Champagne region.

Metodo tradizionale or **classico** (Ital) See **méthode traditionelle**.

Millésime (Fr) The vintage year (eg. 2005).

Monopole (Fr) A vineyard solely owned by a single grower, eg. Clos de Tart in Burgundy.

Mostgewicht (Ger) "Must weight". The density or specific gravity of the grape juice, ascertained with a hydrometer, is the way of measuring its sugar content. The unit of measurement is the degree **Oechsle**.

Muffa nobile (Ital) Noble rot or botrytis. See **botrytized**.

Must Unfermented grape juice.

Mutage (Fr) The arresting of the fermentation by adding spirit to the must. The process by which most fortified wines are made.

Négociant (Fr) A merchant or shipper.

Oechsle (Ger) The specific gravity, therefore sweetness, of German **must** is measured by the method invented by Ferdinand Oechsle (1774–1852). Each gram by which a litre of grape juice is heavier than a litre of water is one degree Oechsle. The number of degrees Oechsle divided by eight is the potential alcoholic content of the wine.

Oenologist (Fr) Oenologist or winemaking consultant.

Offene Weine (Ger) Wines served "open" in a large glass in a café or restaurant.

Ortsteil (Ger) A suburb or part of a larger community with a standing independent from its village. For example, Erbach in the Rheingau is an Ortsteil of the town of Eltville. Certain famous estates (eg. Schloss Vollrads) are allowed to omit the names of their villages from their labels.

Ovals Barrels of any size with oval, rather than round, ends, kept permanently in one place and not moved around the cellar – the German rather than the French tradition.

Passito (Ital) Wine made from grapes dried (either on mats in sheds or in direct sunlight) to concentrate them; strong and usually sweet.

Perlwein (Ger) Slightly fizzy **tafelwein**, often artificially carbonated under pressure. A small measure of acidic carbon dioxide freshens up dull wines.

Pièce (Fr) The standard Burgundy barrel for ageing the wine, holds 228 litres.

Plafond Limite de Classement (PLC) (Fr) A neat dodge for allowing producers to exceed the legal yields for their appellation. Each vintage an extra amount is agreed, often 20 per cent.

Podere (Ital) A farm or wine estate.

Pomace (US) The solid matter – skins, pips, and stems – left after pressing.

Porte-greffe (Fr) Rootstock of phylloxera-resistant vine onto which the desired variety is grafted.

Premier cru (Fr) Legally defined term in Bordeaux and Burgundy, but with different meaning in each. See **grand cru**.

En Primeur (Fr) The system by which wines are sold to consumers before bottling.

Propriétaire (Fr) Owner.

Qualitätswein bestimmter Anbaugebiete (QbA) (Ger) "Quality wine of a designated region". The category of wine above **tafelwein** and **landwein** but below **QmP**. It must be from one of the 13 **anbaugebiete** (unblended), from approved grapes, reach a certain level of ripeness before **chaptalization**, and pass an analytical and tasting test to gain an AP number. In certain underripe vintages, a high proportion of German wine comes into this category, and can be very satisfactory, although never reaching the distinction of QmP wine.

Qualitätswein mit Prädikat (QmP) (Ger) "Quality wine with special attributes" is the awkward official description of all the finest German wines, beginning with the **Kabinett** category and rising in sweetness, body and value to **TBA**. QmP wines must originate in a single **bereich** and are certified at each stage of their career from the vineyard on.

Quinta (Port) Estate.

Quintale (Ital) 100 kilos; used to calculate yields, as in 100 quintali per hectare (roughly equivalent to 70 hectolitres per hectare).

Rebsorte (Ger) Grape variety.

Recioto (Ital) Similar to **Amarone** but with a small amount of residual sweetness.

Récolte (Fr) Harvest.

Regisseur (Fr) Estate manager.

Rendement (Fr) Yield, usually measured in hectolitres per hectare or in grams per bunch.

Restsüsse (Ger) "Residual sugar": the sugar remaining unfermented in a wine at bottling, whether fermentation has stopped naturally or been stopped artificially. In a **TBA** it may reach astonishing figures of more than 200 grams a litre, with very little of the sugar converted to alcohol.

Riserva, riserva speciale (Ital) Wines that have been matured for a statutory number of years (the speciale is older). Except in Piedmont and the Chianti zone, the terms are gradually falling into disuse.

Rosato (Ital) Rosé.

Rosso (Ital) Red.

Rotling (Ger) Pale red wine from mixed red and white grapes.

Rotwein (Ger) Red wine.

Rovere (Ital) Oak (as in barrel).

Säure (Ger) Acidity (measured in units per 1,000 of tartaric acid). The essential balancing agent to the sweetness in German (or any) wine. As a rule of thumb, a well-balanced wine has approximately one unit per 1,000 (ml) of acid for each ten degrees **Oechsle**. Thus an 80-degree Oechsle wine needs an acidity of approximately 8.0.

Schaumwein (Ger) Sparkling wine – a general term for low priced fizz. Quality sparkling wines are called **Sekt**.

Schillerwein (Ger) A pale red (**Rotling**) of **QbA** or **QmP** status, produced only in Württemberg.

Schoppenweine (Ger) Another term for **offene weine** – wine served "open" in a large glass.

Secco (Ital) Dry.

Sekt (Ger) Germany's quality sparkling wine, subject to similar controls as **QbA** wines.

Sélection de Grains Nobles (Fr) Scrupulous selection of **botrytized** grapes to give an ultra-sweet dessert wine; found in Alsace and Anjou.

Skin contact Alas, not that, but a reference to leaving the white-wine juice mixed with the skins before separating them. Some white wines gain good flavours from a few hours maceration with their skins, if healthy, before fermentation. Now out of favour, because of **whole-cluster pressing**.

Solera (Sp) System of fractional blending: the oldest barrel gets topped up with the next oldest, and so on. Used especially for sherry.

Spätlese (Ger) Literally "late-gathered". The **QmP** category above **Kabinett** and below **Auslese**, with wines of a higher alcoholic degree and greater body and "vinosity" than Kabinetts. May be considerably sweeter but not necessarily so, but many now fermented out to dryness. Tasting panels establish a consensus of what constitutes proper Spätlese style in each vintage and region.

Spitzen (Ger) "Top", a favourite German term, whether applied to a vineyard, a grower, or a vintage.

Spumante (Ital) Sparkling.

Stravecchio (Ital) Very old (a term regulated under DOC rules, not permitted elsewhere).

Stück (Ger) The standard traditional oak cask of the Rhine, holding 1,200 litres or about 133 cases. There are also doppelstücke (double), halbstücke (half), and viertel (quarter) stücke.

Superiore (Ital) Superior in any one of a number of ways specifically designated by DOC rules; for example, high alcoholic degree.

Süssreserve (Ger) Unfermented grape juice with all its natural sweetness, held in reserve for "back-blending" with dry, fully fermented wines to arrive at the winemaker's ideal of a balanced wine. This sweetening (which also lowers the alcoholic content) is often overdone, but a judicious hint of extra sweetness can enhance fruity flavours, and make an average wine more attractive. The practice is eschewed by many but not all leading estates.

Tafelwein (Ger) "Table wine", the humblest category of German wine. (Without the prefix Deutsche it might not be German, however Gothic the label.) The origin, alcohol content, and grape varieties are all controlled, but Tafelwein is never more than a light wine for quenching thirst.

Taille (Fr) Pruning.

Tenementi or **tenuta** (Ital) Holding or estate.

Tonneau (Fr) The measure in which Bordeaux wine is still bought from the chateau (900 litres, or four barriques, or 100 dozen bottles).

Trocken (Ger) "Dry" – the official category for wines with less than nine grams of unfermented sugar per litre.

Trockenbeerenauslese (TBA) (Ger) "Selected dried grapes". Ironically, the precise opposite of the last entry, the "dry" here referring to the state of the overripe grapes when picked in a shrivelled state from noble rot and desiccation on the vine. Such is the concentration of sugar, acid, and flavours that **Oechsle** readings of TBA **must** can reach more than 300 degrees. TBA wines are reluctant to ferment and rarely exceed seven degrees alcohol, the remaining intense sweetness acting as a natural preservative and slowing down maturation for many years. Some TBAs from as far back as 1893 are still eminently drinkable.

Uva (Ital) Grape.

Vecchio (Ital) Old.

Vendemmia (Ital) The vintage. It can also be used in place of **annata** on labels. "Vendemmia Tardiva" is a late-harvested but usually not **botrytized** wine.

Vendange Tardive (Fr) Late harvested wine, usually lightly sweet. A specialiy of Alsace.

Verband Deutscher Prädikats-und Qualitätsweingüter (VDP) (Ger) An association of premium growers.

Vieilles Vignes (Fr) Old vines. A term that would benefit from regulation, since there is no agreed age at which a vineyard becomes "old".

Vigna, vigneto (Ital) Vineyard.

Vignaiolo or **viticoltore** (Ital) Grape-grower.

Vin or **vino santo** (Ital) Wine made from grapes dried indoors over winter and aged for many years in small casks. Usually sweet.

Vino cotto (Ital) Cooked (concentrated) wine.

Vino novello (Ital) The wine of the current year, now used in the same sense as Beaujolais Nouveau.

Vino da pasto (Ital) Everyday wine.

Vino da tavola (Ital) The regulation term for non-DOC wines, the equivalent of French vin de table.

Vite (Ital) Vine.

Viticulteur (Fr) Wine-grower.

Weingut (Ger) Wine estate. The term may only be used by growers who grow all their own grapes.

Weinprobe (Ger) Winetasting.

Weinstein (Ger) The deposit of potassium tartrate crystals forming a glittering rock-like lining to old barrels.

Weissherbst (Ger) A rosé wine of **QbA** or **QmP** status made from red grapes of a single variety, the specialty of Baden, Württemberg, and the Pfalz.

Whole-cluster pressing The practice of pressing white grapes, stems and all, as soon as they arrive at the winery. The advantage is a greater freshness in the wine; the drawbacks are, qualitatively, a possible loss of complexity, and, economically, a need for more presses because the stems take up so much room.

Winzer (Ger) Wine-grower.

Winzergenossenschaft, Winzerverein (Ger) Cooperative.

Index